Sunset

WESTERN
GARDEN
BOOK

By the Editors of Sunset Books and Sunset Magazine

SUNSET PUBLISHING CORPORATION • MENLO PARK, CALIFORNIA

Blake Garden, Kensington, California

Sunset Books
President and Publisher: Susan J. Maruyama
Director, Finance & Business Affairs: Gary Loebner
Director, Manufacturing & Sales Service: Lorinda Reichert
Director, Sales & Marketing: Richard A. Smeby
Editorial Director: Kenneth Winchester

***Sunset Western Garden Book* Staff**
Editor: Kathleen Norris Brenzel
Contributing Editors
   The West's 24 Climate Zones: Jim McCausland
   A Guide to Plant Selection: Lauren Bonar Swezey
   Western Plant Encyclopedia: John R. Dunmire, Joseph F. Williamson
   Practical Gardening Dictionary: Lance Walheim
Contributors: Philip Edinger, Suzanne Normand Eyre, Lynn Ocone,
   Joyce Kerr Reeder
Book Production Manager: Lory Day

Sunset Publishing Corporation
Chairman: Jim Nelson
President/Chief Executive Officer: Robin Wolaner
Chief Financial Officer: James E. Mitchell
Publisher: Stephen J. Seabolt
Circulation Director: Robert I. Gursha
Editor, *Sunset Magazine:* William R. Marken

This 40th Anniversary Edition of the *Sunset Western Garden Book*
was revised and produced by
Weldon Owen Reference, Inc.
President: John Owen
Publisher: Roger Smoothy
Managing Editor: Hazel White
Senior Editor and Indexer: Carolyn McGovern
Editors: Fran Haselsteiner, Fran Taylor, Darren Ward
Art Director, Design and Production Manager: Alice Rogers
Concept Design: Alex R. Arthur
Computer Production Manager: Brynn Breuner
Computer Production: Phoebe Bixler, Elaine Holland, Liz Marken,
   Rob Roehrick
Map Design and Cartography: Reineck & Reineck, San Francisco
Botanical Illustrator: Mimi Osborne
Gardening Illustrator: Bill Oetinger
Photography Editor: Ann Leyhe
Horticultural Stylist: Jane Hudon

For Special Sales, bulk orders and premium sales information, call Sunset Custom Publishing and Special Sales Services at **(415) 324-5547**.

Cover photograph: Fremontodendron *'California Glory',* Saxon Holt
Title page photograph: Spring border, Saxon Holt
Endpapers photograph, hardcover edition: Salvia officinalis,
   Marion Brenner

Foreword

This extensively revised edition of the *Sunset Western Garden Book* evolved out of several illustrious predecessors dating back to the 1930s. All of them have focused on plants and seasonal gardening activities that are uniquely suited to the high mountains, low deserts, warm valleys, or foggy coasts of this largely arid area between the Pacific Ocean and the eastern slopes of the Rocky Mountains.

Our 40th Anniversary Edition represents the first major revision since 1967. It contains the best information from previous books, but much of the text is new and reflects the latest thinking on gardening in the West, with its growing population and increasingly stretched natural resources.

In the opening chapter, "The Spirit of Western Gardening," photographs depict new plants and fresh designs that make western gardens distinctive. "A Guide to Plant Selection" lists plants that perform well in specific situations; new color photographs show hundreds of choices. Both chapters recognize recent trends in landscaping with plants that are adapted to the natural landscape.

New four-color maps outline the West's 24 climate zones and provide topographical information for the first time. Small inset maps describe weather conditions that influence local gardening in each of the West's five major population centers (Seattle, Portland, San Francisco, Los Angeles, and San Diego). Throughout the climate zones chapter, new color photographs bring to life the peculiarities of western terrain and climates that determine how we garden and the plants we can grow.

To reflect the changing marketplace for plants, we've expanded the encyclopedia by 30 pages and added to the thousands of plants listed some 76 genera, 168 species, and countless strains and varieties that have become more available in recent years, many of them from countries with climates similar to our own.

A comprehensive new "Practical Gardening Dictionary" describes gardening terms and techniques in an alphabetical and easily accessible format. It contains the latest advice on common western concerns—landscaping for wildfire protection and for water conservation, for example—and on increasingly universal concerns such as managing garden pests in environmentally friendly ways.

The *Sunset Western Garden Book* continues to recognize gardening as an art, a science, and an adventure into the natural world. We think you'll find this new version easier to use than any of its predecessors and hope that it will guide you successfully in your gardening efforts.

For their valuable assistance and continuing goodwill, we thank our consultants, listed on page 623. Special thanks also to Joseph F. Williamson and John R. Dunmire, who broke new ground with the 1967 edition, for their contributions to this 40th Anniversary Edition.

Kathleen N. Brenzel
Editor

CONTENTS

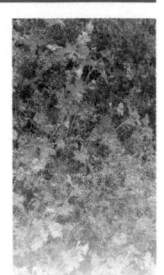

WESTERN PLANT ENCYCLOPEDIA

PRACTICAL GARDENING DICTIONARY

RESOURCE DIRECTORY

INDEXES

THE *Spirit* OF
WESTERN GARDENING

What is the "spirit of western gardening"? As you will see in the pages that follow, it's a pioneering attitude, a willingness to try new plants and fresh designs, to explore new techniques for growing plants and caring for them, or to display one-of-a-kind garden art in delightful new ways. It's the process of making our gardens as refreshingly casual, innovative—even zany—as we are.

But it's also a readiness to connect with nature, to create gardens that reflect or complement the West's natural landscapes. It's a desire to show respect for our planet's limited resources by using less water and fewer chemicals to grow often-healthier plants, while providing food and shelter for wildlife. And it's the ability to draw on our western heritage when choosing plants or deciding on a garden's style.

This spirit shows in our gardens. Whether they're quiet refuges, backyard playgrounds, or carefully decorated outdoor living rooms, they often look as though they could exist nowhere else but in the West.

Roses, pink foxglove, and silver artemisia fill a casual harborside garden in Newport Beach, California *(above)*. Old-fashioned hollyhocks lap at an adobe garden wall in Santa Fe, New Mexico *(opposite)*.

GARDEN PLANTS
from Here, There, and Everywhere

Westerners benefit from a diverse gardening heritage. In the 18th century, Spanish missionaries introduced olive trees, pepper trees, and figs. In the 19th century, explorers brought such exotic imports as dragon trees from the Canary Islands and birds of paradise from South Africa.

Today, progressive growers and nurseries continue to expand the possibilities. Each year they offer us new hybrids, new selections of old standbys, and more exotic plants from foreign lands, as well as a rich palette of native plants that can thrive in our backyards. As a result, at a neighborhood nursery in Los Angeles, we might find centuries-old imports like grapes and more recent imports like blue hibiscus offered alongside familiar California native plants like poppies and oaks.

Introductions from Western Nurseries

New hybrids are making their way into western gardens. At this nursery in Santa Barbara, California, nurseryman Randy Baldwin looks over spiky-leafed New Zealand flax, one of many plants being grown and tested. The best selections will be offered for sale.

Our Own Western Natives

Known to Native Americans centuries before European settlers arrived, West Coast native plants thrive with little care and are increasingly found in contemporary gardens. The bright yellow flowers of a flannel bush take center stage in this exuberant meadow garden at Strybing Arboretum and Botanical Gardens in San Francisco. An evergreen shrub with leathery leaves, it survives on rainfall alone and is unfazed by hot summer sun. Deep orange California poppies and perky Pacific Coast irises mingle in the floral carpet around it. The poppies flourish with or without supplemental water, while irises prefer occasional summer water. Both perennials naturalize, making them excellent candidates for open gardens where they can spread freely.

Camellia
Asia

Eucalyptus
Australia

Freesia
South Africa

Imports from Other Lands

A New Zealand tea tree, with clouds of breathtaking, hot pink blooms, makes a bold entry statement in this Berkeley, California, garden. It's one of a myriad of plants introduced into the West from other countries that have similar winter-wet, summer-dry climates. Shown at right are favored plants from five other regions of the world, and climates ranging from temperate to tropical, that are now at home in the West.

Alstroemeria
South America

Old Favorites from Yesterday's Gardens

Many old favorites are finding new fans among western gardeners. This shrubby Austrian Copper rose (**Rosa foetida** 'Bicolor'), which has petals that are orange red on the inside and yellow on the outside, is very old: the first published information on it dates back to the 1500s, although it was known for hundreds of years prior. It now brings brilliant springtime color to this New Mexico garden.

Plumeria
Mexico, Caribbean

ARTISTRY
and Invention

Western gardens reveal the exuberant spirit of their makers. Whether orderly or casual, productive or whimsical, romantic or dramatic, our gardens are playgrounds for self-expression, extensions of our personalities.

Western gardeners are an adventurous lot. We build trellises that bend vines according to our whims. We're willing to experiment with tougher new plants. And nature's ways in the West inspire and challenge us; given water shortages, intense sunlight, alkaline soil, desert winds, tight spaces, or temperature extremes, we respond with innovative designs. The results are often spectacular, unique, and rewarding.

Artful Innovation

Many western gardens are showcases for bold works of art. Sculptures like Elizabeth Rose's "The Swimmer," a steel nude shown bathing in a pond in Berkeley, California, add playfulness and a bright splash of "can't-miss-it" color to gardens.

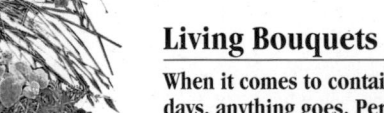

Globe Trellises

Garden trellises need never be purely functional. These 8-foot-tall metal globes, designed by Topher Delaney, are also sculptural; they're draped with wisteria, which bears pendulous lavender flowers in spring. For added drama in the evening, light fixtures in front of each trellis can bathe the vines in a blue glow.

Living Bouquets

When it comes to container planting these days, anything goes. Perennials, grasses, even shrubs now combine in such artful ways that they take on the look of a flower-filled border. This strawberry pot displays soft grasses for texture and perennials for color. In the top of the pot, the arching pink seed heads of purple fountain grass and soft golden spikes of needle grass form a spray behind the mounding velvety gray-green foliage of *Helichrysum petiolare*. Pockets are planted with blue fescue, *Nierembergia* 'Purple Robe', and white sweet alyssum.

Bountiful Border

Edibles are a frequent choice of gardeners who want to grow plants that are both attractive and flavorful. Once grown in kitchen gardens outside the back door, they are now decidedly at home in flower beds. In the California garden pictured below, designed by Rosalind Creasy, annual flowers, perennial herbs, and seasonal vegetables combine. Edible color accents are blood red chard stems, rose-purple chive flowers, nodding blue borage flowers, and cheery pansies.

Stylish Duo: Grasses and Perennials

Grasses are no longer just for lawns or prairies. In this garden, designed by Suzanne Porter, the sun-splashed flower spikes of giant feather grass rise gracefully above colorful companions in a planted pocket. Its perennial partners are New Zealand flax, with striped cream, green, and apricot swordlike leaves, yellow-flowering coreopsis (*Coreopsis auriculata* 'Nana'), and blue-spiked salvia. Clumping blue oat grass accents diagonal corners.

WESTERN GARDENS
Reflect the Region

The natural beauty of the West plays a powerful role in shaping our gardens. Whether against the dramatic backdrop of red rock cliffs in Sedona, Arizona, or in view of the ocean on Santa Barbara's riviera, western gardens reflect the unique topography, soils, and climate of the areas in which we live. Many of our garden plants have evolved naturally on the hills and in the fields and valleys around us. While some gardeners still hope to reshape the desert into a lush oasis, many choose a more natural approach, opting to mimic the surroundings with harmonious plantings.

The gardens shown here, imbued with a refreshing sense of place, combine native or naturally adapted plants with structural materials that echo the intrinsic beauty of thcir regions. Some of them are even designed so that they visually jump their boundaries and embrace the surrounding landscape.

Wild for Wildflowers

This colorful jumble of wildflowers, in an untamed garden in Northern California, looks as though it could have been lifted intact from a planted-by-nature hillside nearby. Sunny orange California poppies surround the dainty white and pink flowers of perennial Santa Barbara daisies. Low mats of blooming plants grow from rock crevices, enhancing the wild look.

Green as the Northwest Woods

This serene garden on the Lakewold estate in Tacoma, Washington, is green most of the year. But in spring, it erupts with pink and white blooms, from dogwoods to rhododendrons, azaleas to tulips. Boxwood parterres add to the garden's formal look.

California Casual

A "classic California landscape of Mediterranean heritage" best describes this garden in Napa Valley, California, designed by Jack Chandler. Borrowing from the history of the garden's original Italian owners, Chandler has created a romantic space that caresses the senses in traditional Mediterranean style; plants play a key role in providing the pleasures of sight, sound, and smell. Fountain grass captures light in its rosy plumes and ripples gently in the slightest breeze. Lavender perfumes the air, and blue hibiscus adds bright spots of color. All complement the vineyards and dry, oak-studded hills beyond the garden's walls.

Southwestern Room with a View

Colorful islands of heat-resistant plants ornament this outdoor room in New Mexico. The low wall and see-through doors invite the Southwest scenery in, while giving structure to the relaxed plantings of yellow-flowering verbascum *(foreground)*, red penstemon, and golden yarrow and gray lamb's ears beyond the curving path.

Inspired by the Coast

Framed by soft gray-green olive trees and edged with a hedge of dark green myoporum, this Southern California garden, designed by Ray Sodomka, makes a serene transition from the home it surrounds to the neighboring wetlands. Its sand dune, dotted with boulders and planted with rosemary, lavender, statice, and clumps of fountain grass, mimics the coast's muted natural dunes.

13

Rocky Mountain Rustic

Against the scenic backdrop of split-rail fences, fields, and distant mountains, this border planting near Aspen, Colorado, has the light, lacy look of a meadow in bloom. Plants include blue and yellow pansies, white ox-eye daisy, deep blue *Campanula glomerata*, and tall, purplish dame's rocket. Another favorite perennial for Rocky Mountain gardens is columbine, pictured below.

Desert at the Door

Though natural beauty draws people to the West, that beauty is often the first thing to go when new houses are built. This house in Tucson, Arizona, touches the land lightly. The owners positioned and built it to incorporate as many of the existing native plants on the site as possible. Then they filled in their garden with more native and desert-compatible plants. Along the entry walk, splashes of color come from self-sowing, unthirsty plants like white blackfoot daisy in the foreground, lavender pink *Verbena gooddingii,* and tall Parry's penstemon. Paths of the native decomposed granite merge with the desert beyond.

The West's 24 CLIMATE ZONES

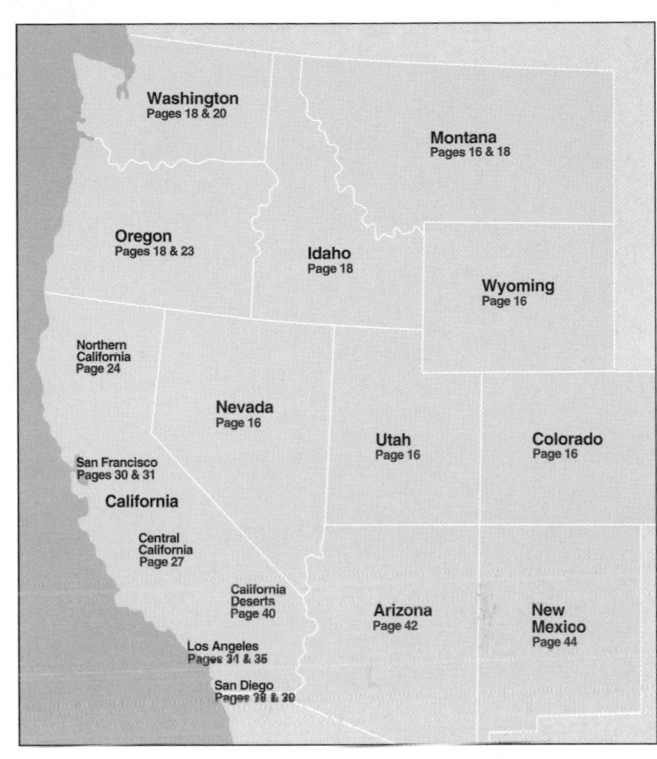

To find your garden's climate zone, start with this locator map and then turn to the page listed for your area. If you garden in a microclimate—a windy passage, thermal belt, cold pocket, hilltop, or canyon that's too small to register on the maps—adjust your climate zone accordingly.

In this book, we've assigned climate zones to almost every listed plant. If you've been gardening long, you know why: some plants can't handle winter cold, while others require it; some suffer in coastal humidity, while others depend on damp air—and so it goes. Six important factors determine each of our two dozen climate zones:

Latitude. Generally, the farther a spot is from the equator, the longer and colder are its winters. Also, as you move toward the poles, length of daylight increases in summer and decreases in winter.

Elevation. High gardens get longer and colder winters, and lower night temperatures all year.

Ocean influence. Weather that blows in off the Pacific Ocean tends to be humid, mild, and laden with precipitation in the cool season.

Continental air influence. The North American continent originates its own weather, which—compared with coastal climates—is colder in winter, hotter in summer, and more likely to get precipitation any time of year. The farther inland you live, the stronger this continental influence.

Mountains and hills. These land formations determine whether areas beyond will be influenced most by marine air or by continental air. The Coast Ranges take some

marine influence out of the air that passes eastward over them. The Sierra-Cascades and Southern California's interior mountains further weaken marine influence. East of the Rocky Mountains, continental and arctic air dominate. In the opposite order, first the Rockies, then the interior ranges, and finally the Coast Ranges reduce the westward influence of continental air.

Local terrain. South-facing slopes get more solar heat than flat land; north-facing slopes get less. Slope also affects air flow:

Why Don't We Use USDA Climate Zones?

The U.S. Department of Agriculture employs a climate zone scheme based on winter minimum temperatures. It provides a useful plant hardiness index, but it has some important drawbacks; for example, it puts the Olympic rain forest into a zone with parts of the Sonoran Desert. Our zone scheme considers winter minimums too, but it also factors in summer highs, length of growing season, humidity, and rainfall patterns to give a more accurate picture of what will grow where. Our thanks to the University of California and the many people and institutions who helped us create and refine it.

warm air rises, cold air sinks. Because hillsides are never as cold in winter as the hilltops above them or the lower ground around them, they're called thermal belts. Lowlands into which cold air flows are called cold-air basins.

Descriptions of climate zones accompany the maps. Zones are numbered from harshest (Zone 1) to mildest (Zone 24) and presented by region—from north to south. Throughout this book, a plant's climate adaptability is indicated by zone numbers.

Growing Season

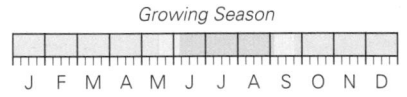

Each zone's growing season—the average number of days between the last frost in spring and the first frost in fall—is shown as a dark green band on a bar below the zone description. The light green parts of the bands indicate shoulder seasons, when light frosts could occur but wouldn't likely bother cool-season crops. Extra-mild zones along the California coast have no shoulder season, since they rarely have killing frosts (28°F or below).

Growing seasons don't tell the whole story. Zone 3 has a shorter average growing season than Zone 2, for example, but its higher year-round temperatures make it a more favorable climate for plants that need extra heat.

Nevada, Montana, Wyoming, Utah, Colorado

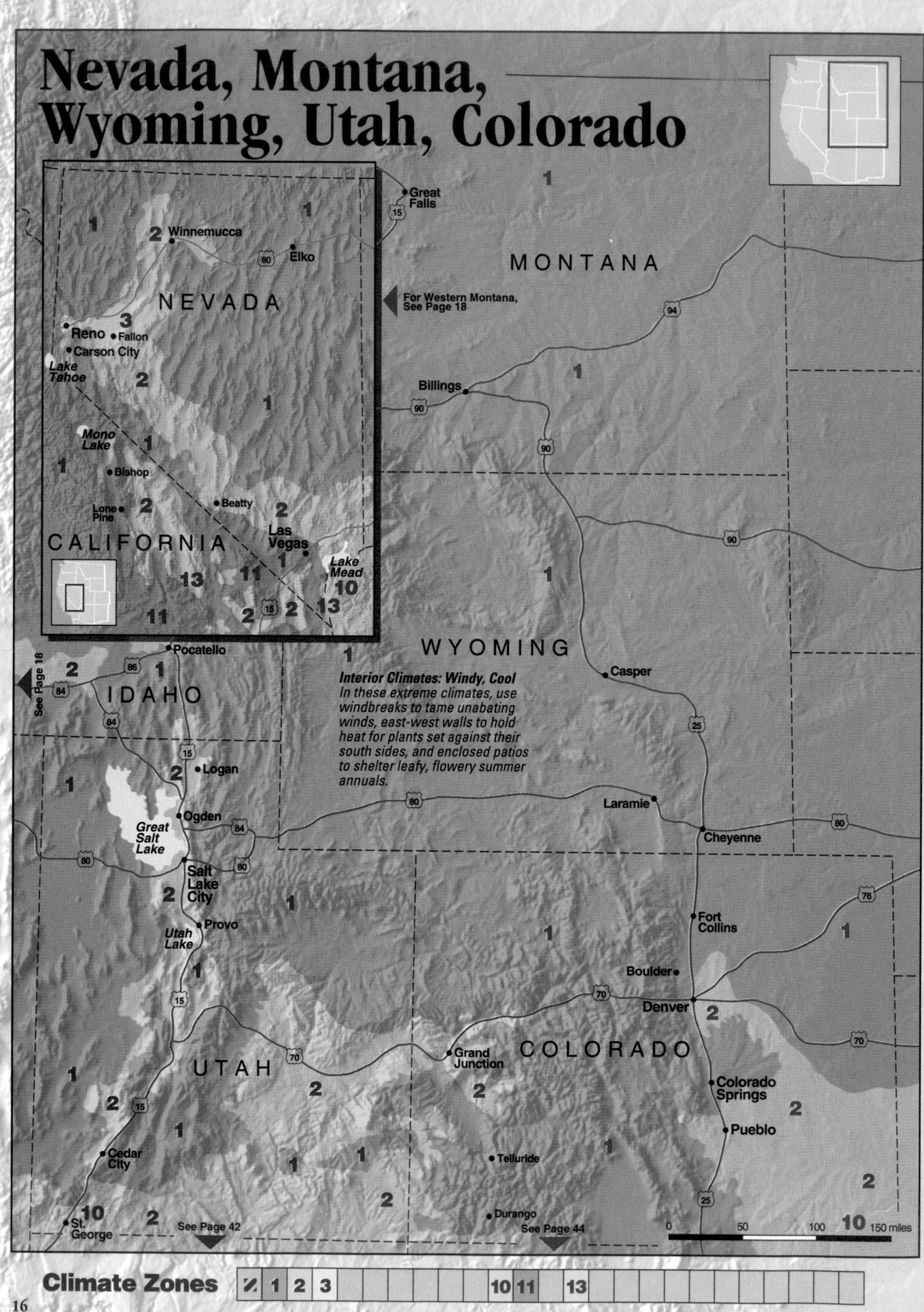

Great Falls

MONTANA

For Western Montana,
See Page 18

Winnemucca

Elko

NEVADA

Reno •Fallon
Carson City

*Lake
Tahoe*

*Mono
Lake*

•Bishop

Lone•
Pine

•Beatty

Las
Vegas

*Lake
Mead*

CALIFORNIA

Billings

Casper

Interior Climates: Windy, Cool
*In these extreme climates, use
windbreaks to tame unabating
winds, east-west walls to hold
heat for plants set against their
south sides, and enclosed patios
to shelter leafy, flowery summer
annuals.*

WYOMING

Pocatello

See Page 18

IDAHO

•Logan

•Ogden

*Great
Salt
Lake*

Salt
Lake
City

Provo•

*Utah
Lake*

Laramie

Cheyenne

Fort
Collins

Boulder•

Denver

COLORADO

Grand
Junction

UTAH

•Cedar
City

•Telluride

Colorado
Springs

•Pueblo

10
St.
George

See Page 42

•Durango

See Page 44

0   50   100   **10** 150 miles

Climate Zones   🖊 **1 2 3**   **10 11   13**

ZONE 1 Coldest Winters in the West

Zones 1, 2, and 3 are the snowy parts of the West—the regions where snow falls and stays on the ground (for a day, a week, or all winter) every year. Of the three snowy-winter climates, Zone 1 is by far the coldest.

The extreme winter cold of regions in Zone 1 can be caused by any or all of the three factors that create cold winters: latitude, influence of the continental air mass, and elevation (the higher you go, the colder it gets).

Growing Season

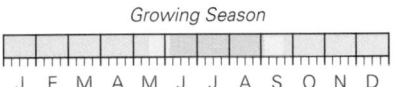

J F M A M J J A S O N D

In this zone, gardeners plant with a 75- to 150-day growing season in mind, though frosts can occur any night of the year. The zone's longer, more reliable growing seasons usually occur where large bodies of water, like Flathead Lake in Montana, moderate the winter cold.

Where Frost Is Never Far Away

Nestled in the Rocky Mountains, the town of Edwards, Colorado, has Zone 1 written all over it. High elevation, snow that's predictable, and a short growing season often combine to create a breathtaking background for a relatively small usable plant palette.

ZONE 2 Second-Coldest Western Climate

Here, as in Zone 1, snow is to be expected in winter. The chief difference between Zones 1 and 2 is that the record low temperatures and the average annual lows are lower in Zone 1 than in Zone 2. The difference is crucial: 'Sierra Beauty' and 'McIntosh' apples, for example, grow well in Zone 2, but not in Zone 1.

In Zone 2, windbreaks, trees planted for shelter, and heavy mulches can make it possible to grow plants that would otherwise perish from the effects of wind, cold, and winter sun. In addition, areas of Utah sheltered by the Wasatch Range and moderated by Great Salt Lake have milder winters than surrounding areas.

In the northerly latitudes and interior areas where the continental air mass rules supreme, determining which areas lie in Zone 2 and which lie in Zone 1 is mostly a matter of elevation. Notice that Zone 2 includes parts of the Snake River of Idaho, as well as the Grande Ronde and Burnt rivers of Oregon. It also extends along the Columbia and Spokane rivers in eastern Washington and to the lakes region of the Idaho panhandle. In Colorado, Zone 2 comprises the river valleys of the western portion of the state and the low-elevation plains in the southeast corner. Zone 2 includes most of the high territory of New Mexico; only a small portion of the state lies in Zone 1. The Zone 2 areas in California and Arizona are at higher elevations, which are nevertheless not as cold as the

higher areas of Zone 1. During a 20-year period in Zone 2, annual low temperatures ranged from $-3°$ to $-34°F.$

Growing Season

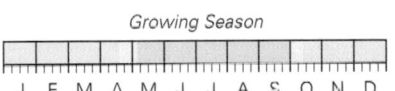

J F M A M J J A S O N D

High Interior Gardening

A meadow of thyme softens rock edges at Ohme Gardens in Wenatchee, Washington. As a ground cover, thyme is tough enough to take all the cold, ice, and snow that this part of Zone 2 can deliver and resilient enough to bounce back every spring.

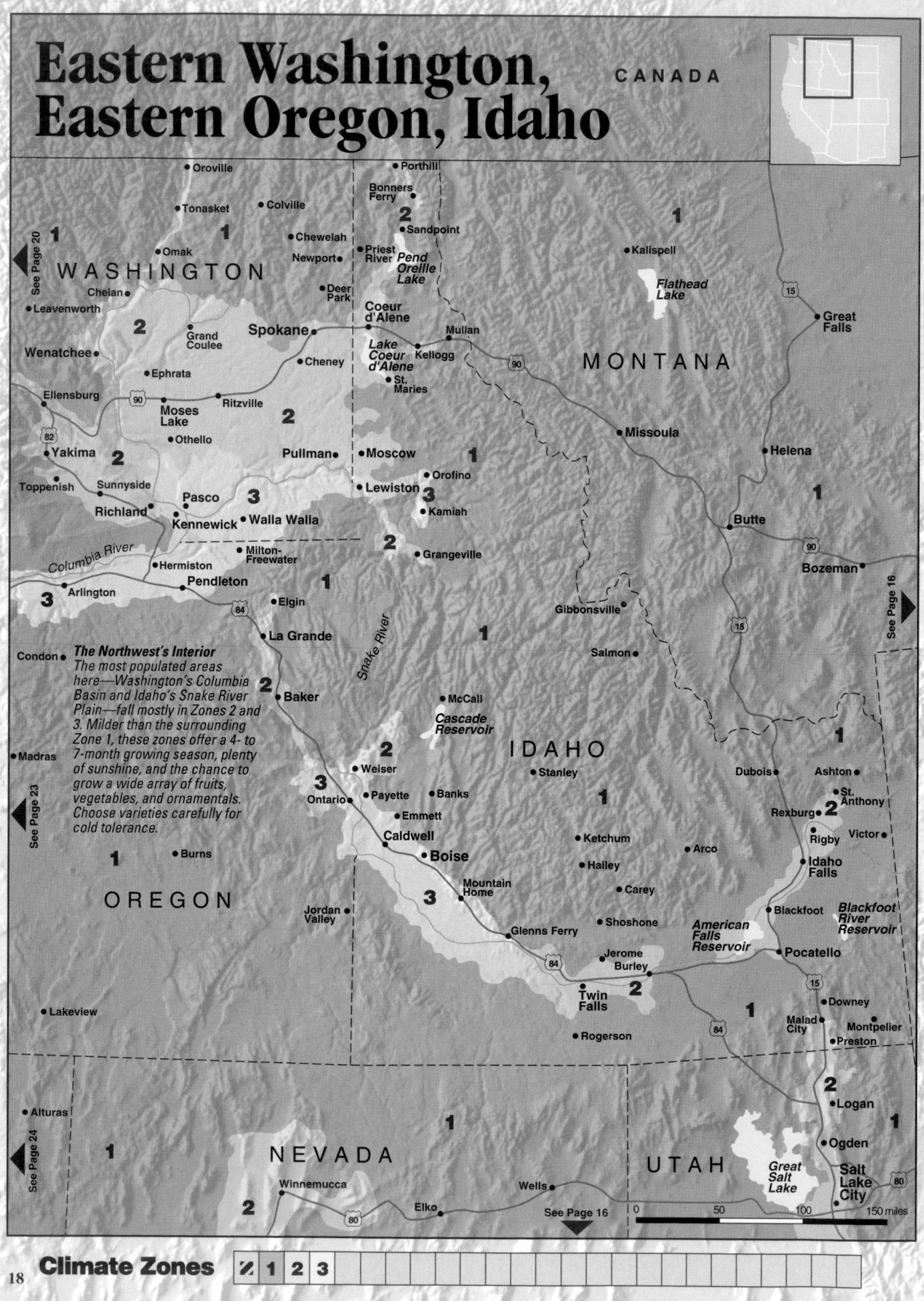

Eastern Washington, Eastern Oregon, Idaho

CANADA

The Northwest's Interior
The most populated areas here—Washington's Columbia Basin and Idaho's Snake River Plain—fall mostly in Zones 2 and 3. Milder than the surrounding Zone 1, these zones offer a 4- to 7-month growing season, plenty of sunshine, and the chance to grow a wide array of fruits, vegetables, and ornamentals. Choose varieties carefully for cold tolerance.

WASHINGTON

OREGON

IDAHO

MONTANA

NEVADA

UTAH

See Page 20
See Page 23
See Page 24
See Page 16
See Page 16

Oroville
Porthill
Bonners Ferry
Tonasket
Colville
Sandpoint
Kalispell
Chewelah
Newport
Omak
Priest River
Pend Oreille Lake
Flathead Lake
Great Falls
Chelan
Deer Park
Leavenworth
Coeur d'Alene
Mullan
Grand Coulee
Spokane
Lake Coeur d'Alene
Kellogg
Wenatchee
Cheney
St. Maries
Ephrata
Missoula
Helena
Ellensburg
Moses Lake
Ritzville
Othello
Pullman
Moscow
Yakima
Orofino
Butte
Toppenish
Sunnyside
Pasco
Lewiston
Kamiah
Bozeman
Richland
Kennewick
Walla Walla
Grangeville
Columbia River
Milton-Freewater
Hermiston
Gibbonsville
Arlington
Pendleton
Salmon
Elgin
Snake River
Condon
La Grande
Madras
Baker
McCall
Cascade Reservoir
Stanley
Dubois
Ashton
St. Anthony
Weiser
Banks
Rexburg
Victor
Payette
Rigby
Emmett
Idaho Falls
Burns
Caldwell
Ketchum
Arco
Blackfoot River Reservoir
Boise
Hailey
Blackfoot
Mountain Home
Carey
American Falls Reservoir
Jordan Valley
Shoshone
Pocatello
Glenns Ferry
Jerome
Burley
Downey
Lakeview
Twin Falls
Malad City
Montpelier
Rogerson
Preston
Logan
Alturas
Ogden
Great Salt Lake
Salt Lake City
Winnemucca
Wells
Elko

See Page 16

0   50   100   150 miles

Climate Zones   1 2 3

ZONE **3** Mildest of High-Elevation and Interior Climates

Cold Country's Banana Belt

Sheltered from Columbia Gorge winds by rows of poplars, commercial peach orchards *(above)* thrive in Zone 3, getting enough winter chill to set fruit and enough summer heat to ripen it. Columbine's exquisite flower *(below)* belies its toughness; some species are native to the intermountain West.

This is the mildest of the snowy-winter climates. East of the Cascades in the Northwest, the Zone 3 areas are the ones that are often called "banana belts." Of course, the only place you can grow the real, fruiting banana satisfactorily outdoors is in tropical climates. But the comparatively mild winter lows of Zone 3 allow gardeners to grow such plants as English boxwood and winter jasmine.

The portion of Zone 3 from the Hood River to Lewiston is slightly lower in elevation than the surrounding Zone 2. The lower elevation, combined with the influence of Pacific air that spills over the Cascades and through the Columbia Gorge, moderates most winters. Much planting is based on winter lows of 10° to 15°F. In an occasional winter, arctic air forces temperatures much lower. Such winters limit the selection of broad-leafed evergreens.

Absolute cold is not so much the enemy here as drying winds that dehydrate plants growing in frozen soil. Wind protection, mulching, shade, and careful late-autumn watering will help you grow many borderline evergreens.

In California, the Zone 3 areas often happen to be the lowest parts of the high mountains—where many cabin owners keep gardens. The zone also includes the Reno area of Nevada.

Over a 20-year period, minimum temperatures in Zone 3 ranged from 13° to −24°F. While growing seasons can be shorter in Zone 3 than in Zone 2, winter minimum temperatures are always higher in Zone 3. In Walla Walla, Washington, the growing season lasts longer than in much of Zone 3—almost 220 days.

Growing Season

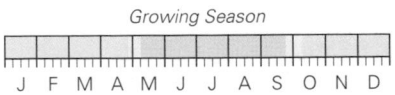

J F M A M J J A S O N D

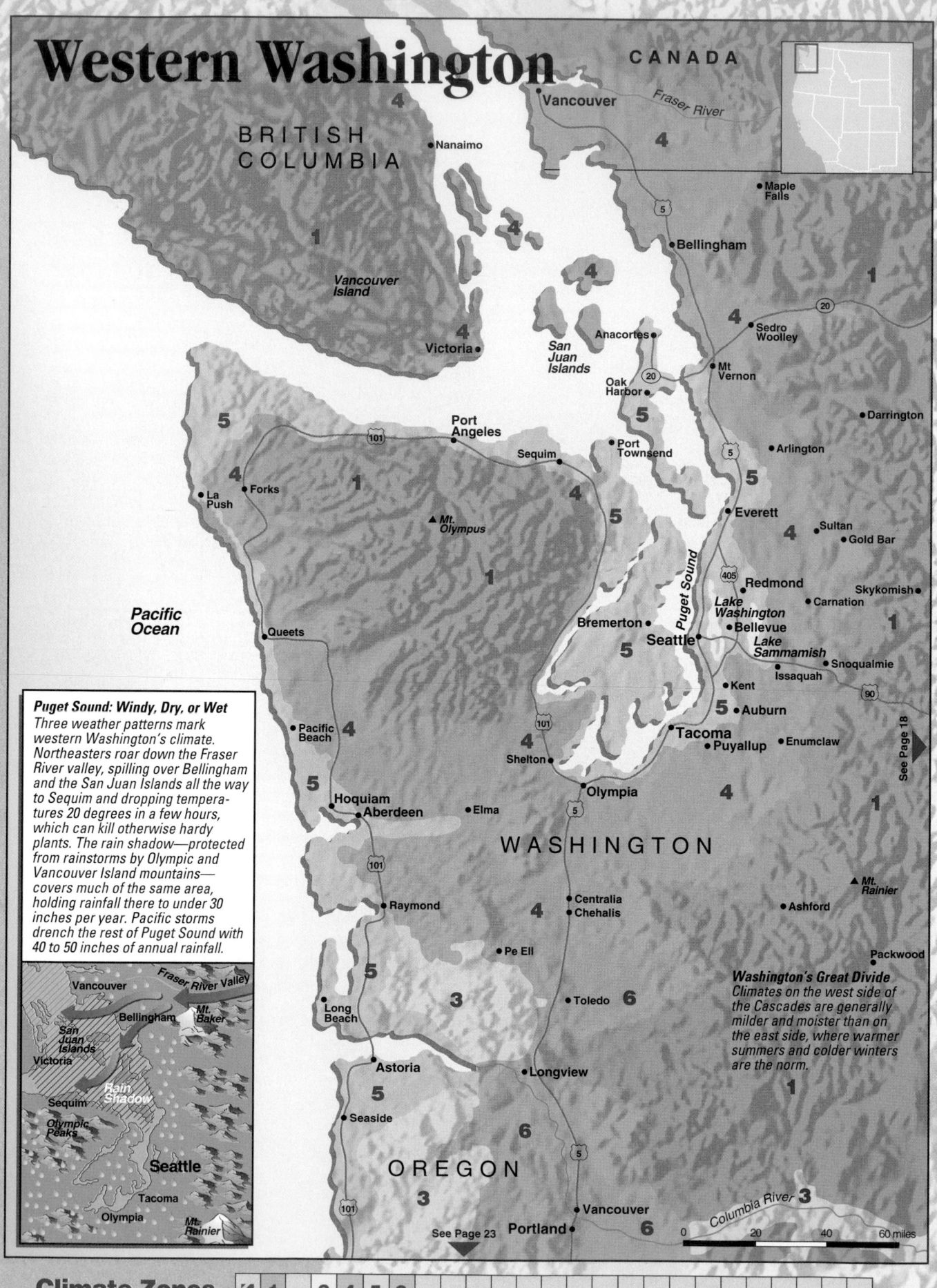

Western Washington

CANADA

Fraser River

Vancouver

BRITISH COLUMBIA

4

4

Nanaimo

Vancouver Island

1

Victoria

4

4

4

San Juan Islands

Anacortes

5

Maple Falls

Bellingham

4

Sedro Woolley

Mt Vernon

Oak Harbor

5

Darrington

Arlington

5

Port Angeles

1

Sequim

Port Townsend

5

5

Everett

Sultan

Gold Bar

4

La Push
Forks

4

5

▲ *Mt. Olympus*

1

4

5

Puget Sound

Redmond

Skykomish

Carnation

Lake Washington

Bellevue

1

Pacific Ocean

Queets

Bremerton

Seattle

Lake Sammamish

5

Snoqualmie

Issaquah

Kent

90

Pacific Beach

4

5

Auburn

Enumclaw

5

Tacoma

Puyallup

Shelton

4

5

Hoquiam
Aberdeen

Elma

Olympia

4

WASHINGTON

Ashford

▲ *Mt. Rainier*

Raymond

Centralia
Chehalis

4

Pe Ell

Packwood

5

3

Toledo

6

Long Beach

Longview

5

Astoria

Seaside

6

OREGON

3

Vancouver

6

Portland

Columbia River 3

3

Puget Sound: Windy, Dry, or Wet

Three weather patterns mark western Washington's climate. Northeasters roar down the Fraser River valley, spilling over Bellingham and the San Juan Islands all the way to Sequim and dropping temperatures 20 degrees in a few hours, which can kill otherwise hardy plants. The rain shadow—protected from rainstorms by Olympic and Vancouver Island mountains— covers much of the same area, holding rainfall there to under 30 inches per year. Pacific storms drench the rest of Puget Sound with 40 to 50 inches of annual rainfall.

Washington's Great Divide

Climates on the west side of the Cascades are generally milder and moister than on the east side, where warmer summers and colder winters are the norm.

Vancouver

Fraser River Valley

Bellingham

Mt. Baker

San Juan Islands

Victoria

Rain Shadow

Sequim

Olympic Peaks

Seattle

Tacoma

Olympia

Mt. Rainier

See Page 18

See Page 23

0   20   40   60 miles

20   **Climate Zones**   ⧄ 1   3 4 5 6

ZONE 4   Cold-Winter Parts of Western Washington and British Columbia

One of the smallest climate zones in the West, Zone 4 is the region west of the Cascades whose climate gets considerable influence from the Pacific Ocean and Puget Sound—but also from the continental air mass, or higher elevation, or both. The zone touches salt water only in Skagit, San Juan, and Whatcom counties and British Columbia, so the influence of marine air is less powerful than in other western zones.

Zone 4 differs from neighboring Zone 5 in that it has extremely low winter temperatures more frequently, a shorter growing season, and, in most locations, considerably more rainfall. No zone grows better perennials and bulbs; people who like woodland plants and rock plants love Zone 4.

Zones 4 and 5 can be found in the same neighborhood, a fact that explains much of the familiar northwestern talk about warm or cold gardens. Over a 20-year period, average winter lows in Zone 4 ranged from 19° down to −7°F.

Tulip Country

Washington's Skagit Valley has just the right soil and climate for growing commercial tulip crops, which wouldn't do as well in warmer climates. On the other hand, some of the tenderer rhododendrons that Seattle grows would freeze here.

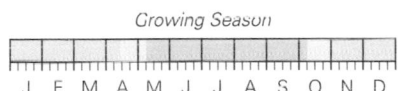

Growing Season

J F M A M J J A S O N D

ZONE 5   Marine Influence Along the Northwest Coast and Puget Sound

Mild ocean air brings relatively warm winters to this area, which is on the same latitude as Duluth, Minnesota, and Bangor, Maine. The region is one of the world's great centers of rhododendron culture and rock gardens.

Over a 20-year period, minimum temperatures ranged from 28° to 1°F. The occasional big freeze, with temperatures plummeting to near 0°F, does considerable damage if it comes very early or very late, when plants are not conditioned for such cold. But these occasional big freezes should not serve as the gauge of hardiness

Waterside Gardening

These astilbes and dogwoods thrive in a woodland garden near Lake Washington. The climate in Zone 5 is much like that of southern England, and the gardens here have benefited from England's long and successful search for more varied garden plants.

required for plants here, for even normally tough native plants have been killed or injured by such freezes.

Many waterside areas show a very low heat accumulation in the summer. To grow heat-loving plants, pick out the hottest spots for them—a south wall or a west wall sheltered from cold winds will almost always supply such heat—and select peach and tomato varieties with low heat needs. The mildness in these areas favors flowering plants: It stretches out the bloom season of everything from fuchsias to calendulas.

The lowlands around Puget Sound and along the coast were once covered with forest, so native woodland plants like trillium, piggy-back plant, and a host of ferns thrive here, as do shade-tolerant trees like vine maples and dogwoods.

Growing Season

J F M A M J J A S O N D

ZONE 6 Willamette Valley

Warmer summers help distinguish the Willamette Valley climate from the climate of Zone 5. In the north, the Willamette can also have a much longer growing season: 279 days in Portland. The Coast Range tempers the coastal winds and somewhat reduces the rainfall, but the climate of the valley is still essentially maritime much of the year. This means that it gets much less winter cold and less summer heat than zones east of the Cascades.

This zone also stretches north along the Columbia River between Portland and Longview, then up the Cowlitz River a few miles.

Average lows are similar to those of Zone 5—even slightly colder in some places—but summer high temperatures average 5° to 9°F warmer, warm enough to put sugar in the 'Elberta' peaches and to speed the growth of such evergreens as abelia and nandina. The long, mild growing season has made the Willamette Valley one

Growing Fields for Trees

The Portland area's long growing season, deep soil, and pronounced winter chill make it nearly perfect for growing nursery stock. These young shade trees in view of Mount Hood *(below)* will be dug and shipped to nurseries all over the United States.

Coated with Ice

Ice on plants, caused by ice storms blowing into Portland from cold eastern areas, is sublimely beautiful. But its weight can break tree branches and flatten meadow grasses against the ground, as shown here.

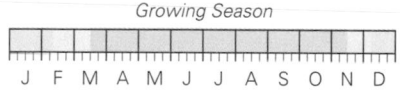

Growing Season

J F M A M J J A S O N D

of the West's best-known growing areas for berries, hazelnuts, and nursery stock. Many of the West's (and the nation's) fruit and shade trees, deciduous shrubs, and broadleafed evergreens start life here.

Any mention of this zone must include roses and rhododendrons, both of which attain near-perfection here. Broad-leafed evergreens generally are at their best; choice azaleas and pieris join rhododendrons as the basic landscaping shrubs.

You'll encounter the zone's only anomaly east of Portland, where icy winter winds blow down out of the Columbia.

All in a Portland Dell

Rhododendrons are among the broadleafed evergreens that mark Zone 6. They're shown off in Portland's Crystal Springs Rhododendron Garden *(above)*.

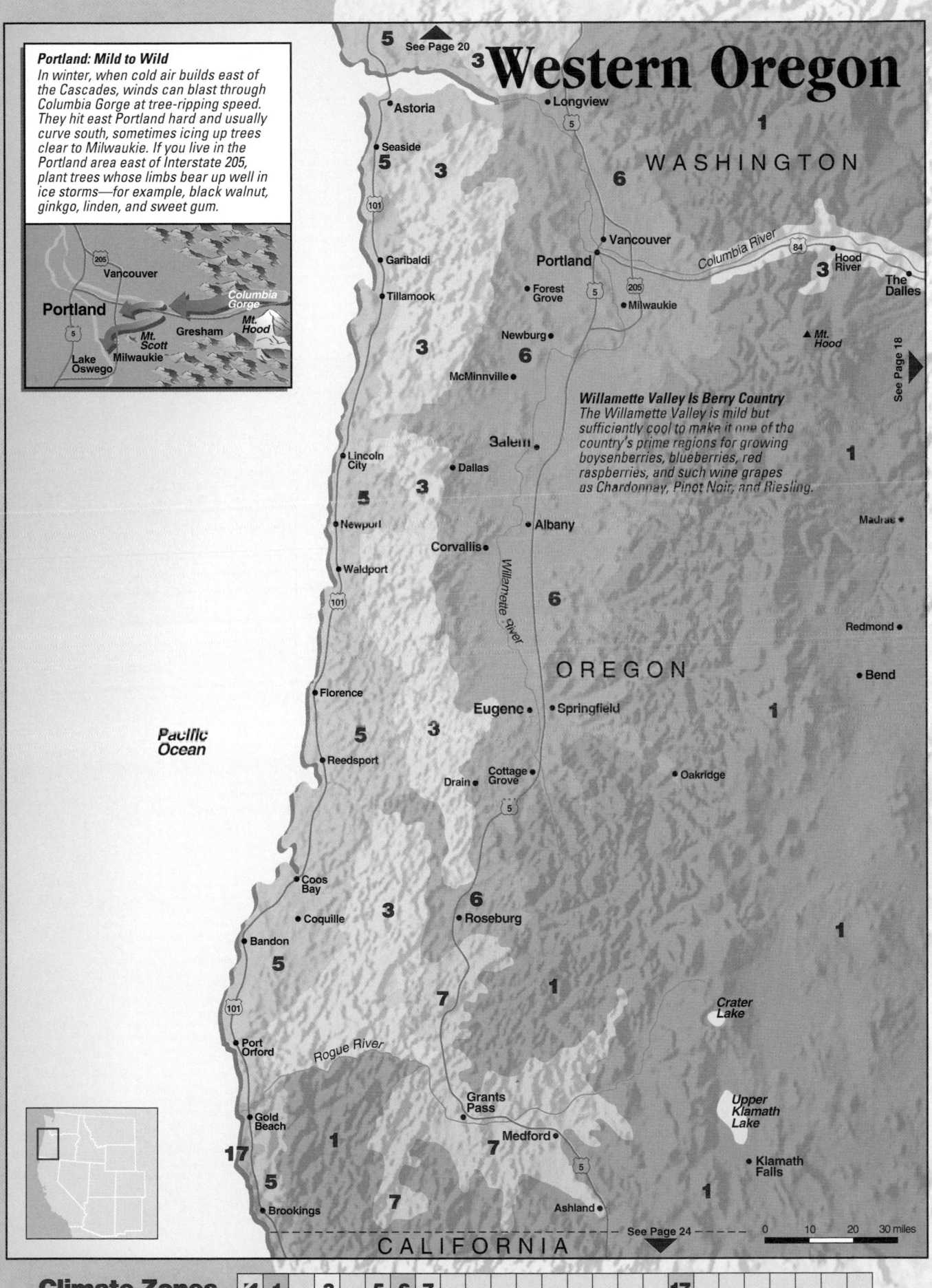

See Page 20

Western Oregon

Portland: Mild to Wild
In winter, when cold air builds east of the Cascades, winds can blast through Columbia Gorge at tree-ripping speed. They hit east Portland hard and usually curve south, sometimes icing up trees clear to Milwaukie. If you live in the Portland area east of Interstate 205, plant trees whose limbs bear up well in ice storms—for example, black walnut, ginkgo, linden, and sweet gum.

Vancouver
Portland
Lake Oswego
Milwaukie
Gresham
Mt. Scott
Mt. Hood
Columbia Gorge
205
5

5

3

WASHINGTON

1

Longview

6

Astoria

5
Seaside

3

Garibaldi

Tillamook

Vancouver
Portland
Forest Grove
Milwaukie

Newburg

McMinnville

3

6

Columbia River

Hood River
3
The Dalles

Mt. Hood

See Page 18

Willamette Valley Is Berry Country
The Willamette Valley is mild but sufficiently cool to make it one of the country's prime regions for growing boysenberries, blueberries, red raspberries, and such wine grapes as Chardonnay, Pinot Noir, and Riesling.

Salem

Dallas

Lincoln City
5

3

Newport

Waldport

Corvallis

Albany

6

Willamette River

1

Madras

OREGON

Redmond

Bend

Florence

5

Reedsport

3

Eugene
Springfield

1

Cottage Grove
Drain

Oakridge

Coos Bay

Coquille

3

Roseburg
6

Bandon

5

7

1

Crater Lake

Port Orford

Rogue River

Gold Beach

17

1

Upper Klamath Lake

Grants Pass

Medford
7

5

7

Ashland

1

Klamath Falls

1

Brookings

Pacific Ocean

See Page 24

0   10   20   30 miles

CALIFORNIA

Climate Zones 1   3   5 6 7   17

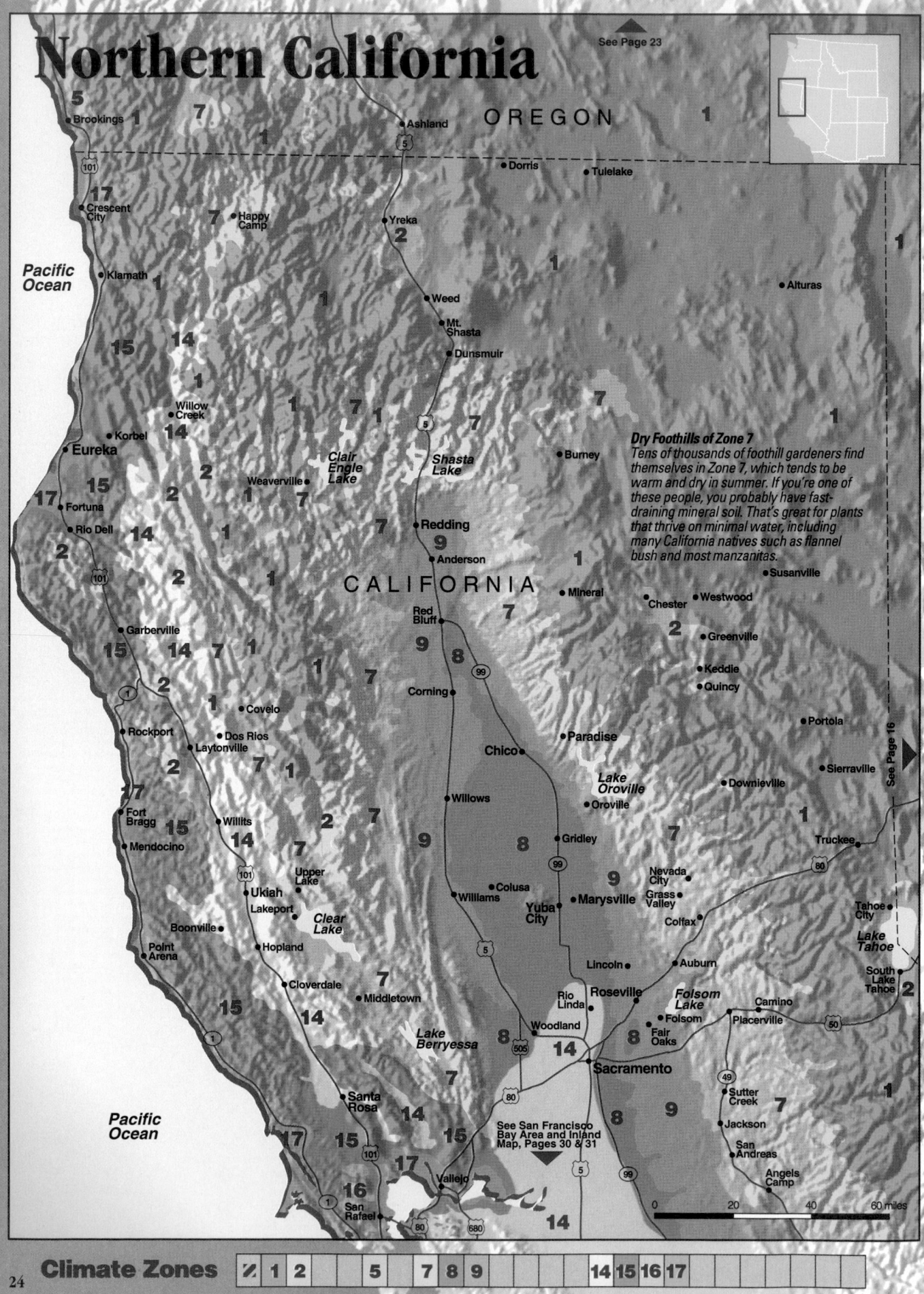

Northern California

See Page 23

OREGON

5
Brookings 1   7   • Ashland   1

1

Dorris •   • Tulelake

17
• Crescent City

7   • Happy Camp   • Yreka   2

Pacific Ocean

• Klamath   1   1   • Weed   • Alturas

15   14   • Mt. Shasta

1   • Dunsmuir

• Willow Creek

14   • Korbel   1   7   1   7   • Burney

Eureka   2   • Weaverville   *Clair Engle Lake*   *Shasta Lake*

15   2   1   7

17   • Fortuna   14   7   • Redding

• Rio Dell   1   9

2   2   • Anderson   1   • Mineral

C A L I F O R N I A

Dry Foothills of Zone 7
Tens of thousands of foothill gardeners find themselves in Zone 7, which tends to be warm and dry in summer. If you're one of these people, you probably have fast-draining mineral soil. That's great for plants that thrive on minimal water, including many California natives such as flannel bush and most manzanitas.

• Susanville

• Chester • Westwood

2   • Greenville

• Garberville   14   7   1   Red Bluff   7   • Keddie

15   9   8   • Quincy

2   1   7   99   • Portola

• Covelo   Corning •   • Paradise

• Rockport   14   7   1   • Downieville   • Sierraville

• Dos Rios   Chico •

2   • Laytonville   *Lake Oroville*

7   1   • Willows   • Oroville   1

7   • Truckee

• Fort Bragg   15   • Willits   14   2   9   8   • Gridley   Nevada City   80

• Mendocino   7   9   • Colusa   Grass Valley

Upper Lake   • Williams   • Marysville   • Colfax   Tahoe City

• **Ukiah**   Yuba City   *Lake Tahoe*

Lakeport   *Clear Lake*

• Boonville   • Lincoln   • Auburn   South Lake Tahoe   2

Point Arena   • Hopland   • Roseville   *Folsom Lake*   • Camino

15   7   Rio Linda   • Folsom   • Placerville   50

• Cloverdale   • Middletown   Woodland   8   Fair Oaks

14   *Lake Berryessa*   505   14   49

15   • Santa Rosa   7   **Sacramento**   • Sutter Creek   7

17   14   8   9   • Jackson

15   15   See San Francisco Bay Area and Inland Map, Pages 30 & 31   • San Andreas

17   99

16   • Vallejo   • Angels Camp

Pacific Ocean   • San Rafael   80   680   14

0   20   40   60 miles

See San Francisco Bay Area and Inland Map, Pages 30 & 31

Climate Zones | / | 1 | 2 | | 5 | | 7 | 8 | 9 | | 14 | 15 | 16 | 17 |

ZONE **7** California's Digger Pine Belt and Oregon's Rogue River Valley

At Home in the Foothills

Digger pines *(left)*, also called foothill or gray pines, mark much of Zone 7. Often you'll find them mixed with oaks, ponderosa pines, and even knobcone pines.

Zone 7 encompasses several thousand square miles in the regions west of the Sierra Nevada and Cascade ranges. Because of the influence of latitude, this climate is found at low elevations in a valley in Oregon (the Rogue Valley) but at middle elevations in California (the low mountains, most of which can be identified by native digger pines).

Hot summers and mild but pronounced winters give this area sharply defined seasons without severe winter cold or enervating humidity. The climate pleases plants that require a marked seasonal pattern to do well — peony, iris, lilac, and flowering cherry, for example. Deciduous fruit trees that require a marked seasonal pattern do well also; the region is noted for its pears, apples, peaches, and cherries.

Gardeners in a few spots around the San Francisco Bay will be surprised to find their gardens mapped in Zone 7, even though there isn't a digger pine to be seen. These are hilltop and ridge-top areas that are too high (and hence too cold in winter) to be included in milder Zones 15 and 16.

For such a big area, it is impossible to state exact low temperatures. But at weather-recording stations in Zone 7, the typical winter lows range from 23° to 9°F, and the record lows vary from 15° to −1°F.

Wild and Tamed Native Oaks

Valley oaks *(top)* dot grassy, rolling foothills in many parts of Zone 7. You can garden under native oaks if you limit your palette to plants that don't need summer water, such as airy grasses, sedges, and *Salvia (above)*.

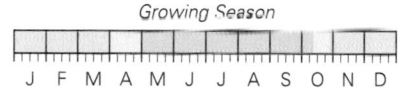

Growing Season

J F M A M J J A S O N D

ZONE **8** Cold-Air Basins of California's Central Valley

Only a shade of difference exists between Zone 8 and Zone 9, but it's an important difference — crucial in some cases. Zone 9 is a thermal belt, meaning that cold air can flow from it to lower ground — and that lower ground is found here in Zone 8. Citrus furnish the most meaningful illustration. Lemons, oranges, and grapefruit, which flourish in Zone 9, cannot be grown commercially in Zone 8 because the winter nights are frequently cold enough to injure the fruit or the trees; the trees would need regular heating to deliver decent crops. The same winter cold can damage many garden plants.

Zone 8 differs from Zone 14, which it joins near the latitudes of north Sacramento and Modesto, in that Zone 14 occasionally gets some marine influence. Low temperatures in Zone 8 over a 20-year period ranged from 29° to 13°F. Certain features that Zones 8 and 9 share are described under Zone 9.

Orchard Country

Cold air rolls off Zone 9 hillsides on winter nights and pools in the colder flatlands — Zone 8 — below. Fruit trees that need chill, like these apple trees near Winters, grow best in the valleys.

Growing Season

J F M A M J J A S O N D

ZONE 9 Thermal Belts of California's Central Valley

As cited in the description of Zone 8, the biggest readily apparent difference between Zones 8 and 9 is that Zone 9, a thermal belt, is a safer climate for citrus than Zone 8, which is a cold-air basin. The same distinction, thermal belt versus cold-air basin, determines which species and varieties—hibiscus, melaleuca, pittosporum, and other plants—are recommended for Zone 9 but not for Zone 8.

Zones 8 and 9 have the following features in common: summer daytime temperatures are high, sunshine is almost constant during the growing season, and growing seasons are long. Deciduous fruits and vegetables of nearly every kind thrive in these long, hot summers; winter cold is just adequate to satisfy the dormancy requirements of the fruit trees. Fiercely cold, piercing north winds blow for several days at a time in winter, but they are more distressing to gardeners than to garden plants. You can minimize them with windbreaks.

Tule fogs (dense fogs that rise from the ground on cold, clear nights) appear and stay for hours or days during winter. The fogs usually hug the ground at night and rise to 800 to 1,000 feet by afternoon.

Heat-loving plants such as oleander and crape myrtle perform at their peak in Zones 8 and 9 (and 14). Plants that like summer coolness and humidity demand some fussing; careful gardeners accommodate them by providing filtered shade from tall trees and plenty of moisture. In Zone 9, winter lows over a 20-year period ranged from 28° to 18°F.

Growing Season

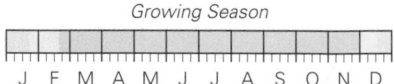

J F M A M J J A S O N D

For Zones 10 to 13, an area that includes the Southwest deserts, turn to pages 41–43.

True Heat-Lovers

Oleanders love heat and thrive in the interior valleys of Zones 8 and 9. But they don't do well where winter temperatures regularly plummet, preferring climates that are moderated by marine air.

The Tule Fog

Zone 9 hills rise into the clear air above the fog-shrouded flatlands of surrounding Zone 8. In winter, dense tule fogs can blanket both Zones 8 and 9 by afternoon, closing roads throughout the Central Valley. The picture above was taken near Bakersfield.

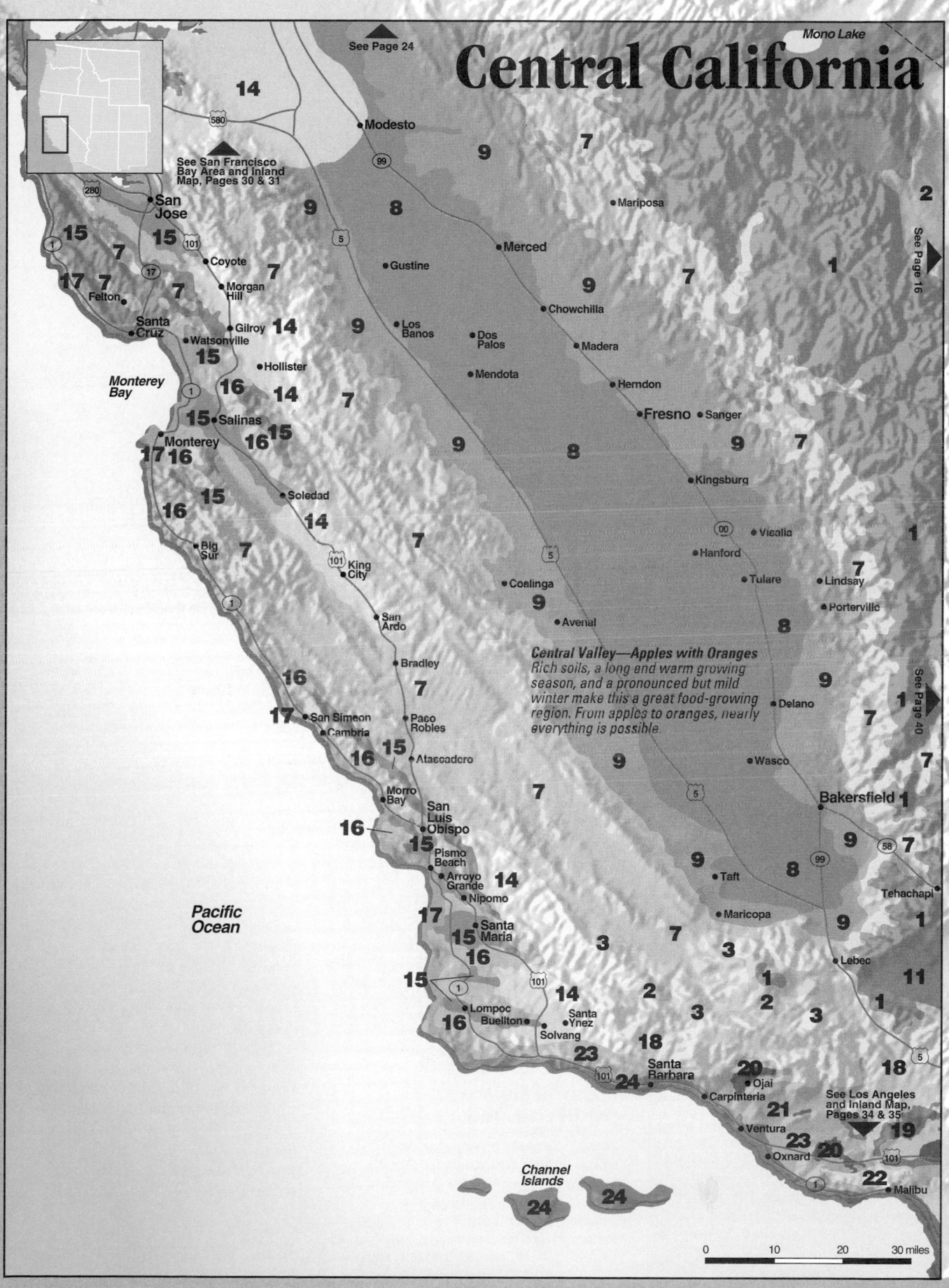

Central California

See Page 24

Mono Lake

14

580

Modesto

9 **7**

See San Francisco Bay Area and Inland Map, Pages 30 & 31

2

San Jose

8

Mariposa

15 **15**

7

9 Merced **1**

17 **7** **7** Coyote **9** **7**

Felton **7** Morgan Hill

Santa Cruz **14** Gustine Los Banos Chowchilla

Watsonville Gilroy **9** Dos Palos Madera

15 Hollister Mendota **9** Herndon

16 **14** **7** Fresno Sanger

Monterey Bay Salinas **15** **8** **9** **7**

17 **16** **16** **15** Kingsburg

Soledad **14** Vicalia **1**

15 **9** Hanford **7**

16 Big Sur **7** King City **8** Coalinga **9** Tulare Lindsay

9 Avenal Porterville

San Ardo **8**

Bradley

16 **7**

Central Valley—Apples with Oranges
Rich soils, a long and warm growing
season, and a pronounced but mild
winter make this a great food-growing
region. From apples to oranges, nearly
everything is possible.

Delano **9** **1**

17 San Simeon Cambria Paso Robles **7**

15 Atascadero **9** Wasco **7**

16 **7**

Morro Bay **7** Bakersfield **1**

San Luis Obispo **9** **58** **7**

16 **8** **99**

15 Pismo Beach **9** Taft **8**

Arroyo Grande **14** Tehachapi

Nipomo **7** Maricopa **9**

17 **3** **1**

15 Santa Maria **3** **3** Lebec **11**

16 **2** **1**

15 **14** **3** **2** **1** **18**

Lompoc Buellton Santa Ynez **3**

16 Solvang **18**

23 See Los Angeles and Inland Map, Pages 34 & 35

24 Santa Barbara **20**

Ojai **19**

Carpinteria **21**

Ventura **23**

Pacific Ocean

Oxnard **20** **22**

Channel Islands Malibu

24 **24**

0   10   20   30 miles

Climate Zones ⬜ 1 2 3   7 8 9   11   14 15 16 17 18 19 20 21 22 23 24

ZONE 14 Northern California's Inland Areas with Some Ocean Influence

Marine air moderates parts of Zone 14 that otherwise would be colder in winter and hotter in summer. The gap in Northern California's Coast Ranges created by San Francisco and San Pablo bays allows marine air to spill much farther inland than it can anywhere else. The same thing happens, but the penetration is not as deep, in the Salinas Valley. Zone 14 also includes the cold-winter valley floors, canyons, and land troughs in the Coast Ranges from Santa Barbara County to Mendocino County.

The milder-winter, marine-influenced areas in Zone 14 and the cold-winter inland valleys within Zone 14 differ in humidity. For example, lowland parts of Contra Costa County are more humid than Sacramento.

Fruits that need winter chilling do well here, as do shrubs needing summer heat (oleander, gardenia). Over a 20-year period, this area had lows ranging from 26° to 16°F. Weather bureau records show all-time lows ranging from 20° down to 11°F.

Perfect for Vineyards

Vineyards blanket much of the land in Napa and Sonoma counties, producing hefty crops for wineries. The valley floors here are designated Zone 14.

Growing Season

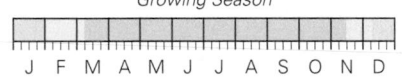

J F M A M J J A S O N D

ZONE 15 Chilly Winters Along the Coast Range

Zones 15 and 16 are areas of Central and Northern California that are influenced by marine air approximately 85 percent of the time and by inland air 15 percent of the time. Note that although Zone 16 is within the Northern California coastal climate area, its winters are milder because the areas in this zone are in thermal belts (explained on page 15). The cold-winter areas that make up Zone 15 lie in cold-air basins, on hilltops above the thermal belts, or far enough north that plant performance dictates a Zone 15 designation.

Many plants recommended for Zone 15 are not suggested for Zone 14 because they must have a moister atmosphere, cooler summers, milder winters, or all three conditions. On the other hand, Zone 15 still receives enough winter chilling to favor some of the cold-winter specialties, such as herbaceous peonies (not recommended for Zones 16 and 17).

Most of this zone gets a nagging afternoon wind in summer. Trees and dense shrubs planted on the windward side of a garden can disperse it, and a neighborhood full of trees can successfully keep it above the rooftops. Low temperatures over a 20-year period ranged from 28° to 21°F, and record lows range from 26° to 16°F.

Plenty of Moist Air, but Dry Air, Too

Zone 15 is moist enough for coast redwoods *(above left)* to thrive. Yet it's warm and dry enough to grow agave and cacti *(left)*. Both plantings were photographed at Sunset's Menlo Park headquarters; the redwoods, now towering more than 80 feet tall, were planted in 1952 from 7-gallon cans.

Growing Season

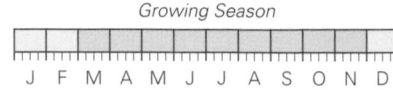

J F M A M J J A S O N D

ZONE 16 Central and Northern California Coast Thermal Belts

This benign climate exists in patches and strips along the Coast Ranges from western Santa Barbara County north to northern Marin County. It's one of Northern California's finest horticultural climates. It consists of thermal belts (slopes from which cold air drains) in the coastal climate area, which is dominated by ocean weather about 85 percent of the time and by inland weather about 15 percent.

Typical lows in Zone 16 over a 20-year period ranged from 32° to 19°F. The lowest recorded temperatures range from 25° to 18°F. This zone gets more heat in summer than Zone 17, which is dominated by maritime air, and has warmer winters than Zone 15. That's a happy combination for gardening.

A summer afternoon wind is an integral part of this climate. Plant trees and shrubs on the windward side of your garden to help disperse it.

Growing Season

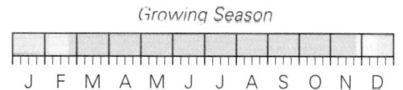

J F M A M J J A S O N D

Warm Slopes with a View

Parts of Zone 16, such as the Oakland-Berkeley hills *(left)*, practically never see a white frost. This zone gets more heat in summer than Zone 17 and has warmer winters than Zone 15—great for subtropicals like ginger lily *(below)*.

ZONE 17 Marine Effects in Northern California

The climate in this zone features cool, wet, almost frostless winters and cool summers with frequent fog or wind. On most days and in most places, the fog tends to come in high and fast, creating a cooling and humidifying blanket between the sun and the earth, reducing the intensity of the light and sunshine. Some heat-loving plants (citrus, hibiscus, gardenia) don't get enough heat to fruit or flower reliably.

In a 20-year period, the lowest winter temperatures in Zone 17 ranged from 36° to 23°F. The lowest temperatures on record at the various weather stations range from 30° to 20°F. Of further interest in this heat-starved climate are the highs of summer, normally in the 60° to 75°F range. The average highest temperature of 12 weather stations in Zone 17 is only 97°F. In all the other Northern California climate zones, average highest temperatures on record are in the 104° to 116°F range.

Growing Season

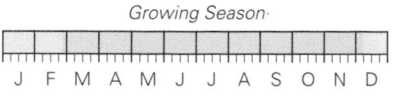

J F M A M J J A S O N D

Smell the Sea, See the Aloes

Zone 17's climate is dominated by the ocean about 98 percent of the time. You can see salt water from most areas in Zone 17, such as Pacific Grove, where mounding aloes and agaves with tall flower spikes bloom at the water's edge. This climate also favors fuchsias and commercially grown artichokes, Brussels sprouts, and Easter lilies.

29

San Francisco Bay Area and Inland

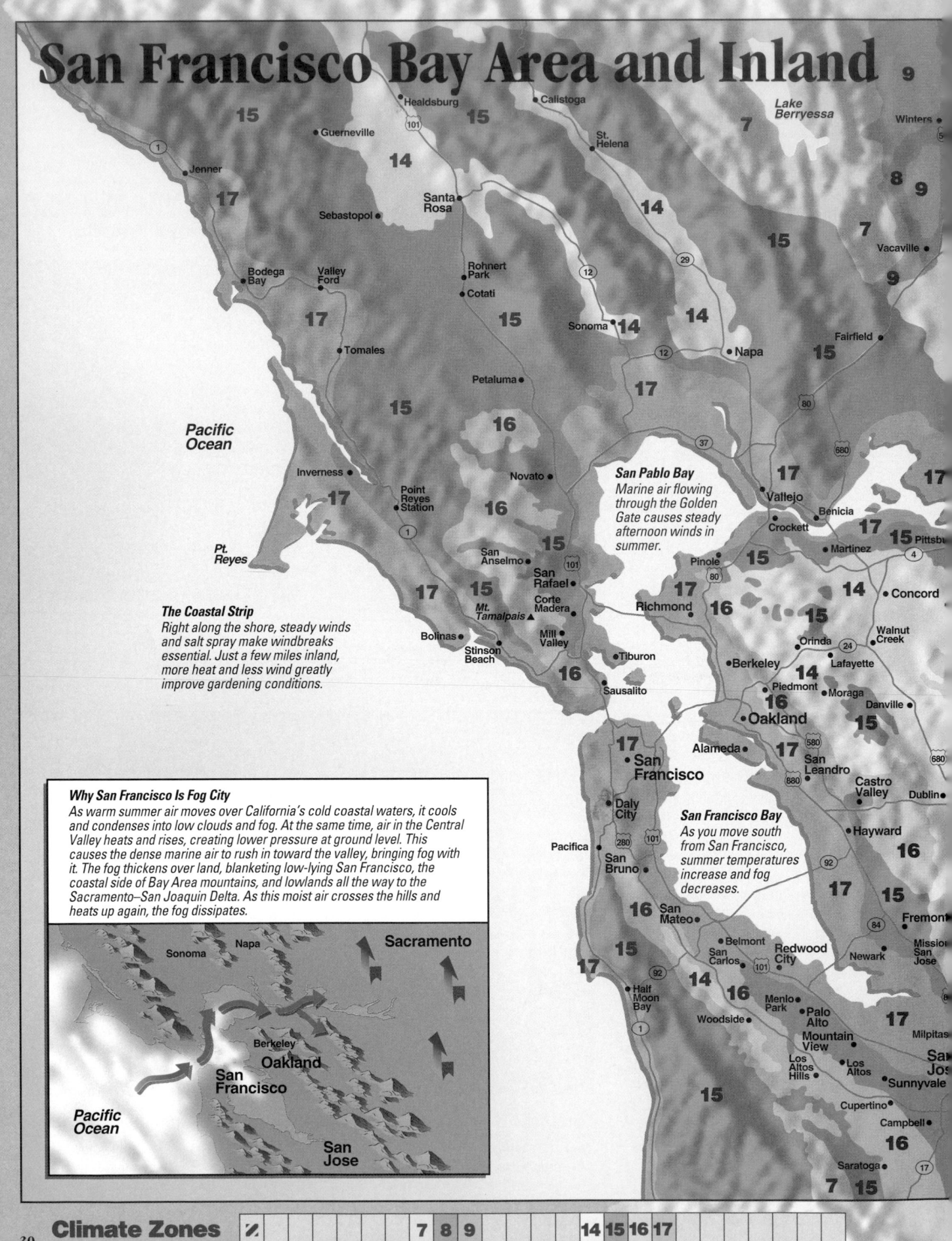

Pacific Ocean

15
Jenner
17
Bodega Bay
Valley Ford
17
Tomales
15

Guerneville
Healdsburg
14
Sebastopol
Santa Rosa
15
Rohnert Park
Cotati
15
Petaluma
16
15
Inverness
Point Reyes Station
16
San Anselmo
15
San Rafael
17
Corte Madera
Mt. Tamalpais ▲
Bolinas
16
Mill Valley
Stinson Beach
16
Sausalito

Calistoga
St. Helena
14
14
Sonoma 14
12
Napa
17
15

9
Lake Berryessa
Winters
7
8 9
9
7
Vacaville
9
Fairfield
15
80

Novato

San Pablo Bay
Marine air flowing through the Golden Gate causes steady afternoon winds in summer.

37
Vallejo
Benicia
Crockett
Pinole
80
Richmond
17
16
15
Martinez
4
14
Concord
15
Walnut Creek
Orinda
24
Lafayette
Berkeley
14
Piedmont
16
Moraga
Danville
Oakland
15
Alameda
17
San Leandro
580
Castro Valley
Dublin
680
680
17
17 15 Pittsbu

17

The Coastal Strip
Right along the shore, steady winds and salt spray make windbreaks essential. Just a few miles inland, more heat and less wind greatly improve gardening conditions.

17
San Francisco
Daly City
Pacifica
San Bruno
280
101
16
San Mateo
15
17
Half Moon Bay
Woodside
1
92
14
16
Menlo Park
Palo Alto
Mountain View
Los Altos Hills
Los Altos
15
Belmont
San Carlos
Redwood City
101
Newark
Hayward
16
17
15
Fremont
Mission San Jose
17
Milpitas
Sa
Jos
Sunnyvale
Cupertino
Campbell
16
Saratoga
7 15
17

Why San Francisco Is Fog City
As warm summer air moves over California's cold coastal waters, it cools and condenses into low clouds and fog. At the same time, air in the Central Valley heats and rises, creating lower pressure at ground level. This causes the dense marine air to rush in toward the valley, bringing fog with it. The fog thickens over land, blanketing low-lying San Francisco, the coastal side of Bay Area mountains, and lowlands all the way to the Sacramento–San Joaquin Delta. As this moist air crosses the hills and heats up again, the fog dissipates.

San Francisco Bay
As you move south from San Francisco, summer temperatures increase and fog decreases.

Sonoma
Napa
Sacramento
Berkeley
Oakland
San Francisco
Pacific Ocean
San Jose

Climate Zones

						7	8	9				14	15	16	17						

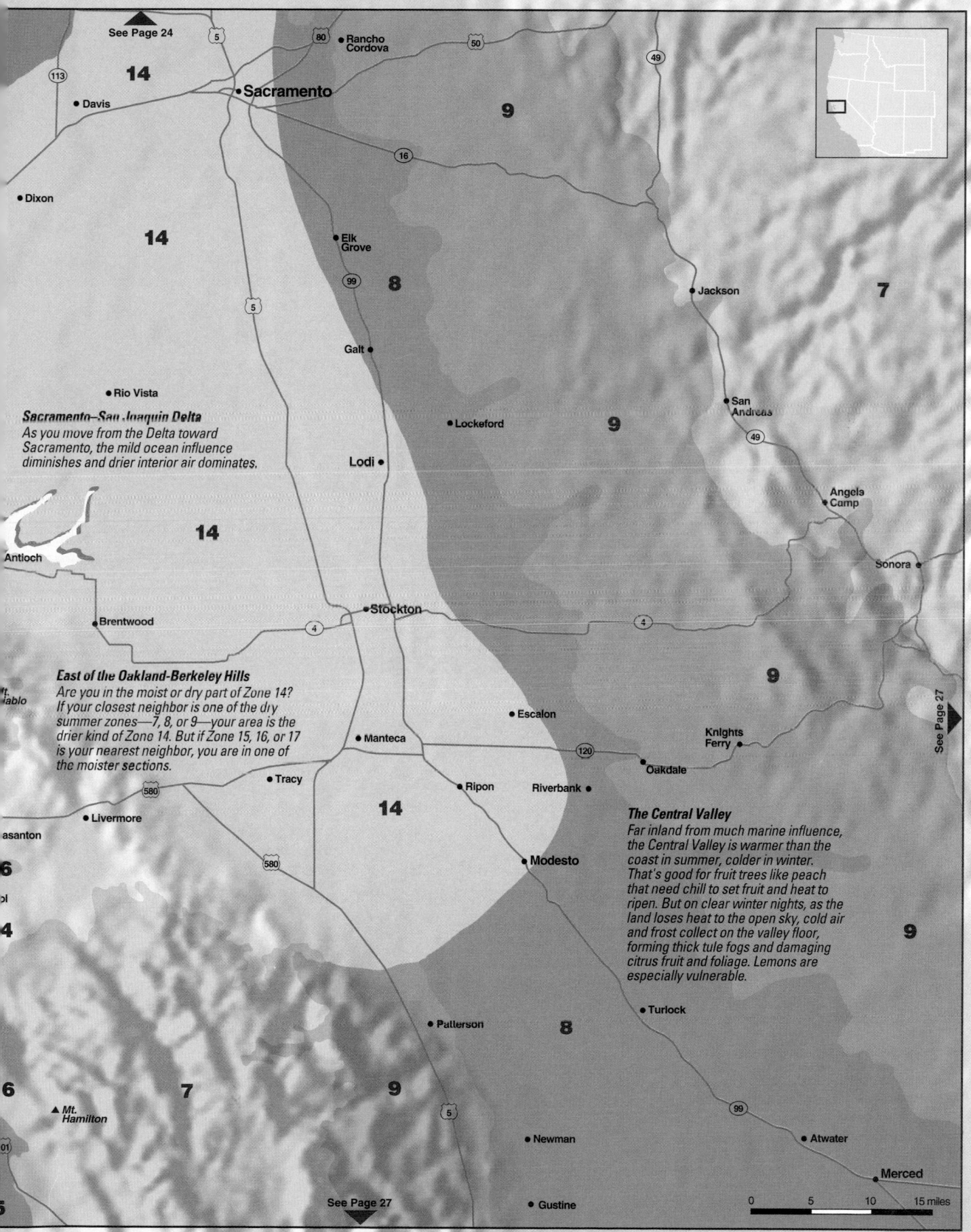

See Page 24

14

113

5

• Davis

80 Rancho Cordova

50

49

• Sacramento

9

• Dixon

16

14

• Elk Grove

99

8

7

• Jackson

• Galt

• Rio Vista

Sacramento–San Joaquin Delta
As you move from the Delta toward Sacramento, the mild ocean influence diminishes and drier interior air dominates.

• Lockeford

9

5

• San Andreas

49

Lodi •

• Angels Camp

Antioch

14

• Sonora

• Brentwood

• Stockton

4

4

See Page 27

East of the Oakland–Berkeley Hills
Are you in the moist or dry part of Zone 14? If your closest neighbor is one of the dry summer zones—7, 8, or 9—your area is the drier kind of Zone 14. But if Zone 15, 16, or 17 is your nearest neighbor, you are in one of the moister sections.

Mt. Diablo

• Escalon

9

Knights Ferry

• Manteca

120

• Oakdale

6

580

• Tracy

• Ripon

Riverbank •

The Central Valley
Far inland from much marine influence, the Central Valley is warmer than the coast in summer, colder in winter. That's good for fruit trees like peach that need chill to set fruit and heat to ripen. But on clear winter nights, as the land loses heat to the open sky, cold air and frost collect on the valley floor, forming thick tule fogs and damaging citrus fruit and foliage. Lemons are especially vulnerable.

Pleasanton

• Livermore

4

580

14

• Modesto

9

6

7

• Turlock

▲ Mt. Hamilton

• Patterson

8

01

9

5

• Newman

• Atwater

• Merced

5

See Page 27

• Gustine

0   5   10   15 miles

ZONE 18 — Above and Below the Thermal Belts in Southern California's Interior Valleys

Zones 18 and 19 are classified as interior climates. This means that the major influence on climate is the continental air mass; the ocean determines the climate no more than 15 percent of the time.

Many of the valley floors of Zone 18 were once regions where apricot, peach, apple, and walnut orchards flourished, but the orchards have now given way to homes. Although the climate supplies enough winter chill for some plants that need it, it is not too cold for many of the hardier subtropicals like cymbidiums. It is too hot, too cold, and too dry for fuchsias but cold enough for tree peonies and many apple varieties, and mild enough for a number of avocado varieties. Zone 18 never supplied much commercial citrus (frosty nights called for too much heating), but home gardeners who can tolerate occasional minor fruit loss can grow citrus here.

Over a 20-year period, winter lows ranged from 28° to 10°F. The all-time lows recorded by different weather stations in Zone 18 ranged from 22° to 7°F.

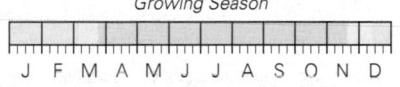

Growing Season

J F M A M J J A S O N D

Chilly Hilltops and Valleys

Zone 18 hilltops, like this one laced with houses, get more cold in winter and warmth in summer than the thermal belts (slopes and hillsides from which cold air drains) that make up Zone 19. Hilltops and cold-air basins get frost, thermal belts don't.

ZONE 19 — Thermal Belts Around Southern California's Interior Valleys

Like that of Zone 18, the climate in this zone is little influenced by the ocean. Both zones, then, have a poor climate for such plants as fuchsias, rhododendrons, and tuberous begonias. Many sections of Zone 19 have always been prime citrus country—especially for those kinds that need extra summer heat in order to grow sweet fruit. Likewise, macadamia nuts and most avocados can be grown here.

The Western Plant Encyclopedia cites many ornamental plants for Zone 19 that

The Southland's Warm Slopes

Douglas iris, California poppies, and yellow meadowfoam splash the landscape with spring color at Rancho Santa Ana Botanic Garden in warm, dry Claremont, California. This garden also contains a wealth of evergreen natives, including ceanothus and manzanitas, that remain unscathed when winter temperatures drop into the 20s.

are not recommended for Zone 18, because of the milder winters in Zone 19. Plants that grow here, but not in Zone 18, include bougainvillea, bouvardia, calocephalus, Cape chestnut *(Calodendrum),* flame pea *(Chorizema),* several kinds of coral tree *(Erythrina),* leucocoryne, livistona palms, Mexican blue and San Jose hesper palms *(Brahea armata, B. brandegeei),* giant Burmese honeysuckle, myoporum, several of the more tender pittosporums, and lady palm *(Rhapis excelsa).*

Winter lows over a 20-year period ranged from 27° to 22°F, and the all-time lows at different weather stations range from 23° to 17°F. These are considerably higher than the temperatures in neighboring Zone 18.

Growing Season

J F M A M J J A S O N D

ZONE 20 Cool Winters in Southern California's Sections of Occasional Ocean Influence

In Zones 20 and 21, the same relative pattern prevails as in Zones 18 and 19. The even-numbered zone is the climate made up of cold-air basins and hilltops, and the odd-numbered one comprises thermal belts. The difference is that Zones 20 and 21 get weather influenced by both maritime air and interior air. In these transitional areas, climate boundaries often move 20 miles in 24 hours with the movements of these air masses.

Because of the greater ocean influence, this climate supports a wide variety of plants. You can see the range of them at the Los Angeles State and County Arboretum in Arcadia. Winter lows over a 20-year period ranged from 28° to 23°F. Record lows at various weather stations range from 21° to 14°F

Caution: Colliding Air Masses

In Zone 20 (but bordering Zone 21), the Los Angeles Arboretum is influenced by both marine and interior air. The result: everything from birches to palms grows here, as do relatively tender tropical trees like jacaranda, Moreton Bay fig, and tabebuia.

Growing Season

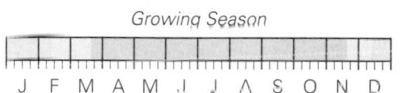

J F M A M J J A S O N D

ZONE 21 Thermal Belts in Southern California's Sections of Occasional Ocean Influence

Where Oranges Meet Lilacs

Cold air drains from slopes above the Santa Clarita River near Moorpark, California, making them perfect for growing oranges *(left)*. Thermal belts such as these make it possible to grow plants in Zone 21 that would be too tender for Zone 20. Zone 21 is just cold enough for some lilacs. Varieties bred to grow and bloom with less winter chill than most lilacs require grow at Descanso Gardens in La Cañada–Flintridge *(below)*.

The combination of weather influences described for Zone 20 applies to Zone 21 as well. Your garden can be in ocean air or a high fog one day and in a mass of interior air (perhaps a drying Santa Ana wind from the desert) the next day.

Because temperatures never dip very far below 30°F, this is fine citrus-growing country. At the same time, it's also the mildest zone that gets enough winter chilling for most forms of lilacs and certain other plants.

Over a 20-year period, winter lows at the weather-recording stations in Zone 21 ranged from 36° to 23°F. Record lows range from 27° to 17°F.

Growing Season

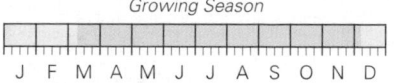

J F M A M J J A S O N D

Los Angeles and Inland

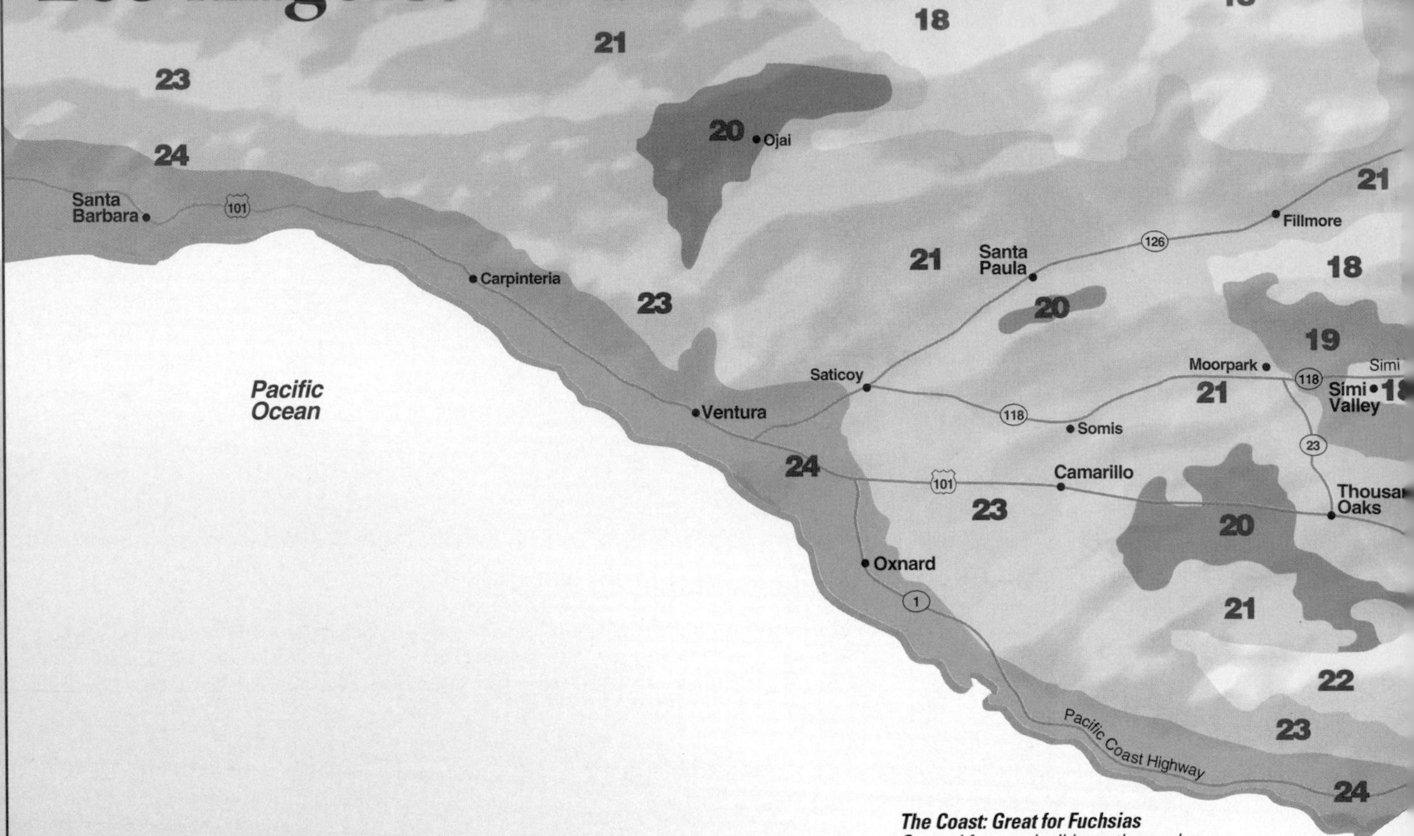

See Page 27

3

18

18

21

23

24

20 • Ojai

21

Santa Barbara •

101

• Carpinteria

21

Santa Paula

Fillmore

126

18

19

Simi

20

Saticoy

Moorpark

118

Simi • 18
Valley

Pacific Ocean

• Ventura

118

21

• Somis

23

Thousand Oaks

24

Camarillo

20

101

23

• Oxnard

21

1

22

23

Pacific Coast Highway

24

The Coast: Great for Fuchsias
Coastal fogs and mild weather make Zone 24 Southern California's best fuchsia and tuberous begonia climate. Scores of less well known plants from Chile, New Zealand, the Canary Islands, and the moister parts of South Africa do well here for the same reason.

Tracking the Santa Anas
Every fall and winter, the Santa Ana wind revs up as the interior's cold, heavy air flows downhill toward the Southern California coast. As this air loses elevation, it compresses, heats up, dries out, and roars ferociously through the passes behind Los Angeles and San Bernardino. Cajon Pass and Soledad Canyon are two main routes, although the wind is named for Santa Ana Canyon. When the Santa Ana wind hits the Los Angeles basin, it's so hot and dry that it desiccates plants. Sprinklers, windbreaks, and row covers help protect them. Santa Anas usually play out near the coast, though sometimes they blow clear to Santa Catalina Island. They reach as far north as Oxnard and as far south as San Diego.

Climate Zones

| ⊘ | 2 | 3 | | | | | | | 11 | | 18 | 19 | 20 | 21 | 22 | 23 | 24 |

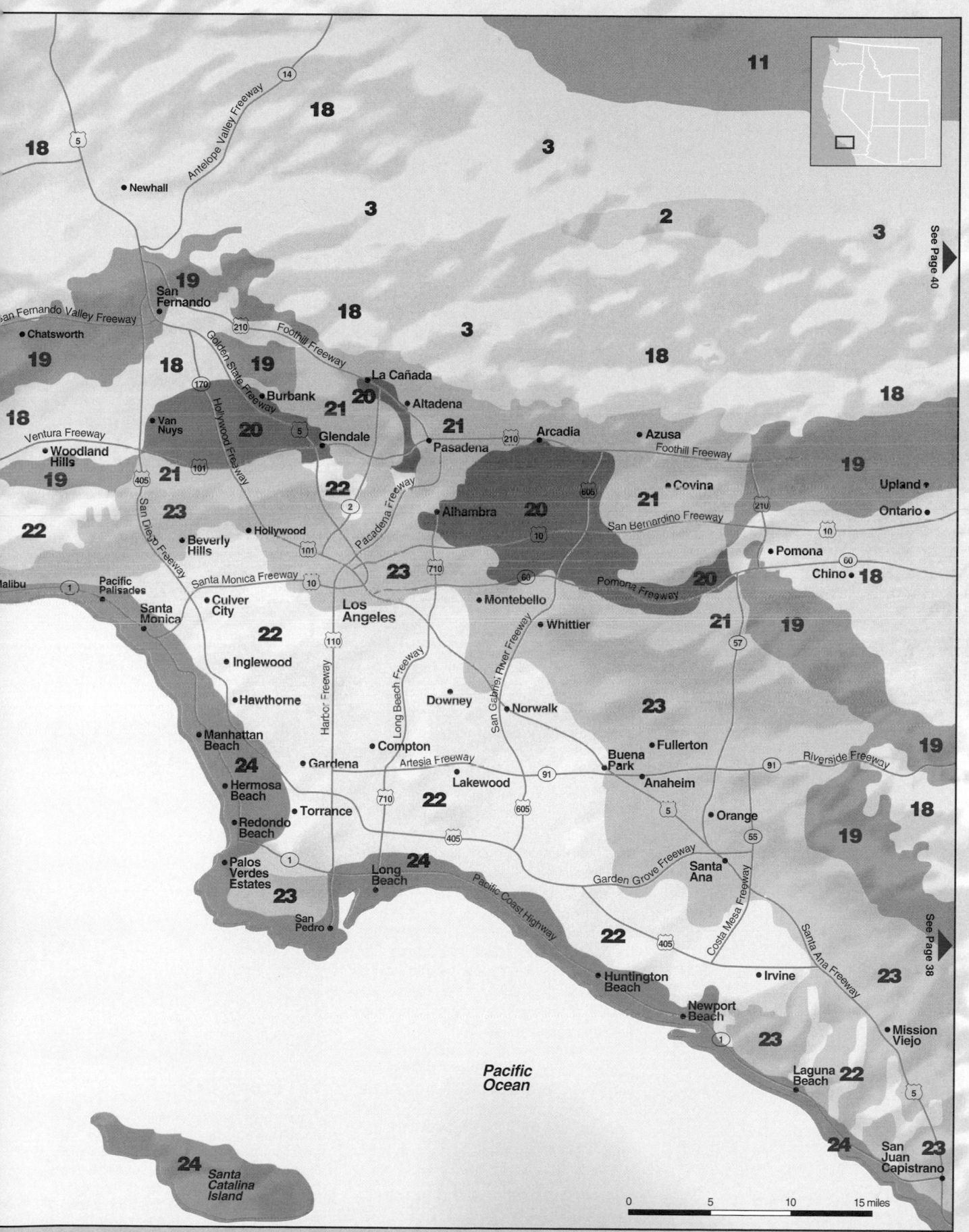

11

18

18 🛣14

3

• Newhall

3

2

3

See Page 40 ►

19
San
Fernando

ean Fernando Valley Freeway

18

3

• Chatsworth

210

Foothill Freeway

19

19

18

Golden State Freeway

19

La Cañada

3

• Altadena

18

18

170
• Burbank

21

20

19

Ventura Freeway

Hollywood Freeway

18

• Van
Nuys

20

5

Glendale

21

210

• Arcadia

• Azusa

Foothill Freeway

18

• Woodland
Hills

21

Pasadena

20

• Covina

19

Upland •

19

23

22

San Diego Freeway

Pasadena Freeway

Pasadena Freeway

20

605

21

San Bernardino Freeway

210

Ontario •

• Alhambra

10

10

Malibu

1

Pacific
Palisades

• Hollywood

101

• Beverly
Hills

Santa Monica Freeway

23

710

60

Pomona Freeway

• Pomona

20

60

Chino • **18**

22

Santa
Monica

10

• Culver
City

22

Los
Angeles

• Montebello

21

19

57

110

• Inglewood

San Gabriel River Freeway

• Whittier

• Hawthorne

Long Beach Freeway

Harbor Freeway

• Downey

• Norwalk

23

• Fullerton

19

• Manhattan
Beach

• Gardena

Artesia Freeway

91

Buena
Park

91

Riverside Freeway

24

• Compton

• Lakewood

Anaheim

18

• Hermosa
Beach

710

22

605

5

• Orange

19

• Torrance

• Redondo
Beach

405

55

Santa
Ana

Costa Mesa Freeway

Santa Ana Freeway

• Palos
Verdes
Estates

1

24
Long
Beach

Garden Grove Freeway

See Page 38 ►

23

San Pedro •

Pacific Coast Highway

22

405

• Irvine

23

• Huntington
Beach

Newport
Beach

23

• Mission
Viejo

1

Pacific
Ocean

Laguna
Beach

22

5

24
Santa
Catalina
Island

24

San
Juan
Capistrano

23

0   5   10   15 miles

ZONE 22 Cold-Winter Portions of Southern California's Coastal Climate

Areas falling in Zone 22 have a coastal climate (they are influenced by the ocean approximately 85 percent of the time). When temperatures drop in winter, these cold-air basins or hilltops above the air-drained slopes have lower winter temperatures than those in neighboring Zone 23.

Actually, the winters are so mild here that lows are not significant, seldom falling below 28°F. Annual winter lows recorded over 20 years ranged from 24° to 21°F.

Gardeners who plant under overhangs or tree canopies can grow subtropical plants that would otherwise be burned by a rare frost. Such plants include bananas, tree ferns, and the like. The lack of a pronounced chilling period during the winter limits the use of such deciduous woody plants as flowering cherry and lilac. Many herbaceous perennials from colder regions fail here because the winters are too warm for them to go dormant.

Growing Season

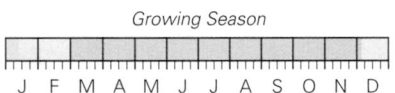

J F M A M J J A S O N D

Orange County's Coastal Canyons

Coastal canyons—narrow, steep-sided valleys that jut inland from the coast—are numerous in Orange County. The canyon floors, where cold air settles in winter, are in Zone 22, while the higher ground on either side falls into warmer Zone 23. Plants that thrive on the slopes can freeze in the canyon below.

ZONE 23 Thermal Belts of Southern California's Coastal Climate

One of the most favored areas in North America for growing subtropical plants, Zone 23 has always been Southern California's best zone for avocados. Frosts don't amount to much here, because 85 percent of the time, Pacific Ocean weather dominates; interior air rules only 15 percent of the time. A notorious portion of this 15 percent consists of those days when hot, dry Santa Ana winds blow.

Zone 23 lacks either the summer heat or the winter cold necessary to grow pears, most apples, and most peaches. But it enjoys more heat than Zone 24. Gardenias and oleanders, for example, are recommended for Zone 23, but not for Zone 24.

Temperatures are mild here, but severe winters descend at times, resulting in a surprising spread of minimum temperatures. Over a 20-year period, lows ranged from 38° to 23°F. In recorded history, lows range from 28° to 23°F.

Growing Season

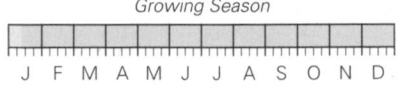

J F M A M J J A S O N D

The Protea Belt

Proteas are grown commercially in Zone 23, both as nursery stock and for their huge, long-lasting flowers, like the pincushions above. Cacti and fountain grass get plenty of sun in this garden in the Hollywood Hills *(far left)*, and more warmth than they would in Zone 24.

ZONE 24 — Marine Influence Along the Southern California Coast

Stretched along Southern California's beaches, this climate zone is almost completely dominated by the ocean. Where the beach runs along high cliffs or palisades, Zone 24 extends only to that barrier. But where hills are low or nonexistent, it runs inland several miles.

This zone has a mild marine climate (milder than Northern California's maritime Zone 17), because south of Point Conception, the Pacific is comparatively warm. The winters are mild, the summers cool, and the air seldom really dry. On many days, the sun doesn't break through the high overcast until afternoon. Very tender plants like fuchsias find a good home here; they get along fine with only moderate summer heat. In this climate, gardens that include such plants as figs, rubber trees, and scheffleras can become jungles.

Morning Coastal Fogs

In summer, high fog is one of Zone 24's regular features, rolling in off the ocean in the morning and burning off during the day *(below)*. It stretches the season for wildflowers, like these California poppies dotting a meadow at Santa Barbara Botanic Garden.

Zone 24 is coldest at the mouths of canyons that channel cold air down from the mountains on clear winter nights. Several such canyons between Laguna Beach and San Clemente are visible on the map. Numerous smaller ones touch the coast between San Clemente and the Mexican border. Partly because of the unusually low temperatures created by this canyon action, the range of winter lows in Zone 24 is broader than you might think. In a 20-year period, lows ranged from 44° to 24°F. The all-time record lows of different stations range from 33° to 20°F. In other words, some weather stations in Zone 24 have never recorded a freezing temperature.

The all-time high temperatures here are interesting because they help define the total climate, but they aren't greatly significant in terms of plant growth. The average all-time high of weather stations in Zone 24 is 105°F. Compare this with temperatures of Northern California's marine climate, Zone 17, which average 97°F, and Southern California's inland climates—Zone 22 at 111°F, Zone 20 at 114°F, and Zone 18 at 115°F.

Growing Season

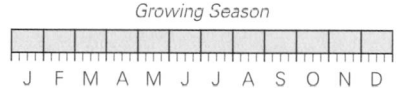

J F M A M J J A S O N D

Southern California Classic

At its best in frost-free Zone 24, bougainvillea can grow rampant where conditions are good *(above)*. This one competes for light, heat, and space with an ornamental asparagus. Both can thrive here on rainfall alone.

San Diego and Environs

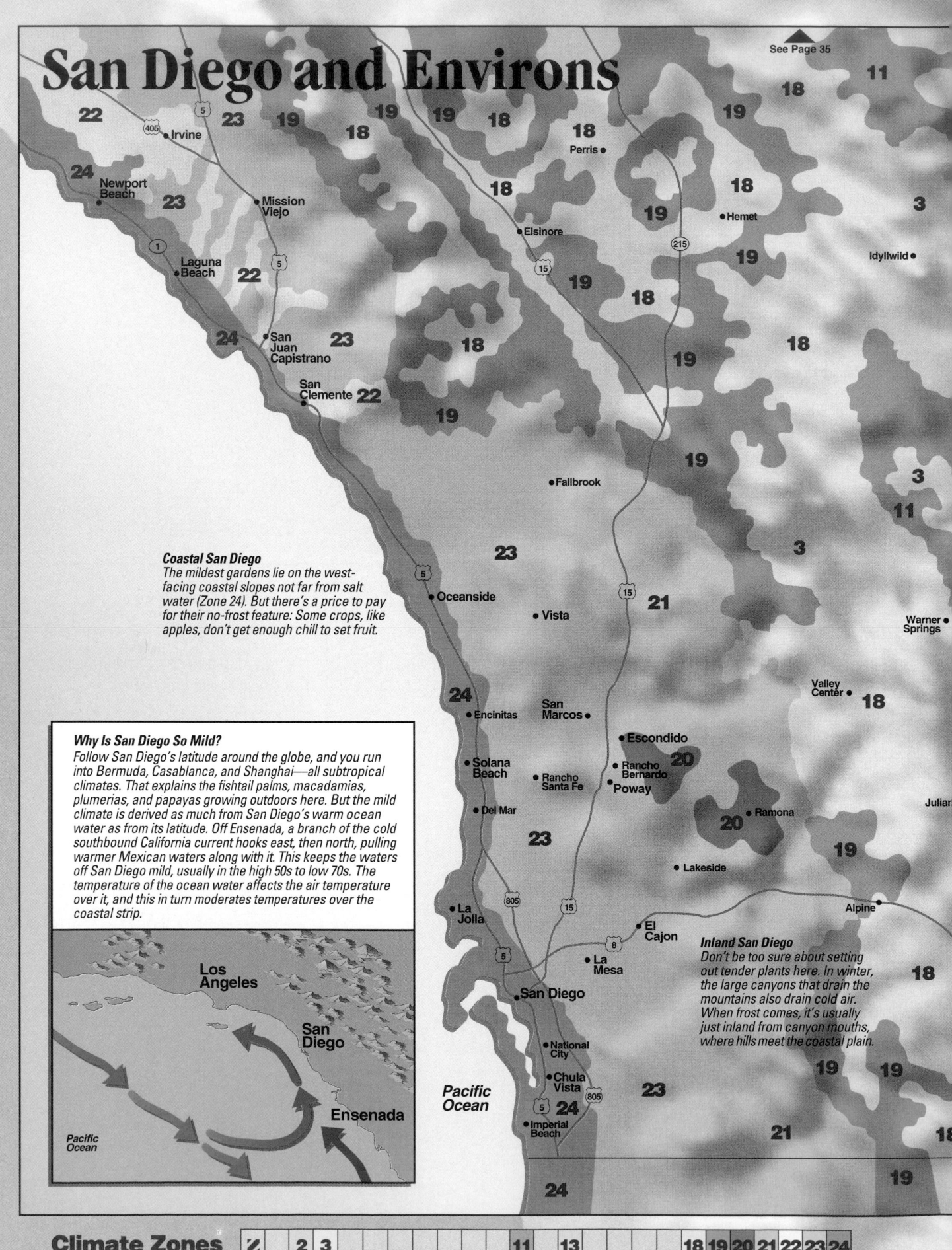

See Page 35

22
23
19
19
19
18
18
11
24
Newport Beach
Irvine
Perris •
18
23
Mission Viejo
18
18
Hemet •
3
22
Laguna Beach
Elsinore •
19
Idyllwild •
24
San Juan Capistrano
23
18
19
19
San Clemente
22
18
19
18
19
19
18
3
Fallbrook •
3
11

Coastal San Diego
The mildest gardens lie on the west-facing coastal slopes not far from salt water (Zone 24). But there's a price to pay for their no-frost feature: Some crops, like apples, don't get enough chill to set fruit.

23
5
• Oceanside
• Vista
21
Warner Springs •
24
Encinitas
San Marcos •
Valley Center •
18
Escondido •
20
Solana Beach
• Rancho Santa Fe
Rancho Bernardo
Poway
Ramona •
20
Juliar
• Del Mar
23
19
• Lakeside

Why Is San Diego So Mild?
Follow San Diego's latitude around the globe, and you run into Bermuda, Casablanca, and Shanghai—all subtropical climates. That explains the fishtail palms, macadamias, plumerias, and papayas growing outdoors here. But the mild climate is derived as much from San Diego's warm ocean water as from its latitude. Off Ensenada, a branch of the cold southbound California current hooks east, then north, pulling warmer Mexican waters along with it. This keeps the waters off San Diego mild, usually in the high 50s to low 70s. The temperature of the ocean water affects the air temperature over it, and this in turn moderates temperatures over the coastal strip.

• La Jolla
805
15
• El Cajon
Alpine
8
• La Mesa
18
San Diego

Inland San Diego
Don't be too sure about setting out tender plants here. In winter, the large canyons that drain the mountains also drain cold air. When frost comes, it's usually just inland from canyon mouths, where hills meet the coastal plain.

Los Angeles
San Diego
• National City
19
19
Ensenada
• Chula Vista
23
Pacific Ocean
5
24
Pacific Ocean
• Imperial Beach
21
18
24
19

Climate Zones | / | 2 | 3 | | | | | | 11 | 13 | | | 18 | 19 | 20 | 21 | 22 | 23 | 24

See Page 40

10

Palm
Springs

13

Palm
Desert

• Indio

11

11

3

11

11

3

13

13

Salton
Sea

13

APPLE ALLEY BAKERY
JULIAN →
APPLE PIE

Coast to Desert
*Drive northeast from the San Diego area
and you'll pass through three very different
climates. Near the coast (Zone 24), such
tender plants as poinsettias, shown here
at Ecke Ranch in Encinitas, thrive outdoors.
In high-elevation Julian (Zone 3), apple
trees get enough winter chill to deliver
hefty crops. In Palm Desert (Zone 13), arid
conditions favor the growth of such tough,
unthirsty heat-lovers as gazania, spiky
ocotillo, and yellow-flowered brittlebush,
shown here at The Living Desert.*

3

13

Brawley •

El
• Centro

8

13

13

See Page 40

13

8

• Calexico

Jacumba

MEXICO

13

0   5   10   15 miles

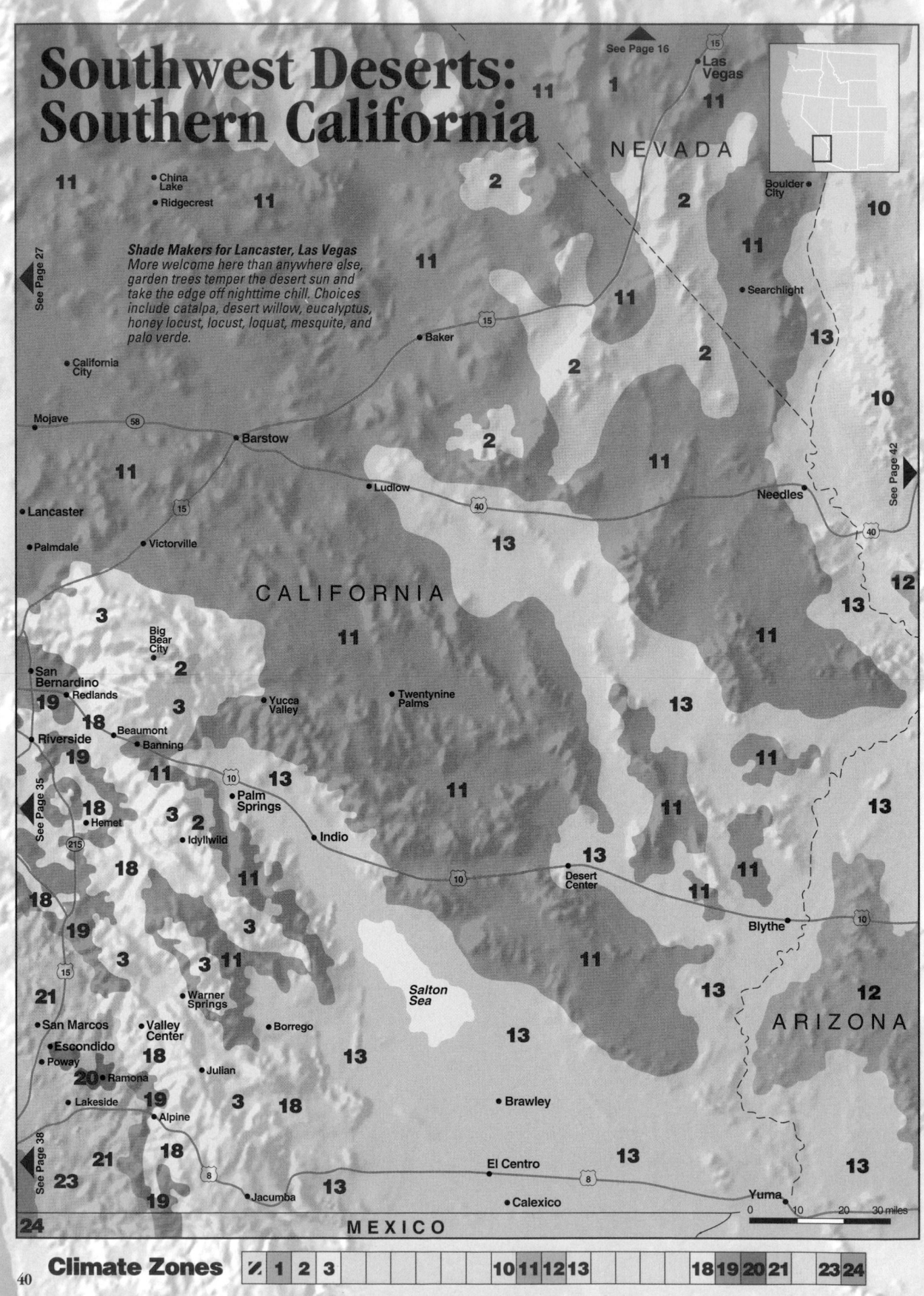

Southwest Deserts: Southern California

See Page 16

11

1

Las Vegas

11

NEVADA

Boulder City

10

2

2

• China Lake

• Ridgecrest

11

11

11

Searchlight

See Page 27

11

2

13

Shade Makers for Lancaster, Las Vegas
More welcome here than anywhere else, garden trees temper the desert sun and take the edge off nighttime chill. Choices include catalpa, desert willow, eucalyptus, honey locust, locust, loquat, mesquite, and palo verde.

11

• Baker

2

2

• California City

Mojave

58

Barstow

2

10

11

• Ludlow

11

See Page 42

Needles

• Lancaster

15

40

13

• Palmdale

• Victorville

12

CALIFORNIA

13

3

11

Big Bear City

San Bernardino

2

• Yucca Valley

• Twentynine Palms

13

19 • Redlands

3

11

18 Beaumont

Riverside • Banning

19

11

10

13

• Palm Springs

11

11

See Page 35

18 • Hemet

3

2

• Idyllwild

• Indio

13

215

11

Desert Center

11

18

3

10

11

18

19

3

Blythe

10

15

3

3 11

11

13

21

• Warner Springs

Salton Sea

12

• San Marcos

• Borrego

ARIZONA

• Escondido

18

13

• Poway

20 • Ramona

• Julian

13

• Brawley

• Lakeside

19

3

18

• Alpine

See Page 38

21

18

13

13

23

8

• El Centro

8

19

13

• Jacumba

• Calexico

Yuma

0   10   20   30 miles

24

MEXICO

Climate Zones ⧄ 1 2 3 | 10 11 12 13 | 18 19 20 21 | 23 24

40

ZONE **10** High Desert of Arizona and New Mexico

Snowy Winters, Peppery Summers

Zone 10 gets enough winter chill to flock pampas grass *(far left)* and let you grow plants that need chilling—lilacs and deciduous fruits, for example. But it also gets plenty of summer heat for growing chilies, shown *(left)* drying on a pole in New Mexico.

This zone consists mostly of the 3,300- to 4,500-foot elevations in parts of Arizona and New Mexico. It also includes parts of southern Utah and southern Nevada. It has a definite winter season; from 75 to more than 100 nights each year have temperatures below 32°F. In the representative towns of Albuquerque, Benson, and Douglas, average winter minimums range from 31° to 24°F. Lows of 25° to 22°F often come in April. The lowest temperature recorded is −17°F.

The cold winter season calls for spring planting and a spring-through-summer growing season. (In neighboring Zones 12 and 13, most planting is done in fall.)

Distinguishing this climate from Zone 11 are more rainfall and less wind. Annual rainfall averages 12 inches, with half of that amount falling in July and August. In the eastern parts of Zone 10 (in the Pecos River drainage), the summer provides more precipitation than does the winter.

Growing Season

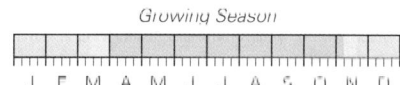

J F M A M J J A S O N D

ZONE **11** Medium to High Desert of California and Southern Nevada

This climate zone shares some similarities with its extremely different neighbors — the cold-winter Zones 1, 2, and 3, and the subtropical low desert, Zone 13. Like Zones 1 to 3, Zone 11 has cold winters, and like Zone 13, it has hot summers. Overall, it is characterized by wide swings in temperature. Hot summer days are followed by cool nights; freezing nights are often followed by daytime temperatures of 60°F. On the average, there are 110 summer days above 90°F, with the highest temperatures recorded hovering between 111° and 117°F. About 85 nights have temperatures below 32°F, with maximum lows between 11° and 0°F.

If soil moisture is inadequate, the characteristic winds and bright sunlight may combine to dry out normally hardy evergreen plants, killing or badly injuring them.

Growing Season

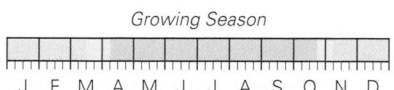

J F M A M J J A S O N D

Water Makes the Difference

Zone 11 is dry: oasis-like Las Vegas gardens *(above)* owe their existence to imported water. Yet wildflowers often make a dazzling show in Antelope Valley in spring *(left)*. Challenges for gardeners in Zone 11? Hot summer days, chilly nights, late spring frosts, and desert winds.

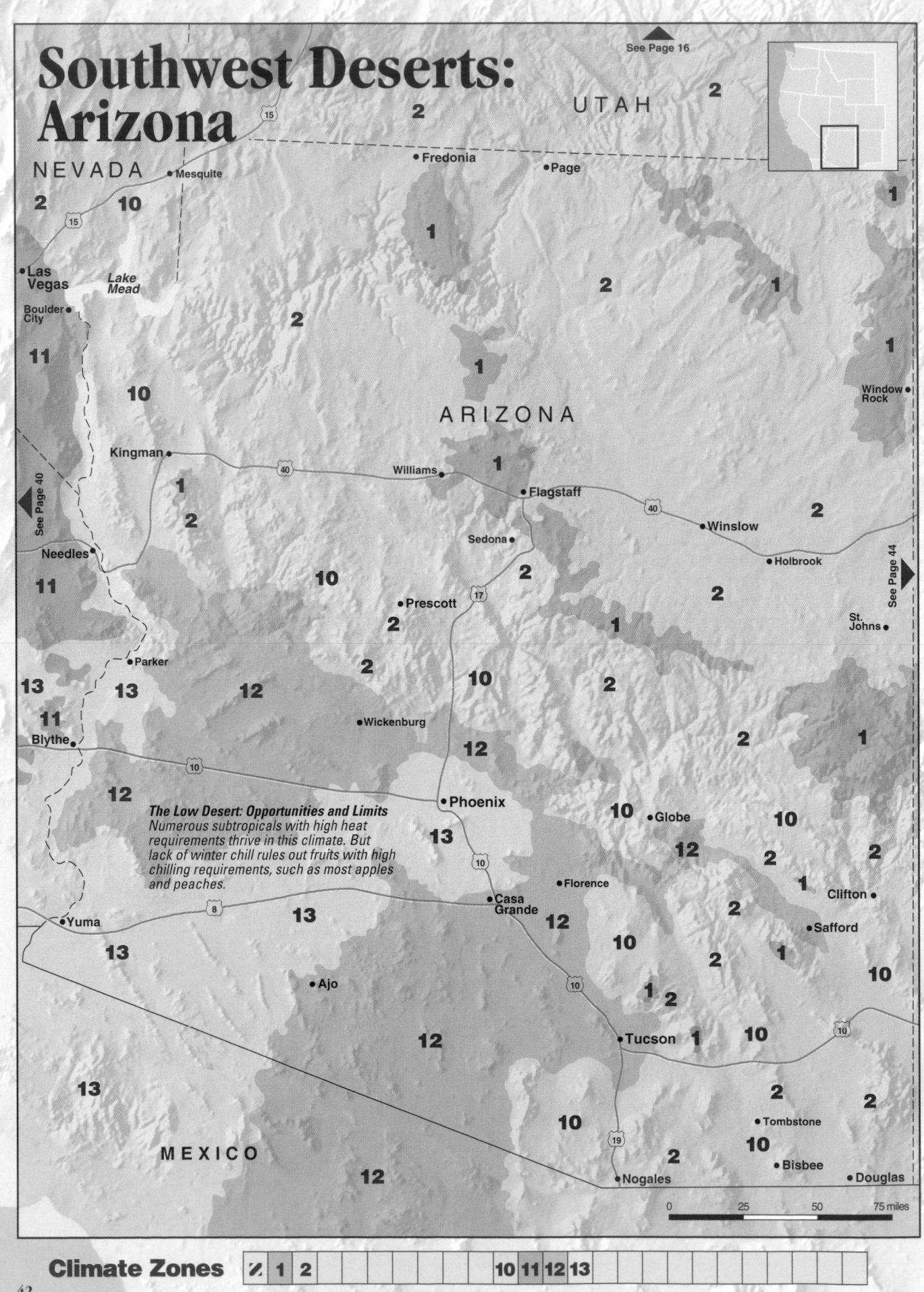

Southwest Deserts: Arizona

See Page 16

UTAH

NEVADA

2

2

Fredonia

Page

1

Mesquite

2   10

2

1

Las Vegas

Lake Mead

1

2

1

Boulder City

11

2

1

10

1

Window Rock

ARIZONA

See Page 40

Kingman

1

Williams

1

2

Flagstaff

2

Winslow

Sedona

Needles

11

10

2

Holbrook

See Page 44

Prescott

2

1

St. Johns

2

2

13   13

12

10

1

Parker

Wickenburg

2

2

1

11

12

Blythe

12

10

Phoenix

10   **Globe**

10

The Low Desert: Opportunities and Limits
Numerous subtropicals with high heat requirements thrive in this climate. But lack of winter chill rules out fruits with high chilling requirements, such as most apples and peaches.

13

12

2

2

Clifton

Florence

2

Safford

Casa Grande

12

10

2

1

13   **Yuma**

13

10

Ajo

1   2

13

12

Tucson

1   10

13

2

2

Tombstone

10

MEXICO

10

Bisbee

2

12

Nogales

Douglas

0   25   50   75 miles

Climate Zones
1   2   10 11 12 13

ZONE 12 Arizona's Intermediate Desert

The crucial difference between Arizona's intermediate desert (Zone 12) and the low desert (Zone 13) is winter cold. But though the intermediate desert averages only 5 more freezing nights than the low desert (20 in Tucson compared with 15 in Phoenix and El Centro), it has harder frosts spread over a longer cold season. Seen another way, Zone 12 averages about 8 months between freezes, 9 months between killing frosts (28°F or lower). Zone 13, on the other hand, averages more than 11 months between killing frosts, when it gets them at all. Extreme low temperatures of 6°F have been recorded in Zone 12. The mean maximums in July and August are 5° or 6°F cooler than the highs of Zone 13.

Many subtropicals that do well in Zone 13 aren't reliably hardy here, but succeed with protection against the extreme winters.

Although winter temperatures are lower than in Zone 13, the total hours of cold are not enough to provide sufficient winter chilling for some deciduous fruits.

From March to May, strong winds (to 40 miles per hour) can damage young tender growth. Windbreaks help. Here, as in Zone 13 and the eastern parts of Zone 10, summer rains are to be expected and can be more dependable than winter rains. And

as in Zone 13, the best season for cool-season crops (salad greens, root vegetables, cabbage family members) starts in September or October.

Growing Season

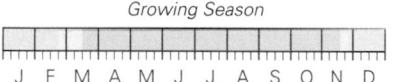

J F M A M J J A S O N D

The Lush Arizona Desert

Saguaro, cholla, and organpipe cacti rise up out of a sea of yellow brittlebush flowers in southern Arizona's intermediate desert. Zone 12 supports a more lush, gardenlike flora than any other desert zone.

ZONE 13 Low or Subtropical Desert Areas

Ranging from below sea level in the Imperial Valley and Death Valley to an elevation of 1,100 feet around Phoenix, Zone 13 is rightly classified as subtropical desert. Average summer maximum temperatures range from 106° to 108°F. Winters are short and mild. Frosts, anticipated from December 1 to February 15, are brief. Although the average minimum winter temperature is 37°F, with just 15 nights below freezing, lows of 19° to 13°F have been recorded.

The gardening year begins in September and October for most vegetable crops and annual flowers, although crops like corn and melons are planted in late winter. Fall-planted crops grow slowly in winter, pick up speed in mid-February, and race through the increasing temperatures of March and April. Spring winds and summer storms are a factor in gardening: the rains help with watering, and dense clouds shield plants from the hot sun.

Subtropicals in California

Winter lows and summer highs exclude some subtropicals from this zone, but ones like bauhinia *(above)*, date palms, and grapefruit thrive here. California fan palms and golden brittlebush bask in the sun in a canyon near Palm Springs *(left)*.

Growing Season*

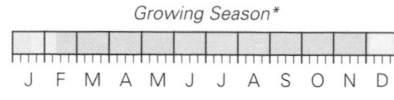

J F M A M J J A S O N D

*heat stops growth in summer

Southwest Deserts: New Mexico

See Page 16

COLORADO

2

1

1

Raton • 1

1

Clayton •

• Farmington

• Tierra Amarilla

2

• Taos

1

2

Clayton •

• Mora

2

• Mosquero

2

1

• Los Alamos

2

• Santa Fe

10

Gallup •

1

1

• Las Vegas

Tucumcari •

40

1

2

Bernalillo •

1

2

Santa Rosa

Albuquerque

10

40

See Page 42

• Los Lunas

1

• Estancia

N E W   M E X I C O

2

10

Fort Sumner

Clovis •

• Socorro

10

1

2

The Faces of Zone 10
In the milder southwest corner of New Mexico, winter temperatures bottom out at 10° to 15°F, while rainfall averages 12 inches. But as you move east, rainfall increases to 16 inches and winter temperatures can drop by 10 degrees or so. In northeastern areas, rainfall remains constant, but winter minimums drop a few more degrees, shortening the growing season.

1

25

• Reserve

1

1

1

2

• Roswell

2

1

1

Lovington •

10

1

10

• Alamogordo

10

• Silver City

10

2

• Carlsbad

Lordsburg •

Deming •

Las Cruces •

10

1

10

10

2

2

10

• El Paso

10

2

TEXAS

2

MEXICO

10

0   25   50   75 miles

10

Climate Zones   1   2   10

44

A Guide to
PLANT SELECTION

The thousands of plants described in the Western Plant Encyclopedia (beginning on page 129) include an infinitely varied assortment of sizes, shapes, textures, and colors. The pleasure of choosing from this rich assortment is available to anyone with a sense of adventure and a bit of earth. But such abundance can sometimes lead to bewilderment. The lists of plants that follow, used with the Western Plant Encyclopedia, will help you to select the right plants, whether you are looking to achieve a special effect with flowers or foliage, tackling a difficult landscape situation, or starting out with the basics.

Entry garden with purple coneflowers and gloriosa daisies

The symbols in the lists will help you choose plants most suitable for your garden. How much sun a plant needs for best performance is shown by one or more of three symbols:

☼ Grows best with unobstructed sunlight all day long or almost all day—except for 1 hour of shade at the beginning or end of a summer day

☽ Needs partial shade—shade for half the day or for at least 3 hours during the hottest part of the day

● Prefers little or no direct sunlight—for example, it does best on the north side of a house or beneath a broad, dense tree

A plant's approximate moisture needs are indicated by one or more of four symbols:

◌ Needs no supplemental watering once established, within 1 or 2 years after it's planted

◐ Tolerates some aridity; give it, for example, three to six soakings during a dry season

● Needs regular irrigation—weekly, or more often during extreme heat

◐◐ Needs a wet or constantly moist soil

A plant's climate adaptability is shown after the ⚡. The zone numbers refer to the climate zones—explained and mapped in The West's 24 Climate Zones—where the plants will grow best. Other information —flower or leaf color, for instance—is explained in legends on the individual lists.

Rudbeckia birta
'Marmalade'

LANDSCAPE PLANTS
with Showy Flowers

Malus 'Liset'

Trees, shrubs, ground covers, and vines are the backbones of the garden, but that doesn't mean they have to take a back seat to showy annuals and perennials. Many permanent landscape plants put on a striking show of blooms, which provide changing interest throughout the year. On this list, plants are arranged by the time of year in which they flower. Use it to plan your garden's floral display according to season and flower color.

Aesculus carnea

Bauhinia

Chionanthus virginicus

SPRING
Trees

Acacia (most)
☼ ◊ ● ✂ ZONES VARY   p. 131

Aesculus
HORSECHESTNUT
NEEDS, ZONES VARY   p. 141

Bauhinia
BRAZILIAN BUTTERFLY TREE
☼ ● ✂ ZONES VARY   p. 179

Catalpa
☼ ● ✂ ALL ZONES   p. 211

Cercidium
PALO VERDE
☼ ◊ ● ✂ 10–14, 18–20   p. 218

Cercis
REDBUD
NEEDS, ZONES VARY   p. 218

Chionanthus virginicus
FRINGE TREE
☼ ● ✂ 1–6, 15–17   p. 224

Cornus
DOGWOOD
☼ ◊ ● ● ✂ ZONES VARY   p. 242

Crataegus
HAWTHORN
☼ ● ✂ 1–12, 14–17   p. 247

Erythrina (some)
CORAL TREE
☼ ● ✂ ZONES VARY   p. 279

Halesia
☼ ● ✂ 2–9, 14–24   p. 315

Laburnum
GOLDENCHAIN TREE
☼ ◊ ● ✂ 1–10, 14–17   p. 345

Magnolia (most deciduous)
☼ ◊ ● ✂ ZONES VARY   p. 365

Malus
CRABAPPLE
☼ ● ✂ 1–21   p. 372

Melaleuca (some)
☼ ◊ ● ✂ ZONES VARY   p. 377

Prunus (flowering)
NEEDS, ZONES VARY   p. 441

Tabebuia chrysotricha
☼ ● ✂ 15, 16, 20–24   p. 500

SPRING
Shrubs

Abutilon (most)
FLOWERING MAPLE
☼ ◊ ● ✂ ZONES VARY   p. 131

Alyogyne huegelii
BLUE HIBISCUS
☼ ● ✂ 15–17, 20–24   p. 149

Berberis
BARBERRY
☼ ◊ ● ● ✂ ALL ZONES   p. 182

Brunfelsia pauciflora
◊ ● ✂ 12–17, 20–24   p. 191

Camellia (many)
◊ ● ✂ 4–9, 12, 14–24   p. 200

Ceanothus
WILD LILAC
☼ ◊ ● ✂ 1–9, 14–24   p. 212

Chaenomeles
FLOWERING QUINCE
☼ ● ✂ 1–21   p. 220

Laburnum

Prunus

Ceanothus thyrsiflorus

For growing symbol explanations, please see page 45.

Cornus florida 'Rubra'

Spring garden with white viburnum

Cistus purpureus

Deutzia gracilis

Exochorda macrantha 'The Bride'

Kalmia latifolia

Choisya ternata
MEXICAN ORANGE
☼ ◑ ◐ ✄ 7–9, 12–24   **p. 225**

Cistus (some)
ROCKROSE
☼ ◊ ◐ ✄ 7–9, 12–24   **p. 229**

Corylopsis
WINTER HAZEL
☼ ◑ ◐ ✄ 4–7, 15–17   **p. 244**

Daphne
NEEDS, ZONES VARY   **p. 258**

Deutzia (some)
☼ ◑ ◐ ✄ 1–11, 14–17   **p. 261**

Erica (most)
HEATH
☼ ◐ ✄ ZONES VARY   **p. 275**

Exochorda
PEARL BUSH
☼ ◐ ✄ 3–9, 14–18   **p. 291**

Forsythia
☼ ◐ ✄ 2–16, 18, 19   **p. 297**

Fremontodendron
FLANNEL BUSH
☼ ◊ ✄ 7–24   **p. 300**

Jasminum (some)
JASMINE
☼ ◑ ◐ ✄ ZONES VARY   **p. 336**

Justicia californica
CHUPAROSA
☼ ◊ ✄ 10–13   **p. 342**

Kalmia latifolia
MOUNTAIN LAUREL
◑ ◐ ✄ 1–7   **p. 343**

Kolkwitzia amabilis
BEAUTY BUSH
☼ ◑ ◐ ✄ 1–11, 14–20   **p. 344**

Leptospermum
TEA TREE
☼ ◊ ◐ ✄ 14–24   **p. 350**

Melaleuca (some)
☼ ◊ ◐ ✄ ZONES VARY   **p. 377**

Michelia figo
BANANA SHRUB
☼ ◑ ◐ ✄ 9, 14–24   **p. 380**

Philadelphus (some)
MOCK ORANGE
☼ ◑ ◐ ✄ ZONES VARY   **p. 413**

Pieris
◑ ◐ ✄ ZONES VARY   **p. 418**

Plumbago auriculata
CAPE PLUMBAGO
☼ ◐ ✄ 8, 9, 12–24   **p. 428**

Rhaphiolepis indica
INDIA HAWTHORN
☼ ◐ ◐ ✄ 8–10, 12–24   **p. 453**

Rhododendron
AZALEA, RHODODENDRON
◑ ◐ ◐ ✄ ZONES VARY   **p. 454**

Ribes (some)
CURRANT, GOOSEBERRY
NEEDS, ZONES VARY   **p. 460**

Rosa
ROSE
NEEDS, ZONES VARY   **p. 462**

Rosmarinus officinalis
ROSEMARY
☼ ◊ ◐ ✄ 4–24   **p. 469**

Sophora secundiflora
TEXAS MOUNTAIN LAUREL
☼ ◑ ◊ ◐ ✄ 8–16, 18–24   **p. 488**

Spiraea (some)
☼ ◑ ◐ ✄ 1–11, 14–21   **p. 490**

Syringa
LILAC
☼ ◐ ◐ ✄ ZONES VARY   **p. 499**

Viburnum (some)
NEEDS, ZONES VARY   **p. 518**

Weigela
☼ ◑ ◐ ✄ 1–11, 14–17   **p. 523**

SPRING
Ground Covers, Vines

Bougainvillea
☼ ◑ ◐ ✄ 22–24   **p. 187**

Clematis (some)
☼ ◐ ✄ 1–6, 15–17   **p. 233**

Clytostoma callistegioides
VIOLET TRUMPET VINE
☼ ◑ ◐ ✄ 9, 12–24   **p. 236**

Delosperma nubigenum
ICE PLANT
☼ ◊ ◐ ✄ ALL ZONES   **p. 260**

Diascia (most)
TWINSPUR
☼ ◑ ◐ ✄ ZONES VARY   **p. 262**

Distictis buccinatoria
BLOOD-RED TRUMPET VINE
☼ ◑ ◐ ✄ 8, 9, 14–24   **p. 265**

Drosanthemum
ICE PLANT
☼ ◐ ✄ 14–24   **p. 268**

Erigeron (some)
FLEABANE
☼ ◑ ◐ ◐ ✄ ZONES VARY   **p. 275**

Melaleuca nesophila

Rhododendron 'Bow Bells'

Rosa 'Belle Story'

Syringa

Clematis

Plant listings continue ▶

Lonicera japonica

Osteospermum fruticosum

Wisteria

Albizia julibrissin

Erythrina

Gelsemium sempervirens
CAROLINA JESSAMINE
☼ ◖ ◗ ◕ ✄ 8–24   **p. 304**

Hardenbergia

☼ ◑ ◖ ◗ ✄ ZONES VARY   **p. 316**

Jasminum (some)
JASMINE
☼ ◑ ◖ ✄ ZONES VARY   **p. 336**

Lampranthus
ICE PLANT
☼ ◯ ◖ ✄ 14–24   **p. 346**

Lonicera (some)
HONEYSUCKLE
☼ ◑ ◖ ✄ ZONES VARY   **p. 360**

Macfadyena unguis-cati
CAT'S CLAW
☼ ◑ ◖ ✄ 8–24   **p. 364**

Oenothera
EVENING PRIMROSE
☼ ◖ ✄ ZONES VARY   **p. 392**

Osteospermum fruticosum
TRAILING AFRICAN DAISY
☼ ◖ ✄ 8, 9, 12–24   **p. 397**

Potentilla (some)
CINQUEFOIL
☼ ◑ ◖ ◗ ✄ ZONES VARY   **p. 435**

Solandra maxima
CUP-OF-GOLD VINE
☼ ◖ ✄ 17, 21–24   **p. 487**

Solanum jasminoides
POTATO VINE
☼ ◑ ◖ ◗ ✄ 8, 9, 12–24   **p. 487**

Vinca
PERIWINKLE
◑ ◕ ◖ ◗ ✄ ZONES VARY   **p. 519**

Wisteria

☼ ◑ ◖ ◗ ✄ ALL ZONES   **p. 523**

SUMMER
Trees

Albizia julibrissin
SILK TREE
☼ ◑ ◖ ✄ 2–23   **p. 144**

Calodendrum capense
CAPE CHESTNUT
☼ ◖ ✄ 19, 21–24   **p. 199**

Cassia leptophylla
GOLD MEDALLION TREE
☼ ◖ ✄ 21–24   **p. 210**

Catalpa

☼ ◖ ✄ ALL ZONES   **p. 211**

Chilopsis linearis
DESERT WILLOW
☼ ◖ ✄ 10–13, 18–21   **p. 223**

Chionanthus retusus
CHINESE FRINGE TREE
☼ ◖ ✄ 2–9, 14–24   **p. 224**

Chitalpa tashkentensis
CHITALPA
☼ ◖ ✄ 3–24   **p. 224**

Cornus kousa
KOUSA DOGWOOD
☼ ◑ ◖ ✄ 3–9, 14, 15, 18, 19 **p. 242**

Erythrina (some)
CORAL TREE
☼ ◖ ✄ ZONES VARY   **p. 279**

Eucalyptus ficifolia
RED-FLOWERING GUM
☼ ◖ ◯ ◖ ✄ SEE CHART   **p. 283**

Jacaranda mimosifolia
JACARANDA
☼ ◖ ✄ 12, 13, 15–24   **p. 336**

Lagerstroemia indica
CRAPE MYRTLE
☼ ◖ ✄ ALL ZONES   **p. 345**

Magnolia grandiflora
SOUTHERN MAGNOLIA
☼ ◑ ◖ ✄ 4–12, 14–24   **p. 367**

Robinia ambigua 'Idahoensis'
IDAHO LOCUST
☼ ◯ ✄ ALL ZONES   **p. 461**

Sophora japonica
JAPANESE PAGODA TREE
☼ ◑ ◖ ✄ ALL ZONES   **p. 488**

Stewartia

☼ ◑ ◖ ◗ ✄ 4–6, 14–17, 20, 21 **p. 493**

Vitex agnus-castus
CHASTE TREE
☼ ◖ ◗ ✄ 4–24   **p. 520**

SUMMER
Shrubs

Abelia

☼ ◑ ◖ ✄ ZONES VARY   **p. 130**

Abutilon
FLOWERING MAPLE
☼ ◑ ◖ ✄ ZONES VARY   **p. 131**

Alyogyne huegelii
BLUE HIBISCUS
☼ ◖ ◗ ✄ 15–17, 20–24   **p. 149**

Brunfelsia pauciflora

◑ ◖ ◗ ✄ 12–17, 20–24   **p. 191**

Buddleia davidii
BUTTERFLY BUSH
☼ ◑ ◖ ◗ ✄ ALL ZONES   **p. 192**

Caesalpinia
BIRD OF PARADISE
☼ ◖ ✄ ZONES VARY   **p. 194**

Magnolia grandiflora

Calodendrum capense

Chitalpa tashkentensis

Eucalyptus ficifolia

Jacaranda mimosifolia

For growing symbol explanations, please see page 45.

Buddleia davidii

Caryopteris clandonensis

Fuchsia

Hebe andersonii

Callistemon
BOTTLEBRUSH
NEEDS VARY, ☀ 8, 9, 12–24   **p. 197**

Calluna vulgaris
SCOTCH HEATHER
☀ ◑ ◐ 2–6, 15–17   **p. 197**

Carpenteria californica
BUSH ANEMONE
☀ ◑ ◐ ◑ 5–9, 14–24   **p. 208**

Caryopteris
BLUEBEARD
☀ ◐ ZONES VARY   **p. 209**

Ceratostigma
PLUMBAGO
☀ ◑ ◐ ◐ ZONES VARY   **p. 217**

Cistus (some)
ROCKROSE
☀ ◐ ◐ 7–9, 12–24   **p. 229**

Clerodendrum
GLORYBOWER
◑ ◐ ZONES VARY   **p. 235**

Clethra
☀ ◑ ◐ ZONES VARY   **p. 235**

Daboecia
IRISH HEATH
☀ ◑ ◐ ZONES VARY   **p. 256**

Deutzia (some)
☀ ◑ ◐ 1–11, 14–17   **p. 261**

Escallonia
☀ ◑ ◐ ◐ MOST ZONES   **p. 280**

Fuchsia
◑ ◐ ◐ ZONES VARY   **p. 300**

Gardenia jasminoides
☀ ◐ ◐ 7–9, 12–16, 18–23   **p. 302**

Grewia occidentalis
LAVENDER STARFLOWER
☀ ◐ 8, 9, 12–24   **p. 313**

Hebe
☀ ◑ ◐ ZONES VARY   **p. 316**

Hibiscus
☀ ◐ ZONES VARY   **p. 322**

Hydrangea
☀ ◑ ◐ ZONES VARY   **p. 327**

Jasminum (some)
JASMINE
☀ ◑ ◐ ZONES VARY   **p. 336**

Justicia carnea
BRAZILIAN PLUME FLOWER
◐ ◐ ◐ 8, 9, 13–24   **p. 342**

Lavandula
LAVENDER
☀ ◐ ZONES VARY   **p. 349**

Lavatera
TREE MALLOW
☀ ◐ ◐ ZONES VARY   **p. 349**

Leucophyllum
TEXAS RANGER
☀ ◐ 7–24   **p. 352**

Melaleuca (some)
☀ ◐ ◐ ZONES VARY   **p. 377**

Nerium oleander
OLEANDER
☀ ◐ ◐ 8–16, 18–24   **p. 390**

Philadelphus (some)
MOCK ORANGE
☀ ◑ ◐ ◐ ZONES VARY   **p. 413**

Phlomis
JERUSALEM SAGE
NEEDS, ZONES VARY   **p. 414**

Potentilla
CINQUEFOIL
☀ ◑ ◐ ◐ ZONES VARY   **p. 435**

Rosa (some)
ROSE
NEEDS, ZONES VARY   **p. 462**

Salvia (several)
SAGE
NEEDS, ZONES VARY   **p. 473**

Spiraea (some)
☀ ◑ ◐ 1–11, 14–21   **p. 490**

Tibouchina urvilleana
PRINCESS FLOWER
☀ ◐ 16, 17, 21–24   **p. 506**

SUMMER
Ground Covers, Vines

Antigonon leptopus
QUEEN'S WREATH
☀ ◐ 12, 13, 18–21   **p. 154**

Bougainvillea
☀ ◑ ◐ 22–24   **p. 187**

Campsis
TRUMPET VINE
☀ ◑ ◐ ZONES VARY   **p. 203**

Clematis (some)
☀ ◐ 1–6, 15–17   **p. 233**

Delosperma cooperi
ICE PLANT
☀ ◐ ◐ ALL ZONES   **p. 260**

Distictis
TRUMPET VINE
☀ ◐ ZONES VARY   **p. 265**

Jasminum nitidum

Lavandula angustifolia

Potentilla fruticosa

Salvia muelleri

Lantana camara

Plant listings continue ▶

Passiflora mollissima

Scaevola

Solanum jasminoides

Sollya heterophylla

Trachelospermum jasminoides

Hibbertia scandens
GUINEA GOLD VINE
☼ ◐ ◉ ✄ 16, 17, 21–24   **p. 322**

Jasminum (some)
JASMINE
☼ ◐ ◉ ✄ ZONES VARY   **p. 336**

Lantana
☼ ◉ ◉ ✄ 8–10, 12–22   **p. 347**

Lonicera
HONEYSUCKLE
☼ ◐ ◉ ✄ ZONES VARY   **p. 360**

Mandevilla
NEEDS, ZONES VARY   **p. 375**

Pandorea jasminoides
BOWER VINE
☼ ◐ ◉ ✄ 16–24   **p. 399**

Passiflora
PASSION VINE
☼ ◉ ✄ ZONES VARY   **p. 401**

Petrea volubilis
QUEEN'S WREATH
☼ ◉ ✄ 19–24   **p. 412**

Plumbago auriculata
CAPE PLUMBAGO
☼ ◉ ✄ 8, 9, 12–24   **p. 428**

Podranea ricasoliana
PINK TRUMPET VINE
☼ ◉ ◉ ✄ 9, 12, 13, 19–24   **p. 431**

Scaevola
☼ ◉ ✄ 8, 9, 14–24   **p. 478**

Solanum jasminoides
POTATO VINE
☼ ◐ ◉ ✄ 8, 9, 12–24   **p. 487**

Sollya heterophylla
AUSTRALIAN BLUEBELL CREEPER
☼ ◐ ◉ ◉ ✄ 8, 9, 14–24   **p. 488**

Trachelospermum jasminoides
STAR JASMINE
☼ ◐ ◉ ✄ 8–24   **p. 509**

Verbena
NEEDS, ZONES VARY   **p. 517**

FALL
Trees

Bauhinia blakeana
HONG KONG ORCHID TREE
☼ ◉ ✄ 13, 19, 21, 23   **p. 179**

Chorisia
FLOSS SILK TREE
☼ ◉ ✄ ZONES VARY   **p. 225**

Erythrina humeana
NATAL CORAL TREE
☼ ◉ ✄ 12, 13, 20–24   **p. 280**

Eucalyptus erythrocorys
RED-CAP GUM
☼ ◊ ◉ ✄ SEE CHART   **p. 283**

Eucalyptus woodwardii
LEMON-FLOWERED GUM
☼ ◊ ◉ ✄ SEE CHART   **p. 287**

Melaleuca (some)
☼ ◊ ◉ ✄ ZONES VARY   **p. 377**

Prunus subhirtella 'Autumnalis'
☼ ◉ ✄ 2–7, 14–20   **p. 440**

FALL
Shrubs

Abelia
☼ ◐ ◉ ✄ ZONES VARY   **p. 130**

Alyogyne huegelii
BLUE HIBISCUS
☼ ◉ ◉ ✄ 15–17, 20–24   **p. 149**

Brugmansia
ANGEL'S TRUMPET
☼ ◐ ◉ ◉ ✄ 16–24   **p. 191**

Buddleia davidii
BUTTERFLY BUSH
☼ ◐ ◉ ◉ ✄ ALL ZONES   **p. 192**

Caesalpinia
BIRD OF PARADISE
☼ ◉ ✄ ZONES VARY   **p. 194**

Camellia sasanqua
◐ ◉ ✄ 4–9, 12, 14–24   **p. 202**

Cassia (some)
SENNA
☼ ◉ ✄ ZONES VARY   **p. 210**

Cleyera japonica
◐ ◉ ✄ 4–6, 8, 9, 14–24   **p. 235**

Escallonia
☼ ◐ ◉ ◉ ✄ MOST ZONES   **p. 280**

Fuchsia
◐ ◉ ◉◉ ✄ ZONES VARY   **p. 300**

Hibiscus (some)
☼ ◉ ✄ ZONES VARY   **p. 322**

Lavatera
TREE MALLOW
☼ ◉ ◉ ✄ ZONES VARY   **p. 349**

Melaleuca (some)
☼ ◊ ◉ ✄ ZONES VARY   **p. 377**

Nerium oleander
OLEANDER
☼ ◊ ◉ ✄ 8–16, 18–24   **p. 390**

Melaleuca nesophila

Brugmansia versicolor 'Charles Grimaldi'

Alyogyne huegelii

Fuchsia

Lavatera thuringiaca

For growing symbol explanations, please see page 45.

Rosa 'Charmian'

Tibouchina urvilleana

Lonicera

Verbena

Bauhinia variegata 'Candida'

Rosa (some)
ROSE
NEEDS, ZONES VARY — **p. 462**

Salvia (some)
SAGE
NEEDS, ZONES VARY — **p. 473**

Tibouchina urvilleana
PRINCESS FLOWER
16, 17, 21–24 — **p. 506**

FALL
Ground Covers, Vines

Antigonon leptopus
QUEEN'S WREATH
12, 13, 18–21 — **p. 154**

Clematis (some)

1–6, 15–17 — **p. 233**

Distictis buccinatoria
BLOOD-RED TRUMPET VINE
8, 9, 14–24 — **p. 265**

Lonicera (some)
HONEYSUCKLE
ZONES VARY — **p. 360**

Mandevilla (some)

ZONES VARY — **p. 375**

Millettia reticulata
EVERGREEN WISTERIA
20–24 — **p. 381**

Plumbago auriculata
CAPE PLUMBAGO
8, 9, 12–24 — **p. 428**

Verbena (some)

NEEDS, ZONES VARY — **p. 517**

WINTER
Trees

Acacia (many)

ZONES VARY — **p. 131**

Bauhinia variegata
PURPLE ORCHID TREE
13, 18–23 — **p. 179**

Erythrina (some)
CORAL TREE
ZONES VARY — **p. 279**

Eucalyptus preissiana
BELL-FRUITED MALLEE
SEE CHART — **p. 285**

Michelia doltsopa

14–24 — **p. 380**

Prunus mume
JAPANESE FLOWERING PLUM
2–9, 12–22 — **p. 443**

WINTER
Shrubs

Acacia
ZONES VARY — **p. 131**

Camellia (many)
4–9, 12, 14–24 — **p. 200**

Cassia (most)
SENNA
ZONES VARY — **p. 210**

Chaenomeles
FLOWERING QUINCE
1–21 — **p. 220**

Chamelaucium uncinatum
GERALDTON WAXFLOWER
8, 9, 12–24 — **p. 221**

Chimonanthus praecox
WINTERSWEET
ZONES VARY — **p. 223**

Daphne (some)

NEEDS, ZONES VARY — **p. 258**

Erica (many)
HEATH
ZONES VARY — **p. 275**

Euphorbia pulcherrima
POINSETTIA
13, 16–24 — **p. 289**

Forsythia

2–16, 18, 19 — **p. 297**

Hamamelis (most)
WITCH HAZEL
ZONES VARY — **p. 316**

Jasminum mesnyi
PRIMROSE JASMINE
4–24 — **p. 337**

Viburnum (some)

NEEDS, ZONES VARY — **p. 518**

WINTER
Ground Covers, Vines

Cephalophyllum 'Red Spike'
RED SPIKE ICE PLANT
8, 9, 11–24 — **p. 217**

Gelsemium sempervirens
CAROLINA JESSAMINE
8–24 — **p. 304**

Hardenbergia

ZONES VARY — **p. 316**

Jasminum (some)
JASMINE
ZONES VARY — **p. 336**

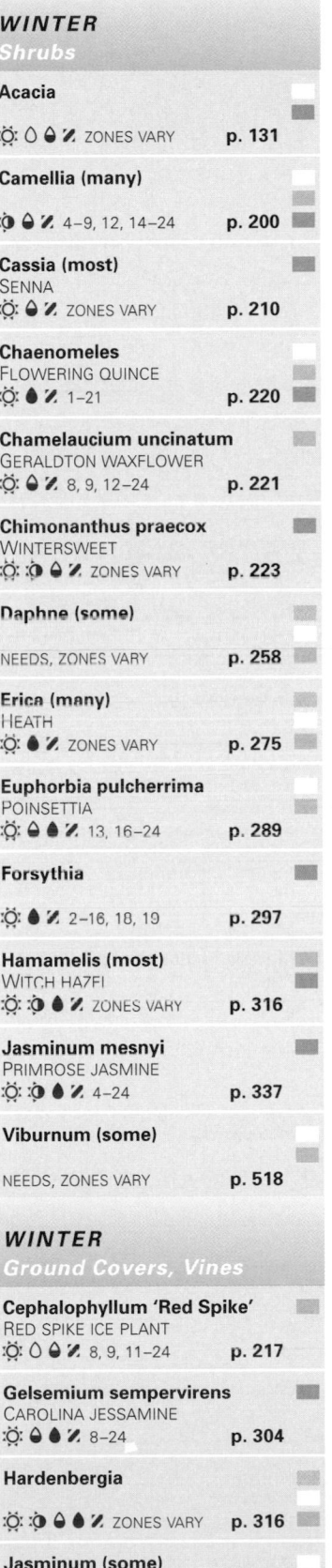

Camellia

Chaenomeles

Daphne odora 'Marginata'

Forsythia

Viburnum tinus

ANNUALS
for Seasonal Color

Flowering annuals provide the quick, showy color that can bring almost instant drama to an otherwise quiet corner of the garden. They come in every size and color imaginable and make delightful fillers between shrubs, as well as colorful companions to perennials. Some plants on this list are biennials or perennials commonly grown as annuals. Cool-season annuals grow best in cool soils and mild temperatures—fall through spring in mild-winter climates. Warm-season annuals are planted after the last frost and generally grow best between late spring and fall. In hot interior climates some annuals grow best from early to late spring.

Lathyrus odoratus

Antirrhinum majus

Calendula officinalis

Campanula medium

Chrysanthemum paludosum

COOL-SEASON ANNUALS

Antirrhinum majus
SNAPDRAGON
☼ ◖ ✂ ALL ZONES — p. 154

Cabbage, kale, flowering
☼ ◑ ◖ ✂ ALL ZONES — p. 194

Calendula officinalis
POT MARIGOLD
☼ ◖ ✂ ALL ZONES — p. 195

Campanula medium
CANTERBURY BELL
☼ ◑ ◖ ✂ 1–9, 14–24 — p. 204

Centaurea cyanus
CORNFLOWER
☼ ◖ ✂ ZONES VARY — p. 216

Chrysanthemum (several)
NEEDS, ZONES VARY — p. 226

Clarkia amoena
GODETIA
☼ ◖ ✂ ALL ZONES — p. 233

Consolida ambigua
LARKSPUR
☼ ◖ ✂ ALL ZONES — p. 239

Cynoglossum amabile
CHINESE FORGET-ME-NOT
☼ ◖ ✂ ALL ZONES — p. 255

Dianthus (some)
☼ ◑ ◖ ✂ ALL ZONES — p. 261

Dimorphotheca
AFRICAN DAISY
☼ ◖ ✂ ALL ZONES — p. 265

Eschscholzia californica
CALIFORNIA POPPY
☼ ◊ ◖ ✂ ALL ZONES — p. 281

Iberis umbellata
GLOBE CANDYTUFT
☼ ◖ ✂ ALL ZONES — p. 329

Lathyrus odoratus
SWEET PEA
☼ ◖ ✂ ALL ZONES — p. 348

Linaria maroccana
TOADFLAX
☼ ◑ ◖ ✂ ALL ZONES — p. 356

Matthiola incana
STOCK
☼ ◑ ◖ ✂ ALL ZONES — p. 376

Myosotis sylvatica
FORGET-ME-NOT
◖ ✂ ALL ZONES — p. 385

Nemesia strumosa
☼ ◖ ✂ ALL ZONES — p. 388

Papaver (some)
POPPY
☼ ◖ ◊ ✂ ZONES VARY — p. 400

Primula (many)
PRIMROSE
☼ ◑ ◑ ◖ ◖ ✂ MOST ZONES — p. 436

Schizanthus pinnatus
POOR MAN'S ORCHID
◑ ◖ ✂ 1–6, 15–17, 21–24 — p. 479

Senecio hybridus
CINERARIA
◑ ◖ ✂ 16, 17, 22–24 — p. 483

Viola
PANSY, VIOLA
☼ ◑ ◖ ✂ ZONES VARY — p. 519

WARM-SEASON ANNUALS

Ageratum houstonianum
FLOSS FLOWER
☼ ◑ ◖ ✂ ALL ZONES — p. 142

VERTICAL BAR: The band indicates blooming season in most zones.

SPRING	
SUMMER	
FALL	
WINTER	

Clarkia amoena

Eschscholzia californica

Nemesia strumosa

Papaver

For growing symbol explanations, please see page 45.

Catharanthus roseus

Celosia

Helichrysum bracteatum

Heliotropium arborescens

Ipomoea

Lobelia erinus

Brachycome iberidifolia
SWAN RIVER DAISY
ALL ZONES　　**p. 189**

Browallia speciosa
AMETHYST FLOWER
ALL ZONES　　**p. 191**

Callistephus chinensis
CHINA ASTER
ALL ZONES　　**p. 197**

Catharanthus roseus
MADAGASCAR PERIWINKLE
ALL ZONES　　**p. 212**

Celosia
COCKSCOMB
ALL ZONES　　**p. 215**

Cleome hasslerana
SPIDER FLOWER
ALL ZONES　　**p. 235**

Convolvulus tricolor
DWARF MORNING GLORY
ALL ZONES　　**p. 239**

Coreopsis tinctoria
CALLIOPSIS
ALL ZONES　　**p. 241**

Cosmos

ALL ZONES　　**p. 245**

Diascia barberae
TWINSPUR
ALL ZONES　　**p. 262**

Eustoma grandiflorum
LISIANTHUS
ALL ZONES　　**p. 290**

Gaillardia pulchella

ALL ZONES　　**p. 302**

Gomphrena
GLOBE AMARANTH
ALL ZONES　　**p. 309**

Gypsophila elegans

ALL ZONES　　**p. 314**

Helianthus annuus
COMMON SUNFLOWER
ALL ZONES　　**p. 318**

Helichrysum bracteatum
STRAWFLOWER
ALL ZONES　　**p. 319**

Heliotropium arborescens
COMMON HELIOTROPE
8–24　　**p. 319**

Impatiens
BALSAM
NEEDS, ZONES VARY　　**p. 330**

Ipomoea
MORNING GLORY
ZONES VARY　　**p. 332**

Lavatera trimestris
ANNUAL MALLOW
ALL ZONES　　**p. 349**

Limonium (some)
SEA LAVENDER
ZONES VARY　　**p. 356**

Lobelia erinus

ALL ZONES　　**p. 359**

Lobularia maritima
SWEET ALYSSUM
ALL ZONES　　**p. 360**

Mimulus hybridus
MONKEY FLOWER
NEEDS VARY, ALL ZONES　　**p. 381**

Nicotiana

ZONES VARY　　**p. 390**

Petunia hybrida
COMMON GARDEN PETUNIA
ALL ZONES　　**p. 412**

Phlox drummondii
ANNUAL PHLOX
ALL ZONES　　**p. 415**

Portulaca grandiflora
MOSS ROSE
ALL ZONES　　**p. 434**

Salpiglossis sinuata
PAINTED TONGUE
ALL ZONES　　**p. 472**

Salvia splendens
SCARLET SAGE
ALL ZONES　　**p. 475**

Sanvitalia procumbens
CREEPING ZINNIA
ALL ZONES　　**p. 476**

Scabiosa atropurpurea
PINCUSHION FLOWER
ALL ZONES　　**p. 478**

Tagetes
MARIGOLD
NEEDS VARY, ALL ZONES　　**p. 500**

Thunbergia alata
BLACK-EYED SUSAN VINE
ALL ZONES　　**p. 505**

Tithonia rotundifolia
MEXICAN SUNFLOWER
ALL ZONES　　**p. 507**

Tropaeolum majus
GARDEN NASTURTIUM
ALL ZONES　　**p. 512**

Verbena

NEEDS VARY, ALL ZONES　　**p. 517**

Zinnia

ALL ZONES　　**p. 528**

Nicotiana

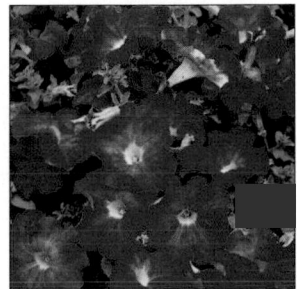
Petunia hybrida

Tagetes tenuifolia 'Lemon Gem'

Thunbergia alata

Verbena

Zinnia elegans
Peter Pan strain

BULBS
and
Bulblike Plants

Some of a garden's showiest flowers appear from bulbs, corms, tubers, rhizomes, and tuberous roots (often lumped together as bulbs). These humble-looking structures store food, allowing the plants to survive underground until it's time to send out shoots and flowers. Bulbs thrive in many different environments. Daffodils and iris, for example, thrive equally well in both desert and mountain regions. Other bulbs have more specific growing needs. You can successfully grow many bulbs out of their range by planting them in containers and growing them indoors (amaryllis is a common example) or by providing a period of chilling in the refrigerator to simulate winter (in mild-winter climates crocus, hyacinths, and tulips should be chilled for 6 weeks).

Freesia

Anemone blanda

Cyclamen persicum

Hyacinthus orientalis

COLOR CODES: Each tint represents a range of colors, not a color match.

BLUE–PURPLE	
WHITE–CREAM	
PINK–RED	
YELLOW–ORANGE	

FALL PLANTED BULBS

Allium
ORNAMENTAL ALLIUM
☀ ◐ ◖ ⚡ ALL ZONES   p. 145

Amaryllis belladonna
NAKED LADY
☀ ◌ ⚡ 4–24   p. 149

Anemone
WINDFLOWER
NEEDS, ZONES VARY   p. 151

Babiana
BABOON FLOWER
☀ ◐ ◖ ◖ ⚡ 4–24   p. 173

Brodiaea
☀ ◌ ⚡ ALL ZONES   p. 190

Chionodoxa
GLORY-OF-THE-SNOW
◐ ◖ ⚡ 1–7, 14–20   p. 224

Crocus
☀ ◐ ◖ ⚡ ALL ZONES   p. 249

Cyclamen (florists' types)
☀ ◐ ◖ ⚡ ZONES VARY   p. 253

Endymion
☀ ◐ ◖ ⚡ ALL ZONES   p. 272

Freesia
☀ ◐ ◖ ⚡ 8, 9, 12–24   p. 300

Fritillaria
FRITILLARY
☀ ◐ ◖ ◖ ⚡ 1–7, 15–17   p. 300

Galanthus
SNOWDROP
☀ ◐ ◖ ⚡ 1–9, 14–17   p. 302

Hippeastrum
AMARYLLIS
☀ ◖ ⚡ 16, 17, 19, 21–24   p. 323

Hyacinthus orientalis
COMMON HYACINTH
☀ ◐ ◖ ⚡ ALL ZONES   p. 326

Ipheion uniflorum
SPRING STAR FLOWER
☀ ◐ ◖ ◖ ⚡ 4–24   p. 331

Iris
NEEDS, ZONES VARY   p. 332

Ixia
AFRICAN CORN LILY
☀ ◖ ⚡ 5–24   p. 336

Leucojum
SNOWFLAKE
◐ ◖ ◖ ⚡ ZONES VARY   p. 352

Lilium
LILY
◐ ◖ ⚡ ALL ZONES   p. 354

Muscari
GRAPE HYACINTH
☀ ◐ ◌ ◖ ⚡ ALL ZONES   p. 384

Narcissus
DAFFODIL
☀ ◐ ◖ ⚡ ALL ZONES   p. 387

Oxalis (some)
NEEDS, ZONES VARY   p. 397

Paeonia (herbaceous)
PEONY
☀ ◐ ◖ ⚡ 1–11, 14–16   p. 398

Puschkinia scilloides
☀ ◐ ◖ ⚡ ALL ZONES   p. 446

Ranunculus asiaticus
PERSIAN RANUNCULUS
☀ ◖ ⚡ ALL ZONES   p. 450

Iris

Narcissus

Lilium Asiatic hybrid

For growing symbol explanations, please see page 45.

Tulipa

Begonia

Dahlia

Gladiolus

Liatris

Rhodohypoxis baurii
☼ ● ✤ 4–7, 14–24   **p. 458**

Rhodophiala bifida
☼ ● ✤ 8, 9, 14–24   **p. 458**

Scilla
SQUILL
☼ ◑ ● ✤ ZONES VARY   **p. 480**

Sparaxis tricolor
HARLEQUIN FLOWER
☼ ● ✤ 9, 12–24   **p. 489**

Triteleia
☼ ◊ ✤ ALL ZONES   **p. 511**

Tritonia crocata
FLAME FREESIA
☼ ● ✤ 9, 13–24   **p. 511**

Tulipa
TULIP
☼ ● ✤ ALL ZONES   **p. 513**

Watsonia pyramidata
☼ ● ● ✤ 4–9, 12–24   **p. 522**

Zantedeschia aethiopica
COMMON CALLA
☼ ◑ ● ● ✤ MOST ZONES   **p. 526**

WINTER-SPRING PLANTED BULBS

Begonia, tuberous
◑ ● ● ✤ 14–24   **p. 182**

Caladium bicolor
FANCY-LEAFED CALADIUM
● ● ✤ 12, 13, 16, 17, 22–24   **p. 194**

Canna
☼ ● ✤ ALL ZONES   **p. 205**

Crocosmia
☼ ◑ ◊ ✤ 5–24   **p. 249**

Cyclamen (florists' types)
☼ ◑ ● ✤ ZONES VARY   **p. 253**

Dahlia
☼ ◑ ● ✤ ZONES VARY   **p. 256**

Gladiolus
☼ ● ✤ ALL ZONES   **p. 307**

Gloriosa rothschildiana
GLORY LILY
☼ ● ✤ 24   **p. 308**

Hippeastrum
AMARYLLIS
◑ ● ● ✤ 16, 17, 19, 21–24   **p. 323**

Homeria collina
☼ ◑ ● ✤ 4–24   **p. 324**

Hymenocallis
☼ ◑ ● ✤ 5, 6, 8, 9, 14–24   **p. 327**

Liatris
GAYFEATHER
☼ ● ● ✤ 1–10, 14–24   **p. 353**

Lilium, Oriental hybrids
☼ ● ✤ ALL ZONES   **p. 355**

Polianthes tuberosa
TUBEROSE
☼ ◑ ● ✤ 15–17, 22–24   **p. 432**

Tigridia pavonia
MEXICAN SHELL FLOWER
☼ ◑ ● ✤ ALL ZONES   **p. 506**

Zantedeschia
CALLA
☼ ◑ ● ● ✤ MOST ZONES   **p. 526**

Zephyranthes
ZEPHYR FLOWER
☼ ● ✤ 1–9, 12–24   **p. 527**

SUMMER PLANTED BULBS

Colchicum
MEADOW SAFFRON
☼ ● ✤ 1–9, 14–24   **p. 237**

Crocus (fall-flowering)
☼ ◑ ● ✤ ALL ZONES   **p. 249**

Cyclamen (except florists' types)
☼ ◑ ● ✤ ZONES VARY   **p. 253**

Lycoris
SPIDER LILY
☼ ◑ ● ✤ ZONES VARY   **p. 363**

Sternbergia lutea
☼ ● ✤ ALL ZONES   **p. 493**

PLANT ANY TIME

Agapanthus
LILY-OF-THE-NILE
☼ ◑ ● ✤ 7–9, 12–24   **p. 141**

Clivia miniata
KAFFIR LILY
● ● ✤ 12–17, 19–24   **p. 236**

Dietes
FORTNIGHT LILY
☼ ◑ ● ● ✤ 8, 9, 12–24   **p. 264**

Hemerocallis
DAYLILY
☼ ◑ ● ✤ ALL ZONES   **p. 320**

Colchicum

Crocus

Agapanthus 'Peter Pan'

Clivia miniata

Hemerocallis

AUTUMN FOLIAGE COLOR

P lants that change leaf color in fall do so in varying degrees, depending on the nature of the plant and the climate it grows in. Generally, the change is less noticeable in mild-winter areas than in cold-winter regions. The plants listed below display a noticeable autumnal foliage change; many are worth planting for that reason alone. Leaf color can be variable within a species, so it's best to shop for plants in fall when their leaves are changing color.

Autumnal planting with maples

COLOR CODES: Each tint represents a range of colors, not a color match. ♣ indicates shrubs that can become small trees.

RED–PURPLE ▇
YELLOW–ORANGE ▇

TREES

Acer (many)
MAPLE
☼ ◐ ◕ ✎ ZONES VARY   **p. 135**

Amelanchier
SERVICEBERRY
☼ ◕ ✎ 1–6   **p. 150**

Cercidiphyllum japonicum
KATSURA TREE
☼ ◑ ◕ ✎ 1–6   **p. 218**

Cercis
REDBUD
NEEDS, ZONES VARY   **p. 218**

Cornus (many)
DOGWOOD
☼ ◑ ◕◕ ✎ ZONES VARY   **p. 242**

Crataegus (some)
HAWTHORN
☼ ◕ ✎ 1–12, 14–17   **p. 247**

Franklinia alatamaha
☼ ◑ ◕ ◕◕ ✎ 2–6, 14–17   **p. 298**

Fraxinus (deciduous)
ASH
NEEDS, ZONES VARY   **p. 298**

Ginkgo biloba
MAIDENHAIR TREE
☼ ◔ ◕ ✎ 1–10, 12, 14–24   **p. 307**

Gleditsia triacanthos
HONEY LOCUST
☼ ◕ ◕ ✎ 1–16,18–20   **p. 308**

Gymnocladus dioica
KENTUCKY COFFEE TREE
☼ ◕ ✎ MOST ZONES   **p. 314**

Halesia
☼ ◕ ✎ 2–9, 14–24   **p. 315**

Koelreuteria bipinnata
CHINESE FLAME TREE
☼ ◕ ✎ 8–24   **p. 344**

Lagerstroemia indica
CRAPE MYRTLE
☼ ◕ ✎ ALL ZONES   **p. 345**

Liquidambar
SWEET GUM
☼ ◕ ✎ ZONES VARY   **p. 357**

Magnolia denudata
YULAN MAGNOLIA
☼ ◑ ◕ ✎ 8, 9, 14–24   **p. 366**

Malus 'Prairifire'
CRABAPPLE
☼ ◕ ✎ 1–21   **p. 374**

Nyssa sylvatica
SOUR GUM
☼ ◕ ◕ ✎ 3–10, 14–21   **p. 392**

Oxydendrum arboreum
SOURWOOD
☼ ◕ ✎ 3–9, 14–17   **p. 397**

Persimmon
NEEDS, ZONES VARY   **p. 412**

Pistacia chinensis
CHINESE PISTACHE
☼ ◔ ◕ ◕ ✎ 4–16, 18–23   **p. 425**

Populus (some)
POPLAR
☼ ◕ ✎ ZONES VARY   **p. 434**

Prunus (deciduous)
NEEDS, ZONES VARY   **p. 439**

Pyrus (deciduous)
ORNAMENTAL PEAR
☼ ◕ ✎ ZONES VARY   **p. 447**

Quercus coccinea
SCARLET OAK
☼ ◔ ◕ ✎ 1–11, 14, 15, 18–20   **p. 448**

For growing symbol explanations, please see page 45.

Cercis canadensis 'Forest Pansy'

Cornus florida

Crataegus

Ginkgo biloba

Gleditsia triacanthos

Lagerstroemia indica

Persimmon

Pistacia chinensis

Quercus kelloggii
CALIFORNIA BLACK OAK
☼ ◐ ◑ ✂ 5–7, 15, 16, 18–21 **p. 448**

Quercus palustris
PIN OAK
☼ ● ✂ ALL ZONES **p. 449**

Quercus phellos
WILLOW OAK
☼ ◐ ● ✂ 1–4, 6–16, 18–21 **p. 449**

Quercus rubra
RED OAK
☼ ● ✂ 1–12, 14–24 **p. 449**

Salix
WILLOW
☼ ●● ✂ ALL ZONES **p. 471**

Sapium sebiferum
CHINESE TALLOW TREE
☼ ● ✂ 8, 9, 12–16, 18–21 **p. 476**

Sassafras albidum
SASSAFRAS
☼ ● ✂ 3–9, 14–17 **p. 477**

Sorbus
MOUNTAIN ASH
☼ ◐ ● ✂ 1–10, 14–17 **p. 489**

Styrax japonicus
JAPANESE SNOWBELL
☼ ◐ ● ✂ 3–10, 14–21 **p. 497**

Zelkova serrata
SAWLEAF ZELKOVA
☼ ● ✂ 3–21 **p. 527**

SHRUBS

Amelanchier
SERVICEBERRY
☼ ● ✂ 1–6 **p. 150** ♣

Berberis thunbergii
JAPANESE BARBERRY
☼ ◐ ●● ✂ ALL ZONES **p. 183**

Blueberry
☼ ●● ✂ 4–6, 17 **p. 186**

Cotinus coggygria
SMOKE TREE
☼ ● ✂ ALL ZONES **p. 245** ♣

Cotoneaster (most deciduous)
☼ ◐ ● ✂ ZONES VARY **p. 245**

Disanthus cercidifolius
☼ ◐ ● ✂ 4–7, 14–17 **p. 265**

Enkianthus
◐ ● ✂ 2–9, 14–21 **p. 272**

Euonymus alata
WINGED EUONYMUS
☼ ◐ ●● ✂ 1–9, 14–16 **p. 288**

Fothergilla
◐ ● ✂ 3–9, 14–17 **p. 297**

Hamamelis
WITCH HAZEL
☼ ◐ ● ✂ ZONES VARY **p. 316** ♣

Hydrangea quercifolia
OAKLEAF HYDRANGEA
☼ ◐ ● ✂ 1–22 **p. 327**

Kerria japonica
☼ ◐ ● ✂ 1–21 **p. 343**

Lagerstroemia indica
CRAPE MYRTLE
☼ ● ✂ ALL ZONES **p. 345**

Magnolia salicifolia
ANISE MAGNOLIA
☼ ● ✂ 2–9, 14–21 **p. 368** ♣

Nandina domestica
HEAVENLY BAMBOO
☼ ◐ ● ◐ ●● ✂ 5–24 **p. 386**

Parrotia persica
PERSIAN PARROTIA
☼ ● ●✂ 4–6, 15–17 **p. 400** ♣

Photinia villosa
☼ ● ● ✂ 1–6 **p. 416** ♣

Punica granatum
POMEGRANATE
☼ ● ✂ 5–23 **p. 445** ♣

Rhododendron
AZALEA, DECIDUOUS
◐ ● ●● ✂ 4–7, 15–17 **p. 458**

Rhus (deciduous)
SUMAC
☼ ◐ ● ✂ ZONES VARY **p. 459** ♣

Spiraea bumalda
☼ ◐ ● ✂ 1–11, 14–21 **p. 491**

Stewartia
☼ ◐ ●● ✂ 4–6, 14–17, 20, 21 **p. 493** ♣

Viburnum (many)
NEEDS, ZONES VARY **p. 518**

VINES

Grape
☼ ◐ ● ✂ ZONES VARY **p. 310**

Parthenocissus
☼ ◐ ● ● ✂ ZONES VARY **p. 401**

Wisteria
☼ ◐ ● ● ✂ ALL ZONES **p. 523**

Populus tremuloides

Pyrus calleryana

Quercus coccinea

Berberis thunbergii 'Rose Glow'

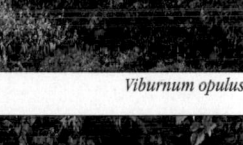
Rhus typhina 'Laciniata'

Viburnum opulus

Parthenocissus quinquefolia

Parthenocissus tricuspidata

57

COLORFUL FRUITS AND BERRIES

Heteromeles arbutifolia

The plants listed below offer a showy display of color in the form of fruit or berries that, depending on the plant, may be red, orange, yellow, purplish, blue, black, or white. Some produce this fruit in addition to striking flowers; others, as a surprise following an inconspicuous blossoming. Pyracantha, toyon, and certain other plants produce fruit that birds find especially attractive. Trees like citrus and persimmon yield prized kitchen crops.

Mandarin orange

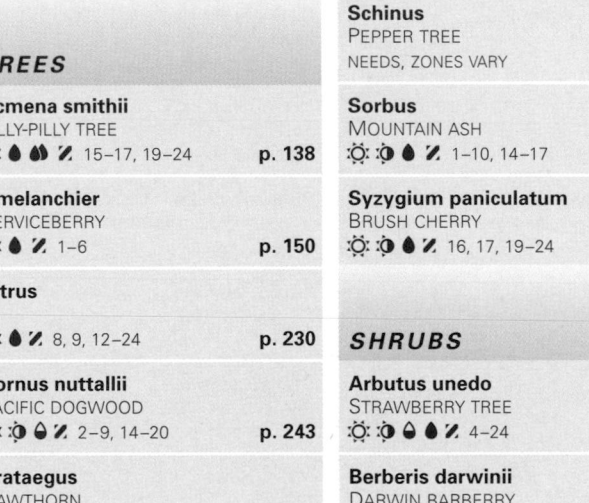

Malus 'Red Jade'

Persimmon

Sambucus mexicana

TREES

Acmena smithii
LILLY-PILLY TREE
☼ ⬤ ⬤ ⚡ 15–17, 19–24   **p. 138**

Amelanchier
SERVICEBERRY
☼ ⬤ ⚡ 1–6   **p. 150**

Citrus
☼ ⬤ ⚡ 8, 9, 12–24   **p. 230**

Cornus nuttallii
PACIFIC DOGWOOD
☼ ◑ ⬤ ⚡ 2–9, 14–20   **p. 243**

Crataegus
HAWTHORN
☼ ⬤ ⚡ 1–12, 14–17   **p. 247**

Eriobotrya japonica
LOQUAT
☼ ◑ ⬤ ⚡ 4–24   **p. 275**

Ilex (many)
HOLLY
☼ ◑ ⬤ ⚡ ZONES VARY   **p. 329**

Koelreuteria
NEEDS, ZONES VARY   **p. 344**

Malus
CRABAPPLE
☼ ⬤ ⚡ 1–21   **p. 372**

Persimmon
NEEDS, ZONES VARY   **p. 412**

Pittosporum rhombifolium
QUEENSLAND PITTOSPORUM
☼ ◑ ⬤ ⬤ ⚡ 12–24   **p. 426**

Sambucus
ELDERBERRY
☼ ◑ ⬤ ⚡ ZONES VARY   **p. 473**

Schinus
PEPPER TREE
NEEDS, ZONES VARY   **p. 479**

Sorbus
MOUNTAIN ASH
☼ ◑ ⬤ ⚡ 1–10, 14–17   **p. 489**

Syzygium paniculatum
BRUSH CHERRY
☼ ◑ ⬤ ⚡ 16, 17, 19–24   **p. 500**

SHRUBS

Arbutus unedo   ♣
STRAWBERRY TREE
☼ ◑ ⬤ ⬤ ⚡ 4–24   **p. 162**

Berberis darwinii
DARWIN BARBERRY
☼ ◑ ⬤ ⬤ ⚡ ALL ZONES   **p. 183**

Berberis thunbergii
JAPANESE BARBERRY
☼ ◑ ⬤ ⬤ ⚡ ALL ZONES   **p. 183**

Berberis wilsoniae
WILSON BARBERRY
☼ ◑ ⬤ ⬤ ⚡ ALL ZONES   **p. 183**

Callicarpa bodinieri
BEAUTYBERRY
☼ ◑ ⬤ ⚡ 3–9, 14–24   **p. 196**

Carissa macrocarpa
NATAL PLUM
☼ ◑ ⬤ ⬤ ⚡ 22–24   **p. 207**

Cestrum
◑ ⬤ ⚡ ZONES VARY   **p. 219**

Clerodendrum trichotomum   ♣
HARLEQUIN GLORYBOWER
☼ ⬤ ⚡ 15–17, 20–24   **p. 235**

Cornus kousa   ♣
KOUSA DOGWOOD
☼ ◑ ⬤ ⚡ 3–9, 14, 15, 18, 19   **p. 242**

SYMBOL: ♣ indicates shrubs that can become small trees.

Sorbus aucuparia

Arbutus unedo 'Elfin King'

Carissa macrocarpa

For growing symbol explanations, please see page 45.

Ilex aquifolium

Mahonia lomariifolia

Nandina domestica

Ochna serrulata

Cornus mas 🌳
CORNELIAN CHERRY
☼ ◑ ◐ ✂ 1–6   p. 242

Corokia cotoneaster
☼ ◑ ◐ ✂ 4–24   p. 243

Corylus 🌳
FILBERT, HAZELNUT
☼ ◐ ✂ 1–9, 14–24   p. 244

Cotoneaster
☼ ◊ ◐ ✂ ZONES VARY   p. 245

Duranta
SKY FLOWER
☼ ◐ ✂ ZONES VARY   p. 268

Elaeagnus
☼ ◑ ◐ ◑ ✂ ZONES VARY   p. 271

Euonymus alata
WINGED EUONYMUS
☼ ◑ ◐ ✂ 1–9, 14–16   p. 288

Euonymus fortunei (some)
☼ ◑ ◐ ✂ 1–17   p. 288

Heteromeles arbutifolia 🌳
TOYON
☼ ◑ ◐ ✂ 5–24   p. 321

Ilex (many) 🌳
HOLLY
☼ ◑ ◐ ✂ ZONES VARY   p. 329

Kolkwitzia amabilis
BEAUTY BUSH
☼ ◑ ◐ ✂ 1–11, 14–20   p. 344

Lonicera (most shrubby types)
HONEYSUCKLE
☼ ◑ ◐ ✂ ZONES VARY   p. 360

Mahonia
NEEDS, ZONES VARY   p. 371

Nandina domestica
HEAVENLY BAMBOO
☼ ◑ ◐ ◊ ◐ ◐ ✂ 5–24   p. 386

Ochna serrulata
MICKEY MOUSE PLANT
◑ ◐ ✂ 14–24   p. 392

Pernettya mucronata
☼ ◑ ◐ ✂ 4–7, 15–17   p. 411

Photinia serrulata 🌳
CHINESE PHOTINIA
☼ ◐ ◐ ✂ 4–16, 18–22   p. 416

Photinia villosa 🌳
☼ ◐ ◐ ✂ 1–6   p. 416

Punica granatum (some) 🌳
POMEGRANATE
☼ ◐ ◐ ✂ 5–24   p. 445

Pyracantha
FIRETHORN
☼ ◑ ◐ ◐ ✂ ZONES VARY   p. 446

Rhaphiolepis
☼ ◑ ◐ ◐ ✂ 8–10, 12–24   p. 453

Rhus typhina 🌳
STAGHORN SUMAC
☼ ◊ ◐ ✂ 1–10, 14–17   p. 460

Ribes (some)
CURRANT, GOOSEBERRY
NEEDS, ZONES VARY   p. 460

Rosa (many, especially rugosas)
ROSE
NEEDS, ZONES VARY   p. 462

Sarcococca ruscifolia
☼ ◑ ◐ ◐ ◑ ✂ 4–9, 14–24   p. 477

Skimmia
◑ ◐ ✂ 4–9, 14–22   p. 486

Solanum pseudocapsicum
JERUSALEM CHERRY
☼ ◑ ◐ ◐ ✂ 23, 24   p. 488

Stranvaesia davidiana 🌳
☼ ◐ ✂ 4–11, 14–17   p. 494

Symphoricarpos
SNOWBERRY
NEEDS, ZONES VARY   p. 498

Ugni molinae
CHILEAN GUAVA
☼ ◑ ◐ ✂ 14–24   p. 514

Vaccinium
◑ ◐ ✂ ZONES VARY   p. 515

Viburnum (many)
NEEDS, ZONES VARY   p. 518

PERENNIALS, VINES

Ampelopsis brevipedunculata
BLUEBERRY CLIMBER
☼ ◑ ◐ ◐ ✂ ALL ZONES   p. 150

Arum italicum
ITALIAN ARUM
◐ ◐ ✂ 4–24   p. 167

Celastrus
BITTERSWEET
☼ ◐ ✂ 1–7   p. 215

Dianella tasmanica
☼ ◑ ◐ ◐ ✂ 8, 9, 14–24   p. 261

Ophiopogon jaburan
☼ ◐ ◐ ◐ ✂ 5–10, 12–24   p. 358

Pyracantha

Rosa 'Cymbeline'

Skimmia

Viburnum plicatum tomentosum 'Mariesii'

Dianella tasmanica

Plants with
COLORED FOLIAGE

Not all color comes from flowers or fruit. The plants listed below offer long-term garden accents in the form of colored leaves: gray or silver, bronze, red, or purple, yellow or gold, blue, and variegated. They can be used to enliven the basic green of other garden foliage, to form contrasting combinations (such as gray and red) with one another, to complement flower colors in season, and to provide eye-catching focal points.

Eucalyptus pulverulenta

Cerastium tomentosum

Artemisia 'Powis Castle'

Santolina chamaecyparissus

Teucrium fruticans

GRAY, SILVER
Trees

Cupressus arizonica glabra
SMOOTH ARIZONA CYPRESS
☼ ◊ ✄ 5, 8–24　　　**p. 252**

Eucalyptus (many)

☼ ◊ ◑ ✄ SEE CHART　　**p. 281**

GRAY, SILVER
Shrubs

Artemisia

☼ ◊ ◑ ✄ ALL ZONES　　**p. 166**

Caryopteris clandonensis (several)
BLUE MIST
☼ ◑ ✄ 1–7, 14–17　　**p. 209**

Cistus (several)
ROCKROSE
☼ ◊ ◑ ✄ 7–9, 12–24　**p. 229**

Convolvulus cneorum
BUSH MORNING GLORY
☼ ◐ ◑ ✄ 7–9, 12–24　**p. 239**

Elaeagnus 'Coral Silver'

☼ ◐ ◑ ◑ ✄ ALL ZONES　**p. 271**

Feijoa sellowiana
PINEAPPLE GUAVA
☼ ◑ ◑ ✄ 7–9, 12–24　**p. 292**

Juniperus (many)
JUNIPER
☼ ◐ ◊ ◑ ◑ ✄ ALL ZONES　**p. 340**

Salvia leucophylla
PURPLE SAGE
☼ ◊ ◑ ✄ 8, 9, 14–17, 19–24　**p. 474**

Santolina chamaecyparissus
LAVENDER COTTON
☼ ◊ ◑ ✄ ALL ZONES　**p. 476**

Teucrium fruticans
BUSH GERMANDER
☼ ◑ ✄ 4–24　　**p. 504**

GRAY, SILVER
Perennials

Achillea (many)
YARROW
☼ ◊ ◑ ✄ ALL ZONES　**p. 138**

Centaurea (perennial)

NEEDS, ZONES VARY　**p. 216**

Cerastium tomentosum
SNOW-IN-SUMMER
☼ ◐ ◑ ◑ ✄ ALL ZONES　**p. 217**

Echeveria (many)

☼ ◐ ◑ ✄ ZONES VARY　**p. 269**

Erysimum 'Bowles Mauve'

☼ ◐ ◑ ✄ 4–6, 14–17, 22, 23　**p. 279**

Euryops

☼ ◑ ✄ 8, 9, 12–24　**p. 290**

Helichrysum petiolare
LICORICE PLANT
☼ ◊ ◑ ✄ 16, 17, 22–24　**p. 319**

Lavandula (most)
LAVENDER
☼ ◑ ✄ ZONES VARY　**p. 349**

Lychnis coronaria
CROWN-PINK
☼ ◐ ◑ ◑ ✄ ALL ZONES　**p. 362**

Origanum dictamnus
CRETE DITTANY
☼ ◑ ✄ 8–24　　**p. 395**

Perovskia 'Blue Spire'
RUSSIAN SAGE
☼ ◑ ✄ ALL ZONES　**p. 412**

For growing symbol explanations, please see page 45.

Echeveria

Helichrysum petiolare

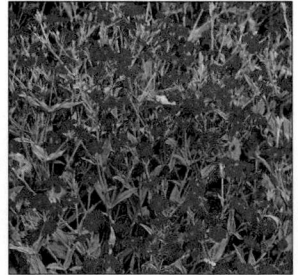

Lychnis coronaria

Achillea
'Moonshine'

Salvia chamaedryoides
☼ ◐ ❍ ⚡ 8, 9, 14–24   **p. 474**

Salvia leucantha
MEXICAN BUSH SAGE
☼ ◐ ❍ ⚡ 10–24   **p. 474**

Sempervivum
HOUSELEEK
☼ ● ❍ ⚡ ALL ZONES   **p. 482**

Stachys byzantina
LAMB'S EARS
☼ ◐ ❍ ⚡ ALL ZONES   **p. 492**

Thymus (several)
THYME
☼ ◐ ❍ ⚡ ALL ZONES   **p. 506**

Verbascum bombyciferum 'Arctic Summer'
☼ ❍ ⚡ ALL ZONES   **p. 517**

Zauschneria
CALIFORNIA FUCHSIA
☼ ◊ ❍ ⚡ 2–10, 12–24   **p. 527**

BRONZE, RED, PURPLE
Trees

Acer palmatum (some)
JAPANESE MAPLE
☼ ◐ ❍ ⚡ 1–10, 12, 14–24   **p. 136**

Acer platanoides (some)
NORWAY MAPLE
☼ ◐ ❍ ⚡ 1–9, 14–17   **p. 137**

Cercis canadensis 'Forest Pansy'
EASTERN REDBUD
☼ ◐ ❍ ⚡ 1–3, 7–20   **p. 218**

Cordyline australis 'Atropurpurea'
BRONZE DRACAENA
☼ ❍ ⚡ 5, 8–11, 14–24   **p. 240**

Cotinus coggygria (some)
SMOKE TREE
☼ ❍ ⚡ ALL ZONES   **p. 245**

Eriobotrya deflexa
BRONZE LOQUAT
☼ ❍ ⚡ 8–24   **p. 275**

Fagus sylvatica (some)
EUROPEAN BEECH
☼ ❍ ❍ ⚡ 1–9, 14–24   **p. 291**

Prunus blireiana
☼ ❍ ⚡ 2–22   **p. 442**

Prunus cerasifera (some)
CHERRY PLUM
☼ ❍ ⚡ 2–22   **p. 442**

BRONZE, RED, PURPLE
Shrubs

Berberis thunbergii (several)
JAPANESE BARBERRY
☼ ◐ ❍ ❍ ⚡ ALL ZONES   **p. 183**

Corylus (several)
FILBERT, HAZELNUT
☼ ◐ ❍ ⚡ 1–9, 14–20   **p. 244**

Dodonaea viscosa 'Purpurea'
PURPLE HOP BUSH
☼ ◐ ◊ ❍ ⚡ 10–13   **p. 266**

Spiraea bumalda (several)
☼ ◐ ❍ ⚡ 1–11, 14–21   **p. 491**

BRONZE, RED, PURPLE
Perennials

Aeonium arboreum 'Atropurpureum'
☼ ◐ ❍ ⚡ 15–17, 20–24   **p. 140**

Ajuga reptans (several)
☼ ◐ ❍ ⚡ ALL ZONES   **p. 144**

Astilbe 'Fanal'
☼ ◐ ❍ ⚡ 2–7, 14–17   **p. 170**

Caladium bicolor
FANCY-LEAFED CALADIUM
● ❍ ⚡ 12, 13, 16, 17, 22–24   **p. 194**

Canna (some)
☼ ❍ ⚡ ALL ZONES   **p. 205**

Euphorbia amygdaloides 'Purpurea'
☼ ❍ ❍ ⚡ 4–24   **p. 289**

Heuchera 'Palace Purple'
☼ ◐ ❍ ⚡ ALL ZONES   **p. 322**

Pennisetum setaceum 'Cupreum'
☼ ◊ ⚡ 8–24   **p. 410**

Phormium tenax (several)
NEW ZEALAND FLAX
☼ ◐ ◊ ❍ ⚡ 7–24   **p. 416**

Sedum spathulifolium 'Purpureum'
☼ ◐ ❍ ⚡ ALL ZONES   **p. 482**

Sedum spurium (some)
☼ ◐ ● ❍ ⚡ ALL ZONES   **p. 482**

YELLOW, GOLD
Trees

Acer shirasawanum 'Aureum'
GOLDEN FULLMOON MAPLE
☼ ◐ ❍ ⚡ 1–6, 14–16   **p. 137**

Chamaecyparis lawsoniana (some)
PORT ORFORD CEDAR
☼ ◐ ❍ ⚡ 4–6, 15–17   **p. 220**

Gleditsia triacanthos 'Sunburst'
SUNBURST HONEY LOCUST
☼ ❍ ⚡ 1–16, 18–20   **p. 308**

Plant listings continue ▶

Salvia leucantha

Stachys byzantina

Acer palmatum 'Ever Red'

Cercis canadensis 'Forest Pansy'

Cotinus coggygria

Berberis thunbergii 'Atropurpurea'

Aeonium arboreum 'Atropurpureum'

Ajuga reptans

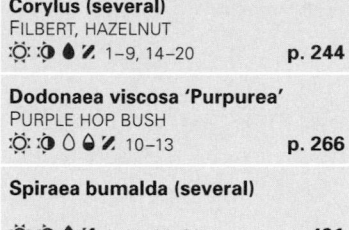

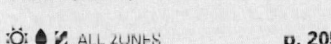

Canna

Heuchera 'Palace Purple'

Chamaecyparis

Chrysanthemum parthenium 'Aureum'

Helichrysum petiolare 'Limelight'

Taxus baccata 'Aurea'

Eucalyptus perriniana

Thuja plicata 'Aurea'

☼ ◐ ◉ ◉ ◍ ⁒ 1–9, 14–24   **p. 505**

YELLOW, GOLD
Shrubs, Perennials

Chamaecyparis (some)

☼ ◐ ◉ ⁒ ZONES VARY   **p. 220**

Chrysanthemum parthenium 'Aureum'

☼ ◐ ◉ ⁒ ALL ZONES   **p. 228**

Coleonema pulchrum 'Sunset Gold'

☼ ◐ ◉ ⁒ 7–9, 14–24   **p. 237**

Helichrysum petiolare 'Limelight'

☼ ◉ ⁒ 16, 17, 22–24   **p. 319**

Hosta (several)
PLANTAIN LILY

◐ ● ◉ ⁒ 1–10, 12–21   **p. 325**

Juniperus (several)
JUNIPER

☼ ◐ ○ ◉ ◉ ⁒ ALL ZONES   **p. 338**

Ligustrum 'Vicaryi'
VICARY GOLDEN PRIVET

☼ ◉ ⁒ ALL ZONES   **p. 354**

Milium effusum 'Aureum'
BOWLES' GOLDEN GRASS

◐ ◉ ⁒ ALL ZONES   **p. 381**

Platycladus orientalis (several)
ORIENTAL ARBORVITAE

☼ ◐ ◉ ⁒ ALL ZONES   **p. 427**

Spiraea bumalda 'Goldflame'

☼ ◐ ◉ ⁒ 1–11, 14–21   **p. 491**

Taxus baccata (several)
ENGLISH YEW

☼ ◐ ● ◉ ⁒ 3–9, 14–24   **p. 502**

Thuja occidentalis 'Rheingold'

☼ ◐ ◉ ◉ ◍ ⁒ MOST ZONES   **p. 505**

Viburnum opulus 'Aureum'

☼ ◐ ◉ ⁒ 1–9, 14–24   **p. 518**

BLUE
Trees

Cedrus atlantica 'Glauca'

☼ ○ ⁒ 2–23   **p. 214**

Chamaecyparis lawsoniana (some)
PORT ORFORD CEDAR

☼ ◐ ◉ ⁒ 4–6, 15–17   **p. 220**

Cunninghamia lanceolata 'Glauca'

☼ ◉ ⁒ 4–6, 14–21   **p. 251**

Eucalyptus (some)

☼ ○ ◉ ⁒ SEE CHART   **p. 281**

Juniperus (some)
JUNIPER

☼ ◐ ○ ◉ ◉ ⁒ ALL ZONES   **p. 338**

Picea pungens (some)
COLORADO SPRUCE

☼ ◐ ◉ ⁒ 1–10, 14–17   **p. 418**

BLUE
Shrubs, Perennials

Chamaecyparis lawsoniana (some)
PORT ORFORD CEDAR

☼ ◐ ◉ ⁒ 4–6, 15–17   **p. 220**

Festuca ovina 'Glauca'
BLUE FESCUE

☼ ◐ ◉ ◉ ⁒ ALL ZONES   **p. 294**

Hosta (several)
PLANTAIN LILY

◐ ● ◉ ⁒ 1–10, 12–21   **p. 325**

Ruta graveolens 'Jackman's Blue'
RUE

☼ ◉ ◉ ⁒ ALL ZONES   **p. 471**

VARIEGATED
Trees

Acer negundo 'Variegatum'
VARIEGATED BOX ELDER

☼ ◐ ◉ ⁒ 1–10, 12–24   **p. 136**

Acer palmatum 'Butterfly'

☼ ◐ ◉ ⁒ 1–10, 12, 14–24   **p. 136**

Cornus florida (several)
FLOWERING DOGWOOD

☼ ◐ ● ◉ ⁒ 1–9, 14–16   **p. 242**

Fagus sylvatica 'Tricolor'
TRICOLOR BEECH

☼ ◉ ◉ ⁒ 1–9, 14–24   **p. 291**

VARIEGATED
Shrubs

Aucuba japonica (several)
JAPANESE AUCUBA

◐ ● ○ ◉ ◉ ⁒ 4–24   **p. 172**

Bougainvillea (some)

☼ ◐ ◉ ⁒ 22–24   **p. 187**

Coprosma repens (several)
MIRROR PLANT

☼ ◐ ◉ ⁒ 15–17, 21–24   **p. 239**

Cotoneaster horizontalis 'Variegatus'

☼ ○ ◉ ⁒ 1–11, 14–24   **p. 246**

Daphne odora 'Marginata'
WINTER DAPHNE

◐ ◉ ⁒ 4–10, 12, 14–24   **p. 259**

Picea pungens

Ruta graveolens 'Jackman's Blue'

Cornus florida 'Welchii'

Daphne odora 'Marginata'

Bougainvillea 'Hawaii'

For growing symbol explanations, please see page 45.

Myrtus communis 'Variegata'

Pittosporum tobira 'Variegata'

Weigela florida 'Variegata'

Actinidia kolomikta

Elaeagnus pungens (some)
SILVERBERRY
☼ ◐ ◗ ◖ ✂ 4–24   **p. 271**

Euonymus (some)
☼ ◐ ◖ ✂ ZONES VARY   **p. 288**

Hydrangea macrophylla 'Tricolor'
GARDEN HYDRANGEA
☼ ◐ ◖ ✂ 2–9, 14–24   **p. 327**

Ilex (several)
HOLLY
☼ ◐ ◖ ✂ ZONES VARY   **p. 329**

Leucothoe fontanesiana 'Rainbow'
◐ ◖ ✂ 4–7, 15–17   **p. 353**

Myrtus communis (several)
TRUE MYRTLE
☼ ◐ ◗ ✂ 8–24   **p. 386**

Osmanthus heterophyllus 'Variegatus'
☼ ◐ ◖ ✂ 3 10, 14 24   **p. 396**

Pieris japonica 'Variegata'
☼ ◐ ◖ ✂ 1–9, 14–17   **p. 418**

Pittosporum tobira 'Variegata'
☼ ◐ ◖ ◖ ✂ 8–24   **p. 426**

Taxus baccata 'Stricta Variegata'
☼ ◐ ● ◖ ✂ 3–9, 14–24   **p. 502**

Viburnum tinus 'Variegatum'
☼ ◐ ◖ ✂ 4–9, 14–23   **p. 519**

Weigela florida 'Variegata'
☼ ◐ ◖ ✂ 1–11, 14–17   **p. 523**

VARIEGATED
Vines, Ground Covers

Actinidia kolomikta
☼ ◐ ◖ ✂ 1–9, 15–17   **p. 139**

Euonymus fortunei (some)
☼ ◐ ◖ ✂ 1–17   **p. 288**

Hedera (some)
IVY
NEEDS, ZONES VARY   **p. 317**

Lonicera japonica 'Aureo-reticulata'
GOLDNET HONEYSUCKLE
☼ ◐ ◖ ✂ 2–24   **p. 361**

Pachysandra terminalis 'Variegata'
◐ ● ◖ ✂ 1–10, 14–21   **p. 398**

Vinca (some)
PERIWINKLE
◐ ● ◖ ✂ ZONES VARY   **p. 519**

VARIEGATED
Perennials, Annuals

Ajuga (several)
CARPET BUGLE
☼ ◐ ◖ ✂ ALL ZONES   **p. 144**

Cabbage, Kale, flowering
☼ ◐ ◖ ✂ ALL ZONES   **pp. 194, 343**

Caladium bicolor
FANCY-LEAFED CALADIUM
● ◖ ✂ 12, 13, 16, 17, 22–24   **p. 194**

Coleus hybridus
COLEUS
◐ ◖ ✂ ALL ZONES   **p. 238**

Glechoma hederacea
GROUND IVY
☼ ◐ ◖ ✂ ALL ZONES   **p. 308**

Helichrysum petiolare 'Variegatum'
☼ ◐ ✂ 16, 17, 22–24   **p. 319**

Hosta (many)
PLANTAIN LILY
☼ ◐ ● ◖ ✂ 1–10, 12–21   **p. 325**

Houttuynia cordata 'Variegata'
☼ ◐ ● ◖ ✂ 1–9, 14–24   **p. 326**

Impatiens, New Guinea hybrids
◐ ◖ ✂ ALL ZONES   **p. 331**

Lamium (several)
DEAD NETTLE
● ◖ ✂ ALL ZONES   **p. 346**

Liriope muscari (some)
LILY TURF
☼ ◐ ● ◖ ◖ ✂ 5–10, 12–24   **p. 358**

Miscanthus sinensis (several)
EULALIA GRASS
☼ ◐ ● ◖ ✂ ALL ZONES   **p. 382**

Pelargonium (several)
GERANIUM
☼ ◐ ◖ ◖ ✂ 8, 9, 12–24   **p. 407**

Phormium tenax (several)
NEW ZEALAND FLAX
☼ ◐ ◗ ◖ ✂ 7–24   **p. 416**

Pulmonaria (several)
LUNGWORT
☼ ● ◖ ✂ 1–9, 14–17   **p. 445**

Salvia officinalis 'Tricolor'
COMMON SAGE
☼ ◖ ✂ ALL ZONES   **p. 475**

Sedum sieboldii 'Variegatum'
☼ ◐ ◖ ✂ 3–24   **p. 482**

Tulbaghia violacea (some)
SOCIETY GARLIC
☼ ◖ ✂ 13–24   **p. 512**

Hedera helix 'Buttercup'

Caladium bicolor

Lamium

Pulmonaria

Tulbaghia violacea

SHOWY PERENNIALS
for Beds and Borders

Diascia rigescens

Year after year, these garden mainstays provide spectacular flowers that inspire artists and photographers to attempt to capture their fleeting beauty. Perennials are distinguished from annuals and biennials by their longevity—they live for more than two years and usually bloom every year. Depending on the plant and the climate, they may be evergreen, or they may die to the ground every winter and regrow from the roots the next spring.

Perennial border

Alstroemeria

Armeria maritima

Aster novi-belgii

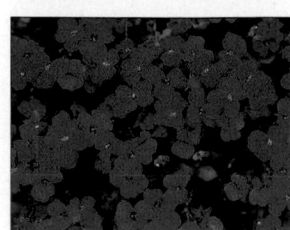

Aubrieta deltoidea

Achillea
YARROW
☼ ◐ ◔ ✂ ALL ZONES — **p.138**

Agastache
GIANT HYSSOP
☼ ◐ ◔ ✂ 4–9, 14–24 — **p. 142**

Alstroemeria
☼ ◔ ✂ 5–9, 14–24 — **p. 148**

Anemone hybrida
JAPANESE ANEMONE
☼ ◐ ◔ ✂ ALL ZONES — **p. 151**

Aquilegia
COLUMBINE
☼ ◐ ◔ ✂ ALL ZONES — **p. 160**

Arctotis (some)
AFRICAN DAISY
☼ ◔ ✂ 7–9, 14–24 — **p. 164**

Arenaria montana
SANDWORT
☼ ◔ ✂ 2–9, 14–24 — **p. 164**

Armeria
THRIFT
☼ ◔ ◔ ✂ ALL ZONES — **p. 165**

Aster
☼ ◔ ✂ ALL ZONES — **p. 170**

Astilbe
FALSE SPIRAEA
☼ ◐ ◔ ✂ 2–7, 14–17 — **p. 170**

Aubrieta deltoidea
COMMON AUBRIETA
☼ ◐ ◔ ✂ 1–9, 14–21 — **p. 171**

Aurinia saxatilis
BASKET-OF-GOLD
☼ ◐ ◔ ✂ ALL ZONES — **p. 172**

Begonia, semperflorens
BEDDING BEGONIAS
☼ ◐ ◔ ✂ 14–24 — **p. 181**

Campanula (some)
BELLFLOWER
☼ ◐ ◔ ✂ ZONES VARY — **p. 203**

Catananche caerulea
CUPID'S DART
☼ ◔ ✂ ALL ZONES — **p. 211**

Cerastium tomentosum
SNOW-IN-SUMMER
☼ ◐ ◔ ◔ ✂ ALL ZONES — **p. 217**

Chrysanthemum
NEEDS, ZONES VARY — **p. 226**

Convallaria majalis
LILY-OF-THE-VALLEY
◐ ◔ ✂ 1–7, 14–20 — **p. 239**

Coreopsis
☼ ◔ ✂ ZONES VARY — **p. 240**

Delphinium
☼ ◔ ✂ ZONES VARY — **p. 260**

Dianthus
PINK
☼ ◐ ◔ ✂ ALL ZONES — **p. 261**

Diascia
TWINSPUR
☼ ◐ ◔ ✂ ZONES VARY — **p. 262**

Dicentra
BLEEDING HEART
◔ ◔ ✂ 1–9, 14–24 — **p. 262**

Dierama
FAIRY WAND
☼ ◔ ✂ 4–24 — **p. 264**

Digitalis
FOXGLOVE
◐ ◔ ✂ ALL ZONES — **p. 264**

Dorycnium hirsutum
☼ ◔ ✂ 8, 9, 14–24 — **p. 267**

For growing symbol explanations, please see page 45.

COLOR CODES: Each tint represents a range of colors, not a color match.

BLUE-PURPLE
WHITE-CREAM
PINK-RED
YELLOW-ORANGE

Campanula persicifolia

Cerastium tomentosum

Chrysanthemum maximum

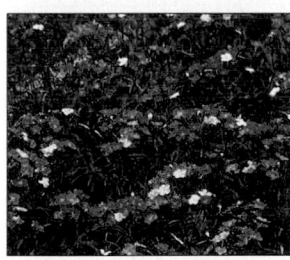

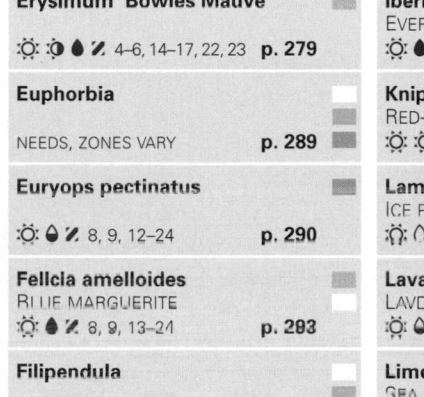

SPECIAL EFFECTS

Echinacea purpurea
PURPLE CONEFLOWER
☼ ◐ ● ⚡ ALL ZONES   p. 269

Echinops exaltatus
GLOBE THISTLE
☼ ◐ ● ⚡ ALL ZONES   p. 270

Erigeron
FLEABANE
NEEDS, ZONES VARY   p. 275

Erodium reichardii
CRANESBILL
☼ ◐ ● ⚡ 7–9, 14–24   p. 278

Eryngium amethystinum
SEA HOLLY
☼ ● ⚡ ALL ZONES   p. 279

Erysimum 'Bowles Mauve'
☼ ◐ ● ⚡ 4–6, 14–17, 22, 23   p. 279

Euphorbia
NEEDS, ZONES VARY   p. 289

Euryops pectinatus
☼ ● ⚡ 8, 9, 12–24   p. 290

Felicia amelloides
BLUE MARGUERITE
☼ ● ⚡ 8, 9, 13–24   p. 293

Filipendula
☼ ◐ ● ⚡ 1–9, 14–24   p. 296

Francoa ramosa
MAIDEN'S WREATH
◐ ● ⚡ 4, 5, 8, 9, 12–24   p. 298

Gaillardia grandiflora
BLANKET FLOWER
☼ ● ⚡ ALL ZONES   p. 301

Gaura lindheimeri
GAURA
☼ ● ⚡ ALL ZONES   p. 304

Gazania
☼ ● ⚡ 8–24   p. 304

Geranium
CRANESBILL
NEEDS, ZONES VARY   p. 305

Gerbera jamesonii
TRANSVAAL DAISY
☼ ◐ ● ⚡ 8, 9, 12–24   p. 306

Geum
☼ ◐ ● ⚡ ALL ZONES   p. 306

Gypsophila
☼ ● ⚡ ZONES VARY   p. 314

Helianthemum nummularium
SUNROSE
☼ ● ⚡ ALL ZONES   p. 318

Heliotropium arborescens
COMMON HELIOTROPE
☼ ◐ ● ⚡ 8–24   p. 319

Helleborus
HELLEBORE
NEEDS, ZONES VARY   p. 319

Hemerocallis
DAYLILY
☼ ◐ ● ⚡ ALL ZONES   p. 320

Heuchera
CORAL BELLS
☼ ◐ ● ● ⚡ ZONES VARY   p. 322

Hunnemannia fumariifolia
MEXICAN TULIP POPPY
☼ ◊ ⚡ ALL ZONES   p. 326

Iberis sempervirens
EVERGREEN CANDYTUFT
☼ ● ⚡ ALL ZONES   p. 329

Kniphofia uvaria
RED-HOT POKER
☼ ◐ ◊ ⚡ 1–9, 14–24   p. 344

Lampranthus
ICE PLANT
☼ ◊ ● ⚡ 14–24   p. 346

Lavandula
LAVENDER
☼ ● ⚡ ZONES VARY   p. 349

Limonium
SEA LAVENDER
☼ ● ⚡ ZONES VARY   p. 356

Linaria purpurea
TOADFLAX
☼ ◐ ● ⚡ ALL ZONES   p. 356

Linum perenne
PERENNIAL BLUE FLAX
☼ ● ⚡ ALL ZONES   p. 357

Lobelia cardinalis
CARDINAL FLOWER
☼ ◐ ● ● ⚡ 1–7, 12–17   p. 359

Lychnis chalcedonica
MALTESE CROSS
☼ ◐ ● ⚡ 1–9, 11–24   p. 362

Macleaya cordata
PLUME POPPY
☼ ● ⚡ ALL ZONES   p. 364

Malva alcea
MALLOW
☼ ● ⚡ ALL ZONES   p. 372

Mimulus
MONKEY FLOWER
NEEDS, ZONES VARY   p. 381

Mirabilis jalapa
FOUR O'CLOCK
☼ ◊ ⚡ 4–24   p. 381

Nemesia fruticans
☼ ● ⚡ 16–24   p. 388

Dorycnium hirsutum

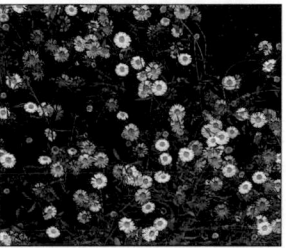
Erigeron karvinskianus

Geranium

Helianthemum nummularium

Heliotropium arborescens 'Black Beauty'

Delphinium

Dianthus

Dicentra spectabilis 'Alba'

Plant listings continue ▶

Penstemon gloxinioides 'Garnet'

Hemerocallis

Lavandula

Oenothera

Nierembergia
CUP FLOWER
☼ ◐ ✱ ZONES VARY   **p. 391**

Oenothera
EVENING PRIMROSE
☼ ◐ ✱ ZONES VARY   **p. 392**

Origanum

NEEDS, ZONES VARY   **p. 395**

Osteospermum
AFRICAN DAISY
☼ ◐ ✱ 8, 9, 12–24   **p. 396**

Paeonia (herbaceous)
PEONY
☼ ◐ ◐ ✱ 1–11, 14–16   **p. 398**

Papaver orientale
ORIENTAL POPPY
☼ ◐ ◐ ✱ 1–17   **p. 400**

Pelargonium
GERANIUM
NEEDS VARY, ✱ 8, 9, 12–24   **p. 407**

Penstemon (many)
BEARD TONGUE
NEEDS, ZONES VARY   **p. 410**

Perovskia 'Blue Spire'
RUSSIAN SAGE
☼ ◐ ✱ ALL ZONES   **p. 412**

Phlomis
JERUSALEM SAGE
NEEDS, ZONES VARY   **p. 414**

Phlox paniculata
SUMMER PHLOX
☼ ◐ ◐ ✱ 1–14, 18–21   **p. 415**

Phlox subulata
MOSS PINK
☼ ◐ ◐ ✱ 1–17   **p. 415**

Phygelius
CAPE FUCHSIA
☼ ◐ ◐ ✱ 4–9, 14–24   **p. 416**

Physostegia virginiana
FALSE DRAGONHEAD
☼ ◐ ◐ ✱ ALL ZONES   **p. 417**

Platycodon grandiflorus
BALLOON FLOWER
☼ ◐ ◐ ✱ ALL ZONES   **p. 427**

Polemonium

◐ ◐ ◐ ◐ ✱ 1–11, 14–17   **p. 431**

Primula (many)
PRIMROSE
☼ ◐ ◐ ◐ ◐ ✱ 1–10, 12–24   **p. 436**

Prunella
SELF-HEAL
☼ ◐ ◐ ✱ ALL ZONES   **p. 439**

Pulmonaria
LUNGWORT
☼ ● ◐ ◐ ✱ 1–9, 14–17   **p. 445**

Rodgersia
☼ ◐ ◐ ◐ ✱ 2–9, 14–17   **p. 461**

Romneya coulteri
MATILIJA POPPY
☼ ◊ ◐ ✱ ALL ZONES   **p. 462**

Rudbeckia

☼ ◐ ✱ ALL ZONES   **p. 469**

Salvia
SAGE
NEEDS, ZONES VARY   **p. 473**

Scabiosa
PINCUSHION FLOWER
☼ ◐ ✱ ZONES VARY   **p. 478**

Scaevola

☼ ◐ ✱ 8, 9, 14–24   **p. 478**

Sedum spectabile (varieties)

☼ ◐ ✱ ALL ZONES   **p. 482**

Sedum telephium (varieties)

☼ ◐ ◐ ✱ ALL ZONES   **p. 482**

Sidalcea malviflora
CHECKERBLOOM
☼ ◐ ✱ 4–9, 14–24   **p. 485**

Silene

NEEDS, ZONES VARY   **p. 485**

Sisyrinchium bellum
BLUE-EYED GRASS
☼ ◐ ◐ ◐ ✱ 4–24   **p. 486**

Stokesia laevis
STOKES ASTER
☼ ◐ ✱ 1–9, 12–24   **p. 494**

Strelitzia reginae
BIRD OF PARADISE
☼ ☼ ◐ ✱ 22–24   **p. 496**

Tagetes lemmonii

☼ ◐ ✱ 8–10, 12–24   **p. 501**

Teucrium chamaedrys
GERMANDER
☼ ◐ ✱ ALL ZONES   **p. 504**

Thalictrum
MEADOW RUE
☼ ◐ ◐ ✱ ALL ZONES   **p. 504**

Thymus
THYME
☼ ◐ ◐ ✱ ALL ZONES   **p. 506**

Trachelium caeruleum

☼ ◐ ✱ 7–9, 14–24   **p. 509**

Tulbaghia

☼ ◐ ✱ 13–24   **p. 512**

Papaver orientale

Prunella

Rudbeckia fulgida 'Goldsturm'

Sisyrinchium bellum

Thalictrum

For growing symbol explanations, please see page 45.

Citrus 'Bearss'

FRAGRANT PLANTS

A garden's fragrance can be as memorable as its appearance; years later, the scent of a particular blossom can evoke a past experience. Flower fragrance is usually most pronounced on warm and humid days and least noticeable when weather is dry and hot. Use fragrant plants in containers on a patio, or plant a favorite fragrance beneath a window so the sweet or spicy aroma can drift into the house.

Aesculus californica

Magnolia

Boronia molloyae

Brugmansia versicolor 'Charles Grimaldi'

Buddleia

Choisya ternata

Gardenia jasminoides 'Radicans'

Daphne burkwoodii

Jasminum nitidum

TREES

Aesculus californica
CALIFORNIA BUCKEYE
☼ ◐ ● ⚡ 4 10, 12, 14 24   **p. 141**

Citrus
☼ ● ⚡ 8, 9, 12–24   **p. 230**

Cladrastis lutea
YELLOW WOOD
☼ ● ⚡ 1–9, 14–16   **p. 233**

Clethra arborea
LILY-OF-THE-VALLEY TREE
☼ ◐ ● ⚡ 15–17, 21–24   **p. 235**

Drimys winteri
WINTER'S BARK
☼ ◐ ● ● ⚡ 8, 9, 14–24   **p. 267**

Elaeagnus angustifolia
RUSSIAN OLIVE
☼ ◐ ● ● ⚡ 1–3, 7–14, 18, 19   **p. 271**

Hymenosporum flavum
SWEETSHADE
☼ ◐ ● ⚡ 8, 9, 14–23   **p. 328**

Magnolia (many)
☼ ◐ ● ⚡ ZONES VARY   **p. 365**

Malus (some)
CRABAPPLE
☼ ● ⚡ 1–21   **p. 372**

Michelia doltsopa
☼ ◐ ● ⚡ 14–24   **p. 380**

Prunus blireiana
FLOWERING PLUM
☼ ● ⚡ 2–22   **p. 442**

Styrax obassia
FRAGRANT SNOWBELL
☼ ◐ ● ⚡ 3–10, 14–21   **p. 497**

SHRUBS

Acacia (several)
☼ ◐ ● ⚡ ZONES VARY   **p. 131**

Azara (some)
◐ ● ⚡ ZONES VARY   **p. 173**

Boronia
◐ ● ⚡ ZONES VARY   **p. 187**

Bouvardia longiflora 'Albatross'
◐ ● ⚡ 12, 13, 16, 17, 19–24   **p. 188**

Brugmansia (several)
ANGEL'S TRUMPET
☼ ◐ ● ● ⚡ 16–24   **p. 191**

Buddleia
☼ ◐ ● ● ⚡ ALL ZONES   **p. 192**

Calycanthus floridus
CAROLINA ALLSPICE
☼ ◐ ● ● ⚡ 1–9, 14–22   **p. 199**

Carissa
☼ ◐ ● ● ⚡ 22–24   **p. 207**

Carpenteria californica
BUSH ANEMONE
☼ ◐ ● ● ⚡ 5–9, 14–24   **p. 208**

Cestrum (some)
◐ ● ⚡ ZONES VARY   **p. 219**

Chimonanthus praecox
WINTERSWEET
☼ ◐ ● ⚡ ZONES VARY   **p. 223**

Choisya ternata
MEXICAN ORANGE
☼ ◐ ● ⚡ 7–9, 12–24   **p. 225**

Plant listings continue ▶

Jasminum polyanthum

Lavandula dentata

Lonicera japonica

Michelia figo

Philadelphus

Clerodendrum bungei
CASHMERE BOUQUET
☼ ◐ ♦ ℀ 5–9, 12–24   **p. 235**

Clethra alnifolia
SUMMERSWEET
☼ ◐ ♦ ℀ 2–6   **p. 235**

Corylopsis
WINTER HAZEL
☼ ◐ ♦ ℀ 4–7, 15–17   **p. 244**

Daphne (many)

NEEDS, ZONES VARY   **p. 258**

Elaeagnus

☼ ◐ ♦ ♦ ℀ ZONES VARY   **p. 271**

Gardenia

☼ ♦♦ ℀ ZONES VARY   **p. 302**

Hamamelis
WITCH HAZEL
☼ ◐ ℀ ZONES VARY   **p. 316**

Jasminum (some)
JASMINE
☼ ◐ ♦ ℀ ZONES VARY   **p. 336**

Lavandula (most)
LAVENDER
☼ ♦ ℀ ZONES VARY   **p. 349**

Lonicera
HONEYSUCKLE
☼ ◐ ♦ ℀ ZONES VARY   **p. 360**

Michelia figo
BANANA SHRUB
☼ ◐ ♦ ℀ 9, 14–24   **p. 380**

Murraya paniculata
ORANGE JESSAMINE
◐ ♦ ℀ 21–24   **p. 384**

Osmanthus (most)

☼ ◐ ♦ ℀ ZONES VARY   **p. 396**

Philadelphus (most)
MOCK ORANGE
☼ ◐ ♦ ℀ ZONES VARY   **p. 413**

Pittosporum (several)

☼ ◐ ♦ ♦ ℀ ZONES VARY   **p. 425**

Plumeria

☼ ◐ ♦ ℀ ZONES VARY   **p. 428**

Rhaphiolepis 'Majestic Beauty'

☼ ◐ ♦ ♦ ℀ 8–10, 12–24   **p. 453**

Rhododendron 'Else Frye'

◐ ♦ ♦♦ ℀ 4–6, 15–17   **p. 455**

Rhododendron 'Fragrantissimum'

☼ ◐ ♦ ♦♦ ℀ 4–6, 15–17   **p. 455**

Rhododendron, Loderi hybrids
◐ ♦ ♦♦ ℀ 4–6, 15–17   **p. 456**

Rhododendron, Maddenii hybrids
◐ ♦ ♦♦ ℀ 15–17   **p. 454**

Rhododendron, Viscosum hybrids
DECIDUOUS AZALEAS
◐ ♦ ♦♦ ℀ 4–6, 15–17   **p. 458**

Ribes odoratum
☼ ◐ ♦ ℀ ALL ZONES   **p. 460**

Rosa (many)
ROSE
NEEDS, ZONES VARY   **p. 462**

Sarcococca
☼ ◐ ● ♦ ♦ ℀ 4–9, 14–24   **p. 476**

Skimmia japonica (esp. males)
◐ ♦ ℀ 4–9, 14–22   **p. 487**

Sophora secundiflora
TEXAS MOUNTAIN LAUREL
☼ ◐ ♦ ♦ ℀ 8–16, 18–24   **p. 488**

Syringa (many)
LILAC
☼ ♦ ♦ ℀ ZONES VARY   **p. 499**

Viburnum (several)

NEEDS, ZONES VARY   **p. 518**

VINES

Beaumontia grandiflora
EASTER LILY VINE
☼ ◐ ♦♦ ℀ 12, 13, 16, 17, 21–24   **p. 180**

Clematis armandii
EVERGREEN CLEMATIS
☼ ♦ ℀ 1–6, 15–17   **p. 233**

Distictis laxiflora
VANILLA TRUMPET VINE
☼ ♦ ℀ 16, 22–24   **p. 265**

Gelsemium sempervirens
CAROLINA JESSAMINE
☼ ♦ ♦ ℀ 8–24   **p. 304**

Hoya carnosa
WAX FLOWER
● ♦ ℀ 15–24   **p. 326**

Ipomoea alba
MOONFLOWER
☼ ♦ ℀ ALL ZONES   **p. 332**

Jasminum (some)
JASMINE
☼ ◐ ♦ ℀ ZONES VARY   **p. 336**

Lonicera (some)
HONEYSUCKLE
☼ ◐ ♦ ℀ ZONES VARY   **p. 360**

Pittosporum tobira

Rosa 'Iceberg'

Passiflora alatocaerulea

Trachelospermum jasminoides

Cosmos atrosanguineus

For growing symbol explanations, please see page 45.

Crinum powellii 'Album'

Dianthus

Iris

Lilium 'Stargazer'

Mandevilla laxa
CHILEAN JASMINE
:☼: ● ❦ ✄ 4–9, 14–21   **p. 375**

Passiflora alatocaerulea
PASSION VINE
:☼: ● ❦ ✄ 12–24   **p. 402**

Stephanotis floribunda
MADAGASCAR JASMINE
:◐: ● ❦ ✄ 23, 24   **p. 493**

Trachelospermum
STAR JASMINE
:☼: :◐: ● ❦ ✄ ZONES VARY   **p. 509**

Wisteria
:☼: :◐: ● ❦ ● ❦ ✄ ALL ZONES   **p. 523**

PERENNIALS, ANNUALS, BULBS

Amaryllis belladonna
NAKED LADY
:☼: ◊ ✄ 4–24   **p. 149**

Centaurea moschata
SWEET SULTAN
:☼: ● ❦ ✄ ALL ZONES   **p. 216**

Convallaria majalis
LILY-OF-THE-VALLEY
:◐: ● ❦ ✄ ZONES 1–7, 14–20   **p. 239**

Cosmos atrosanguineus
CHOCOLATE COSMOS
:☼: ● ❦ ✄ 4–9, 14–24   **p. 245**

Crinum
:☼: :◐: ● ❦ ● ❦ ✄ 8, 9, 12–24   **p. 248**

Crocus chrysanthus
:☼: :◐: ● ❦ ✄ ALL ZONES   **p. 249**

Dianthus (some)
PINK
:☼: :◐: ● ❦ ✄ ALL ZONES   **p. 261**

Erysimum cheiri
WALLFLOWER
:☼: :◐: ● ❦ ● ❦ ✄ 4–6, 14–17, 22, 23 **p. 279**

Freesia (some)
:☼: :◐: ● ❦ ✄ 8, 9, 12–24   **p. 300**

Hedychium coronarium
WHITE GINGER LILY
:◐: ● ❦ ✄ 16, 17, 22–24   **p. 318**

Heliotropium arborescens
COMMON HELIOTROPE
:☼: :◐: ● ✄ 8–24   **p. 319**

Hemerocallis lilioasphodelus
LEMON DAYLILY
:☼: ● ❦ ✄ ALL ZONES   **p. 320**

Hosta plantaginea
FRAGRANT PLANTAIN LILY
:☼: :◐: ● ❦ ● ❦ ✄ 1–10, 12–21   **p. 325**

Hyacinthus
HYACINTH
:☼: :◐: ● ❦ ✄ ALL ZONES   **p. 326**

Hymenocallis
:☼: :◐: ● ❦ ✄ 5, 6, 8, 9, 14–24   **p. 327**

Iberis amara
HYACINTH-FLOWERED CANDYTUFT
:☼: ● ❦ ✄ ALL ZONES   **p. 329**

Ipomoea alba
MOONFLOWER
:☼: ● ❦ ✄ ALL ZONES   **p. 332**

Iris, bearded (some)
:☼: :◐: ● ❦ ✄ ALL ZONES   **p. 333**

Lathyrus odoratus
SWEET PEA
:☼: ● ❦ ✄ ALL ZONES   **p. 348**

Lilium (many)
LILY
:◐: ● ❦ ✄ ALL ZONES   **p. 354**

Matthiola
STOCK
:☼: :◐: ● ❦ ✄ ALL ZONES   **p. 376**

Narcissus (many)
DAFFODIL
:☼: :◐: ● ❦ ✄ ALL ZONES   **p. 387**

Nelumbo
LOTUS
:☼: :◐: ● ❦ ✄ ALL ZONES   **p. 388**

Nicotiana
:☼: :◐: ● ❦ ✄ ZONES VARY   **p. 390**

Paeonia (many)
PEONY
:☼: :◐: ● ❦ ✄ ZONES VARY   **p. 398**

Phlox paniculata (esp. light colors)
SUMMER PHLOX
:☼: :◐: ● ❦ ✄ 1–14, 18–21   **p. 415**

Polianthes tuberosa
TUBEROSE
:☼: :◐: ● ❦ ✄ 15–17, 22–24   **p. 432**

Primula alpicola
MOONLIGHT PRIMROSE
:☼: :◐: ● ● ● ❦ ✄ 1–6, 17   **p. 437**

Primula vulgaris (some)
ENGLISH PRIMROSE
:☼: :◐: ● ● ● ❦ ✄ MOST ZONES   **p. 438**

Reseda odorata
MIGNONETTE
:☼: :◐: ● ❦ ✄ ALL ZONES   **p. 452**

Tropaeolum majus
GARDEN NASTURTIUM
:☼: :◐: ● ❦ ✄ ALL ZONES   **p. 512**

Viola odorata
SWEET VIOLET
:☼: :◐: ● ❦ ✄ ALL ZONES   **p. 520**

Heliotropium arborescens

Nelumbo nucifera

Nicotiana

Phlox paniculata

Tropaeolum majus

SPECIAL EFFECTS

Yucca elata

NATIVE PLANTS

Native plants bring a rich diversity of texture and color to home gardens. Today, they also make sense: they have evolved to survive the climate of a particular region and to live on what nature provides for them. For busy gardeners, they provide the bonus of needing usually minimal upkeep. The following plant list identifies native plants for four western regions—the Pacific Northwest, the Rocky Mountain region, California, and the Southwest. When selecting a plant for your region, keep in mind that although a plant is native, it may not be unthirsty. Plants such as native columbines and quaking aspen come from moist habitats and need plenty of water. All native plants that have been growing in nursery containers need water while they are becoming established in a garden (which can take several years for large trees). Only after plants are established can you cut back on water for those types that thrive naturally with little moisture.

Arbutus menziesii

Chamaecyparis nootkatensis

PACIFIC NORTHWEST
Trees

Abies concolor
WHITE FIR
☀ ◐ ◑ ● ☑ 1–9, 14–24   **p. 130**

Abies lasiocarpa
ALPINE FIR
☀ ◐ ◑ ● ● ☑ 1–9, 14–17   **p. 130**

Acer circinatum
VINE MAPLE
☀ ◐ ● ◑ ☑ 1–6, 14–17   **p. 135**

Arbutus menziesii
MADRONE
☀ ● ☑ 3–7, 14–19   **p. 162**

Calocedrus decurrens
INCENSE CEDAR
☀ ● ☑ 1–12, 14–24   **p. 198**

Chamaecyparis nootkatensis
ALASKA CEDAR
☀ ◐ ● ☑ 4–6, 15–17   **p. 220**

Cornus nuttallii
PACIFIC DOGWOOD
☀ ◐ ● ◑ ☑ 2–9, 14–20   **p. 243**

Fraxinus latifolia
OREGON ASH
☀ ◯ ◑ ● ◑ ☑ 4–24   **p. 299**

Pinus contorta
SHORE PINE
☀ ● ☑ SEE CHART   **p. 421**

Pseudotsuga menziesii
DOUGLAS FIR
☀ ◐ ◯ ● ◑ ☑ 1–10, 14–17   **p. 443**

Quercus garryana
GARRY OAK
☀ ◯ ● ☑ 4–6, 15–17   **p. 448**

Taxus brevifolia
WESTERN YEW
☀ ◐ ● ● ☑ 1–6, 14–17   **p. 502**

Thuja plicata
WESTERN RED CEDAR
☀ ◐ ● ◑ ● ◑ ☑ 1–9, 14–24   **p. 505**

Tsuga mertensiana
MOUNTAIN HEMLOCK
☀ ● ☑ 1–7, 14–17   **p. 512**

PACIFIC NORTHWEST
Shrubs

Acer glabrum
ROCKY MOUNTAIN MAPLE
☀ ◐ ● ☑ 1–3, 10   **p. 136**

Amelanchier alnifolia
SASKATOON
☀ ● ☑ 1–6   **p. 150**

Arctostaphylos media
☀ ● ☑ 4–9, 14–24   **p. 163**

Cornus stolonifera
REDTWIG DOGWOOD
☀ ● ◑ ☑ 1–9, 14–21   **p. 243**

Corylus cornuta californica
WESTERN HAZELNUT
☀ ◐ ● ◑ ☑ 1–9, 14–20   **p. 244**

Garrya issaquahensis
SILKTASSEL
☀ ◐ ● ☑ 4–7, 14–17   **p. 303**

Gaultheria shallon
SALAL
☀ ● ☑ 3–7, 14–17, 21–24   **p. 303**

Holodiscus discolor
OCEAN SPRAY
☀ ● ☑ 1–7, 14–17   **p. 324**

Leucothoe davisiae
SIERRA LAUREL
◐ ● ◑ ☑ 1–7, 15–17   **p. 353**

Mahonia aquifolium
OREGON GRAPE
☀ ◐ ● ◯ ● ☑ 1–21   **p. 371**

For growing symbol explanations, please see page 45.

Tsuga mertensiana

Cornus stolonifera

Corylus cornuta californica

Pinus contorta

Gaultheria shallon

Mahonia aquifolium

Myrica californica

Cornus canadensis

Adiantum aleuticum

Mahonia nervosa
LONGLEAF MAHONIA
● ◐ ● 🌢 ✂ 2–9, 14–17   **p. 371**

Myrica californica
PACIFIC WAX MYRTLE
☼ ◐ ● ✂ 4–6, 14–17, 20–24   **p. 385**

Rhododendron occidentale
WESTERN AZALEA
☼ ◐ ● ✂ 4–9, 14–17, 19–24   **p. 458**

Ribes aureum
GOLDEN CURRANT
☼ ◐ ● ✂ ALL ZONES   **p. 460**

Ribes sanguineum
RED FLOWERING CURRANT
☼ ◐ ○ ● ✂ 4–9, 14–24   **p. 460**

Vaccinium ovatum
EVERGREEN HUCKLEBERRY
◐ ● ✂ 4–7, 14–17   **p. 516**

PACIFIC NORTHWEST
Ground Covers, Vines

Asarum caudatum
WILD GINGER
● ● ✂ 4–6, 14–24   **p. 167**

Cornus canadensis
BUNCHBERRY
● ● ✂ 1–7   **p. 242**

Fragaria chiloensis
WILD STRAWBERRY
☼ ◐ ● ● ✂ 4–24   **p. 298**

Mahonia repens
CREEPING MAHONIA
☼ ◐ ● ✂ 1–21   **p. 371**

Maianthemum dilatatum
FALSE LILY-OF-THE-VALLEY
◐ ○ ✂ 1–9, 14–17   **p. 371**

PACIFIC NORTHWEST
Perennials, Ferns, Grasses

Adiantum aleuticum
FIVE-FINGER FERN
◐ ● ● ✂ 1–9, 14–21   **p. 140**

Aquilegia formosa
WESTERN COLUMBINE
☼ ◐ ● ✂ ALL ZONES   **p. 160**

Blechnum spicant
DEER FERN
● ● ✂ 1–9, 14–17   **p. 185**

Camassia quamash
CAMASS
☼ ● ● ✂ 1–9, 14–17   **p. 200**

Dodecatheon
SHOOTING STAR
☼ ◐ ● ● ✂ ALL ZONES   **p. 266**

Dryas octopetala
☼ ● ✂ 1–6   **p. 268**

Dryopteris expansa
SPREADING WOOD FERN
◐ ● ● ● ✂ 4–9, 14–24   **p. 268**

Erythronium revolutum
◐ ● ● ● ✂ 1–7, 15–17   **p. 280**

Fritillaria lanceolata
CHECKER LILY
☼ ◐ ● ● ✂ 1–7, 15–17   **p. 300**

Iris, Pacific Coast and hybrids
☼ ◐ ● ● ✂ 4–24   **p. 334**

Lewisia
☼ ◐ ● ✂ 1–7, 14–17   **p. 353**

Lilium columbianum
COLUMBIA LILY
◐ ● ✂ ALL ZONES   **p. 355**

Linnaea borealis
TWINFLOWER
☼ ◐ ● ● ✂ 1–7, 14–17   **p. 356**

Polystichum munitum
SWORD FERN
● ● ● ✂ 4–9, 14–24   **p. 433**

Sedum spathulifolium
☼ ◐ ● ✂ ALL ZONES   **p. 482**

Smilacina racemosa
FALSE SOLOMON'S SEAL
☼ ◐ ● ● ✂ 1–7, 14–17   **p. 487**

Tolmiea menziesii
PIGGY-BACK PLANT
☼ ● ● ● ● ✂ 5–9, 12–24   **p. 507**

Trillium ovatum
◐ ● ● ✂ 1–6, 14–17   **p. 511**

Vancouveria
◐ ● ● ✂ ZONES VARY   **p. 516**

ROCKY MOUNTAIN REGION
Trees

Abies concolor
WHITE FIR
☼ ◐ ● ● ✂ 1–9, 14–24   **p. 130**

Betula occidentalis
☼ ● ● ● ✂ 1–3, 10   **p. 184**

Juniperus monosperma
☼ ◐ ○ ● ● ✂ ALL ZONES   **p. 341**

Juniperus scopulorum (some)
☼ ◐ ○ ● ● ✂ ALL ZONES   **p. 341**

Picea pungens
COLORADO SPRUCE
☼ ◐ ● ✂ 1–10, 14–17   **p. 418**

Aquilegia formosa

Dryas octopetala

Iris, Pacific Coast

Lewisia cotyledon

Sedum spathulifolium 'Cape Blanco'

Trillium ovatum

Plant listings continue ▶

Picea pungens

Pinus aristata

Populus acuminata

Pinus (several)
PINE
☼ ◊ ◑ ⁄ SEE CHART   **p. 419**

Populus acuminata
LANCELEAF COTTONWOOD
☼ ◑ ⁄ ALL ZONES   **p. 434**

Populus tremuloides
QUAKING ASPEN
☼ ◑ ⁄ 1–7   **p. 434**

Prunus americana
WILD PLUM
☼ ◑ ◑ ⁄ 1–3, 10   **p. 442**

Pseudotsuga menziesii
DOUGLAS FIR
☼ ◐ ◊ ◑ ⁄ 1–10, 14–17   **p. 443**

ROCKY MOUNTAIN REGION
Shrubs

Acer glabrum
ROCKY MOUNTAIN MAPLE
☼ ◐ ◑ ⁄ 1–3, 10   **p. 136**

Amelanchier alnifolia
SASKATOON
☼ ◑ ⁄ 1–6   **p. 150**

Artemisia tridentata
BIG SAGEBRUSH
☼ ◊ ◑ ⁄ ALL ZONES   **p. 166**

Ceanothus velutinus
TOBACCO BRUSH
☼ ◊ ◑ ⁄ 1–3   **p. 214**

Cercocarpus ledifolius
CURL-LEAF MOUNTAIN MAHOGANY
☼ ◊ ⁄ ALL ZONES   **p. 219**

Cercocarpus montanus

☼ ◊ ⁄ ALL ZONES   **p. 219**

Chrysothamnus nauseosus
RUBBER RABBITBRUSH
☼ ◊ ⁄ 1–3, 10, 11   **p. 228**

Cornus stolonifera
REDTWIG DOGWOOD
☼ ◐ ◑ ◑ ⁄ 1–9, 14–21   **p. 243**

Corylus cornuta californica
WESTERN HAZELNUT
☼ ◐ ◊ ◑ ⁄ 1–9, 14–20   **p. 244**

Cowania mexicana stansburiana
CLIFFROSE
☼ ◑ ⁄ 1–3, 10–13   **p. 246**

Elaeagnus commutata
SILVERBERRY
☼ ◊ ◑ ◑ ⁄ 1–3   **p. 271**

Fallugia paradoxa
APACHE PLUME
☼ ◊ ⁄ 2–23   **p. 292**

Forestiera neomexicana
NEW MEXICAN PRIVET
☼ ◊ ◑ ⁄ ALL ZONES   **p. 297**

Holodiscus dumosus
ROCK SPIRAEA
◐ ◑ ⁄ 1–3, 10   **p. 324**

Juniperus communis
☼ ◐ ◊ ◑ ◑ ⁄ ALL ZONES   **p. 341**

Philadelphus lewisii
WILD MOCK ORANGE
☼ ◐ ◑ ⁄ 1–17   **p. 413**

Prunus besseyi
WESTERN SAND CHERRY
☼ ◑ ◑ ⁄ 1–3, 10   **p. 442**

Quercus gambelii
ROCKY MOUNTAIN WHITE OAK
☼ ◊ ◑ ⁄ 1–3, 10   **p. 448**

Rhus glabra cismontana

☼ ◊ ◑ ⁄ 1–10, 14–17   **p. 459**

Rhus trilobata
SQUAWBUSH
☼ ◊ ◑ ⁄ 1–3, 10   **p. 460**

Ribes aureum
GOLDEN CURRANT
☼ ◐ ◑ ◑ ⁄ ALL ZONES   **p. 460**

Robinia neomexicana
DESERT LOCUST
☼ ◊ ⁄ 1–3, 7–11, 14–24   **p. 461**

Rubus deliciosus
ROCKY MOUNTAIN THIMBLEBERRY
☼ ◐ ◑ ⁄ 1–5, 10   **p. 469**

Shepherdia argentea
SILVER BUFFALOBERRY
☼ ◊ ⁄ 1–3, 7, 10, 14–24   **p. 485**

Symphoricarpos orbiculatus
CORAL BERRY
☼ ◊ ⁄ ALL ZONES   **p. 499**

Yucca baccata
DATIL YUCCA
☼ ◑ ◑ ⁄ ALL ZONES   **p. 525**

ROCKY MOUNTAIN REGION
Ground Covers, Vines

Antennaria dioica
PUSSY TOES
☼ ◐ ◑ ⁄ ALL ZONES   **p. 153**

Arctostaphylos uva-ursi
KINNIKINNICK
☼ ◑ ⁄ 1–9, 14–24   **p. 163**

Calylophus hartwegii

☼ ◐ ◑ ⁄ 1–3, 10–13   **p. 200**

Clematis ligusticifolia

☼ ◑ ⁄ 1–6, 15–17   **p. 234**

Humulus lupulus neomexicanus

☼ ◑ ⁄ ALL ZONES   **p. 326**

Quercus gambelii

Ribes aureum

Antennaria dioica

Campanula rotundifolia

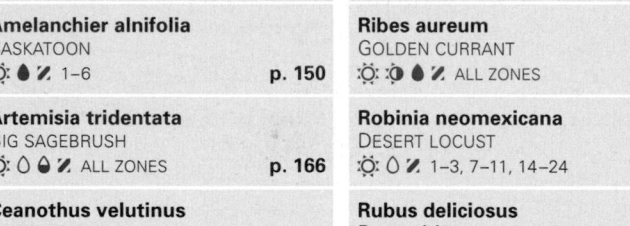

For growing symbol explanations, please see page 45.

SPECIAL EFFECTS

Oenothera berlandieri

Oenothera caespitosa

Penstemon ambiguus

Penstemon strictus

Mahonia repens
CREEPING MAHONIA
☼ ◑ ◌ ✄ 1–21 **p. 371**

Zinnia grandiflora
☼ ◌ ◌ ✄ ALL ZONES **p. 528**

ROCKY MOUNTAIN REGION
Perennials, Ferns

Aquilegia caerulea
ROCKY MOUNTAIN COLUMBINE
☼ ◑ ◌ ✄ ALL ZONES **p. 160**

Callirhoe involucrata
WINE CUPS
☼ ◌ ✄ ALL ZONES **p. 196**

Campanula rotundifolia
BLUEBELL OF SCOTLAND
☼ ◑ ◌ ✄ 1–9, 14–24 **p. 205**

Eriogonum umbellatum
SULFUR FLOWER
☼ ◊ ◌ ✄ ALL ZONES **p. 278**

Geum triflorum
PRAIRIE SMOKE
☼ ◑ ◌ ✄ ALL ZONES **p. 306**

Melampodium leucanthum
BLACKFOOT DAISY
:(): ◌ ✄ 1–3, 10 13 **p. 377**

Monarda fistulosa
☼ ◑ ◌ ◖ ✄ ALL ZONES **p. 382**

Oenothera berlandieri
MEXICAN EVENING PRIMROSE
☼ ◌ ✄ ALL ZONES **p. 392**

Oenothera caespitosa
TUFTED OR WHITE EVENING PRIMROSE
☼ ◌ ✄ 1–3, 7–14, 18–21 **p. 392**

Penstemon ambiguus
PRAIRIE PENSTEMON
☼ ◑ ◌ ✄ 7–15, 18–21 **p. 410**

Penstemon barbatus
☼ ◑ ◌ ✄ ALL ZONES **p. 410**

Penstemon eatonii
FIRECRACKER PENSTEMON
☼ ◑ ◌ ✄ 1–3, 7–13, 18–21 **p. 410**

Penstemon palmeri
☼ ◌ ◌ ✄ 10–13 **p. 410**

Penstemon pinifolius
☼ ◑ ◌ ✄ ALL ZONES **p. 410**

Penstemon strictus
ROCKY MOUNTAIN PENSTEMON
☼ ◑ ◌ ✄ 1–3, 10–13 **p. 411**

Ratibida columnifera
MEXICAN HAT
☼ ◌ ✄ ALL ZONES **p. 451**

CALIFORNIA
Trees

Abies (several)
FIR
☼ ◑ ◌ ◌ ✄ ZONES VARY **p. 130**

Aesculus californica
CALIFORNIA BUCKEYE
☼ ◊ ◌ ✄ 4–10, 12, 14–24 **p. 141**

Arbutus menziesii
MADRONE
☼ ◌ ✄ 3–7, 14–19 **p. 162**

Calocedrus decurrens
INCENSE CEDAR
☼ ◌ ✄ 1–12, 14–24 **p. 198**

Cercis occidentalis
WESTERN REDBUD
☼ ◊ ◌ ✄ 2–24 **p. 218**

Chamaecyparis lawsoniana
PORT ORFORD CEDAR
☼ ◑ ◌ ✄ 4–6, 15–17 **p. 220**

Chamaecyparis nootkatensis
ALASKA CEDAR
☼ ◑ ◌ ✄ 4–6, 15–17 **p. 220**

Cornus nuttallii
PACIFIC DOGWOOD
☼ ◑ ◌ ✄ 2–9, 14–20 **p. 243**

Lithocarpus densiflorus
TANBARK OAK
☼ ◑ ◌ ✄ 4–7, 14–24 **p. 359**

Lyonothamnus floribundus
CATALINA IRONWOOD
☼ ◌ ✄ 15–17, 19–24 **p. 363**

Pinus (several)
PINE
NEEDS, ZONES VARY **p. 419**

Platanus racemosa
CALIFORNIA SYCAMORE
☼ ◌ ✄ 4–24 **p. 426**

Populus fremontii
WESTERN COTTONWOOD
☼ ◌ ✄ 7–24 **p. 434**

Populus tremuloides
QUAKING ASPEN
☼ ◌ ✄ 1–7 **p. 434**

Quercus (many)
OAK
☼ ◊ ◌ ✄ ZONES VARY **p. 447**

Umbellularia californica
CALIFORNIA LAUREL
☼ ◑ ◊ ✄ 4–10, 12–24 **p. 515**

CALIFORNIA
Shrubs

Arctostaphylos (many)
MANZANITA
☼ ◌ ✄ ZONES VARY **p. 162**

Ratibida columnifera

Pinus radiata

Platanus racemosa

Populus tremuloides

Plant listings continue ▶

Arctostaphylos uva-ursi
'Wood's Compact'

Calycanthus occidentalis

Carpenteria californica

Ceanothus 'Ray Hartman'

Cercis occidentalis

Baccharis pilularis
DWARF COYOTE BRUSH
☼ ◌ ◉ ✂ 5–11, 14–24   p. 173

Calycanthus occidentalis
SPICE BUSH
☼ ☼ ◉ ● ◉ ✂ 4–9, 14–22   p. 200

Carpenteria californica
BUSH ANEMONE
☼ ☼ ◌ ◉ ✂ 5–9, 14–24   p. 208

Ceanothus (many)
WILD LILAC
☼ ◌ ◉ ✂ 1–9, 14–24   p. 212

Cercis occidentalis
WESTERN REDBUD
☼ ◌ ◉ ✂ 2–24   p. 218

Cornus stolonifera
REDTWIG DOGWOOD
☼ ● ◉ ● ✂ 1–9, 14–21   p. 243

Dendromecon harfordii
ISLAND BUSH POPPY
☼ ◌ ✂ 5–8, 14–24   p. 260

Eriogonum (many)
WILD BUCKWHEAT
☼ ◌ ◉ ✂ ZONES VARY   p. 278

Fremontodendron (several)
FLANNEL BUSH
☼ ◌ ✂ 7–24   p. 300

Galvezia speciosa
ISLAND BUSH-SNAPDRAGON
☼ ☼ ◌ ✂ 14–24   p. 302

Garrya (several)
SILKTASSEL
NEEDS, ZONES VARY   p. 303

Heteromeles arbutifolia
TOYON
☼ ☼ ◉ ✂ 5–24   p. 321

Lavatera assurgentiflora
TREE MALLOW
☼ ◉ ◉ ✂ 14–24   p. 349

Lupinus arboreus
LUPINE
☼ ◌ ◉ ✂ 14–17, 22–24   p. 362

Mahonia (several)
NEEDS, ZONES VARY   p. 371

Myrica californica
PACIFIC WAX MYRTLE
☼ ◉ ✂ 4–6, 14–17, 20–24   p. 385

Penstemon centranthifolius
SCARLET BUGLER
☼ ☼ ◉ ✂ 7–23   p. 410

Philadelphus lewisii
WILD MOCK ORANGE
☼ ☼ ◉ ✂ 1–17   p. 413

Prunus ilicifolia
HOLLYLEAF CHERRY
☼ ☼ ◌ ◉ ✂ 7–9, 12–24   p. 439

Prunus lyonii
CATALINA CHERRY
☼ ◌ ◉ ✂ 7–9, 12–24   p. 441

Rhamnus californica (several)
COFFEEBERRY
☼ ◌ ◌ ◉ ✂ 4–24   p. 452

Rhododendron occidentale
WESTERN AZALEA
☼ ◉ ◉ ✂ 4–9, 14–17, 19–24   p. 458

Rhus integrifolia
LEMONADE BERRY
☼ ◌ ◉ ✂ 15–17, 20–24   p. 459

Rhus ovata
SUGAR BUSH
☼ ◌ ◉ ✂ 7–24   p. 460

Ribes (several)
CURRANT, GOOSEBERRY
NEEDS, ZONES VARY   p. 460

Salvia clevelandii
☼ ◉ ✂ 10–24   p. 474

Salvia leucophylla
PURPLE SAGE
☼ ◌ ◉ ✂ 8, 9, 14–17, 19–24 p. 474

Sambucus (some)
ELDERBERRY
☼ ☼ ◉ ◉ ✂ ZONES VARY   p. 473

Styrax officinalis californicus
CALIFORNIA STORAX
☼ ☼ ◉ ◉ ✂ 8, 9, 14–24   p. 497

Symphoricarpos albus
COMMON SNOWBERRY
☼ ☼ ◌ ◉ ✂ ALL ZONES   p. 498

Trichostema lanatum
WOOLLY BLUE CURLS
☼ ◌ ✂ 14–24   p. 510

CALIFORNIA
Ground Covers, Vines

Arctostaphylos (many)
MANZANITA
☼ ◉ ✂ ZONES VARY   p. 162

Aristolochia californica
CALIFORNIA DUTCHMAN'S PIPE
☼ ◉ ◉ ✂ 7–9, 14–24   p. 165

Ceanothus (many)
WILD LILAC
☼ ◌ ◉ ✂ 1–9, 14–24   p. 212

Clematis ligusticifolia
☼ ◉ ✂ 1–6, 15–17   p. 234

CALIFORNIA
Perennials, Ferns, Grasses

Achillea millefolium
COMMON YARROW
☼ ◌ ◉ ✂ ALL ZONES   p. 138

Dendromecon harfordii

Eriogonum umbellatum

Philadelphus lewisii

Rhamnus californica
'Eve Case'

Rhus integrifolia

For growing symbol explanations, please see page 45.

Salvia clevelandii

Heuchera

Sambucus callicarpa

Trichostema lanatum

Erigeron glaucus

Aquilegia formosa

Iris, Pacific Coast

Mimulus

Lilium pardalinum

Aquilegia formosa
WESTERN COLUMBINE
☼ ◑ ◔ ✿ ALL ZONES   **p. 160**

Artemisia californica
CALIFORNIA SAGEBRUSH
☼ ○ ◔ ✿ ALL ZONES   **p. 166**

Asarum caudatum
WILD GINGER
● ◑◔ ✿ 4–6, 14–24   **p. 167**

Elymus
LYME GRASS
☼ ◑ ◔ ✿ 8, 9, 14–24   **p. 272**

Erigeron glaucus
BEACH ASTER
☼ ◑ ◔ ✿ 4–6, 15–17, 22–24   **p. 275**

Heuchera
CORAL BELLS
NEEDS, ZONES VARY   **p. 322**

Iris, Pacific Coast and hybrids
☼ ◑ ◔ ◔ ✿ 4–24   **p. 334**

Lilium humboldtii
HUMBOLDT LILY
◑ ◔ ✿ ALL ZONES   **p. 355**

Lilium pardalinum
LEOPARD LILY
◑ ◔ ✿ ALL ZONES   **p. 356**

Mimulus
MONKEY FLOWER
NEEDS, ZONES VARY   **p. 381**

Muhlenbergia rigens
DEER GRASS
☼ ◑ ○ ◔ ✿ 7–24   **p. 384**

Penstemon heterophyllus purdyi
☼ ◑ ◔ ✿ 6–24   **p. 410**

Penstemon spectabilis
ROYAL BEARD TONGUE
☼ ◑ ◔ ✿ 7, 14–23   **p. 411**

Romneya coulteri
MATILIJA POPPY
☼ ○ ◔ ✿ ALL ZONES   **p. 462**

Sidalcea malviflora
CHECKERBLOOM
☼ ◔ ✿ 4–9, 14–24   **p. 485**

Sisyrinchium bellum (many)
BLUE-EYED GRASS
☼ ◑ ◔ ◔ ✿ 4–24   **p. 486**

Sisyrinchium californicum
YELLOW-EYED GRASS
☼ ◑ ◔ ◔ ✿ 4–24   **p. 486**

Stipa pulchra
PURPLE NEEDLE GRASS
☼ ◔ ✿ 5, 7–9, 11, 14–24   **p. 494**

Vancouveria hexandra
◑ ◔ ◔ ✿ 4–6, 14–17   **p. 516**

Plant listings continue ▶

Penstemon heterophyllus purdyi

Sisyrinchium bellum

Vancouveria hexandra

Zauschneria californica latifolia

Cercidium microphyllum

Olneya tesota

Washingtonia

Calliandra californica

Chrysothamnus nauseosus

Vancouveria planipetala
INSIDE-OUT FLOWER
☼ ◐ ◌ ◗ ☇ 4–6, 14–17   p. 516

Zauschneria
CALIFORNIA FUCHSIA
☼ ◌ ◗ ☇ 2–10, 12–24   p. 527

SOUTHWEST
Trees

Acacia constricta
WHITETHORN ACACIA
☼ ◌ ◗ ☇ 10–24   p. 132

Acacia smallii
☼ ◌ ◗ ☇ 8, 9, 12–24   p. 134

Cercidium floridum
BLUE PALO VERDE
☼ ◐ ◗ ☇ 10–14, 18–20   p. 218

Cercidium microphyllum
FOOTHILLS PALO VERDE
☼ ◐ ◗ ☇ 10–14, 18–20   p. 218

Cercidium praecox
SONORAN PALO VERDE
☼ ◐ ◗ ☇ 12, 13, 18–20   p. 218

Chilopsis linearis
DESERT WILLOW
☼ ◗ ☇ 10–13, 18–21   p. 223

Cupressus arizonica
ARIZONA CYPRESS
☼ ◌ ☇ 5, 8–24   p. 252

Lysiloma microphylla thornberi
FEATHER BUSH
☼ ◌ ☇ 10, 12–24   p. 363

Olneya tesota
DESERT IRONWOOD
☼ ◐ ☇ 12, 13   p. 393

Pithecellobium flexicaule
TEXAS EBONY
☼ ◗ ☇ 10–13   p. 425

Platanus wrightii
ARIZONA SYCAMORE
☼ ◗ ☇ 10–12   p. 426

Prosopis
MESQUITE
☼ ◌ ◗ ☇ 10–13   p. 438

Quercus emoryi
EMORY OAK
☼ ◌ ◗ ☇ 10–13   p. 448

Washingtonia
FAN PALM
☼ ◐ ◗ ☇ 8–24   p. 522

SOUTHWEST
Shrubs

Anisacanthus thurberi
DESERT HONEYSUCKLE
☼ ◐ ☇ 8–13, 18, 19   p. 152

Calliandra californica
BAJA FAIRY DUSTER
☼ ◐ ☇ 10–24   p. 196

Calliandra eriophylla
FAIRY DUSTER
☼ ◐ ☇ 10–24   p. 196

Chrysothamnus nauseosus
RUBBER RABBITBRUSH
☼ ◌ ☇ 1–3, 10, 11   p. 228

Cordia boissieri
TEXAS OLIVE
☼ ◐ ◐ ◗ ☇ 8–24   p. 240

Cordia parvifolia
☼ ◐ ◐ ◗ ☇ 8–24   p. 240

Dalea frutescens
BLACK DALEA
☼ ◐ ☇ 12, 13   p. 257

Dalea pulchra
INDIGO BUSH
☼ ◐ ☇ 12, 13   p. 258

Dodonaea viscosa
HOP BUSH
☼ ◐ ◌ ◐ ☇ 7–9, 12–24   p. 266

Encelia farinosa
BRITTLEBUSH
☼ ◐ ☇ 7–10, 14–24   p. 272

Fallugia paradoxa
APACHE PLUME
☼ ◌ ☇ 2–23   p. 292

Justicia californica
CHUPAROSA
☼ ◌ ☇ 10–13   p. 342

Larrea tridentata
CREOSOTE BUSH
☼ ◌ ◐ ☇ 10–13, 19   p. 347

Leucophyllum
TEXAS RANGER
☼ ◐ ☇ 7–24   p. 352

Rhus ovata
SUGAR BUSH
☼ ◌ ◐ ☇ 7–24   p. 460

Rhus trilobata
SQUAWBUSH
☼ ◌ ◐ ☇ 1–3, 10   p. 460

Salvia chamaedryoides
☼ ◐ ☇ 8, 9, 14–24   p. 474

Salvia greggii
AUTUMN SAGE
☼ ◐ ◌ ◐ ☇ 8–24   p. 474

Simmondsia chinensis
JOJOBA
☼ ◐ ☇ 10–13, 19–24   p. 486

Sophora secundiflora
TEXAS MOUNTAIN LAUREL
☼ ◐ ◐ ◌ ◐ ☇ 8–16, 18–24   p. 488

Encelia farinosa

Salvia greggii

Tagetes lemmonii

Tecoma stans

Calylophus hartwegii

For growing symbol explanations, please see page 45.

SPECIAL EFFECTS

Zinnia grandiflora

Agave

Fouquieria splendens

Hesperaloe parviflora

Opuntia

Tagetes lemmonii

☼ ◖ ⚡ 8–10, 12–24   **p. 501**

Tecoma stans

☼ ◖ ⚡ 10, 12, 13, 21–24   **p. 503**

Vauquelinia californica
ARIZONA ROSEWOOD

☼ ◗ ⚡ 10–13   **p. 516**

SOUTHWEST
Ground Covers, Vines

Antigonon leptopus
QUEEN'S WREATH

☼ ◖ ◗ ⚡ 12, 13, 18–21   **p. 154**

Baccharis 'Centennial'

☼ ◖ ⚡ 10–13   **p. 173**

Calylophus hartwegii

☼ ◑ ◖ ◗ ⚡ 1–3, 10–13   **p. 200**

Dalea greggii
TRAILING INDIGO BUSH

☼ ◖ ⚡ 12, 13   **p. 258**

Mascagnia macroptera
YELLOW ORCHID VINE

☼ ◖ ⚡ 12, 21   **p. 375**

Merremia aurea
YELLOW MORNING GLORY

☼ ◖ ⚡ 12–24   **p. 379**

Oenothera berlandieri
MEXICAN EVENING PRIMROSE

☼ ◖ ⚡ ALL ZONES   **p. 392**

Oenothera stubbei
BAJA EVENING PRIMROSE

☼ ◖ ⚡ ALL ZONES   **p. 393**

Zinnia grandiflora

☼ ◖ ◗ ⚡ ALL ZONES   **p. 528**

SOUTHWEST
Grasses, Accent Plants

Agave (many)

NEEDS, ZONES VARY   **p. 142**

Echinocactus (many)
BARREL CACTUS

☼ ◑ ◖ ◗ ⚡ 12–24   **p. 270**

Echinocereus (some)
HEDGEHOG CACTUS

☼ ◖ ⚡ ZONES VARY   **p. 270**

Ferocactus (some)
BARREL CACTUS

☼ ◗ ⚡ 8–24   **p. 293**

Fouquieria splendens
OCOTILLO

☼ ◗ ⚡ 10–13, 18–20   **p. 298**

Hesperaloe parviflora

☼ ◗ ⚡ 10–16, 18–21   **p. 321**

Muhlenbergia dumosa
BAMBOO MUHLY

☼ ◑ ◗ ◖ ⚡ 8–24   **p. 384**

Muhlenbergia rigens
DEER GRASS

☼ ◑ ◖ ◗ ⚡ 7–24   **p. 384**

Opuntia (many)

☼ ◗ ◖ ◗ ⚡ ZONES VARY   **p. 394**

Yucca (many)

☼ ◖ ◗ ⚡ ZONES VARY   **p. 525**

SOUTHWEST
Annuals, Perennials

Baileya multiradiata
DESERT MARIGOLD

☼ ◖ ◗ ⚡ ALL ZONES   **p. 174**

Melampodium leucanthum
BLACKFOOT DAISY

☼ ◖ ⚡ 1–3, 10–13   **p. 377**

Oenothera caespitosa
TUFTED OR WHITE EVENING PRIMROSE

☼ ◖ ⚡ 1–3, 7–14, 18–21   **p. 392**

Penstemon ambiguus
PRAIRIE PENSTEMON

☼ ◑ ◖ ◗ ⚡ 7–15, 18–21   **p. 410**

Penstemon barbatus

☼ ◑ ◖ ◗ ⚡ ALL ZONES   **p. 410**

Penstemon eatonii
FIRECRACKER PENSTEMON

☼ ◑ ◖ ◗ ⚡ 1–3, 7–13, 18–21   **p. 410**

Penstemon parryi
PARRY'S PENSTEMON

☼ ◑ ◖ ◗ ⚡ 12, 13   **p. 410**

Penstemon strictus
ROCKY MOUNTAIN PENSTEMON

☼ ◑ ◖ ◗ ⚡ 1–3, 10–13   **p. 411**

Penstemon superbus

☼ ◑ ◖ ⚡ 12, 13   **p. 411**

Ratibida columnifera
MEXICAN HAT

☼ ◖ ⚡ ALL ZONES   **p. 451**

Salvia farinacea
MEALY-CUP SAGE

☼ ◖ ⚡ ALL ZONES   **p. 474**

Verbena bipinnatifida

☼ ◖ ⚡ ALL ZONES   **p. 517**

Verbena gooddingii

☼ ◖ ◗ ⚡ ALL ZONES   **p. 517**

Baileya multiradiata

Melampodium leucanthum

Penstemon eatonii

Ratibida columnifera

Verbena bipinnatifida

Plants for
ESPALIERS

Iochroma cyaneum

Camellia reticulata 'Shot Silk'

Fruit trees grown against a sunny wall so that crops could be raised early or in marginally warm regions were the first plants to be espaliered—trained so that their branches would grow horizontally. Today, the practice of espaliering has expanded to include ornamentals trained in a formal arrangement or in an irregular pattern to emphasize their natural growth habit. Espaliers are well suited to the narrow space between a walk and wall and to any wall or fence where you want a tracery of branches, foliage, or flowers. The plants listed below are among the easiest to espalier—strong enough to be self-supporting yet flexible enough to be guided.

Apple, 'McIntosh'

Cestrum

Orange

Fig, edible

Abutilon ✻
FLOWERING MAPLE
☼ ◐ ◗ ✓ ZONES VARY   **p. 131**

Acer circinatum ✻
VINE MAPLE
◗ ◗ ✓ 1–6, 14–17   **p. 135**

Apple ✻
☼ ◗ ✓ ALL ZONES   **p. 155** 🍒

Apricot ✻
☼ ◗ ✓ ZONES VARY   **p. 159** 🍒

Bauhinia galpinii ✻
RED BAUHINIA
☼ ◗ ✓ 13, 15, 16, 18–23   **p. 179**

Calliandra haematocephala ✻
PINK POWDER PUFF
☼ ◗ ✓ 22–24   **p. 196**

Callistemon ✻
BOTTLEBRUSH
☼ ◗ ✓ 8, 9, 12–24   **p. 197**

Camellia (some) ✻
◐ ◗ ✓ 4–9, 12, 14–24   **p. 200**

Carissa macrocarpa 'Fancy' ✻
NATAL PLUM
☼ ◐ ◗ ◗ ✓ 22–24   **p. 207** 🍒

Cestrum (some) ✻
◗ ◗ ✓ ZONES VARY   **p. 219** 🍒

Cherry ✻
☼ ◗ ✓ ZONES VARY   **p. 222** 🍒

Citrus ✻
☼ ◗ ✓ 8, 9, 12–24   **p. 230** 🍒

Clianthus puniceus ✻
PARROT BEAK
☼ ◐ ◗ ✓ 8, 9, 14–24   **p. 236**

Cocculus laurifolius
☼ ◐ ● ◗ ✓ 8, 9, 12–24   **p. 236**

Coprosma repens
MIRROR PLANT
☼ ☼ ◗ ✓ 15–17, 21–24   **p. 239**

Cotoneaster lacteus ✻
☼ ○ ◗ ✓ 4–24   **p. 246** 🍒

Elaeagnus (evergreen) ✻
☼ ◐ ● ◗ ✓ ZONES VARY   **p. 271** 🍒

Eriobotrya deflexa ✻
BRONZE LOQUAT
☼ ◐ ◗ ✓ 8–24   **p. 275**

Eriobotrya japonica
LOQUAT
☼ ☼ ◐ ◗ ✓ 4–24   **p. 275** 🍒

Escallonia exoniensis ✻
☼ ◐ ● ◗ ✓ MOST ZONES   **p. 280**

Eucalyptus caesia ✻
☼ ○ ◗ ✓ SEE CHART   **p. 282**

Eucalyptus rhodantha ✻
ROSE MALLEE
☼ ○ ◗ ✓ SEE CHART   **p. 286**

Euonymus fortunei (some)
☼ ◐ ◗ ✓ 1–17   **p. 288** 🍒

Feijoa sellowiana ✻
PINEAPPLE GUAVA
☼ ◐ ◗ ✓ 7–9, 12–24   **p. 292** 🍒

Ficus auriculata
☼ ◗ ✓ 20–24   **p. 294** 🍒

Ficus benjamina
WEEPING CHINESE BANYAN
☼ ◐ ◗ ✓ 13, 23, 24   **p. 294**

SYMBOLS: ✻ indicates plants that bear showy flowers; 🍒 indicates plants that bear showy fruit.

Cotoneaster lacteus

Elaeagnus pungens

Feijoa sellowiana

For growing symbol explanations, please see page 45.

Grewia occidentalis

Magnolia grandiflora

Malus

Ochna serrulata

Fig, edible
☼ ◊ ⚡ 4–9, 12–24   **p. 295**

Gardenia ✳
☼ ◐ ⚡ ZONES VARY   **p. 302**

Grewia occidentalis ✳
LAVENDER STARFLOWER
☼ ◐ ⚡ 8, 9, 12–24   **p. 313**

Griselinia
☼ ◐ ◐ ⚡ 9, 14–17, 20–24   **p. 313**

Hibiscus rosa-sinensis ✳
CHINESE HIBISCUS
☼ ◐ ⚡ 9, 12, 13, 15, 16, 19–24 **p. 323**

Ilex altaclarensis 'Wilsonii'
WILSON HOLLY
☼ ◐ ◐ ⚡ 3–24   **p. 329**

Iochroma cyaneum ✳
☼ ◐ ◐◐ ⚡ 16, 17, 19–24   **p. 331**

Itea ilicifolia ✳
HOLLYLEAF SWEETSPIRE
☼ ◐ ◐ ⚡ 4–24   **p. 335**

Juniperus chinensis 'Torulosa'
HOLLYWOOD JUNIPER
☼ ◐ ◐ ◐ ⚡ ALL ZONES   **p. 340**

Laburnum watereri ✳
☼ ◐ ◐ ⚡ 1–10, 14–17   **p. 345**

Magnolia grandiflora (smallest) ✳
SOUTHERN MAGNOLIA
☼ ◐ ◐ ⚡ 4–12, 14–24   **p. 367**

Malus ✳
CRABAPPLE
☼ ◐ ⚡ 1–21   **p. 372**

Michelia figo ✳
BANANA SHRUB
☼ ◐ ◐ ⚡ 9, 14–24   **p. 380**

Nectarine ✳
☼ ◐ ⚡ ZONES VARY   **p. 403**

Ochna serrulata ✳
MICKEY MOUSE PLANT
◐ ◐ ⚡ 14–24   **p. 392**

Osmanthus fragrans ✳
SWEET OLIVE
☼ ◐ ◐ ⚡ 8, 9, 12–24   **p. 396**

Peach ✳
☼ ◐ ⚡ ZONES VARY   **p. 403**

Pear ✳
☼ ◐ ◐ ⚡ 1–11, 14–18   **p. 407**

Persimmon
NEEDS, ZONES VARY   **p. 412**

Photinia fraseri ✳
☼ ◐ ◐ ⚡ 4–24   **p. 416**

Plum ✳
☼ ◐ ⚡ ZONES VARY   **p. 428**

Podocarpus gracilior
FERN PINE
☼ ◐ ◐ ⚡ 8, 9, 12–24   **p. 431**

Podocarpus macrophyllus
YEW PINE
☼ ◐ ◐ ⚡ 4–9, 12–24   **p. 431**

Prunus (deciduous) ✳
NEEDS, ZONES VARY   **p. 439**

Pyracantha ✳
FIRETHORN
☼ ◐ ◐ ◐ ⚡ ZONES VARY   **p. 446**

Pyrus kawakamii ✳
EVERGREEN PEAR
☼ ◐ ⚡ 8, 9, 12–24   **p. 447**

Rhododendron 'Else Frye' ✳
◐ ◐ ◐◐ ⚡ 4–6, 15–17   **p. 455**

**Rhododendron
'Fragrantissimum'** ✳
◐ ◐ ◐◐ ⚡ 4–6, 15–17   **p. 455**

Rhus integrifolia ✳
LEMONADE BERRY
☼ ◊ ◐ ⚡ 15–17, 20–24   **p. 459**

Rhus laurina ✳
LAUREL SUMAC
☼ ◊ ◐ ⚡ 20–24   **p. 460**

Rhus ovata ✳
SUGAR BUSH
☼ ◊ ◐ ⚡ 7–24   **p. 460**

Sarcococca ruscifolia
☼ ◐ ◐ ◐ ◐ ⚡ 4–9, 14–24 **p. 477**

Sophora secundiflora ✳
TEXAS MOUNTAIN LAUREL
☼ ◐ ◐ ◐ ⚡ 8–16, 18–24   **p. 488**

Tecomaria capensis ✳
CAPE HONEYSUCKLE
☼ ◐ ◐ ⚡ 12, 13, 16, 18–24 **p. 503**

Viburnum burkwoodii ✳
☼ ◐ ◐ ⚡ 1–12, 14–24   **p. 518**

**Viburnum macrocephalum
macrocephalum** ✳
☼ ◐ ◐ ⚡ 1–9, 14–24   **p. 518**

Viburnum plicatum plicatum ✳
JAPANESE SNOWBALL
☼ ◐ ◐ ⚡ 1–9, 14–24   **p. 519**

Xylosma congestum
☼ ◐ ◐ ◐ ◐ ⚡ 8–24   **p. 525**

Pear

Pyracantha

Sophora secundiflora

Viburnum plicatum plicatum

Achillea and Gaillardia

FLOWERS
for Cutting

A large bouquet of fresh flowers is a satisfying reward for your gardening efforts. Many kinds of flowers are good for cutting. The ones listed here will generally last a week in water. Annuals and biennials must be planted every year, although a few, such as larkspur and cosmos, may reseed themselves. Perennials and most bulbs provide flowers for cutting year after year. Peak flower season can come earlier or later than indicated, depending on climate and care.

Consolida ambigua

Antirrhinum majus

Centaurea cyanus

Cosmos bipinnatus

ANNUALS, BIENNIALS

Antirrhinum majus
SNAPDRAGON
☼ ◑ ✂ ALL ZONES   p. 154

Calendula officinalis
POT MARIGOLD
☼ ◑ ✂ ALL ZONES   p. 195

Callistephus chinensis
CHINA ASTER
☼ ◑ ✂ ALL ZONES   p. 197

Centaurea cyanus
CORNFLOWER
☼ ◑ ✂ ALL ZONES   p. 216

Clarkia amoena
GODETIA
☼ ◑ ✂ ALL ZONES   p. 233

Cleome hasslerana
SPIDER FLOWER
☼ ◑ ✂ ALL ZONES   p. 235

Consolida ambigua
LARKSPUR
☼ ◑ ✂ ALL ZONES   p. 239

Cosmos bipinnatus
☼ ◑ ✂ ALL ZONES   p. 245

Dianthus (some)
☼ ◐ ◑ ✂ ALL ZONES   p. 261

Eustoma grandiflorum
LISIANTHUS
☼ ◑ ✂ ALL ZONES   p. 290

Gomphrena globosa
GLOBE AMARANTH
☼ ◐ ◑ ✂ ALL ZONES   p. 309

Gypsophila elegans
☼ ◑ ✂ ALL ZONES   p. 314

Helianthus annuus
COMMON SUNFLOWER
☼ ◑ ◑ ✂ ALL ZONES   p. 318

Helichrysum bracteatum
STRAWFLOWER
☼ ◑ ✂ ALL ZONES   p. 319

Helipterum roseum
PINK AND WHITE EVERLASTING
☼ ◑ ✂ ALL ZONES   p. 319

Lathyrus odoratus
SWEET PEA
☼ ◑ ✂ ALL ZONES   p. 348

Lavatera trimestris
ANNUAL MALLOW
☼ ◑ ◑ ✂ ALL ZONES   p. 349

Limonium sinuatum
☼ ◑ ✂ ALL ZONES   p. 356

Matthiola
STOCK
☼ ◐ ◑ ✂ ALL ZONES   p. 376

Nigella damascena
LOVE-IN-A-MIST
☼ ◐ ◑ ✂ ALL ZONES   p. 391

Phlox drummondii
ANNUAL PHLOX
☼ ◐ ◑ ✂ ALL ZONES   p. 415

Psylliostachys suworowii
☼ ◑ ✂ ALL ZONES   p. 444

Scabiosa (some)
PINCUSHION FLOWER
☼ ◑ ✂ ALL ZONES   p. 478

Tagetes (most)
MARIGOLD
☼ ◑ ✂ ALL ZONES   p. 500

Tithonia rotundifolia
MEXICAN SUNFLOWER
☼ ◑ ✂ ALL ZONES   p. 507

VERTICAL BAR: The green band indicates bloom time (most zones). An empty bar indicates the bloom time varies by variety.

SPRING	
SUMMER	
FALL	
WINTER	

Helianthus annuus

Lathyrus odoratus

Scabiosa atropurpurea

For growing symbol explanations, please see page 45.

Tagetes tenuifolia 'Lemon Gem'

Tithonia rotundifolia

Alstroemeria

Dahlia

Delphinium Magic Fountains strain

Zinnia
☼ ◖◖✂ ALL ZONES   **p. 528**

PERENNIALS, BULBS

Achillea filipendulina
FERNLEAF YARROW
☼ ◌◖◖✂ ALL ZONES   **p. 138**

Achillea millefolium
COMMON YARROW
☼ ◌◖◖✂ ALL ZONES   **p. 138**

Alstroemeria
☼ ◖✂ 5–9, 14–24   **p. 148**

Anemone coronaria
POPPY-FLOWERED ANEMONE
◐ ◖◖✂ ALL ZONES   **p. 151**

Anemone hybrida
JAPANESE ANEMONE
◐ ◖◖✂ ALL ZONES   **p. 151**

Aster
◑ ◖✂ ALL ZONES   **p. 170**

Campanula (some)
BELLFLOWER
☼ ◐ ◖✂ 1–9, 14–24   **p. 203**

Chrysanthemum (some)
NEEDS, ZONES VARY   **p. 226**

Coreopsis (most)
☼ ◖✂ ZONES VARY   **p. 240**

Dahlia
☼ ◐ ◖✂ ALL ZONES   **p. 256**

Delphinium
☼ ◖✂ ZONES VARY   **p. 260**

Dianthus (many)
☼ ◐ ◖✂ ALL ZONES   **p. 261**

Echinacea purpurea
PURPLE CONEFLOWER
☼ ◖◖✂ ALL ZONES   **p. 269**

Freesia
☼ ◐ ◖◖✂ 8, 9, 12–24   **p. 300**

Gaillardia grandiflora
BLANKET FLOWER
☼ ◖✂ ALL ZONES   **p. 301**

Gerbera jamesonii
TRANSVAAL DAISY
☼ ◖✂ 8, 9, 12–24   **p. 306**

Gladiolus
☼ ◖✂ ALL ZONES   **p. 307**

Gypsophila paniculata
BABY'S BREATH
☼ ◖✂ 1–10, 14–16, 18–21   **p. 314**

Iris
NEEDS, ZONES VARY   **p. 332**

Lavandula
LAVENDER
☼ ◖✂ ZONES VARY   **p. 349**

Liatris
GAYFEATHER
☼ ◖◖✂ 1–10, 14–24   **p. 353**

Lilium
LILY
☼ ◖◖✂ ALL ZONES   **p. 354**

Limonium perezii
☼ ◖✂ 13, 15–17, 20–24   **p. 356**

Narcissus
DAFFODIL
☼ ◐ ◖◖✂ ALL ZONES   **p. 387**

Phlox paniculata
SUMMER PHLOX
☼ ◐ ◖◖✂ 1–14, 18–21   **p. 415**

Platycodon grandiflorus
BALLOON FLOWER
☼ ◐ ◖◖✂ ALL ZONES   **p. 427**

Polianthes tuberosa
TUBEROSE
☼ ◐ ◖◖✂ 15–17, 22–24   **p. 432**

Ranunculus asiaticus
PERSIAN RANUNCULUS
☼ ◖✂ ALL ZONES   **p. 450**

Rudbeckia hirta
GLORIOSA DAISY
☼ ◖✂ ALL ZONES   **p. 470**

Scabiosa (some)
PINCUSHION FLOWER
☼ ◖✂ ZONES VARY   **p. 478**

Stokesia laevis
STOKES ASTER
☼ ◖✂ 1–9, 12–24   **p. 494**

Thalictrum aquilegifolium
MEADOW RUE
◐ ◖◖✂ ALL ZONES   **p. 504**

Tritonia
☼ ◖✂ 9, 13–24   **p. 511**

Tulipa
TULIP
☼ ◖✂ ALL ZONES   **p. 513**

Veronica spicata
SPEEDWELL
☼ ◖✂ ALL ZONES   **p. 518**

Zantedeschia
CALLA
☼ ◐ ◖◖◖✂ MOST ZONES   **p. 526**

Gerbera jamesonii

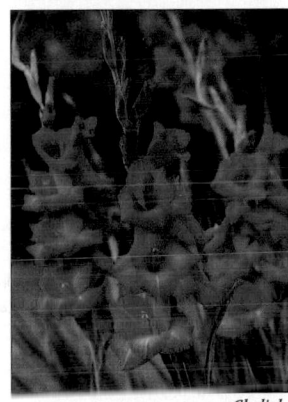
Gladiolus

Liatris spicata

Platycodon grandiflorus

Echinacea purpurea

Hummingbird at fuchsia

Plants That Attract
BUTTERFLIES AND HUMMINGBIRDS

Passiflora alatocaerulea

Butterflies and hummingbirds are welcome visitors to most gardens. Choose the right plants and you can encourage them to stay a while. Butterfly larvae (caterpillars) need food plants; adult butterflies need nectar plants. Sunny areas such as meadows that are sheltered from the wind and contain such amenities as leaf litter, rock crevices, brush piles, damp places, and even weeds are the most welcoming of gardens for butterflies. When you choose plants, keep in mind that not every plant will attract butterflies in every region. And never use pesticides, unless you can target the specific pest without harming the butterflies. Hummingbirds ingest half their weight in food every day. Flowering plants provide nectar; spiders and insects supply protein. Hummingbirds visit a huge array of plants. The ones listed are some of their favorites.

Linaria purpurea

Artichoke

Diascia

Helianthus

Cassia

Aster novi-belgii 'Carnival'

BUTTERFLY LARVAE
Annuals, Perennials, Grasses

Alcea rosea
HOLLYHOCK
☼ ● ✚ ALL ZONES — p. 144

Antirrhinum majus
SNAPDRAGON
☼ ● ✚ ALL ZONES — p. 154

Artichoke
☼ ● ✚ ZONES VARY — p. 166

Asclepias (esp. natives)
☼ ● ● ✚ ZONES VARY — p. 167

Aster
☼ ● ✚ ALL ZONES — p. 170

Broccoli, Cabbage, Mustard
☼ ● ✚ ALL ZONES — pp. 190, 194, 385

Diascia
TWINSPUR
☼ ◐ ● ✚ ZONES VARY — p. 262

Dicentra
BLEEDING HEART
● ● ✚ 1–9, 14–24 — p. 262

Digitalis purpurea
COMMON FOXGLOVE
◐ ● ✚ ALL ZONES — p. 265

Foeniculum vulgare
COMMON FENNEL
☼ ◊ ✚ ALL ZONES — p. 297

Geum
☼ ◐ ● ✚ ALL ZONES — p. 306

Helianthus
SUNFLOWER
☼ ● ● ✚ ALL ZONES — p. 318

Heliotropium arborescens
COMMON HELIOTROPE
☼ ◐ ● ✚ 8–24 — p. 319

Linaria purpurea
TOADFLAX
☼ ◐ ● ✚ ALL ZONES — p. 356

Lupinus
LUPINE
NEEDS, ZONES VARY — p. 362

Penstemon
BEARD TONGUE
NEEDS, ZONES VARY — p. 410

Sidalcea malviflora
CHECKERBLOOM
☼ ● ✚ 4–9, 14–24 — p. 485

Tropaeolum majus
GARDEN NASTURTIUM
☼ ◐ ● ✚ ALL ZONES — p. 512

Veronica
SPEEDWELL
☼ ● ✚ ALL ZONES — p. 517

BUTTERFLY LARVAE
Ground Covers, Vines

Passiflora
PASSION VINE
☼ ● ✚ ZONES VARY — p. 401

For growing symbol explanations, please see page 45.

Holodiscus discolor

Hibiscus

Ribes

Mimulus aurantiacus

Rosa 'Leander'

Strawberry

☼ ◑ ◐ ✂ ALL ZONES   p. 494

Wisteria

☼ ◑ ◐ ◐ ✂ ALL ZONES   p. 523

BUTTERFLY LARVAE
Shrubs

Cassia
SENNA
☼ ◐ ✂ ZONES VARY   p. 210

Ceanothus
WILD LILAC
☼ ◊ ◐ ✂ 1–9, 14–24   p. 212

Eriogonum
WILD BUCKWHEAT
☼ ◊ ◐ ✂ ZONES VARY   p. 278

Hibiscus

☼ ◐ ✂ ZONES VARY   p. 322

Holodiscus discolor
OCEAN SPRAY
☼ ◐ ✂ 1–7, 14–17   p. 324

Lavatera
TREE MALLOW
☼ ◐ ◐ ✂ ZONES VARY   p. 349

Malva
MALLOW
☼ ◐ ✂ ALL ZONES   p. 372

Mimulus aurantiacus
STICKY MONKEY FLOWER
☼ ◑ ◐ ✂ 8, 9, 14–24   p. 381

Plumbago auriculata
CAPE PLUMBAGO
☼ ◐ ✂ 8, 9, 12–24   p. 428

Rhamnus californica
COFFEEBERRY
☼ ◑ ◊ ◐ ✂ 4–24   p. 452

Ribes
CURRANT, GOOSEBERRY
NEEDS, ZONES VARY   p. 460

Rosa
ROSE
NEEDS, ZONES VARY   p. 462

Spiraea

☼ ◑ ◐ ✂ 1–11, 14–21   p. 490

Viburnum

NEEDS, ZONES VARY   p. 518

BUTTERFLY LARVAE
Trees

Aesculus
HORSECHESTNUT
NEEDS, ZONES VARY   p. 141

Arbutus menziesii
MADRONE
☼ ◊ ◐ ✂ 3–7, 14–19   p. 162

Betula
BIRCH
☼ ◐ ◐ ◑ ✂ ZONES VARY   p. 183

Celtis
HACKBERRY
☼ ◑ ◐ ✂ ZONES VARY   p. 216

Citrus
☼ ◐ ✂ 8, 9, 12–24   p. 230

Cornus
DOGWOOD
NEEDS, ZONES VARY   p. 242

Crataegus
HAWTHORN
☼ ◐ ✂ 1–12, 14–17   p. 247

Malus
CRABAPPLE
☼ ◐ ✂ 1–21   p. 372

Pinus
PINE
NEEDS, ZONES VARY   p. 419

Platanus
PLANE TREE, SYCAMORE
☼ ◐ ✂ ZONES VARY   p. 426

Populus
POPLAR
☼ ◐ ✂ ZONES VARY   p. 434

Prosopis
MESQUITE
☼ ◊ ◐ ✂ 10–13   p. 438

Prunus

NEEDS, ZONES VARY   p. 439

Pseudotsuga menziesii
DOUGLAS FIR
☼ ◑ ◊ ◐ ✂ 1–10, 14–17   p. 443

Quercus
OAK
☼ ◊ ◐ ✂ ZONES VARY   p. 447

Salix
WILLOW
☼ ◐ ◑ ✂ ALL ZONES   p. 471

ADULT BUTTERFLIES
Annuals, Perennials, Grasses

Achillea
YARROW
☼ ◊ ◐ ✂ ALL ZONES   p. 138

Agapanthus
LILY-OF-THE-NILE
☼ ◐ ◐ ✂ 7–9, 12–24   p. 141

Antirrhinum majus
SNAPDRAGON
☼ ◐ ✂ ALL ZONES   p. 154

Cornus

Platanus

Pseudotsuga menziesii

Quercus

Plant listings continue ▶

SPECIAL EFFECTS

Armeria

Centranthus ruber

Cosmos

Eryngium amethystinum

Aquilegia
COLUMBINE
☼ ◐ ◔ ✄ ALL ZONES   **p. 160**

Armeria
THRIFT, SEA PINK
☼ ◔ ◔ ✄ ALL ZONES   **p. 165**

Asclepias tuberosa
BUTTERFLY WEED
☼ ◐ ◔ ✄ ALL ZONES   **p. 168**

Aster
☼ ◔ ✄ ALL ZONES   **p. 170**

Astilbe
FALSE SPIRAEA
☼ ◐ ◔ ✄ 2–7, 14–17   **p. 170**

Borago officinalis
BORAGE
☼ ◐ ● ◔ ◔ ✄ ALL ZONES   **p. 187**

Bouvardia
NEEDS, ZONES VARY   **p. 188**

Catananche caerulea
CUPID'S DART
☼ ◔ ✄ ALL ZONES   **p. 211**

Centranthus ruber
JUPITER'S BEARD
☼ ◐ ● ◔ ◔ ◔ ✄ 7–9, 12–24   **p. 216**

Chrysanthemum maximum
SHASTA DAISY
☼ ◐ ◔ ✄ ALL ZONES   **p. 226**

Coreopsis
☼ ◔ ✄ ZONES VARY   **p. 240**

Cosmos
☼ ◔ ✄ ZONES VARY   **p. 245**

Cynoglossum
NEEDS, ZONES VARY   **p. 255**

Delphinium
☼ ◔ ✄ ZONES VARY   **p. 260**

Dianthus
PINK
☼ ◐ ◔ ✄ ALL ZONES   **p. 261**

Echinacea purpurea
PURPLE CONEFLOWER
☼ ◐ ◔ ✄ ALL ZONES   **p. 269**

Echinops exaltatus
GLOBE THISTLE
☼ ◔ ◔ ✄ ALL ZONES   **p. 270**

Erigeron
FLEABANE
☼ ◐ ◔ ◔ ✄ ZONES VARY   **p. 275**

Eryngium amethystinum
SEA HOLLY
☼ ◔ ✄ ALL ZONES   **p. 279**

Erysimum cheiri
WALLFLOWER
☼ ◐ ◔ ✄ 4–6, 14–17, 22, 23   **p. 279**

Gaillardia grandiflora
BLANKET FLOWER
☼ ◔ ✄ ALL ZONES   **p. 301**

Heliotropium arborescens
COMMON HELIOTROPE
☼ ◐ ◔ ✄ 8–24   **p. 319**

Iberis
CANDYTUFT
☼ ◔ ✄ ALL ZONES   **p. 329**

Lathyrus odoratus
SWEET PEA
☼ ◔ ✄ ALL ZONES   **p. 348**

Liatris
GAYFEATHER
☼ ◔ ◔ ✄ 1–10, 14–24   **p. 353**

Lobelia
NEEDS, ZONES VARY   **p. 359**

Lobularia maritima
SWEET ALYSSUM
☼ ◐ ◔ ✄ ALL ZONES   **p. 360**

Monarda
BEE BALM, OSWEGO TEA
☼ ◐ ◔ ● ✄ ALL ZONES   **p. 382**

Origanum vulgare
OREGANO
☼ ◔ ✄ ALL ZONES   **p. 395**

Penstemon
BEARD TONGUE
NEEDS, ZONES VARY   **p. 410**

Phlox
☼ ◐ ◔ ✄ ZONES VARY   **p. 414**

Ranunculus
NEEDS VARY, ALL ZONES   **p. 450**

Rudbeckia hirta
GLORIOSA DAISY
☼ ◔ ✄ ALL ZONES   **p. 470**

Salvia
SAGE
NEEDS, ZONES VARY   **p. 473**

Scabiosa
PINCUSHION FLOWER
☼ ◔ ✄ ZONES VARY   **p. 478**

Sedum (tall)
STONECROP
NEEDS, ZONES VARY   **p. 481**

Solidago
GOLDENROD
☼ ◐ ◔ ✄ ALL ZONES   **p. 488**

Tagetes
MARIGOLD
NEEDS, ZONES VARY   **p. 500**

For growing symbol explanations, please see page 45.

Erysimum cheiri

Lathyrus odoratus

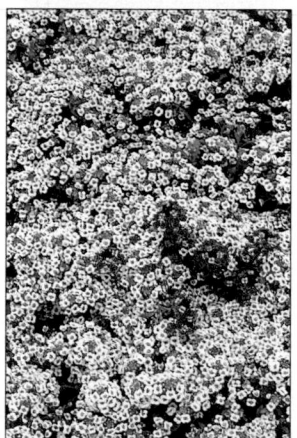

Lobularia maritima

*Rudbeckia hirta
'Marmalade'*

Salvia clevelandii

Buddleia

Choisya ternata

Heteromeles arbutifolia

Lantana

Verbena bonariensis

☼ ◐ ◢ 8–24   **p. 517**

ADULT BUTTERFLIES
Shrubs

Abelia

☼ ◐ ◐ ◢ ZONES VARY   **p. 130**

Arctostaphylos
MANZANITA
☼ ◐ ◢ ZONES VARY   **p. 162**

Buddleia

☼ ◐ ◐ ◐ ◢ ALL ZONES   **p. 192**

Calluna vulgaris
SCOTCH HEATHER
☼ ◐ ◢ 2–6, 15–17   **p. 197**

Caryopteris
BLUEBEARD
☼ ◐ ◢ ZONES VARY   **p. 209**

Ceanothus
WILD LILAC
☼ ◊ ◢ 1–9, 14–24   **p. 212**

Choisya ternata
MEXICAN ORANGE
☼ ◐ ◐ ◢ 7–9, 12–24   **p. 225**

Clethra alnifolia
SUMMERSWEET
☼ ◐ ◐ ◢ 2–6   **p. 235**

Eriogonum (some)
WILD BUCKWHEAT
☼ ◊ ◐ ◢ ZONES VARY   **p. 278**

Escallonia

☼ ◐ ◐ ◐ ◢ 4–9, 14–17, 20–24   **p. 280**

Grewia occidentalis
LAVENDER STARFLOWER
☼ ◐ ◢ 8, 9, 12–24   **p. 313**

Hebe

☼ ◐ ◐ ◢ ZONES VARY   **p. 316**

Heteromeles arbutifolia
TOYON
☼ ◐ ◢ 5–24   **p. 321**

Lantana

☼ ◐ ◐ ◢ 8–10, 12–22   **p. 347**

Lavandula
LAVENDER
☼ ◐ ◢ ZONES VARY   **p. 349**

Lonicera
HONEYSUCKLE
☼ ◐ ◐ ◢ ZONES VARY   **p. 360**

Mahonia

NEEDS, ZONES VARY   **p. 371**

Philadelphus (single-flowered)
MOCK ORANGE
☼ ◐ ◐ ◢ ZONES VARY   **p. 413**

Potentilla
CINQUEFOIL
☼ ◐ ◐ ◐ ◢ ZONES VARY   **p. 435**

Rhamnus californica
COFFEEBERRY
☼ ◐ ◊ ◐ ◢ 4–24   **p. 452**

Rhododendron

◐ ◐ ◐ ◢ ZONES VARY   **p. 454**

Rhus trilobata
SQUAWBUSH
☼ ◊ ◐ ◢ 1–3, 10   **p. 460**

Ribes
CURRANT, GOOSEBERRY
NEEDS, ZONES VARY   **p. 460**

Rosmarinus officinalis
ROSEMARY
☼ ◊ ◐ ◢ 4–24   **p. 469**

Sambucus
ELDERBERRY
☼ ◐ ◐ ◢ ZONES VARY   **p. 473**

Spiraea

☼ ◐ ◐ ◢ 1–11, 14–21   **p. 490**

Syringa
LILAC
☼ ◐ ◐ ◢ ZONES VARY   **p. 499**

Vaccinium

◐ ◐ ◢ ZONES VARY   **p. 515**

Zauschneria
CALIFORNIA FUCHSIA
☼ ◊ ◐ ◢ 2–10, 12–24   **p. 527**

ADULT BUTTERFLIES
Trees

Acer
MAPLE
☼ ◐ ◐ ◢ ZONES VARY   **p. 135**

Aesculus
HORSECHESTNUT
NEEDS, ZONES VARY   **p. 141**

Apple

☼ ◊ ◐ ◢ ALL ZONES   **p. 155**

Arbutus menziesii
MADRONE
☼ ◐ ◢ 3–7, 14–19   **p. 162**

Citrus
ORANGE
☼ ◐ ◢ 8, 9, 12–24   **p. 231**

Salix
WILLOW
☼ ◐ ◢ ALL ZONES   **p. 471**

Mahonia aquifolium

Philadelphus

Rhus trilobata

Aesculus carnea

Plant listings continue ▶

Vitex

Cleome hasslerana

Iris

Kniphofia uvaria

Crocosmia crocosmiiflora

Vitex
CHASTE TREE
☼ ◖ ● ✄ ZONES VARY   p. 520

HUMMINGBIRDS
Annuals, Perennials, Bulbs

Alcea rosea
HOLLYHOCK
☼ ● ✄ ALL ZONES   p. 144

Aquilegia
COLUMBINE
☼ ◖ ● ✄ ALL ZONES   p. 160

Asclepias tuberosa
BUTTERFLY WEED
☼ ● ✄ ALL ZONES   p. 168

Clarkia
☼ ● ✄ ALL ZONES   p. 233

Cleome hasslerana
SPIDER FLOWER
☼ ● ✄ ALL ZONES   p. 235

Crocosmia crocosmiiflora
MONTBRETIA
☼ ◖ ◗ ✄ 5–24   p. 249

Delphinium
☼ ● ✄ ZONES VARY   p. 260

Digitalis
FOXGLOVE
◖ ● ✄ ALL ZONES   p. 264

Gladiolus
☼ ● ✄ ALL ZONES   p. 307

Heuchera
CORAL BELLS
☼ ◖ ● ● ✄ ZONES VARY   p. 322

Ipomopsis aggregata
☼ ◗ ✄ ALL ZONES   p. 332

Iris
NEEDS, ZONES VARY   p. 332

Kniphofia uvaria
RED-HOT POKER
☼ ◖ ◗ ✄ 1–9, 14–24   p. 344

Leonotis leonurus
LION'S TAIL
☼ ◗ ● ✄ 8–24   p. 350

Lilium columbianum
COLUMBIA LILY
◖ ● ✄ ALL ZONES   p. 355

Lobelia cardinalis
CARDINAL FLOWER
☼ ◖ ● ● ✄ 1–7, 12–17   p. 359

Lobelia laxiflora
☼ ◖ ● ✄ 7–9, 12–24   p. 360

Lupinus
LUPINE
NEEDS, ZONES VARY   p. 362

Mimulus
MONKEY FLOWER
NEEDS, ZONES VARY   p. 381

Monarda
BEE BALM, OSWEGO TEA
☼ ◖ ● ● ✄ ALL ZONES   p. 382

Pelargonium
GERANIUM
☼ ◖ ● ● ✄ 8, 9, 12–24   p. 407

Penstemon (many)
BEARD TONGUE
NEEDS, ZONES VARY   p. 410

Salvia (many)
SAGE
NEEDS, ZONES VARY   p. 473

Strelitzia reginae
BIRD OF PARADISE
☼ ◖ ● ✄ 22–24   p. 496

Veronica
SPEEDWELL
☼ ● ✄ ALL ZONES   p. 517

Zauschneria
CALIFORNIA FUCHSIA
☼ ◗ ● ✄ 2–10, 12–24   p. 527

Zinnia
☼ ● ● ✄ ALL ZONES   p. 528

HUMMINGBIRDS
Ground Covers, Vines

Bean, scarlet runner
☼ ● ✄ ALL ZONES   p. 180

Campsis
TRUMPET VINE
☼ ◖ ● ✄ ZONES VARY   p. 203

Clematis ligusticifolia
☼ ● ✄ 1–6, 15–17   p. 234

Ipomoea quamoclit
CARDINAL CLIMBER
☼ ● ✄ ALL ZONES   p. 332

Lantana montevidensis
☼ ● ● ✄ 8–10, 12–22   p. 347

Pyrostegia venusta
FLAME VINE
☼ ◗ ● ✄ 13, 16, 21–24   p. 447

HUMMINGBIRDS
Shrubs, Succulents

Abutilon
FLOWERING MAPLE
☼ ◖ ● ● ✄ ZONES VARY   p. 131

Leonotis leonurus

Lupinus

Penstemon

Pelargonium

Salvia leucantha

For growing symbol explanations, please see page 45.

Strelitzia reginae

Zauschneria californica

Campsis radicans

Grevillea

Justicia

Acacia

☼ ○ ◐ ⚞ ZONES VARY — p. 131

Aloe

☼ ◑ ◐ ⚞ 8, 9, 12–24 — p. 147

Arbutus unedo
STRAWBERRY TREE

☼ ◑ ◐ ◐ ⚞ 4–24 — p. 162

Arctostaphylos
MANZANITA

☼ ◐ ⚞ ZONES VARY — p. 162

Bouvardia ternifolia

◑ ◐ ⚞ 8–10, 12–24 — p. 189

Buddleia

☼ ◑ ◐ ◐ ⚞ ALL ZONES — p. 192

Caesalpinia

☼ ◐ ⚞ ZONES VARY — p. 194

Calliandra

☼ ○ ◐ ⚞ ZONES VARY — p. 196

Callistemon citrinus
LEMON BOTTLEBRUSH

☼ ◐ ⚞ 8, 9, 12–24 — p. 197

Ceanothus
WILD LILAC

☼ ○ ⚞ 1–9, 14–24 — p. 212

Cercis occidentalis
WESTERN REDBUD

☼ ○ ◐ ⚞ 2–24 — p. 218

Cestrum

◑ ◐ ⚞ ZONES VARY — p. 219

Chaenomeles
FLOWERING QUINCE

☼ ◐ ⚞ 1–21 — p. 220

Correa
AUSTRALIAN FUCHSIA

☼ ◑ ◐ ⚞ 14–24 — p. 243

Cotoneaster

☼ ○ ◐ ⚞ ZONES VARY — p. 245

Feijoa sellowiana
PINEAPPLE GUAVA

☼ ◐ ⚞ 7–9, 12–24 — p. 292

Fuchsia

◑ ◐ ◐ ⚞ ZONES VARY — p. 300

Grevillea (red-flowered)

NEEDS, ZONES VARY — p. 312

Heteromeles arbutifolia
TOYON

☼ ◐ ⚞ 5–24 — p. 321

Hibiscus

☼ ◐ ⚞ ZONES VARY — p. 322

Justicia (several)

NEEDS, ZONES VARY — p. 342

Kolkwitzia amabilis
BEAUTY BUSH

☼ ◑ ◐ ⚞ 1–11, 14–20 — p. 344

Lavandula (many)
LAVENDER

☼ ◐ ⚞ ZONES VARY — p. 349

Leucophyllum
TEXAS RANGER

☼ ◐ ⚞ 7–24 — p. 352

Lonicera
HONEYSUCKLE

☼ ◑ ◐ ◐ ⚞ ZONES VARY — p. 360

Ribes sanguineum
RED FLOWERING CURRANT

☼ ◑ ○ ◐ ⚞ 4–9, 14–24 — p. 460

Ribes speciosum
FUCHSIA FLOWERING GOOSEBERRY

☼ ◑ ◐ ⚞ 8, 9, 14–24 — p. 460

Sambucus
ELDERBERRY

☼ ◑ ◐ ⚞ ZONES VARY — p. 473

Syringa
LILAC

☼ ◐ ⚞ ZONES VARY — p. 499

Tecoma stans
YELLOW BELLS

☼ ◐ ⚞ 10, 12, 13, 21–24 — p. 503

Tecomaria capensis
CAPE HONEYSUCKLE

☼ ◑ ◐ ⚞ 12, 13, 16, 18–24 — p. 503

Weigela

☼ ◑ ◐ ⚞ 1–11, 14–17 — p. 523

HUMMINGBIRDS
Trees

Aesculus
HORSECHESTNUT
NEEDS, ZONES VARY — p. 141

Albizia julibrissin
SILK TREE

☼ ◑ ◐ ⚞ 2–23 — p. 144

Chilopsis linearis
DESERT WILLOW

☼ ◐ ⚞ 10–13, 18–21 — p. 223

Erythrina
CORAL TREE

☼ ◐ ⚞ ZONES VARY — p. 279

Eucalyptus

☼ ○ ◐ ⚞ SEE CHART — p. 281

Lavandula

Weigela

Albizia julibrissin

Erythrina

Eucalyptus ficifolia

Scaevola 'Mauve Clusters'

Plants to Use Near

SWIMMING POOLS

Plants chosen to landscape swimming pool areas must meet two requirements. Branches, foliage, and flowers should be smooth—not bristly, prickly, sharp, or thorny so as to annoy or injure pool users. The plants also should be as litter-free as possible; what litter they produce should be too large to pass into the pool's filter. The plants listed here will meet these specifications.

Poolside garden

Fatsia japonica

Lavandula angustifolia

Pittosporum tobira 'Wheeler's Dwarf'

TREES

Plant	Zones	Page
Acacia stenophylla SHOESTRING ACACIA	8, 9, 12–24	p. 134
Cordyline	NEEDS, ZONES VARY	p. 240
Dracaena	ZONES VARY	p. 267
Ensete	13, 15–24	p. 273
Ficus auriculata	20–24	p. 294
Firmiana simplex CHINESE PARASOL TREE	5, 6, 8, 9, 12–24	p. 296
Geijera parviflora AUSTRALIAN WILLOW	8, 9, 12–24	p. 304
Palms	NEEDS, ZONES VARY	p. 398
Schefflera	ZONES VARY	p. 478
Tree ferns	NEEDS, ZONES VARY	p. 510

SHRUBS

Plant	Zones	Page
Baccharis 'Centennial'	10–13	p. 173
Camellia	4–9, 12, 14–24	p. 200
Carissa macrocarpa NATAL PLUM	22–24	p. 207
Fatsia japonica JAPANESE ARALIA	4–9, 13–24	p. 292
Griselinia	9, 14–17, 20–24	p. 313
Juniperus JUNIPER	ALL ZONES	p. 338
Lantana	8–10, 12–22	p. 347
Lavandula LAVENDER	ZONES VARY	p. 349
Pittosporum tobira 'Wheeler's Dwarf'	8–24	p. 426
Rhaphiolepis	8–10, 12–24	p. 453
Ternstroemia gymnanthera	4–9, 12–24	p. 503
Viburnum davidii	4–9, 14–24	p. 518

GROUND COVERS, VINES

Plant	Zones	Page
Beaumontia grandiflora EASTER LILY VINE	12, 13, 16, 17, 21–24	p. 180

Rhaphiolepis indica

Solandra maxima

Agave attenuata

For growing symbol explanations, please see page 45.

Anigozanthos flavidus

Canna

Hemerocallis

Dymondia margaretae

☼ ◐ ◐ ✂ 15–24   **p. 269**

Fatshedera lizei

☼ ◑ ● ◐ ◐ ✂ 4–10, 12–24   **p. 292**

Lantana montevidensis

☼ ◐ ◐ ✂ 8–10, 12–24   **p. 347**

Scaevola

☼ ◐ ◐ ✂ 8, 9, 14–24   **p. 478**

Solandra maxima
CUP-OF-GOLD VINE
☼ ◐ ✂ 17, 21–24   **p. 487**

Tetrastigma voinieranum

◑ ◐ ✂ 13, 17, 20–24   **p. 503**

Zoysia tenuifolia
KOREAN GRASS
☼ ◑ ◐ ◐ ✂ 8, 9, 12–24   **p. 528**

PERENNIALS

Agapanthus
LILY-OF-THE-NILE
☼ ◑ ◐ ✂ 7–9, 12–24   **p. 141**

Agave attenuata

◑ ◐ ◐◐ ✂ 20–24   **p. 142**

Aloe

☼ ◑ ◐ ✂ 8, 9, 12–24   **p. 147**

Alstroemeria, evergreen hybrids

☼ ◐ ✂ 5–9, 14–24   **p. 148**

Anigozanthos flavidus
KANGAROO PAW
☼ ◐ ✂ 12, 13, 15–24   **p. 152**

Armeria
THRIFT
☼ ◐ ◐ ✂ ALL ZONES   **p. 165**

Artemisia 'Powis Castle'

☼ ◯ ◐ ✂ ALL ZONES   **p. 166**

Aspidistra elatior
CAST-IRON PLANT
◑ ● ◐ ✂ 4–10, 12–24   **p. 169**

Canna

☼ ◐ ✂ ALL ZONES   **p. 205**

Colocasia esculenta
ELEPHANT'S EAR
◑ ◐ ✂ ZONES VARY   **p. 238**

Coreopsis

☼ ◐ ✂ ZONES VARY   **p. 240**

Cyperus

☼ ◑ ● ◐◐ ✂ ZONES VARY   **p. 255**

Dianella tasmanica

☼ ◑ ◐ ◐ ✂ 8, 9, 14–24   **p. 261**

Dietes
FORTNIGHT LILY
☼ ◑ ◐ ● ◐ ✂ 8, 9, 12–24   **p. 264**

Erysimum 'Bowles Mauve'

☼ ◑ ◐ ✂ 4–6, 14–17, 22, 23   **p. 279**

Gaillardia

☼ ◐ ✂ ALL ZONES   **p. 301**

Gazania

☼ ◐ ✂ 8–24   **p. 304**

Hemerocallis
DAYLILY
☼ ◑ ◐ ✂ ALL ZONES   **p. 320**

Hesperaloe parviflora

☼ ◯ ✂ 10–16, 18–21   **p. 321**

Kniphofia uvaria
RED-HOT POKER
☼ ◑ ◯ ✂ 1–9, 14–24   **p. 344**

Limonium perezii

☼ ◐ ✂ 13, 15–17, 20–24   **p. 356**

Liriope
LILY TURF
☼ ◑ ● ◐◐ ✂ 5–10, 12–24   **p. 358**

Ophiopogon

☼ ◑ ● ◐ ◐◐ ✂ 5–10, 12–24   **p. 358**

Philodendron (treelike types)

◑ ● ◐◐ ✂ 8, 9, 12–24   **p. 414**

Phlomis
JERUSALEM SAGE
☼ ◐ ✂ ZONES VARY   **p. 414**

Phormium
NEW ZEALAND FLAX
☼ ◑ ◯ ◐ ◐ ✂ 7–24   **p. 415**

Santolina

☼ ◯ ◐ ✂ ALL ZONES   **p. 476**

Strelitzia
BIRD OF PARADISE
☼ ◑ ◐ ✂ ZONES VARY   **p. 496**

Tulbaghia violacea
SOCIETY GARLIC
☼ ◐ ✂ 13–14   **p. 512**

Yucca (some)

☼ ◐ ◐ ✂ ZONES VARY   **p. 525**

Hesperaloe parviflora

Kniphofia uvaria

Limonium perezii

Yucca aloifolia

Good Choices for
ROCK GARDENS

Acer palmatum 'Dissectum'

S mall or tiny shrubs, miniature bulbous plants, annuals and perennials that form low tufts or creeping mats of foliage— these are the choices listed here for planting in rock gardens. Classic European rock gardens and alpine landscapes can be re-created in the cool Pacific Northwest, but to produce the same effect in Southern California calls for a different assortment of plants. Read the climate zone adaptations carefully.

Helianthemum nummularium

Picea glauca

Pinus mugo mugo

Erica cinerea

Cistus salviifolius

TREES

Abies balsamea 'Nana'
DWARF BALSAM FIR
☼ ◑ ✚ 3–7, 15–17   **p. 130**

Acer palmatum (dwarf)
JAPANESE MAPLE
☼ ◑ ◑ ✚ 1–10, 12, 14–24   **p. 136**

Betula pendula 'Trost's Dwarf'
☼ ◑ ◑◑ ✚ 1–12, 14–24   **p. 184**

Cedrus deodara (dwarf)
DEODAR CEDAR
☼ ◊ ✚ 2–12, 14–24   **p. 215**

Chamaecyparis obtusa (dwarf)
HINOKI FALSE CYPRESS
☼ ◑ ◑ ✚ 4–6, 15–17   **p. 220**

Picea (many dwarf types)
SPRUCE
NEEDS, ZONES VARY   **p. 417**

Pinus densiflora 'Umbraculifera'
TANYOSHO PINE
☼ ◊ ◑ ✚ SEE CHART   **p. 421**

Pinus edulis
PIÑON
☼ ◊ ✚ SEE CHART   **p. 421**

Pinus monophylla
SINGLELEAF PIÑON PINE
☼ ◊ ◑ ✚ SEE CHART   **p. 422**

Pinus mugo mugo
MUGHO PINE
☼ ◊ ◑ ✚ SEE CHART   **p. 423**

Pinus strobus 'Nana'
DWARF WHITE PINE
☼ ◑ ✚ SEE CHART   **p. 424**

Pinus sylvestris (several)
DWARF SCOTCH PINE
☼ ◊ ◑ ✚ SEE CHART   **p. 424**

Tsuga canadensis (dwarf)
CANADA HEMLOCK
☼ ◑ ✚ 3–7, 17   **p. 512**

SHRUBS, SHRUBLETS

Calluna vulgaris (dwarf)
SCOTCH HEATHER
☼ ◑ ✚ 2–6, 15–17   **p. 197**

Calocephalus brownii
CUSHION BUSH
☼ ◊ ◑ ✚ 16, 17, 19, 21–24   **p. 198**

Cistus (some)
ROCKROSE
☼ ◊ ◑ ✚ 7–9, 12–24   **p. 229**

Cotoneaster (dwarf)
☼ ◊ ◑ ✚ ZONES VARY   **p. 245**

Daboecia cantabrica
IRISH HEATH
☼ ◑ ◑ ✚ 3–9, 14–24   **p. 256**

Erica (dwarf)
HEATH
☼ ◑ ✚ ZONES VARY   **p. 275**

Gaultheria (most)
◑ ◑ ✚ ZONES VARY   **p. 303**

Genista (several dwarf types)
DWARF BROOM
☼ ◊ ✚ ZONES VARY   **p. 304**

Halimium
☼ ◑ ✚ 7–9, 12–24   **p. 316**

Hebe (several dwarf types)
☼ ◑ ◑ ✚ ZONES VARY   **p. 316**

Helianthemum nummularium
SUNROSE
☼ ◑ ✚ ALL ZONES   **p. 318**

Gaultheria

Hebe

Teucrium chamaedrys

For growing symbol explanations, please see page 45.

Hypericum coris
ST. JOHNSWORT
☼ ◑ ◔ ◕ ✎ 4–24 p. 328

Ilex crenata (several dwarf types)
DWARF JAPANESE HOLLY
☼ ◑ ◕ ✎ 2–9, 14–24 p. 330

Jasminum parkeri
DWARF JASMINE
☼ ◑ ◕ ✎ 5–9, 12–24 p. 337

Juniperus (many dwarf types)
JUNIPER
☼ ◑ ◔ ◔ ◕ ✎ ALL ZONES p. 338

Pieris japonica (dwarf)
LILY-OF-THE-VALLEY SHRUB
☼ ◕ ✎ 1–9, 14–17 p. 418

Pimelea prostrata
☼ ◑ ◕ ✎ 4–7, 14–17 p. 419

Rhododendron
AZALEA, DWARF SATSUKI
☼ ◕ ◔ ✎ 4–9, 14–24 p. 458

Rhododendron (several dwarf types)
◑ ◕ ◔ ✎ ZONES VARY p. 454

Teucrium (low-growing)
GERMANDER
☼ ◕ ✎ ZONES VARY p. 504

Vaccinium vitis-idaea minus
LINGONBERRY
◑ ◕ ✎ 2–7, 14–17 p. 516

PERENNIALS

Acaena
SHEEP BUR
☼ ◑ ◕ ✎ 4–9, 14–24 p. 135

Achillea (dwarf)
YARROW
☼ ◔ ◕ ✎ ALL ZONES p. 138

Aeonium
☼ ◑ ◕ ✎ 15–17, 20–24 p. 140

Aethionema
STONECRESS
☼ ◑ ◕ ✎ 1–9, 14–21 p. 141

Ajuga genevensis
CARPET BUGLE
☼ ◑ ◕ ✎ ALL ZONES p. 144

Androsace
ROCK JASMINE
☼ ◕ ✎ 1–6, 14–17 p. 151

Anemone pulsatilla
EUROPEAN PASQUE FLOWER
☼ ◑ ◕ ✎ 1–6, 15–17 p. 151

Antennaria dioica
PUSSY TOES
☼ ◕ ◔ ✎ ALL ZONES p. 153

Acaena

Aeonium urbicum

Androsace sarmentosa

Aquilegia (dwarf)
COLUMBINE
☼ ◑ ◕ ✎ ALL ZONES p. 160

Arabis
ROCKCRESS
☼ ◕ ✎ ZONES VARY p. 161

Arenaria
SANDWORT
NEEDS VARY, ✎ 2–9, 14–24 p. 164

Armeria
THRIFT, SEA PINK
☼ ◕ ✎ ALL ZONES p. 165

Aster alpinus
☼ ◕ ✎ ALL ZONES p. 170

Aubrieta deltoidea
COMMON AUBRIETA
☼ ◑ ◕ ✎ 1–9, 14–21 p. 171

Aurinia saxatilis
BASKET-OF-GOLD
☼ ◑ ◕ ✎ ALL ZONES p. 172

Campanula (smallest)
BELLFLOWER
☼ ◑ ◕ ✎ 1–9, 14–24 p. 203

Cerastium tomentosum
SNOW-IN-SUMMER
☼ ◑ ◕ ◔ ✎ ALL ZONES p. 217

Delosperma
ICE PLANT
☼ ◔ ◕ ✎ ZONES VARY p. 260

Dianthus (smallest)
PINK
☼ ◑ ◕ ✎ ALL ZONES p. 261

Dodecatheon
SHOOTING STAR
☼ ◑ ◕ ✎ ALL ZONES p. 266

Draba
☼ ◕ ✎ 1–7 p. 267

Dryas
☼ ◕ ✎ 1–6 p. 268

Echeveria (many)
☼ ◑ ◕ ✎ ZONES VARY p. 269

Erigeron (dwarf)
FLEABANE
☼ ◑ ◕ ◔ ✎ ZONES VARY p. 275

Eriogonum (dwarf)
WILD BUCKWHEAT
☼ ◔ ◕ ✎ ZONES VARY p. 278

Erodium reichardii
CRANESBILL
☼ ◑ ◕ ✎ 7–9, 14–24 p. 278

Euphorbia myrsinites
☼ ◕ ✎ ALL ZONES p. 289

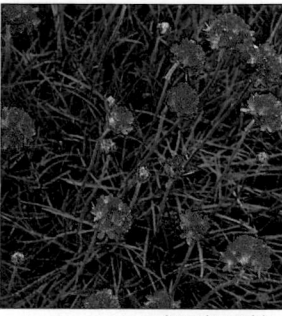

Armeria maritima

Campanula portenschlagiana

Echeveria

Erigeron

Euphorbia myrsinites

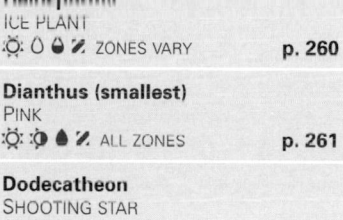
Plant listings continue ▶

Geranium

Heuchera

Lewisia

Lithodora diffusa

Gentiana
GENTIAN
☼ ◑ ◐ ✔ 1–6, 14–17   **p. 305**

Geranium (smallest)
CRANESBILL
NEEDS, ZONES VARY   **p. 305**

Gypsophila (several dwarf types)
☼ ◐ ✔ ZONES VARY   **p. 314**

Herniaria glabra
GREEN CARPET
☼ ◑ ◐ ◐ ✔ ALL ZONES   **p. 321**

Heuchera
CORAL BELLS
☼ ◑ ◐ ◐ ✔ ZONES VARY   **p. 322**

Iberis sempervirens
EVERGREEN CANDYTUFT
☼ ◐ ✔ ALL ZONES   **p. 329**

Lewisia
☼ ◑ ◐ ✔ 1–7, 14–17   **p. 353**

Lithodora diffusa
☼ ◑ ◐ ✔ 5–7, 14–17   **p. 359**

Origanum (low-growing)
☼ ◐ ✔ ZONES VARY   **p. 395**

Papaver burseri
ALPINE POPPY
☼ ◐ ◐ ✔ ALL ZONES   **p. 400**

**Penstemon
(subshrubs or mat-forming)**
☼ ◑ ◐ ✔ ZONES VARY   **p. 410**

Phlox (trailing or creeping)
☼ ◑ ◐ ✔ ZONES VARY   **p. 414**

Pleione
◐ ◐ ✔ 5–9, 14–24   **p. 427**

Polemonium reptans
◑ ◐ ◐ ◐ ✔ 1–11, 14–17   **p. 431**

Primula (most)
☼ ◑ ◐ ◐ ◐ ✔ 1–10, 12–24   **p. 436**

Saponaria ocymoides
☼ ◐ ✔ ALL ZONES   **p. 476**

Saxifraga
SAXIFRAGE
NEEDS, ZONES VARY   **p. 477**

Sedum (many)
STONECROP
NEEDS, ZONES VARY   **p. 481**

Sempervivum
HOUSELEEK
☼ ◐ ◐ ✔ ALL ZONES   **p. 482**

Senecio (some)
NEEDS, ZONES VARY   **p. 482**

Silene acaulis
CUSHION PINK
☼ ◑ ◐ ✔ 1–11, 14–16, 18–21   **p. 485**

Sisyrinchium (smallest)
☼ ◑ ◐ ◐ ✔ 4–24   **p. 486**

Thymus
THYME
☼ ◑ ◐ ✔ ALL ZONES   **p. 506**

Veronica (mat-forming)
SPEEDWELL
☼ ◐ ✔ ALL ZONES   **p. 517**

BULBS, BULBLIKE PLANTS

Allium (smallest)
ORNAMENTAL ALLIUM
☼ ◑ ◐ ✔ ALL ZONES   **p. 145**

Chionodoxa
GLORY-OF-THE-SNOW
◑ ◐ ✔ 1–7, 14–20   **p. 224**

Crocus
☼ ◑ ◐ ✔ ALL ZONES   **p. 249**

Cyclamen (except C. persicum)
☼ ◑ ◐ ✔ 1–9, 14–24   **p. 253**

Freesia
☼ ◑ ◐ ✔ 8, 9, 12–24   **p. 300**

Galanthus
SNOWDROP
☼ ◑ ◐ ✔ 1–9, 14–17   **p. 302**

Iris (smallest)
NEEDS, ZONES VARY   **p. 332**

Muscari
GRAPE HYACINTH
☼ ◑ ◐ ◐ ✔ ALL ZONES   **p. 384**

Narcissus (small)
DAFFODIL
☼ ◑ ◐ ✔ ALL ZONES   **p. 387**

Sternbergia lutea
☼ ◐ ✔ ALL ZONES   **p. 493**

Tritonia
☼ ◐ ✔ 9, 13–24   **p. 511**

Tulipa (species only)
TULIP
☼ ◐ ✔ ALL ZONES   **p. 513**

Zephyranthes
ZEPHYR FLOWER, FAIRY LILY
☼ ◐ ✔ 1–9, 12–24   **p. 527**

Saponaria ocymoides

Sisyrinchium bellum

Veronica

Crocus

Muscari

For growing symbol explanations, please see page 45.

Hedera with *Rhaphiolepis*

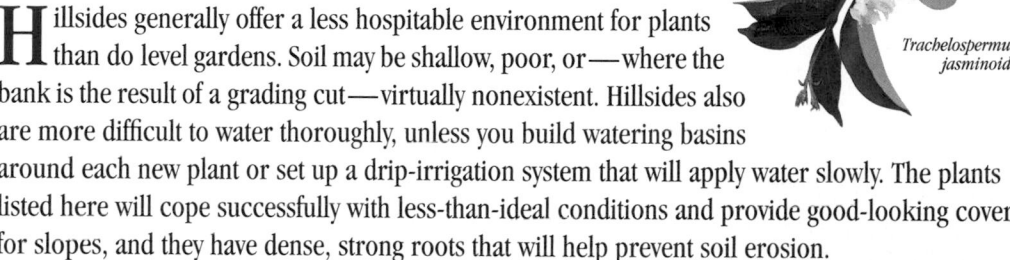
Trachelospermum jasminoides

Plants for
EROSION CONTROL

Hillsides generally offer a less hospitable environment for plants than do level gardens. Soil may be shallow, poor, or—where the bank is the result of a grading cut—virtually nonexistent. Hillsides also are more difficult to water thoroughly, unless you build watering basins around each new plant or set up a drip-irrigation system that will apply water slowly. The plants listed here will cope successfully with less-than-ideal conditions and provide good-looking cover for slopes, and they have dense, strong roots that will help prevent soil erosion.

Cistus

Echium fastuosum

Lantana

SHRUBS

Ceanothus
WILD LILAC
☼ ◐ ♦ ✂ 1–9, 14–24   **p. 212**

Cistus (sandy soil or coastal)
ROCKROSE
☼ ◐ ♦ ✂ 7 9, 12–24   **p. 229**

Coprosma kirkii
☼ ◐ ♦ ✂ 14–17, 21–24   **p. 239**

Cotoneaster
☼ ◐ ♦ ✂ ZONES VARY   **p. 245**

Echium fastuosum
PRIDE OF MADEIRA
☼ ◐ ♦♦ ✂ 14–24   **p. 270**

Eriogonum fasciculatum
CALIFORNIA BUCKWHEAT
☼ ◐ ♦ ✂ 8, 9, 12–24   **p. 278**

Hypericum calycinum
CREEPING ST. JOHNSWORT
☼ ☼ ◐ ♦♦ ✂ 2–24   **p. 328**

Juniperus (ground covers)
JUNIPER
☼ ☼ ◐ ♦ ♦♦ ✂ ALL ZONES   **p. 338**

Lantana
☼ ◐ ♦♦ ✂ 8–10, 12–22   **p. 347**

Mahonia repens
CREEPING MAHONIA
☼ ☼ ◐ ♦ ✂ 1–21   **p. 371**

Rhamnus crocea ilicifolia
HOLLYLEAF REDBERRY
☼ ◐ ✂ 7–16, 18–21   **p. 453**

Rhus (several)
SUMAC
☼ ◐ ♦ ✂ ZONES VARY   **p. 459**

Ribes viburnifolium
EVERGREEN CURRANT
☼ ☼ ◐ ♦ ✂ 8, 9, 14–24   **p. 461**

Rosa rugosa
RAMANAS ROSE
☼ ◐ ♦ ♦♦ ✂ ALL ZONES   **p. 468**

Rosmarinus officinalis
ROSEMARY
☼ ◐ ♦ ✂ 4–24   **p. 469**

Symphoricarpos
SNOWBERRY
NEEDS, ZONES VARY   **p. 498**

VINES

Hedera
IVY
☼ ☼ ● ◐ ♦ ♦♦ ✂ ZONES VARY   **p. 317**

Lonicera japonica
JAPANESE HONEYSUCKLE
☼ ☼ ◐ ♦ ✂ 2–24   **p. 361**

Trachelospermum
STAR JASMINE
☼ ☼ ◐ ♦ ✂ ZONES VARY   **p. 509**

PERENNIALS, GROUND COVERS

Coronilla varia
CROWN VETCH
☼ ☼ ◐ ♦ ✂ ALL ZONES   **p. 243**

Malephora
ICE PLANT
☼ ◐ ✂ ZONES VARY   **p. 372**

Polygonum cuspidatum compactum
☼ ♦ ✂ ALL ZONES   **p. 432**

Vinca
PERIWINKLE
☼ ● ♦ ✂ ZONES VARY   **p. 519**

Rosmarinus officinalis

Lonicera japonica

Vinca minor 'Bowles' Variety

For growing symbol explanations, please see page 45.

Acer circinatum

Plants That
TOLERATE SHADE

S hady spots, whether created by leafy trees, north-facing walls, or an overhead structure, are darker and cooler than sunny locations. Many plants that thrive in sunlight and warmth fail to perform in the different environment that shade provides. In the lists below are trees, shrubs, ground covers, vines, perennials, bulbs, and annuals that thrive in part or full shade.

Redwood bench in shade

SYMBOL: �֎ indicates plants that bear showy flowers.

Arbutus unedo

Laurus nobilis

Podocarpus henkelii

Abutilon

TREES

Acer circinatum
VINE MAPLE
☼ ◑ ◐ ⚡ 1–6, 14–17   **p. 135**

Acer palmatum
JAPANESE MAPLE
☼ ◑ ◐ ⚡ 1–10, 12, 14–24   **p. 136**

Arbutus unedo   �֎
STRAWBERRY TREE
☼ ◑ ◐ ◑ ⚡ 4–24   **p. 162**

Davidia involucrata   ✖
DOVE TREE
☼ ◑ ◐ ⚡ 4–9, 14–21   **p. 259**

Laurus nobilis
SWEET BAY
☼ ◑ ◐ ⚡ 5–9, 12–24   **p. 349**

Palms (some)
NEEDS, ZONES VARY   **p. 398**

Podocarpus
☼ ◑ ◐ ⚡ ZONES VARY   **p. 431**

Schefflera
☼ ◑ ◐ ⚡ ZONES VARY   **p. 478**

Tree ferns
NEEDS, ZONES VARY   **p. 510**

SHRUBS

Abutilon   ✖
FLOWERING MAPLE
☼ ◑ ◐ ⚡ ZONES VARY   **p. 131**

Aucuba japonica
JAPANESE AUCUBA
◑ ● ◊ ◐ ◑ ⚡ 4–24   **p. 172**

Azara   ✖
◑ ◐ ⚡ ZONES VARY   **p. 173**

Brunfelsia pauciflora   ✖
◑ ◐ ⚡ 12–17, 20–24   **p. 191**

Buxus
BOXWOOD
☼ ◑ ● ◐ ⚡ ZONES VARY   **p. 193**

Camellia   ✖
◑ ◐ ⚡ 4–9, 12, 14–24   **p. 200**

Carpenteria californica   ✖
BUSH ANEMONE
☼ ◑ ◊ ◐ ⚡ 5–9, 14–24   **p. 208**

Cleyera japonica   ✖
◑ ◐ ⚡ 4–6, 8, 9, 14–24   **p. 235**

Cocculus laurifolius
☼ ◑ ● ◐ ⚡ 8, 9, 12–24   **p. 236**

Coprosma repens
MIRROR PLANT
☼ ◑ ◐ ⚡ 15–17, 21–24   **p. 239**

Cordyline stricta   ✖
◑ ● ◐ ◐ ⚡ 13, 16, 17, 20–24   **p. 240**

Cycadaceae
CYCADS
◑ ◐ ⚡ ZONES VARY   **p. 253**

Daphne odora   ✖
WINTER DAPHNE
◑ ◐ ⚡ 4–10, 12, 14–24   **p. 258**

Enkianthus   ✖
◑ ◐ ⚡ 2–9, 14–21   **p. 272**

Euonymus fortunei
☼ ◑ ◐ ⚡ 1–17   **p. 288**

For growing symbol explanations, please see page 45.

Brunfelsia pauciflora

Camellia

Carpenteria californica

Cycadaceae

Fatsia japonica
JAPANESE ARALIA
4–9, 13–24 · p. 292

Fuchsia ✳

ZONES VARY · p. 300

Gardenia jasminoides ✳

7–9, 12–16, 18–23 · p. 302

Gaultheria ✳

ZONES VARY · p. 303

Griselinia lucida

9, 14–17, 20–24 · p. 313

Hydrangea ✳

ZONES VARY · p. 327

Fuchsia

Ilex
HOLLY
ZONES VARY · p. 329

Kalmia latifolia ✳
MOUNTAIN LAUREL
1, 7, 16, 17 · p. 343

Kalmiopsis leachiana ✳

4–6, 14–17 · p. 343

Leucothoe ✳

NEEDS, ZONES VARY · p. 352

Loropetalum chinense ✳

6–9, 14–24 · p. 361

Mahonia ✳

NEEDS, ZONES VARY · p. 371

Nandina domestica ✳
HEAVENLY BAMBOO
5–24 · p. 386

Osmanthus

ZONES VARY · p. 396

Philodendron selloum

8, 9, 12–24 · p. 414

Pieris ✳

ZONES VARY · p. 418

Pittosporum ✳

ZONES VARY · p. 425

Rhapis
LADY PALM
ZONES VARY · p. 453

Rhododendron ✳
AZALEA, RHODODENDRON
ZONES VARY · p. 454

Gardenia jasminoides

Hydrangea macrophylla

Pieris forrestii

Sarcococca
4–9, 14–24 · p. 476

Skimmia ✳

4–9, 14–22 · p. 486

Symphoricarpos (some) ✳
SNOWBERRY
NEEDS, ZONES VARY · p. 498

Ternstroemia gymnanthera

4–9, 12–24 · p. 503

Vaccinium ✳

ZONES VARY · p. 515

Viburnum (evergreen) ✳

NEEDS, ZONES VARY · p. 518

GROUND COVERS, VINES

Cissus (some)

NEEDS, ZONES VARY · p. 228

Fatshedera lizei

4–10, 12–24 · p. 292

Fragaria chiloensis ✳
WILD STRAWBERRY
4–24 · p. 298

Glechoma hederacea
GROUND IVY
ALL ZONES · p. 308

Hedera
IVY
NEEDS, ZONES VARY · p. 317

Houttuynia cordata

1–9, 14–24 · p. 325

Monstera deliciosa
SPLIT-LEAF PHILODENDRON
16, 17, 21–24 · p. 382

Pachysandra terminalis ✳
JAPANESE SPURGE
1–10, 14–21 · p. 398

Parthenocissus

ZONES VARY · p. 401

Rhoicissus capensis
EVERGREEN GRAPE
16, 17, 21–24 · p. 459

Trachelospermum jasminoides ✳
STAR JASMINE
8–24 · p. 509

Vinca ✳
PERIWINKLE
ZONES VARY · p. 519

Pittosporum rhombifolium

Skimmia japonica

Vaccinium ovatum

Hedera colchica

Parthenocissus tricuspidata

Plant listings continue ▶

Alchemilla mollis

Astilbe

Begonia foliosa 'Miniata'

Calceolaria integrifolia

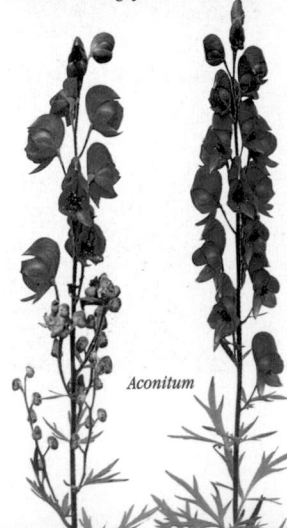

Aconitum

PERENNIALS, BULBS, ANNUALS

Acanthus mollis ☀
BEAR'S BREECH
☼ ◐ ◑ ● ◢ 4–24   **p. 135**

Aconitum ☀
MONKSHOOD
● ◐◐ ◢ 1–9, 14–21   **p. 138**

Ajuga ☀
CARPET BUGLE
☼ ☼ ● ◢ ALL ZONES   **p. 144**

Alchemilla ☀
LADY'S-MANTLE
NEEDS, ZONES VARY   **p. 145**

Anemone ☀
WINDFLOWER
NEEDS, ZONES VARY   **p. 151**

Aquilegia ☀
COLUMBINE
☼ ☼ ● ◢ ALL ZONES   **p. 160**

Arum ☀
● ● ◢ 4–24   **p. 167**

Asarum caudatum ☀
WILD GINGER
● ◐◐ ◢ 4–6, 14–24   **p. 167**

Aspidistra elatior
CAST-IRON PLANT
☼ ● ● ◢ 4–10, 12–24   **p. 169**

Astilbe ☀
FALSE SPIRAEA
☼ ☼ ● ◢ 2–7, 14–17   **p. 170**

Begonia ☀
☼ ● ● ◐◐ ◢ 14–24   **p. 181**

Bergenia ☀
☼ ☼ ● ● ◢ 1–9, 12–24   **p. 183**

Billbergia ☀
☼ ● ◐◐ ◢ 12, 13, 16–24   **p. 184**

Browallia ☀
AMETHYST FLOWER
☼ ● ◢ ALL ZONES   **p. 191**

Brunnera macrophylla ☀
BRUNNERA
☼ ☼ ● ● ◢ ALL ZONES   **p. 192**

Caladium bicolor
FANCY-LEAFED CALADIUM
● ◐◐ ◢ 12, 13, 16, 17, 22–24   **p. 194**

Calceolaria (most) ☀
NEEDS, ZONES VARY   **p. 195**

Campanula (some) ☀
BELLFLOWER
☼ ☼ ● ◢ 1–9, 14–24   **p. 203**

Clivia miniata ☀
KAFFIR LILY
● ● ◢ 12–17, 19–24   **p. 236**

Coleus hybridus ☀
COLEUS
☼ ● ◐◐ ◢ ALL ZONES   **p. 238**

Colocasia esculenta
ELEPHANT'S EAR
☼ ● ◐◐ ◢ ALL ZONES   **p. 238**

Convallaria majalis ☀
LILY-OF-THE-VALLEY
☼ ● ◢ 1–7, 14–20   **p. 239**

Corydalis ☀
☼ ● ◢ 4–9, 14–24   **p. 244**

Cotula squalida ☀
NEW ZEALAND BRASS BUTTONS
☼ ☼ ● ◢ 4–9, 14–24   **p. 246**

Crassula
☼ ● ◐ ◢ 8, 9, 12–24   **p. 247**

Cyclamen ☀
☼ ● ● ◢ ZONES VARY   **p. 253**

Cymbidium ☀
☼ ● ◢ ALL ZONES   **p. 254**

Dianella tasmanica ☀
☼ ☼ ● ◐◐ ◢ 8, 9, 14–24   **p. 261**

Dicentra (most) ☀
BLEEDING HEART
● ● ◢ 1–9, 14–24   **p. 262**

Digitalis ☀
FOXGLOVE
☼ ● ◢ ALL ZONES   **p. 264**

Doronicum ☀
LEOPARD'S BANE
☼ ● ◢ 1–7, 14–17   **p. 266**

Duchesnea indica ☀
INDIAN MOCK STRAWBERRY
☼ ☼ ● ● ◢ ALL ZONES   **p. 268**

Endymion ☀
☼ ☼ ● ◢ ALL ZONES   **p. 272**

Epimedium ☀
☼ ● ◢ 1–9, 14–17   **p. 273**

Erythronium ☀
☼ ● ● ◐◐ ◢ 1–7, 15–17   **p. 280**

Ferns
NEEDS, ZONES VARY   **p. 293**

Filipendula ☀
☼ ☼ ● ◢ 1–9, 14–24   **p. 296**

Campanula portenschlagiana

Clivia miniata

Digitalis purpurea Foxy strain

Francoa sonchifolia

For growing symbol explanations, please see page 45.

Helleborus orientalis

Geranium 'Johnson's Blue'

Hosta

Lamium maculatum

Impatiens

Lilium Asiatic hybrid

Francoa ✳
MAIDEN'S WREATH
☽ ◖ ◢ ✌ 4, 5, 8, 9, 12–24   **p. 298**

Galax urceolata ✳
☽ ● ◢ ✌ 1–6   **p. 302**

Galium odoratum ✳
SWEET WOODRUFF
● ◖◢ ✌ 1–6, 15–17   **p. 302**

Gentiana ✳
GENTIAN
☼ ☽ ◖◢ ✌ 1–6, 14–17   **p. 305**

Geranium (some) ✳
CRANESBILL
NEEDS, ZONES VARY   **p. 305**

Helleborus ✳
HELLEBORE
NEEDS, ZONES VARY   **p. 319**

Heuchera ✳
CORAL BELLS
NEEDS, ZONES VARY   **p. 322**

Hosta ✳
PLANTAIN LILY
☼ ☽ ● ◢ ✌ 1–10, 12–21   **p. 325**

Impatiens (most) ✳
NEEDS, ZONES VARY   **p. 330**

Iris foetidissima ✳
GLADWIN IRIS
☼ ☽ ● ◢ ✌ ALL ZONES   **p. 335**

Iris, crested ✳
☼ ☽ ◢ ✌ 17, 20, 24   **p. 335**

Lamium maculatum ✳
DEAD NETTLE
● ◖◢ ✌ ALL ZONES   **p. 346**

Ligularia ✳
☼ ☽ ● ◢ ✌ ZONES VARY   **p. 353**

Lilium ✳
LILY
☽ ◢ ✌ ALL ZONES   **p. 354**

Liriope ✳
LILY TURF
☼ ☽ ● ◢ ◖◢ ✌ 5–10, 12–24   **p. 358**

Lobelia (most) ✳
NEEDS, ZONES VARY   **p. 359**

Lysimachia nummularia ✳
MONEYWORT
☽ ● ◢ ✌ 1–9, 14–24   **p. 363**

Mimulus hybridus ✳
● ◢ ✌ ALL ZONES   **p. 381**

Myosotis ✳
FORGET-ME-NOT
☽ ◢ ✌ ALL ZONES   **p. 385**

Ophiopogon ✳
☼ ☽ ● ◢ ◖◢ ✌ 5–10, 12–24   **p. 358**

Oxalis ✳
NEEDS, ZONES VARY   **p. 397**

Polemonium ✳
☽ ● ◢ ◖◢ ✌ 1–11, 14–17   **p. 431**

Polygonatum ✳
SOLOMON'S SEAL
● ◖◢ ✌ 1–7, 15–17   **p. 432**

Primula ✳
PRIMROSE
☼ ☽ ● ◢ ◖◢ ✌ 1–10, 12–24   **p. 436**

Pulmonaria ✳
LUNGWORT
☼ ● ◢◢ ✌ 1–9, 14–17   **p. 445**

Rehmannia elata ✳
☼ ☽ ● ◢ ✌ 7–10, 12–24   **p. 452**

Saxifraga ✳
SAXIFRAGE
NEEDS, ZONES VARY   **p. 477**

Senecio hybridus ✳
CINERARIA
☽ ● ◢ ✌ 16, 17, 22–24   **p. 483**

Sisyrinchium bellum ✳
BLUE-EYED GRASS
☼ ☽ ◢ ● ◢ ✌ 4–24   **p. 486**

Smilacina racemosa ✳
FALSE SOLOMON'S SEAL
☼ ☽ ● ◢ ✌ 1–7, 14–17   **p. 487**

Soleirolia soleirolii ✳
BABY'S TEARS
☼ ● ◢ ◖◢ ✌ 4–24   **p. 488**

Thalictrum ✳
MEADOW RUE
☼ ◢ ✌ ALL ZONES   **p. 504**

Tolmiea menziesii ✳
PIGGY-BACK PLANT
☼ ● ◢ ◖◢ ✌ 5–9, 12–24   **p. 507**

Tradescantia ✳
☽ ● ◢ ◖◢ ✌ ZONES VARY   **p. 510**

Trillium ✳
WAKE ROBIN
☼ ● ◢ ✌ ZONES VARY   **p. 511**

Trollius ✳
GLOBEFLOWER
☼ ● ◢ ✌ ALL ZONES   **p. 512**

Vancouveria ✳
NEEDS, ZONES VARY   **p. 516**

Viola ✳
VIOLA, PANSY
☼ ☽ ◢ ✌ ZONES VARY   **p. 519**

Polygonatum odoratum

Rehmannia elata

Senecio hybridus

Tradescantia

Viola

Plants for
ARID GARDENS

Eucalyptus ficifolia

Fremontodendron californicum

Much of the West has a short annual rainy season followed by many dry months in which plants receive no water except what is supplied artificially. In periodically recurring drought years, in which rainfall is far below normal, water available for gardens may be severely limited. Fortunately, many fine plants, once they are established in the garden, will thrive with little or no water during the normal dry season. Here are some proven performers.

Olea europaea

SYMBOLS: ❋ indicates plants that bear showy flowers; ♣ indicates shrubs that can become small trees.

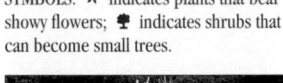

Aesculus californica

Cupressus macrocarpa

Ceratonia siliqua

TREES

Acacia (many) ❋
☼ ◐ ❍ ✿ ZONES VARY   p. 131

Aesculus californica ❋
CALIFORNIA BUCKEYE
☼ ◐ ❍ ✿ 4–10, 12, 14–24   p. 141

Arbutus 'Marina' ❋
☼ ◐ ❍ ✿ 8, 9, 14–24   p. 162

Brachychiton ❋
☼ ◐ ✿ ZONES VARY   p. 189

Calocedrus decurrens
INCENSE CEDAR
☼ ◐ ✿ 1–12, 14–24   p. 198

Cassia leptophylla ❋
GOLD MEDALLION TREE
☼ ◐ ✿ 21–24   p. 210

Casuarina
BEEFWOOD
☼ ◐ ✿ 8, 9, 12–24   p. 211

Cedrus
CEDAR
☼ ◐ ✿ ZONES VARY   p. 214

Celtis
HACKBERRY
☼ ◐ ◐ ✿ ZONES VARY   p. 216

Ceratonia siliqua
CAROB
☼ ◐ ✿ 9, 13–16, 18–24   p. 217

Cercidium ❋
PALO VERDE
☼ ◐ ◐ ✿ 10–14, 18–20   p. 218

Chilopsis linearis ❋
DESERT WILLOW
☼ ◐ ✿ 10–13, 18–21   p. 223

Chitalpa tashkentensis ❋
CHITALPA
☼ ◐ ✿ 3–24   p. 224

Cupressus
CYPRESS
☼ ◐ ✿ ZONES VARY   p. 252

Elaeagnus angustifolia
RUSSIAN OLIVE
☼ ◐ ◐ ◐ ✿ 1–3, 7–14, 18, 19   p. 271

Eucalyptus (most) ❋
☼ ◐ ◐ ✿ SEE CHART   p. 281

Fraxinus (most)
ASH
NEEDS, ZONES VARY   p. 298

Geijera parviflora
AUSTRALIAN WILLOW
☼ ◐ ◐ ✿ 8, 9, 12–24   p. 304

Grevillea robusta ❋
SILK OAK
☼ ◐ ◐ ✿ 8, 9, 12–24   p. 313

Gymnocladus dioica
KENTUCKY COFFEE TREE
☼ ◐ ✿ 1–3, 7–10, 12–16, 18–21   p. 314

Koelreuteria paniculata ❋
GOLDENRAIN TREE
☼ ◐ ◐ ✿ 2–21   p. 344

Lagerstroemia indica ❋
CRAPE MYRTLE
☼ ◐ ✿ ALL ZONES   p. 345

Laurus nobilis ❋
SWEET BAY
☼ ◐ ◐ ✿ 5–9, 12–24   p. 349

Olea europaea
OLIVE
☼ ◐ ✿ 8, 9, 11–24   p. 393

Olneya tesota ❋
DESERT IRONWOOD
☼ ◐ ✿ 12, 13   p. 393

Parkinsonia aculeata

Lagerstroemia indica 'Rosea'

Quercus

For growing symbol explanations, please see page 45.

SPECIAL SITUATIONS

Arctostaphylos densiflora

Artemisia 'Powis Castle'

Baccharis pilularis 'Twin Peaks'

Buddleia davidii 'Maroon'

Parkinsonia aculeata	✳
MEXICAN PALO VERDE	
☼ ◐ ∦ 8–24	**p. 400**
Pinus (most)	
PINE	
☼ ◐ ● ∦ SEE CHART	**p. 419**
Pistacia	
PISTACHE	
NEEDS, ZONES VARY	**p. 425**
Pithecellobium flexicaule	✳
TEXAS EBONY	
☼ ● ∦ 10–13	**p. 425**
Prosopis	✳
MESQUITE	
☼ ◐ ● ∦ 10–13	**p. 438**
Quercus	
OAK	
☼ ◐ ● ∦ ZONES VARY	**p. 447**
Rhus lancea	
AFRICAN SUMAC	
☼ ● ∦ 8, 9, 12–24	**p. 460**
Robinia	✳
LOCUST	
☼ ◐ ∦ ZONES VARY	**p. 461**
Schinus terebinthifolius	
BRAZILIAN PEPPER TREE	
☼ ● ∦ 13, 15–17, 19–24	**p. 479**
Sophora japonica	✳
JAPANESE PAGODA TREE	
☼ ◐ ● ∦ ALL ZONES	**p. 488**
Tilia tomentosa	
SILVER LINDEN	
☼ ◐ ● ∦ 1–21	**p. 507**
Tristania conferta	
BRISBANE BOX	
☼ ◐ ● ∦ 19–24	**p. 511**

SHRUBS

Acacia (many)	✳
☼ ◐ ● ∦ ZONES VARY	**p. 131**
Alyogyne huegelii	✳
BLUE HIBISCUS	
☼ ● ● ∦ 15–17, 20–24	**p. 149**
Anisacanthus thurberi	✳
DESERT HONEYSUCKLE	
☼ ● ∦ 8–13, 18, 19	**p. 152**
Anisodontea	✳
CAPE MALLOW	
☼ ◐ ● ∦ 14–24	**p. 152**
Arbutus unedo	✳ ♣
STRAWBERRY TREE	
☼ ◐ ● ● ∦ 4–24	**p. 162**
Arctostaphylos	✳
MANZANITA	
☼ ● ∦ ZONES VARY	**p. 162**

Artemisia	
☼ ◐ ● ∦ ALL ZONES	**p. 166**
Atriplex	
SALTBUSH	
☼ ● ∦ ZONES VARY	**p. 171**
Baccharis	
NEEDS, ZONES VARY	**p. 173**
Buddleia davidii	✳
BUTTERFLY BUSH	
☼ ◐ ● ● ∦ ALL ZONES	**p. 192**
Caesalpinia	✳
☼ ● ∦ ZONES VARY	**p. 194**
Calliandra (most)	✳
NEEDS, ZONES VARY	**p. 196**
Callistemon (most)	✳ ♣
BOTTLEBRUSH	
☼ ● ∦ 8, 9, 12–24	**p. 197**
Caragana arborescens	✳ ♣
SIBERIAN PEASHRUB	
☼ ● ∦ 1–21	**p. 206**
Caryopteris clandonensis	✳
BLUE MIST	
☼ ● ∦ 1–7, 14–17	**p. 209**
Cassia (some)	✳
SENNA	
☼ ● ∦ ZONES VARY	**p. 210**
Ceanothus	✳
WILD LILAC	
☼ ● ∦ 1–9, 14–24	**p. 212**
Cercis occidentalis	✳ ♣
WESTERN REDBUD	
☼ ◐ ● ∦ 2–24	**p. 218**
Cercocarpus	♣
MOUNTAIN MAHOGANY	
☼ ◐ ∦ ZONES VARY	**p. 219**
Chamaerops humilis	♣
MEDITERRANEAN FAN PALM	
☼ ● ● ∦ 4–24	**p. 221**
Chamelaucium uncinatum	✳
GERALDTON WAXFLOWER	
☼ ● ∦ 8, 9, 12–24	**p. 221**
Cistus	✳
ROCKROSE	
☼ ◐ ∦ 7–9, 12–24	**p. 229**
Convolvulus cneorum	✳
BUSH MORNING GLORY	
☼ ◐ ● ∦ 7–9, 12–24	**p. 239**
Coprosma (most)	
☼ ◐ ● ∦ ZONES VARY	**p. 239**
Cordia	✳ ♣
☼ ◐ ● ● ∦ 8–24	**p. 240**

Cassia

Cistus purpureus

Cordia boissieri

Cytisus

Plant listings continue ▶

Dendromecon

Dodonaea viscosa

Echium

Escallonia

Correa ☼
AUSTRALIAN FUCHSIA
☼ ◐ ● ◢ 14–24　　　　p. 243

Cotinus coggygria ☼
SMOKE TREE 🌳
☼ ● ◢ ALL ZONES　　p. 245

Cotoneaster ☼
☼ ◐ ● ◢ ZONES VARY　p. 245

Cytisus ☼
BROOM
☼ ◐ ◢ ZONES VARY　　p. 256

Dalea ☼
🌳
☼ ● ◢ 12, 13　　　　p. 257

Dendromecon ☼
BUSH POPPY
☼ ◐ ◢ 5–8, 14–24　　p. 260

Dodonaea viscosa 🌳
HOP BUSH
☼ ◑ ◐ ● ◢ 7–9, 12–24　p. 266

Echium ☼
☼ ● ● ◢ ZONES VARY　p. 270

Elaeagnus (some) ☼
☼ ◑ ◐ ● ◢ ZONES VARY　p. 271

Encelia farinosa ☼
BRITTLEBUSH
☼ ● ◢ 7–10, 14–24　　p. 272

Eremophila ☼
EMU BUSH
☼ ● ◢ 8, 9, 14–24　　p. 274

Eriogonum ☼
WILD BUCKWHEAT
☼ ◐ ● ◢ ZONES VARY　p. 278

Escallonia ☼
☼ ◑ ◐ ● ◢ 4–9, 14–17, 20–24　p. 280

Euryops ☼
☼ ● ◢ 8, 9, 12–24　　p. 290

Fallugia paradoxa ☼
APACHE PLUME
☼ ◐ ◢ 2–23　　　　p. 292

Feijoa sellowiana ☼
PINEAPPLE GUAVA 🌳
☼ ● ● ◢ 7–9, 12–24　p. 292

Fremontodendron ☼
FLANNEL BUSH
☼ ◐ ◢ 7–24　　　　p. 300

Galvezia speciosa ☼
ISLAND BUSH SNAPDRAGON
☼ ◑ ● ◢ 14–24　　　p. 302

Garrya (some) ☼
SILKTASSEL
NEEDS, ZONES VARY　p. 303

Genista ☼
BROOM
☼ ◐ ◢ ZONES VARY　　p. 304

Grevillea (most) ☼
NEEDS, ZONES VARY　p. 312

Hakea ☼
🌳
☼ ◐ ◢ 9, 12–17, 19–24　p. 315

Heteromeles arbutifolia ☼
TOYON 🌳
☼ ◑ ● ◢ 5–24　　　p. 321

Juniperus (some) ☼
JUNIPER 🌳
☼ ◑ ◐ ● ● ◢ ALL ZONES　p. 338

Justicia (some) ☼
NEEDS, ZONES VARY　p. 342

Lantana ☼
☼ ● ● ◢ 8–10, 12–22　p. 347

Lavandula ☼
LAVENDER
☼ ● ◢ ZONES VARY　　p. 349

Lavatera ☼
TREE MALLOW
☼ ● ● ◢ ZONES VARY　p. 349

Leonotis leonurus ☼
LION'S TAIL
☼ ◐ ● ◢ 8–24　　　p. 350

Leptospermum ☼
TEA TREE 🌳
☼ ◐ ● ◢ 14–24　　　p. 350

Leucophyllum ☼
TEXAS RANGER
☼ ● ◢ 7–24　　　　p. 352

Lysiloma microphylla thornberi ☼
FEATHER BUSH 🌳
☼ ◐ ◢ 10, 12–24　　p. 363

Mahonia (most) ☼
NEEDS, ZONES VARY　p. 371

Melaleuca (most) ☼
🌳
☼ ◐ ● ◢ ZONES VARY　p. 377

Myrica californica 🌳
PACIFIC WAX MYRTLE
☼ ● ◢ 4–6, 14–17, 20–24　p. 385

Myrsine africana ☼
AFRICAN BOXWOOD
☼ ◐ ● ◢ 8, 9, 14–24　p. 386

Myrtus ☼
MYRTLE
☼ ◑ ◐ ◢ 8–24　　　p. 386

Nandina domestica ☼
HEAVENLY BAMBOO
☼ ◑ ● ◐ ● ● ◢ 5–24　p. 386

Juniperus chinensis

Grevillea
'Constance'

*Lavandula
angustifolia*
'Hidcote'

Lavatera assurgentiflora

For growing symbol explanations, please see page 45.

Leonotis leonurus

Myrtus

Plumbago auriculata

Portulacaria afra

Rosmarinus officinalis

Nerium oleander ❋ 🌳
OLEANDER
☀ 🌑 💧 8–16, 18–24   p. 390

Phlomis ❋
JERUSALEM SAGE
NEEDS, ZONES VARY   p. 414

Photinia serrulata ❋ 🌳
CHINESE PHOTINIA
☀ 🌑 💧 4–16, 18–22   p. 416

Pittosporum ❋ 🌳
☀ 🌓 🌑 💧 ZONES VARY   p. 425

Plumbago auriculata ❋
CAPE PLUMBAGO
☀ 🌑 💧 8, 9, 12–24   p. 428

Portulacaria afra ❋
ELEPHANT'S FOOD
☀ 🌓 🌑 🌑 💧 13, 16, 17, 22–24   p. 435

Prunus ilicifolia ❋ 🌳
HOLLYLEAF CHERRY
☀ 🌓 🌑 🌑 💧 7–9, 12–24   p. 439

Prunus lyonii ❋ 🌳
CATALINA CHERRY
☀ 🌑 💧 7–9, 12–24   p. 441

Punica granatum ❋ 🌳
POMEGRANATE
☀ 🌑 💧 5–24   p. 445

Pyracantha ❋
FIRETHORN
☀ 🌑 💧 ZONES VARY   p. 446

Rhamnus (most) 🌳
NEEDS, ZONES VARY   p. 452

Rhaphiolepis ❋
☀ 🌓 🌑 🌑 💧 8–10, 12–24   p. 453

Rhus ❋ 🌳
SUMAC
☀ 🌑 💧 ZONES VARY   p. 459

Ribes (most) ❋
CURRANT, GOOSEBERRY
NEEDS, ZONES VARY   p. 460

Rosa rugosa ❋
RAMANAS ROSE
☀ 🌓 🌑 💧 ALL ZONES   p. 468

Rosmarinus officinalis ❋
ROSEMARY
☀ 🌑 💧 4–24   p. 469

Rubus ❋
BRAMBLE
☀ 🌓 💧 ZONES VARY   p. 469

Ruellia (some) ❋
NEEDS, ZONES VARY   p. 470

Salvia (most) ❋
SAGE
NEEDS, ZONES VARY   p. 473

Santolina chamaecyparissus ❋
LAVENDER COTTON
☀ 🌑 💧 ALL ZONES   p. 476

Simmondsia chinensis
JOJOBA
☀ 🌑 💧 10–13, 19–24   p. 486

Sollya heterophylla ❋
AUSTRALIAN BLUEBELL CREEPER
☀ 🌓 🌑 🌑 💧 8, 9, 14–24   p. 488

Sophora secundiflora ❋ 🌳
TEXAS MOUNTAIN LAUREL
☀ 🌑 💧 8–16, 18–24   p. 488

Tamarix (some) ❋ 🌳
TAMARISK
☀ 🌑 💧 ZONES VARY   p. 501

Tecoma stans ❋ 🌳
YELLOW BELLS
☀ 🌑 💧 10, 12, 13, 21–24   p. 503

Teucrium ❋
GERMANDER
☀ 🌑 💧 ZONES VARY   p. 504

Trichostema lanatum ❋
WOOLLY BLUE CURLS
☀ 🌑 💧 14–24   p. 510

Vauquelinia californica ❋ 🌳
ARIZONA ROSEWOOD
☀ 🌑 💧 10–13   p. 516

Vitex agnus-castus ❋ 🌳
CHASTE TREE
☀ 🌑 💧 4–24   p. 520

Westringia fruticosa ❋
☀ 🌑 🌑 💧 8, 9, 14–24   p. 523

Xylosma congestum 🌳
☀ 🌓 🌑 🌑 💧 8–24   p. 525

GROUND COVERS, VINES

Acacia redolens ❋
🌑 🌑 💧 8, 9, 12–24   p. 134

Antigonon leptopus ❋
QUEEN'S WREATH
☀ 🌑 💧 12, 13, 18–21   p. 154

Aptenia cordifolia 'Red Apple' ❋
☀ 🌑 💧 17, 21–24   p. 160

Arctostaphylos uva-ursi ❋
KINNIKINNICK
☀ 🌑 💧 1–9, 14–24   p. 163

Bougainvillea ❋
☀ 🌓 🌑 💧 22–24   p. 187

Calylophus hartwegii ❋
☀ 🌑 💧 1–3, 10–13   p. 200

Salvia leucantha

Tecoma stans

Trichostema lanatum

Aptenia cordifolia 'Red Apple'

Bougainvillea

Plant listings continue ▶

101

Convolvulus mauritanicus

Gazania

Thymus pseudolanuginosus

Achillea taygetea

Agave vilmoriniana

Cerastium tomentosum ✳
SNOW-IN-SUMMER
☼ ◐ ◓ ◑ ✂ ALL ZONES   **p. 217**

Ceratostigma plumbaginoides ✳
DWARF PLUMBAGO
☼ ◐ ◓ ◑ ✂ 2–10, 14–24   **p. 218**

Cissus incisa
☼ ◊ ✂ 12, 13   **p. 229**

Convolvulus mauritanicus ✳
GROUND MORNING GLORY
☼ ◐ ◑ ✂ 4–9, 12–24   **p. 239**

Dalea greggii ✳
TRAILING INDIGO BUSH
☼ ◑ ✂ 12, 13   **p. 258**

Delosperma ✳
ICE PLANT
☼ ◊ ◓ ◑ ✂ ZONES VARY   **p. 260**

Gazania ✳
☼ ◑ ✂ 8–24   **p. 304**

Gelsemium sempervirens ✳
CAROLINA JESSAMINE
☼ ◑ ◑ ✂ 8–24   **p. 304**

Helianthemum nummularium ✳
SUNROSE
☼ ◑ ✂ ALL ZONES   **p. 318**

Ipomoea acuminata ✳
BLUE DAWN FLOWER
☼ ◑ ✂ 8, 9, 12–24   **p. 332**

Lampranthus ✳
ICE PLANT
☼ ◊ ◑ ✂ 14–24   **p. 346**

Lantana montevidensis ✳
☼ ◑ ◑ ✂ 8–10, 12–22   **p. 347**

Macfadyena unguis-cati ✳
CAT'S CLAW
☼ ◐ ◑ ✂ 8–24   **p. 364**

Malephora ✳
ICE PLANT
☼ ◊ ✂ ZONES VARY   **p. 372**

Mascagnia ✳
ORCHID VINE
☼ ◑ ✂ 12–24   **p. 375**

Merremia aurea ✳
YELLOW MORNING GLORY
☼ ◑ ✂ 12–24   **p. 379**

Myoporum parvifolium ✳
☼ ◑ ◑ ✂ 8, 9, 12–16, 18–24   **p. 385**

Phyla nodiflora ✳
LIPPIA
☼ ◑ ◑ ✂ 8–24   **p. 416**

Podranea ricasoliana ✳
PINK TRUMPET VINE
☼ ◑ ◑ ✂ 9, 12, 13, 19–24   **p. 431**

Polygonum aubertii ✳
SILVER LACE VINE
☼ ◐ ◓ ◑ ✂ ALL ZONES   **p. 432**

Rosa banksiae ✳
LADY BANKS' ROSE
☼ ◐ ◑ ✂ 4–24   **p. 467**

Rosmarinus officinalis (dwarf) ✳
ROSEMARY
☼ ◊ ◑ ✂ 4–24   **p. 469**

Thymus ✳
THYME
☼ ◐ ◑ ✂ ALL ZONES   **p. 506**

Verbena (most) ✳
NEEDS, ZONES VARY   **p. 517**

Wisteria ✳
☼ ◐ ◓ ◑ ✂ ALL ZONES   **p. 523**

PERENNIALS, BULBS, ANNUALS, ACCENTS

Achillea ✳
YARROW
☼ ◊ ◑ ✂ ALL ZONES   **p. 138**

Agapanthus ✳
LILY-OF-THE-NILE
☼ ◐ ◑ ✂ 7–9, 12–24   **p. 141**

Agave ✳
☼ ◐ ◑ ✂ ZONES VARY   **p. 142**

Aloe (most) ✳
☼ ◐ ◑ ✂ 8, 9, 12–24   **p. 147**

Amaryllis belladonna ✳
NAKED LADY
☼ ◊ ✂ 4–24   **p. 149**

Anigozanthos ✳
KANGAROO PAW
☼ ◑ ✂ 12, 13, 15–24   **p. 152**

Antennaria dioica ✳
PUSSY TOES
☼ ◐ ◑ ✂ ALL ZONES   **p. 153**

Artemisia
☼ ◊ ◑ ✂ ALL ZONES   **p. 166**

Babiana ✳
BABOON FLOWER
☼ ◐ ◑ ◑ ✂ 4–24   **p. 173**

Baileya multiradiata ✳
DESERT MARIGOLD
☼ ◑ ◑ ✂ ALL ZONES   **p. 174**

Centranthus ruber ✳
JUPITER'S BEARD
☼ ◐ ◑ ◊ ◑ ◑ ✂ 7–9, 12–24   **p. 216**

Coreopsis ✳
☼ ◑ ✂ ZONES VARY   **p. 240**

Aloe

Anigozanthos flavidus

Coreopsis lanceolata

Euphorbia characias wulfenii

Centranthus ruber

For growing symbol explanations, please see page 45.

Gaillardia

Geranium incanum

Kniphofia uvaria

Linum perenne lewisii

Oenothera

Dasylirion wheeleri ✳
DESERT SPOON
☼ ◐ ✂ 10–24　　p. 259

Dietes ✳
FORTNIGHT LILY
☼ ◐ ◒ ◒ ✂ 8, 9, 12–24　　p. 264

Echeveria (most) ✳
☼ ◐ ◒ ✂ ZONES VARY　　p. 269

Euphorbia (most) ✳
NEEDS, ZONES VARY　　p. 289

Festuca ovina 'Glauca' ✳
BLUE FESCUE
☼ ◐ ◒ ◒ ✂ ALL ZONES　　p. 294

Gaillardia ✳
☼ ◒ ✂ ALL ZONES　　p. 301

Gaura lindheimeri ✳
GAURA
☼ ◒ ✂ ALL ZONES　　p. 304

Geranium incanum ✳
☼ ◐ ◒ ✂ 14–24　　p. 305

Hesperaloe parviflora ✳
☼ ◊ ✂ 10–10, 18–21　　p. 321

Iris, bearded ✳
☼ ◐ ◒ ✂ ALL ZONES　　p. 333

Kniphofia uvaria ✳
RED-HOT POKER
☼ ◐ ◊ ✂ 1–9, 14–24　　p. 344

Liatris ✳
GAYFEATHER
☼ ◒ ◒ ✂ 1–10, 14–24　　p. 353

Limonium perezii ✳
☼ ◒ ✂ 13, 15–17, 20–24　　p. 356

Linum ✳
FLAX
☼ ◒ ✂ ALL ZONES　　p. 357

Lobelia laxiflora ✳
☼ ◐ ◒ ✂ 7–9, 12–24　　p. 360

Melampodium leucanthum ✳
BLACKFOOT DAISY
☼ ◒ ✂ 1–3, 10–13　　p. 377

Mimulus aurantiacus ✳
STICKY MONKEY FLOWER
☼ ◐ ◒ ✂ 8, 9, 14–24　　p. 381

Muhlenbergia ✳
☼ ◐ ◊ ◒ ✂ ZONES VARY　　p. 384

Oenothera ✳
EVENING PRIMROSE
☼ ◒ ✂ ZONES VARY　　p. 392

Pennisetum setaceum ✳
FOUNTAIN GRASS
☼ ◊ ✂ 8–24　　p. 410

Penstemon (many) ✳
BEARD TONGUE
☼ ◐ ◒ ✂ ZONES VARY　　p. 410

Perovskia 'Blue Spire' ✳
RUSSIAN SAGE
☼ ◒ ✂ ALL ZONES　　p. 412

Phormium ✳
NEW ZEALAND FLAX
☼ ◐ ◊ ◊ ◒ ✂ 7–24　　p. 415

Romneya coulteri ✳
MATILIJA POPPY
☼ ◊ ◒ ✂ ALL ZONES　　p. 462

Salvia (most) ✳
SAGE
NEEDS, ZONES VARY　　p. 473

Santolina ✳
☼ ◊ ◒ ✂ ALL ZONES　　p. 476

Sedum (many) ✳
STONECROP
☼ ◐ ● ◊ ✂ ZONES VARY　　p. 481

Sisyrinchium bellum ✳
BLUE-EYED GRASS
☼ ◐ ◒ ◒ ✂ 4–24　　p. 488

Stachys byzantina ✳
LAMB'S EARS
☼ ◒ ◒ ✂ ALL ZONES　　p. 492

Stipa (some) ✳
NEEDS, ZONES VARY　　p. 493

Tagetes lemmonii ✳
MARIGOLD
☼ ◒ ✂ 8–10, 12–24　　p. 501

Tithonia rotundifolia ✳
MEXICAN SUNFLOWER
☼ ◒ ✂ ALL ZONES　　p. 507

Verbascum ✳
MULLEIN
☼ ◒ ✂ ALL ZONES　　p. 517

Verbena (most) ✳
NEEDS, ZONES VARY　　p. 517

Watsonia ✳
☼ ◒ ● ✂ 4–9, 12–24　　p. 522

Yucca (most) ✳
☼ ◒ ● ✂ ZONES VARY　　p. 525

Zauschneria ✳
CALIFORNIA FUCHSIA
☼ ◊ ◒ ✂ 2–10, 12–24　　p. 527

Zinnia grandiflora ✳
☼ ◒ ◒ ✂ ALL ZONES　　p. 528

Pennisetum setaceum

Perovskia 'Blue Spire'

Salvia coccinea

Watsonia

SPECIAL SITUATIONS

Plants for
UNDER OAKS

The West is home to many centuries-old native oaks that are valued for their majestic beauty. Unfortunately, these same oaks have suffered the consequences of development and inappropriate watering and landscaping around them. The following list will help you select plants that don't demand lots of water, so are suitable for planting beneath these grand trees. Some are sun lovers but will tolerate filtered light. A few cautions: Do not plant, irrigate, or disturb the soil within 10 feet of the trunk, and avoid injuring the roots. Keep lawn outside the drip line. Plant sparingly; use drip irrigation or soaker hoses, not sprinklers. Avoid planting under declining oaks.

Oak planting with Santa Barbara daisy

Holodiscus discolor

Grevillea rosmarinifolia

Nerium oleander

Cistus crispus

SHRUBS

Arctostaphylos
MANZANITA
☼ ◑ ✿ ZONES VARY   p. 162

Berberis darwinii
DARWIN BARBERRY
☼ ◑ ◐ ◑ ✿ ALL ZONES   p. 183

Carpenteria californica
BUSH ANEMONE
☼ ◑ ◐ ◑ ✿ 5–9, 14–24   p. 208

Ceanothus
WILD LILAC
☼ ◐ ◑ ✿ 1–9, 14–24   p. 212

Cistus (some)
ROCKROSE
☼ ◐ ◑ ✿ 7–9, 12–24   p. 229

Eriogonum
WILD BUCKWHEAT
☼ ◐ ◑ ✿ ZONES VARY   p. 278

Galvezia speciosa
ISLAND BUSH SNAPDRAGON
☼ ◑ ◐ ✿ 14–24   p. 302

Garrya
SILKTASSEL
NEEDS, ZONES VARY   p. 303

Grevillea rosmarinifolia
ROSEMARY GREVILLEA
☼ ◐ ◑ ✿ 8, 9, 12–24   p. 313

Holodiscus discolor
OCEAN SPRAY
◑ ◐ ✿ 1–7, 14–17   p. 324

Mahonia

NEEDS, ZONES VARY   p. 371

Myrica californica
PACIFIC WAX MYRTLE
☼ ◑ ◐ ✿ 4–6, 14–17, 20–24   p. 385

Myrtus communis
TRUE MYRTLE
☼ ◑ ◐ ✿ 8–24   p. 386

Nandina domestica
HEAVENLY BAMBOO
☼ ◑ ◐ ● ◐ ◑ ✿ 5–24   p. 386

Nerium oleander
OLEANDER
☼ ◑ ◐ ✿ 8–16, 18–24   p. 390

Plumbago auriculata
CAPE PLUMBAGO
☼ ◐ ◑ ✿ 8, 9, 12–24   p. 428

Rhamnus (most)

NEEDS, ZONES VARY   p. 452

Rhus integrifolia
LEMONADE BERRY
☼ ◐ ◑ ✿ 15–17, 20–24   p. 459

Rhus ovata
SUGAR BUSH
☼ ◐ ◑ ✿ 7–24   p. 460

Ribes (drought-tolerant)
CURRANT, GOOSEBERRY
NEEDS, ZONES VARY   p. 460

Teucrium
GERMANDER
☼ ◐ ◑ ✿ ZONES VARY   p. 504

Viburnum tinus
LAURUSTINUS
☼ ◑ ◐ ✿ 4–10, 12, 13, 14–23   p. 519

GROUND COVERS

Baccharis pilularis 'Twin Peaks'
DWARF COYOTE BRUSH
☼ ◐ ◑ ✿ 5–11, 14–24   p. 173

Cistus (some)
ROCKROSE
☼ ◐ ◑ ✿ 7–9, 12–24   p. 229

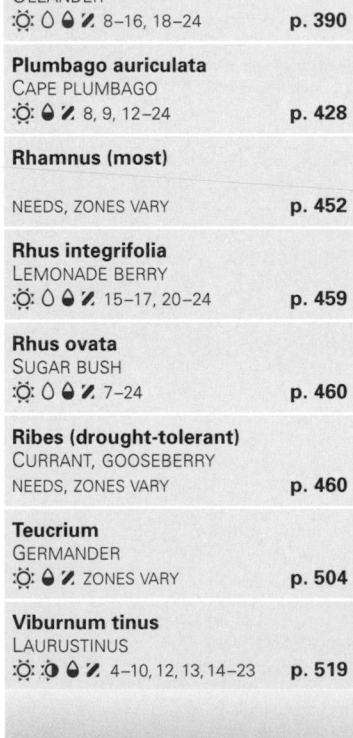

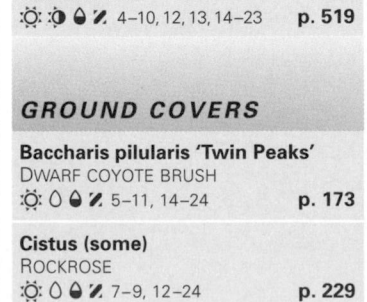

Bergenia crassifolia

Cotoneaster

Rosmarinus officinalis

Artemisia 'Powis Castle'

For growing symbol explanations, please see page 45.

SPECIAL SITUATIONS

Coprosma kirkii
☼ ☽ ◑ ◐ ⚡ 14–17, 21–24   **p. 239**

Correa
AUSTRALIAN FUCHSIA
☼ ☽ ◑ ◐ ⚡ 14–24   **p. 243**

Cotoneaster
☼ ○ ◐ ⚡ ZONES VARY   **p. 245**

Fragaria chiloensis
WILD STRAWBERRY
☼ ☽ ◑ ◐ ● ⚡ 4–24   **p. 298**

Juniperus
JUNIPER
☼ ☽ ○ ◑ ◐ ● ⚡ ALL ZONES   **p. 338**

Mahonia repens
CREEPING MAHONIA
☼ ☽ ◑ ⚡ 1–21   **p. 371**

Polygonum capitatum
☼ ☽ ◑ ◐ ⚡ 8, 9, 12–24   **p. 432**

Ribes viburnifolium
EVERGREEN CURRANT
☼ ☽ ◑ ⚡ 8, 9, 14–24   **p. 461**

Rosmarinus officinalis
ROSEMARY
☼ ○ ◐ ⚡ 4–24   **p. 469**

PERENNIALS

Achillea tomentosa
WOOLLY YARROW
☼ ☽ ○ ◐ ⚡ ALL ZONES   **p. 138**

Aloe
☼ ☽ ◑ ⚡ 8, 9, 12–24   **p. 147**

Artemisia
☼ ○ ◐ ⚡ ALL ZONES   **p. 166**

Bergenia crassifolia
WINTER-BLOOMING BERGENIA
☼ ☽ ◑ ◐ ⚡ 1–9, 12–24   **p. 183**

Dryopteris arguta
CALIFORNIA WOOD FERN
☽ ● ◑ ◐ ⚡ 4–9, 14–24   **p. 268**

Erigeron karvinskianus
SANTA BARBARA DAISY
☼ ☽ ◑ ◐ ⚡ 8, 9, 12–24   **p. 275**

Eschscholzia californica
CALIFORNIA POPPY
☼ ○ ◐ ⚡ ALL ZONES   **p. 281**

Hemerocallis
DAYLILY
☼ ☽ ◑ ◐ ⚡ ALL ZONES   **p. 320**

Heuchera
CORAL BELLS
☼ ☽ ◑ ◐ ⚡ ZONES VARY   **p. 322**

Iris, Pacific Coast and hybrids
☼ ☽ ◑ ◐ ⚡ 4–24   **p. 334**

Kniphofia uvaria
RED-HOT POKER
☼ ☽ ○ ◑ ⚡ 1–9, 14–24   **p. 344**

Limonium perezii
☼ ◑ ⚡ 13, 15–17, 20–24   **p. 356**

Muhlenbergia rigens
DEER GRASS
☼ ☽ ○ ◑ ⚡ 7–24   **p. 384**

Nepeta faassenii
CATMINT
☼ ☽ ◑ ◐ ⚡ ALL ZONES   **p. 389**

Nephrolepis cordifolia
SOUTHERN SWORD FERN
☼ ● ◑ ◐ ⚡ 8, 9, 12–24   **p. 389**

Oenothera
EVENING PRIMROSE
☼ ◑ ⚡ ZONES VARY   **p. 392**

Origanum
NEEDS, ZONES VARY   **p. 395**

Pennisetum setaceum 'Cupreum'
☼ ○ ⚡ 8–24   **p. 410**

Penstemon (some)
BEARD TONGUE
☼ ☽ ◑ ⚡ ZONES VARY   **p. 410**

Polystichum munitum
SWORD FERN
● ◑ ⚡ 4–9, 14–24   **p. 433**

Romneya coulteri
MATILIJA POPPY
☼ ○ ◑ ⚡ ALL ZONES   **p. 462**

Salvia (most)
SAGE
☼ ◑ ⚡ ZONES VARY   **p. 473**

Santolina chamaecyparissus
LAVENDER COTTON
☼ ○ ◑ ⚡ ALL ZONES   **p. 476**

Sedum (most)
STONECROP
☼ ☽ ● ◑ ⚡ ZONES VARY   **p. 481**

Sisyrinchium bellum
BLUE-EYED GRASS
☼ ☽ ◑ ◐ ⚡ 4–24   **p. 486**

Stipa pulchra
PURPLE NEEDLE GRASS
☼ ◑ ⚡ 5, 7–9, 11, 14–24   **p. 494**

Thymus
THYME
☼ ☽ ◑ ⚡ ALL ZONES   **p. 506**

Zauschneria
CALIFORNIA FUCHSIA
☼ ○ ◑ ⚡ 2–10, 12–24   **p. 527**

Dryopteris arguta

Eschscholzia californica

Hemerocallis

Heuchera sanguinea

Nephrolepis cordifolia

Nepeta faassenii

Polystichum munitum

Romneya coulteri

Albizia julibrissin

Plants That
RESIST DEER

Browsing deer are charming to watch, but they can do considerable damage to gardens. There are various ways to discourage or repel deer; another solution is to grow plants that deer will find unpalatable. However, deer in different areas seem to have somewhat different tastes. To complicate the picture further, young plants may be eaten but older ones left alone; plants untouched in spring may be eaten in fall. As a final frustration, tastes change: what deer pass by one year they may find irresistible the next. Despite these variables, a number of plants can be considered "best bets" in deer country. These are listed below.

Acer palmatum 'Sango Kaku'

Ginkgo biloba

Melaleuca linariifolia

TREES

Abies
FIR
☼ ❊ ◐ ♦ ⚡ ZONES VARY   p. 130

Acacia   ❊
☼ ◐ ♦ ⚡ ZONES VARY   p. 131

Acer circinatum   ❦
VINE MAPLE
☼ ❊ ◐ ♦ ⚡ 1–6, 14–17   p. 135

Acer palmatum   ❦
JAPANESE MAPLE
☼ ❊ ◐ ♦ ⚡ 1–10, 12, 14–24   p. 136

Albizia
NEEDS, ZONES VARY   p. 144

Callistemon
BOTTLEBRUSH
☼ ◐ ♦ ⚡ 8, 9, 12–24   p. 197

Cedrus
CEDAR
☼ ◐ ♦ ⚡ ZONES VARY   p. 214

Celtis
HACKBERRY
☼ ❊ ◐ ♦ ⚡ ZONES VARY   p. 216

Ceratonia siliqua
CAROB
☼ ◐ ♦ ⚡ 9, 13–16, 18–24   p. 217

Cercis occidentalis   ❦
WESTERN REDBUD
☼ ◐ ♦ ⚡ 2–24   p. 218

Chamaecyparis
FALSE CYPRESS
☼ ❊ ◐ ♦ ⚡ ZONES VARY   p. 220

Crataegus
HAWTHORN
☼ ◐ ♦ ⚡ 1–12, 14–17   p. 247

Cupressus
CYPRESS
☼ ◐ ⚡ ZONES VARY   p. 252

Eucalyptus (some)   ❦
☼ ◐ ♦ ⚡ SEE CHART   p. 281

Fig, edible
☼ ◐ ⚡ 4–9, 12–24   p. 295

Fraxinus   ❦
ASH   ▦
NEEDS, ZONES VARY   p. 298

Ginkgo biloba
MAIDENHAIR TREE
☼ ◐ ♦ ⚡ 1–10, 12, 14–24   p. 307

Magnolia
☼ ❊ ♦ ⚡ ZONES VARY   p. 365

Maytenus boaria
MAYTEN TREE
☼ ◐ ♦ ⚡ 8, 9, 14–21   p. 376

Melaleuca
☼ ◐ ♦ ⚡ ZONES VARY   p. 377

Olea europaea
OLIVE
☼ ◐ ⚡ 8, 9, 11–24   p. 393

Palms
NEEDS, ZONES VARY   p. 398

Picea
SPRUCE
NEEDS, ZONES VARY   p. 417

Pinus
PINE
NEEDS, ZONES VARY   p. 419

Podocarpus
☼ ❊ ♦ ⚡ ZONES VARY   p. 431

SYMBOLS: ❦ indicates plants that are eaten in some areas; ❊ indicates plants whose flowers are sometimes eaten; ▦ indicates plants that must be protected when young.

Browsing deer

Olea europaea

Picea

For growing symbol explanations, please see page 45.

Pinus sabiniana

Alyogyne huegelii

Aesculus californica

Pseudotsuga menziesii
DOUGLAS FIR
☼ ◐ ◊ ● ✓ 1–10, 14–17   **p. 443**

Quercus   ⌗
OAK
☼ ◊ ● ✓ ZONES VARY   **p. 447**

Sequoia sempervirens
COAST REDWOOD
☼ ◐ ● ● ✓ 4–9, 14–24   **p. 483**

Tamarix
TAMARISK
☼ ◊ ● ✓ ZONES VARY   **p. 501**

Umbellularia californica
CALIFORNIA LAUREL
☼ ◐ ◊ ✓ 4–10, 12–24   **p. 515**

SHRUBS

Abelia grandiflora
GLOSSY ABELIA
☼ ◐ ● ✓ 5–24   **p. 130**

Aesculus californica
CALIFORNIA BUCKEYE
☼ ◊ ● ✓ 4–10, 12, 14–24   **p. 141**

Alyogyne huegelii
BLUE HIBISCUS
☼ ● ● ✓ 15–17, 20–24   **p. 149**

Anisodontea
CAPE MALLOW
☼ ● ● ✓ 14–24   **p. 152**

Arctostaphylos   ✿
MANZANITA
☼ ● ● ✓ ZONES VARY   **p. 162**

Bamboo
☼ ◐ ● ✓ ZONES VARY   **p. 174**

Berberis   ✿
BARBERRY
☼ ◐ ● ● ✓ ALL ZONES   **p. 182**

Buddleia
☼ ◐ ● ● ✓ ALL ZONES   **p. 192**

Buxus
BOXWOOD
☼ ◐ ● ● ✓ ZONES VARY   **p. 193**

Callistemon
BOTTLEBRUSH
☼ ● ✓ 8, 9, 12–24   **p. 197**

Calluna vulgaris
SCOTCH HEATHER
☼ ● ✓ 2–6, 15–17   **p. 197**

Carpenteria californica
BUSH ANEMONE
☼ ◐ ● ● ✓ 5–9, 14–24   **p. 208**

Cassia
SENNA
☼ ● ✓ ZONES VARY   **p. 210**

Ceanothus 'Blue Jeans'
☼ ◊ ● ✓ 1–9, 14–24   **p. 213**

Ceanothus 'Julia Phelps'
☼ ◊ ● ✓ 1–9, 14–24   **p. 214**

Chaenomeles
FLOWERING QUINCE
☼ ● ✓ 1–21   **p. 220**

Choisya ternata
MEXICAN ORANGE
☼ ◐ ● ✓ 7–9, 12–24   **p. 225**

Cistus (most)   ✿❄
ROCKROSE
☼ ◊ ● ✓ 7–9, 12–24   **p. 229**

Coleonema and Diosma
BREATH OF HEAVEN
☼ ◐ ● ✓ 7–9, 14–24   **p. 237**

Coprosma
NEEDS, ZONES VARY   **p. 239**

Corokia cotoneaster
☼ ◐ ● ✓ 4–24   **p. 243**

Correa
AUSTRALIAN FUCHSIA
☼ ◐ ● ✓ 14–24   **p. 243**

Cotoneaster   ✿
☼ ◊ ● ✓ ZONES VARY   **p. 245**

Daphne
NEEDS, ZONES VARY   **p. 258**

Dendromecon
BUSH POPPY
☼ ◊ ✓ 5–8, 14–24   **p. 260**

Dodonaea viscosa   ✿
HOP BUSH
☼ ◐ ◊ ● ✓ 7–9, 12–24   **p. 266**

Elaeagnus
☼ ◐ ● ● ✓ ZONES VARY   **p. 271**

Erica
HEATH
☼ ● ✓ ZONES VARY   **p. 275**

Eriogonum
WILD BUCKWHEAT
☼ ◊ ● ✓ ZONES VARY   **p. 278**

Escallonia
☼ ◐ ● ● ✓ 4–9, 14–17, 20–24 **p. 280**

Feijoa sellowiana
PINEAPPLE GUAVA
☼ ◐ ● ✓ 7–9, 12–24   **p. 292**

Fremontodendron   ✿
FLANNEL BUSH
☼ ◊ ✓ 7–24   **p. 300**

Plant listings continue ▶

Anisodontea

Arctostaphylos densiflora 'Howard McMinn'

Corokia cotoneaster

Dendromecon harfordii

Eriogonum

Fremontodendron 'California Glory'

SPECIAL SITUATIONS

Grevillea 'Canberra'

Lavatera thuringiaca

Leonotis leonurus

Lantana 'Radiation'

Nerium oleander

Gaultheria shallon
SALAL
☼ ◐ ❍ ✂ 3–7, 14–17, 21–24   **p. 303**

Grevillea

NEEDS, ZONES VARY   **p. 312**

Hakea suaveolens
SWEET HAKEA
☼ ◊ ✂ 9, 12–17, 19–24   **p. 315**

Heteromeles arbutifolia 🍃
TOYON
☼ ◑ ❍ ✂ 5–24   **p. 321**

Hypericum
ST. JOHNSWORT
☼ ◑ ❍ ◐ ✂ 4–24   **p. 328**

Ilex
HOLLY
☼ ◑ ❍ ✂ ZONES VARY   **p. 329**

Juniperus
JUNIPER
☼ ◑ ❍ ❍ ◐ ✂ ALL ZONES   **p. 338**

Kerria japonica

☼ ◑ ❍ ✂ 1–21   **p. 343**

Lantana

☼ ❍ ◐ ✂ 8–10, 12–22   **p. 347**

Lavandula (some) 🍃
LAVENDER
☼ ❍ ✂ ZONES VARY   **p. 349**

Lavatera
TREE MALLOW
☼ ❍ ◐ ✂ ZONES VARY   **p. 349**

Leonotis leonurus
LION'S TAIL
☼ ◊ ❍ ✂ 8–24   **p. 350**

Leptospermum
TEA TREE
☼ ◊ ❍ ✂ 14–24   **p. 350**

Mahonia 🍃

NEEDS, ZONES VARY   **p. 371**

Myoporum

☼ ❍ ◐ ✂ ZONES VARY   **p. 385**

Myrica californica 🍃
PACIFIC WAX MYRTLE
☼ ❍ ✂ 4–6, 14–17, 20–24   **p. 385**

Myrtus communis
TRUE MYRTLE
☼ ◑ ◊ ✂ 8–24   **p. 386**

Nandina domestica 🍃
HEAVENLY BAMBOO
☼ ◑ ● ❍ ◐ ✂ 5–24   **p. 386**

Nerium oleander
OLEANDER
☼ ◊ ❍ ✂ 8–16, 18–24   **p. 390**

Plumbago auriculata
CAPE PLUMBAGO
☼ ❍ ✂ 8, 9, 12–24   **p. 428**

Potentilla 🍃
CINQUEFOIL
☼ ◑ ❍ ◐ ✂ ZONES VARY   **p. 435**

Pyracantha 🍃 🔲
FIRETHORN
☼ ❍ ◐ ✂ ZONES VARY   **p. 446**

Rhododendron (not azaleas)

◑ ❍ ◐ ◐ ✂ ZONES VARY   **p. 454**

Rhus
SUMAC
☼ ❍ ◊ ✂ ZONES VARY   **p. 459**

Ribes 🍃
CURRANT, GOOSEBERRY
NEEDS, ZONES VARY   **p. 460**

Rosmarinus officinalis
ROSEMARY
☼ ◊ ❍ ◐ ✂ 4–24   **p. 469**

Salvia 🍃
SAGE
NEEDS, ZONES VARY   **p. 473**

Sarcococca
☼ ◑ ● ❍ ◐ ✂ 4–9, 14–24   **p. 476**

Syringa 🍃
LILAC
☼ ◑ ❍ ✂ ZONES VARY   **p. 499**

Teucrium
GERMANDER
☼ ❍ ◐ ✂ ZONES VARY   **p. 504**

Tibouchina urvilleana
PRINCESS FLOWER
☼ ◑ ❍ ◐ ✂ 16, 17, 21–24   **p. 506**

Trichostema lanatum
WOOLLY BLUE CURLS
☼ ◊ ✂ 14–24   **p. 510**

Vaccinium ovatum
EVERGREEN HUCKLEBERRY
☼ ❍ ◐ ✂ 4–7, 14–17   **p. 516**

Viburnum

NEEDS, ZONES VARY   **p. 518**

Westringia fruticosa

☼ ❍ ◐ ✂ 8, 9, 14–24   **p. 523**

GROUND COVERS, VINES

Ajuga
CARPET BUGLE
☼ ◑ ● ◐ ✂ ALL ZONES   **p. 144**

Asteriscus maritimus

☼ ◊ ✂ 9, 15–24   **p. 170**

Rhododendron

Vaccinium ovatum

Ceratostigma plumbaginoides

Gazania 'Burgundy'

Hedera helix

For growing symbol explanations, please see page 45.

Osteospermum fruticosum

Sollya heterophylla

Acanthus mollis

Achillea millefolium hybrid

Aster frikartii

Bougainvillea
☼ ◐ ◌ ◕ ⚡ 22–24   **p. 187**

Ceratostigma plumbaginoides
DWARF PLUMBAGO
☼ ◐ ◕ ◌ ⚡ 2–10, 14–24   **p. 218**

Fragaria chiloensis ✿
WILD STRAWBERRY
☼ ◐ ◕ ◌ ⚡ 4–24   **p. 298**

Gazania
☼ ◕ ⚡ 8–24   **p. 304**

Gelsemium sempervirens
CAROLINA JESSAMINE
☼ ◕ ◌ ⚡ 8–24   **p. 304**

Hedera helix ✿
ENGLISH IVY
☼ ◐ ● ◕ ◌ ⚡ ALL ZONES   **p. 317**

Hibbertia scandens
GUINEA GOLD VINE
☼ ◐ ◕ ⚡ 16, 17, 21–24   **p. 322**

Jasminum ✿
JASMINE
☼ ◐ ◕ ⚡ ZONES VARY   **p. 336**

Lantana montevidensis
☼ ◕ ◌ 8–10, 12–22   **p. 347**

Osteospermum fruticosum
TRAILING AFRICAN DAISY
☼ ◕ ⚡ 8, 9, 12–24   **p. 397**

Pachysandra terminalis
JAPANESE SPURGE
◕ ● ◕ ⚡ 1–10, 14–21   **p. 398**

Scaevola
☼ ◕ ⚡ 8, 9, 14–24   **p. 478**

Solanum jasminoides
POTATO VINE
☼ ◐ ◕ ◌ ⚡ 8, 9, 12–24   **p. 487**

Sollya heterophylla
AUSTRALIAN BLUEBELL CREEPER
☼ ◐ ◕ ◌ ⚡ 8, 9, 14–24   **p. 488**

Tecomaria capensis
CAPE HONEYSUCKLE
☼ ◐ ◕ ⚡ 12, 13, 16, 18–24   **p. 503**

Vinca
PERIWINKLE
◐ ● ◕ ⚡ ZONES VARY   **p. 519**

Wisteria
☼ ◐ ◕ ◌ ⚡ ALL ZONES   **p. 523**

PERENNIALS, BULBS

Acanthus mollis
BEAR'S BREECH
☼ ◐ ◕ ◌ ⚡ 4–24   **p. 135**

Achillea
YARROW
☼ ◌ ◕ ◌ ⚡ ALL ZONES   **p. 138**

Agave
NEEDS, ZONES VARY   **p. 142**

Aloe
☼ ◐ ◕ ⚡ 8, 9, 12–24   **p. 147**

Amaryllis belladonna
NAKED LADY
☼ ◌ ◕ ⚡ 4–24   **p. 149**

Aquilegia
COLUMBINE
☼ ◐ ◕ ◌ ⚡ ALL ZONES   **p. 160**

Armeria
THRIFT
☼ ◕ ◌ ⚡ ALL ZONES   **p. 165**

Artemisia
☼ ◌ ◕ ⚡ ALL ZONES   **p. 166**

Aster
☼ ◕ ⚡ ALL ZONES   **p. 170**

Astilbe
FALSE SPIRAEA
☼ ◐ ◕ ⚡ 2–7 14–17   **p. 170**

Begonia, tuberous
◐ ● ◕ ⚡ 14–24   **p. 182**

Brachycome
SWAN RIVER DAISY
☼ ◕ ⚡ ZONES VARY   **p. 189**

Campanula poscharskyana
SERBIAN BELLFLOWER
☼ ◐ ◕ ⚡ 1–9, 10–12, 14–24   **p. 205**

Carex
SEDGE
☼ ◐ ◕ ◌ ⚡ 4–9, 14–24   **p. 206**

Centaurea ✿
NEEDS, ZONES VARY   **p. 216**

Centranthus ruber
JUPITER'S BEARD
☼ ◐ ● ◌ ◕ ◌ ⚡ 7–9, 12–24   **p. 216**

Cerastium tomentosum
SNOW-IN-SUMMER
☼ ◐ ◕ ◌ ⚡ ALL ZONES   **p. 217**

Chrysanthemum frutescens ✤
MARGUERITE
☼ ◕ ⚡ 14–24   **p. 226**

Coreopsis
☼ ◕ ⚡ ZONES VARY   **p. 240**

Crocosmia
☼ ◐ ◌ ⚡ 5–24   **p. 249**

Astilbe arendsii hybrid

Brachycome

Aquilegia McKana hybrid

Campanula poscharskyana

Carex

Plant listings continue ▶

Erysimum 'Bowles Mauve'

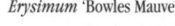

Erodium reichardii

Eschscholzia californica

Euphorbia martinii

Hemerocallis

Crocus
☼ ☼ ◗ ✂ ALL ZONES — p. 249

Cyclamen
☼ ☼ ◗ ✂ ZONES VARY — p. 253

Dahlia
☼ ☼ ◗ ✂ ALL ZONES — p. 256

Dicentra
BLEEDING HEART
● ◗ ✂ 1–9, 14–24 — p. 262

Dietes vegeta
☼ ☼ ◗ ◗ ✂ 8, 9, 12–24 — p. 264

Digitalis
FOXGLOVE
☼ ◗ ✂ ALL ZONES — p. 264

Echinacea purpurea
PURPLE CONEFLOWER
☼ ◗ ◗ ✂ ALL ZONES — p. 269

Echium fastuosum
PRIDE OF MADEIRA
☼ ◗ ◗ ✂ 14–24 — p. 270

Erigeron
FLEABANE
☼ ☼ ◗ ◗ ✂ ZONES VARY — p. 275

Erodium reichardii
CRANESBILL
☼ ☼ ◗ ✂ 7–9, 14–24 — p. 278

Erysimum 'Bowles Mauve'
☼ ☼ ◗ ◗ ✂ 4–6, 14–17, 22, 23 — p. 279

Erysimum cheiri
WALLFLOWER
☼ ☼ ◗ ◗ ✂ 4–6, 14–17, 22, 23 — p. 279

Eschscholzia californica
CALIFORNIA POPPY
☼ ◊ ◗ ✂ ALL ZONES — p. 281

Euphorbia
NEEDS, ZONES VARY — p. 289

Euryops
☼ ◗ ✂ 8, 9, 12–24 — p. 290

Felicia amelloides
BLUE MARGUERITE
☼ ◗ ✂ 8, 9, 13–24 — p. 293

Ferns
NEEDS, ZONES VARY — p. 293

Festuca ovina 'Glauca'
BLUE FESCUE
☼ ☼ ◗ ◗ ✂ ALL ZONES — p. 294

Freesia
☼ ◗ ◗ ✂ 8, 9, 12–24 — p. 300

Gaillardia grandiflora
BLANKET FLOWER
☼ ◗ ✂ ALL ZONES — p. 301

Geranium
CRANESBILL
NEEDS, ZONES VARY — p. 305

Helichrysum
☼ ◊ ◗ ✂ ZONES VARY — p. 319

Helleborus
HELLEBORE
NEEDS, ZONES VARY — p. 319

Hemerocallis
DAYLILY
☼ ☼ ◗ ✂ ALL ZONES — p. 320

Herbs (except basil)
NEEDS, ZONES VARY — p. 320

Iberis
CANDYTUFT
☼ ◗ ✂ ALL ZONES — p. 329

Iris
NEEDS, ZONES VARY — p. 332

Ixia
AFRICAN CORN LILY
☼ ◗ ✂ 5–24 — p. 336

Kniphofia uvaria
RED-HOT POKER
☼ ◊ ◗ ✂ 1–9, 14–24 — p. 344

Lamium maculatum
DEAD NETTLE
● ◗ ✂ ALL ZONES — p. 346

Limonium
SEA LAVENDER
☼ ◗ ✂ ZONES VARY — p. 356

Liriope and Ophiopogon
LILY TURF
☼ ◗ ● ◗ ◗ ✂ 5–10, 12–24 — p. 358

Lithodora diffusa
☼ ☼ ◗ ✂ 5–7, 14–17 — p. 359

Lupinus
LUPINE
NEEDS, ZONES VARY — p. 362

Lychnis coronaria
CROWN-PINK
☼ ☼ ◗ ✂ ALL ZONES — p. 362

Mimulus
MONKEY FLOWER
NEEDS, ZONES VARY — p. 381

Miscanthus sinensis
EULALIA GRASS
☼ ☼ ● ◗ ✂ ALL ZONES — p. 382

Monarda
BEE BALM
☼ ☼ ◗ ◗ ✂ ALL ZONES — p. 382

Kniphofia uvaria

Origanum laevigatum 'Hopley's'

Pennisetum setaceum

Penstemon gloxinioides

Phormium hybrid

For growing symbol explanations, please see page 45.

Romneya coulteri

Santolina chamaecyparissus

Stachys byzantina

Tagetes lemmonii

Myosotis scorpioides
☼ ● ⚡ ALL ZONES — p. 385

Narcissus
DAFFODIL
☼ ◐ ● ⚡ ALL ZONES — p. 387

Nepeta
☼ ● ● ⚡ ALL ZONES — p. 389

Origanum
NEEDS, ZONES VARY — p. 395

Papaver orientale
ORIENTAL POPPY
☼ ● ● ⚡ 1–17 — p. 400

Pennisetum setaceum
☼ ◊ ⚡ 8–24 — p. 410

Penstemon ❦
BEARD TONGUE
NEEDS, ZONES VARY — p. 410

Phlomis fruticosa
☼ ◐ ● ⚡ 4–24 — p. 414

Phlox subulata
MOSS PINK
☼ ◐ ● ⚡ 1–17 — p. 415

Phormium
NEW ZEALAND FLAX
☼ ◐ ◊ ● ● ⚡ 7–24 — p. 415

Romneya coulteri ❦
MATILIJA POPPY
☼ ◊ ● ⚡ ALL ZONES — p. 462

Rudbeckia hirta
GLORIOSA DAISY
☼ ● ⚡ ALL ZONES — p. 470

Santolina
☼ ◊ ● ⚡ ALL ZONES — p. 476

Saxifraga
SAXIFRAGE
NEEDS, ZONES VARY — p. 477

Scabiosa (some) ❦
PINCUSHION FLOWER
☼ ● ⚡ ZONES VARY — p. 478

Scilla
SQUILL
☼ ◐ ● ⚡ ZONES VARY — p. 480

Sisyrinchium
☼ ◐ ● ● ⚡ 4–24 — p. 486

Stachys byzantina
LAMB'S EARS
☼ ◐ ● ⚡ ALL ZONES — p. 492

Stipa
FEATHER GRASS
NEEDS, ZONES VARY — p. 493

Tagetes lemmonii
☼ ● ⚡ 8–10, 12–24 — p. 501

Thymus
THYME
☼ ◐ ● ⚡ ALL ZONES — p. 506

Tulbaghia violacea
SOCIETY GARLIC
☼ ● ⚡ 13–24 — p. 512

Verbena ❦
NEEDS, ZONES VARY — p. 517

Veronica
SPEEDWELL
☼ ● ⚡ ALL ZONES — p. 517

Viola odorata
SWEET VIOLET
☼ ◐ ● ⚡ ALL ZONES — p. 520

Zantedeschia
CALLA
☼ ◐ ● ●● ⚡ 5, 6, 8, 9, 14–24 — p. 526

Zauschneria
CALIFORNIA FUCHSIA
☼ ◊ ● ⚡ 2–10, 12–24 — p. 527

ANNUALS

Ageratum houstonianum
FLOSS FLOWER
☼ ◐ ● ⚡ ALL ZONES — p. 142

Campanula medium
CANTERBURY BELL
☼ ◐ ● ⚡ 1–9, 14–24 — p. 204

Catharanthus roseus
MADAGASCAR PERIWINKLE
☼ ◐ ● ⚡ ALL ZONES — p. 212

Clarkia amoena
GODETIA
☼ ● ⚡ ALL ZONES — p. 233

Impatiens ❦
BALSAM
NEEDS VARY, ALL ZONES — p. 330

Lupinus (some)
LUPINE
NEEDS, ZONES VARY — p. 362

Myosotis sylvatica
☼ ◐ ● ⚡ ALL ZONES — p. 385

Papaver rhoeas
SHIRLEY POPPY
☼ ● ● ⚡ ALL ZONES — p. 400

Scabiosa (some)
PINCUSHION FLOWER
☼ ● ⚡ ALL ZONES — p. 478

Senecio hybridus
CINERARIA
☼ ● ● ⚡ ALL ZONES — p. 483

Thymus

Clarkia amoena

Impatiens

Myosotis sylvatica

Scabiosa

Eucalyptus ficifolia

Melaleuca linariifolia

Plants for
WINDY AREAS

Callistemon

Whether you live on the coast or in inland areas, strong winds can wreak havoc on plants. Wind causes water stress in plants by increasing transpiration and evaporation from leaves. A gale-force wind can defoliate or uproot plants, or snap off branches with such force that stems or trunks can split. The plants listed below are tough enough to withstand strong winds, while still providing plenty of ornamental value in the garden. Where just a genus name appears, all species of that genus are appropriate for windy areas.

Metrosideros excelsus

TREES

Acacia (some)
☼ ◊ ◐ ✄ ZONES VARY   **p. 131**

Arbutus
NEEDS, ZONES VARY   **p. 162**

Chilopsis linearis
DESERT WILLOW
☼ ◐ ✄ 10–13, 18–21   **p. 223**

Cupressus
CYPRESS
☼ ◊ ✄ ZONES VARY   **p. 252**

Eucalyptus (most)
☼ ◊ ◐ ✄ SEE CHART   **p. 281**

Ficus rubiginosa
RUSTYLEAF FIG
☼ ◑ ◐ ✄ 18–24   **p. 295**

Fraxinus 'Fan West'
☼ ◐ ✄ 1–14   **p. 299**

Fraxinus velutina 'Rio Grande'
FAN-TEX ASH
☼ ◊ ◐ ✄ 8–24   **p. 299**

Ligustrum lucidum
GLOSSY PRIVET
☼ ◑ ◐ ✄ 5, 6, 8–24   **p. 354**

Melaleuca (most)
☼ ◊ ◐ ✄ ZONES VARY   **p. 377**

Metrosideros excelsus
NEW ZEALAND CHRISTMAS TREE
☼ ◊ ◐ ✄ 17, 23, 24   **p. 380**

Olea europaea
OLIVE
☼ ◊ ✄ 8, 9, 11–24   **p. 393**

Palms
NEEDS, ZONES VARY   **p. 398**

Parkinsonia aculeata
MEXICAN PALO VERDE
☼ ◐ ✄ 8–24   **p. 400**

Pinus (many)
PINE
NEEDS, ZONES VARY   **p. 419**

Quercus ilex
HOLLY OAK
☼ ◊ ◐ ✄ 4–24   **p. 448**

Quercus virginiana
SOUTHERN LIVE OAK
☼ ◐ ✄ 4–24   **p. 449**

Tamarix
TAMARISK
☼ ◊ ◐ ✄ ZONES VARY   **p. 501**

Thuja occidentalis
AMERICAN ARBORVITAE
☼ ☼ ◐ ◐ ◑ ✄ MOST ZONES   **p. 505**

SHRUBS

Arctostaphylos
MANZANITA
☼ ◐ ✄ ZONES VARY   **p. 162**

Artemisia
☼ ◊ ◐ ✄ ALL ZONES   **p. 166**

Berberis
BARBERRY
☼ ◑ ◐ ◐ ✄ ALL ZONES   **p. 182**

Buxus
BOXWOOD
☼ ◑ ● ◐ ✄ ZONES VARY   **p. 193**

Callistemon
BOTTLEBRUSH
☼ ◐ ✄ 8, 9, 12–24   **p. 197**

Ceanothus impressus

Chamaecyparis pisifera

Cistus hybridus

Cotoneaster microphyllus

Olea europaea

Buxus sempervirens 'Suffruticosa'

For growing symbol explanations, please see page 45.

Echium

Escallonia langleyensis

Juniperus chinensis 'Torulosa'

Lavatera thuringiaca 'Barnsley'

Leptospermum scoparium

Carissa
☼ ◐ ◖ ● ✂ 22–24　　　　**p. 207**

Ceanothus
WILD LILAC
☼ ◖ ● ✂ 1–9, 14–24　　　**p. 212**

Chamaecyparis
FALSE CYPRESS
☼ ◐ ● ✂ ZONES VARY　　　**p. 220**

Cistus
ROCKROSE
☼ ◖ ● ✂ 7–9, 12–24　　　**p. 229**

Coprosma
NEEDS, ZONES VARY　　　**p. 239**

Correa
AUSTRALIAN FUCHSIA
☼ ◐ ● ✂ 14–24　　　　**p. 243**

Cotoneaster
☼ ◖ ● ✂ ZONES VARY　　　**p. 245**

Dodonaea viscosa
HOP BUSH
☼ ◐ ◖ ● ✂ 7–9, 12–24　　**p. 266**

Echium
☼ ◖ ● ✂ ZONES VARY　　　**p. 270**

Elaeagnus
☼ ◐ ◖ ● ✂ ZONES VARY　　**p. 271**

Escallonia
☼ ◐ ◖ ● ✂ 4–9, 14–17, 20–24 **p. 280**

Euonymus japonica
EVERGREEN EUONYMUS
☼ ◐ ● ✂ 2–20　　　　**p. 288**

Griselinia littoralis
☼ ◐ ● ✂ 9, 14–17, 20–24　**p. 313**

Hakea suaveolens
SWEET HAKEA
☼ ◖ ✂ 9, 12–17, 19–24　**p. 315**

Juniperus
JUNIPER
☼ ◐ ◖ ● ◖ ● ✂ ALL ZONES **p. 338**

Laurus nobilis
SWEET BAY
☼ ◐ ● ✂ 5–9, 12–24　　**p. 349**

Lavandula
LAVENDER
☼ ● ✂ ZONES VARY　　　**p. 349**

Lavatera
TREE MALLOW
☼ ● ● ✂ ZONES VARY　　**p. 349**

Leptospermum
TEA TREE
☼ ◖ ● ✂ 14–24　　　　**p. 350**

Leucophyllum
TEXAS RANGER
☼ ● ✂ 7–24　　　　**p. 352**

Ligustrum japonicum 'Texanum'
☼ ◐ ● ✂ 4–24　　　　**p. 354**

Lupinus arboreus
LUPINE
☼ ◖ ● ✂ 14–17, 22–24　**p. 362**

Myoporum (some)
☼ ◖ ● ✂ ZONES VARY　　**p. 385**

Myrica californica
PACIFIC WAX MYRTLE
☼ ◖ ● ✂ 4–6, 14–17, 20–24 **p. 385**

Nandina domestica
HEAVENLY BAMBOO
☼ ◐ ◖ ● ◖ ● ✂ 5–24　　**p. 386**

Nerium oleander
OLEANDER
☼ ◖ ● ✂ 8–16, 18–24　　**p. 390**

Pittosporum (most)
☼ ◐ ◖ ● ✂ ZONES VARY　**p. 425**

Prunus (evergreen)
NEEDS, ZONES VARY　　　**p. 400**

Pyracantha
FIRETHORN
☼ ◖ ● ✂ ZONES VARY　　**p. 446**

Rhamnus (some)
NEEDS, ZONES VARY　　　**p. 452**

Rhaphiolepis (most)
☼ ◐ ◖ ● ● ✂ 8–10, 12–24 **p. 453**

Rhus (some)
SUMAC
☼ ◖ ● ✂ ZONES VARY　　**p. 459**

Rosmarinus officinalis
ROSEMARY
☼ ◖ ● ● ✂ 4–24　　　　**p. 469**

Westringia fruticosa
☼ ● ● ✂ 8, 9, 14–24　　**p. 523**

Xylosma congestum
☼ ◐ ● ● ✂ 8–24　　　**p. 525**

GROUND COVERS, VINES

Abronia
SAND VERBENA
☼ ◖ ● ✂ 4, 5, 17, 24　　**p. 131**

Arctotheca calendula
CAPE WEED
☼ ◖ ● ✂ 8, 9, 13–24　　**p. 164**

Ligustrum japonicum 'Texanum'

Lupinus arboreus

Nandina domestica

Pittosporum tobira

Prunus lusitanica

Plant listings continue ▶

Bougainvillea

Delosperma cooperi

Lantana montevidensis

Carex elata 'Bowles Golden'

Chrysanthemum frutescens

Eriogonum

Asteriscus maritimus

☼ ◐ ✿ 9, 15–24   **p. 170**

Baccharis pilularis
DWARF COYOTE BRUSH
☼ ◐ ● ✿ 5–11, 14–24   **p. 173**

Bougainvillea

☼ ◐ ● ✿ 22–24   **p. 187**

Carpobrotus
ICE PLANT
☼ ● ✿ 12–24   **p. 208**

Delosperma
ICE PLANT
☼ ◐ ● ✿ ZONES VARY   **p. 260**

Drosanthemum

☼ ● ✿ 14–24   **p. 268**

Lampranthus
ICE PLANT
☼ ◐ ● ✿ 14–24   **p. 346**

Lantana

☼ ● ● ✿ 8–10, 12–22   **p. 347**

Muehlenbeckia complexa
MATTRESS VINE
☼ ◐ ● ✿ 8, 9, 14–24   **p. 384**

Osteospermum fruticosum
TRAILING AFRICAN DAISY
☼ ● ✿ 8, 9, 12–24   **p. 397**

Tecomaria capensis
CAPE HONEYSUCKLE
☼ ◐ ● ✿ 12, 13, 16, 18–24   **p. 503**

PERENNIALS, ACCENT PLANTS

Agapanthus
LILY-OF-THE-NILE
☼ ◐ ● ✿ 7–9, 12–24   **p. 141**

Agave

☼ ◐ ● ✿ ZONES VARY   **p. 142**

Aloe

☼ ◐ ● ✿ 8, 9, 12–24   **p. 147**

Asparagus densiflorus 'Sprengeri'
SPRENGER ASPARAGUS
☼ ◐ ● ● ✿ 12–24   **p. 168**

Calocephalus brownii
CUSHION BUSH
☼ ● ● ✿ 16, 17, 19, 21–24   **p. 198**

Carex
SEDGE
☼ ● ● ✿ 4–9, 14–24   **p. 206**

Cerastium tomentosum
SNOW-IN-SUMMER
☼ ◐ ● ● ✿ ALL ZONES   **p. 217**

Chrysanthemum frutescens
MARGUERITE
☼ ● ✿ 14–24   **p. 226**

Crassula argentea
JADE PLANT
☼ ◐ ● ◐ ✿ 8, 9, 12–24   **p. 247**

Dudleya
☼ ◐ ● ✿ 12, 13, 16, 17, 21–24 **p. 268**

Erigeron glaucus
BEACH ASTER
☼ ◐ ● ✿ 4–6, 15–17, 22–24   **p. 275**

Eriogonum
WILD BUCKWHEAT
☼ ◐ ● ✿ ZONES VARY   **p. 278**

Erysimum
WALLFLOWER
☼ ◐ ● ● ✿ ZONES VARY   **p. 279**

Euphorbia

NEEDS, ZONES VARY   **p. 289**

Euryops

☼ ● ✿ 8, 9, 12–24   **p. 290**

Felicia amelloides
BLUE MARGUERITE
☼ ● ✿ 8, 9, 13–24   **p. 293**

Hemerocallis
DAYLILY
☼ ◐ ● ✿ ALL ZONES   **p. 320**

Kniphofia uvaria
RED-HOT POKER
☼ ◐ ● ✿ 1–9, 14–24   **p. 344**

Limonium perezii

☼ ● ✿ 13, 15–17, 20–24   **p. 356**

Pelargonium
GERANIUM
☼ ◐ ● ● ✿ 8, 9, 12–24   **p. 407**

Phlomis
JERUSALEM SAGE
☼ ● ✿ ZONES VARY   **p. 414**

Phormium
NEW ZEALAND FLAX
☼ ◐ ◐ ● ✿ 7–24   **p. 415**

Salvia
SAGE
NEEDS, ZONES VARY   **p. 473**

Santolina

☼ ◐ ● ✿ ALL ZONES   **p. 476**

Yucca

☼ ◐ ● ✿ ZONES VARY   **p. 525**

Zauschneria
CALIFORNIA FUCHSIA
☼ ◐ ● ✿ 2–10, 12–24   **p. 527**

Euphorbia seguierana niciciana

Euryops pectinatus 'Viridis'

Kniphofia uvaria

Phlomis russeliana

Agapanthus 'Peter Pan'

For growing symbol explanations, please see page 45.

GROUND COVERS
and Lawn Substitutes

Epimedium at base of tree

Lawn, the best-known ground cover, is unsurpassed as a surface to walk and play on. But where foot traffic is infrequent or undesirable, many other plants can offer much of a lawn's neatness and uniformity with considerably less maintenance. Ground covers run the gamut of foliage textures and colors, and many are noted for their colorful flowers. Some spread by underground runners or root as they grow. Others grow from clumps and must be planted close together to achieve the effect of a ground cover. Not all of them are low mats; some are knee-high or even taller. The taller ones function as barriers rather than as the green bridge a lawn provides.

Alchemilla mollis

Antennaria dioica

Arctostaphylos uva-ursi

Artemisia stellerana 'Silver Brocade'

GROUND COVERS

Abelia grandiflora 'Prostrata' 🌿
☀️ 🌤️ 💧 5–24   p. 130

Achillea tomentosa 🌿
WOOLLY YARROW
☀️ 🌤️ ○ 💧 ALL ZONES   p. 138

Ajuga reptans 🌿
CARPET BUGLE
☀️ 🌤️ 💧 ALL ZONES   p. 144

Alchemilla 🌿
LADY'S-MANTLE
☀️ 🌤️ 💧 ZONES VARY   p. 145

Antennaria dioica 🌿
PUSSY TOES
☀️ 💧 💧 ALL ZONES   p. 153

Aptenia cordifolia 'Red Apple' 🌿
☀️ 💧 💧 17, 21–24   p. 160

Arabis 🌿
ROCKCRESS
☀️ 💧 💧 ZONES VARY   p. 161

Arctostaphylos (several) 🌿
MANZANITA
☀️ 💧 💧 ZONES VARY   p. 162

Arctotheca calendula 🌿
CAPE WEED
☀️ ○ 💧 💧 8, 9, 13–24   p. 164

Arctotis (some) 🌿
AFRICAN DAISY
☀️ 💧 💧 7–9, 14–24   p. 164

Arenaria 🌿
SANDWORT
NEEDS VARY, 💧 2–9, 14–24   p. 164

Artemisia (several) 🌿
☀️ ○ 💧 ALL ZONES   p. 166

Asarum caudatum 🌿
WILD GINGER
● ● 💧 💧 4–6, 14–24   p. 167

Astilbe chinensis 'Pumila' 🌿
☀️ 🌤️ ● ● 💧 2–7, 14–17   p. 170

Atriplex semibaccata 🌿
AUSTRALIAN SALTBUSH
☀️ 💧 💧 8–10, 12–24   p. 171

Baccharis pilularis 🌿
DWARF COYOTE BRUSH
☀️ ○ 💧 💧 5–11, 14–24   p. 173

Bergenia 🌿
☀️ 🌤️ ● ● 💧 1–9, 12–24   p. 183

Bougainvillea 🍃
☀️ 🌤️ 💧 💧 22–24   p. 187

Calluna vulgaris (some) 🌿
SCOTCH HEATHER
☀️ 💧 💧 2–6, 15–17   p. 197

Camellia sasanqua (some) 🌿
🌤️ 💧 💧 4–9, 12, 14–24   p. 202

Campanula (some) 🌿
BELLFLOWER
☀️ 🌤️ 💧 💧 1–9, 14–24   p. 203

Carex comans 🌿
NEW ZEALAND HAIR SEDGE
☀️ 🌤️ ● ● 💧 4–9, 14–24   p. 206

Carissa macrocarpa (some) 🌿
NATAL PLUM
☀️ 🌤️ ● 💧 💧 22–24   p. 207

Carpobrotus 🌿
ICE PLANT
☀️ 💧 💧 12–24   p. 208

Ceanothus (some) 🌿
WILD LILAC
☀️ ○ 💧 💧 1–9, 14–24   p. 212

SYMBOLS: The symbols indicate whether a plant is a shrub 🌿, perennial 🌿, or vine 🍃.

Ajuga reptans

Asarum caudatum

Bergenia

Plant listings continue ▶

Carex comans

Convolvulus mauritanicus

Cornus canadensis

Corydalis lutea

Diascia 'Ruby Field'

Cephalophyllum 'Red Spike'
RED SPIKE ICE PLANT
☼ ◐ ❋ ✂ 8, 9, 11–24   **p. 217**

Cerastium tomentosum
SNOW-IN-SUMMER
☼ ◐ ❋ ✂ ALL ZONES   **p. 217**

Ceratostigma plumbaginoides
DWARF PLUMBAGO
☼ ◐ ❋ ✂ 2–10, 14–24   **p. 218**

Cissus (some)
NEEDS, ZONES VARY   **p. 228**

Cistus (some)
ROCKROSE
☼ ◐ ✂ 7–9, 12–24   **p. 229**

Convolvulus mauritanicus
GROUND MORNING GLORY
☼ ◐ ❋ 4–9, 12–24   **p. 239**

Coprosma kirkii
☼ ◐ ❋ ✂ 14–17, 21–24   **p. 239**

Cornus canadensis
BUNCHBERRY
● ❋ ✂ 1–7   **p. 242**

Correa pulchella
☼ ◐ ❋ ✂ 14–24   **p. 244**

Corydalis
◐ ❋ ✂ 4–9, 14–24   **p. 244**

Cotoneaster (some)
☼ ◐ ❋ ✂ ZONES VARY   **p. 245**

Cotula squalida
NEW ZEALAND BRASS BUTTONS
☼ ◐ ❋ ✂ 4–9, 14–24   **p. 246**

Cymbalaria muralis
KENILWORTH IVY
● ❋ ✂ 3–24   **p. 254**

Dampiera diversifolia
☼ ❋ ✂ 15–24   **p. 258**

Delosperma
ICE PLANT
☼ ◐ ❋ ✂ ZONES VARY   **p. 260**

Diascia
TWINSPUR
☼ ◐ ❋ ✂ ZONES VARY   **p. 262**

Drosanthemum
☼ ❋ ✂ 14–24   **p. 268**

Dryas
☼ ❋ ✂ 1–6   **p. 268**

Duchesnea indica
INDIAN MOCK STRAWBERRY
☼ ◐ ❋ ✂ ALL ZONES   **p. 268**

Dymondia margaretae
☼ ❋ ✂ 15–24   **p. 269**

Epimedium
◐ ❋ ✂ 1–9, 14–17   **p. 273**

Erica (some)
HEATH
☼ ❋ ✂ ZONES VARY   **p. 275**

Erigeron karvinskianus
SANTA BARBARA DAISY
☼ ◐ ❋ ✂ 8, 9, 12–24   **p. 275**

Erodium reichardii
CRANESBILL
☼ ◐ ❋ ✂ 7–9, 14–24   **p. 278**

Euonymus fortunei (varieties)
WINTER CREEPER
☼ ◐ ❋ ✂ 1–17   **p. 288**

Festuca
FESCUE
☼ ◐ ❋ ✂ ALL ZONES   **p. 293**

Fragaria chiloensis
WILD STRAWBERRY
☼ ◐ ❋ ✂ 4–24   **p. 298**

Galium odoratum
SWEET WOODRUFF
● ❋ ◐ ✂ 1–6, 15–17   **p. 302**

Gaultheria (some)
◐ ❋ ✂ ZONES VARY   **p. 303**

Gazania
☼ ❋ ✂ 8–24   **p. 304**

Gelsemium sempervirens
CAROLINA JESSAMINE
☼ ❋ ✂ 8–24   **p. 304**

Genista (some)
BROOM
☼ ◐ ✂ ZONES VARY   **p. 304**

Geranium
CRANESBILL
NEEDS, ZONES VARY   **p. 305**

Glechoma hederacea
GROUND IVY
☼ ◐ ● ❋ ✂ ALL ZONES   **p. 308**

Gypsophila repens
☼ ❋ ✂ 1–11, 14–16, 18–21   **p. 314**

Halimium
☼ ❋ ✂ 7–9, 12–24   **p. 316**

Hedera
IVY
NEEDS, ZONES VARY   **p. 317**

Helianthemum nummularium
SUNROSE
☼ ❋ ✂ ALL ZONES   **p. 318**

Epimedium

Euonymus fortunei

Festuca cinerea

Fragaria chiloensis

Galium odoratum

For growing symbol explanations, please see page 45.

Lonicera japonica

Helianthemum nummularium

Houttuynia cordata 'Variegata'

Lantana

Lysimachia nummularia

Hibbertia scandens
GUINEA GOLD VINE
☼ ◐ ● ✔ 16, 17, 21–24   p. 322

Houttuynia cordata 'Variegata'
☼ ◐ ● ◖ ✔ 1–9, 14–24   p. 325

Hypericum (low-growing)
ST. JOHNSWORT
☼ ◐ ● ● ✔ 4–24   p. 328

Jasminum (some)
JASMINE
☼ ◐ ● ✔ ZONES VARY   p. 336

Juniperus (low-growing)
JUNIPER
☼ ◐ ◊ ● ● ✔ ALL ZONES   p. 338

Lamium maculatum (several)
DEAD NETTLE
● ◖ ✔ ALL ZONES   p. 346

Lampranthus
ICE PLANT
☼ ◊ ● ✔ 14–24   p. 346

Lantana (some)
☼ ● ● ✔ 8–10, 12–22   p. 347

Laurentia fluviatilis
BLUE STAR CREEPER
☼ ◊ ● ✔ 4, 5, 8, 9, 14–24   p. 348

Leucothoe fontanesiana
DROOPING LEUCOTHOE
◖ ✔ 4–7, 15–17   p. 353

Liriope spicata
CREEPING LILY TURF
☼ ◐ ● ● ◖ ✔ ALL ZONES   p. 358

Lonicera japonica
JAPANESE HONEYSUCKLE
☼ ◐ ● ✔ 2–24   p. 361

Lotus berthelotii
PARROT'S BEAK
☼ ◐ ● ✔ 9, 15–24   p. 361

Lysimachia
☼ ◐ ● ● ✔ ZONES VARY   p. 363

Mahonia (some)
NEEDS, ZONES VARY   p. 371

Malephora
ICE PLANT
☼ ◊ ✔ ZONES VARY   p. 372

Mazus reptans
☼ ◐ ● ✔ 14–24   p. 376

Muehlenbeckia
WIRE VINE
☼ ◐ ● ✔ ZONES VARY   p. 384

Myoporum parvifolium
☼ ◐ ● ● ✔ 8, 9, 12–16, 18–24   p. 385

Nepeta faassenii
CATMINT
☼ ◐ ● ● ✔ ALL ZONES   p. 389

Nierembergia
CUP FLOWER
☼ ● ✔ ZONES VARY   p. 391

Oenothera (many)
EVENING PRIMROSE
☼ ● ✔ ZONES VARY   p. 392

Ophiopogon japonicus
MONDO GRASS
☼ ◐ ● ● ◖ ✔ 5–10, 12–24   p. 358

Origanum (many)
NEEDS, ZONES VARY   p. 395

Oscularia
☼ ● ✔ 15–24   p. 396

Osteospermum fruticosum
TRAILING AFRICAN DAISY
☼ ● ✔ 8, 9, 12–24   p. 397

Oxalis oregana
REDWOOD SORREL
● ◐ ● ✔ 4–9, 14–24   p. 397

Pachysandra terminalis
JAPANESE SPURGE
☼ ◐ ● ◖ ✔ 1–10, 14–21   p. 398

Paxistima canbyi
☼ ◐ ● ● ✔ 1–10, 14–21   p. 402

Pelargonium peltatum
IVY GERANIUM
☼ ◐ ● ● ✔ 8, 9, 12–24   p. 400

Penstemon (low-growing)
BEARD TONGUE
☼ ◐ ● ● ✔ ZONES VARY   p. 410

Phlox (mat-forming)
☼ ◐ ● ✔ ZONES VARY   p. 414

Plecostachys serpyllifolia
☼ ● ✔ 8, 9, 14–24   p. 427

Polygonum (several)
KNOTWEED
NEEDS, ZONES VARY   p. 432

Potentilla (several)
CINQUEFOIL
☼ ◐ ● ✔ ZONES VARY   p. 435

Pratia angulata
☼ ◐ ● ● ● ✔ 4–9, 14–24   p. 436

Prunella
SELF-HEAL
☼ ◐ ● ✔ ALL ZONES   p. 439

Pulmonaria (several)
LUNGWORT
◐ ● ● ✔ 1–9, 14–17   p. 445

Nepeta faassenii

Ophiopogon japonicus

Oenothera berlandieri 'Siskiyou'

Oxalis oregana

Phlox subulata

Plant listings continue ▶

BASIC LANDSCAPING

117

Potentilla

Rosmarinus officinalis 'Prostratus'

Pratia angulata

Sarcococca hookerana humilis

Soleirolia soleirolii

Pyracantha (low-growing)
FIRETHORN
☼ ◑ ◐ ☀ ✂ ZONES VARY   **p. 446**

Ranunculus repens 'Pleniflorus'
CREEPING BUTTERCUP
◑ ● ● ◐ ALL ZONES   **p. 450**

Rhoicissus capensis
EVERGREEN GRAPE
☼ ◑ ◐ ✂ 16, 17, 21–24   **p. 459**

Ribes viburnifolium
EVERGREEN CURRANT
☼ ◑ ◯ ◐ ✂ 8, 9, 14–24   **p. 461**

Rosmarinus officinalis (low)
ROSEMARY
☼ ◯ ◐ ✂ 4–24   **p. 469**

Rubus pentalobus
☼ ◑ ◐ ✂ 4–6, 14–17   **p. 469**

Sagina subulata
IRISH MOSS, SCOTCH MOSS
☼ ◑ ◐ ✂ 1–11, 14–24   **p. 471**

Saponaria ocymoides
☼ ◐ ✂ ALL ZONES   **p. 476**

Sarcococca hookerana humilis
◑ ● ◐ ◐ ✂ 4–9, 14–24   **p. 477**

Saxifraga
SAXIFRAGE
NEEDS, ZONES VARY   **p. 477**

Scaevola
☼ ◐ ✂ 8, 9, 14–24   **p. 478**

Sedum (many)
STONECROP
NEEDS, ZONES VARY   **p. 481**

Senecio mandraliscae
NEEDS VARY, ✂ 12, 13, 16, 17, 21–24   **p. 483**

Senecio serpens
☼ ◑ ◐ ◐ ✂ 16, 17, 21–24   **p. 483**

Soleirolia soleirolii
BABY'S TEARS
◑ ● ◐ ◐ ◐ ✂ 4–24   **p. 488**

Sollya heterophylla
AUSTRALIAN BLUEBELL CREEPER
☼ ◑ ◐ ◐ ✂ 8, 9, 14–24   **p. 488**

Taxus baccata 'Repandens'
SPREADING ENGLISH YEW
☼ ◑ ◐ ● ✂ 3–9, 14–24   **p. 502**

Tetrastigma voinieranum
◐ ◐ ✂ 13, 17, 20–24   **p. 503**

Teucrium chamaedrys
GERMANDER
☼ ◐ ✂ ALL ZONES   **p. 504**

Thymus
THYME
☼ ◑ ◐ ✂ ALL ZONES   **p. 506**

Tolmiea menziesii
PIGGY-BACK PLANT
◑ ● ◐ ◐ ◐ ✂ 5–9, 12–24   **p. 507**

Trachelospermum
STAR JASMINE
☼ ◑ ◐ ◐ ✂ ZONES VARY   **p. 509**

Vaccinium vitis-idaea
COWBERRY
◑ ◐ ✂ 2–7, 14–17   **p. 516**

Vancouveria
◑ ◐ ◐ ✂ ZONES VARY   **p. 516**

Verbena
NEEDS, ZONES VARY   **p. 517**

Veronica (several)
SPEEDWELL
☼ ◐ ✂ ALL ZONES   **p. 517**

Vinca
PERIWINKLE
◑ ● ◐ ✂ ZONES VARY   **p. 519**

Viola (several)
VIOLET
☼ ◐ ✂ ZONES VARY   **p. 519**

WALK-ON LAWN SUBSTITUTES

Arenaria
SANDWORT
NEEDS VARY, ✂ 2–9, 14–24   **p. 164**

Carex flacca
BLUE SEDGE
☼ ◑ ◐ ◐ ✂ 4–9, 14–24   **p. 206**

Chamaemelum nobile
CHAMOMILE
☼ ◐ ◐ ✂ ALL ZONES   **p. 221**

Cotula squalida
NEW ZEALAND BRASS BUTTONS
☼ ◑ ◐ ✂ 4–9, 14–24   **p. 246**

Hippocrepis comosa (mat-forming)
☼ ◐ ✂ 8–24   **p. 324**

Laurentia fluviatilis
BLUE STAR CREEPER
☼ ◐ ◐ ✂ 4, 5, 8, 9, 14–24   **p. 348**

Phyla nodiflora
LIPPIA
☼ ◐ ◐ ✂ 8–24   **p. 416**

Sagina subulata (mat-forming)
IRISH MOSS, SCOTCH MOSS
☼ ◑ ◐ ✂ 1–11, 14–24   **p. 471**

Zoysia tenuifolia
KOREAN GRASS
☼ ◑ ◐ ◐ ◐ ✂ 8, 9, 12–24   **p. 528**

Teucrium chamaedrys

Thymus praecox arcticus

Vancouveria planipetala

Vinca minor

Chamaemelum nobile

For growing symbol explanations, please see page 45.

Bougainvillea and nasturtium

VINES

and Vinelike Plants

Vines are some of the most tractable of plants. Unlike shrubs and trees, which have fairly inflexible growth habits, most vines can be guided to grow where you want them to. You can train a vine to grow upward or outward (or both) on a flat, vertical surface; up and around a post or tree trunk; or up and over a pergola. Many will perform alternative duty as a ground cover.

Though vines are all flexible and long limbed, they climb in different manners: some with tendrils, some by twining, some by clinging. Some have no means of attachment at all; they will climb only if you tie them to a support.

Lonicera sempervirens

Clytostoma callistegioides

Distictis buccinatoria

EVERGREEN

Plant	Common name	Zones	Page
Anemopaegma chamberlaynii ✱	YELLOW TRUMPET VINE	15–17, 19, 21–24	p. 151
Beaumontia grandiflora ✱	EASTER LILY VINE	12, 13, 16, 17, 21–24	p. 180
Bougainvillea ✱		22–24	p. 187
Cissus		NEEDS, ZONES VARY	p. 228
Clematis armandii ✱	EVERGREEN CLEMATIS	1–6, 15–17	p. 233
Clerodendrum thomsoniae ✱	BLEEDING HEART GLORYBOWER	22–24	p. 235
Clytostoma callistegioides ✱	VIOLET TRUMPET VINE	9, 12–24	p. 236
Distictis ✱	TRUMPET VINE	ZONES VARY	p. 265
Euonymus fortunei		1–17	p. 288
Ficus pumila	CREEPING FIG	8–24	p. 295
Gelsemium sempervirens ✱	CAROLINA JESSAMINE	8–24	p. 304
Hardenbergia ✱		ZONES VARY	p. 316
Hedera (many)	IVY	NEEDS, ZONES VARY	p. 317
Hibbertia scandens ✱	GUINEA GOLD VINE	16, 17, 21–24	p. 322
Jasminum (several) ✱	JASMINE	ZONES VARY	p. 336
Lapageria rosea ✱	CHILEAN BELLFLOWER	5, 6, 15–17, 23, 24	p. 347
Lonicera (several) ✱	HONEYSUCKLE	ZONES VARY	p. 360
Macfadyena unguis-cati ✱	CAT'S CLAW	8–24	p. 364
Mandevilla 'Alice du Pont' ✱		21–24	p. 375
Millettia reticulata ✱	EVERGREEN WISTERIA	20–24	p. 381
Muehlenbeckia complexa	MATTRESS VINE	8, 9, 14–24	p. 384
Pandorea ✱		16–24	p. 399
Passiflora ✱	PASSION VINE	ZONES VARY	p. 401
Petrea volubilis ✱	QUEEN'S WREATH	19–24	p. 412
Plumbago auriculata ✱	CAPE PLUMBAGO	8, 9, 12–24	p. 428

SYMBOLS: ✱ indicates vines that bear showy flowers; ⟳ indicates perennial vines that are grown as annuals.

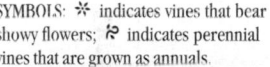

Pandorea jasminoides

Passiflora caerulea

Stephanotis floribunda

Plant listings continue ▶

Thunbergia gregorii

Trachelospermum jasminoides

Akebia quinata

Clematis

Parthenocissus tricuspidata

Podranea ricasoliana ✳
PINK TRUMPET VINE
☼ ● ● ⚡ 9, 12, 13, 19–24   **p. 431**

Polygonum aubertii ✳
SILVER LACE VINE
☼ ● ● ⚡ 8, 9, 13–24   **p. 432**

Pyrostegia venusta ✳
FLAME VINE
☼ ◐ ● ⚡ 13, 16, 21–24   **p. 447**

Rhoicissus capensis ✳
EVERGREEN GRAPE
☼ ◐ ● ⚡ 16, 17, 21–24   **p.459**

Solandra maxima ✳
CUP-OF-GOLD VINE
☼ ● ⚡ 17, 21–24   **p. 487**

Solanum jasminoides ✳
POTATO VINE
☼ ◐ ● ● ⚡ 8, 9, 12–24   **p. 487**

Stephanotis floribunda ✳
MADAGASCAR JASMINE
◐ ● ⚡ 23, 24   **p. 493**

Stigmaphyllon ciliatum ✳
ORCHID VINE
◐ ● ● ⚡ 19–24   **p. 493**

Tecomaria capensis ✳
CAPE HONEYSUCKLE
☼ ◐ ● ● ⚡ 12, 13, 16, 18–24   **p. 503**

Thunbergia ✳
☼ ◐ ● ⚡ ZONES VARY   **p. 505**

Trachelospermum ✳
STAR JASMINE
☼ ◐ ● ● ⚡ ZONES VARY   **p. 509**

DECIDUOUS

Actinidia
KIWI
☼ ◐ ● ● ⚡ ZONES VARY   **p. 139**

Akebia quinata ✳
FIVELEAF AKEBIA
☼ ◐ ● ● ● ⚡ ALL ZONES   **p. 144**

Ampelopsis brevipedunculata
BLUEBERRY CLIMBER
☼ ◐ ● ● ● ⚡ ALL ZONES   **p. 150**

Antigonon leptopus ✳
QUEEN'S WREATH
☼ ● ● ● ⚡ 12, 13, 18–21   **p. 154**

Campsis ✳
TRUMPET VINE
☼ ● ● ⚡ ZONES VARY   **p. 203**

Celastrus
BITTERSWEET
☼ ● ⚡ 1–7   **p. 215**

Clematis (most) ✳
☼ ● ⚡ 1–6, 15–17   **p. 233**

Grape
☼ ● ⚡ ZONES VARY   **p. 310**

Humulus lupulus ✳
COMMON HOP
☼ ● ⚡ ALL ZONES   **p. 326**

Hydrangea anomala ✳
CLIMBING HYDRANGEA
☼ ◐ ● ⚡ 1–21   **p. 327**

Ipomoea ✳
MORNING GLORY
☼ ● ⚡ ZONES VARY   **p. 332**

Mandevilla laxa ✳
CHILEAN JASMINE
☼ ● ⚡ 4–9, 14–21   **p. 375**

Parthenocissus
☼ ◐ ● ● ⚡ ZONES VARY   **p. 401**

Rosa (climbers) ✳
ROSE
NEEDS, ZONES VARY   **p. 462**

Solanum wendlandii ✳
COSTA RICAN NIGHTSHADE
☼ ◐ ● ● ⚡ 16, 21–24   **p. 488**

Vigna caracalla ✳
SNAIL VINE
☼ ● ⚡ 12–24   **p. 519**

Wisteria ✳
☼ ◐ ● ● ⚡ ALL ZONES   **p. 523**

ANNUALS

Asarina ✳
CLIMBING SNAPDRAGON
☼ ◐ ● ⚡ ALL ZONES   **p. 167**

Bean, scarlet runner ✳
☼ ● ⚡ ALL ZONES   **p. 180**

Cardiospermum halicacabum ✳
LOVE-IN-A-PUFF
☼ ● ● ⚡ ALL ZONES   **p. 206**

Cobaea scandens ✳
CUP-AND-SAUCER VINE
☼ ● ⚡ ALL ZONES   **p. 236**

Dolichos lablab ✳
HYACINTH BEAN
☼ ● ⚡ ALL ZONES   **p. 266**

Ipomoea (some) ✳
MORNING GLORY
☼ ● ⚡ ZONES VARY   **p. 332**

Lathyrus odoratus ✳
SWEET PEA
☼ ● ⚡ ALL ZONES   **p. 348**

Tropaeolum ✳
NASTURTIUM
☼ ◐ ● ⚡ ALL ZONES   **p. 512**

Vigna caracalla

Wisteria floribunda

Ipomoea

Tropaeolum majus

Tropaeolum peregrinum

For growing symbol explanations, please see page 45.

Nandina domestica

Chaenomeles

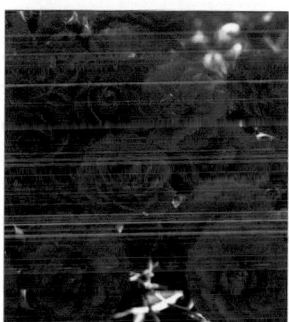

Rosa 'Showbiz'

Abelia grandiflora

Arbutus unedo

Plants for
HEDGES AND SCREENS

Plants that have foliage from the ground up are good candidates for providing a screen in your landscape. Some are knee-high shrublets, mainly useful for edging a walk or path; others are large shrubby trees that, grouped closely, can block an objectionable view or direct your attention to a focal point in the garden. Shearing can transform some plants into formal hedges.

DECIDUOUS

Berberis (some)
BARBERRY
☼ ◑ ◐ ◗ ✄ ALL ZONES   p. 182

Carpinus betulus ♦♦♦
EUROPEAN HORNBEAM
☼ ◗ ✄ 3–9, 14–17   p. 208

Chaenomeles
FLOWERING QUINCE
☼ ◗ ✄ 1–21   p. 220

Crataegus monogyna ♦♦♦
HAWTHORN
☼ ◗ ✄ 1–12, 14–17   p. 248

Elaeagnus angustifolia
RUSSIAN OLIVE
☼ ◑ ◐ ◗ ✄ 1–3, 7–14, 18, 19   p. 271

Ligustrum (some) ♦♦♦
PRIVET
☼ ◑ ◗ ✄ ZONES VARY   p. 354

Rhamnus frangula 'Columnaris' ♦♦♦
TALLHEDGE BUCKTHORN
☼ ◑ ◐ ◗ ✄ 1–7, 10–13   p. 453

Rosa (shrub)
ROSE
NEEDS, ZONES VARY   p. 466

Salix purpurea 'Gracilis'
DWARF PURPLE OSIER
☼ ◐ ◗ ✄ ALL ZONES   p. 472

Viburnum opulus 'Nanum'
EUROPEAN CRANBERRY BUSH
☼ ◑ ◗ ✄ 1–9, 14–24   p. 518

Weigela
☼ ◑ ◗ ✄ 1–11, 14–17   p. 523

EVERGREEN

Abelia grandiflora
GLOSSY ABELIA
☼ ◑ ◗ ✄ 5–24   p. 130

Arbutus unedo
STRAWBERRY TREE
☼ ◑ ◐ ◗ ✄ 4–24   p. 162

Bamboo (many)
☼ ◗ ✄ ZONES VARY   p. 174

Berberis (some)
BARBERRY
☼ ◑ ◗ ◐ ◗ ✄ ALL ZONES   p. 182

Buxus ♦♦♦
BOXWOOD
☼ ◑ ◐ ◗ ✄ ZONES VARY   p. 193

Callistemon (some) ♦♦♦
BOTTLEBRUSH
☼ ◗ ✄ 8, 9, 12–24   p. 197

Carissa ♦♦♦
☼ ◑ ◐ ◗ ✄ 22–24   p. 207

Chamaecyparis lawsoniana (several)
☼ ◑ ◐ ◗ ✄ 4–6, 15–17   p. 220

Choisya ternata
MEXICAN ORANGE
☼ ◑ ◐ ◗ ✄ 7–9, 12–24   p. 225

Cocculus laurifolius
☼ ◑ ◐ ◗ ✄ 8, 9, 12–24   p. 236

Cotoneaster (some)
☼ ◐ ◗ ✄ ZONES VARY   p. 245

Cupressus (most) ♦♦♦
CYPRESS
☼ ◐ ✄ ZONES VARY   p. 252

Dodonaea viscosa
HOP BUSH
☼ ◑ ◐ ◐ ◗ ✄ 7–9, 12–24   p. 266

Elaeagnus (some) ♦♦♦
☼ ◑ ◐ ◗ ✄ ZONES VARY   p. 271

Escallonia ♦♦♦
☼ ◑ ◐ ◐ ◗ ✄ 4–9, 14–17, 20–24   p. 280

SYMBOL: ♦♦♦ indicates plants that can be clipped into formal hedges.

Callistemon citrinus

Choisya ternata

Escallonia exoniensis 'Fradesii'

Grewia occidentalis

Plant listings continue ▶

Hibiscus rosa-sinensis

Ilex

Leptospermum

Ligustrum japonicum

Myrtus communis

Euonymus (most)
☼ ◑ ◐ ✿ ZONES VARY   p. 288

Feijoa sellowiana
PINEAPPLE GUAVA
☼ ◐ ◐ ✿ 7–9, 12–24   p. 292

Gardenia jasminoides
☼ ◐ ✿ 7–9, 12–16, 18–23   p. 302

Garrya elliptica
COAST SILKTASSEL
☼ ◑ ◐ ◐ ✿ 5–9, 14–21   p. 303

Grevillea rosmarinifolia
ROSEMARY GREVILLEA
☼ ◐ ◐ ✿ 8, 9, 12–24   p. 313

Grewia occidentalis
LAVENDER STARFLOWER
☼ ◐ ✿ 8, 9, 12–24   p. 313

Heteromeles arbutifolia
TOYON
☼ ◑ ◐ ◐ ✿ 5–24   p. 321

Hibiscus rosa-sinensis
CHINESE HIBISCUS
☼ ◐ ✿ 9, 12, 13, 15, 16, 19–24   p. 323

Ilex
HOLLY
☼ ◑ ◐ ◐ ✿ ZONES VARY   p. 329

Juniperus (shrub, columnar)
JUNIPER
☼ ◑ ◐ ◐ ◐ ✿ ALL ZONES   p. 338

Leptospermum (most)
TEA TREE
☼ ◐ ◐ ✿ 14–24   p. 350

Leucophyllum frutescens
TEXAS RANGER
☼ ◐ ✿ 7–24   p. 352

Ligustrum (some)
PRIVET
☼ ◑ ◐ ◐ ✿ ZONES VARY   p. 354

Mahonia (tall)
NEEDS, ZONES VARY   p. 371

Murraya paniculata
ORANGE JESSAMINE
◑ ◐ ✿ 21–24   p. 384

Myrica californica
PACIFIC WAX MYRTLE
☼ ◐ ✿ 4–6, 14–17, 20–24   p. 385

Myrsine africana
AFRICAN BOXWOOD
☼ ◑ ◐ ◐ ✿ 8, 9, 14–24   p. 386

Myrtus communis
TRUE MYRTLE
☼ ◑ ◐ ✿ 8–24   p. 386

Nandina domestica
HEAVENLY BAMBOO
☼ ◑ ◐ ◐ ◐ ◐ ✿ 5–24   p. 386

Nerium oleander
OLEANDER
☼ ◐ ◐ ✿ 8–16, 18–24   p. 390

Osmanthus (several)
☼ ◑ ◐ ◐ ✿ ZONES VARY   p. 396

Photinia
☼ ◐ ◐ ✿ ZONES VARY   p. 416

Pittosporum (several)
☼ ◑ ◐ ◐ ✿ ZONES VARY   p. 425

Podocarpus
☼ ◑ ◐ ◐ ✿ ZONES VARY   p. 431

Prunus (evergreen)
NEEDS, ZONES VARY   p. 439

Pyracantha
FIRETHORN
☼ ◐ ◐ ✿ ZONES VARY   p. 446

Rhamnus alaternus
ITALIAN BUCKTHORN
☼ ◑ ◐ ◐ ◐ ✿ 4–24   p. 452

Rhaphiolepis
☼ ◑ ◐ ◐ ✿ 8–10, 12–24   p. 453

Rosmarinus officinalis
ROSEMARY
☼ ◐ ◐ ✿ 4–24   p. 469

Syzygium paniculatum
BRUSH CHERRY
☼ ◑ ◐ ◐ ✿ 16, 17, 19–24   p. 500

Taxus
YEW
☼ ◑ ● ◐ ◐ ✿ 3–9, 14–24   p. 502

Tecomaria capensis
CAPE HONEYSUCKLE
☼ ◐ ◐ ✿ 12, 13, 16, 18–24   p. 503

Thevetia
☼ ◐ ✿ ZONES VARY   p. 504

Thuja
ARBORVITAE
☼ ◑ ◐ ◐ ◐ ◐ ✿ ZONES VARY   p. 505

Umbellularia californica
CALIFORNIA LAUREL
☼ ◐ ◐ ✿ 4–10, 12–24   p. 515

Vaccinium ovatum
EVERGREEN HUCKLEBERRY
◑ ◐ ✿ 4–7, 14–17   p. 516

Viburnum (several)
NEEDS, ZONES VARY   p. 518

Xylosma congestum
☼ ◐ ◐ ◐ ✿ 8–24   p. 525

Photinia fraseri

Nerium oleander

Tecomaria capensis

Viburnum tinus

Xylosma congestum

For growing symbol explanations, please see page 45.

Woodland at Butchart Gardens

TREES

Acer griseum

Acer davidii

The best trees are well suited to their sites. Patio trees are generally small, as trees go, and look good at close range. Many have showy displays of flowers, fruit, or both; some have striking fall foliage or decorative bark. All are "well mannered": root systems are not likely to crack pavement; branches do not shed lots of leaves or drop messy fruit to litter or stain patios.

All patio trees are fine candidates for garden planting, but the list of garden trees includes others not suitable as patio trees. Some may shed leaves or fruit that would require frequent cleanup on a patio but pose no problem in a garden. Others may have roots that could crack paving.

Large landscape trees are generally too massive for small gardens, but are worth planting where there is room for them to grow. Some of them make fine windbreaks.

PATIO TREES
Deciduous

Acer buergeranum
TRIDENT MAPLE
☼ ◐ ◖ ✄ 4–9, 14–17, 20, 21   **p. 135**

Acer circinatum
VINE MAPLE
☼ ◐ ◖ ✄ 1–6, 14–17   **p. 135**

Acer davidii
DAVID'S MAPLE
☼ ◐ ◖ ✄ 1–6, 15–17, 20, 21   **p. 136**

Acer ginnala
AMUR MAPLE
☼ ◐ ◖ ✄ 1–9, 14–16   **p. 136**

Acer griseum
PAPERBARK MAPLE
☼ ◐ ◖ ✄ 1–9, 14–21   **p. 136**

Acer palmatum
JAPANESE MAPLE
☼ ◐ ◖ ✄ 1–10, 12, 14–24   **p. 136**

Amelanchier
SERVICEBERRY
☼ ◖ ✄ 1–6   **p. 150**

Bauhinia blakeana
HONG KONG ORCHID TREE
☼ ◖ ✄ 13, 19, 21, 23   **p. 179**

Bauhinia forficata
BRAZILIAN BUTTERFLY TREE
☼ ◐ ◖ ✄ 9, 12–23   **p. 179**

Bauhinia variegata
PURPLE ORCHID TREE
☼ ◖ ✄ 13, 18–23   **p. 179**

Cercidium
PALO VERDE
☼ ◖ ◖ ✄ 10–14, 18–20   **p. 218**

Cercis
REDBUD
NEEDS, ZONES VARY   **p. 218**

Chilopsis linearis
DESERT WILLOW
☼ ◖ ✄ 10–13, 18–21   **p. 223**

Chionanthus
FRINGE TREE
☼ ◖ ✄ ZONES VARY   **p. 224**

Chitalpa tashkentensis
CHITALPA
☼ ◖ ✄ 3–24   **p. 224**

Chorisia speciosa
☼ ◖ ✄ 12–24   **p. 225**

Cladrastis lutea
YELLOW WOOD
☼ ◖ ✄ 1–9, 14–16   **p. 233**

Cornus florida
FLOWERING DOGWOOD
☼ ◐ ◖ ✄ 1–9, 14–16   **p. 242**

Cornus kousa
KOUSA DOGWOOD
☼ ◐ ◖ ✄ 3–9, 14, 15, 18, 19   **p. 242**

Corylus (most)
FILBERT, HAZELNUT
☼ ◐ ◖ ✄ 1–9, 14–20   **p. 244**

Cotinus coggygria
SMOKE TREE
☼ ◖ ✄ ALL ZONES   **p. 245**

Crataegus
HAWTHORN
☼ ◖ ✄ 1–12, 14–17   **p. 247**

Davidia involucrata
DOVE TREE
☼ ◐ ◖ ✄ 4–9, 14–21   **p. 259**

Erythrina (most)
CORAL TREE
☼ ◖ ✄ ZONES VARY   **p. 279**

Franklinia alatamaha
☼ ◐ ◖ ◖ ✄ 2–6, 14–17   **p. 298**

SYMBOL: ▐◀ indicates plants whose roots may be invasive or break concrete.

Chilopsis linearis

Chionanthus retusus

Chitalpa tashkentensis

Plant listings continue ▶

Cornus kousa

Cotinus coggygria

Crataegus laevigata 'Paul's Scarlet'

Erythrina falcata

Halesia carolina
SILVER BELL
☼ ◑ ♦ ✂ 2–9, 14–24   **p. 315**

Koelreuteria

NEEDS, ZONES VARY   **p. 344**

Lagerstroemia indica hybrids
CRAPE MYRTLE
☼ ♦ ✂ ALL ZONES   **p. 345**

Lysiloma microphylla thornberi
FEATHER BUSH
☼ ◊ ✂ 10, 12–24   **p. 363**

Magnolia (small)

☼ ◑ ♦ ✂ ZONES VARY   **p. 365**

Malus
CRABAPPLE
☼ ♦ ✂ 1–21   **p. 372**

Oxydendrum arboreum
SOURWOOD
☼ ♦ ✂ 3–9, 14–17   **p. 397**

Parrotia persica
PERSIAN PARROTIA
☼ ♦ ♦ ✂ 4–6, 15–17   **p. 400**

Pistacia chinensis
CHINESE PISTACHE
☼ ◊ ♦ ♦ ✂ 4–16, 18–23   **p. 425**

Prunus
FLOWERING CHERRY
☼ ♦ ♦ ✂ 4–6, 15–17   **p. 441**

Prunus cerasifera 'Purple Pony'

☼ ♦ ✂ 2–22   **p. 442**

Prunus mume
JAPANESE FLOWERING PLUM
☼ ♦ ✂ 2–9, 12–22   **p. 443**

Pyrus
ORNAMENTAL PEAR
☼ ♦ ✂ ZONES VARY   **p. 447**

Sapium sebiferum
CHINESE TALLOW TREE
☼ ♦ ✂ 8, 9, 12–16, 18–21   **p. 476**

Stewartia (small)

☼ ◑ ♦ ♦ ✂ 4–6, 14–17, 20, 21   **p. 493**

Tabebuia

☼ ♦ ✂ 15, 16, 20–24   **p. 500**

PATIO TREES
Evergreen

Acacia aneura
MULGA
☼ ◊ ♦ ✂ 8, 9, 12–24   **p. 132**

Acacia craspedocarpa

☼ ◊ ♦ ✂ 8, 9, 12–24   **p. 132**

Acacia podalyriifolia
PEARL ACACIA
☼ ◊ ♦ ✂ 8, 9, 13–24   **p. 133**

Cassia leptophylla
GOLD MEDALLION TREE
☼ ♦ ✂ 21–24   **p. 210**

Citrus
☼ ♦ ✂ 8, 9, 12–24   **p. 230**

Clethra arborea
LILY-OF-THE-VALLEY TREE
☼ ◑ ♦ ✂ 15–17, 21–24   **p. 235**

Cocculus laurifolius

☼ ◑ ♦ ♦ ✂ 8, 9, 12–24   **p. 236**

Cordia boissieri
TEXAS OLIVE
☼ ◑ ♦ ♦ ✂ 8–24   **p. 240**

Cupressus (some)
CYPRESS
☼ ♦ ✂ ZONES VARY   **p. 252**

Dodonaea viscosa
HOP BUSH
☼ ◑ ◊ ♦ ✂ 7–9, 12–24   **p. 266**

Drimys winteri
WINTER'S BARK
☼ ♦ ♦ ✂ 8, 9, 14–24   **p. 267**

Eriobotrya deflexa
BRONZE LOQUAT
☼ ◑ ♦ ✂ 8–24   **p. 275**

Eucalyptus campaspe
SILVER-TOPPED GIMLET
☼ ◊ ♦ ✂ SEE CHART   **p. 282**

Eucalyptus formanii

☼ ◊ ♦ ✂ SEE CHART   **p. 283**

Eucalyptus leucoxylon 'Rosea'

☼ ◊ ♦ ✂ SEE CHART   **p. 284**

Eucalyptus spathulata
SWAMP MALLEE
☼ ◊ ♦ ✂ SEE CHART   **p. 286**

Eucalyptus torquata
CORAL GUM
☼ ◊ ♦ ✂ SEE CHART   **p. 286**

Geijera parviflora
AUSTRALIAN WILLOW
☼ ◊ ♦ ✂ 8, 9, 12–24   **p. 304**

Hakea laurina
PINCUSHION TREE
☼ ◊ ✂ 9, 12–17, 19–24   **p. 315**

Heteromeles arbutifolia
TOYON
☼ ◑ ♦ ✂ 5–24   **p. 321**

Laurus nobilis 'Saratoga'
SWEET BAY
☼ ◑ ♦ ✂ 5–9, 12–24   **p. 349**

Lagerstroemia indica

Prunus

Sapium sebiferum

Cassia leptophylla

Dodonaea viscosa
'Purpurea'

For growing symbol explanations, please see page 45.

*Laurus nobilis
'Saratoga'*

Heteromeles arbutifolia

Nerium oleander

Thevetia thevetioides

Albizia julibrissin

Leptospermum laevigatum
AUSTRALIAN TEA TREE
☼ ◊ ● ⚡ 14–24   **p. 351**

Ligustrum lucidum
GLOSSY PRIVET
☼ ◐ ● ⚡ 5, 6, 18–24   **p. 354**

Melaleuca quinquenervia
CAJEPUT TREE
☼ ◊ ● ⚡ 9, 13, 15–17, 20–24   **p. 377**

Michelia doltsopa
☼ ◐ ● ⚡ 14–24   **p. 380**

Nerium oleander
OLEANDER
☼ ● ⚡ 8–16, 18–24   **p. 390**

Olea europaea (fruitless)
OLIVE
☼ ◊ ⚡ 8, 9, 11–24   **p. 393**

Osmanthus fragrans
SWEET OLIVE
☼ ◐ ● ⚡ 8, 9, 12–24   **p. 396**

Palms (some)
NEEDS, ZONES VARY   **p. 398**

Podocarpus gracilior
FERN PINE
☼ ◐ ● ⚡ 8, 9, 12–24   **p. 431**

Pyrus
ORNAMENTAL PEAR
☼ ● ⚡ ZONES VARY   **p. 447**

Rhaphiolepis 'Majestic Beauty'
☼ ◐ ● ● ⚡ 8–10, 12–24   **p. 453**

Rhus lancea
AFRICAN SUMAC
☼ ◊ ● ● ⚡ 8, 9, 12–24   **p. 460**

Schefflera actinophylla
QUEENSLAND UMBRELLA TREE
☼ ◐ ● ⚡ 21–24   **p. 478**

Schefflera pueckleri
☼ ◐ ● ⚡ 19–24   **p. 479**

Schinus terebinthifolius
BRAZILIAN PEPPER TREE
☼ ● ⚡ 13, 15–17, 19–24   **p. 479**

Sophora secundiflora
TEXAS MOUNTAIN LAUREL
☼ ◐ ● ● ⚡ 8–16, 18–24   **p. 488**

Stenocarpus sinuatus
FIREWHEEL TREE
☼ ● ● ⚡ 16, 17, 20–24   **p. 492**

Thevetia thevetioides
GIANT THEVETIA
☼ ● ⚡ 12, 13, 22–24   **p. 504**

Tristania laurina
☼ ◊ ● ⚡ 19–24   **p. 511**

Xylosma congestum
☼ ◐ ● ● ⚡ 8–24   **p. 525**

SMALL TO MEDIUM GARDEN TREES
Deciduous

Albizia julibrissin
SILK TREE
☼ ◐ ● ⚡ 2–23   **p. 144**

Betula   ⧄
BIRCH
☼ ● ●● ⚡ ZONES VARY   **p. 183**

Brachychiton
☼ ◊ ⚡ ZONES VARY   **p. 189**

Calodendrum capense
CAPE CHESTNUT
☼ ● ⚡ 19, 21–24   **p. 199**

Carpinus
HORNBEAM
☼ ● ⚡ ZONES VARY   **p. 208**

Celtis
HACKBERRY
☼ ◐ ● ⚡ ZONES VARY   **p. 216**

Cercidiphyllum japonicum
KATSURA TREE
☼ ◐ ● ⚡ 1–6   **p. 218**

Chilopsis linearis
DESERT WILLOW
☼ ◊ ⚡ 10–13, 18–21   **p. 223**

Fraxinus angustifolia 'Raywood'
RAYWOOD ASH
☼ ● ⚡ 3–9, 12–24   **p. 299**

Fraxinus holotricha
☼ ● ⚡ 4–24   **p. 299**

Fraxinus velutina
ARIZONA ASH
☼ ● ⚡ 8, 9, 10–24   **p. 299**

Gleditsia triacanthos   ⧄
HONEY LOCUST
☼ ◊ ● ⚡ 1–16, 18–20   **p. 308**

Laburnum
GOLDENCHAIN TREE
☼ ◐ ● ⚡ 1–10, 14–17   **p. 345**

Magnolia (many)
☼ ◐ ● ⚡ ZONES VARY   **p. 365**

Morus alba   ⧄
WHITE MULBERRY
☼ ● ● ⚡ ALL ZONES   **p. 383**

Nyssa sylvatica
SOUR GUM
☼ ◊ ● ⚡ 3–10, 14–21   **p. 392**

Parkinsonia aculeata
MEXICAN PALO VERDE
☼ ◊ ⚡ 8–24   **p. 400**

Xylosma congestum

Brachychiton acerifolius

Laburnum

Magnolia soulangiana

Plant listings continue ▶

Persimmon

Punica granatum

Populus tremuloides

Styrax japonicus

Tilia cordata

| **Persimmon** | |
| NEEDS, ZONES VARY | **p. 412** |

Populus tremuloides	ℝ
QUAKING ASPEN	
☼ ◐ ✿ 1–7	**p. 434**

Prosopis	
MESQUITE	
☼ ◊ ◐ ✿ 10–13	**p. 438**

Prunus	
FLOWERING PEACH	
☼ ◐ ✿ 2–24	**p. 441**

Punica granatum	
POMEGRANATE	
☼ ◐ ✿ 5–24	**p. 445**

Sophora japonica	
JAPANESE PAGODA TREE	
☼ ◑ ◊ ◐ ✿ ALL ZONES	**p. 488**

Sorbus aucuparia	
EUROPEAN MOUNTAIN ASH	
☼ ◑ ◐ ✿ 1–10	**p. 489**

| **Styrax** | |
| NEEDS, ZONES VARY | **p. 497** |

Tilia cordata	
LITTLE-LEAF LINDEN	
☼ ◐ ✿ 1–17	**p. 507**

Tilia euchlora	
CRIMEAN LINDEN	
☼ ◐ ✿ 1–17	**p. 507**

Tipuana tipu	
TIPU TREE	
☼ ◐ ✿ 13–16, 18–24	**p. 507**

Vitex agnus-castus	
CHASTE TREE	
☼ ◐ ✿ 4–24	**p. 520**

SMALL TO MEDIUM GARDEN TREES
Evergreen

Acacia baileyana	
BAILEY ACACIA	
☼ ◊ ◐ ✿ 7–9, 13–24	**p. 132**

Acacia cognata	
BOWER WATTLE	
☼ ◊ ◐ ✿ 16–24	**p. 132**

Acacia pendula	
WEEPING ACACIA	
☼ ◊ ◐ ✿ 13–24	**p. 133**

| **Acacia smallii** | |
| ☼ ◊ ◐ ✿ 8, 9, 12–24 | **p. 134** |

Acacia stenophylla	
SHOESTRING ACACIA	
☼ ◊ ◐ ✿ 8, 9, 12–24	**p. 134**

| **Acer paxii** | |
| ☼ ◐ ◐ ✿ 8, 9, 14–24 | **p. 137** |

Agonis flexuosa	
PEPPERMINT TREE	
☼ ◐ ✿ 15–17, 20–24	**p. 143**

| **Arbutus 'Marina'** | |
| ☼ ◐ ◐ ✿ 8, 9, 14–24 | **p. 162** |

Arbutus unedo	
STRAWBERRY TREE	
☼ ◑ ◐ ◐ ✿ 4–24	**p. 162**

| **Arctostaphylos manzanita 'Dr. Hurd'** | |
| ☼ ◐ ✿ 4–9, 14–24 | **p. 163** |

Brugmansia	
ANGEL'S TRUMPET	
☼ ◑ ● ◐ ✿ 16–24	**p. 191**

Callistemon citrinus	
LEMON BOTTLEBRUSH	
☼ ◐ ✿ 8, 9, 12–24	**p. 197**

Callistemon viminalis	
WEEPING BOTTLEBRUSH	
☼ ◐ ✿ 14–24	**p. 197**

Ceratonia siliqua	ℝ
CAROB	
☼ ◐ ✿ 9, 13–16, 18–24	**p. 217**

Cornus capitata	
EVERGREEN DOGWOOD	
☼ ◑ ◐ ◐ ✿ 8, 9, 14–20	**p. 242**

Crinodendron patagua	
LILY-OF-THE-VALLEY TREE	
☼ ◐◐ ✿ 14–24	**p. 248**

Eriobotrya japonica	
LOQUAT	
☼ ◑ ◐ ✿ 4–24	**p. 275**

| **Erythrina falcata** | |
| ☼ ◐ ✿ 19–24 | **p. 280** |

Eucalyptus cornuta	
YATE	
☼ ◊ ◐ ✿ SEE CHART	**p. 282**

Eucalyptus ficifolia	
RED-FLOWERING GUM	
☼ ◊ ◐ ✿ SEE CHART	**p. 283**

Eucalyptus microtheca	
COOLIBAH	
☼ ◊ ◐ ✿ SEE CHART	**p. 284**

Eucalyptus nicholii	
NICHOL'S WILLOW-LEAFED PEPPERMINT	
☼ ◊ ◐ ✿ SEE CHART	**p. 284**

Eucalyptus polyanthemos	
SILVER DOLLAR GUM	
☼ ◊ ◐ ✿ SEE CHART	**p. 285**

Ficus benjamina	
WEEPING CHINESE BANYAN	
☼ ◑ ● ◐ ✿ 13, 23, 24	**p. 294**

Ficus microcarpa	
INDIAN LAUREL FIG	
☼ ◐ ✿ 9, 13, 16–24	**p. 295**

Brugmansia

Callistemon citrinus

Cornus capitata

Ilex

Eucalyptus ficifolia

For growing symbol explanations, please see page 45.

Maytenus boaria

Pittosporum eugenioides

Ginkgo biloba

Ficus rubiginosa
RUSTYLEAF FIG
☼ ◐ ● ● ⚡ 18–24   **p. 295**

Garrya elliptica 'James Roof'
COAST SILKTASSEL
☼ ◐ ● ⚡ 5–9, 14–21   **p. 303**

Hymenosporum flavum
SWEETSHADE
☼ ◐ ● ● ⚡ 8, 9, 14–23   **p. 328**

Ilex (many)
HOLLY
☼ ◐ ● ● ⚡ ZONES VARY   **p. 329**

Lagunaria patersonii
PRIMROSE TREE
☼ ● ● ⚡ 13, 15–24   **p. 346**

Luma apiculata
☼ ● ● ● ⚡ 14–24   **p. 362**

Magnolia (some)   ◪
☼ ◐ ● ● ⚡ ZONES VARY   **p. 365**

Maytenus boaria
MAYTEN TREE
☼ ● ● ⚡ 8, 9, 14–21   **p. 376**

Melaleuca linariifolia
FLAXLEAF PAPERBARK
☼ ○ ● ● ⚡ 9, 13–24   **p. 377**

Metrosideros excelsus   ◪
NEW ZEALAND CHRISTMAS TREE
☼ ○ ● ● ⚡ 17, 23, 24   **p. 380**

Olneya tesota
DESERT IRONWOOD
☼ ○ ⚡ 12, 13   **p. 393**

Pinus contorta
SHORE PINE
☼ ● ● ⚡ SEE CHART   **p. 421**

Pithecellobium flexicaule
TEXAS EBONY
☼ ● ● ⚡ 10–13   **p. 425**

Pittosporum (several)
☼ ◐ ● ● ⚡ ZONES VARY   **p. 425**

Prunus caroliniana
CAROLINA LAUREL CHERRY
☼ ○ ● ⚡ 7–24   **p. 439**

Tristania conferta
BRISBANE BOX
☼ ○ ● ● ⚡ 19–24   **p. 511**

Umbellularia californica
CALIFORNIA LAUREL
☼ ◐ ○ ● ⚡ 4–10, 12–24   **p. 515**

LARGE LANDSCAPE TREES
Deciduous

Acer rubrum
SCARLET MAPLE
☼ ◐ ● ● ⚡ 1–9, 14–17   **p. 137**

Fagus sylvatica
EUROPEAN BEECH
☼ ● ● ⚡ 1–9, 14–24   **p. 291**

Ginkgo biloba
MAIDENHAIR TREE
☼ ○ ● ● ⚡ 1–10, 12, 14–24   **p. 307**

Jacaranda mimosifolia
JACARANDA
☼ ● ⚡ 12, 13, 15–24   **p. 336**

Liquidambar   ◪
SWEET GUM
☼ ● ⚡ ZONES VARY   **p. 357**

Liriodendron tulipifera
TULIP TREE
☼ ● ⚡ 1–12, 14–23   **p. 357**

Platanus
SYCAMORE
☼ ● ⚡ ZONES VARY   **p. 426**

Quercus (many)
OAK
☼ ○ ● ⚡ ZONES VARY   **p. 447**

Robinia ambigua 'Idahoensis'   ◪
IDAHO LOCUST
☼ ○ ⚡ ALL ZONES   **p. 461**

Robinia pseudoacacia   ◪
BLACK LOCUST
☼ ○ ⚡ ALL ZONES   **p. 461**

Zelkova serrata
SAWLEAF ZELKOVA
☼ ● ⚡ 3–21   **p. 527**

LARGE LANDSCAPE TREES
Evergreen

Castanospermum australe
MORETON BAY CHESTNUT
☼ ● ● ⚡ 18–22   **p. 211**

Cedrus
CEDAR
☼ ○ ⚡ ZONES VARY   **p. 214**

Cinnamomum camphora   ◪
CAMPHOR TREE
☼ ● ● ⚡ 8, 9, 12–24   **p. 228**

Pinus eldarica
AFGHAN PINE
☼ ○ ● ● ⚡ SEE CHART   **p. 421**

Pinus nigra
AUSTRIAN BLACK PINE
☼ ○ ● ⚡ SEE CHART   **p. 423**

Pinus pinea
ITALIAN STONE PINE
☼ ○ ● ⚡ SEE CHART   **p. 423**

Pinus thunbergiana
JAPANESE BLACK PINE
☼ ○ ● ⚡ SEE CHART   **p. 424**

Pinus wallichiana
HIMALAYAN WHITE PINE
☼ ○ ● ⚡ SEE CHART   **p. 424**

Jacaranda mimosifolia

Liquidambar

Robinia ambigua 'Idahoensis'

Cinnamomum camphora

Plant listings continue ▶

Quercus agrifolia

Quercus suber

Elaeagnus angustifolia

Populus nigra 'Italica'

Tsuga canadensis

Quercus agrifolia
COAST LIVE OAK
☼ ◊ ● ⚡ 5, 7–24   **p. 448**

Quercus ilex
HOLLY OAK
☼ ◊ ● ⚡ 4–24   **p. 448**

Quercus suber
CORK OAK
☼ ◊ ● ⚡ 8–16, 18–23   **p. 449**

Quercus virginiana
SOUTHERN LIVE OAK
☼ ● ⚡ 4–24   **p. 449**

Sequoia sempervirens
COAST REDWOOD
☼ ● ● ● ⚡ 4–9, 14–24   **p. 483**

Tsuga canadensis
CANADA HEMLOCK
☼ ● ⚡ 3–7, 17   **p. 512**

TREES FOR WINDBREAKS
Deciduous

Acer campestre
HEDGE MAPLE
☼ ● ● ⚡ 1–9, 14   **p. 135**

Broussonetia papyrifera
PAPER MULBERRY
☼ ◊ ⚡ 3–24   **p. 191**

Elaeagnus angustifolia
RUSSIAN OLIVE
☼ ● ● ● ⚡ 1–3, 7–14, 18, 19 **p. 271**

Maclura pomifera
OSAGE ORANGE
☼ ◊ ⚡ ALL ZONES   **p. 365**

Populus alba 'Pyramidalis' ⟡
BOLLEANA POPLAR
☼ ● ⚡ ALL ZONES   **p. 434**

Populus fremontii ⟡
WESTERN COTTONWOOD
☼ ● ⚡ 7–24   **p. 434**

Populus nigra 'Italica' ⟡
LOMBARDY POPLAR
☼ ● ⚡ ALL ZONES   **p. 434**

Prosopis glandulosa torreyana
HONEY MESQUITE
☼ ◊ ● ⚡ 10–13   **p. 438**

Tamarix ⟡
TAMARISK
☼ ◊ ● ⚡ ZONES VARY   **p. 501**

Ulmus pumila ⟡
SIBERIAN ELM
☼ ● ⚡ ALL ZONES   **p. 515**

TREES FOR WINDBREAKS
Evergreen

Acacia craspedocarpa

☼ ◊ ● ⚡ 8, 9, 12–24   **p. 132**

Acacia melanoxylon
BLACKWOOD ACACIA
☼ ◊ ● ⚡ 8, 9, 13–24   **p. 133**

Calocedrus decurrens
INCENSE CEDAR
☼ ● ⚡ 1–12, 14–24   **p. 198**

Casuarina
BEEFWOOD
☼ ◊ ⚡ 8, 9, 12–24   **p. 211**

Chamaecyparis lawsoniana
PORT ORFORD CEDAR
☼ ☼ ● ⚡ 4–6, 15–17   **p. 220**

Cupressus (most)
CYPRESS
☼ ● ⚡ ZONES VARY   **p. 252**

Eucalyptus (many)
☼ ◊ ● ⚡ SEE CHART   **p. 281**

Griselinia littoralis

☼ ☼ ● ⚡ 9, 14–17, 20–24   **p. 313**

Lagunaria patersonii
PRIMROSE TREE
☼ ◊ ⚡ 13, 15–24   **p. 346**

Ligustrum lucidum
GLOSSY PRIVET
☼ ☼ ● ⚡ 5, 6, 8–24   **p. 354**

Melaleuca quinquenervia
CAJEPUT TREE
☼ ◊ ● ⚡ 9, 13, 15–17, 20–24 **p. 377**

Metrosideros excelsus ⟡
NEW ZEALAND CHRISTMAS TREE
☼ ● ⚡ 17, 23, 24   **p. 380**

Picea abies
NORWAY SPRUCE
☼ ☼ ● ⚡ 1–6, 14–17   **p. 417**

Pinus (many)
PINE
☼ ◊ ● ⚡ SEE CHART   **p. 419**

Pittosporum (except ⟡
P. phillyraeoides)
☼ ◊ ● ⚡ ZONES VARY   **p. 425**

Pseudotsuga menziesii
DOUGLAS FIR
☼ ◊ ● ● ⚡ 1–10, 14–17   **p. 443**

Schinus molle ⟡
CALIFORNIA PEPPER TREE
☼ ◊ ⚡ 8, 9, 12–24   **p. 479**

Sequoia sempervirens
COAST REDWOOD
☼ ● ● ● ⚡ 4–9, 14–24   **p. 483**

Tamarix aphylla ⟡
ATHEL TREE
☼ ◊ ● ⚡ 7–24   **p. 501**

Thuja plicata
WESTERN RED CEDAR
☼ ● ● ● ● ⚡ 1–9, 14–24   **p. 505**

Calocedrus decurrens

Cupressus macrocarpa

Pinus contorta

Pseudotsuga menziesii

Schinus molle

For growing symbol explanations, please see page 45.

Western Plant
ENCYCLOPEDIA

The vast spectrum of plants sold in western nurseries—from the asters and bachelor's buttons of old-fashioned cottage gardens to such landscape curiosities as the velvety-flowered kangaroo paws from Australia—is described in this encyclopedia. Many of the 6,000 plants included here are widely available throughout the West; others are common in only one region and rare elsewhere.

Chitalpa tashkentensis

The plants appear in alphabetical order under their scientific name (genus and species). The exceptions are common fruits, vegetables, and berries, which appear under their common name (apple, for example). If you know only a plant's common name, look up that name; you'll find the page number cross-reference to the plant entry.

Scientific plant names are based on *Hortus Third* (New York: Macmillan, 1976) and the more recent *New Royal Horticultural Society Dictionary of Gardening* (London: Macmillan; New York: Stockton Press, 1992). Where the two authorities differ, we give both names with cross-references. We also have consulted local plant indexes. Some of these names may be unfamiliar, but their use will make it easier for gardeners to speak a common language. (For help in understanding scientific plant names, see the Resource Directory, page 604.)

The sample entry below illustrates the format used throughout the encyclopedia. For the convenience of plant shoppers, former (and perhaps more familiar) scientific names are shown in parentheses after the scientific name and are also cross-referenced. Next comes the plant's common name, followed by the family name, listed in italics. The plant type is described in a few words on the next line.

Climate adaptability is shown in the line that begins with ⚡. The zone numbers refer to the climate zones—explained and mapped in The West's 24 Climate Zones—where the plants will grow. For instance, "Zones 14–24" gives the inclusive zones for which the

plant is recommended. "All zones" means the plant will grow in the entire West.

Plant exposure is shown by one or more of three symbols indicating how much sun a plant needs for best performance. ☼ means the plant grows best with unobstructed sunlight all day long or almost all day—you can overlook an hour or so of shade at the beginning or end of a summer day. ◐ means that the plant needs partial shade—shade for half the day or for at least 3 hours during the hottest part of the day. ● indicates that a plant prefers little or no direct sunlight—for example, it does best on the north side of a house or beneath a broad, dense tree.

A plant's approximate moisture needs are indicated by one or more of four symbols. ◊ means the plant needs no supplemental watering once established, within 1 or 2 years after planting. ◖ means the plant tolerates some aridity; give it, for example, three to six soakings during a dry season. ● means the plant needs regular irrigation—weekly for some plants or more often (perhaps even daily) during extreme heat. ●● indicates that the plant needs a wet or constantly moist soil. Additional advice follows the exposure and moisture symbols.

If a plant, or any of its parts, is known to be poisonous, the toxicity is described in the last line next to the symbol ◈. Plants not marked with this symbol may have poisonous parts, but their toxicity is not well known.

The drawings that accompany the entries give a general idea of the appearance of one or more members of a genus; not all members of the genus will necessarily look alike. Read the descriptions of the individual species.

Plant families are also included in the alphabetical listings. A family name may be omitted if only one member of the family is given in the plant encyclopedia; in these instances, the listed plant adequately illustrates family characteristics. When authorities differ on the appropriate names for certain plant families, we list both.

Throughout the encyclopedia you will find color boxes that highlight advice on selecting plants ▭, planting and culture tips ▭, landscape and kitchen ideas ▭, harvesting tips ▭, and surprising facts ▭.

ALOYSIA triphylla
(Lippia citriodora)

LEMON VERBENA

Verbenaceae

DECIDUOUS OR PARTIALLY EVERGREEN HERB-SHRUB

⚡ ZONES 9, 10, 12–24

☼ FULL SUN

● REGULAR WATER

Aloysia triphylla

A

AARON'S BEARD. See HYPERICUM calycinum   **p. 328**

ABELIA

Caprifoliaceae

SHRUBS

✔ ZONES VARY BY SPECIES

☼ ◑ BEST IN SUN, TOLERATE SOME SHADE

◐ MODERATE WATER

Abelia grandiflora

Graceful, arching branches densely clothed with oval, usually glossy leaves ½–1½ in. long; bronzy new growth. Tubular or bell-shaped flowers in clusters at ends of branches or among leaves. Though small, blossoms are plentiful enough to be showy, mostly during summer and early fall. When blooms drop, they usually leave purplish or copper-colored sepals that provide color into the fall months. Leaves also may take on bronzy tints in fall.

To keep the shrub's graceful form, prune selectively; don't shear. The more stems you cut to the ground in winter or early spring, the more open and arching next year's growth will be.

Abelias are adaptable plants, useful in shrub borders, as space dividers and visual barriers, and near house walls; lower kinds are good bank or ground covers.

A. floribunda. MEXICAN ABELIA. Evergreen. Zones 8, 9, 12–24. Severely damaged at 20°F. Usually 3–6 ft. tall, sometimes 10 ft. Arching, reddish stems are downy or hairy. Pendulous tubular flowers, 1½ in. long, reddish purple, single or in clusters. Usually summer blooming but often in full bloom in January. Needs partial shade in hot-summer areas.

A. grandiflora. GLOSSY ABELIA. Evergreen to partially deciduous. Zones 5–24. Hybrid of two species from China. Best known and most popular of the abelias. Grows to 8 ft. tall or taller; spreads to 5 ft. or more. Flowers white or faintly tinged pink, June–October.

A. g. 'Edward Goucher' (A. gaucheri). Like *A. grandiflora,* evergreen in milder climates to nearly deciduous at 15°F. Lower growing (to 3–5 ft.) and lacier than *A. grandiflora.* Small lilac pink flowers with orange throats make a showy display, June–October.

At 0°F, both *A. grandiflora* and *A. g.* 'Edward Goucher' freeze to the ground but usually recover to bloom the same year, making graceful border plants 10–15 in. tall.

A. g. 'Francis Mason'. Low, densely branched shrub with pink flowers; leaves variegated with yellow. Blooms June–October.

A. g. 'Prostrata'. Occasionally partially deciduous even in mildest climates. Low-growing (1½–2 ft.), spreading variety useful as ground cover, bank planting, low foreground shrub. For massing, set 3–4 ft. apart. Blooms June–October.

A. g. 'Sherwoodii'. Smaller and more compact than *A. grandiflora;* grows 3–4 ft. tall, 5 ft. wide. Blooms June–October.

ABELMOSCHUS moschatus

SILK FLOWER

Malvaceae

ANNUAL

✔ ALL ZONES

☼ ◑ FULL SUN BUT WILL BLOOM IN SHADE

◐ MODERATE WATER

Abelmoschus moschatus

Bushy plant about 1½ ft. tall and wide, with deep green, deeply cut leaves. Five-petaled, 3–4½-in. flowers, cherry red or pink with white centers, resemble tropical hibiscus. Likes good garden soil, heat, and full sun but will bloom in shade.

Grow from seed; flowering begins 100 days after sowing and continues up to frost or cold weather. Can be grown as house plant in a 6-in. pot.

ABIES

FIR

Pinaceae

EVERGREEN TREES

✔ ZONES VARY BY SPECIES

☼ ◑ FULL SUN OR LIGHT SHADE

◐ ● MOST TOLERATE ARIDITY; SOME NEED WATER

Abies concolor

In nature, firs are tall, erect, symmetrical trees with uniformly spaced branch whorls. Large cones are held erect; they shatter after ripening, leaving a spiky stalk. Most (but not all) native firs are high mountain plants that grow best in or near their natural environments. They grow slowly if at all in hot, dry, windy areas at low elevations, though firs from some other parts of the world do well in warm, dry climates.

Christmas tree farms grow native firs for cutting, and nurseries in the Northwest and Northern California grow a few species for the living Christmas tree trade. Licensed collectors in the Northwest dig picturesque, contorted firs at high elevations near the timberline and market them through nurseries as "alpine conifers." Use these in rock gardens; small specimens are good container or bonsai subjects. Birds are attracted by fir seeds.

A. amabilis. SILVER FIR, CASCADE FIR. Zones 1–7, 15–17. Native to southern Alaska south through Coast Ranges and Cascades of Washington and Oregon. Tall tree in the wilds, smaller (20–50 ft.) in lowland gardens in the Pacific Northwest. Dark green needles, silvery beneath, curve upward along the branches. Give it room to grow.

A. balsamea. BALSAM FIR. Zones 3–7, 15–17. Native to eastern American mountains. Only the dwarf variety 'Nana' is occasionally sold in the West. Interesting rock garden subject. Slow-growing, dense, dark green cushion; give partial shade, ample water.

A. bracteata (A. venusta). SANTA LUCIA FIR, BRISTLECONE FIR. Zones 8, 9, 14–21. From steep, rocky slopes on the seaward side of the Santa Lucia Mountains, Monterey County, California. A tall tree (70 ft. in 50 years), with spreading (15–20 ft.) lower branches and slender steeplelike crown. Stiff, 1½–2½-in.-long needles are dark green above, with white lines beneath; needle points are unusually sharp. Roundish cones are unique—about 4 in. long, with a long, slender, pointed bract on each cone scale. Exceptionally tolerant of heat and aridity.

A. concolor. WHITE FIR. Zones 1–9, 14–24. Native to mountains of southern Oregon, California, southern Rocky Mountains, Baja California. One of the big five in the timber belt of the Sierra Nevada, along with ponderosa pine, sugar pine, incense cedar, and Douglas fir. It's a popular Christmas tree and one of the most commonly grown native firs in western gardens. Needs no irrigation where it's native; some elsewhere.

Large, symmetrical tree in its native range and in the Northwest. Slower growing in California gardens; has reached 30 ft. in as many years in lowland California. Best as container plant in Southern California. Bluish green, 1–2-in.-long needles. Some consider the variety 'Candicans', with bluish white foliage, to be the "bluest" of all conifers.

A. grandis. LOWLAND FIR, GRAND FIR. Zones 1–9, 14–17. From British Columbia inland to Montana, southward to Sonoma County, California. In California it grows near the ocean along Highway 1. Many Northwest gardeners live and garden successfully under this fir; they prune it high. It's one of the largest firs, reaching to 300 ft. (lower in cultivation). Handsome, deep green, 1–1½-in.-long needles in two rows along branches; glossy above, white lines beneath.

A. koreana. KOREAN FIR. Zones 3–9, 14–24. Native to Korea. Slow-growing, compact, pyramidal tree seldom over 30 ft. Shiny, short green needles. Sets cones on young, small trees. Variety 'Aurea', with gold-green foliage, is even smaller, slower growing.

A. lasiocarpa. ALPINE FIR. Zones 1–9, 14–17. Native to Alaska, south through the high Cascades of Washington and Oregon; nearly throughout the Rocky Mountains. Narrow, steeple-shaped tree, 60–90 ft. tall in good soil in moist areas. Bluish green, 1–1½-in.-long needles.

Best known in gardens as an "alpine conifer," it is dug near timberline and sold in nurseries. Extremely slow growing in California gardens. Allow 15–20-ft. spread in Northwest gardens as it usually doesn't hold its narrow shape in cultivation.

A. l. arizonica. CORK FIR. Zones 1–9, 14–17. Native to San Francisco Peaks, Arizona, at 8,500-ft. elevation. Interesting creamy white, thick, corky bark. Very handsome as a youngster. Good bonsai.

A. magnifica. RED FIR. Zones 1–7. Native to the mountains of southern Oregon, California's Sierra Nevada south to Kern County, and the Coast Ranges south to Lake County. This is the "silver tip" fir of the California cut Christmas tree trade. Tall and stately, with symmetrical, horizontal, rather short branches. New growth silvery gray. Mature needles blue green, 1 in. long; curve upward on upper limbs, in two rows on lower branches. Hard to grow at low elevations.

A. nordmanniana. NORDMANN FIR. Zones 1–11, 14–24. Native to the Caucasus, Asia Minor, Greece. Vigorous, densely foliaged fir, 30–50 ft. tall and 20 ft. wide in cultivation. Dark green, shiny, ¾–1½-in.-long needles, with whitish bands beneath, densely cover branches.

More adaptable to California gardens than native firs, becoming a symmetrical, densely branched cone. Needs adequate water; will submit to long-term container growing.

A. pinsapo. SPANISH FIR. Zones 5–11, 14–24. Native to Spain. Very slow growing, to 25 ft. in 40 years. In Southern California, good dwarf effect for years. Dense, symmetrical form; it's sometimes taken for a spruce. Stiff, deep green, ½–¾-in.-long needles are set uniformly around branches. Variety 'Glauca' is blue gray.

A. procera (A. nobilis). NOBLE FIR. Zones 1–7, 15–17. Native to the Siskiyou Mountains of California, northern mountains of Oregon and Washington. Similar to California's red fir in appearance; grown in Northwest nurseries as a live Christmas tree. Grows 90–200 ft. tall in wilds, almost as tall in Northwest gardens. Short, stiff branches; blue-green, 1-in.-long needles. Large cones with extended bracts as in *A. bracteata*.

ABRONIA

SAND VERBENA

Nyctaginaceae

PERENNIALS AND ANNUALS

☀ ZONES 4, 5, 17, 24

☼ FULL SUN

◊ ● LITTLE OR NO WATERING

Abronia latifolia

Not a true verbena. Oval to roundish, very thick, fleshy leaves. Small, tubular, fragrant flowers in headlike clusters. *A. latifolia* and *A. umbellata* are naturally suited for holding sand in beach gardens.

Grow all species from seed. Seeds are hard to find; you may be able to buy them from wildflower specialists.

A. latifolia. YELLOW SAND VERBENA. Perennial. Native to seacoast, British Columbia to Santa Barbara. Thick leaves 1½ in. long and as wide; under ideal conditions plants form leafy mats up to 3 ft. across. The whole plant is gummy enough to become encrusted with sand or dust. Bright yellow flowers May–October. Sow seeds in flats, in pots, or in light, well-drained, sandy soil. Scraping or peeling off each seed's papery covering should facilitate germination.

A. umbellata. PINK SAND VERBENA. Perennial. Native to coasts, British Columbia to Baja California. Creeping, slender, fleshy, often reddish stems 1 ft. long or more. Leaves 1–2 in. long, not quite as wide. Rosy pink flowers bloom almost all year. Grow as *A. latifolia*.

A. villosa. Annual but will live 2–3 years with summer water. Desert native that thrives in heat, aridity. Resembles *A. umbellata*, but plant is hairy and somewhat sticky. Sow fall or spring.

FOR INFORMATION ON SELECTING PLANTS

PLEASE SEE PAGES 45–128

ABUTILON

FLOWERING MAPLE, CHINESE BELLFLOWER, CHINESE LANTERN

Malvaceae

EVERGREEN VINE-SHRUBS

☀ ZONES VARY BY SPECIES

☼ ◑ FULL SUN ON COAST, PARTIAL SHADE INLAND

● MODERATE WATER

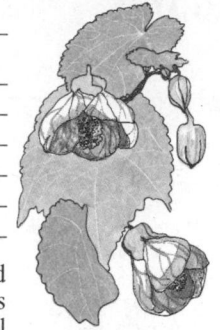

Abutilon hybridum

Mostly native to South America. Planted primarily for the pleasure provided by its flowers. Growth rapid, coarse, and rangy; control by pinching out branch tips.

Can be trained as standards or espaliers, but best as loose, informal espalier. In cold climates it can be used as container plant indoors in winter, out on terrace in summer. Gets whitefly and scale insects; control both with malathion or light oil spray.

A. hybridum. Zones 8, 9, 12–24. The best-known flowering maple. Upright, arching growth to 8–10 ft., with equal spread. Broad maplelike leaves. Drooping bell-like flowers in white, yellow, pink, and red. Main blooming season April–June, but white and yellow forms seem to bloom almost continuously.

A. megapotamicum. Zones 8, 9, 12–24. Vigorous growth to 10 ft. and as wide. Leaves are arrowlike, 1½–3 in. long. May–September, flowers resembling red-and-yellow lanterns gaily decorate the long, rangy branches. This vine-shrub is more graceful in detail than in entirety but can be trained to an interesting pattern. Good hanging basket plant. 'Marianne' has superior form; 'Variegata' has leaves mottled with yellow; 'Victory' is compact and floriferous with small, deep yellow flowers.

A. pictum 'Thompsonii'. Zones 8, 9, 12–24. Similar to *A. hybridum* but foliage strikingly variegated with creamy yellow. Blooms almost continuously, bearing pale orange bells veined with red.

A. vitifolium (Corynabutilon vitifolium). Zones 5, 6, 15–17. To 15 ft. Gray-green maplelike leaves to 6 in. or longer. Summer flowers lilac blue to white, 2½–3 in. wide, borne singly or clustered on long stalks. Needs high humidity.

ABYSSINIAN BANANA. See ENSETE ventricosum	**p. 273**
ABYSSINIAN SWORD LILY. See GLADIOLUS callianthus	**p. 307**

ACACIA

Fabaceae (Leguminosae)

EVERGREEN OR DECIDUOUS SHRUBS OR TREES

☀ ZONES VARY BY SPECIES

☼ FULL SUN

◊ ● NO WATER ON COAST, SOME INLAND

▶ SEE CHART NEXT PAGE

Acacia baileyana

Native to the tropics or warm regions of the world, notably Australia, Mexico, and our southwestern states. Of the many species tested over the last 150 years nearly 30 serve beautifully and functionally in California and Arizona landscapes; new species are continually under test.

Of species in use today several offer fountains of clear yellow flowers in January and February. Some are quite fragrant when in bloom. Many decorate and protect hillsides, banks, freeway landscapes. Some serve well in beach plantings. All are attractive to birds. Those listed in chart are evergreen, except where noted.

Acacia melanoxylon

Most nurseries sell only a few of the many acacia species, but you can easily grow acacias from seed you collect yourself or order from a specialist.

ACACIA

NAME	ZONES	HEIGHT	SPREAD	LEAVES	FLOWERS	COMMENTS
Acacia abyssinica	13–24	20–25 ft.	20–25 ft.	Finely divided, feathery. Evergreen in mildest climates	Yellow puff balls on short stems. Spring	Slow growth to spreading, flat-topped silhouette. Grow as single- or multitrunked tree or big shrub
A. adunca WALLANGARA WATTLE	8, 9, 12–24	12–25 ft.	10–15 ft.	Narrow, deep green to bluish, 6 in. long	Orange-yellow puffballs in large clusters. Fall, winter, spring	Compact growth
A. aneura MULGA	8, 9, 12–24	To 20 ft.	To 12 ft.	Small, silvery gray, undivided	Yellow rods. Spring	Evergreen small patio tree. Definitely gray. Clean, hardy, trouble free under desert conditions. Avoid needle-leafed forms
A. armata KANGAROO THORN	13–24	10–15 ft.	10–12 ft.	Light green, waxy, 1-in.-long leaves on thorny branches	Yellow, single, ¼-in.-wide balls. Feb.–Mar.	Blooms when young. Used as pot plant in cold areas. Thorniness makes it a real barrier plant
A. baileyana BAILEY ACACIA (often called MIMOSA as cut flowers)	7–9, 13–24; borderline, 6	20–30 ft.	20–40 ft.	Feathery, finely cut, blue-gray	Yellow, in clusters. Fragrant. Profuse in Jan.–Feb.	Most commonly planted and one of hardiest. Wonderful tree on banks when grown as multitrunked shrub-tree
A. b. 'Purpurea' PURPLE-LEAF ACACIA	8, 9, 14–24	20–30 ft.	20–30 ft.	Same, except for lavender to purple new growth	Same	Cut back to encourage new growth, prolong foliage color
A. boormanii SNOWY RIVER WATTLE	8, 9, 12–24	10–15 ft.	6–15 ft.	Narrow, gray-green, 2–3 in. long	Bright yellow, fragrant puffs at branch ends. Dec.–Mar.	Can sucker to form thickets. Tolerates winter wet
A. cognata (**A. subporosa**) BOWER WATTLE, RIVER WATTLE	16–24	20–30 ft.	20–30 ft.	Narrow, drooping, bright green, to 4 in. long	Paired pale yellow puffs. Spring	Graceful weeping tree. 'Emerald Cascade' and 'Emerald Showers' are selections. Damaged at 20°F
A. constricta WHITE THORN MESCAT ACACIA	10–24	10–18 ft.	To 18 ft.	Tiny, feathery	Yellow, fragrant. Summer	Open, spiny, deciduous shrub. Valuable in natural desert landscape for texture, size, summer flowers
A. craspedocarpa	8, 9, 12–24	To 18 ft.	To 10 ft.	Roundish, thick, gray	Yellow rods. Late winter, spring	Tolerates desert soils, drought, neglect. Dense foliage makes good screen. Broad, flat, wrinkled seedpods are decorative
A. cultriformis KNIFE ACACIA	13–24	10–15 ft.	10–15 ft.	Silvery gray, shaped like 1-in.-long paring knife blades	Yellow, in clusters. Mar.	Naturally a multistemmed tree. Barrier or screen. Useful on banks, slopes
A. cyanophylla (see **A. saligna**)						
A. cyclopis	8, 9, 13–24	10–15 ft.	15–20 ft.	Dark green, narrow, to 3½ in. long	Bright yellow, single or clustered; inconspicuous. Spring	Screening plant along highways. Very drought resistant. Good for hedges. Pods open to show unusual seeds—black with red rings surrounding them
A. dealbata (**A. decurrens dealbata**)	8, 9, 14–24; borderline, 6	To 50 ft.	40–50 ft.	Feathery, silvery gray	Similar to *A. baileyana*	Twigs and young branches also silvery gray; attractive. Very fast growing
A. decora GRACEFUL WATTLE	13–24	6–8 ft.	6–8 ft.	Rather narrow, 2 in. long, curved, bluish	Yellow balls in 2-in.-long clusters. Mass display in spring	Screening. Can be used as trimmed hedge 5 ft. high

ACACIA

NAME	ZONES	HEIGHT	SPREAD	LEAVES	FLOWERS	COMMENTS
A. decurrens (A. decurrens mollis) (plants offered are often the similar **A. mearnsii**) GREEN WATTLE	8, 9, 14–24; borderline, 6	To 50 ft.	40–50 ft.	Feathery, dark green	Yellow, in clusters. Feb.–Mar.	Longer lived than *A. baileyana*; more tolerant of wind and water. Invasive roots, litter rule it out of small gardens
A. drummondii DRUMMOND WATTLE	15–24	3–6 ft.	4–6 ft.	Tiny, fernlike, sparse, dark green	Inch-long, bright yellow rods. Winter	Attractive drought-tolerant shrub. Tender to frost while young
A. farnesiana SWEET ACACIA (see also **A. smallii**)	13–24 (see comments)	To 20 ft.	15–25 ft.	Deciduous, feathery, finely divided. Branches thorny	Deep yellow, fragrant balls most of the year. May freeze in cold snaps	Needs frost-free location in Zone 13. Can freeze to stump in Zone 12. Better for desert is similar *A. smallii*, often sold as *A. farnesiana*
A. flexifolia BENT-LEAF WATTLE	8–9, 14–24	6–8 ft.	6–8 ft.	Inch-long, upward-pointing, gray-green	Fragrant, pale yellow. Winter	Drought tolerant, hardy to 20°F
A. glaucoptera CLAY WATTLE, QUEEN WATTLE	16–24	1½–5 ft.	6–9 ft.	Odd, flat, winged stems are blue-green tinted red	Small yellow flower puffs not important	Odd foliage; new growth purplish red. Tender to frost
A. iteaphylla FLINDERS RANGE WATTLE	14–24	9–15 ft.	9–18 ft.	Narrow, pale blue-gray leaves to 4 in. New growth pinkish to purplish	Profuse, pale yellow. Late summer to spring	Tolerates drought. Useful screen plant
A. longifolia (often sold as **A. latifolia**) SYDNEY GOLDEN WATTLE	8, 9, 14–24	To 20 ft.	To 20 ft.	Bright green, 3–6 in. long	Golden yellow, loose 2½-in.-long spikes along branches in late winter, early spring	Usually big, rounded, billowy shrub. Very fast growing; very tolerant. Used as road screening against dust and headlights. Good soil binder near the beach (winds make it prostrate). Short lived (20–30 years)
A. melanoxylon BLACKWOOD ACACIA, BLACK ACACIA	8, 9, 13–24	To 40 ft.	To 20 ft.	Dark green, 2–4 in. long	Creamy to straw color, in short clusters. Mar.–Apr.	Fast, dense, upright growth. Can be pruned as ball or standard. Roots, litter, brittle branches a problem in confined areas. Thrives in California's Central Valley, as well as in salt breezes beside San Francisco Bay
A. minuta (see **A. smallii**)						
A. notabilis	12–24	To 10 ft.	To 10 ft.	Leathery, blue-green, 2–5 in. long	Bright yellow balls. Spring	Clean, sharp lines, blue-green color, flower display make this a good dense screen in desert
A. pendula WEEPING ACACIA, WEEPING MYALL	13–24	To 25 ft.	To 15 ft.	Blue-gray, to 4 in. long, on long weeping branches	Yellow, in pairs or clusters. Blooms erratically in Apr., May	Beautiful weeping tree. Perfect for cascading from behind wall. Interesting structural form as mature individual. Makes graceful espalier. Slow grower, seldom looks good in container
A. podalyriifolia PEARL ACACIA	8, 9, 13–24	10–20 ft.	12–15 ft.	Roundish, 1½ in. long, silvery gray, soft and satiny to touch	Light yellow, fluffy, in long clusters. Nov.–Mar.	Shrub or can be trained as rounded, open-headed tree. Excellent for patio use. Good winter color. Won't tolerate summer watering. Prune heavily after flowering to keep it compact
A. pravissima OVENS WATTLE	12–24	12–20 ft	12–20 ft.	Short, triangular, gray-green leaves tightly packed along branches	Heavy crop, bright yellow, scented. Winter, spring	Endures frost, heat, wind, marine exposure

A

ACACIA

NAME	ZONES	HEIGHT	SPREAD	LEAVES	FLOWERS	COMMENTS
A. redolens, (A. ongerup, A. redolens 'Prostrata')	8, 9, 12–24	1–2 ft.	15 ft.	Narrow, gray-green, leathery	Puffy yellow balls. Spring	Ground cover for banks, large areas of poor soil. Endures drought, heat. 'Ongerup' and A. melanoxylon 'Ongerup' similar or identical
A. retinodes (often sold as A. floribunda) WATER WATTLE, FLORIBUNDA ACACIA	8, 9, 13–24; borderline, 5, 6	To 20 ft.	To 20 ft.	Yellow-green, to 5 in. long	Yellow, small heads in clusters. Blooms most of year near coast	Quick screen. Can be a pendulous, see-through tree. Tends to get leggy. The only acacia with chance of survival in Seattle if mild winters come four in a row
A. rigidula BLACKBRUSH ACACIA	10–13	10–15 ft.	10–15 ft.	Deep green, rounded leaflets	Fragrant, pale yellow, 2–3-in. spikes; practically glow on a bright spring day. Mar.–Apr.	Slower growing than other acacias. Naturally a multistemmed tree. To train as single-stemmed tree, pull off suckers at base
A. salicina WILLOW ACACIA, AUSTRALIAN WILLOW	8, 9, 12–24	20–40 ft.	To 15 ft.	Dark green, narrow, to 3 in. long	Cream-colored balls. Blooms most of year; heaviest in fall and winter	Fast-growing tree with semiweeping habit. Water moderately to control growth; prune to keep open, prevent wind damage. Don't overwater. Best with one side of tree always dry
A. saligna (A. cyanophylla) BLUE-LEAF WATTLE	8, 9, 13–24	20–30 ft.	15–20 ft.	Narrow, blue-green, 6–12 in. long	Nearly orange balls in clusters. Heavy bloom Mar., Apr.	Screen for privacy or wind control. Multitrunked big shrub or tree
A. schaffneri	8, 9, 12–24	To 18 ft.	To 20 ft.	Finely divided, deciduous, closely set along branches	Yellow balls, fragrant. Spring	Exotic form with curving branches like green tentacles. Prune to form trunk and shape branches. Short thorns hidden in leaves
A. smallii (A. minuta)	8, 9, 12–24	Variable; to 30–35 ft.	15–25 ft.	Finely divided, deciduous. Thorny branches	Yellow, fragrant puff balls. Spring	Often sold as A. farnesiana, which is cold-tender. Plant A. smallii where frost occurs
A. stenophylla SHOESTRING ACACIA	8, 9, 12–24	To 30 ft.	To 20 ft.	Long (to 16 in.), narrow, drooping pale leaves contrast with maroon new bark	Creamy, 1/2-in. balls. Late winter, spring	Fast-growing, open, weeping tree. Makes wonderful shadows on walls, provides lightest shade for flowers
A. subporosa (see A. cognata)						
A. verticillata	14–24	To 15 ft.	To 15 ft.	Dark green, needlelike leaves, 3/4 in. long, in whorls. Looks like an airy conifer	Pale yellow in 1-in.-long spikes. Apr.–May	Good low hedge in wind. Unpruned, it develops open form with many spreading, twisting trunks. Sheared, it grows dense and full. Good at beach; resists oak root fungus

The acacias differ widely in foliage and growth habit. Some have feathery, much divided leaves; others have flattened leafstalks that fulfill the function of leaves. Many start life with feathery leaves and later develop leathery ones.

Larger-growing acacia species may end up as shrubs or trees depending on how they are pruned in youth. Remove the lead shoot and the plant grows as a shrub; remove the lower branches and it will be treelike. Stake the tree types until they are deeply anchored; deep, infrequent watering encourages deep rooting and better anchorage.

Prune large trees to open interiors to reduce dieback of shaded branches and prevent wind damage. Thin by removing branches entirely to the trunk.

Many acacias are relatively short lived—20–30 years. But if a tree grows to 20 ft. high in 3 years, the short life can be accepted.

Many acacias become chlorotic where water is bad and salts accumulate, as do many other plants in such soil.

The blackwood acacia (*A. melanoxylon*) has aggressive roots, lifts sidewalks, splits easily, and suckers. In shallow soil or where roots compete it is a bad actor. Yet in the right place it is well behaved and beautiful, vigorous, and dependable under difficult conditions of poor soil, wind, and drought.

ANXIOUS TO PLEASE IN ALL WAYS BUT ONE

Few plants in the mild West give as much service as acacias do. They need little or no water (none on coasts, just a bit in interior lowlands). You can prune them (they respond nicely to it) or not prune them. They seldom suffer any kind of pest damage. They can tolerate—and actually help subdue—regular winds. Their only weakness is in their flowers' contribution to the color spectrum. All that any of the species listed in the accompanying chart can offer is some shade of yellow (whitish through medium yellow to orangish).

ACAENA

SHEEP BUR

Rosaceae

PERENNIALS

☘ ZONES 4–9, 14–24

☼ ◑ SUN OR PARTIAL SHADE

● REGULAR WATER

Acaena microphylla

The two New Zealand natives described below form large, loose mats of attractive gray-green or pale green leaves that are divided into leaflets. Grow from seed or divisions in spring. Rather slow to establish; burn in hot sun. Plant 6–12 in. apart. Use in areas where a gray-green, loose, fine-textured mat is wanted—beside paths, in filtered shade beneath trees, in rock gardens. Can take some foot traffic. Remove burrs, which look messy and stick to clothing and pets.

A. buchananii. Has dense, silky, whitish green leaves, each with 11–13 round, small leaflets with scalloped edges.

A. microphylla. NEW ZEALAND BUR. Pale green leaves similar to above but larger and almost without hairs; 7–13 leaflets per leaf.

ACALYPHA

Euphorbiaceae

EVERGREEN TROPICAL SHRUBS

☘ ZONES 21–23

◑ PARTIAL SHADE

● MODERATE WATER

Acalypha hispida

All three of the species described are tropical and quite tender; *A. wilkesiana* can be used as an annual.

A. hispida. CHENILLE PLANT. Native to the East Indies. Needs tropical climate. Best in plastic-covered outdoor rooms. Control size by pinching and pruning; can grow to a bulky 10 ft. Heavy, rich green leaves to 8 in. wide. Flowers hang in 1½-ft.-long clusters resembling tassels of crimson chenille. Blooms most heavily in June; scattered bloom all year. Good house plant with heavy pruning.

A. pendula. FIRETAIL. Resembles *A. hispida* in flower form but plant is much smaller; shorter tassels droop from trailing branches. Good in hanging basket.

A. wilkesiana (A. tricolor). COPPER LEAF. Native to South Pacific islands. Foliage more colorful than many flowers. Used as an annual, substituting for flowers from September to frost. Leaves to 8 in.; may be bronzy green mottled with shades of red and purple, red with crimson and bronze, or green edged with crimson and stippled with orange and red. In a warm, sheltered spot it can grow as a shrub to 6 ft. or more. Best in container with fast-draining potting mix, kept slightly dry through winter.

Acanthaceae. The acanthus family consists of herbs and shrubs, generally from warm or tropical areas. Many have showy flowers or foliage. Examples are *Acanthus mollis*, *Aphelandra squarrosa*, and *Thunbergia*.

ACANTHUS mollis

BEAR'S BREECH

Acanthaceae

PERENNIAL

☘ ZONES 4–24

☼ ◑ LIGHT SHADE; SUN IN COASTAL AREAS

◐ ● SOME WATER IN SUMMER

Acanthus mollis

Native to southern Europe. Fast-growing, spreading plant with basal clusters of hand-

some, deeply lobed and cut, shining dark green leaves to 2 ft. long. Rigid 1½-ft. spikes of tubular whitish, lilac, or rose flowers with spiny green or purplish bracts top 2–3-ft. stems. Blooms late spring or early summer. Variety 'Oak Leaf' is very similar to species; 'Latifolius' has larger leaves, is hardier.

Cut back after flowering. To keep foliage through summer, cut off flower stalks and soak roots occasionally. Bait for slugs and snails. Divide clumps between October and March. Plant where it can be confined; roots travel underground, making the plant difficult to eradicate. Effective with bamboo, large-leafed ferns. Best in moist, shady situations but will also grow in dry, sunny spots.

ACCA sellowiana. See FEIJOA sellowiana   p. 292

ACER

MAPLE

Aceraceae

DECIDUOUS OR EVERGREEN TREES OR SHRUBS

☘ ZONES VARY BY SPECIES

☼ ◑ FULL SUN OR PARTIAL SHADE

● OCCASIONAL DEEP WATERINGS

Acer palmatum

When you talk about maples, you're talking about many trees—large and midsize deciduous shade trees; smaller evergreen and deciduous trees; and dainty, picturesque shrub-trees. In general, maples are highly favored in the Pacific Northwest, in the intermountain areas, and, to a lesser extent, in Northern California; with a few exceptions they are not adapted to Southern California or the Southwest's desert areas. Practically all maples in Southern California show marginal leafburn after mid-June and lack the fall color of maples in colder areas.

The larger maples have extensive fibrous root systems that take water and nutrients from the topsoil. The great canopy of leaves calls for a steady, constant supply of water—not necessarily frequent watering but constantly available water throughout the root zone. Occasional deep watering and periodic feeding will help keep roots down.

A. buergeranum. TRIDENT MAPLE. Deciduous tree. Zones 4–9, 14–17, 20, 21. Native to China, Japan. Grows 20–25 ft. high. Roundish crown of 3-in.-wide glossy, three-lobed leaves that are pale beneath. Fall color usually red, sometimes orange or yellow. Low, spreading growth; stake and prune to make it branch high. A decorative, useful patio tree and favorite bonsai subject.

A. campestre. HEDGE MAPLE. Deciduous tree. Zones 1–9, 14. Native to Europe, western Asia. Slow growing to 70 ft., seldom over 30 ft. in cultivation. Forms an especially dense, compact, rounded head in the Northwest; thinner in California. Leaves 2–4 in. wide, with three to five lobes, dull green above; turn yellow in fall. 'Queen Elizabeth' has glossier foliage, more erect habit.

A. capillipes. Deciduous tree. Zones 1–9, 12, 14–24. Native to Japan. Moderate growth rate to 30 ft. Young branches red, turning brown with white stripes with age. Young leaves red; leafstalks and midribs red. Leaves shallowly three-lobed, 3–5 in. long; turn scarlet in fall.

A. cappadocicum. COLISEUM MAPLE. Deciduous tree. Zones 1–6. Native to western Asia. Known here in its variety 'Rubrum', RED COLISEUM MAPLE. Grows to 35 ft.; forms compact, rounded crown. Leaves with five to seven lobes, 5½ in. wide. Bright red spring foliage turns rich dark green.

A. circinatum. VINE MAPLE. Deciduous shrub or small tree. Zones 1–6, 14–17. Native to moist woods, stream banks in coastal mountains of British Columbia south to Northern California. Crooked, sprawling, and vinelike in the forest shade, with many stems from the base; single-trunked small tree 5–35 ft. high in full sun. Loses its vinelike characteristics in open situations. Leaves with 5 to 11 lobes, 2–6 in. wide and as long, light green turning orange, scarlet, or yellow in the fall. New spring foliage usually has reddish tints. Tiny reddish purple flowers in clusters, April–May, followed by paired winged seeds that look like little red bow ties among the green leaves. One of the most airy and delicate western natives. The rare variety 'Monroe' has finely cut leaves.

Let it go untrimmed to make natural bowers, ideal settings for ferns and woodland flowers. Use under a canopy of tall conifers where its blazing fall color offers brilliant contrast. Can be espaliered against shady side of a wall. Its contorted leafless branches make an intricate pattern in winter. Select in fall to get best autumn color.

A. davidii. DAVID'S MAPLE. Deciduous tree. Zones 1–6, 15–17, 20, 21. Native to central China. This 20–35-ft.-high maple is distinctive on several counts. Bark is shiny green striped with silvery white, particularly striking in winter. Leaves are glossy green, oval or lobed, 2–7 in. long, 1½–4 in. wide, deeply veined. New foliage bronze tinted; fall color of bright yellow, red orange, and purple. Clustered greenish yellow flowers showy in April or May.

Acer davidii

A. ginnala. AMUR MAPLE. Deciduous shrub or small tree. Zones 1–9, 14–16. Native to Manchuria, north China, Japan. To 20 ft. high. Three-lobed, toothed leaves to 3 in. long, 2 in. wide. Striking red fall color. Clusters of small, fragrant yellowish flowers in early spring are followed by handsome bright red, winged seeds. Comes into its own in the coldest areas of the West. Grown as staked, trained single tree or multiple-trunked tall shrub. 'Flame', 15–20 ft. tall, shows fiery red fall color.

A. glabrum. ROCKY MOUNTAIN MAPLE. Deciduous shrub or small tree. Zones 1–3, 10. Leaves 2–5 in. wide, three- to five-lobed or divided into three leaflets, borne on dark red twigs. Fruit tinged red. Fall foliage yellow. Multitrunked clumps may be only 6 ft. tall or up to 30 ft. under ideal conditions. Needs well-drained soil and ample moisture.

A. griseum. PAPERBARK MAPLE. Deciduous tree. Zones 1–9, 14–21. Native to China. Grows to 25 ft. or higher with narrow to rounded crown. In winter it makes a striking silhouette with bare branches angling out and up from main trunk and reddish bark peeling away in paper-thin sheets. Late to leaf out in spring; leaves are divided into three coarsely toothed leaflets 1½–2½ in. long, dark green above, silvery below. Inconspicuous red flowers in spring develop into showy winged seeds. Foliage turns brilliant red in fall.

A. japonicum. FULLMOON MAPLE. Deciduous shrub or small tree. Zones 1–6, 14–16. Native to Japan. To 20–30 ft. Nearly round, 2–5-in.-long leaves cut into 7–11 lobes. The varieties obtainable are small, slow growing, and best placed as shrubs.

A. j. 'Aconitifolium'. FERNLEAF FULLMOON MAPLE. Leaves are deeply cut, almost to leafstalk; each lobe is also cut and toothed. Fine fall color where adapted.

A. j. 'Aureum'. GOLDEN FULLMOON MAPLE. See A. shirasawanum 'Aureum'

A. macrophyllum. BIGLEAF MAPLE. Deciduous tree. Zones 4–17. Native to stream banks, moist canyons, Alaska to foothills of California. Broad-topped, dense shade tree 30–95 ft. high—too big for a small garden or a street tree. Large three- to five-lobed leaves are 6–15 in. wide, sometimes bigger on young, vigorous sapling growth; leaves turn from medium green to yellow in fall. Small greenish yellow flowers in drooping clusters, April–May, followed by clusters of paired winged seeds that look rather like tawny, drooping butterflies. Yellow fall color spectacular in cool areas. Resistant to oak root fungus.

Acer macrophyllum

A. morrisonense. FORMOSAN MAPLE, MT. MORRISON MAPLE. Deciduous tree. Zones 4–6, 15–17. Native to Taiwan (Formosa). Fast, upright growth rounding with age; probably 30–40 ft. Greenish bark striped white. New growth red in early spring, foliage red in fall. Summer foliage light green, red leafstalks; three-lobed leaves, 5 in. long, 4 in. wide. Needs ample water, good soil.

A. negundo. BOX ELDER. Deciduous tree. Zones 1–10, 12–24. Native to most of United States. Where you can grow other maples of your choice, this is a weed tree of many faults—it seeds readily, hosts box elder bugs, suckers badly, and is subject to breakage. Fast growing to 60 ft., usually less. Leaves divided into three to five (or seven to nine) oval, 2–5-in.-long leaflets with toothed margins; yellow in fall.

A. n. 'Flamingo'. Has white and pink leaf markings.

A. n. 'Variegatum'. VARIEGATED BOX ELDER. Not as large or weedy as the species. Combination of green and creamy white leaves stands out in any situation. Large, pendant clusters of white fruit are spectacular.

A. nigrum. BLACK MAPLE. Zones 1–10, 14–20. Similar to sugar maple (*A. saccharum*), but more resistant to heat and drought. Light green leaves turn yellow in fall. 'Greencolumn' can reach 65 ft. tall, 25 ft. wide.

A. oblongum. EVERGREEN MAPLE. Evergreen or partially evergreen tree. Zones 8–10, 12, 14–24. Native to the Himalayas and China. Reaches 20–25 ft. high and almost as wide; branches tend to sweep outward and upward. Slender, shiny, deep green leaves, no lobes. New growth attractive bronzy pink in spring. Loses all leaves in sharp cold.

A. o. biauritum. See A. paxii

A. palmatum. JAPANESE MAPLE. Deciduous shrub or tree. Zones 1–10, 12, 14–24. Native to Japan and Korea. Slow growing to 20 ft.; normally many stemmed. Most airy and delicate of all maples. Leaves 2–4 in. long, deeply cut into five to nine toothed lobes. All-year interest: young spring growth is glowing red; summer's leaves are soft green; fall foliage is scarlet, orange, or yellow. Slender leafless branches in greens and reds provide winter pattern. Resistant to oak root fungus.

Grafted garden varieties are popular (the list below includes only the best known of dozens available), but common seedlings have uncommon grace and usefulness: they are more rugged, faster growing, and more drought tolerant, and they stand more sun and wind than named forms do. Japanese maples thrive everywhere in the Northwest, where they make good small street trees. They can be grown with success in California if given shelter from hot, dry, or constant winds. Filtered shade is best but full sun can be satisfactory. In California consider the local soil and water; wherever azaleas are difficult and suffer from salt buildup in the soil, Japanese maples will show burn on leaf edges. Give same watering treatment as azaleas—flood occasionally to leach out salts.

Used effectively on north and east walls, in patios and entryways, as small lawn trees. Attractive in groves (like birches) as woodland planting; for natural effect, set out plants of different sizes with varying spacing. Good under oaks, as background for ferns and azaleas, alongside pools. Invaluable in tubs and for bonsai. Japanese maple is inclined to grow in flat, horizontal planes, so pruning to accentuate this growth habit is easy. Prune to plane downward when given a water foreground.

The grafted garden forms are usually smaller than seedlings, more weeping and spreading, brighter in foliage color, and more finely cut in leaf. In California, it seems that the more finely cut the leaf, the greater the leafburn problem. Some of the best are

'Atropurpureum'. RED JAPANESE MAPLE. Purplish or bronze to bronzy green leaves, brighter in sun. Holds color all summer.

'Bloodgood'. Vigorous, upright growth to 15 ft. Deep red spring and summer foliage, scarlet in fall. Bark blackish red.

'Bonfire'. Orange-pink spring and fall foliage; twisted trunk, short branches, drooping branchlets.

'Burgundy Lace'. Leaves more deeply cut than those of 'Atropurpureum'; branchlets bright green.

'Butterfly'. Small (to 7-ft.) shrub with small bluish green leaves edged in white. Cut out growth that reverts to plain green.

'Crimson Queen'. Small, shrubby, with finely cut leaves that hold color all summer, turn scarlet before dropping off in fall.

'Dissectum' ('Dissectum Viridis'). LACELEAF JAPANESE MAPLE. Small shrub with drooping branches, green bark; pale green, finely divided leaves turn gold in autumn.

'Ever Red' ('Dissectum Atropurpureum'). Small mounding shrub with weeping branches. Finely divided, purple-tinged, lacy foliage turns crimson in fall.

'Filiferum Purpureum'. Mounding shrub to 10 ft. with threadlike leaf segments opening dark red and aging bronzy green.

'Garnet'. Similar to 'Crimson Queen' and 'Ever Red'; somewhat more vigorous grower.

'Ornatum' ('Dissectum Atropurpureum'). RED LACELEAF JAPANESE MAPLE. Like 'Dissectum' but with red leaves turning brighter red in autumn.

'Oshio Beni'. Like 'Atropurpureum' but more vigorous; has long, arching branches.

'Sango Kaku' ('Senkaki'). CORAL BARK MAPLE. Vigorous, upright, treelike. Fall foliage yellow. Twigs, branches striking coral red in winter.

JAPANESE MAPLES IN CONTAINERS

These lovely little shrub-trees make grand container plants, especially if you choose varieties that stay small. Give them soil that holds moisture but drains fast. Water often enough that the plants can maintain fresh and vital leaf tissue. And supply a constant level of nutrients through the in-leaf months; slow-release fertilizer serves this purpose well. Display the plants in a partly shaded spot that's as wind-free as possible.

A. paxii (A. oblongum biauritum). Evergreen tree. Zones 8, 9, 14–24. To 30 ft. Leaves usually three-lobed, occasionally oval or mitten shaped. Slow growth; compact head of dense foliage.

A. platanoides. NORWAY MAPLE. Deciduous tree. Zones 1–9, 14–17. Native to Europe, western Asia. Broad-crowned, densely foliaged tree to 50–60 ft. Leaves five-lobed, 3–5 in. wide, deep green above, paler beneath; turn yellow in fall. Showy clusters of small, greenish yellow flowers in early spring. Very adaptable, tolerating many soil and environmental conditions. Once a widely recommended street tree but now objected to where aphids cause honeydew drip and sooty mold. Voracious root system deep down and at surface also a problem. Here are some of the best horticultural varieties (purple-leafed forms perform poorly in alkaline soils unless soil is conditioned):

'Cavalier'. Compact, round headed, to 30 ft.

'Cleveland' and 'Cleveland II'. Shapely, compact, well-formed trees about 50 ft. tall.

'Columnare'. Slower grower, narrower form than the species.

'Crimson King'. Holds purple foliage color until leaves drop. Slower growing than the species. Fine in Northwest and California foothills.

'Deborah'. Like 'Schwedler' but faster growing, straighter.

'Drummondii'. Leaves are edged with silvery white; unusual and striking.

'Faassen's Black'. Pyramidal in shape, with dark purple leaves.

'Globe'. Slow growing with dense, round crown; eventual height 20–25 ft.

'Green Lace'. Finely cut, dark green leaves; moderate growth rate to 40 ft.

'Jade Glen'. Vigorous, straight-growing form with bright yellow fall color.

'Parkway'. Essentially a broader tree than 'Columnare', with a dense canopy.

'Royal Red Leaf'. Another good red- or purple-leafed form.

'Schwedler' or 'Schwedleri'. Purplish red leaves in spring turn to dark bronzy green, gold in autumn.

'Summershade'. Fast-growing, upright, heat-resistant selection.

A. pseudoplatanus. SYCAMORE MAPLE. Deciduous tree. Zones 1–9, 14–20. Native to Europe, western Asia. Moderate growth to 40 ft. or more. Leaves 3–5 in. wide, five-lobed, thick, prominently veined, dark green above, pale below. No particular fall color. The variety 'Atropurpureum' ('Spaethii') has leaves that are rich purple underneath.

A. rubrum. SCARLET MAPLE, RED MAPLE. Deciduous tree. Zones 1–9, 14–17. Native to eastern United States. Fairly fast growth to 40 ft. or more, with 20-ft. spread. Faster growing than Norway or sycamore maples. Red twigs, branchlets, and buds; quite showy flowers. Fruit dull red. Leaves 2–4 in. long, with three to five lobes, shiny green above, pale beneath; brilliant scarlet fall color in frosty areas. Rates

Acer rubrum

high in Pacific Northwest, where several selected forms are available. Needs careful watering in Zone 14.

'Armstrong' and 'Armstrong II'. Tall, very narrow trees with good red fall color.

'Autumn Radiance'. Broad oval form, orange-red fall color.

'Bowhall'. Tall, narrow, cone shaped, with orange-red foliage color in fall.

'Columnare'. Tall, broadly columnar.

'Gerling'. Broadly pyramidal, to 35 ft. with 20-ft. spread.

'Karpick'. Narrow grower with red twigs, yellow to red fall color.

'Northwood'. Rounded form. Extremely cold hardy.

'October Glory'. Tall, round-headed tree; last to turn color in fall.

'Red Sunset'. Upright, vigorous branching pattern.

'Scarlet Sentinel'. Columnar, fast-growing form.

'Schlesingeri'. Tall, broad, fast growing, with regular form; orange-red fall color.

'Shade King'. Very fast grower to 50 ft. Pale green foliage turns bright red in fall.

'Tilford'. Nearly globe-shaped crown if grown in the open; pyramidal when crowded.

'V. J. Drake'. Unusual fall color; leaf borders turn red and violet while center is still green. Leaves eventually turn completely red.

A. saccharinum. SILVER MAPLE. Deciduous tree. Zones 1–9, 12, 14–24. Native to eastern United States. Grows fast to 40–100 ft. with equal spread. Open form, with semipendulous branches; casts fairly open shade. Bark silvery gray except on oldest wood. Leaves 3–6 in. wide, five-lobed, light green above, silvery beneath. In Northwest, fall color is a mixture of scarlet, orange, and yellow—often in same leaf. Aggressive roots hard on sidewalks, sewers.

You pay a penalty for the advantage of fast growth: weak wood and narrow crotch angles make this tree break easily. Many rate it the least desirable of maples. Unusually susceptible to aphids and cottony scale. Suffers from chlorosis in alkaline soils. Nevertheless, it is often planted for fast growth and graceful habit.

A. s. 'Silver Queen'. Fast growing, more upright than the species, seedless. Bright gold fall color.

A. s. 'Wieri' (A. s. 'Laciniatum'). WIER MAPLE, CUTLEAF SILVER MAPLE. Same as species but leaves are much more finely cut; provides open shade.

A. saccharum. SUGAR MAPLE. Deciduous tree. Zones 1–10, 14–20. From eastern United States; in the Northeast it's the source of maple sugar. Moderate growth to 60 ft. and more. Stout branches with upward sweep form fairly compact crown. Leaves 3–6 in. wide, with three to five lobes, green above, pale below. Spectacular fall color in cold-winter areas—yellow and orange to deep red and scarlet. Varieties include 'Arrowhead' (erect pyramid); 'Bonfire' (tall, spreading, bright red fall color); 'Commemoration' (heavy leaf texture; orange, yellow, red fall color); 'Green Mountain' (tolerant of heat and drought); 'Legacy' (fast growing, multi-hued in fall); 'Monumentale' (narrow, erect); and 'Seneca Chief' (narrow form, orange to yellow fall color).

A. s. grandidentatum (A. grandidentatum). WASATCH MAPLE, BIGTOOTH MAPLE, ROCKY MOUNTAIN SUGAR MAPLE. Leaves with three to five lobes and large blunt teeth. Grows as shrub or 20–30-ft. tree. Brilliant fall color in tones of yellow, orange, rose red. In nature, it grows in canyons and on stream banks. In gardens it requires well-drained soil on the dry side.

A. shirasawanum 'Aureum'. GOLDEN FULLMOON MAPLE. Deciduous shrub or small tree. Zones 1–6, 14–16. Leaves open pale gold in spring and remain a pale chartreuse yellow all summer.

A. tataricum. TATARIAN MAPLE. Zones 1–6, 14–16. Resembles *A. ginnala* in size and habit. Leaves toothed, lobed only on young plants, 2–3½ in. long. Winged seeds red in summer, showy; fall color yellow to reddish brown. Extremely hardy.

A. truncatum. Deciduous tree. Zones 1–9, 14–23. Native to China. Grows fairly rapidly to 25 ft. Like a small Norway maple with more deeply lobed leaves to 4 in. wide. Expanding leaves are purplish red, summer leaves green, autumn leaves dark purplish red. A good lawn or patio tree.

A

Aceraceae. The maple family consists of deciduous, rarely evergreen, trees and shrubs with paired opposite leaves and paired, winged seeds.

ACHILLEA

YARROW	
Asteraceae (Compositae)	
PERENNIALS	
⚭ ALL ZONES	
☼ FULL SUN	
◊ ◌ NO WATER, OR JUST A LITTLE	

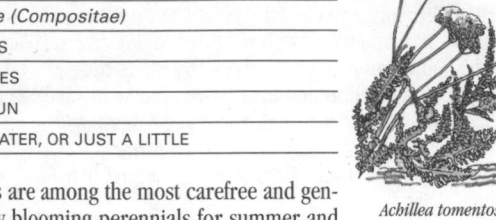

Achillea tomentosa

Yarrows are among the most carefree and generously blooming perennials for summer and early fall, several being equally useful in the garden and as cut flowers (taller kinds may be cut and dried for winter bouquets). Leaves are gray or green, bitter-aromatic, usually finely divided (some with toothed edges). Flower heads usually in flattish clusters. Yarrows need only routine care: some watering (though they endure drought once established), cutting back after bloom, dividing when clumps get crowded.

A. ageratifolia. GREEK YARROW. Native to Balkan region. Low mats of silvery leaves, toothed or nearly smooth edged. White flower clusters ½–1 in. across on stems 4–10 in. tall.

A. clavennae. SILVERY YARROW. Mats of silvery gray, silky leaves, lobed somewhat like chrysanthemum leaves. Loose, flat-topped clusters of ½–¾-in.-wide ivory white flower heads on 5–10-in.-high stems. Often sold as *A. argentea*. Combines beautifully with *Festuca ovina* 'Glauca', yellow sunroses *(Helianthemum),* creeping yellow-flowered sedums.

A. filipendulina. FERNLEAF YARROW. Tall, erect plants 4–5 ft. high, with deep green, fernlike leaves. Bright yellow flower heads in large, flat-topped clusters. Dried or fresh, they are good for flower arrangements. Several horticultural varieties are available. 'Gold Plate', a tall plant, has flower clusters up to 6 in. wide; 'Coronation Gold', to about 3 ft., also has large flower clusters. Combine these tall yarrows in borders with clumps of delphiniums, red-hot poker *(Kniphofia uvaria),* and Shasta daisies.

A. kellereri. Gray-green ferny leaves on a low (6-in.) plant. Clusters of flower heads look like tiny, white daisies with yellow centers.

A. millefolium. COMMON YARROW, MILFOIL. This species may spread a bit or grow erect to 3 ft. Narrow, fernlike, green or gray-green leaves on 3-ft. stems. White flower clusters grow on long stems. *A. m.* 'Rosea' has rosy flower heads. One of the more successful garden varieties is 'Fire King'. It grows to about 3 ft.; has gray foliage and dark reddish flowers; and is good for dry, hot situations. 'Cerise Queen' has brighter red flowers. Hybrids, many of them named, have extended the color range. Summer Pastels and Debutante show lighter shades of white and cream to yellow and red; they can grow from seed. Galaxy exhibits deeper colors. A form from California's Channel Islands has pink flowers.

A LAWN-MEADOW DOTTED WITH WILDFLOWERS

That's the effect you get with common yarrow *(Achillea millefolium)* treated as a sometimes-mowed ground cover. Install in spring, like this: Prepare soil as for a new lawn. Use ½ lb. of seed per 1,000 sq. ft. Mix it with an equal amount of sand and broadcast the mix with a handheld spreader. Press seeds in with a lawn roller. Mow 2 to 8 times a year (the less often you mow, the more flowers can form). Use a rotary mower at a 3–4 in. setting. Water during the dry season as needed.

A. 'Moonshine'. Upright growth to 2 ft. Gray-green foliage and light yellow flowers. Like *A. taygetea* but flowers are deeper yellow.

A. ptarmica. Erect plant up to 2 ft. high. Narrow leaves with finely toothed edges. White flower heads in rather open, flattish clusters. 'The Pearl' has double flowers.

A. taygetea. Native to the Levant. Grows to 1½ ft. Gray-green, divided leaves 3–4 in. long. Dense clusters of bright yellow flower heads fade to primrose yellow—excellent contrast in color shades until it's time to shear off old stalks. Good cut flowers.

A. tomentosa. WOOLLY YARROW. Makes a flat, spreading mat of fernlike, deep green, hairy leaves. Golden flower heads in flat clusters top 6–10-in. stems in summer. 'Primrose Beauty' has pale yellow flowers; 'King George' has cream flowers. A good edging and a neat ground cover for sunny or partly shaded small areas; used in rock gardens. Shear off dead flowers to leave attractive green mat.

ACHIMENES

Gesneriaceae	
TENDER PERENNIALS USED AS ANNUALS OR INDOORS	
⚭ ALL ZONES	
● SHADE	
◌◌ CAREFUL, FREQUENT WATER	

Achimenes

Native to tropical America. Related to African violet and gloxinia; and requires similar treatment. Plants 1–2 ft. high, some trailing. Slender stems; roundish, crisp, bright to dark green, hairy leaves. Flaring tubular flowers, 1–3 in. across, in pink, blue, lavender, orchid, purple.

Grow as house plant, in greenhouse or lathhouse, or on patio protected from direct sun and wind. Plant rhizomes March–April, placing ½–1 in. deep in moist peat moss and sand. Keep in light shade at 60°F. When 3 in. high, set 6–12 plants in 6–7-in. fern pot or hanging basket, in potting mix of equal parts peat moss, perlite, leaf mold. In fall, cure and dry rhizomes. Store in cool, dry place over winter; repot in spring.

ACIDANTHERA bicolor. See GLADIOLUS callianthus p. 307

ACMENA smithii (Eugenia smithii)

LILLY-PILLY TREE	
Myrtaceae	
EVERGREEN LARGE SHRUB OR SMALL TREE	
⚭ ZONES 15–17, 19–24	
☼ FULL SUN	
◌◌ REGULAR TO MUCH WATER	

Acmena smithii

Big feature is its dramatic show of clustered white, lavender, or lavender pink, ¼–½-in.-wide, edible berries in winter; they last a long time. If trained, can grow as tree to 10–25 ft. high. Awkward in growth unless trained. Shiny, pinkish green to green, 3-in.-long leaves. Many small white flowers in clusters at branch tips. Takes normal good garden care but is at its best with deep, rich soil and ample water.

ACONITUM

ACONITE, MONKSHOOD	
Ranunculaceae	
PERENNIALS	
⚭ ZONES 1–9, 14–21	
● SHADE	
◌◌ AMPLE WATER; NEVER LET DRY OUT	
◊ ALL PARTS ARE POISONOUS	

Aconitum napellus

Leaves, usually lobed, in basal clusters. Flowers shaped like hoods or helmets, along tall spikes. Monkshood has a definite place in rich soil under trees, at the back of flower beds, or even at the edge of a shaded bog garden. Substitute for delphinium in shade. Combines effectively with ferns, thalictrum, Japanese anemone *(Anemone hybrida)*, astilbe, hosta, and francoa.

Hard to establish in warm, dry climates. Sow seeds in spring; or sow in late summer or early fall for bloom the next year. Divide in early spring or late fall, or leave undivided for years. Completely dormant in winter; mark site.

A. carmichaelii (A. fischeri). Native to central China. Densely leafy stems 2–4 ft. high. Leaves leathery, dark green, lobed and coarsely toothed. Blooms in fall; deep purple-blue flowers form dense, branching clusters 4–8 in. long. Variety 'Wilsonii' grows 6–8 ft. high, has more open flower clusters 10–18 in. long.

A. henryi (A. bicolor) 'Sparks'. Grows 4–5 ft. tall, with dark purple-blue flowers on a widely branching plant.

A. napellus. GARDEN MONKSHOOD. Native to Europe. Upright leafy plants 2–5 ft. high. Leaves 2–5 in. wide, divided into narrow lobes. Flowers usually blue or violet, in spikelike clusters.

ACORUS gramineus

Araceae	
PERENNIAL	
✂ ALL ZONES	
☼ FULL SUN	
💧 MUCH WATER	

Acorus gramineus

Native to Japan, northern Asia. Related to callas, but fans of grasslike leaves more nearly resemble miniature tufts of iris. Flowers are inconspicuous. 'Ogon' has rich golden yellow leaves. 'Pusillus' is tiny, its green leaves seldom more than 1 in. long. It is used in planting miniature landscapes and dish gardens. 'Variegatus', with white edged, ¼-in.-wide leaves to 1¼ ft. long, can be planted in bog gardens or at pool edges. 'Variegatus' is also useful with collections of grasses, bamboos, or sword-leafed plants among gravel and boulders.

ACTINIDIA

Actinidiaceae	
DECIDUOUS VINES	
✂ ZONES VARY BY SPECIES	
☼ ☽ FULL SUN OR PARTIAL SHADE	
💧 MODERATE WATER	

Actinidia deliciosa

Native to eastern Asia. Handsome foliage. Plant in rich soil. Give moderate water and feed often. Supply sturdy supports for them to twine upon, such as a trellis, an arbor, or a patio overhead. You can also train them to cover walls and fences; guide and tie vines to the support as necessary. Thin occasionally to shape or to control pattern.

In winter, prune and shape plant for form and fruit production. Shape to one or two main trunks; cut out closely parallel or crossing branches. Fruit is borne on shoots from year-old or older wood; cut out shoots that have fruited for three years and shorten younger shoots, leaving from three to seven buds beyond previous summer's fruit. In summer, shorten overlong shoots and unwind shoots that twine around main branches.

A. arguta. HARDY KIWI. Zones 1–10, 12, 14–24. Much like *A. deliciosa* but with smaller leaves, flowers; fruit 1–1½ in. long, fuzzless (eat skin and all). Female varieties 'Ananasnaja' and 'Hood River' need male varieties for pollen. The rare variety 'Issai' is self-fertile. Fruiting is satisfactory even in mild winters.

A. deliciosa (A. chinensis). KIWI, CHINESE GOOSEBERRY VINE. Zones 4–9, 12, 14–24. Twines and leans to 30 ft. if not curbed. Leaves 5–8 in. long, roundish, rich dark green above, velvety white below. New growth often has rich red fuzz. Flowers (May) 1–1½ in. wide, opening creamy and fading to buff. Fruit egg size, roughly egg shaped, covered with

brown fuzz. Green flesh edible and delicious, with hints of melon, strawberry, banana. Although single plants are ornamental, you need both a male and a female plant for fruit. The best female (fruiting) varieties are 'Chico' and 'Hayward' (similar, possibly identical varieties); 'Vincent' needs little winter chill and is a good variety for the mildest winter climates. 'Tomuri' is pollenizer for 'Vincent'.

Harvest fruit in latest October or November. Store at refrigerator temperature in plastic bags. Ripen fruit at room temperature as needed.

A. kolomikta. Zones 1–9, 15–17. Rapid growth to 15 ft. or more to produce a wondrous foliage mass made up of heart-shaped, 3–5-in.-long, variegated leaves. Some leaves are all white, some are green splashed with white, and others have rose, pink, or even red variegation.

ADENIUM obesum

Apocynaceae	
SHRUB, USUALLY GROWN IN CONTAINER INDOORS	
✂ CAN BE KEPT OUTDOORS IN ZONES 23, 24	
☼ FULL SUN	
💧 AMPLE WATER DURING GROWTH	
☠ MILKY SAP IS POISONOUS	

Adenium obesum

Twisted branches grow from huge, fleshy, half-buried trunk or rootstock. Leaves sparse; plant leafless for long periods. Clustered saucer-shaped blossoms are deep pink, 2 in. or more across. Cannot take frost or winter chill and cold soil. Needs heat, light, perfect drainage, ample summer water during growth, no water during dormancy; in short, this is a plant for careful enthusiasts and collectors. In bloom, extremely showy; in eastern tropical Africa, where it is native, it is known as desert rose or desert azalea.

ADENOPHORA liliifolia

LADY BELLS	
Campanulaceae (Lobeliaceae)	
PERENNIAL	
✂ ZONES 1–9, 14–24	
☼ ☽ FULL SUN OR PARTIAL SHADE	
💧 MODERATE WATER	

Adenophora liliifolia

Grows to 18 in., with roundish or heart-shaped lower leaves and branching clusters of hanging, bell-shaped blue flowers in midsummer. Fragrant. Resembles a midsize campanula. Sometimes used in meadow or woodland edge plantings.

ADENOSTOMA

Rosaceae	
EVERGREEN SHRUBS	
✂ ZONES VARY BY SPECIES	
☼ FULL SUN	
⬦ NO WATER ONCE ESTABLISHED	

Adenostoma fasciculatum

These evergreen shrubs resemble heather more than roses. They tolerate heat, aridity, and poor rocky soil.

A. fasciculatum. CHAMISE, GREASEWOOD. Zones 14–16, 18–24. Leaves tiny, needlelike, clustered. Flowers tiny, white, in dense 2–5-in. clusters. Ordinarily a sparse shrub to 12 ft. tall, but a prostrate form is available. Used in native plantings.

A. sparsifolium. RED SHANKS. Zones 14–16, 18–21. To 18 ft., with shredding red bark. Needles not clustered; flower clusters somewhat longer and more open than *A. fasciculatum.*

A

ADIANTUM

MAIDENHAIR FERN	
Polypodiaceae	
FERNS	
✄ ZONES VARY BY SPECIES	
☼ ● PARTIAL OR FULL SHADE	
💧 LOTS OF WATER	

Adiantum aleuticum

Most are native to tropics; some are western natives. Stems thin, wiry, and dark; fronds finely cut; leaflets mostly fan shaped, bright green, thin textured. Plants need shade, steady moisture, and soil rich in organic matter. Leaves of even hardy varieties die back in hard frosts. Kinds listed as tender or indoor plants sometimes succeed in sheltered places or lanais in mild-winter areas. Protect from snails and slugs.

A. aleuticum (A. aleuticum pedatum). FIVE-FINGER FERN, WESTERN MAIDENHAIR. Zones 1–9, 14–21. North America. Fronds fork to make a fingerlike pattern atop slender 1–2½-ft. stems. General effect airy and fresh; excellent in containers or shaded beds.

A. capillus-veneris. SOUTHERN MAIDENHAIR. Zones 5–9, 14–24. Native to North America. To 1½ ft. tall, fronds twice divided but not forked.

A. hispidulum. ROSY MAIDENHAIR. Tropics of Asia, Africa. Indoor or greenhouse plant. To 1 ft. tall. Young fronds rosy brown, turning medium green, shaped somewhat like five-finger fern (*A. aleuticum*).

A. jordanii. CALIFORNIA MAIDENHAIR. Zones 5–9, 14–24. Native to California, southern Oregon. Twice-divided fronds to 2 ft. tall.

A. peruvianum. SILVER DOLLAR MAIDENHAIR. Indoor or greenhouse plant. Peru. To 1½ ft. or more in height. Segments of leaves quite large, to 2 in. wide.

A. raddianum (A. cuneatum, A. decorum). Tender fern for indoors or greenhouse. Brazil. Fronds cut three or four times, 15–18 in. long. Many named varieties differing in texture and compactness. Grow in pots; move outdoors to a sheltered, shaded patio in summer. Varieties commonly sold are 'Fritz-Luthii', 'Gracillimum' (most finely cut), and 'Pacific Maid'.

A. tenerum. Indoors or greenhouse. New World tropics. Long, broad fronds arch gracefully, are finely divided into many deeply cut segments ½–¾ in. wide. Plant sold as *A. t.* 'Wrightii' is similar or identical.

AECHMEA

Bromeliaceae	
BROMELIADS	
✄ OUTDOORS, ZONES 22–24; OR INDOORS	
● SHADE	
💧 UNIQUE WATER NEEDS AND MECHANICS	

Aechmea fasciata

In frost-free areas, grow in pots, in hanging baskets, or in moss fastened in crotches of trees—always in shaded places with good air circulation. Indoors or outdoors, soil should be fast draining but moisture retentive. Apply water every 1–2 weeks into cups within leaves. Put water on soil when it's really dry to the touch. Bromeliad specialists list dozens of species and varieties, and new hybrids appear frequently.

A. chantinii. Rosettes of leaves 1–3 ft. long, green to gray green banded with silver or darker green. Tall flower clusters have orange, pink, or red bracts; yellow-and-red flowers; white or blue fruit.

A. fasciata. Gray-green leaves crossbanded with silvery white. From the center grows a cluster of rosy pink flower bracts in which nestle pale blue flowers that change to deep rose. 'Silver King' has unusually silvery leaves; leaves of 'Marginata' are edged with creamy white bands.

A. 'Foster's Favorite'. Hybrid with bright wine red, lacquered leaves about 1 ft. long. Drooping, spikelike flower clusters in coral red and blue. 'Royal Wine', another hybrid, forms an open rosette of somewhat leathery, glossy, light green leaves that are burgundy red beneath. Orange-and-blue flowers are borne in drooping clusters.

A. fulgens. Green leaves dusted with gray, 12–16 in. long, 2–3 in. wide. Flower cluster usually above the leaves; blossoms red, blue, and blue violet. *A. f. discolor* has brownish red or violet red leaves, usually faintly striped. Many hybrids.

A. pectinata. Stiff rosettes up to 3 ft.; leaves to 3 in. wide, strongly marked pink or red at bloom time. Flowers whitish and green.

A. weilbachii. Shiny leaves, green or suffused with red tones, in 2–3-ft.-wide rosettes. Dull red, 1½-ft. flower stalk has orange-red berries tipped with lilac.

AEGOPODIUM podagraria

BISHOP'S WEED, GOUT WEED	
Apiaceae (Umbelliferae)	
DECIDUOUS PERENNIAL	
✄ ZONES 1–7	
☼ ● PARTIAL OR FULL SHADE	
💧 MODERATE WATER	

Aegopodium podagraria

Very vigorous ground cover. Spreads by creeping underground rootstocks, may become invasive; best if contained behind underground barrier of wood, concrete, or heavy tar paper. Many light green, divided leaves make a low (to 6 in.), dense mass; leaflets are ½–3 in. long. To keep it low and even, mow it two or three times a year.

A. p. 'Variegatum'. The most widely planted form. Commonly used in intermountain regions (Salt Lake City, Denver). Leaflets are edged white, giving a luminous effect in shade. Pull plants that revert to solid green leaves.

AEONIUM

Crassulaceae	
SUCCULENTS	
✄ ZONES 15–17, 20–24	
☼ ☼ FULL SUN NEAR COAST, PARTIAL SHADE INLAND	
💧 INFREQUENT BUT DEEP WATERING	

Aeonium arboreum

Among the most useful succulents for decorative effects, in pots or in the ground. All have a sculpturesque quality.

A. arboreum. Branched stems to 3 ft. tall, each branch with a 6–8-in.-wide rosette of light green, lightly fringed, fleshy leaves. Yellow flowers in long clusters. Variety 'Atropurpureum', with dark purple rosettes, is more striking and more widely grown than *A. arboreum*. Rosettes of 'Zwartkop' are nearly black.

A. decorum. Bushy, rounded, many-branched plants to 10 in., each branch ending in a 2-in. rosette. Fleshy, reddish-tinted leaves with red edges. Neat, compact. Pink flowers.

A. floribundum. Hybrid between *A. simsii* and *A. spathulatum;* 1-ft. cushion with 2–3-in. rosettes of medium green, fleshy leaves streaked with darker green. Abundant yellow flowers in spring.

A. haworthii. Free branching, shrubby, to 2 ft., with blue-green, red-edged rosettes 2–3 in. wide. White flowers.

A. 'Pseudotabulaeforme'. Smooth, flat, light green rosettes to 10 in. wide. Makes offsets freely.

A. simsii (A. caespitosum). Low, dense, spreading, very leafy, 6 in. tall. Bright green leaf rosettes. Yellow flowers.

A. urbicum. "Dinner platter" rosettes to 8–10 in. wide. Long, narrow, light green leaves, loosely arranged, have reddish edges.

AESCULUS

HORSECHESTNUT
Hippocastanaceae
DECIDUOUS TREES OR LARGE SHRUBS
ZONES VARY BY SPECIES
FULL SUN
WATER NEEDS VARY BY SPECIES
SEEDS OF ALL ARE SLIGHTLY TOXIC

Aesculus carnea

Leaves are divided fanwise into large, toothed leaflets. Flowers, in long, dense, showy clusters at the ends of branches, attract hummingbirds. Leathery fruit capsules enclose glossy seeds.

A. californica. CALIFORNIA BUCKEYE. Zones 4–10, 12, 14–24. Native to dry slopes and canyons below 4,000-ft. elevation in Coast Ranges and Sierra Nevada foothills.

Shrub or small tree, often with several stems to 10–20 ft. or taller. Very wide spreading (give it room). New foliage pale apple green; mature leaves have five to seven rich green, 3–6-in.-long leaflets. Striking sight in April or May when fragrant, creamy flower plumes make it a giant candelabrum. Large, pear-shaped fruits—with green covering splitting to reveal large, brown, shiny seeds—are favorites for fall flower arrangements. Seeds sprout freely; seedlings make unusual bonsai subjects.

In the wild, *A. californica* drops its leaves very early—by July—but if given water will hold them until fall. After leaf drop, the tree presents an interesting silhouette—silvery trunk, branches, branchlets.

A. carnea. RED HORSECHESTNUT. Zones 1–10, 12, 14–17. Hybrid between *A. hippocastanum* and *A. pavia*. To 40 ft. high and 30 ft. wide. Round headed with large, dark green leaves, each divided fanwise into five leaflets; casts dense shade. In April–May, bears hundreds of 8-in.-long plumes of soft pink to red flowers; 'Briotii' has rosy crimson flowers; 'O'Neill Red' has single flowers of bright red.

Plants of *A. carnea* are smaller than *A. hippocastanum* and easier to accommodate in small gardens; they need summer water.

A. hippocastanum. COMMON HORSECHESTNUT. Zones 1–10, 12, 14–17. To 60 ft. high with a 40-ft. spread, this bulky, densely foliaged tree gives heavy shade. Needs summer water. Leaves divided fanwise into five to seven toothed, 4–10-in.-long leaflets. Spectacular spring flower show: ivory blooms with pink markings in 1 ft. long plumes. Invasive roots can break up walks. 'Baumannii' has double flowers, sets no seeds.

A. pavia. RED BUCKEYE. Zones 3–9, 14–24. Bulky shrub or tree to 12 ft., with narrow, erect 10-in. clusters of bright red, rarely yellow, flowers. Regular water.

AETHIONEMA

STONECRESS
Brassicaceae (Cruciferae)
PERENNIALS
ZONES 1–9, 14–21
FULL SUN
INFREQUENT WATER

Aethionema warleyense

Native to Mediterranean region and Asia Minor. Choice shrublets, attractive in or out of bloom, best adapted to colder climates; a favorite among rock gardeners. Grow best in a light, porous soil with considerable lime. Bloom late spring to summer. Deadhead flowers.

A. schistosum. Erect, unbranched stems 5–10 in. high, densely clothed with narrow, slate blue, ½-in.-long leaves. Fragrant, rose-colored flowers; petals about ¼ in. long.

A. warleyense (A. 'Warley Rose'). Hybrid form; neat, compact plant to 8 in. high. Pink flowers in dense clusters. Widely used; only one planted to any extent in warmer climates.

AFRICAN BOXWOOD. See MYRSINE africana **p. 386**
AFRICAN CORN LILY. See IXIA **p. 336**
AFRICAN DAISY. See ARCTOTIS, DIMORPHOTHECA, OSTEOSPERMUM **pp. 164, 265, 396**
AFRICAN IRIS. See DIETES **p. 264**
AFRICAN LINDEN. See SPARMANNIA africana **p. 489**
AFRICAN VIOLET. See SAINTPAULIA ionantha **p. 471**

AGAPANTHUS

LILY-OF-THE-NILE
Amaryllidaceae
EVERGREEN OR DECIDUOUS PERENNIALS
ZONES 7–9, 12–24
FULL SUN OR PARTIAL SHADE
OCCASIONAL GROWING-SEASON WATER

Agapanthus orientalis

Adaptable. Will grow in full sun or in as little as 3 hours of sun a day. Best in loamy soil but will grow in heavy soils; thrives with ample water during growing season, but established plants can grow and bloom without watering. Divide infrequently; every 5 or 6 years is usually sufficient. In cold-winter areas, lift and store over winter and replant in spring. Superb container plant. Good near pools.

A. africanus. Evergreen. Leaves shorter, narrower than those of *A. orientalis;* flower stalks shorter (to 1½ ft. tall) with fewer flowers (20–50 to a cluster). Blue flowers midsummer to early fall. Often sold as *A. umbellatus.*

A. campanulatus. Deciduous, to 3 ft., with drooping dark blue flowers. The white form is 'Albus'.

A. Headbourne hybrids. Deciduous, 2–2½ ft. tall, cold hardy (with mulching) in western Washington and Oregon.

A. 'Henryi'. Resembles 'Peter Pan' but has white flowers.

A. inapertus. Deciduous. Deep blue tubular flowers droop from a 4–5-ft. stalk.

A. orientalis. Evergreen. Most commonly planted. Broad, arching leaves in big clumps. Stems to 4–5 ft. tall bear up to 100 blue flowers. There are white ('Albus'), double ('Flore Pleno'), and giant blue varieties. Often sold as *A. africanus, A. umbellatus.*

A. 'Peter Pan'. Evergreen. Outstanding free-blooming dwarf variety. Foliage clumps are 8–12 in. tall; clustered blue flowers top 1–1½-ft. stems.

A. 'Queen Anne'. Evergreen. Foliage clump 12–15 in. tall; leaves narrow. Flower stalks 2 ft. tall; flowers medium blue over a long summer season.

A. 'Rancho White'. Evergreen. Foliage clump 1–1½ ft. tall; leaves broad. Flower stalks 1½–2 ft. tall carry heavy clusters of white flowers. Also known as 'Dwarf White' and 'Rancho'. 'Peter Pan Albus' is similar or identical.

Selections with intensely deep blue flowers are 'Elaine', 'Ellamae', 'Mood Indigo', and 'Storm Cloud'.

AGAPANTHUS AND FRIENDS

Agapanthus, a reliable producer of bold and pretty summertime flowers, combines well in garden beds with other substantial, easy-care performers. For instance, try it with belladonna lily or naked lady *(Amaryllis belladonna)* and marigolds. Some other good companions are *Phlox paniculata* and poker plant *(Kniphofia uvaria)*. In bouquets, use cut agapanthus flowers with the blooms of sea lavender *(Limonium perezii)*.

A

AGAPETES serpens
(Pentapterygium serpens)

Ericaceae

EVERGREEN SHRUB

✿ ZONES 15–17, 23, 24

☼ PARTIAL SHADE

💧 GENEROUS WATER

Agapetes serpens

Arching, drooping branches to 3 ft. or more rise from a swollen, tuber-like base. Narrow leaves ½–1 in. long crowd in two rows along branches. Lanternlike, inch-long flowers, red marked with deeper red chevrons, hang under the branches in spring. A blueberry relative, it needs acid planting mix. Odd, showy hanging basket plant. Also attractive planted above retaining wall or on high bank where viewers can see stripings on flowers. Native to moderate elevations in Himalayas.

AGASTACHE

GIANT HYSSOP

Lamiaceae (Labiatae)

PERENNIALS

✿ ZONES 4–9, 14–24

☼ ☽ FULL SUN OR PARTIAL SHADE

💧 MODERATE WATER

Agastache foeniculum

Aromatic perennials somewhat resembling salvias, with whorls of purple, blue, or yellow flowers forming spikelike clusters.

A. barberi. Zones 8, 9, 14–24. Woody-based perennial to 2 ft. with 2-in. leaves and reddish purple flowers. 'Firebird' has coppery orange-red flowers, 'Tutti-Frutti', purple ones.

A. foeniculum. ANISE HYSSOP. Zones 4–24. Erect, narrow clumping perennial to 5 ft., with anise- or licorice-scented foliage and dense clusters of lilac blue flowers. Decorative and useful in perennial borders or herb gardens.

AGATHAEA coelestis. See FELICIA amelloides　　　　**p. 293**

Agavaceae. The agave family contains rosette-forming, sometimes treelike plants generally from dry regions. Flower clusters are spikes or spikelike; leaves often contain tough fibers.

AGAVE

Agavaceae

SUCCULENTS

✿ ZONES VARY BY SPECIES

☼ ☽ FULL SUN OR PARTIAL SHADE

💧 INFREQUENT WATER, EXCEPT AS NOTED

Agave attenuata

Succulents, mostly gigantic, with large clumps of fleshy, strap-shaped leaves. The flower clusters are big but not colorful. After flowering—which may not occur for years—the foliage clump dies, usually leaving behind suckers that make new plants. The plants shrivel from serious drought but plump up again when watered or rained on.

A. americana. CENTURY PLANT. Zones 10, 12–24. Leaves to 6 ft. long, with hooked spines along the edges and a wicked spine at the tip; blue-green in color. Be sure you really want one before planting it: the bulk and spines make it formidable to remove. After 10 years or more, the plant produces a branched, 15–40-ft. flower stalk bearing yellowish green flowers. There are several varieties with yellow- or white-striped leaves.

A. attenuata. Zones 20–24. Leaves 2½ ft. long, soft green or gray-green, fleshy, somewhat translucent, without spines. Makes clumps to 5 ft.

across; older plants develop a stout trunk to 5 ft. tall. Greenish yellow flowers dense on arching spikes to 12–14 ft. long. Will take poor soil but does best in rich soil with ample water. Protect from frost and hot sun. Statuesque container plant. Good near ocean or pool.

A. filifera. Zones 12–24. Rosettes less than 2 ft. wide; leaves are narrow, dark green, lined with white, and edged with long white threads.

A. parryi huachucensis. Zones 10, 12–24. Gray-green, 2–3-ft.-wide rosettes resemble giant artichokes. Tips of leaves fiercely spined. Makes offsets freely.

A. victoriae-reginae. Zones 10, 12, 13, 15–17, 21–24. Clumps only a foot or so across. The many dark green leaves are 6 in. long, 2 in. wide, stiff, thick, with narrow white lines. Slow growing; will stand in pot or ground 20 years before flowering (greenish flowers on tall stalks), and then die.

A. vilmoriniana (A. mayoensis). OCTOPUS AGAVE. Zones 12–24. Pale green or yellowish green rosettes up to 6 ft. wide. Leaves 3–4 in. wide, fleshy, deeply channeled above, with a single long spine at the end. Arching, twisted leaves give plant look of an octopus or a huge spider. Very handsome in containers.

AGERATUM houstonianum

FLOSS FLOWER

Asteraceae (Compositae)

ANNUAL

✿ ALL ZONES IF PLANTING TIMES FOLLOWED

☼ ☽ FULL SUN OR PARTIAL SHADE

💧 REGULAR WATER

Ageratum houstonianum

Reliable favorite for summer and fall color in borders and containers. The lavender blue–flowered varieties combine with flowers of almost any color or shape. Leaves roundish, usually heart shaped at the base, soft green, hairy. Tiny lavender blue, white, or pink tassel-like flowers in dense clusters. Dwarf varieties make excellent edgings or pattern plantings with other low-growing annuals.

Plant in sun except in hot-summer climates, where filtered shade is better. Rich, moist soil is best. In mild-winter areas plant in late summer for fall color. Easy to transplant even when in bloom. Effective combinations: lavender blue ageratum with salmon pink annual phlox, Madagascar periwinkle (*Catharanthus,* once known as *Vinca rosea*) in pink shades, or dwarf yellow marigolds *(Tagetes)*.

Dwarf lavender blue varieties (4–6 in. tall) include 'Blue Blazer', 'Blue Danube' ('Blue Puffs'), 'Blue Surf', and 'Royal Delft'. 'Blue Mink' and 'North Sea' are somewhat taller (9–12 in.). Pink-flowered 'Pink Powderpuffs' is 9 in. tall; 'Summer Snow', also 9 in. tall, has white blooms.

AGLAONEMA

Araceae

PERENNIAL HOUSE PLANTS

☽ ● TOLERATES VERY LOW LIGHT

💧 FREQUENT WATER

Aglaonema modestum

Tropical plants valued mostly for their ornamental foliage. Flowers resemble small, greenish white callas. Need a rich, porous potting mix; thrive with lots of water but will get along with small amounts. Cut stems will grow a long time in a glass of water. Exudation from leaf tips, especially of *A. modestum,* spots wood finishes (as on tabletops).

Among the best plants for poorly lighted situations. In fact, few plants can get by on as little light as aglaonema; *A. modestum* is especially tolerant of low light.

A. commutatum. Grows to 2 ft. Deep green leaves to 6 in. long, 2 in. across, with pale green markings on veins. Flowers followed by inch-long clusters of yellow to red berries. *A. c. maculatum,* with many irregular, gray-green stripes on leaves, is the most common. 'Pseudobracteatum',

1–2 ft. tall, has white leafstalks and deep green leaves marked with pale green and creamy yellow. 'Treubii' has narrow leaves heavily marked with silvery gray.

A. costatum. Slow-growing, low plant with broad, deep green leaves spotted white and a broad white stripe along the midrib. *A. c.* 'Foxii' is similar or identical.

A. crispum (A. roebelenii). Robust plant with leathery leaves to 10 in. long, 5 in. wide, dark green with pale green markings. Sometimes sold as *A.* 'Pewter'.

A. modestum. CHINESE EVERGREEN. A serviceable, easily grown plant, in time forming substantial clumps with several stems 2–3 ft. high. Shiny dark green leaves to 1½ ft. long, 5 in. wide. Often sold as *A. simplex*.

A. 'Silver King' and **'Silver Queen'.** Both are heavy producers of narrow, dark green leaves strongly marked with silver. Both grow to 2 ft. 'Silver King' has larger leaves than 'Silver Queen'.

AGONIS

Myrtaceae	
EVERGREEN TREES OR LARGE SHRUBS	
☀ ZONES 15–17, 20–24	
☼ FULL SUN	
◐ REQUIRES VERY LITTLE WATER	

Native to Australia. Very tolerant of different soil types and watering practices. Related to *Leptospermum* and *Melaleuca*.

A. flexuosa. PEPPERMINT TREE, AUSTRALIAN WILLOW MYRTLE. One of the best small trees for California gardens where temperatures stay above 27°F. Will freeze to the ground at 25°F; in the Sacramento Valley it has come back from the stump. Spreading, medium–fast growing to 25–35 ft. Narrow, willowlike leaves to 6 in. long densely clothe the weeping branches. Leaves smell like peppermint when crushed. Small white flowers carried abundantly in June. Use it in a lawn, train it as an espalier, or use it as a tub plant.

A. juniperina. JUNIPER MYRTLE. More open and finely textured than *A. flexuosa* but grows to about the same height. Narrow, ¼–½-in.-long soft green leaves. Bears fluffy white flower clusters, summer to November.

Agonis flexuosa

AGROPYRON

WHEATGRASS	
Poaceae (Gramineae)	
LAWN GRASSES	
☀ ZONES 1–3, 10	
☼ FULL SUN	
◐ MONTHLY SOAKINGS	

Two kinds of wheatgrass, both basically pasture grasses, make reasonably attractive lawns in Rocky Mountains and on high plains. They can survive with 8–18 in. of rainfall per year, but when planted close and mowed at 2 in. they should be soaked to 18–20 in. every 30 days. Plant 2 lbs. per 1,000 sq. ft.

A. cristatum. CRESTED WHEATGRASS. Bunching grass rather than sod-forming grass. Fairway strain, used for low-maintenance, low-irrigation lawns, is shorter, denser, and finer than common kind.

A. smithii. WESTERN WHEATGRASS. Forms sod, but slowly. Tolerates great heat, cold, moderately alkaline soil.

Agropyron smithii

FOR INFORMATION ON YOUR CLIMATE ZONE

PLEASE SEE PAGES 15–44

AGROSTEMMA githago

CORN COCKLE	
Caryophyllaceae	
ANNUAL	
☀ ALL ZONES	
☼ FULL SUN	
◐ MODERATE WATER	
◊ ALL PARTS ARE POISONOUS IF EATEN	

The species is an attractive weed of roadside and grain field. Variety 'Milas' is a superior plant with 3-in. flowers of deep purplish pink, lined and spotted with deep purple and centered with a white eye. Stems 6–12 in. long make it a good cut flower. Plants wispy but sturdy, 2–3 ft. tall. Sow seed in spring or early summer for summer and fall bloom in most climates; sow in fall for winter–spring bloom in warmest climates. Mass at rear of border, among shrubs, or in front of fence or hedge.

Agrostemma githago

AGROSTIS

BENT, BENT GRASS	
Poaceae (Gramineae)	
LAWN GRASSES	
☀ ALL ZONES	
☼ FULL SUN	
◐ FREQUENT WATER	

All except redtop make beautiful velvety lawns under proper conditions and with constant care. They need frequent close mowing, frequent feeding, occasional topdressing, and much water. In hot weather they succumb to fungal diseases. In San Francisco Bay Area, bent grasses (planted intentionally or distributed by birds) tend to dominate bluegrasses and fescues. Best putting greens are of bent grass.

Agrostis stolonifera

A. gigantea. REDTOP. Coarser than other bents, not generally used in lawns. Has been used as quick-sprouting nurse grass in mixtures or for winter overseeding of Bermuda and other winter-dormant grasses.

A. stolonifera. CREEPING BENT. Premium lawn but requires the most care, including frequent mowing to ½ in. tall with special mower. Seed-grown strains include Emerald, Penncross, and Seaside. In some areas you can buy sprigs or sod of choice strains, Congressional, Old Orchard.

A. tenuis. COLONIAL BENT. More erect than creeping bent; somewhat easier to care for but still fussy. Astoria and Highland are best-known strains; the latter is tougher, hardier, more disease resistant. Mow to ¾ in.

AILANTHUS altissima
(A. glandulosa)

TREE-OF-HEAVEN	
Simaroubaceae	
DECIDUOUS TREE	
☀ ALL ZONES	
☼ FULL SUN	
○ NO WATER ONCE ESTABLISHED	

Native to China. Planted in the 1800s in California's gold country, where it now runs wild. Fast growth to 50 ft. Leaves 1–3 ft. long are divided into 13–25 leaflets 3–5 in. long. Inconspicuous greenish flowers are usually followed by handsome clusters of red-brown, winged seed pods in late summer and fall; great for dried arrangements. Often condemned as a weed tree because it suckers profusely and self-seeds, it must be praised for its ability to create beauty and shade under adverse conditions— aridity, hot winds, extreme air pollution, and every type of difficult soil.

Ailanthus altissima

A

AIR PLANT. See KALANCHOE pinnata   p. 343

Aizoaceae. This family of succulent plants includes all the ice plants and most of the so-called living stones.

AJUGA

CARPET BUGLE

Lamiaceae (Labiatae)

PERENNIALS

▨ ALL ZONES

☼ ☽ FULL SUN OR PARTIAL SHADE

◑ REGULAR WATER

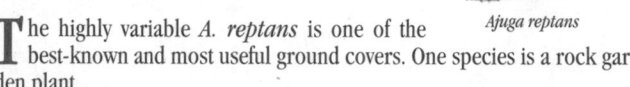
Ajuga reptans

The highly variable *A. reptans* is one of the best-known and most useful ground covers. One species is a rock garden plant.

A. genevensis. Rock garden plant 5–14 in. high, no runners. Grayish, hairy stems and coarse-toothed leaves to 3 in. long. Flowers in blue spikes; rose and white forms are also sold.

A. pyramidalis. Erect plants 2–10 in. high; do not spread by runners. Stems, with long grayish hairs, have many roundish 1½–4-in.-long leaves. Violet blue flowers are not obvious among the large leaves. Variety 'Metallica Crispa' has reddish brown leaves with a metallic glint.

A. reptans. The popular ground cover ajuga. Spreads quickly by runners, making a mat of dark green leaves that grow 2–3 in. wide in full sun, 3–4 in. wide in part shade. Bears mostly blue flowers in 4–6-in.-high spikes. Many varieties are available; some are sold under several names.

All the varieties of *A. reptans* listed below make thick carpets of lustrous leaves, enhanced from spring to early summer with spikes of showy flowers. Plant in spring or early fall 6–12 in. apart, 1½ ft. for the big ones. Give full sun to partial shade; in full sun, those with bronze or metallic tints keep color best. Feed in spring or late summer. Water every 7–10 days in summer. Mow or trim off old flower spikes. Subject to root-knot nematodes; also subject to rot and fungal diseases where drainage or air circulation is poor.

Varieties listed below as giant and jungle ajugas are sold under many names, the green ones as 'Crispa' and the purplish or bronzy ones as 'Metallica Crispa', 'Bronze Ripple', or 'Rubra' (these are not the same as *A. pyramidalis* 'Metallica Crispa'). All have blue flowers.

'Burgundy Lace' ('Burgundy Glow'). Variety of *A. reptans* with reddish purple foliage variegated with white and pink.

'Giant Bronze'. Deep metallic bronze leaves larger, more vigorous, and crisper than those of *A. reptans*. To 6 in. tall in sun, 9 in. tall in shade.

'Giant Green'. Like 'Giant Bronze' but leaves are bright green.

'Jungle Bronze'. Large, rounded, wavy-edged leaves of bronzy tone, in clumps; tall growing. Flowers on 8–10-in.-high spikes.

'Jungle Green'. Largest-leafed ajuga—rounded, crisp edged, and green. Less mounding than 'Jungle Bronze'.

'Purpurea'. Similar to *A. reptans* but with bronze or purple tint in leaves. Leaves often slightly larger. Often sold as 'Atropurpurea'.

'Variegata'. Leaves edged and splotched with creamy yellow.

AKEBIA quinata

FIVELEAF AKEBIA

Lardizabalaceae

DECIDUOUS VINE, EVERGREEN IN MILD WINTERS

▨ ALL ZONES

☼ ☽ ● SUN OR SHADE

◑ REGULAR WATER

Akebia quinata

Native to Japan, China, and Korea. Twines to 15–20 ft. Grows fast in mild regions, slower where winters are cold. Dainty leaves on 3–5-in. stalks, each divided into five deep green leaflets 2–3 in. long, notched at tips. Clusters of quaint dull purple flowers in spring are more a surprise than a show. The edible fruit, if produced, looks like a thick, 2½–4-in.-long, purplish sausage.

Give support for climbing; keep under control. Benefits from annual pruning. Recovers quickly when cut to the ground. For a tracery effect on post or column, prune out all but two or three basal stems.

A. trifoliata. THREELEAF AKEBIA. Like the above but with three instead of five leaflets per leaf.

ALASKA CEDAR. See CHAMAECYPARIS nootkatensis   p. 220

ALBIZIA (Albizzia)

Fabaceae (Leguminosae)

DECIDUOUS TO SEMIEVERGREEN TREES

▨ ZONES VARY BY SPECIES

☼ ☽ SUN OR PARTIAL SHADE

◑◑ WATER NEEDS VARY BY SPECIES

Albizia julibrissin

These trees have twice-divided, finely textured foliage and powder-puff flowers that are attractive to birds.

A. distachya (A. lophantha). PLUME ALBIZIA. Semievergreen. Zones 15–17, 22–24. Native to Australia. Not as hardy as the better-known *A. julibrissin*. In California coastal areas it often naturalizes. Needs no irrigation; will grow in pure sand at beach. Fast growing to 20 ft. Foliage is dark velvety green compared to the light yellowish green of *A. julibrissin*, but it too is fernlike. The flowers in late spring are greenish yellow in fluffy, 2-in.-long spikes. Best as a temporary screen at beach while slower permanent planting develops. Gets shabby-looking inland.

A. julibrissin. SILK TREE. Deciduous. Zones 2–23. Native to Asia from Iran to Japan. This is the mimosa of eastern United States. Rapid growth to 40 ft. with wider spread. Can be headed back to make a 10–20-ft. umbrella. Pink, fluffy flowers like pincushions on ferny-leafed branches in summer. Light-sensitive leaves fold at night. The variety 'Rosea' has richer pink flowers and is considered hardier.

Does best with high summer heat. One of the best sellers in inland valleys of Southern California. With ample water grows fast; on skimpy irrigation usually survives but grows slowly, looks yellowish.

Silk tree is an excellent small shade tree with a unique flat-topped shape that makes a true canopy for a patio. Because of its undulating form and flowers held above the foliage, it's especially beautiful when viewed from above, as from a deck or hilltop. Somewhat of a problem to get started as a high-headed tree. Must be staked and trained; with the thumb, rub out buds that start too low. Best planted from containers established at least 1 year; bare-root plants need skillful planting, watering.

Silk tree is most attractive in its natural growth habit—as a multiple-stemmed tree. Filtered shade permits growth of lawn and shrubs beneath. Despite litter of fallen leaves, flowers, and pods, a good patio plant.

ALCEA rosea (Althaea rosea)

HOLLYHOCK

Malvaceae

BIENNIAL OR SHORT-LIVED PERENNIAL

▨ ALL ZONES

☼ FULL SUN

◑ REGULAR WATER

Alcea rosea

This old-fashioned favorite has its place against a fence or wall or at the back of a border. Old single varieties can reach 9 ft.; newer strains and selections are shorter. Big, rough, roundish heart-shaped leaves more or less lobed; single, semidouble, or double flowers 3–6 in. wide in white, pink, rose, red, purple, creamy yellow, apricot. Summer bloom. Chater's Double is a fine perennial strain; 6-ft. spires have 5–6-in. flowers. So-called annual strains (biennials treated as annuals) bloom first year from seed sown in early spring: Summer Carnival strain is 5–6 ft. tall with double 4-in. flowers; Majorette strain is 2½ ft. tall with 3–4-in. flowers; Pinafore strain (mixed colors) branches freely from base, has five to eight bloom stalks per plant.

Destroy rust-infected leaves as soon as disease appears. Bait to protect from snails and slugs.

MAKE HOLLYHOCKS BLOOM TWICE

In July, after blooms fade, cut off hollyhock flower stems just above the ground. Continue to feed and water the plants. Roots will push out another flush of growth, which will rebloom in September. This technique demands a lot from the plants, so give them the best growing conditions you can: feed two or three times during the regular growing season, and water as needed all along.

ALCHEMILLA

LADY'S-MANTLE	
Rosaceae	
PERENNIALS	
☀ ZONES VARY BY SPECIES	
☼ ● TOLERATE SUN IN COOL-SUMMER CLIMATES	
● REGULAR WATER	

Alchemilla mollis

Rounded pale green lobed leaves have a silvery look; after rain or overhead watering they hold beads of water on their surfaces. Flowers are yellowish green, in large branched clusters, individually inconspicuous but attractive as a mass. Useful for edgings in shady places, as ground cover and as soothing contrast to brightly colored flowers.

A. ellenbeckii. Zones 14–24. Creeping, rooting stems, with leaves less than 1 inch wide. Attractive small-scale ground cover for damp shade.

A. mollis. Zones 2–9, 14–24. To 2 ft. or more, with equal spread, and leaves up to 6 in. across.

ALDER. See ALNUS	**p. 146**
ALDER BUCKTHORN. See RHAMNUS frangula	**p. 453**
ALEXANDRA PALM. See ARCHONTOPHOENIX alexandrae	**p. 162**
ALGERIAN IVY. See HEDERA canariensis	**p. 317**

ALLIUM

ORNAMENTAL ALLIUM	
Liliaceae	
BULBS	
☀ ALL ZONES	
☼ ☼ FULL SUN OR PARTIAL SHADE	
● AMPLE WATER DURING GROWTH	

About 500 species, all from the Northern Hemisphere, many from mountains of the West. Relatives of the edible onion, peerless as cut flowers (fresh or dried) and useful in borders; smaller

Allium giganteum

kinds are effective in rock gardens. Most ornamental alliums are hardy, sun loving, easy to grow; they thrive in deep, rich, sandy loam. Plant bulbs in fall. Lift and divide only after they become crowded. Alliums bear small flowers in compact or loose roundish clusters at ends of leafless stems 6 in.–5 ft. tall or more. Many are delightfully fragrant; those with onion odor must be bruised or cut to give it off. Flowers from late spring through summer, in white and shades of pink, rose, violet, red, blue, yellow.

A. aflatunense. Round clusters of lilac flowers on stems 2½–5 ft. tall. Resembles *A. giganteum* but with smaller (2–3-in.) flower clusters; blooms late May.

A. albopilosum. See A. christophii

A. atropurpureum. Stems to 2½ ft. tall carry 2-in. clusters of dark purple to nearly black flowers in May or June.

A. caeruleum (A. azureum). BLUE ALLIUM. Cornflower blue flowers in dense, round clusters 2 in. across on 1-ft. stems. June bloom.

A. carinatum pulchellum (A. pulchellum). Tight clusters of reddish purple flowers on 2-ft. stems, May or June.

A. cepa. See Onion

A. christophii (A. albopilosum). STAR OF PERSIA. Distinctive. Very large clusters (6–12 in. across) of lavender to deep lilac, starlike flowers with metallic sheen. June bloom. Stems 12–15 in. tall. Leaves to 1½ ft. long, white and hairy beneath. Dried flower cluster looks like an elegant ornament.

A. giganteum. GIANT ALLIUM. Spectacular ball-like clusters of bright lilac flowers on stems 5 ft. or more tall. Leaves 1½ ft. long, 2 in. wide. July bloom.

A. karataviense. TURKESTAN ALLIUM. Large, dense, round flower clusters in May, varying in color from pinkish to beige to reddish lilac. Broad, flat, recurved leaves, 2–5 in. across.

A. moly. GOLDEN GARLIC. Bright, shining, yellow flowers in open clusters on 9–18-in.-tall stems. June bloom. Flat leaves 2 in. wide, almost as long as flower stems

A. narcissiflorum. Foot-tall stems with loose clusters of ½-in. bell-shaped, bright rose flowers, May or June.

A. neapolitanum. Spreading clusters of large white flowers on 1-ft. stems bloom in May. Leaves 1 in. wide. Variety 'Grandiflorum' is larger, blooms earlier. A form of 'Grandiflorum' listed as 'Cowanii' is considered superior. Grown commercially as cut flowers; pot plant in cold climates.

A. ostrowskianum (A. oreophilum ostrowskianum). Large, loose clusters of rose-colored flowers in June on 8–12-in. stems; two to three narrow, gray-green leaves. Variety 'Zwanenburg' has deep carmine red flowers, 6-in. stems. Good for rock gardens, cutting.

A. porrum. See Leek

A. pulchellum. See A. carinatum pulchellum

A. rosenbachianum. Similar to *A. giganteum* but slightly smaller; blooms earlier.

A. sativum. See Garlic

A. schoenoprasum. See Chives

A. scorodoprasum. See Garlic

A. sphaerocephalum. DRUMSTICKS, ROUND-HEADED GARLIC. Tight, dense, spherical red-purple flower clusters on 2-ft. stems, May or June. Spreads freely.

A. tuberosum. CHINESE CHIVES, GARLIC CHIVES, ORIENTAL GARLIC. Spreads by tuberous rootstocks and by seeds. Clumps of gray-green, flat leaves ¼ in. wide, 1 ft. long or less. Abundance of 1–1½-ft.-tall stalks bear clusters of white flowers in summer. Flowers have scent of violets, are excellent for fresh or dry arrangements. Leaves have mild garlic flavor, are useful in salads and cooked dishes. Grow like chives. Dormant in winter.

A. unifolium. California native with extremely handsome, satiny, lavender pink flowers on 1–2-ft. stems. June bloom.

Allium tuberosum

ALLOPLECTUS nummularia (Hypocyrta nummularia)

GOLDFISH PLANT

Gesneriaceae

INDOOR CONTAINER PLANT

● SHADE

💧 FREQUENT WATER

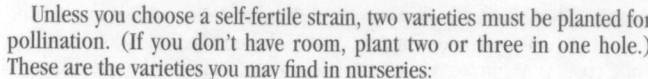

Alloplectus nummularia

Related to African violet, with similar cultural needs. Foot-long, arching branches closely set with shiny oval or roundish leaves to 2½ in. long. Flowers about 1 in. long, orange, puffy, and roundish, pinched at tip into pursed mouth like that of goldfish.

With ample warmth and humidity this plant will bloom year-round. Easy to root from tip cuttings; stems may root when in contact with damp soil mix. Because of arching, trailing growth, best in hanging pot.

ALLSPICE, CAROLINA. See CALYCANTHUS floridus p. 199

ALMOND

Rosaceae

DECIDUOUS TREES

🌿 ZONES 8–10, 12–16, 19–21

☼ FULL SUN

💧 INFREQUENT, DEEP WATERING

As trees, almonds are nearly as hardy as peaches, but as nut producers they are more exacting in climate adaptation. Zones listed are for best nut production. Frost during the trees' early blooming period cuts the crop, and if they escape that, a late (April) frost will destroy small fruits that are forming. Nuts will not develop properly in areas with cool summers and high humidity. To experiment in areas where frost is a hazard, choose late-blooming varieties.

Almond

Tree grows to 20–30 ft. high, erect when young, spreading and dome shaped in age. Leaves 3–5 in. long, pale green with gray tinge. Flowers 1–2 in. across, palest pink or white. Fruit looks like a leathery, flattened, undersized green peach. The hull splits to reveal the pit, which is the almond that you harvest.

Harvest almonds when hulls split. At this stage you may need to knock nuts from trees or pick them off ground. Remove leathery hull and spread hulled nuts in sun for day or two to dry. To test for adequate dryness, shake nuts—kernels should rattle in shells. Store dried nuts indoors.

Almonds do well in any type of soil except heavy, poorly drained soil, where they are subject to root rot. Need deep soil—at least 6 ft. Almonds need spraying to control mites, which cause premature yellowing and falling of leaves and may also cause weakening or eventual death. Brown rot makes fruit rot and harden; it also attacks twigs, killing them back and forming cankers on main trunk and branches.

Unless you choose a self-fertile strain, two varieties must be planted for pollination. (If you don't have room, plant two or three in one hole.) These are the varieties you may find in nurseries:

'All-in-One'. Semidwarf tree blooms with 'Texas' and 'Nonpareil'. Medium to large sweet, soft-shell nuts, September–October. Self-fertile.

'Carmel'. A regular heavy bearer of small nuts with good flavor. Pollinates 'Nonpareil' and 'Texas'.

'Garden Prince'. Dwarf tree with showy pink bloom and medium-size, soft-shell nuts. Self-fertile.

'Hall' ('Hall's Hardy'). Hard-shell nut of good size and quality. Pink bloom comes late—an advantage in late-frost regions. Tree is as hardy as a peach. Partially self-fertile but better with 'Jordanolo' or 'Texas' as pollinators.

'Jordanolo'. High-quality nut but subject to bud failure in areas of extreme summer heat. 'Ne Plus Ultra' and 'Nonpareil' are pollinators.

'Kapareil'. Small, soft-shell nuts. Pollinator for 'Nonpareil'.

'Ne Plus Ultra'. Large kernels in attractive soft shells. Pollinator for 'Nonpareil'.

'Nonpareil'. Best all-around variety. Easily shelled by hand. Some bud failure in very hot summer regions. Pollinate with 'Jordanolo', 'Ne Plus Ultra', 'Kapareil'.

'Texas' ('Mission'). Small, semihard-shell nut. Regular, heavy producer. Late bloomer, one of safest for cold-winter, late-frost areas. Use 'Nonpareil' or 'Hall' as pollinators. For ornamental relatives, see *Prunus*.

ALMOND, FLOWERING. See PRUNUS triloba p. 443

ALNUS

ALDER

Betulaceae

DECIDUOUS TREES

🌿 ZONES VARY BY SPECIES

☼ ☽ ● ANY EXPOSURE

💧 AMPLE WATER (OR GROW IT BESIDE A CREEK)

Alnus rhombifolia

Moisture loving; of remarkably rapid growth In all species, clusters of tassel-like, greenish yellow male flower catkins give interesting display before leaf-out. Female flowers develop into small woody cones that decorate bare branches in winter; these delight flower arrangers. Seeds attract birds. Roots are invasive—less troublesome if deep watering practices are followed.

A. cordata. ITALIAN ALDER. Zones 8, 9, 14–24. Native to Italy, Corsica. Young growth vertical; older trees to 40 ft., spreading to 25 ft. Heart-shaped, 4-in. leaves, glossy rich green above, paler beneath. Short deciduous period. More restrained than *A. rhombifolia*. Favored in Southwest, except high desert.

A. glutinosa. BLACK ALDER. Zones 1–10, 14–24. Native to Europe, North Africa, Asia. Not as fast growing as *A. rhombifolia*. Probably best as multistemmed tree. Grows to 70 ft. Roundish, 2–4-in., coarsely toothed leaves, dark lustrous green. Makes dense mass from ground up. Good for screen.

A. oregona (A. rubra). RED ALDER. Zones 4–6, 15–17. Native to stream banks and marshy places. Most common alder of lowlands in Pacific Northwest. Ranges from Alaska south to Santa Cruz County, California; rarely found more than 10 miles from coast in California. Grows to 90 ft. high but usually 45–50 ft. Attractive smooth, light gray bark. Dark green, 2–4-in. leaves, rust colored and hairy beneath; coarsely toothed margins are rolled under. Can take surprising amount of brackish water and is useful wherever underground water is somewhat saline. Generally disliked in Northwest because it's a favorite of tent caterpillars.

A. rhombifolia. WHITE ALDER. Zones 1–9, 14–21. Native along streams throughout most of California's foothills except along coast; mountains of Oregon, Washington, British Columbia, and Idaho. Very fast growing to 50–90 ft., with 40-ft. spread. Very tolerant of heat and wind. Spreading or ascending branches often pendulous at tips. Coarsely toothed, 2½–4½-in. leaves dark green above, paler green beneath. In its native areas it's susceptible to tent caterpillars.

A. tenuifolia. MOUNTAIN ALDER, THINLEAF ALDER. Zones 1–3, 10. Shrub or small tree to 20–25 ft. Extremely hardy to cold.

ALOCASIA

| ELEPHANT'S EAR |
| Araceae |
| PERENNIALS |
| 🗲 OUTDOORS, ZONES 22–24; OR INDOORS |
| ☼ FILTERED SUNLIGHT |
| ◖ LOTS OF WATER |
| ◈ PLANT JUICES ARE POISONOUS |

Alocasia macrorrhiza

Native to tropical Asia. Handsome, lush plants for tropical effects. Flowers like those of calla (*Zantedeschia*). Plant in wind-protected places or indoors. Provide ample organic matter in soil and light, frequent feedings. Tropical plant specialists sell many kinds with leaves in coppery and purplish tones, often with striking white veins.

A. amazonica. AFRICAN MASK. House plant. Leathery, deep bronzy green leaves to 16 in. long have wavy edges, heavy white main veins.

A. macrorrhiza. Evergreen at 29°F; loses leaves at lower temperatures but comes back in spring if frosts not too severe. Large, arrow-shaped leaves to 2 ft. or longer, on stalks to 5 ft. tall, form a dome-shaped plant 4 ft. across. Tiny flowers on spike surrounded by greenish white bract. Flowers followed by reddish fruit, giving spike the look of corn on the cob.

A. odora. Similar to *A. macrorrhiza* but not quite as hardy. Flowers fragrant.

ALOE

| Liliaceae |
| SUCCULENTS |
| 🗲 ZONES 8, 9, 12–24 |
| ☼☀ FULL SUN; LIGHT SHADE INLAND |
| ◖ INFREQUENT, DEEP WATERING |
| ◈ LATEX BENEATH THE SKIN IS IRRITANT |

Aloe arborescens

Aloes range from 6-in. miniatures to trees; all form clumps of fleshy, pointed leaves and bear branched or unbranched clusters of orange, yellow, cream, or red flowers. Most are South African. Showy, easy to grow, needing little or no watering, they rate among Southern California's most valuable ornamentals. Most kinds make outstanding container plants. Some species in bloom every month; biggest show February–September. Leaves may be green or gray-green, often strikingly banded or streaked with contrasting colors. Aloes grow easily in well-drained soil in reasonably frost-free areas. Where winters are cooler, grow in pots and shelter from frosts. Aloes listed here are only a few of the many kinds.

A. arborescens. TREE ALOE. Older clumps may reach 18 ft. Branching stems carry big clumps of gray-green, spiny-edged leaves. Flowers (December–February) in long, spiky clusters, bright vermilion to clear yellow. Withstands salt spray. Tolerates shade. Foliage damaged at 29°F, but plants have survived 17°F. Not reliably hardy in Zone 12.

A. aristata. Dwarf species for pots, edging, ground covers. Reaches 8–12 in. tall and wide. Rosettes densely packed with 4-in.-long, ¾-in.-wide leaves ending in whiplike threads. Flowers orange red in 1–1½-ft.-tall clusters, winter.

A. bainesii. Slow-growing tree with heavy, forking trunk and branches. Rosettes of 2–3-ft. leaves, spikes of rose pink flowers on 1½–2-ft. stalks. Used for stately, sculpturesque pattern in landscape. Tender to frost.

A. barbadensis. See A. vera

A. brevifolia. Low clumps of blunt, thick, gray-green, spiny-edged leaves 3 in. long. Clusters of red flowers, 20 in. tall, intermittent all year.

A. ciliaris. Climbing, sprawling, with pencil-thick stems to 10 ft. long. Leaves small, thick, soft green. Long-stalked, 3–6-in. flower clusters with 20–30 green- or yellow-tipped scarlet flowers, intermittent all year. Takes some shade, little frost.

A. distans. JEWELED ALOE. Running, rooting, branching stems make clumps of 6-in., fleshy, blue-green leaves with scattered whitish spots and white teeth along edges. Forked flower stems, 1½–2 ft. tall, carry clusters of red flowers.

A. nobilis. Dark green leaves edged with small hooked teeth grow in rosettes to 1 ft. across and about as tall. Clustered orange-red flowers appear on 2-ft. stalks in June, last for 6 weeks. Good container subject—takes limited root space.

A. plicatilis. Slow growing, with thick, forking trunks crowned with fans (not rosettes) of smooth, gray-green, foot-long leaves. Clusters of 1½-ft. scarlet flowers. Sculpturesque container plant when young; reaches 3–5 ft. in 10 years. Tender.

A. saponaria. Short-stemmed, broad clumps. Broad, thick, 8-in.-long leaves variegated with white spots. Clumps spread rapidly and may become bound together—dig up too-thick clumps and separate them. Branched flower stalk 1½–2½ ft. tall. Orange-red to shrimp pink flowers over long period.

Aloe saponaria

A. striata. CORAL ALOE. Leaves broad, 20 in. long, spineless, gray green, with narrow pinkish red edge. They grow in rosettes 2 ft. wide on short trunk. Brilliant coral pink to orange flowers in branched clusters, February–May. Handsome, tailored plant. Protect from hot sun in desert.

A. variegata. PARTRIDGE-BREAST ALOE, TIGER ALOE. Foot-high, triangular rosette of fleshy, triangular, dark green, 5-in.-long leaves strikingly banded and edged with white. Loose flower clusters of pink to dull red flowers intermittent all year.

A. vera (A. barbadensis). MEDICINAL ALOE, BARBADOS ALOE. Clustering rosettes of narrow, fleshy, stiffly upright leaves 1–2 ft. long. Yellow flowers in dense spike atop 3-ft. stalk. Favorite folk medicine plant used to treat burns, bites, inflammation, and a host of other ills. One of best for Zones 12, 13. Survives without extra water but needs some to look good.

ALONSOA

| MASK FLOWER |
| Scrophulariaceae |
| PERENNIALS OFTEN GROWN AS ANNUALS |
| 🗲 ZONES 23, 24 |
| ☼☀ FULL SUN OR PARTIAL SHADE |
| ◖ REGULAR WATER |

Alonsoa warscewiczii

Barely hardy in the mildest climates, mask flowers are usually grown as summer bedding plants, as fillers in the perennial border, or as indoor or outdoor container plants. Sprawling or erect to 3 ft., freely branching, with wispy foliage and open clusters of oddly shaped, roundish flowers. All are fairly easy to grow from seed, blooming the first year if started early and continuing to frost or cold weather.

A. linearis. Flowers brick red.

A. meridionalis. Flowers are orange to dark red, somewhat less than 1 in. wide. Firestone Jewels strain has flowers ranging from white through yellow to salmon, pink, and red. 'Shell Pink' and 'Salmon' are offered as plants.

A. warscewiczii. Flowers scarlet to peach with dark eyes, to ½ in. across.

A

ALOYSIA triphylla
(Lippia citriodora)

LEMON VERBENA

Verbenaceae

DECIDUOUS OR PARTIALLY EVERGREEN HERB-SHRUB

ZONES 9, 10, 12–24

FULL SUN

REGULAR WATER

Aloysia triphylla

Borderline hardy as far north as Seattle if planted against warm wall. Legginess is the natural state of this plant; it's the herb that grew like a gangling shrub in grandmother's garden. Prized for its lemon-scented leaves. Grows to 6 ft. or taller; narrow leaves to 3 in. long are arranged in whorls of three or four along branches. Bears open clusters of very small lilac or whitish flowers in summer. By pinch-pruning you can shape it to give interesting tracery against wall. Or let it grow among lower plants to hide its legginess.

In cold climates, grow it as a house plant (pinch frequently) and let it spend warm months out of doors. When you read of the scent of verbena in literature about the antebellum South, lemon verbena is the plant being described.

This genus contains another species, *A. wrightii*, that is native to desert mountains from California to Texas and northern Mexico. Its common name is oreganillo ("little oregano"). It is occasionally used as flavoring or as tea.

LEMON VERBENA LEAVES FOR FRAGRANCE AND FLAVOR

This plant is prized for its lemon-scented leaves, which scent the area around them in the garden. The long, shiny leaves add lemony flavor to teas and iced drinks. Dry the leaves for potpourri. When making apple jelly, try placing a big fresh leaf in the bottom of each glass or jar. For all these purposes, pick the fresh-looking leaves from near the top of the stem.

ALPINIA

Zingiberaceae

PERENNIALS WITH RHIZOMES

EVERGREEN IN ZONES 22–24

LIGHT SHADE

LOTS OF WATER

Alpinia zerumbet

Roots hardy to about 15°F. Die down in winter in Zones 15–17. Need wind-free exposure, good soil. In order to bloom, alpinia must be established at least 2 years. Remove flowered canes yearly.

A. sanderae. VARIEGATED GINGER. To 3–4 ft. tall, with 8-in.-long leaves striped with white. Rarely flowers. A good container plant.

A. zerumbet (A. nutans, A. speciosa). SHELL GINGER, SHELL FLOWER. Native to tropical Asia and Polynesia. Grandest of gingers, best all-year appearance. To 8–9 ft. tall. Leaves shiny, 2 ft. long, 5 in. wide, with distinct parallel veins; grow on stems that are maroon at maturity. Waxy white or pinkish, shell-like, fragrant flowers marked red, purple, brown, in pendant clusters on arching stems in late summer.

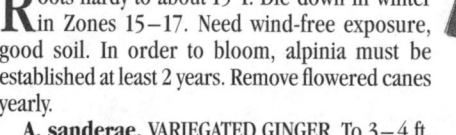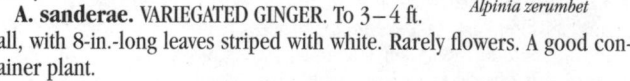

ALSOPHILA australis, A. cooperi. See CYATHEA cooperi   p. 253

ALSTROEMERIA

Liliaceae

PERENNIALS

ZONES 5–9, 14–24

FULL SUN

MODERATE WATER

CAUSES DERMATITIS IN ALLERGIC PEOPLE

Alstroemeria aurantiaca

Ligtu hybrids bloom on leafy stems 2–5 ft. tall, topped with broad, loose clusters of azalealike flowers in beautiful colors—orange, yellow, and shades of pink, rose, red, lilac, and creamy white to white; many are streaked and speckled with darker colors. Masses of color in borders from May to midsummer. Long-lasting cut flowers. Tops wither after bloom; flowerless shoots dry up even sooner.

Evergreen hybrids (Cordu, Meyer) have a long bloom season if spent flowering stems are pulled, not cut. Colors include white to pink, red, lilac, and purple, usually bicolored and spotted.

A few nurseries offer 3–4-ft.-tall Peruvian Lily (*A. aurea, A. aurantiaca*). 'Orange King' has orange-yellow, brown-spotted flowers; 'Lutea' has yellow flowers, 'Splendens' red. *A. psittacina (A. pulchella)* is 1–1½ ft. tall, more or less evergreen, with dark red flowers tipped green and spotted deep purple. It can be invasive.

Best in cool, moist, deep, sandy to medium loam. Plant roots in fall; if you buy alstroemeria in a gallon can, you can plant it outdoors any time in mild-winter climates. Set roots 6–8 in. deep, 1 ft. apart; handle brittle roots gently. Leave clumps undisturbed for many years because they reestablish slowly after transplanting. You can easily start alstroemerias by sowing seed where the plants are to grow or in individual pots for later transplanting. Sow in fall, winter, or earliest spring. All are hardy in cold-winter climates if planted at proper depth and kept mulched in winter. Ligtu hybrids can be allowed to dry off after bloom. Evergreen kinds must be watered for continued bloom. Cool summers prolong bloom.

PICK ALSTROEMERIA FLOWERS IN A SPECIAL WAY

When you pick flowers of the evergreen kinds of alstroemeria, don't cut them. Instead, grasp each flower stem several inches above the soil and gently twist and pull upward to break the stem's base cleanly away from the rhizome. Cutting slows growth, but this technique encourages new bud growth and flower production. The best times to pick are in the cool months of spring and fall, when the plants are growing best.

ALTERNANTHERA ficoidea

Amaranthaceae

PERENNIAL TREATED AS ANNUAL

ALL ZONES

FULL SUN

MODERATE WATER

Alternanthera ficoidea 'Bettzickiana'

Colorful foliage somewhat resembles that of coleus. Plants grow 6–12 in. tall and should be planted 4–10 in. apart for colorful effect. Where winters are cold, plant only after soil warms up. Keep low and compact by shearing. Grow from cuttings. Often sold as *A. bettzickiana*. 'Aurea Nana' is low grower with yellow-splotched foliage. 'Bettzickiana' has spoon-shaped leaves with red and yellow markings. 'Magnifica' is a red bronze dwarf. 'Parrot Feather' and 'Versicolor' have broad green leaves with yellow markings and pink veins.

ALTHAEA rosea. See ALCEA rosea   p. 144

ALYOGYNE huegelii (Hibiscus huegelii)

BLUE HIBISCUS

Malvaceae

EVERGREEN SHRUB

ZONES 15–17, 20–24

FULL SUN

LITTLE TO MODERATE WATER

Alyogyne huegelii

Upright growth to 5–8 ft. Foliage deeply cut, dark green, rough textured. Flowers 4–5 in. across, lilac blue to deep purple, with glossy petals. Blooms off and on throughout year; individual flowers last 2–3 days. Hardy to about 23°F. Pinch or prune as needed to keep it compact. Variable from seed. 'Santa Cruz' is good deep blue selection. 'Monterey Bay' is even bluer.

ALYSSUM

Brassicaceae (Cruciferae)

PERENNIALS

ALL ZONES

FULL SUN OR JUST A LITTLE SHADE

LITTLE WATER

Alyssum montanum

Mostly native to Mediterranean region. Mounding plants or shrublets that brighten spring borders and rock gardens with their cheerful bloom. They thrive in poor, rocky soil.

A. montanum. Stems up to 8 in. high; leaves gray, hairy (denser on underside); flowers yellow, fragrant, in dense short clusters.

A. saxatile. See Aurinia saxatilis

A. wulfenianum. Prostrate and trailing, with fleshy, silvery leaves and sheets of pale yellow flowers.

Amaranthaceae. The amaranth family largely consists of herbaceous plants, many of them weedy. Flowers are small and chaffy, often effective when massed.

AMARANTHUS

AMARANTH

Amaranthaceae

ANNUALS

ALL ZONES

FULL SUN OR PARTIAL SHADE

MODERATE WATER

Amaranthus caudatus

Coarse, sometimes weedy plants; a few ornamental kinds are grown for their brightly colored foliage or flowers. Sow seed in early summer—soil temperature must be above 70°F for germination.

Picked when young and tender, leaves and stems of many species (even some of the weedy ones) can be cooked like spinach, taking its place in hot weather. Some species have seeds that look like sesame seeds, have a high protein content, and can be used as grain.

A. caudatus. LOVE-LIES-BLEEDING, TASSEL FLOWER. Sturdy, branching plant 3–8 ft. high; leaves 2–10 in. long, ½–4 in. wide. Red flowers in drooping, tassel-like clusters. A curiosity rather than a pretty plant. One of the amaranths that produce grain.

A. hybridus erythrostachys. PRINCE'S FEATHER. To 5 ft. high with leaves 1–6 in. long, ½–3 in. wide, usually reddish. Flowers red or brownish red in many-branched clusters. Some strains grown as spinach substitute or for grain.

A. tricolor. JOSEPH'S COAT. Branching plant 1–4 ft. high. Leaves 2½–6 in. long, 2–4 in. wide, blotched in shades of red and green. Selections such as 'Early Splendor', 'Flaming Fountain', and 'Molten Fire' bear masses of yellow to scarlet foliage at tops of main stems and principal branches. Green-leafed strains used as spinach substitute under the name "tampala."

AMARCRINUM memoria-corsii (A. 'Howardii')

Amaryllidaceae

BULB

ZONES 8, 9, 12–24

SUN OR PARTIAL SHADE

MODERATE WATER

Amarcrinum memoria-corsii

Can be grown as an indoor/outdoor plant or as a house plant. Hybrid between *Crinum moorei* and belladonna lily (*Amaryllis belladonna*). Flowering stems to 4 ft. carry very large clusters of soft pink, funnel-shaped, very fragrant, long lasting flowers resembling belladonna lily. With year-round water, plant stays evergreen in mild climates. If no moisture is available, it simply endures until water comes, then starts growth and bloom. Scarce in nurseries; get offset bulbs from a friend. Be especially careful to protect from snails and slugs.

Amaryllidaceae. The amaryllis family consists of herbaceous plants with strap-shaped leaves, bulbous or rhizomatous rootstocks, and clustered flowers (rarely a single flower) on top of a leafless stem.

AMARYLLIS belladonna (Brunsvigia rosea)

BELLADONNA LILY, NAKED LADY

Amaryllidaceae

BULB

ZONES 4–24

FULL SUN

GROWS AND BLOOMS ON NATURE'S BOUNTY

BULBS ARE POISONOUS

Amaryllis belladonna

Hardy in mild-winter areas; needs protected southern exposure and warm, dry summer to bloom in western Oregon and Washington. Native to South Africa. Bold, straplike leaves in clumps 2–3 ft. across in fall and winter; dormant late spring and early summer. In August, clusters of 4–12 trumpet-shaped, rosy pink, fragrant flowers bloom on top of bare, reddish brown stalks 2–3 ft. tall. Will grow in almost any soil with no irrigation at all; very long lived. Plant right after bloom; set bulb top even with ground level. Lift and divide clumps infrequently; may not bloom for several years if disturbed at wrong time. For plants with common name amaryllis see *Hippeastrum*.

A. hallii. See Lycoris squamigera

AMELANCHIER

JUNEBERRY, SHADBLOW, SERVICEBERRY

Rosaceae

DECIDUOUS SHRUBS OR SMALL TREES

⚘ ZONES 1–6

☼ FULL SUN

● MODERATE WATER

Amelanchier laevis

Drooping clusters of white or pinkish flowers in early spring are showy but short lived. Purplish new foliage turns deep green, then yellow and red in fall. Small dark blue fruits, popular with birds, taste like blueberries. Roots not aggressive; shade not dense. Plant against dark background to show off flowers, form, fall color. Give sun, ordinary good soil, moderate water. Serviceberry is often pronounced "sarvisberry."

A. alnifolia. SASKATOON. Shrub or small tree to 20 ft., spreading by rhizomes. Native to western Canada and mountainous parts of the West.

A. canadensis. Narrowish big shrub or small tree to 25 ft., with short, erect flower clusters.

A. laevis. Narrow shrub or small tree to 40 ft., with nodding or drooping flower clusters. 'Cumulus' has regular form, yellow-orange to red fall color.

| AMERICAN SWEET GUM. See LIQUIDAMBAR styraciflua | p. 357 |
| AMETHYST FLOWER. See BROWALLIA | p. 191 |

AMPELOPSIS brevipedunculata

BLUEBERRY CLIMBER

Vitaceae

DECIDUOUS VINE

⚘ ALL ZONES

☼ ◑ ● ANY EXPOSURE

● MODERATE WATER

Ampelopsis brevipedunculata

Strong, rampant climber with twining tendrils. To 20 ft. Large, handsome, three-lobed, 2½–5-in.-wide leaves are dark green. In warm climates, leaves turn red and partially drop in fall; more leaves come out, redden, and drop all winter. Many clusters of small grapelike berries turn from greenish ivory to brilliant metallic blue in late summer and fall. Needs strong support. Superb on concrete and rock walls or as shade plant on arbors. Attracts birds. The variety 'Elegans' has leaves variegated with white and pink. Smaller, less vigorous, and less hardy than the species, it is a splendid hanging basket plant.

Boston ivy and Virginia creeper, formerly included in genus *Ampelopsis*, are now placed under genus *Parthenocissus* because, unlike *Ampelopsis*, both have disks at ends of their tendrils.

AMSONIA tabernaemontana

BLUE STAR FLOWER

Apocynaceae

PERENNIAL

⚘ ZONES 3–24

☼ FULL SUN

● INFREQUENT WATER

Amsonia tabernaemontana

This milkweed relative from the southeastern United States forms a tight clump of 2–3-ft. stems closely set with narrow, willowlike leaves and topped by nodding clusters of small, star-shaped, pale blue flowers. A tough plant, it will endure ordinary soil and occasional lapses in watering. Flowers look good with yellow and orange daisylike flowers.

AMUR CHOKECHERRY. See PRUNUS maackii — p. 442

Anacardiaceae. The cashew family includes evergreen or deciduous trees, shrubs, and vines with small, unshowy, but often profuse flowers. Foliage is attractive; fruits are sometimes showy or edible. Many have poisonous or irritating sap. Mango and poison oak indicate the diversity of the family.

ANACYCLUS depressus (A. pyrethrum depressus)

MOUNT ATLAS DAISY

Asteraceae (Compositae)

PERENNIAL

⚘ ALL ZONES

☼ FULL SUN

● INFREQUENT WATER

Anacyclus depressus

Slowly forms dense, spreading mat somewhat like chamomile. Grayish leaves finely divided. Single daisylike flowers to 2 in. across, with yellow center disks and white ray-type petals (red on reverse side). Blooms in summer. Good in sunny, dry, hot rock gardens. Generally hardy but may freeze in extremely severe winters or rot in cold, wet, heavy soil.

ANAGALLIS

PIMPERNEL

Primulaceae

ANNUALS OR PERENNIALS

⚘ ALL ZONES

☼ FULL SUN

● ● ◐ ● MUCH OR LITTLE WATER

Anagallis monelli linifolia

Two species sometimes seen, one a weed. Less aggressive kinds attractive in rock gardens with sunroses (*Helianthemum*), sedums, snow-in-summer (*Cerastium*).

A. arvensis. SCARLET PIMPERNEL. Annual. Low-growing weed with ¼-in. flowers of brick red. *A. a. caerulea* has deep blue, larger flowers.

A. monelli. Perennial or biennial to 1½ ft., with ¾-in. flowers of bright blue. *A. m.* 'Pacific Blue' is a superior selection. *A. m.* 'Phillipsii' is compact, 1 ft. tall; *A. m. linifolia* has narrower leaves than *A. monelli*.

ANCHUSA

Boraginaceae

ANNUALS, BIENNIALS, OR PERENNIALS

⚘ ZONES VARY BY SPECIES

☼ FULL SUN

● VERY LITTLE WATER NEEDED

Anchusa capensis

Related to forget-me-not (*Myosotis*) but larger and showier, anchusas are worth growing for vibrant blue color. These rate high for purest blue among the easier plants.

A. azurea (A. italica). Perennial. All zones. Coarse, open, spreading, 3–5 ft. tall. Leaves 6 in. or longer, covered with bristly hairs. Clusters of bright blue blossoms, ½–¾ in. across, bloom in summer and fall. Horticultural forms include 'Dropmore', gentian blue; 'Opal', sky blue; and 'Loddon Royalist' (a newer variety), rich blue. Not for small areas: once established, it is difficult to eradicate.

A. capensis. CAPE FORGET-ME-NOT, SUMMER FORGET-ME-NOT. Zones 7–24. Native of South Africa. Hardy annual or biennial, 1½ ft. high; leaves narrow, to 5 in. long, ½ in. wide. Flowers bright blue, white throated, ¼ in. across, in clusters 2 in. long. Use for vivid clean blue in summer borders with marigolds (*Tagetes*), petunias.

A

ANDROSACE

ROCK JASMINE

Primulaceae

PERENNIALS

◿ ZONES 1–6, 14–17

☼ FULL SUN

◖ MODERATE WATER

Androsace lanuginosa

Choice rock garden miniatures grown mostly by alpine plant specialists. All types require perfect drainage and are best adapted to gravelly banks in rock gardens. Protect from more aggressive rockery plants such as alyssum, arabis, aubrieta. Rarely succeed in warm-winter areas.

A. lanuginosa. Trailing plant forms mats 3 ft. across. Silvery leaves to ¾ in. long, covered with silky white hairs. Pink flowers in dense clusters on 2-in. stems. *A. l. leichtlinii* has white flowers with crimson eyes.

A. primuloides. Trailing; forms 4-in.-long runners. Leaves ½–2 in. long in rosettes covered with silvery hairs. Flowers pink, to ½ in. across, in clusters on 5-in. stems.

A. sarmentosa. Spreads by runners. Leaves to 1½ in. long, in rosettes, covered with silvery hairs when young. Flowers rose colored, ¼ in. across, in clusters on stems 5 in. tall. *A. s. chumbyi* forms dense clump, has woolly leaves.

ANEMONE

WINDFLOWER, ANEMONE

Ranunculaceae

PERENNIALS WITH TUBEROUS OR FIBROUS ROOTS

◿ ZONES VARY BY SPECIES

☼ ◑ ◖ EXPOSURE NEEDS VARY BY SPECIES

◖ ◗ REGULAR WATER; TAKE SOME ARIDITY

◈ ALL PARTS ARE POISONOUS

Anemone blanda

A rich and varied group of plants ranging in size from alpine rock garden miniatures to tall Japanese anemones grown in borders; bloom extends from very early spring to fall, depending on species.

The first three species listed below are grown from tubers. Plant them in a spot that gets some shade every day. Set out tubers October or November; in cold-winter areas, wait until spring to set out *A. coronaria* and *A. fulgens.* (Or, if planting in November, mulch with 6–8 in. of leaf mold or peat moss after first hard frost.) In warmer climates, some soak tubers of *A. coronaria* for a few hours before planting.

Plant tubers 1–2 in. deep, 8–12 in. apart, in rich, light, well-drained garden loam. Or start in flats of damp sand; set out in garden when leaves are a few inches tall. Keep soil moist. Protect from birds until leaves toughen. In high-rainfall areas, excess moisture induces rot.

A. blanda. Zones 1–9, 14–23. Stems rise 2–8 in. from tuberous roots. Finely divided leaves covered with soft hairs. In spring, one sky blue flower, 1–1½ in. across, on each stem. Often confused with *A. apennina,* which has more pointed leaf segments. Grow with and among Japanese maples, azaleas, and other light shrubbery in partial shade. Associate with miniature daffodils, tulips, and scillas; or grow in pots. Some selections have 2-in. flowers on 10–12-in. plants. 'Blue Star' is blue, 'Pink Star' pink, 'Radar' purplish red, and 'White Splendor' white.

A. coronaria. POPPY-FLOWERED ANEMONE. All zones. Common large-flowered, showy anemone valued for cutting and for spectacular color in spring borders. Finely divided green leaves. Flowers red, blue, tones and mixtures of

Anemone coronaria

these colors, and white, 1½–2½ in. across, borne singly on 6–18-in. stems. Tuberous rooted. Most popular strains are De Caen (with single flowers) and St. Brigid (with semidouble to double flowers). Grow in partial shade.

A. fulgens. SCARLET WINDFLOWER. Zones 1–9, 14–24. To 1 ft. from tuberous roots. Leaves entirely or slightly divided. Flowers 2½ in. across, brilliant scarlet with black stamens. St. Bavo strain comes in unusual color range including pink and rusty coral. Partial shade.

A. hybrida (A. japonica, A. hupehensis japonica). JAPANESE ANEMONE. All zones. A long-lived, fibrous-rooted perennial indispensable for fall color in partial shade. Graceful, branching stems 2–4 ft. high rise from clump of dark green, three- to five-lobed leaves covered with soft hairs. Flowers semidouble, in white, silvery pink, or rose. Many named varieties. Slow to establish but once started spreads readily if roots not disturbed. Mulch in fall where winters are extremely severe. Increase by divisions in fall or early spring or by root cuttings in spring. May need staking. Effective in clumps in front of tall shrubbery or under high-branching trees.

A. nemorosa. WOOD ANEMONE. Zones 3–9, 14–24. To 1 ft., with creeping rhizomes, deeply cut leaves, and inch-wide white (rarely pinkish or blue) flowers held above the foliage. Shade. Spreads slowly to make an attractive woodland ground cover. Many named varieties exist; 'Allenii' has large blue flowers, and there are double forms.

A. oregana (A. quinquefolia oregana). Zones 3–7, 15–17. Resembles *A. nemorosa,* with white, pink, or blue flowers. Partial shade. Native to Northern California and the Northwest.

A. pulsatilla. EUROPEAN PASQUE FLOWER. Zones 1–6, 15–17. Attractive alpine plant forming 9–12-in.-high clumps. Fernlike, silky-hairy leaves, 4–6 in. long, appear after flowers. Blossoms in April and May: bell shaped, to 2½ in. across, blue to reddish purple, with golden stamens. Handsome seed clusters like feathery, smoky gray pompoms. This hardy plant is best adapted to cool, moist climates; rarely succeeds in warm, dry areas. Sun or partial shade. Sow seed or make divisions in spring.

A. vitifolia robustissima. Zones 1–7, 15–17. Vigorous plant to 6 ft. tall with single pink flowers. Resembles *A. hybrida* on a larger scale. Plant in partial shade. True name is probably *A. tomentosa.*

WHICH SIDE OF AN ANEMONE BULB IS UP?

Locating the top side of an anemone tuber can be difficult because of its irregular shape. The important sign to look for is the depressed scar left by the base of last year's stem (sometimes you really have to search for it); plant the tuber with the scarred side up.

ANEMOPAEGMA chamberlaynii (Bignonia chamberlaynii)

YELLOW TRUMPET VINE

Bignoniaceae

EVERGREEN VINE

◿ ZONES 15–17, 19, 21–24

☼ ◑ FULL SUN OR PARTIAL SHADE

◖ MODERATE WATER

Anemopaegma chamberlaynii

Climbs by unbranched tendrils. Leaves divided into two leaflets to 7 in. long. Flowers yellow, trumpet shaped, 3 in. long, in clusters longer than the leaves. Summer blooming. Often confused with *Macfadyena (Doxantha) unguis-cati. Anemopaegma* has larger leaflets (7 in., compared to 2 in.); paler yellow flowers with purple or white markings in the throat; and coiling, unbranched tendrils instead of branched tendrils with little hooks (like cat's claws) at the ends. *Macfadyena* can fasten itself to nearly any surface, clinging by its claws; *Anemopaegma* needs something to cling to.

A

ANETHUM graveolens

DILL

Apiaceae (Umbelliferae)

ANNUAL HERB

☒ ALL ZONES

☼ FULL SUN

⬤ INFREQUENT WATER

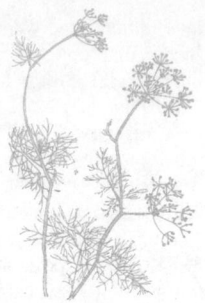

Anethum graveolens

To 3–4 ft. Soft, feathery leaves; umbrellalike, 6-in.-wide clusters of small yellow flowers. Seeds and leaves have pungent fragrance. Sow seed where plants are to be grown; for constant supply, sow several times during spring and summer. Thin seedlings to 1½ ft. apart. Sprouts and grows better in spring than summer. An easy way to grow it in a casual garden is to let a few plants go to seed. Seedlings appear here and there at odd times and can be pulled and chopped as "dill weed." Use seeds in pickling and vinegar; use fresh or dried leaves on lamb chops and in salads, stews, sauces.

ANGELICA archangelica

ANGELICA

Apiaceae (Umbelliferae)

BIENNIAL

☒ ALL ZONES

◑ PARTIAL SHADE

⬤ MOIST SOIL

Angelica archangelica

To 6 ft. Tropical-looking plant with divided and toothed, yellow-green leaves 2–3 ft. long. Greenish white flowers in large umbrellalike clusters. Grow in moist, rich, slightly acid soil in partial shade. Cut flowers before buds open to prolong plant's life. Propagate from seed sown as soon as ripe in fall. Use to flavor wines; hollow stems may be candied.

ANGEL'S HAIR. See ARTEMISIA schmidtiana	**p. 166**
ANGEL'S TEARS. See NARCISSUS triandrus, SOLEIROLIA soleirolii	**pp. 388, 488**

ANIGOZANTHOS

KANGAROO PAW

Haemodoraceae

EVERGREEN PERENNIALS

☒ ZONES 12, 13, 15–24

☼ FULL SUN

⬤ REGULAR WATER DURING FLOWERING

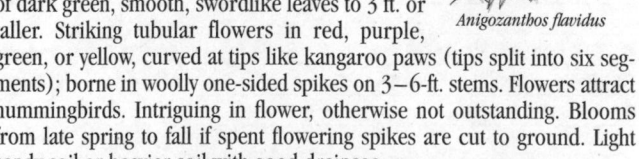

Anigozanthos flavidus

Native to open eucalyptus forests in western Australia. From thick rootstocks grow clumps of dark green, smooth, swordlike leaves to 3 ft. or taller. Striking tubular flowers in red, purple, green, or yellow, curved at tips like kangaroo paws (tips split into six segments); borne in woolly one-sided spikes on 3–6-ft. stems. Flowers attract hummingbirds. Intriguing in flower, otherwise not outstanding. Blooms from late spring to fall if spent flowering spikes are cut to ground. Light sandy soil or heavier soil with good drainage.

A. flavidus (A. flavida). Branching stems to 5 ft. Tubular, curved, hairy flowers 1–1½ in. long, yellow-green tinged with red. Colors of named hybrids range from deep rust red to pure yellow, with many shades of orange between. Named hybrids bloom heavily and are superior garden plants.

A. manglesii. Unbranched green stems to 3 ft., thickly covered with red hairs. Flowers brilliant deep green, red at base, woolly on outside, 3 in. long.

ANISACANTHUS thurberi

DESERT HONEYSUCKLE

Acanthaceae

EVERGREEN OR DECIDUOUS SHRUB

☒ ZONES 8–13, 18, 19

☼ FULL SUN

⬤ INFREQUENT, DEEP WATERING

Anisacanthus thurberi

Native to Arizona, New Mexico, Texas, northern Mexico. In mild-winter areas grows to 3–5 ft. with stout branches. Looks best when treated as perennial, cut to ground in winter either by frost or by pruning shears. Valued for its long, spring–summer season of color. Tubular, 1½-in.-long, yellow-orange flowers in spikes; light green leaves, 1½–2 in. long and ½ in. wide. Plants sold under this name may be *Justicia leonardii;* these have bright red flowers and leaves to 6 in. long.

ANISE. See PIMPINELLA anisum	**p. 419**

ANISODONTEA

CAPE MALLOW

Malvaceae

EVERGREEN SHRUBS

☒ ZONES 14–24

☼ FULL SUN

◯ ⬤ LITTLE TO NO WATER ONCE ESTABLISHED

Anisodontea hypomandarum

These quick-growing South Africans are notable for producing vast quantities of flowers over a long period. Growth is rounded, rather open but freely branching, with small lobed leaves. Flowers are shaped like miniature individual hollyhock flowers and are borne throughout mild weather, year-round in mildest climates. Use in shrub perennial borders or in large containers.

A. capensis. Grows to 6 ft., with 1-in. lobed leaves and 1-in. flowers of purplish pink, with deeper veining and a dark basal spot. Probably identical to *A. hypomandarum.*

A. hypomandarum. To 6 ft. or more, with 1½-in. leaves and inch-wide pink flowers with dark veins and eyes. Flowering is continuous and profuse. Sometimes trained as single-trunk standards. 'Tara's Pink' has larger leaves and larger, lighter flowers.

A. scabrosa. To 6 ft., with aromatic leaves 2½–3 in. long and deep rosy purple flowers with darker eye spots.

Annonaceae. The annona family consists primarily of tropical trees and shrubs; many have edible fruit, but only a very few are hardy in the West.

ANNONA cherimola

CHERIMOYA

Annonaceae

BRIEFLY DECIDUOUS LARGE SHRUB OR SMALL TREE

☒ ZONES 21–24

☼ FULL SUN

⬤ AMPLE WATER

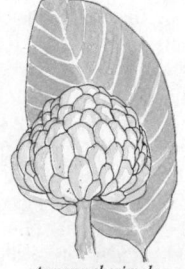

Annona cherimola

Hardy to about 25°F. Grows fast first 3–4 years, then slows to make 15-ft. tree with 15–20-ft. spread. After tree has developed for 4–5 years, prune annually to produce bearing wood. Leaves dull green above, velvety-hairy beneath, 4–10 in. long; leaves drop in late spring. Thick, fleshy, 1-in., brownish or yellow, hairy flowers with a fruity fragrance begin opening about time of leaf drops and continue forming for 3–4 months. Pleasant near terrace.

To ensure fruit set, gather pollen on a brush and transfer it to the stigma of a freshly opened flower.

Large green fruits weigh ½–1½ lbs. Skin of most varieties looks like short overlapping leaves; some show knobby warts. Pick when fruit turns to yellowish green, then store in refrigerator until skin turns brownish green to brown. Skin is tender and thin. Handle fruit carefully. Creamy white flesh contains large black seeds. Flesh is almost custardlike; eat it with a spoon.

ANNUAL MALLOW. See LAVATERA trimestris p. 349

ANREDERA cordifolia (Boussingaultia baselloides)

MADEIRA VINE

Basellaceae

PERENNIAL VINE

ZONES 4–24

FULL SUN

MODERATE WATER

Anredera cordifolia

In Zones 4–10 treat as you would dahlias: dig in fall and store tubers over winter. Heart-shaped green leaves 1–3 in. long. Fragrant white flowers in foot-long spikes in late summer, fall. Climbs by twining; may reach 20 ft. in one season. Small tubers form where leaves join stems. Old-fashioned plant useful for summer screening of decks or other sitting areas. Can run rampant in mildest coastal climates.

ANTENNARIA dioica

PUSSY TOES

Asteraceae (Compositae)

PERENNIAL

ALL ZONES

FULL SUN

LITTLE TO MODERATE WATER

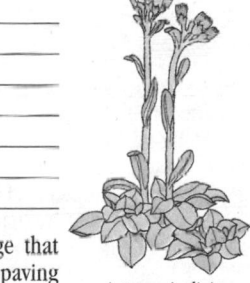
Antennaria dioica

Forms inch-high mats of woolly foliage that slowly spread among rocks, between paving stones, or at front of border. Furry puffs of flowers are pinkish white, deep pink in the variety 'Rubra'. Extremely hardy to cold; will withstand some light foot traffic.

ANTHEMIS

Asteraceae (Compositae)

EVERGREEN PERENNIALS

ALL ZONES

FULL SUN

REGULAR WATER

Anthemis tinctoria

Aromatic foliage, especially when bruised. Leaves divided into many segments. Flowers daisylike or buttonlike. Some are weedy, but the following species are choice garden plants.

A. carpatica (A. cretica carpatica). Green to gray-green mounds with 1½-in. white, yellow-centered daisies on 6-in. stems.

A. marschalliana (A. biebersteiniana). Rounded plant 1 ft. tall and as wide, with finely cut, fernlike, silvery leaves and 1-in. brilliant yellow, daisylike blooms.

A. nobilis. See Chamaemelum nobile

A. punctata cupaniana. Foot-tall, spreading mounds of silvery foliage topped by a long show of white daisies.

A. tinctoria. GOLDEN MARGUERITE. Erect, shrubby. Grows to 2–3 ft. Angular stems. Light green, much-divided leaves. Golden yellow, daisylike flowers, to 2 in. across, bloom in summer and fall. Average water. Grow from seed, stem cuttings, or divisions in fall or spring. Summer border plant. Varieties include 'Beauty of Grallagh', golden orange flowers; 'E. C. Buxton', white with yellow centers; 'Kelwayi', golden yellow; 'Moonlight', soft, pale yellow.

ANTHRISCUS cerefolium

CHERVIL

Apiaceae (Umbelliferae)

ANNUAL CULINARY HERB

ALL ZONES

PARTIAL SHADE

REGULAR WATER

Anthriscus cerefolium

Grows 1–2 ft. Finely cut, fernlike leaves resembling parsley; white flowers. Use like parsley, fresh or dried; flavor milder than parsley. Grow from seed in raised bed near kitchen door, in box near barbecue, or in vegetable garden. Quickly goes to seed in hot weather. Keep flower clusters cut to encourage vegetative growth.

ANTHURIUM

Araceae

PERENNIAL INDOOR AND GREENHOUSE PLANTS

NO DIRECT SUN

HEAVY WATERING; NEEDS HUMIDITY

Anthurium andraeanum

Native to tropical American rain forests. Exotic anthuriums with handsome dark green leaves and lustrous flower bracts in vivid red, luscious pinks, or white are no more difficult to grow as house plants than are some orchids.

The higher the humidity, the better. Anthurium leaves lose shiny texture and may die if humidity drops below 50 percent for more than a few days. Keep pots on trays of moist gravel, in bathroom, or under polyethylene cover. Sponge or spray leaves several times daily. For good bloom, plant by window with good light but no direct sun. Generally grow best in 80–90°F temperatures but will get along in normal house temperature (low 70s). Growth stops below 65°F, is damaged below 50°F. Protect from drafts. Pot anthuriums in coarse, porous mix of leaf mold, sandy soil, and shredded osmunda. Give light feeding every 4 weeks.

A. andraeanum. Dark green, oblong leaves to 1 ft. long and 6 in. wide, heart shaped at base. Flower bracts spreading, heart shaped, to 6 in. long, surrounding yellow, callalike flower spike. Flower bracts, in shades of red, rose, pink, and white, shine as though lacquered. Bloom more or less continuously—plant may have from four to six flowers during the year. Flowers last 6 weeks on plant, 4 weeks after cut.

A. crystallinum. Leaves, up to 1½ ft. long, 1 ft. wide, are deep green with striking white veining. Flowers unexciting, with small, narrow, greenish bracts. Many similar anthuriums exist in florist trade; plants offered as *A. crystallinum* may be *A. clarinervium, A. magnificum,* or some other species.

A. scandens. Climbing or trailing plant to 2 ft., with 3-in.-long tapered oval leaves and small, fragrant greenish flowers, translucent lilac berries.

A. scherzeranum. Slow-growing, compact plant to 2 ft. Dark green leaves 8 in. long, 2 in. wide. Flower bracts broad, 3 in. long, deep red varying to rose, salmon, white. Yellow flower spikes spirally coiled. Easier to handle than *A. andraeanum* and often thrives under ordinary, good house plant conditions.

A

ANTIGONON leptopus

ROSA DE MONTANA, QUEEN'S WREATH,
CORAL VINE

Polygonaceae

DECIDUOUS VINE

✿ ZONES 12, 13, 18–21; WIND SHELTERED IN 22–24

☼ FULL SUN

◐◖ LITTLE TO MODERATE WATER

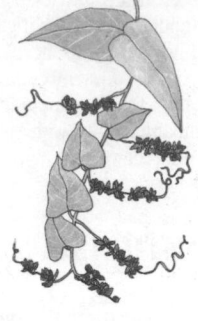

Antigonon leptopus

This native of Mexico must have been loved by many to earn such colorful common names. Plant revels in high summer heat, sun, moderate water. Evergreen in warm-winter areas. Fast growing, climbing by tendrils to 40 ft. Foliage—dark green, 3–5-in.-long, heart-shaped or arrow-shaped leaves—is open and airy. Small rose pink flowers to 1½ in. long are carried in long, trailing sprays from midsummer to fall. In cold winters, leaves fall and most of top dies. Recovers quickly. Treat as perennial. Where winter temperatures drop below 25°F protect roots with mulch. There is a rare white variety 'Album', and a hot rose pink—nearly red—variety named 'Baja Red'; from seed the color of the latter is variable, but the best are as red as 'Barbara Karst' bougainvillea.

A wonderful vine in the low deserts of California and Arizona. In those climates it can grow without irrigation, but it may die back to ground in summer. Elsewhere give it hottest spot in garden. Let it shade patio or terrace; drape its foliage and blossom sprays along eaves, fence, or garden wall.

ANTIRRHINUM majus

SNAPDRAGON

Scrophulariaceae

PERENNIAL USUALLY TREATED AS ANNUAL

✿ ALL ZONES

☼ FULL SUN

◖ REGULAR WATER

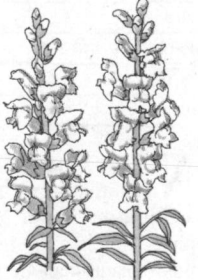

Antirrhinum majus

Among best flowers for sunny borders and cutting, reaching greatest perfection in spring and early summer—in winter and spring in warm-winter, hot-summer regions. Individual flower of basic snapdragon has five lobes, which are divided into unequal upper and lower "jaws"; slight pinch at sides of flower will make dragon open its jaws. Later developments include double flowers; the bell-shaped kind, with round, open flowers; and the azalea-shaped bloom, which is a doubled bellflower.

Snapping snapdragons in tall (2½–3-ft.) range include Pocket and Topper strains (single flowers) and Double Supreme strain. Intermediate (12–20 in.) are Cinderella, Coronette, Minaret, 'Princess White with Purple Eye', Sprite, and Tahiti. Dwarfs (6–8 in.) include Dwarf Bedding Floral Carpet, Kim, Kolibri, and Royal Carpet.

FIVE WAYS TO AVOID SNAPDRAGON RUST

Snapdragons, like lawns, roses, and hollyhocks, can fall victim to rust (orange pustules on undersides of leaves). Here are five ways to avoid or minimize it: Start with rust-resistant varieties (even that's not foolproof). Keep plants well watered. Avoid overhead watering (or do it only in the morning or on sunny days). Feed regularly. If necessary, change planting locations from one year to the next.

Bell-flowered or penstemon-flowered strains include Bright Butterflies and Wedding Bells (both 2½ ft.); Little Darling and Liberty Bell (both

15 in.); and Pixie (6–8 in.). Azalea-flowered (double bell-shaped) strains are Madame Butterfly (2½ ft.) and Sweetheart (1 ft.).

Sow seed in flats from late summer to early spring for later transplanting or buy started plants at nursery. Set out plants in early fall in mild-winter areas, spring in colder sections. If snapdragons set out in early fall reach bud stage before night temperatures drop below 50°F, they will start blooming in winter and continue until weather gets hot.

Valuable cut flowers. Tall and intermediate forms are splendid vertical accents in borders with delphinium, iris, daylily *(Hemerocallis)*, peach-leafed bluebell *(Campanula persicifolia)*, Oriental poppy. Dwarf kinds effective as edgings and in rock gardens and raised beds, or pots.

APACHE PLUME. See FALLUGIA paradoxa p. 292

APHELANDRA squarrosa

Acanthaceae

EVERGREEN HOUSE PLANT

◑● PARTIAL OR FULL SHADE

◖ REGULAR WATER

Aphelandra squarrosa

Native to Mexico, South America. Popular for leaves and flowers. Large, 8–12-in.-long, dark green leaves strikingly veined with white. Green-tipped yellow flowers and waxy, golden yellow flower bracts make colorful upright spikes at tips of stems. Variety 'Louisae' is best known, but newer varieties 'Apollo White' and 'Dania' are more compact and show more white venation. To make plants bushy, cut stems back to one or two pairs of leaves after flowering. Give plant routine house plant culture. Place it where it gets morning (or filtered) sun. Occasionally used outdoors in protected spots in Southern California gardens.

Apiaceae. This family, also known as Umbelliferae, comprises nearly 3,000 plants, most of them annuals and perennials. All have flowers in umbels—flat- or round-topped clusters whose individual flower stems all originate at a single point. Many are vegetables (carrot, parsnip, celery, fennel) or aromatic herbs (parsley, coriander, dill). Others are grown for ornament *(Eryngium amethystinum, Trachymene coerulea)*.

Apocynaceae. The dogbane family contains shrubs, trees, and vines with milky, often poisonous sap. Flowers are often showy and fragrant, as in frangipani *(Plumeria rubra)* and oleander *(Nerium oleander)*.

Aponogetonaceae. Only the following genus is of importance in this small family of aquatic plants.

APONOGETON distachyus

CAPE PONDWEED, WATER HAWTHORN

Aponogetonaceae

AQUATIC PLANT

✿ ALL ZONES

☼◑ FULL SUN OR PARTIAL SHADE

◖◖ LIVES IN WATER

Aponogeton distachyus

Native to South Africa. Like miniature water lily, it produces floating leaves from submerged tuber. Leaves are long and narrow; ⅓-in.-long white, fragrant flowers stand above water in double-branched clusters.

In hot-summer climates, blooms in cool weather and is dormant in hottest weather; where winters are cold, blooms in summer and is dormant in winter. Same culture as water lily *(Nymphaea);* will bloom in shade.

APPLE

Rosaceae

DECIDUOUS FRUIT TREES

◩ ALL ZONES

☼ FULL SUN

◐ ◑ WATER DURING LONG DRY PERIODS

▶ SEE CHART NEXT PAGE

Apple

Most widely adapted deciduous fruit, grown in every western climate. Mild winters of the low desert and the marine and coastal climates of Southern California do not provide enough winter cold for most standard varieties. Since nursery customers often insist on the popular varieties they see on fruit stands, varieties are sold in areas unfavorable to best performance. In Southern California, Phoenix, and Tucson, nurseries often offer varieties for customers who live in nearby higher elevations. For this reason, the apple chart indicates where some varieties perform best as well as where they are sold. For ornamental relatives, see *Malus.*

All apples require pollination. Most will set adequate fruit on their own pollen but will set more fruit if pollinated by another variety. Certain varieties (triploids) do not produce fertile pollen and will not fertilize either their own flowers or those of other apples. If a pollinating variety grows in your neighborhood, you need not plant one yourself.

If you have a tree that is not bearing, graft a branch of another variety onto it or place fresh flower bouquets from another variety (in can of water) at base of tree. Don't use 'Gravenstein', 'Winesap', or any other triploid (pollen-sterile) tree to pollinate an unfruitful tree.

The apple needs sun and, for best production, some water. Don't crowd it into partially shaded places. To have more than one variety in limited space, buy multiple-variety trees or dwarf trees.

Multiple-variety trees have three to five varieties grafted onto a single trunk and rootstock; they may be standard, dwarf, or semidwarf. You get not only a selection of varieties but also pollination, if needed.

In choosing varieties, remember that good apples are not necessarily red. Skin color is not an indicator of quality or taste. Red varieties are widely sold only because red apples have sales appeal. Make sure that eye appeal, slight taste preference, or name doesn't influence you to choose a difficult-to-grow variety. For example, if to your taste 'Golden Delicious' and 'Red Delicious' are nearly equal, consider differences in growing them. 'Golden Delicious' produces fruit without pollinator and comes into bearing earlier. It keeps well, while 'Red Delicious' becomes mealy if not stored at 35–40°F or lower. And it can be used for cooking, while 'Red Delicious' is strictly an eating apple.

If you want perfect fruit, the apple tree will need much care; however, as an ornamental tree it has more character, better form, and longer life than most deciduous fruit trees. It does best in deep soil but gets by in many imperfect situations, including heavy soils. Codling moth is the universal insect pest of apples; to control it, spray with diazinon, malathion, or carbaryl as soon as petals have fallen and repeat according to label instructions or recommendations of local farm advisors. Apple maggot is a serious pest in some areas and is spreading; check with local authorities to find out if it is a problem where you live. If so, spray in midsummer, with later sprays at 2-week intervals until 2 weeks before harvest.

Dwarf and spur apples. True dwarf apples (5–8 ft. in height and spread) are made by grafting standard apples on dwarfing rootstocks such as M9 and P22. These trees take up little room but have shallow roots; they need the support of a fence, wall, or sturdy trellis to stand against wind and rain. They also need good soil and extra care in feeding and watering.

Genetic dwarf apples are naturally small (5–8 ft.) even when grafted on standard, nondwarfing rootstocks. 'Garden Delicious' is an example.

Semidwarf trees are larger than true dwarfs but smaller than standard trees. They bear bigger crops than dwarfs and take up less space than standards. Many commercial orchards get high yields by using semidwarf trees and planting them close together. Semidwarf rootstocks reduce tree size by approximately the following factors: EM 26 and EM VIIA are about half normal size; they may be espaliered or trellised if planted 12–16 ft. apart and allowed to grow 10–12 ft. tall. Trees on MM 106 are approximately 65 percent of normal height; those on MM 111 are 75 percent of normal height.

Rarely, growers offer trees dwarfed by double-working—grafting a piece of M9 trunk on vigorous rootstock, then grafting a bearing variety on this "interstock." The resulting dwarf is somewhat larger than a true dwarf tree and has much more vigorous roots.

Apples bear flowers and fruit on spurs—short branches that grow from 2-year or older wood. Spurs normally begin to appear only after tree has grown in place 3–5 years. On spur-type apples, spurs form earlier (within 2 years after planting) and grow closer together on shorter branches, giving more apples per foot of branch. Spur apples are natural or genetic semidwarfs about two-thirds the size of normal apple trees when they are grafted on ordinary rootstocks. They can be further dwarfed by grafting onto dwarfing rootstocks; M VIIA and M 26 give smallest trees, MM 106 and MM 111 somewhat larger ones.

APPLES THAT NEED LITTLE WINTER CHILL

To grow and fruit properly, most apple varieties require between 900 and 1,200 hours of temperatures below 45°F. Most areas of Southern California don't regularly get that cold for that length of time. But these apples thrive in the southland's mild-winter climate zones 18–24: 'Anna' (needs only 150 hours of chilling), 'Dorsett Golden' (250 hours), 'Gordon' (250 hours), and 'Fuji' (300 hours).

Training and pruning apple trees. Careful early training and some annual pruning and shaping are necessary to keep apple trees manageable in size, healthy, and productive. Most home and orchard apples grow on vase-shaped trees—broad, spreading, with three (sometimes more) main scaffold branches arising from a 2½–3-ft.-tall trunk. These branches should not arise at the same point; select ones that are evenly spaced around trunk and at least 8 or 9 in. apart. As tree grows, prune out crossing branches and overvigorous branches growing toward center of tree.

Spur apples and apples on semidwarfing rootstocks are often trained as central-leader or pyramidal trees. Side branches grow outward from central trunk to form symmetrical pyramid, with tiers of branches that grow shorter toward top of plant. Keep branches from growing directly above and close to lower branches; upper ones will shade lower ones out. Keep side branches from outgrowing the leader and secondary side branches from outstripping primary branches. If branches grow at a narrow angle to leader, spread them to a 45° angle with heavy wire or wood-and-nail spreaders.

Dwarf trees can grow as pyramids; as single-stem trees with fruiting spurs along main trunk; or as espaliers tied to wood or wire frames, fences, or other supports.

Apples' fruiting spurs remain productive for up to 20 years. Pruning of mature trees consists of removing weak, dead, or poorly placed branches and twigs to encourage development of strong new growth and to permit sunlight to reach into tree, where it will encourage spur growth and discourage mildew.

FOR GROWING SYMBOL EXPLANATIONS

PLEASE SEE PAGE 129

APPLE

A

VARIETY	ZONES	RIPENING DATE	FRUIT	COMMENTS
'Adina'	18–24	Early Aug.	Large, round, fragrant, dark red. Firm, sweet, creamy white flesh with cinnamon overtones	Needs little winter chill (350 hours) to bear. Requires a pollinator
'Anna'	7–24	Early summer. Sometimes a later, light crop	Large, pale green blushed red. Sweet with some acid. Crisp, stores well	Produces at young age. Needs very little winter chill to bear. Use 'Ein Shemer' or 'Dorsett Golden' as pollinator. Good annual bearer
'Arkansas Black'	1–3, 10–11	Oct., Nov.	Medium-size. Dark, deep red. Hard-crisp	Best after storage for two months. 'Arkansas Black Spur' is spurred variation
'Ashmead's Kernel'	4–17	Late	Medium-size, red-orange blush over rough yellow-green skin	Good disease resistance
'Beverly Hills'	18–24. One of best for Southern California coast	Early	Small to medium, yellow, splashed and striped red. Tender, somewhat tart. Fair quality. Somewhat resembles 'McIntosh'	Definitely for cool areas. Will not develop good quality in hot interiors
'Braeburn'	1–9, 14–16	Mid-Oct.	Medium-size, golden red. Crisp, sweet-tart flavor	Fruit drops in hot climates. Thin fruit to prevent biennial cropping
'Chehalis'	4–6	Mid-Sept.–early Oct.	Large, yellow-green. Soft, but bakes well. Mild flavor, melting flesh; good in salads	Like 'Golden Delicious' but resists scab in western Washington, Oregon. Poor keeper
'Cox Orange Pippin'	7, 14–16	Late Sept.	Medium-size, dull orange-red. Flesh yellow, firm, juicy. Flavor superb. English dessert favorite	Susceptible to scab and cracking. Dense growth; thin out branches. Dislikes extreme cold, heat, low humidity. Worth trying for its unique flavor
'Delicious' ('Red Delicious')	Sold wherever apples will grow. Best in 2, 3, 7	Midseason to late	Everybody recognizes pointed blossom end with five knobs. Color varies with strain and garden climate; best where days are bright and warm, nights cool. Often older, striped kinds have better flavor than highly colored commercial strains	Many strains that vary in ripening season, depth and uniformity of coloring. 'Crimson Spur' popular home variety. Highly susceptible to scab, this apple is difficult for home gardeners in Zones 4–6. Needs pollinator; 'Golden Delicious' good
'Discovery'	4–6	Aug.	Red stripes over yellow. Good for sauces	Best west of Cascades. Sometimes cracks in stem end
'Dorsett Golden'	13, 17–24	Early summer	Medium to large. Yellow or greenish yellow skin. Sweet. Keeps a few weeks	Seedling of 'Golden Delicious' from Bermuda. Needs no winter chill. Good pollinator for 'Anna'
'Earligold'	4–9	Early July	Light yellow, medium-size. Tart, juicy, crisp	One of best very early apples. Long season for summer apple
'Ein Shemer'	13, 17–24	Early summer	Yellow to greenish yellow. Medium-size. Juicy, crisp, mildly acid	Needs very little winter chill. Pollinates 'Anna'
'Elstar'	4–7, 15–17	Mid-Sept.	Small to medium, red and yellow. Excellent, tart flavor. One of the best pie and sauce apples; also bakes well	Grows best west of Cascades, poorly in hot climates. Bears in alternate years

APPLE

VARIETY	ZONES	RIPENING DATE	FRUIT	COMMENTS
'Empire'	2, 3, 6, 7, 14–16	Late midseason	'McIntosh'-'Delicious' cross. Small to medium, roundish, dark red. Flesh creamy white, juicy, crisp, aromatic, subacid. Stores well	Good tree structure, annual bearer
'Enterprise'	1–9, 14–16	Late Oct.	Medium-size, red blush, firm, sweet, keeps well	Immune to scab but subject to preharvest fruit drop
'Fiesta'	1–9, 14–16	Late Sept.	Larger and better flavored than 'Cox Orange Pippin', and doesn't crack. Firm; red stripes	Productive; no preharvest drops
'Fuji'	7–9, 14–16	Late Oct.	Tapered form, red stripes. Medium to large, firm, very sweet, excellent flavor, good keeper	Heavy bearer. Needs long season. Keeps well at room temperature
'Gala'	4–9, 14–16	Early midseason	Medium-size, beautiful red on yellow color. Firm, crisp, yellow flesh. Juicy, very sweet. Stores well	Vigorous, heavy bearer with long, supple branches that break easily. Provide support, if necessary
'Garden Delicious'	1–3, 6–9, 14–20	Late summer	Medium to large, golden green, red blush	Genetic dwarf 6–8 ft. tall and as wide
'Ginger Gold'	1–9, 14–16	Late Aug.	Large, yellow, smooth, tapered. Crisp, firm, flavorful	Spreading, a tip bearer, susceptible to mildew. Annually productive
'Golden Delicious' ('Yellow Delicious')	1–3, 7–11, 14–24	Midseason to late	Clear yellow; similar in shape to 'Delicious', with less prominent knobs. Highly aromatic, crisp, excellent for eating and cooking	Not related to 'Red Delicious'; different taste, habit. Spurred types available: 'Goldspur', 'Yelospur'. 'Prime Gold' is rust-resistant variety. Excellent pollinator for many other varieties
'Golden Supreme'	1–11, 14–17	Midseason	Medium large, yellow with some red blush. Smooth, excellent flavor. Two weeks earlier than 'Golden Delicious'	Very vigorous upright tree. Tends to bear every other year. Thinning fruits early will help overcome heavy bearing, cause of biennial cropping
'Gordon'	18–24	July–Oct.	Large, greenish yellow blushed red. Sweet-tart. Long blooming, bearing periods	Tree vigorous, upright, semidwarf. Many closely spaced spurs. Low chill
'Granny Smith'	6–11, 14–16. Late ripening and scab limit use, 4–6	Late Aug., mid-Sept.; much later in cool-summer areas	Large, bright to yellowish green, firm fleshed, tart	Australian favorite before it came to U.S. Stores well, makes good pies, sauce
'Gravenstein'	Widely sold in 4–11, 14–24. Best in 15–17	Early to midseason	Brilliant red stripes over deep yellow. Crisp, aromatic, juicy. Excellent for eating; makes applesauce with character	Justly famous variety of California's north coast apple district. 'Red Gravenstein' is more highly colored. Needs pollinator and will not pollinate other apple varieties. Susceptible to mildew Zones 4–6
'Holland' ('Summer Champion')	20–24	Early to mid-Oct.	Very large, dark strawberry red. Firm, smooth, juicy. Stores well	Bears at early age
'Idared'	4–6, 15–17	Oct.	Bright red apple with firm white flesh, tart at picking time	Stores well and flavor sweetens in storage. Early, annual heavy bearer
'Jonagold'	2–9, 14–16	Mid-Sept.–early Oct.	Large; heavy red striping over yellow. Firm, subacid, juicy, fine flavor, resembles 'Jonathan'. Stores well. A frequent taste-test favorite	Productive, medium-size tree. Heavy bearer. Needs pollinator (don't use 'Golden Delicious', one of its parents); will not pollinate other varieties

APPLE

VARIETY	ZONES	RIPENING DATE	FRUIT	COMMENTS
'Jonathan'	Sold everywhere. Best in 2, 3, 7	Early fall. Midseason	Small to medium, round-oblong. High-colored red. Juicy, moderately tart, crackling crisp, sprightly	All-purpose apple. Subject to mildew, somewhat resistant to scab
'Liberty'	4–9, 14–16	Late Sept., early Oct.	Medium-size, elongated, heavy red blush. Fine sweet-tart flavor. Crisp, dessert quality	Productive annual bearer. Immune to scab; can get mildew west of Cascades. Resists rust, fireblight
'Macoun'	1–7, 15, 16	Mid-Oct.	Medium-size, red striped on green ground. Sweet, crisp, and juicy. Tasty for dessert and good cooking. A frequent taste-test winner	Large, upright trees fairly resistant to mildew, scab. Thin for good fruit size. Drops badly when ripe
'McIntosh' ('Red McIntosh')	2–6, 14–16	Late midseason	Medium to large. Bright red, nearly round. Snowy white, tender flesh. Tart, excellent	Excellent apple for garden if given good care. 'Double Red McIntosh' and 'Nured McIntosh' have high color. Drops badly when ripe
'Melrose'	1–7, 15, 16	Late Oct.	Medium to large, roundish, red striped deeper red. Flesh white, mildly subacid, aromatic	Cross between 'Jonathan' and 'Delicious'. Exceptional storage, good dessert apple. Somewhat mildew resistant. Considered one of the best
'Mollie's Delicious'	8, 9, 14–20	Aug.	Large, light yellow blushed red. Light yellow flesh, aromatic, juicy, sweet. Stores well	Bears early, needs little winter chill. No pollinator required
'Mutsu'	4–9, 15, 16	Late Oct.	Medium, greenish yellow to yellow blushed red. Flesh white, very crisp, somewhat more tart than 'Golden Delicious'. Frequent taste-test winner in the Northwest regions	Good dessert and cooking apple with long storage life. Tree exceptionally large and vigorous. Needs pollinator. Tends to get bitter pit
'Newtown Pippin' ('Yellow Newtown', 'Yellow Pippin')	1–11, 13–22. Susceptible to mildew, 4–6	Late	Large, green. Crisp and tart, fair for eating, excellent for cooking	Large, vigorous tree
'Northern Spy' ('Red Spy')	1–3, 6, 7. Best in cold-winter areas	Late	Large, red. Tender, fine-grained flesh. Apple epicure's delight for sprightly flavor	Slow to reach bearing age. Needs pollinator. Keeps well
'Pettingill'	23, 24	Midseason to late	Large, red-blushed green to red, thick-skinned. Firm, white, tasty, moderately acid flesh	Large, upright, productive tree with very low chilling requirement. Regular bearer
'Redfree'	4–9, 14–17	Late Aug.	Red, firm, crisp, medium-size, good flavor	Heavy bearer, immune to scab
'Red Gold'	2, 3, 7–9, 14–17	Early fall	Medium-size, slightly oblong, glossy red with yellowish, mild flesh. Juicy. Keeps well	Vigorous hybrid between 'Red Delicious' and 'Golden Delicious'
'Rome Beauty' ('Red Rome')	3, 7, 10, 11	Late midseason	Large, round, smooth, red. Greenish white flesh. Outstanding baking apple, but indifferent for eating fresh	Early bearer. 'Red Rome' is all-over red kind most frequently sold. Blooms late, escapes frost
'Sierra Beauty'	2, 3, 6–9, 14–16	Early Oct.	Large, yellow with red stripes. Firm, sweet-tart. Keeps well. Exceptionally attractive	Needs little winter chill

APPLE

VARIETY	ZONES	RIPENING DATE	FRUIT	COMMENTS
'Spartan'	4–7, 15, 16	Midseason to late	Small to medium, dark red with purplish bloom. Crisp flesh, excellent flavor. Frequent taste-test winner	Equals 'McIntosh' in flavor. Tree habit good; heavy bearing necessitates thinning
'Spitzenberg' ('Esopus Spitzenberg')	1–7	Late	Medium to large, red-dotted yellow. Crisp, fine-grained, tangy, spicy	Old favorite, best in cold-winter areas. Subject to fireblight, mildew
'Stayman' (often called 'Winesap')	1–7, 10, 11. Susceptible to scab	Latest	Medium to large, round. Lively flavor. Fine-grained, firm, juicy. 'Stayman' is large, red with green and russet dots. 'Winesap' is smaller, all red	Old-timer that remains top favorite. 'Stayman' is a 'Winesap' cross
'Summerred'	4–7, 15, 16	Late Aug.	Medium-size, bright red; tart and good chiefly for cooking until fully ripe, then good dessert quality too	Consistent annual bearer for western Oregon and Washington. Goes overripe too fast in hot-summer climates
'Sunrise'	1–9, 14–16	Early Aug.	Small, red stripes on yellow. Firm, sweet flavor. Short storage life	Spreading tree that produces many branches. Annual producer
'Tropical Beauty'	18–24	Aug.	Medium to large, bright red, juicy white flesh. Mild, sweet flavor	Pollination not required. Production enhanced if it grows near 'Adina'
'Valmore'	8, 9, 18–24	Aug.	Large, red blushed yellow. Flesh yellowish white, aromatic, good for cooking, eating	Will fruit in warm areas with little winter chill
'Wealthy' ('Red Wealthy', 'Double Red Wealthy')	1–7	Midseason	Medium to large, rough, red. Flesh white veined pink, firm, tart, juicy. Good cooking variety	Small, cold-hardy tree that tends to alternate bearing. Not for hot climates
'William's Pride'	1–7	Early Aug.	Medium-size, red	Moderate-size tree. One of the best early red apples
'Winter Banana'	4–9, 14–24	Midseason	Large, attractive, pale yellow blushed pink, waxy finish. Tender, tangy, aromatic	Accepts mild winters. Needs pollinator. There is a 'Spur Winter Banana'
'Winter Pearmain' ('White Winter Pearmain')	20–24	Midseason	Medium to large. Pale greenish yellow skin with pink blush. Excellent flavor, tender flesh, fine-grained. All-purpose	Performs better than standard cold-winter varieties in Southern California. Needs pollinator

APRICOT

Rosaceae

DECIDUOUS FRUIT TREES

ZONES VARY BY VARIETY

FULL SUN

INFREQUENT, DEEP WATERING

Apricot

Apricots can be grown throughout the West, with these limitations: because they bloom early in the season, they will not fruit in regions with late frosts; in cool, humid coastal areas, tree and fruit are unusually subject to brown rot and blight; in mild-winter areas of Southern California, only varieties with low requirements for winter chill will do well. Apricots are good dual-purpose fruit and shade trees, easy to maintain. They can also be trained as espaliers. Your county agent or farm advisor can give you a local timetable and directions for spraying apricots (essential dates: during dormant season, before and after flowering, and at red-bud stage). To get big apricots, do this: in midspring, thin excess fruit from branches, leaving 2–4 in. between individual apricots.

Apricots bear most fruit on short fruit spurs that form on the previous year's growth and remain fruitful for about 4 years. The goal of pruning should be to conserve enough new growth (which will produce spurs) to replace old, exhausted spurs, which should be cut out.

Here's a list of varieties sold at nurseries. Many are available on dwarf and semidwarf rootstocks. Some varieties need a pollinator, as indicated. For ornamental relatives, see *Prunus*.

'Aprigold'. Zones 2, 3, 6–9, 12–16, 18–23. Good-quality, full-size fruit. Genetic (natural) dwarf 4–6 ft. tall, 6–8 ft. wide. ▶

'Autumn Royal'. Zones 2, 3, 6–9, 12–16, 18–23. Resembles 'Royal' but fruit ripens in September; only autumn-ripening apricot tree.

'Blenril'. Zones 2, 3, 6. Like 'Royal' in quality. Needs pollinator (any variety except 'Riland').

'Chinese' ('Mormon'). Zones 1–3, 6. Late bloom, hardy tree; good production in late-frost and cold-winter regions.

'Early Gold' ('Early Golden', 'Earligold'). Zones 8–12, 14–23. Early-fruiting variety that needs little winter chill.

'Floragold'. Zones 2, 3, 6–24. Early-ripening, full-size fruit grows on genetic (natural) semidwarf tree (about half the size of normal apricot tree).

'Golden Amber'. Zones 2, 3, 6–9, 12–16, 18–23. Resembles 'Royal' but blooms over month-long period; fruit ripens over similar period from mid-June to mid-July.

'Goldrich'. Zones 2–6. Good-quality fruit on hardy, cold-resistant tree. Needs pollinator.

'King'. Zones 8–9, 12–16, 18–23. Early ripening, very large, very highly colored. Hard to pollinate; 'Perfection' does best job.

'Moongold'. Zones 1–3. Plum-size, golden, sweet, sprightly fruit. Developed for coldest winter climates.

'Moorpark'. Zones 2, 3, 6–11, 14–16. Very large fruit, fine flavor. Color develops unevenly. Good home dessert or drying variety, poor canner.

'Newcastle'. Zones 10–12, 20–23. Good Southern California variety; needs little winter chilling.

'Perfection' ('Goldbeck'). Zones 2–9, 12–16, 18–23. Fruit very large but flavor only mediocre. Chilling requirement low; tree hardy. Needs pollinator (any variety except 'Reeves').

'Puget Gold'. Zones 4–6. Consistent bearer in Puget Sound area; fairly tolerant of apricot diseases. Medium-size fruit in early August. Flavor good, low in acid.

'Redsweet'. Zones 12–16, 18–23. Highly colored, very early ripening fruit. Needs early-blooming pollinator ('Nugget' or 'Perfection').

'Riland'. Zones 2, 3, 6. Early-ripening, highly colored, roundish fruit. Needs pollinator.

'Rival'. Zones 2–6. Large, oval orange fruit blushed red. Needs early-flowering pollinator ('Perfection').

'Royal', 'Blenheim'. Zones 2, 3, 6–23. Regardless of how labeled in nurseries, these are either two identical varieties or one variety under two names. Standard variety in California's apricot regions. Good for canning or drying.

'Royalty'. Zones 2, 3, 6–9, 12–23. Extra-large fruit on heavy, wind-resistant spurs. Early bearing.

'Snowball'. Zones 14–16, 18–23. Early ripening; white skin with pink blush, white flesh.

'Sun-Glow'. Zones 2–6. Highly colored, early fruit. Hardy tree with extra-hardy fruit buds.

'Sungold'. Zones 1–3. Plum-size, slightly flattened, bright orange, sweet, mild fruit. Developed for coldest winter climates.

'Tilton'. Zones 1–8, 10, 11, 18, 20. Higher chilling requirement than for 'Royal' but less subject to brown rot and sunburn.

'Wenatchee' ('Wenatchee Moorpark'). Zones 2, 3, 6. Large fruit, excellent flavor.

APTENIA cordifolia
(Mesembryanthemum cordifolium)

Aizoaceae

SHRUBBY PERENNIAL

◪ ZONES 17, 21–24

☼ FULL SUN

◖ VERY LITTLE WATER

Aptenia cordifolia

Ice plant relative with trailing stems to 2 ft. long and profusion of inch-wide, heart-shaped or oval, bright green, fleshy leaves. Purplish red,

inch-wide ice plant flowers in spring and summer. Though fleshy, looks less like ice plant than most. Use as trailer in rock garden, on slope or wall, or in hanging pot. *A. c.* 'Variegata' has white-bordered leaves. 'Red Apple', hybrid with *Platythyra haeckeliana,* has brighter red flowers, is good ground cover.

Aquifoliaceae. The holly family contains evergreen trees or shrubs with berrylike fruit. *Ilex* (holly) is the only important genus.

AQUILEGIA

COLUMBINE

Ranunculaceae

PERENNIALS

◪ ALL ZONES

☼ ◗ FULL SUN OR FILTERED SHADE

◖ MODERATE WATER

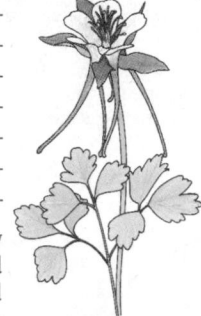
Aquilegia McKana Giant

Columbines have a fairylike, woodland quality with their lacy foliage and beautifully posed flowers in exquisite pastels, deeper shades, and white. Erect, branching, 2 in.–4 ft. high. Fresh green, divided leaves reminiscent of maidenhair fern. Bloom in spring, early summer. Flowers to 3 in. across, erect or nodding, often with sepals and petals in contrasting colors; usually have backward-projecting, nectar-bearing spurs. Some kinds have large flowers and very long spurs; these have an airier look than short-spurred kinds or double-flowered strains, although the latter make bolder color mass.

Preferred tall hybrid strains are graceful, long-spurred McKana Giants and double-flowering Spring Song. Lower-growing strains are Biedermeier and Dragonfly (1 ft.); long-spurred Music (1½ ft.); and single to double, upward-facing Fairyland (15 in.).

All columbines are hardy. Cut back old stems for second crop of flowers; leave some seed if you want plants to self-sow. All kinds of columbines attract hummingbirds. Subject to leaf miners, aphids, and red spider mites but usually require only routine care. Replace old plants about every 3 years.

A. alpina. ALPINE COLUMBINE. Native of the Alps. Grows 12–16 in. high. Flowers blue, to 2 in. across, with straight or curved spurs 1 in. long.

A. caerulea. ROCKY MOUNTAIN COLUMBINE. State flower of Colorado. 1½–3 ft. high. Flowers erect, 2 in. or more across, blue and white. Spurs straight or spreading, to 2 in. long. This species hybridized with *A. chrysantha* and others to produce many long-spurred hybrids. Best in filtered shade and moist soil.

A. chrysantha. GOLDEN or GOLDEN-SPURRED COLUMBINE. Native to Arizona, New Mexico, and adjacent Mexico. Large, many-branched plant to 3–4 ft. One of showiest species. Leaflets densely covered with soft hairs beneath. Flowers erect, 1½–3 in. across, clear yellow; spurs slender, 2–2½ in. long.

A. flabellata. Native to Japan. Stocky 9-inch plant with lilac blue and creamy white flowers in early spring. Good rock garden plant. *A. f.* 'Nana' is even shorter.

A. formosa. WESTERN COLUMBINE. Native to Utah and California to Alaska. Grows 1½–3 ft. high. Flowers nodding, 1½–2 in. across, red and yellow; spurs stout and straight, red. Good in woodland garden; allow to form seeds, which are relished by song sparrows, juncos, and other small birds. *A. f. truncata* is sometimes sold as *A. californica;* it is a tall columbine with red spurs, orange petals, and yellow sepals.

A. longissima. Native to southwest Texas and northern Mexico; 2½–3 ft. tall. Similar to *A. chrysantha.* Flowers numerous, erect, pale yellow; spurs very narrow, drooping, 4–6 in. long.

A. saximontana. In effect a miniature *A. caerulea,* 4–8 in. tall.

A. vulgaris. EUROPEAN COLUMBINE. Naturalized in eastern United States. Grows to 1–2½ ft. Flowers nodding, up to 2 in. across, in blue, purple, or white; short, knobby spurs about ¾ in. long.

ARABIS

ROCKCRESS

Brassicaceae (Cruciferae)

PERENNIALS

✎ ALL ZONES, EXCEPT AS NOTED

☼ FULL SUN

◐ MODERATE WATER

Arabis caucasica

Low-growing, spreading plants for edgings, rock gardens, ground covers, pattern plantings. All kinds have attractive year-round foliage and clusters of white, pink, or rose purple flowers in spring.

A. alpina. MOUNTAIN ROCKCRESS. Zones 1–7. Low, tufted plant, rough-hairy, with leafy stems 4–10 in. high and basal leaves in clusters. White flowers in dense, short clusters. Variety 'Rosea', 6 in. high, has pink flowers; 'Variegata' has variegated leaves. Plants sold as *A. alpina* are often really *A. caucasica*.

A. blepharophylla. CALIFORNIA ROCKCRESS, ROSE CRESS. Zones 5, 6, 15–17. Native to rocky hillsides and ridges near sea, Marin County to Monterey County, California. Tufted perennial 4–8 in. high. Basal leaves 1–2¾ in. long. Rose purple flowers, fragrant, ½–¾ in. wide, in short, dense clusters. Blooms March and April. Rock plant in nature, equally adapted to well-drained spot in rock garden. Also good container plant.

A. caucasica (A. albida). WALL ROCKCRESS. Native Mediterranean region to Iran. Dependable old favorite. Forms mat of gray leaves to 6 in. high. White, ½-in. flowers almost cover plants in early spring. Excellent ground cover and base planting for spring-flowering bulbs such as daffodils and paper-white narcissus. Companion for *Aurinia saxatilis* and *Aubrieta deltoidea*.

A. c. 'Variegata'. Has gray leaves with creamy white margins. 'Floreplena' has double flowers; 'Rosabella' and 'Pink Charm' have pink blooms. Latter two are popular rock garden plants in colder climates. Start plants from cuttings or sow seeds in spring or fall. Provide some shade in hot, dry areas. Short lived where winters are warm.

A. ferdinandi-coburgii. Tight clumps to 4 in. Commonest form is 'Variegata', with leaves heavily edged and splashed with white.

A. sturii. Dense, fist-size cushions of small bright green leaves eventually grow into small mats. Clusters of white flowers on 2–3-in. stems in early spring. Some consider it one of the 50 finest rock garden plants.

Araceae. The arum family contains plants ranging from tuberous or rhizomatous perennials to shrubby or climbing tropical foliage plants. Leaves are often highly ornamental; while variable in shape, they tend to be arrowlike. Inconspicuous flowers cluster tightly on a club-shaped spadix within an often showy leaflike bract (spathe). Examples are anthurium, calla *(Zantedeschia)*, and philodendron. Sap of many is highly irritating to mouth and throat.

ARALIA

Araliaceae

DECIDUOUS SHRUB-TREES

✎ ZONES 2–24

☼◐ FULL SUN OR PARTIAL SHADE

◐ MODERATE WATER

Aralia chinensis

Striking bold-leafed plants that may eventually grow to 25–30 ft. under ideal conditions. Often shrublike and multistemmed (because of suckering habit), especially in colder areas where they may grow to 10 ft. Branches are nearly vertical or slightly spreading, usually very spiny. Huge leaves, clustered at ends of branches and divided into many leaflets, have effective pattern value.

White flowers, small but in such large, branched clusters that they are showy in midsummer, are followed by purplish berrylike fruit.

Not good near swimming pools because of spines; even leafstalks are sometimes prickly. Protect plants from wind to avoid burning foliage.

A. chinensis. CHINESE ANGELICA. Only moderately spiny. Leaves 2–3 ft. long, divided into 2–6-in.-long toothed leaflets without stalks. Flower clusters grow 1–2 ft. wide.

A. elata. JAPANESE ANGELICA TREE. Native to northeast Asia. Similar to *A. chinensis* but leaflets are narrower, have fewer teeth. *A. e.* 'Variegata' has leaflets strikingly bordered with creamy white.

A. elegantissima. See Schefflera elegantissima

A. papyrifera. See Tetrapanax papyriferus

A. sieboldii. JAPANESE ARALIA. See Fatsia japonica

Araliaceae. The aralia family of herbaceous and woody plants is marked by leaves that are divided fanwise into leaflets or veined in pattern like the fingers of a hand. Individually tiny flowers are in round clusters or in large compound clusters. Examples are English ivy, Japanese aralia *(Fatsia japonica)*, and schefflera.

ARAUCARIA

Araucariaceae

EVERGREEN TREES

✎ ZONES VARY BY SPECIES

☼ FULL SUN

◐ REGULAR WATER

Araucaria araucana

These strange-looking conifers, prominent skyline trees in many parks and old estates in California, provide distinctive silhouette with their evenly spread tiers of stiff branches. Most have stiff, closely overlapping, dark to bright green leaves. All do well in a wide range of soils with adequate drainage.

These trees serve well as skyline trees, but they become so towering that they need the space they would have in a park. And they are not trees to sit under—with age they bear large, spiny, 10–15-lb. cones that fall with a crash. They thrive in containers for several years, even in desert areas.

A. araucana (A. imbricata). MONKEY PUZZLE TREE. Zones 4–9, 14–24. Native to Chile. Arboreal oddity with heavy, spreading branches and ropelike branchlets closely set with sharp-pointed dark green leaves. Hardiest of araucarias. Slow growing in youth, it eventually reaches 70–90 ft.

A. bidwillii. BUNYA-BUNYA. Zones 7–9, 12–24. Native to Australia. Probably most widely planted araucaria in both coastal and valley areas of California. Moderate growth to 80 ft.; broadly rounded crown supplies dense shade. Two kinds of leaves: juvenile leaves are glossy, rather narrow, ¾–2 in. long, stiff, more or less spreading in two rows; mature leaves are oval, ½ in. long, rather woody, spirally arranged and overlapping along branches. Unusual house plant; very tough and tolerant of low light.

A. heterophylla (A. excelsa). NORFOLK ISLAND PINE. Zones 17, 21–24. Moderate growth rate to 100 ft., of pyramidal shape. Juvenile leaves rather narrow, ½ in. long, curved and with sharp points; mature leaves somewhat triangular and densely overlapping. Can be held in containers for many years—outdoors in mild climates, indoors anywhere.

Araucaria heterophylla

Araucariaceae. Coniferous trees with symmetrical branching habit and leaves that vary from needlelike to broad and leathery. *Araucaria* is the only representative in this book.

A

ARAUJIA sericofera

WHITE BLADDER FLOWER

Asclepiadaceae

EVERGREEN OR PARTIALLY DECIDUOUS VINE

⚡ ZONES 8, 9, 14–24

☀ ◗ FULL SUN OR PARTIAL SHADE

◖ ◖ ◖ LITTLE OR MUCH WATER

Araujia sericofera

Native to Brazil. Woody vine that sometimes spontaneously pops up in gardens from windborne, silky-tufted seeds. Becomes weedy, massive tangle in year or two. Leaves tend to drop at base. Twines 20–30 ft. in one season. Leaves 2–4 in. long, glossy dark green above, whitish beneath. White or pinkish bell-shaped flowers, 1–1½ in. wide, followed by long, flat, leathery fruit. Not first-class vine. Used for quick temporary screen in poor soil, windy places.

ARBORVITAE. See PLATYCLADUS orientalis, THUJA   pp. 427, 505

ARBUTUS

Ericaceae

EVERGREEN TREES AND SHRUB-TREES

⚡ ZONES VARY BY SPECIES

☀ FULL SUN, EXCEPT AS NOTED

◖ ◖ WATER NEEDS VARY BY SPECIES

The species *A. menziesii* is a western native; *A. andrachne* and *A. unedo* come from the Mediterranean. *A.* 'Marina' is of uncertain origin.

Arbutus unedo

A. andrachne. Evergreen large shrub or tree to 20–40 ft. Zones 8, 9, 14–24. Resembles madrone, but with smaller, less shiny leaves. Peeling bark is beautiful. Eastern Mediterranean native; not as difficult to grow as madrone. From little to regular watering.

A. 'Marina'. Evergreen tree to 40 ft., usually less. Zones 8, 9, 14–24. Hybrid of uncertain parentage. Resembles *A. unedo* but has larger leaves, rosy pink flowers in the fall. Good garden substitute for madrone. Little to regular water.

A. menziesii. MADRONE, MADRONA. Evergreen tree or large shrub. Zones 3–7, 14–19. Native from British Columbia to Southern California in Coast Ranges, occasionally in middle elevations of Sierra Nevada. Mature height ranges from 20 to 100 ft. Forms broad, round head almost as wide as tall. In groves, plants are more slender. Main feature is smooth, reddish brown bark that peels in thin flakes. Leathery, 3–6-in.-long leaves are shiny dark green on top, dull gray green beneath. In spring, large clusters of white to pinkish, bell-shaped flowers at branch ends. These are followed in early fall by clusters of brilliant red-and-orange, rough-coated berries that remain on tree most of winter if birds don't get them.

If you live in madrone country and have a tree in your garden, treasure it. Its requirements in gardens outside its native area are exacting: it must have fast drainage and nonalkaline water. Water just enough to keep plants going until they are established, and then give only infrequent and deep watering.

A. unedo. STRAWBERRY TREE. Evergreen shrub-tree. Zones 4–24. Native to southern Europe, Ireland. Damaged in severe winters in Zones 4–7 but worth risk. Remarkably good performance in wide range of climates and soils, from desert to seashore. In California, one of the best lawn or raised-bed trees. It tolerates wind at the beach and takes from little to regular watering. Sun or part shade; full shade in desert.

Slow to moderate growth to 8–35 ft. with equal spread. Normally has basal suckers, stem sprouts. Can be pruned, not sheared, to make open-crowned tree. Or plant several and leave unpruned to make screen. Trunk and branches have rich red-brown shreddy bark; tend to become twisted and gnarled in age. Dark green, handsome, red-stemmed leaves are oblong and 2–3 in. long. Clusters of small, white or greenish white, urn-shaped flowers and round, red-and-yellow, ¾-in. fruit, somewhat strawberrylike in texture, appear at the same time in fall and winter; fruit is edible but mealy and nearly tasteless.

A. u. 'Compacta' is a smaller shrub but still larger than *A. u.* 'Elfin King', a picturesque, contorted true dwarf form (not over 5 ft. tall at 10 years of age) that flowers and fruits nearly continuously. 'Elfin King' is a splendid container plant or show plant for small entry garden.

A. u. 'Oktoberfest' is a 6- to 8-ft. shrub with deep pink flowers.

MADRONE OR MADRONA?

Those are the two ways people in *Arbutus menziesii* territory say the common name for this shrub-tree. But curiously, they do it backward from what a linguist might expect. North of the Siskiyou mountain range, a land that was settled by English-speaking people, the tree is called by its Spanish name, madrona, while in California, where the Spanish peppered the land with names like Monterey, San Bernardino, and Vallejo, people call it just plain madrone (with two syllables).

ARCHONTOPHOENIX

Arecaceae (Palmae)

PALMS

⚡ OUTDOORS, ZONES 21–24; OR INDOORS

☀ ◗ FULL SUN OR PARTIAL SHADE

◖ MODERATE WATER

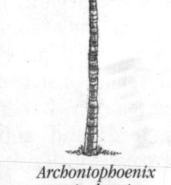

Called bangalow or piccabeen palms in Australia. They grow to 50 ft. or more, with 10–15-ft. spread. Handsome, stately, difficult to transplant when large. Where winds are strong, plant in lee of buildings to prevent damage. Young trees can't take frost; mature plants may stand 28°F. They tolerate shade and can grow many years grouped under tall trees. Old leaves shed cleanly, leaving smooth green trunks. Feathery leaves on mature trees 8–10 ft. long, green above, gray green beneath.

Archontophoenix cunninghamiana

A. alexandrae. ALEXANDRA PALM. Trunk enlarged toward base.

A. cunninghamiana (Seaforthia elegans). KING PALM. More common than *A. alexandrae*. Trunk not prominently enlarged at base. Clustered amethyst flowers are handsome. Highly recommended for nearly frost-free areas.

ARCTANTHEMUM. See CHRYSANTHEMUM arcticum   p. 226

ARCTOSTAPHYLOS

MANZANITA

Ericaceae

EVERGREEN SHRUBS

⚡ ZONES VARY BY SPECIES

☀ FULL SUN

◖ SOME WATER

Large group of western natives ranging in size from creepers to full-size shrubs to small trees. Waxy, bell-like flowers and fruit like tiny apples. Most are characterized by (and admired for) crooked branches with smooth red to purple bark. Shrubs attract birds.

Arctostaphylos densiflora

Low-growing ground cover manzanitas do best in loose soils that drain rapidly. They tolerate heavier soils. Taller ground covers (especially those that spread by rooting branches) and most shrub and tree forms must have loose, well-drained soil.

The first summer after planting, water every 4–7 days, depending on weather. In warm-summer areas, established plants in well-drained soil generally thrive on once-a-month watering; in heavy soil, they need less frequent watering. You may be able to water only once or twice a summer. Control growth by frequent pinching during growing season.

Blooming season is not noted in the following list unless it differs from general February–March–April sequence.

A. 'Austin Hill'. Resembles *A. manzanita* 'Dr. Hurd' but smaller (to 8 ft.), with similar burgundy-colored bark, good garden-water tolerance.

A. bakeri 'Louis Edmunds'. Zones 4–9, 14–17. Upright shrub to 5–6 ft. tall. Gray-green foliage. Pink flowers in hanging clusters. Good garden-water tolerance.

A. columbiana. HAIRY MANZANITA. Zones 4–6, 15–17. Native to low coastal mountains, central California to British Columbia. Form propagated and sold in northwestern nurseries is called 'Oregon Hybrid'. Low-growing, compact shrub with reddish bark, gray-green leaves 3 in. long, white flowers, and red-cheeked summer fruit. Useful plant, tough enough for highway landscaping in western Oregon and Washington.

A. densiflora. VINE HILL MANZANITA. Zones 7–9, 14–21. Native to Sonoma County, California. All varieties except 'Sentinel' grow low and spreading; outer branches take root when they touch soil. Main stems slender and crooked. Bark of trunks and branches smooth, reddish black. Leaves light or dark green, glossy, small, in ½–1 in. range. Flowers white or pink. In bank planting, low types do best on east- or northeast-facing slopes, in loose soil with good drainage.

A. d. 'Harmony'. Very similar to 'Howard McMinn' (see next) but somewhat taller and broader. Less well known but considered best form by some specialists. Pinkish white flowers.

A. d. 'Howard McMinn'. Grows in mound to 5–6 ft. tall (usually much less); spreads as much as 7 ft. in 5 years. If tips pruned after flowering, plant becomes as dense as sheared Kurume azalea. (Don't prune tips of prostrate branches.) Flowers whitish pink.

A. d. 'Sentinel'. An upright form to 6 ft. or more and spreading to 8 ft. Light green, downy leaves. Can be trained as small tree by selecting dominant stem or stems and removing others. Sensitive to salt burn, root rots.

A. edmundsii. LITTLE SUR MANZANITA. Zones 6–9, 14–24. Low-growing manzanitas from coastal Monterey County, California. Five varieties are grown from cuttings. 'Danville' is 4–24 in. tall, to 12 ft. wide, with roundish, light green, inch-long leaves on red stems and pink flowers in December and January. 'Carmel Sur' has exceptionally good form—gray-green, neat-looking foliage; soft pink flowers—and is fast growing and very garden-water tolerant. 'Indian Hill' appreciates light shade. 'Little Sur' has dense, flat growth (new growth bronze); pointed leaves with reddish margins; slow growth rate; and soft pink flowers in March–April. Good hillside planting. 'Parvifolia' has exceptionally shiny foliage and showy pink flowers. New growth is rich bronze in color.

A. 'Emerald Carpet'. Zones 6–9, 14–24. Dense, uniform carpet 9–14 in. tall, mounding slightly higher after many years. Leaves roundish oval; ½ in. long; bright green in hottest, driest weather. Small pink flowers in March–April, not showy. In hot interior valleys needs deep irrigation every 2–3 weeks. One of greenest, most uniform manzanitas.

A. franciscana. Zones 6–9, 14–24. Grows to 2½ ft., spreads slowly to 7 ft. (in 15 years). Native to San Francisco but nearly extinct there. White flowers.

A. glauca. Zones 4–9, 14–24. Spreading shrub to 15 ft. tall, 20 ft. wide, with dark reddish brown bark and 3-in. blue-gray leaves. Large, branched clusters carry pink to white flowers.

A. hookeri. MONTEREY MANZANITA. Zones 6–9, 14–24. Native to Monterey Peninsula. Slow growing to form dense mounds 1½–4 ft. high, spreading to 6 ft. and more. Oval, ¾-in.-long, bright green, glossy leaves. Flowers white to pinkish; fruit bright red, shiny; bark red brown, smooth. Good on hillsides.

A. h. 'Monterey Carpet'. Compact growth; foot-high ground cover spreads by rooting branches to 12 ft.

A. h. 'Wayside'. Taller growing, to 4 ft., while spreading to 8 ft. and more. Trailing branches take root. May be slow to fill in; eventually dense, attractive mound.

A. insularis. ISLAND MANZANITA. Zones 16–24. Large, dense shrub to 10–15 ft., with bright green leaves and white flowers in large drooping clusters. Midwinter bloom. 'Canyon Sparkles' is a compact selection.

A. 'John Dourley'. One of the best of the newer selections, it grows to 3 ft. tall by 8 ft. wide, with gray-green foliage (new growth bronze) and white, pink-tinged flowers. Good garden-water tolerance.

A. manzanita. COMMON MANZANITA. Tall shrub or treelike shrub. Zones 4–9, 14–24. Native to inner Coast Ranges, Sierra Nevada foothills. Widely adapted. Grows 6–20 ft. high, spreads 4–10 ft. wide. Crooked picturesque branching habit; purplish red bark. Shiny bright green to dull green, broadly oval leaves, ¾–1½ in. long. Flowers white to pink in open, drooping clusters. Fruit white turning to deep red.

A. m. 'Dr. Hurd'. Treelike form to 15 ft. tall, as wide or wider. Mahogany bark; large, light green leaves; white flowers January–March.

A. media. Zones 4–9, 14–24. May be a natural hybrid of *A. uva-ursi* and *A. columbiana*. As far as gardener is concerned, it's a higher-growing *A. uva-ursi* (to 2 ft.) with brighter red branches and leathery dark green leaves. Spreads faster than *A. uva-ursi*.

A. nummularia. FORT BRAGG MANZANITA. Zones 14–24. Densely foliaged, low-growing (6–18 in., rarely taller) shrub with small bright green leaves, small white flowers. Attractive but considered difficult outside its native north coastal California forests. Needs good drainage, acid soil, and shade except near coast.

A. 'Pacific Mist'. Zones 7–9, 14–24. Grows to 2½ ft. high. Spreading stems turn upward near ends. Bark is deep reddish brown. Narrow leaves gray green. Sparse bloom white. Needs pinching to force branching, but eventually it forms a good, dense ground cover.

A GREEN CARPET ON A STEEP SLOPE

Sometimes a slope needs to be covered with something low and green, but the site is too steep for a lawn. What to do? One good answer is to use dependable, bank-covering manzanitas: *Arctostaphylos* 'Emerald Carpet' or *A. uva-ursi*. The latter has prettier flowers. It comes in six named varieties, each with its own set of attributes.

A. pajaroensis. PAJARO MANZANITA. Zones 14–24. Grows 3–8 ft., with broader spread. Leaves open bronzy, turning bluish green. Flowers pink to white. 'Paradise' is a choice selection with long-lasting bronze foliage color and pink flowers. 'Warren Roberts' is similar, but leaves are more bluish and new growth is darker bronze.

A. pumila. DUNE MANZANITA. Zone 17. Native to dunes around Monterey Bay, California. Spreading, prostrate habit, to 1–2½ ft. high. Roots freely where branches touch ground. Leaves dull green, narrowish, ½–1 in. long. Short, dense clusters of small white to pink flowers. Good ground cover in sandy soil near coast.

A. 'Sunset'. Zones 6–9, 14–24. Natural hybrid between *A. hookeri* and *A. pajaroensis* from Monterey County, California. New foliage coppery red, turning bright green. Makes mound 4–5 ft. tall by 4–6 ft. wide. Pinkish white flowers in March–April.

A. uva-ursi. BEARBERRY, KINNIKINNICK. Zones 1–9, 14–24. Native from San Mateo County, California, north to Alaska. Also widespread in other northern latitudes. Long a popular ground cover in Pacific Northwest and intermontane areas. Prostrate form, spreading and rooting as it creeps to 15 ft. wide; glossy, bright green, leathery leaves to 1 in., turning red in winter. Flowers white or pinkish. Fruit bright red or pink. A most useful plant in Northwest: good for ground cover on slopes, and as trailing mat on wall, with mugho pines, yews. Slowness in starting allows weeds to form: mulch with peat moss or sawdust to keep them down and to keep soil moist for root growth and rooting of branches. Good on hillsides. ▶

A

A. u. 'Alaska'. Flat grower with small, round, dark green leaves.

A. u. 'Massachusetts'. Like 'Alaska', this is small leafed, flat growing. Good resistance to leaf spot and leaf gall in Northwest.

A. u. 'Point Reyes'. Dark green leaves are closely set along branches. More tolerant of heat and drought than *A. u.* 'Radiant'.

A. u. 'Radiant'. Leaves lighter green than those of *A. u.* 'Point Reyes', more widely spaced. Heavy crop of large, bright red fruit in autumn, lasting into winter; sometimes fails to fruit if pollinating insects not active at bloom time.

A. u. 'Wood's Compact'. Compact grower, with red branches densely clad with dark green leaves. Pink flowers.

A. u. 'Wood's Red'. Quarter-inch bright red berries, reliably produced, distinguish this selection. Grows best in Northwest or Northern California.

ARCTOTHECA calendula

CAPE WEED

Asteraceae (Compositae)

EVERGREEN PERENNIAL

❚ ZONES 8, 9, 13–24

☼ FULL SUN

◐ ● LITTLE OR NO WATER ONCE ESTABLISHED

Arctotheca calendula

Rapidly spreading ground cover, less than 1 ft. tall, with yellow daisy flowers 2 in. across most of year, peaking March through June. Gray-green, deeply divided leaves. Not fussy about soil. Space 1½ ft. apart for fast cover. Some frost damage in high 20s, but recovers quickly. Not for small areas; good on hillsides.

ARCTOTIS

AFRICAN DAISY

Asteraceae (Compositae)

ANNUALS AND PERENNIALS

❚ ZONES 7–9, 14–24

☼ FULL SUN

● WATER DURING ACTIVE GROWTH

Arctotis acaulis

Annuals and perennials, the latter usually grown as annuals. "African daisy" can refer to any of several plants; names and identities of the plants are often confused, even by seed companies and nurseries. *Arctotis* species have lobed leaves that are rough, hairy, or woolly; their flower heads usually have a contrasting ring of color around central eye. *Dimorphotheca* species (commonly used for mass flower color in winter) are annuals with smooth green foliage; their flowers are in the yellow-orange-salmon range or are white. Trailing ground cover African daisies and woody, shrubby white, yellow, or purple African daisies are *Osteospermum*.

A. acaulis. Perennial. Spreading, stemless clumps of leaves; flower heads to 3½ in. wide on 6-in.-long stalks are yellow with purplish black centers.

A. breviscapa. Annual, somewhat smaller than *A. acaulis,* with orange-yellow, brown-centered flowers.

A. hybrids. Most garden plants are hybrids 1–1½ ft. tall. 3-in. flowers come in white, pink, red, purplish, cream, yellow, and orange, usually with a dark ring around the nearly black eyespot. In mild climates plants grow in winter and early spring and bloom from spring into early summer, with scattered bloom occurring later. They will self-sow but tend to revert to orange. You can perpetuate colors you like by taking cuttings. Plants survive as perennials in mildest climates but bloom best in their first year.

A. stoechadifolia grandis. Bushy annual to 2 ft., with gray-green, slightly hairy leaves and 3-in. white daisies in which yellow ring surrounds deep blue central eye.

ARDISIA

MARLBERRY

Myrsinaceae

EVERGREEN SHRUBS OR SHRUBLETS

❚ ZONES VARY BY SPECIES

● SHADE

💧 FREQUENT WATER

Ardisia japonica

Of the 150 species of evergreen shrubs in this genus, only the following two are widely grown in the West. Valued for foliage, beadlike fruits.

A. crenata (A. crenulata, A. crispa). Usually grown indoors. Most familiar as 1½-ft. single-stemmed potted plant. In large tub it can reach 4 ft. with nearly equal spread. In spring, spirelike clusters of tiny (¼-in.) white or pinkish flowers are carried above shiny, wavy-edged, 3-in.-long leaves. Flowers are followed by brilliant scarlet fruit in autumn and usually through winter. Routine house plant care.

A. japonica. Zones 5, 6, 15–17. Low shrub that spreads as ground cover by rhizomes to produce succession of upright branches 6–18 in. high. Makes quality ground cover in shade. Needs ample water. Leathery, bright green leaves (4 in. long) are clustered at tips of branches. Forms with white or gold leaf variegation are sometimes sold. White, ¼-in. flowers, two to six in cluster, appear in fall, followed by small (¼-in.), round, bright red fruits that last into winter.

Arecaceae. It's difficult to generalize about any plant family as large and widespread as palms. Generally speaking, they have single, unbranched trunks of considerable height; some grow in clusters, though, and some are dwarf or stemless. The leaves are usually divided into many leaflets, either like ribs of a fan (fan palms) or like a feather, with many parallel leaflets growing outward from a long central stem (feather palms). But some palms have undivided leaves. This family was formerly called Palmae. See also Palms.

ARECA lutescens. See CHRYSALIDOCARPUS lutescens   **p. 226**

ARECASTRUM romanzoffianum. See SYAGRUS romanzoffianum   **p. 498**

ARENARIA

SANDWORT

Caryophyllaceae

PERENNIAL GROUND COVERS

❚ ZONES 2–9, 14–24

☼ ◑ ● EXPOSURE NEEDS VARY BY SPECIES

💧 💧 MODERATE TO AMPLE WATER

Arenaria montana

Low evergreen plants carpet ground with dense mats of mosslike foliage, have small white flowers in late spring and summer. They are often used as lawn substitutes, between stepping stones, or for velvety green patches in rock gardens. Can be invasive; hard to eradicate in well-watered gardens.

A. balearica. CORSICAN SANDWORT. Forms dense mat to 3 in. high. Leaves oval, thick, glossy, to ⅛ in. long. Grows best in shade with lots of water. Adapted to planting in small areas—for example, to cover soil of container-grown tree.

A. montana. Grows 2–4 in. high; weak stems up to 1 ft. long, usually covered with soft hairs. Leaves grayish, ½–¾ in. long. White flowers, 1 in. across, profuse in June. Good plant to let trail over sunny rock or tumble over low wall. Moderate water requirements.

A. verna (A. v. caespitosa). See Sagina subulata

ARGEMONE

PRICKLY POPPY

Papaveraceae

ANNUALS OR BIENNIALS

✓ ALL ZONES

☼ FULL SUN

◊ NO WATER ONCE ESTABLISHED

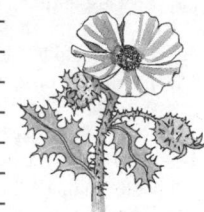
Argemone mexicana

Prickly-leafed and prickly-stemmed plants with large, showy poppy flowers. Native to desert or dry areas, Wyoming to Mexico and west to California. Grow easily from seed sown where plants are to bloom or from seed sown in pots; transplant gently. Need sun and good drainage. Bloom mostly in summer. To 3 ft.

A. intermedia. See A. polyanthemos
A. mexicana. Annual. Yellow to orange flowers.
A. platyceras. Annual. White flowers. Most common kind.
A. polyanthemos (A. intermedia). Annual or biennial. White flowers.

ARGYRANTHEMUM. See CHRYSANTHEMUM frutescens p. 226

ARISTEA ecklonii

Iridaceae

PERENNIAL

✓ ZONES 8, 9, 12–24

☼ ☽ FULL SUN OR PARTIAL SHADE

◊ MODERATE WATER

Aristea ecklonii

Swordlike evergreen leaves form 2-ft. clumps, above which rise winged, flattened, 2½-ft. branching flower stalks that bear bright blue six-petaled flowers less than an inch wide. Individual flowers are short lived, but new ones appear over a long season. Remove spent flower stems to prevent aggressive self-sowing.

ARISTOLOCHIA

Aristolochiaceae

DECIDUOUS OR EVERGREEN VINES

✓ ZONES VARY BY SPECIES

☼ ☽ ● EXPOSURE NEEDS VARY BY SPECIES

◊ ALL RESPOND WELL TO AMPLE WATER

Aristolochia elegans

Curiously shaped flowers in rather sober colors resemble curved pipes with flared bowls or birds with bent necks.

A. californica. CALIFORNIA DUTCHMAN'S PIPE. Deciduous. Zones 7–9, 14–24. Native to Coast Ranges and Sierra Nevada foothills of Northern California. Will cover 8-by-12-ft. screen with some training or climb by long thin shoots 10–16 ft. into nearby tree.

Flower display before leaves, late January to April. Pendulous, 1-in.-long flowers are cream colored with red-purple veins at maturity. Bright green, heart-shaped leaves to 5 in. long. Grows from seed or from the rooted shoots around base of vine. Interesting and useful where many less hardy vines would freeze. Accepts any soil but needs partial shade and ample moisture.

A. durior (A. macrophylla). DUTCHMAN'S PIPE. Deciduous. All zones. Native to eastern United States. Will cover 15 by 20 ft. in one season. Easily grown from seed. Large, 6–14-in.-long, kidney-shaped, deep green glossy leaves are carried in shinglelike pattern to form dense cover on trellis. Blooms June and July; flower is yellowish green, 3-in. curved tube that flares into three brownish purple lobes about 1 in. wide; flowers almost hidden by leaves. Thrives in full sun or heavy shade. No special

care. Generous feeding and watering will speed growth. Cut back in winter if too heavy. Short lived in warm-winter areas. Will not stand strong winds.

A. elegans (A. littoralis). CALICO FLOWER. Outdoors in Zones 23, 24; house or greenhouse plant elsewhere. Twining evergreen vine to 6 ft. or more. Wiry, slender stems; heart-shaped leaves 3 in. long. Whitish buds shaped like little pelicans open to 3-in.-wide, heart-shaped flowers of deep purple veined creamy white. Needs rich soil, moisture, partial shade.

Aristolochiaceae. This family includes *Aristolochia* and *Asarum,* the wild gingers. All display odd-shaped flowers in low-key colors.

ARMERIA

THRIFT, SEA PINK

Plumbaginaceae

HARDY EVERGREEN PERENNIALS

✓ ALL ZONES

☼ FULL SUN

◊ ◊ LITTLE TO MODERATE WATER

Armeria maritima

Narrow, stiff leaves grow in compact tufts or basal rosettes; small white, pink, rose, or red flowers in dense globular heads from early spring to late fall. Sturdy, dependable plants for edging walks or borders and for tidy mounds in rock gardens or raised beds. Attractive in containers. Need excellent soil drainage. Shear flowers after bloom. Feed once a year with slow-acting fertilizer. Propagate by divisions or from seeds in spring or fall.

A. alliacea. Leaf clumps 2–6 in. tall produce 8–16-in. flowering stalks with bright pink flowers. 'Leucantha' has white flowers. Somewhat less hardy than other species.

A. girardii (A. juncea, A. setacea). Low, dense mounds of narrow, needlelike foliage produce lavender pink flowers in spring. Reblooms if old flowers are removed.

A. juniperifolia (A. caespitosa). Stiff, needle-shaped leaves ½ in. long in low, extremely compact rosettes. Flowers rose pink or white in dense, round clusters on 2-in. stems. This little mountain native is very touchy about drainage; apply mulch of fine gravel around plants to prevent basal stem rot, especially in summer.

A. maritima (Statice armeria, Armeria vulgaris). COMMON THRIFT. Tufted mounds spreading to 1 ft. with 6-in.-long, stiff, grasslike leaves. Small white to rose pink flowers in tight, round clusters at top of 6–10-in. stalks. Blooms almost all year along coast; flowers profusely in spring in other areas. 'Bloodstone' (rose red) and 'Cotton Tail' (white) are selections.

ARRHENATHERUM elatius bulbosum 'Variegatum'

BULBOUS OAT GRASS

Poaceae (Gramineae)

PERENNIAL

✓ ZONES 1–7

☼ ☽ SUN OR PARTIAL SHADE

◊ MODERATE WATER

Arrhenatherum elatius bulbosum 'Variegatum'

With its 6–12-in. narrow leaves boldly edged and striped in white, it is attractive in the perennial border or large rock garden and can brighten a dark place under trees or big shrubs.

PRACTICAL GARDENING DICTIONARY
PLEASE SEE PAGES 529–592

A

ARTEMISIA

Asteraceae (Compositae)

EVERGREEN OR DECIDUOUS SHRUBS, PERENNIALS

☘ ALL ZONES

☼ FULL SUN

◐ ◉ IN BORDERS, BEST WITH A LITTLE WATER

Artemisia abrotanum

Several species are valuable for interesting leaf patterns and silvery gray or white aromatic foliage; others are aromatic herbs. Most kinds excellent for use in mixed border where white or silvery leaves soften harsh reds or oranges and blend beautifully with blues, lavenders, and pinks. Divide in spring and fall.

A. abrotanum. SOUTHERNWOOD, OLD MAN. Deciduous shrub. To 3–5 ft. Beautiful lemon-scented, green, feathery foliage; yellowish white flower heads. Use for pleasantly scented foliage in shrub border. Hang sprigs in closet to discourage moths. Burn a few leaves on stove to kill cooking odors.

A. absinthium. COMMON WORMWOOD. Evergreen woody perennial. To 2–4 ft. Silvery gray, finely divided leaves with bitter taste, pungent odor. Minute yellow flowers. Keep pruned to get better-shaped plant. Divide every 3 years. Background shrub; good gray feature in flower border, particularly fine with delphiniums. 'Lambrook Silver' is an 18-inch form with especially finely cut, silver white leaves.

A. arborescens. Woody-based perennial or shrub 3 ft. or a little more in height, 2 ft. wide, with silvery white, very finely cut foliage. Most attractive but more tender than other artemisias.

A. californica. CALIFORNIA SAGEBRUSH. Native to coast, Northern California to Baja California. Finely divided grayish white leaves on stems 1½–5 ft. tall. Drought tolerant once established; loses leaves in extreme drought. 'Canyon Gray' and 'Montara' are superior selections.

A. cana. Native east of the Sierra-Cascade divide. Evergreen shrub 1½–3 ft. tall with narrow, silvery green leaves. Extremely hardy to drought, cold.

A. caucasica. SILVER SPREADER. Evergreen shrublet 3–6 in. tall, spreading to 2 ft. in width. Silky, silvery green foliage; small yellow flowers. Bank or ground cover. Needs good drainage. Takes extremes of heat and cold. Plant 1–2 ft. apart.

A. dracunculus. FRENCH TARRAGON, TRUE TARRAGON. Perennial. To 1–2 ft.; spreads slowly by creeping rhizomes. Creeping habit. Shiny dark green, narrow leaves are very aromatic. Woody stems; flowers greenish white in branched clusters. Dies to ground in winter. Attractive container plant. Cut sprigs in June for seasoning vinegar. Use fresh or dried leaves to season salads, egg and cheese dishes, fish. Divide plant every 3 or 4 years to keep it vigorous. Propagate by divisions or by cuttings. Plants grown from seed are not true culinary tarragon.

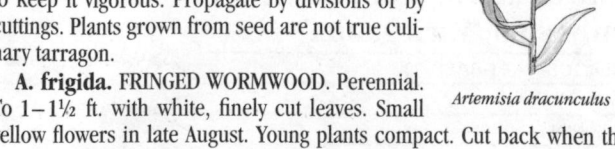
Artemisia dracunculus

A. frigida. FRINGED WORMWOOD. Perennial. To 1–1½ ft. with white, finely cut leaves. Small yellow flowers in late August. Young plants compact. Cut back when they become rangy.

A. lactiflora. WHITE MUGWORT. Border perennial. Tall, straight column to 4–5 ft. One of few artemisias with attractive flowers: creamy white in large, branched, 1½-ft. sprays, August–September. Leaves dark green with broad, tooth-edged lobes.

A. ludoviciana albula (A. albula). SILVER KING ARTEMISIA. Bushy perennial. To 2–3½ ft., with slender, spreading branches and silvery white, 2-in. leaves. The lower leaves have three to five lobes; the upper ones are narrow and unlobed. Cut foliage useful in arrangements.

A. pontica. ROMAN WORMWOOD. Shrub. To 4 ft. Feathery, silver gray leaves. Heads of nodding, whitish yellow flowers in long, open, branched clusters. Leaves used in sachets.

A. 'Powis Castle'. A hybrid, with *A. absinthium* as a probable parent. Silvery, lacy mound to 3 ft. tall, 6 ft. wide. Splendid background plant for bright flowers and tough enough to use as a bank or berm cover.

A. pycnocephala. SANDHILL SAGE. Shrubby perennial. Native to beaches of Northern California. Erect, rounded, somewhat spreading; 1–2 ft. tall. Soft, silvery white or gray leaves, crowded, divided into narrow lobes. Very small yellow flowers. Remove flower spikes as they open to keep plants compact. Becomes unkempt with age. Replace every 2 years. 'David's Choice' is a compact 1 ft. tall, 3 ft. wide.

A. schmidtiana. ANGEL'S HAIR. Perennial. Forms dome, 2 ft. high and 1 ft. wide, of woolly, silvery white, finely cut leaves. Flowers insignificant. Variety 'Silver Mound' is 1 ft. high.

A. stellerana. BEACH WORMWOOD, OLD WOMAN, DUSTY MILLER. Woody perennial. Dense, silvery gray plant to 2½ ft. with 1–4-in. lobed leaves. Hardier than *Senecio cineraria* (another dusty miller), this artemisia is often used in its place in colder climates. Yellow flowers in spikelike clusters. 'Silver Brocade' is a superior, densely growing selection.

A. tridentata. BIG SAGEBRUSH. Evergreen shrub. Native to Great Basin region of the West. Grows 1½–15 ft. high. Many branches. Narrow, hairy gray leaves ¾ in. long, usually with three teeth at tip, very aromatic. Insignificant flowers. Sagebrush that gives pungent fragrance for which western deserts are known. Of limited landscape use but grows easily in any sunny, well-drained spot.

ARTICHOKE

Asteraceae (Compositae)

PERENNIAL VEGETABLE WITH LANDSCAPE VALUE

☘ ZONES VARY; SEE BELOW

☼ FULL SUN

◉ WATER OFTEN TO PRODUCE CROP

Artichoke

In Zones 8, 9, 14–24, grow as dependable perennial crop. Anywhere else, plant in spring when offered and hope for the best—you'll get foliage, maybe flowers, and a crop if you're lucky. A big ferny-looking plant with irregular, somewhat fountainlike form to 4 ft. high, 6–8 ft. wide. Leaves are silvery green. Big flower buds form at tops of stalks: they are the artichokes you cook and eat. If not cut, buds open into spectacular purple-blue, 6-in. thistlelike flowers that can be cut for arrangements. (They serve best if cut just before flowers are fully open.)

In California's cool-summer coast (Zone 17), where it is grown commercially, artichoke can be both a handsome ornamental plant and a producer of fine, tender artichokes from September to May or all year. In Zones 8, 9, 14–16, 18–24, plant grows luxuriantly at least from spring through fall, and edible buds come as extra dividend in early summer only. In colder winter climates roots and shoots must be protected in winter to keep them alive. Can succeed in desert with afternoon shade or shade cloth protection.

TWO ARTICHOKE CROPS IN A SEASON

In California's artichoke country (Zone 17) you can encourage a second crop from your artichoke plants as soon as you harvest the last bud of the first crop: Cut the main stalk off an inch above ground. New sprouts at the base will grow faster and produce sooner than the uncut plant would. Typically, this cut is made in June, and the growth that follows produces a second crop in fall.

Plant dormant roots or plants from containers in winter or early spring, setting root shanks vertically with buds or shoots just above soil line. Space plants 4–6 ft. apart in full sun. After growth starts, water thoroughly once a week, wetting entire root system. If grown only for ornamental value, can tolerate much drought, going dormant in summer heat. Spray to control aphids; after buds start to form, use just strong jet sprays of water to blast off aphids (no insecticides then). Bait to control snails and slugs. For gopher control, plant in raised beds with wire-mesh bottoms or in large containers. Harvest buds while they are still tight and plump. Cut off old stalks near ground level when leaves begin to yellow. In cold-winter areas, cut tops to 1 ft. in fall, tie them over root crown, and mulch heavily to protect from frost.

ARUGULA

ROQUETTE, RUGOLA

Brassicaceae (Cruciferae)

EDIBLE ANNUAL

☙ ALL ZONES

☼ FULL SUN

● MODERATE WATER

Arugula

Leaves of this weedy plant supply 1–4-in.-long leaves, like small mustard leaves, that give a nutty zing to green salads. Pick small leaves; the bigger ones have sharp taste. Grows to 3 ft. high. Start from seed in winter or spring. Reseeds.

ARUM

Araceae

PERENNIALS WITH TUBEROUS ROOTS

☙ ZONES 4–24

● SHADE

● AMPLE WATER DURING SUMMER

◊ ALL PLANT PARTS ARE INJURIOUS

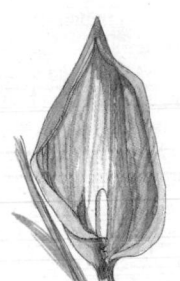
Arum italicum

Arrow-shaped or heart-shaped leaves. Curious callalike blossoms on short stalks. Flower bract half encloses thick, fleshy spike, which bears tiny flowers. Use in shady flower borders where hardy, as indoor plants in cold-winter climates.

A. cornutum. See Sauromatum

A. italicum. ITALIAN ARUM. Arrow-shaped leaves, 8 in. long and wide. Very short stem; white or greenish white (sometimes purple-spotted) flowers in spring and early summer. Bract first stands erect, then folds over and conceals short yellow spike. Dense clusters of bright red fruit follow. Lasting long after leaves have faded, these are the most conspicuous feature of the plant. They resemble small, bright red ears of shucked corn. In variety 'Pictum', leaves are veined with white.

A. palaestinum. BLACK CALLA. Leaves 6–8 in. long. The arrow-shaped flower bract, about the same length, greenish outside, blackish purple inside, has a curved back that reveals the blackish purple spike; spring and early summer.

A. pictum. Light green, heart-shaped, 10-in.-long leaves on 10-in. stalks appear in spring. Flower bract is violet, green at base. Spike purplish black.

ARUNDINARIA. See BAMBOO   **p. 174**

ARUNDO donax

GIANT REED

Poaceae (Gramineae)

PERENNIAL

☙ ALL ZONES

☼ FULL SUN

● MOIST SOIL

Arundo donax

One of largest grasses, planted for bold effects in garden fringe areas or by watersides. Also planted in hot-summer climates as quick windbreak or for erosion control. Often called a bamboo. Strong, somewhat woody stems, 6–20 ft.

high. Leaves to 2 ft. long, flat, 3 in. wide. Flowers in rather narrow, erect clusters to 2 ft. high. *A. d.* 'Versicolor' (*A. d.* 'Variegata') has leaves with white or yellowish stripes. Needs rich, moist soil. Protect roots with mulch in cold-winter areas. Cut out dead stems and thin occasionally to get look-through quality. Extremely invasive; plant only where you can control it. Can become a pest in irrigation ditches. Stems have some utility as plant stakes or, if woven together with wire, as fencing or shade canopy.

ASARINA

CLIMBING SNAPDRAGON, CHICKABIDDY

Scrophulariaceae

TENDER PERENNIALS OFTEN GROWN AS ANNUALS

☙ ALL ZONES AS ANNUALS, 17–24 AS PERENNIALS

☼ ☼ TOLERATES FULL SUN IN ZONES 17, 24

● REGULAR WATER

Asarina antirrhinifolia

Climbing, sprawling, or trailing tender perennials with tubular flowers that flare at the mouth like snapdragons (a close relative). Plants from early sowings will bloom in late spring and through the summer. Grow them on a trellis or brushy twigs or in window boxes or hanging pots. They can also trail over a wall or serve as a small-scale ground cover.

A. antirrhinifolia. Flowers are lavender to purple, 1 in. long, with white throats marked yellow. A mixed-color seed strain offers red-and-yellow or blue-and-white flowers.

A. barclaiana. Vigorous grower to 8–10 ft., with white to pink or purple flowers. 'Angel's Trumpet' has 2 in. pink flowers.

A. scandens. Resembles *A. barclaiana,* with flowers that range from white to pink and dark blue.

ASARUM caudatum

WILD GINGER

Aristolochiaceae

PERENNIAL

☙ ZONES 4–6, 14–24

● SHADE

●● AMPLE WATER

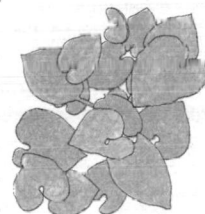
Asarum caudatum

Native to woods of Coast Ranges, mainly in redwood belt from Santa Cruz Mountains to Del Norte County, north to British Columbia. Remarkably handsome ground cover for shade, forming a lush, lustrous dark green carpet of heart-shaped leaves 2–7 in. across, 7–10 in. high. Reddish brown flowers, bell shaped with long tails, produced close to ground under leaves; bloom in spring.

Grows in average soil with heavy watering but spreads faster and is more luxuriant in rich soil with ample humus. Start from divisions or from container-grown plants. Protect from slugs and snails.

Asclepiadaceae. Best-known family members are the milkweeds (*Asclepias*), but other garden plants also belong to this group, among them many succulents and some perennials and vines, including *Stephanotis*.

ASCLEPIAS

Asclepiadaceae

PERENNIALS OR SHRUBS

☙ ZONES VARY BY SPECIES

☼ FULL SUN

●● OCCASIONAL TO REGULAR WATER

◊ ALL PARTS OF MANY ASCLEPIAS ARE POISONOUS

Asclepias fruticosa

Milkweeds are best-known representatives. Just a few are grown as garden plants. ▶

A

A. fruticosa (Gomphocarpus fruticosus) and A. physocarpa (G. physocarpus). SWAN PLANT, GOOSE PLANT. Shrubby perennials. Zones 14–24. These two very similar plants sometimes volunteer in gardens. Plants are occasionally sold for fat, puffy, pale green inflated seed pods with curving stems like swans' necks. Fruits have coverings of soft, fleshy prickles. Stripped of leaves and dried, stems make striking arrangements. Plants are narrowly upright, 3–6 ft. tall, and the many stems are clothed with gray-green, willowlike leaves. Flowers are not showy.

A. tuberosa. BUTTERFLY WEED. All zones. Many stems to 3 ft. rise every year from perennial root. Broad clusters of bright orange flowers appear in midsummer, attracting swarms of butterflies. Prefers good drainage and little summer water. Native to eastern United States. Flowers of Gay Butterflies strain yellow to red.

ASH. See FRAXINUS	**p. 298**
ASH, MOUNTAIN. See SORBUS	**p. 489**

ASPARAGUS, EDIBLE

Liliaceae

PERENNIAL VEGETABLE

✴ ALL ZONES

☼ FULL SUN

◐ LOTS OF WATER

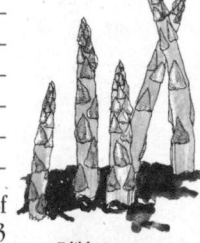

Edible Asparagus

One of most permanent and dependable of home garden vegetables. Plants take 2–3 years to come into full production but then furnish delicious spears every spring for 10–15 years. They take up considerable space but do so in the grand manner: plants are tall, feathery, graceful, highly ornamental. Use asparagus along sunny fence or as background for flowers or vegetables.

Seeds grow into strong young plants in one season (sow in spring), but roots are far more widely used. Set out seedlings or roots (not wilted, no smaller than an adult's hand) in fall or winter (mild climates), or in early spring (cold winters). Make trenches 1 ft. wide and 8–10 in. deep. Space trenches 4–6 ft. apart. Heap loose, manure-enriched soil at bottoms of trenches and soak. Space plants 1 ft. apart, setting them so that tops are 6–8 in. below surface. Spread roots out evenly. Cover with 2 in. of soil and water again.

As young plants grow, gradually fill in trench, taking care not to cover growing tips. Soak deeply whenever soil begins to dry out at root depth. Don't harvest any spears the first year; object at this time is to build big root mass. When plants turn brown in late fall or early winter, cut stems to ground. In cold-winter areas, permit dead stalks to stand until spring; they will help trap and hold snow, which will furnish protection to root crowns.

HOW TO BLANCH ASPARAGUS

Fresh white asparagus is a delicacy. It's not a special variety; blanching makes it white. In early spring before spears emerge, mound soil 8 in. high over a row of asparagus. When tips emerge from the top of the mounded soil, push a long-handled knife into the base of the mound to cut each spear well below the surface. Pull cut shoots out by the tips. Level mounds after the harvest season.

The following spring you can cut your first spears; cut only for 4–6 weeks or until appearance of thin spears indicates that roots are nearing exhaustion. Then permit plants to grow. Cultivate, feed, and irrigate heavily. The third year you should be able to cut spears for 8–10 weeks. Spears are ready to cut when they are 5–8 in. long. Thrust knife down at 45° angle to soil; flat cutting may injure adjacent developing spears. If asparagus beetle appears during cutting season, control with rotenone or (carefully noting

label precautions) malathion. After cutting season, spray with any all-purpose insecticide.

Asparagus seed and roots are sold as "traditional" ('Martha Washington' and others) and "all-male" ('Jersey Giant' and others). The latter kinds are bred to produce more and larger spears because they don't have to put energy into seed production. Such varieties still produce an occasional female plant.

ASPARAGUS, ORNAMENTAL

Liliaceae

PERENNIALS

✴ OUTDOORS, ZONES 12–24; OR INDOORS

☼ ◐ FULL SUN OR PARTIAL SHADE

◐ ● BEST WITH REGULAR WATER

Asparagus densiflorus 'Sprengeri'

There are about 150 kinds of asparagus besides the edible one—all members of the lily family. Best known of ornamental kinds is the fern asparagus *(A. setaceus),* which is not a true fern. Although valued mostly for handsome foliage of unusual textural quality, some of these species have small but fragrant flowers and colorful berries. Green foliage sprays are made up of what look like leaves. Needlelike or broader, these are actually short branches called cladodes. The true leaves are inconspicuous dry scales.

Most ornamental asparagus look greenest in partial shade but thrive in sun near coast. Leaves turn yellow in dense shade. Plant in well-drained soil to which peat moss or ground bark has been added. Because of fleshy roots, plants can go for periods without water, but grow better when it is ample. Feed in spring with complete fertilizer. Trim out old shoots to make room for new growth. Will survive light frosts but may be killed to ground by severe cold. After frost, plants often come back from roots.

A. asparagoides. SMILAX ASPARAGUS. Much-branched vine with spineless stems to 20 ft. or more. Often seen in older gardens. Leaves to 1 in. long, sharp pointed, stiffish, glossy grass green. Small, fragrant white flowers in spring followed by blue berries. Birds feed on berries, drop seeds that sprout at random about the garden. (Plant also self-sows readily.) Roots are clusters of fleshy thongs and are nearly immortal, surviving long drought and sprouting when rains come. Foliage sprays prized for table decoration. If it gets little water, plant dies back in summer, revives with fall rains. Becomes tangled mass unless trained. Variety 'Myrtifolius', commonly called baby smilax, is a more graceful form with smaller leaves.

A. crispus. BASKET ASPARAGUS. Airy, graceful plant for hanging baskets. Drooping, zigzag stems have bright green, three-angled leaves in whorls of three. Often sold as *A. scandens* 'Deflexus'.

A. densiflorus 'Myers'. MYERS ASPARAGUS. Plants send up several to many stiffly upright stems to 2 ft. or more, densely clothed with needlelike deep green leaves. Plants have fluffy look. Good in containers. A little less hardy than Sprenger asparagus. Sometimes sold as *A. meyeri* or *A. myersii.*

A. d. 'Sprengeri'. SPRENGER ASPARAGUS. Arching or drooping stems 3–6 ft. long. Shiny, bright green needlelike leaves, 1 in. long, in bundles. Bright red berries. Popular for hanging baskets or containers, indoors and out. Train on trellis; climbs by means of small hooked prickles. Used as billowy ground cover where temperatures stay above 24°F. Takes full sun as well as partial shade; grows in ordinary or even poor soil. Will tolerate dryness of indoors but needs bright light. Sometimes sold as *A. sprengeri.* Form sold as *A. d.* 'Sprengeri Compacta' or *A. sarmentosus* 'Compacta' is denser with shorter stems.

A. falcatus. SICKLE-THORN ASPARAGUS. Derives common name from curved thorns along stems by which it climbs to 40 ft. in its native area (in gardens usually grows to 10 ft.). Leaves 2–3 in. long in clusters of three to five at ends of branches. Tiny, white, fragrant flowers in loose clusters. Brown berries. Grows rapidly. Excellent foliage mass to cover fence or wall or to provide shade for a pergola or lathhouse. Foliage resembles that of *Podocarpus macrophyllus.*

A. **macowanii.** See A. retrofractus

A. **meyeri, A. myersii.** See A. densiflorus 'Myers'

A. **officinalis.** See Asparagus, Edible

A. **plumosus.** See A. setaceus

A. **retrofractus.** Erect, shrubby, slightly climbing, very tender. Slender, silvery gray stems grow slowly to 8–10 ft. high. Leaves threadlike, 1 in. long, in fluffy, rich green tufts. Clusters of small white flowers. Handsome in containers; useful in flower arrangements. Cut foliage lasts 10 days out of water, several weeks in water.

A. **sarmentosus.** See A. densiflorus 'Sprengeri'

A. **scandens.** BASKET ASPARAGUS. Slender, branching vine climbing to 6 ft. Deep green needlelike leaves on zigzag, drooping stems. Greenish white flowers ⅛ in. long. Scarlet berries.

A. **scandens 'Deflexus'.** See A. crispus

A. **setaceus (A. plumosus).** FERN ASPARAGUS. Branching woody vine climbs by wiry, spiny stems to 10–20 ft. Tiny threadlike leaves form feathery dark green sprays that resemble fern fronds. Tiny white flowers. Berries purple black. Dense, fine-textured foliage mass useful as screen against walls, fences. Florists use foliage as fillers in bouquets; holds up better than delicate ferns. Sometimes called emerald feather. Dwarf variety 'Nanus' is good in containers. 'Pyramidalis' has upswept, windblown look, is less vigorous than common fern asparagus.

A. **sprengeri.** See A. densiflorus 'Sprengeri'

ASPEN. See POPULUS	**p. 434**
ASPEN DAISY. See ERIGERON speciosus macranthus	**p. 275**
ASPERULA odorata. See GALIUM odoratum	**p. 302**

ASPHODELINE lutea

YELLOW ASPHODEL, KING'S SPEAR

Liliaceae

PERENNIAL

✀ ALL ZONES

☼ ◑ FULL SUN OR PARTIAL SHADE

● REGULAR WATER

Asphodeline lutea

This rhizomatous perennial has clumps of dark green, grassy 12-in. leaves. The 3-ft. flower stalk is topped in spring by an 8-in. narrow cluster of yellow, fragrant flowers a little more than 1 in. across. These peer from a shag of buff or reddish brown bracts. Use it in perennial borders.

ASPIDISTRA elatior (A. lurida)

CAST-IRON PLANT

Liliaceae

EVERGREEN PERENNIAL

✀ ZONES 4–10, 12–24; OR INDOORS

◐ ● TOLERATES VERY LOW LIGHT

● MODERATE WATER

Aspidistra elatior

Sturdy, long-lived foliage plant remarkable for its ability to thrive under conditions unacceptable to most kinds of plants. Leaf blades 1–2½ ft. long, 3–4 in. wide, tough, glossy dark green and arching, with distinct parallel veins; each blade is supported by a 6–8-in.-long grooved leafstalk. Inconspicuous brownish flowers bloom in spring close to ground. Although extremely tolerant, requiring minimal care, aspidistra grows best in porous soil enriched with organic matter and responds to feeding in spring and summer. Will grow in dark, shaded areas (under decks or stairs) anywhere, as well as in filtered sun—except in Zones 12 and 13, where it takes full shade only. Keep leaves dust

free and glossy by hosing them off, or clean with a soft brush or cloth. Variegated form (*A. elatior* 'Variegata'), with leaves striped with white, loses its variegation if it is planted in soil that's too rich.

ASPIDIUM capense. See RUMOHRA adiantiformis	**p. 470**

ASPLENIUM

Polypodiaceae

FERNS

✀ ZONES VARY BY SPECIES

● SHADE

◐◐ WATER LIBERALLY

Asplenium bulbiferum

Widespread and variable group. These resemble each other only in botanical details and need for shade and liberal watering. Once called spleenwort for alleged medicinal value.

A. **bulbiferum.** MOTHER FERN. Outdoors in Zones 14 (protected), 15–17, 20–24; house plant elsewhere. From New Zealand. Graceful, very finely cut light green fronds to 4 ft. tall. Fronds produce plantlets that can be removed and planted. Heavy or medium shade. Hardy to 26°F. Watch for snails and slugs.

A. **daucifolium (A. viviparum).** House plant. Similar to *A. bulbiferum* but smaller (to 2 ft.), with more finely divided fronds. Also makes plantlets.

A. **nidus (A. nidus-avis).** BIRD'S NEST FERN. House plant. Tender fern with showy, apple green, undivided fronds to 4 ft. long, 8 in. wide, growing upright in cluster. Striking foliage plant; best as container plant to be grown indoors in winter, on shady patio in summer. One snail or slug can ruin a frond.

Asplenium nidus

ASTARTEA fascicularis

Myrtaceae

EVERGREEN SHRUB

✀ ZONES 15–24

☼ ◑ FULL SUN OR PARTIAL SHADE

◔ ONCE ESTABLISHED, NEEDS NO WATER

Astartea fascicularis

Related to *Leptospermum* but with smaller leaves and flowers. 'Bremer Bay' grows to 3 ft. or taller and is somewhat wider, with short, narrow, needlelike leaves in bundles thickly arranged along the stems. Flowers are ⅓ in. across, white or pinkish, and borne in incredible profusion over a very long period, with the heaviest bloom in winter. Branches last well when cut. 'Prostrate Form' is a few inches tall, 3 ft. wide. 'Winter Pink' resembles 'Bremer Bay', but its deeper pink flowers are more concentrated over a shorter season in winter and early spring.

ASTELIA nervosa chathamica (A. chathamica)

SILVER SPEAR

Liliaceae

PERENNIAL

✀ ZONES 16, 17, 19–24

☼ ◑ FULL SUN OR PARTIAL SHADE

● MODERATE WATER

Astelia nervosa chathamica

This unusual New Zealand perennial forms clumps of 3–4-ft. leaves 2–4 in. wide. Leaves are silky and silvery. The plant suggests a rather narrow, erect, and quite harmless century plant or yucca. Flowers are small and cream colored, in branched clusters 20 in. tall. Orange berries rarely seen. It affords a handsome contrast to low, mounding plants or billowing grasses and makes a striking centerpiece in a big container of mixed perennials. Must have good drainage.

ASTER

Asteraceae (Compositae)	
PERENNIALS	
✎ ALL ZONES	
☼ FULL SUN	
● REGULAR WATER	

Aster frikartii

There are more than 600 species of true asters, ranging from alpine kinds forming compact mounds 6 in. high to open-branching plants 6 ft. tall. Flowers come in white or shades of blue, red, pink, lavender, or purple, mostly with yellow centers. Most asters bloom in summer and fall; some hybrids start flowering in spring. Taller asters are invaluable for abundant color in large borders or among shrubs. Large sprays effective in arrangements. Compact dwarf or cushion types make tidy edgings, mounds of color in rock gardens, good container plants.

Adapted to most soils. Most luxuriant in fertile soil. Resistant to insects and diseases, except for mildew on leaves in late fall. Strong-growing asters have invasive roots, need control. Divide clumps yearly in late fall or early spring. Replant vigorous young divisions from outside of clump; discard old center. Divide smaller, tufted, less vigorously growing kinds every 2 years.

A. alpinus. Mounding plant 6–12 in. tall. Leaves ½–5 in. long, mostly in basal tuft. Several stems grow from basal clump, each carrying one violet blue flower 1½–2 in. across; May–June bloom. Best in cold-winter areas.

A. amellus. ITALIAN ASTER. Sturdy, hairy plant to 2 ft. Branching stems with violet, yellow-centered flowers 2 in. across.

A. ericoides. HEATH ASTER. Grows 1½–3 ft. tall, with a wispy look and a profusion of tiny white (rarely bluish or pink) flowers.

A. frikartii. One of the finest, most useful and widely adapted perennials. Hybrid between *A. amellus* and *A. thomsonii,* a hairy-leafed, lilac-flowered, 3-ft. species native to the Himalayas. Abundant clear lavender to violet blue single flowers are 2½ in. across. Open, spreading growth to 2 ft. high. Blooms May–October—almost all year in mild-winter areas if dead flowers are removed regularly. 'Wonder of Stafa' and 'Mönch' are lavender blue favorites.

A. fruticosus. See Felicia fruticosa

A. novae-angliae. NEW ENGLAND ASTER. Stout-stemmed plant to 3–5 ft. with hairy leaves to 5 in. long. Flowers deep purple, 2 in. across. Good in wet areas.

A. novi-belgii. NEW YORK ASTER. To 3 ft., similar to New England aster but with smooth leaves. Full clusters of bright blue-violet flowers.

Michaelmas daisy is the name applied to hybrids of *A. novae-angliae* and *A. novi-belgii.* They are tall (3–4 ft.), graceful, branching plants. Many horticultural varieties with flowers in white, pale to deep pink, rose, red, and many shades of blue, violet, and purple.

Oregon-Pacific asters, hybrids between a dwarf species native to the West and some well-known Michaelmas daisies, are splendid garden plants. Dwarf, intermediate, and taller forms range in height from under 1 ft. to 2½ ft. Compact, floriferous, blooming late spring to fall. Many named varieties available in white, blue, lavender, purple, rose, pink, cream.

A. tataricus. A giant (to 5–7 ft.) with 2-ft. leaves and sheaves of inch-wide blue flower heads in flat clusters late in the season.

A. yunnanensis 'Napsbury'. An improved garden variety of this Chinese species. Leaves dark green in basal tufts. Stems to 1½ ft., each bearing a single lavender blue, orange-centered flower. Blooms in summer.

For the common annual or China aster, sold in six-packs at nurseries, see *Callistephus.*

Asteraceae. The sunflower or daisy family, one of the largest plant families, is characterized by flowers borne in tight clusters (heads). In the most familiar form, these heads contain two types of flowers—small, tightly clustered disk flowers in the center of the head, and larger, strap-shaped ray flowers around the edge. The sunflower is a familiar example. The family was formerly called Compositae.

ASTERISCUS

Asteraceae (Compositae)	
PERENNIALS	
✎ ZONES VARY BY SPECIES	
☼ FULL SUN	
○ NO WATER ONCE ESTABLISHED	

Asteriscus maritimus

Leafy, nearly shrubby daisies from the Mediterranean and the Canary Islands. Showy yellow flowers contrast with silky leaves. Use with other Mediterranean plants.

A. maritimus (Odontospermum maritimum). Zones 9, 15–24. Evergreen ground cover to 1 ft. tall, 4 ft. wide, with silvery green foliage and 1½-in. golden yellow flowers. Sometimes called gold coin. Tough, tolerant plant for most soils; tolerates seaside conditions.

A. sericeus (Nauplius sericeus). CANARY ISLAND DAISY. Zones 16, 17, 19–24. Shrubbier and less sprawling than *A. maritimus,* with silky, silvery leaves that set off the bright yellow flowers for a gold and silver effect. The foliage has an odd odor when brushed, and old leaves tend to blacken and adhere to the stems. If groomed, *A. sericeus* makes a striking container plant.

ASTILBE

FALSE SPIRAEA, MEADOW SWEET	
Saxifragaceae	
PERENNIALS	
✎ ZONES 2–7, 14–17; SHORT LIVED IN 8, 9, 18–24	
☼ ◑ FULL SUN OR PARTIAL SHADE	
●● MOIST BUT NOT BOGGY SOIL	

Astilbe arendsii

Valued for light, airy quality of plumelike flower clusters and attractive foliage, ability to provide color from May through July. Leaves divided, with toothed or cut leaflets; leaves in some species simply lobed with cut margins. Small white, pink, or red flowers in graceful, branching clusters held on slender, wiry stems 6 in.–3 ft. or higher.

Most astilbes sold in nurseries are hybrids. These are usually called *A. arendsii.* There are many varieties, but most nurseries stock only a few. Some of best are 'Avalanche', 2 ft., white flowers; 'Betsy Cuperus', 2½ ft., pale pink flowers; 'Deutschland', 2 ft., creamy white flowers; 'Fanal', 2 ft., bronzy foliage, garnet red flowers; 'Glow', 2 ft., ruby red flowers; 'Rheinland', 2 ft., bright pink flowers; 'Straussenfeder', 2½ ft., drooping, arching, coral pink flowers.

Plant in sun or partial shade in Zones 2–7, 14–17; in shade in Zones 8, 9, 18–24. Combine in shade gardens with columbine, meadow rue, plantain lily, bergenia; in sunnier situations with peonies, delphiniums, iris. Often planted at edge of pools. Good in pots and tubs. Needs cool, moist soil rich in humus. Cut back after flowering. Divide clumps every 4–5 years.

A. chinensis 'Pumila'. Low mats of leaves make 4-in.-deep ground cover. In summer, lilac pink flower clusters to 12–15 in.

A. simplicifolia 'Sprite'. Foot-tall clumps of bronzy green foliage are topped in summer by branching, somewhat drooping clusters of shell pink flowers.

A. taquetii. To 4 ft. tall, with pinkish purple flowers in erect, dense clusters. Blooms late summer. 'Superba' is best form.

A

ASTRANTIA

MASTERWORT

Apiaceae (Umbelliferae)

PERENNIALS

⚡ ZONES 4–9, 14–24

☼:◐ FULL SUN OR PARTIAL SHADE

⬤ REGULAR WATER

Astrantia major

Winter dormant, with leafy stems 2½–3 ft. tall. Flowers in dense, tight clusters surrounded by papery bracts resemble pincushions or, superficially, daisies. Flowers are attractive in arrangements and can be dried for winter use. Plants are useful in woodland gardens.

A. major. Grows to 32 in., with inch-wide clusters of white and green or white and pink flowers.

A. maxima. Slightly larger than *A. major*, with pink flowers.

ATHANASIA parviflora (Hymenolepis parviflora)

COULTER BUSH

Asteraceae (Compositae)

EVERGREEN SHRUB

⚡ ZONES 16–24

☼ FULL SUN

⬤ LITTLE SUMMER WATERING ONCE ESTABLISHED

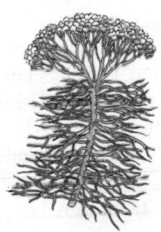

Athanasia parviflora

This South African shrub grows 3 ft. tall, 4 ft. wide, with finely cut silvery leaves. Yellow flowers are small but are in dense, branched clusters well above the foliage in spring and summer. Plant somewhat resembles a silvery-leafed marguerite daisy, while the flowers look like yarrow.

ATHEL TREE. See TAMARIX aphylla p. 501

ATHYRIUM

Polypodiaceae

FERNS

⚡ ZONES 1–9, 14–24

⬤ SHADE

⬤⬤ MOIST SOIL

Athyrium filix-femina

Evergreen in mildest areas, these ferns turn brown after repeated frosts. Leave dead fronds on plant to provide mulch and to shelter emerging fronds in early spring, then cut back. Prefer rich, damp soil and shade. Propagate by dividing old clumps in early spring.

A. filix-femina. LADY FERN. Grows to 4 ft. or more. Rootstock rises up on older plants to make short trunk. Vertical effect; narrow at bottom, spreading at top. Thin fronds, finely divided. Vigorous; can be invasive. Specialists stock many varieties with oddly cut and feathered fronds.

A. nipponicum 'Pictum' (A. goeringianum 'Pictum'). JAPANESE PAINTED FERN. Fronds grow to 1½ ft. long, making a tight, slowly spreading clump. Leaflets are purplish at base, then lavender, then silvery greenish gray toward ends.

FOR INFORMATION ON SELECTING PLANTS

PLEASE SEE PAGES 45–128

ATRIPLEX

SALTBUSH

Chenopodiaceae

EVERGREEN OR DECIDUOUS SHRUBS

⚡ ZONES VARY BY SPECIES

☼ FULL SUN

⬤ VERY LITTLE WATER

Atriplex hymenelytra

Unusually tolerant of direct seashore conditions or highly alkaline desert soils. Saltbushes are mostly grown for their gray or silvery foliage; flowers and seeds attract birds.

A. barklayana. Zones 16–24. Dwarf saltbush from Baja California forms a dense 18-in. mound 4 ft. across. Inch-long leaves are covered with white powder. Needs little or no summer water once established.

A. canescens. FOUR-WING SALTBUSH. Evergreen. Zones 2–24. Native throughout much of arid section of West. Dense growth 3–6 ft. high, spreading to 4–8 ft. Narrow gray leaves ½–2 in. long.

A. hymenelytra. DESERT HOLLY. Evergreen (everwhitish). Zones 3, 7–14, 18, 19. Native to deserts of Southern California, western Arizona, southern Nevada, southwestern Utah. Compact shrub 1–3 ft. high with whitish branches and silvery, deeply toothed roundish leaves, to 1½ in. long. Has Christmas holly look—in white. Much used for decorations. Outside native range, needs very fast drainage. Water heavily February–May only.

A. lentiformis. QUAIL BUSH. Deciduous. Zones 7–14, 18, 19. Native to alkali wastes in California valleys and deserts and east to Nevada, Utah, and New Mexico. Densely branched, sometimes spiny shrub, 3–10 ft. high, 6–12 ft. wide. Oval, bluish gray leaves ½–2 in. long. Useful as salt-tolerant hedge or windbreak.

A. l. breweri. BREWER SALTBUSH. Almost evergreen. Zones 8, 9, 12–24. Native to California coast south of San Francisco Bay, inland to Riverside County. Like quail bush but not spiny. Grows 5–7 ft. high, 6–8 ft. wide; can be hedge sheared. Useful gray plant on ocean front. Will grow in reclaimed marine soil.

A. nummularia. Evergreen. Zones 15–24. Dense, rounded, nearly white evergreen shrub to 6 ft. It will grow in sun or light shade and endure summer drought, winter flooding, and alkaline soil.

A. semibaccata. AUSTRALIAN SALTBUSH. Evergreen. Zones 8–10, 12–24. Excellent gray-green ground cover spreading to 1–6 ft. and more. Forms dense, foot-tall mat of ½–1½-in.-long leaves. Deep rooted. Plant 3 ft. apart for solid cover.

AUBRIETA deltoidea

COMMON AUBRIETA

Brassicaceae (Cruciferae)

PERENNIAL

⚡ ZONES 1–9, 14–21

☼:◐ FULL SUN OR LIGHT SHADE

⬤ WATER BEFORE AND DURING BLOOM

Aubrieta deltoidea

Native from eastern Mediterranean region to Iran. Low, spreading, mat-forming perennial—familiar sight in Northwest and high-elevation rock gardens, where it is often seen in bloom in early spring, with basket-of-gold, rockcress *(Arabis),* perennial candytuft *(Iberis),* and *Phlox subulata.* Ideal for chinks in dry stone walls or between patio flagstones. Grows 2–6 in. high, 1–1½ ft. across. Small gray-green leaves with a few teeth at top. Tiny rose to deep red, pale to deep lilac, or purple flowers. 'Novalis Blue' is a fine seed-grown variety.

Needs water before and during bloom. Takes some drought later on. After bloom, shear off flowers before they set seed. Don't cut back more than half—always keep some foliage. After trimming, top-dress with mixture of gritty soil and bone meal. Sow seeds in late spring for blooms the following spring. Difficult to divide clumps; make cuttings in late summer.

A

AUCUBA japonica

JAPANESE AUCUBA

Cornaceae

EVERGREEN SHRUB

✂ ZONES 4–24

☼ ● PERFORMS WELL IN DEEP SHADE

◊ ◖ ● ANY WATERING REGIME OKAY

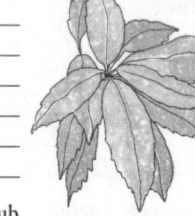

Aucuba japonica

Native from Himalayas to Japan. Important shrub to western gardeners. Seedlings vary in leaf form and variegations; many varieties offered. Standard green-leafed aucuba grows at moderate rate to 6–10 (sometimes 15) ft. and almost as wide. Can be kept lower by pruning. Buxom shrub, densely clothed with polished, dark green, toothed leaves 3–8 in. long, 1½–3 in. wide.

Minute, dark maroon flowers in March are followed by clusters of bright red, ¾-in. berries from October to February. Both sexes must be planted to ensure fruit crop.

Green-leafed varieties are 'Longifolia' ('Salicifolia'), narrow willowlike leaves (female); 'Nana', dwarf to about 3 ft. (female); 'Serratifolia', long leaves, coarsely toothed edges (female).

Variegated varieties (usually slower growing) are 'Crotonifolia', leaves heavily splashed with white and gold (male); 'Fructu Albo', leaves variegated with white, berries pale pinkish buff (female); 'Picturata' ('Aureomaculata'), leaves centered with golden yellow, edged with dark green dotted yellow (female); 'Sulphur', green leaves with broad yellow edge (female); 'Variegata', gold dust plant, best-known aucuba, dark green leaves spotted with yellow (male or female). 'Mr. Goldstrike' has heavier gold splashings.

Tolerant of wide range of soils but will grow better and look better if poor or heavy soils are improved. Requires shade from hot sun, accepts deep shade. Tolerates low light level under trees, competes successfully with tree roots. Gets mealybug and mites. Prune to control height or form by cutting back to a leaf joint (node).

All aucubas make choice tub plants for shady patio or in the house. Use variegated forms to light up dark corners. Associate with ferns, hydrangeas.

AURICULA. See PRIMULA auricula   p. 437

AURINIA saxatilis (Alyssum saxatile)

BASKET-OF-GOLD

Brassicaceae (Cruciferae)

PERENNIAL

✂ ALL ZONES

☼ ◐ FULL SUN OR LIGHT SHADE

● MODERATE WATER

Aurinia saxatilis

Stems 8–12 in. high; leaves gray, 2–5 in. long. Dense clusters of tiny golden yellow flowers in spring and early summer. Use as foreground plant in borders, in rock gardens, atop walls. Shear lightly (not more than half) right after bloom. Generally hardy but may be killed in extremely cold winters. Self-sows readily. Varieties include 'Citrina' ('Lutea'), with pale yellow flowers; 'Compacta', dwarf, tight growing; 'Plena' ('Flore Pleno'), double flowered; 'Silver Queen', compact, with pale yellow flowers; 'Sunnyborder Apricot', with apricot-shaded flowers.

AUSTRALIAN BLUEBELL CREEPER. See SOLLYA heterophylla   p. 488

AUSTRALIAN FLAME TREE. See BRACHYCHITON acerifolius   p. 189

AUSTRALIAN FUCHSIA. See CORREA   p. 243

AUSTRALIAN TEA TREE. See LEPTOSPERMUM laevigatum   p. 351

AUSTRALIAN TREE FERN. See CYATHEA cooperi   p. 253

AUSTRALIAN WILLOW. See GEIJERA parviflora   p. 304

AUSTRIAN BRIER. See ROSA foetida   p. 468

AVOCADO

Lauraceae

EVERGREEN TREES

✂ ZONES VARY BY VARIETY

☼ FULL SUN

● LIGHT, FREQUENT WATERING

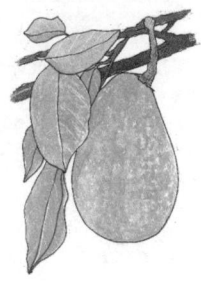

Avocado

In California, two races of avocados are grown: Mexican and Guatemalan. (Widely planted 'Fuerte' is thought to be hybrid of the two.) Guatemalan varieties find ideal climate protected from direct wind in Zones 19, 21, 23, and 24. Mexican varieties, bearing smaller, less attractive fruit, are hardier and grow in Zones 9, 16–24. Although avocados are hardy to 20–24°F, flowers form in winter, and temperatures much below freezing destroy crop. Resistant to oak root fungus. Avocados tend to bear crops in cycles, producing heavy crop one year, light crop the next. (Light crop is generally enough for home gardener.)

When using in landscape, remember that most varieties will grow to 30 ft. and spread wider (although tree size can be controlled by pruning). Tree should have best of protection from winds. It drops leaves quite heavily all year. Wide-spreading branches with heavy foliage make dense shade beneath, creating a good garden area for potted plants that need shade. St. Augustine grass will grow beneath avocado trees.

The all-important factor in growing avocados is good drainage. High water table in winter rainy season is often fatal, even in well-drained soils. Build wide basin for watering; let fallen leaves build up there to provide mulch. Most roots are in top 2 ft. of soil, so water lightly and frequently enough to keep that layer moist but not wet (fast drainage is important). Give heavy irrigation every third or fourth time to wash out any excess accumulated salts. This will minimize salt burn. Fertilize lightly. Control chlorosis with iron sulfate or iron chelate.

Fruit of all varieties in following list has thin, pliable, smooth skin unless otherwise noted.

'Bacon'. Mexican. Zones 9, 16, 17, 19–24. Upright grower. Medium-size green fruit of good quality, November–March. Regular annual crop. Produces when young.

'Duke'. Mexican. Zones 16–22. Large tree. Medium to large green fruit, September–November.

'Fuerte'. Hybrid. Zones 20–24. Large tree; best-known avocado. Early flowers subject to frost in borderline areas. Medium-size green fruit of high quality, November–June.

'Gwen'. Guatemalan. Zones 19–24. Tree to 20 ft. tall, narrow. Black-skinned fruit ripens February–November.

'Hass'. Guatemalan. Zones 16, 17, 19, 21, 23, 24. Large, spreading tree. Medium to large dark purple (almost black) fruit, April–October. Pebbly skin, thick but pliable.

'Jim'. Mexican. Zones 19–24. Upright growth. Medium-size fruit with thin green skin. Bears young and regularly, October–January.

'Mexicola'. Mexican. Zones 9, 16–22. Good garden avocado but fruit too small for commercial market. Probably hardiest. Consistent bearer of small, dark purple fruit with thin, tender skin and outstanding nutty flavor, August–October.

'Pinkerton'. Guatemalan. Zones 19–24. Large tree with heavy annual production of large green fruit. Main crop January–April.

'Reed'. Guatemalan. Zones 21–24. Slender upright grower. Medium to large, round, rough-skinned fruit. Bears most years, July–September.

'Rincon'. Guatemalan. Zones 19–24. Low-growing tree. Small green fruit with large seed, ripens January–April. Smooth skin, medium thick, pliable.

'Santana'. Mexican. Zones 9, 19–24. Resembles 'Zutano' but slightly larger; heavy bearer winter–early spring.

'Whitsell'. Guatemalan. Zones 19–24. Tree 10–12 ft. tall. Large black-skinned fruit, February–November. Tends to bear in alternate seasons.

'Wurtz'. Guatemalan. Small tree (8–10 ft. tall) with slender weeping branches. Medium-size green fruit in summer; bears young but is not an annual bearer. For small garden or large containers. Often sold as 'Dwarf', 'Littlecado', and 'Minicado'.

'Zutano'. Mexican. Zones 9, 19–24. Upright grower. Pear-shaped fruits, 'Fuerte' size, green, good quality, October–February. In Southern California, tends to get "end spot" (brown scaly area at tip of fruit).

WHAT CAUSES FINGERLING AVOCADOS?

Often called "cukes" or "cocktail avocados," small fingerling fruits form after the embryo of a pollinated flower dies. Drying winds or sudden heat can cause this to happen, especially on 'Fuerte' or Mexican-type avocado trees. Pick mature fingerling avocados and let them ripen. They're always seedless. Try peeling and cutting them in half, and serve them with a dip on top as an hors d'oeuvre.

AZALEA. See RHODODENDRON   p. 454

AZARA

Flacourtiaceae
EVERGREEN SHRUBS
ZONES VARY BY SPECIES
PARTIAL SHADE
REGULAR WATER

Azara microphylla

Best-known species is *A. microphylla*. Its flat branching habit and neatly arranged leaves make it natural for espalier or as free-standing silhouette against wall. Other three species are quite different, but all four have sweetly fragrant yellow flowers that smell like chocolate to some, vanilla to others.

All azaras need protection from hot afternoon sun. All need ample water, fast-draining soil, and regular fertilizing.

A. dentata. Zones 15–17. Large shrub or small tree to 15 ft. Inch-wide, toothed, rounded shiny leaves. Dense branching, rounded shape make it useful for screen or hedge. Fluffy yellow spring flowers highly fragrant. Tolerates considerable shade.

A. lanceolata. LANCELEAF AZARA. Zones 15–17. Large, spreading shrub to 20 ft. Equal to *A. microphylla* in pattern value but with much larger leaves, more lush effect. Leaves mostly 2½ in. long, rather narrow. Foliage bright yellowish green. April flowers pale yellow, in short clusters.

A. microphylla. BOXLEAF AZARA. Zones 5–9, 14–24. Slow growing when small, fast when established; to 12–18 ft., spreading 8–12 ft. When old, treelike to 30 ft.

Arching branches spread fanlike to give definite two-dimensional effect. May become leggy and awkward unless controlled; tip-prune young branches. Shiny dark green leaves, roundish, ½–¾ in. long. Flowers yellow, fragrant, in short clusters, February–March.

A. petiolaris (A. gilliesii). Zones 15–17. Large shrub to 15–20 ft. but easily trained into single-stemmed tree. Deep green, lustrous, oval to roundish leaves, 1½–3 in. long, look somewhat like holly leaves and hang from branches like aspen. Nodding, 1-in.-long clusters of bright yellow, tiny flowers, February–March.

AZTEC LILY. See SPREKELIA formosissima   p. 491

BABACO. See CARICA heilbornii   p. 207

BABIANA

BABOON FLOWER
Iridaceae
CORMS
ZONES 4–24
FULL SUN OR VERY LIGHT SHADE
WATER DURING GROWTH

Babiana stricta

Native to South Africa. Spikes of freesialike flowers in blue, lavender, red, cream, and white bloom in March (California) to June (Northwest). Leaves are strongly ribbed, usually hairy, set edgewise to stem. Plant corms 4 in. deep, 3 in. apart, along border edge, paths, in rock gardens; also in deep pots. Ample water during growth, less after leaves turn yellow. In mild climates leave in ground several years. In coldest areas lift and store corms like gladiolus.

B. rubrocyanea. Spikes to 5–6 in. with six or seven flowers to a spike. Bottom half of each flower deep red, upper half royal blue.

B. stricta. Very attractive. Royal blue flowers on 1-ft. stems. Leaves 6 in. high. Varieties in purple, lavender, white, and blue and white.

BABY BLUE EYES. See NEMOPHILA menziesii   p. 388

BABY'S BREATH. See GYPSOPHILA paniculata   p. 314

BABY SNAPDRAGON. See LINARIA maroccana   p. 356

BABY'S TEARS. See SOLEIROLIA soleirolii   p. 488

BACCHARIS

Asteraceae (Compositae)
EVERGREEN SHRUBS
ZONES VARY BY SPECIES
FULL SUN ONLY
WATER NEEDS VARY BY CLIMATE

Baccharis pilularis

All grow in difficult growing conditions. Some are useful landscape plants as ground or bank cover in rugged areas.

B. 'Centennial'. Zones 10–13. Hybrid between *B. pilularis* and *B. sarothroides*. Grows 5 ft. wide, half as tall, with narrow leaves and tufted tan seed capsules in spring. Tolerates desert heat; resists root rot caused by water molds.

B. pilularis. DWARF COYOTE BRUSH. Zones 5–11, 14–24. Native to California coast, Sonoma to Monterey counties. Remarkable climate and soil adaptation. Near the coast it thrives with no water at all; inland it looks better with monthly watering. In California's high desert, it's the most dependable of all ground covers. Everywhere, it's a very valuable, very dependable bank and flatland cover for low-maintenance areas in sun.

Makes dense, rather billowy, bright green mat, 8–24 in. high and spreading to 6 ft. or more. Small, ½-in., toothed leaves are closely set on many branches. Needs shearing back once a year in early spring before new growth starts. Cut out old arching branches and thin to rejuvenate. Feed with a nitrogen fertilizer immediately after cutting back. Male and female flowers, borne on different plants, are of no interest. Female plants produce cottony seeds that can make a mess when blown by wind. The plants available in most nurseries are produced by cuttings from male plants. 'Twin Peaks' ('Twin Peaks #2') has small, dark green leaves and moderate growth rate. 'Pigeon Point' has larger and lighter green leaves and grows faster (9 ft. wide in 4 years); can make a 2–3-ft. hedge.

B. sarothroides. DESERT BROOM. Zones 10–13. Nearly leafless but branches are bright green throughout year. Grows 6–7 ft. tall; can be clipped to 2–3 ft. Female plants covered with cottony fluff of seeds in late fall and winter. Can take good or poor drainage. Useful for erosion control, replanting disturbed land, or natural landscape in desert regions.

B

BACHELOR'S BUTTON. See CENTAUREA cyanus   p. 216

BALSAM PEAR. See MOMORDICA charantia   p. 382

BAECKEA

Myrtaceae

EVERGREEN SHRUBS

🌡 ZONES 15–24

☀ ☼ SUN OR LIGHT SHADE

◖ LITTLE WATER ONCE ESTABLISHED

Baeckea ramossissima prostrata

Australian shrubs with tiny needlelike leaves and a profusion of small white to pink flowers resembling miniature tea tree (*Leptospermum*) blossoms.

B. ramossissima prostrata. Grows 3 in. tall and spreads 2–3 ft. Flowers white to pale pink.

B. virgata. Reaches 8 ft. or more, with a profusion of white, honey-scented flowers in spring and summer.

BAILEYA multiradiata

DESERT MARIGOLD

Asteraceae (Compositae)

ANNUAL, PERENNIAL

🌡 ALL ZONES; BEST IN DESERT

☀ FULL SUN ONLY

◖ ◗ WATER IF DESERT RAINS FAIL

Baileya multiradiata

Western desert native displays inch-wide, bright yellow flower heads above gray foliage on 1–1½-ft. plants. Basic bloom period spring through fall; year-round bloom from self-sown seedlings is possible in low desert. Sow seed fall or spring, rake in, and water thoroughly. Keep moist until seeds sprout; then reduce watering to 1 or 2 times a week. Thin to 1½ ft. apart. To prolong bloom, water every week or two.

BALD CYPRESS. See TAXODIUM distichum   **p. 502**

BALLOON FLOWER. See PLATYCODON grandiflorus   **p. 427**

BALLOTA pseudodictamnus

Lamiaceae (Labiatae)

SHRUBBY PERENNIAL

🌡 ZONES 8, 9, 14–24

☀ FULL SUN

◖ INFREQUENT WATER

Ballota pseudodictamnus

Perennial of dense, rounded growth habit to 18–20 in. with opposite pairs of roundish, inch-wide, furry gray-green leaves. Whorls of small white flowers are less important than foliage and habit. Use in mixed perennial beds or bank plantings. Looks good with lavender, Jerusalem sage, and other Mediterranean perennials. Cut back hard in spring before new growth starts.

BALSAM. See IMPATIENS balsamina   **p. 331**

Balsaminaceae. The touch-me-not family embraces herbaceous or shrubby plants with juicy stems, irregular flowers with spurs, and explosive seed capsules. Impatiens is the only important member.

BAMBOO

Poaceae (Gramineae)

GIANT GRASSES

🌡 SEE CHART FOR HARDINESS

☀ ☼ FULL SUN OR PARTIAL SHADE

◖ WATER DURING FAST GROWTH

▶ SEE CHART

Bambusa multiplex

Large, woody stems (culms) divided into sections (internodes) by obvious joints (nodes). Upper nodes produce buds that develop into branches; these, in larger bamboos, divide into secondary branches that bear leaves. Bamboos spread by underground stems (rhizomes) that, like the aboveground culms, are jointed and carry buds. Manner in which rhizomes grow explains difference between running and clump bamboos.

In running bamboos (*Arundinaria, Chimonobambusa, Phyllostachys, Pseudosasa, Sasa, Semiarundinaria,* and *Shibataea*), underground stems grow rapidly to varying distances from parent plant before sending up new vertical shoots. These bamboos eventually form large patches or groves unless spread is curbed. They are generally fairly hardy plants from temperate regions in China and Japan.

In clump bamboos (*Bambusa, Chusquea, Fargesia, Otatea*), underground stems grow only a short distance before sending up new stems. These form clumps that slowly expand around the edges. Most are tropical or subtropical.

See chart for hardiness. Figures indicate temperatures at which leaf damage occurs. Stems and rhizomes may be considerably hardier.

Plant container-grown bamboos at any time of year. Best time to propagate from existing clumps is just before growth begins in spring; divide hardy kinds in March or early April, tropical ones in May or early June. (Transplanting at other times is possible, but risk of losing divisions is high in summer heat or winter chill and wet soil.) Cut or saw divisions with roots and at least three connected culms. If divisions are large, cut back tops to balance loss of roots and rhizomes. Foliage may wilt or wither, but culms will send out new leaves.

Rhizome cutting is another means of propagation. In clump bamboos, this cutting consists of the rooted base of a culm; in running bamboos, it is a foot-long length of rhizome with roots and buds. Plant in rich mix with ample organic material added.

Bambusa oldhamii

Culms of all bamboos have already attained their maximum diameter when they poke through ground; in mature plants, they usually reach their maximum height within a month. Many do become increasingly leafy in subsequent years, but not taller. Plants are evergreen, but there is considerable dropping of older leaves; old plantings develop nearly weedproof mulch of dead leaves. Individual canes live for several years but eventually die and should be cut out.

Mature bamboos grow phenomenally fast during their brief growth period—culms of giant types may increase in length by several feet a day. Don't expect such quick growth the first year after transplanting, though. Giant timber bamboo, for example, needs 3–5 years to build up a rhizome system capable of supporting culms that grow several feet a day; growth during early years will be less impressive. To get fast growth and great size, water frequently and feed once a month with high-nitrogen or lawn fertilizer; to restrict size and spread, water and feed less. Once established, plants tolerate considerable drought, but rhizomes will not spread into dry soil (or into water). The accompanying chart lists two heights for each bamboo. "Controlled Height" means average height under dry conditions with little feeding, or with rhizome spread controlled by barriers. "Uncontrolled Height" refers to plants growing under best conditions without confinement.

▶ page 178

BAMBOO

For explanation of height, see page 174; for Roman numerals I, II, III, and IV, see page 178. Hardiness is temperature at which leaf damage occurs.

NAME	ALSO SOLD AS	CONTROLLED (UNCONTROLLED) HEIGHT	GROWTH HABIT	STEM DIAMETER	HARDINESS	COMMENTS (GROWTH HABIT, CHARACTERISTICS, USES)
Arundinaria amabilis TONKIN CANE, TEASTICK BAMBOO		20–25 ft. (50 ft.)	Running	2½ in.	10°F	III. Erect, thick-walled canes with small nodes. Beautiful, useful for wood
Bambusa beecheyana BEECHEY BAMBOO	*Sinocalamus beecheyanus*	12–20 ft. (20–40 ft.)	Clump	4–5 in.	15°F	IV. Culms arch strongly for broad, graceful effect. Tropical looking. Scarce
B. multiplex	*B. glaucescens*	8–10 ft. (15–25 ft.)	Clump	1½ in.	15°F	II. Branches from base to top. Dense growth. Hedges, screens. Less common than its varieties described below
B. m. 'Alphonse Karr' ALPHONSE KARR BAMBOO		8–10 ft. (15–35 ft.)	Clump	½–1 in.	15°F	II. Similar to above, but culms are brilliantly striped green on yellow. New culms pinkish and green
B. m. 'Fernleaf' FERNLEAF BAMBOO	*B. nana, B. disticha*	6–10 ft. (10–20 ft.)	Clump	½ in.	15°F	II. Closely spaced leaves, 10–20 to twig, give ferny look. Loses this look, grows coarser with rich soil, ample water
B. m. 'Golden Goddess' GOLDEN GODDESS BAMBOO		6–8 ft. (6–10 ft.)	Clump	½ in.	15°F	II. Graceful, dense, arching growth. Good container or screen plant. Give tops room to spread
B. m. riviereorum CHINESE GODDESS BAMBOO		4–6 ft. (6–8 ft.)	Clump	¼ in.	15°F	II. Solid culms arch gracefully. Tiny leaves in lacy, ferny sprays
B. m. 'Silverstripe'		20 ft. (40 ft.)	Clump	1½ in.	15°F	II. Most vigorous of hedge bamboo varieties. Leaves have white stripes; occasional white stripes on culms
B. oldhamii OLDHAM BAMBOO, CLUMPING GIANT TIMBER BAMBOO	*Sinocalamus oldhamii*	15–25 ft. (20–55 ft.)	Clump	4 in.	15°F	IV. Densely foliaged, erect clumps make it good plant for big, dense screens. Or use single plant for imposing vertical mass. Commonest big bamboo in Southern California
B. textilis		15–20 ft. (20–40 ft.)	Clump	2 in.	13°F	II or IV. Handsome, erect, reasonably hardy, rare. New culms blue green, sheaths green to orange
B. tuldoides PUNTING POLE BAMBOO		15–20 ft. (20–55 ft.)	Clump	2 in.	15°F	IV. Prolific producer of slender, erect culms. Best as single plant
B. ventricosa BUDDHA'S BELLY BAMBOO		3–6 ft. (15–30 ft.)	Clump	2 in.	20°F	II or IV. Stays small, produces swollen culms that give it its name only when confined in tubs or grown in poor, dryish soil. Otherwise a giant bamboo with straight culms
B. vulgaris vittata		15–25 ft. (to 50 ft.)	Clump	4 in.	30°F	IV. Yellow culms have vertical green stripes. Used in well-lit interiors and mildest coastal areas. Striking color. Rare
Chimonobambusa marmorea MARBLED BAMBOO (sometimes sold as "dwarf black bamboo")	*Arundinaria marmorea*	2–4 ft. (4–6 ft.)	Running	¼ in.	20°F	III. New culm sheaths marbled cream and purplish. Older culms nearly black. Densely leafy; makes first-class hedge plant if roots are curbed

BAMBOO

NAME	ALSO SOLD AS	CONTROLLED (UNCONTROLLED) HEIGHT	GROWTH HABIT	STEM DIAMETER	HARDINESS	COMMENTS (GROWTH HABIT, CHARACTERISTICS, USES)
C. quadrangularis SQUARE-STEM BAMBOO	*Bambusa quadrangularis*	10–15 ft. (20–30 ft.)	Running	1 in.	15°F	III. Squarish culms have prominent joints, carry heavy whorls of branches. Valued for vertical effect
Chusquea coronalis		8–12 ft. (12–15 ft.)	Clump	¾ in.	28°F	IV. Arching culms bear masses of tiny leaves on short whorled branches. Exceptionally attractive. Sun or light shade. Rare
Fargesia murielae	*Sinarundinaria murielae*	6–8 ft. (15 ft.)	Clump	¾ in.	−20°F	II. One of two hardiest bamboos for U.S. Light, airy, narrow clump, arching and drooping at top. Rare
F. nitida FOUNTAIN BAMBOO	*Sinarundinaria nitida*	6–8 ft. (15–20 ft.)	Clump	¾ in.	0°F	II. Light, airy, graceful, narrow clump, arching and drooping at top. Greenish purple culms mature to deep purplish black. Needs shade to look its best. Rare
Indocalamus tessellata	*Arundinaria ragamowskii*	2–3 ft. (3–6 ft.)	Running	¼ in.	0°F	Resembles *Sasa palmata*, but much lower growth, much longer leaves (2 ft.). Rapid spreader, best in shade. Rare
Otatea acuminata aztecorum MEXICAN WEEPING BAMBOO	*Yushania aztecorum, Arthrostylidium longifolium*	8–10 ft. (20 ft.)	Clump	1½ in.	15°F	II. Extremely narrow leaves (6 in. by ⅛ in.) give lacy look. Foliage masses bend nearly to ground. Fairly drought resistant when established. Rare
Phyllostachys aurea GOLDEN BAMBOO		6–10 ft. (10–20 ft.)	Running	2 in.	0°F	III. Erect, stiff culms, usually with crowded joints at base—good identifying mark. Dense foliage makes it good screen or hedge. Can take much drought but looks better with ample water. Good choice for growing in tubs
P. aureosulcata YELLOW GROOVE BAMBOO		12–15 ft. (15–25 ft.)	Running	1½ in.	−20°F	III. Like more slender, more open golden bamboo. Young culms green with pronounced yellowish groove. One of two hardiest bamboos
P. bambusoides GIANT TIMBER BAMBOO, JAPANESE TIMBER BAMBOO	*P. reticulata*	15–35 ft. (25–45 ft.)	Running	6 in.	0°F	IV. Once commonest of large, hardy timber bamboos. Most perished during blooming period in 1960s–1970s. New plants from seed are available. Makes beautiful groves if lowest branches are trimmed off
P. b. 'Castillon'	*P. castillonis*	10–15 ft. (15–20 ft.)	Running	2 in.	0°F	III. Yellow culms show green stripe above each branch cluster. Rare
P. heterocycla pubescens MOSO BAMBOO	*P. edulis*	20–40 ft. (40–60 ft.)	Running	8 in.	5°F	IV. Largest of running timber bamboos. Gray-green, heavy culms; small, feathery leaves. Rare and hard to establish
P. meyeri		10–20 ft. (20–30 ft.)	Running	2 in.	−4°F	III. Somewhat like *P. aurea* but lacks crowded basal joints. Hardy to cold
P. nigra BLACK BAMBOO		4–8 ft. (10–15 ft.)	Running	1½ in.	0°F	III. New culms green, turning black in second year (rarely olive green dotted black). Best in afternoon shade where summers are hot
P. n. 'Henon'		50 ft. (to 54 ft.)	Running	3½ in.	0°F	III. Much larger than black bamboo. Culms whitish green, not changing to black, rough to touch

B

BAMBOO

NAME	ALSO SOLD AS	CONTROLLED (UNCONTROLLED) HEIGHT	GROWTH HABIT	STEM DIAMETER	HARDINESS	COMMENTS (GROWTH HABIT, CHARACTERISTICS, USES)
Pleioblastus argenteostriata		2–3 ft. (3–4 ft.)	Running	¼ in.	10°F	I. Good light-colored ground cover for shade. Looks best cut back every year. White stripes on leaves
P. chino vaginata 'Variegata'		2–3 ft. (3–4 ft.)	Running	⅜ in.	10°F	I. Graceful, densely foliaged. Slender leaves striped white. Sun or light shade
P. distichus DWARF FERNLEAF BAMBOO	*Sasa disticha*	1–2 ft. (2–3 ft.)	Running	⅛ in.	10°F	I. Delicate in appearance. Tiny, two-ranked ferny leaves. Rampant; cut back to ground if rank or stemmy
P. pygmaea	*Sasa pygmaea*	½–1 ft. (1–1½ ft.)	Running	⅛ in.	0°F	I. Aggressive spreader; good bank holder and erosion control. Can be mowed every few years to keep it from growing stemmy and unattractive
P. simonii SIMON BAMBOO, MEDAKE	*Arundinaria simonii*	10 ft. (20 ft.)	Running	1½ in.	0°F	III. Vertical growth pattern, moderate spreader. Screens, hedges; garden stakes
P. s. variegatus		10 ft. (20 ft.)	Running	1½ in.	0°F	III. Like *P. simonii* but some leaves have white striping
P. variegata DWARF WHITESTRIPE BAMBOO	*Sasa variegata, S. fortunei*	1–2 ft. (2–3 ft.)	Running	¼ in.	−10°F	I. Fast spreader; curb rhizomes. Use in tubs or as deep ground cover. Sun or light shade
P. viridistriatus	*Arundinaria auricoma*	1–2 ft. (2½ ft.)	Running	¼ in.	0°F	I. Leaves 8 in. long, 1½ in. wide are strikingly variegated green and gold
Pseudosasa japonica ARROW BAMBOO	*Arundinaria japonica*	6–10 ft. (10–18 ft.)	Running	¾ in.	0°F	III. Stiffly erect culms with one branch at each joint. Leaves large, with long, pointed tails. Rampant thick hedge in mild-winter climates; slow spreader where winters are cold, making dense, erect clumps
Sasa palmata PALMATE BAMBOO	Sometimes sold as *S. senanensis*	4–5 ft. (8–12 ft.)	Running	⅜ in.	0°F	In class by itself. Grows bigger in Zones 4–6 and 15–17 than in 18–24. Broad, handsome leaves (to 15 in. long by 4 in. wide) spread fingerlike from stem and branch tips. Rampant spreader; curb it
S. tessellata	*Arundinaria ragamowskii*	2–3 ft. (3–6 ft.)	Running	¼ in.	0°F	Resembles *S. palmata*, but much lower growth, much longer leaves (to 2 ft.). Slow spreader, best in shade. Rare
S. veitchii		2–3 ft. (2–3 ft.)	Running	¼ in.	0°F	I. Rampant spreader with large (7-in.-by-1-in.) dark green leaves that turn whitish buff all around the edges in autumn for variegated effect. Appropriate in Japanese gardens if curbed
Semiarundinaria fastuosa NARIHIRA BAMBOO		8–10 ft. (12–25 ft.)	Running	1¼ in.	−4°F	II or III. Rigidly upright growth. Slow spreader easily kept to a clump. Planted closely, makes tall, narrow, dense hedge or windbreak
Shibataea kumasaca		2–3 ft. (5–6 ft.)	Running	¼ in.	10°F	III. Slow spreading, makes compact clumps of unbamboolike appearance. Leaves are short and broad (4 in. by 1 in.), distinctly stalked. Needs acid soil

Difficult to mass-produce and little known, most bamboos are hard to find in nurseries. Inquire about specialists in your area. The American Bamboo Society has chapters in the Northwest, in Northern California, and in Southern California. Society members often propagate rare varieties for sales in connection with their meetings. Arboretum and botanical garden sales are another source. Plants may be offered under the principal name listed or under one of the synonyms. Plant names change so frequently that vendors cannot always keep up.

Phyllostachys aurea

In the case of bamboo, disregard the rule of never buying root-bound plants: the more crowded the plant in the container, the faster its growth when planted. Both running and clump types grow well when roots are confined.

Scale, mealybugs, and aphids are occasionally found on bamboo but seldom do any harm; if they secrete honeydew in bothersome amounts, spray with malathion. To control mites, release predatory mites.

The chart classifies each bamboo by habit of growth, which, of course, determines its use in the garden. In Group I are the dwarf or low-growing ground cover types. These can be used for erosion control or, in small clumps (carefully confined in a long section of flue tile), in border or rock garden. Group II includes clump bamboos with fountainlike habit of growth. These have widest use in landscaping. They require no more space than the average strong-growing shrub. Clipped, they make hedges or screens that won't spread much into surrounding soil. When unclipped, they line up as informal screens or grow singly to show off their graceful form.

Bamboos in Group III are running bamboos of moderate size and more or less vertical growth. Use them as screens, hedges, or (if curbed) alone. Group IV includes the giant bamboos. Use running kinds for groves or for Oriental effects on a grand scale. Clumping kinds have a tropical look, especially if they are used with broad-leafed tropical plants. All may be thinned and clipped to show off culms. Thin clumps or groves by cutting out old or dead culms at the base.

Some of the smaller bamboos bloom on some of their stalks every year and continue to grow. Some bloom partially and at erratic intervals. Some have never been known to bloom. Others bloom heavily, set seed, and die. Giant timber bamboo (*Phyllostachys bambusoides*) and other species of *Phyllostachys* bloom at rare intervals of 30–60 years, produce flowers for a long period, and become enfeebled. They may recover very slowly or die. There is evidence that very heavy feeding and watering may speed their recovery.

Bamboos are not recommended for year-round indoor culture, but container-grown plants can spend extended periods indoors in cool, bright rooms. You can revive plants by taking them outdoors, but it is important to avoid sudden changes in temperature and light.

There are several ways to eliminate unwanted bamboo. Digging it out with mattock and spade is the surest method, though sometimes difficult.

Phyllostachys nigra

Rhizomes are generally not deep, but they may be widespread. Remove them all or regrowth will occur. Starve out roots by cutting off all shoots before they exceed 2 ft. in height; repeat as needed—probably many times over the course of a year. Contact foliage sprays that kill leaves have the same effect as removing culms. Translocation weed killers have only a temporary effect on bamboo. Soil sterilants will kill the plants; repeat treatments may be necessary. Avoid damaging roots of nearby plants, and beware of runoff to other parts of the garden.

FOR INFORMATION ON YOUR CLIMATE ZONE

PLEASE SEE PAGES 15–44

CREEPING BAMBOO CAN BE CONTAINED

Make 1½-ft.-deep barriers with strips of galvanized sheet metal or with poured concrete, or plant in long flue tiles or bottomless oil drums. You can limit spread by periodically inserting a spade down to its full depth around the clump. New shoots break off easily; they do not resprout. Another way to limit spread of large running bamboos: Dig a foot-deep trench around plant and sever any rhizomes that grow into it; the trench will fill with a loose mulch of leaves. Sift through leaves with gloved hands to find roving rhizomes.

BANKSIA

Proteaceae

EVERGREEN SHRUBS OR TREES

ZONES 15–24

FULL SUN

TOLERATE SOME ARIDITY

Banksia ericifolia

Few of the many banksia species are in cultivation, although botanical gardens sometimes offer plants at plant sales. Leaves are usually long and narrow, sometimes spectacularly saw-toothed. Individually small flowers appear in dense round or cylindrical cones (often spectacular) and are followed by long-lasting woody seed cones. Flowers are rich in nectar. Plants subject to root rot fungi and require perfect drainage. Most can withstand long dry periods once established. Treat chlorosis with iron.

B. ericifolia. HEATH BANKSIA. Medium to large shrub with short, needlelike leaves and 6–8-in. cylindrical clusters of orange to red flowers. Tolerates coastal winds.

B. integrifolia. TREE BANKSIA. Medium-size tree with narrow leaves to 6 in. long, 2 in. wide, with smooth or slightly toothed edges. Pale yellow flower clusters can reach 6 in. Highly tolerant of coastal sand and wind.

BAPTISIA australis

FALSE INDIGO, WILD INDIGO

Fabaceae (Leguminosae)

PERENNIAL

ALL ZONES

FULL SUN

TAPROOT ENABLES IT TO SURVIVE DRYNESS

Baptisia australis

Native to eastern and southern United States. Somewhat like bush lupine in habit. Grows 3–6 ft. tall, with bluish green, deeply cut leaves. Spikes of small, indigo blue, sweet pea–shaped flowers appear in early summer, followed by inflated seedpods; both flowers and pods are interesting in arrangements. Cut back spent flowers for repeat bloom. Specialists carry seed.

BARBERRY. See **BERBERIS**   **p. 182**

BARLERIA obtusa

Acanthaceae

EVERGREEN SHRUB

⚡ ZONES 16–24

☼ ◑ LIGHT SHADE; FULL SUN IN FOG BELT

💧 REGULAR WATER

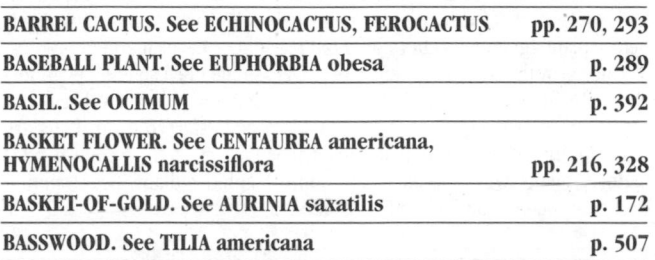

Barleria obtusa

Shrub to 3 ft. tall with dark green, 3-in. leaves and loose clusters of blue, 1½-in. flowers in winter and spring. It likes rich soil and even moisture when in full growth. Pinch to keep compact. Sometimes grown as indoor/outdoor or house plant in cold-winter areas.

BARREL CACTUS. See ECHINOCACTUS, FEROCACTUS	**pp. 270, 293**
BASEBALL PLANT. See EUPHORBIA obesa	**p. 289**
BASIL. See OCIMUM	**p. 392**
BASKET FLOWER. See CENTAUREA americana, HYMENOCALLIS narcissiflora	**pp. 216, 328**
BASKET-OF-GOLD. See AURINIA saxatilis	**p. 172**
BASSWOOD. See TILIA americana	**p. 507**

BAUERA rubioides

Baueraceae

EVERGREEN SHRUB

⚡ ZONES 15–24

☼ ◑ PARTIAL SHADE; FULL SUN IN FOG BELT

💧 REGULAR WATER

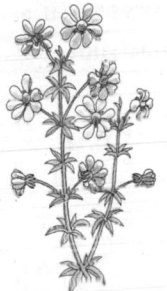

Bauera rubioides

A mounding, spreading, graceful shrub to 2 ft. tall and 5 ft. wide, with tiny needlelike leaves and a profusion of small, dangling white or pinkish flowers throughout much of the year, heaviest in late winter and spring. It can arch over rocks or low fence, or half trail down a lightly shaded bank. Roots from cuttings.

BAUHINIA

BRAZILIAN BUTTERFLY TREE

Fabaceae (Leguminosae)

EVERGREEN OR DECIDUOUS TREES, SHRUBS

⚡ ZONES VARY BY SPECIES

☼ B. FORFICATA TOLERATES JUST A LITTLE SHADE

💧 MODERATE WATER

Bauhinia forficata

These flamboyant flowering plants have a very special place in Hawaii and mild-winter areas of California and Arizona. They vary greatly by species and climate. Common to all garden bauhinias are twin "leaves," actually twin lobes.

B. blakeana. HONG KONG ORCHID TREE. Partially deciduous for short period. Zones 13, 19, 21, 23. Native to southern China. Flowers are shaped like some orchids; colors range from cranberry maroon through purple and rose to orchid pink, often in same blossom. Flowers are much larger (5½–6 in. wide) than those of other bauhinias; also unlike others, they appear in late fall to spring. Gray-green leaves tend to drop off around bloom time but not completely. Umbrella-type growth habit. To 20 ft. high.

B. forficata. BRAZILIAN BUTTERFLY TREE. Evergreen to deciduous large shrub or tree. Zones 9, 12–23. Native to Brazil. Probably hardiest bauhinia. In spring and through summer, bears narrow-petaled, creamy white flowers to 3 in. wide. Deep green leaves, more pointed lobes than others. Grows to 20 ft., often with twisting, leaning trunk, picturesque angled branches. Short, sharp thorns at branch joints. Good canopy for

patio. In hot, dry climate, give some afternoon shade; if unshaded, blooms tend to shrivel during day. Often sold as *B. corniculata* or *B. candicans*.

B. galpinii (B. punctata). RED BAUHINIA. Evergreen to semideciduous shrub. Zones 13, 15, 16, 18–23. Native to South and tropical Africa. Brick red to orange flowers, as spectacular as bougainvillea. Sprawling, half-climbing, with 15-ft. spread. Best as espalier on warm wall. With hard pruning, can make splendid flowering bonsai for large pot or box.

B. variegata. PURPLE ORCHID TREE. Partially to wholly deciduous. Zones 13, 18–23. Native to India, China. Most frequently planted. Hardy to 22°F. Spectacular street trees where spring is warm and stays warm. Wonderful show of light pink to orchid purple, broad-petaled, 2–3-in.-wide flowers, usually January to April. Light green, broad-lobed leaves generally drop in midwinter. Produces huge crop of messy-looking beans after blooming. Trim beans off if you wish—trimming brings new growth earlier. Inclined to grow as shrub with many stems. Staked and pruned, becomes attractive 20–35-ft. tree. Commonly sold as *B. purpurea*.

B. v. 'Candida'. WHITE ORCHID TREE. Like *B. variegata*. White flowers.

BAY. See LAURUS, UMBELLULARIA californica	**pp. 349, 515**
BAYBERRY. See MYRICA pensylvanica	**p. 386**
BEACH ASTER. See ERIGERON glaucus	**p. 275**
BEACH WORMWOOD. See ARTEMISIA stellerana	**p. 166**
BEAD PLANT. See NERTERA granadensis	**p. 390**

BEAN, BROAD

FAVA BEAN, HORSE BEAN

Fabaceae (Leguminosae)

ANNUAL

⚡ ALL ZONES

☼ FULL SUN

💧 MODERATE WATER

⚠ SOME PEOPLE HAVE SEVERE REACTIONS

Fava Bean

This bean (actually a giant vetch) was known in ancient and medieval times; it is a Mediterranean plant, while all other familiar beans are New World plants. It is an annual of bushy growth to 2–4 ft. Best known in coastal climates. You can cook and eat immature pods like edible-pod peas; prepare immature and mature seeds in same way as green or dry limas.

Unlike true beans, this is a cool-season plant. In cold-winter areas, plant as early in spring as soil can be worked. In mild coastal climates, plant in fall for late-winter or early-spring ripening. Matures in 120–150 days, depending on temperature. Space rows 1½–2½ ft. apart. Plant seeds 1 in. deep, 4–5 in. apart; thin to 8–10 in. apart. Watch for and control aphids.

Most people can safely eat fava beans, though a very few (principally of Mediterranean ancestry) have an enzyme deficiency that can cause severe reactions to the beans and even the pollen.

BEAN, DRY

Fabaceae (Leguminosae)

ANNUAL

⚡ ALL ZONES

☼ FULL SUN

💧 BEGIN WATERING AFTER SEEDLINGS EMERGE

Same culture as bush form of snap bean. Let pods remain on bush until they turn dry or begin to shatter; thresh beans from pods, dry, store to soak and cook later. 'Pinto', 'Red Kidney', and 'White Marrowfat' belong to this group.

Dry Bean

B

BEAN, LIMA

Fabaceae (Leguminosae)

ANNUAL

✂ ALL ZONES

☼ FULL SUN

◐ BEGIN WATERING AFTER SEEDLINGS EMERGE

Lima Bean

Like snap beans (which they resemble), limas come in either bush or vine (pole) form. They develop slower than string beans—bush types require 65–75 days, pole kinds 78–95 days—and do not produce as reliably in extremely dry, hot weather. They must be shelled before cooking—a tedious chore but worth it if you like fresh limas. Among bush types, 'Burpee's Improved Bush', 'Henderson Bush', and 'Fordhook 242' are outstanding; the last two are especially useful in hot-summer areas. 'Prizetaker' and 'King of the Garden' are fine, large-seeded climbing forms; 'Small White Lima' or 'Sieva', usually grown for drying, gives heavy yields of shelled beans. Grow like snap beans.

BEAN, SCARLET RUNNER

Fabaceae (Leguminosae)

ANNUAL TWINING VINE

✂ ALL ZONES

☼ FULL SUN

◐ BEGIN WATERING AFTER SEEDLINGS EMERGE

Scarlet Runner Bean

Showy and ornamental with bright scarlet flowers in slender clusters and with bright green leaves divided into three roundish, 3–5-in.-long leaflets. Use to cover fences, arbors, outbuildings; provides quick shade on porches. Pink- and white-flowered varieties exist.

Flowers are followed by flattened, very dark green pods that are edible and tasty when young but toughen as they reach full size. Beans from older pods can be shelled for cooking like green limas. Culture is same as for snap beans.

GROW A BEAN TEPEE

From July to September, children can play in the cool, shady confines of a scarlet runner bean tepee. Place a vertical 10-ft. center pole 18 in. deep in the soil. Pack it in well. Place bases of at least four 10-ft.-long bamboo poles (or other skinny wooden sticks) 4½ ft. out from base of center pole and tie their tops together 6–12 in. below top of center pole. In a circle just outside pole bases, plant the beans 1 in. deep and 1–3 in. apart. Train the vines up the outside of the tepee, keeping main stems out of its interior.

BEAN, SNAP

STRING BEAN, GREEN BEAN

Fabaceae (Leguminosae)

ANNUAL

✂ ALL ZONES

☼ FULL SUN

◐ BEGIN WATERING AFTER SEEDLINGS EMERGE

Snap Bean

Of all beans, the snap bean is the most widely planted and most useful for home gardens. Snap beans have tender, fleshy pods with little fiber; they may be green, yellow (wax beans), or

purple ('Royalty'). Purple kinds turn green in cooking. Plants grow as self-supporting bushes (bush beans) or as climbing vines (pole beans). Bush types bear earlier, but vines are more productive. Plants resemble scarlet runner bean, but white or purple flowers are not showy.

Plant seeds as soon as soil is warm, in full sun and good soil. These seeds must push heavy seed leaves through soil, so see that it is reasonably loose and open. Plant seeds of bush types an inch deep and 1–3 in. apart in rows, with 2–3 ft. between rows. Pole beans can be managed in a number of ways: set three or four 8-ft. poles in the ground and tie together at top in wigwam fashion; or set single poles 3 or 4 ft. apart and sow six or eight beans around each, thinning to three or four strongest seedlings; or insert poles 1 or 2 ft. apart in rows and sow seeds as you would bush beans; or sow along sunny wall, fence, or trellis and train vines on web of light string supported by wire or heavy twine. Moisten ground thoroughly before planting; do not water again until seedlings have emerged.

Once growth starts, keep soil moist. Occasional deep soaking is preferable to frequent light sprinklings, which may encourage mildew. Feed after plants are in active growth and again when pods start to form. Pods are ready in 50–70 days, according to variety. Pick every 5–7 days; if pods mature, plants will stop bearing. Control aphids, diabrotica (spotted cucumber beetle), and whiteflies as needed.

BEAUCARNEA recurvata

PONYTAIL, BOTTLE PALM

Agavaceae

SUCCULENT SHRUB OR TREE

✂ ZONES 13, 16–24; OR INDOORS

☼ FULL SUN

◐ INFREQUENT, DEEP WATERING

Beaucarnea recurvata

Base of trunk is greatly swollen. On young plants it resembles a big onion sitting on soil; on old trees in the ground, it can be a woody mass several feet across. Leaves cluster at ends of branches in dense tufts; arching and drooping, they measure 3 ft. or more in length, ¾ in. wide. Very old trees may produce inconspicuous clusters of creamy white flowers.

Outdoors, give plants sun, well-drained soil, and infrequent deep watering. They do exceptionally well as house plants when given good light and are not overwatered. Mature plants have endured temperatures to 18°F; young plants in containers freeze to death in the low 20s. Plants moved from indoors to permanent garden locations outdoors should have gradually increasing exposure to sun and low temperatures.

BEAUMONTIA grandiflora

HERALD'S TRUMPET, EASTER LILY VINE

Apocynaceae

EVERGREEN VINE

✂ ZONES 12, 13, 16, 17, 21–24

☼ ◑ FULL SUN OR A LITTLE SHADE

◐◐ AMPLE WATER

Beaumontia grandiflora

Climbs by arching, semitwining branches to as much as 30 ft. and spreads as wide. Large, dark green, 6–9-in., oval to roundish leaves, smooth and shiny above, slightly downy beneath, furnish lush tropical look. From April until September, bears trumpet-shaped,

5-in.-long, green-veined, fragrant white flowers that look like Easter lilies. Needs deep, rich soil, ample water, and heavy feeding. Prune after flowering to keep it in scale, but preserve good proportion of 2- and 3-year-old wood; flowers are not borne on new growth. Makes big espalier on warm wall sheltered from wind. Or train along eaves of house; give it a sturdy support. Good near swimming pools. Hardy to 28°F.

BEET

Chenopodiaceae
BIENNIAL GROWN AS ANNUAL
☑ ALL ZONES
☼ FULL SUN
◉ FREQUENT WATER

Beet

To have fresh beets all summer, plant seeds in short rows at monthly intervals, starting as soon as soil can be worked in spring. Best in sun; where summers are very hot, plant to mature before or after extreme heat. Cover seeds with ¼ in. of compost, sand, or vermiculite to prevent caking. Sow seeds 1 in. apart; thin to 2 in. while plants are small; the thinnings—tops and roots—are edible. To keep roots tender, water often in dry weather. Feed plants at 3–4-week intervals for speedy growth. Begin harvesting when beets are 1 in. wide; complete harvesting before beets exceed 3 in.—larger ones are woody.

Round, red varieties include 'Detroit Dark Red' and 'Crosby's Egyptian' (old favorites) as well as many newer ones. Novelties include 'Cylindra' and 'Forma Nova' (with long, cylindrical roots); there are also golden yellow and white varieties.

BEGONIA

Begoniaceae
PERENNIALS
☑ ZONES 14–24; OR TREAT AS ANNUALS
◐ ◉ BEST IN FILTERED SHADE
◉ MOIST SOIL AND HUMID AIR

Tuberous Begonia

Perennials, sometimes shrubby, grown for textured, multicolored foliage, saucer-sized flowers, or lacy clusters of smaller flowers. Outdoors, most grow best in pots in the ground or in hanging baskets in filtered shade with rich, porous, fast-draining soil, consistent but light feeding, and enough water to keep soil moist but not soggy. Most thrive as indoor plants, in greenhouse, or under lath. Some prefer terrarium conditions. Almost all require at least moderate humidity. (During hot, dry summers, set pots in moist, pebble-filled saucers.)

Most can be propagated easily from leaf, stem, or rhizome cuttings. They also grow from dust-fine seed. Of the many hundreds of species and varieties, relatively few are sold widely.

Begonia enthusiasts group or classify the different kinds by growth habit, which coincidentally groups them by their care needs.

Cane-type begonias. They get their name from their stems, which grow tall and woody and have prominent bamboolike joints. The group includes so-called angel-wing begonias. These erect plants have multiple stems,

some reaching 5 ft. or more under the right conditions. Most bloom profusely with large clusters of white, pink, orange, or red flowers early spring through autumn. Some are everblooming. When roots fill 4-inch pots, plants can be placed in large containers or in the ground. Position plants where they will get plenty of light, some sun, and no wind. They may require staking. Protect from heavy frosts. Old canes that have grown barren should be pruned to two leaf joints in early spring to stimulate new growth.

B. 'Irene Nuss'. Dark red-and-green leaves and huge drooping clusters of coral pink flowers.

Hiemalis begonias. Usually sold as Rieger begonias. Bushy, compact; profuse bloomers and outstanding outdoor or indoor plants. Flowers average about 2 in. across and appear over a long season that includes winter. On well-grown plants, green leaves and stems are all but invisible beneath a blanket of bloom. Give indoor plants plenty of light in winter. In summer, keep out of hot noonday sun. Water thoroughly when top inch of soil is dry. Don't sprinkle leaves. Plant may get rangy, an indication of approaching dormancy; if they do, cut stems to 4-in. stubs.

Multiflora begonias. Bushy, compact plants 1–1½ ft. tall. Profuse bloom in carmine, scarlet, orange, yellow, apricot, salmon, pink. Includes Nonstop.

Rex begonias. With their bold, multicolored leaves, these are probably the most striking of all foliage begonias. While many named varieties are grown by collectors, easier-to-find unnamed seedling plants are almost as decorative. The leaves grow from a rhizome; see "Rhizomatous begonias" for care. In addition, rex begonias should get high humidity (at least 50 percent) to do their best. Provide it by misting with a spray bottle, placing pots on wet pebbles in a tray, or keeping plants in greenhouse. When rhizome grows too far past edge of pot for your taste, either repot into slightly larger container or cut off rhizome end inside pot edge. Old rhizome will branch and grow new leaves. Make rhizome cuttings of the piece you remove and root in mixture of half peat moss, half perlite.

Rex Begonia

Rhizomatous begonias. Like rex begonias, these grow from a rhizome, a usually creeping stem-type structure at or near soil level. Although some have handsome flowers, they are grown primarily for foliage, which varies in color and texture among species and varieties. The group includes so-called star begonias, named for their leaf shape. Rhizomatous begonias perform well as house plants: give them bright light through a window and water only when the top inch or so of soil is dry. Plant them in wide, shallow pots. They flower from winter through summer, the season varying among specific plants. White to pink flowers appear in clusters on erect stems above the foliage. Rhizomes will grow over edge of pot, eventually forming a ball-shaped plant; if you wish, cut rhizomes back to pot. The old rhizome will branch and grow new leaves. Root the pieces of rhizome in mixture of half peat moss, half perlite.

B. masoniana. IRON CROSS BEGONIA. Large puckered leaves; known for chocolate brown pattern resembling Maltese cross on green background. Flowers insignificant.

Semperflorens begonias. Fibrous or bedding begonias. Dwarf (6–8 in.) and taller (10–12 in.) strains grown in garden beds or containers as if annuals, producing lots of small flowers spring through fall in a white-through-red range. Foliage can be green, red, bronze, or variegated. In mild climates, can overwinter, live for years. Thrives in full sun along coast. Prefers broken shade inland, but dark-foliaged kinds will take sun if well watered.

Shrublike begonias. This large class is marked by multiple stems that are soft and green rather than bamboolike as in the cane-type group. Grown for both foliage and flowers. Leaves are very interesting—some are heavily textured; others grow white or red "hairs"; still others develop a soft, feltlike coating. Most grow upright and bushy, but others are less erect and make suitable subjects for hanging baskets. Flowers in shades of pink, red, white, and peach can come any time, depending on species or variety. Care consists of repotting into larger container as the plant outgrows its pot. Some shrublike begonias can get very large—as tall as 8 ft. They require ample moisture—water when soil begins to dry on surface. Prune to shape; pinch tips to encourage branching.

B. 'Digswelliana'. Shrublike plant, 2–3 ft. high, with glossy leaves 2–4 in. long. Red flowers in clusters bloom almost continuously spring–fall.

B. foliosa. Inch-long leaves packed tightly on twiggy plant give fernlike look. Stems arch or droop to 3 ft. Flowers are small, white to red. 'Miniata' has rose pink to rose red flowers.

B. 'Richmondensis.' Exceeds 2 ft. tall with arching stems carrying deep green, shiny, crisp leaves with red undersides. Vivid pink to crimson flowers develop from darker buds. Big and sturdy. Tolerant of sun and wind.

Trailing or climbing begonias. These have stems that trail or climb, depending on how you train them. They are suited to hanging basket culture or planting in the ground where well protected.

B. solananthera. Glossy light green leaves; fragrant white flowers with red centers.

Tuberous begonias. Among the best-known begonias in the West are these magnificent large-flowered hybrids that grow from tubers. Types range from plants with saucer-size blooms and a few upright stems to multistemmed hanging basket types covered with flowers. Except for some rare kinds, they are summer- and fall-blooming in almost any flower color except blue.

Grow tuberous begonias in filtered shade, such as under lath or in the open with eastern exposure. For best bloom, mist with water several times a day unless you live in foggy coastal area. Watch for fuzzy white spots on leaves, which signal powdery mildew. In fall, when leaves begin to yellow and wilt, reduce watering. When stems have fallen off the plant on their own, lift tuber; shake off dirt; dry tuber in the sun for 3 days; and store in cool, dry place, such as a garden shed or garage, with its label until spring, when little pink buds will become visible. Then begin the process again. In April and May you can buy small seedling plants and plant them directly in pots.

Strains are sold as hanging or upright. The former bloom more profusely; the latter have larger flowers. Colors are white, red, pink, yellow, and peach; shapes are frilly (carnation), formal double (camellia), and tight-centered (rose). Some have petal edges in contrasting colors (picotee). Popular strains are Double Trumpet (improved rose form), Prima Donna (improved camellia), and Hanging Sensation.

BELAMCANDA chinensis

BLACKBERRY LILY
Iridaceae
PERENNIAL WITH RHIZOME
☀ ALL ZONES
☼ ◑ SUN OR PARTIAL SHADE
◗ REGULAR WATER

Belamcanda chinensis

Common name derives from cluster of shining black seeds exposed when capsules split. Sword-shaped, irislike leaves 1 in. wide. Flowers 1½–2 in. across, orange dotted with red, on 2–3-ft. branching stems; bloom over long period in August, September. Plant rhizomes 1 in. deep in porous soil. Effective in clumps in border. Seed capsules make unique arrangements.

BELLADONNA LILY. See AMARYLLIS belladonna	p. 149
BELLFLOWER. See CAMPANULA	p. 203

BELLIS perennis

ENGLISH DAISY
Asteraceae (Compositae)
PERENNIAL OFTEN TREATED AS ANNUAL
☀ ALL ZONES
☼ ◑ FULL SUN; LIGHT SHADE IN WARM AREAS
◐ ● MODERATE TO LOTS OF WATER

Bellis perennis

Native to Europe and Mediterranean region. The original English daisies are the kind you sometimes see growing in lawns. Plump, fully double ones sold in nurseries are horticultural varieties. Rosettes of dark green leaves 1–2 in. long. Pink, rose, red, or white double flowers on 3–6-in. stems, in spring and early summer. Meadow plant; needs good soil, much moisture, light shade in warm areas, full sun near coast. Edging or bedding plant; effective with bulbs.

BELLS-OF-IRELAND. See MOLUCCELLA laevis	p. 382
BELOPERONE. See JUSTICIA	p. 342
BENT, BENT GRASS. See AGROSTIS	p. 143

Berberidaceae. The barberry family contains both shrubs and herbaceous perennials. Barberry and nandina are typical of the former; *Epimedium* and *Vancouveria*, the latter.

BERBERIS

BARBERRY
Berberidaceae
DECIDUOUS AND EVERGREEN SHRUBS
☀ ALL ZONES
☼ ◑ SUN OR LIGHT SHADE
◐ ● LITTLE TO MODERATE WATER

Berberis darwinii

Approximate hardiness of each species, deciduous and evergreen, is given in descriptions below. Ability of barberries, especially the deciduous species, to take punishment in climate and soil extremes makes them worth attention in all "hard" climates. Barberries require no more than ordinary garden care. Vigorous growers can take a lot of cutting back for growth renewal; if plants are left to their own devices, some of inner branches die and plants become ratty. The following list omits details about bloom time, flower color, and spines unless the plant lacks the typical yellow spring flowers and spiny branches of the genus.

B. buxifolia. MAGELLAN BARBERRY. Evergreen. Hardy to 0°F. Rather rigid upright growth to 6 ft. and as wide. Leaves small, leathery, to 1 in. long. Flowers orange yellow. Berries dark purple, one or two at each leaf cluster.

FOR GROWING SYMBOL EXPLANATIONS
PLEASE SEE PAGE 129

B. b. nana. To 1½ ft. high and 2 ft. wide. Use to control foot traffic or plant where yellow bloom in evergreen is important. (There is an even lower-growing variety, 'Pygmaea'.)

B. chenaultii. Evergreen. Hardy to 0°F. Slow growing, low (to 4 ft.), with arching branches. Leaves dark green, spine toothed, 1–1½ in. long. Flowers bright yellow. Low barrier hedge, foreground planting.

B. darwinii. DARWIN BARBERRY. Evergreen. Hardy to 10°F. Showiest barberry. Fountainlike growth to 5–10 ft. high and 4–7 ft. wide. Leaves small (1 in.), crisp, dark green, hollylike. Orange-yellow flowers are so thick along branches that it's difficult to see foliage. Berries dark blue and numerous—popular with birds. Wonderful as background for Oregon grape (*Mahonia aquifolium*). Spreads by underground runners.

B. gladwynensis 'William Penn'. Evergreen, partially deciduous around 0–10°F. Resembles *B. julianae* in size and general effect, but with broader, glossier leaves; faster growing. Good show of bright yellow flowers.

B. irwinii (B. stenophylla irwinii). Hybrid. Evergreen. Hardy to 0°F. Graceful, fountainlike growth habit to 1½ ft. high. Attractive foliage: narrow, dark green, 1-in.-long leaves.

B. julianae. WINTERGREEN BARBERRY. Evergreen or semideciduous. Hardy to 0°F, but foliage damaged by winter cold. Dense, upright, to 6 ft., with slightly angled branches. Very leathery, spine-toothed, 3-in.-long, dark green leaves. Fruit bluish black. Reddish fall color. One of the thorniest—formidable as barrier hedge.

B. linearifolia. 'Orange King'. Evergreen shrub to 5 ft. Hardy to 10°F. Open growth habit, with narrow, glossy, 2-in. leaves and short clusters of deep orange flowers.

B. mentorensis. Hybrid. Evergreen to about −5°F. Semideciduous to deciduous in colder weather. Hardy to −20°F. Stands hot, dry weather. Rather compact growth to 7 ft. and as wide. Easy to maintain as hedge at any height. Leaves dark green, 1 in. long; beautiful red fall color in cold climates. Berries dull dark red.

B. stenophylla. ROSEMARY BARBERRY. Evergreen garden hybrids. Hardy to 0°F. Leaves narrow, ½–1 in. long, with rolled-in edges, spiny tip. Best known of many varieties is 'Corallina Compacta', coral barberry, 1½ ft. tall, with nodding clusters of bright orange flowers. Rock garden, foreground.

B. thunbergii. JAPANESE BARBERRY. Deciduous. Hardy to −20°F. Graceful growth habit with slender, arching, spiny branches; if not sheared, usually reaches 4–6 ft. tall with equal spread. Dense foliage with roundish, ½–1½-in.-long leaves, deep green above, paler beneath, turning to yellow, orange, and red before they fall. Beadlike, bright red berries stud branches in fall and through winter. Hedge, barrier planting, or single shrub.

B. t. 'Atropurpurea'. RED-LEAF JAPANESE BARBERRY. Foliage bronzy red to purplish red all summer. Must have sun to develop color.

B. t. 'Aurea'. Bright golden yellow foliage, best in full sun. Will tolerate light shade. Slow growing to 1½–2 ft.

B. t. 'Cherry Bomb'. Resembles 'Crimson Pygmy', but taller (to 4 ft.), with large leaves and more open growth.

B. t. 'Crimson Pygmy' (B. t. 'Atropurpurea Nana'). Hardy to −10°F. Selected miniature form, generally less than 1½ ft. high and 2½ ft. wide as 10-year-old. Mature leaves bronzy blood red; new leaves bright red. Must have sun to develop color.

B. t. 'Kobold'. Extra-dwarf bright green variety of Japanese barberry. Like 'Crimson Pygmy' in habit but fuller and rounder.

B. t. 'Rose Glow'. New foliage marbled bronzy red and pinkish white, deepening to rose and bronze. Colors best in full sun or lightest shade.

B. t. 'Sparkle'. To 5 ft. tall and 4–6 ft. wide, with rich green foliage that turns vivid yellow, orange, and red in fall.

B. verruculosa. WARTY BARBERRY. Evergreen. Hardy to 0°F. Neat, tailored shrub with informal elegance. Can reach 3–4 ft. tall but can be held to 1½ ft. without becoming clumpy. Perky, glossy dark green, 1-in.-long leaves are whitish beneath. In fall and winter a red leaf develops as highlight here and there in green foliage. Berries black with purplish bloom. Very choice and easy to use on banks, in foreground of shrubbery, or in front of leggy rhododendrons or azaleas.

B. wilsoniae. WILSON BARBERRY. Deciduous, partially evergreen in mild climates. Hardy to 5°F. Moderate growth to 6 ft. high and as wide, but can be held to 3–4-ft. hedge. Fine-textured foliage, with light green, roundish, ½–1-in. leaves. Small yellow flowers in dense clusters. Beautiful coral to salmon red berries. Handsome barrier hedge.

BERCKMAN DWARF ARBORVITAE. See PLATYCLADUS orientalis p. 427

BERGENIA

Saxifragaceae

PERENNIALS, EVERGREEN EXCEPT IN COLDEST AREAS

☑ ZONES 1–9, 12–24

☼ ◑ PARTIAL SHADE; FULL SUN ON COAST

◓ ◒ TO MAKE THEM LOOK VERDANT, WATER THEM

Bergenia crassifolia

Native to Himalayas and mountains of China. Thick rootstocks; large, glossy green leaves. Thick leafless stalks, 1–1½ ft. high, bear graceful nodding clusters of small white, pink, or rose flowers. Ornamental foliage an all-year asset. Strong, substantial textural quality in borders, under trees, as bold-patterned ground cover. Effective with ferns, hellebores, hostas, and as foreground planting for *Fatsia japonica*, aucubas, rhododendrons.

Best performance in partial shade but will take full sun in cool coastal climates. *B. cordifolia* and *B. crassifolia* endure neglect, poor soil, cold, but respond to good soil, regular watering, feeding, grooming. Cut back yearly to prevent legginess. Divide crowded clumps; replant vigorous divisions. Bait for snails and slugs.

B. ciliata (B. ligulata). Choicest, most elegant. To 1 ft. Lustrous, light green leaves to 1 ft. long and wide, smooth on edges but fringed with soft hairs; young leaves bronzy. White, rose, or purplish flowers bloom late spring, summer. Slightly tender; leaves burn in severe frost. Plants sold under this name may be garden hybrids.

B. cordifolia. HEARTLEAF BERGENIA. Leaves glossy, roundish, heart shaped at base, with wavy, toothed edges. In spring, rose or lilac flowers in pendulous clusters partially hidden by large leaves. Plant grows to 20 in.

B. crassifolia. WINTER-BLOOMING BERGENIA. Best-known bergenia. Leaves dark green, 8 in. or more across, with wavy, sparsely toothed edges. Flowers rose, lilac, or purple, in dense clusters on erect stems standing well above leaves. Plants 20 in. high. Blooms January, February.

BERMUDA, BERMUDA GRASS. See CYNODON dactylon	**p. 254**
BERMUDA BUTTERCUP. See OXALIS pes-caprae	**p. 397**
BETHLEHEM SAGE. See PULMONARIA saccharata	**p. 445**

BETULA

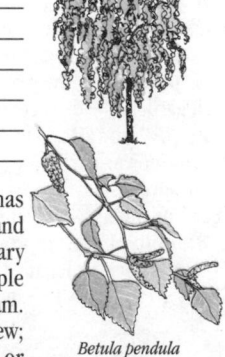

BIRCH

Betulaceae

DECIDUOUS TREES

☑ ZONES VARY BY SPECIES

☼ FULL SUN

◓ ◒ NATIVE TO RAINY-SUMMER CLIMATES

The white-barked European white birch has relatives that resemble it in graceful habit and small-scale, finely toothed leaves, but which vary in size and bark color. All birches need ample water at all times and a regular feeding program. All are susceptible to aphids that drip honeydew; for that reason, these are not trees for a patio or

Betula pendula

to park a car under. Bronze birch borer can be a problem in the northern Rocky Mountain states; leaf miners in Oregon. Generally too greedy for lawns. Poor tolerance of drought. On all birches small conelike fruit hangs on branches through the winter. ▶

B

B. albo-sinensis. Zones 1–11, 14–24. Western China. Tall tree (to 100 ft.) grown chiefly for beautiful pinkish brown to coppery bark covered with gray powdery bloom. Leaves 3 in. long. Variety *B. a. septentrionalis* has flaking bark that is orange to orange brown.

B. jacquemontii (B. utilis jacquemontii). Zones 3–11, 14–17. Northern India. Tall, narrow tree with brilliant white bark. Grows about 2 ft. a year to 40 ft., then more slowly to an eventual 60 ft. Seedlings vary in bark color; buy grafted trees.

B. maximowicziana. MONARCH BIRCH. Zones 3–9, 14–24. Native to Japan. Fast growing; open growth when young. Can reach 80–100 ft. Bark flaking, orange brown, eventually gray or white. Leaves large (up to 6 in. long), turning bright yellow in fall.

B. nigra. RIVER BIRCH, RED BIRCH. All zones. Native to eastern half of United States. Very fast growth in first years; eventually reaches 50–90 ft. Pyramidal form. Trunk often forks near ground, but tree can be trained to single stem. Young bark is pinkish, very smooth, and shiny. On older trees bark flakes and curls in cinnamon brown to blackish sheets. Diamond-shaped leaves, 1–3 in. long, are bright glossy green above, silvery below. Needs ample moisture. 'Heritage' is more erect, has tan bark.

B. occidentalis (B. fontinalis). Zones 1–3, 10. Large shrub or clumping small tree to 12–15 ft. Bark smooth, shiny, cinnamon brown. Leaves 2 in. long, turning pale clear yellow in fall. A native streamside tree, it likes moisture but needs good drainage as well.

B. papyrifera. CANOE BIRCH, PAPER BIRCH. Zones 1–6. Native to northern part of North America. Similar to *B. pendula* but taller (to 100 ft.), more open, less weeping. Trunk creamy white. Bark peels off in papery layers. Leaves are larger (to 4 in. long), more sparse.

B. pendula. EUROPEAN WHITE BIRCH. Zones 1–12, 14–24. Native from Europe to Asia Minor. Widely planted in western United States. Delicate and lacy. Upright branching with weeping side branches. Average mature tree 30–40 ft. high, spreading to half its height. Bark on twigs and young branches is golden brown. Bark on trunk and main limbs becomes white, marked with black clefts; oldest bark at base is blackish gray. Rich green, glossy leaves to 2½ in. long, diamond shaped, with slender tapered point. Often sold as weeping birch, although trees vary somewhat in habit and young trees show little inclination to weep.

European white birch has many uses. Its form and color are enhanced by dark background of pines. Dramatic when night-lighted. Lends itself to planting in grove formation, some single trees, some grouped. Trees of unequal sizes, planted with unequal spacing, suggest a natural setting. Trees grown in clumps of several trunks are available.

B. p. 'Dalecarlica' (B. p. 'Laciniata'). CUTLEAF WEEPING BIRCH. Leaves deeply cut. Branches strongly weeping; graceful open tree. Weeping forms are more affected by dry, hot weather than species. Foliage shows stress by late summer.

B. p. 'Fastigiata' (B. alba 'Fastigiata'). PYRAMIDAL WHITE BIRCH. Branches upright; habit somewhat like that of Lombardy poplar. Excellent screening tree.

B. p. 'Purpurea' (B. alba 'Purpurea'). PURPLE BIRCH. Twigs purple black. New foliage rich purple maroon, fading to purplish green in summer; striking effect against white bark. Best in cool to cold climates.

B. p. 'Trost's Dwarf'. True 3-ft.-by-3-ft. dwarf for bonsai, container, rock garden. Needs excellent drainage.

B. p. 'Youngii'. YOUNG'S WEEPING BIRCH. Slender branches hang straight down. Form like weeping mulberry's, but tree is more graceful. Decorative display tree. Trunk must be staked to desired height. Same climate limitations as that of *B. p.* 'Dalecarlica'.

B. platyphylla japonica. JAPANESE WHITE BIRCH. Zones 1–11, 14–24. Native to Japan. Fast growth to 40–50 ft.; narrow, open habit. Glossy green leaves to 3 in. long turn yellow in fall. Bark white.

Betulaceae. The birch family includes deciduous trees and shrubs with inconspicuous flowers in tight clusters (catkins). Representatives are alder, birch, filbert, and hornbeam.

Bignoniaceae. The bignonia family includes vines (mostly), trees, shrubs, and (rarely) perennials or annuals—all with trumpet-shaped, often two-lipped flowers. The family gets its name from the genus *Bignonia,* which once included most of the trumpet vines; though most of these have been reclassified, they are often still sold as *Bignonia.* Listed below are the older names, followed by the new:

B. chamberlaynii. See Anemopaegma chamberlaynii
B. cherere. See Distictis buccinatoria
B. chinensis. See Campsis grandiflora
B. jasminoides. See Pandorea jasminoides
B. radicans. See Campsis radicans
B. speciosa. See Clytostoma callistegioides
B. tweediana. See Macfadyena unguis-cati
B. venusta. See Pyrostegia venusta
B. violacea. See Clytostoma callistegioides

BILLBERGIA

Bromeliaceae

EVERGREEN PERENNIALS

🌡 ZONES 12, 13, 16–24; OR INDOORS

☼ FILTERED SHADE

💧 💧 AMPLE WATER DURING WARM WEATHER

Billbergia nutans

This pineapple relative is native to Brazil, where the plants grow as epiphytes on trees. Stiff, spiny-toothed leaves in basal clusters. Showy bracts and tubular flowers in drooping clusters. Usually grown in containers for display indoors or on patios. In Southern California, often grown under trees as an easy ground cover; in borders; or on limbs of trees or bark slabs, with roots wrapped in sphagnum moss and leaf mold. Excellent cut flowers.

Pot in light, porous mixture of sand, ground bark, or leaf mold. Need little water in winter, when growth is slow; large amounts during active growth in warm weather. Usually hold water in funnel-like center of leaf rosette, which acts as reservoir. When grown as house plants, give plenty of light and sun. Increase by cutting off suckers from base of plant. Specialists in bromeliads list dozens of varieties.

B. nutans. QUEEN'S TEARS. Most commonly grown. Spiny green leaves to 1½ ft. long. Long spikes of rosy red bracts; drooping flowers with green petals edged deep blue. Vigorous. Makes offsets freely; easy to grow and propagate.

B. pyramidalis. Leaves to 3 ft. long, 2½ in. wide, with spiny-toothed margins. Flowers with red, violet-tipped petals and bright red bracts in dense spikes 4 in. long.

B. sanderana. Leaves leathery, to 1 ft. long, spiny toothed, dotted with white. Loose, nodding, 10-in.-long clusters of flowers with blue petals, yellowish green at the base; blue-tipped sepals, rose-colored bracts.

BLACKBERRY

Rosaceae

BERRY-PRODUCING VINES

✄ ZONES VARY BY VARIETY

☼ FULL SUN

💧 WATER DURING GROWING SEASON

Blackberry

The West has its own special kinds of blackberries, most of which are trailing types, while midwestern and eastern blackberries are hardy, upright, and stiff caned. For ornamental relatives, see *Rubus*. The wild blackberry of the Pacific Northwest and Northern California has contributed its rich, sprightly flavor to several varieties. Each has its own pattern of climate adaptation. Leaves are divided fanwise, often with thorny stalks and midribs. All blackberries require deep soil, full sun, and ample water through the growing season.

Trailing types are best grown on some kind of trellis. Pruning must follow growth habit. Roots are perennial but canes are biennial, appearing and growing one year, flowering and fruiting the second. Where grown on trellis, train only 1-year-old canes on it, and in August, after harvest, remove all canes that have fruited (cut canes to the ground). The canes of the current season, those growing beneath the trellis, should now be trained onto it; thin out all but 12–16 canes and prune to 6–8 ft. These will produce side branches during remainder of growing season. Cut side branches back to 1 ft. In early spring, with new spring growth, small branches grow from the side branches. These bear fruit. Thin out semi-upright varieties to four to eight canes, prune at 5–6 ft., and spread fanwise on trellis. Upright varieties need no trellis but are easier to handle when tied to a wire about 2½ ft. above ground. Select three or four canes and tip them at 2½–3 ft. to force side growth. Tie where canes cross wire.

To control red-berry mite (mostly affecting the 'Himalaya' and 'Evergreen' varieties), spider mites, and whitefly, spray in winter and again as buds are about to break, with a dormant spray containing lime sulfur. Spray with malathion as leaves unfold and again a month later.

Fertilize established plantings with commercial fertilizer according to manufacturer's label. In Northwest, feed at blossom time. Best results in California if you split yearly amount into three applications: before new growth starts, again in midspring, and again in midsummer. Keep down weeds. Pull out suckers. Above all, don't let plants get away from you.

These varieties are available in western nurseries (all are trailing types except where noted otherwise):

'Boysen' and 'Thornless Boysen'. All zones; not reliably hardy in Zone 1 but come through winter if canes are left on ground and covered with snow or with straw mulch. Popular for high yield and flavor—eaten fresh, cooked, or frozen. Berries are reddish, large (1¼ in. long, 1 in. thick), soft, sweet-tart; have a delightful aroma. Berries carry dusty bloom, are not shiny.

'Cascade'. Best in Zones 4–6, 16, 17. Some grown Zones 20–24. Not adapted in Zones 10–13. Not reliably hardy in Zones 1–3. Berries bright, deep red, almost black (red when cooked), about 1 in. long, ½ in. thick, with classic wild blackberry flavor. Tender and very juicy; a poor shipper but an excellent garden variety.

'Evergreen' and 'Thornless Evergreen'. This is the commercial blackberry in Zones 4–6. Not reliably hardy in Zones 1–3. Grown in Zones 15–17 where quantity is important. Strong canes, semierect growth. Bushes vigorous with heavy crops of large (1½-in.-long, ¾-in.-thick), exceptionally firm, black, sweet berries. Seeds large.

'Himalaya'. Grown in Zones 14–17 for long harvest season—mid-July to October. Seldom sold but has escaped and grows wild wherever adapted. Can be prodigious, spreading pest. Extremely vigorous, semierect canes grow 20–30 ft. in one season. Berries shiny jet black, medium size (1 in. long, ¾ in. thick). Seeds medium large.

'Logan' and 'Thornless Logan'. Same climate adaptation as 'Boysen'. Berries (1¼ in. long, ¾ in. thick) are light reddish, not darkening when ripe, with fine hairs that dull color. Flavor tarter than 'Boysen'; excellent for canning and pies.

'Marion'. Zones 7–9, 14–24. Similar to 'Olallie' in berry size and quality but better adapted in Zones 4–6. Climate adaptation same as 'Cascade'.

'Nectar'. Identical to 'Boysen'.

'Olallie'. Zones 7–9, 14–24. Better adapted in California than in its Oregon homeland. Berries large (1½ in. long, ¾ in. thick), shiny black, firm, sweeter than 'Cascade' but with some wild blackberry sprightliness.

'Smoothstem'. Zones 4–9, 14–17. Semierect canes 8–10 ft. long. Fruit large, blunt, jet black. Productive; poor shipper but good home variety. Thornless.

'Tay' or 'Tayberry'. Zones 4–9, 14–17. Hybrid between blackberry and raspberry. Long, trailing, thorny vines. Heavy bearer of mild-flavored, dark red to purple-black, 1½-in. fruit. Bears earlier than other blackberries.

'Thornfree'. Zones 4–9, 14–17. Semierect thornless canes 7–8 ft. long. Tart, shiny black berries are medium large. Heavy bearing.

'Young' and 'Thornless Young'. Climate adaptation similar to 'Boysen' but not as productive in all climates. Berry same size and color as 'Boysen' but shiny and somewhat sweeter.

BLECHNUM (Lomaria)

Polypodiaceae

EVERGREEN FERNS

✄ ZONES VARY BY SPECIES

● MOIST, SHADY LOCATIONS

💧 REGULAR WATER

Blechnum spicant

These ferns are noted for their symmetrical, formal appearance. Emerging fronds are often reddish or brown.

B. brasiliense. Zones 19, 21–24. Dwarf tree fern reaching only 4 ft. in height. Nearly erect fronds in compact clusters. Variety 'Crispum' has elegantly ruffled fronds, reddish when young.

B. gibbum. Zones 19, 21–24. Dwarf tree fern with wide-spreading crown of fronds atop slender trunk eventually 3 ft. high. 'Moorei' has wider, more leathery leaflets; is more attractive in winter. Avoid overhead water.

B. penna-marina. Zones 15–17, 20–24; with protection, Zones 4–6. Spreads slowly to make patches of refined 4–8-in. fronds in cool, moist, sheltered places; can be used as house plant.

B. spicant. DEER FERN, DEER TONGUE FERN. Zones 1–9, 14–17. Native to Northern California and Northwest. Produces fronds of two kinds. Sterile fronds are narrow, dark glossy green, spreading or angled, 1–3 ft. tall; fertile fronds are stiffly erect, very narrow, with narrow, widely spaced leaflets. Deep shade, moisture, woodsy soil.

BLEEDING HEART. See DICENTRA   **p. 262**

BLETILLA striata
(B. hyacinthina)

CHINESE GROUND ORCHID

Orchidaceae

TERRESTRIAL ORCHID

☘ ZONES 4–9, 12–24

☼ UNDER HIGH-BRANCHING TREES OR LATH

💧 FREQUENT WATER DURING GROWTH

Bletilla striata

A terrestrial orchid native to China and Japan. Lavender, cattleya-like, 1–2-in. flowers, up to a dozen on 1½–2-ft. stem, produced for about 6 weeks beginning in May or June. Pale green, plaited leaves, 3–6 to a plant. *B. s.* 'Alba' is a white-flowered form.

Plant the tuberlike roots outdoors in early spring in all but coldest areas of West for spring and early summer bloom. Hardy to about 20°F (to 10°F if roots are protected). Dies back to ground each winter. Mulch with straw in cold climates. In time will develop large clumps if grown in light shade and in a moist soil rich in humus. Can be divided in early spring before growth starts, but don't do it too often; blooms best when crowded. Plant in pot or in ground under high-branching trees or under lath.

BLOODLEAF. See IRESINE herbstii	**p. 332**
BLOOD LILY. See HAEMANTHUS katherinae	**p. 315**
BLOOD-RED TRUMPET VINE. See DISTICTIS buccinatoria	**p. 265**
BLOODROOT. See SANGUINARIA canadensis	**p. 473**
BLUEBEARD. See CARYOPTERIS	**p. 209**
BLUEBELL. See ENDYMION, SCILLA	**pp. 272, 480**

BLUEBERRY

Ericaceae

DECIDUOUS SHRUB

☘ ZONES 4–6, 17; WITH CARE, 2, 3, 7–9, 14–16

☼ FULL SUN

💧 FREQUENT WATER

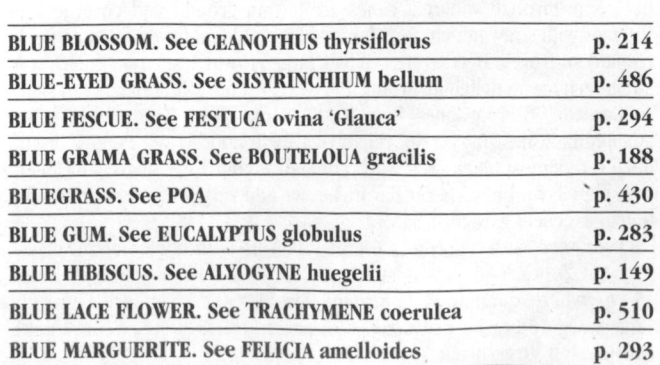

Blueberry

Native to eastern United States. For ornamental relatives, see *Vaccinium*. Thrive under conditions that suit rhododendrons and azaleas, to which they are related. Need sun and cool, moist, acid soil that drains well. In the "special-care" zones listed above, either create acid soil conditions or grow plants in straight peat moss or ground bark.

Blueberries contribute more than fruit to garden: they are handsome plants for hedge or shrub border. Most varieties grow upright to 6 ft. or more; a few are rather sprawling and under 5 ft. Leaves, to 3 in. long, are bronze when new, then dark green, turning scarlet or yellow in fall. Spring flowers tiny, white to pinkish, urn shaped. Fruit very decorative in summer. Plant 3 ft. apart as informal hedge; in larger plantings, as shrubs, space 4–5 ft. apart. Commercial growers allow 6–8 ft. or even more between plants.

Plant two varieties for better pollination. Shallow roots benefit from 4–6-in.-thick mulch of sawdust, ground bark, or the like. Water frequently. Use acid-forming fertilizers. In California you may need to use iron sulfate or iron chelate to correct chlorosis.

Prune to prevent overbearing. Plants shape themselves but often produce so many fruit buds that fruit is undersize and growth of plants slows down. Keep first-year plants from bearing by stripping off flowers. On older plants, cut back ends of twigs to point where fruit buds are widely spaced. Or simply remove some of oldest branches each year. Remove all weak shoots.

The following varieties have proved themselves in home gardens. Choose for long harvest season. Plant at least two for each season ("early" means ripening early to mid-June; "midseason" means early to mid-July; "late" means late July into August). Allow two plants for each member of your family. Although all varieties are sold in Northwest and Northern California, growers especially recommend these for California: 'Berkeley', 'Bluecrop', 'Dixi', 'Earliblue', 'Jersey'.

'Atlantic'. Late. Sprawling habit. Large light blue berries.

'Berkeley'. Midseason to late. Open, spreading, tall. Large light berries.

'Bluecrop'. Midseason. Erect, tall growth. Large berries. Excellent flavor. Attractive shrub.

'Blueray'. Midseason. Vigorous, tall. Large, highly flavored, crisp berries. Attractive shrub.

'Collins'. Early to midseason. Erect, attractive bush. Small clusters of large, very tasty fruit.

'Concord'. Midseason. Upright to spreading growth. Attractive. Large berry, tart flavored until fully ripe.

'Coville'. Late. Tall, open, spreading. Unusually large leaves. Very attractive. Long clusters of very large light blue berries.

'Dixi'. Late. Not attractive plant—tall and open. Needs heavy pruning. Berries, among largest and tastiest, are medium blue, firm and sweet.

'Earliblue'. Early to midseason. Tall, erect. Large, heavy leaves. Large berries of excellent flavor.

'Ivanhoe'. Early to midseason. Large dark berries—firm, crisp, tart.

'Jersey'. Midseason to late. Tall, erect growing. Large light blue berries. Very bland. Yellow fall and winter color.

'Pemberton'. Very vigorous, tall. Berries large, dark blue, of good dessert quality.

'Rancocas'. Early to midseason. Tall, erect, open, arching habit. Excellent shrub. Leaves smaller than most. Needs heavy pruning. Berries mild and sweet. Dependable old-timer.

'Rubel'. Early to late. Erect, tall growth. Berries firm and tart. Needs pruning to produce large berries.

'Stanley'. Early to midseason. Erect, medium tall. Attractive foliage. One of tastiest—firm, aromatic berries with spicy flavor.

'Weymouth'. Very early. Ripens all berries quickly. Erect, medium height. Large dark blue berries of fair quality; lack aroma.

Dwarf varieties include 'Northblue' (3 ft.), 'North Country' (2 ft.), and 'Northsky' (1½ ft.); all are extremely hardy.

A BLUEBERRY FOR MILD CLIMATES AND CONTAINERS

Rabbiteye blueberries are selections of *Vaccinium ashei*, a native of the Southeast, and they can be grown in Southern California. Unlike most blueberries, these tolerate heat, but they do have the same need for acid soil. 'Sharpblue', bearing in April or May, is the only self-fertile kind; others need cross-pollination. 'Bluebelle', 'Southland', and 'Tifblue' ripen in May and June.

BLUE BLOSSOM. See CEANOTHUS thyrsiflorus	**p. 214**
BLUE-EYED GRASS. See SISYRINCHIUM bellum	**p. 486**
BLUE FESCUE. See FESTUCA ovina 'Glauca'	**p. 294**
BLUE GRAMA GRASS. See BOUTELOUA gracilis	**p. 188**
BLUEGRASS. See POA	**p. 430**
BLUE GUM. See EUCALYPTUS globulus	**p. 283**
BLUE HIBISCUS. See ALYOGYNE huegelii	**p. 149**
BLUE LACE FLOWER. See TRACHYMENE coerulea	**p. 510**
BLUE MARGUERITE. See FELICIA amelloides	**p. 293**

BOLTONIA asteroides

Asteraceae (Compositae)

PERENNIAL

☀ ALL ZONES

☀ ◑ FULL SUN OR LIGHT SHADE

◐ REGULAR WATER

Boltonia asteroides

Tall stems bear broad, mounded clusters of small white to blue flowers that much resemble Michaelmas daisies *(Aster)*. With adequate water plants can reach 6 ft. or more. The variety 'Snowbank' is somewhat more compact (5 ft.), and has larger flowers of a clearer white. In poor soil and with reduced water plants survive but may bloom feebly on 2-ft. stems.

Bombacaceae. This tropical family of trees and shrubs contains one genus grown in the mild-winter West: *Chorisia*. Both species of *Chorisia* have showy flowers.

Boraginaceae. The borage family consists of annuals and perennials (rarely shrubs or trees), most of which have small flowers in coiled clusters that straighten as bloom progresses. Forget-me-not *(Myosotis)* is a familiar example.

BORAGO officinalis

BORAGE

Boraginaceae

ANNUAL HERB

☀ ALL ZONES

☀ ◑ ◐ SUN OR SHADE

◐◐ WATER TO PRODUCE LEAVES FOR HARVEST

Borago officinalis

Grows 1–3 ft. high. Bristly, gray-green leaves up to 4–6 in. long are edible, with a cucumberlike flavor. Blue, saucer-shaped, nodding flowers in leafy clusters on branched stems.

Tolerates poor soil. Grows large, needs lots of room. Seeds itself freely but doesn't transplant easily. Good no-watering ground cover and soil binder. Use small tender leaves in salads; you can also pickle them or cook them as greens. Cut flowers for arrangements or use as an attractive garnish.

BORONIA

Rutaceae

EVERGREEN SHRUBS

☀ ZONES VARY BY SPECIES

☀ ◑ SUN OR LIGHT SHADE

◐ FUSSY ABOUT TOO MUCH OR TOO LITTLE WATER

Boronia megastigma

Small shrubs from Australia. Finely divided leaves with needlelike leaflets give plants a wispy look. Attractive but relatively short lived. They need well-drained, slightly acid, sandy or

light loamy soil, and careful watering; they can never completely dry or stay wet at root for any length of time and survive.

B. crenulata. Zones 16–24. Compact shrub 2–3 ft. tall, 3–4 ft. wide, with tiny dark green leaves and small pink flowers over a long season. Regular water.

B. heterophylla. RED BORONIA. Zones 16–24. Dense grower to 6–8 ft., with finely cut foliage and a heavy showing of deep pink flowers opening from red buds. Flowers are intensely fragrant and last well when cut. Regular water.

B. megastigma. BROWN BORONIA. Zones 15–17, 20–24. Only 1–2 ft. tall, with nodding, ½-in., bell-shaped flowers, brown lined with yellow. Powerful, pleasant scent combines freesia, orange blossom, and other fragrances; blooms February–March. Count on replacing it every 2 or 3 years from seed or cuttings. Will last longer if grown in light potting mix in containers.

B. molloyae (B. elatior). PINK BORONIA, TALL BORONIA. Zones 15–17. Grows to 4–6 ft. Clouds of ¼-in., bell-shaped, pink to rose flowers in spring. Cut back severely after flowering.

BOUGAINVILLEA

Nyctaginaceae

EVERGREEN SHRUBBY VINES

☀ ZONES 22–24; SEE BELOW FOR USE IN FROST ZONES

☀ ◑ FULL SUN, LIGHT SHADE IN HOTTEST AREAS

◐ LITTLE WATER ONCE ESTABLISHED

Bougainvillea 'San Diego Red'

Reliably hardy in nearest we have to tropical climate (Zones 22–24), yet widely and satisfyingly grown in zones of minimum frost: 12, 13, 15–17, 19, 21. Use has even extended into Zones 5 and 6 of Northwest, thanks to low-growing shrubby types that can be purchased in full bloom in gallon cans and grown as container plants. They are used on terrace or patio as summer annual and moved into protected area over winter. Where frosts are routine, vines should be given protected warm wall or warmest spot in garden. If vines get by first winter or two they will be big enough to take most winter damage and recover. In any case, flower production comes so quickly that replacement is not a real deterrent.

PLANTING A BOUGAINVILLEA?

Watch those roots—they're fragile and do not knit easily. Here is how to keep the root ball intact during planting. Put the plant in an extra-wide planting hole, can and all. Insert blades of sharp, needle-nose shears into one of the drain holes and cut all the way around the can's bottom. Slide the detached bottom out from under the can. Then, make a cut down one side of can from the top to bottom. Make another cut on the opposite side. Fill in with soil around the root ball. Slide the two detached pieces up and out.

Bougainvillea's vibrant colors come not from its small inconspicuous flowers, but from the three large bracts that surround them. Vines make dense cover of medium-size, medium green leaves. Vigor and growth habit vary by species and variety. Plant in sun (in light shade in hottest areas) in early spring (after frosts), to give longest possible growing time before next frost.

Supply sturdy supports and keep shoots tied up so they won't whip in wind and strong gusts won't shred leaves against sharp thorns along stems.

Fertilize in spring and summer. Water normally while plants are growing fast; then ease off temporarily in midsummer to promote better flowering. Don't be afraid to prune—to renew plant, shape, or direct growth. Prune heavily in spring after frost. On wall-grown plants, nip back long stems during growing season to produce more flowering wood. Shrubby kinds or heavily pruned plants make good self-supporting container shrubs for terrace or patio. Without support and with occasional corrective pruning, bougainvillea can make broad, sprawling shrub, bank and ground cover, or hanging basket plant.

Double-flowering kinds can look messy because they hold faded flowers for a long time.

All of the following are tall-growing vines except those noted as shrubs.

'Afterglow'. Yellow orange; heavy bloom. Open growth, sparse foliage.

'Barbara Karst'. Bright red in sun, bluish crimson in shade; blooms young and for long period. Vigorous growth. Likes heat of desert. Fast comeback after frost.

'Betty Hendry' ('Indian Maid'). Basically red but with touches of yellow and purple. Blooms young and for a long period.

B. brasiliensis. See B. spectabilis

'Brilliant Variegated'. Spreading, mounding shrub. Leaves variegated with gray green and silver. Brick red flowers. Often used in hanging baskets, pots.

'California Gold' ('Sunset'). Close to pale yellow. Blooms young.

'Camarillo Festival'. Hot pink to gold blend.

'Cherry Blossom'. Double-flowered rose pink, with white to pale green centers.

'Crimson Jewel'. Vigorous shrubby, sprawling plant. Good in containers, as shrub, or as sunny bank cover. Lower growth, better color than 'Temple Fire'. Heavy bloom, long season.

'Crimson Lake'. See 'Mrs. Butt'

'Don Mario'. Large, vigorous vine with huge clusters of deep purple red blooms.

'Hawaii'. ('Raspberry Ice'). Shrubby, mounding, spreading. Leaves have golden yellow margins. New leaves tinged red. Flowers red. Good hanging basket plant. Regardless of its tropical name, it's one of the hardiest.

'Isabel Greensmith'. Flowers variously described as orange, red orange, or red with yellow tinting.

'Jamaica White'. Bracts white, veined light green. Blooms young. Moderately vigorous.

'James Walker'. Big reddish purple flowers on big vine.

'La Jolla'. Bright red bracts, compact, shrubby habit. Good shrub, container plant.

'Lavender Queen'. An improved *B. spectabilis,* with bigger bracts, heavier bloom.

'Manila Red'. Many rows of magenta red bracts make heavy clusters of double-looking bloom.

'Mary Palmer's Enchantment'. Very vigorous, large-growing vine with pure white bracts.

'Mrs. Butt' ('Crimson Lake'). Old-fashioned variety with good crimson color. Needs lots of heat for bloom. Moderately vigorous.

'Orange King'. Bronzy orange. Open growth. Needs long summer, no frost.

'Pink Tiara'. Abundant pale pink to rose flowers over long season.

'Raspberry Ice'. See 'Hawaii'

'Rosea'. Large rose red bracts on large vine.

'Rosenka'. Can be held to shrub proportions if occasional wild shoot is pruned out. Gold flowers age pink.

'San Diego Red' ('San Diego', 'Scarlett O'Hara'). One of best on all counts: large, deep green leaves that hold well in cold winters; deep red bracts over long season; hardiness equal to old-fashioned purple kind. Vigorous, high climbing. Can be trained to tree form by staking and pruning.

'Southern Rose'. Lavender rose to pink.

B. spectabilis (B. brasiliensis). Hardy and vigorous. Blooms well in cool summers. Purple flowers. Best for Zones 16, 17.

'Tahitian Dawn'. Big vine with gold bracts aging to rosy purple.

'Tahitian Maid'. Extra rows of bracts give double effect to blush pink clusters.

'Temple Fire'. Shrublike growth to 4 ft. high, 6 ft. wide. Partially deciduous. Bronze red.

'Texas Dawn'. Choice, vigorous pink. Purplish pink bracts in large sprays.

'Torch Glow'. An oddity: an erect, multistemmed plant to 6 ft. It needs no support. Reddish pink flowers close to stems are partially hidden by foliage.

'White Madonna'. Pure white bracts.

BOULDER RASPBERRY. See RUBUS deliciosus	**p. 469**
BOUSSINGAULTIA. See ANREDERA cordifolia	**p. 153**

BOUTELOUA gracilis

BLUE GRAMA GRASS

Poaceae (Gramineae)

BUNCHING GRASS

⚡ ZONES 1–3

☼ FULL SUN

💧 VERY LITTLE WATER

Bouteloua gracilis

Pasture grass used for low-maintenance, low-water-use lawns in sunny, arid, alkaline regions of Rocky Mountains and high plains. Hardy throughout this area. Bunching rather than sod forming, it nevertheless makes fair lawn if sown at 1 lb. per 1,000 sq. ft. Sow in fall to take advantage of winter rain, snow. Water to depth of 1 ft. while it is becoming established; thereafter it can get along with virtually no irrigation. Mow at 1½ in.

BOUVARDIA

Rubiaceae

EVERGREEN SHRUBS

⚡ ZONES VARY BY SPECIES

◐ PARTIAL SHADE

💧 WATER NEEDS VARY BY SPECIES

Bouvardia longiflora

Native to Arizona, New Mexico, Mexico, and Central America. Loose, often straggling growth habit. Showy clusters of tubular flowers; *B. longiflora* 'Albatross' has fragrant blossoms but is also the most tender and looks poorest after flowers are gone. The nonfragrant red-flowered types are hardier, easier to grow.

B. glaberrima. Zones 8–10, 12–24. Native to mountain canyons in southern Arizona, New Mexico. To 3 ft. tall, shrubby but dying back at tops in cold weather. Smooth green leaves 1–3 in. long. Clustered inch-long, tubular, red (rarely pink or white) flowers. Tolerates aridity.

> ### GOOD IN BOUQUETS, SMELLS LIKE JASMINE
> Cutting the flowering stems of a *Bouvardia longiflora* helps stimulate new growth—the more you cut, the more new stems the plant is inclined to produce. Make the cuts right above a leaf, or cut entire stems back to their bases. White flowers are attractive in bouquets.

B. longiflora 'Albatross' (B. humboldtii 'Albatross'). Zones 12, 13, 16, 17, 19–24. Fragrant, snow white, 3-in.-long, tubular flowers in loose clusters on a weak-stemmed shrub, 2–3 ft. high with paired 2-in. leaves. Blossoms appear at almost any time. Pinch out stem tips to make bushier. Grow in tubs or boxes in rich, fast-draining soil mix. Ample water. The variety 'Stephanie' is more compact and floriferous.

B. ternifolia (B. jacquinii). Zones 8–10, 12–24. A 6-ft.-tall shrub with 2-in. leaves in whorls of three or four. Red, 1-in.-long, tubular flowers in loose clusters at ends of branches. Selected forms are pink, rose, coral, red. Tolerates aridity.

BRACHYCHITON (Sterculia)

Sterculiaceae

EVERGREEN TO PARTLY OR WHOLLY DECIDUOUS TREES

ZONES VARY BY SPECIES

FULL SUN

NO WATER ONCE ESTABLISHED

Native to Australia. All have woody, canoe-shaped fruits that delight flower arrangers but are merely litter to some gardeners.

B. acerifolius (Sterculia acerifolia). FLAME TREE, AUSTRALIAN FLAME TREE. Deciduous for brief period. Zones 16–21, 23. When at its best, a most spectacular red-flowering tree reaching 60 ft. or more. Hardy to 25°F. Strong, heavy, smooth trunk, usually green. Leaves are handsome, glossy, bright green, 10-in.-wide fans, deeply lobed. Showiest flowering season usually May to June. Tree wholly or partially covered with great clusters of small, ³/₄-in., tubular, red or orange-red bells. Leaves drop before flowers appear in portion of tree that blooms.

Brachychiton populneus

B. populneus (Sterculia diversifolia). BOTTLE TREE. Evergreen. Zones 12–24. Moderate growth to 30–50 ft., 30-ft. spread. Common name from very heavy trunk, broad at base, tapering quickly. Leaves (2–3 in. long), a fresh green year-round, give general effect of poplar. They shimmer in breeze like aspens. Clusters of small, bell-shaped, white flowers in May and June noticeable close up; 2¹/₂–3-in. woody fruits that follow are noticeable in litter they produce. Appreciated in low and intermediate deserts, where it is frequently used as a shade tree and as a screen or high, wide windbreak. Susceptible to Texas root rot.

BRACHYCOME

SWAN RIVER DAISY

Asteraceae (Compositae)

ANNUALS AND PERENNIALS

ZONES VARY BY SPECIES

FULL SUN

REGULAR WATER

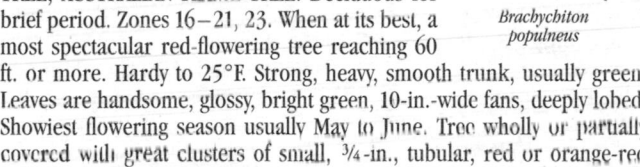

Brachycome iberidifolia

Neat, charming Australian daisies make mounds 1 ft. tall, 1¹/₂ ft. across, with finely divided leaves and a profusion of inch-wide daisies in spring and summer. Use in rock garden, at front of border, in containers or raised beds.

B. iberidifolia. Annual. All zones. Flowers are blue, white, or pink. Sow seed where plants are to grow.

B. multifida. Perennial. Zones 14–24. Very similar to *B. iberidifolia* but perennial. Blue most common color. Propagate by cuttings.

Many similar species and varieties may be encountered in various shades of blue or pink.

BRACHYSEMA lanceolatum

SCIMITAR SHRUB, SWAN RIVER PEA SHRUB

Fabaceae (Leguminosae)

EVERGREEN SHRUB

ZONES 8, 9, 12–24

FULL SUN

LITTLE WATER ONCE ESTABLISHED

Brachysema lanceolatum

Unusual flowers have earned it its common names and place in gardens. Blooms are bright red and shaped like sweet peas, but with inch-long pairs of petals (keels) shaped like scimitars. Never makes great show of flowers, but it's rarely out of bloom. To 3 ft. or more, loosely formed, erect in growth, spreading in age. Leaves narrow, to 4 in. long, dark green above, silvery beneath. Prune by thinning out old, straggly stems. Best with fast drainage, in sandy soil. Don't pamper; go light with fertilizers.

BRAHEA (Erythea)

Arecaceae (Palmae)

PALMS

ZONES VARY BY SPECIES

FULL SUN

NO WATER ONCE ESTABLISHED

Brahea armata

These fan palms from Mexico are somewhat like the more familiar washingtonias in appearance, but with important differences. All tolerate aridity.

B. armata. MEXICAN BLUE PALM. Zones 10, 12–17, 19–24. Grows slowly to 40 ft., top spreading 6–8 ft. Leaves silvery blue, almost white. Conspicuous creamy flowers. Hardy to 18°F and takes heat and wind.

B. brandegeei. SAN JOSE HESPER PALM. Zones 19, 21–24. Slow grower with slender, flexible trunk. Eventually tall; reaches 125 ft. in its native Baja California. Trunk sheds leaves when old. Three leaves 3 ft. long are light gray green. Hardy to 26°F.

B. edulis. GUADALUPE PALM. Zones 12–24. From Guadalupe Island off Baja California. Like *B. armata* but leaves are light green; flowers less conspicuous. Slow grower to 30 ft., stout trunked. Old leaves drop, leaving the naked, elephant-hide trunk ringed with scars. Hardy to below 20°F; takes beach and desert conditions.

B. elegans. FRANCESCHI PALM. Zones 13–17, 19–24. Slowest growing of braheas; develops a trunk very slowly and reaches only 15 ft. Leaves gray green. From northern Mexico; hardy to 22°F.

Brassicaceae. The mustard or cress family contains many food plants and ornamentals as well as a number of weeds. The notable characteristic is a 4-petaled flower resembling cross. Familiar members include all the cabbage group, radishes, turnips, stocks, and sweet alyssum (*Lobularia*). This family was formerly called Cruciferae.

B

BRIMEURA amethystina (Hyacinthus amethystinus)

Liliaceae

BULB

✔ ALL ZONES

☼ FULL SUN

◊ NO WATER ONCE ESTABLISHED

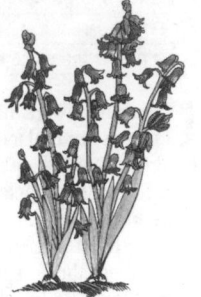

Brimeura amethystina

Bulbs, leaf rosettes exactly resemble small hyacinths. For rock gardens or naturalizing. Plants bloom in spring, bearing loose spikes of clear blue bells with paler blue streaks on 6–8-in.-tall stems. Plant in mid- to late autumn, 2 in. deep, 3 in. apart. Mulch in areas where winters are very cold.

BRIZA maxima

RATTLESNAKE GRASS, QUAKING GRASS

Poaceae (Gramineae)

ANNUAL

✔ ALL ZONES

☼ FULL SUN

◊ NO WATER ONCE ESTABLISHED

Briza maxima

Native to Mediterranean region. Ornamental grass of delicate, graceful form; used effectively in dry arrangements and bouquets. Grows 1–2 ft. high. Leaves are ¼ in. wide, to 6 in. long. Clusters of nodding, seed-bearing spikelets, ½ in. long (or longer), papery and straw colored when dry, dangle on threadlike stems. Spikelets resemble rattlesnake rattles. Scatter seed where plants are to grow; thin seedlings to 1 ft. apart. Often grows wild along roadsides, in fields. *B. media* is similar but perennial.

BROCCOLI

Brassicaceae (Cruciferae)

BIENNIALS GROWN AS ANNUALS

✔ ALL ZONES

☼ FULL SUN

● REGULAR WATER

Broccoli

Among cole crops (cabbage and its close relatives) best all-round for home gardener; bears over long season, is not difficult to grow. Grows to 4 ft. and has branching habit. Central stalk bears cluster of green flower buds that may reach 6 in. in diameter. When central cluster is removed, side branches will lengthen and produce smaller clusters. Good varieties are 'Calabrese', 'Cleopatra', 'De Cicco', 'Italian Green Sprouting'.

Broccoli is a cool-season plant that tends to bolt into flower when temperatures are high, so plant it to mature during cool weather. In mild climates plant in late summer, fall, or winter for winter or early spring crops. In cold-winter areas set out young plants about 2 weeks before last frost.

Young plants resist frost but not hard freezes. Good guide to planting time is appearance of young plants in nurseries. Young plants ready to be planted take 4–6 weeks to develop from seed. One pack of seed will produce far more plants than even the largest home garden can handle, so save surplus seed for later plantings. A dozen plants will supply a family.

Choose a sunny location; space plants 1½–2 ft. apart in rows and leave 3 ft. between rows. Keep plants growing vigorously with regular deep irrigation and one to two feedings of commercial fertilizer before heads start to form. Cut heads before clustered buds begin to open. Include 5–6 in. of edible stalk and leaves. Watch for and control aphids and cabbage worm.

BRODIAEA

Liliaceae

CORMS

✔ ALL ZONES

☼ FULL SUN

◊ NO WATER ONCE ESTABLISHED

Brodiaea elegans

Many are natives of the Pacific Coast, where they bloom in sunny fields and meadows in spring and early summer. Few grasslike leaves; a cluster of funnel-shaped or tubular, ½–2-in.-long flowers tops the stem. In nature they are often found in adobe soil, in areas where it rains heavily in winter and early spring and corms completely dry out in summer. In gardens give similar conditions (no dry-season watering). Where plants must take summer watering, plant in sandy or gritty soil. Plant corms 2–3 in. deep. In cold-winter areas grow in containers or mulch to protect from freezing and thawing.

Brodiaea includes many plants now listed under different names. Cross-references below will guide you to appropriate entries under *Dichelostemma* and *Triteleia*.

B. capitata. See Dichelostemma pulchellum

B. coronaria (B. grandiflora). HARVEST BRODIAEA. Clusters of dark blue, inch-long flowers on 6–10-in. stems. Late spring, early summer bloom.

B. elegans. HARVEST BRODIAEA. Similar to B. *coronaria*, but taller (to 16 in.). Often seen as *B. grandiflora* or *B. coronaria*.

B. grandiflora. See B. coronaria. Another plant known by same name is *Triteleia grandiflora*.

B. hyacinthina. See Triteleia hyacinthina

B. ida-maia. See Dichelostemma ida-maia

B. ixioides. See Triteleia ixioides

B. lactea. See Triteleia hyacinthina

B. laxa. See Triteleia laxa

B. lutea. See Triteleia ixioides

B. minor. Dark blue flowers on stems that may be 3–4 in. long, rarely 1 ft. long.

B. 'Queen Fabiola'. See Triteleia 'Queen Fabiola'

B. tubergenii. See Triteleia tubergenii

B. uniflora. See Ipheion uniflorum

BROMELIA balansae

HEART OF FLAME

Bromeliaceae

PERENNIAL

✔ ZONES 19–24

☼ FULL SUN

● REGULAR WATER

Bromelia balansae

Pineapple relative. Forms impressive cluster of 30–50 arching, saw-toothed leaves, glossy dark green above, whitish beneath. To 4 ft. tall, 4–6 ft. across. Center leaves turn bright scarlet in spring or early summer. From this center rises a stalk bearing a spike of rose-colored flowers margined with white. Needs warm nights to perform satisfactorily. Almost any soil if drainage is good. Feed lightly once or twice in summer.

Bromeliaceae. The bromelia, or pineapple, family; all its members are called bromeliads. Most bromeliads are stemless perennials with clustered leaves and showy flowers in unbranched or branched clusters. Leaves of many kinds are handsomely marked, and the flower clusters gain beauty from colorful bracts. Pineapple, the best-known example, is sometimes grown as a house plant.

In most areas of the West, bromeliads are considered choice house plants. Kinds most often grown indoors are, in their native homes, epiphytes: plants that perch on trees or rocks and gain their sustenance from rain and from whatever leaf mold gathers around their roots. These often have cupped leaf bases that hold water between rains. In mildest areas of the West, many of these epiphytes grow well outdoors in sheltered places.

A few bromeliads (*Puya* is the best known) are desert plants that resemble yuccas and thrive in the same conditions.

FASTEN A BROMELIAD TO A TREE BRANCH
In Zones 15–17, 19–24, bromeliad fanciers sometimes fasten these vibrant, junglelike plants to tree branches, packing sphagnum moss around the roots to hold moisture and encourage root growth. More often these plants are kept in pots of loose, fast-draining, highly organic growing mix. Feed lightly but infrequently and keep central cups filled with water.

BRONZE DRACAENA. See CORDYLINE australis 'Atropurpurea' p. 240

BROOM. See CYTISUS, GENISTA,
SPARTIUM junceum   pp. 256, 304, 490

BROUSSONETIA papyrifera

PAPER MULBERRY
Moraceae
DECIDUOUS TREE
☘ ZONES 3–24
☼ FULL SUN
◯ NO WATER ONCE ESTABLISHED

Broussonetia papyrifera

Valuable as shade tree where soil and climate limit choice. Takes stony, sterile, or alkaline soils, strong winds, desert heat. Hardy in all but coldest areas. Moderate growth to 50 ft., with dense, broad crown to 40 ft. across. Smooth, gray bark. Heart-shaped, 4–8-in., rough leaves, gray and velvety beneath; edges toothed, often lobed when young. Male flowers, catkins; female, rounded heads. Suckering habit can be problem in highly cultivated gardens. Seldom suckers in desert. Good in rough bank plantings. Common name comes from inner bark, used for making paper and Polynesian tapa cloth. Has been sold as *Morus papyrifera*.

BROWALLIA

AMETHYST FLOWER
Solanaceae
ANNUALS, SOMETIMES LIVING OVER AS PERENNIALS
☘ ALL ZONES
☼ WARM SHADE OR FILTERED SUNLIGHT
● REGULAR WATER

Browallia speciosa

Choice plant for connoisseur of blue flowers. Bears one-sided clusters of lobelia-like blooms ½–2 in. long and just as wide in brilliant blue, violet, or white; blue flowers are more striking because of contrasting

white eye or throat. Blooms profusely in warm shade or filtered sunlight. Graceful in hanging basket or pots. Fine cut flower.

Sow seeds in early spring for summer bloom, in fall for winter color indoors or in greenhouses. Plants need warmth, regular moisture. You can lift vigorous plants in fall, cut back, and pot; new growth will produce flowers through winter in warm spot. Rarely sold as plants in nurseries; get seeds from specialists.

B. americana. Branching, 1–2 ft. high; roundish leaves. Violet or blue flowers ½ in. long, ½ in. across, borne among leaves. 'Sapphire', dwarf compact variety, dark blue with white eye, is very free blooming. This species and its variety is often listed in catalogs as *B. elata* and *B. elata* 'Sapphire'.

B. speciosa. Lives over as perennial in mild-winter climates. Sprawling, to 1–2 ft. high. Flowers dark purple above, pale lilac beneath, 1½–2 in. across. 'Blue Bells Improved', lavender blue, grows 10 in. tall, needs no pinching to make it branch. 'Marine Bells' has deep indigo flowers, 'Silver Bells' white flowers.

BRUGMANSIA (Datura)

ANGEL'S TRUMPET
Solanaceae
EVERGREEN SHRUBS
☘ ZONES 16–24
☼ ☼ ● SUN OR SHADE; WIND-SHELTERED
◗ WATER DURING GROWTH AND BLOOM SEASON
❧ FLOWERS AND SEEDS POISONOUS IF EATEN

Brugmansia candida

Related to the annual or perennial jimsonweeds, or thorn apples (*Datura*). All kinds sold have tubular flowers. These shrubs will astonish your visitors.

All are large shrubs that can be trained as small trees. Expect frost damage and unattractive winter appearance. Prune in early spring after last frost. Cut back branchlets to one or two buds. (Tubbed plants can be wintered indoors with a little light and very little water.)

Large of leaf and flower, these are dominating shrubs and should be brought into garden with that in mind. *B. candida*, white-flowered angel's trumpet, is showy in moonlight.

B. arborea. Plants usually offered under this name are either *B. candida* or *B. suaveolens*. The true *B. arborea* has smaller flowers.

B. candida. Native to Peru. Fast and rank growing with soft, pulpy growth to 10–15 ft. (6 ft. or more in one season). Dull green, large leaves in the 8–12-in. range. Heavy, single or double white trumpets, 8 in. or more long, are fragrant, especially at night. They appear in summer and fall, often as late as November or December in warm, sheltered gardens.

B. sanguinea. Native to Peru. Fast growing to 12–15 ft. Leaves bright green to 8 in. long. Trumpets, orange red with yellow veinings, about 10 in. long, hang straight down bell fashion from new growth. Rare.

B. suaveolens. Native to Brazil. Similar to *B. candida*, but leaves and flowers are somewhat larger and flowers less fragrant.

B. versicolor. To 15 ft. tall. Flowers white or peach colored. Named versions of uncertain origin include 'Charles Grimaldi' (pale orange yellow) and 'Frosty Pink' (cream deepening to pink).

BRUNFELSIA pauciflora calycina (B. calycina)

Solanaceae
EVERGREEN SHRUBS
☘ ZONES 12–17, 20–24
☼ PARTIAL SHADE; PROTECT FROM FULL SUN
◗ AMPLE WATER

Brunfelsia pauciflora 'Floribunda'

In all but warmest locations these shrubs lose most of their foliage for short period. Upright or spreading, to about

B

3 ft. Oval, 3–4-in.-long leaves dark green above, pale green below. Rich dark purple tubular flowers, several in a cluster, flare to 2 in. wide; bloom comes in spring, early summer.

Brunfelsias are handsome plants that deserve extra attention. Give them rich, well-drained soil mix on acid side. Give iron in Zones 12, 13, to prevent chlorosis. Protect from full sun for best foliage and flower. Provide constant supply of water; feed through growing season. Prune in spring to remove scraggly growth and to shape.

Brunfelsia pauciflora 'Floribunda'

Use where you can admire spectacular flower show. Brunfelsias grow well in containers.

B. p. 'Eximia' (B. c. eximia). Somewhat dwarfed, compact version of *B. p.* 'Floribunda', a more widely planted variety. Flowers are a bit smaller but more generously produced.

B. p. 'Floribunda'. YESTERDAY-TODAY-AND-TOMORROW. Common name comes from quick color change of blossoms: purple ("yesterday"), lavender ("today"), white ("tomorrow"). Flowers profusely displayed all over plant. In partial shade will reach 10 ft. or more with several stems from base. (May be held to 3 ft. by pruning.)

B. p. 'Macrantha' (B. floribunda 'Lindeniana', B. grandiflora). Differs markedly from above. The most tender. More slender growing; larger leaves, often 8 in. long, 2½ in. wide. Flowers 2–4 in. across, deep purple with lavender zone bordering white throat.

BRUNNERA macrophylla

BRUNNERA

Boraginaceae

PERENNIAL

⚡ ALL ZONES

☼ ◑ PARTIAL SHADE; SUN OR PART SHADE ON COAST

◐ ◗ MOIST SOIL; TOLERATES SOME DRYNESS

Brunnera macrophylla

Reaches 1½ ft. tall; leaves heart shaped, dark green, 3–4 in. wide. There is also a rare variety with white-edged leaves. In spring, *Brunnera* produces airy clusters of tiny, clear blue, forget-me-not flowers with yellow centers. Uses: informal ground cover under high-branching deciduous trees; among spring-flowering shrubs such as forsythia, deciduous magnolias; filler between newly planted evergreen shrubs. Freely self-sows once established. Planted seeds often difficult to germinate (try freezing them before sowing). Increase by dividing clumps in fall.

BRUNSVIGIA rosea. See AMARYLLIS belladonna	**p. 149**
BRUSH CHERRY, AUSTRALIAN BRUSH CHERRY. See SYZYGIUM paniculatum	**p. 500**

BRUSSELS SPROUTS

Brassicaceae (Cruciferae)

ANNUAL

⚡ ALL ZONES EXCEPT IN CONDITIONS NOTED BELOW

☼ FULL SUN

◐ REGULAR WATER

Brussels Sprouts

A cabbage relative of unusual appearance. Mature plant has crown of fairly large leaves, and its tall stem is completely covered with tiny sprouts. Fairly easy to grow where summers are not too hot, long, or dry. 'Jade Cross Hybrid' is easiest to grow and most heat tolerant; 'Long Island Improved' ('Catskill') is standard market variety. You may have to grow your own from seed. Sow outdoors or in flats in

April; transplant young plants in June or early July to sunny place. Sprouts are ready in fall. In mild climates plant in fall or winter for winter and spring use.

Treat the same as broccoli. When big leaves start to turn yellow, begin picking. Snap off little sprouts from bottom first—best when slightly smaller than golf ball. Leave little sprouts on upper stem to mature. After picking, remove only leaves below harvested sprouts. A single plant will yield from 50 to 100 sprouts.

BUCHLOE dactyloides

BUFFALO GRASS

Poaceae (Gramineae)

PERENNIAL GRASS

⚡ ZONES 1–3, 10, 11

☼ FULL SUN

◐ VERY LITTLE WATER

Buchloe dactyloides

Makes a low-maintenance, low-water-need lawn. Slow to sprout and fill in, it spreads rapidly by surface runners once established and makes matted, reasonably dense turf that takes hard wear and looks fairly good with very little summer water. Needs sun. Gray green from late spring to hard frost, straw colored through late fall and winter. Runners can invade surrounding garden beds. Given minimum water, it grows to 4 in. tall and requires little or no mowing. More water means higher growth, some mowing. Sow 2 lbs. per 1,000 sq. ft. Soak occasionally to 1 ft. while grass is getting started. To start from sod, in spring, plant 4-in.-wide plugs 3–4 ft. apart on prepared soil; cover should be complete in 2 seasons.

BUCKEYE. See AESCULUS californica	**p. 141**
BUCKTHORN. See RHAMNUS	**p. 452**
BUCKWHEAT. See ERIOGONUM	**p. 278**

BUDDLEIA

Loganiaceae

EVERGREEN OR DECIDUOUS SHRUBS OR SMALL TREES

⚡ ALL ZONES

☼ ◑ SUN OR LIGHT SHADE

◐ ◗ WATER ENOUGH TO MAINTAIN GROWTH

Buddleia davidii

Many species known; all have some charm in either flower color or fragrance, but only two species are readily available.

B. alternifolia. FOUNTAIN BUTTERFLY BUSH. Deciduous shrub or small tree. It can reach 12 ft. or more, with arching, willowlike branches rather thinly clothed with 1–4-in.-long leaves, dark dull green above, gray and hairy beneath. Blooms in spring from previous year's growth; profuse small clusters of mildly fragrant, lilac purple flowers make sweeping wands of color. Tolerates many soils; does very well in poor, dry gravels. Prune after bloom: remove some of oldest wood down to within few inches of ground. Or train up into small single- or multiple-trunked tree. So trained, it somewhat resembles a small weeping willow.

B. davidii. BUTTERFLY BUSH, SUMMER LILAC. Deciduous or semievergreen shrub. Fast, rank growth each spring and summer to 3, 4, or even 10 ft. Leaves tapering, 4–12 in. long, dark green above, white and felted beneath. In midsummer, small fragrant flowers (lilac with orange eye) appear in dense, arching, spikelike, slender clusters 6–12 in. long or more, at branch ends. Butterflies often visit flowers.

Needs good drainage and enough water to maintain growth but little else. In cold climates, the soft wood freezes nearly to ground but roots are hardy.

Many varieties are obtainable, differing mostly in flower color; colors include pink, lilac, blue, purple, and white.

BULBINELLA floribunda (B. robusta, B. setosa)

Liliaceae

PERENNIAL WITH TUBEROUS ROOTSTOCK

☀ ☽ ZONES 14–24

☼ ☽ PARTIAL SHADE IN HOT-SUMMER AREAS

💧 WATER IN SPRING; KEEP ON DRY SIDE IN SUMMER

Bulbinella floribunda

Native to South Africa. Valuable for winter color, forming large clump of 20–26-in., narrow, floppy leaves topped in January–February with 4-in.-long spikes of clear yellow flowers. Similar to poker plant *(Kniphofia)* but spikes are shorter and less pointed, and individual flowers are bell shaped, not tubular. Splendid cut flower. Low-maintenance borders—makes colonies in rather short time. Any soil if well drained. Pull off old, dry foliage after bloom. Divide crowded clumps. Easy to grow from seed sown in spring.

BUTIA capitata

PINDO PALM

Arecaceae (Palmae)

PALM

☀ ZONES 8, 9, 12–24

☼ ☽ SUN OR LIGHT SHADE

💧 REGULAR WATER

Butia capitata

Native to Brazil, Uruguay, Argentina. Slow-growing, very hardy palm to 10–20 ft. Trunk heavy, patterned with stubs of old leaves; tree is more attractive if stubs are trimmed to the same length. Feathery, gray-green arching leaves. Very small flowers, yellow to red edible fruits. Hardy to 15°F. Slow growth.

HOW TO MAKE A BUDDLEIA BEHAVE

In summer and early fall, a well-maintained *Buddleia davidii* plant looks like a big, handsome fountain of arching, flower-laden branches. But neglected or poorly handled plants can look like brush piles, with branches uneven and crisscrossed. To keep the plant orderly and attractive, cut it back yearly to about 3 ft. (or lower). Do the cutting after fall flowering in Zones 4–9, 12–24; in spring in Zones 1–3, 10, 11. The brand-new shoots that follow such a pruning will, on their own, make an attractive fountain-form display the following summer.

Buxaceae. The boxwood family comprises principally evergreen shrubs with inconspicuous flowers (fragrant in *Sarcococca*). Members include *Buxus, Pachysandra,* and *Sarcococca.*

BUXUS

BOXWOOD, BOX

Buxaceae

EVERGREEN SHRUBS OR SMALL TREES

☀ ZONES VARY BY SPECIES

☼ ☽ ● FULL SUN OR SHADE

💧 LOOKS BEST IF WATERED IN SUMMER

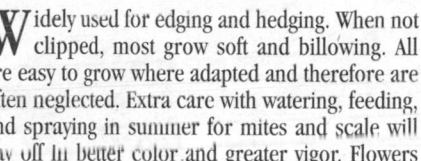
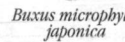

Buxus microphylla japonica

Widely used for edging and hedging. When not clipped, most grow soft and billowing. All are easy to grow where adapted and therefore are often neglected. Extra care with watering, feeding, and spraying in summer for mites and scale will pay off in better color and greater vigor. Flowers quite inconspicuous.

B. harlandii. Zones 8–24. The boxwood sold by this name in California, commonly called Korean boxwood, does not fit description of the true species *B. harlandii* and differs from both Japanese boxwood and true Korean boxwood. Leaves are narrower and brighter green than those of Japanese boxwood, and plant appears better suited to colder areas of California.

B. microphylla. This species is rarely planted. Its widely planted varieties include the following:

B. m. japonica. JAPANESE BOXWOOD. Zones 8–24. Hardy to 0°F. but poor winter appearance in cold areas. It takes California's dry heat and alkaline soil—conditions that rule out English boxwood. Compact foliage (small, 1/3–1-in., round-tipped leaves) is lively bright green in summer, brown or bronze in winter in many areas. Grows slowly to 4–6 ft. if not pruned, making a pleasing informal green shrub. Most often clipped as low or medium hedge or shaped into globes, tiers, pyramids in containers. Can be held to 6-in. height as a hedge or border edging.

B. m. j. 'Compacta'. Extra-dwarf plant with tiny leaves. Slow growing; good rock garden plant.

B. m. j. 'Green Beauty'. Zones 3–24. Hardier than common Japanese boxwood (to –10°F), holds its deep green color in coldest weather and is considerably greener than *B. m. japonica* in summer heat.

B. m. j. 'Winter Gem'. Zones 2–24. Hardiest of Japanese boxwoods.

B. m. koreana. KOREAN BOXWOOD. All zones. Hardy to –18°F. Slower and lower growing than Japanese boxwood. Leaves smaller (1/4–1/2 in.). This should not be confused with "Korean boxwood" or *Buxus harlandii* commonly sold in California. *B. m. koreana* is noted for its hardiness and will live where others freeze out. It is slower growing and smaller in leaf than the plant sold as *B. harlandii.*

B. sempervirens. COMMON BOXWOOD, ENGLISH BOXWOOD. Zones 3–6, 15–17. Dies out in alkaline soils, hot-summer areas. Will grow to height of 15–20 ft. with equal spread. Dense foliage of medium-size, lustrous, dark green, oval leaves. Dwarf form *B. s.* 'Suffruticosa' is best known; the taller-growing varieties are used in Northwest.

B. s. 'Suffruticosa'. TRUE DWARF BOXWOOD. Slower growing than others, to 4–5 ft. but generally clipped lower. Small leaves, dense form and texture. There's a silver-edged variegated form.

C

CABBAGE

Brassicaceae (Cruciferae)

ANNUALS OR BIENNIALS GROWN AS ANNUALS

✎ ALL ZONES

☼ ☽ TOLERATE LIGHT SHADE IN HOT CLIMATES

◖ NEVER LET PLANTS WILT

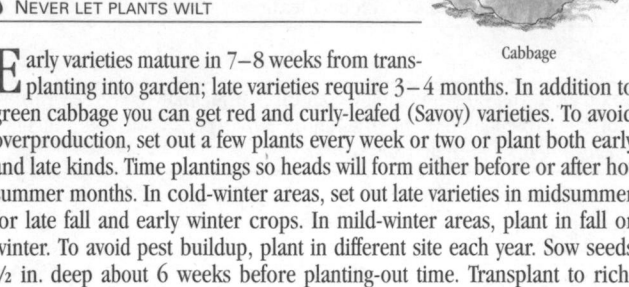

Cabbage

Early varieties mature in 7–8 weeks from trans-planting into garden; late varieties require 3–4 months. In addition to green cabbage you can get red and curly-leafed (Savoy) varieties. To avoid overproduction, set out a few plants every week or two or plant both early and late kinds. Time plantings so heads will form either before or after hot summer months. In cold-winter areas, set out late varieties in midsummer for late fall and early winter crops. In mild-winter areas, plant in fall or winter. To avoid pest buildup, plant in different site each year. Sow seeds ½ in. deep about 6 weeks before planting-out time. Transplant to rich, moist soil, spacing plants 2–2½ ft. apart. Give frequent light applications of nitrogen fertilizer. Mulch helps keep soil moist and cool. Control aphids and green cabbage worm. Light frost doesn't hurt cabbage, but harvest and store before heavy freezes occur. For ornamental relatives, see Cabbage, Flowering.

CABBAGE, FLOWERING

Brassicaceae (Cruciferae)

ANNUALS OR BIENNIALS GROWN AS ANNUALS

✎ ALL ZONES

☼ ☽ BEST IN FULL SUN, TOLERATE SOME SHADE

◖ REGULAR WATER

Flowering Cabbage

Flowering cabbage and flowering kale are grown for their highly ornamental, highly colored leaf rosettes, which look like giant peonies in deep blue green marbled and edged with white, cream, rose, or purple. Kale differs from cabbage in that its head is slightly looser and its leaf edges are more heavily fringed. Both appreciate same soil, care, and timing as conventional cabbage. Their 10-in. "flowers" are spectacular in cool-season garden. Plant 15–18 in. apart in open-ground beds, singly in 8-in. pots, or several in a large container. Colors are strongest after first frosts touch plants. Single rosette cut and placed on spike holder in bowl makes striking harvest arrangement. Foliage is sold as salad savory; it is edible raw or cooked and is highly decorative as a salad garnish.

CABBAGE PALM. See SABAL palmetto p. 471

Cactaceae. The cactus family contains a huge number of succulent plants (see also Succulents). Generally leafless, they have stems modified into cylinders, pads, or joints that store water in times of drought. Thick skin reduces evaporation, and most species have spines to protect plants against browsing animals. Flowers are usually large and brightly colored; fruit may also be colorful and is sometimes edible.

All (with one doubtful exception) are native to the Americas—from Canada to Argentina, from sea level into high mountains, in deserts or in dripping tropical rain forests. Many are native to drier parts of the West.

Cacti range in height from a few inches to 50 ft. Larger species are used to create desert landscapes. Smaller species are grown in pots or, if sufficiently hardy, in rock gardens. Many are easy-care, showy house or greenhouse plants. Large landscaping types require full sun, well-drained soil. Water newly planted cacti very little; roots are subject to rot before they begin active growth. In 4–6 weeks, when new roots are active, water thoroughly; then let soil dry before watering again. Reduce watering in fall to allow plants to go dormant. Feed monthly in spring, summer. For some larger kinds appropriate for garden use, see *Carnegiea gigantea,*

Cephalocereus senilis, Cereus peruvianus, Echinocactus, Echinocereus, Espostoa lanata, Ferocactus, Lemaireocereus thurberi, Opuntia.

Smaller cacti for pot or rock garden culture usually have interesting forms and brightly colored flowers. Feed and water plants well during warm weather for good display; taper off on fertilizer to encourage winter dormancy. Use fast-draining soil mix. See *Chamaecereus sylvestri, Coryphantha vivipara, Echinopsis, Lobivia, Lobivopsis, Mammillaria.*

Showiest in flower are tropical cacti that grow as epiphytes on trees or rocks. These need rich soil with much humus, frequent feeding and watering, partial shade, and protection from frost. Grow in lathhouse or greenhouse, or handle as outdoor/indoor plants. See *Epiphyllum, Rhipsalidopsis, Schlumbergera.*

CAESALPINIA (Poinciana)

Fabaceae (Leguminosae)

EVERGREEN OR DECIDUOUS SHRUBS OR SMALL TREES

✎ ZONES VARY BY SPECIES

☼ FULL SUN

◖ INFREQUENT, DEEP WATERING

◈ PODS AND SEEDS CAUSE SERIOUS ILLNESS

Caesalpinia gilliesii

Caesalpinias grow quickly and easily in hot sun with light, well-drained soil and infrequent, deep watering.

C. gilliesii (Poinciana gilliesii). BIRD OF PARADISE BUSH. Deciduous or evergreen shrub or small tree. Zones 8–16, 18–23; occasionally seen in Zones 6, 7. Tough, interesting, fast growing to 10 ft., with finely cut, filmy foliage on rather open, angular branch structure. Drops leaves in cold winters. Blooms all summer; clusters of yellow flowers adorned with protruding, bright red, 4–5-in.-long stamens. Flowers attract hummingbirds.

C. mexicana. MEXICAN BIRD OF PARADISE. Evergreen shrub or small tree. Zones 12–16, 18–23. Moderately fast growth to 10–12 ft.; may be pruned to 6–8 ft. Foliage coarser than that of *C. pulcherrima.* Blooms year-round except in coldest months, bearing lemon yellow flower clusters 6 in. long, 4 in. thick.

C. pulcherrima (Poinciana pulcherrima). RED BIRD OF PARADISE. Tropical deciduous shrub. Zones 12–16, 18–23. Fast, dense growth to 10 ft. tall, 10 ft. wide. Dark green leaves with many ¾-in.-long leaflets. Blooms throughout warm weather; flowers orange or red (rarely yellow), clustered, with long red stamens. May be evergreen in mild winters. Useful for quick screening. Freezes to ground in colder areas but rebounds quickly in spring. Even if it doesn't freeze back, you can cut it back to ground in early spring to make more compact mound.

CAJEPUT TREE. See MELALEUCA quinquenervia p. 377

CALADIUM bicolor

FANCY-LEAFED CALADIUM

Araceae

TUBEROUS-ROOTED PERENNIAL

✎ ZONES 12, 13, 16, 17, 22–24; OR INDOORS

◖ SHADE

◖◖ CAREFUL, FREQUENT WATERING

◈ JUICES CAN CAUSE SWELLING IN MOUTH, THROAT

Caladium bicolor

Native to tropical America. Not grown for flowers. Entire show comes from large, arrow-shaped, long-stalked, almost translucent leaves colored in bands and blotches of red, rose, pink, white, silver, bronze, and green. Most varieties sold in nurseries derived from *C. bicolor*—usually 2 ft. tall, occasionally 4 ft. Caladiums need warm shade, daytime temperature of 70°F. Best in Zones 23, 24; in all zones as

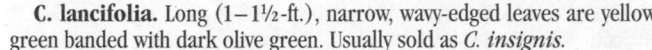

summer pot plants on sheltered patios or in borders; bring in in winter. Combine with ferns, coleus, alocasias, colocasias, and tuberous begonias.

Same pot culture as that for tuberous begonias. Start tubers indoors in March, outdoors in May. Pot in mix of equal parts coarse sand, leaf mold, and ground bark or peat moss. Use 5-in. pot for 2½-in. tuber, 7-in. pot for 1 large or 2 small tubers. Fill pot halfway with mix; stir in heaping teaspoon of fish meal. Add 1 in. of mix, set tuber with knobby side up, cover with 2 in. of mix. Water thoroughly.

To plant in ground, replace top 6 in. of existing soil with same mix as for pots. Place 1 tbsp. of fish meal in bottom of each hole; proceed as described above. Keep soil moist, not wet. Provide more moisture as leaves develop. Syringe overhead every day or two during active growth. Feed with liquid fish fertilizer once a week, starting when leaves appear. Bait for slugs and snails. Gradually withhold water when leaves start to die down. In about a month, lift tubers, remove most of soil, dry in semishade for 10 days. Dust tubers with insecticide-fungicide preparation; store for winter in dry peat moss or vermiculite at temperature between 50° and 60°F.

C. esculentum. See Colocasia esculenta

CALAMAGROSTIS
acutifolia 'Stricta'

FEATHER REED GRASS	
Poaceae (Gramineae)	
PERENNIAL	
☀ ALL ZONES	
☼ FULL SUN	
🌢 REGULAR WATER	

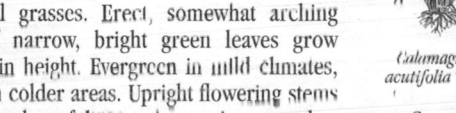
Calamagrostis acutifolia 'Stricta'

One of the most effective and handsome ornamental grasses. Erect, somewhat arching clumps of narrow, bright green leaves grow 1½–4 ft. in height. Evergreen in mild climates, partly so in colder areas. Upright flowering stems rise 3–4 ft. above foliage in late spring or early summer. Green with purplish tones, they age to golden yellow, then buff by winter.

CALAMONDIN. See CITRUS, Sour-Acid Mandarin Oranges p. 232

CALATHEA

Marantaceae	
INDOOR AND GREENHOUSE PLANTS	
● SHADE	
🌢 REGULAR WATER	

Calathea zebrina

Native to tropical America or Africa. Calatheas are usually called marantas, to which they are closely related and from which they differ only in technical aspects. Interesting plants for indoor decoration in winter, outdoor use in summer. Ornamental leaves, beautifully marked in various shades of green, white, and pink, arranged in basal tufts. Flowers of most are inconspicuous and of no consequence. Need warm atmosphere (not under 55°F) and shade, although good light necessary for rich leaf color. Porous potting mix, perfect drainage; stagnant conditions harmful. Wet leaves frequently. Repot as often as necessary to avoid root-bound condition.

C. crocata. ETERNAL FLAME. Leaves 6 in. long, 1–1½ in. wide, dark green above, purple beneath. Spikes 2 in. long, consisting of bright orange flower bracts that look like little torches. Clump has several shoots; each shoot dies after blooming, but new ones appear to keep up the show. Variable performance as house plant; subject to mites in low humidity. Does better in greenhouse.

c. insignis. Striking, 3–7 ft. in native rain forest, lower in cultivation, with 1–1½-ft.-long, yellow-green leaves striped olive green.

C. lancifolia. Long (1–1½-ft.), narrow, wavy-edged leaves are yellow green banded with dark olive green. Usually sold as *C. insignis*.

C. louisae. To 3 ft. Foot-long dark green leaves heavily feathered with gray green along midrib.

C. makoyana. Showy, 2–4 ft. high. Leaves with areas of olive green or cream above, pink blotches beneath. Silver featherings on rest of upper surface, corresponding cream-colored area underneath.

C. ornata. Sturdy, 1½–3 ft. high. Leaves 2–3 ft. long, rich green above, purplish red beneath. Juvenile leaves usually pink striped between veins; intermediate foliage striped white. Variety 'Roseo-lineata' has pink and white stripes at angle to midrib.

C. zebrina. ZEBRA PLANT. Compact plant to 1–3 ft. high. Ellipse-shaped leaves reach 1–2 ft. long, almost half as wide. Upper surfaces are velvety green with alternating bars of pale yellow green and olive green extending outward from midrib; undersides are purplish red.

CALCEOLARIA

Scrophulariaceae	
PERENNIALS	
☀ ZONES VARY BY SPECIES	
☼ ◐ ● EXPOSURE NEEDS VARY BY SPECIES	
🌢 REGULAR WATER	

Calceolaria integrifolia

Native Mexico to Chile. Loose clusters of small pouchlike or slipperlike flowers, usually yellow but sometimes red bronze or spotted with red or orange brown. Bloom in spring and summer. Plants much branched, often woody stemmed and shrubby, 8 in.–6 ft. high, with dark green, crinkly leaves.

C. arachnoidea. Zones 16, 17, 21–24. Rosettes of white, woolly leaves produce 1–2-ft. stems with clusters of small purple flowers. Partial shade.

C. biflora. Zones 5–9, 14–24. Rosettes of 3-in. leaves produce leafless stems topped by yellow flowers ('Goldcrest') or yellow flowers heavily spotted with red ('John Innes'). Partial shade.

C. herbeohybrida. Zones 14–24 as bedding plant or pot plant in shade; house plant in sun. This is florists' calceolaria, with masses of inch-long yellow to velvety red flowers, often spotted and marbled. Usually grown from seed sown in spring or summer in light, porous soil; plants ready for final potting or planting out in fall. Can reach a height of 2½ ft., but the most popular strains are the lower-growing Multiflora Nana and Multiflora, which grow 9–15 in. tall. Plants are usually discarded after flowering but sometimes live over. Strain called Anytime tolerates high temperatures better than other strains; start it indoors in late winter for summer bloom.

C. integrifolia. Zones 14–24. Shrubby plant 1½–6 ft. high. Leaves about 3 in. long and 1 in. wide. Clusters of yellow to red-brown, unspotted flowers ½ in. across. Will grow in full sun; takes heat, light frost. Borders, pots, hanging baskets. Best bloom when root-bound. Good cut flower. Variety 'Golden Nugget' most commonly sold; vigorous, 1½–2 ft., clear golden yellow flowers spring to fall. 'Russet' and 'Kentish Hero' have orange-red to brown flowers.

CALENDULA officinalis

CALENDULA, POT MARIGOLD	
Asteraceae (Compositae)	
ANNUAL	
☀ ALL ZONES	
☼ FULL SUN	
🌢 MODERATE WATER	

Calendula officinalis

Sure, easy color from late fall through spring in mild-winter areas; spring to midsummer in colder climates. Besides familiar daisylike, orange and bright yellow double blooms 2½–4½ in. across, calendulas come in more subtle shades of apricot, cream, and soft yellow. Plants somewhat branching, 1–2 ft. high. Leaves are long, narrow, round on ends, slightly sticky, and aromatic. Plants effective in masses of single colors in borders and parking strips, along drives, in containers. Long-lasting cut flowers.

Sow seed in place or in flats in late summer or early fall in mild-winter climates, spring elsewhere. Or buy seedlings at nurseries. Adapts to most soils if drainage is fast. Remove spent flowers to prolong bloom. Although it is an excellent pot plant, the common name is actually derived from the plant's earlier use as a "pot herb"—a vegetable to be used in the cooking pot.

Dwarf strains (12–15 in.) include Bon Bon (earliest), Dwarf Gem, and Fiesta (Fiesta Gitana). Taller (1½–2 ft.) are Kablouna (pompom centers with looser edges), Pacific Beauty, and Radio (quilled, "cactus" blooms).

CALLIANDRA

Fabaceae (Leguminosae)
EVERGREEN SHRUBS
☀ ZONES VARY BY SPECIES
☼ SUN AND WARMTH
◐ ◑ ● WATER NEEDS VARY BY SPECIES

Group of 250 or more species represented here by a flame bush, a pink powder puff, and fairy dusters—all showy, spreading shrubs.

Calliandra tweedii

C. californica. BAJA FAIRY DUSTER. Zones 10–24. Although similar to *C. eriophylla,* foliage is more luxuriant. Blooms through warm part of year if given some supplemental summer water.

C. eriophylla. FAIRY DUSTER, FALSE MESQUITE. Zones 10–24. Native from California's Imperial and eastern San Diego counties east to Texas; south into Baja California. Open growth to 3 ft. tall, 4–5 ft. wide. Leaves finely cut into tiny leaflets. Flower clusters show pink to red stamens in fluffy balls to 1½ in. across, February or March. Needs no irrigation at all.

C. haematocephala (C. inaequilatera). PINK POWDER PUFF. Zones 22–24. Native to Bolivia. Grows fast to 10 ft. or more with equal spread. Its beauty has carried it into harsher areas than Zones 22–24: in Zones 13 and 16–21 it requires special protection of overhang or warm sunny wall. In form, it's a natural espalier. Foliage not as feathery as that of *C. tweedii;* leaflets longer, broader, and darker—glossy copper when new, turning to dark metallic green. Big puffs (2–3 in. across) of silky stamens, watermelon pink, are produced October–March. There is a rare white-flowered form. Needs light soil and plenty of water.

C. tweedii. TRINIDAD FLAME BUSH, BRAZILIAN FLAME BUSH. Best in Zones 22–24; satisfactory in Zones 15–21; freezes back but recovers in Zones 7–9, 12–14. Graceful, picturesque structure to 6–8 ft. tall, 5–8 ft. wide. Leaves, lacy and fernlike, divided into many tiny leaflets, scarcely hide branches. Flower clusters show as bright crimson pompoms at branch ends, February to fall. Not fussy about soil. Once established, it needs no water at all. Prune to thin and also to retain an interesting branch pattern. Often sold as *C. guildingii.*

CALLICARPA

BEAUTYBERRY
Verbenaceae
DECIDUOUS SHRUBS
☀ ZONES VARY BY SPECIES
☼ ☼ SUN OR LIGHT SHADE
● MODERATE WATER

Callicarpa bodinieri

Graceful shrubs with arching branches. Small, tight clusters of lilac flowers followed by long-lasting, tight clusters of lavender to violet purple small, round fruits that last well into winter. Fall foliage color is attractive. Bloom and fruit on new wood; prune in spring. In coldest winters may freeze back to the ground but come back from roots.

C. americana. Zones 4–9, 14–24. To 6 ft., with leaves to 6 in. long that turn purplish in fall. Fruits are purple.

C. bodinieri. Zones 3–9, 14–24. Grows to 6 ft. or more, with willow-like leaves that turn pink or orange to purple in fall. Berries are violet. 'Profusion' is a select, heavy-fruiting variety.

C. dichotoma. Zones 3–9, 14–24. To 6 ft. Resembles a smaller, finer-textured *C. bodinieri.* 'Issai' is a select variety.

C. japonica. Zones 3–9, 14–24. To 3–5 ft., with deep reddish purple fall foliage, pink flowers, and purple fruits. 'Leucocarpa' has white fruits.

CALLIRHOE involucrata

POPPY MALLOW, WINE CUPS
Malvaceae
PERENNIAL
☀ ALL ZONES
☼ FULL SUN
● TOLERATES SOME ARIDITY ONCE ESTABLISHED

Callirhoe involucrata

Thick, fleshy root produces a spreading plant 6 in. tall by 2–3 ft. wide, with roundish, deeply cut leaves and quantities of 2-in. purplish red mallow flowers during hot weather. Needs good drainage but survives in poor soil and intense heat. Useful on hot slopes or areas that get little attention.

CALLISIA

Commelinaceae
INDOOR PLANTS IN HANGING POTS
● SHADE
● REGULAR WATER

Callisia elegans

They look like, and are related to, wandering Jews (*Tradescantia* and *Zebrina*); they may be brought outdoors in warm season. For care, see *Tradescantia albiflora.*

C. elegans. Stems spread or reach upward instead of drooping, usually much less than maximum of 2 ft. Leaves thick, semisucculent, 3 in. long by 1 in. wide. Upper surfaces dark olive green with white pinstripes running lengthwise; undersides purple. Small flowers, not often seen.

C. fragrans. Leaves to 10 in. long make big rosettes that resemble loose-knit hen and chicks (*Echeveria*). Long runners produce miniatures of parent at tips. Makes massive hanging basket plant that is impressive rather than attractive. Branched clusters of fragrant flowers seldom produced. Offsets can be detached and set in shallow trays of water, the rosettes resting on pebbles or other support. They will root and grow for several months with no further attention, tolerating low light, dryness.

C. repens. This creeping, trailing plant is often sold as *Tradescantia* or as 'Little Jewel'. Closely spaced, thick, fleshy, shiny, bright green leaves an inch long or less make it attractive hanging pot plant. Small flowers bloom infrequently.

CALLISTEMON

BOTTLEBRUSH	
Myrtaceae	
EVERGREEN SHRUBS OR TREES	
▨ ZONES 8, 9, 12–24	
☼ FULL SUN	
◗ NEED LITTLE WATER, EXCEPT WHERE NOTED	

Callistemon citrinus

Native to Australia. Colorful flowers in dense spikes or round clusters consisting principally of long, bristlelike stamens—hence the common name. Flowers followed by woody capsules that persist for years and sometimes look like bands of beads pressed into bark. Generally tolerant of saline-alkaline soils but sometimes suffer from chlorosis. Often severely damaged at 20°F. Fast growing, easy to train. Quick wall cover as informal espaliers. Several can be trained as small trees. Some can be used in formal clipped hedges or as informal screens or windbreaks. A few can be trained as ground covers.

Many kinds are being sold under names whose identification is uncertain. Some plants sold as *Callistemon* may be melaleucas, which are closely related.

C. citrinus (C. lanceolatus). LEMON BOTTLEBRUSH. Best-selling bottlebrush; most tolerant of heat, cold, and adverse soils (can be troubled with chlorosis in Zones 12 and 13). Massive shrub to 10–15 ft., but with staking and pruning in youth easily trained into narrowish, round-headed, 20–25-ft. tree. Nurseries offer it as shrub, espalier, or tree. Narrow, 3-in.-long leaves coppery in new growth, then vivid green. Bright red, 6-in.-long brushes appear in cycles throughout year. Hummingbirds love flowers.

Variable plant when grown from seed. Cutting-grown selections with good flower size and color are *C. c.* 'Improved' and *C. c.* 'Splendens'. *C. c.* 'Compacta' is smaller (4 ft. by 4 ft. at 3 years), with smaller spikes. *C. c.* 'Violaceus' ('Jeffersii') is smaller (to 6 ft. tall, 4 ft. wide), stiffer in branching, with narrower, shorter leaves and reddish purple flowers fading to lavender. 'Mauve Mist' is nearly identical, possibly taller (to 10 ft.).

C. linearis. NARROW-LEAFED BOTTLEBRUSH. Shrubby, 6–8 ft. tall (sometimes to 15 ft.), 5 ft. wide, with narrow, 2–5-in.-long leaves. Bright crimson brushes 5 in. long in summer.

C. pachyphyllus viridis. Stiff-branched, spreading shrub to 6–7 ft. Leaves nearly as narrow and stiff as pine needles. Flower spikes are bright apple green against dark green foliage.

C. rigidus. STIFF BOTTLEBRUSH. Erect, sparse, rigid shrub or small tree to 20 ft. with 10-ft. spread. Leaves sharp pointed, gray green (sometimes purplish). Red flower brushes 2½–4½ in. long, spring and summer. Seed capsules prominent. Least graceful bottlebrush.

C. salignus. WHITE BOTTLEBRUSH. Shrub or tree to 20–25 ft. Dense crown of foliage. New growth bright pink to copper. Willowy leaves 2–3 in. long. Flowers pale yellow to cream colored in 1½–3-in. clusters. Train as small shade tree or plant 4–5 ft. apart as hedge.

C. viminalis. WEEPING BOTTLEBRUSH. Shrub or small tree with pendulous branches. Fast growing to 20–30 ft. with 15-ft. spread. Leaves narrow, light green, 6 in. long. Bright red brushes May–July; scattered bloom throughout year. Needs ample water. Not for windy, dry areas. May be damaged by cold winters in Zones 8, 9, 12, 13. As tree, needs staking, thinning of surplus

Callistemon viminalis

branches to prevent tangled, top-heavy growth. Inclined toward sparseness because leaves tend to grow only at ends of long, hanging branches. 'Captain Cook' is dwarf variety useful as border, low hedge, or screen plant. 'Little John' is a superior dwarf form, 3 ft. tall and wide, with dense growth pattern and blood red flowers in fall, winter, and spring. 'McCaskillii' is denser in habit than others, more vigorous, and better in flower color and form. Variety sold as 'Dwarf' resembles 'McCaskillii'.

CALLISTEPHUS chinensis

CHINA ASTER	
Asteraceae (Compositae)	
ANNUAL	
▨ ALL ZONES	
☼ FULL SUN	
◗ REGULAR WATER; AVOID OVERWATERING	

Callistephus chinensis

Splendid cut flower and effective bedding plant when well grown and free of disease. Plants 1–3 ft. high. Some kinds are branching; others (developed mainly for florists) have strong stems and no side shoots. Leaves deeply toothed or lobed. Summer is bloom season. Many different flower forms: quilled, curled, incurved, ribbonlike, or interlaced rays; some have crested centers. Varieties classified as peony-flowered, pompom, anemone-flowered, ostrich feather. Colors range from white to pastel pink, rose pink, lavender, lavender blue, violet, purple, crimson, wine, and scarlet.

Plant in rich, loamy or sandy soil. After frosts, sow seed in place or set out plants started in flats. Keep growth steady; sudden checks in growth are harmful. Subject to aster yellows, a viral disease carried by leafhoppers. Discard infected plants. Spray or dust to control leafhoppers. All but wilt-resistant types are subject to aster wilt or stem rot, caused by parasitic fungus that lives in soil and is transmitted through roots into plants. Overwatering produces ideal condition for diseases, especially in heavy soil. Never plant in same location in successive years.

CALLUNA vulgaris

SCOTCH HEATHER	
Ericaceae	
EVERGREEN SHRUB	
▨ ZONES 2–6, 15–17	
☼ FULL SUN	
◗ MODERATE WATER	

Calluna vulgaris

This, the true and only Scotch heather, has crowded, tiny, scalelike, dark green leaves and one-sided spikes of bell-shaped, rosy pink flowers. Garden varieties (far more common than wild kind) include dwarf ground cover and rock garden plants ranging from 2–4 in. to 2–3 ft. tall. Taller varieties make good backgrounds for lower kinds and are attractive cut flowers. Flower colors include white, pale to deep pink, lavender, and purple. Foliage—paler and deeper greens, yellow, chartreuse, gray, or russet—often changes color in winter. Most bloom in mid- to late summer; a few bloom into late fall. To prune, shear off faded flowers and branch tips immediately after bloom (with latest-flowering varieties, delay pruning until March).

Heathers thrive in sandy, peaty, fast-draining soil. In Northwest, where they are best adapted, they require little or no fertilizing. Where watering must be frequent, light feeding with acid plant food—once in February or March, a second time in June—will encourage good growth and bloom.

Here are a few of the scores of varieties obtainable from specialists:

'Alba Jae'. Sprawler to 18 in. Summer–fall, has bright green leaves, white flowers.

▶

C

'Alba Plena'. Loose, medium green mound to 1 ft. Double white flowers, August–September. Fast growing.

'Aurea'. Spreading, twiggy, 8–12-in. plant with gold foliage turning russet in winter. Sparse purple bloom, August–September.

'Aureafolia'. Upright, to 1½–2 ft. Chartreuse foliage, tinged gold in summer. White flowers, August–September.

'Blazeaway'. Pale foliage with apricot tints, emerging bronzy. Lavender flowers, summer–fall.

'Corbett Red'. Compact grower with dark green foliage. Violet red flowers, summer–fall.

GOOD HOBBY PLANTS

Scotch heathers come in a stimulating range of colors and textures. If you carefully choose varieties, you can have bloom from June to November. Combine them with heaths *(Erica)* for year-round bloom, or plant them among other acid-loving plants (rhododendron, pieris, huckleberry) for contrasting texture.

'County Wicklow'. Mounding, 9–18 in., medium green. Pink double flowers from white buds, August–October.

'Dainty Bess'. Tiny gray leaves form mat 2–4 in. tall. Lavender flowers, August–September; shapes itself to rocks, crevices.

'Darkness'. Dark green foliage; dark purple flowers, summer–fall.

'David Eason'. Spreading mound, 1–1½ ft. Light green foliage; reddish purple flowers, October–November.

'Else Frye'. Erect plant to 2 ft. Medium green foliage; double white flowers, July–August.

'Foxii Nana'. Small mound to 6 in. Dark green foliage; purple flowers, August–September. A dwarf pincushion.

'Goldsworth Crimson'. Mounding, 1½–2 ft. Dark or smoky green foliage; crimson flowers October–November.

'H. E. Beale'. Loose mound to 2 ft. Dark green foliage; soft pink double flowers, August–October. Long spikes are good for cutting.

'J. H. Hamilton'. Prostrate, bushy, to 9 in. Deep green foliage; profuse double pink bloom, August–September.

'Mair's Variety'. Erect, 2–3 ft. Medium green foliage; white flowers, July–September. Easy to grow, good background.

'Martha Herman'. Compact, with lime green leaves. White flowers, summer–fall.

'Minima Prostrata'. Nearly flat habit. Foliage dark green in summer, bronze in winter. Flowers, light rose purple, summer–fall.

'Mrs. Pat'. Bushy, to 8 in. Light green foliage; pink new growth. Light purple flowers, July–September.

'Mrs. Ronald Gray'. Creeping mound, to 3 in. Dark green foliage; reddish purple flowers, August–September. Excellent ground cover.

'Mullion'. Tight mound to 9 in. Dark green foliage, rosy purple flowers, August–September. Fine ground cover.

'Nana'. Low, spreading, to 4 in. Dark green foliage; purple flowers, July–September. Often called carpet heather.

'Nana Compacta'. Tight mound to 4 in. Medium green. Purple flowers, July–September. Pincushion heather for rockery.

'Roma'. Compact, to 9 in. Dark green foliage; deep pink flowers, August–October.

'Searlei'. Bushy, 1–1½ ft. Yellow-green feathery foliage. White flowers, August–October.

'Silver King', 'Silver Knight', 'Silver Queen'. Varieties with light gray-green foliage and pink flowers blooming summer–fall.

'Tib'. Rounded, bushy, to 1–1½ ft. Medium green foliage; deepest rosy purple double flowers, August–September.

CALOCEDRUS decurrens (Libocedrus decurrens)

INCENSE CEDAR

Cupressaceae

EVERGREEN TREE

✂ ZONES 1–12, 14–24

☀ CAN GROW UP OUT OF SHADE INTO FULL SUN

💧 WATER THROUGH FIRST 4–5 DRY SEASONS

Calocedrus decurrens

Native to the mountains of southern Oregon, California, western Nevada; northern Baja California. Unlike most of its native associates—white fir, Douglas fir, sugar pine—it adapts to many western climates. Symmetrical tree to 75–90 ft. with dense, narrow, pyramidal crown; trunk with reddish brown bark. Rich green foliage in flat sprays. Tree gives pungent fragrance to garden in warm weather. Small, yellowish brown to reddish brown cones that, when open, look like ducks' bills.

Although slow growing at first, it may grow 2 ft. per year when established. Takes blazing summer heat. Tolerates poor soils. Good tree to make green wall, high screen, windbreak. Common on the Yosemite Valley floor, this tree has been seen by millions.

CALOCEPHALUS brownii (Leucophyta brownii)

CUSHION BUSH

Asteraceae (Compositae)

EVERGREEN SHRUBBY PERENNIAL

✂ ZONES 16, 17, 19, 21–24; BEST IN ZONES 17, 24

☀ FULL SUN

💧 AVOID OVERWATERING

Calocephalus brownii

Native to Australia, Tasmania. Silvery white throughout, this unusual mounding plant is at its best when buffeted by winds and exposed to salt air and spray. Tiny threadlike leaves, ⅛ in. long, pressed tightly against wiry, branching stems. Grows 3 ft. tall, equally broad. Flower heads button shaped, ½ in. across, in clusters. Stunning high ground cover or rock garden plant. Effective in large planters with succulents. Fresh or dried foliage attractive in arrangements. Sandy or gravelly soil, fast drainage. Cut out dead wood on older plants.

CALOCHORTUS

Liliaceae

BULBS

✂ ZONES VARY; SEE BELOW

☀ FULL SUN

💧 KEEP MOIST IN WINTER, SPRING; DRY IN SUMMER

Beautiful western natives, most numerous in California. Of most interest to hobbyists willing to give more than ordinary care. It's best to plant kinds native to your area or to an area with similar climate, so the following descriptions identify the native growing region of each species.

Calochortus venustus

Bulbs can be difficult to find; check mail-order suppliers of rare bulbs. You may grow them in cans or boxes, plunge into ground in fall. Mix very coarse sand and loam into the soil; then set tips of bulbs 2–3 in. deep. Lift after spring bloom to dry out in summer.

198

There are three flower forms. Globe tulips or fairy lanterns have three to five nodding flowers to a stalk, and petals turn inward to form a globe. Star tulips have erect, cup-shaped flowers, often with tips of petals rolled outward; some of these, called cat's ears or pussy ears, have long, straight hairs on inner flower surfaces. Most striking are mariposa lilies, whose erect, branching, 10–24-in. stems hold big, colorful, cup-shaped flowers. Leaves scanty, long, grasslike.

Here are kinds most often available for sale:

C. albus. WHITE GLOBE LILY, FAIRY LANTERN. Coast Ranges, Sierra Nevada foothills. Stems 2 ft. tall; white, 1¼-in. flowers, March–May.

C. amabilis. GOLDEN FAIRY LANTERN. Northern Coast Ranges. Stems are 15 in. tall; flowers 1¼ in. long, deep yellow often tinged brown, March–May.

C. amoenus. PURPLE GLOBE TULIP. Sierra Nevada foothills. Rosy purple lanterns, 1¼ in. long, on 8–16-in. stems, April–June.

C. clavatus. Coast Ranges, Sierra Nevada foothills. Mariposa lily with yellow flowers sometimes marked brownish red, 2–3 in. wide, on stems to 3 ft. Blooms April–June.

C. luteus (C. luteus citrinus). Coast Ranges, Sierra Nevada foothills. Yellow, 2½-in. mariposa lilies on 1–1½-ft. stems, April–June.

C. maweanus. See C. tolmiei

C. nuttallii. SEGO LILY. Eastern Montana, south to New Mexico and Arizona. State flower of Utah. Flowers white, marked lilac or purple, 2–3 in. wide, on stems 1½ ft. tall. Early summer bloom.

C. splendens. LILAC MARIPOSA. Coast Ranges, Northern California to Baja California. Deep lilac, 2-in. flowers, sometimes with purple centers, on 1–2-ft. stems. Early summer bloom.

C. tolmiei (C. maweanus). CAT'S EARS, PUSSY EARS. Mountains of Oregon, Northern California. White to cream flowers often tinged pinkish or purplish, 1½ in. wide, fringed and furry on inner surfaces. Weak stems to 16 in. Spring blooming.

C. uniflorus (C. lilacinus). STAR TULIP. Northern California coast and Coast Ranges, southern Oregon. Lilac flowers 1 in. long, 1½ in. wide, on 4-in. stems. Spring blooming.

C. venustus. WHITE MARIPOSA LILY. Central and Southern California Coast Ranges, central Sierra Nevada. Flowers 3–3½ in. wide, white or yellow to purple, dark red, often with peacock eye at base of petals. Stems 10 in. tall, often much taller. May–July bloom.

C. vestae. Northern California Coast Ranges. White through pink and lilac to rose, centered with red-brown peacock eye banded in yellow. Lily flowers are 1½ in. wide and carried on 1–1½ ft. stems in late spring and early summer.

CALODENDRUM capense

CAPE CHESTNUT	
Rutaceae	
BRIEFLY DECIDUOUS TREE	
⚘ ZONES 19, 21–24; WORTH RISKING IN 15, 16	
☼ FULL SUN	
⬤ ROOT ZONE SHOULD NOT GO COMPLETELY DRY	

Native to South Africa. Broad crowned, 25–40 ft. Noteworthy for profuse display of spikes of rosy lilac, 1½-in.-long flowers. Whole flower cluster measures 10–12 in. high by as much across and extends well above foliage, giving effect of candelabrum. Generally blooms from May into

Calodendrum capense

July. Seldom flowers when young. Slow growing. Leaves are light to medium green, oval, to 6 in. Time of flowering and deciduous period varies by location and season. Plant it out of prevailing wind. Light, sandy soils are not to its liking.

CALONYCTION aculeatum. See IPOMOEA alba   p. 332

CALOTHAMNUS

NET BUSH	
Myrtaceae	
EVERGREEN SHRUBS	
⚘ ZONES 8, 9, 12–24	
☼ FULL SUN	
⬤ TOLERATE SOME ARIDITY	

Calothamnus quadrifidus

Native to western Australia. Related to bottlebrush *(Callistemon)* and probably adapted to same climates. Tolerate heat, wind, salt breeze, and poor soil if drainage is good (expect root rot if it is not). Needlelike leaves densely clothe rather spreading branches. Flowers that somewhat resemble one-sided bottlebrushes grow along branches, rather close to wood. Sporadic bloom all year. Prune hard after flowering to keep plants from getting straggly. Woody, unattractive in age.

Of the many species introduced, these two are being grown by nurseries:

C. quadrifidus. Grows 6–8 ft. high. Dark green leaves, ½–1 in. long. Short clusters of dark red flowers.

C. villosus (C. villosus prostratus). To 4 ft. Leaves ½ in. long, covered with soft hairs. Long, deep red flower clusters.

CALTHA palustris

MARSH MARIGOLD	
Ranunculaceae	
PERENNIAL	
⚘ ALL ZONES	
☼ ◑ ⬤ ANY EXPOSURE	
⬤ BOG OR MARSH PLANT IN NATURE	
⚘ ANY PART CAN CAUSE INFLAMMATION, PAIN	

Caltha palustris

Native to eastern United States, Europe, Asia. Up to 2 ft. tall, well adapted to edges of pools, ponds, streams, other moist situations. With sufficient water it can be grown in borders, but must not dry out in summer. Good with bog irises, moisture-loving ferns. Green leaves 2–7 in. across; vivid yellow flowers are 2 in. across, in clusters. Lush, glossy foliage gives an almost tropical effect. Plant is vigorous; increase by divisions or sow seed in boggy soil. There is a double-flowered form.

Calycanthaceae. The calycanthus family contains shrubs with paired opposite leaves and flowers that somewhat resemble small water lilies—each bloom has an indefinite number of segments not easily defined as petals or sepals. *Calycanthus* and *Chimonanthus praecox* are typical.

CALYCANTHUS

Calycanthaceae	
DECIDUOUS SHRUBS	
⚘ ZONES VARY BY SPECIES	
☼ ◑ ⬤ ANY EXPOSURE	
⬤ REGULAR WATER	
⚘ SEEDS CAN PRODUCE CONVULSIONS	

Calycanthus occidentalis

Deciduous shrubs, represented in western gardens by a western and an eastern native. Flowers worthwhile for fragrance, form. Bulky shrubs with lush foliage.

C. floridus. CAROLINA ALLSPICE. Hardy in Zones 1–9, 14–22. Native Virginia to Florida. Stiffly branched shrub to 10 ft. tall, 5–8 ft. wide. Leaves oval to 5 in., glossy dark green above, grayish green beneath. Flowers, 2 in. wide, maroon brown, with strawberrylike fragrance, carried at ends of leafy branchlets May–July, depending on climate and exposure. Blooms followed by brownish, pear-shaped capsules, fragrant when crushed. ▶

C

C. occidentalis. SPICE BUSH. Zones 4–9, 14–22. Native along streams, moist slopes in California Coast Ranges and Sierra Nevada foothills. To 4–12 ft. high. Leaves 2–6 in. long, 1–2 in. wide, bright green, turning yellow in fall. Reddish brown flowers to 2 in. across, resembling small water lilies, appear April–August depending on climate. Both flowers and bruised leaves have fragrance of old wine barrel. Can be trained into multistemmed small tree but is most useful as a background shrub or medium to tall screen. Easily grown from seed.

CALYLOPHUS hartwegii

Onagraceae	
PERENNIAL	
☀ ☽	ZONES 1–3, 10–13
☀ ☽	FULL SUN OR PARTIAL SHADE
○	TOLERATES SOME ARIDITY

An evening primrose look-alike, this perennial grows 8 in. tall, 2 ft. across, and spreads by underground rhizomes. Yellow 1-in. flowers appear over a long season. Plants are dormant in winter, when stems may be cut back.

Calylophus hartwegii

CALYTRIX

Myrtaceae	
EVERGREEN SHRUBS	
☀ ☽	ZONES 15–24
☀ ☽	FULL SUN OR LIGHT SHADE
○	TOLERATE SOME ARIDITY ONCE ESTABLISHED

These Australian shrubs have tiny evergreen leaves and a profusion of small but showy star-shaped flowers. They need excellent drainage and should be kept compact by pruning after bloom. They can be used for low-maintenance plantings or for screening.

Calytrix alpestris

C. alpestris. SNOW MYRTLE. Grows to a graceful, open 6-ft.-tall and -wide shrub, with pink buds opening to white flowers.

C. tetragona. FRINGE MYRTLE. A 3–6-ft. shrub with white or pink flowers followed by calyxes that age to deep red or purple for prolonged color. Choice cut flower.

CAMASSIA

CAMASS	
Liliaceae	
BULBS	
☀	ZONES 1–9, 14–17
☀	FULL SUN
●●	HEAVY WATERING DURING GROWTH

Most species native to moist meadows, marshes, fields in Northern California and Northwest. Starlike, slender-petaled blossoms are carried on spikes in late spring, early summer; grasslike basal leaves dry quickly after bloom. Plant in moist situation, fairly heavy soil, where bulbs can remain undisturbed for many years. Set bulbs 4 in. deep, 6 in. apart. To avoid premature rooting, plant after weather cools in fall.

Camassia quamash

C. cusickii. Dense clusters of pale blue flowers on stems 2–3 ft. tall.

C. leichtlinii. Large, handsome clusters of creamy white flowers on stems 2–4 ft. tall. *C. l. suksdorfii* is attractive blue form. 'Alba' has whiter flowers than species, and 'Plena' has double greenish yellow blooms.

C. quamash (C. esculenta). Loose clusters of deep blue flowers on 1–2-ft. stems; flowers of 'Orion' are deeper blue, those of 'San Juan Form' deeper still.

CAMELLIA

Theaceae	
EVERGREEN SHRUBS OR SMALL TREES	
☀	ZONES 4–9, 12, 14–24
☼	BEST OUT OF STRONG SUN
○	NEED WATER WHEN YOUNG

Native to eastern and southern Asia. There are over 3,000 named kinds; range in color, size, and form is remarkable.

Camellia hiemalis

The following pages briefly discuss the cultural requirements of camellias and describe some of the lesser-known species as well as the widely distributed old favorites and new varieties. The plant descriptions include the unique cultural needs of species and varieties; general cultural requirements appear below.

Camellias need well-drained soil rich in organic material. Never plant camellias so trunk base is below soil line, and never permit soil to wash over and cover this base. Keep roots cool with 2-in.-thick mulch.

Camellias make outstanding container plants—especially in wooden tubs and barrel halves. As a general rule, plant gallon-size camellias into 12–14-in.-wide tubs, 5-gallon ones into 16–18-in. tubs. Fill with a planting mix containing 50 percent or more organic material.

Camellias thrive and bloom best when sheltered from strong, hot sun and drying winds, though some species and varieties are more sun tolerant than others. Tall old plants in old gardens prove that camellias can thrive in full sun when they are mature enough to have roots shaded by heavy canopy of leaves. Young plants will grow better and bear more attractive flowers if grown under partial shade of tall trees, under lath cover, or on north side of a building. A few camellias need shade at any age.

Established plants (over 3 years old and vigorous) can survive on natural rainfall. If your water is high in salts and you irrigate your camellias, leach out accumulated salts with deep soaking—twice in summer—to dissolve harmful salts and carry them deep below the root zone.

Fertilize with a commercial acid plant food. Generally, time to feed is in weeks and months following bloom; read fertilizer label for complete instructions. Don't use more than called for. Better to cut amounts in half and feed twice as frequently. Don't feed sick plants. Poor drainage and water or soil with excess salts are the main troublemakers. Best cure is to move plant into aboveground bed of pure ground bark or peat moss until it recovers.

Scorched or yellowed areas in center of leaves are usually due to sunburn. Burned leaf edges, excessive leaf drop, or corky spots usually indicate overfertilizing. Yellow leaves with green veins are signs of chlorosis. Check drainage, leach, and treat with iron or iron chelates.

One disease may be serious: camellia petal blight. Flowers rapidly turn ugly brown. Browning at edges of petals (especially whites and pale pinks) may be caused by sun or wind, but if brown rapidly runs into center of flower, suspect petal blight. Sanitation is the best control. Pick up all fallen flowers and petals, pick off all infected flowers from plants, and dispose of in covered trash bin; encourage neighbors to do the same. Remove mulch (if you use one), haul it away, and replace with fresh one; a deep mulch (4–5 in.) helps keep spores of fungus from reaching the air.

Some flower bud dropping may be natural phenomenon; many camellias set more buds than they can open. Bud drop can be caused by overwatering, but more often by underwatering, especially during summer. It can also be caused by spells of very low humidity.

Some varieties bear too many flowers. To get nicest display from them, remove buds in midsummer like this: from branch-end clusters remove all but one or two round flower buds (leaf buds are slender); along stems, remove enough to leave single flower bud for each 2–4 in. of branch.

Prune right after flowering or during summer and fall. Remove dead or weak wood and thin when growth is so dense that flowers have no room to open properly. Prune at will to get form you want. Shorten lower branches to encourage upright growth. Cut back top growth to flatten lanky shrubs. Make cut just above scar that terminates previous year's growth (often a slightly thickened, somewhat rough area where bark texture and color change slightly). A cut just above this point will usually force three or four dormant buds into growth.

C. chrysantha. GOLDEN CAMELLIA. Tall, vigorous, open grower with large (6 in. or longer), glossy, net-veined leaves and 2–2½-in. golden yellow flowers. Hybridizers use it to enlarge the camellia color palette.

C. granthamiana. Becomes a big shrub or small tree of rather open growth with leathery, glossy, heavily veined, and crinkled leaves 2–6 in. long. Flowers large (to 6 in. or more), white, single, often with fluted or folded ("rabbit-ear") petals and a heavy central tuft of bright yellow stamens. Flowers open in October, November, and December from large, brown, scaly, silky-haired buds. A cross between this species and *C. reticulata* produced 'China Lady', which looks like a big pink *C. granthamiana*. It has been the parent of several other remarkable seedling camellias. Needs excellent drainage; avoid overwatering.

C. hiemalis. Includes number of varieties formerly listed as Sasanquas but differing in their later and longer bloom and heavier-textured flowers. Four good examples:

'Chansonette'. Vigorous, spreading growth. Large, bright pink, formal double flowers with frilled petals.

'Shishi-Gashira'. One of the most useful and ornamental shrubs. Low growing with arching branches that in time pile up tier on tier to make compact, dark green, glossy-leafed plant. Leaves rather small for camellia, giving medium-fine foliage texture. Flowers rose red, semidouble to double, 2–2½ in. wide, heavily borne over long season—October–March in good year. Full sun or shade.

'Showa-No-Sakae'. Faster growing, more open than 'Shishi-Gashira'; willowy, arching branches. Semidouble to double flowers of soft pink, occasionally marked with white. Try this as espalier or in hanging basket.

'Showa Supreme'. Very similar to above but has somewhat larger flowers of peony form.

Higo camellias. These camellias, bred for 200 years in Japan but only now attracting attention in the United States, are probably varieties of *C. japonica* They are generally compact plants with dense, heavy foliage and thick-petaled single flowers with broad, full brush of stamens in the center. In ideal Higo camellia, mass of stamens should be at least half the diameter of flower. Colors include white, pink, red; both solid and variegated. Many named varieties are already available in this country, and more are likely to appear.

C. japonica. To most gardeners this is the camellia. Naturally a large shrub or small tree but variable in size, growth rate, and habit. Hundred-year-old plants in California reach 20 ft. high and equally wide, and larger plants exist, but most gardeners can consider camellias to be 6–12-ft. shrubs. Many are lower growing.

Here are 17 varieties that are old standbys with western gardeners. Easily obtainable, inexpensive, and handsome even in comparison with some of the newest introductions, they are plants for both beginners and advanced gardeners.

In the list, seasons of bloom are labeled "early," "midseason," and "late." In California "early" means October–January; "midseason" is January–March; "late," March–May. In the Northwest, "early" means December–February; "midseason," March and April; "late," May.

Flower size is also noted for each variety. A "very large" flower is over 5 in. across; "large," 4–5 in.; "medium large," 3½–4 in.; "medium," 3–3½ in.; "small," 2½–3 in.; "miniature," 2½ in. or less.

'Adolphe Audusson'. Midseason. Very large, dark red, semidouble flowers, heavily borne on a medium-size, symmetrical, vigorous shrub. Hardy.

'Adolphe Audusson Variegated' is identical but heavily marbled white on red.

'Alba Plena.' Early. Brought from China in 1792 and still a favorite large, white, formal double. Slow, bushy growth. Early bloom a disadvantage in cold or rainy areas. Protect flowers from rain and wind.

'Berenice Boddy'. Midseason. Medium semidouble, light pink with deeper shading. Vigorous upright growth. One of the most cold hardy.

'Covina'. Midseason–late. Medium, rose red, semidouble to rose-form flowers on a compact plant. Highly sun tolerant.

'Daikagura'. Early–late. Large, rose red, peony-type flowers on a dense, upright bush. Very long bloom season. 'Daikagura Variegated' is similar but has rose red flowers marbled with white.

'Debutante'. Early–midseason. Medium-large, peony-form flowers of light pink. Profusely blooming. Vigorous upright growth.

'Elegans' ('Chandler'). Also known as 'Chandleri Elegans'. Early–midseason. Very large anemone-form camellia with rose pink petals and smaller petals called petaloids, the latter often marked white. Slow growth and spreading, arching branches make it a natural for espalier. Stake to provide height, and don't remove main shoot; it may be very slow to resume upward growth. A 100-year-old-plus variety that remains a favorite. Its offspring resemble it in every way except flower color: 'C. M. Wilson', pale pink; 'Shiro Chan', white, sometimes faintly marked with pink; and 'Elegans (Chandler) Variegated', heavily marbled rose pink and white. A solid rose pink form is called 'Francine'. 'Elegans Champagne' has creamy-centered white flowers. 'Elegans Splendor' is blush pink edged white.

'Glen 40' ('Coquetti'). Midseason–late. Large formal double of deep red. One of best reds for corsages. Slow, compact, upright growth. Handsome even out of flower. Hardy; very good in containers.

'Herme' ('Jordan's Pride'). Midseason. Medium-large, semidouble flowers are pink, irregularly bordered white and streaked deep pink. Sometimes has all solid pink flowers on certain branches. Free blooming, dependable.

'Kramer's Supreme'. Midseason. Very large, deep, full peony-form flowers of deep, clear red. Some people can detect a faint fragrance. Unusually vigorous, compact, upright. Takes some sun.

'Kumasaka'. Midseason–late. Medium large, rose form to peony form, rose pink. Vigorous, compact, upright growth and remarkably heavy flower production make it choice landscape plant. Hardy. Takes morning sun.

'Magnoliaeflora'. Midseason. Medium semidouble flowers of pale pink. Many blossoms, good cut flower. Medium grower of compact yet spreading form. Hardy.

'Mathotiana'. Midseason–late. Very large, rose form to formal double, deep crimson, sometimes with purplish cast. Vigorous upright grower. Takes cold and stands up well in hot-summer areas. Does not grow very well along the southern California coast.

'Mrs. Charles Cobb'. Midseason–late. Large semidouble to peony-form flowers in deep red. Freely flowering. Compact plant with dense foliage. Best in warmer areas.

'Pope Pius IX' ('Prince Eugene Napoleon'). Midseason. A cherry red, medium-large formal double. Medium, compact, upright growth.

'Purity'. Late. White, medium, rose form to formal double, usually showing a few stamens. Vigorous upright plant. Late bloom often escapes rain damage.

'Wildfire'. Early–midseason. Medium, semidouble, orange-red flowers. Vigorous, upright plant.

The preceding 17 are the old classics in the camellia world. The following, all introduced since 1950, may supplant them in time:

Flower Forms of *Camellia japonica*

Single

Semidouble

Formal Double

Peony Form

Anemone Form

Rose Form

'Carter's Sunburst'. Early—late. Large to very large pale pink flowers striped deeper pink. Semidouble to peony-form to formal double flowers on medium, compact plants.

'Drama Girl'. Midseason. Huge semidouble flowers of deep salmon rose pink. Vigorous, open, pendulous growth.

'Grand Slam'. Midseason. Large to very large flowers in glowing deep red. Semidouble to peony form. There is a variegated form.

'Guilio Nuccio'. Midseason. Coral rose, very large semidouble flowers with inner petals fluted in "rabbit-ear" effect. Unusual depth and substance. Vigorous upright growth. Many consider this variety to be the world's finest camellia. Variegated, fringed forms are available.

'Mrs. D. W. Davis'. Midseason. Spectacular, very large, somewhat cup-shaped flowers of palest blush pink open from egg-sized buds. Vigorous, upright, compact plant with very handsome broad leaves.

'Nuccio's Gem'. Midseason. Medium to large, perfectly formed full formal double, white. Strong, full, upright grower.

'Nuccio's Jewel'. Midseason—late. Large loose to full peony-form flowers are white with pink edging on petals.

'Nuccio's Pearl'. Midseason. Medium-size, full formal double flowers are white, with a rim of deep pink outer petals.

'Silver Waves'. Early—midseason. Large, semidouble white flowers have wavy-edged petals.

'Swan Lake'. Midseason—late. Very large, white, formal double to peony-form flower. Vigorous upright growth.

'Tiffany'. Midseason—late. Very large, warm pink flowers. Rose form to loose, irregular semidouble. Vigorous, upright shrub.

'Tom Knudsen'. Early—midseason. Medium to large dark red flowers with deeper red veining. Formal to peony to rose form.

C. lutchuensis. Limber-branched shrub to 10 ft. with tiny (1½-in.-long, ½-in.-wide) leaves and profusion of tiny white flowers with strong, pleasant fragrance. Being used as parent to introduce fragrance to larger camellias. Long, pliant branches make it an easily trained espalier.

C. reticulata. Some of the biggest and most spectacular camellia flowers occur in this species, and likely as not they appear on some of the lankiest and least graceful plants.

Plants differ somewhat according to variety, but generally speaking they are rather gaunt and open shrubs that eventually become trees of considerable size—possibly 35–50 ft. tall. In gardens consider them 10-ft.-tall shrubs, 8 ft. wide. Leaves also variable but tend to be dull green, leathery, and strongly net-veined.

Camellia reticulata

Culture is quite similar to that of other camellias, except that the plants seem intolerant of heavy pruning. This, in addition to their natural lankiness and size, makes them difficult to place in garden. They are at their best in light shade of old oaks, where they should stand alone with plenty of room to develop. They are good container subjects while young, but are not handsome out of bloom. They develop better form and heavier foliage in open ground. In Zones 4–6, grow them in containers so you can move them into winter protection, or plant beneath overhang or near wall.

Best-known varieties have very large, semidouble flowers with deeply fluted and curled inner petals. These inner petals give great depth to flower. All bloom January—May in California, March—May in Northwest. The following varieties are the best choices for garden use:

'Buddha'. Rose pink flower of very large size; inner petals unusually erect and wavy. Gaunt, open; fast growth.

'Butterfly Wings'. Loose, semidouble flower of great size (reported up to 9 in. across), rose pink; petals broad and wavy. Growth open, rather narrow.

'Captain Rawes'. Reddish rose pink semidouble flowers of large size. Vigorous bushy plant with good foliage. Hardiest of Reticulatas.

'Chang's Temple'. True variety is large, open-centered, deep rose flower, with center petals notched and fluted. 'Cornelian' (see below) is sometimes sold as 'Chang's Temple'.

'Cornelian'. Large, deep, irregular peony-form flowers with wavy petals, rosy pink to red, heavily variegated with white. Vigorous plant with big leaves; leaves are usually marked with white. This variety is often sold as

'Chang's Temple' (see description above) or as 'Lion Head'. The true 'Lion Head' is not found in American gardens.

'Crimson Robe'. Very large, bright red, semidouble flowers. Petals firm textured and wavy. Vigorous plant of better appearance than most Reticulatas.

'Purple Gown'. Large, purplish red, peony-form to formal double flowers. Compact plant with best growth habit and foliage in the group.

'Shot Silk'. Large, loose, semidouble flowers of brilliant pink with iridescent finish that sparkles in sunlight. Fast, rather open growth.

'Tali Queen'. Very large, deep reddish pink flowers of loose semidouble form with heavily crinkled petals. Plant form and foliage very good. This plant is often sold as 'Noble Pearl'; true 'Noble Pearl' is not available in this country.

C. rusticana. SNOW CAMELLIA. A race of small-flowered camellias from a cold, extremely snowy part of Japan. Flowers may be white, pink, or red, and single to double in form. Plants tend to be spreading, and branches are remarkably supple. They are not any hardier than *C. japonica* and are generally considered to be a subspecies (*C. j. rusticana*).

C. saluenensis. Shrub of dense leafy growth to 10–15 ft. tall. Leaves elliptic, rather narrow, pointed, thick textured, 1½–2½ in. long and half as wide. Flowers are bell shaped and rather small, varying in color from white to fairly deep pink. Flowering is in early spring. Not of great value in itself, it has brought floriferousness, hardiness, and graceful appearance to a large group of its hybrids.

CAMELLIA BLOOMS FOR CHRISTMAS

These 12 favorite varieties supply flowers in December, in time for holiday decorating and gift-giving: white—'Alba Plena', 'Nuccio's Gem'; pink and coral pink—'Chandleri Elegans', 'Coral Delight', 'Debutante', 'Magnoliaflora'; red or orange red—'Adolph Audusson Variegated', 'Daikagura', 'Freedom Bell', 'Shishi Gashira', 'Wildfire', and 'Yuletide', a Sasanqua.

C. sasanqua. Useful broad-leafed evergreens for espaliers, ground covers, informal hedges, screening, containers, and bonsai. Vary in form from upright and densely bushy to spreading and vinelike. Leaves dark green, shiny, 1½–3½ in. long, a third as wide. Flowers heavily produced in autumn and early winter, short lived, rather flimsy, but so numerous that plants make a show for months. Some are lightly fragrant.

Most Sasanquas tolerate much sun, and some thrive in full hot sun if soil is right and watering ample. They take drought very well. The Sasanquas are perfectly hardy in camellia areas of Pacific Northwest, but flowers are too often damaged by fall and winter rains and frost to call them successful.

'Apple Blossom'. Single white flowers blushed with pink, from pink buds. Spreading plant.

'Cleopatra'. Rose pink semidouble flowers with narrow, curving petals. Growth is erect, fairly compact. Takes clipping well.

'Hana Jiman'. Large semidouble flowers white, edged pink. Fast, open growth; good espalier.

'Jean May'. Large double, shell pink. Compact, upright grower with exceptionally glossy foliage.

'Kanjiro'. Large semidouble flowers of rose pink shading to rose red at petal edges. Erect growth habit.

'Mine-No-Yuki' ('White Doves'). Large, white, peony-form double. Drops many buds. Spreading, willowy growth; effective espalier.

'Momozono-Nishiki'. Large semidouble flowers are rose, shaded white. Twisted petals.

'Narumigata'. Large, single, cupped flowers, white tinged pink.

'Setsugekka'. Large, white, semidouble flowers with fluted petals. Considerable substance to flowers; cut sprays hold well in water. Shrub's growth is upright and rather bushy.

'Tanya'. Deep rose pink single flowers. Tolerates much sun. Good ground cover.

'Yuletide'. Profusion of small, single, bright red flowers on dense, compact, upright plant.

C. sinensis (Thea sinensis). TEA. In the West the tea plant grows as dense round shrub to 15 ft. with leathery, dull, dark green leaves to 5 in. long. Fall flowers are white, small (1½ in. across), and fragrant. Takes well to pruning. Can be trimmed as hedge. Tea can be grown in California but has never been a major crop for economic reasons.

C. vernalis. Certain camellias once classed as Sasanquas have been placed here because they bloom later than Sasanquas, are denser in growth, shinier in leaf, and have firmer-textured flowers. They are generally sold as Sasanquas. Best-known varieties are

'Dawn'. Single to semidouble, small white flowers blushed pink. Dense, upright shrub of unusual hardiness.

'Hiryu'. Deep red, small, rose form. Dense, upright plant. 'Hiryu Nishiki' has white markings on flowers.

Hybrid camellias. The term as used here refers to camellias that are hybrids between two or more species. Several hundred of these hybrids have been introduced, and a few can be found with a little looking. The first wave of hybridizing utilized *C. japonica* and *C. saluenensis;* this cross gave plants of generally good garden form that resembled *C. japonica* in foliage and produced abundant medium-size flowers. Most hybridizing efforts now involve *C. reticulata.* These new hybrids are more spectacular in flower and should be considered separately. (See *C. japonica* for explanations of bloom season and flower size terminology.)

Hybrids involving *C. saluenensis* or other small-flowered species and varieties:

'Coral Delight'. Midseason. Coral pink semidouble flowers form garlands along the branches. Slow grower.

'Donation'. Midseason. Large semidouble flowers of orchid pink borne all along stems. Blooms young and heavily, on vigorous, upright, compact plant with slightly pendulous branches. Quite resistant to cold and sun. Appreciates a little shade in hot, dry areas. There is a variegated form.

'E. G. Waterhouse'. Midseason–late. Medium, full, formal double of excellent form. Light pink flowers heavily produced on vigorous, upright shrub.

'Fragrant Pink'. Midseason. Cross between *C. j. rusticana* and *C. lutchuensis* has loose peony-form flowers on spreading bush. Flowers small, deep pink, very fragrant.

'Freedom Bell'. Midseason. Small to medium, semidouble, bell-shaped blooms of dark red open beneath branches.

'J. C. Williams'. Early–late. Medium single, cup-shaped flowers of phlox pink over very long season. Vigorous upright shrub with rather pendulous branches. This and the similar 'Mary Christian' and 'St. Ewe' are good plants for the Northwest.

Hybrids involving *C. reticulata:*

'Flower Girl'. Early–midseason. Large to very large, semidouble to peony-form flowers of bright pink. Vigorous, upright growth. Profuse flowering and small leaves come from its Sasanqua parent, big flowers from its Reticulata ancestor.

'Francie L.'. Midseason–late. Very large semidouble flowers with upright, wavy petals. Deep rose pink.

'Valentine Day'. Midseason–late. Large to very large, salmon pink, formal double flowers. Fast, upright grower.

'Valley Knudsen'. Midseason–late. Large to very large, deep orchid pink semidouble to loose peony form. Compact upright growth.

CAMPANULA

BELLFLOWER

Campanulaceae (Lobeliaceae)

MOSTLY PERENNIALS; SOME BIENNIALS OR ANNUALS

✿ MOSTLY ZONES 1–9, 14–24

☼ ◑ FULL SUN ON COAST, FILTERED SHADE INLAND

● MOIST SOIL DURING DRY MONTHS

▶ SEE CHART NEXT PAGE

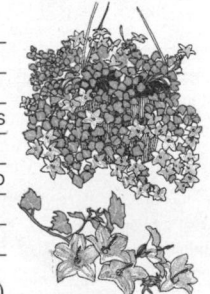

Campanula isophylla

Vast and varied group (nearly 300 species) encompassing trailers, creeping or tufted miniatures, and erect kinds 1–6 ft. tall. Flowers generally bell shaped, but some star shaped, cup shaped, or round and flat. Usually blue, lavender, violet, purple, or white; some pink. Bloom period from spring to fall.

Uses for campanulas are as varied as the plants. Gemlike miniatures deserve special settings—close-up situations in rock gardens, niches in dry walls, raised beds, containers. Trailing kinds are ideal for hanging pots or baskets, wall crevices; vigorous spreading growers serve well as ground covers. Upright growers are valuable in borders, for cutting, occasionally in containers.

In general, campanulas grow best in good, well-drained soil. Most species are fairly easy to grow from seed sown in flats in spring or early summer, transplanted to garden in fall for bloom the following year; also may be increased by cuttings or divisions. Divide clumps in fall every 3–4 years; some may need yearly division. Low-growing kinds especially attractive to snails, slugs.

Campanulaceae. The campanula or bellflower family contains perennials or biennials, typically with bell-shaped or saucer-shaped flowers in shades of blue to purple, lilac, and white. This family includes plants formerly grouped under Lobeliaceae.

CAMPHOR TREE. See CINNAMOMUM camphora   p. 228

CAMPSIS

TRUMPET CREEPER, TRUMPET VINE

Bignoniaceae

DECIDUOUS VINES

✿ ZONES VARY BY SPECIES

☼ ◑ FULL SUN OR PARTIAL SHADE

● MODERATE WATER

Campsis radicans

Vigorous climbers that cling to wood, brick, and stucco surfaces with aerial rootlets. Unless thinned, old plants sometimes become top heavy and pull away from supporting surface. Will spread through garden and into neighbor's by suckering roots. If you try to dig up suckers, any remaining piece of root will grow another plant. Can be trained as big shrub or flowering hedge if branches are shortened after first year's growth. Use for large-scale effects, quick summer screen. All produce open, arching sprays of trumpet-shaped flowers in August and September.

C. grandiflora (Bignonia chinensis). CHINESE TRUMPET CREEPER. Zones 2–12, 14–21. Not as vigorous, large, or hardy as the American native *C. radicans,* but with slightly larger, more open scarlet flowers. Leaves divided into seven to nine leaflets, each 2½ in. long.

C. radicans (Bignonia radicans). COMMON TRUMPET CREEPER. Zones 1–21. Native to eastern United States. Most used in cold-winter areas. Deep freeze will kill to ground but new stems grow quickly. Leaves divided into 9–11 toothed leaflets, each 2½ in. long. Flowers, growing in clusters of 6–12, are 3-in.-long orange tubes with scarlet lobes that flare to 2 in. wide. Grows fast to 40 ft. or more, bursting with health and vigor. There is a rare, yellow-flowered variety, 'Flava'.

C. tagliabuana. All zones. Hybrid between the two above species. 'Mme. Galen', best-known variety, has attractive salmon red flowers. 'Crimson Trumpet' bears pure red blooms.

CANARY BIRD BUSH. See CROTALARIA agatiflora   p. 249

CANARY BIRD FLOWER. See TROPAEOLUM peregrinum   p. 512

CANARY ISLAND BROOM. See GENISTA canariensis   p. 305

CANARY ISLAND DAISY. See ASTERISCUS sericeus   p. 170

CANDLE BUSH. See CASSIA alata   p. 210

CANDOLLEA cuneiformis. See HIBBERTIA cuneiformis   p. 322

CAMPANULA

NAME, TYPE	GROWTH HABIT, SIZE	FOLIAGE	FLOWERS	USES, COMMENTS
Campanula alpestris (**C. allionii**) Perennial	Rosettes spring from creeping rhizome stems 2–5 in. long	Leaves 2 in. long in rosettes	1¾ in. long, erect or horizontal, blue or white. Summer	Rock gardens, borders, edging
C. barbata Short-lived perennial or biennial	Clumps of erect stems, 4–18 in. high	Leaves mostly at base of stem, 2–5 in. long, narrow, hairy	Bell-shaped, lilac blue, bearded inside, 1 in. long, nodding. Few near top of each stem. Summer	Foreground in borders, rock gardens. Tap rooted; needs good drainage. White forms may appear from seed
C. carpatica (**C. turbinata**) TUSSOCK BELLFLOWER Perennial	Compact leafy tufts, stems branching and spreading. Usually about 8 in. tall, may reach 12–18 in.	Leaves smooth, bright green, wavy, toothed, 1–1½ in. long	Open bell- or cup-shaped, blue or white, 1–2 in. across, single and erect on stems above foliage. Late spring	Rock gardens, foreground in borders, edging. Variable in flower size and color. 'Blue Chips' and 'White Chips' good dwarf varieties. Easily grown from seed; sometimes sold as 'Blue Clips', 'White Clips'
C. elatines garganica (**C. garganica**) Perennial	Low (3–6 in. high), with outward spreading stems	Small, gray or green, sharply toothed, heart-shaped leaves	Flat, star-shaped, violet blue. One or a few at top of stem. June to fall	Rock gardens. Usually sold as *C. garganica*. Somewhat like a miniature, prostrate *C. poscharskyana*
C. fragilis Perennial	Vinelike, trailing flower stems 12–16 in. long. Dies back to a tight basal rosette of leaves	Glossy oval leaves 1 in. across	Star-shaped, blue with white centers, 1½ in. across, in leaf joints at ends of branches. Late summer and fall	Choice spots in rock gardens or walls. Hanging containers. A plant for collectors, specialists
C. glomerata Perennial	Upright, with erect side branches to 1–2 ft.	Basal leaves broad, wavy-edged. Stem leaves broad, toothed. Both somewhat hairy	Narrow, bell-shaped, flaring at the mouth, 1 in. long, blue-violet, tightly clustered at tops of stems. June–July	Shaded borders or large rock gardens. Plants have proportionately more foliage than flowers. Seed-grown strains Superba and Alba are deepest purple and white respectively
C. isophylla ITALIAN BELLFLOWER, STAR OF BETHLEHEM Perennial	Trailing or hanging stems to 2 ft. long	Leaves heart-shaped, light green, toothed, 1–1½ in. long and wide	Pale blue, star-shaped, 1 in. wide, profuse in late summer and fall. Variety 'Alba' most popular, has white flowers, larger than the above. Variety 'Mayi' has gray, soft-hairy leaves, large lavender blue flowers	Hanging baskets, wall pots, tops of walls, rock gardens. Choice ground cover for small areas on slopes in mild-winter climates. Filtered shade. Hardy San Francisco and south; in Southern California, best near coast; indoor/outdoor plant in cold-winter areas. Grow from cuttings or from seed of Kristal strain, which blooms first year from winter sowing indoors
C. lactiflora Perennial	Erect, branching, leafy, 3½–5 ft. tall	Oblong, pointed, toothed leaves 2–3 in. long	Broadly bell-shaped to star-shaped, 1 in. long, white to pale blue in drooping clusters at ends of branches. June–Sept.	Rear of borders in sun or partial shade. Needs no dry-season watering. Endures even dry shade and is long lived
C. medium CANTERBURY BELL, CUP-AND-SAUCER Biennial or annual	Sturdy, hairy, leafy, with erect stems 2½–4 ft. tall	Basal leaves 6–10 in.; stem leaves 3–5 in., wavy-margined	Bell-shaped or urn-shaped, 1–2 in. across, single or double, held upright in long, loose open clusters. Purple, violet, blue, lavender, pink, white. May–July. 'Calycanthema' has a broad, colored calyx	Sow seed in May or June for bloom next year, or set out plants from nursery 15–18 in. apart. Good for cutting. 'Calycanthema', commonly called cup-and-saucer, is very popular. Annual variety with bell-shaped flowers (not cup-and-saucer) blooms in 6 months from seed
C. persicifolia PEACH-LEAFED BLUEBELL Perennial	Strong-growing, slender, erect stems 2–3 ft. tall. Plants leafy at base	Basal leaves smooth edged, green, 4–8 in. long. Stem leaves 2–4 in. long, shaped like leaves of peach tree	Open, cup-shaped, about 1 in. across, held erect on short side shoots on sturdy stems. Blue, pink, or white. June–Aug.	Choice plant for borders. Easy to grow from seed sown in late spring. 'Telham Beauty', old but still popular, has 3-in. blue flowers. 'Blue Gardenia' and 'White Pearl' have double flowers
C. portenschlagiana (**C. muralis**) DALMATIAN BELLFLOWER Perennial	Low, leafy, mounding mats 4–7 in. high	Roundish, heart-shaped, deep green leaves with deeply toothed, slightly wavy edges	Flaring bell-shaped, violet blue flowers to 1 in. long; 2 or 3 on each semierect stem. May–Aug., sometimes blooming again in fall	Fine plant for edging or as small-scale ground cover. In warm regions best in partial shade. Spreads moderately fast; is sturdy, permanent, and not invasive. Easily increased by dividing. 'Resholt' variety has deeper blue flowers

CAMPANULA

NAME, TYPE	GROWTH HABIT, SIZE	FOLIAGE	FLOWERS	USES, COMMENTS
C. poscharskyana SERBIAN BELLFLOWER Perennial	Spreading, many branched, leafy, with semiupright flowering stems 1 ft. tall or taller	Long heart-shaped, irregularly toothed, slightly hairy leaves 1–3½ in. long, ¾–3 in. wide	Star-shaped, ½–1 in. across, blue-lilac or lavender. Spring to early summer	Very vigorous. Shaded border near pools, shaded rock gardens, with fuchsias and begonias. Needs little water; takes sun near coast. Small area ground cover. Unlike other campanulas, thrives even in Zones 10–12
C. pyramidalis CHIMNEY BELLFLOWER Biennial or short-lived perennial	Sturdy upright stems, unbranched or branched at base, 4–6 ft. tall	Leaves nearly heart-shaped, about 2 in. long, with long stalks	Flat, saucer-shaped blue or white flowers, over 1 in. long, in dense spikes. July–Sept.	Back of perennial borders, bays in big shrubbery borders, containers. Stake early to keep stems straight. In cold-winter climates mulch around plants
C. rapunculoides ROVER BELLFLOWER Perennial	Clumps of long-stemmed leaves send up 3-ft. spires of blue-purple bells	Leaves medium green, large, heart-shaped at base	Funnel-shaped flowers, 1 in. long. Sometimes pale blue or white	Tough, invasive plant, useful in difficult soils, climates. Don't plant near delicate subjects
C. rotundifolia BLUEBELL OF SCOTLAND, HAREBELL Perennial	Upright or spreading, simple or with many branches, 6–20 in. tall	Leaves green or sometimes slightly grayish. Basal leaves roundish, long-stalked, 1 in. across. Stem leaves grasslike, 2–3 in. long. May dry up before blooming time	Broad, bell-shaped, bright blue, 1 in. across, one or a few nodding in open clusters. July–Aug.	Flower color variable, sometimes in lavender, purple, or white shades. Rock gardens, borders, naturalized under deciduous trees. Self-sows in favorable situations

---

CANDYTUFT. See IBERIS   **p. 329**

CANNA

Cannaceae

TUBEROUS-ROOTED PERENNIALS

✓ ALL ZONES

☼ FULL SUN

◐ HEAVY WATERING DURING BLOOM

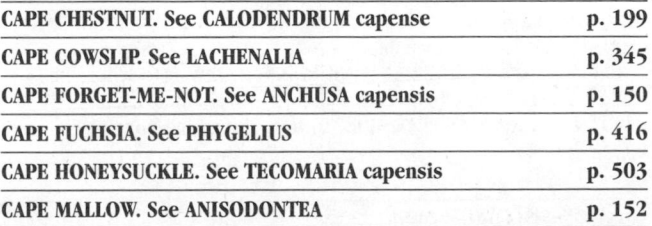

Canna

Native to tropics and subtropics. Best adapted to warm-summer climates; in Zones 1–3, lift and store the roots over winter. An old favorite that can add a tropical touch in the right place. Large, rich green to bronzy red leaves resemble those of banana (*Musa*) or ti plants (*Cordyline terminalis*). Flowers reminiscent of ginger lilies (*Hedychium*) bloom on 3–6-ft. stalks in summer, fall. A dozen or more varieties come in a wide range of sizes and shapes, in white, ivory, shades of yellow, orange, pink, apricot, coral, salmon, and red. Bicolors include 'Cleopatra', with flowers strikingly streaked and spotted red on yellow. Low-growing strains are Grand Opera (26 in.), Pfitzer's Dwarf (2½–3 ft.), and Seven Dwarfs (1½ ft.); grow the last from seed.

Most effective in groups of single colors against plain background. Grow in borders, near poolside (with good drainage), in large pots or tubs on terrace or patio. Leaves useful in arrangements; cut flowers do not keep well. Plant rootstocks in spring after frosts, in rich, loose soil. Set 5 in. deep, 10 in. apart. Remove faded flowers after bloom. After all flower clusters have bloomed, cut stalk to ground.

CANTALOUPE. See MELON, MUSKMELON, CANTALOUPE   **p. 378**

CANTERBURY BELL. See CAMPANULA medium   **p. 204**

CANTUA buxifolia

MAGIC FLOWER, SACRED FLOWER OF THE INCAS

Polemoniaceae

EVERGREEN SHRUB

✓ ZONES 16–24

☼ PARTIAL SHADE

◐ NO WATER ONCE ESTABLISHED

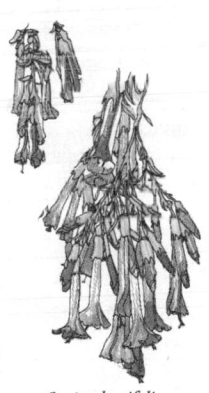

Cantua buxifolia

Native of Peru, Bolivia, and northern Chile. Scraggly open growth to 6–10 ft. Small leaves 1 in. long or less. Magnificent blossoms come sporadically during year; 4-in., tubular, rose or cerise red flowers with yellow stripes appear in terminal clusters, bending branches with their weight. There is a form with yellow flowers and a dwarf ('Hot Pants') with rose pink flowers.

Give light soil. Needs support of stake or trellis. Young plants effective in hanging baskets. Or grow in tub and hide plant when it's out of bloom. Prune after flowering.

CAPE CHESTNUT. See CALODENDRUM capense	**p. 199**
CAPE COWSLIP. See LACHENALIA	**p. 345**
CAPE FORGET-ME-NOT. See ANCHUSA capensis	**p. 150**
CAPE FUCHSIA. See PHYGELIUS	**p. 416**
CAPE HONEYSUCKLE. See TECOMARIA capensis	**p. 503**
CAPE MALLOW. See ANISODONTEA	**p. 152**

FOR INFORMATION ON SELECTING PLANTS
PLEASE SEE PAGES 45–128

CAPE MARIGOLD. See DIMORPHOTHECA, OSTEOSPERMUM	pp. 265, 396
CAPE PONDWEED. See APONOGETON distachyus	p. 154
CAPE PRIMROSE. See STREPTOCARPUS	p. 496
CAPER. See CAPPARIS spinosa	p. 206
CAPE WEED. See ARCTOTHECA calendula	p. 164

Capparaceae. The caper family includes *Capparis,* the caper plant, and *Cleome hasslerana,* the spider flower.

CAPPARIS spinosa

CAPER

Capparaceae

DECIDUOUS SHRUB

☣ ZONES 8, 9, 12–24

☼ FULL SUN

◐ LITTLE WATER

Capparis spinosa

N ative to Mediterranean. Habit varies from sprawling semivine to dense, rounded shrub to 5 ft. Leaves deep green, nearly round, up to 2 in. across (usually less) on sprawling, vinelike, sometimes spiny branches. White, 2–3-in. flowers with showy brushes of lavender stamens rise on long stalks from every leaf base, open at dawn and close in late afternoon. Unopened buds are pickled as commercial capers.

Propagate from cuttings or seed (slow to sprout and grow). Tolerates poor soil but needs good drainage. Grow as ground cover, garden curiosity; or let it spill over a wall.

Caprifoliaceae. The honeysuckle family of shrubs and vines contains many ornamentals in addition to honeysuckle (*Lonicera);* among them are *Abelia, Viburnum,* and *Weigela.*

CARAGANA

PEASHRUB

Fabaceae (Leguminosae)

DECIDUOUS SHRUBS OR SMALL TREES

☣ ZONES 1–21

☼ FULL SUN

◐ TOLERATE SOME ARIDITY

Caragana arborescens

N ative to Russia, Manchuria, Siberia. Leaves divided into small leaflets. Spring flowers shaped like bright yellow sweet peas. Useful where choice is limited by cold, heat, wind, bright sun; nearly indestructible in desert, mountain climates. Use as windbreak, clipped hedge, cover for wildlife.

C. arborescens. SIBERIAN PEASHRUB. Fast growing to 20 ft., with 15-ft. spread. Leaves to 3 in. long, each with four to six pairs of leaflets.

C. frutex. RUSSIAN PEASHRUB. To 10 ft.; leaves have one or two pairs of 1-in. leaflets.

CARAWAY. See CARUM carvi	p. 209
CARDINAL CLIMBER. See IPOMOEA quamoclit	p. 332
CARDINAL FLOWER. See LOBELIA cardinalis	p. 359

CARDIOSPERMUM halicacabum

BALLOON VINE, LOVE-IN-A-PUFF

Sapindaceae

PERENNIAL VINE OFTEN GROWN AS ANNUAL

☣ ALL ZONES AS ANNUAL; 14–24 AS PERENNIAL

☼ ◐ FULL SUN OR LIGHT SHADE

◐ MODERATE WATER

Cardiospermum halicacabum

F ast-growing vine climbing by tendrils. Leaves are divided into deeply toothed leaflets. Small white flowers are followed by inch-wide inflated seed capsules like tiny balloons. Fast, dense growth makes vines useful as temporary screen or cover for chain-link fence. In warm regions, sow seed in place. Where summers are short, start seed indoors.

CARDOON

Asteraceae (Compositae)

PERENNIAL

☣ ZONES 8, 9, 12–24

☼ FULL SUN

◐ REGULAR WATER

Cardoon

V egetable closely related to artichoke but grown for edible leafstalks rather than for flower buds. For climate, soil, and other requirements, see Artichoke. To prepare leaves for harvest, blanch them by gathering them together, tying them up, and wrapping with paper to exclude light. Allow 1 month's blanching before harvest. To cook, cut heavy leaf midribs into 3–4-in. lengths, parboil until tender, then fry; or serve boiled with butter or other sauce. As ornamental, makes large (to 8 ft. or more), striking, gray-green plant that naturalizes in mild-winter climates. Size, spininess rule it out in small gardens. Purple artichokelike flowers attractive cut and dried. Can escape and become weed.

CAREX

SEDGE

Cyperaceae

PERENNIALS

☣ ZONES 4–9, 14–24

☼ ◐ SUN ON COAST, PARTIAL SHADE INLAND

◐◐ CONSTANTLY MOIST SOIL

Carex buchananii

G rasslike, clumping plants grown for foliage effect in borders, rock gardens, containers, water gardens. Long, narrow evergreen leaves are often striped or oddly colored. Specialists offer many varieties.

C. buchananii. LEATHER LEAF SEDGE. Curly-tipped, arching blades 2–3 ft. tall make clumps of striking reddish bronze. Use with gray foliage or with deep greens.

C. comans (C. albula). NEW ZEALAND HAIR SEDGE. Dense, finely textured clumps of narrow leaves are silvery green. Leaves, usually 1 ft. long, may reach 6 ft., and on slopes look like flowing water. Also sold as 'Frosty Curls'. 'Bronze' is similar but has coppery brown leaves.

C. conica 'Marginata'. A 6-in. dwarf sedge with white-margined leaves.

C. elata 'Bowles Golden'. Clumps up to 2 ft. have narrow leaves that emerge bright yellow in spring and hold some color until late summer. Needs much moisture; will grow in water.

C. flacca (C. glauca). BLUE SEDGE. Creeping perennial with blue-gray grasslike foliage 6–12 in. tall; evergreen only in mildest climates. Tolerant of many soils and irrigation schemes; best in moist soil. Not invasive but spreads slowly and can be clipped like a lawn. Endures light foot traffic, moderate shade, competition with tree roots.

C. morrowii expallida (C. m. 'Variegata'). VARIEGATED JAPANESE SEDGE. Drooping leaves striped with green and white make 1-ft. mound. Edging plant; single clumps attractive among rocks. *C. m.* 'Aurea-variegata' has gold-striped leaves. It is known also as *C. m.* 'Goldband'.

CARICA

Caricaceae

EVERGREEN LARGE SHRUBS OR SMALL TREES

⚡ ZONES VARY BY SPECIES

☼ BENEFIT FROM REFLECTED HEAT IN WINTER

💧 AMPLE WATER DURING WARM WEATHER

Carica pubescens

All need excellent drainage, warmth. The key to success is choosing the right location. Root rot in cold, wet soil is the principal cause of failure, so locate plants on south slope or south side of house where winter sun can heat soil.

C. heilbornii. BABACO. Zones 19–24. Native to higher elevations in the Andes. Resembles a dwarfish (5–8-ft.-tall) papaya. Foot-long, seedless fruit's color and texture resemble those of crenshaw melon. Full sun near coast, some afternoon shade inland. Often sold as *C. pentagona.*

C. papaya. PAPAYA. Zones 21, 23, 24; or in greenhouse. Native to tropical America. Grow three to five trees in a group; you need male and female trees for fruit production. Tree grows 20–25 ft. tall, with a straight trunk topped by crown of broad (to 2 ft.), fanlike, deeply lobed leaves on 2-ft.-long stems. Cream-colored flowers are inconspicuous; trees bear fruit when young. To get most fruit, don't attempt to grow papaya as permanent tree. Keep a few plants coming along each year, and destroy old ones. Give plants ample water and fertilizer in warm weather. Grow from seeds saved from fruit, or start with purchased plants.

C. pubescens. MOUNTAIN PAPAYA. Zones 21–24. Native to mountains of Colombia and Ecuador. Generally grown as a shrub, though it resembles a many-trunked, upright tree to 10–12 ft. Foliage borne in dense clusters at tops of trunks. Elaborately lobed, foot-wide leaves are fanlike, veined, sandpapery, dark green above, lighter beneath. Inconspicuous cream-colored flowers. Fruit small, edible when cooked. Male and female plants needed for fruit set.

CARISSA

Apocynaceae

EVERGREEN SHRUBS

⚡ ZONES 22–24; SEE BELOW

☼ ◑ TOLERATE SOME SHADE; FRUIT BEST IN SUN

◐ 💧 LITTLE WATER NEAR COAST, REGULAR INLAND

Carissa macrocarpa

Their rightful climates are Zones 22–24, but so many gardeners find carissa appealing that these shrubs are grown in Zones 12, 13, 16–21—far beyond safe limits. Excellent in ocean wind, salt spray. Easy to grow. Accept variety of soils, exposures. Prune to control erratic growth.

C. edulis. Native to Africa. Differs from widely grown *C. macrocarpa* in several ways. Shrubby or somewhat vinelike to 10 ft.; will grow to 30 ft. high and as wide. Glossy, bright green, red-tinged leaves to 2 in. long. Bears large clusters of pure white, fragrant flowers, opening from pink buds. Cherry-size fruit changes from green to red to purplish black as it ripens.

C. macrocarpa (C. grandiflora). NATAL PLUM. Native to South Africa. Fast-growing, strong, upright, rounding shrub of rather loose habit to 5–7 ft. (occasionally to 18 ft.). Lustrous, leathery, rich green, 3-in. oval leaves. Spines along branches and at end of each twig. White flowers, almost as fragrant as star jasmine and of same five-petaled star shape but larger (to 2 in. wide), appear throughout year, followed by fruit. Flowers, green fruit, and ripe fruit often appear together. Use as screen or hedge. Prune heavily for formal hedges, lightly for informal screen. Strong growth, spines dis-

courage trespassers. Don't plant near walkways, where spines can be annoying to passersby. If you grow Natal plum outside Zones 22–24, give it same favorite spot you'd give bougainvillea—a warm wall facing south or west, preferably with overhang to keep off frost. It may also be grown as an indoor plant in good light.

C. m. 'Boxwood Beauty'. Exceptionally compact growth to 2 ft. and as wide. Deep green leaves, like a large-leafed boxwood. Excellent for hedging and shaping. No thorns.

C. m. 'Fancy'. Upright grower to 6 ft. Unusually large fruit, good show of flowers. Use as lightly pruned screen.

C. m. 'Green Carpet'. Low growing to 1–1½ ft., spreading to 4 ft. or more. Smaller leaves than those of *C. macrocarpa.* Excellent ground cover.

C. m. 'Horizontalis'. To 1½–2 ft., spreading, trailing. Dense foliage.

C. m. 'Minima'. Slow growth to 1–1½ ft. tall, 2 ft. wide. Leaves and flowers both tiny.

C. m. 'Prostrata'. Vigorous, to about 2 ft. and spreading. Good ground cover. Prune out growth that tends upright. Can be trained as espalier.

C. m. 'Ruby Point'. Upright grower to 6 ft. New leaves hold their red color through the growing season.

C. m. 'Tomlinson'. Dwarf, compact growth to 2–2½ ft. high, 3 ft. wide. Shiny mahogany-tinted foliage, large flowers, wine-colored fruit. No thorns. Slow growing. Use as tub plant or for foundation plantings.

C. m. 'Tuttle' (C. m. 'Nana Compacta Tuttlei'). To 2–3 ft. high, 3–5 ft. wide. Compact, dense foliage. Heavy producer of flowers and fruit. Used as ground cover.

CARISSA'S TASTY FRUIT

Carissa macrocarpa, a plant of considerable beauty and function, also offers tasty and useful oval fruits. Pick them when they are 1–2 in. long and red. They're good eaten out of hand or in salads (skin and all). When people describe the taste, they most often use the word "cranberry." If you can pick enough at one time, you can make jelly, sauce, or pie from them. While picking, be wary of the plant's spines.

CARMEL CREEPER. See CEANOTHUS griseus horizontalis   **p. 213**

CARNATION. See DIANTHUS caryophyllus   **p. 262**

CARNEGIEA gigantea

SAGUARO

Cactaceae

GIANT CACTUS

⚡ ZONES 12, 13, 18–21

☼ FULL SUN

◊ NO WATER ONCE ESTABLISHED

Carnegiea gigantea

Native to northern Mexico, Arizona, California. Columnar and branching, with prominent ribs that give it fluted appearance. Grows very slowly to 50 ft. Spines light brown, ½–3 in. long.

Mature plants bloom in May, bearing white, single flowers 4–5 in. long (state flower of Arizona). Night blooming. Oval, edible fruit, sometimes mistaken for flowers, splits open to show red pulp within. Stays pot size or garden size for many years.

CAROB. See CERATONIA siliqua   **p. 217**

CAROLINA ALLSPICE. See CALYCANTHUS floridus   **p. 199**

CAROLINA JESSAMINE. See GELSEMIUM sempervirens   **p. 304**

CAROLINA LAUREL CHERRY. See PRUNUS caroliniana   **p. 439**

CARPENTERIA californica

BUSH ANEMONE

Philadelphiaceae (Saxifragaceae)

EVERGREEN SHRUB

✿ ZONES 5–9, 14–24

☼ ☽ FULL SUN OR PARTIAL SHADE

◗ ● NO WATER ON COAST, SOME INLAND

Carpenteria californica

Native to California, localized in Sierra Nevada foothills between Kings and San Joaquin rivers in Fresno County. Slow growing to 3–6 ft., with many stems arising from base. Older bark light colored and peeling, new shoots purplish. Leaves thick, narrow, dark green above and whitish beneath, 2–4½ in. long. Flowers white, anemonelike, 1½–3 in. wide, with a slight, pleasant fragrance. Blooms May–August. Resistant to oak root fungus.

This attractive native with rather formal look accepts ordinary garden conditions. Inspect new growth occasionally for pest infestation; wash off aphids that could disfigure plants. Spray as new leaves form. Prune after flowering to restrain growth or shape.

CARPET BUGLE. See AJUGA   p. 144

CARPINUS

HORNBEAM

Betulaceae

DECIDUOUS TREES

✿ ZONES VARY BY SPECIES

☼ FULL SUN

● REGULAR WATER

Hardy, well-behaved, relatively small shade trees. Long life and good habits as street trees. Retain leaves well into winter. Fruit—small, hard nutlets in leaflike bracts—is carried in attractive drooping clusters.

Carpinus betulus

C. betulus. EUROPEAN HORNBEAM. Zones 3–9, 14–17. Moderate growth to 40 ft. Dense pyramidal form, eventually becoming broad with drooping outer branches. Dark green, toothed leaves, 2–5 in. long. Fall color yellow or dark red in cold winters. Fruit clusters to 5 in. long. Subject to scale insect infestations. Can be clipped into hedge or screen. Variety 'Fastigiata' is narrow column in youth, dense pyramid in maturity; it is the variety commonly sold.

C. caroliniana. AMERICAN HORNBEAM. Zones 1–9, 14–17. Native from Florida to Texas, north to Virginia, southern Illinois. Moderate growth to round-headed, 25–30-ft. tree. Bark is smooth and gray. Dark green leaves, 1–3 in. long, with toothed edges. In fall, leaves turn mottled yellow and red. Fruit clusters 1½–4 in. long.

CARPOBROTUS

ICE PLANT

Aizoaceae

SUCCULENT PERENNIALS OR SUBSHRUBS

✿ ZONES 12–24

☼ FULL SUN

● USUALLY NO WATER ONCE ESTABLISHED

Carpobrotus chilensis

Coarse-leafed, trailing plants useful for binding sand at the beach and for covering sunny banks (but not steep banks, since their weight when waterlogged could cause them to slide). Can develop patches of dieback if severely stressed by lack of water or nitrogen during growth season. Scale insects can be a problem.

C. chilensis (Mesembryanthemum aequilaterale). Native along coast, Oregon to Baja California. The straight, three-sided, fleshy leaves are 2 in. long; flowers lightly fragrant, rosy purple. Summer bloom.

C. edulis (Mesembryanthemum edule). From South Africa. Leaves curved, 4–5 in. long. Flowers pale yellow to rose. Fruit edible but not particularly good.

CARRION FLOWER. See STAPELIA   p. 492

CARROT

Apiaceae (Umbelliferae)

BIENNIALS GROWN AS ANNUALS

✿ ALL ZONES

☼ FULL SUN

● MAINTAIN EVEN SOIL MOISTURE

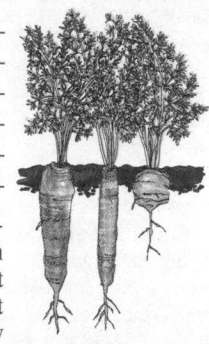

Carrot

The variety to plant depends on the soil's condition: carrots reach smooth perfection only in good-textured soil free of stones and clods. Plant long market kinds only if you can give them a foot of this ideal, light soil. If you can provide only a few inches, plant half-long varieties such as 'Nantes' and 'Chantenay' or miniatures 'Amstel', 'Lady Finger', or 'Short 'n Sweet'.

Sow thickly in rows at least 1 ft. apart. Soil should be fine enough for root development and loose enough so crusting can't check sprouting of seeds. If crust should form, keep soil soft by sprinkling. Too much nitrogen or a lot of manure will make excessive top growth and cause forking of roots. Maintain even soil moisture: alternating dry and wet conditions cause split roots. To grow successive plantings, sow seed when previous planting is up and growing; in cold-winter climates, make last sowing 70 days before anticipated killing frost. When tops are 1–2 in. high, thin plants to 1½ in. apart; thin again if roots begin to crowd. After first thinning, apply narrow band of commercial fertilizer 2 in. out from the row. Begin harvest when carrots reach finger size. In mild-winter climates, carrots store well in the ground; dig as needed.

CARROT THINNINGS TO EAT

Carrot harvesting actually starts with thinning—the removal of excess seedlings when the tops are about 1–2 in. tall to make space for others to grow. Steam the tiny carrots in butter. Or chop the entire miniature plants, tops and all; add to tossed salads for a fresh surprise.

CARROT WOOD. See CUPANIOPSIS anacardioides   p. 251

CARTHAMUS tinctorius

SAFFLOWER, FALSE SAFFRON

Asteraceae (Compositae)

ANNUAL

✿ ALL ZONES

☼ FULL SUN

● INFREQUENT WATER

Carthamus tinctorius

This relative of the thistles is ornamental as well as useful. Erect, spiny-leafed stems, 1–3 ft. tall, bear orange-yellow flower heads above leafy bracts; inner bracts are spiny. Durable cut flower, fresh or dried. Grown commercially for oil extracted from the seeds. The dried flowers have been used for seasoning in place of true saffron, which they somewhat resemble in color and flavor. Sow seeds in place in spring after frosts. An ornamental spineless safflower is also available.

CARUM carvi

CARAWAY

Apiaceae (Umbelliferae)

BIENNIAL HERB

☒ ALL ZONES

☼ FULL SUN

◐ REGULAR WATER

Carum carvi

Mound of carrotlike leaves, 1–2 ft. high, in first year. Umbrellalike clusters of white flowers rise above foliage in second year. Plant dies after seeds ripen in midsummer. Start from seed sown in place in fall or spring. Thrives in well-drained soil. Thin seedlings to 1½ ft. To harvest seed, pick dry heads and rub off seeds. Sift to remove chaff, dry thoroughly, and store in jars. Use dried seeds for flavoring pickles, vegetables, cookies, rye bread.

CARYA illinoensis
(Carya pecan)

PECAN

Juglandaceae

DECIDUOUS TREE

☒ ZONES 4–10, 12–16, 18–23; SEE BELOW

☼ FULL SUN

◐ OCCASIONAL DEEP WATERINGS IN HOT SUMMERS

Carya illinoensis

Native to southern and central United States. Graceful, shapely tree to 70 ft. tall and equally wide. May be grown in Zones 4–10, 12–16, 18–23 as ornamental; Zones 8–10, 12–14, 18–20 for good nut crop. Foliage like that of English walnut but prettier, with more (11–17) leaflets that are narrower and longer (4–7 in.); foliage pattern finer textured, shade lighter. Resistant to oak root fungus.

Needs well-drained, deep soils (6–10 ft. deep). Won't stand salinity. In zinc-deficient desert soils, prevent or cure pecan rosette (abnormal clumps of twigs) with zinc sulfate sprays or soil treatment. Prune to shape or to remove dead wood. Select varieties by climate: 'F. W. Anderson' (self-fertile) is good for San Joaquin Valley; 'Mahan' (self-fertile) thrives in low desert; 'Western Schley' fruits over wide range of climates, needs pollinator. 'Wichita' is good pollinator for 'Western Schley', bears good nuts very young. 'Barton', 'Burkett', 'Choctaw', 'Mohawk', 'Stuart', 'Success', and many others also sold. Of these, 'Burkett' needs pollinator.

To plant, set out bare-root trees in winter. Dig deep holes to accommodate the long taproot; position bud union above soil level. Firm soil about roots, water thoroughly, and irrigate every 1–2 weeks the first year.

Caryophyllaceae. The pink family includes many garden annuals and perennials as well as a few weeds. Leaves are borne in opposite pairs at joints that are often swollen; leaves are often joined together at their bases. Pinks and carnations are typical representatives, along with *Cerastium* and *Lychnis*.

CARYOPTERIS

BLUEBEARD

Verbenaceae

DECIDUOUS SHRUBS

☒ ZONES VARY BY SPECIES

☼ FULL SUN

◐ INFREQUENT WATER

Caryopteris clandonensis

Valued for contribution of cool blue to flower border from August to frost. Generally grown as shrubby perennials. If plant not frozen back in winter, cut back nearly to ground in spring. Cut it back after each wave of bloom for flowers from July to frosts.

C. clandonensis. BLUE MIST. Zones 1–7, 14–17. Low growing to 2-ft.-by-2-ft. mound of narrow, 3-in.-long leaves. Clusters of small blue flowers top upper parts of stems. Selected forms 'Azure' and 'Heavenly Blue' have deep blue flowers. 'Dark Knight' and 'Longwood Blue' have deep blue flowers and silvery foliage. 'Worcester Gold' has yellow leaves, blue flowers.

C. incana (C. mastacanthus). COMMON BLUEBEARD, BLUE SPIRAEA. Zones 1–7, 14–17. Taller growing than *C. clandonensis*, to 3–4 ft., with lavender blue flowers.

C. odorata. HIMALAYAN BLUEBEARD. Zones 3–7, 14–17. Grows to 8 ft. tall, 5 ft. wide, with shiny green foliage and purplish pink flower clusters at branch ends.

CARYOTA

FISHTAIL PALM

Arecaceae (Palmae)

PALMS

☒ ZONES 23, 24; OR INDOORS

☼ PARTIAL SHADE

◐ MODERATE WATER

Caryota ochlandra

Feather palms with finely divided leaves, the leaflets flattened and split at tips like fish tails. Tender. Native to southeast Asia, where they grow in full sun. Indoors, need as much light as possible.

C. mitis. CLUSTERED FISHTAIL PALM. Slow grower to 20–25 ft. Basal offshoots eventually form clustered trunks. Foliage light green. Very tender; thrives only in ideal environment.

C. ochlandra. CANTON FISHTAIL PALM. Will probably reach 25 ft. Medium dark green leaves. Hardiest of the caryotas, it has survived to 26°F.

C. urens. FISHTAIL WINE PALM. Single-stemmed palm to 100 ft. in Asia, to 15–20 ft. here with careful protection. If temperatures go below 32°F, it's certain to die. Dark green leaves. Avoid handling fruit with bare hands; invisible crystals can cause severe itching.

CASCARA sagrada. See RHAMNUS purshiana	p. 453
CASHMERE BOUQUET. See CLERODENDRUM bungei	p. 235

CASIMIROA edulis

WHITE SAPOTE

Rutaceae

EVERGREEN TREE; SOMETIMES DECIDUOUS

☒ ZONES 15, 16, 22–24

☼ FULL SUN

◐ REGULAR WATER

Casimiroa edulis

Beautiful tropical tree that will withstand more cold than most avocados, does well wherever lemons are grown. To 50 ft. Keep it to almost any height by pinching out terminal bud, creating wide umbrellalike form. Prune off lower branches. Luxuriant, glossy green leaves divided fanwise into three to seven oval, 3–5-in.-long leaflets.

Tree bears heavy crop of 3–4-in., round, pale green to yellow fruits. Flavor is described in many ways: similar to peach but more bland, like banana but sweeter, like ripe pear in rich syrup, like custard with banana-peach flavor. Consistency of custard. Fruit ripens August through November. Overripe fruit becomes slightly bitter. Pick when firm ripe, at which point it is mellow and sweet. Mature tree may produce several hundred pounds of fruit, far more than any one family can use. Cleanup becomes a chore, so plant where dropping fruit can be raked up or get lost in a ground cover. Goes deciduous for short time—when hit by frost or in June—when tree can become completely bare for brief period. ▶

209

Needs consistent feeding. Budded trees give best fruit and are grown in limited quantities; 'Coleman', 'Pike', 'Wilson', and 'Suebelle' are all good.

CASSIA

SENNA

Fabaceae (Leguminosae)

EVERGREEN OR DECIDUOUS SHRUBS OR TREES

✎ ZONES VARY BY SPECIES

☼ FULL SUN

💧 INFREQUENT, DEEP WATERING

Cassia artemisioides

These shrubs and trees from many lands provide a great number of landscaping choices for Southern California and Arizona. "Yellow" and "golden" are the words for cassia. Flowers may be yellow, bright yellow, egg-yolk yellow, deep yellow, gold. *C. excelsa* and *C. leptophylla* will grow in lawns where drainage is fast. Many species have been reclassified as *Senna*.

Flowering dates in the following list are approximate. Many species will bloom almost any time or scatter bloom over a long period.

C. alata (Senna alata). CANDLE BUSH. Deciduous shrub. Zone 23. Native to tropics. Grows 8–12 ft. tall and spreads wider. Golden yellow flowers (1 in. wide) in big spikelike clusters, November–January. Leaves divided into 12–28 leaflets 2½ in. long. Prune hard after bloom.

C. artemisioides (Senna artemisioides). FEATHERY CASSIA. Evergreen shrub. Zones 8, 9, 12–16, 18–23. Native to Australia. Attractive, light, and airy structure to 3–5 ft. Leaves are gray, divided into six to eight needlelike, 1-in.-long leaflets. Flowers (¾ in.) sulfur yellow, five to eight in a cluster, January–April, often into summer. Prune lightly after flowering to eliminate heavy setting of seed. Needs no water once established.

C. bicapsularis (Senna bicapsularis). Evergreen shrub. Zones 13, 22–24. Native to tropics. To 10 ft. Recovers after killed to ground by frost. Yellow, ½-in.-wide flowers in spikelike clusters, October–February, if not cut short by frost. Prune severely after flowering. Leaflets roundish, rather thick, six to ten to a leaf.

C. candolleana (Senna candolleana). Evergreen shrub. Zones 12–24. To 5–6 ft. Showy golden yellow flowers in fall.

C. corymbosa (Senna corymbosa). FLOWERY SENNA. Large evergreen shrub. Zones 12, 13, 21–24. Native to Argentina. Naturalizes. To 10 ft. Yellow flowers in rounded clusters, spring to fall. Dark green leaves with six narrow, oblong, 1–2-in. leaflets. Prune severely after flowering. For small garden, less rank-growing *C. tomentosa* is better.

C. didymobotrya. Evergreen shrub. Zones 13, 22–24. Native to east Africa. Naturalizes. Rangy grower to 10 ft. Leaflets 2 in. long, 8–16 pairs per leaf. Yellow, 1½-in.-wide flowers in upright, dense clusters (to 1 ft.), December–April. Thrives in heat. Smelly but attractive plant for large wild gardens. Also sold as *Senna didymobotrya* and *C. nairobensis*.

C. excelsa (C. fistula). CROWN OF GOLD TREE. Partially evergreen tree. Zones 12, 13, 19–24. Native to Argentina. Grows fast to 25–30 ft. Leaves divided into 10–20 pairs of 1-in.-long leaflets. Large bright yellow flowers in 12–16-in.-long clusters, late summer, early fall. Prune hard after flowering. Needs moisture in growing season.

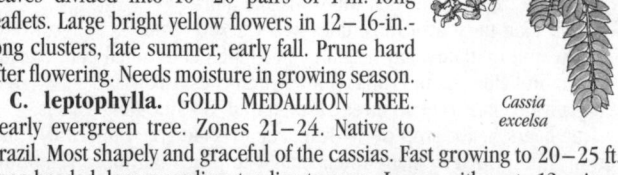

Cassia excelsa

C. leptophylla. GOLD MEDALLION TREE. Nearly evergreen tree. Zones 21–24. Native to Brazil. Most shapely and graceful of the cassias. Fast growing to 20–25 ft.; open headed, low spreading, tending to weep. Leaves with up to 12 pairs of narrow leaflets. Deep yellow flowers to 3 in. wide, in 6–8-in.-long spikes through July–August; scattered blooms later. Prune as for *C. excelsa*.

C. multijuga (Senna multijuga). Evergreen tree. Zones 22–24. Native to Brazil. Heavy-foliaged, much-branched tree to 15–20 ft. Somewhat brittle. Yellow, 2-in.-wide flowers in clusters in late summer and fall. Leaves have 18–40 pairs of rather narrow leaflets that grow to ¾ in. long. Prune as for *C. excelsa*.

C. nemophila (C. eremophila). Zones 12–24. Resembles *C. artemisioides* but has green rather than gray foliage and takes cold somewhat better.

C. phyllodenia. Evergreen shrub. Zones 11–24. Grows rapidly to 5–6 ft. tall. Leaves are narrow, curved, silvery gray. Sulfur yellow flowers appear over a long season—December through April in Phoenix. Needs no feeding. Prune only to shape or remove dead wood.

C. splendida (Senna splendida). GOLDEN WONDER SENNA. Evergreen shrub. Zones 12, 13, 21–24. Native to Brazil. This name has been applied to a number of cassias of varying growth habits. To 10–12 ft. high and about as wide.

Orange-yellow, 1½-in.-wide flowers in loose clusters at branch ends, November–January. Other plantings of cassias with this name, with bright yellow flowers, are strongly horizontal in branch pattern, 5–8 ft. high, spreading to 12 ft. wide. All must be severely pruned after flowering.

C. sturtii (Senna sturtii). Evergreen shrub. Zones 12–14. Native to Australia. Leaves with two to five pairs of narrow, inch-long leaflets. Bushy, 3–6-ft., gray-green shrub with clustered bright yellow flowers. Longer bloom than *C. artemisioides*, neater plant.

C. surattensis (C. glauca or Senna surattensis). Evergreen shrub. Zones 19–24. Grows fast to 6–8 ft. and spreads wider. Bright yellow flowers (¾ in. wide) in small clusters at branch ends, nearly all year. Roundish, 1½-in.-long leaflets, 12–20 to each leaf. Does not need to be pruned heavily. One of best for small gardens.

C. tomentosa (Senna multiglandulosa). WOOLLY SENNA. Evergreen shrub. Zones 13, 17, 22–24. Native to Mexico and South America. Vigorous, rank growth to 12–15 ft. Leaves divided into 12–16 leaflets, each 2½ in. long, that are green above, white and hairy beneath. Deep yellow flowers in upright clusters at ends of branches in winter, early spring. Prune hard after flowering.

CASTANEA

CHESTNUT

Fagaceae

DECIDUOUS TREES

✎ ZONES 2–9, 14–17

☼ FULL SUN

💧 OCCASIONAL DEEP WATERINGS

Castanea mollissima

The American chestnut (*C. dentata*) has become nearly extinct as a result of a fungal disease. However, two other chestnuts are available in the West. They have handsome dark to bright green foliage. Creamy white, small flowers in long (8–10-in.), slim catkins make quite a display in June or July. The large edible nuts are enclosed in prickly burrs. These are wonderful dense shade trees where there is space to accommodate them, as at large country places.

C. mollissima. CHINESE CHESTNUT. Native to China, Korea. Grows to 60 ft. with rounded crown that may spread to 40 ft. Leaves 3–7 in. long, with coarsely toothed edges. Most nursery trees are grown from seed, not cuttings; hence, nuts are variable but generally of good quality. Single trees bear lightly or not at all. Plant two or more to ensure cross-pollination and you'll get a substantial crop. Intolerant of alkaline soil conditions.

C. sativa. SPANISH CHESTNUT. Native to southern Europe, north Africa, western Asia. Larger, broader tree than *C. mollissima*. Can reach 100 ft. in height with greater spread, but usually a 40–60-ft. tree in gardens. Leaves 4–9 in. long, with sharply toothed edges. Produces large chestnuts of excellent quality; these are the nuts usually sold in markets. Size, litter, and disagreeable odor of pollen make it a tree for wide-open spaces. Resistant to oak root fungus.

Dunstan hybrid chestnuts. Zones 2–9, 14–24. These are offspring of American and Chinese chestnut parents, with characteristics intermediate between the two (the American chestnut is—or was—a tall, broad timber tree with small but very sweet nuts). The hybrids seem resistant to the blight and produce nuts equal to Spanish chestnuts in size and sweeter in flavor.

CASTANOSPERMUM australe

MORETON BAY CHESTNUT

Fabaceae (Leguminosae)

EVERGREEN TREE

✂ ZONES 18–22

☼ FULL SUN

⬤ TOLERATES SOME ARIDITY

Castanospermum australe

Native to Australia. Beautiful in foliage; spectacular in flower. To 50–60 ft. tall, nearly as wide. Large, shiny, dark green leaves are divided into 11–15 leaflets about 1½ by 5 in. Flowers bright red and yellow, in stiff spikes about 8 in. long. They grow from twigs, branches, and main trunk in summer. Seeds like chestnuts are occasionally roasted and eaten but don't taste very good.

CAST-IRON PLANT. See ASPIDISTRA elatior	**p. 169**
CASTOR BEAN. See RICINUS communis	**p. 461**

CASUARINA

BEEFWOOD, SHE-OAK

Casuarinaceae

EVERGREEN TREES

✂ ZONES 8, 9, 12–24

☼ FULL SUN

⬤ NO WATER ONCE ESTABLISHED

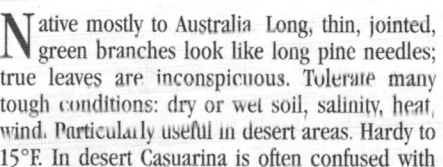

Casuarina stricta

Native mostly to Australia. Long, thin, jointed, green branches look like long pine needles; true leaves are inconspicuous. Tolerate many tough conditions: dry or wet soil, salinity, heat, wind. Particularly useful in desert areas. Hardy to 15°F. In desert Casuarina is often confused with Athel tamarisk (*Tamarix aphylla*) because of similar foliage. Distinctive difference: the casuarina's conelike fruit.

C. cunninghamiana. RIVER SHE-OAK. Tallest and largest. To 70 ft. Finest texture, with dark green branches.

C. equisetifolia. HORSETAIL TREE. Fast grower to 40–60 ft., 20 ft. wide. Has pendulous, gray-green branches. Plant sold under this name may be *C. cunninghamiana* or hybrid between it and *C. glauca*.

C. stricta (C. verticillata). MOUNTAIN or DROOPING SHE-OAK, COAST BEEFWOOD. Fast grower to 20–35 ft. Darkest green foliage and largest cones (1 in.). Makes beautiful silhouette against sky. Attractive street tree. Good at seashore.

CATALINA CHERRY. See PRUNUS lyonii	**p. 441**
CATALINA IRONWOOD. See LYONOTHAMNUS floribundus	**p. 363**
CATALINA PERFUME. See RIBES viburnifolium	**p. 461**

CATALPA

Bignoniaceae

DECIDUOUS TREES

✂ ALL ZONES

☼ FULL SUN

⬤ TAKE SOME ARIDITY

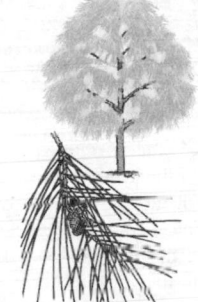

Catalpa speciosa

Catalpas are among the few truly hardy deciduous trees that can compete in flower and leaf with the subtropicals of Southern California. Large, upright clusters of trumpet-shaped, 2-in.-wide flowers, pure white, striped and marked with yellow and soft brown, are displayed in late spring and summer above large, bold, heart-shaped leaves. Flowers are followed by long, bean-shaped seed capsules, sometimes called Indian beans or Indian stogies.

Unusually well adapted to extremes of heat and cold and to soils throughout the West. Where winds are strong, should be planted in lee of taller trees or buildings to protect leaves from wind damage. Some gardeners object to litter of fallen flowers in summer and seed capsules in autumn. Plants need shaping while young, seldom develop a well-established dominant shoot. Shorten side branches as tree grows. When branching begins at the desired height, remove lower branches.

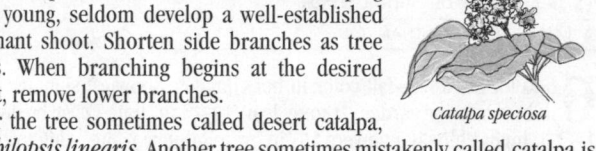

Catalpa speciosa

For the tree sometimes called desert catalpa, see *Chilopsis linearis*. Another tree sometimes mistakenly called catalpa is the very similar *Paulownia tomentosa*, or empress tree, with lavender flowers. *Paulownia* shows flower buds in winter; catalpa does not.

C. bignonioides. COMMON CATALPA, INDIAN BEAN. Native to southeastern United States. Generally smaller than *C. speciosa*, 20–50 ft. according to climate or soil, with somewhat smaller spread. Leaves 5–8 in. long, often in whorls, give odd odor when crushed. The variety 'Aurea' has yellow leaves. Resistant to oak root fungus.

C. b. 'Nana'. UMBRELLA CATALPA. A dense globe form usually grafted high on *C. bignonioides*. Almost always sold as *C. bungei*. It never blooms. Cut it back to keep it in scale.

C. erubescens 'Purpurea'. Young leaves and branchlets of this catalpa are deep blackish purple, turning purple-toned green in summer.

C. speciosa. WESTERN CATALPA. Native southern Illinois to Arkansas. Round headed; 40–70 ft. tall. Leaves 6–12 in. long; no odor when crushed. Fewer flowers per cluster than for *C. bignonioides*. Most widely distributed in the West. Early training and pruning will give tall trunk and umbrella shaped crown.

CATANANCHE caerulea

CUPID'S DART

Asteraceae (Compositae)

PERENNIAL

✂ ALL ZONES

☼ FULL SUN

⬤ TOLERATES SOME ARIDITY

Catananche caerulea

Sturdy, free-flowering plant for summer borders and arrangements. Leaves gray green, 8–12 in. long, mostly at base of stem. Lavender blue, 2-in. flower heads reminiscent of cornflowers are surrounded by strawlike, shining bracts. Stems 2 ft. tall. Flowers may be dried for use in bouquets. Remove faded flowers to prolong bloom. 'Alba' is a white variety.

CATHA edulis

KHAT

Celastraceae

EVERGREEN SHRUB

✂ ZONES 12, 13, 16–24

☼ FULL SUN

⬤ TOLERATES SOME ARIDITY

Catha edulis

Valued for all-year foliage beauty. Bronzy green, shiny, oval, 2–4-in.-long, slightly toothed leaves take on reddish tints through fall and winter. Grown as spreading shrub to 8 ft. tall; old plants in parks are more than 20 ft. tall. Pinch or prune to keep compact. Effective as espalier. Red stems and bark add interest. Medium-size leaves make good transition between small-scale foliage and large leaves, such as those of loquat. Very small white flowers. Needs fast drainage but not rich soil. Does well in poor soil, dry situations, or coastal winds.

CATHARANTHUS roseus (Vinca rosea)

MADAGASCAR PERIWINKLE

Apocynaceae

PERENNIAL OFTEN GROWN AS ANNUAL

☑ ALL ZONES

☼ ◑ FULL SUN OR PARTIAL SHADE

◐ LOOKS THIRSTIER THAN IT IS

Catharanthus roseus

Good for summer–fall color in hot climates. Showiest summer flower in hot, interior gardens. Glossy leaves 1–3 in. long cover bushy plant 1–2 ft. high. Phloxlike flowers 1½ in. wide in pure white, white with rose or red eye, blush pink, or bright rose. The Little series grows a compact 8–10 in. Creeping strains, including the Carpet series, grow 4–8 in. tall, 1½ ft. wide. Will bloom first season from seed sown early indoors, in greenhouse or cold frame. Nurseries sell plants in late spring. Self-sows readily.

Continues to flower after zinnias and marigolds have gone, until Thanksgiving if weather stays mild. Lives over in frostless areas but may look ragged in winter. In coastal areas, blooms in hot late summer.

CATTLEYA

Orchidaceae

EPIPHYTIC ORCHIDS

◑ BRIGHT INDOOR LIGHT

◐ REGULAR WATER

Cattleya

Native to tropical America. Most popular and best known of orchids. Showy flowers are used for corsages.

Species, varieties, and hybrids are too numerous to list here. All have pseudobulbs, 1–3 in. thick, bearing leathery leaves and a stem topped with one to four or more flowers. Plants range from a few inches tall to 2 ft. or more. Commercial growers offer wide range of flower colors—lavender and purple; white; semialbas (white with colored lip) including some novelties such as yellow, orange, red, green, bronze (many of these are crosses between *Cattleya* and other genera).

All cattleyas grow best in greenhouse where temperature, humidity, and light can be readily controlled. However, you can also grow them as house plants. Main requirements: (1) warm temperature (60°F at night, 70°F or higher during the day); (2) relatively high humidity—50–60 percent or more; (3) good light—20–40 percent of outside light with protection from hot midday sun. (Color of orchid foliage should be light green and leaves should be erect. When light intensity is too low, leaves turn dark green and new growth becomes soft.) Also see Orchidaceae.

CAULIFLOWER

Brassicaceae (Cruciferae)

ANNUAL OR BIENNIAL GROWN AS ANNUAL

☑ ALL ZONES

☼ FULL SUN

◐ REGULAR WATER

Cauliflower

Related to broccoli and cabbage; has similar cultural requirements but is more difficult to grow. Easiest in cool,

humid coastal regions; where summers are dry and hot, grow it to harvest well before or well after midsummer. Home gardeners usually plant one of the several 'Snowball' varieties or hybrids such as 'Early White Hybrid' and 'Snow Crown Hybrid'. An unusual variety is 'Purple Head', a large plant with a deep purple head that turns green in cooking. 'Romanesco' makes cone-shaped heads of light green flowerets that are less tightly packed than those of other cauliflowers. Considered to have a fine flavor. 'Cauli-Broc' Hybrid', a cross between cauliflower and broccoli, has a light green curd with a flavor resembling that of both parents.

Grow cauliflower like broccoli. Start with small plants. Space them 18–20 in. apart in rows 3 ft. apart. Be sure to keep plants actively growing; any check during transplanting or later growth is likely to cause premature setting of undersized heads. When heads first appear, tie up the large leaves around them to keep them white. Harvest heads as soon as they reach full size. 'Ravella Hybrid' is self-blanching; leaves curl over developing head without assistance.

CEANOTHUS

WILD LILAC

Rhamnaceae

EVERGREEN SHRUBS, SMALL TREES, GROUND COVERS

☑ ZONES 1–9, 14–24; SEE BELOW

☼ FULL SUN

◐ ◑ NO WATER NEAR COAST, SOME INLAND

▶ SEE CHART

Ceanothus gloriosus

Some species grow in eastern United States, Rocky Mountains, the Northwest, and Mexico, but most are native to California. They range in flower color from white through all shades of blue to deep violet blue. They all flower in spring, mostly in March or April. In descriptions on chart, time of flowering is not indicated unless it is unusual. New varieties (most of them propagated from selected wild plants) appear frequently, and old varieties disappear from nurseries. For the widest choice deal with a specialist in western natives. In Zones 1–3, 8, 9, stay with varieties locally tested and sold.

Ceanothus sometimes get aphids and whitefly, but these are easy to control. As a group, ceanothus plants don't live very long; 5–10 years is typical.

Ceanothus griseus horizontalis

THE BEST CARE FOR CEANOTHUS?

Take a tip from nature. Almost all kinds of ceanothus can succumb to root rot caused by water mold organisms. This doesn't happen in the wild because the plants grow on rocky slopes and go without surface water all summer. But in the garden, water's a major factor. If possible, plant ceanothus beyond reach of sprinklers or drip emitters, and water them by hose through the first dry season only.

FOR INFORMATION ON YOUR CLIMATE ZONE

PLEASE SEE PAGES 15–44

CEANOTHUS

SPECIES OR VARIETY	SIZE	FOLIAGE	FLOWERS	COMMENTS
Ceanothus 'Blue Jeans'	7–9 ft. tall, 7–9 ft. wide	Dark green, leathery leaves	Profuse, pale powder blue clusters	Tolerates heavy soil, drought, summer water. Shear after bloom for low-water-use hedge
C. 'Centennial'	2 ft. tall, 10 ft. wide	Small, shiny dark green leaves	Very dark blue, in short clusters	More heat resistant than *C. griseus horizontalis*
C. 'Concha'	6–7 ft. tall, 6–8 ft. wide	Densely clad in dark green 1-in. leaves	Dark blue 1-in. clusters	One of the best. Tolerates summer water. Hardy to 15°F
C. 'Dark Star'	5–6 ft. tall, 8–10 ft. wide	Tiny (¼-in.), dark green leaves	Dark cobalt blue 1½-in. clusters	Similar to 'Julia Phelps', maybe better. Deerproof
C. fendleri	From prostrate to 6 ft.	1-in. gray-green leaves, partially evergreen or deciduous	Bluish white	Native to Rocky Mountains. Hardy in Zones 1–3
C. 'Frosty Blue'	6–9 ft. tall, 8–10 ft. wide	Dark green ½-in. leaves. Dense	Deep blue, white-frosted, 2½–3-in. spikelike clusters	Flowers shimmer with white. Sturdy stems. Can be shaped as small tree
C. 'Gentian Plume'	10–20 ft. tall, 12–20 ft. wide	Dark green 2½-in. leaves	Dark blue 10-in. spikelike clusters	Leggy when young; pinching helps. If stems get so long that plants "fall apart," prune them
C. gloriosus POINT REYES CEANOTHUS	1–1½ ft. tall, 12–16 ft. wide	Dark green, oval 1-in. leaves, tough and spiny	Mostly light blue 1-in. clusters	Much used in Zones 4–6. Does not do well in summer heat of Zones 7, 14, 18–21
C. g. 'Anchor Bay'	1–1½ ft. tall, 6–8 ft. wide	Very dense	Somewhat deeper blue than above	Dense foliage holds down weeds
C. g. exaltatus 'Emily Brown'	2–3 ft. tall, 8–12 ft. wide	Dark green, hollylike 1-in. leaves	Dark violet blue 1-in. clusters	Stands heavy soil, water near coast
C. g. porrectus	3–4 ft. tall, 6–8 ft. wide	Dark green, hollylike ½-in. leaves	Medium dark blue 1-in. clusters	Dense growth but sparse bloom
C. griseus horizontalis CARMEL CREEPER	1½–2½ ft. tall, 5–15 ft. wide	Glossy, oval, 2-in., bright green leaves	Light blue 1-in. clusters	Some sold under this name may be 'Hurricane Point'. Sometimes winter-damaged in Zones 4–7, 14
C. g. h. 'Hurricane Point'	2–3 ft. tall, to 36 ft. wide	Glossy, oval 2-in. leaves	Pale blue 1-in. clusters	Very fast, somewhat rank grower. Deer love this and the other forms of *C. griseus*
C. g. h. 'Yankee Point'	2–3 ft. tall, 8–10 ft. wide	Glossy, dark green 1½-in. leaves	Medium blue 1-in. clusters	One of best ground-covering kinds. Looks refined
C. g. 'Louis Edmunds'	5–6 ft. tall, 9–20 ft. wide	Bright glossy green 1-in. leaves	Medium sea blue 1-in. clusters	Stands heavy soil, water
C. g. 'Santa Ana'	4–5 ft. tall, 10–15 ft. wide	Rich dark green ½-in. leaves	Dark midnight blue 1-in. clusters	Small leaves, somewhat brushy stems, but beautiful flowers
C. hearstiorum	6 in. tall, 6–8 ft. wide	Bumpy 1½-in. leaves	Medium blue 1-in. clusters	One of flattest, but lets in weeds. Spreads from center like a star. Variable performance; not dependable
C. impressus SANTA BARBARA CEANOTHUS	6–9 ft. tall, 10–15 ft. wide	Dense mass of dark green ½-in. leaves	Lovely dark blue 1-in. clusters	Temperamental; does best near coast
C. 'Joyce Coulter'	2–5 ft. tall, 10–12 ft. wide	Medium green 1-in. leaves	Medium blue 3–5-in. spikelike clusters	Grows as mound rather than ground cover

▶

CEANOTHUS

SPECIES OR VARIETY	SIZE	FOLIAGE	FLOWERS	COMMENTS
C. 'Julia Phelps'	4½–7 ft. tall, 7–9 ft. wide	Small (½-in.), dark green leaves	Dark indigo blue 1-in. clusters	One of best colors, best bloomers
C. maritimus	1–3 ft. tall, 3–8 ft. wide	Blue-green to grayish ½-in. leaves, typically gray or white beneath	White to pale lavender ½-in. clusters	Height and color vary greatly. 'Frosty Dawn' has darker blue flowers. 'Point Sierra' is more tolerant of interior heat
C. 'Owlswood Blue'	8–10 ft. tall, 10–12 ft. wide	Dark green, oval 2½-in. leaves	Dark blue 4–6-in. spikelike clusters	Reliable, heavy bloom
C. prostratus SQUAW CARPET, MAHALA MATS	Prostrate; to 8 ft. wide	Leathery, toothed, light green leaves, ½–1 in. long	Deep to light blue clusters	Blooms Apr.–June. Useful in native range (higher elevations in northern Sierra Nevada), nearly impossible elsewhere. *C. p. occidentalis,* from northern Coast Ranges, is rare, difficult
C. 'Ray Hartman'	12–20 ft. tall, 15–20 ft. wide	Big (2–3-in.), dark green leaves	Medium blue 3–5-in. spikelike clusters	Can be trained as small tree
C. rigidus 'Snowball'	6 ft. tall, 12–16 ft. wide	Dark green ½-in. leaves	White puffs, ¾ in. wide	Handsome, dense, mounding
C. 'Sierra Blue'	10–12 ft. tall, 8–10 ft. wide	Glossy, medium green 1½-in. leaves	Bright medium blue 6–8-in. spikelike clusters	Very fast grower; weedy first few years
C. thyrsiflorus BLUE BLOSSOM	6–21 ft. tall, 8–30 ft. wide	Green, glossy leaves to 2 in.	Light to dark blue 3-in. spikelike clusters	One of the hardiest evergreen ceanothus. *C. t. repens* is a prostrate form
C. t. 'Skylark'	3–6 ft. tall, 5 ft. wide	Glossy, medium green 2-in. leaves	Dark blue clusters; profuse bloom over a long season	Tolerates summer water
C. t. 'Snow Flurry'	6–10 ft. tall, 8–12 ft. wide	Rich green 2-in. leaves	Profuse pure white clusters	
C. velutinus TOBACCO BRUSH	3–8 ft. tall, 3–8 ft. wide	Glossy, aromatic leaves 3 in. long	White, late in season	Useful in native plantings in cold climates. Zones 1–3

CEDRELA

Meliaceae

DECIDUOUS TREES

☀ ZONES VARY BY SPECIES

☼ FULL SUN

◐ REGULAR WATER

Cedrela sinensis

Flower in spring. Leaves with many leaflets, somewhat like those of *Ailanthus altissima* (tree of heaven).

C. fissilis. Zones 16, 17, 22–24. Native to Central and South America. Smooth-trunked, round-headed tree grows to 50 ft. or more. Beautiful old street trees in Santa Barbara. Yellowish, velvety flowers in dense, drooping clusters followed by star-shaped, woody capsules containing winged seeds; much prized for dry arrangements.

C. sinensis (Toona sinensis). Zones 2–9, 14–24. Native to China. Slow to medium growth to 50 ft. Long, pendulous clusters of white flowers appear in April and May, followed by capsules similar to those of *C. fissilis.* Prized for beauty of new growth—tinted in shades of cream, soft pink, and rose. Suckers freely.

FOR GROWING SYMBOL EXPLANATIONS
PLEASE SEE PAGE 129

CEDRUS

CEDAR

Pinaceae

EVERGREEN TREES

☀ ZONES VARY BY SPECIES

☼ FULL SUN

○ NO WATER ONCE ESTABLISHED

Cedrus atlantica

These conifers, the true cedars, are among the most widely grown conifers in the West. Cedars bear needles in tufted clusters. Cone scales, like those of firs, fall from tree, leaving a spiky core behind. Male catkins produce prodigious amounts of pollen that may cover you with yellow dust on a windy day. All are deep rooted and aridity tolerant once established.

C. atlantica (C. libani atlantica). ATLAS CEDAR. Zones 2–23. Native to Algeria. Slow to moderate growth to 60 ft. and more. Open, angular growth in youth. Branches usually get too long and heavy on young trees unless tips are pinched out or cut back. In Zones 2–7, branches of any age tend to break in heavy snows. Growth naturally less open with age. Less spreading than other true cedars, but still needs 30-ft. circle.

Needles, less than 1 in. long, are bluish green. Varieties: *C. a.* 'Aurea', needles with yellowish tint; *C. a.* 'Glauca', silvery blue; *C. a.* 'Glauca Pendula', weeping form with blue needles; *C. a.* 'Pendula', vertically drooping branches. Untrained, spreading, informally branching plants are sold as "rustics."

C. brevifolia. CYPRUS (or CYPRIAN) CEDAR. Zones 5–24. Native to island of Cyprus. Resembles *C. libani* but is a smaller tree (to 50 ft.) with shorter needles (¼–½ in.) and smaller cones. Sometimes considered variety of *C. libani*. Very slow growing.

C. deodara. DEODAR CEDAR. Zones 2–12, 14–24. Native to the Himalayas. Fast growing to 80 ft., with 40-ft. spread at ground level. Lower branches sweep down to ground, then upward. Upper branches openly spaced, graceful. Nodding tip identifies it in skyline. Softer, lighter texture than other cedars. Planted in small lawn, it soon overpowers area. You can control spread of tree by cutting new growth of side branches halfway back in late spring. This pruning also makes tree more dense.

Cedrus deodara

Although deodars sold by nurseries are very similar in form, many variations occur in a group of seedlings—from scarecrowlike forms to compact low shrubs. Following three variations are propagated by cuttings or grafting: 'Aurea', with yellow new foliage turning golden green in summer; 'Descanso Dwarf' ('Compacta'), a slow-growing form reaching 15 ft. in 20 years; and 'Pendula' ('Prostrata'), which grows flat on ground or will drapé over rock or wall. Deodar cedar can be pruned to grow as spreading low or high shrub. Annual late-spring pruning will keep it in the shape you want.

C. libani. CEDAR OF LEBANON. Zones 2–24. Native to Asia Minor. To 80 ft., but slow growing—to 15 ft. in 15 years. Variable in growth habit. Usually a dense, narrow pyramid in youth. In young trees, needles, less than 1 in. long, are brightest green of the cedars; in old trees, they are dark gray green. Spreads picturesquely as it matures to become majestic skyline tree with long horizontal arms and irregular crown. Rather scarce and expensive because of time to reach salable size. Routine garden care. No pruning needed. 'Sargentii' or 'Pendula Sargentii' grows even more slowly, has a short trunk and crowded, weeping branches; choice container or rock garden plant. 'Pendula' is a slow-growing, weeping form.

Celastraceae. This family of evergreen or deciduous woody plants has undistinguished flowers, but fruit is often brightly colored. *Celastrus* and *Euonymus* are examples.

CELASTRUS

BITTERSWEET	
Celastraceae	
DECIDUOUS VINES	
🌿 ZONES 1–7	
☀ FULL SUN	
💧 REGULAR WATER	

Celastrus scandens

Grown principally for clusters of handsome summer fruit—yellow to orange capsules that split open to display brilliant red-coated seeds inside. Branches bearing fruit are much prized for indoor arrangements. Since birds seem uninterested in fruit, display extends into winter.

Vigorous and twining with ropelike branches; need support. Will become tangled mass of intertwining branches unless pruned constantly. Cut out fruiting branches in winter; pinch out tips of vigorous branches in summer.

C. orbiculatus. To 30–40 ft. Leaves roundish, toothed, to 4 in. Fruit on short side shoots is partially obscured until leaves fall.

C. rosthornianus (C. loeseneri). CHINESE BITTERSWEET. To 20 ft. with dark green, oval leaves to 5 in. long. Fruit heavily borne.

C. scandens. AMERICAN BITTERSWEET. Native to eastern United States. To 10–20 ft. Leaves very light green, oval, toothed, to 4 in. Fruit in scattered dense clusters is held above leaves, looks showy before foliage falls.

Male and female flowers on different plants. To get fruit, plant one male plant with the female plants.

CELERIAC

Apiaceae (Umbelliferae)	
BIENNIAL GROWN AS ANNUAL	
🌿 ALL ZONES	
☀ FULL SUN	
💧 REGULAR WATER	

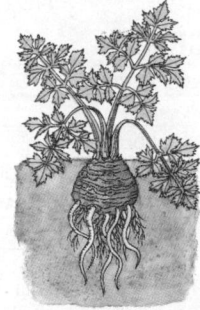
Celeriac

A form of celery grown for its large, rounded, edible roots rather than for leafstalks; is usually displayed in markets as "celery root." Roots are peeled, then cooked or used raw in salads.

Growth requirements are same as for celery. Grow plants 6–8 in. apart in rows spaced 1½–2 ft. apart. Harvest when roots are 3 in. across or larger—in about 120 days. 'Giant Prague' is the recommended variety.

CELERY

Apiaceae (Umbelliferae)	
BIENNIAL GROWN AS ANNUAL	
🌿 ALL ZONES	
☀ FULL SUN	
💧 FREQUENT, THOROUGH WATERING	

Celery

Plant seeds in flats in early spring. Where winters are mild, start in summer and grow as winter crop. Seedlings are slow to reach planting size; save time, purchase seedlings. Plant seedlings 6 in. apart in rows 2 ft. apart. Enrich planting soil with fertilizer. Every 2–3 weeks apply liquid fertilizer with irrigation water. Work some soil up around plants as they grow to keep them upright and whiten stalks. Or blanch by setting bottomless milk carton, tar paper cylinder, or similar device over plants to exclude light from stalks (leaves must have sunlight). Or use unblanched (green). Bait to control snails and slugs; use fungicide to control blight.

CELERY ROOT. See CELERIAC   p. 215

CELOSIA

COCKSCOMB, CHINESE WOOLFLOWER	
Amaranthaceae	
ANNUALS	
🌿 ALL ZONES; BEST IN ZONES 8–14, 18, 19	
☀ FULL SUN	
💧 LITTLE SUMMER WATER EXCEPT IN DESERTS	

Celosia 'Cristata'

Richly colored tropical plants, some with flower clusters in bizarre shapes. Although attractive in cut arrangements with other flowers, in gardens celosias are most effective by themselves. Cut blooms can be dried for winter bouquets. Sow seed in place in late spring or early summer, or set out started plants.

There are two kinds of cockscombs, both derived from a silvery white–flowered species, *C. argentea*, which has narrow leaves 2 in. long or more. One group, the plume cockscombs (often sold as *C.* 'Plumosa'), has plumy flower clusters. Some of these, like Chinese woolflower (sometimes sold as *C.* 'Childsii'), have plumy flower clusters that look like tangled masses of yarn. Flowers come in brilliant shades of pink, orange red, gold, crimson. You can get 2½–3-ft.-high forms or dwarf, more compact varieties. The latter grow about 1 ft. high and bear heavily branched plumes.

The other group is the crested cockscombs (often sold as *C.* 'Cristata'). These have velvety, fan-shaped flower clusters, often much contorted and fluted. Flowers are yellow, orange, crimson, purple, and red. Tall kinds grow to 3 ft., dwarf varieties to 10 in. high.

CELTIS

HACKBERRY

Ulmaceae

DECIDUOUS TREES

ZONES VARY BY SPECIES

FULL SUN OR SOME SHADE

TOLERATE SOME ARIDITY

Celtis occidentalis

Related to elms and similar to them in most details, but smaller. All have virtue of deep rooting; old trees in narrow planting strips expand in trunk diameter and nearly fill strips without surface roots or any sign of heaving the sidewalk or curb. Bare-root plants, especially in larger sizes, sometimes fail to leaf out. Buy in containers or try for small bare-root trees with big root systems. Especially good in windy locations, though young trees should be staked until well established. Trees will take wind, desert heat, and alkaline soil.

Street or lawn trees, even near buildings or paving. All have inconspicuous flowers. Only pest problem of note seems to be occasional aphid attack. In Zones 1–3, 10–13, insects cause leaf gall on hackberry trees. Attractive to birds.

C. australis. EUROPEAN HACKBERRY. Zones 8–16, 18–20. Moderate grower to 40 ft. in 14–15 years. In youth, branches are more upright than those of other hackberries. Never as wide spreading as *C. occidentalis;* dark green leaves, 2–5 in. long, more coarsely toothed and more sharply pointed. Has shorter deciduous period than *C. occidentalis.*

C. occidentalis. COMMON HACKBERRY. All zones. Native to eastern United States. Grows to form rounded crown 50 ft. high or more and nearly as wide. Branches are spreading and sometimes pendulous. Leaves oval, bright green, 2–5 in. long, finely toothed on edges. Tree does not leaf out until April or later. In Zones 10–13, it lives longer than and is superior to commonly planted "Chinese elm" (actually the Siberian elm, *Ulmus pumila*). Resistant to oak root fungus. Tolerates heat, wind, alkaline soil, urban pollution.

C. pallida. DESERT HACKBERRY, GRANJENO. Zones 10–13. Shrub or small tree. Dense, spiny growth to 18 ft.; leaves 1 in. or less in length. Small orange berries. Useful in desert regions as honey source or bird food, for screen or barrier planting, or for erosion control.

C. reticulata (C. douglasii). WESTERN HACKBERRY. Zones 1–3, 10–13. Native to eastern Washington and through intermontane area to Utah, and in mountains of Arizona and Southern California. Worthwhile ornamental tree in those regions. Grows 25–30 ft. high with similar spread. Has somewhat pendulous branches. Oval leaves to 2½ in. long, margins toothed, pale beneath, strongly veined. Tiny red or brown berries eaten by birds.

C. sinensis. CHINESE HACKBERRY, YUNNAN HACKBERRY. Zones 8–16, 18–20. Similar in growth habit to *C. occidentalis,* but smaller. Leaves to 4 in. long, smoother and glossier than those of other hackberries, with scallop-toothed edges.

CENTAUREA

Asteraceae (Compositae)

PERENNIALS AND ANNUALS

ZONES VARY BY SPECIES

FULL SUN

MODERATE WATER, EXCEPT AS NOTED

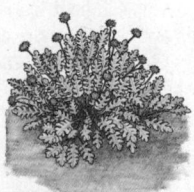

Centaurea cineraria

Out of some 500 species, only dozen or so widely cultivated. Of these, annuals (cornflower and sweet sultan) are grown mainly for cut flowers; perennial kinds used principally for soft, silvery foliage. All are relatively easy to grow. For best performance add lime to acid soils. Sow seeds of annuals in spring or fall. Set out plants of perennial kinds any time, preferably in spring or fall; also sow seed, make cuttings in summer.

C. americana. BASKET FLOWER. All zones. Annual to 5–6 ft. Native to central and southwestern United States. Leaves rather rough, oval, to 4 in. long. Flower heads to 4 in. wide are rose pink, paler toward center. Good in arrangements, fresh or dried.

C. cineraria (C. candidissima). DUSTY MILLER. Zones 8–24. (This common name applied to many plants with whitish foliage. Also see *C. gymnocarpa, Senecio cineraria.*) Compact perennial to 1 ft. or more. Velvety white leaves, mostly in basal clump, are strap shaped, with broad, roundish lobes. Solitary 1-in. flower heads (purple, occasionally yellow) in summer. Trim back after flowering. Most popular of dusty millers in California. Attracts bees.

C. cyanus. CORNFLOWER, BACHELOR'S BUTTON. All zones. Annual. To 1–2½ ft., branching if given sufficient space. Narrow, gray-green leaves, 2–3 in. long. Flower heads 1–1½ in. across, blue, pink, rose, wine red, and white. Blue varieties are traditional favorites for boutonnieres. 'Jubilee Gem' is bushy, compact, 1 ft. tall, with deep blue flowers; Polka Dot strain has all cornflower colors on 16-in. plants. Sow seed in early spring in cold-winter areas, late summer or fall where winters are mild.

C. gymnocarpa. DUSTY MILLER. Zones 8–24. Perennial. Now considered a form of *C. cineraria.* 1–3-ft. plant; white, feltlike leaves, somewhat resembling those of *C. cineraria* but more finely divided. Usually two or three purple flower heads at ends of leafy branches. Trim plants after bloom. Needs no water once established.

C. hypoleuca 'John Coutts'. Zones 1–9, 14–24. Resembles *C. montana* but has deeply lobed leaves and deep rose flower heads.

C. montana. Zones 1–9, 14–24. Perennial. Clumps 1½–2 ft. tall and as wide, with grayish green leaves to 7 in. long. Flowers resembling ragged 3-in. blue cornflowers top the stems. Use in perennial borders. Water regularly. Protect from snails. Divide every other year.

C. moschata. SWEET SULTAN. All zones. Annual. Erect, branching at base, to 2 ft.; Imperialis strain to 3 ft. Green, deeply toothed leaves; thistle-like, 2-in. flower heads mostly in shades of lilac through rose, sometimes white or yellow. Musklike fragrance. Splendid cut flower. Sow seed directly on soil in spring or set out as transplants. Needs lots of heat; no overhead water.

CENTRANTHUS ruber (Valeriana rubra)

JUPITER'S BEARD, RED VALERIAN

Valerianaceae

PERENNIAL

ZONES 7–9, 12–24

SUN OR SHADE

LOOKS BEST WITH SOME WATER

Centranthus ruber

Rank, invasive, and much maligned. Used correctly, it's hard to beat for long, showy bloom in difficult situations. Bushy, to 3 ft. high. Bluish green leaves 4 in. long. Small, deep crimson to pale pink flowers about ½ in. long, in dense terminal clusters. Blooms late spring, early summer. Variety 'Albus' is white.

Use in fringe areas of garden, on rough slopes, banks, and walls; in streetside areas far from hose. Naturalized in many parts of West. White variety especially attractive with large beds of daylilies. Good cut flower. Will grow in poor, dry soil; accepts almost any condition except damp shade. Self-sows prolifically because of small dandelionlike parachutes on seeds. Cut off old flowering stems to shape plant and prolong bloom.

CENTURY PLANT. See AGAVE *americana*   p. 142

CEPHALOCEREUS senilis

OLD MAN CACTUS

Cactaceae

CACTUS

🌡 ZONES 21–24

☼ FULL SUN

◐ ◒ LITTLE OR NO WATER

Cephalocereus senilis

Native to Mexico. Slender, columnar cactus growing slowly to 40 ft., usually much less. Covered with long, grayish white hairs. Yellow, 1½-in. spines. Old plants have 2-in.-long rose-colored flowers in April. Night blooming. Protect from hard frosts. Good pot plant; older plants striking in cactus garden. Indoors, give it southern light.

CEPHALOPHYLLUM 'Red Spike'

RED SPIKE ICE PLANT

Aizoaceae

SUCCULENT PERENNIAL

🌡 ZONES 8, 9, 11–24

☼ FULL SUN

◐ ◒ SOME SUMMER WATER IN ZONES 11–13

Cephalophyllum
'Red Spike'

Clumping plant 3–5 in. high, slowly spreading to 15–18 in. wide. Spiky, bronzy red leaves point straight up. Bright cerise red, 2-in.-wide flowers in winter, with scattering of bloom at other seasons. Often sold as *Cylindrophyllum speciosum*. Plant 6–12 in. apart for ground cover. Draws bees.

CEPHALOTAXUS

PLUM YEW

Cephalotaxaceae

EVERGREEN SHRUBS OR TREES

🌡 ZONES 4–9, 14–17

☼◐ PARTIAL SHADE IN HOT-SUMMER AREAS

◒ MODERATE WATER

Cephalotaxus harringtonia

Related to yews (*Taxus*), differing in larger, brighter green needles and (on female plants only) larger fruit that resembles small green or brown plums. Plum yews grow slowly and like acid to neutral soil.

C. fortunei. CHINESE PLUM YEW. Big shrub or small tree to 10 ft. tall (rarely more), with soft, needlelike leaves up to 3½ in. long, ⅛ in. wide.

C. harringtonia. Spreading shrub or small tree with needles 1–2½ in. long. The variety 'Fastigiata' is the only one available in the West; narrow and erect, it resembles Irish yew (*Taxus baccata* 'Stricta').

CERASTIUM tomentosum

SNOW-IN-SUMMER

Caryophyllaceae

PERENNIAL

🌡 ALL ZONES

☼◐ FULL SUN OR PARTIAL SHADE

◒◒ WATER OFTEN FOR FAST GROWTH

Cerastium tomentosum

Low-growing plant that performs equally well in mild and cold climates, coastal or desert areas. Spreading, dense, tufty mats of silvery gray, ¾-in.-long leaves. Masses of snow white flowers, ½–¾ in. across, in early summer. Plant grows to about 6–8 in. high, spreads 2–3 ft. in 1 year.

In warmest areas give light shade. Any soil as long as drainage is good: standing water causes root rot. Set divisions or plants 1–1½ ft. apart, or sow seed. Feed 2 or 3 times a year to speed growth. Shear off faded flower clusters. May look a bit shabby in cold winters but revives rapidly in spring. Divide in fall or early spring.

CERASTIUM—THE "ALL ZONES" HERO

You can grow cerastium anywhere in the West. But avoid extensive planting in prominent situations because it's not as long lived as some ground covers. Use it as a ground cover on sunny banks or on level ground; let it cascade from the top of a wall. Or plant it in patterns with other low perennials, in rock gardens, along edging paths or driveways, between stepping stones or bulbs.

CERATONIA siliqua

CAROB, ST. JOHN'S BREAD

Fabaceae (Leguminosae)

EVERGREEN LARGE SHRUB OR SMALL TREE

🌡 ZONES 9, 13–16, 18–24

☼ FULL SUN

◒ INFREQUENT, DEEP WATERING

Ceratonia siliqua

Native to eastern Mediterranean region. Often multistemmed, it maintains bushy form with branches to ground when allowed to grow naturally. Use this way as big hedge, informal or trimmed. Trained as tree, with lower branches removed, it grows at moderate rate to become dense and round headed, up to 30–40 ft. tall and as wide. Will reach 20 ft. in 10 years. As street tree it needs more than normal space since roots will break sidewalks.

Foliage is dark green with a sparkle, unusually dense. Individual leaves are divided into 4–10 round leaflets averaging about 2 in. long. Small red flowers in spring. Female trees produce (and drop) abundant 1-ft.-long flattened, dark brown, leathery pods. Rich in sugar, the pods are milled to a fine powder and sold in health food stores as chocolate substitute.

Give young trees winter protection first year or two. Hardy to 18°F. Carob is subject to root crown rot and should be watered infrequently and deeply. Once established, needs no summer water. Resistant to oak root fungus. If raised as fruit, needs water.

CERATOSTIGMA

Plumbaginaceae

EVERGREEN SUBSHRUBS OR PERENNIALS

🌡 ZONES VARY BY SPECIES

☼◐ FULL SUN OR PARTIAL SHADE

◒◒ STAND INCONSISTENT WATERING

Ceratostigma plumbaginoides

All are best treated as perennials, cut back each winter even in frost-free areas. Valued for clusters of rich deep blue, phloxlike flowers that bloom in summer to late fall, when garden needs cool hues.

C. abyssinicum. Zones 8, 9, 14–24. Resembles *C. griffithii*, with slightly longer flowers of bright blue.

C. griffithii. BURMESE PLUMBAGO. Zones 4–9, 14–24. Similar to *C. willmottianum* in hardiness and appearance but more compact and lower growing (2½–3 ft.). Displays its brilliant blue flowers somewhat later, from July into late fall.

▶

C. plumbaginoides. DWARF PLUMBAGO. Zones 2–10, 14–24. A perennial wiry-stemmed ground cover 6–12 in. high. In loose soil and where growing season is long, spreads rapidly by underground stems, eventually covering large areas. Bronzy green to dark green leaves, 3 in. long, turn reddish brown with frosts. Intense blue, ½-in.-wide flowers from July until first frosts. When plants show signs of aging, remove old crowns and replace with rooted stems. Although hardy in extreme cold and fluctuating winter temperatures, it will not bloom well unless it has a long growing season. Most effective in early or midautumn, when blue flowers contrast with red autumn foliage. Often sold as *Plumbago larpentae.*

C. willmottianum. CHINESE PLUMBAGO. Zones 4–9, 14–24. Grows as airy mass of wiry stems to 2–4 ft. high and as wide. Deep green leaves, roundish to oval, 2 in. long; turn yellow or red and drop quickly after frost. Bright blue, ½-in.-wide flowers, June–November. Very similar to *C. griffithii* but with larger, more diamond-shaped leaves with tapering tips.

For pale blue–flowered Cape plumbago, see *Plumbago auriculata.*

CERATOZAMIA mexicana

Zamiaceae

CYCAD

☑ ZONES 21–24

☼ PARTIAL SHADE

◗ REGULAR WATER

Ceratozamia mexicana

Related to *Cycas revoluta* and similar in appearance. Trunk usually a foot high, 4–6 ft. in great age, a foot thick. Very slow growing. Leaves in whorl, 3–6 ft. long, divided featherwise into 15–20 pairs of foot-long, inch-wide leaflets. Striking in containers or protected place in open ground. Protect from frosts.

CERCIDIPHYLLUM japonicum

KATSURA TREE

Cercidiphyllaceae

DECIDUOUS TREE

☑ ZONES 1–6; IN SOME SHADE, 14–16, 18–20

☼ ◑ FULL SUN OR PARTIAL SHADE

◗ AMPLE WATER DURING GROWING SEASON

Cercidiphyllum japonicum

Native to Japan. A tree of many virtues where adapted. Light and dainty branch and leaf pattern. Foliage, always fresh looking, shows tints of red throughout growing season—brilliant red or yellow in fall, especially if watered infrequently at end of summer. Needs protection, such as under high branches, from hot sun and dry winds.

Rather slow growing, eventually to 40 ft. or more. Varying growth habits: some have single trunk; most have multiple trunks angled upward and outward. Nearly round, 2–4-in. leaves neatly spaced in pairs along arching branches. Mature leaves are dark blue green above, grayish beneath. Flowers inconspicuous. There is a weeping form, known as 'Pendulum' or 'Pendula'.

CERCIDIUM

PALO VERDE

Fabaceae (Leguminosae)

DECIDUOUS TREES

☑ ZONES 10–14, 18–20

☼ FULL SUN

◐ ◗ TOLERATE ARIDITY, BUT BETTER WITH WATER

Cercidium floridum

The common name "palo verde" (Spanish for "green tree") covers four desert trees—Mexican palo verde (see *Parkinsonia aculeata*),

blue palo verde, littleleaf palo verde, and Sonoran palo verde. All species attract birds.

C. floridum (C. torreyanum). BLUE PALO VERDE. Native to deserts of Southern California, Arizona, Baja California. Beautifies desert and the garden oases that have been planted there. In gardens it grows fast to 30 ft. and as wide. In spring, 2–4½-in.-long clusters of small, bright yellow flowers almost hide the branches. When out of bloom, shows intricate pattern of bluish green, spiny branches, branchlets, and leafstalks. (Leaves—each with one to three pairs of smooth, tiny leaflets—are shed early, leaving leafstalks to provide lightly filtered shade.)

C. microphyllum. LITTLELEAF PALO VERDE, FOOTHILLS PALO VERDE. Native to eastern San Bernardino County, California; Arizona; Sonoran Desert; Baja California. Similar to blue palo verde but bark and leaves (with 4–12 pairs of hairy leaflets) are yellowish green; flowers are paler yellow, in 1-in.-long clusters.

C. praecox (C. plurifoliolatum). SONORAN PALO VERDE. Native Sonoran Desert to South America. Umbrella form, lime green trunk. Tender in Zones 10, 11, colder parts of 12.

CERCIS

REDBUD

Fabaceae (Leguminosae)

DECIDUOUS SHRUBS OR TREES

☑ ZONES VARY BY SPECIES

☼ FULL SUN, EXCEPT AS NOTED

◗ REGULAR WATER, EXCEPT C. OCCIDENTALIS

Cercis occidentalis

Five redbuds are grown in the West: two western natives, one eastern native, one from Europe, one from China. Early spring flowers, sweet pea shaped, small, bloom in clusters; where tree is adapted, blossoms are borne in great profusion on bare twigs, branches, sometimes even on main trunk. Flowers are followed by clusters of flat pods. Attractive broad, rounded leaves are heart shaped at base. All give fall color with first frosts.

C. canadensis. EASTERN REDBUD. Zones 1–3, 7–20. Native of eastern United States. Largest and fastest growing of available species where adapted. To 25–35 ft. tall. Most apt to take tree form. Round headed but with horizontally tiered branches in age. Rich green, 3–6-in.-long leaves have pointed tips. Small (½-in.-long), rosy pink flowers clothe bare brown branches in early spring. Valuable for filling the gap between the early-flowering fruit trees (flowering peach, flowering plum), and the crabapples and late-flowering cherries. Varieties are 'Alba' (white flowers); 'Flame' (double flowers); 'Forest Pansy' (purple foliage, needs some shade in hot climates); 'Oklahoma' (wine red flowers and thick, glossy, heat-resistant leaves); and 'Rubye Atkinson' (pure pink flowers).

C. canadensis mexicana (C. mexicana). Includes plants from many sources in Mexico. Most widely distributed is a form with a single trunk to 15 ft., and leathery blue-green leaves and pinkish purple flowers. Hardy in Zones 4–24.

C. chinensis. CHINESE REDBUD. Zones 4–20. Native to China, Japan. Seen mostly as light, open shrub to 10–12 ft. Flower clusters (3–5 in. long) are deep rose, almost rosy purple. Leaves are sometimes glossier and brighter green than those of *C. canadensis,* with transparent line around the edge. Spectacular tree in high deserts of Arizona. 'Avondale' is a superior form with deep purple flowers.

C. occidentalis. WESTERN REDBUD. Zones 2–24. Native to California, Arizona, Utah, but predominantly in California foothills below 4,000 ft. Shrub or small tree 10–18 ft. in height and spread. Usually grows several trunks from base. All-year interest. In spring it delivers 3-week display of brilliant magenta flowers, ½ in. long. Summer foliage of handsome blue-green, 3-in. leaves, notched or rounded at tip; interspersed are newly forming seed pods in brilliant magenta. In fall, whole plant turns light yellow or red. In winter, bare branches in picturesque pattern hold reddish brown seed pods. Excellent for dry, seldom watered banks. Water regularly in first year or two to speed growth. Thereafter, needs no water on coast; some inland. Profuse flower production only where winter temperatures drop to 28°F or lower. Resistant to oak root fungus.

C. reniformis. Zones 2–9, 14–24. Native to Southwest. Leaves leathery, blue green, 2–3 in. wide, with rounded or notched tips. Flowers as in *C. canadensis;* variety 'Alba', with white flowers, is sold in West.

C. siliquastrum. JUDAS TREE. Zones 2–19. Native to Europe and western Asia. Generally of shrubby habit to 25 ft., occasionally a taller, slender tree with single trunk. Flowers are purplish rose, ½ in. long. Large 3–5-in. leaves, deeply heart shaped at base, rounded or notched at tip. Occasionally damaged by late frosts in Northwest. Resistant to oak root fungus.

CERCOCARPUS

MOUNTAIN MAHOGANY	
Rosaceae	
EVERGREEN, DECIDUOUS TALL SHRUBS, SMALL TREES	
☀ ZONES VARY BY SPECIES	
☼ FULL SUN	
○ NO WATER ONCE ESTABLISHED	

Cercocarpus betuloides

Natives of western mountains and foothills. Several have a most attractive open structure and branching pattern. Distinguished in fall by long-lasting small fruit topped by a long, twisted, feathery, tail-like plume that sparkles in sunlight. About 20 kinds are native to the West, but the following are most widespread:

C. betuloides. HARDTACK, MOUNTAIN IRONWOOD, SWEET BRUSH. Zones 6–24. Evergreen, native to dry slopes and foothills below 6,000-ft. elevation, southwestern Oregon, California, northern Baja California. Generally a shrub 5–12 ft. high. Can form small tree with wide-spreading crown of arching branches to 20 ft. Wedge-shaped, ½–1-in. leaves clustered on short spurs; leaves are dark green above, pale beneath, with feathery veining and toothed edges.

C. intricatus (C. ledifolius intricatus). Zones 1–3, 7, 9–11, 14–16, 18–24. Evergreen shrub. Slow growth from 3 to 9 ft., with intricate branching and tiny inrolled leaves, green above, gray underneath.

C. ledifolius. CURL-LEAF MOUNTAIN MAHOGANY. All zones. Evergreen, native to dry mountain slopes, 4,000–9,000-ft. elevation, throughout the western states from eastern slopes of Sierra Nevada–Cascade divide to Rockies. In warmer western part of its range, it is about the same size as *C. betuloides;* in highest, coldest part of range, it is a very slow growing, excellent hedge or small tree of character. Leaves leathery, ½–1 in. long, resinous, dark green above, white beneath, with inrolled edges.

C. montanus. All zones; most useful in Zones 1–2, 10. Deciduous shrub, usually 4–6 ft. tall and as wide, rarely to 8–9 ft. Leaves 1–2 in. long, white beneath. Useful in dry places, coldest climates.

CEREUS peruvianus (C. uruguayanus)

Cactaceae	
CACTUS	
☀ ZONES 16, 17, 21–24	
☼ FULL SUN	
○ TOLERATES SOME ARIDITY	

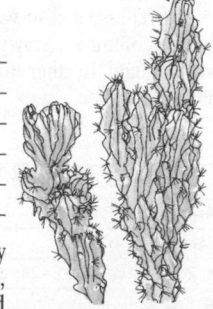

Cereus peruvianus 'Monstrosus'

Tall, branching, treelike cactus eventually reaching 30–50 ft. Striking bluish green, especially when young; ribbed with scattered spines. Flowers white, 6–7 in. long, 5 in. across, in June. Night blooming. Striking outline; effective in large containers. Protect from hard frosts. Variety 'Monstrosus' is smaller, slower growing than species, with ribs irregularly broken up into knobs and crests.

CEROPEGIA woodii

ROSARY VINE	
Asclepiadaceae	
SUCCULENT	
☀ ZONES 21–24; OR INDOORS	
☼ PARTIAL SHADE	
● REGULAR WATER	

Ceropegia woodii

From South Africa. Little vine with hanging or trailing thin stems growing from tuberous base. Paired heart-shaped leaves—thick and succulent, ⅔ in. long, dark green marbled white. Little tubers that form on stems can be used to start new plants. Flowers small, dull pink or purplish, not showy but interesting in structure. Best in pots; stems may trail in thin curtain or be trained on small trellis. Give some shade and regular watering.

Other ceropegias are available from specialists: some are shrubby, some vining, and others stiffly succulent; but all of them have fascinating flower structure.

CESTRUM

Solanaceae	
EVERGREEN SHRUBS	
☀ ZONES VARY BY SPECIES	
☼ PARTIAL SHADE	
● REGULAR WATER	
◊ FRUIT AND SAP ARE POISONOUS	

Cestrum elegans

All have showy, tubular flowers. Flowers and fruit attract birds. Fast growing, inclined to be rangy and top-heavy unless consistently pruned. Best in warm, sheltered spot. Feed generously. Add organic soil amendments before planting. Nip back consistently to maintain compact form and cut back severely after flowering or fruiting. In climates specified below, plants may freeze back in heavy frosts but will recover quickly.

C. aurantiacum. ORANGE CESTRUM. Zones 16, 17, 21–24. Native to Guatemala. Rare and handsome. To 8 ft. Brilliant show of clustered 1-in.-long, orange flowers in late spring, summer, followed by white berries. Deep green, oval, 4-in. leaves. Tall growing; best used as vine or espalier.

C. elegans (C. purpureum). RED CESTRUM. Zones 13, 17, 19–24. Shrub or semiclimber to 10 ft. or higher, with arching branches, deep green 4-in. leaves. Masses of purplish red, 1-in.-long flowers in spring and summer, followed by red berries. Good espalier. 'Smithii' has pink flowers.

C. nocturnum. NIGHT JESSAMINE. Zones 13, 16–24. Native to West Indies. Evergreen shrub to 12 ft. with 4–8-in.-long leaves and clusters of creamy white flowers in summer; white berries. Powerfully fragrant at night—too powerful for some people.

C. parqui. WILLOW-LEAFED JESSAMINE. Zones 13–24. Native to Chile. To 6–10 ft. tall with many branches from base. Dense foliage of willowlike leaves, 3–6 in. long. Greenish yellow, 1-in.-long summer flowers in clusters. Berries dark violet brown. Not as attractive as other species in form, flowers, or fruit, but its perfume is potent. Leaves blacken in light frost. Best used where winter appearance is unimportant. In cold-winter areas, protect roots with mulch and use as perennial.

CESTRUMS FOR HUMMINGBIRDS

All cestrums come from the American tropics, and all have tubular flowers that attract the Americas' native nectar feeder, the hummingbird. Cestrum is a Pan-American plant to serve a Pan-American bird. But the plant doesn't limit its avian favors: warblers pierce the flowers to drink the nectar and mockingbirds eat the berries.

CHAENOMELES

FLOWERING QUINCE

Rosaceae

DECIDUOUS SHRUBS

✿ ZONES 1–21

☼ FULL SUN

◗ REGULAR WATER DURING GROWING SEASON

Chaenomeles

Flowering quinces are among the first shrubs to bloom each year. As early as January you can take a budded stem or two indoors, place it in water in a warm window, and watch buds break into bloom. The plants are picturesque, practically indestructible shrubs of varying growth habit. Shiny green leaves are red tinged when young. Branches are attractive when out of leaf—strong in line, with an oriental feeling. Some flowering quinces grow to 10 ft. and spread wider; some are compact and low growing. Most are thorny; a few thornless. Some bear small quincelike fruit. All are useful as hedges and barriers.

All are easy to grow. Tolerant of extremes in cold and heat, light to heavy soil. May suffer from chlorosis in alkaline soils (use iron chelate or iron sulfate). May bloom reluctantly in warm-winter areas. Prune any time to shape, limit growth, or gain special effects. Good time to prune is in bud and bloom season. (Use cut branches for indoor arrangements.) New growth that follows will bear next year's flowers. Flowers attract birds.

The following list of choice varieties notes both height and flower color. Tall types are 6 ft. and over; low are 2–3 ft. All are garden hybrids (some formerly called *Cydonia*); specialists can furnish even more varieties.

'Apple Blossom'. Tall. White and pink.

'Cameo'. Low, compact. Double, soft apricot pink.

'Contorta'. Low. White to pink; twisted branches. Good as bonsai.

'Corallina' ('Coral Glow'). Tall. Reddish orange.

'Coral Sea'. Tall. Large, coral pink.

'Enchantress'. Tall. Large, shell pink.

'Falconet Charlot'. Tall, thornless. Double salmon pink.

'Hollandia'. Tall. Large red flowers, reblooms in fall.

'Jet Trail'. Low. Pure white.

'Low-n-White'. Low, spreading. White.

'Minerva'. Low, spreading. Cherry red.

'Nivalis'. Tall. Large, pure white.

'Orange Delight' ('Maulei'). Low, spreading. Orange to orange red.

'Pink Beauty'. Tall. Purplish pink.

'Pink Lady'. Low. Rose pink blooms from deeper-colored buds.

'Red Ruffles'. Tall. Almost thornless. Large, ruffled, red.

'Rowallane'. Darkest red flowers on a 3–4-ft. shrub.

'Snow'. Tall. Large, pure white.

'Stanford Red'. Low, almost thornless. Tomato red.

'Super Red'. Tall, upright. Large, bright red.

'Texas Scarlet'. Low. Tomato red.

'Toyo Nishiki'. Tall. Pink, white, pink and white, red all on same branch.

CHAIN FERN. See WOODWARDIA fimbriata   **p. 524**

CHAMAECEREUS sylvestri (Echinops chamaecereus)

PEANUT CACTUS

Cactaceae

CACTUS

✿ ZONES 8–10, 12–24

☼ FULL SUN

◗ WATER DURING GROWTH AND BLOOM

Chamaecereus sylvestri

Native to Argentina. The cylindrical, ribbed, spiny, 2–3-in. joints of this dwarf cactus fall off easily and root just as easily. Profusely blooming in spring and early summer; even tiny rooted joints bloom. Flowers bright scarlet, almost 3 in. long. Great favorite with children.

CHAMAECYPARIS

FALSE CYPRESS

Cupressaceae

EVERGREEN SHRUBS OR TREES

✿ ZONES VARY BY SPECIES

☼ ☼ FULL SUN OR PARTIAL SHADE

◗ MODERATE WATER

Chamaecyparis lawsoniana

All of the many varieties sold are forms of five species—two western natives, two from Japan, and one from the eastern United States. New varieties appear each year, while older ones lose market share. Many closely resemble each other and are often mislabeled.

Susceptible to root rot in heavy soils; give them fast drainage. Dead foliage often appears on inner, older wood. Much of this is normal aging, but mites can be a cause. A strong jet from the hose will clear out mites and much of the dead foliage.

Many dwarf and variegated kinds are available, providing a rich source of bonsai and rock garden material. When the plants are grown in containers or cold frames, climate and soil requirements are less of a consideration.

C. lawsoniana. PORT ORFORD CEDAR, LAWSON CYPRESS. Best in Zones 4–6; satisfactory in Zones 15–17; poor to satisfactory in Zones 7–9, 14, 18–21 (best in partial shade). In Zones 2–3, foliage burns in cold wind and hot sun. An important timber tree of southern Oregon and Northern California. The 60-ft. pyramidal tree of the wilds with lacy, drooping foliage sprays is seldom seen in gardens. Blue-green forms include 'Allumii' (slow growing to 30 ft.); 'Ellwoodii', dense, compact growth to 6–8 ft.; and 'Wisselii', to 15–18 ft., with twisted, irregular growth. Golden-leafed plants are 'Golden King', 'Lutea', and 'Stewartii', conical plants to 30 ft. or more.

C. nootkatensis. NOOTKA CYPRESS, ALASKA CEDAR. Zones 4–6, 15–17. Pyramidal tree to 80 ft., coarser than *C. lawsoniana;* stands greater cold, poorer soil. 'Pendula', a weeping form, slowly grows to 10 ft., possibly to 30 ft.

C. obtusa. HINOKI FALSE CYPRESS. Zones 4–6, 15–17; the dwarf forms are worth coddling elsewhere. There are dozens of golden, dwarf, and fern-leafed forms but two varieties are the most important in landscaping: 'Gracilis', slender hinoki cypress, of slender, upright growth to 20 ft. with nodding branch tips; and 'Nana Gracilis', a miniature of the former to 4 ft. in height.

C. pisifera. SAWARA FALSE CYPRESS. Zones 4–6, 15–17. Japanese tree to 20–30 ft., rarely seen except in its garden varieties. 'Cyano-Viridis' ('Boulevard') is a slow, dense bush to 6–8 ft., with silvery blue-green foliage. 'Filifera', to 8 ft., has drooping, threadlike branchlets; 'Filifera Aurea', similar branchlets in yellow.

C. thyoides. WHITE CEDAR. Zones 4–6, 15–17. Eastern U.S. timber tree is represented in western gardens by two varieties: 'Andelyensis', a dense, columnar, gray-green shrub to 10 ft., turning bronze in cold weather; and 'Heather Bun', broader than the above, turning intense plum purple in winter.

CHAMAEDOREA

Arecaceae (Palmae)

PALMS

✿ ZONES 16, 17, 22–24; OR INDOORS

◗ SHADE

◗◗ AMPLE WATER WITH GOOD DRAINAGE

Chamaedorea elegans

Small, feather type. Generally slow growing. Some have single trunks, others clustered trunks. Leaves variable in shape. Good on shaded patio.

C. cataractarum. Single-stemmed palm growing slowly to 4–5 ft.; trunk speckled. Older plants take some frost.

C. costaricana. If well fed and liberally watered, develops fairly fast into bamboolike clumps of 8–10-ft. trunks. Good pot palm; will eventually need good-sized container. Lacy, feathery leaves 3–4 ft. long.

C. elegans. Often called parlor palm. The best indoor chamaedorea, tolerating crowded roots, poor light. Single stemmed; grows very slowly to eventual 3–4 ft. Occasionally douse tops of potted plants with water. Feed regularly. Groom by removing old leafstalks. Repot every 2–3 years, carefully washing off old soil and replacing with good potting mix. Plant three or more in container for effective display. Widely sold as *Neanthe bella.*

C. ernesti-augustii. Slow growing to 5 ft., with dark green leaves shaped like fish tails.

C. erumpens. Cluster-forming, bamboolike dwarf with drooping leaves. Slow grower to 4–5 ft.

C. geonomiformis. Fine palm for pots. Grows slowly to 4 ft. Broad oblong leaves are not feathery, but are deeply split at tips like fish tails.

C. glaucifolia. Slow growing to 8 ft. or more. Finely textured, feathery leaves, 4–6 ft. long, with bluish green tint on both sides (most marked on underside).

C. klotzschiana. Single-trunk palm, growing slowly to 4–5 ft. Handsome, dark green, feathery leaves. Hardy to 28°F.

C. microspadix. Cluster palm with slender, ringed stems to 8 ft. Feathery leaves. One of hardier kinds, it takes very light frost.

C. radicalis. Slow-growing, single-stemmed plant to 4 ft. tall. Boldly patterned dark green leaves. Interesting, colorful seed formation. Will take temperatures down to a range of 22–28°F.

C. seifrizii. Cluster palm of dense, compact growth to 8–10 ft. Feathery leaves with narrow leaflets. Takes 28°F.

C. tenella. Single trunk to 3–4 ft. Dark bluish green leaves are exceptionally strong, large, and broad; undivided but deeply cleft at ends.

C. tepejilote. Single trunk ringed with swollen joints like those of bamboo. Moderate growth to 10 ft.; leaves 4 ft. long, feathery.

CHAMAEMELUM nobile (Anthemis nobilis)

CHAMOMILE

Asteraceae (Compositae)

EVERGREEN PERENNIAL

🗺 ALL ZONES

☼ ◐ FULL SUN OR PARTIAL SHADE

🌢 MODERATE WATER

Chamaemelum nobile

Forms soft-textured, spreading, 3–12-in. mat of bright light green, finely cut, aromatic leaves. Most commonly grown form has small yellow buttons of summer-blooming flower heads; some forms have little daisylike flower heads. Makes lawn substitute if mowed or sheared occasionally. 'Treneague' is a nonflowering variety that needs no mowing. Also used between stepping stones. Plant divisions 1 ft. apart.

Chamomile tea is made from dried flower heads, but sweeter, more flavorful tea comes from flowers of *Matricaria recutita (M. chamomilla).*

CHAMAEROPS humilis

MEDITERRANEAN FAN PALM

Arecaceae (Palmae)

PALM TREE

🗺 ZONES 4–24

☼ FULL SUN

🌢 🌢 SUMMER WATER SPEEDS GROWTH

Chamaerops humilis

Probably hardiest palm; has survived 6°F. Clumps slowly develop from offshoots, curving to height of 20 ft.; may also reach 20 ft. wide.

Growth extremely slow in Portland and Seattle. Leaves green to bluish green. Versatile: Use in containers, mass under trees, grow as impenetrable hedge. Wind resistant.

CHAMELAUCIUM uncinatum

GERALDTON WAXFLOWER

Myrtaceae

EVERGREEN SHRUB

🗺 ZONES 8, 9, 12–24

☼ FULL SUN

🌢 INFREQUENT BUT DEEP WATERING IN SUMMER

Chamelaucium uncinatum

Native to Australia. Bright green, needlelike leaves and showy sprays of winter-blooming, pale pink or rosy, ½-in. flowers are cherished for flower arrangements of long-lasting beauty. Light and airy, loose and sprawling, fast growth to 6–8 ft. (10–12 ft. when staked) with equal spread. Looks somewhat like loose-growing heather. Very old plants have interesting twisted trunks and shaggy bark. Sometimes sold as *C. ciliatum.*

Plant on dry, sunny bank or in cutting garden in fast-draining soil. Or combine with plants that don't require regular summer watering, such as *Cassia artemisioides* or rosemary. Prune freely for arrangements or cut back after flowering. Seedling plants vary. Select in bloom to get color you want. Variety 'Vista' has large pink flowers. 'University' ('University Red') is deep reddish purple. 'Lady Stephanie' is light pink.

CHAMISE. See ADENOSTOMA fasciculatum	**p. 139**
CHAMOMILE. See CHAMAEMELUM nobile, MATRICARIA recutita	**pp. 221, 376**
CHARD. See SWISS CHARD	**p. 498**

CHASMANTHE aethiopica

Iridaceae

CORM

🗺 ZONES 15–24

☼ ◐ FULL SUN OR PARTIAL SHADE

🌢 NO WATER ONCE ESTABLISHED

Chasmanthe aethiopica

Fans of 2-ft. light green swordlike leaves of this South African plant appear shortly after first rains. One-sided, 2–3-ft., narrow spikes of bright orange red follow in late winter or early spring. Plants are fairly hardy, but frost may damage flower buds. Extremely showy plant in a dull season. Cut faded flower stems to prevent self-sowing. Corms multiply rapidly; dig and divide every 2–3 years.

CHASMANTHIUM latifolium (Uniola latifolia)

SEA OATS, BAMBOO GRASS

Poaceae (Gramineae)

PERENNIAL GRASS

🗺 ALL ZONES

☼ ◐ PARTIAL SHADE IN HOT-SUMMER AREAS

🌢 REGULAR WATER

Chasmanthium latifolium

Ornamental grass clumping with broad, bamboolike leaves topped by arching flowering stems, 2–5 ft. tall, carrying showers of silvery green flower spikelets that resemble flattened clusters of oats (or flattened armadillos). Flowering stems dry to an attractive greenish straw color and look good in dried arrangements. Clumps broaden slowly and are not aggressive like bamboo. Leaves turn brown in winter, when plants should be cut back near the ground. Divide clumps when they become overgrown and bloom drops off. Stake if flowering stems sprawl too far.

CHASTE TREE. See VITEX   **p. 520**

CHAYOTE

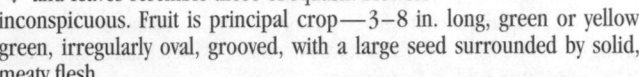

Cucurbitaceae

ANNUAL OR PERENNIAL VINE

⚡ ANNUAL IN ALL ZONES; PERENNIAL, 14–16, 19–24

☼ FULL SUN

💧 REGULAR WATER

Chayote

Vine with edible fruit, related to squash. Vine and leaves resemble those of squash. Flowers inconspicuous. Fruit is principal crop—3–8 in. long, green or yellow green, irregularly oval, grooved, with a large seed surrounded by solid, meaty flesh.

Needs rich soil. Climbs by tendrils; provide fence or trellis. Buy fruit at store in fall and allow to sprout; plant whole fruit edgewise, sprouted end at lowest point, narrow end exposed. If shoot is long, cut it back to 1–2 in. Plant two or more vines to assure pollination. Plant in February or March; in area where roots may freeze, plant in 5-gallon can or tub and store plant until after frost. Plants can produce 20–30-ft. vine in first year, 40–50-ft. vine in second. Tops die down in frost. Bloom starts when day length shortens in fall; fruit is ready in a month.

CHAYOTE FRUIT—BOIL IT OR BAKE IT

When boiled or baked, the chayote fruit's seed and firm flesh taste something like summer squash. A well-grown plant can produce 200 or more fruits. The vine's large, fleshy, tuberous roots are also edible.

CHECKERBERRY. See GAULTHERIA procumbens   **p. 303**

CHECKER LILY. See FRITILLARIA   **p. 300**

CHEIRANTHUS. See ERYSIMUM   **p. 279**

CHENILLE PLANT. See ACALYPHA hispida   **p. 135**

Chenopodiaceae. The goosefoot family contains many annuals and perennials (some of them weeds) and a few shrubs. Flowers are inconspicuous. Many will tolerate salty or alkaline soil, and some are useful food plants, notably beet and spinach.

CHENOPODIUM

Chenopodiaceae

ANNUALS

⚡ ZONES VARY BY SPECIES

☼ FULL SUN

💧 REGULAR WATER

Chenopodium quinoa

Most are weeds; some species have use as food. The plants often have a strong odor. The flowers of *Chenopodium* are greenish and insignificant.

C. album. PIGWEED, LAMB'S QUARTERS. Annual. All zones. Tall weed with leaves to 4 in. long; whitish underneath, smooth pale green above. Leaves can be cooked like spinach.

C. ambrosioides. EPAZOTE, MEXICAN TEA. All zones as annual; Zones 8, 9, 14–24 as perennial. Strongly scented leaves to 5 in. long, deeply cut or toothed. Sometimes grown in gardens or collected from the roadside as seasoning for Mexican dishes.

C. quinoa. QUINOA. Annual. All zones. To 5 ft. tall, with dense flower and seed clusters. A traditional grain of the Andes. Individual seeds look like sesame seeds; they are rinsed to remove surface bitterness, then cooked like rice. Protein content is high. Cannot tolerate high temperatures at blooming or seed setting. Needs short days to bloom; can tolerate light frost. Thrives on 10 in. of water during the growing season. Plant in May or June and harvest in fall. Excellent production in high valleys in the Rocky Mountains. Strains that yield at sea level are obtainable.

CHERIMOYA. See ANNONA cherimola   **p. 152**

CHERRY

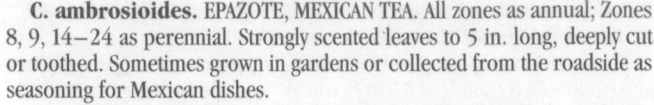

Rosaceae

DECIDUOUS TREES

⚡ ZONES VARY BY TYPE

☼ FULL SUN

💧 REGULAR, DEEP WATERING

Fruiting Cherry

Both the sweet and sour cherries are useful and attractive trees in the home garden.

Sweet cherries. Most common market type and most widely known in the West. Trees 30–35 ft. tall, as broad in some varieties; at their best in deep, well-drained soil in Zones 2, 6, 7, 14, 15. They have high chilling requirement (need many winter hours below 45°F) and are therefore not adapted to mild-winter areas of Southern California or low desert.

Two trees are usually needed to produce fruit, and second tree must be chosen with care. No combination of these will produce fruit: 'Bing', 'Lambert', 'Royal Ann'. These varieties will pollinate any other cherry: 'Black Tartarian', 'Corum', 'Deacon', 'Republican', 'Sam', 'Stella', and 'Van'. However, because 'Lambert' blooms late, it is pollinated best by 'Republican'.

'Glacier', 'Lapins', 'Stella', and 'Sunburst' are self-fertile (a lone tree will bear).

Fruiting spurs are long lived, do not need to be renewed by pruning. Prune trees only to maintain good structure and shape. Fruit appears in late spring in warm areas, early summer in Northwest. Birds everywhere like sweet cherries. Protect with manufactured netting. For control of brown rot and blossom blight, spray with a copper spray just as leaves fall in autumn, then with a fungicide when first blooms appear and weekly during bloom. To control mites, spray with a miticide in spring before buds open.

Varieties:

'Berryessa'. Fruit resembles 'Royal Ann', but larger. Less likely to produce double fruit in hot weather.

'Bing'. Top quality. Large, dark red, meaty fruit of fine flavor. Midseason.

'Black Tartarian'. Fruit smaller than 'Bing', purplish black, firm, sweet. Ripens early.

'Chinook'. Fruit resembles 'Bing', ripens 4–10 days earlier.

'Corum'. Light-colored fruit with colorless juice, whitish flesh. Excellent flavor. Ripens 7 days before 'Royal Ann'.

'Deacon'. Large tree. Large to midsize, firm, black fruit. Sweet, pleasant flavor. Ripens 7 days before 'Bing'.

'Early Burlat'. Like 'Bing'; ripens 2 weeks earlier.

'Early Ruby'. Dark red, purple-fleshed early cherry that performs well in all sweet cherry areas. Needs pollinator (see list above); 'Black Tartarian', 'Royal Ann', 'Van' are all good.

'Glacier'. Large dark cherry, 5 days ahead of 'Bing' and tastes better. Self-fertile.

'Hardy Giant'. Dark red fruit resembles 'Bing'. Good pollinator, especially for 'Lambert'.

'Jubilee'. Resembles 'Bing', but fruit larger. Fewer double fruits.

'Kansas Sweet' ('Hansen'). Large red cherry with semisweet flavor. Late ripening.

'Lambert'. Very large, black, late-ripening fruit, very firm. Flavor more sprightly than 'Bing'.

'Lapins'. Resembles 'Bing' but is self-fertile.

'Mona'. Resembles 'Black Tartarian', but larger. Ripens very early.

'Olympus'. Dark cherry, ripens after 'Bing'. Smaller fruit, larger crop. Pollinate with sour cherry 'Montmorency'.

'Rainier'. Has yellow skin with pink blush; ripens a few days before 'Bing'.

'Republican' ('Black Republican', 'Black Oregon'). Large, spreading tree. Small, round, purplish black fruit with dark juice, tender yet crisp texture. Good flavor. Late season.

'Royal Ann' ('Napoleon'). Large, spreading tree, very productive. Light yellow fruit with pink blush; tender, crisp. Sprightly flavor. Midseason.

'Sam'. Vigorous tree. Large, firm, black fruit. Excellent flavor.

'Stella'. Dark red fruit like 'Lambert'; ripens a few days later. Self-fertile and good pollinator for other cherries.

'Sunburst'. Self-fertile cross between 'Stella' and 'Van'. Early ripening. Large black fruit, good tree structure.

'Sunset'. Very late dark red cherry; late ripening lessens danger of cracking in late spring rains.

'Utah Giant'. Ripens with 'Bing' but is larger, sweeter; develops sweetness even before fully ripe. Holds color when processed. Pollinate with 'Van' or 'Stella'.

'Van'. Heavy-bearing tree. Shiny black fruit, firmer and slightly smaller than 'Bing'. Good flavor. Ripens earlier than 'Bing' in Northwest, right with it in California.

Sour cherries. Sour cherries are spreading, garden-size trees to 20 ft., best grown in Zones 1–9, 14–17 in well-drained soil. Sour cherries are self-fertile and are reasonably good pollinators for sweet cherries. 'Montmorency' and 'Early Richmond' are preferred varieties with small, bright red, soft, juicy, sweet-tart fruit. 'English Morello' is darker, with tarter fruit and red juice. 'Meteor' has fruit like 'Montmorency', but it's a smaller tree. 'North Star', with red to dark red skin and yellow, sour flesh, is a small, very hardy tree.

CHICORY

Asteraceae (Compositae)

PERENNIAL

☀ ALL ZONES, BUT DIFFICULT IN HOT-SUMMER AREAS

☀ FULL SUN

💧 MODERATE WATER

Chicory

Botanically known as *Cichorium intybus*. Dried ground roots can be roasted and used as substitute for coffee. Wild form grows as 3–6-ft. perennial roadside weed in much of West and is recognized by its pretty sky blue flowers. Grown for its leaves, it's known as chicory, endive, or curly endive; grown for its blanched sprouts, it's known as Belgian or French endive, endive hearts, or witloof ("white leaf"). For culture, see Endive.

Radicchio is the name given to a number of red-leafed chicories grown for salads. 'Rossa de Verona', or 'Rouge de Verone', is the best known. It makes lettucelike heads that color to a deep rosy red as weather grows cold in autumn or winter. Slight bitterness lessens as color deepens. Sow in early

summer to mature in cold weather. Sow seeds of the similar 'Giulio' in spring to harvest in summer, 'Cesare' in midsummer for fall, winter harvest.

CHILOPSIS linearis

DESERT WILLOW, DESERT CATALPA

Bignoniaceae

DECIDUOUS LARGE SHRUB OR SMALL TREE

☀ ZONES 10–13, 18–21

☀ FULL SUN

💧 TOLERATES SOME ARIDITY

Chilopsis linearis

Native to desert washes and stream beds below 5,000 ft. Open and airy when trained as small tree. At first grows fast (to 3 ft. in a season), then slows down, leveling off at about 25 ft. With age it develops shaggy bark and twisting trunks somewhat like Australian tea tree (*Leptospermum laevigatum*). Drops leaves early, holds a heavy crop of catalpalike fruit through winter, and can look shaggy. But pruning can make it very handsome.

Long, narrow, 2–5-in. leaves. Flowers look somewhat like catalpa's, trumpet shaped with crimped lobes. Flower color—pink, white, rose, or lavender, marked with purple—varies among seedlings. Nurseries select most colorful. Flowers appear in spring and often through fall; attract birds. Gallon-size plants bear in first year. 'Burgundy' has deep purplish red flowers.

CHIMONANTHUS praecox
(C. fragrans, Meratia praecox)

WINTERSWEET

Calycanthaceae

DECIDUOUS SHRUB

☀ ZONES DETERMINE BLOOM TIME

☀☀ AFTERNOON SUN PROTECTION IN HOT AREAS

💧 OCCASIONAL DEEP WATERINGS IN SUMMER

Chimonanthus praecox

Native to China and Japan. Needs some winter cold. Tall, open, growing slowly to 10–15 ft. high and 6–8 ft. wide, having many basal stems. Keep lower by pruning while in flower. Or prune as small tree by removing excess stems. Leaves medium green, tapering, 3–6 in. long and half as wide. Flowers on leafless stems, 1 in. across; outer sepals pale yellow, inner sepals chocolate colored, smaller. February–March, blooms in Zones 4–7; December–May, in Zones 8, 9, 14–17. Plant where its winter fragrance can be enjoyed. Some possible locations: near a much-used service entrance or path, near a bedroom window.

CHINESE CABBAGE

Brassicaceae (Cruciferae)

BIENNIAL GROWN AS ANNUAL

☘ ALL ZONES

☼ FULL SUN

💧 REGULAR WATER

Chinese Cabbage

Makes head somewhat looser than usual cabbage; sometimes called celery cabbage. Raw or cooked, it has more delicate flavor than cabbage. There are two kinds: pe-tsai, with tall, narrow heads; and wong bok, with short, broad heads. Favored pe-tsai variety is 'Michihli'; wong bok varieties include 'Springtime', 'Summertime', and 'Wintertime' (early to late maturing). Definitely cool-season crop; very prone to bolt to seed in hot weather or in long days of spring and early summer. In Zones 1–6, 10, 11, plant seeds directly in open ground in July; in August or September in other areas. Sow seeds thinly in rows 2–2½ ft. apart and thin plants to 1½–2 ft. apart. Heads should be ready in 70–80 days.

CHIONANTHUS

FRINGE TREE

Oleaceae

DECIDUOUS TREES

☘ ZONES VARY BY SPECIES

☼ FULL SUN

💧 MODERATE WATER

Chionanthus retusus

Earn common name from narrow, fringelike, white petals on flowers that are borne in impressive, ample, lacy clusters. There are male and female trees. If both are present, female plants produce fruit like small dark olives in clusters. Male trees have larger flowers. Broad leaves turn deep yellow in fall.

C. retusus. CHINESE FRINGE TREE. Zones 2–9, 14–24. Generally smaller growing than *C. virginicus*—to 20 ft. Leaves 2–4 in. long. Flower clusters to 4 in. long in June and July. In bloom this is a magnificent tree, something like a tremendous white lilac.

C. virginicus. FRINGE TREE. Zones 1–6, 15–17. Native Pennsylvania to Florida and Texas. Grows to 30 ft. where well adapted. Leaves and flower clusters are twice as big as those of *C. retusus,* and it blooms earlier (May). Fragrant.

In Zones 1–6, the most you can hope for is 12 ft. in 10 years; the plant is best used as a very slow growing, airy shrub (it blooms profusely when only 2–3 ft. tall). In these zones it is one of the last deciduous plants to leaf out in spring; flowers are more greenish than white.

Chionanthus virginicus

CHIONODOXA

GLORY-OF-THE-SNOW

Liliaceae

BULBS

☘ ZONES 1–7, 14–20

☼ PARTIAL SHADE

💧 REGULAR WATER

Chionodoxa luciliae

Native to alpine meadows in Asia Minor. Charming small bulbous plants 4–6 in. high; among first to bloom in spring. Narrow basal leaves, two or three to each flower stalk. Blue or white, short, tubular, open flowers in loose spikes. Plant bulbs 3 in. deep in September or October in half shade; keep moist. Under favorable conditions, plants self-sow freely.

C. luciliae. Most generally available. About ten brilliant blue, white-centered, starlike flowers on 6-in. stalks. 'Alba' offers larger white flowers; 'Gigantea' has larger leaves, larger flowers of violet blue with white throat.

C. sardensis. Deep, true gentian blue flowers with very small white eye.

CHITALPA tashkentensis

CHITALPA

Bignoniaceae

DECIDUOUS TREE

☘ ZONES 3–24

☼ FULL SUN

💧 TOLERATES SOME ARIDITY

Chitalpa tashkentensis

Fast growing to 20–30 ft. and as wide, this tree combines the larger flowers of its *Catalpa bignonioides* parent with the desert toughness and color of *Chilopsis linearis,* the other parent. Leaves are 4–5 in. long, an inch wide. Clusters of frilly trumpet-shaped flowers appear over a long season. 'Pink Dawn' has pink flowers, 'Morning Cloud' white ones.

CHIVES

Liliaceae

SMALL, CLUMP-FORMING PERENNIAL

☘ ALL ZONES

☼☽ FULL SUN OR SOME SHADE

💧💧 BEST IN MOIST SOIL

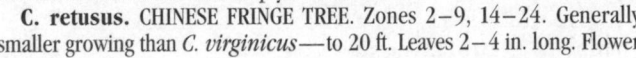

Chives

Leaves are grasslike in general appearance but round and hollow in cross section. Clumps may reach 2 ft. in height but are usually shorter. Cloverlike, rose purple spring flowers are carried in clusters atop thin stems. Plant is pretty enough to use as edging in sunny or lightly shaded flower border or herb garden. Does best in moist, fairly rich soil. May be increased by divisions or grown from seed. Evergreen (or nearly so) in mild regions; goes dormant where winters are severe, but small divisions may be potted in rich soil and grown on kitchen windowsill. Chop or snip leaves; use as garnish or add to salads, cream cheese, cottage cheese, egg dishes, gravies, and soups for delicate onionlike flavor. For garlic chives (Chinese chives), see *Allium tuberosum.*

CHLOROPHYTUM

Liliaceae

INDOOR PLANTS, GROUND COVERS

ZONES VARY BY SPECIES

PARTIAL OR FULL SHADE

REGULAR WATER

Lily relatives with clumps of attractive evergreen foliage and small white or greenish flowers in long clusters.

Chlorophytum comosum

C. bichetii. Indoor plant. Slow growing to an eventual 8–10 in. tall, 1½ ft. across. Leaves dark green with white stripes, shorter and relatively broader than those of *C. comosum,* gracefully recurved. Small white flowers on 8-in. stalks. Does not make runners. Light to heavy shade. Water only when dry; feed occasionally to maintain good leaf color.

C. comosum. SPIDER PLANT. Evergreen perennial. Indoor plant; outdoor ground cover in Zones 15–17, 19–24. Native to Africa. Shade-loving plant forms 1–3-ft.-high clumps of soft, curving leaves like long, broad grass blades. 'Variegatum' and 'Vittatum', striped white, are popular. Flowers white, ½ in. long, in loose, leafy-tipped spikes standing above foliage. Greatest attraction: miniature duplicates of mother plant, complete with root, at end of curved stems (as with strawberry plant offsets); these offsets can be cut off, potted individually. Excellent, easily grown house plant for fully lighted window, greenhouse. Ground cover or hanging basket plant in partial shade. As ground cover, set 2 ft. apart in diamond pattern. Plants will fill in area in same year. Often sold as *C. capense.*

CHOISYA ternata

MEXICAN ORANGE

Rutaceae

EVERGREEN SHRUB

GOOD IN ZONES 7–9, 12–24; BORDERLINE, 4–6

FULL SUN NEAR COAST, LIGHT SHADE INLAND

INFREQUENT BUT DEEP WATERING

Choisya ternata

Hardy to 15°F. Fast growing to 6–8 ft. high and as wide. Lustrous yellow-green leaves held toward end of branches are divided into fans of three leaflets (to 3 in. long); fans give shrub dense, massive look but with highlights and shadows. Clusters of fragrant white flowers, somewhat like small orange blossoms, open in very early spring and bloom continuously into April, intermittently through summer. Appealing to bees. Sometimes called mock orange.

Use as attractive informal hedge or screen. Mass to fill large spaces. Prune throughout growing season to shape and thin out branches, thereby forcing replacement wood from inside plant. Cut freely for decoration when in bloom.

Gets straggly and bears few flowers in too much shade. It's touchy about soil conditions. Difficult in alkaline soils or where water is high in salts. Under such conditions, prepare special soil mix as for azaleas. Often suffers from pests and soil problems in Zones 18–24. Subject to root rot and crown rot if drainage is not fast. Subject to damage from sucking insects and mites. New foliage of the variety 'Sundance' is yellow, gradually turns green.

CHOKECHERRY. See PRUNUS *virginiana*   p. 443

CHORISIA

FLOSS SILK TREE

Bombacaceae

EVERGREEN TO BRIEFLY DECIDUOUS TREES

ZONES VARY BY SPECIES

FULL SUN

ONCE ESTABLISHED, WATER MONTHLY

Chorisia speciosa

Native to South America. Heavy trunks studded with thick, heavy spines. Young trunks are green, becoming gray with age. Leaves divided into leaflets like fingers of a hand; leaves fall during autumn flowering or whenever winter temperatures drop below 27°F. In late summer reduce watering of established trees to encourage more flowers.

Flowers large and showy, somewhat resembling narrow-petaled hibiscus. Fast drainage and controlled watering are keys to success.

C. insignis. WHITE FLOSS SILK TREE. Zones 12, 13, 15–24. To 50 ft. tall. Flowers white to pale yellow, 5–6 in. across. Blooms from fall into winter; flowering stopped by frost.

C. speciosa. Zones 12–24. Grows 3–5 ft. a year for first few years, then slowly to 30–60 ft. tall. Flowers are pink, purplish rose, or burgundy. Two grafted kinds are obtainable: 'Los Angeles Beautiful' has wine red flowers, and 'Majestic Beauty' has rich pink flowers.

CHORIZEMA

FLAME PEA

Fabaceae (Leguminosae)

EVERGREEN SHRUBS

ZONES 15–17, 19–24

FLOWER COLOR MORE INTENSE IN PART SHADE

MODERATE WATER

Chorizema cordatum

Native to Australia. Hardy to about 24°F. Both species present riotous, gaudy display of clustered, sweet pea–shaped flowers in blended orange and purplish red, February–June. Fast growing, with slender, graceful branches.

Left to go their own way, they are attractive spilling over wall, on banks, in containers, or hanging baskets. Pruned, pinched, and cut back severely after flowering, they make compact 2-ft. shrubs for ground cover, edging, or flower border. Source of late-winter color.

C. cordatum. HEART-LEAF FLAME PEA. Grows 3–5 ft. high, sometimes more under ideal conditions. Dark green leaves 1–2 in. long, with small prickly teeth along the edges. Species sometimes erroneously sold as *C. ilicifolium.*

C. ilicifolium. HOLLY FLAME PEA. Low, spreading shrub grows to 2–3 ft. high. Oval, ¾–1-in. leaves are similar to those of *C. cordatum,* but edges are wavy and have long, prickly teeth; vaguely resemble holly leaves.

CHRISTMAS BERRY. See HETEROMELES *arbutifolia*   p. 321

CHRISTMAS CACTUS. See SCHLUMBERGERA *bridgesii*   p. 480

CHRISTMAS FERN. See POLYSTICHUM *acrostichoides*   p. 433

CHRISTMAS ROSE. See HELLEBORUS *niger*   p. 320

C

CHRYSALIDOCARPUS
lutescens

Arecaceae (Palmae)

PALM

🌡 ZONES 23, 24; OR INDOORS

☼ ◐ FULL SUN NEAR COAST

💧 REGULAR WATER

Clumping feather palm of slow growth to 10–15 ft. Graceful plant with smooth trunks and yellowish green leaves. In Zone 23, grow in frost-free, shady, sheltered spot. Gets spider mites when grown indoors. Tricky to maintain, but a lovely palm. Often sold as *Areca lutescens*.

Chrysalidocarpus lutescens

CHRYSANTHEMUM

Asteraceae (Compositae)

PERENNIALS AND ANNUALS

🌡 ALL ZONES, EXCEPT AS NOTED

☼ BEST IN FULL SUN, EXCEPT AS NOTED

💧 REGULAR WATER, EXCEPT AS NOTED

There are about 160 species of chrysanthemum, mostly native to China, Japan, and Europe. Included are some of most popular and useful of garden plants—top favorite being *C. morifolium*, whose modern descendants are known as florists' chrysanthemums. Botanists have split *Chrysanthemum* into many new genera. Growers may be slow to use new names, but some have begun. We list the new names immediately after the old.

Chrysanthemum frutescens

C. arcticum (Arctanthemum arcticum). ARCTIC CHRYSANTHEMUM. Very hardy autumn-blooming perennial, forming clump with stems 6–12 in. high. Spoon-shaped leaves, usually three-lobed, 1–3 in. long, leathery in texture. White or pinkish flower heads 1–2 in. across. Developed from this species is a group of hybrids known as Northland daisies, with single flowers 3 in. across or more, in shades of pink, rose, rosy purple, and yellow. *C. arcticum* itself is primarily rock garden plant. Taller-growing varieties serve best in borders.

C. balsamita (Tanacetum balsamita). COSTMARY. Weedy 2–4-ft. perennial with sweet-scented foliage that justifies its presence in herb garden (use leaves in salads and sachets). If leggy stems are cut back, gray-green basal leaves with tiny scalloped margins can make herb garden edging. Divide clumps and reset divisions in late summer or fall.

C. carinatum. SUMMER CHRYSANTHEMUM, TRICOLOR CHRYSANTHEMUM. Summer- and fall-blooming annual, growing 1–3 ft. high, about 3 ft. wide. In mild-winter climates, blooms winter and spring. Deeply cut foliage; showy, single, daisylike, 2-in.-wide flower heads in purple, orange, scarlet, salmon, rose, yellow, and white, with contrasting bands around dark center. Satisfactory, long-lasting cut flowers. Sow seeds in spring either in pots or in open ground. Where winters are mild, do sowing in fall. Court Jesters is an excellent strain. Light or heavy soil; grows wild in sand dunes along sections of Southern California coast.

C. coccineum (Pyrethrum roseum, Tanacetum coccineum). PYRETHRUM, PAINTED DAISY. Bushy perennial to 2–3 ft. with very finely divided, bright green leaves and single, daisylike, long-stemmed flowers in pink, red, and white. Also available in double and anemone-flowered forms. Starts blooming in April in mild-winter climates, in May or June in colder areas; if cut back, blooms again in late summer. Excellent for cutting, borders. Needs summer heat to perform well. Divide clumps or sow seeds in spring. Double forms may not come true from seed; they may revert to single flowers.

C. coronarium. CROWN DAISY. Annual. To 2½ ft., with light green, coarsely cut leaves and yellow daisies. A Mediterranean native, it is some-

times seen naturalized on roadsides. A variety is the vegetable known as shungiku, chop-suey greens, or edible chrysanthemum. It can be cooked like spinach.

C. frutescens (Argyranthemum frutescens). MARGUERITE, PARIS DAISY. Zones 14–24. Short-lived perennial grown as annual in cold climates. Bright green, coarsely divided leaves; abundant daisylike flowers, 1½–2½ in. across, in white, yellow, or pink. 'Snow White', double anemone type, has pure white flowers, more restrained growth habit than species; 'White Lady' and 'Pink Lady' have buttonlike flower heads; 'Silver Leaf' has gray-green leaves and masses of white flowers that are much smaller than those of regular marguerite. 'Dwarf White' and 'Dwarf Yellow' are smaller growers. All kinds, but particularly familiar white and yellow marguerites, are splendid for containers and for quick effects in borders, mass displays in new gardens.

Small plants set out in spring will grow 4 ft. across by summer. In buying plants, avoid large, vigorous-looking ones with large leaves—they will bloom sparsely. Also avoid plants showing signs of fasciation (flattening or widening of stems) near crown.

Plant in light soil. Marguerites grow exceptionally well near coast; with sufficient water and good drainage, they also succeed inland but may freeze in cold winters. For continued bloom prune lightly at frequent intervals. Do not prune older plants severely—they seldom produce new growth from hardened wood. Replace every 2–3 years with new plants. Few pests but subject to leaf miner, to thrips (which reduce flower quality), and—on old plants—to root galls and nematodes.

C. gayanum (Pyrethropsis gayana). Zones 14–24. Shrubby perennial. 1½ ft. tall, 4 ft. wide, with finely cut gray-green foliage and 1½-in. pink daisy flowers with dark centers. Long bloom season, heaviest late winter, early spring. Needs only occasional watering.

C. hosmariense (Pyrethropsis hosmariensis). Zones 4–24. Perennial. To 8 in. tall, 2 ft. wide, with white daisies over a long season, heaviest in winter. Silvery, finely cut foliage. Needs little water.

C. leucanthemum (Leucanthemum vulgare). OX-EYE DAISY, COMMON DAISY. Perennial. To 2 ft., with bright green foliage and white, yellow-centered daisies. European native naturalized in many places.

C. maximum (C. superbum, Leucanthemum maximum). SHASTA DAISY. Useful perennial for summer and fall bloom in all climates. Original 2–4-ft.-tall Shasta daisy, with coarse, leathery leaves and gold-centered, white flower heads 2–4 in. across, has been largely superseded by varieties with larger, better-formed, longer-blooming flowers. They are available in single, double, quilled, and shaggy-flowered forms. All are white, but two show a touch of yellow. Some bloom May–October. Shasta daisies are splendid in borders and cut arrangements.

Following are some of the varieties available in nurseries:

'Esther Read', most popular double white, longest bloom; 'Marconi', large frilly double; 'Aglaya', similar to 'Marconi', longest blooming season; 'Alaska', big, old-fashioned single; 'Horace Read', 4-in.-wide, dahlialike flower; 'Majestic', large yellow-centered flower; 'Thomas Killin', 6-in.-wide (largest) yellow-centered flower.

'Cobham's Gold' has distinctive flowers in yellow-tinted, off-white shade. 'Canarybird', another yellow, is dwarf, with attractive dark green foliage.

Most popular varieties for cut flowers are 'Esther Read', 'Majestic', 'Aglaya', and 'Thomas Killin'.

Shasta daisies are easy to grow from seed. Catalogs offer many strains, including Roggli Super Giant (single) and Diener's Strain (double). 'Marconi' (double), also available in seed, nearly always blooms double. 'Silver Princess' (also called 'Little Princess' and 'Little Miss Muffet') is 12–15-in. dwarf single. 'Snow Lady' (single), an All-America winner, 10–12 in. tall, begins to bloom in 5 months from seed, then blooms nearly continuously.

Set out divisions of Shasta daisies in fall or early spring, container-grown plants any time. Thrive in fairly rich, moist, well-drained soil. Prefer sun, but do well in partial shade in hot-summer climates; double-flowered kinds hold up better in very light shade. In coldest regions, mulch around plants but do not smother foliage. Divide clumps every 2–3 years in early spring (or in fall in mild-winter areas). Shasta daisies are generally easy to grow but have a few problems. Disease called "gall" causes root crown to split into many weak, poorly rooted growing points that soon die. Dig out and dispose of affected plants; sterilize soil before planting in same spot. Bait to control snails and slugs.

Shasta daisies in well-drained soils can take plenty of water, especially before and during bloom; at this time apply liquid fertilizer to encourage large flowers.

C. morifolium (Dendranthema grandiflorum). FLORISTS' CHRYSANTHEMUM. The most useful of all autumn-blooming perennials for borders, containers, and cutting, and the most versatile and varied of all chrysanthemum species, available in many flower forms, colors, plant and flower sizes, and growth habits. Colors include yellow, red, pink, orange, bronze, purple, and lavender, as well as multicolors. Following are flower forms as designated by chrysanthemum hobbyists:

Chrysanthemum morifolium

Anemone. One or more rows of rays with large raised center disk or cushion. Center disk may be same color as rays or different. (Disbud to encourage very large flowers.)

Brush. Narrow, rolled rays give brush or soft cactus dahlia effect.

Decorative. Long, broad rays overlap in shingle effect to form broad, full flower.

Incurve. Big double flowers with broad rays curving upward and inward.

Irregular curve. Like above, but with looser, more softly curving rays.

Laciniated. Fully double, with rays fringed and cut at tips in carnation effect.

Pompom. Globular, neat, compact flowers with flat, fluted, or quilled rays. Usually small, they can reach 5 in. with disbudding.

Quill. Long, narrow rolled rays; like spider but less droopy.

Reflex. Big double flowers with rays that curl in, out, and sideways, creating shaggy effect.

Semidouble. Somewhat like single or daisy, but with two, three, or four rows of rays around a yellow center.

Single or daisy. Single row of rays around a yellow center. May be large or small, with broad or narrow rays.

Spider. Long, curling, tubular rays ending in fish-hook curved tips.

Spoon. Tubular rays flatten at tip to make little disks, sometimes in colors that contrast with body of flower.

Garden culture. It's easy to grow chrysanthemums, not so easy to grow prize-winning chrysanthemums. The latter need more water, feeding, pinching, pruning, grooming, and pest control than most perennials.

Plant in good, well-drained garden soil improved by organic matter and a complete fertilizer dug in 2 or 3 weeks before planting. In hot climates, provide shade from afternoon sun. Don't plant near large trees or hedges with invasive roots.

Set out young plants (rooted cuttings or vigorous, single-stem divisions) in early spring. When dividing clumps, take divisions from outside; discard woody centers. Water deeply at intervals determined by your soil structure—frequently in porous soils, less often in heavy soils. Too little water causes woody stems and loss of lower leaves; overwatering causes leaves to yellow, then blacken and drop. Stems are attacked by borers in desert areas. Aphids are the only notable pest in all areas. Good way to avoid them is to feed plants with systemic insecticide/fertilizer combination.

Feed plants in ground two or three times during the growing season; make last application with low-nitrogen fertilizer not less than 2 weeks before bloom.

Sturdy plants and big flowers are result of frequent pinching, which should begin at planting time with removal of new plant's tip. Lateral shoots will form; select one to four of these for continued growth. Continue pinching all summer, nipping top pair of leaves on every shoot that reaches 5 in. in length. On some early-blooming cushion varieties, or in coldest

regions, pinching should be stopped earlier. Stake plants to keep them upright. To produce huge blooms, remove all flower buds except for one or two in each cluster—this is called disbudding.

Pot culture. Pot rooted cuttings February–April, using porous, fibrous, moisture-holding planting mix. Move plants to larger pots as growth requires—don't let them become root-bound. Pinch as directed above; stake as required. Plants need water daily in warm weather, every other day in cool conditions. Feed with liquid fertilizer every 7–10 days until buds show color.

Care after bloom. Cut back plants to within 8 in. of ground. Where soils are heavy and likely to remain wet in winter, dig clumps with soil intact and set on top of ground in inconspicuous place. Cover with sand or sawdust if you wish. Take cuttings from early to late spring (up until May for some varieties), or when shoots are 3–4 in. long. As new shoots develop, you can make additional cuttings of them. In cold-winter areas, store in cold frame or mulch with light, noncompacting material like excelsior.

Off-season, potted chrysanthemums. Florists and stores sell potted chrysanthemums in bloom every day of the year, even though by nature a chrysanthemum blooms in late summer or fall. Growers force these plants to bloom out of season by subjecting them to artificial day lengths, using lights and dark cloths. You can plunge the potted flowering plants right into a garden bed or border for an immediate (but expensive) display, or you can enjoy them in the house while the flowers remain fresh and then plant them out. Either way, they will not bloom again at the same off-season time the next year. Instead, they will revert to their natural inclination and commence fall bloom once again.

Cut off flowers when they fade, leaving stems about 6–8 in. long. Remove soil clump from pot and break apart the several individual plants that were grown in the pot. Plant these individual plants. When new growth shows from the roots, cut off remainder of old flower stems.

C. multicaule (Coleostephus myconis). Annual. Broad-rayed, buttery yellow daisies 2½ in. across rise in spring above 6–8-in.-wide mats of bright green, fleshy foliage. Blooms best in cool weather; usually sold in fall, winter, early spring from six-packs or pots. Plants may live over a second year in cool coastal climates. Give them sun, average soil, water.

> ### BUTTER YELLOW DAISIES
> *Chrysanthemum multicaule* makes a great companion for bulbs in pots. Try it with Dutch iris—plant three bulbs in an 18-in. pot in October, and in the spaces between the bulbs plant three chrysanthemums from a six-pack. In March and April this pairing will give you a beautiful display of butter yellow and Wedgwood blue.

C. nipponicum (Nipponanthemum nipponicum). Zones 3–9, 14–24. Perennial. Resembling large (to 3 ft.), rounded, shrubby Shasta daisy with a dense mass of nearly succulent bright green leaves. White daisy flowers on long stems form in late fall (October–November). Needs adequate water all summer to prevent lower foliage from browning. Cut back after bloom.

C. pacificum (Pyrethrum marginatum, Dendranthema pacificum). GOLD AND SILVER CHRYSANTHEMUM. Prohibited in some areas as a host to white rust of chrysanthemum. Semitrailing, semishrubby perennial with stems to 2–3 ft., densely clad in lobed dark green leaves apparently edged white (woolly white undersides show at edges). Late in the year broad clusters of yellow flowers appear; lacking rays, they resemble clustered brass buttons. Used as a bank or ground cover or at the front of the perennial border. A tough plant, but without regular summer water lower leaves will die off. Cut back to new growth after bloom.

C. paludosum (Leucanthemum paludosum). Annual, sometimes living over for a second bloom season. Flowers look like miniature Shasta daisies. White daisy flower heads 1–1½ in. wide on 8–10-in. stems above dark green, deeply toothed leaves. For care, see *C. multicaule.*

C. parthenium. FEVERFEW. Compact, leafy, aggressive perennial once favored in Victorian gardens. Leaves have strong odor, offensive to some. Named varieties range from 1 to 3 ft. tall. 'Golden Ball' has bright yellow flower heads and no rays; 'Silver Ball' is completely double with only the white rays showing. In 'Aureum', commonly sold in flats as 'Golden Feather', chartreuse-colored foliage is principal attraction. Sow seeds in spring for bloom by midsummer, or divide in fall or spring (in cold climates). Can also grow from cuttings. Full sun or light shade.

C. ptarmiciflorum (Tanacetum ptarmiciflorum). DUSTY MILLER, SILVER LACE. All zones as annual; Zones 16, 17, 19–24 as perennial. To 6–10 in. tall, 8–10 in. wide. Very finely cut, silvery white leaves. Where hardy, produces white daisy flowers on 1½-ft. stems.

C. rubellum (Dendranthema zawadskii). A 2-ft. perennial with finely cut leaves and pink flowers over a long blooming season beginning in late summer. 'Clara Curtis' is the best-known variety.

C. weyrichii (Dendranthema weyrichii). Mat-forming perennial for rock garden. Leaves finely cut. Pink daisies appear just above foliage.

CHRYSANTHEMUM BASKET FOR A FALL SHOW

In late May or early June plant five rooted cuttings of small-flowered varieties in a 10-in. hanging basket or three in an 8-in. one. At planting time and during growth, pinch out tips to force side branching. Keep in full sun in cool climates, light shade inland. In late summer, train outer stems downward by tying them down sides of container.

CHRYSOLARIX. See PSEUDOLARIX kaempferi   **p. 443**

CHRYSOTHAMNUS nauseosus

RUBBER RABBITBRUSH, GRAY RABBITBRUSH
Asteraceae (Compositae)
DECIDUOUS SHRUB
✂ ZONES 1–3, 10, 11
☼ FULL SUN
◊ NO WATER ONCE ESTABLISHED

Chrysothamnus nauseosus

Native to high desert, intermountain, and Rocky Mountain areas. Shrub to 6 ft., with narrow gray-green leaves that usually drop by flowering time in late summer, early autumn. Masses of golden yellow, fluffy flowers in broad, flat-topped clusters. Use in low-maintenance gardens, native plant gardens.

CHUPAROSA. See JUSTICIA californica	**p. 342**
CICHORIUM intybus. See CHICORY	**p. 223**
CIDER GUM. See EUCALYPTUS gunnii	**p. 283**
CIGAR PLANT. See CUPHEA ignea	**p. 252**
CILANTRO. See CORIANDRUM sativum	**p. 241**

CIMICIFUGA

BUGBANE
Ranunculaceae
PERENNIALS
✂ ZONES 1–7, 17
☼ ● TOLERATE CONSIDERABLE SUN
◖ REGULAR WATER

Cimicifuga racemosa

Stately, upright, slim spikes of small white flowers grow from clumps of shiny, dark green leaves divided into many 1½–3-in.-long, deeply toothed leaflets. Flowers late summer to fall. Handsome among large ferns in woodland garden. Best in rich, well-drained, moist soil. Will take considerable sun with ample water. Clumps can remain undisturbed for many years. Divide in fall or (in cold areas) in early spring before growth starts. Dried seed clusters useful in flower arrangements.

C. japonica. White flowers on purplish black stalks, 3–4 ft. tall.

C. racemosa. BLACK SNAKEROOT. Flower spikes grow to 7 ft.

C. simplex. KAMCHATKA BUGBANE. Flower spikes to 3–5 ft.

CINERARIA. See SENECIO hybridus   **p. 483**

CINNAMOMUM

Lauraceae
EVERGREEN TREES
✂ ZONES VARY BY SPECIES
☼ FULL SUN
◖ INFREQUENT, DEEP WATERING

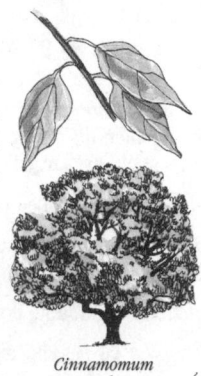

Cinnamomum camphora

Slow to moderate growth rate; trees eventually reach considerable size. Both species have aromatic leaves that smell like camphor when crushed. Good for large lawns, but competitive root system makes them poor choice for garden beds. Thrive in hot-summer areas where winter temperatures stay above 20°F.

Not much bothered by pests, but subject to a root rot—verticillium wilt. Symptoms: wilting and dying of twigs, branches, entire center of tree, or entire tree. Wood in twigs or branches shows brownish discoloration. Trees most susceptible after wet winters or if planted in poorly drained soil. No cure is known, though trees often outgrow the problem. To treat, cut out damaged branches. Fertilize trees with nitrogen fertilizer and water deeply.

C. camphora. CAMPHOR TREE. Zones 8, 9, 12–24. Native to China, Japan. A delight to the eye in every season. Winter foliage is shiny yellow green. In early spring new foliage may be pink, red, or bronze, depending on tree. Usually strong structure, heavy trunk, and heavy, upright, spreading limbs. Beautiful in rain, when trunks look black. Grows slowly to 50 ft. or more with wider spread. Leaves 2½–5 in. long. Drops leaves quite heavily in March; flowers, fruits, and twigs drop later. Clusters of tiny, fragrant, yellow flowers in profusion in May, followed by small blackish fruits.

C. glanduliferum. NEPAL CAMPHOR TREE. Zones 15–17, 19–24. Native to Himalayas. Differs in having larger, richer green, more leathery leaves. Nepal camphor tree is more upright in branching habit than *C. camphora*, slightly more tender, and apparently faster growing.

CINQUEFOIL. See POTENTILLA   **p. 435**

CISSUS

Vitaceae
EVERGREEN VINES
✂ ZONES VARY BY SPECIES
☼ FULL SUN, EXCEPT AS NOTED
◊ ◖ ● WATER NEEDS VARY BY SPECIES

Cissus antarctica

Most climb by tendrils. Related to Virginia creeper, Boston ivy, and grape, they are distinguished for their foliage. Easy to grow. Not fussy about soil, water, or fertilizer. Flowers inconspicuous. Useful near swimming pools.

C. antarctica. KANGAROO TREEBINE. Zones 16–24. Native to Australia. A graceful vine, vigorous once established. To 10 ft. Medium green, shiny leaves, 2–3½ in. long and almost as wide, with toothed edges. In the ground, needs no water once established. Good tub plant indoors or out, in sun or shade, for climbing up or tumbling down; for trellis, wall, or hillside.

C. capensis. See Rhoicissus capensis

C. discolor. Indoor and greenhouse plant. Climbing, but usually grown in hanging pots. Leaves 4–6 in. long, oval, toothed, with showy pink and silver markings; maroon on lower surface. Leaves resemble those of rex begonia in color and texture. Species needs warmth, semishade, humidity, ample water.

C. hypoglauca. Zones 13–24. Native to Australia. Rapid growth to 15 ft. in one season. Eventually climbs to 30–50 ft. Leaves highly polished, divided into five roundish, leathery leaflets 3 in. long; foliage strong in texture with bronzy color tones. New growth covered with rust-colored fuzz. Use in same way as *C. antarctica.* Makes good bank cover in sun or light shade; will control erosion. Needs little or no water.

C. incisa (C. trifoliolata). Zones 12, 13. Hardy deciduous vine with small, almost succulent, ivy-shaped leaves, 1–2 in. wide. Very fast growing. Good on trellis or rough wall or scrambling over rocks. Needs no irrigation, but looks cool and woodsy.

C. quadrangula (C. quadrangularis). Indoor and greenhouse plant. Succulent vine, usually grown in hanging baskets. Generally leafless, with fleshy, jointed, thick, four-angled or winged stems that climb or trail several feet. Occasional leaves oval or three-lobed, 2 in. long. Odd rather than pretty, *C. quadrangula* is easy to grow with water, good light, good drainage.

C. rhombifolia. GRAPE IVY. Zones 13, 15, 16, 21–24 (needs all-year warmth). Native to South America. To 20 ft. Beautiful dark green foliage. Leaves divided into diamond-shaped leaflets 1–4 in. long, with sharp-toothed edges; show bronze overtones because of reddish hairs on veins beneath. Widely used indoors. Outdoors, it grows to good size and can be trained on trellis, pergola, or driftwood branches. Grows in sun or fairly deep shade, tolerating low light intensity indoors. In the ground it needs some water. The variety 'Mandaiana' is more upright and compact than the species, with larger, more substantial leaflets. 'Ellen Danica' has leaflets shallowly lobed like an oak leaf; it grows more compactly than grape ivy and has darker green, less lustrous leaves.

C. striata. Zones 13–24. Native to South America. To 20 ft. In effect a miniature Virginia creeper, with small, leathery leaves divided into three to five leaflets, each 1–3 in. long. Stems reddish. Use as ground or wall cover, to make long traceries against plain surfaces or to spill over wall. Sun or shade; needs some water. Useful and beautiful.

C. voinieriana. See Tetrastigma voinieriana

Cistaceae. Members of the rockrose family grown in the West are evergreen shrubs with flowers that look something like single roses—small in *Helianthemum nummularium,* large in *Cistus.* Individual flowers are short lived but appear over a long season.

CISTUS

ROCKROSE

Cistaceae

EVERGREEN SHRUBS

✿ ZONES 7–9, 12–24; BORDERLINE IN ZONES 4–6

☼ FULL SUN

◊ ● LITTLE OR NO WATER ONCE ESTABLISHED

Cistus purpureus

Native to Mediterranean region. Hardy to 15°F. Producers of showy spring flowers, rockroses are sun loving, fast growing, tolerant of aridity. Often planted in fire-hazard areas. They accept poor, dry soil and will take cold ocean winds, salt spray, or desert heat. Rockroses should have well-drained soil if they are to be watered. To keep plants vigorous and neat, cut out a few old stems from time to time. Tip-pinch young plants to thicken growth, or give a light overall shearing to new growth.

When planting in area that will not be irrigated, don't plant root-bound plants. Cut circling roots and spread out the mass so roots can grow down to lower soil levels.

Use as dry-bank cover, massed by themselves or interplanted with ceanothus, wild buckwheat *(Eriogonum),* or sunroses *(Helianthemum nummularium).* Taller kinds make good informal screens or low dividers. Useful in big rock gardens, in rough areas along drives and roads, or in sunny wild areas. They can reduce erosion.

C. albidus. WHITE-LEAVED ROCKROSE. To 4 ft. tall, 8 ft. wide, with furry gray leaves and 2-in. flowers of bright purplish pink in spring, often with repeat bloom in fall.

C. corbariensis. See C. hybridus

C. crispus. To 3 ft. tall, 5 ft. wide with furry, wavy-edged gray-green leaves, purple-pink flowers. 'Santa Cruz' is similar, with a longer bloom season.

C. 'Doris Hibberson'. Compact, to 3 ft. tall and as wide. Gray-green foliage. Leaves 1–2 in. long, oval. Clear pink, 3-in.-wide flowers with crinkled silky petals in June, July. Flowers blend with other flower colors better than do blooms of commonly grown *C. purpureus.*

C. hybridus (C. corbariensis). WHITE ROCKROSE. Spreading growth to 2–5 ft. high and almost as wide. Leaves to 2 in. long, gray green, crinkly; fragrant on warm days. Flowers 1½ in. across, white with yellow centers, in late spring. Widely grown.

C. incanus (C. villosus). Bushy plant 3–5 ft. tall and equally wide. Oval 1–3-in.-long leaves densely covered with down. Flowers purplish pink, 2–2½ in. across, in late spring and early summer. *C. i. creticus (C. creticus)* is similar, but with wavy-edged leaves.

C. ladanifer (C. ladaniferus maculatus). CRIMSON-SPOT ROCKROSE. Compact, to 3–5 ft. high, with equal spread. Leaves to 4 in. long, dark green above, lighter green beneath, fragrant. White, 3-in.-wide flowers with dark crimson spot at base of each petal, June–July. There is an unspotted white form, 'Albiflorus'. Plant formerly known as *C. palhinhae* is now *C. l. latifolius,* a lower-growing (2-ft.) plant with larger (3–4-in.) pure white flowers. 'Blanche' (2 ft.) and 'Frank Birch' (6–8 ft.), both with very large (4-in.) pure white flowers, are considered hybrids between this species and its variety.

C. laurifolius. Stiff, erect growth to 5 ft., with 3-in. dark green leaves with pale undersides. White flowers 2–2½ in. wide in long-stalked clusters of three or more.

C. 'Peggy Sammons'. To 6 ft., with gray-green leaves and pink flowers. Heavy bloomer.

C. purpureus. ORCHID ROCKROSE. Compact grower to 4 ft. tall and wide, often shorter and wider where constant ocean winds keep plants low. Leaves 1–2 in. long, dark green above, gray and hairy beneath. Reddish purple, 3-in.-wide flowers with red spot at base of each petal, June–July. Very fine where cool winds and salt spray limit choice of plants.

C. salviifolius. SAGELEAF ROCKROSE. Wide-spreading shrub to 2 ft. high and 6 ft. across. Leaves light gray green, about 1 in. long, crinkly, veined, crisp looking. Flowers 1½ in. wide, white with yellow spots at base of petals, very profuse in late spring. Good bank or ground cover for rough situations. Usually sold as *C. villosus* 'Prostratus'.

C. skanbergii. Low, broad bush 3 ft. tall and 8 ft. wide. Gray-green leaves; pure pink, 1-in. flowers in great profusion in late spring.

C. 'Sunset'. Dense, spreading growth to 2 ft. tall, 6–8 ft. wide. Leaves are gray green, flowers dark magenta pink. Long bloom period.

C. 'Victor Reiter'. Stiffly erect plant to 3–4 ft., with gray-green leaves and hot pink, pale-centered flowers 2–2½ in. across.

C. villosus. See C. incanus

C. villosus 'Prostratus'. See C. salviifolius

C. 'Warley Rose'. Grows 1 ft. tall, 4 ft. wide, with dark green leaves and purplish pink flowers.

CITRON. See CITRUS, Miscellaneous · · · · · · · · · · · · · · · p. 232

FOR INFORMATION ON YOUR CLIMATE ZONE
PLEASE SEE PAGES 15–44

CITRUS

Rutaceae

EVERGREEN TREES AND SHRUBS

✿ ZONES 8, 9, 12–24; OR INDOORS

☼ FULL SUN

● DO NOT LET ROOT ZONE BECOME DRY OR SOGGY

Orange

As landscaping plants, they offer year-round attractive form and glossy deep green foliage, fragrant flowers, and decorative fruit in season. If you want quality fruit, your choice of varieties will depend on the total amount of heat available through the fruit-developing period (need varies according to type) and on the winter cold in your zone. Choice and use are also determined by whether plants are standard trees or dwarfs. Citrus flowers draw bees.

Heat requirements. Lemons and limes need the least heat and will produce usable fruit in cool-summer areas (where winter temperatures are not too low). 'Valencia' orange has higher heat requirement and greater frost tolerance. Navel oranges need even more heat, but their fruit development period is shorter than that of 'Valencia'; a tree will produce palatable fruit between winter frosts if summer heat is high. Navel, therefore, is a good selection for Zones 8, 9, 12, 13. Mandarin oranges (tangerine group) need high heat for top flavor. Grapefruit develops full flavor only in areas of prolonged high heat.

Hardiness. Citrus of one kind or another are grown in every Arizona and California climate where winter temperatures do not fall much below 20°F. From least hardy to hardiest, they rank generally in this order: 'Mexican' lime (28°F), limequat, grapefruit, pummelo, regular lemon, tangelo and tangor, 'Bearss' lime, sweet orange, most mandarin oranges (tangerines), 'Rangpur' lime and 'Improved Meyer' lemon, 'Owari' mandarin, sour orange, orangequat, kumquat, calamondin (20°F).

Standard or dwarf. Practically all citrus sold have been budded or grafted on an understock. Standard trees (20–30 ft. tall and as wide) are grown on a variety of understocks. Dwarf trees are grown on understocks of trifoliate orange *(Poncirus trifoliata)* or Hiryu (Flying Dragon); the latter is a naturally dwarf, contorted, spiny form of trifoliate orange (variety *P. t.* 'Monstrosa'). Trifoliate orange understocks produce trees 4–10 ft. tall (some may eventually reach 15–20 ft.); Hiryu produces even smaller trees (5–7 ft. at 13 years old).

Check citrus periodically for suckers (branches that arise below the graft line) and remove them before they compete with (or overwhelm) the desired variety.

Drainage. First requirement is fast drainage. If soil drains slowly, don't attempt to plant citrus in it regardless of how you condition it. In poorly drained soil, plant above soil level in raised beds or by mounding up soil around plant. Drainage in average soil, and water retention in very light soil, will be improved by digging in a 4–6-in. layer of peat moss, sawdust, or ground bark to depth of 1 ft.

Watering. Citrus need moist soil, but never freestanding water. They need air in the soil. Danger from overwatering is greatest in clay soil where air spaces are minute. In soil with proper drainage, water newly planted trees almost as frequently as trees in containers—twice a week in normal summer weather, more frequently during hot spells. Water established trees every other week. In clay soils, space watering intervals so top part of soil dries between irrigations. Don't let tree reach wilting point.

If you build basins, make them wider than spread of branches. Citrus roots extend out twice as far as the distance from the trunk to branch ends. Keep trunk dry by starting basin 6 in. or more from trunk. When you water, be sure to wet entire root zone (that is, wet to depth of 4 ft.).

Mulching. Since citrus roots grow near surface as well as deeper, a mulch over soil is beneficial. Use a 2–3-in.-deep layer of sawdust or the like, or large pebbles or gravel.

Fertilizing. Give 1–1½ lbs. of actual nitrogen to a mature tree each year. (To get pounds of "actual nitrogen," multiply percentage of total nitrogen, as stated on label, times weight of fertilizer.) It's best to apply one-third in late winter, one-third in June, and one-third in August. Spread fertilizer beneath and well beyond branch spread of tree, and water in deeply. Use a high-nitrogen formula.

Citrus may suffer from iron chlorosis or zinc deficiency. Chlorosis (yellowing leaves with dark green veins) may also be caused by excess water, so check your irrigation practice. Treat with chelated iron or iron sulfate. Zinc deficiency shows up as a yellowish blotch or mottle between leaf veins. Control with zinc foliar sprays. Commercial products containing both iron chelates and zinc are available as sprays.

Pests and diseases. Citrus can get aphids, mites, scale insects, and mealybugs. If these pests' natural enemies fail to handle the infestations, and if jets of water fail to keep the pests in check, spray with appropriate chemicals. If scale remains troublesome, spray with light oil in early spring. Bait or spray for snails and slugs whenever necessary, especially during warm-night spells of winter and spring.

Copper bands, available in some areas, will keep snails out of trees. Where it is legal to do so (in Southern California), colonize citrus groves with decollate snails, which prey on the garden snail.

Weirdly deformed fruit (especially lemons) is caused by the citrus bud mite. Control by a light summer oil spray in spring and in fall; spray only in fall in hot-summer areas. Reduce harmful insect populations by keeping ants out of trees with sticky bands on trunks. (Ants prey on natural insect predators of the mites.)

The few fungus ailments of citrus occur in poorly drained soil. Water molds, causing root rot, show up in yellowing and dropping foliage. Best control is to correct your watering schedule.

Brown rot gummosis usually occurs in older trees at base of trunk. Keep base of trunk dry; trim and clean the oozing wounds, removing decayed bark to a point where discolored wood does not show. Paint areas with Bordeaux paste mixture.

Sunburn. Citrus bark sunburns in hot-sun areas. Trunks should be wrapped (paper trunk bands are available commercially). When heavy pruning exposes trunks or limbs, protect bark with whitewash or latex paint. Common latex wall paint in tan or brown, similar to bark color, is satisfactory.

Pruning. Commercial trees are allowed to carry branches right to ground. Production is heaviest on lower branches. Growers prune only to remove twiggy growth and weak branches or, in young plant, to nip back wild growth and balance plant. You can prune garden trees to shape as desired; espaliers of citrus are traditional. Lemons and sour oranges are often planted close and pruned as hedges. Many citrus are thorny, so wear gloves and long-sleeved shirt when picking fruit or pruning.

Citrus in containers. Daily watering may be necessary in hot weather. Containers should have diameter of at least 1½ ft.

Citrus indoors. Gardeners in warm-summer/cold-winter areas can grow citrus in containers, bringing plants indoors for winter protection. A cool greenhouse is best, but a basement area with good bright light is satisfactory. Use very little water.

GRAPEFRUITS

'Marsh Seedless'. The West's main commercial type. Large light yellow fruit. Ripens 18 months after bloom—late November to June in desert areas. Needs highest, most prolonged summer heat for top-quality fruit, but even out of best climate it's a beautiful tree. Standard tree grows to 30 ft. or more; on dwarf rootstock, less than half as high. Large glossy leaves.

'Melogold' and 'Oroblanco'. Hybrids between grapefruit and pummelo, these resemble grapefruit in appearance, are generally sweeter than grapefruit, and require less heat to produce palatable fruit. 'Oroblanco' is somewhat sweeter and has a thicker rind. 'Melogold' has a thinner rind and a flavor more like grapefruit. They ripen November–February in hotter regions, March–April on the coast.

'Ruby' ('Redblush', 'Ruby Red'). Pink grapefruit. Red-blushed skin and pinkish flesh. Does not color well except in desert.

'Star Ruby'. Resembles 'Ruby', with deeper color in peel and flesh. Needs less heat to ripen.

LEMONS

'Eureka'. The standard lemon of markets. Bears throughout year. Not as vigorous as 'Lisbon' lemon. Somewhat open growth, branches with few thorns. As a dwarf it's dense with large, dark leaves. New growth is bronzy purple. Height 20 ft.; less as dwarf.

Lemon

'Improved Meyer'. This strain supposedly has more resistance to infection and virus diseases than older 'Meyer' lemons; it has been propagated from stock that is free of disease that the older strain harbored and could pass on to other citrus. Other than that, it should be like the original. Fruit is quite different from commercial lemon—rounder, thin skinned, more orange in color. Tangy aroma, very juicy, but less acidic than standard lemon. Bears fruit all year round, at early age. Tree is not a dwarf on its own roots. Will grow to 12 ft. with a 15-ft. spread. On dwarf rootstock it's half that size.

'Lisbon'. Vigorous growth, thorny, upright, denser than 'Eureka', to 20–25 ft. Can be trimmed up into highly decorative small tree. Fruit practically identical to 'Eureka'. Ripens mostly in fall, but some ripening all year. More resistant to cold than 'Eureka' and better adapted to high heat. Best lemon for Arizona.

'Ponderosa'. A novelty. Bears huge, rough lemons with thick, coarse skin; 2-lb. fruits not unusual. Mild lemon flavor. Bears at early age, frequently in gallon-can size. Main crop in winter, with some fruit through year. Open, angular branching; large leaves widely spaced. To 8–10 ft.; dwarf size, 4–6 ft.

'Sungold'. Attractive semidwarf (to 14 ft. tall, 8 ft. wide) lemon with green-striped yellow fruit and leaves mottled with white and cream.

'Villa Franca'. Generally similar to 'Eureka' but tree is larger, more vigorous, and has denser foliage and thornier branches. Fruit is similar to 'Eureka'. Sold in Arizona to grow in Zones 12 and 13; not common in California.

LIMES

'Bearss'. Best lime for California gardens. Succeeds where oranges are successful. Tree is quite angular and open when young but forms dense round crown to 15–20 ft. when mature (half that size on dwarf rootstock). It's thorny and inclined to drop many leaves in winter. Young fruit green, light yellow when ripe, almost size of lemon. When fully ripe it is especially juicy. Seedless. Main crop winter to late spring, some fruit all year.

'Mexican'. The standard bartender's lime—small, green to yellow green. Grow it in Zones 21–23. Grows to 12–15 ft. with upright twiggy branches.

LIMEQUATS

'Eustis'. Hybrid of 'Mexican' lime and kumquat. Fruit is the shape and size of a jumbo olive, light yellow when ripe. Flavor and aroma of lime; provides fresh lime flavor in regions too frosty for true limes. Rind edible. Ripens late fall and winter. Some fruit all year. Tree is shrublike, angular branching, twiggy, and rather open. Dwarf plant excellent in container.

'Tavares'. Plant is more compact, fuller, shapelier than 'Eustis'. Fruit is larger, long oval in shape, heavily borne. Lime flavor weak in overripe fruit.

MANDARIN ORANGES (TANGERINES)

'Clementine'. Algerian tangerine. Fruit a little larger than 'Dancy', fewer seeds, ripens November–December. Fruit remains on tree, juicy and sweet, for months. Grows to 12 ft., semiopen with vertical, spreading, somewhat willowy branches. Seems to develop full flavor in areas too cool for a good 'Dancy'. 'Clementine' usually bears light crops unless planted with another variety for pollination.

'Dancy'. The standard tangerine in markets before Christmas. Fruit smaller and seedier than other mandarins. Best flavor in Zones 12 and 13 but good in Zones 21–23. Ripens December–January. Holds well on tree.

Upright tree with erect branches. Dwarf tree handsome in container or as espalier.

'Encore'. Light orange, thin-skinned fruit ripens in summer, holds until fall. Quality good. Erect tree with slender branches and narrow leaves.

'Fairchild'. Hybrid between 'Clementine' mandarin and 'Orlando' tangelo. Medium-size, deep orange fruit peels easily, is juicy and tasty, has many seeds. Ripens November–December. Small, compact tree bears every year. Needs another variety nearby for pollination.

'Fremont'. Hybrid between 'Clementine' and an Oriental mandarin called Ponkan. Medium-size, bright orange fruit ripens December–January. Flavor good. Tree tends to bear in alternate years; thin fruit when unusually heavy.

'Honey'. Hybrid between 'King' and 'Willow' mandarin. Small, seedy fruit with rich, sweet flavor. Tends to bear heavily in alternate years. Vigorous tree. Not the same as 'Murcott', a Florida variety often sold in markets as 'Honey'.

'Kara'. Hybrid between 'King' and 'Owari'. Fruit large (2½ in.) for mandarin. Tart-sweet, aromatic flavor when ripened in warm interior climates. Ripens January and February in Zones 12, 13; March to May and June in Zones 8, 9, 14, 15, 18–23. From one season to another may be very seedy or nearly seedless. Tree form resembles 'Owari'. Spreading, often drooping branches with large leaves. Grows to a rounded 15–20 ft., half that size as dwarf.

'Kinnow'. Hybrid between 'King' and 'Willow' mandarin. Medium-size fruit has rich, aromatic flavor. Stores well on tree. Ripens January–May. Handsome tree—columnar, dense, very symmetrical to 20 ft. (dwarf will reach 10 ft.). Densely foliaged with slender leaves. Good in any citrus climate.

'Mediterranean' ('Willow Leaf'). The important mandarin of the Mediterranean region. Sweet, aromatic fruit ripens in spring. Tree spreading, with thin, willowy branches and narrow leaves.

'Owari'. Owari Satsuma. Source of imported canned mandarins. Sweet, delicate flavor; nearly seedless, medium to large fruit. Loose skin. Earliest mandarin to ripen—October to Christmas. Quickly overripens if left on tree but keeps well in cool storage. Standard trees are spreading, to 10–15 ft. high. Dwarf trees can be used as 6-ft. shrubs. Open, angular growth in early age, then more compact. Not suited to desert.

'Wilking'. From same parents as 'Honey' and 'Kinnow'. Small to medium fruit with relatively thin rind; very juicy with rich, distinctive flavor. Fruit stores well on tree. Tree is rounded, medium height, and nearly thornless; tends to bear heavily in alternate years.

ORANGES

The commercial oranges of the West are typified by the 'Washington' navel and the 'Valencia'. In the following list, 'Washington' and the other navel varieties are described first, then 'Valencia' and its counterparts, and finally the other, lesser-known oranges.

'Washington' navel. Widely adapted except in desert regions; best in warm interiors. Standard tree is 20–25-ft. globe. On dwarf stock it becomes 8-ft. mound. Bears December–February.

'Robertson' navel. Variant of 'Washington' navel. Fruit identical but earlier by 2–3 weeks. Tends to carry fruit in clusters. Tree generally smaller in size than 'Washington'. Has same climate adaptation. Dwarf trees produce amazing amounts of fruit.

'Skaggs Bonanza'. Another variant of 'Washington'. Fruit colors and ripens earlier; tree comes into bearing at younger age. Very heavy bearing.

'Summernavel'. Fruit much like 'Washington'. Sometimes fails to color as well, but flavor is good. Later ripening—well into summer months. Tree is more openly branched, with much larger leaves than 'Washington'. A dwarf tree will cover area bigger than 8 ft. square quite rapidly.

In some seasons, navel oranges are subject to split navels. This seems unrelated to culture, generally occurring when weather conditions favor fast fruit development. To keep tree in even growth, avoid excess fertilizer. Watch leaf color: yellowish leaves are signs of nitrogen need; dark green, lush leaves with burned tips or edges indicate too much nitrogen.

'Valencia'. The juice orange of stores. Most widely planted orange in the world, widely adapted in California. Poor risk in Arizona; if planted there, select a warm location or provide some protection to fruit, which must winter on tree. One of Arizona Sweets (see below) would be safer selection. 'Valencia' oranges mature in summer and store on tree for months, improving in sweetness. Tree vigorous and fuller growing than 'Washington' navel, both as standard and dwarf.

'Seedless Valencia'. Variant of 'Valencia'. Fruit size, quality, and season are same. May not bear as prolifically.

Arizona Sweets. These are a group of varieties grown in Arizona. 'Diller', 'Hamlin', 'Marrs', and 'Pineapple' are the principal ones.

'Diller'. Small to medium oranges with few seeds, high-quality juice. Ripen November–December (before heavy frost). Vigorous, large, dense tree with large leaves.

'Hamlin'. Similar to 'Diller', with mid-size fruit; not as hardy.

'Marrs'. Early-ripening, tasty, low-acid fruit on a naturally semidwarf tree. Bears young.

'Pineapple'. Early-ripening, mid-size fruit of excellent flavor.

'Shamouti' ('Palestine Jaffa'). Originated in Palestine and considered there to be finest orange. Large, seedless, no navel. Not a commercial orange in California because not sufficiently superior to 'Washington' navel. Grown on dwarf rootstock for home gardeners because of beauty in form and foliage. It's wider than tall. Leaves larger than navel. Heavy crop of fruit in early spring.

'Trovita'. Originated from seedling of 'Washington' navel. Thin skinned and about navel size, but without navel. Ripens in early spring. Apparently requires less heat than other sweet oranges and develops good-quality fruit near—not on—coast. Nevertheless, it tolerates heat well enough to pass as one of the Arizona Sweets. Dwarf tree has 'Washington' navel look with handsome dark green leaves.

Blood oranges. These are characterized by red pigmentation in flesh, juice, and (to a lesser degree) rind. Flavor is excellent, with raspberry overtones. Generally speaking, they thrive wherever oranges produce good fruit. Pigmentation varies with local microclimates and weather.

'Moro'. Deep red flesh with touch of red on rind. No rind pigmentation near coast. Bears January–April.

'Sanguinelli'. Red-skinned fruit; flesh inside streaked with red. Bears February–May.

'Tarocco'. Red or red-suffused pulp, pink to red juice. Color varies. The less heat, the more color. Good quality in cooler areas. Ripens late spring. Tree is very vigorous and open growing, with long, willowy, vinelike branches. Dwarf tree makes ideal espalier.

KUMQUATS (FORTUNELLA)

Very hardy. May not flower or fruit in cold-winter citrus climates but always worthwhile for form and foliage. Leaves bright green, 3 in. long, oval, pointed. White flowers have rich orange blossom perfume. Edible rind is sweet; flesh is tart. Fruit is candied, preserved whole, or used in marmalade or jelly. Expect regular fruit production only in warm-summer areas. Plant size variable (6–25 ft.) when grown on its own roots. On dwarf rootstock, a compact, dense shrub-tree to 4 ft. In pots or tubs, admirably suited for patio or garden.

F. crassifolia. MEIWA KUMQUAT. Fruit round; larger, somewhat sweeter than *F. margarita*. Tree less hardy.

F. margarita. NAGAMI KUMQUAT. Fruit oval, bright orange, about 1 in. in diameter.

SOUR-ACID MANDARIN ORANGES

Calamondin. Fruit looks like tiny (¾–1½-in.) orange. Hundreds hang from tall, columnar plant (8–10-ft., even as dwarf). Most attractive in containers. Flesh is tender, juicy, sour, with a few small seeds. Primary use is as an ornamental; not a fruit to eat fresh. Skin and flesh good in marmalades.

'Otaheite' orange. Natural dwarf only a few feet tall. Usually grown indoors as decorative pot plant. Not true orange. Will bear very young. Fruit is orange to reddish orange, small, round, rough skinned, insipid in flavor. About as hardy as lemon.

'Rangpur'. Commonly called Rangpur lime, probably not lime at all. Fruit looks and peels like a mandarin, does not have lime taste. Less acid than lemon but with flavor overtones that make it a rich, interesting base for punches and mixed drinks. Good landscape tree, vigorous, sturdy,

bushy. Fast growth to 15 ft. and as wide (as dwarf, to 8 ft.). Dense when pruned, open otherwise. Fruits colorful as ornaments, hang on tree throughout year. Has wide climate tolerance.

TANGELOS

'Minneola'. Hybrid of 'Dancy' tangerine and grapefruit. Fruit is bright orange red, smooth, large. Flavor similar to tangerine. Few seeds. Ripens February–March. Stores on tree for two months. Tree not as large or dense as grapefruit. Leaves 3½–5 in. long, pointed. Thrives in citrus areas.

'Orlando'. Fruit medium–large, looks like a flattened orange. Rind is orange, adheres to orange-colored flesh. Very juicy, mildly sweet, matures early in season. Tree is similar to 'Minneola' but with distinctively cupped leaves; less vigorous but more resistant to cold.

'Sampson'. Hybrid of tangerine and grapefruit, but fruit more like small, golden grapefruit with orange-red pulp. Best for juice and marmalades. Ripens February–April. Standard tree is vigorous, fast growing to 30 ft. Form similar to that of grapefruit. Most decorative as dwarf tree. Dark green, oval, 2–3-in. leaves. Best in Zones 14–16, 20–23. Subject to sunburn in desert areas.

MULTIPLE-VARIETY CITRUS PLANTS

The nursery offerings go by such names as cocktail citrus, salad citrus, and citrus medley. On these plants that bear multiple kinds of fruit, several varieties (usually two or three) have been budded onto one stem. Such plants save space, but you must continually cut back the vigorous growers (limes, lemons, pummelos, grapefruits) so the weaker ones (oranges, mandarins, tangerines) can survive.

TANGORS

'Temple'. Tangerine-orange hybrid. High-quality fruit in Zone 13. Flattened, deep bright orange fruit is loose skinned and easy to peel. Pulp tender textured, orange, juicy; "different" but good flavor (not too sweet). Ripens in early spring. Tree to 12 ft. high with greater spread; bushy and thorny. To a wide 6 ft. on dwarf stock. Leaves are similar to mandarin's, smaller and narrower than orange's.

MISCELLANEOUS

Sour orange, Seville orange *(Citrus aurantium)*. Makes large hedges, street trees, lawn trees. Fragrant flowers. Spectacular orange-red, 3-in. fruits in clusters. Fruit is bitter and makes excellent bitter marmalade. Tree grows to 20–30 ft. with 15–20-ft. spread; dense foliage. Plant 6–10 ft. apart for tall screen, 3–4 ft. apart (prune heavily) for hedge.

'Bouquet', 'Bouquet des Fleurs'. Commonly called Bouquet orange, another very hardy sour orange. Big shrub or small tree to 8–10 ft. Graceful foliage, dark green. Used as hedge or windbreak. Flowers unusually large and extremely fragrant. Fruit small, bitter, used only in marmalades.

'Chinotto' orange. Smaller in all dimensions than other sour oranges. Dense, bushy, round headed, with closely set, small, almost myrtlelike leaves. Very slow growing to 7–10 ft. tall. Formal appearance, often rounded high on stem and clipped. Makes an ideal tub plant. Fruit is ornamental, small, round, bright orange; it is used in Europe for candying. Often sold as myrtle-leaf orange.

'Etrog' citron. Attractive foliage. Fruit is small, oblong, yellow, fragrant, and unusually lumpy on the surface. Peel usually candied.

'Nippon' orangequat. Hybrid between kumquat and 'Owari' mandarin. Fruit larger than kumquat, with sweet rind and mild-flavored pulp; can be eaten whole. Fruit borne winter–spring holds well, makes plant a fine tubbed ornamental.

'Chandler' pummelo. The pummelo (pomelo, shaddock) is probably one parent of the grapefruit. The fruit is huge and thick skinned, with firm, relatively dry pulp; it has not proven popular in this country. 'Chandler', with pinkish flesh, is flavorful, moderately juicy. To eat, peel fruit, separate segments, then remove membrane surrounding segments.

Trifoliate orange *(Poncirus trifoliata)*. Deciduous shrub or small tree to 15 ft., with spiny branches; typically fragrant flowers; and hard, bitter, yellow fruit. Fruit is inedible, but plant is useful as dwarfing understock and as a parent in breeding hardy citrus. Rarely grown as an ornamental oddity or as an impenetrable hedge.

CLADRASTIS lutea

YELLOW WOOD

Fabaceae (Leguminosae)

DECIDUOUS TREE

✂ ZONES 1–9, 14–16

☼ FULL SUN

💧 MODERATE WATER

Cladrastis lutea

Native to Kentucky, Tennessee, and North Carolina. Slow growing to 30–35 ft. with broad, rounded head half as wide as tree is high. Divided 8–12-in.-wide leaves. Bright green in summer, brilliant yellow in fall, they look like those of English walnut.

May not flower until 10 years old and may skip bloom some years, but spectacular when it does. In May or early June it produces long (6–10-in.) clusters of white, very fragrant flowers that resemble wisteria blossoms. ('Rosea' is a pink-flowered kind.) Blooms followed by flat, 3–4-in.-long seedpods. Useful and attractive as terrace, patio, or lawn tree even if it never blooms.

Prune when young to shorten side branches. Remove lower branches entirely when tree has height you want.

CLARKIA (includes Godetia)

Onagraceae

ANNUALS

✂ ALL ZONES

☼ FULL SUN

💧 KEEP SOIL MOIST FROM SEEDING TO FLOWERING

Clarkia amoena

Native to western South and North America; especially numerous in California. They grow in the cool season, bloom in spring and early summer. Attractive in mixed borders or in mass displays, alone or with love-in-a-mist (*Nigella damascena*), cornflower (*Centaurea cyanus*), violas, sweet alyssum (*Lobularia maritima*). Cut branches keep for several days; cut when top bud opens (others open successively).

Sow seed in place in fall (mild-winter areas) or spring. Seedlings difficult to transplant, but volunteer seedlings grow very well. Best in sandy soil without added fertilizer.

C. amoena (Godetia amoena, G. grandiflora). FAREWELL-TO-SPRING, GODETIA. Native California to British Columbia. Two wild forms: coarse stemmed and sprawling, 4–5 in. high; slender stemmed, 1½–2½ ft. high. Tapered leaves are ½–2 in. long. On both forms, upright buds open into cup-shaped, slightly flaring, pink or lavender flowers, 2 in. across, usually blotched or penciled in crimson. Although seeds of named varieties are rarely sold in United States (more available in England), strains of mixed colors are easy to find. Dwarf Gem grows 10 in. tall; Tall Upright reaches 2–3 ft.

C. concinna. RED-RIBBONS. California native. To 1½ ft. tall. Deep pink to lavender flowers with three-lobed, fan-shaped petals. Leaves rounded, ½–2 in. long. May be found in wildflower seed mixes.

C. pulchella. Native to Pacific Northwest. Slender, upright, mostly unbranched, 1–1½ ft. high. Stems reddish; leaves narrow, 1–2 in. long, sparse. Flowers single, with four petals; petals taper to clawlike base, are three-lobed at tip. There are semidouble and dwarf forms. Some garden clarkias probably hybrids between *C. pulchella* and *C. unguiculata*.

C. unguiculata (*C. elegans*). CLARKIA, MOUNTAIN GARLAND. Erect, to 1–4 ft. Reddish stems, 1–1¾-in.-long leaves, 1-in.-wide flowers in rose, purple, white. Some varieties have double white, orange, salmon, crimson,

purple, rose, pink, and creamy yellow flowers. Double-flowered kinds are ones usually sold in seed packets.

CLEMATIS

Ranunculaceae

DECIDUOUS OR EVERGREEN VINES

✂ ALL ZONES; BEST IN 1–6, 15–17

☼ ROOTS NEED TO BE COOL; TOPS IN SUN

💧 ROOTS NEED REGULAR MOISTURE

Clematis armandii

Most of the 200-odd species are deciduous vines; the evergreen *C. armandii* and a few interesting freestanding or sprawling perennials and small shrubs are exceptions. All have attractive flowers, and most are spectacular. The flowers are followed by fluffy clusters of seeds with tails, often quite effective in flower arrangements. Leaves of deciduous kinds are dark green, usually divided into leaflets; leafstalks twist and curl to hold plant to its support.

Clematis are not demanding, but their few specific requirements should be met. Plant vine types next to trellis, tree trunk, or open framework to give stems support for twining. Give them rich, loose, fast-draining soil; add generous quantities of peat moss, ground bark, and the like. Add lime only where soil tests indicate calcium deficiency.

To provide cool area for roots, add mulch, place large flat rock over soil, plant shallow-rooted ground cover over the root area, or plant in shade of small shrub or evergreen vine and stake so the top can catch sun. Put in support when planting and tie up stems at once. Stems are easily broken, so protect them with wire netting if child or dog traffic is heavy. Clematis need constant moisture and nutrients to make their great rush of growth; apply a complete liquid fertilizer monthly during the growing season.

Pruning clematis sounds complicated, but it need not be; plants are forgiving and will quickly repair mistakes. Do remember that dormant wood can look dead, and take care not to make accidental cuts. Watch for healthy buds at leaf bases and preserve them. The basic objective is to get the greatest number of flowers on the shapeliest plant.

The type of pruning you do depends on when your plants flower. If you don't know what kind you have, watch them for a year to see when they bloom; then prune accordingly.

Spring-blooming clematis bloom only on the previous year's wood. Cut back a month after flowering to restrict sprawl, preserving main branches.

Summer- and fall-blooming clematis bloom on wood produced in the spring. Cut back in late fall after flowering or in early spring as buds swell. For the first 2–3 years, cut to within 6–12 in. of the ground, or to 2–3 buds; to 2 ft. or less on older plants.

Clematis that bloom in spring and again in summer or fall bloom on old wood in spring, new wood later. Do only light, corrective pruning in fall or early spring; pinch or lightly shape portions that have bloomed to stimulate low branching and avoid a bare base.

Cut flowers are choice for indoors (float in bowl). Burn cut stems with match to make flowers last longer. Unless otherwise specified, flowers are 4–6 in. across.

C. alpina. To 8–12 ft., with dangling flowers borne singly on long stalks. Flowers have four spreading, pointed petal-like sepals and an inner cup of smaller modified stamens. Flowers may be blue, white, purple, pink, or red, depending on variety. 'Willy', pale pink, is best known. 'Helsingborg' is dark blue, 'Pamela Jackman' lavender blue.

C. armandii. EVERGREEN CLEMATIS. Native to China. Leaves burn badly at tips where soil or water contains excess salts. Fast growing to 20 ft. Leaves divided into three glossy dark green leaflets, 3–5 in. long; they droop downward to create strongly textured pattern. Glistening white, 2½-in.-wide, fragrant flowers in large, branched clusters, March–April.

Slow to start; races when established. Needs constant pruning after flowering to prevent tangling and buildup of dead thatch on inner parts of vine. Keep and tie up stems you want, and cut out all others. Frequent pinching will hold foliage to eye level. ▶

Train along fence tops or rails, roof gables. Allow to climb tall trees. Trained on substantial frame, makes privacy screen if not allowed to become bare at base.

There is a light pink–flowered form, *C. a.* 'Hendersoni Rubra'.

C. chrysocoma. Native to western China. To 6–8 ft. or more in height; fairly open. Young branches, leaves, and flower stalks covered with yellow down. Flowers long stalked, white, shaded pink, 2 in. wide, in clusters from old wood in spring, with later flowers following from new wood. Will take considerable shade.

C. davidiana. See C. heracleifolia davidiana

C. dioscoreifolia (C. paniculata). SWEET AUTUMN CLEMATIS. Native to Japan. Tall, vigorous, forming billowy masses of 1-in.-wide, creamy white, fragrant flowers in late summer and fall. Dark green, glossy leaves divided into three to five oval, 1–2½-in.-long leaflets. After bloom or in early spring, prune year's growth to one or two buds. Good privacy screen, arbor cover.

C. florida 'Sieboldii' (C. f. 'Bicolor'). Flowers 3–4 in. across, with a central puff of purple petal-like stamens. Vine is a somewhat delicate 8–12 ft. Not as rugged as other clematis but a striking flower.

C. heracleifolia davidiana (C. davidiana). Native to China. Half-woody perennial to 4 ft. high. Deep green leaves divided into 3 broad, oval, 3–6-in.-long leaflets. Dense clusters of 1-in.-long, tubular, medium to deep blue, fragrant flowers, July–August. Use in perennial or shrub border.

C. integrifolia. Native to Europe and Asia. Semishrubby perennial to 3 ft. with dark green, undivided, 2–4-in.-long leaves and nodding, urn-shaped, 1½-in.-long blue flowers, June–July. Prune after bloom.

C. jackmanii. Series of hybrids between forms of *C. lanuginosa* and *C. viticella*. All are vigorous plants of rapid growth to 10 ft. or more in one season. The best known of the older large-flowered hybrids is known simply as *C. jackmanii*. It has a profusion of 4–5-in. rich purple flowers with four sepals. Blooms heavily from June to July and later. Newer hybrids have larger flowers with more sepals, but none blooms as profusely. *C. j.* 'Comtesse de Bouchaud' has silvery rose pink flowers; *C. j.* 'Mme. Edouard Andre', purplish red blossoms. All flower on new wood; all do best with severe pruning in early spring as buds begin to swell. Species freezes to ground in cold-winter areas. (For more on large-flowered hybrid clematis, see discussion below.)

C. lanuginosa. Native to China. A parent of many of the finest large-flowered hybrids. Grows only to about 6–9 ft. but produces magnificent display of large (6-in.) lilac to white flowers, May–July. Best known for its variety *C. l.* 'Candida', with 8-in. white flowers and light yellow stamens. Blooms on new and old wood. In favorable climates will bloom March–April. Prune only to remove dead or weak growth in early spring. Then, after first flush of flowers, cut back flowered portions promptly for another crop later in the summer.

C. lasiantha. This native of the California chaparral blooms earlier, is less showy than other California species, needs little summer water.

C. lawsoniana. Thought to be hybrid of *C. lanuginosa* and *C. patens*. To 6–10 ft. Large (6–9 in.) flowers, rosy purple and dark veined. Its best-known form is *C. l.* 'Henryi', which bears tremendous 8-in. flowers, white with dark stamens, June–August.

C. ligusticifolia. Native to much of the West. High-climbing (to 20 ft. or more), deciduous vine much like *C. dioscoreifolia* in habit and flowering. Slightly fragrant flowers in spring, summer; attractive seed heads.

C. macropetala. DOWNY CLEMATIS. Native to China, Siberia. Variable in size, may reach 6–10 ft. high. In early spring, produces 4-in. lavender to powder blue flowers that look double; they resemble ballet skirts. Blooms are followed by showy bronzy pink, silvery-tailed seed clusters. *C. m.* 'Markham Pink' has lavender pink flowers. Prune lightly in February to remove weak shoots and limit vigorous growth to sound wood.

C. montana. ANEMONE CLEMATIS. Native to Himalayas, China. Vigorous to 20 ft. or more. Extremely hardy, easy to grow. Massive early spring display of 2–2½-in. anemonelike flowers,

Clematis montana

opening white, turning pink. Flowers on old wood, so can be heavily thinned or pruned immediately after flowering to rejuvenate or reduce size.

C. m. 'Rubens'. To 15–25 ft. Foliage is bronzy green, new growth crimson. Fragrant flowers, rose red to pink, are carried throughout vine.

C. m. 'Tetrarose'. Considered more vigorous than *C. m.* 'Rubens'.

C. 'Nelly Moser'. Mauve sepals marked by dark red stripe in center of each.

C. paniculata. See C. dioscoreifolia

C. 'Ramona'. Lavender blue; classic for planting with yellow or coppery climbing roses.

C. tangutica. GOLDEN CLEMATIS. Native to Mongolia, northern China. To 10–15 ft., with gray-green, finely divided leaves. Bright yellow, 2–4-in., nodding, lantern-shaped flowers in great profusion from July to fall. They are followed by handsome, silvery-tailed seed clusters. Prune the same as *C. dioscoreifolia*.

C. texensis. SCARLET CLEMATIS. Native to Texas. Fast growing to 6–10 ft. Dense bluish green foliage. Bright scarlet, urn-shaped flowers to 1 in. long, July–August. Has not done well in Seattle but flourishes in Reno. More tolerant of dry soils than most clematis.

C. viticella. Native to southern Europe, western Asia. To 12–15 ft. Purple or rose purple, 2-in. flowers, June–August. Very hardy. Named varieties include 'Mme. Julia Correvon', rosy red, and 'Polish Spirit', deep purple-blue with red center.

CLASSIC TRELLIS PLANT GOES CASUAL

In winter, plant a bare-root clematis plant in a clay or wood hanging basket containing rich, loose, fast-draining soil mix (hold mix in pot with piece of window screen over drain hole). Keep plant in filtered shade or morning sun. Don't skimp on water or fertilizer. Spectacular, 4–5-in. flowers will spill over edge 5 months after planting. Late every winter, shorten stems to 6–12 in.

Large-flowered hybrid clematis. Although well over a hundred varieties of large-flowered hybrid clematis are being grown today, your local nursery is not likely to offer more than a dozen of the old favorites. Mail-order catalogs remain the best source for collectors seeking the newest. Flowers on some of these may reach 10 in. in width.

Here are varieties to choose from—old favorites first, then newer offerings:

White. 'Henryi' and *C. lanuginosa* 'Candida' are standard. 'Marie Boisselot' or 'Mme. Le Coultre' (large, flat, round flowers) and 'Gillian Blades' (huge, star-shaped flowers) are newer.

Pink. 'Comtesse de Bouchaud', the standard pink, has these rivals: 'Charissima' (veined pink with deeper bars); 'Hagley Hybrid' ('Pink Chiffon'), shell pink with pointed sepals; and 'Lincoln Star' (pink with paler edges).

Red. Red clematis have deep purplish red flowers that are best displayed where the sun can shine through them, as on the top of a fence. 'Mme. Edouard Andre', 'Ernest Markham', and 'Red Cardinal' are standards. 'Ville de Lyon' has full, rounded, velvety flowers; 'Niobe' is the darkest red of all.

Blue violet. Mid-blue 'Ramona' is always popular. Other varieties are: 'Edo Murasaki' (deep blue); 'General Sikorski' (huge, with faint red bar); 'Lady Betty Balfour' (dark blue); 'Mrs. Cholmondeley' (big, veined sky blue); 'Piccadilly' (purplish blue); 'Prince Philip' (huge purplish blue with ruffled edges); and 'Will Goodwin' (lavender to sky blue).

Purple. *C. jackmanii* is the most popular purple. Others are 'Gypsy Queen' (deepest purple); 'Jackmanii Superba' (larger, somewhat redder than *C. jackmanii*); 'Mrs. N. Thompson' (deep bluish purple with red bar); and 'Richard Pennell' (rosy purple).

Bicolor. 'Nelly Moser' (pink with reddish bar) is deservedly one of the most popular clematis. 'Carnaby' (white with a red bar) and 'Dr. Ruppel' (pink with red bar) are newer, splashier.

Double. Fully double, roselike blooms in early summer on old wood are usually followed later by single or semidouble flowers on new wood. 'Belle of Woking' is silvery blue; 'Duchess of Edinburgh', white; 'Mrs. P. T. James', deep blue; 'Teshio', lavender; and 'Vyvyan Pennell', deep blue with lavender blue center.

CLEOME hasslerana (C. spinosa)

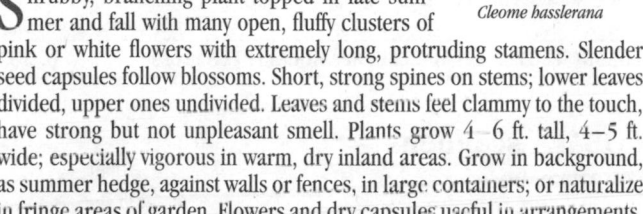

SPIDER FLOWER

Capparaceae

ANNUAL

✔ ALL ZONES

☼ FULL SUN

💧 KEEP ON DRY SIDE OR PLANT GETS TOO VIGOROUS

Cleome hasslerana

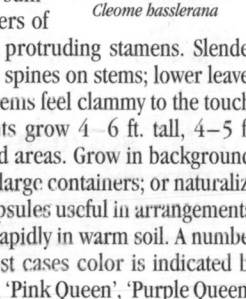

Shrubby, branching plant topped in late summer and fall with many open, fluffy clusters of pink or white flowers with extremely long, protruding stamens. Slender seed capsules follow blossoms. Short, strong spines on stems; lower leaves divided, upper ones undivided. Leaves and stems feel clammy to the touch, have strong but not unpleasant smell. Plants grow 4–6 ft. tall, 4–5 ft. wide; especially vigorous in warm, dry inland areas. Grow in background, as summer hedge, against walls or fences, in large containers; or naturalize in fringe areas of garden. Flowers and dry capsules useful in arrangements.

Sow seeds in place in spring; they sprout rapidly in warm soil. A number of varieties can be grown from seed. In most cases color is indicated by variety name: 'Cherry Queen', 'Mauve Queen', 'Pink Queen', 'Purple Queen', 'Rose Queen', and 'Ruby Queen'. 'Helen Campbell' is snow white.

CLERODENDRUM

GLORYBOWER

Verbenaceae

EVERGREEN OR DECIDUOUS SHRUBS OR TREES

✔ ZONES VARY BY SPECIES

☼ PARTIAL SHADE

💧 MODERATE WATER

Clerodendrum thomsoniae

Some are outdoor plants; others are house plants. Though they are relatively little known, all have showy, brightly colored flowers.

C. bungei (C. foetidum). CASHMERE BOUQUET. Evergreen shrub. Zones 5–9, 12–24. Native to China. Grows rapidly to 6 ft. tall; soft wooded. Prune severely in spring and pinch back through growing season to make 2–3-ft. compact shrub. Spreads by suckers, eventually forming thicket if not restrained. Big leaves (to 1 ft.), broadly oval with toothed edges, dark green above, with rusty fuzz beneath; ill smelling when crushed. Delightfully fragrant flowers in summer: ¾ in. wide, rosy red, in loose clusters to 8 in. across. Plant where its appearance, except in flowering season, is not important. It is resistant to oak root fungus.

C. fragrans pleniflorum (C. philippinum plenifolium). Evergreen to partly deciduous shrub. Zones 8, 9, 12–24. Coarse shrub spreading freely by root suckers unless confined. To 5–8 ft. (much less in containers), with 10-in. leaves like those of *C. bungei*. Flowers pale pink, double, in broad clusters that resemble florist's hydrangea; sweet, clean fragrance.

C. thomsoniae (C. balfouri). BLEEDING HEART GLORYBOWER. Evergreen shrubby vine. In most protected spots of Zones 22–24; indoor/outdoor pot plant elsewhere. Native to west Africa. Leaves oval, 4–7 in. long, dark green, shiny, distinctly ribbed. Flowers are a study in color contrast—scarlet 1-in. tubes surrounded by large (¾-in.-long) white calyxes, carried in flattish 5-in.-wide clusters, August–October. Will flower in 6-in. pot. Can grow to 6 ft. or more if left untrimmed. Give support for twining. Needs rich, loose soil mix, plenty of water with good drainage. Prune after flowering.

C. trichotomum. HARLEQUIN GLORYBOWER. Deciduous shrub-tree. In Zones 5, 6, may freeze to ground and come back from roots; adapted to Zones 15–17, 20–24. Native to Japan. Grows with many stems from base to 10–15 ft. or more. Leaves oval, to 5 in. long, dark green, soft, hairy. Fragrant clusters of white, tubular flowers almost twice as long as prominent, fleshy, ½-in.-long scarlet calyxes. Late-summer bloom. Calyxes hang on and contrast pleasingly with turquoise or blue-green, metallic-looking fruit. *C. t. fargesii*, from China, is somewhat hardier and smaller; it has smooth leaves and green calyxes that later turn pink. Routine care. Give room to spread at top and plant under it to hide its legginess.

C. ugandense. Evergreen shrub. Zones 9, 14–24. To 10 ft. (usually much less), with glossy dark green, 4-in.-long leaves and 1-in.-long flowers with one violet blue petal and four pale blue ones. Pistil and stamens arch outward and upward.

CLETHRA

Clethraceae

DECIDUOUS SHRUBS AND EVERGREEN TREES

✔ ZONES VARY BY SPECIES

☼ ◐ SUN; PARTIAL SHADE IN HOT-SUMMER AREAS

💧 MODERATE WATER

Clethra arborea

Distinctive plants with definite climate and soil preferences. Small five-lobed flowers clustered at the branch tips.

C. alnifolia. SUMMERSWEET, SWEET PEPPER-BUSH. Deciduous shrub. Zones 2–6. Native to eastern United States. To 10 ft. high with thin, strong branches forming vertical pattern. Spreads slowly by suckers into broad clumps. Dark green leaves, 2–4 in. long and half as wide, have toothed edges. Leafs out very late, in mid-May. Blooms in late summer: each branch tip carries several 4–6-in.-long spires of tiny, gleaming white flowers, spicily perfumed. Grows best in soils where rhododendrons thrive. Full sun in cool gardens, some shade where summers are warm. *C. a.* 'Pinkspire' has deep pink flowers; *C. a.* 'Rosea', pale pink blooms.

C. arborea. LILY-OF-THE-VALLEY TREE. Evergreen tree. Zones 15–17, 21–24. Native to Madeira. Beautiful small tree. Grows at moderate rate to 20 ft., rather stiffly upright with 10-ft. spread. Densely clothed with glossy, bronzy green, 4-in.-long leaves. White flowers in upright, branched clusters resemble lily-of-the-valley, even in their fragrance. They appear in late summer.

Leaf tips burn with frost, but plant comes back from old wood or from roots when damaged.

Easy to grow in soils where azaleas or rhododendrons thrive. Where salts build up, condition soil with peat moss or ground bark and make sure drainage is fast. Needs abundant moisture. If necessary, spray for red spider mites in summer. For another lily-of-the-valley tree, see *Crinodendron patagua*.

C. barbinervis. JAPANESE SWEET SHRUB. Deciduous shrub. Zones 5–9, 14–24. Slow grower to 15–18 ft., with sharply toothed leaves that turn bright yellow in fall. Drooping 4–6-in. clusters of fragrant white flowers in summer.

CLEYERA japonica (Eurya ochnacea)

Theaceae

EVERGREEN SHRUB

✔ ZONES 4–6, 8, 9, 14–24

☼ PARTIAL SHADE

💧 TOLERATES SOME ARIDITY

Native to Japan and southeast Asia. Handsome foliage shrub related to camellia. Similar in

Cleyera japonica

character to *Ternstroemia gymnanthera.* Grows at moderate rate to 15 ft. tall and as wide, with graceful, spreading, arching branches. New leaves are beautiful deep brownish red. Mature leaves, 3–6 in. long, are glossy dark green with reddish midrib. Small clusters of fragrant, creamy white flowers, September–October, are followed by small, dark red, puffy berries that last through winter. Flowers and berries are attractive but not showy, don't form on young plants. 'Tricolor' *(C. fortunei)* has yellow and rose variegation on its foliage.

CLIANTHUS puniceus

PARROT BEAK

Fabaceae (Leguminosae)

EVERGREEN SHRUBLIKE VINE

ZONES 8, 9, 14–24

FULL SUN ON COAST, PARTIAL SHADE INLAND

AMPLE WATER THROUGH BLOOMING SEASON

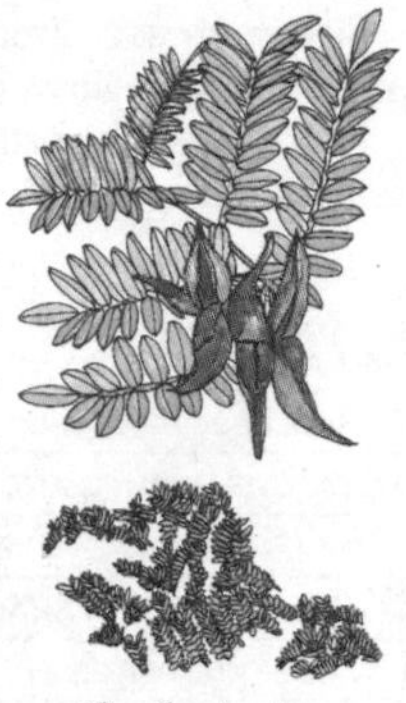

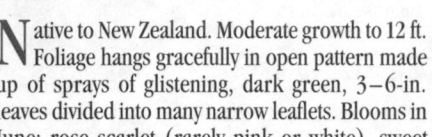

Clianthus puniceus

Native to New Zealand. Moderate growth to 12 ft. Foliage hangs gracefully in open pattern made up of sprays of glistening, dark green, 3–6-in. leaves divided into many narrow leaflets. Blooms in June: rose scarlet (rarely pink or white), sweet pea–shaped flowers with 3-in. parrot-beak keels swing downward between leaves. Pods that follow are 3 in. long. Train as espalier or on support to bring out full beauty of leaves and flowers. Routine garden care. If soil is heavy, mix in organic soil amendment. Watch for snails and spider mites.

CLIFF-BRAKE. See PELLAEA **p. 409**

CLIFF ROSE. See COWANIA mexicana stansburiana **p. 246**

CLIMBING LILY. See GLORIOSA rothschildiana **p. 308**

CLIVIA miniata

Amaryllidaceae

TUBEROUS-ROOTED EVERGREEN PERENNIAL

ZONES 12–17, 19–24

BEST WITH NO DIRECT SUN

REGULAR WATER

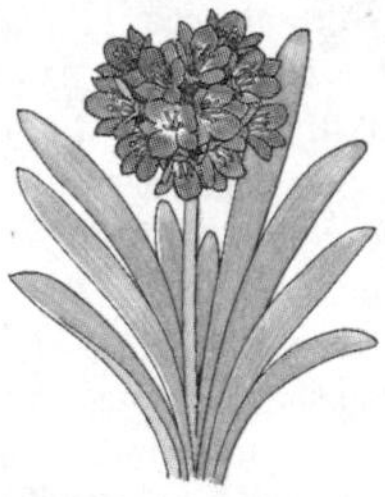

Clivia miniata

Native to South Africa. Striking member of amaryllis family with brilliant clusters of orange, funnel-shaped flowers rising from dense clumps of dark green, strap-shaped, 1½-ft.-long leaves. Blooming period is December–April; most bloom March–April. Ornamental red berries follow flowers. French and Belgian hybrids have very wide, dark green leaves and yellow to deep red orange blooms on thick, rigid stalks. 'Flame' is an exceptionally hot orange red. Solomone Hybrids have pale to deep yellow flowers.

In frostless areas or well-protected parts of garden, clivias are handsome in shaded borders with ferns, azaleas, other shade plants. Superb in containers; grow indoors in cold climates. Plant with top of tuber just above soil line. Let clumps grow undisturbed for years. Container plants bloom best with regular fertilizing, crowded roots. Still commonly known as kaffir lily in some areas.

CLOVE PINK. See DIANTHUS caryophyllus **p. 262**

CLOVER. See TRIFOLIUM **p. 510**

FOR GROWING SYMBOL EXPLANATIONS
PLEASE SEE PAGE 129

CLYTOSTOMA callistegioides

VIOLET TRUMPET VINE

Bignoniaceae

EVERGREEN VINE

EVERGREEN IN ZONES 9, 12–24

FULL SUN OR PARTIAL SHADE

MODERATE WATER

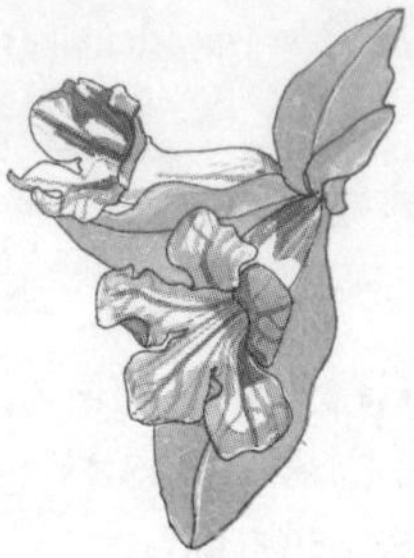

Clytostoma callistegioides

Tops hardy to 20°F, roots to 10°F. Strong growing; will clamber over anything by tendrils. Needs support on walls. Extended terminal shoots hang down in curtain effect. Leaves divided into two glossy, dark green leaflets with wavy margins. Trumpet-shaped flowers in violet, lavender, or pale purple, 3 in. long and nearly as wide at the top, in sprays at end of shoots, late spring to fall. Prune in late winter to discipline growth, prevent tangling. At other times of year, remove unwanted long runners and spent flower sprays. Formerly *Bignonia violacea, B. speciosa.*

COARSE-FLOWERED MALLEE. See EUCALYPTUS grossa **p. 283**

COBAEA scandens

CUP-AND-SAUCER VINE

Polemoniaceae

TENDER PERENNIAL GROWN AS ANNUAL

ALL ZONES

FULL SUN

REGULAR WATER

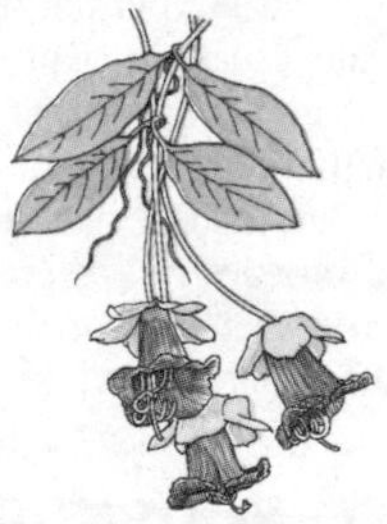

Cobaea scandens

Native of Mexico. Extremely vigorous growth to 25 ft. Bell-shaped flowers are first greenish, then violet or rose purple; there is also a white-flowered form. Called cup-and-saucer vine because 2-in.-long cup of petals sits in large, green, saucerlike calyx. Leaves divided into two or three pairs of oval, 4-in. leaflets. At ends of leaves are curling tendrils that enable vine to climb rough surfaces without support.

The hard-coated seeds may rot if sown out of doors in cool weather. Start seeds indoors in 4-in. pots; notch seeds with knife and press edgewise into moistened potting mix. Barely cover seeds. Keep moist but not wet; transplant to warm, sunny location when weather warms up. Blooms first year from seed. In mild winters it lives from year to year, eventually reaching more than 40 ft. in length and blooming heavily from May until October. When growing it near the coast, plant it out of ocean wind.

COBRA LILY. See DARLINGTONIA californica **p. 259**

COCCULUS laurifolius

Menispermaceae

EVERGREEN SHRUB OR SMALL TREE

ZONES 8, 9, 12–24

ANY EXPOSURE

PREFERS MOISTURE

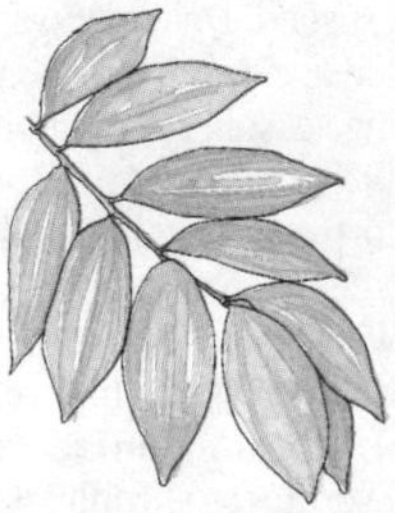

Cocculus laurifolius

Native to Himalayas. Grows slowly at first, then moderately rapidly to 25 ft. or more. Can be kept lower by pruning or may be trained as espalier. Usually multistemmed shrub with arching, spreading growth as wide as high. Staked and trained as tree, it takes on umbrella shape. Leaves shiny, leathery, oblong to 6 in., with three strongly marked veins running from base to tip. Useful as screen or background plant. Long, willowy branches are as easily led and trained as vines; fastened to a trellis, they make an effective screen.

CODIAEUM variegatum

CROTON

Euphorbiaceae

HOUSE PLANT OR ANNUAL

🗓 ZONE 24 AS ANNUAL; OR INDOORS

☼ ● BRIGHT GREENHOUSE; SHADE OUTDOORS

💧💧 REGULAR TO AMPLE WATER

Codiaeum variegatum

Grown principally for coloring of large, leathery, glossy leaves, which may be green, yellow, red, purple, bronze, pink, or almost any combination of these. Leaves may be oval, lance shaped, or very narrow; straight edged or lobed. Dozens of named forms combine these differing features. Can reach 6 ft. or more but is usually seen as single-stemmed plant 6–24 in. tall. It performs best in a warm, bright, humid greenhouse.

COFFEA arabica

COFFEE

Rubiaceae

EVERGREEN SHRUB

🗓 ZONES 21–24; OR INDOORS

● SHADE OUTDOORS

💧 REGULAR WATER

Coffea arabica

Native to east Africa. The coffee tree of commerce is sold as a handsome container plant for patio, lanai, and large well-lit rooms. It's an upright shrub to 15 ft. with evenly spaced tiers of branches, clothed with shining, dark green, oval leaves to 6 in. long. Small (¾ in.), fragrant white flowers are clustered near leaf bases. They are followed by ½-in. fruits that start green and finally turn purple or red. Each contains two seeds—coffee beans. Grow in container, using same potting mixes and culture as for camellias. Must be protected from frosts.

COIX lacryma-jobi

JOB'S TEARS

Poaceae (Gramineae)

PERENNIAL GRASS; ANNUAL IN COLDER CLIMATES

🗓 ZONES 12–24

☼ ◑ FULL SUN OR PARTIAL SHADE

💧 REGULAR WATER

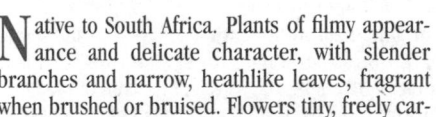

Coix lacryma-jobi

A curiosity grown for its ornamental "beads." Loose growing with smooth, prominently jointed stems to 6 ft. Sword-shaped leaves to 2 ft. long, 1½ in. wide. Outside covering of female flower hardens as seed ripens; becomes shiny, ¼–1½-in. bead in pearly white, gray, or violet. String into bracelets. Cut stems for winter arrangements before seeds dry and shatter.

COLCHICUM

MEADOW SAFFRON, AUTUMN CROCUS

Liliaceae

CORMS

🗓 ZONES 1–9, 14–24

☼ FULL SUN

💧 REGULAR WATER IN SPRING, SPARING IN SUMMER

❀ ALL PARTS ARE HIGHLY POISONOUS

Colchicum

Mediterranean plants. Many species; sometimes called autumn crocus, but not true crocuses. Shining, brown-skinned, thick-scaled corms send up clusters of long-tubed, flaring, lavender pink, rose purple, or white flowers to 4 in. across in late summer, whether corms are sitting in dish on windowsill or planted in soil. When planted out, broad, 6–12-in.-long leaves show in spring and then die long before flower cluster rises from ground. Best planted where they need not be disturbed more often than every 3 years or so. Corms available during brief dormant period in July and August. The two best varieties are 'The Giant', single lavender, and 'Waterlily', double violet. Plant with tips 3–4 in. under soil surface. To plant in bowls, set upright on 1–2 in. of pebbles or in special fiber sold for this purpose, and fill with water to base of corms

---

AUTUMN CROCUS IN A LAWN

Autumn crocus can add little clusters of lavender pink to a lawn in September. How to create such a picture: in midsummer, peel back small pieces of sod, plant corms in well-amended soil beneath, then lay sod back down and water well. For a more permanent splash of color every spring, plant purple Dutch crocus in fall.

COLEONEMA and DIOSMA

BREATH OF HEAVEN

Rutaceae

EVERGREEN SHRUBS

🗓 ZONES 7–9, 14–24

☼ ◑ TALLER GROWTH IN LIGHT SHADE

💧 REGULAR WATER; AVOID OVERWATERING

Coleonema pulchrum

Native to South Africa. Plants of filmy appearance and delicate character, with slender branches and narrow, heathlike leaves, fragrant when brushed or bruised. Flowers tiny, freely carried over long season in winter and spring, with scattered bloom to be expected at any time. You will find plants in nurseries under either *Coleonema* or *Diosma*. Actually, your choice amounts to a white- or a pink-flowering breath of heaven.

Plant in light soil. Fast drainage is a must. To control size and promote compactness, shear lightly after main bloom is over. For even more filmy look, thin out some interior stems.

Good on banks or hillsides, along paths where you can break off and bruise a twig to enjoy the foliage's fragrance. Frequently used next to buildings, though a little wispy for such use.

C. album. WHITE BREATH OF HEAVEN. Grows to 5 ft. or more and as wide. White flowers. Almost universally sold as either *Diosma reevesii* or *D. alba.*

C. pulchrum. PINK BREATH OF HEAVEN, PINK DIOSMA. Grows to 5 ft., occasionally to 10 ft. Flowers pink. Often sold as *Diosma pulchra.* 'Sunset Gold' has yellow foliage, grows 1½ ft. tall, 4 ft. wide.

Diosma ericoides. BREATH OF HEAVEN. Introduced into California in 1890. However, most plants sold under this name now are *Coleonema album.* Has similar form and white flowers.

COLEUS hybridus

COLEUS
Lamiaceae (Labiatae)
PERENNIAL TREATED AS ANNUAL OR INDOOR PLANT
☀ ALL ZONES
☼ BEST IN STRONG, INDIRECT LIGHT OR THIN SHADE
⬥ AMPLE WATER

Coleus hybridus

Native to tropics. Often sold as *C. blumei*. Grown for brilliantly colored leaves; blue flower spikes are attractive but spoil shape of plant and are best pinched out in bud. Leaves may be 3–6 in. long in large-leafed strains (1½–2 ft. tall), 1–1½ in. long in dwarf (1-ft.) strains. Colors include green, chartreuse, yellow, buff, salmon, orange, red, purple, brown, often with many colors on one leaf.

Giant Exhibition and Oriental Splendor are large-leafed strains. Carefree is dwarf, self-branching, with deeply lobed and ruffled 1–1½-in. leaves. Salicifolius has crowded, long, narrow leaves; plant resembles foot-high feather duster. Named cutting-grown varieties exist, but most plants are grown from seed.

Useful for summer borders and as indoor/outdoor container and hanging basket plants. Plant in spring. Easy from seed sown indoors or, with protection, out of doors in warm weather. Easy from cuttings, which root in water as well as other media. Needs rich, loose, well-drained soil, warmth. Feed regularly with high-nitrogen fertilizer. Pinch stems often to encourage branching and compact habit; remove flower buds to ensure vigorous growth. Recently renamed *Solenostemon scutellarioides*.

COLLARDS. See KALE	p. 343

COLLINSIA heterophylla (C. bicolor)

CHINESE HOUSES
Scrophulariaceae
ANNUAL
☀ ALL ZONES
☼ FULL SUN
⬥ MOIST SOIL

Collinsia heterophylla

Native to California. Rather uncommon plant; blooms spring to early summer, with snapdragonlike flowers to 1 in. long held in tiers at top of 1–2-ft.-tall, somewhat hairy stems. Upper lip of flower white, lower one rose or violet. Leaves oblong, to 2 in. long. Gives light, dainty effect in front of borders, scattered under deciduous trees, or as ground cover for bulbs. Sow seed in place in fall or spring in rich, moist soil. Self-sows under favorable conditions.

COLOCASIA esculenta (Caladium esculentum)

TARO, ELEPHANT'S EAR
Araceae
TUBEROUS-ROOTED PERENNIAL
☀ ALL ZONES; SEE BELOW
☼ BEST IN WARM, FILTERED SHADE
⬥⬥ HEAVY WATERING
◈ JUICES CAN CAUSE SWELLING IN MOUTH, THROAT

Colocasia esculenta

Evergreen only in Zones 23, 24 (tops freeze at 30°F); grows as herbaceous perennial in Zones 12, 16–22, where tubers may be left in ground. In Zones 1–12, 14, 15, grow in containers or lift and store tubers over winter. Native to tropical Asia and Polynesia. Fast growing to 6 ft. Mammoth, heart-shaped, gray-green leaves add lush effect to any tropical planting within one season. Flowers resemble giant callas but are seldom seen. Effective with tree ferns, araliads, ginger, strelitzia. Handsome in large tub, raised beds, near swimming pools.

Protect from wind, which tears leaves. Feed lightly once a month in growing season.

The starchy roots are a staple food in Hawaii and the Pacific area in general; taro is occasionally grown for food production by Hawaiians and Californians of Pacific Island descent.

COLONIAL BENT. See AGROSTIS tenuis	p. 143
COLUMBINE. See AQUILEGIA	p. 160

COMAROSTAPHYLIS diversifolia

SUMMER HOLLY
Ericaceae
EVERGREEN SHRUB OR SMALL TREE
☀ ZONES 7–9, 14–24
☼ ☼ SUN ON COAST; PARTIAL SHADE INLAND
⬥ TOLERATES SOME ARIDITY

Native to coastal Southern California and Baja California. Rather formal growth to 6 ft. as shrub, 18 ft. as small tree. Gray bark. Leathery, 1–3-in.-long leaves, shiny dark green above, white and hairy beneath, with inrolled margins. (Variety *C. d. planifolia* has flat leaves.) Small, white, manzanitalike flowers, April–May, followed by clusters of red, warty berries similar to those of madrone.

Comarostaphylis diversifolia

COMFREY. See SYMPHYTUM officinale	p. 499

Commelinaceae. The spiderwort family is composed of herbaceous perennials, often fleshy, mostly tropical or subtropical. Wandering Jew (*Tradescantia albiflora* and *Zebrina pendula*) and spiderwort (*Tradescantia virginiana*) are familiar examples. Flowers generally have three rounded petals.

COMPASS BARREL CACTUS. See FEROCACTUS cylindraceus	p. 293
Compositae. See Asteraceae	p. 170
CONFEDERATE ROSE. See HIBISCUS mutabilis	p. 322

CONRADINA verticillata

CUMBERLAND ROSEMARY
Lamiaceae (Labiatae)
SHRUBBY PERENNIAL
☀ ZONES 4–9, 14–17
☼ FULL SUN
⬥ REGULAR WATER

Conradina verticillata

Aromatic, freely branching plant that roots from trailing branches to make a small-scale ground cover. Leaves are narrow, resembling rosemary (*Rosmarinus*). Lavender pink flowers top the 12–15-in. plants in early summer.

PRACTICAL GARDENING DICTIONARY

PLEASE SEE PAGES 529–592

CONSOLIDA ambigua
(Delphinium ajacis)

LARKSPUR, ANNUAL DELPHINIUM

Ranunculaceae

ANNUAL

✄ ALL ZONES

☼ FULL SUN

● MODERATE WATER

◆ ENTIRE PLANT, ESPECIALLY SEEDS, IS TOXIC

Consolida ambigua

Native to southern Europe. Upright, 1–5 ft. tall, with deeply cut leaves; blossom spikes densely set with 1–1½-in.-wide flowers (most are double) in white, blue-and-white, or shades of blue, lilac, pink, rose, salmon, carmine. Best bloom in cooler spring and early summer months. Giant Imperial strain has many 4–5-ft. vertical stalks compactly placed. Regal strain has 4–5-ft. base-branching stems, thick spikes of large flowers similar to perennial delphiniums. Super Imperial strain is base branching, has large flowers in 1½-ft. cone-shaped spikes. Steeplechase is base branching, has biggest double flowers on 4–5-ft. spikes, and is heat resistant. Sow seed where plants are to grow; fall planting is best except in heavy, slow-draining soils. Cover seed with ⅛ in. soil, thin plants to avoid crowding, get biggest flowers.

CONVALLARIA majalis

LILY-OF-THE-VALLEY

Liliaceae

PERENNIAL GROWN FROM PIP

✄ ZONES 1–7, 14–20

◐ PARTIAL SHADE

● REGULAR WATER

◆ ALL PARTS ARE POISONOUS

Convallaria majalis

Small, fragrant, drooping, waxy white, bell-shaped, spring-blooming flowers on 6–8-in. stems rising above two broad basal leaves. Ground cover; use as carpet between camellias, rhododendrons, pieris, under deciduous trees or high-branching, not-too-dense evergreen trees.

Plant clumps or single pips (upright small rootstocks) in November or December in Zones 4–7, 14–20; in September or October in Zones 1–3. Give rich soil with ample humus. Set clumps 1–2 ft. apart, single pips 4–5 in. apart, 1½ in. deep. Cover yearly with leaf mold, peat moss, or ground bark. Large, prechilled forcing pips, available in December and January (even in mild-climate areas), can be potted for bloom indoors. After bloom, plunge pots in ground in cool, shaded area. When dormant, either remove plants from pots and plant in garden, or wash soil off pips and store in plastic bags in vegetable compartment of refrigerator until December or January; then either pot for bloom indoors or plant in garden.

Convolvulaceae. The morning glory family contains climbing or trailing plants, usually with funnel-shaped flowers. Morning glories (*Convolvulus* and *Ipomoea*) are typical examples.

CONVOLVULUS

Convolvulaceae

EVERGREEN SHRUBS AND PERENNIALS; ANNUALS

✄ ZONES VARY BY SPECIES

☼◐ MORE COMPACT IN FULL SUN

● TOLERATE SOME ARIDITY

Convolvulus cneorum

All species have funnel-shaped flowers much like morning glories. In fact, common vining morning glories (*Ipomoea*) are sometimes sold as *Convolvulus*.

C. cneorum. BUSH MORNING GLORY. Evergreen shrub. Best in Zones 7–9, 12–24; marginal in Zones 5, 6. Native to southern Europe. Rapid growing to 2–4 ft. and as wide. Silky-smooth, silvery gray, lance-shaped leaves 1–2½ in. long. White or pink-tinted morning glories with yellow throats open from pink buds, May–September. Give light soil and fast drainage. Prune severely to renew plant; can get leggy if left alone.

C. mauritanicus (C. sabatius). GROUND MORNING GLORY. Evergreen perennial. Zones 4–9, 12–24. Native to Africa. Grows 1–2 ft. high with branches trailing to spread of 3 ft. or more. Soft, hairy, gray-green, roundish leaves ½–1½ in. long. Flowers lavender blue, 1–2 in. wide, June–November. Grows well in light, gravelly soil with good drainage but will take clay soil if not overwatered. Tends to become woody; prevent by trimming in late winter. Use on dry banks as ground cover (plant 3 ft. apart), or group with sunroses (*Helianthemum*) or cerastium.

C. tricolor. DWARF MORNING GLORY. Summer annual. All zones. Native to southern Europe. Bushy, branching, somewhat trailing plants to 1 ft. high and 2 ft. wide. Small, narrow leaves. Flowers, 1½ in. across, variable in color but usually blue with yellow throat. Nick tough seed coats with knife and plant in place when soil has warmed up. Use as edging, against low trellis, or at top of wall. 'Blue Flash' and Rainbow Flash (mixed colors) grow 6 in. tall.

COPPER LEAF. See ACALYPHA wilkesiana   p. 135

COPROSMA

Rubiaceae

EVERGREEN SHRUBS, GROUND COVERS

✄ ZONES VARY BY SPECIES

☼◐ FULL SUN OR PARTIAL SHADE

● MOST TAKE SOME ARIDITY

Coprosma repens

Native to New Zealand. All are valuable for ease of maintenance in difficult situations and for handsome, glossy foliage.

C. 'Coppershine'. Zones 8, 9, 14–17, 21–24. Rounded shrub to 6 ft. with equal spread; fast growing while young. Leaves 1–1¾ in. long, half as wide, leathery, polished bright green heavily shaded with coppery brown; new growth even more heavily tinted, and entire plant bright copper in winter. Good medium-size hedge, screen.

C. kirkii. Zones 14–17, 21–24. Spreading shrub to 2–3 ft. high or nearly prostrate, with long, straight stems slanting outward from base. Tough, medium-height ground cover or bank cover. Leaves, closely set on stems, are yellow green, small (½–1 in. long), narrow. Grows in wide range of soils. Prune regularly to keep dense. Tolerates sea wind, salt spray.

C. pumila. Zones 8, 9, 14–24. Spreading, mounding shrub to 2–2½ ft. tall, eventually 8 ft. wide. Leaves bright shining green, roundish oval, to ¾ in. long. Plant 2–2½ ft. apart for ground cover in 3 years. Cut out upwardly growing branches. 'Verde Vista' (*C.* 'Prostrata') is best variety.

C. repens (C. baueri). MIRROR PLANT. Zones 15–17, 21–24. Rapid growth to 10 ft. with 6-ft. spread. Open, straggly shrub if neglected but beautiful plant when cared for. You can't imagine shinier, glossier leaves: they're dark to light green, 3 in. long, oval or oblong. Inconspicuous greenish or white flowers often followed by small yellow or orange fruit.

Three variegated forms are grown: 'Argentea' is blotched with white, 'Variegata' with yellowish green; 'Marble Queen' grows only 2 to 3 ft. tall, has striking white variegation.

Two prunings a year will keep it dense and at any height desired. Where shrub receives ocean wind, no pruning is necessary. Except in beach areas, give it part shade; water generously. Use as hedge, screen, wall shrub, informal espalier.

CORAL BELLS. See HEUCHERA sanguinea   p. 322

CORAL BERRY. See SYMPHORICARPOS orbiculatus   p. 499

CORDIA

Boraginaceae

EVERGREEN SHRUBS OR SMALL TREES

☘ ZONES 8–24

☼ ◑ FULL SUN OR PARTIAL SHADE

◐ ● INFREQUENT WATER OR REGULAR WATER

Cordia boissieri

Native to Texas, Baja California, and Mexico; adapted to low and intermediate deserts. Hardy to 15°F; leaves freeze, but plants recover.

C. boissieri. TEXAS OLIVE. Oval, grayish green, rough-surfaced leaves to 5 in. long. White flowers with yellow throats, 2½ in. wide, in clusters April–May and continuing over long season. May bloom again in autumn. Can be kept pruned as a low (3–5-ft.) shrub or allowed to reach 8–10 ft. With training, can be made into a small tree.

C. parvifolia. Native of Baja California. Smaller shrub with smaller white flowers. Tolerates heat and aridity.

CORDYLINE

Agavaceae

EVERGREEN PALMLIKE SHRUBS OR TREES

☘ ZONES VARY BY SPECIES

☼ ◑ ● EXPOSURE NEEDS VARY BY SPECIES

◐ ◑ ● WATER NEEDS VARY BY SPECIES

Cordyline australis

Woody plants with swordlike leaves, related to yuccas and agaves but usually ranked with palms in nurseries and in landscape. Good next to swimming pools. Often sold as *Dracaena;* for true *Dracaena,* see that entry.

C. australis (Dracaena australis). Zones 5, 8–11, 14–24. Full sun. Tolerates some aridity. In youth, fountain of 3-ft.-long, narrow (2–5-in.-wide), swordlike leaves. Upper leaves are erect; lower leaves arch and droop. In maturity, 20–30-ft. tree, branching high on trunk, rather stiff looking (like Joshua tree). Fragrant, ¼-in. flowers in late spring are carried in long, branching clusters.

For more graceful plant, cut back when young to force multiple trunks. Or plant in clumps of six to eight; each year, cut a few back to ground until all develop multiple trunks. Hardiest of cordylines, to 15°F or lower. Grows fastest in soil deep enough for big, carrotlike root. Used for tropical effects, with boulders and gravel for desert look, near seashore.

C. a. 'Atropurpurea'. BRONZE DRACAENA. Like the above, but with bronzy red foliage. Slower growth. Combine with gray or warm yellowish green to bring out color.

C. 'Baueri'. Zones 8, 9, 14–24. To 8–10 ft. high, with 2-ft.-long swordlike leaves of deep purple red. Needs full sun, occasional water.

C. indivisa. BLUE DRACAENA. Zones 16, 17, 20–24. Full sun. Trunk to 25 ft., topped with crown of rather stiff, huge leaves (6 ft. long, 6 in. wide). White flowers in 4-ft.-long clusters. Plant in groups of varying heights. Hardy to 26°F. Tolerates aridity and seaside conditions.

C. stricta. Zones 13, 16, 17, 20–24. Needs ample water, shade except near coast. Takes desert heat with ample water in shade. Slender stems clustered at base or branching low with branches quite erect. Swordlike, 2-ft.-long leaves are dark green with hint of purple. Lavender flowers in

large, branched clusters, very decorative in spring. Will grow to 15 ft. but can be kept lower by cutting tall canes to ground. New canes replace them. Long cuttings stuck in ground will root quickly. Hardy to 26°F. Fine container plant indoors or out; good for tall, tropical-looking background in narrow, shaded areas, lanais, or side gardens.

C. terminalis. TI PLANT. Zones 21–24 or indoors. Plants are usually started from "logs"—sections of stem imported from Hawaii. Lay short lengths in peat moss–sand mixture, covering about one-half their diameter. Keep moist. When shoots grow out and root, cut them off and pot them. Take ordinary indoor care; plant tolerates low light intensity. Plant has many named forms with red, yellow, or variegated leaves. White, foot-long flower clusters. Outdoors it reaches 6–8 ft. in special, frost-free locations where it receives regular water and soil stays warm.

COREOPSIS

Asteraceae (Compositae)

PERENNIALS AND ANNUALS

☘ ZONES VARY BY SPECIES

☼ FULL SUN

◐ VERY LITTLE WATER ONCE ESTABLISHED

Coreopsis tinctoria

Easily grown members of sunflower family yielding profusion of yellow, orange, maroon, or reddish flowers from late spring to fall. Both annual and perennial kinds are easy to propagate—annuals from seed sown in place (full sun) or in pots, perennials from seed or division of root crown. Tend to self-sow; seeds attract birds.

C. auriculata 'Nana'. Perennial. Evergreen to semievergreen in Zones 17–24; deciduous in Zones 1–16. Makes 5–6-in.-high mat of leaves 2–5 in. long. Under ideal conditions, it will spread by stolons to form a 2-ft.-wide clump in a year. Bright orange-yellow flower heads, 1–2½ in. wide, rise well above foliage. Long and profuse blooming season from spring to fall if you remove faded flowers. Best used in foreground of taller plants, in border, or as edging.

C. gigantea. Perennial. Zones 16, 17, 21–24. Native to coastal Southern California, Baja California. Thick, succulent trunks 3 ft. tall (rarely to 10 ft.) hold a few branches tipped with clusters of fernlike leaves. Clusters of 3-in. yellow daisies appear in spring. Showy in seaside plant collection; rarely sold in nurseries.

C. grandiflora. COREOPSIS. Perennial. All zones. Grows 1–2 ft. high, spreading to 3 ft.; leaves narrow, dark green, three- to five-lobed. Bright yellow, 2½–3-in.-wide flowers bloom all summer, carried on long slender stems high above foliage. Variety 'Sunburst' has large, semidouble flowers; it will bloom the first year from seed sown early in spring, then spread by self-sowing. 'Early Sunrise' is similar and even earlier to bloom. Both are tough enough for use in roadside beautification.

GROOMING COREOPSIS

Early in the flowering season you can easily groom coreopsis by cutting off spent flowers with a pair of one-hand pruning shears. But by summer the dead flowers can outnumber the new until they're too much for one-hand shears. Cut back the waves of dead flowers with hedge shears. Such whole-sale removals can bring on successive bloom.

C. lanceolata. COREOPSIS. Perennial. All zones. Grows 1–2 ft. high. Leaves somewhat hairy, narrow, mostly in tuft near base. Flower heads 1½–2 in. across, yellow, on pale green stems. Some leaves on lower stem have a few lobes. When well established, will persist year after year. Excellent cut flower.

C. maritima. Perennial. Zones 14–24. Native to coast of Southern California. Sometimes called sea dahlia. Grows 1–3 ft. high from tuberous taproot. Stems are hollow; leaves somewhat succulent, divided into very narrow lobes. Clear yellow, 2½–4-in. flower heads on 9–12-in.-long stems bloom in spring. Borders, naturalizing, striking cut flowers.

C. rosea. Perennial. All zones. Finely textured plant 1½–2 ft. tall with pink, yellow-centered daisylike flowers from summer to fall. Unlike other species, prefers moist soil.

C. tinctoria. ANNUAL COREOPSIS, CALLIOPSIS. Annual. All zones. Slender, upright, 1½–3 ft. tall with wiry stems; much like cosmos in growth habit. Leaves and stems smooth. Flowers similar to perennial coreopsis, in yellow, orange, maroon, bronze, and reddish, banded with contrasting colors; purple-brown centers. Dwarf and double varieties. Sow seed in place in full sun and dryish soil.

C. verticillata. Perennial. Zones 14–24. Plant is 2½–3 ft. tall, half as broad. Many erect or slightly leaning stems carry many whorls of finely divided, very narrow leaves. At top are 2-in. bright yellow daisies, freely borne over long summer and autumn season. One of the most tolerant of drought, neglect. 'Moonbeam', 1½–2 ft. tall, has pale yellow flowers; 'Zagreb', 1 ft. tall, has golden yellow flowers.

CORIANDRUM sativum

CORIANDER, CHINESE PARSLEY, CILANTRO
Apiaceae (Umbelliferae)
ANNUAL HERB
ALL ZONES
FULL SUN
REGULAR WATER

Grows 12–15 in. high. Delicate fernlike foliage; flat clusters of pinkish white flowers. Aromatic seeds crushed before use as seasoning for sausage, beans, stews, cookies, wines. Young leaves used in salads, soups, poultry recipes, and variety of Mexican and Chinese dishes. Grow in good, well-drained soil. Start from seed (including coriander seed sold in grocery stores); grows quickly, self-sows.

Coriandrum sativum

CORN

Poaceae (Gramineae)
ANNUALS
ALL ZONES
FULL SUN—ALWAYS
SPECIAL WATERING TIMES; SEE BELOW

Sweet corn is the one cereal crop that home gardeners are likely to grow; it requires considerable space but is still well worth growing. Once most sweet corn is picked, its sugar changes to starch very quickly; only by rushing ears from garden directly to boiling water can you capture full sweetness. Supersweet varieties of corn are actually sweeter than standard kinds and maintain their sweetness longer after harvest because of a gene that increases the quantity of sugar and slows its conversion to starch. A very few people find these varieties too sweet.

Sweet Corn

Corn needs heat, but suitable early hybrid varieties will grow even in cool-summer areas of the Northwest.

Corn is widely adapted but grows best in deep, rich soils; good drainage is important. Give full sun. Sow seed 2 weeks after average date of last frost, and make three or four more plantings at 2-week intervals; or plant early, midseason, and late varieties. Plant corn in blocks of short rows rather than single long rows; pollination is by wind, and unless good supply of pollen falls on silks, ears will be poorly filled. Don't plant popcorn near sweet corn; pollen of one kind can affect characteristics of other. For the same reason, some supersweet varieties have to be grown at a distance from other varieties. Either plant in rows 3 ft. apart and thin seedlings to stand 1 ft. apart, or plant in "hills" (actually clumps) 3 ft. apart each way. Place six or seven seeds in each hill and thin to three strongest plants. Give plants ample water and one feeding when stalks are 7–8 in. tall. Make certain that you apply good deep watering that thoroughly wets entire root zone just as tassel emerges from stalk; repeat again when silk forms. Don't remove suckers that appear.

FOR THE TASTIEST EAR OF CORN

Check your crop when ears are plump and silks have withered; pull back husks and try popping a kernel with your thumb. Generally, corn is ready to eat 3 weeks after silks first appear. Kernels should squirt milky juice; watery juice means that corn is immature. Doughy consistency indicates overmaturity. Elderly homegrown sweet corn is no better than corn you buy in supermarkets.

Corn earworm is the principal insect pest. There is no simple control. Most gardeners expect some harvested ears to show worm damage at the silk ends, and they just cut off those ends. The prevention (it's tedious) goes like this: Three days after silks appear, use a medicine dropper to put 20 drops of mineral oil on the base of each ear's silks. Repeat every 3 days until silks turn brown.

Ornamental corn. Annual. Some kinds of corn are grown for the beauty of their shelled ears rather than for their eating qualities. Calico, Indian, Squaw, and rainbow corn are some names given to strains that have brightly colored kernels—red, brown, blue, gray, black, yellow, and many mixtures of these colors. Grow like sweet corn, but let ears ripen fully; silks will be withered, husks will turn straw color, and kernels will be firm. Cut ear from plant, including 1½ in. of stalk below ear; pull back husks (leave attached to ears) and dry thoroughly. Grow well away from late sweet corn; mix of pollen can affect its flavor.

Ornamental Corn

Zea mays japonica includes several kinds of corn grown for ornamental foliage; one occasionally sold is 'Gracilis', a dwarf corn with bright green leaves striped white.

Popcorn. Annual. Grow and harvest popcorn just like ornamental corn described above. When ears are thoroughly dry, rub kernels off cobs and store in dry place. White and yellow popcorn resemble other corn in appearance. Strawberry popcorn, grown either for popping or for its ornamental value, has stubby, fat, strawberrylike ears packed with red kernels.

Popcorn

Cornaceae. The dogwood family consists of trees and shrubs with clustered inconspicuous flowers (sometimes surrounded by showy bracts) and berrylike fruit. *Aucuba japonica* and *Cornus* are examples.

CORNELIAN CHERRY. See CORNUS mas	p. 242
CORNFLOWER. See CENTAUREA cyanus	p. 216
CORN PLANT. See DRACAENA fragrans	p. 267

FOR INFORMATION ON SELECTING PLANTS

PLEASE SEE PAGES 45–128

CORNUS

DOGWOOD

Cornaceae

DECIDUOUS SHRUBS OR TREES (WITH EXCEPTIONS)

ZONES VARY BY SPECIES

GROUND COVER NEEDS SHADE

REGULAR WATER, EXCEPT AS NOTED

Cornus florida

All offer attractive foliage and flowers; some have spectacular fruit and winter bark. Many have bright fall foliage.

C. alba. TATARIAN DOGWOOD. Shrub. Zones 1–9, 14–24. In cold-winter areas its bare, blood red twigs are colorful against snow. Upright to about 10 ft. high; wide spreading, eventually producing thicket of many stems. Branches densely clothed with 2½–5-in.-long leaves to 2½ in. wide, deep, rich green above, lighter beneath; red in fall. Small, fragrant, creamy white flowers in 1–2-in.-wide, flattish clusters in April, May. Bluish white to whitish small fruits. Leaves of 'Gouchaultii' have yellow borders suffused with pink. Variety 'Argenteomarginata' (*C.* 'Elegantissima') has showy green-and-white leaves on red stems.

C. a. 'Sibirica'. SIBERIAN DOGWOOD. Less rampant than species; grows to about 7 ft. high with 5-ft. spread. Gleaming coral red branches in winter.

In both *C. alba* and *C. a.* 'Sibirica', new wood is brightest; cut back in spring to force new growth.

C. alternifolia. PAGODA DOGWOOD. Shrub or small tree. Zones 1–6. Multitrunked, to 20 ft. high. Strong horizontal branching pattern makes attractive winter silhouette. Light green leaves turn red in fall. Small clusters of creamy spring flowers are not showy. Blue-black fruit follows.

C. canadensis. BUNCHBERRY. Deciduous carpet plant. Zones 1–7; difficult but possible in Zones 8, 9, 14–16. Native Northern California to Alaska and eastward. It's difficult to believe this 6–9-in. perennial is related to dogwoods when you see it under trees by lakes and streams in Northwest. Creeping rootstocks send up stems topped by whorls of four to six oval or roundish, 1–2-in.-long leaves; deep rich green, they turn yellow in fall, die down in winter.

Plants bloom in May or June, bearing small, compact clusters of tiny flowers surrounded by (usually) four oval, ½–¾-in.-long, pure white bracts. Clusters of small, shiny, bright red fruit in August and September.

For shade in cool, moist climates, in acid soil with generous amounts of humus or rotten wood. Considered hard to establish, but when transplanted with piece of rotten log with bark attached, it establishes readily. Excellent companion plant for rhododendrons, ferns, trilliums, lilies.

C. capitata. EVERGREEN DOGWOOD. Large shrub or small tree. Zones 8, 9, 14–20. From Himalayas. Hardy to 15°F. Not reliably evergreen in cold weather. In mild winters it often loses half its leaves. Moderate growth to 20–30 ft. high, eventually with equal spread. Green to grayish green leaves, 2–4 in. long by ¾–1¾ in. wide; some turn red or purplish in fall.

Unless grown from cuttings, trees don't flower until about 8–10 years old, but when they do they are delightful. Small flower cluster is surrounded by four to six creamy to pale yellow, 1½–2-in.-long bracts in May and June. Large, fleshy, reddish purple fruit in October and November can be a litter problem, though birds may do some cleaning up for you.

C. controversa. GIANT DOGWOOD. Tree. Zones 3–9, 14, 18, 19. From the Orient. Hardy to 5°F. Resembles big shrubby dogwoods in leaves, flowers, and fruit but grows rapidly into magnificent 40–60-ft. tree with picturesque horizontal branches. Luxuriant 3–6-in.-long oval leaves, 2–3 in. wide, are dark green above, silvery green beneath, glowing red in fall. Creamy white flowers are not spectacular but so abundant in May they give good show. They form in fluffy, flattish clusters 3–7 in. wide. Shiny, bluish black, ½-in.-wide fruit, enjoyed by birds, ripens in August and September. Plant in full sun for most flowers and best fall color. Keep soil moist.

C. 'Eddie's White Wonder'. Tree. Zones 2–9, 14–20. Hybrid between *C. florida* and *C. nuttallii;* taller, more erect than former, twiggier than latter. Blooms in May, with four- or five-bracted flower clusters. Easier to transplant than western native *C. nuttallii.*

C. florida. FLOWERING DOGWOOD, EASTERN DOGWOOD. Tree. Zones 1–9, 14–16. Native to eastern United States. To 20 ft. high. Most commonly planted flowering dogwood in Northwest and mountain areas and much a part of spring flower display. In hot climates, shade or whitewash trunk to prevent sunburn, borer attacks. Plant in raised bed where soils are heavy.

In its horizontal branching pattern, it somewhat resembles our western native, *C. nuttallii,* but gray twigs at branch ends tend to be upright. It usually has shorter trunk. Small flower clusters are surrounded by four roundish, 2–4-in.-wide, white bracts with notched tips. Bracts form in autumn; in harsh, dry winters, tips may wither, preventing inflorescence from opening fully. Flowers almost cover tree in May before leaves expand. Oval leaves, 2–6 in. long by 2½ in. wide, are bright green above, lighter beneath; they turn glowing red before they fall. Clusters of small, oval, scarlet fruit last into winter or until birds eat them.

C. f. 'Cherokee Chief'. Deep rosy red bracts, paler at base.

C. f. 'Cherokee Princess'. Gives unusually heavy display of white blooms.

C. f. 'Cloud Nine'. Blooms young and heavily. Tolerates Southern California heat and lack of winter chill better than other varieties. Blooms better in cold climates than other kinds of *C. florida.*

C. f. 'Pendula'. Drooping branches give it weeping look.

C. f. 'Pink Flame'. Leaves green and cream, deepening to dark green and red. Bracts pink.

C. f. 'Rainbow'. Leaves strongly marked bright yellow on green. Heavy bloomer, large bracts.

C. f. 'Rubra'. Long-time favorite for its pink or rose bracts.

C. f. 'Welchii'. TRICOLOR DOGWOOD. Best known for its variegated, 4-in.-long leaves of creamy white, pink, deep rose, and green throughout spring and summer; leaves turn deep rose to almost red in fall. Rather inconspicuous pinkish to white bracts are not profuse. Does best with some shade.

C. kousa. KOUSA DOGWOOD. Large shrub or small tree. Zones 3–9, 14, 15, 18, 19. Native to Japan and Korea. Later blooming (June–July) than other flowering dogwoods. Can be big multi-stemmed shrub or (with training) small tree to 20 ft. or higher. Delicate limb structure and spreading, dense horizontal growth habit. Lustrous, medium green leaves, 4 in. long, have rusty brown hairs at base of veins on undersurface. Yellow and scarlet fall color.

Cornus kousa

Flowers along tops of branches show above leaves. Creamy white, slender-pointed, 2–3-in.-long, rather narrow bracts surround flower cluster, turn pink along edges. In October, red fruit hangs below branches like big strawberries. 'Milky Way' is more floriferous and has pure white bracts. 'Summer Stars' blooms later and is lavish in bloom. 'Rosabella' has pink bracts.

HEALTHY TREE DOGWOODS

Wanted: a tree dogwood that will make a beautiful color display in the Pacific Northwest every year and not come down with some tree disease. If that's your quest, the place to look is among the many forms of *Cornus kousa.* These trees, from China, Japan, and Korea, don't succumb to the diseases that make life so difficult for the American tree species *C. florida* and *C. nuttallii.*

C. k. chinensis. Native to China, has larger leaves and larger bracts.

C. mas. CORNELIAN CHERRY. Shrub or tree. Zones 1–6. Native to southern Europe and Asia. One of earliest dogwoods to bloom, it shows mass of clustered small yellow blossoms on bare twigs in February and

March. It's usually an airy, twiggy shrub but can be trained as 15–20-ft. small tree. Oval leaves, 2–4 in. long, shiny green turning to yellow; some forms turn red in fall. Autumn color is enhanced by clusters of bright scarlet, ¾-in.-long fruit that hangs on from September until birds get it. Fruit is edible and is frequently used in making preserves. Tolerates alkaline soils.

C. nuttallii. PACIFIC DOGWOOD, WESTERN DOGWOOD. Tree. Zones 2–9, 14–20. Native to Pacific Northwest and Northern California. One of our most spectacular natives when it wears its gleaming white bracts on bare branches in April or May. Often there's a second flowering with leaves in September. Unfortunately, it's not as easy to grow in gardens as Eastern dogwood (*C. florida*). It reacts unfavorably to routine garden watering, fertilizing, pruning; injury to its tender bark provides entrance for insects and diseases. But if you give plants exceptionally good drainage and infrequent summer watering, and plant under high-branching trees so bark will not sunburn, you have a chance of success.

Where adapted, this tree will grow to 50 ft. or taller with 20-ft. spread, with one trunk or several. Gray-barked branches grow in pleasing horizontal pattern, attractive in winter. Oval, 3–5-in.-long leaves are rich green above, grayish green beneath; they turn to beautiful yellows, pinks, and reds in fall. The four to eight bracts are 2–3 in. long, roundish, rounded or pointed at tips, white or tinged with pink. Decorative red to orange-red fruit in buttonlike clusters forms in fall.

C. n. 'Colrigo Giant'. Low-branching but erect habit, vigorous, heavy trunked, with profusion of 6-in. flower heads. Named for Columbia River Gorge, where parent plant was found. Often sold as 'Corigo Giant'.

C. n. 'Goldspot'. Leaves splashed with creamy yellow. Blooms when only 2 ft. tall. Bracts are larger than those of species. Long (2-month) flowering season, often with some fall bloom.

C. rutgersensis. STELLAR DOGWOOD. Zones 3–9, 14, 15, 18, 19. These hybrids between *C. florida* and *C. kousa* have greater resistance to diseases than *C. florida*. They are single-stemmed, low-branching trees to 20 ft., blooming between *C. florida* and *C. kousa*. Flower bracts resemble those of *C. florida* and are produced with the leaves in early summer. Fall foliage is brilliant red. 'Stellar Pink' has pink bracts; 'Aurora', 'Galaxy', and 'Ruth Ellen', broad-bracted white flowers; 'Constellation', narrower white bracts.

C. sanguinea. BLOODTWIG DOGWOOD. Shrub. Zones 1–7. Big show comes in fall with dark blood red foliage and in winter with bare, purplish to dark red twigs and branches. Prune severely in spring to produce new branches and twigs for winter color. Grows as big multistemmed shrub to 12 ft. high, about 8 ft. wide. Dark green leaves 1½–3 in. long. June flowers are greenish white in 2-in.-wide clusters. Black fruit.

C. stolonifera (C. sericea). REDTWIG DOGWOOD, RED-OSIER DOGWOOD. Shrub. Zones 1–9, 14–21. Native to moist places, Northern California to Alaska and eastward. Another dogwood with brilliant show of red fall color and bright red winter twigs. Not only thrives in coldest mountainous areas of West, but also throughout California—even intermediate valleys of Southern California if given frequent watering. Grows rapidly as big multistemmed shrub to 15 ft. high or more. Spreads widely by creeping underground stems and rooting branches. Tolerates shade. To control, use a spade to cut off roots that have gone too far. Cut off branches that touch ground. Small, creamy white flowers in 2-in.-wide clusters appear among leaves (oval, 1½–2½ in. long, fresh deep green in color) throughout the summer months and into fall. Fruit is white or bluish.

Use this adaptable native as a space filler on moist ground or plant along property line as a screen.

C. s. baileyi. Grows 6–8 ft. tall; exceptionally bright red twigs in winter. *C. s. coloradensis*, Colorado redtwig, is shorter (5–6 ft.), and twigs are not such a bright red.

C. s. 'Flaviramea'. YELLOWTWIG DOGWOOD. Has yellow twigs and branches.

C. s. 'Isanti'. A compact 5 ft. tall.

C. s. 'Kelseyi' (C. s. 'Nana'). Dwarf seldom over 1½ ft. tall. Bright red stems.

COROKIA cotoneaster

Cornaceae
EVERGREEN SHRUB
ZONES 4–24
FULL SUN OR PARTIAL SHADE
MODERATE WATER

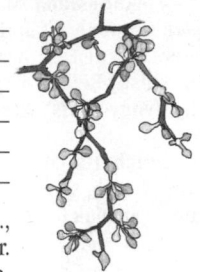
Corokia cotoneaster

Native to New Zealand. Slow growing to 10 ft., but usually seen as 2–4-ft. plant in container. Intricate branch pattern made up of many slim, contorted, interlaced, nearly black branches. Sparse foliage; leaves ¾ in. long, dark glossy green above, white underneath. Tiny, starlike, ½-in., yellow flowers in spring, followed by small orange fruits on older plants. Tolerates alkaline soil, seaside conditions. Thrives in container with fast-draining mix. Night lighting from beneath emphasizes bizarre zigzag branch pattern, which can be further emphasized by pruning.

CORONILLA varia

CROWN VETCH
Fabaceae (Leguminosae)
PERENNIAL GROUND COVER
ALL ZONES
BEST IN FULL SUN, TOLERATES SOME SHADE
WATER IN SPRING AND SUMMER

Coronilla varia

Related to peas, beans, and clovers. Creeping roots and rhizomes make it tenacious ground cover with straggling stems to 2 ft. Leaves made up of 11–25 oval leaflets, ½–¾ in. long. Lavender pink flowers in 1-in. clusters soon become bundles of brown, slender, fingerlike seedpods. Goes dormant and looks ratty during coldest weather. In spring, mow, feed, and water it several times, and it will make a lush green summer cover. Too invasive and rank for flower beds. Use for covering banks and remote places. Once established, difficult to eliminate. Variety 'Penngift' is widely sold in cold-winter climates.

CORREA

AUSTRALIAN FUCHSIA
Rutaceae
EVERGREEN SHRUBS
ZONES 14–24
BEST IN FULL SUN; NO REFLECTED HEAT
TOLERATE SOME ARIDITY

Correa pulchella

Flower form may suggest fuchsia, but in all other ways these plants are far from fuchsialike. Low to medium height, usually dense and spreading. Leaves small (to 1 in.), roundish, densely felted underneath; shrubs have a gray or gray-green color that contrasts subtly with other grays and distinctly with dark greens. All are valued for their long winter flowering season, normally November–April. Small (½–¾-in.) flowers are individually handsome but not showy; they hang down along branches like small bells. ▶

IT'S EASY TO KILL CORREAS WITH KINDNESS

Correas do well in poor, rocky soil but must have fast drainage. They're easy to kill with kindness—overwatering and overfeeding. Use as ground covers on banks or slopes. Attractive in large containers placed where flowers can be enjoyed close up.

C. backhousiana. More successful in Southern California than *C. pul-chella.* Growth habit upright and rather sprawling to 4–5 ft. and as wide. Flowers chartreuse. Often sold as *C. magnifica.*

C. 'Dusky Bells'. Low-growing (2-ft.), broad plant with deep red flowers.

C. 'Ivory Bells'. Resembles *C.* 'Dusky Bells' but with creamy white flowers.

C. pulchella. Most widely grown correa in Northern California. To 2–2½ ft. high, spreading as wide as 8 ft. Leaves green above, gray green below. Light pink flowers. 'Orange Flame' has small orange flowers.

CORTADERIA selloana

PAMPAS GRASS

Poaceae (Gramineae)

EVERGREEN GIANT ORNAMENTAL GRASS

ZONES 4–24

FULL SUN

TAKES THE DRIEST TO THE WETTEST

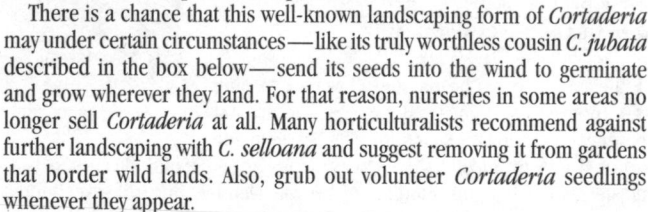
Cortaderia selloana

Native to Argentina. Very fast growing in rich soil in mild climates; from gallon-can size to 8 ft. in one season. Established, may reach 20 ft. in height. Each plant is a fountain of saw-toothed, grassy leaves above which, in late summer, rise long stalks bearing 1–3-ft., white to chamois or pink flower plumes.

There is a chance that this well-known landscaping form of *Cortaderia* may under certain circumstances—like its truly worthless cousin *C. jubata* described in the box below—send its seeds into the wind to germinate and grow wherever they land. For that reason, nurseries in some areas no longer sell *Cortaderia* at all. Many horticulturalists recommend against further landscaping with *C. selloana* and suggest removing it from gardens that border wild lands. Also, grub out volunteer *Cortaderia* seedlings whenever they appear.

THE HORRID COUSIN OF PAMPAS GRASS

Jubata grass (*Cortaderia jubata*), a relative of pampas grass, has become a serious weed on the California coast. It seeds itself freely and crowds out native plants. Leaves are much shorter than those of pampas grass, making jubata's skinnier plumes stand higher above the foliage. Jubata grass bears fewer plumes per plant.

CORYDALIS

Fumariaceae

PERENNIALS

ZONES 4–9, 14–24

PARTIAL SHADE

MOIST, NOT SOGGY, SOIL

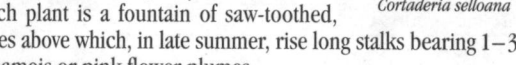
Corydalis lutea

Handsome clumps of dainty divided leaves much like those of bleeding heart (to which it is closely related) or maidenhair fern. Clusters of small, spurred flowers, usually yellow. Plant in rich, moist soil. Effective in rock crevices, in open woodland, near pool or streamside. Combine with ferns, columbine, bleeding heart, primroses. Divide clumps or sow seed in spring or fall. Plants self-sow in garden.

C. cheilanthifolia. Hardy Chinese native, 8–10 in. high, with fernlike green foliage. Clusters of yellow, ½-in.-long flowers in May and June.

C. lutea. Native to southern Europe. To 15 in. tall. Masses of gray-green foliage on many stems. Golden yellow, ¾-in.-long, short-spurred flowers throughout summer.

CORYLOPSIS

WINTER HAZEL

Hamamelidaceae

DECIDUOUS SHRUBS

ZONES 4–7, 15–17

WIND-SHELTERED LOCATION

REGULAR WATER

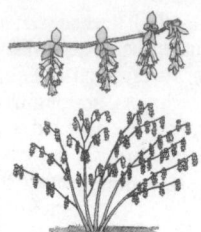
Corylopsis spicata

Valued for show of soft yellow, fragrant flowers that come on bare branches in March or earlier. New leaves that follow bloom are often tinged pink before they turn bright green; they're roundish, somewhat resembling filbert (hazelnut) leaves. Slow growing to 8–15 ft. and as wide. Make rather open structure with attractive, delicate branching pattern.

Give same soil type as for rhododendrons. Use in shrub border, edge of woodland.

C. glabrescens. FRAGRANT WINTER HAZEL. Larger than other species, can reach 15 ft.

C. pauciflora. BUTTERCUP WINTER HAZEL. Flowers are primrose yellow, ¾ in., bell shaped, in drooping clusters of two or three. Leaves 1–3 in. long, with sharply toothed edges. Grows 8–10 ft. tall.

C. sinensis. To 15 ft., with 3-in. clusters of yellow flowers, purple fall foliage.

C. spicata. SPIKE WINTER HAZEL. Flowers are pale yellow, ½ in., bell shaped, in 1½-in.-long drooping clusters of 6–12. Leaves to 4 in. long, with toothed edges. Grows 8–10 ft. tall.

CORYLUS

FILBERT, HAZELNUT

Betulaceae

DECIDUOUS SHRUBS OR TREES

ZONES 1–9, 14–20

FULL SUN OR PARTIAL SHADE

MODERATE WATER

Corylus avellana 'Fusco-rubra'

Filberts are usually thought of as trees grown for their edible nuts (see Filbert), but the following types are grown as ornamentals; one is a western native.

C. avellana. EUROPEAN FILBERT. Shrub. Not as widely grown as its two varieties described below. To 10–15 ft. high and wide; leaves broad, roundish, 3–4 in. long, turning yellow in fall. Ornamental greenish yellow male flower catkins hang on all winter, turn yellow in earliest spring before leaves appear. Roundish nuts of good flavor enclosed by two irregularly lobed bracts.

C. a. 'Contorta'. HARRY LAUDER'S WALKING STICK. Fantastically gnarled and twisted branches and twigs. Takes well to container culture and lends itself to display as curiosity. Will grow to 8–10 ft. Leaves smaller than those of species.

C. a. 'Fusco-rubra' (C. a. 'Atropurpurea'). Identical to species except for its handsome purple leaf color.

C. colurna. TURKISH HAZEL. Tree. To 75 ft. tall, 30 ft. wide, with 5-in. leaves and clustered nuts smaller than filberts. Extremely cold hardy. Attractive tree in its own right, and a parent of hybrids (with *C. avellana*) called trazels.

C. cornuta californica. WESTERN HAZELNUT. Shrub. Native to damp slopes below 7,000-ft. elevation, northern Coast Ranges and Sierra Nevada of California, north to British Columbia. Open, spreading, multistemmed, 5–12 ft. high. Roundish, somewhat hairy, 1½–3-in.-long leaves with coarsely toothed edges turn bright yellow in fall. Like *C. avellana*, has decorative male flower catkins. Nuts small, kernels flavorful; enveloped in leafy husk with long, drawn-out beak.

C. maxima. See Filbert

C. m. 'Purpurea'. Tree or shrub. Makes handsome, well-structured, small tree to 20 ft. or suckering shrub to 12–15 ft. Roundish leaves 2–6 in. long, dark purple in spring and summer. Burns quite badly in Southern California's hot-summer areas.

CORYNABUTILON vitifolium. See ABUTILON vitifolium   **p. 131**

CORYNOCARPUS laevigata

NEW ZEALAND LAUREL

Corynocarpaceae

EVERGREEN SHRUB OR SMALL TREE

⚡ ZONES 16, 17, 23, 24; BEST IN ZONES 17, 24

☼ ◑ FULL SUN OR PARTIAL SHADE

● REGULAR WATER

◈ FRUIT IS EXTREMELY POISONOUS

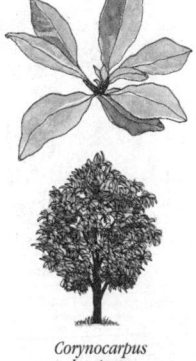

Corynocarpus laevigata

Handsome, upright, to 20–40 ft. high. Beautiful dark green, very glossy, leathery leaves, oblong to 7 in. by 2 in. wide. Flowers noticeable but of no importance—tiny, whitish, in 3–8-in.-long upright clusters. Fruit orange, oblong, 1 in. long. Good in containers. Slow growing; keeps attractive form for years. Use as screen or large hedge, background. Good in sheltered areas, entryways, under overhangs.

CORYPHANTHA vivipara

Cactaceae

LITTLE CACTUS

⚡ ALL ZONES

☼ FULL SUN

◖◗ LITTLE TO MUCH WATER IN GROWING SEASON

Coryphantha vivipara

Native Alberta to north Texas. Has single or clustered globular, 2-in. bodies covered with little knobs bearing white spines. Flowers purple, showy, to 2 in. long. One of hardiest forms of cactus, taking temperatures far below zero. Usually sold as *Mammillaria vivipara*.

COSMOS

Asteraceae (Compositae)

PERENNIALS AND ANNUALS

⚡ ALL ZONES, EXCEPT AS NOTED

☼ FULL SUN

● TOLERATE SOME ARIDITY

Cosmos bipinnatus

Native to tropical America, mostly Mexico. Showy summer- and fall-blooming plants, open and branching in habit, with bright green divided leaves and daisylike flowers in many colors and forms (single, double, crested, and frilled). Heights vary from 2½ to 8 ft. Use for mass color in borders or background, or as filler among shrubs. Useful in arrangements if flowers are cut when freshly opened and placed immediately in deep cool water. Sow seed in open ground from spring to summer, or set out transplants from flats. Plant in not-too-rich soil. Plants self-sow freely, attract birds.

C. atrosanguineus. CHOCOLATE COSMOS. Zones 4–9, 14–24. Tuberous-rooted perennial to 2–2½ ft., with coarsely cut foliage and deep brownish red cosmos flowers nearly 2 in. wide. These are produced in late summer and fall and have a strong perfume of chocolate (or vanilla). Attractive with silvery-foliaged plants. In cold-winter areas tubers may be dug and stored over winter like dahlias.

C. bipinnatus. Annual flowers in white and shades of pink, rose, lavender, purple, or crimson, with tufted yellow centers. Heights up to 8 ft. Modern improved cosmos include Sensation strain, 3–6 ft. tall, earlier blooming than old-fashioned tall kinds. Sensation varieties are 'Dazzler' (crimson) and 'Radiance' (rose with red center); white and pink are also available. 'Candystripe' has smaller (3-in.) white-and-rose flowers; blooms even earlier on smaller plants. Seashell strain has rolled, quilled ray florets like long, narrow cones.

C. sulphureus. YELLOW COSMOS. Annual. Grows to 7 ft., with yellow or golden yellow flowers with yellow centers. Tends to become weedy looking at end of season. Klondike strain grows 3–4 ft. tall, with 2-in. semidouble flowers ranging from scarlet orange to yellow. Dwarf Klondike or Sunny strain is 1½ ft. tall, with 1½-in. flowers.

COSTMARY. See CHRYSANTHEMUM balsamita   **p. 226**

COTINUS coggygria (Rhus cotinus)

SMOKE TREE

Anacardiaceae

DECIDUOUS SHRUB OR TREE

⚡ ALL ZONES; ESPECIALLY VALUABLE IN 1–3, 10, 11

☼ FULL SUN

● TOLERATES SOME ARIDITY

Cotinus coggygria

Unusual shrub-tree creating broad, urn-shaped mass usually as wide as it is high—eventually to 25 ft. Roundish leaves 1½–3 in. long; bluish green in summer, yellow to orange red in fall. Dramatic puffs of purple to lavender "smoke" come from large, loose clusters of fading flowers: as tiny greenish blossoms fade, stalks of sterile flowers elongate and become clothed with fuzzy purple hairs.

At its best under stress in poor or rocky soil. When grown in cultivated gardens, must have fast drainage and infrequent watering to avoid root rot. Resistant to oak root fungus.

C. c. 'Purpureus'. has purple leaves that gradually turn to green, and richer purple smoke puffs. *C. c.* 'Royal Purple' retains purple leaves through the summer.

A less widely grown American species is *Cotinus obovatus*, American smoke tree. Somewhat larger than others, with larger leaves. Fall color equally striking. For another smoke tree, see *Dalea spinosa*.

COTONEASTER

Rosaceae

EVERGREEN, SEMIEVERGREEN, DECIDUOUS SHRUBS

⚡ ZONES VARY BY SPECIES

☼ FULL SUN

◯ ● LITTLE OR NO WATER ONCE ESTABLISHED

Cotoneaster buxifolius

They range from ground covers to stiffly upright, small shrubs to tall-growing (20-ft.) shrubs of fountainlike growth with graceful, arching branches. All grow vigorously and thrive with little or no maintenance. In fact, they look better and produce better crops of fall and winter berries if planted on dry slopes—where they can reduce erosion—or in poor soil rather than rich, moist garden soil. Spring bloom; flowers white or pinkish, resembling tiny single roses, not showy but pretty because of their abundance.

While some medium and tall growers can be sheared, they look best when allowed to maintain natural fountain shapes. Prune only to enhance graceful arch of branches. Keep medium growers looking young by pruning out portion of oldest wood each year. Prune ground covers to remove dead or awkward branches. Give flat growers room to spread. Don't plant near walk or drive where branch ends will need stubbing.

Cotoneasters are useful, if not striking shrubs, and can be attractive in the proper setting. Some are especially attractive in form and branching pattern (*C. congestus, C. horizontalis*), while others are notable for colorful, long-lasting fruit (*C. lacteus, C. microphyllus*). Trailing varieties make excellent ground cover plants. Low horizontal kinds die out in desert heat.

C. acutifolius. PEKING COTONEASTER. Deciduous. Zones 1–3. To 10 ft. tall and as wide, with glossy green foliage turning red in fall. Fruit is black. Useful as hedge or screen.

C. adpressus praecox. Deciduous. All zones. To 1½ ft. tall, 6 ft. wide, with shiny leaves turning maroon red in fall, a profusion of bright red ½-in. fruit. Bank or ground cover. Tolerates some shade. *C. adpressus* is similar, somewhat smaller.

C. apiculatus. CRANBERRY COTONEASTER. Deciduous. All zones. Dense grower to 3 ft. tall, 6 ft. wide, with small round leaves turning deep red in autumn. Fruit is size of large cranberry, in clusters. Can take some shade. Use as bank cover, hedge, background planting.

C. buxifolius. Evergreen or semievergreen. Zones 4–24. Small gray leaves clothe 3–6-ft. arching stems. Bright red berries. Often sold as *C. glaucophyllus*.

C. congestus (*C. microphyllus glacialis*). PYRENEES COTONEASTER. Evergreen. Zones 2–24. Slow grower to 3 ft., with dense, downward-curving branches, tiny dark green leaves, small, bright red fruit. Use in containers, rock gardens, above walls.

C. dammeri (*C. humifusus*). BEARBERRY COTONEASTER. Evergreen. All zones. Fast, prostrate growth to 3–6 in. tall, 10 ft. wide. Branches root along ground. Leaves are bright, glossy green; fruit bright red. Many varieties differ somewhat in height, rate of growth. 'Coral Beauty' is 6 in. tall; 'Eichholz', 10–12 in. tall with a scattering of red-orange leaves in fall; 'Lowfast', 12 in. tall; 'Skogsholmen', 1½ ft. tall. All are good ground covers in sun or partial shade and can drape over walls, cascade down slopes. *C.* 'Lowfast' is similar in appearance and uses; it is a fast grower to 1 ft. tall, 15 ft. wide.

C. divaricatus. SPREADING COTONEASTER. Deciduous. All zones. Stiff growth to 6 ft. tall and wide. Dark green leaves closely set on branches turn orange red in fall. Egg-shaped bright red fruits are ½ in. long. Informal hedge, screen, bank planting.

C. horizontalis. ROCK COTONEASTER. Deciduous. Zones 1–11, 14–24. Can be 2–3 ft. tall, 15 ft. wide, with stiff horizontal branches and many branchlets set in herringbone pattern. Leaves are small, round, bright green; turn orange and red before falling. Out of leaf very briefly. Showy red fruit. Effective when given enough room to spread; ugly when branches must be cut short to accommodate traffic. Fine bank cover or low traffic barrier. *C. h. perpusillus* is smaller, more compact. 'Variegatus' has leaves edged in white.

Cotoneaster horizontalis

C. lacteus (*C. parneyi*). Evergreen. Zones 4–24. Graceful, arching habit to 8 ft. or more, with dark green leaves 2 in. long, clustered white flowers, and a heavy crop of long-lasting red fruit in 2–3-in. clusters. Best as informal hedge screen, or espalier. Can be clipped as formal hedge, but form suffers.

C. microphyllus. ROCKSPRAY COTONEASTER. Evergreen. Zones 2–9, 14–24. Its horizontal branches trail and root to 6 ft.; secondary branches grow erect to 2 or 3 ft. Leaves are very small (⅓ in.), dark green, gray beneath. Fruit is rosy red. *C. m. thymifolius* has even tinier leaves, with edges rolled under. It is a smaller plant. Both are effective in rock gardens, on banks.

Cotoneaster lacteus

C. multiflorus. Deciduous. All zones. Grows 6–10 ft. tall as spreading shrub or small tree with graceful arching and trailing branches. Dark green leaves are 2½ in. long. Clustered white flowers are showier than those of other cotoneasters. Pinkish red fruits follow.

C. salicifolius. WILLOWLEAF COTONEASTER. Evergreen or semievergreen. Zones 2–24. An erect, spreading shrub to 15–18 ft., with narrow, dark green leaves 1–3½ in. long and bright red fruits. Graceful screening or background plant but can self-sow and become invasive.

Better known are the trailing forms used as ground cover. 'Emerald Carpet' is 12–15 in. tall, to 8 ft. wide, with compact habit and small leaves. 'Herbstfeuer' ('Autumn Fire') is lower growing (to 6 in.). 'Repens' is similar in appearance. It is sometimes grafted to a tall stem of some other cotoneaster species and used as a weeping tree.

COTTONWOOD. See POPULUS p. 434

COTULA squalida (Leptinella squalida)

NEW ZEALAND BRASS BUTTONS

Asteraceae (Compositae)

EVERGREEN PERENNIAL GROUND COVER

ZONES 4–9, 14–24

FULL SUN OR PARTIAL SHADE

MODERATE WATER

Cotula squalida

Grows only a few inches high, but branches creep to 1 ft. or more. Leaves are soft, hairy, fernlike, bronzy green. Flowers are like yellow brass buttons about ¼ in. across. Calyxlike bracts below heads fit tightly against "buttons." Can be increased by planting divisions.

COTYLEDON

Crassulaceae

SUCCULENTS

ZONES VARY BY SPECIES

BEST IN LIGHT SHADE

LITTLE OR NO WATER

Cotyledon orbiculata

Various sizes and appearances. Easily grown from cuttings and handsome in containers, raised beds, or open ground beds.

C. orbiculata. Zones 16, 17, 21–24. Shrubby, compact, to 3 ft. tall. Opposing pairs of fleshy leaves are 2–3 in. long, rounded, gray green to nearly white, narrowly edged red. Green-leafed forms are available. Flower stems rise above plant and carry clusters of orange, bell-shaped, drooping flowers in summer. Good landscaping shrub in mild climates and well-drained soils. Splendid container plant.

C. undulata. Zones 17, 23, 24. Striking 1½-ft. plant with broad, thick leaves thickly dusted with pure white powder. Leaf edges wavy. Flowers (spring and early summer) orange, drooping, clustered. Overhead watering washes off powder.

COWANIA mexicana stansburiana

CLIFF ROSE

Rosaceae

EVERGREEN SHRUB

ZONES 1–3, 10–13

FULL SUN

INFREQUENT WATER

Cowania mexicana stansburiana

Native to California's Mojave Desert, Nevada, Arizona, Utah, Colorado, New Mexico, and Mexico. Much-branched, straggly shrub to 6 ft. high and as wide. Tiny, ½-in., deeply toothed leaves. Flowers like miniature single roses, just ½ in. wide, creamy or sulfur yellow, rarely white, in April–June. Moment of glory comes after bloom, when many very tiny fruits with long, plumy tails soften shrub to feathery haze.

CRABAPPLE

Rosaceae

DECIDUOUS FRUIT TREE

ZONES 1–9, 11–21

FULL SUN

MODERATE WATER

Crabapple is a small, usually tart apple. Many kinds are valued more for their springtime flowers than for their fruit; these are flowering crabapples, described under *Malus*. Crabapple varieties grown mostly for fruit (used for jelly making and pickling) are infrequently sold at western nurseries. Of several that may be sold, most popular is 'Transcendent', with red-cheeked yellow apples to 2 in. wide. Ripens in late summer. For culture, see Apple.

Crabapple

CRASPEDIA globosa

DRUMSTICKS

Asteraceae (Compositae)

PERENNIAL

ZONES 8, 9, 14–24

FULL SUN

REGULAR WATER

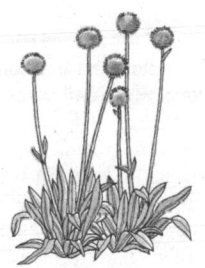

Craspedia globosa

Odd, attractive, offbeat Australian daisy in 8–12-in. clumps. Silvery leaves send up 2-ft. stalks, each topped by a 1-in. globe of tiny yellow flowers. Bloom may occur at any time of the year, and flowers are useful, fresh or dry, in arrangements.

CRASSULA

Crassulaceae

SUCCULENTS

ZONES 8, 9, 12–24; OR INDOORS

PRODUCE FLOWERS IN SUN

NO WATER ONCE ESTABLISHED

Crassula argentea

Mostly from South Africa. Provide overhead protection in Zones 8, 9, 12–15, 18–21. All have succulent foliage and many have strange geometric forms.

C. arborescens. A shrubby, heavy-branched plant very like jade plant, but with gray-green, red-edged, red-dotted leaves. Flowers (usually seen only on old plants) are star shaped, white fading to pink. Good change of pace from jade plant; smaller and slower growing.

C. argentea. JADE PLANT. Top-notch house plant, large container plant, landscaping shrub in mildest climates. Sometimes sold as *C. portulacea*. Stout trunk, sturdy limbs even on small plants—and plant will stay small in small container. Can reach 9 ft. in time but is usually shorter.

Leaves are thick, oblong, fleshy pads 1–2 in. long, glossy bright green, sometimes with red-tinged edges. 'Crosby's Dwarf' is a low, compact grower; variegated kinds are 'Sunset' (yellow tinged red) and 'Tricolor' (green, white, and pinkish). Clusters of pink, star-shaped flowers form in profusion, November–April. Good near swimming pools.

C. corymbulosa. Low growing, to 6–30 in. Slightly branched, with rosettes of long, triangular, fleshy leaves; leaves are dark red when plant is grown in full sun and poor soil. Tiny white flowers.

C. falcata. Grows to 4 ft. high. Fleshy, gray-green, sickle-shaped leaves are vertically arranged in two rows on stems. Dense clusters of scarlet flowers appear in late summer.

C. lactea. Spreading, semishrubby plant 1–2 ft. tall. Fleshy dark green leaves; white flowers in 4–6-in. clusters, October–December. Grows in shade, even dense shade. Fine rock garden plant.

C. lycopodioides. Leafy, branching, erect stems to 1 ft. high, closely packed with tiny green leaves in four rows; effect is that of braided watch chain or of some strange green coral. Very small greenish flowers. Easy and useful in miniature and dish gardens.

Crassula falcata

C. 'Morgan's Pink'. Fine miniature hybrid. Densely packed, fleshy leaves in tight cluster to 4 in. tall. Big, brushlike clusters of pink flowers are nearly as big as the plant. Spring bloom.

C. multicava. Dark green, spreading ground cover or hanging plant. Light pink, mosquitolike flowers in loose clusters, late winter, spring. Rampant grower in sun or shade, in any soil.

C. pyramidalis. Interesting oddity to 3–4 in. high; flat, triangular leaves closely packed in four rows give plant squarish cross section.

C. schmidtii. Mat-forming, spreading plant to 4 in. tall with long, slender, rich green leaves. Small, heavily borne, clustered flowers, dark rose or purplish, in winter and spring. Good pot or rock garden plant.

C. tetragona. Upright plants with treelike habit, 1–2 ft. high. Leaves narrow, 1 in. long. Flowers white. Widely used in dish gardens to suggest miniature pine trees.

Crassulaceae. This large family of usually herbaceous (rarely shrubby) plants is familiar through sedums, sempervivums, and a host of other familiar succulents. Leaves are often in rosettes, as in the familiar hen and chicks (*Echeveria*).

CRATAEGUS

HAWTHORN

Rosaceae

DECIDUOUS TREES

ZONES 1–12, 14–17

FULL SUN

KEEP ON DRY SIDE TO AVOID RANK GROWTH

These trees, members of the rose family, are known for their pretty spring flowers and showy fruit in summer, fall. They have thorny branches and need some pruning to thin out excess twiggy growth. They attract bees, birds.

Crataegus laevigata

Keep aphids in check. Fireblight makes entire branches die back quickly; cut out blighted branches well below dead part and wash pruning tools with disinfectant after each cut.

C. ambigua. RUSSIAN HAWTHORN. Moderate growth to 15–25 ft. Vase form, twisting branches give attractive silhouette. Leaves to 2½ in. long, deeply cut. White flowers, much small red fruit. Extremely winter hardy.

C. 'Autumn Glory'. Hybrid origin. Vigorous growth to 25 ft. with 15-ft. spread. Twiggy, dense. Dark green leaves similar to those of *C. laevigata* but more leathery. Clusters of single white flowers in spring. Very large, glossy, bright red fruit, autumn into winter. Type most susceptible to fireblight. ▶

247

C

C. crus-galli. COCKSPUR THORN. Wide-spreading tree to 30 ft. Stiff thorns to 3 in. long. Smooth, glossy, dark green, toothed leaves. White flowers. Dull orange-red fruit. Good red and yellow fall color.

C. laevigata (C. oxyacantha). ENGLISH HAWTHORN. Native to Europe and North Africa. Moderate growth to 18–25 ft. with 15–20-ft. spread. Leaves similar to those of *C. monogyna* but lobes are toothed. Best known through its varieties: 'Paul's Scarlet', clusters of double rose to red flowers; 'Double White'; 'Double Pink'. Doubles set little fruit. 'Crimson Cloud' ('Superba') has bright red single flowers with white centers, bright red fruit.

C. lavallei (C. carrierei). CARRIERE HAWTHORN. Hybrid origin. To 25 ft. with 15–20-ft. spread. More erect and open branching than other hawthorns, with less twiggy growth. Very handsome. Leaves dark green, leathery, 2–4 in. long, toothed; turn bronze red after first sharp frost and hang on well into winter. White flowers in spring followed by loose clusters of large orange to red fruit that last all winter. Fruit is messy on walks.

C. mollis. DOWNY HAWTHORN. Big, broad tree to 30 ft.; looks like mature apple tree. Leaves to 4 in. long, lobed, toothed, covered with down. Flowers white, 1 in. wide. Red fruit 1 in. across, also downy; fruit doesn't last on tree as long as that of other species, but has value in jelly making.

C. monogyna. Native to Europe, North Africa, and western Asia. Classic hawthorn of English countryside for hedges and boundary plantings. Represented in western nurseries by variety 'Stricta'. Narrow growth habit to 30 ft. tall and 8 ft. wide. Plant 5 ft. apart for dense, narrow screen or barrier. Leaves 2 in. long, with three to seven deep, smooth-edged lobes. Flowers white. Small red fruit in clusters, rather difficult to see.

C. oxyacantha. See *C. laevigata*

C. phaenopyrum (C. cordata). WASHINGTON THORN. Native to southeastern United States. Moderate growth to 25 ft. with 20-ft. spread. Light and open limb structure. Glossy leaves 2–3 in. long with three to five sharp-pointed lobes (like some maples); foliage turns beautiful orange and red in fall. Small white flowers in broad clusters in late spring or early summer. Shiny red fruit in autumn hangs on well into winter. More graceful and delicate than other hawthorns, and preferred street or lawn tree. Least susceptible to fireblight.

C. pinnatifida. Native to northeastern Asia. To 20 ft. high, 10–12 ft. wide. Leaves lobed like those of *C. laevigata* but bigger and thicker; they turn red in fall. Tree has more open, upright habit than *C. laevigata*. Flowers white, ¾ in. wide, in 3-in. clusters. Fruit slightly smaller than that of *C. lavallei*.

C. 'Toba'. Canadian hybrid of great cold tolerance. To 20 ft. Leaves similar to those of *C. lavallei*. White flowers age to pink. Sets few large fruit.

C. viridis. GREEN HAWTHORN. Moderate growth to 25–30 ft., with broad, spreading crown. Leaves yellowish in fall, not showy. Clustered white flowers followed by red fruit.

CRESS, GARDEN

Brassicaceae (Cruciferae)

SUMMER ANNUAL

ALL ZONES

FULL SUN OR PARTIAL SHADE

REGULAR TO AMPLE WATER

It is sometimes called pepper grass and tastes like watercress. Easy to grow as long as weather is cool. Sow seed as early in spring as possible.

Garden Cress

Plant in rich, moist soil. Make rows 1 ft. apart; thin plants to 3 in. apart (eat thinnings). Cress matures fast; make successive sowings every 2 weeks up to middle of May. Where frosts are mild, sow through fall and winter. Try growing garden cress in shallow pots of soil or planting mix in sunny kitchen window. It sprouts in a few days, can be harvested (with scissors) in 2–3 weeks. Or grow it by sprinkling seeds on pads of wet cheesecloth; keep damp until harvest in 2 weeks.

CRETE DITTANY. See ORIGANUM dictamnus   p. 395

CRINODENDRON

Elaeocarpaceae

EVERGREEN TREES

ZONES 14–24

FULL SUN

WET, REGULARLY SPRINKLED LOCATION

Crinodendron patagua

Little-known evergreen shrub-trees with leathery leaves, somewhat stiff growth habit, and attractive flowers. Native to Chile.

C. hookerianum. Zones 5, 6, 16, 17. Big shrub or small tree to 25 ft. Stiff branches clothed with narrow, sharply toothed leaves; drooping red flowers 1 in. long open from buds resembling cherries. Easy to propagate from cuttings but hard to grow. Needs good drainage, cool summers, high humidity. Spider mites are a constant problem.

C. patagua (C. dependens, Tricuspidaria dependens). LILY-OF-THE-VALLEY TREE. Somewhat like evergreen oak in general appearance; sometimes called flowering oak. Grows at moderate rate to 25 ft. and almost as wide, with upright branching and a rounded crown. Leaves 2½ in. long, ½–1 in. wide, dark green above, gray green beneath, with irregularly toothed edges.

In June and July, sometimes into October, it wears hundreds of ¾-in.-long, white, bell-shaped flowers. These are followed by numerous attractive cream and red seed capsules that drop and can be messy on paving. Tends to grow in shrublike fashion, or some branches turn down while others stick up. Early staking and pruning important. Prune out brushy growth toward center; remove branches that tend to hang down. In lawn, water deeply once a month to discourage surface rooting. For another lily-of-the-valley tree, see *Clethra*.

CRINUM

Liliaceae

BULBS

ZONES 8, 9, 12–24; OR INDOORS

FULL SUN OR PARTIAL SHADE

REGULAR TO AMPLE WATER

ALL PARTS ARE TOXIC

Distinguished from their near relative amaryllis by long, slender flower tube that is longer than flower segments. Long-stalked cluster of lily-shaped, 4–6-in.-long, fragrant flowers rises in spring or summer from persistent clump of long, strap-shaped or sword-shaped leaves. Bulbs large, rather slender, tapering to stemlike neck; thick, fleshy roots. Bulbs generally available (from specialists) all year, but spring or fall planting is preferred.

Crinum powellii

Provide soil with plenty of humus. Set bulbs 6 in. under surface; give ample space to develop. Divide infrequently. Bait for snails. In colder sections, mulch heavily in winter; move plants in containers into frostproof place. Plant in sheltered, sunny locations in Zones 8, 9, 12–22.

Plantings of crinum are excellent for tropical effects. Mail-order nurseries offer a wide selection.

C. bulbispermum (C. longifolium). Long, narrow, twisting gray-green leaves tend to lie on the ground. Flowers are deep pink.

C. 'Ellen Bosanquet'. Leaves are broad, bright green. Flowers are deep rose, nearly red.

C. moorei. Large bulbs with 6–8-in. diameter and stemlike neck 1 ft. long or more. Long, thin, wavy-edged, bright green leaves. Bell-shaped pinkish red flowers.

C. powellii. Resembles *C. moorei* (one of its parents) but has dark rose-colored flowers. The variety 'Album' is a good pure white form, vigorous enough to serve as a tall ground cover in shade.

CROCOSMIA

Iridaceae

CORMS

✿ ZONES 5–24

☼ ◑ FULL SUN ON COAST, PARTIAL SHADE INLAND

◌ NO WATER ONCE ESTABLISHED

Crocosmia crocosmiiflora

Native to tropical and southern Africa. Formerly called tritonia and related to freesia, ixia, sparaxis. Sword-shaped leaves in basal clumps. Small orange, red, yellow flowers bloom in summer on branched stems. Useful for splashes of garden color and for cutting. In colder climates, provide sheltered location and winter mulch.

C. crocosmiiflora (Tritonia crocosmiiflora). MONTBRETIA. A favorite for generations, montbretias can still be seen in older gardens where they have spread freely, as though native, producing orange-crimson flowers 1½–2 in. across on 3–4-ft. stems. Sword-shaped leaves to 3 ft., ½–1 in. wide. Many once-common named forms in yellow, orange, cream, and near scarlet are making a comeback. Good for naturalizing on slopes or in fringe areas.

C. hybrids. Sturdy plants with branching spikes of large flowers. Often called Masoniorum Hybrids. 'Lucifer' is 4 ft. tall, with bright red flowers. 'Solfatare', to 2 ft., has bronze-tinted foliage and pale orange-yellow flowers.

C. masoniorum. From South Africa. Leaves 2½ ft. long, 2 in. wide. Flowers flaming orange to orange scarlet, 1½ in. across, borne in dense, one-sided clusters on 2½–3-ft. stems that arch over at the top. Buds open slowly from base to tip of clusters, and old flowers drop cleanly from stems. Flowers last about 2 weeks when cut.

Crocosmia masoniorum

CROCUS

Iridaceae

CORMS

✿ ALL ZONES, BUT MOST PREFER COLDER CLIMATES

☼ ◑ FULL SUN OR PARTIAL SHADE

● WATER DURING GROWTH AND BLOOM

Leaves are basal and grasslike—often with silvery midrib—and appear before, with, or after flowers, depending on species. Flowers with long stemlike tubes and flaring or cup-shaped petals are 1½–3 in. long; the short (true) stems are hidden underground.

Crocus vernus

Most crocus bloom in earliest spring or late winter, but some species bloom August–November, the flowers rising from bare earth weeks or days after planting. Mass them for best effect. Attractive in rock gardens,

between stepping stones, in containers. Set corms 2–3 in. deep in light, porous soil. Protect from gophers. Divide every 3–4 years.

C. ancyrensis. Flowers golden yellow, small, very early.

C. angustifolius. CLOTH OF GOLD CROCUS. Formerly *C. susianus*. Orange-gold, starlike flowers with dark brown center stripe. January–February bloom, March in cold climates.

C. chrysanthus. Orange yellow, sweet scented. Hybrids and selections of this plant range from white and cream through the yellows and blues, often marked with deeper color. Usually even more freely flowering than Dutch crocus but with smaller flowers. Spring bloom. Popular varieties are 'Blue Pearl', palest blue; 'Cream Beauty', pale yellow; 'E. P. Bowles', yellow with purple featherings; 'Ladykiller', outside purple edged white, inside white feathered purple; 'Princess Beatrix', blue with yellow center; and 'Snow Bunting', pure white.

C. imperati. Bright lilac inside, buff veined purple outside, saucer shaped. Early spring.

C. kotschyanus. Formerly *C. zonatus*. Pinkish lavender or lilac. September bloom.

C. sativus. SAFFRON CROCUS. Lilac. Orange-red stigma is true saffron of commerce. Interesting rather than showy. Autumn. To harvest saffron, pluck the stigmas as soon as flowers open, dry them, and store them in glass or plastic vials. Stigmas from a dozen flowers will season a good-size paella or similar dish. To get continued good yield of saffron, divide corms as soon as leaves turn brown; replant in fresh or improved soil. Mark planting site with low-growing ground cover so you won't dig up dormant bulbs.

C. sieberi. Delicate lavender blue with golden throat. One of earliest.

C. speciosus. Showy blue-violet flowers in October. Lavender and mauve varieties available. Fast increase by seed and division. Showiest autumn-flowering crocus.

C. tomasinianus. Slender buds; star-shaped, silvery lavender-blue flowers, sometimes with dark blotch at tips of segments. Very early—January or February in milder climates.

C. vernus. DUTCH CROCUS. Familiar crocus in shades of white, yellow, lavender, and purple, often penciled and streaked. February–April (depending on climate). Most vigorous crocus, and only one widely sold in all areas.

CROTALARIA agatiflora

CANARY BIRD BUSH

Fabaceae (Leguminosae)

EVERGREEN SHRUB

✿ ZONES 13, 15–24

☼ ◑ FULL SUN OR PARTIAL SHADE

● REGULAR WATER

☣ ENTIRE PLANT IS POISONOUS

Crotalaria agatiflora

Native to east Africa. Recovers quickly after frost damage. Fast, rank growth to 12 ft. and as wide unless frequently pruned (which it should be). Common name is well earned: unique 1½-in. flowers are strung along flower spike (to 14 in. long) like so many chartreuse birds. Heaviest bloom in summer or fall, but in frost-free areas it blooms intermittently for 10 months. Foliage is pleasing gray green, with leaves divided into 3-in.-long leaflets.

Yellow green flowers harmonize with most colors. Try with red geraniums, zinnias, or coral tree (*Erythrina*), or with yellow-flowered shrubs for long succession of bloom. Prune 2 or 3 times a year to correct open, weak-stemmed growth, condense and improve outline, and control size.

CROTON. See CODIAEUM *variegatum*   **p. 237**

FOR INFORMATION ON YOUR CLIMATE ZONE
PLEASE SEE PAGES 15–44

CROWEA exalata

Rutaceae

EVERGREEN SHRUB

☒ ZONES 16, 17, 19, 21–24

☼ ☽ LIGHT SHADE IN HOT AREAS

⬤ MODERATE WATER

Crowea exalata

Native to Australia. Small (3-ft.) shrub with narrow, dark green 1–2-in. leaves and deep rose pink star-shaped flowers a little less than 1 in. wide. Flowering is nearly continuous. Needs good drainage. Remains compact with light pruning. Takes full sun if roots are kept cool and moist.

CRYPTANTHUS zonatus

Bromeliaceae

PERENNIAL

☒ ZONES 17, 23, 24; OR INDOORS

⬤ BEST IN HEAVY SHADE

⬤ MODERATE WATER

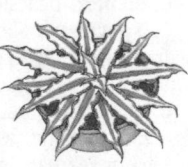
Cryptanthus zonatus

Native to Brazil. Grown for showy leaves in spreading, low-growing clusters to 1½ ft. wide, usually less. Individual leaves wavy, dark brownish red, banded crosswise with green, brown, or white. Unimportant little white flowers grow among leaves. Pot in equal parts coarse sand, ground bark or peat moss, and shredded osmunda. Most effective in mass or mixed plantings, terrariums.

C. bivittatus is similar to *C. zonatus* in cultural needs and general appearance, but has green leaves with lengthwise stripes of creamy white. Many other striped and banded species and hybrids are available from specialists.

CRYPTOCARYA rubra

Lauraceae

EVERGREEN TREE

☒ ZONES 14–17, 20–24

☼ FULL SUN

⬤ MODERATE WATER

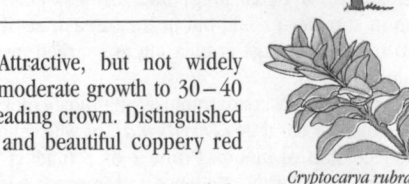
Cryptocarya rubra

Native to Chile. Attractive, but not widely planted. Slow to moderate growth to 30–40 ft. Dense, slightly spreading crown. Distinguished by rich brown bark and beautiful coppery red new foliage.

When mature, the 2–3-in.-long, roundish, thick-textured leaves are very glossy dark green above, bluish green beneath. Leaves are spicily fragrant when crushed. Inconspicuous flowers are followed by fragrant, whitish fruit with a pink blush. Occasionally planted as a street tree in California. Stake and prune unless multiple trunk is desired. Occasional frost damage in Zones 14–16.

CRYPTOMERIA japonica

JAPANESE CRYPTOMERIA

Taxodiaceae

EVERGREEN TREE

☒ ZONES 4–9, 14–24

☼ FULL SUN

⬤ MODERATE WATER

Cryptomeria japonica

Graceful conifer, fast growing (3–4 ft. a year) in youth. Eventually skyline tree with straight columnar trunk; thin red-brown bark peeling in strips. Foliage soft bright green to bluish green in growing season, brownish purple in cold weather. Branches, slightly pendulous, are clothed with ½–1-in.-long needlelike leaves. Roundish, red-brown cones ¾–1 in. wide. These trees are sometimes used in closely planted groves for a Japanese garden effect. Resistant to oak root fungus.

C. j. 'Elegans'. PLUME CEDAR, PLUME CRYPTOMERIA. Quite unlike species. Feathery, grayish green, soft-textured foliage. Turns rich coppery red or purplish in winter. Grows slowly into broad-based, dense pyramid, 20–60 ft. high. Trunks on old trees may lean or curve. For Oriental effect, prune out some branches to give tiered look. For most effective display, give it space.

C. j. 'Lobbii Nana' (C. j. 'Lobbii'). Upright, dwarf, very slow to 4 ft. Foliage dark green.

C. j. 'Pygmaea' (C. j. 'Nana'). DWARF CRYPTOMERIA. Bushy dwarf 1½–2 ft. high, 2½ ft. wide. Dark green, needlelike leaves, twisted branches.

C. j. 'Vilmoriniana'. Slow-growing dwarf to about 1–2 ft. Fluffy gray-green summer foliage turns bronze during late fall and winter. Rock garden or container plant.

CTENANTHE

Marantaceae

HOUSE PLANTS

☒ ON PATIOS IN ZONES 23, 24; OR INDOORS

☽ PARTIAL SHADE

⬤⬤ AMPLE WATER

Ctenanthe compressa

Leaves are big feature; they may be short stalked, set along stem, or long stalked, rising from base only. Insignificant white flowers form under bracts in spikes at ends of branches. Use with other tropical foliage plants such as philodendron, alocasia, tree ferns. Plant in rich, moist soil; feed with liquid fertilizer.

C. 'Burle Marx'. Grows to 15 in. Leaves gray green above, feathered with dark green; maroon underneath. Leafstalks maroon. Tender; best grown as house plant, even in mild Zones 23, 24.

C. compressa. BAMBURANTA. Plants to 2–3 ft. high. Leathery leaves are oblong, lopsided, to about 15 in. long, waxy green on top, gray green beneath, held at angle on top of wiry stems. Often sold as *Bamburanta arnoldiana*.

C. lubbersiana (Maranta lubbersiana). To 2 ft. Yellow, 8-in. leaves with green markings.

C. oppenheimiana. GIANT BAMBURANTA. Compact, branching, 3–5 ft. high. Narrow, leathery leaves, dark green banded with silver above, purple beneath, set at angle on downy stalks. *C. o.* 'Tricolor' has showy cream patches with its other colors.

FOR GROWING SYMBOL EXPLANATIONS
PLEASE SEE PAGE 129

CTENITIS pentangularis

Polypodiaceae

FERN

ZONES 17, 21–24

PARTIAL OR FULL SHADE

LITTLE TO MODERATE WATER

Ctenitis pentangularis

Native to New Zealand. This low-growing fern makes dense clumps of triangular, finely cut fronds. Will take moderately dry conditions and temperatures down to 26°F.

CUCUMBER

Cucurbitaceae

ANNUAL VINES

ALL ZONES

FULL SUN

MAINTAIN EVEN SOIL MOISTURE

Cucumber

Each vine needs at least 25 sq. ft., but you can use a fence or trellis to conserve space. Both warm soil to sprout seeds and warmth for pollination are required.

There are long, smooth, green, slicing cucumbers; numerous small pickling cucumbers; and roundish, yellow, mild-flavored lemon cucumbers. Novelties include Oriental varieties (long, slim, very mild), Armenian cucumber (actually a long, curving, pale green, ribbed melon with cucumber look and mild cucumber flavor), and English greenhouse cucumber. English greenhouse cucumbers must be grown in greenhouse to avoid pollination by bees, with subsequent loss of form and flavor; when well grown they are mildest of all cucumbers.

Bush cucumbers—varieties with compact vines—take up little garden space. Burpless varieties resemble hothouse cucumbers in shape and mild flavor but can be grown out of doors. Pickling cucumbers should be picked as soon as they have reached the proper size—tiny for sweet pickles (gherkins), larger for dills or pickle slices. They grow too large very quickly.

'Sweet Success' has quality of greenhouse cucumber but can be grown outdoors. Flowers are all female, but plants need no pollinator. Grow on trellis for long, straight cucumbers.

Plant seeds in sunny spot 1 or 2 weeks after average date of last frost. To grow cucumbers on trellis, plant seeds 1 in. deep and 1–3 ft. apart and permit main stem to reach top of support. Pick while young to ensure continued production.

FRENCH CORNICHON PICKLES

For a gourmet pickle, buy seed of French cornichons from a specialty seed dealer. Plant when soil warms and all danger of frost is past. Plants require full sun, fertile soil, and consistent moisture. It's best to grow these little cucumbers on a trellis or in a 3-ft.-tall cage (two seedlings to a 14-in.-diameter cage). As plants mature, check them daily for fruit. For pickling, take fruits when they are 1–2 in. long. Larger fruits, 2–2½ in., are best for eating fresh.

CUCUMBER TREE. See MAGNOLIA acuminata   p. 366

Cucurbitaceae. The gourd family as seen in western gardens consists of annual vines with yellow or white flowers and large, fleshy, seedy fruits—cucumbers, gourds, melons, pumpkins, and squash.

CUNNINGHAMIA lanceolata

CHINA FIR

Taxodiaceae

EVERGREEN TREE

ZONES 4–6, 14–21

FULL SUN

MODERATE WATER

Cunninghamia lanceolata

Native to China. Picturesque conifer with heavy trunk; stout, whorled branches; and drooping branchlets. Grows at moderate rate to 30 ft. with 20-ft. spread. Stiff, needlelike, sharp-pointed leaves are 1½–2½ in. long, green above, whitish beneath. Brown cones (1–2 in.) interesting but not profuse. Among palest of needled evergreens in spring and summer; turns red bronze in cold winters. Needs protection from hot, dry wind in summer and cold winds in winter. Becomes less attractive as it ages. Prune out dead branchlets. *C. l.* 'Glauca' is more widely grown and hardier than *C. lanceolata*. Its foliage is striking gray blue.

CUP-AND-SAUCER. See CAMPANULA medium   p. 204

CUP-AND-SAUCER VINE. See COBAEA scandens   p. 236

CUPANIOPSIS anacardioides

CARROT WOOD

Sapindaceae

EVERGREEN TREE

ZONES 16–24

FULL SUN

TOLERATES WET SOIL

Cupaniopsis anacardioides

Native to Australia. Slow to moderate growth to 40 ft.; glossy dark green leaves divided into six to ten leathery, 4-in. long leaflets. Tolerates salt laden soil, salt winds at the coast, and hot, dry winds inland. Generally neat, never chlorotic in appearance. As they approach maturity, trees may produce marble-size, leathery, yellow to orange fruit that splits but does not squash or stain. Some trees fruit heavily enough to be an annoyance, while others never fruit, for reasons not understood. Some feel that young trees selected for unusual vigor and broader than usual leaflets will produce less fruit than others; another theory is that trees under stress tend to develop more female flowers, hence more fruit. It is also believed that thinning out the tree every 2 years or so will result in production of young, nonfruiting wood. For several years, at least, an attractive, well-behaved tree. Consider underplanting with a ground cover deep enough to swallow the fruit drop. If you do so, be prepared to pull volunteer seedlings when they appear. Many landscape architects feel that the tree's virtues outweigh its faults.

CUP FLOWER. See NIEREMBERGIA   p. 391

CUPHEA

Lythraceae

SHRUBBY PERENNIALS OR DWARF SHRUBS

ZONES 16, 17, 21–24; OR SUMMER ANNUAL

POTTED PLANTS BEST IN LIGHT SHADE

HEAVY WATERING

Cuphea ignea

Native to Mexico, Guatemala. Interesting for summer color in small beds, as formal edging for border, along paths, in containers. Pinch tips for compact growth; severely cut back older plants in late fall or early spring. Easy from cuttings.

C. hyssopifolia. FALSE HEATHER. Compact shrublet 6 in.–2 ft. tall, with flexible, leafy branchlets. Leaves evergreen, ½–¾ in. long, very narrow. Tiny summer flowers in pink, purple, or white are scarcely half as long as leaves. White form most useful.

C. ignea. CIGAR PLANT. Leafy, compact, 1 ft. high and wide. Leaves narrow, dark green, 1–1½ in. long. Flowers tubular, ¾ in. long, bright red with white tip and dark ring at end (hence name "cigar plant"). Blooms summer and fall.

CUPID'S DART. See CATANANCHE caerulea	**p. 211**
CUP-OF-GOLD VINE. See SOLANDRA maxima	**p. 487**

Cupressaceae. The cypress family differs from the pine and yew families in having leaves that are usually reduced to scales and cones with few scales. Cones may even be berrylike, as in junipers.

CUPRESSOCYPARIS leylandii

Cupressaceae

EVERGREEN TREE

✿ ZONES 3–24

☼ FULL SUN

● MODERATE WATER

Cupressocyparis leylandii

Hybrid between *Chamaecyparis nootkatensis* and *Cupressus macrocarpa*. Grows very fast (from cuttings to 15–20 ft. in 5 years). Most planted as quick screening. However, some 10-year-old plantings have become open and floppy with age. Long, slender, upright branches of flattened, gray-green foliage sprays give youthful tree narrow pyramidal form. Produces small cones composed of scales. Accepts wide variety of soil and climate, strong wind; in warm-summer climates, loses stiff, upright habit and is subject to coryneum canker fungus. 'Naylor's Blue' has grayish blue foliage; 'Castlewellan' has golden yellow new growth and a narrow, erect habit; 'Emerald Isle' has bright green foliage on plants 20–25 ft. tall, 6–8 ft. wide.

CUPRESSUS

CYPRESS

Cupressaceae

EVERGREEN TREES

✿ ZONES VARY BY SPECIES

☼ FULL SUN

◊ NO WATER ONCE ESTABLISHED

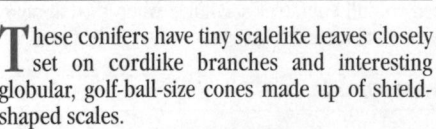

Cupressus arizonica

These conifers have tiny scalelike leaves closely set on cordlike branches and interesting globular, golf-ball-size cones made up of shield-shaped scales.

C. arizonica. ARIZONA CYPRESS. Zones 5, 8–24. This plant and *C. a. glabra* (often sold as *C. glabra*), SMOOTH ARIZONA CYPRESS, are at their best in hot interior climates, where they are useful as quick windbreaks. Native to central Arizona. To 40 ft., spreading to 20 ft. Seedlings variable, with foliage ranging from green to blue gray or silvery. Arizona cypress has rough bark; smooth Arizona cypress has smooth cherry red bark. Selected forms include 'Blue Pyramid', a dense blue-gray pyramid to 20–25 ft; 'Gareei', with silvery blue-green foliage; and 'Pyramidalis', compact and symmetrical.

C. forbesii. TECATE CYPRESS. Zones 8–14, 18–20. Native to Santa Ana Mountains, Orange County; and mountains of San Diego County, California. Low-branching tree to 20 ft., with cherry red bark and green foliage. Very

fast growing—in fact, it may get too top heavy for size of root system. Needs to be kept on dry side for wind resistance. Useful as hedge or screen.

C. macrocarpa. MONTEREY CYPRESS. Zone 17. Native to California's Monterey Peninsula. Beautiful tree to 40 ft. or more, with rich bright green foliage. Narrow and pyramidal in youth, spreading and picturesque in age or in windy coastal conditions. Away from cool coastal winds is very subject to coryneum canker fungus, for which there is no cure. Look for foliage that first turns yellow, then deep reddish brown, and falls off slowly. Destroy infected trees. Fast-growing windbreak tree in coastal conditions.

'Golden Pillar' is a slow-growing, large, pyramidal shrub. Foliage is golden yellow in sun, yellow green in partial shade.

C. sempervirens. ITALIAN CYPRESS. Zones 4–24; best in Zones 8–15, 18–20. Native to southern Europe, western Asia. Species itself, with horizontal branches and dark green foliage, is seldom sold. *C. s.* 'Stricta' (*C. s.* 'Fastigiata'), columnar Italian cypress, and *C. s.* 'Glauca', blue Italian cypress (really blue green), are classic Mediterranean cypresses. They eventually grow into dense, narrow, columnar trees to 60 ft. *C. s.* 'Swane's Golden' (narrowly columnar) has golden yellow new growth.

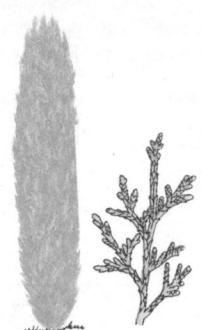

Cupressus sempervirens

CURRANT

Saxifragaceae

DECIDUOUS SHRUBS

✿ ALL ZONES; BEST IN ZONES 1–6, 17

☼ ◐ ● FULL SUN ON COAST, SHADE INLAND

● REGULAR WATER

Currant

Many-stemmed shrubs to 3–5 ft. high and equally broad, depending on vigor and variety. Attractive foliage of lobed and toothed leaves to 3 in. wide.

Flowers, yellowish in drooping clusters, are followed by clusters of red or white fruit in early summer. Leaves drop rather early in fall. Currants bear at base of year-old wood and on spurs on 2- and 3-year wood. Prune so that you keep balance of 1-, 2-, and 3-year canes; prune out older canes and weak growth. 'Red Lake', 'Perfection', and 'Cherry' are preferred varieties.

In some areas it is illegal to plant currants, which may be hosts to white pine blister rust. Ask county agent or nursery about requirements in your area. Do not grow where water or soil is high in sodium.

Black currant, once illegal as the favored host of the pine rust, is now available in a rust-resistant hybrid named 'Consort'. Fruit production is heavy; fruit is blackish purple and has a distinctive flavor with a suggestion of blackberry. It may be used in preserves or sauces.

For ornamental relatives, see *Ribes*.

CUSHION BUSH. See CALOCEPHALUS brownii	**p. 198**
CUSHION PINK. See SILENE acaulis	**p. 485**

CYANOTIS

Commelinaceae

EVERGREEN PERENNIALS GROWN INDOORS

◔ BRIGHT INDOOR LIGHT

● MODERATE WATER

Cyanotis somaliensis

Related to wandering Jews (*Tradescantia albiflora* and *Zebrina pendula*), they resemble them but have shorter stems, fleshier, more succulent leaves, and noticeable covering of soft "fur." Give them fairly rich, loose planting mix. Propagate by cuttings.

C. kewensis. TEDDY BEAR. Leaves 1–1½ in. long, coated with brown "fur." Small three-petaled flowers are purplish red.

C. somaliensis. PUSSY EARS. Stems somewhat longer than above (to 9–10 in.), leaves covered with white "fur," flowers blue.

CYATHEA cooperi

AUSTRALIAN TREE FERN

Cyatheaceae

TREE FERN

⚥ ZONES 15–24

☼ ◑ PARTIAL SHADE; FULL SUN IN FOG BELT

● REGULAR WATER

Cyathea cooperi

Fastest growing of the fairly hardy tree ferns. Often sold as *Alsophila australis, A. cooperi,* or *Sphaeropteris cooperi.* Can grow from 1-ft. to 6-ft. spread in a year, eventually to 20 ft. tall. Broad fronds are finely cut, bright green, to a spread of 12 ft. Brownish hair on leafstalks and leaf undersurfaces can irritate skin; wear long sleeves, hat, neckcloth when grooming plants. Hardy to possibly 20°F, but with damage to fronds. Reasonably safe in sheltered places along the coast and in warm coastal valleys.

Cycadaceae. This is the best-known family in Cycadales, an order of slow-growing evergreen plants with large, firm, palmlike or fernlike leaves and conelike fruit. Most people think of them as a kind of palm.

Most are native to tropical regions. Some are subtropical, and among these, some are hardy enough to grow out of doors in mild-winter climates.

In addition to *Cycas revoluta*, cycads include *Ceratozamia mexicana, Dioon,* and *Zamia pumila* (members of a related family, Zamiaceae).

CYCAS revoluta

SAGO PALM

Cycadaceae

CYCAD

⚥ ZONES 8–24

◑ PARTIAL SHADE

● REGULAR WATER

Cycas revoluta

In youth (2–3 ft. tall), has airy, lacy appearance of ferns; with age (grows very slowly to as high as 10 ft.), looks more like palm. But it is neither—it is a primitive, cone-bearing plant related to conifers. From central point at top of single trunk (sometimes several trunks), featherlike leaves grow out in rosettes. Leaves are 2–3 ft. long (larger on very old plants), divided into many narrow, leathery, dark glossy green segments. Makes offsets (new plants attached to parent).

Choice container or bonsai plant; useful for tropical look. Tough, tolerant house or patio plant. Hardiest (to 15°F), most widely grown cycad.

CYCLAMEN

Primulaceae

TUBEROUS-ROOTED PERENNIALS

⚥ ZONES VARY BY SPECIES

☼ ◑ FULL SUN OR PARTIAL SHADE

● KEEP SOIL MOIST DURING GROWTH

Cyclamen persicum

Grown for pretty white, pink, rose, or red flowers that resemble shooting stars. Attractive leaves in basal clumps. Zones and uses for large-flowered florists' cyclamen (*C. persicum*) are given under that name. All other types are small flowered, hardy, best adapted in Zones 1–9, 14–24. They bloom as described in listing below,

and all lose leaves during part of year. Leaves may appear before or with flowers. Use hardy types in rock gardens; in naturalized clumps under trees; as carpets under camellias, rhododendrons, and large, noninvasive ferns. Or grow them in pots out of direct sun.

All kinds of cyclamen grow best in fairly rich, porous soil with lots of humus. Plant tubers 6–10 in. apart; cover with ½ in. soil. (Florists' cyclamen is an exception to usual planting practice; upper half of tuber should protrude above soil level.) Best planting time is dormant period, June–August—except for florists' cyclamen, which is always sold as a potted plant rather than a tuber and is available in most seasons (although most are sold in late fall or during the winter–spring blooming period). Top-dress annually with light application of potting soil with complete fertilizer added, being careful not to cover top of tuber. Do not cultivate around roots.

The smaller hardy cyclamen grow well under native oaks; they can tolerate a summer resting period.

Cyclamen grow readily from seed; small-flowered hardy species take several years to bloom. Older strains of florists' cyclamen needed 15–18 months from seed to bloom; newer strains can bloom in as little as 7 months. Grown out of doors in open ground, cyclamen often self-sow.

C. atkinsii. Crimson flowers on 4–6-in. stems; deep green, silver-mottled leaves. Also pink, white varieties. January–March.

C. cilicium. Pale pink, purple-blotched, fragrant flowers on 2–6-in. stems; mottled leaves. September–January. There is a white-flowered variety, 'Album'.

C. coum. Deep crimson rose flowers on 4–6-in. stems; round, deep green leaves. White, pink varieties. January–March.

C. europaeum. See C. purpurascens

C. hederifolium (C. neapolitanum). Large light green leaves marbled silver and white. Rose pink flowers bloom on 3–4-in. stems, August–September. Also white variety. One of most vigorous and easiest to grow; very reliable in cold-winter climates. Set tubers a foot apart.

> ### AVOID WILD BULBS
> As a buyer of species cyclamen (any kind other than *C. persicum*), you should check to ascertain that the bulbs are commercially grown and not taken from the wild. Many bulb species are endangered and fast disappearing in their native habitats. Look for labels that mention "Holland" or "cultivated." In addition to cyclamen species, bulbs that have been dug in the wild for sale in the United States include *Eranthis, Galanthus, Leucojum,* and species *Narcissus.*

C. persicum. Wild ancestor of florists' cyclamen. Original species has deep to pale pink or white, 2-in. fragrant flowers on 6-in. stems. Selective breeding has given large-flowered florists' cyclamen (the old favorites) and, more recently, smaller strains. Fragrance has disappeared, with rare exceptions.

Florists' cyclamen grows outdoors in Zones 16–24. Blooms late fall to spring, flowers crimson, red, salmon, purple, or white on 6–8-in. stems. Kidney-shaped dark green leaves. Good choice for color in places occupied by tuberous begonias in summer. Must have shade in warm summer climates. Plants will lose leaves and go dormant in hot weather, but usually survive if drainage is good and soil not waterlogged.

Dwarf or miniature florists' cyclamens are popular; they are half or three-quarter-size replicas of standards. Careful gardeners can get these to bloom in 7–8 months from seed. Miniature strains (profuse show of 1½-in. flowers on 6–8-in. plants) include fragrant Dwarf Fragrance and Mirabelle strains.

C. purpurascens (C. europaeum). Distinctly fragrant crimson flowers, July–August, on 5–6-in. stems. Bright green leaves mottled silvery white; almost evergreen.

C. repandum. Bright crimson flowers with long, narrow petals on 5–6-in. stems, spring; rich green, ivy-shaped leaves, marbled silver, toothed on edges.

CYMBALARIA

Scrophulariaceae

SMALL CREEPING PERENNIAL PLANTS

🗷 ZONES 3–24

● SHADE

◗ REGULAR WATER

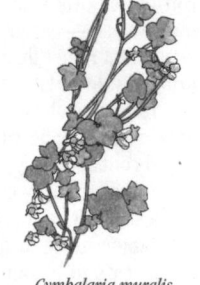

Cymbalaria muralis

Related to snapdragons. Unshowy, but they have their uses as small-scale ground covers in cool, shady places or as decorations for terrarium or hanging basket. In ground, can be invasive.

C. aequitriloba. Inch-deep mat that looks like small-scale dichondra. Leaves have three to five slight lobes. Purple, snapdragon-shaped flowers are pretty but too tiny to make a show. Use as moss substitute.

C. muralis (Linaria cymbalaria). KENILWORTH IVY. Perennial usually growing as annual. Dainty creeper that may appear uninvited in shadier parts of garden, sometimes even sprouting in chinks of stone or brick wall. Trailing stems root at joints. Leaves 1 in. wide or less, smooth, with three to seven toothlike lobes. Small lilac blue flowers carried singly on stalks a little longer than leaves.

CYMBIDIUM

Orchidaceae

TERRESTRIAL ORCHIDS

🗷 ALL ZONES; SEE BELOW

◐ BEST WITH 50 PERCENT SHADE

◗ KEEP SOIL MOIST DURING GROWTH

Miniature
Cymbidium

Native to high altitudes in southeast Asia, where rainfall is heavy and nights cool. Very popular because of their relatively easy culture. Except in frost-free areas, grow plants in containers in lathhouse, greenhouse, or under overhang or high-branching tree. For added enjoyment bring indoors when in flower. Excellent cut flower. Long, narrow, grasslike foliage forms sheath around short, stout, oval pseudobulbs. Long-lasting flowers grow on erect or arching spikes. Standard types usually bloom from February to early May. Bloom season for miniatures starts in September, is heaviest November–January.

For best bloom, give as much light as possible without burning foliage. Plants do well under plastic cloth shading or under lath. Let leaf color be your guide: plants with yellow-green leaves generally flower best; dark green foliage means too much shade. (During flowering period, give plants shade to prolong bloom life, keep flowers from fading.)

SOIL MIX FOR CYMBIDIUMS

If the store where you buy your cymbidiums doesn't offer a packaged cymbidium soil mix, here's a good one you can make: 2 parts redwood bark or sawdust, 2 parts peat moss, 1 part sand. Add a 4-in. pot of complete, dry fertilizer to each wheelbarrow of mix. Packaged or homemade, the medium should drain fast and still retain moisture.

Plants prefer 45–55°F night temperature, rising to as high as 80–90°F during day. They'll stand temperatures as low as 28°F for short time only; therefore, where there's danger of harder frosts, protect plants with covering of polyethylene film. Flower spikes are more tender than other plant tissues.

Keep potting medium moist when new growth is developing and maturing—usually March–September. In winter, water just enough to keep bulbs from shriveling. On hot summer days, syringe foliage early in day.

Feed with complete liquid fertilizer high in nitrogen every 10 days to 2 weeks, January–July. Use low-nitrogen fertilizer August–December.

Transplant potted plants when bulbs fill pots. When dividing plants, keep minimum of three healthy bulbs (with foliage) in each division. Dust cuts with sulfur or paint them with tree seal to discourage rot. Watch for slugs and snails at all times.

Most cymbidium growers list only hybrids in their catalogs—large-flowered varieties with white, pink, yellow, green, or bronze blooms. Most have yellow throat, dark red markings on lip. Large-flowered forms produce dozen or more 4½–5-in. flowers per stem. Miniature varieties, about a quarter the size of large-flowered forms, are popular for their size, free-blooming qualities, flower color.

CYMBOPOGON citratus

LEMON GRASS

Poaceae (Gramineae)

TENDER PERENNIAL

🗷 ZONE 16, 17, 23, 24

☼ FULL SUN

◗ REGULAR WATER

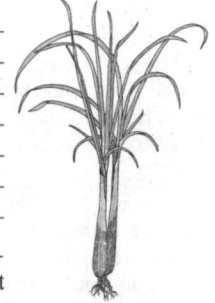

All parts of the plant are strongly lemon-scented and are widely used as an ingredient in southeast Asian cooking. Lemon grass is occasionally grown in gardens, where it sometimes

Cymbopogon citratus

lives over in the mildest winters of the warmer California climates. It is safer to pot up a division and keep it indoors or in a greenhouse over winter. Clumps of inch-wide leaves grow 2–3 ft. tall. Sheathing leaf bases are nearly bulbous in appearance.

CYNODON dactylon

BERMUDA GRASS, BERMUDA

Poaceae (Gramineae)

LAWN GRASS

🗷 ZONES 8, 9, 12–24

☼ FULL SUN

◐◗ WATER LESS THAN MOST LAWN GRASSES

Subtropical fine-textured grass that spreads rapidly by surface and underground runners.

Cynodon dactylon

Tolerates heat, and looks good if well maintained. It turns brown in winter; some varieties stay green longer than others, and most stay green longer if well fed. Bermuda grass can be overseeded with cool-season grasses or dyed green for winter color. Needs sun and should be cut low; ½ in. is desirable. Needs thatching—removal of matted layer of old stems and stolons beneath the leaves—to look its best.

Common Bermuda is good minimum-maintenance lawn for large area. Needs feeding, careful and frequent mowing to remove seed spikes. Roots invade shrubbery and flower beds if not carefully confined. Can become extremely difficult to eradicate. Plant from hulled seed or sprigs.

Hybrid Bermudas are finer in texture and better in color than common kind. They crowd out common Bermuda in time but are harder to overseed with rye, bluegrass, or red fescue. Help them stay green in winter by feeding in September and October and by removing thatch. Useful in areas with short dormant season. Grow from sprigs (stolons), plugs, or sod.

'Santa Ana'. Deep green, coarse, smog resistant. Takes hard wear; holds color late.

'Tifdwarf'. Extremely low and dense; takes very close mowing. Slower to establish than others, but slower to spread where it's not wanted. Useful as small-scale ground cover on banks, among rocks.

'Tifgreen'. Fine textured, deep blue green, dense. Few seed spikes, sterile seeds. Takes close mowing; preferred for putting greens.

'Tifway'. Low growth, fine texture, stiff blades, dark green, dense, wear resistant. Slow to start. Sterile (no seeds).

'U-3'. More finely textured than common Bermuda but with obvious and unattractive seed spikes. Very tough. Grow from sprigs; not dependable from seed, tending to revert to mixture of many types. Not up to other hybrids in quality.

CYNOGLOSSUM

Boraginaceae

PERENNIALS; BIENNIALS TREATED AS ANNUALS

🌿 ZONES VARY BY SPECIES

☼ ◐ ● EXPOSURE NEEDS VARY BY SPECIES

◊ ◐ ● WATER NEEDS VARY BY SPECIES

Cynoglossum amabile

Bedding, border, or wild garden plants with blue, white, or pink flowers like forget-me-nots, to which they are related.

C. amabile. CHINESE FORGET-ME-NOT. Biennial grown as annual. All zones. Plant is 1½–2 ft. tall. Leaves grayish green, soft, hairy, lance shaped. Loose sprays of rich blue, pink, or white flowers, larger than forget-me-nots, appear in spring, into summer where weather is cool. 'Firmament', widely available, most popular variety, has rich blue flowers on compact, 1½-ft -high plants. Combine with snapdragons, godetias, candytuft, clarkia, violas; especially effective with white, yellow, pink, salmon, or coral flowers.

Blooms first year from seed sown (preferably where plants are to grow) in fall or early spring. Hardy except in most severe winters. Sun, regular watering.

C. grande. WESTERN HOUND'S TONGUE. Perennial. Zones 4–9, 14–24. Native to Coast Ranges and Sierra Nevada slopes below 4,000 ft. Leaves hairy, mostly basal, spreading, 6–12 in. long. Flowers blue, ⅓–½ in. across, white in center, March–June. Plants 1–2½ ft. tall; die back in summer to heavy underground root. Choose a shaded, woodsy site with cool soil and little or no summer water.

Cyperaceae. Members of the sedge family superficially resemble grasses, but their stems are usually three-sided and their leaves are arranged in three ranks. They generally grow in wet places; *Carex* and *Cyperus* are examples.

CYPERUS

Cyperaceae

PERENNIALS

🌿 ZONES VARY BY SPECIES

☼ ◐ ● ANY EXPOSURE

◐ BOG PLANTS IN NATURE

Cyperus papyrus

These are sedges—grasslike plants distinguished from true grasses by three-angled, solid stems and very different flowering parts. Valued for striking form, silhouette, shadow pattern.

Most cyperus grow in rich, moist soil or with roots submerged in water, in sun or shade. Groom plants by removing dead or broken stems; divide and replant vigorous ones when clump becomes too large, saving smaller, outside divisions and discarding overgrown centers. In cold climates, pot up divisions and keep them over the winter as house plants.

C. albostriatus (C. diffusus). Zones 14–24. Resembles *C. alternifolius*, but tends to be less hardy, shorter (to 20 in.), with broader leaves and lusher, softer appearance. Vigorous, invasive; best used in contained space.

C. alternifolius. UMBRELLA PLANT. Zones 8, 9, 12–24. Narrow, firm, spreading leaves arranged like ribs of umbrella at tops of 2–4-ft. stems. Flowers in dry, greenish brown clusters. Dwarf form is *C. a.* 'Gracilis' (*C. a.* 'Nanus'). Grows in or out of water. Effective near pools, in pots or planters, or in dry stream beds or small rock gardens. Self-sows. Can become weedy, take over a small pool.

C. isocladus (C. haspan). DWARF PAPYRUS. Zones 16, 17, 23, 24. Flowers and long, thin leaves combine to make filmy brown and green clusters on slender stems about 1½ ft. high. Sink in pots in water gardens where slender leafless stems will not lose delicately shaped design among larger and coarser plants. Use in oriental gardens.

C. papyrus. PAPYRUS. Zones 16, 17, 23, 24. Tall, graceful, dark green stems 6–10 ft. high, topped with clusters of green threadlike parts to 1½ ft. long (longer than small leaves at base of cluster). Will grow quickly in 2 in. of water in shallow pool, or can be potted and placed on bricks or inverted pot in deeper water. Protect from strong wind. Also grows well in rich, moist soil out of water. Used by flower arrangers.

CYPHOMANDRA betacea (C. crassicaulis)

TREE TOMATO, TAMARILLO

Solanaceae

EVERGREEN OR PARTIALLY EVERGREEN SHRUB

🌿 ZONES 14–24; OR INDOORS

☼ ◐ FULL SUN OR PARTIAL SHADE

● MODERATE WATER

Cyphomandra betacea

Fast growth to 10–12 ft. Treelike habit. Pointed oval leaves 4–10 in. long. Summer and fall flowers small, pinkish. Winter fruit is red, 2–3 in. long, egg shaped, edible; has acid, slightly tomato-like flavor. If you find the fruit too tart, try stewing it with a little sugar, as the Australians do. Grow from seed like tomato. Shelter from frost; overhead protection in Zones 14, 15, 18–21. Spray to control sucking insects.

CYPRESS. See *Cupressus.* True cypresses are all *Cupressus;* many plants erroneously called cypress are under *Chamaecyparis* and *Taxodium.*

CYPRESS VINE. See IPOMOEA quamoclit   p. 332

Cypripedium. For tropical and subtropical orchids sold under this name, see *Paphiopedilum.* True cypripediums, the hardy lady's slipper orchids, are rare or endangered in the wild and extremely difficult to maintain in gardens. Most are collected from wild stands and seldom survive.

CYRTANTHUS mackenii

Amaryllidaceae

BULB

🌿 ZONES 16–24; OR INDOORS

◐ PARTIAL SHADE

● WATER REGULARLY DURING GROWTH

Cyrtanthus mackenii

South African native. Foot-long, narrow (⅓-in.-wide) leaves have somewhat wavy edges. Tubular, curved, 2-in.-long white flowers nod in loose clusters at ends of stems. Blooms in spring. There are also cream- and yellow-flowered forms and hybrids in coral, orange, and red shades. Plants grow actively throughout year, produce numerous offsets. Grow them in well-drained acid soil. Plant in sheltered situations in Zones 16–22. If grown in pots, plants will need annual repotting. At that time, remove small bulblets and pot them up for bloom in 1½–2 years. For *C. purpureus*, see *Vallota speciosa.*

D

CYRTOMIUM falcatum

HOLLY FERN

Polypodiaceae

FERN

◪ ZONES 16, 17, 22–24

◐ ● PARTIAL OR FULL SHADE

💧 AMPLE WATER

Cyrtomium falcatum

Coarse-textured but handsome fern, 2–3 ft. tall, sometimes taller. Leaflets large, dark green, glossy, leathery. Takes indoor conditions well and thrives outside in milder areas. Hardy to 25°F. Take care not to plant too deeply. The variety 'Rochfordianum' has fringed leaflets.

CYTISUS

BROOM

Fabaceae (Leguminosae)

EVERGREEN, SEMIEVERGREEN, DECIDUOUS SHRUBS

◪ ZONES VARY BY SPECIES

☼ FULL SUN

◌ NO WATER ONCE ESTABLISHED

Cytisus battandieri

Most widely planted brooms belong here, but look for Spanish broom under *Spartium junceum*, other choice shrubs under *Genista*. Deciduous or evergreen shrubs (many nearly leafless, but with green or gray-green stems). Sweet pea–shaped flowers, often fragrant. Plants tolerate wind, seashore conditions, and rocky, infertile soil. Where soil is highly alkaline, give them iron sulfate. Prune after bloom to keep to reasonable size and form, lessen production of unsightly seedpods.

C. battandieri. ATLAS BROOM. Semievergreen or deciduous. Zones 5, 6. Fast growth to 12–15 ft. high and as wide. Can be trained as small tree. Leaves divided into three roundish leaflets to 3½ in. long, 1½ in. wide, covered with silvery, silky hairs. Fragrant, clear yellow flowers in spikelike 5-in. clusters at branch ends, June–September.

C. canariensis (Genista canariensis). CANARY ISLAND BROOM. Evergreen. Zones 8, 9, 12–24. Damaged at 15°F but recovers quickly. Many-branched, upright shrub to 6–8 ft. high, 5–6 ft. wide. Bright green leaves divided into ½-in. leaflets. Bright yellow, fragrant flowers in short clusters at ends of branches, spring and summer.

THE BAD-NEWS BROOMS

Three species of broom—*Cytisus canariensis*, *C. scoparius*, and *Spartium junceum*—escaped from landscapes starting in the early part of the 20th century, and their legion of seedlings is now taking over sections of low-elevation wild land in California and the Northwest. The lesson (a little late): if you live anywhere near open land and you desire broom plants, use one of the species that has better manners.

C. kewensis. KEW BROOM. Dwarf evergreen shrublet. Best in Zones 4–6; less vigorous but satisfactory in Zones 16, 17. Low (less than 1 ft. high), spreading with trailing branches to 4 ft. or more. Creamy white, ½-in. flowers, April–May. Tiny leaves. Branches will cascade.

C. lydia. See Genista lydia

C. praecox. WARMINSTER BROOM. Zones 2–9, 12–22. Deciduous. Compact growth with many slender stems to 3–5 ft. high and 4–6 ft. wide. Mounding mass of pale yellow to creamy white flowers, March–April in south, April–May in north. Small leaves fall early. Effective as informal screen or hedge, along drives, paths, garden steps. 'Allgold', slightly taller, has bright yellow flowers; 'Hollandia', pink ones. 'Moonlight', formerly considered *C. praecox* variety, is now thought to be form of *C. scoparius*.

C. purgans. PROVENCE BROOM. Zones 4–6. Deciduous. Dense, mounding growth to 3 ft. high with equal spread. Silky, hairy leaves roundish, ¼–½ in. long. Fragrant, chrome yellow flowers, May–July.

C. racemosus. See C. spachianus

C. scoparius. SCOTCH BROOM. Evergreen. Zones 4–9, 14–22. This one has given all brooms a bad name. Upright growing mass of wandlike green stems (often leafless or nearly so) may reach 10 ft. Golden yellow, ¾-in. flowers, spring and early summer.

Much less aggressive are lower-growing, more colorful forms. Most of these grow 5–8 ft. tall: 'Burkwoodii', red touched yellow; 'Carla', pink and crimson lined white; 'Dorothy Walpole', rose pink and crimson; 'Lena', lemon yellow and red; 'Lilac Time', lilac pink, compact; 'Lord Lambourne', scarlet and cream; 'Minstead', white flushed lilac and deep purple; 'Moonlight', pale yellow, compact; 'Pomona', orange and apricot; 'St. Mary's', white; 'San Francisco' and 'Stanford', red.

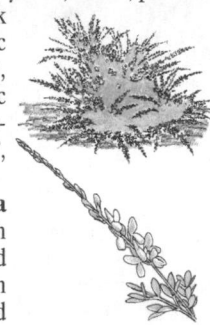

C. spachianus (C. racemosus, Genista racemosa). Zones 7–9, 11–24. Similar in growth habit to *C. canariensis* but with larger leaflets and longer, looser spikes of yellow, fragrant flowers in late spring. Naturalizes where adapted. Often sold as *Genista fragrans*.

Cytisus spachianus

DABOECIA

IRISH HEATH

Ericaceae

SMALL EVERGREEN SHRUBS OF HEATHER FAMILY

◪ ZONES VARY BY SPECIES

☼ ◐ TOLERATE FULL SUN NEAR COAST

● REGULAR WATER

Daboecia cantabrica

Give them acid, fast-draining soil. These shrubs are most useful on hillsides and in rock gardens or wild gardens.

D. azorica. Zones 8, 9, 14–24. Mounds to 6–10 in. Closely set, bright green leaves ¼ in. long, broader than those of other heaths and heathers. Egg-shaped, rosy red flowers ½ in. long on spikelike clusters, April–May, occasionally in fall.

D. cantabrica. Zones 3–9, 14–24. Erect stems make slightly spreading plant 1½–2 ft. tall. Larger leaves than those of *D. azorica*. Pinkish purple, ½-in., egg-shaped flowers in narrow 3–5-in. clusters, June–October (April–October in warmer areas). Cut back in fall to keep compact. Varieties include 'Alba', white; 'Praegerae', pure pink; 'Rosea', deep pink. 'William Buchanan' is a prostrate grower with reddish purple flowers; 'William Buchanan Gold' is similar but with some yellow variegation in the foliage.

DAFFODIL. See NARCISSUS p. 387

DAHLBERG DAISY. See DYSSODIA tenuiloba p. 269

DAHLIA

Asteraceae (Compositae)

TUBEROUS-ROOTED PERENNIALS

◪ ALL ZONES, EXCEPT AS NOTED

☼ ◐ LIGHT AFTERNOON SHADE IN HOTTEST AREAS

● REGULAR WATER

Native to Mexico, Guatemala. Through centuries of hybridizing and selection, dahlias have become tremendously diversified, available in numerous flower types and in all colors but

Dahlia Hybrid

Decorative and Cactus Dahlias

| Informal Decorative | Formal Decorative | Cactus | Semicactus | Single | Collarette | Ball | Anemone | Pompom |

true blue. Sketches illustrate types based on flower form as classified by American Dahlia Society.

Bush and bedding dahlias grow from 15 in. to over 6 ft. high. The tall bush forms are useful as summer hedges, screens, and fillers among shrubs; lower kinds give mass color in borders and containers. Modern dahlias, with their strong stems, long-lasting blooms that face outward or upward, and substantial, attractive foliage, are striking cut flowers. Leaves are generally divided into many large, deep green leaflets.

Planting. Most dahlias are started from tubers. Plant them after frost is past and soil is warm. Several weeks before planting, dig soil 1 ft. deep and work in ground bark, composted redwood sawdust, or peat moss; also add coarse sand to heavy soils.

Dig holes 1 ft. deep and 3 ft. apart for most varieties; space largest kinds 4–5 ft. apart, smaller ones 1–2 ft. If you use fertilizer at planting time, thoroughly mix ¼ cup of complete fertilizer in bottom of hole, then add 4 in. of plain soil. Drive 5 ft. stake into hole, place tuber horizontally, 2 in. from stake, with eye pointing toward it. Cover tuber with 3 in. of soil. Water thoroughly if no rains are expected. As shoots grow, gradually fill hole with soil.

For tall dahlias, plant seeds early indoors; transplant seedlings into garden beds after frosts are over. In climates where ground freezes in winter, dig and store tubers, as described below, the following fall and thereafter. In other regions, tubers may remain in place as long as drainage is excellent and ground does not freeze deeply. Plants will survive in most of California and the Northwest west of the Cascades; elsewhere in the Northwest, mulch with 4 in. of straw or similar material.

For dwarf dahlias, sow seed in place after soil is warm, or buy and plant started seedlings from the nursery. Dwarf dahlias are best replaced each year, but you may dig and store tubers or overwinter them as you would with tall dahlias.

Thinning, pinching. On tall-growing types, thin to strongest shoot or two shoots (you can make cuttings of removed shoots). When remaining shoots have three sets of leaves, pinch off tips just above top set; two side shoots develop from each pair of leaves. For large flowers, remove all but terminal buds on side shoots. Smaller-flowered dahlias, such as miniatures, pompoms, singles, or dwarfs, need only first pinching.

Plant care. Start watering regularly after shoots are above ground, and continue throughout active growth. Dahlias planted in enriched soil don't need additional food. If soil lacks nutrients, side-dress plants with fertilizer high in phosphates and potash when first flower buds appear. Avoid high-nitrogen fertilizers: they result in soft growth, weak stems, tubers liable to rot in storage. Mulch to keep down weeds and to eliminate cultivating, which may injure feeder roots. Bait for snails and slugs.

Cut flowers. Pick nearly mature flowers in early morning or evening. Immediately place cut stems in 2–3 in. of hot water; let stand in gradually cooling water for several hours or overnight.

Lifting, storing. After tops turn yellow or are frosted, cut stalks to 4 in. above ground. Dig around plant 1 ft. from center, carefully pry up clump with spading fork, shake off loose soil, and let clump dry in sun for several hours. From that point, follow either of two methods:

Method 1: divide clumps immediately (as described under method 2). This saves storage space. Freshly dug tubers are easy to cut; it is easy to recognize eyes or growth buds at this time. Dust cut surfaces with sulfur to prevent rot; bury tubers in sand, sawdust, or vermiculite; and store through winter in cool (40–45°F), dry place.

Method 2: leave clumps intact; cover them with dry sand, sawdust, peat moss, perlite, or vermiculite; store in cool, dry place. There is less danger of shrinkage with this storage method. About 2–4 weeks before planting in spring, separate tubers by cutting stalks with sharp knife; leave 1 in. of stalk attached to each tuber. Tuber must have eye or bud in order to produce new plant. Place tubers in moist sand to encourage development of sprouts.

D. imperialis. TREE DAHLIA. Zones 4–6, 8, 9, 14–24. A 10–20-ft. multistemmed tree grows each year from permanent roots; in late fall, 4–8-in. lavender, daisy-type flowers with yellow centers are produced at branch ends. Leaves composed of many leaflets. Frosts kill tops completely; cut back to ground afterward. If tree dahlia bloomed longer or remained evergreen, it would be a valued landscape plant, but annual live-and-die cycle relegates it to tall novelty class. Seldom sold in nurseries. Grow from cuttings taken near tops of stems (or from side shoots) in fall; root in containers of moist sand kept in protected place over winter. Or dig root clump and divide in fall. Full sun or half shade. *D. excelsa, D. maxonii* are similar.

DAIS cotinifolia

POMPON TREE
Thymelaeaceae
BRIEFLY DECIDUOUS SHRUB OR SMALL TREE
☀ ZONES 16–24
☼ FULL SUN
● REGULAR WATER

Dais cotinifolia

Native to South Africa. Worthwhile flowering shrub or small tree, somewhat like crape myrtle in size and shape. Slow growing to 12 ft. with 10-ft. spread. Flower clusters resembling 1½-in. balls of pink shredded coconut are carried at ends of twigs in June and July. Flowers remain after fading and are then rather unsightly. Bluish green leaves to 2½ in. long drop in sharp frosts. By nature a multitrunked shrub-tree, it looks best trained to single trunk. Unusually tolerant of heat. Will stand reflected light and heat of pavement and walls.

DAISY TREE. See MONTANOA p. 383

DALEA

Fabaceae (Leguminosae)
EVERGREEN OR DECIDUOUS SHRUBS OR TREES
☀ ZONES 12, 13
☼ FULL SUN
● PERFORM WELL AT EDGE OF IRRIGATION

Evergreen or deciduous shrubs or trees with finely divided leaves and clusters of sweet pea–shaped flowers.

Dalea spinosa

D. frutescens. BLACK DALEA. Evergreen shrub 1–3 ft. tall and as wide. Round clusters of purple flowers open in late summer, fall. ▶

D. greggii. TRAILING INDIGO BUSH. Fast-growing (to 3 ft. wide in 1½ years), evergreen prostrate shrub with pearl gray foliage, clusters of tiny (smaller than ½-in.) purple flowers in spring and early summer. Excellent ground cover for desert; tolerates heat, desert soil, aridity when established. Unappealing to rabbits. To get fast growth, water deeply every 2 weeks.

D. oaxacana. Deciduous shrub to 1–1½ ft. tall. Tiny, finely divided gray-green leaves drop in fall, just after tiny purple flowers fade. Useful in furnishing some shade to such heat-sensitive ground covers as red spike ice plant (*Cephalophyllum*).

D. pulchra. INDIGO BUSH. Evergreen shrub 3–5 ft. tall, equally wide. Silvery green foliage and clustered purple flowers at branch ends in spring. Prune to fatten. Infrequent summer watering will prevent partial leaf drop.

D. spinosa. SMOKE TREE. Deciduous. Native to desert washes below 1,500 ft. in Southern California, Arizona, Baja California. The few small leaves drop early. When tree is out of leaf, intricate network of gray, spiny branches resembles cloud of smoke. Good show of fragrant violet blue flowers, April–June (flower branches make choice dry arrangements).

Useful in natural desert gardens. Usually grows to 12 ft., but with summer water grows in bursts to as much as 30 ft. Easily grown from seed sown in warm weather. Sow in place or in small container and plant out.

DAMPIERA diversifolia

Goodeniaceae

PERENNIAL GROUND COVER

✿ ZONES 15–24

☼ FULL SUN

● REGULAR WATER

Dampiera diversifolia

Prostrate plant spreading by suckers and rooting from trailing stems. Leaves evergreen, narrowly oval, up to 1 in. long. In spring and summer, many small, dark blue flowers appear at end of new growth to produce circle effect. Spreads steadily in loose, well-drained soil, but not invasive or weedy.

DANDELION
(Taraxacum officinale)

Asteraceae (Compositae)

PERENNIAL

✿ ALL ZONES

☼ FULL SUN

● REGULAR WATER

Cultivated Dandelion

A weed in lawns and flower beds, it can also be a cultivated edible-leaf crop. Seeds sold in packets. Cultivated forms have been selected for larger, thicker leaves than those of common weed form. Tie leaves together to blanch interiors; eat like endive. Add tender leaves to mixed green salads; boil thick leaves like collards or other greens.

DAPHNE

Thymelaeaceae

EVERGREEN, SEMIEVERGREEN, DECIDUOUS SHRUBS

✿ ZONES VARY BY SPECIES

☼ ◑ EXPOSURE NEEDS VARY BY SPECIES

● MOST NEED LITTLE WATER

⬥ ALL PARTS, ESPECIALLY FRUITS, ARE POISONOUS

Daphne odora 'Marginata'

Of the many kinds, three (*D. burkwoodii*, *D. cneorum*, *D. odora*) are widely grown in West; most of the others are choice rock garden subjects with limited distribution in the nursery trade. Although some daphnes are easier to grow than others, all require fast-draining soil and careful summer watering. They are far more temperamental in California than in Northwest.

D. burkwoodii. Evergreen or semievergreen to deciduous. Zones 3–6, 14–17. Erect, compact growth to 3–4 ft.; closely set, narrow leaves and numerous small clusters of fragrant flowers (white fading to pink) around branch ends in late spring and again in late summer. Sun or light shade; little water. Use in shrub borders, at woodland edge, as foundation planting.

D. b. 'Carol Mackie'. Resembles the above, but has gold-edged leaves. White flowers open from white buds.

D. b. 'Somerset'. Similar to species, but larger (4–5 ft.), with pink flowers in May and June.

D. cneorum. GARLAND DAPHNE. Evergreen. Zones 2–9, 14–17. Matting and spreading; less than 1 ft. high and 3 ft. wide. Good container plant. Trailing branches covered with narrow, 1-in.-long, dark green leaves. Clusters of fragrant rosy pink flowers appear in April and May. Choice rock garden plant; give it partial shade in warm areas, full sun in cool-summer areas, and little water. After bloom is through, top-dress with mix of peat moss and sand to keep roots cool and induce additional rooting of trailing stems.

Varieties include 'Eximia', lower growing than the species and with larger flowers; 'Pygmaea Alba', 3 in. tall, 1 ft. wide, with white flowers; 'Ruby Glow', with larger, more deeply colored flowers and with late-summer rebloom; and 'Variegata', with gold-edged leaves.

D. genkwa. LILAC DAPHNE. Deciduous. Best in Zones 4–6, 16, 17. Erect, open growth to 3–4 ft. high and as wide. Before leaves expand, clusters of lilac blue, scentless flowers wreathe branches, making foot-long wands of blossoms. White fruit follows flowers. Leaves are oval, 2 in. long. Use in rock garden, shrub border. Full sun or partial shade, little water.

D. mantensiana. Evergreen. Zones 4–6, 15–17. Grows slowly to 1½ ft., spreading to 3 ft. Clusters of perfumed purple flowers at branch tips, May–June (and often through summer). Densely branched and well foliaged, it can be used in same way as low-growing azaleas. Leaves narrow, to 1¼ in. long. Little water; full sun or light shade.

D. mezereum. FEBRUARY DAPHNE. Deciduous. Zones 1–7, 14–17. Rather gawky, stiffly twigged, erect growth to 4 ft. with roundish, 2–3-in.-long, thin leaves. Should be planted in groups. Sun to partial shade, little water. Fragrant reddish purple flowers in short stalkless clusters are carried along branches in February before leaf-out and continue until April. May go dormant by late July or August. Clusters of red fruit follow flowers.

D. m. 'Alba'. Same as above but with white flowers, yellow fruit; not as rangy in growth.

D. odora. WINTER DAPHNE. Evergreen. Zones 4–10, 12, 14–24. So much loved, so prized for the pervasive, pre-spring fragrance of its flowers that it continues to be widely planted in spite of its unpredictable behavior. Very neat, handsome plant usually to about 4 ft. high and spreading wider; occasionally grows 8–10 ft. high. Rather narrow, 3-in.-long leaves are thick and glossy. Charming flowers of pink to deep red on outside, with creamy pink throats, appear in nosegay clusters at ends of branches, February–March.

D. odora needs much air around its roots, so plant in porous soil. Dig planting hole twice as wide as root ball and 1½ times as deep. Refill with 1 part soil, 1 part fine sand, 2 parts ground bark. To create ideal drainage: before refilling hole, drill through bottom until you hit a better-draining soil layer. Refill that chimney with mixture, too. Set top of root ball higher than soil surface. If you grow it in a container, use the same mix.

In Zones 18–24, transplanting an existing *D. odora* often fails; digging cuts roots, plant suffers, water molds get at it. Transplanting works in Zones 4–9, 14–17.

Plant this daphne where it can get at least 3 hours of shade a day. If possible, shade soil around roots with living ground cover. A pH of 7.0 is right for it (important in Zones 4–6). Feed right after bloom with complete fertilizer but not acid plant food.

During dry season, water as infrequently as plant will allow. Little or no water in summer increases flowering next spring and helps prevent death from water molds.

D. o. 'Alba'. Plain green leaves, white flowers. Terminal growth sometimes distorted by fasciation (cockscomb-like growths).

D. o. 'Leucanthe'. Vigorous and relatively disease resistant, with dark green leaves and a profusion of pale pink flowers with white interiors.

D. o. 'Marginata' ('Aureo-Marginata'). More widely grown than species. Leaves are edged with band of yellow.

DAPHNE PRUNING? IT'S SPECIAL

Correct the shape of a *D. odora* by cutting late-winter flower clusters to wear as corsages or to show. Make cuts to outfacing buds to promote spreading, to infacing ones to promote upward growth. Cut stems of deciduous kinds for bouquets while they are in bud: put them in water indoors and buds will open.

DARLINGTONIA californica

CALIFORNIA PITCHER PLANT, COBRA LILY

Sarraceniaceae

NOVELTY PERENNIAL

⚡ ZONES 4–7, 14–17

☼ ◑ FULL SUN OR PARTIAL SHADE

💧 KEEP SOIL MOIST AT ALL TIMES

Darlingtonia californica

Native to bogs in mountains of Northern California and Oregon. Grow in containers in sunny spot indoors or in greenhouse. Interesting for its unusual leaves and habit of digesting insects. Plant grows in clumps of 1–2-ft., tubelike, yellow-green, veiny leaves, hooded at top. Hood has translucent spots. At mouth opening are two flared lobes, often reddish in color. Insects are lured into this leafy trap by sticky glands. Once insects are inside, downward pointing hairs prevent escape. Insects fall to base of leaf and decay; when they reach a soluble state, they become protein food absorbed by plant's cells.

Striking flowers, nodding at ends of 2½–4-ft. stems, appear April–June. Long, slender, pale green sepals; shorter dark purple petals. Blooms followed by mahogany brown seed capsules.

Pot in live sphagnum moss. Water overhead. Dry fertilizer, saline water are harmful. Collected plants are packaged and sold in a few nurseries and specialty shops, generally from October through June. They rarely thrive beyond a season or two.

DARMERA peltata
(Peltiphyllum peltatum)

UMBRELLA PLANT, INDIAN RHUBARB

Saxifragaceae

PERENNIAL

⚡ ZONES 1–7, 14–20

◑ PARTIAL SHADE

💧 HEAVY WATERING

Darmera peltata

Native to mountains of Northern California and southern Oregon. Large, round clusters of pink flowers appear on bare stalks to 6 ft. tall in spring. Shield-shaped leaves 1–2 ft. wide appear later on 2–6-ft. stalks. Stout rhizomes to 2 in. thick grow in damp ground or even into streams. A spectacular plant for pond, stream, or damp, cool woodland site.

FOR INFORMATION ON SELECTING PLANTS

PLEASE SEE PAGES 45–128

DASYLIRION

SOTOL

Agavaceae

EVERGREEN SHRUBS

⚡ ZONES VARY BY SPECIES

☼ FULL SUN

◐ NO WATER ONCE ESTABLISHED

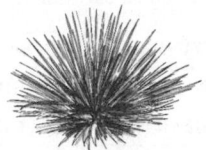

Dasylirion wheeleri

Native to deserts and mountains of the Southwest. Clumps of narrow grassy leaves spring from a woody base that can with age grow into a treelike trunk. Tiny greenish white flowers are tightly clustered on a tall narrow spike. Use in desert landscapes with other desert plants.

D. longissima. MEXICAN GRASS TREE. Zones 12–24. Mexico native. Narrow leaves may reach 6 ft. Trunk is slow to form, but may reach 10 ft.

D. wheeleri. DESERT SPOON, SOTOL. Zones 10–24, most widely used in 10–13. Spiky, bluish gray leaves to 3 ft. are stiffer than those of *D. longissima*. Inch-wide leaves slowly build a trunk to 3 ft. tall, covered with dried, drooping shag of old leaves. Base of each leaf broadens where it joins the trunk to form a long-handled spoon prized in arrangements. Eventually produces tiny flowers on tall, slender spike (9–15 ft. tall).

DATE PALM. See PHOENIX	**p. 415**
DATURA. See BRUGMANSIA	**p. 191**
DAUBENTONIA tripetii. See SESBANIA tripetii	**p. 484**

DAVALLIA trichomanoides

SQUIRREL'S FOOT FERN

Polypodiaceae

FERN

⚡ ZONES 17, 23, 24; OR INDOORS

◑ PARTIAL SHADE

◐ 💧 WATER LESS THAN OTHER FERNS

Davallia trichomanoides

Very finely divided fronds to 1 ft. long, 6 in. wide, rise from light reddish brown, furry rhizomes (like squirrel's feet) that creep over soil surface. Hardy to 30°F; can be used in mild-winter areas as small-scale ground cover in partly shaded areas. Best use in any climate is as hanging basket plant. Use light, fast-draining soil mix. Feed occasionally. For similar fern, see *Humata tyermannii*.

DAVIDIA involucrata

DOVE TREE

Nyssaceae

DECIDUOUS TREE

⚡ ZONES 4–9, 14–21

☼ ◑ FULL SUN ON COAST, PARTIAL SHADE INLAND

💧 REGULAR WATER

Davidia involucrata

Native to China. Tree to 35 ft. in Pacific Northwest (higher in California), with rounded crown and strong branching pattern. Has clean look in and out of leaf. When it flowers in May, general effect is that of white doves resting among green leaves—or as some say, like handkerchiefs drying on branches. Because leaves are already out at bloom time, blossoms aren't as showy as smaller flowers of deciduous fruit trees.

Leaves are vivid green, 3–6 in. long, roundish to heart shaped. Small, clustered, red-anthered flowers are carried between two large, unequal, white or creamy white bracts; one 6 in. long, other about 4 in. Brown fruit about the size of a golf ball hangs on tree well into winter. ▸

Plant it by itself; it should not compete with other flowering trees. Nice in front of dark conifers where vivid green and white stand out.

DELOSPERMA

ICE PLANT

Aizoaceae

SUCCULENTS

ZONES VARY BY SPECIES

FULL SUN

NO WATER NEAR COAST, SOME WATER INLAND

Delosperma 'Alba'

The huge group called *Delosperma* includes a useful ground cover and two of the hardiest ice plants. All thrive in full sun with good drainage and just enough water to keep them looking bright and fresh.

D. 'Alba'. WHITE TRAILING ICE PLANT. Zones 12–24. Dwarf, spreading, rooting freely from stems. Good ground and bank cover with lively green, fleshy, roundish leaves and small white flowers that attract bees. Plant 1 ft. apart for quick cover.

D. cooperi. All zones. One of the two hardiest ice plants. Grows 5 in. tall, 2 ft. wide. Brilliant, shining purple flowers bloom all summer long. Tolerates 0°F if protected by snow or mulch.

D. nubigenum. All zones. Hardiest of all ice plants, it has withstood −25°F. Barely 1 in. high, spreading to 3 ft. Fleshy, cylindrical, bright green leaves turn red in fall, green up again in spring. Bright golden yellow flowers, 1–1½ in. wide, blanket plants in spring. Effective rock garden plant in mountain climates.

DELPHINIUM

Ranunculaceae

PERENNIALS, SOME TREATED AS ANNUALS

ZONES VARY BY SPECIES

FULL SUN

REGULAR WATER

Delphinium elatum

Most people associate delphiniums with blue flowers, but color range also includes white and shades of red, pink, lavender, purple, and yellow. Leaves are lobed or fanlike, variously cut and divided. Taller hybrids offer rich colors in elegant spirelike form. All kinds are effective in borders and make good cut flowers; lower-growing kinds serve well as container plants. Blossoms attract birds.

All kinds are easy to grow from seed. In mild-winter areas, sow fresh seed in flats or pots of light soil mix in July or August; set out transplants in October for bloom in late spring and early summer. (In mild-winter climates, most perennial forms are short lived, often treated as annuals.) In cold climates, refrigerate summer-harvested seed in airtight containers until time to sow. Sow seed in March or April, set out transplants in June or July for first bloom by September (and more bloom the following summer).

Delphiniums need rich, porous soil, and regular fertilizing. Improve poor or heavy soils by blending in soil conditioners. Add lime to strongly acid soils. Work small handful of superphosphate into bottom of hole before setting out plant. Be careful not to cover root crown. Protect from snails, slugs.

D. ajacis. See Consolida ambigua

D. belladonna. Sturdy, bushy perennial. Zones 1–9, 14–24. To 3–4 ft. Deeply cut leaves; short-stemmed, airy flower clusters. Varieties: 'Belladonna', light blue; 'Bellamosum', dark blue; 'Casa Blanca', white; 'Cliveden Beauty', deep turquoise blue. All have flowers 1½–2 in. across, are longer lived than tall hybrids listed under *D. elatum*.

D. cardinale. SCARLET LARKSPUR. Perennial. Zones 14–24. Native to California coastal mountains, Monterey County south. Erect stems grow 3–6 ft. tall from deep, thick, woody roots. Leaves 3–9 in. wide, with deep, narrow lobes. Flowers 1 in. across, with scarlet calyx and spur and yellow, scarlet-tipped petals; May–June bloom. Sow seed early for first-year bloom.

D. elatum. CANDLE DELPHINIUM, CANDLE LARKSPUR. Perennial. Zones 1–10, 14–24. Along with *D. cheilanthum* and others, this 3–6-ft. Siberian species, with small dark or dull purple flowers, is parent of modern tall-growing delphinium strains such as spectacular Pacific strain.

Pacific strain delphinium hybrids (also called Giant Pacific, Pacific Hybrids, and Pacific Coast Hybrids) grow up to 8 ft. tall, come in selected color series such as 'Summer Skies', light blue; 'Blue Bird', medium blue; 'Blue Jay', medium to dark blue; 'Galahad', clear white with white center; 'Percival', white with black center. Other purple, lavender, pink named varieties also sold.

Like Pacific strain but shorter (2–2½ ft. tall) are the Blue Fountains, Blue Springs, and Magic Fountains strains. Even shorter is the Stand Up strain (15–20 in.). These shorter strains seldom require staking.

Other strains have flowers in shades of lilac pink to deep raspberry rose, clear lilac, lavender, royal purple, and darkest violet. Wrexham strain, tall growing with large spikes, was developed in England. Grow as annuals in Zones 12, 13. For annual delphiniums (larkspurs), see *Consolida ambigua*.

D. grandiflorum (D. chinense). CHINESE or BOUQUET DELPHINIUM. Short-lived perennial treated as biennial or annual. All zones. Bushy, branching, 1 ft. tall or less. Varieties include 'Dwarf Blue Mirror', 1 ft., upward-facing flowers of deep blue; and 'Tom Thumb', 8 in. tall, pure gentian blue flowers.

D. nudicaule. SCARLET LARKSPUR. Perennial. Zones 5–7, 14–24. Native of Northern California, southwestern Oregon. Slender plant to 1–3 ft. tall. Leaves long stalked, mostly basal, broadly divided. Flowers few, long spurred, red. Sun or half shade; best in woodland situations.

DENDROMECON

BUSH POPPY

Papaveraceae

EVERGREEN SHRUBS

ZONES 5–8, 14–24

BEST IN FULL SUN

THRIVE IN DRY SOIL ONCE ESTABLISHED

Have been grown in Zone 5 as south-wall shrubs. Both species here give showy display of bright yellow, 2-in.-wide, poppylike flowers. Use for banks and roadsides, with other native shrubs.

Dendromecon harfordii

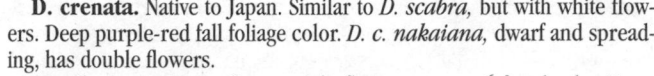
D. harfordii (D. rigida harfordii). ISLAND BUSH POPPY. Native to Santa Cruz and Santa Rosa islands off coast of Southern California. Rounded or spreading large shrub or small tree to 20 ft. Leaves deep green, to 3 in. long, half as wide. Free flowering April–July; scattered bloom throughout year. Prune to thin or shape after bloom.

D. rigida. BUSH POPPY. Native to dry chaparral in lower elevations in California. Untidy growing wild. Freely branched shrub 2–8 ft. tall, with shredding, yellowish gray or white bark. Thick, veiny, gray-green leaves 1–4 in. long. Flowers March–June. Prune back to 2 ft. after flowering.

DEODAR CEDAR. See CEDRUS deodara p. 215

DESCHAMPSIA

TUFTED HAIR GRASS	
Poaceae (Gramineae)	
PERENNIAL GRASSES	
✄ ALL ZONES	
☼ ☽ FULL SUN OR PARTIAL SHADE	
◖ ● STAY EVERGREEN WITH WATER	

Deschampsia caespitosa vivipara

Tufted hair grass is native to much of North America, but most garden varieties are imports from European nurseries. The native California form is quite tolerant of aridity and shade, with dark green foliage clumps 1½–2 ft. tall obscured by fine clouds of yellow blossoms in spring. These fade to gray by summer. A good ground cover under native oaks. *D. holciformis*, Pacific hair grass, is darker green, finer in texture, and less water independent.

D. caespitosa vivipara. Darkest green foliage and odd inflorescences that produce plantlets instead of flowers. These droop to the ground.

D. c. 'Bronzeschleier' ('Bronzy Veil') and *D. c.* 'Goldgehaenge' have bronzy yellow and golden yellow 3-ft. inflorescences.

DESERT BROOM. See BACCHARIS sarothroides — p. 173

DESERT HOLLY. See ATRIPLEX hymenelytra — p. 171

DESERT HONEYSUCKLE. See ANISACANTHUS thurberi — p. 152

DESERT IRONWOOD. See OLNEYA tesota — p. 393

DESERT MARIGOLD. See BAILEYA multiradiata — p. 174

DESERT OLIVE. See FORESTIERA neomexicana — p. 297

DESERT SPOON. See DASYLIRION wheeleri — p. 259

DESERT WILLOW. See CHILOPSIS linearis — p. 223

DEUTZIA

Saxifragaceae	
DECIDUOUS FLOWERING SHRUBS	
✄ ZONES 1–11, 14–17	
☼ ☽ FULL SUN OR LIGHT SHADE	
● REGULAR WATER	

Deutzia rosea

They are best used among evergreens, where they can make a show when in flower, then blend back in with other greenery during the rest of the year. Their May flowering coincides with that of late-spring bulbs such as tulips and Dutch iris.

Prune after flowering. With low- or medium-growing kinds, cut some of oldest stems to ground every other year. Prune tall-growing kinds severely by cutting back wood that has flowered. Cut to outward-facing side branches.

D. crenata. Native to Japan. Similar to *D. scabra*, but with white flowers. Deep purple-red fall foliage color. *D. c. nakaiana*, dwarf and spreading, has double flowers.

D. elegantissima. Bears pink flowers on a 6-ft. shrub. *D. e.* 'Rosealind', 4–5 ft. tall and spreading, has deep rose flowers.

D. gracilis. SLENDER DEUTZIA. Native to Japan. To 6 ft. or less. Many slender stems arch gracefully, carry bright green, 2½-in., sharply toothed leaves and clusters of snowy white flowers. The variety 'Nikko' grows only 1–2 ft. tall by 5 ft. wide and can be used as a ground cover.

D. hybrida 'Pink-a-Boo'. Erect shrub to 6–8 ft. tall, 6 ft. wide, with large clusters of pink flowers.

D. rosea. Hybrid. Low-growing shrub (to 3–4 ft.), with finely toothed, 1–3-in.-long leaves. Flowers pinkish outside, white inside, in short clusters.

D. scabra. Native to Japan, China. This plant and its varieties are robust shrubs 7–10 ft. tall. Leaves oval, 3 in. long, dull green, roughish to touch, with scallop-toothed edges. May–June flowers white or pinkish, in narrow, upright clusters. Best-known variety is *D. s.* 'Pride of Rochester', with large clusters of small, double, frilled flowers, rosy purple outside.

DIANELLA tasmanica

Liliaceae	
PERENNIAL	
✄ ZONES 0, 9, 14–24	
☼ ☽ PARTIAL SHADE; FULL SUN ALONG COAST	
● ●● FRUITS WELL WITH AMPLE WATER	

Dianella tasmanica

Fibrous-rooted plant with sturdy, swordlike leaves to 4–5 ft. Small, pale blue, summer-blooming flowers in loose clusters on straight, slender stalks, followed by glistening turquoise blue berries lasting 2 months or longer. Grow in partial shade (full sun along coast). Provide rich, porous soil and routine feeding. Attractive near swimming pools.

DIANTHUS

PINK	
Caryophyllaceae	
PERENNIALS, BIENNIALS, AND ANNUALS	
✄ ALL ZONES	
☼ ☽ LIGHT AFTERNOON SHADE IN HOT AREAS	
● REGULAR WATER	

Dianthus caryophyllus

Over 300 species and extremely large number of hybrids, many with high garden value. Most kinds form attractive evergreen mats or tufts of grasslike green, gray-green, blue-green, or blue-gray leaves. Single or double flowers in white and shades of pink, rose, red, yellow, and orange bloom in spring or summer, sometimes until frost. Many have rich, spicy fragrance.

Among dianthus are appealing border favorites such as cottage pink and sweet William, highly prized cut flowers such as carnation (clove pink), and rock garden miniatures. Many excellent named varieties not mentioned here are available locally.

All kinds of dianthus thrive in light, fast-draining soil. Carnations, sweet William, and cottage pinks need fairly rich soil; rock garden or alpine types require gritty growing medium, with added lime if soil is acid. Avoid overwatering. Shear off faded blooms. Sow seed of annual kinds in flats or directly in garden. Propagate perennial kinds by cuttings made from tips of growing shoots, by division or layering, or from seed.

Carnations and sweet William are subject to rust and fusarium wilt.

D. barbatus. SWEET WILLIAM. Vigorous biennial often grown as annual. Sturdy stems 10–20 in. high; leaves are flat, light to dark green, 1½–3 in. long. Dense clusters of white, pink, rose, red, purplish, or bicolored flowers, about ½ in. across, set among leafy bracts; not very fragrant. Sow seed in late spring for bloom following year. Double-flowered and dwarf (8–10-in.-tall) strains are obtainable from seed. Roundabout and Summer Beauty strains (1 ft.) bloom the first year from seed. Indian Carpet is only 6 in. tall.

D. caryophyllus. CARNATION, CLOVE PINK. Perennial. There are two distinct categories of carnations: florists' and border types. Both have double flowers, bluish green leaves, and branching, leafy stems often becoming woody at base.

Border carnations are bushier and more compact than florist type, 12–14 in. high. Flowers 2–2½ in. wide, fragrant, are borne in profusion. Effective as shrub border edgings, in mixed flower border, and in containers. Hybrid carnations grown from seed are usually treated as annuals, but often live over. 'Juliet' makes compact, foot-tall clumps with long production of 2½-in. scarlet flowers; 'Luminette', 2 ft. tall, is similar. Pixie Delight strain also is similar but includes full range of carnation colors. Knight series has strong stems, blooms in 5 months from seed; Bambino strain is a little slower to bloom. There is also a strain called simply Hanging Mixed, with pink- or red-flowered plants that sprawl or hang from pot or window box.

Florists' carnations are grown commercially in greenhouses, outdoors in gardens in mild-winter areas. Greenhouse-grown plants reach 4 ft., have fragrant flowers 3 in. wide in many colors—white, shades of pink and red, orange, purple, yellow; some are variegated. For large flowers, leave only terminal bloom on each stem, pinching out all other buds down to fifth joint, below which new flowering stems will develop. Stake to prevent sprawling. Start with strong cuttings taken from the most vigorous plants of selected named varieties. Sturdy plants conceal supports, look quite tidy.

D. chinensis. CHINESE PINK, RAINBOW PINK. Biennial or short-lived perennial; most varieties grown as annuals. Erect, 6–30 in. high; stems branch only at top. Stem leaves narrow, 1–3 in. long, ½ in. wide, hairy on margins. Basal leaves usually gone by flowering time. Flowers about 1 in. across, rose lilac with deeper colored eye; lack fragrance. Modern strains are compact (1 ft. tall or less) domes covered with bright flowers in white, pink, red, and all variations and combinations of those colors. 'Fire Carpet' is a brilliant solid red; 'Snowfire', white with a red eye. Telstar is an extra dwarf (6–8-in.) strain. Petals are deeply fringed on some, smooth edged on others. Some flowers have intricately marked eyes. Sow directly in ground in spring, in full sun, for summer bloom. Pick off faded flowers with their bases to prolong bloom.

THE STRONGLY FRAGRANT KINDS OF DIANTHUS

In addition to cheerful colors and striking patterns, most dianthus offer a strong, spicy, clovelike scent. The following are especially known for their nice nose: border carnations, *D. deltoides*, *D. gratianopolitanus*, *D. plumarius*, *D.* 'Rose Bowl', *D.* 'Tiny Rubies'.

D. deltoides. MAIDEN PINK. Hardy perennial forming loose mats. Flowering stems 8–12 in. high, with short leaves. Flowers, about ¾ in. across, borne at end of forked stems; petals sharp toothed, light or dark rose to purple or white, spotted with lighter colors. Blooms in summer, sometimes again in fall. Useful, showy ground or bank covers.

Named varieties include 'Vampire', deep red; 'Zing', bright scarlet; 'Zing Rose', rose red. Microchip is a mixture including pinks, reds, and whites, often with contrasting eyes. Although these bloom in just a few weeks from seed, they are still hardy perennials.

D. gratianopolitanus (D. caesius). CHEDDAR PINK. Perennial. Neat, compact mounds of blue-gray foliage on weak, branching stems up to 1 ft. long. Flowering stems erect, 3–12 in. high. Very fragrant pink blooms with toothed petals, May–June.

D. 'Little Joe'. Perennial. Irresistible little plant forming clump of deep blue-gray foliage 4–6 in. high and about 6 in. across. Crimson single flowers bloom from May to November if dead blooms are removed. Especially effective with rock garden campanulas.

D. plumarius. COTTAGE PINK. Perennial. Charming, almost legendary plant, cultivated for hundreds of years, used in developing many hybrids. Typically has loosely matted gray-green foliage. Flowering stems 10–18 in. tall; flowers spicily fragrant, single or double, with petals more or less fringed, in rose, pink, or white with dark centers. Highly prized are old laced pinks, with spicy-scented white flowers in which each petal is outlined in red or pink. Blooms from June to October. Indispensable edging for borders or for peony or rose beds. Perfect in small arrangements and old-fashioned bouquets.

D. 'Rose Bowl'. Perennial. Gray-green, very narrow leaves form tight mat 2–3 in. high. Richly fragrant, cerise rose flowers 1 in. across on 6-in. stems. Blooms almost continuously if spent blooms are removed regularly.

D. 'Spotty'. Resembles the above, but the pink flowers are heavily spotted with white.

D. 'Tiny Rubies'. Perennial. Tufts of gray foliage to 3 in. high, spreading to 4 in. Small, double, fragrant ruby red flowers in early summer. This and other dwarf kinds of dianthus are among longest lived, most attractive rock garden subjects and small-scale ground covers, with fresh-looking foliage at all seasons.

Diapensiaceae. The diapensia family contains a few perennials and tiny shrubs native to northern parts of the globe. Some, such as *Galax urceolata* and *Shortia*, are useful in shady gardens or rock gardens.

DIASCIA

TWINSPUR
Scrophulariaceae
PERENNIALS AND ANNUALS
✿ ZONES VARY BY SPECIES
☼ ◑ PARTIAL SHADE IN HOT-SUMMER AREAS
◑ INFREQUENT WATER

Diascia barberae

South African natives with rich salmon to coral pink flowers, each with two prominent spurs on back. Flowers in spikelike clusters at ends of stems. Use in rock gardens, borders, pots. Perennial sorts may die in winter if planted in heavy, wet soil.

D. barberae. Annual. All zones. Slender stems 6–12 in. tall. Sow seed directly in ground.

D. cordata. Perennial. Zones 7–9, 14–24. Low green mat with 10-in. sprays of salmon pink. Summer blooming.

D. fetcaniensis. Resembles 'Ruby Field' but is somewhat larger.

D. integerrima. Perennial. Zones 7–9, 14–24. Smooth gray foliage, rose pink flowers. To 1½ ft. tall.

D. rigescens. Perennial. Zones 7–9, 14–24. Sprawling stems make 2-ft.-wide clumps; turn up at ends to display 6–8-in. spikes of rich pink. Spring and summer bloom. Cut out old stems.

D. 'Ruby Field'. Perennial. Zones 7–9, 14–24. Similar to *D. cordata*, with longer bloom season. Hybrid between *D. barberae* and *D. cordata*.

D. vigilis. Perennial. Zones 7–9, 14–24. Grows to 20 in., with fleshy green leaves and light pink flowers over a long season.

DICENTRA

BLEEDING HEART
Fumariaceae
PERENNIALS
✿ ZONES 1–9, 14–24
● SHADE
◑ REGULAR WATER

Dicentra spectabilis

Short lived in mild-winter areas. Graceful, divided, fernlike foliage. Dainty flowers, usually heart shaped, in pink,

rose, or white on leafless stems. Combine handsomely with ferns, begonias, primroses, fuchsias, bergenias, hellebores. In general, dicentras need rich, light, moist, porous soil. Never let water stand around roots. Since foliage dies down in winter, mark clumps to avoid digging into roots in dormant season.

D. chrysantha. GOLDEN EARDROPS. Native to inner Coast Ranges and Sierra Nevada foothills of California. Erect perennial with sparse, blue-gray, divided leaves on stout, hollow, 4–5-ft. stems. Flowers golden yellow, short spurred, held upright in large clusters. Requires warmth, good drainage, not-too-rich soil. Has deep taproot, needs no water during flowering in spring and summer. Seed available from wildflower specialists.

D. eximia. FRINGED BLEEDING HEART. Native of northeastern United States. Forms tidy, nonspreading clumps 1–1½ ft. high. Leaves at base of plant, blue gray, more finely divided than those of *D. formosa*. Deep rose pink flowers with short, rounded spurs bloom May–August. Cut back in July or August for second growth and occasional repeat bloom. Variety 'Alba' has white flowers. 'Bountiful' has deep blue-green foliage and fuchsia red flowers. 'Zestful' has light green leaves and rose pink flowers throughout much of the year in mild-winter climates.

D. formosa. WESTERN BLEEDING HEART. Native to moist woods along Pacific coast. Leafless flower stalks 8–18 in. high, with clusters of pendulous pale or deep rose flowers on reddish stems, April–June. Blue-green foliage. Variety 'Sweetheart', beautiful white flowers, light green leaves, blooms May–October. 'Tuolumne Rose' has large blue-green leaves and tall clusters of large rose pink blooms. *D. f. oregana*, native of Siskiyou Mountains in southern Oregon and Northern California, grows about 8 in high, has translucent blue-green leaves, cream-colored flowers with rosy-tipped petals.

D. 'Luxuriant'. Hybrid of *D. eximia* and *D. peregrina*. Extremely vigorous. Dark blue-green foliage. Flowers are as dark as those of *D. eximia* 'Bountiful', even in full sun. Foliage mass 10 in. tall, flower spikes 18–20 in. high.

D. spectabilis. COMMON BLEEDING HEART. Native of Japan. Old garden favorite, showiest bleeding heart. Leafy-stemmed plants 2–3 ft. high. Leaves soft green, largest of all dicentras. In late spring, rose pink, pendulous, heart-shaped flowers, 1 in. or more long, with protruding white petals, borne on one side of arching stems. 'Alba' ('Pantaloons') is a lovely pure white form. Beautiful with maidenhair ferns and in arrangements with tulips and lilacs. In Southwest, you can sometimes establish bleeding heart permanently in cool moist spot in foothill canyons, but usual practice is to plant new roots in ground or container each year and discard plants in early summer after blooming. These dormant roots—fleshy and sometimes even woody—are available in late fall, winter, and earliest spring. Plant as soon as they become available in your area.

DICHELOSTEMMA

Amaryllidaceae

CORMS

ALL ZONES

BEST IN FULL SUN, TOLERATE SOME SHADE

NO DRY-SEASON WATERING

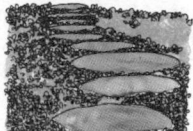

Dichelostemma ida-maia

Western natives usually sold as species of *Brodiaea*, and still considered brodiaeas by many botanists. See *Brodiaea* for culture. All have few, narrow, grassy leaves.

D. ida-maia (Brevoortia or Brodiaea ida-maia). FIRECRACKER FLOWER. Clusters of 6–20 or more pendulous, tubular, scarlet flowers tipped green. Blooms May–July. To 3 ft. Good dry-summer woodland plant.

D. pulchellum (D. capitatum, Brodiaea capitata). BLUE DICKS, WILD HYACINTH. Deep blue or violet blue flowers in tight, headlike cluster surrounded with purplish bracts. Blooms March–May. To 2 ft. Thrives in poor soils, summer-baked locations. Pretty spring flowers for sunny banks.

DICHONDRA micrantha

Convolvulaceae

GROUND COVER

ZONES 8–10, 12–24

FULL SUN OR PARTIAL SHADE

REGULAR OR HEAVY WATER

Dichondra micrantha

Ground-hugging plant that spreads by rooting surface runners. Small, round leaves look like miniature water lily pads. In shade and with heavy feeding and watering it can grow to 6 in. tall. It generally needs frequent mowing, but in sun and in areas subject to foot traffic—as between stepping stones—it stays low and seldom, if ever, needs mowing. Often sold as *D. carolinensis* or *D. repens*.

> ### DICHONDRA, THE FORMER LAWN
>
> In the mid–20th century, dichondra was widely hailed (and much planted) as a lawn in the mild West. Its several-decade popularity utterly delighted the flea beetles of the region. They especially loved to feed on big panels of the plant. History has since shown that the plant's best uses are in limited space: on small plots of ground, between stepping stones in a walk or terrace.

DICKSONIA

Dicksoniaceae

TREE FERNS

ZONES VARY BY SPECIES

SHADE; TAKE SUN IN ZONES 17, 24

FREQUENT WATER DURING HOT DRY WEATHER

Dicksonia antarctica

Hardy, slow growing, from Southern Hemisphere. Easy to transplant and establish. See Ferns for culture.

D. antarctica. TASMANIAN TREE FERN. Zones 8, 9, 14–17, 19–24. Native to southeastern Australia, Tasmania. Hardiest of tree ferns; well-established plants tolerate 20°F. Thick, red-brown, fuzzy trunk grows slowly to 15 ft. From top of trunk grow many arching, 3–6-ft. fronds; mature fronds are more finely cut than those of Australian tree fern (*Cyathea*). Stands full sun in coastal gardens.

D. squarrosa. Zones 17, 23, 24. Native to New Zealand. Slender, dark trunk grows slowly to 20 ft. tall. Flat crown of 8-ft.-long, stiff, leathery fronds. Much less frequently grown than *D. antarctica*.

Dicksoniaceae. The dicksonia family of tree ferns differs from the other tree fern family, Cyatheaceae, but only in technical details. One representative is *Dicksonia*.

DICTAMNUS albus

GAS PLANT, FRAXINELLA

Rutaceae

PERENNIAL

ZONES 1–9

FULL SUN OR PARTIAL SHADE

REGULAR WATER

Sturdy, long lived, extremely permanent in colder climates. Needs little care once established. Forms clumps 2½–4 ft. high. Strong

Dictamnus albus

D

lemony odor when rubbed or brushed against. Attractive, glossy, olive green leaves with 9–11 leaflets, each 1–3 in. long. Spikelike clusters of white flowers about 1 in. long with prominent greenish stamens, June–July. Worth growing from seed (a slow process). There are varieties that grow taller and more robust than species, with pink and rosy purple flowers and darker green leaves.

Effective in borders; combine white-flowered kind with yellow daylily, Siberian iris, taller campanulas. Good cut flower. Divide infrequently; divisions take 2–3 years before making a show. Propagate from seed sown in fall or spring or from root cuttings in spring. Common name, "gas plant," derives from this phenomenon: if lighted match is held near flowers on warm, still evenings, volatile oil exuded from glands on that part of plant will ignite and burn briefly.

DIDISCUS coeruleus. See TRACHYMENE coerulea   **p. 510**

DIEFFENBACHIA

DUMB CANE
Araceae
EVERGREEN INDOOR FOLIAGE PLANTS
☼ AMPLE NORTHERN LIGHT
◑ WATER WHEN SOIL SURFACE FEELS DRY
◈ SAP BURNS MOUTH, MAY PARALYZE VOCAL CORDS

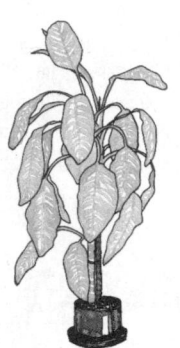

Dieffenbachia amoena

Striking variegated leaves. Colors vary from dark green to yellow green and chartreuse, with variegations in white or pale cream. Small plants generally have single stems, while older plants may develop multiple stems. Flowers like odd, narrow callas form on mature plants.

Turn pot occasionally. If plant gets leggy, air-layer it or root cuttings in water. Old, leggy plants, cut back to 6 in. above soil line, usually resprout with multiple stems. Repot when roots begin pushing plant up in pot. Once repotted, plant usually sends out new basal shoots. Potting soil should drain freely. Feed bimonthly in spring and summer with half-strength liquid fertilizer. Underfed, underwatered plants show amazingly strong hold on life, recovering from severe wilting when better conditions come. They will not withstand constant overwatering, and sudden change from low to high light level will burn leaves. However, you can move plants into sheltered patio or lanai in summer.

D. amoena. To 6 ft. or more. Broad, dark green, 1½-ft.-long leaves with narrow, white, slanting stripes on either side of midrib.

D. bausei. Grows to 3 ft. or more in height, with 1-ft. greenish yellow leaves with deep green blotches and white flecks.

D. 'Exotica'. Compact with small leaves. Leaves have dull green edges and much creamy white variegation. Midrib is creamy white.

D. maculata (D. picta). To 6 ft. or taller. Wide, oval, green leaves, 10 in. or more in length, have greenish white dots and patches.

D. m. 'Rudolph Roehrs'. To 6 ft., with 10-in. leaves of pale chartreuse, blotched with ivory and edged with green.

D. m. 'Superba'. Foliage thicker and slightly more durable than that of species; more creamy white dots and patches.

DIERAMA

FAIRY WAND
Iridaceae
CORMS
◿ ZONES 4–24
☼ FULL SUN
◑ REGULAR WATER DURING ACTIVE GROWTH

Dierama pulcherrimum

Native to South Africa. Swordlike 2-ft. leaves; slender, tough, arching stems 4–7 ft. tall, topped with pendulous, bell-shaped, mauve, purple, or white flowers. Effective against background of dark green shrubs or at edge of pool where graceful form can be displayed. Plant in moist soil. When dividing clumps, include several corms in each division.

D. pendulum. Flowers white, lavender pink, or mauve, 1 in. long, March–April.

D. pulcherrimum. Leaves very stiff. Flowers bright purple to almost white, 1½ in. long, May–June.

DIETES (Moraea)

FORTNIGHT LILY, AFRICAN IRIS
Iridaceae
EVERGREEN PERENNIALS GROWING FROM RHIZOMES
◿ ZONES 8, 9, 12–24
☼ ◑ FULL SUN OR PARTIAL SHADE
◒ ◈ BLOOM MORE FREELY WITH REGULAR WATER

Dietes vegeta

Fan-shaped clumps of narrow, stiff, irislike leaves. Flowers like miniature Japanese iris appear on branched stalks throughout spring, summer, and fall, sometimes well into winter in mild areas. Each flower lasts only a day but is quickly replaced by another. Bloom bursts seem to come at 2-week intervals—hence the name "fortnight lily." Break off forming seedpods to increase flower production and prevent volunteer plants. Effective near swimming pools.

Plant in any fairly good soil. Divide overgrown clumps in autumn or winter.

D. bicolor. To 2 ft. Flowers light yellow, about 2 in. wide, with maroon blotches. Cut flower stems to ground after blossoms fade.

D. hybrids. 'Lemon Drops' and 'Orange Drops' are occasionally seen. These resemble *D. vegeta,* but flowers are creamy, with conspicuous yellow or orange blotches.

D. vegeta (D. iridioides, Moraea iridioides). To 4 ft., with 3-in.-wide, waxy white flowers with orange-and-brown blotch, purple stippling. 'Johnsonii' is robust variety with large leaves and flowers. Break off old blossoms individually to prevent self-sowing and prolong bloom, but don't cut off long, branching flower stems (these last from year to year). Instead, cut back to lower leaf joint near base of plant. Excellent in permanent landscape plantings with pebbles, rocks, substantial shrubs.

DIGITALIS

FOXGLOVE
Scrophulariaceae
PERENNIALS OR BIENNIALS
◿ ALL ZONES
◐ LIGHT SHADE
◑ REGULAR WATER
◈ ALL PARTS ARE POISONOUS

Digitalis purpurea

Erect plants 2–8 ft. high with tubular flowers shaped like fingers of glove in purple, yellow, white, pastels. Hairy, gray-green leaves grow in clumps at base of plant. Use foxgloves for vertical display among shrubs or with ferns, taller campanulas, meadow rue. Bloom May–September; hummingbirds like the flowers.

Plant in rich soil. Set out plants in fall for bloom following spring, summer. Sow seed in spring. Bait for snails, slugs. After first flowering, cut main spike; side shoots develop, bloom until September. Plants self-sow freely.

D. ferruginea. RUSTY FOXGLOVE. Biennial or perennial with very leafy stems to 6 ft. Leaves deeply veined. Flowers ¾–1¼ in. long, yellowish, netted with rusty red, in long, dense spikes.

D. grandiflora (D. ambigua). YELLOW FOXGLOVE. Biennial or perennial. Hairy-leafed plant 2–3 ft. high. Toothed leaves wrap around stem. Large flowers, 2–3 in. long, yellowish marked with brown.

D. mertonensis. True perennial with 2–3-ft. spikes of odd yet attractive coppery rose blooms. Though hybrid between two species, it comes true from seed.

D. purpurea. COMMON FOXGLOVE. Biennial, sometimes perennial. Naturalizes in shaded places. Variable, appears in many garden forms. Bold, erect, to 4 ft. high or more. Clumps of large, rough, woolly, light green leaves. Stem leaves short stalked, becoming smaller toward top of plant; these leaves are source of digitalis, a valued but highly poisonous medicinal drug. Flowers 2–3 in. long, pendulous, purple, spotted on lower, paler side, borne in one-sided, 1–2-ft.-long spikes. Several garden strains: Excelsior, 5 ft., has fuller spikes than species, with flowers more horizontally held to show off interior spotting; Foxy, 3 ft., performs as an annual, blooming in 5 months from seed; Gloxiniiflora, 4 ft., has flowers that are individually larger and open wider than the species; Monstrosa, 3 ft., has an unusual trait: the topmost flower of each spike is open or bowl shaped and 3 in. wide; Shirley is a tall (6-ft.), robust strain in full range of colors. Volunteer foxglove seedlings are frequently white or light colors.

FOXGLOVES—SHOWY TOWERS

Flowers on spikes 3 ft. tall or more add charm and dimension to a garden. And foxgloves are perhaps the easiest of the towering flowering plants. An especially showy use for these plants is to fill a boxwood-edged flower bed with just one kind. Set the plants 1 ft. apart. Or mass them at the back of perennial borders.

DIMORPHOTHECA

AFRICAN DAISY, CAPE MARIGOLD

Asteraceae (Compositae)

ANNUALS

☰ ALL ZONES; BETTER INLAND THAN COASTAL

☼ FULL SUN

◐ TAKE SOME ARIDITY

Dimorphotheca sinuata

Gay, free-blooming plants with daisy flowers, unsurpassed for winter and spring color in dry, warm-winter areas. Broadcast seed in late summer or early fall where plants are to grow. Best in light soil. Flowers close when shaded, during heavy overcast, and at night. Use in broad masses as ground cover, in borders and parking strips, along rural roadsides, as filler among low shrubs.

D. barberae. See Osteospermum barberae

D. ecklonis. See Osteospermum ecklonis

D. fruticosa. See Osteospermum fruticosum

D. pluvialis (D. annua). Branched stems 4–16 in. high. Leaves to 3½ in. long, 1 in. wide, coarsely toothed. Flower heads 1–2 in. across; rays white above, violet or purple beneath; yellow center. Variety 'Glistening White', dwarf form with flower heads 4 in. across, is especially desirable.

D. sinuata. Best known of annual African daisies. Plants 4–12 in. high. Leaves narrow, 2–3 in. long, with a few teeth or shallow indentations. Flower heads 1½ in. across, with orange-yellow rays, sometimes deep violet at base, and yellow center. Hybrids between this species and *D. pluvialis* come in white and shades of yellow, orange, apricot, and salmon, often with contrasting dark centers.

Excellent for winter–spring color in Zones 10–13; reseeds yearly. Needs some supplemental water October–March if winter rains don't come. Leave area dry over summer. Usually sold as *D. aurantiaca.*

For other plants known as African daisy, see *Arctotis, Osteospermum.*

DIOON

Zamiaceae

CYCADS

☰ ZONES VARY BY SPECIES

◐ PARTIAL SHADE

◕ REGULAR WATER

Dioon edule

In general, resemble *Cycas revoluta* and take same culture. Dioons are more tender and less frequently sold, even slower in growth.

D. edule. Zones 12, 13, 17, 19–24. Very slow. Eventually forms cylindrical trunk 6–10 in. wide, 3 ft. high. Leaves spreading, slightly arching, 3–5 ft. long, made of many leaflets toothed at tips or smooth edged. Leaves dusty blue green, soft, feathery on young plants; darker green, more rigid, hard, shiny on mature plants.

D. spinulosum. Zones 21–24. Slow growth to 12 ft. Leaves to 5 ft. long, with up to 100 narrow, spine-toothed, dark green, 6–8-in.-long leaflets. Protect from frosts.

DISANTHUS cercidifolius

Hamamelidaceae

DECIDUOUS SHRUB

☰ ZONES 4–7, 14–17

☼◐ SUN OR LIGHT SHADE

◕ REGULAR WATER

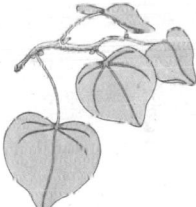

Disanthus cercidifolius

Shrub 10–12 ft. tall, somewhat narrower with nearly round, smooth, bluish green leaves 2–4 in. wide. Flowers are tiny, purplish, inconspicuous. Plant grown for its splendid fall color—deep red with orange tints.

DISTICTIS

Bignoniaceae

EVERGREEN VINES

☰ ZONES VARY BY SPECIES

☼◐ FULL SUN OR PARTIAL SHADE

◕ REGULAR WATER

Distictis buccinatoria

Spectacular vines for milder climates. Climb by tendrils and have trumpet-shaped flowers. To 20–30 ft. tall. Hardy to 24°F.

D. buccinatoria (Bignonia cherere, Phaedranthus buccinatorius). BLOOD-RED TRUMPET VINE. Zones 8, 9, 14–24. Leaves have two oblong to oval leaflets 2–4 in. long. Clusters of 4-in.-long, trumpet-shaped flowers stand out well from vine. Color is orange red fading to bluish red, with yellow throat. Flowers appear in bursts throughout year when weather warms. Effective on fence, high wall, arbor. Prune yearly to keep under control. Give protected site in interior valleys. Generously feed and water young plants until established.

D. laxiflora (D. lactiflora, D. cinerea). VANILLA TRUMPET VINE. Zones 16, 22–24. Native to Mexico. More restrained than most trumpet vines and requires less pruning. Leaves, with two or three deep green, oblong, 2½-in.-long leaflets, make attractive pattern all year. The 3½-in.-long vanilla-scented trumpets, violet at first, fading to lavender and white, appear in generous clusters throughout warmer months, sometimes giving 8 months of bloom.

D. 'Rivers'. ROYAL TRUMPET VINE. Zones 16, 22–24. Plants sold under this name have larger leaves and flowers than other kinds and are much more vigorous. Substantial, glossy deep green leaves give them better winter appearance. Purple trumpets (to 5 in.) marked orange inside. Grows a little more slowly than *D. buccinatoria;* easier to keep neat. Sometimes labeled *D. riversii.*

Distictis 'Rivers'

DIZYGOTHECA elegantissima. See SCHEFFLERA elegantissima p. 478

DODECATHEON

SHOOTING STAR
Primulaceae
PERENNIALS
✂ ALL ZONES
☀ ◑ FULL SUN OR PARTIAL SHADE
💧 REGULAR WATER DURING GROWTH AND BLOOM

Dodecatheon hendersonii

Mostly native to West. Spring flowers somewhat like small cyclamen, few to many in cluster on leafless stem ranging from a few inches to 2 ft. tall. Colors of many species range from white to pink, lavender to magenta. Pale green leaves in basal rosettes dry up in summer heat. Need porous, rich, well-drained soil. Let soil dry out after bloom.

Rarely available in nurseries. Buy seed from specialists in native plant seeds or gather from wild plants. Grow species native to your area; not all are hardy everywhere. Western *D. hendersonii* has leaves to 6 in., 3–15 white to magenta flowers on 1½-ft. stalks.

DODONAEA

HOP BUSH, HOPSEED BUSH
Sapindaceae
EVERGREEN SHRUBS
✂ ZONES VARY BY SPECIES
☀ ◑ FULL SUN OR LIGHT SHADE
◊ 💧 LITTLE OR NO WATER ONCE ESTABLISHED

Tough, tolerant shrubs mostly from Australia, although the most common species, *D. viscosa,* is native to our own Southwest as well as many other parts of the world. All tolerate wind, poor soil, heat. Foliage may be finely divided and fernlike or undivided. Flowers are insignificant, but seedpods are often showy and long lasting.

Dodonaea viscosa

D. adenophora, D. microzyga. Zones 8, 9, 14–24. Plants sold under these names are probably forms of *D. tenuifolia.* Spreading shrub 3–10 ft. tall with finely cut leaves and very showy red fruits.

D. boroniifolia. Zones 8, 9, 14–24. Grows 1½–6 ft. tall, with spreading branches and shiny, dark green, finely cut leaves 1½ in. long. Fruiting capsules ¾ in. wide are pink to purplish red.

D. multijuga. Zones 8, 9, 14–24. Shrub to 6 ft., with finely cut leaves and showy red fruits.

D. viscosa. Zones 7–9, 12–24. Native to Arizona and elsewhere in warmer parts of the world. Fast growing, with many upright stems to 12–15 ft. high, spreading almost as wide (can be trained to tree form by cutting out all but single stem). Willowlike green leaves to 4 in. long.

Most popular variety is 'Purpurea', purple hop bush, selected form with rich bronzy green leaves that turn deeper in winter. Seedlings vary greatly in color; variety 'Saratoga' (grown from cuttings) is uniformly rich purple. Plant purple-leafed kinds in full sun to retain rich coloration; they will turn green in shade. Clusters of flowers are insignificant. Creamy to pinkish winged seedpods attractive in late summer.

Can be pruned as hedge or espalier or planted 6–8 ft. apart and left unpruned to become big informal screen. Its biggest asset is probably its wide cultural tolerance: it takes any kind of soil, ocean winds, dry desert heat. It's quite tolerant to aridity when established but will also take ample water (grows well in flower beds).

Native Arizona green form (Zones 10–13) is useful plant for the desert —hardier to cold and deeper rooted than the purple-leafed form. Pinkish orange, papery seeds stand out better against green foliage. With little water, stays a compact 6–8-ft. shrub; with more water, quickly grows to 15 ft.

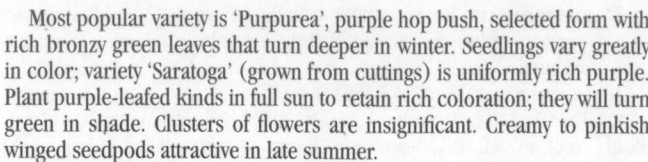

> ### DODONAEA MAKES HEDGES AND SCREENS
> This no-water-needed evergreen shrub serves beautifully as a clipped hedge or an unclipped screen. Growth is fast and uniform, maintenance easy. Set plants 3 ft. apart in a row to make a clipped hedge or 6 ft. apart to make a tall, wide, unpruned screen.

DOG-TOOTH VIOLET. See ERYTHRONIUM dens-canis	p. 280
DOGWOOD. See CORNUS	p. 242

DOLICHOS

Fabaceae (Leguminosae)
PERENNIAL TWINING VINES
✂ ZONES VARY BY SPECIES
☀ FULL SUN
💧 REGULAR WATER

Dolichos lablab

These twining vines produce dense cover of light green leaves divided like fans into three leaflets.

D. lablab. HYACINTH BEAN. Perennial vine usually grown as annual. All zones. Fast to 10 ft. Broad, oval leaflets to 3–6 in. long. Sweet pea–shaped purple or white flowers in loose clusters on long stems stand out from foliage. Flowers followed by velvety, beanlike pods to 2½ in. long. Grow plants like string beans for quick screening. Needs good drainage.

D. lignosus (Dipogon australis). AUSTRALIAN PEA VINE. Zones 16, 17, 21–24. Somewhat woody vine with small, triangular, 1½-in.-long leaflets and small rose purple flowers clustered at ends of long stalks. Evergreen in mild winters. Grow from seed and train on trellis or frame for summer screen. Grows to 10 ft. or more.

DORONICUM

LEOPARD'S BANE
Asteraceae (Compositae)
PERENNIALS
✂ ZONES 1–7, 14–17
◑ PARTIAL SHADE
💧 REGULAR WATER

Doronicum cordatum

Showy, bright yellow, daisylike flowers on long stems rise in early spring from mounds of dense, dark green, usually heart-shaped leaves. Divide clumps every 2–3 years; young plants bloom best.

Use in groups under high-branching deciduous trees; combine with white, purple, or lavender tulips, blue violas or forget-me-nots; use in front of purple lilacs or with hellebores at edge of woodland or shade border. Good cut flowers.

D. cordatum (D. caucasicum). Flower heads 2 in. across, borne singly on 1–1½-ft. stems. Increases by stolons. Variety 'Magnificum' more robust than species, with larger flowers; 'Finesse' has 3-in. flowers.

D. plantagineum. PLANTAIN LEOPARD'S BANE. Grows from tuberous rhizomes. Stout stems 2–5 ft. tall; rather coarse foliage. Early blooming; flowers 2–4 in. across, few to a stem. Best in wild garden.

DOROTHEANTHUS bellidiformis

LIVINGSTONE DAISY	
Aizoaceae	
SUCCULENT ANNUAL	
✂ ALL ZONES	
☼ FULL SUN	
◗ MODERATE WATER	

*Dorotheanthus
bellidiformis*

Ice plant, but unlike most others, an annual. Pretty and useful temporary carpet in poor, dry soil. Trailing, a few inches high, with fleshy, bright green leaves and daisylike, 2-in. flowers in white, pink, orange, red. Sow seed in warm weather. Comes into bloom quickly. Draws bees.

DORYCNIUM hirsutum

Fabaceae (Leguminosae)	
EVERGREEN SHRUB	
✂ ZONES 8, 9, 14–24	
☼ FULL SUN	
○ NO WATER ONCE ESTABLISHED	

Dorycnium hirsutum

Shrub or shrubby perennial to 2 ft. tall, with dense foliage of furry gray-white leaves divided into three leaflets less than 1 in. long. White flowers with pink tints are borne in cloverlike heads. Useful for silvery white effects.

DOUGLAS FIR. See PSEUDOTSUGA menziesii   p. 443

DOVE TREE. See DAVIDIA involucrata   p. 259

DOXANTHA unguis-cati. See MACFADYENA unguis-cati   p. 364

DRABA

Brassicaceae (Cruciferae)	
ROCK GARDEN PERENNIALS	
✂ ZONES 1–7	
☼ FULL SUN	
◗ DON'T MISS A WATERING	

Draba aizoides

Out of a probable 300 species from the mountains and subarctic regions of the world, only a few can be mentioned. All are low matforming or cushion-forming plants with tightly clustered, tiny leaves in rosettes and yellow flowers (rarely white) in short, spikelike clusters. All require perfect drainage and, although they can endure great cold, dislike soggy soil. Use in rock gardens.

D. aizoides. Tufts of tiny rosettes make clumps 2–4 in. across. Flowering stems to 4 in. hold four to ten or more bright yellow, four-petaled flowers.

D. oligosperma. One of the more than dozen species native to the Rocky Mountain area, it makes silvery mats up to 1 ft. wide topped with yellow flowers.

DRACAENA

Agavaceae	
EVERGREEN, SMALL PALMLIKE TREES	
✂ ZONES VARY BY SPECIES	
☼ ◑ FULL SUN OR PARTIAL SHADE	
◗ TOLERATE SOME ARIDITY	

Dracaena draco

Essentially foliage plants, grown in house or on lanais; certain kinds can be grown outdoors, as noted below. Some show graceful fountain forms with broad, curved, ribbonlike leaves, occasionally striped with chartreuse or white. Some have very stiff, swordlike leaves. Almost never flower as house plants. In containers, water only when top ½–1 in. of soil is dry.

D. australis. See Cordyline australis

D. deremensis. Zone 24, protected from wind. Native to tropical Africa. Most commonly sold is variety 'Warneckii': erect, slow growing to an eventual 15 ft., with 2-ft.-long, 2-in.-wide leaves in rich green striped white and gray. 'Bausei' is green with white center stripe; 'Longii' has broader white center stripe; 'Janet Craig' has broad, dark green leaves. Compact versions of 'Janet Craig' and 'Warneckii' exist.

D. draco. DRAGON TREE. Zones 16, 17, 21–24. Native to Canary Islands. Stout trunk with upward-reaching or spreading branches topped by clusters of heavy, 2-ft.-long, sword-shaped leaves. Grows slowly to 20 ft. high and as wide. Makes odd but interesting silhouette. Clusters of greenish white flowers form at branch ends. After blossoms drop, stemmy clusters remain. Trim them off to keep plants neat.

D. fragrans. CORN PLANT. Zones 21, 23, 24, protected from wind. Native to west Africa. Upright, eventually to 20 ft. high, but slow growing. Heavy, ribbonlike, blue-green leaves to 3 ft. long, 4 in. wide. (Typical plant in 8 in. pot will bear leaves about 1½ ft. long.) Variety 'Massangeana' has broad yellow stripe in center of leaf. Other striped varieties are 'Lindenii' and 'Victoriae'.

D. marginata. Zones 21, 23, 24, protected from wind. Very easy to grow, very popular. Slender, erect, smooth gray stems to an eventual 12 ft carry chevron markings where old leaves have fallen. Stems topped by crowns of narrow, leathery leaves to 2 ft. long, ½ in. wide. Leaves are deep glossy green with narrow margin of purplish red. If plant grows too tall, cut off crown and reroot it. New crowns will appear on old stem. 'Tricolor' ('Candy Cane') adds narrow gold stripe to green and red.

Dracaena marginata

D. sanderana. Zones 21, 23, 24, protected from wind. Native to west Africa. Neat and upright, to a possible 6–10 ft., somewhat resembling young corn plant. Strap-shaped, 9-in.-long leaves striped with white.

For other plants often called dracaena, see *Cordyline*.

DRAGON TREE. See DRACAENA draco   p. 267

DRIMYS winteri

WINTER'S BARK	
Winteraceae	
SMALL EVERGREEN TREE	
✂ ZONES 8, 9, 14–24	
☼ ◑ ● TAKES SOME SUN NEAR COAST, SHADE INLAND	
◗ REGULAR WATER	

Drimys winteri

Native to southern Chile and Argentina. Slender, to 25 ft. Distinguished chiefly for clean foliage and dignified presence. Stems and branches, which

D

tend to droop gracefully, are mahogany red with aromatic bark. Bright green, leathery, fragrant leaves are elliptical, 5–10 in. long. Small clusters of jasmine-scented, creamy white flowers about 1 in. wide, appear in winter and spring. Usually multistemmed but easily trained to single trunk. May require pruning from time to time to maintain outline of pleasing symmetry. Provide good soil drainage.

DROSANTHEMUM

Aizoaceae

SUCCULENT PERENNIALS

⚘ ZONES 14–24

☼ BEST IN FULL SUN

💧 LITTLE OR NO WATER, ESPECIALLY NEAR COAST

Drosanthemum floribundum

The two ice plants described here are often confused with each other, although they are quite different. In both, leaves are covered by glistening dots that look like tiny ice crystals. And both have typical ice plant flowers with many narrow petals. Both endure poor soil.

D. floribundum. ROSEA ICE PLANT. Grows to 6 in. tall, but stems trail to considerable length or drape over rocks, walls. Best ice plant for reducing erosion on steep slopes. Pale pink, ¾-in.-wide flowers make sheets of color in late spring, early summer. Bees are fond of them.

D. hispidum. To 2 ft. tall, 3 ft. wide, less inclined to stem-root than is *D. floribundum.* Showy, 1-in. purple flowers in late spring, early summer. *D. floribundum* is often sold as *D. hispidum.*

DRUMSTICKS. See ALLIUM sphaerocephalum, CRASPEDIA globosa   **pp. 145, 247**

DRYAS

Rosaceae

PERENNIALS

⚘ ZONES 1–6

☼ FULL SUN

💧 WATER LESS THAN MOST PERENNIALS

Dryas octopetala

Choice plants for rock gardens. Evergreen or partially so; somewhat shrubby at base, forming carpet of leafy creeping stems. Shiny white or yellow strawberrylike flowers, May–July; ornamental seed capsules with silvery white tails.

D. drummondii. To 4 in. high. Leaves oblong, 1½ in. long, white and woolly beneath. Flowers nodding, bright yellow, ¾ in. across.

D. octopetala. Leaves 1 in. long. Flowers white, 1½ in. across, erect. Mats up to 2–3 ft. high.

D. suendermannii. Hybrid between two species above. Leaves oblong, 1–1½ in. long, thick textured, similar to oak leaves. Flowers yellowish in bud, white in full bloom, nodding.

DRYOPTERIS

WOOD FERN

Polypodiaceae

FERNS

⚘ ZONES 4–9, 14–24

☼ ● PARTIAL TO FULL SHADE

💧 💧 LITTLE TO REGULAR WATER

Dryopteris expansa

Native to many parts of world. Two natives of western United States and one exotic species are sometimes sold.

D. arguta. COASTAL or CALIFORNIA WOOD FERN. Native of Washington to Southern California. Dark green, finely cut, airy fronds to 2½ ft. tall. Not easy to grow in gardens; best naturalized in woods. Avoid overwatering.

D. erythrosora. Native to China, Japan. One of few ferns with seasonal color value: fronds are reddish when young, deep green in late spring, summer. Spreading, 1½–2 ft. tall.

D. expansa (D. dilatata). SPREADING WOOD FERN. Native to much of Northern Hemisphere, including western United States. Fronds 1–3 ft. tall, even more finely cut than those of *D. arguta.* Named varieties sometimes seen in northwestern nurseries. In Southern California, best in pots.

DUCHESNEA indica

INDIAN MOCK STRAWBERRY

Rosaceae

PERENNIAL GROUND COVER

⚘ ALL ZONES

☼ ◑ ● ANY EXPOSURE

💧 LITTLE WATER

Duchesnea indica

Grows like strawberry, with trailing stems that root firmly along ground. Bright green, long-stalked leaves with three leaflets. Yellow, ½-in. flowers are followed by red, ½-in., insipid-tasting fruit that stands above foliage rather than under leaves as in true strawberry. Grows readily without much care. Best used as ground cover among open shrubs or small trees. Plant 1–1½ ft. apart. In well-watered garden, can become rampant invader. Attracts birds.

DUDLEYA

Crassulaceae

ROSETTE-FORMING SUCCULENTS

⚘ ZONES 12, 13, 16, 17, 21–24

☼ FULL SUN

💧 TOLERATE SOME ARIDITY

Dudleya brittonii

Native to California, Arizona, Baja California. About 40 species are known, and some of these are common on California's coastal cliffs or inland hills. Best known in cultivation is *D. brittonii* (from Baja California), with 1½-ft.-wide leaf rosettes on stems that gradually lengthen into 1–2-ft. trunks. Leaves fleshy, covered with a heavy coat of chalky powder that can be rubbed off. Striking plant when well grown; needs bright light and shelter from rain, hail, and frost. Best under glass or plastic roof. Others are valued for use in containers, rock gardens, low borders. *D. caespitosa* (Southern California) and *D. farinosa* (Northern California) are familiar sea-cliff plants; both are sometimes called cliff lettuce.

DUMB CANE. See DIEFFENBACHIA   **p. 264**

DURANTA

Verbenaceae

EVERGREEN SHRUBS

⚘ ZONES VARY BY SPECIES

☼ FULL SUN

💧 CONSTANT MOISTURE

☠ DURANTA REPENS BERRIES ARE POISONOUS

Duranta repens

Glossy green leaves arranged in pairs or whorls along stem. Attractive blue flowers in clusters attract butterflies in summer, are followed by bunches of yellow berrylike fruit. Many plants sold as *D. stenostachya* are actually *D. repens.* Distinguishing characteristics described below. Valued for summer flowers and fruit. Use as quick, tall screen. Thrive in hot-summer areas. Need continual thinning and pruning to stay under control.

D. repens (D. erecta, D. plumieri). SKY FLOWER, GOLDEN DEW-DROP, PIGEON BERRY. Zones 13, 16, 17, 21–24. Native to southern Florida, West Indies, Mexico to Brazil. Fast growing to 10–25 ft. Tends to form multistemmed clumps; branches often drooping and vinelike. Stems may or may not have sharp spines. Oval to roundish leaves are 1–2 in. long, rounded or pointed at tip. Tubular, violet blue flowers flare to less than ½ in. wide. Fruit clusters 1–6 in. long. 'Alba' has white flowers.

D. stenostachya. BRAZILIAN SKY FLOWER. Zones 13, 16, 21–23. Not as hardy as *D. repens;* seems to require more heat and is not at its best in Zones 17, 24. Makes neater, more compact shrub than *D. repens,* usually growing to about 4–6 ft. (under ideal conditions, 15 ft.). Stems are spineless. Leaves are larger (3–8 in. long) than those of *D. repens* and taper to long, slender point. Lavender blue flowers are also somewhat larger; fruit clusters grow to 1 ft. long.

DUSTY MILLER. This name is given to a number of plants with gray foliage. The dusty miller of one region may be unknown in another. Among many dusty millers are *Artemisia stellerana, Centaurea cineraria, C. gymnocarpa, Chrysanthemum ptarmiciflorum, Lychnis coronaria,* and *Senecto cineraria.*

DUTCHMAN'S PIPE. See ARISTOLOCHIA durior   p. 165

DYMONDIA margaretae

Asteraceae (Compositae)
EVERGREEN PERENNIAL
✷ ZONES 15–24
☼ FULL SUN
◐ ● TAKES ARIDITY OR REGULAR WATER

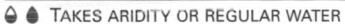

Dymondia margaretae

Ground cover. Native to South Africa. Grows in tight mats 2–3 in. deep; spreads slowly by offsets. Narrow (⅛-in.) leaves are 2–3 in. long, deep grayish green above and rolled at the edges to show cottony white undersides. Summer flowers are yellow, 1–1½-in.-wide daisies half buried in the foliage. Deep roots give established plants considerable tolerance of aridity, but plants spread faster if watered. Use between paving blocks and stepping stones, in rock gardens; can take light foot traffic.

DYSSODIA tenuiloba
(Thymophylla tenuiloba)

DAHLBERG DAISY, GOLDEN FLEECE
Asteraceae (Compositae)
SUMMER ANNUAL; MAY LIVE OVER AS PERENNIAL
✷ ZONES 8–14, 18–20
☼ FULL SUN
◐ ● WATER LESS THAN MOST ANNUALS

Dyssodia tenuiloba

Southwest native. To 1 ft. high. Divided, threadlike leaves make dark green background for yellow flower heads, which look much like miniature golden marguerites. Use for massed display or pockets of color. Start in flats or plant in place, preferably in sandy soil. Blooms early summer to fall, to early winter in warm climates. Pull out plants that get ragged with age.

EASTER CACTUS. See RHIPSALIDOPSIS gaertneri   p. 454

EASTER LILY CACTUS. See ECHINOPSIS   p. 270

EASTER LILY VINE. See BEAUMONTIA grandiflora   p. 180

ECHEVERIA

Crassulaceae
SUCCULENTS
✷ ZONES VARY BY SPECIES
☼ ◐ FULL SUN OR PARTIAL SHADE
● TOLERATE ARIDITY; MAY NEED SUMMER WATER

Echeveria agavoides

All form rosettes of fleshy green or gray-green leaves, often marked or overlaid with deeper colors. Bell-shaped, nodding flowers, usually pink, red, or yellow, on long, slender, sometimes branched clusters. Good in rock gardens.

E. agavoides (Urbinia agavoides). Zones 8, 9, 12–24. Rosettes 6–8 in. across, with stiff, fleshy, smooth, bright green, sharp-pointed leaves that may be marked deep reddish brown at tips and edges. Flower stalks to 1½ ft. bear small red-and-yellow blooms.

E. crenulata. Zones 17, 21–24. Loose rosettes on short, thick stems. Pale green or white-powdered leaves to 1 ft. long and 6 in. wide, with wavy, crimped, purplish red edges. Flower clusters to 3 ft. high, with a few yellow-and-red flowers. Striking plant. Shelter from hottest sun; water frequently in summer.

E. elegans. HEN AND CHICKS. Zones 8, 9, 12–24. Tight, grayish white rosettes to 4 in. across, spreading freely by offsets. Flowers pink, lined yellow, in clusters to 8 in. long. Common, useful for pattern planting, edging, containers. Can burn in hot summer sun.

E. hybrids. Zones 8, 9, 12–24. Generally have large, loose rosettes of big leaves on single or branched stems. Leaves are crimped, waved, wattled, or heavily shaded with red, bronze, or purple. All are splendid pot plants; they do well in open ground in mild coastal gardens. Among them are 'Arlie Wright', with large, open rosettes of wavy-edged, pinkish leaves; 'Cameo', with large blue-gray leaves, each centered with a large raised lump of the same color; and 'Perle von Nürnberg', with pearly lavender blue foliage. Smaller, with short, close-set leaves, is 'Doris Taylor'; its leaves are densely covered with short hairs. Showy, nodding flowers are red and yellow.

E. imbricata. HEN AND CHICKS. Zones 8, 9, 12–24. Rosettes 4–6 in. across, saucer-shaped, gray green. Loose clusters of small, bell-shaped, orange-red flowers. Makes offsets very freely. Probably most common hen and chicks in California gardens.

Echeveria imbricata

E. secunda. HEN AND CHICKS. Zones 8, 9, 14–24. Gray- or blue-green rosettes, to 4 in. across. Makes offsets freely. *E. s. glauca (E. glauca),* its leaves faintly edged purple red, forms purplish blue-green rosettes.

E. setosa. Zones 17, 23, 24. Dense rosettes to 4 in. across are dark green, densely covered with white, stiff hairs. Flowers red, tipped with yellow. Good choice for rock gardens, shallow containers. Very tender.

ECHINACEA purpurea
(Rudbeckia purpurea)

PURPLE CONEFLOWER
Asteraceae (Compositae)
PERENNIAL
✷ ALL ZONES
☼ FULL SUN
◐ ● SOME ARIDITY; BEST WITH REGULAR WATER

Echinacea purpurea

Coarse, stiff plant, forming large clumps of erect stems 4–5 ft. tall. Leaves oblong, 3–8 in. long. Showy flower heads with drooping purple rays and dark purple centers bloom over long period in late summer. Rosy pink 'Bright Star' and 'White Swan' are selected varieties with 3–4-in. flowers on 2–2½-ft. plants. Use on outskirts of garden or in wide borders with other robust perennials such as Shasta daisies, sunflowers, Michaelmas daisies. Divide clumps in spring or fall.

E

E

ECHINOCACTUS

BARREL CACTUS

Cactaceae

PERENNIALS

☀ ZONES 12–24

☀ ◗ SOME SUMMER SHADE IN HOTTEST DESERT

◖ WATER EVERY TWO WEEKS DURING SUMMER

Echinocactus grusonii

Numerous kinds of large, cylindrical cacti with prominent ribs and stout thorns. Many native to Southwest. Best known in gardens is *E. grusonii,* golden barrel, a Mexican cactus of slow growth to 4 ft. high, 2½ ft. in diameter, with showy, stiff, yellow, 3-in. spines and yellow, 1½–2-in. flowers at top of plant in April–May. It needs protection from hard frosts. Provide frost protection with improvised canopies of branches.

ECHINOCEREUS

HEDGEHOG CACTUS

Cactaceae

PERENNIALS

☀ ZONES VARY BY SPECIES

☀ FULL SUN

◖ TAKE MUCH ARIDITY WHEN ESTABLISHED

Echinocereus engelmannii

Nearly 50 species of hedgehog cactus grow in the southwestern United States and northern Mexico, with some growing at fairly high elevations in Utah and Colorado, where they are subject to freezing temperatures. All have cylindrical, ribbed bodies in clumps; showy red, yellow, purple, or white flowers with many rows of petals; and fleshy fruit, edible in some species. Although hardy to cold in most zones, and often seen in collections, they are used in landscaping chiefly in desert or interior mountain gardens.

E. engelmannii. Zones 2, 3, 7, 10–24. Clumps grow to 3 ft. wide, 2 ft. tall. Flowers are 2–3 in. wide, lavender to deep purplish red. Inch-long red fruits are edible.

E. triglochidiatus. CLARET CUP. Zones 2, 3, 10, 11, 14, 18–23. Dense mounds, sometimes with hundreds of stems to 16 in. tall, each stem to 5 in. thick. Flowers are 3½ in. wide, orange to red, the inch-long fruit pink to red.

ECHINOPS exaltatus

GLOBE THISTLE

Asteraceae (Compositae)

PERENNIAL

☀ ALL ZONES

☀ FULL SUN

◖ ◗ LOOKS BEST WITH MODERATE WATER

Echinops exaltatus

Rugged-looking, erect, rigidly branched plant 3–4 ft. high. Coarse, prickly, deeply cut, gray-green leaves. Small steel blue flowers in round heads 2 in. across, midsummer to late fall. 'Taplow Blue' is desirable selected form. Flowers are long lasting when cut and hold color when dry. Plants often mistakenly sold under names of *E. ritro* and *E. sphaerocephalus. E. banaticus* 'Blue Glow' is similar.

Plant in soil with good drainage. Established plants tolerate dry periods. Grow from divisions in spring or fall, or sow seed in flats or open ground in spring. Color and interesting form complement yellow and orange rudbeckias, heleniums; combine well with Michaelmas daisies and phlox.

ECHINOPSIS

EASTER LILY CACTUS, SEA URCHIN CACTUS

Cactaceae

PERENNIALS

☀ ZONES 16, 17, 21–24; OR INDOORS

☀ FULL SUN; INDOORS IN SUNNY WINDOW

◖ REGULAR WATER SPRING THROUGH FALL

Echinopsis

Small (6–10-in.-high), cylindrical or globular cacti from South America, generally grown in pots. Big, long-tubed, many-petaled flowers in shades of white, yellow, pink, and red can reach 6–8 in. long. Free blooming in summer if given good light, frequent feeding, fast-draining soil. Many kinds, all showy and easy to grow. Give little or no water in winter.

E. chamaecereus. See Chamaecereus silvestri

E. eyriesii. Cylindrical plant 6–12 in. tall, with dark spines and large (8–10-in.-long, 2–4-in.-wide) white flowers. Eventually forms clumps.

E. hamatacantha. Round plant to 4 in. tall with 3-in. red to yellow flowers.

ECHIUM

Boraginaceae

BIENNIALS OR SHRUBBY PERENNIALS

☀ ZONES VARY BY SPECIES

☀ FULL SUN

◖ ◗ LITTLE WATER AT COAST, MODERATE INLAND

◗ ECHIUM VULGARE IS POISONOUS

Echium fastuosum

Striking form and flower clusters. All do well in dry, poor soil but need good drainage. All are excellent for seacoast gardens. No summer water at all in Zones 15–17, 22–24; need weekly summer watering in Zones 14, 18–21. All types attract bees.

E. fastuosum (E. candicans). PRIDE OF MADEIRA. Shrubby perennial. Zones 14–24. Large, picturesque plant with many coarse, heavy branches 3–6 ft. high. Hairy, gray-green, narrow leaves form roundish, irregular mounds at ends of stems. Great spikelike clusters of bluish purple, ½-in.-long flowers stand out dramatically, well above foliage, May–June. Branch tips and developing flower spikes may be killed by March frosts in inland areas. Use for bold effects against walls, at back of wide flower border, and on slopes. Very effective with *Limonium perezii*. Prune lightly to keep plant bushy. Cut off faded flower spikes.

E. pininana. Short-lived shrubby perennial. Zones 16, 17, 22–24. Tall (to 18 ft.), sparsely branched. Stems packed with long, narrow, bristly gray-green leaves and topped with long spikelike clusters of blue flowers. Rarely sold but occasionally seen in old gardens near coast.

E. vulgare. Biennial grown as an annual. All zones. Blooms first year if sown early autumn, winter, or earliest spring. Grows 1–3 ft. tall. Leaves covered with stiff white bristles; blue, white, or pink flowers in spikelike clusters. Endures aridity, poor soil. Seeds freely and can become a pest if seedlings are not hoed out.

E. wildpretii. TOWER OF JEWELS. Biennial. Zones 15–17, 21–24. Striking plant, 4–10 ft. high. Spends its first year as attractive, roundish mass of long, narrow leaves covered with silvery gray hairs. In its second year it starts to grow. By mid- or late spring it will form thick column of rose to rose red flowers, 6–10 ft. high and a foot or more thick. When all the countless little flowers have faded, the plant dies, leaving behind a vast amount of seed. If resulting seedlings are not hoed out, these may be grown to flower the next year. An interesting oddity.

PRACTICAL GARDENING DICTIONARY

PLEASE SEE PAGES 529–592

EDELWEISS. See LEONTOPODIUM alpinum   p. 350

EGGPLANT

Solanaceae

ANNUALS

✔ ALL ZONES

☼ FULL SUN

💧 WATER WHEN SOIL AT ROOTS IS DRY

Eggplant 'Black Beauty'

Few vegetable plants are handsomer than egg-plant. Bushes resemble little trees, 2–3 ft. high and equally wide. Big leaves (usually lobed) are purple tinged; drooping violet flowers are 1½ in. across. And, of course, big purple fruit is spectacular. Plants are effective in large containers or raised beds; a well-spaced row of them makes distinguished border between vegetable and flower garden. Most people plant large roundish or oval varieties such as 'Black Beauty', 'Burpee Hybrid', or 'Early Beauty'; the Japanese, who prefer their eggplant small and very tender, prefer long, slender variety usually sold as 'Japanese'. Specialists in imported vegetable seeds offer numerous colored varieties, including the full-sized 'White Beauty' and a host of smaller varieties in a range of sizes (down to ½ in.) and colors—yellow, red, green. Some of the smaller ones genuinely resemble eggs. All are edible as well as attractive.

Can be grown from seed (sow indoors 8–10 weeks before date of last expected frost), but starting from nursery-grown plants is much easier. Set plants out in sun in spring when frosts are over and soil is warm. Space 3 ft. apart in loose, fertile soil. Feed once every 6 weeks with commercial fertilizer. Keep weeds out. Prevent too much fruit setting by pinching out some terminal growth and some blossoms; three to six large fruits per plant will result.

If you enjoy tiny whole eggplants, allow plants to produce freely. Harvest fruits after they develop some color but never wait until they lose their glossy shine. Dust or spray to control aphids and whiteflies. For ornamental relatives, see *Solanum.*

EGLANTINE. See ROSA eglanteria   p. 467

EICHHORNIA crassipes

WATER HYACINTH

Pontederiaceae

AQUATIC PLANT

✔ ZONES 8, 9, 13–24

☼ FULL SUN

💧 PONDS OR POOLS

Eichhornia crassipes

Native to tropical America. Floating leaves and feathery roots. Leaves ½–5 in. wide, nearly circular in shape; leaf stems inflated. Blooms showy, lilac blue, about 2 in. long. Upper petals with yellow spot in center, in many-flowered spikes. Can become pest; do not turn it loose in natural or large bodies of water. Needs warmth to flower profusely.

Elaeagnaceae. This family contains trees and shrubs with a coating of tiny silvery or brown scales on leaves (and sometimes on flowers) and with small, tart-tasting, single-seeded fruits. Most are tough plants from arid or semiarid climates.

ELAEAGNUS

Elaeagnaceae

DECIDUOUS, EVERGREEN SHRUBS AND SMALL TREES

✔ ZONES VARY BY SPECIES

☼ ☼ FULL SUN OR PARTIAL SHADE

💧 💧 LITTLE TO REGULAR WATER

Elaeagnus pungens

All are splendid screen plants. All grow fast when young, becoming dense, full, firm, and tough—and they do it with little upkeep. All tolerate seashore conditions, heat, and wind. Established plants need no water. Plant 10–12 ft. apart for screening.

Foliage is distinguished in evergreen forms by silvery (sometimes brown) dots that cover leaves, reflecting sunlight to give plants a special sparkle. Deciduous kinds have silvery gray leaves. Small, insignificant, but usually fragrant flowers are followed by decorative fruit, usually red with silvery flecks. Evergreen kinds bloom in fall; in addition to their prime role as screen plants, they are useful as natural espaliers, clipped hedges, or high bank covers.

E. angustifolia. RUSSIAN OLIVE. Small deciduous tree. Zones 1–3, 7–14, 18, 19. To 20 ft. high, but can be clipped as medium-height hedge. Angular trunk and branches (sometimes thorny) are covered with shredding dark brown bark that is picturesque in winter. Bark contrasts with willowlike, 2-in.-long, silvery gray leaves. Small, very fragrant greenish yellow flowers in early summer are followed by berrylike fruit that resembles miniature olives. Can take almost any amount of punishment in interior. Does poorly and is out of character in mild-winter, cool-summer climates. Resistant to oak root fungus. Good background plant, barrier.

E. commutata. SILVERBERRY. Deciduous shrub. Zones 1–3. Native to Canada, northern plains, and Rocky Mountains. To 12 ft. with slender, open form, red-brown branches, silvery leaves. Tiny, fragrant flowers followed by dry, silvery berries that are good bird food.

E. 'Coral Silver'. Large shrub, evergreen in Zones 19–24, deciduous or partially deciduous elsewhere. All zones. Has unusually bright gray foliage, coral red berries in fall.

E. ebbingei (E. macrophylla 'Ebbingei'). Evergreen shrub. Zones 5–24. More upright (to 10–12 ft.) than *E. pungens,* with thornless branches. Leaves 2–4 in. long, silvery on both sides when young, are later dark green above and silvery beneath. Tiny, fragrant, silvery flowers. Red fruit makes good jelly. 'Gilt Edge' has striking yellow margins on its leaves.

E. multiflora. Deciduous shrub. Zones 2–24. To 6 ft.; leaves silvery green above, silvery and brown below. Small, fragrant flowers followed by attractive, ½-in.-long, bright orange-red berries on 1-in. stalks. Fruit is edible but tart, much loved by birds.

E. pungens. SILVERBERRY. Large evergreen shrub. Zones 4–24. Has rather rigid, sprawling, angular habit of growth to height of 6–15 ft.; can be kept lower and denser by pruning. Grayish green, 1–3-in.-long leaves have wavy edges and brown tinting from rusty dots. Branches are spiny, also covered with rusty dots. Overall color of shrub is olive drab. Oval fruit, ½ in. long, red with silver dust. Tough container plant in reflected heat, wind. Variegated forms listed below are more widespread than the plain olive drab variety and have a brighter, lighter look in the landscape. Both kinds make effective barrier plantings: growth is dense and twiggy, and spininess is a help, yet plant is not aggressively spiny.

E. p. 'Fruitlandii'. Zones 5–24. Leaves large, silvery.

E. p. 'Maculata'. GOLDEN ELAEAGNUS. Leaves have gold blotch in center.

E. p. 'Marginata'. SILVER-EDGE ELAEAGNUS. Leaves have silvery white margins.

E. p. 'Variegata'. YELLOW-EDGE ELAEAGNUS. Leaves have yellowish white margins.

ELDERBERRY. See SAMBUCUS   p. 473

ELEPHANT'S EAR. See ALOCASIA, COLOCASIA esculenta   pp. 147, 238

E

ELYMUS

LYME GRASS

Poaceae (Gramineae)

PERENNIAL GRASSES

✂ ZONES 8, 9, 14–24

☼ ◑ SUN OR LIGHT SHADE

◑ TOLERATE ARIDITY IN COASTAL CONDITIONS

Elymus arenarius
'Glaucus'

Of the many lyme grasses (which are also known as wild ryes) the following two are most widely grown for blue-gray foliage. (Some botanists prefer the name *Leymus*.)

E. arenarius 'Glaucus'. BLUE LYME GRASS. Vigorous clumps of gray-blue foliage are topped by inconspicuous flower clusters. Plants tolerate sand or clay. Remains evergreen with some supplemental summer water. Good soil binder; may need curbing.

E. condensatus 'Canyon Prince'. Native to San Miguel Island off the Southern California coast. Outstanding blue-gray grass with powdery blue flower plumes held 2–3 ft. above the blue-gray foliage.

ENCELIA

Asteraceae (Compositae)

DECIDUOUS SHRUBS

✂ ZONES 7–10, 14–24

☼ FULL SUN

◑ OCCASIONAL WATER INLAND

Encelia farinosa

Much-branched shrubs to 5 ft. or more, with scattered leaves that tend to drop in drought and loose showers of yellow daisylike flowers. Useful for out-of-the-way places beyond irrigation.

E. californica. Green leaves to 2½ in., with brown-centered flower heads to nearly 3 in.

E. farinosa. BRITTLEBUSH, INCIENSO. Aromatic shrub with silvery leaves and a profusion of somewhat smaller yellow- or brown-centered flowers.

ENDIVE

Asteraceae (Compositae)

FALL OR LATE-SUMMER ANNUAL

✂ ALL ZONES

☼ FULL SUN

◑ REGULAR WATER

Endive

Botanically known as *Cichorium endivia*. This species includes curly endive and broad-leafed endive (escarole). Forms rosette of leaves. Tolerates more heat than lettuce, grows faster in cold weather. Sow in late summer for maturity during rainy season (in cold-winter areas, sow seed June to August). Endive matures in 90–95 days. Space plants 10–12 in. apart in rows 15–18 in. apart. When plants have reached full size, pull outer leaves over center and tie them up; center leaves will blanch to yellow or white. 'Green Curled' is standard curly endive; 'Broad-leaved Batavian' is best broad-leafed kind. Belgian or French endives are the blanched sprouts from roots of a kind of chicory. Roots are dug after a summer's growth, then stored in the dark to sprout. See Chicory.

ENDYMION
(Scilla, Hyacinthoides)

ENGLISH AND SPANISH BLUEBELLS, WOOD HYACINTH

Liliaceae

BULBS

✂ ALL ZONES

☼ ◑ FULL SUN OR PARTIAL SHADE

◑ IN DRY-WINTER AREAS, WATER FROM OCTOBER ON

Endymion non-scriptus

These are still popularly known as scilla, but the current botanical name is *Hyacinthoides*. They resemble hyacinths but are taller, with looser flower clusters and fewer, narrower leaves. Most dealers still sell them as scilla. Plant informal drifts among tall shrubs, under deciduous trees, among low-growing perennials. Let bulbs dry out through summer. They thrive in pots and are good for cutting.

E. hispanicus (Scilla campanulata, S. hispanica). SPANISH BLUEBELL. Most widely planted. Prolific, vigorous, with sturdy 20-in. stems bearing 12 or more nodding bells about ¾ in. long. Blue is most popular color, 'Excelsior' (deep blue) most popular variety. There are also white, pink, rose forms. Plant in fall—3 in. deep in mild climates, to 6 in. deep where winters are severe. Flowers appear in spring.

E. non-scriptus (Scilla nonscripta). ENGLISH BLUEBELL, WOOD HYACINTH. Flowers narrower and smaller than those of Spanish bluebell, on 1-ft. spikes. Culture same as for *E. hispanicus*.

NATURALIZING A BLUEBELL PLANTING

Broadcast a handful of bulbs over an area and plant them where they fall. For a realistic effect, before planting rearrange the bulbs so they are closest together at one end of a group or toward the center—as though the colony originated at one spot and gradually increased outward. Mostly space bulbs about 6 in. apart.

ENKIANTHUS

Ericaceae

DECIDUOUS SHRUBS

✂ ZONES 2–9, 14–21

◑ LIGHT SHADE

◑ SHOULD NEVER DRY OUT

Enkianthus campanulatus

Native to Japan. Upright stems with tiers of nearly horizontal branches, narrow in youth, broad in age, but always good looking. Leaves, whorled or crowded at branch ends, turn orange or red in autumn. Nodding, bell-shaped flowers in clusters. Grow in well-drained soil to which plenty of peat moss or ground bark has been added. Prune only to remove dead or broken branches. Plant with other acid-loving plants, in location where silhouette and fall color can be effective.

E. campanulatus. Slow-growing, handsome shrub to 20 ft. in 20 years (10 ft. by 4 ft. wide in 10 years). Bluish green leaves, 1½–3 in. long, turn brilliant red in fall. In May, pendulous clusters of yellow-green, red-veined, ½-in.-long bells hang below leaves. *E. c. palibinii* has deep red flowers; its variety 'Albiflorus' has white blooms.

E. cernuus. Seldom over 10 ft. tall, with 1–2-in.-long leaves. White flowers. Not as well known as *E. c. rubens*, which has translucent deep red flowers in May.

E. perulatus. Grows to 6–8 ft. high. Roundish, 1–2-in.-long leaves; exceptionally good scarlet fall color. Nodding clusters of small white flowers open before leaves emerge.

ENSETE

Musaceae

LARGE, PALMLIKE PERENNIALS

ZONES 13, 15–24; SEE BELOW

FULL SUN OR PARTIAL SHADE

WATER FREQUENTLY TO SPEED GROWTH

Ensete ventricosum

Evergreen in Zones 17, 19–24; die back each cold winter, regrow in spring in Zones 13, 15, 16, 18. They are also container plants to grow outdoors in summer, indoors or in greenhouse over winter. Good near swimming pools.

E. ventricosum (Musa ensete). ABYSSINIAN BANANA. Lush, tropical-looking, dark green leaves 10–20 ft. long, 2–4 ft. wide, with stout midribs, grow out in arching form from single vertical stem, 6–20 ft. high. Fast growing. Leaves easily shredded by winds, so plant in wind-sheltered place. Flowers typically form 2–5 years after planting; plant dies to roots after flowering. Possible then to grow new plants from shoots at crown, but easier to discard, replace with new nursery plants. Flowers (inconspicuous) form within cylinder of bronze red bracts at end of stem.

E. v. 'Maurelii'. Similar to *E. ventricosum,* but leaves are tinged with red on upper surface, especially along edges. Leafstalks are dark red. Stems grow 12–15 ft. high. 'Montbeliardii' is less squat than 'Maurelii'.

EPAULETTE TREE. See PTEROSTYRAX hispidus   p. 445

EPAZOTE. See CHENOPODIUM ambrosioides   p. 222

EPIDENDRUM

Orchidaceae

EPIPHYTIC OR TERRESTRIAL ORCHIDS

ZONES 17, 21–24; OR INDOORS

FULL SUN OR PARTIAL SHADE; SEE BELOW

ROUTINE WATERING, HIGH HUMIDITY

Epidendrum obrienianum

All are easy to grow. Most species bear large clusters of blooms. On the whole they take same culture as cattleya. Those with hard, round pseudobulbs and thick, leathery leaves are tolerant of sun and aridity. Softer-textured (reed-stemmed) plants with thin, stemlike pseudobulbs do best with more shade and year-round moisture. Both types grow in ground bark or other orchid media.

Reed-stemmed types need abundance of sun to flower but also coolness and shade at roots. Mulch plants in ground beds. If sun is too hot, foliage turns bright red and burns. Tip growth will burn at 28°F; plants are killed to ground at about 22°F. In cold-winter areas, grow reed-stemmed plants in pots and move them indoors in winter.

Feed regularly with mild liquid fertilizer during growing season. Feed plants grown in pure ground bark at every other watering with high-nitrogen liquid fertilizer. Feed plants grown in other media monthly. When blooms fade, cut flower stem back to within one or two joints above soil.

E. cochleatum. Native to tropical America. Pear-shaped pseudobulbs 2–5 in. high, with one or more leaves as long as or longer than pseudobulb. Erect flower stem bears five to ten 2–3-in.-wide flowers. Narrow, twisted, yellow-green sepals and petals; purplish black lip (shaped like cockleshell) with lighter veins. Blooms at various times. Hardy to 25°F; grows outdoors in mildest winter climates.

E. ibaguense (E. radicans). Native to Colombia. Erect, 2–4-ft., reed-like leafy stems. Dense, globular clusters of 1–1½-in. orange-yellow flow-

ers with fringed lips are held at tips of slender stems well above foliage. Bloom season varies. Numerous hybrids in shades of yellow, orange, pink, red, lavender, and white, generally sold by color rather than by name.

E. obrienianum. Best known of reed-stemmed hybrids. Dense clusters of vivid red flowers, each the shape of miniature cattleya orchid, carried on slender stems 1–2 ft. above foliage.

EPILOBIUM. See ZAUSCHNERIA   p. 527

EPIMEDIUM

Berberidaceae

EVERGREEN PERENNIALS

ZONES 1–9, 14–17

PARTIAL SHADE

NEEDS SOME SUMMER WATER

Epimedium grandiflorum

Low-growing evergreen or nearly evergreen plants with creeping underground stems. Leathery, divided leaves on thin, wiry stems. Heart-shaped leaflets up to 3 in. long are bronzy pink in spring, green in summer, bronzy in fall. In spring, loose spikes of small, waxy flowers in pink, red, creamy yellow, or white. Use as ground cover under trees or among rhododendrons, azaleas, camellias; good in large rock gardens. Adaptable to containers. Foliage, flowers long lasting in arrangements. Divide large clumps in spring or fall by cutting through tough roots with sharp spade.

E. grandiflorum. BISHOP'S HAT, LONGSPUR EPIMEDIUM. About 1 ft. high. Flowers 1–2 in. across, shaped like bishop's hat; outer sepals red, inner sepals pale violet, petals white with long spurs. Varieties have white, pinkish, or violet flowers. 'Rose Queen', bearing crimson flowers with white-tipped spurs, is outstanding variety.

E. pinnatum. Grows 12–15 in. high. Yellow flowers are ⅔ in. across, with red petals and protruding stamens. *E. p. colchicum* (often sold as *E. p. elegans*) is larger, with showier flowers.

E. rubrum. To 1 ft. Flowers, borne in showy clusters, have bright crimson sepals, pale yellow or white, slipperlike petals, upward-curving spurs. Rosy pink 'Pink Queen' and white 'Snow Queen' are desirable varieties offered in specialty nurseries.

EPIPHYLLUM

ORCHID CACTUS

Cactaceae

PERENNIALS

ZONES 8, 9, 14–24, WITH PROTECTION; OR INDOORS

BEST UNDER LATH IN SUMMER OR UNDER TREES

REGULAR WATER IN SUMMER, LITTLE IN WINTER

Epiphyllum Hybrid

Growers use *Epiphyllum* to cover a wide range of plants—epiphyllum itself and a number of crosses with related plants. All are tropical (not desert) cacti, and most grow on tree branches as epiphytes, like some orchids. Grow them in pots indoors; in Zones 8, 9, 14–24 in lathhouse or shade. They need rich, quick-draining soil with plenty of sand and leaf mold, peat moss, or ground bark. Cuttings are easy to root in spring or summer. Permit the base of the cutting to dry for a day or two before potting it up. Overwatering and poor drainage cause bud drop.

In winter, epiphyllums need protection from frost. Most have arching (to 2 ft. high), trailing stems and look best in hanging pots, tubs, or baskets. Stems are long, flat, smooth, quite spineless, and usually notched along edges. Flowers range from medium size to very large (up to 10 in. across); color range includes white, cream, yellow, pink, rose, lavender, scarlet, and orange. Many varieties have blends of two or more colors. April–June bloom season. Feed with low-nitrogen fertilizer before and after bloom.

E

EPIPREMNUM aureum (Pothos aureus, Raphidophora aurea, Scindapsus aureus)

POTHOS

Araceae

EVERGREEN CLIMBING PERENNIAL GROWN INDOORS

◐ ● PARTIAL OR FULL SHADE

● REGULAR WATER

Epipremnum aureum

Related to philodendron and similar in appearance. Takes same treatment as climbing philodendrons. Flowers are inconspicuous. Oval, leathery leaves 2–4 in. long, bright green splashed or marbled with yellow. (In greenhouse and with plenty of root room, becomes big vine with deeply cut, 2–2½-ft.-long leaves.) Attractive trailer for pots, window boxes, large terrariums.

EPISCIA

FLAME VIOLET

Gesneriaceae

INDOOR PLANTS RELATED TO AFRICAN VIOLET

◐ BRIGHT INDOOR LIGHT

◖ AMPLE WATER

Episcia cupreata

Low-growing plants spread by strawberrylike runners with new plants at tips; excellent display in hanging pots. Leaves 2–5 in. long, 1–3 in. wide; typically oval, velvety, beautifully colored. Flowers somewhat resemble African violets, appear at scattered intervals through the year. Plants bloom best in high humidity of greenhouse but will grow as house plants with no direct sun.

E. cupreata. Red flowers. *E. c. viridifolia* has green leaves with creamy veins; 'Metallica', olive green leaves with pale stripes, red edges; 'Chocolate Soldier', chocolate brown, silver-veined leaves; and 'Silver Sheen', silver leaves with darker margins.

EQUISETUM hyemale

HORSETAIL

Equisetaceae

PERENNIAL

✔ ALL ZONES

☼ ◖ FULL SUN OR PARTIAL SHADE

◖ MARSHY AREAS OR POOLS

Equisetum hyemale

Rushlike survivor of Carboniferous age. Slender, hollow, 4-ft. stems are bright green with black-and-ash-colored ring at each joint. Spores borne in conelike spikes at end of stem. Several species, but *E. hyemale* most common. Called horsetail because many of the species have bushy look from many whorls of slender, jointed green stems that radiate out from joints of main stem.

Although horsetail is effective in some garden situations, especially near water, use it with caution: it is extremely invasive and difficult to get rid of. Best confined to containers. In open ground, root-prune unwanted shoots rigorously and constantly.

Miniature *E. scirpoides* is similar, but only 6 to 8 in. tall.

FOR INFORMATION ON SELECTING PLANTS
PLEASE SEE PAGES 45–128

ERANTHIS hyemalis

WINTER ACONITE

Ranunculaceae

TUBER

✔ ZONES 1–9, 14–17

☼ PARTIAL SHADE

● REGULAR WATER

Eranthis hyemalis

Charming buttercuplike plant 2–8 in. high, blooming in early spring. Single yellow flowers up to 1½ in. wide, with five to nine petal-like sepals; each bloom sits on a single, deeply lobed, bright green leaf that looks like a ruff. Round basal leaves divided into narrow lobes appear immediately after flowers. Ideal companions for other small bulbs or bulblike plants that bloom at same time, such as snowdrop *(Galanthus nivalis)* and Siberian squill *(Scilla sibirica)*. Plant tubers in August or early September before they shrivel. If tubers are dry, plump up in wet sand before planting. When dividing, separate into small clumps rather than single tubers. Plant tubers 3 in. deep, 4 in. apart, in moist, porous soil.

EREMOPHILA

EMU BUSH

Myoporaceae

EVERGREEN SHRUBS

✔ ZONES 8, 9, 14–24

☼ FULL SUN

◖ TOLERATE SOME ARIDITY

Eremophila laani

Of about 180 species of these Australian shrubs, just a few are grown in California. All tolerate aridity, wind, poor soil, and heat, but like good drainage.

E. glabra. COMMON EMU BUSH. Creeping or upright to 5 ft. wide, possibly 9 ft., with narrow leaves and tubular flowers over 1 in. long in yellow, orange, or red.

E. laani. Small to medium (6-ft.) bush with narrow, 2-in., gray-green leaves and white, pink, or red flowers. 'Roger's Pink' has clear pink flowers in summer, with a scattering throughout the year.

E. maculata. SPOTTED EMU BUSH. Grows 3 ft. tall, twice as wide. Dense growth of narrow leaves and a heavy winter and spring crop of dark red, yellow, orange, or pink flowers, with a scattering throughout the year. 'Aurea' has lighter green leaves and yellow flowers.

EREMURUS

FOXTAIL LILY, DESERT CANDLE

Liliaceae

PERENNIALS

✔ ZONES 1–9

☼ FULL SUN

◖ TOLERATE SOME ARIDITY

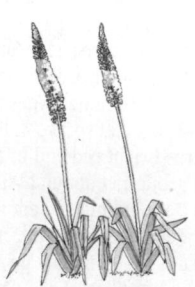

Eremurus himalaicus

Imposing lily relatives with spirelike flowering stems 4–9 ft. tall. Bell-shaped white, pink, or yellow flowers, ½–1 in. wide, massed closely in graceful, pointed spikes. Plants bloom in late spring, early summer. Strap-shaped basal leaves in rosettes appear in early spring, fade away after bloom in summer. Magnificent in large borders against background of dark green foliage, wall, or solid fence. Dramatic in arrangements; cut when lowest flowers on spike open. Plant in rich, fast-draining soil. Handle thick, brittle roots carefully; they tend to rot when bruised or broken. When leaves die down, mark spot; don't disturb roots.

E. himalaicus. Leaves bright green, to 1½ ft. long. Flowers white, about 1 in. across, in 2-ft. spikes on tall stems to 3 ft. or more.

E. robustus. Leaves about 2 ft. long, in dense basal rosettes. Stems 8–9 ft. high, topped with 2–3-ft. spikes of clear pink flowers lightly veined with brown.

E. Shelford hybrids. To 4–5 ft. tall; flowers in white and shades of buff, pink, yellow, and orange.

ERICA

HEATH

Ericaceae

EVERGREEN SHRUBS

ZONES VARY BY SPECIES

FULL SUN

CONSISTENT, CAREFUL WATERING

SEE CHART NEXT PAGE

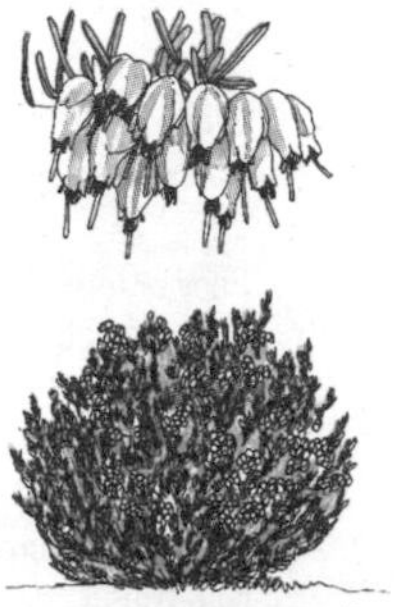

Erica carnea 'Springwood'

Evergreen shrubs with small, needlelike leaves and abundant bell-shaped, urn-shaped, or tubular flowers, usually small. Hardiest kinds, native to northern and western Europe, are widely used as shrubs or ground cover plants in cool-summer, humid regions of California and Northwest. Good on slopes. South African species are tender to frost; where temperatures dip below 28°F, they are most safely grown in containers and given shelter. They are about as hardy as fuchsias. A third group of heaths, native to Mediterranean and southern Europe, is intermediate in hardiness. All attract bees. Taller ones can be used as screens.

All need excellent drainage and most need acid soil (exceptions noted in chart). Sandy soil with peat moss and compost added is ideal; heavy clay is usually fatal. They are not heavy feeders; annual sifting of compost may be enough. If plants lose color, give light feeding of acid plant food in early spring or apply iron sulfate. No standing water on roots, and no absolute dryness. Near coast where air is moist, watering intervals are longer than in inland areas. Inland, give them light shade or afternoon shade. Prune after bloom by cutting back wood that has flowered; don't cut back into leafless wood. In suitable climates (as in Zones 4–6), fanciers may plant heather gardens for a Persian-carpet effect. With careful selection of varieties of both *Erica* and *Calluna,* you can have color year-round.

Ericaceae. The heath family contains shrubs and trees with rounded, bell-shaped, tubular, or irregular flowers, often showy, and fruits that are either capsules or berries. All share a preference, if not always a need, for acid soil with ample water and excellent aeration (a few plants from dry-summer climates are exceptions). Many are fine garden plants; azalea and rhododendron *(Rhododendron),* blueberry, heath *(Erica),* and heather *(Calluna vulgaris)* are examples.

ERIGERON

FLEABANE

Asteraceae (Compositae)

PERENNIALS

ZONES VARY BY SPECIES

SUN OR LIGHT SHADE

MODERATE WATER; SOME TAKE ARIDITY

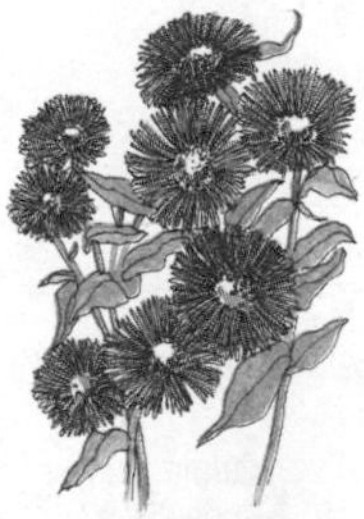

Erigeron speciosus

Free-blooming plants with daisylike flowers; similar to closely related Michaelmas daisy *(Aster),* except that erigeron's flower heads have threadlike rays in two or more rows rather than broader rays in a single row. White, pink, lavender, or violet flowers, usually with yellow centers, early summer into fall. Sandy soil. Cut back after flowering to prolong bloom. Rock garden species need especially fast drainage.

E. glaucus. BEACH ASTER, SEASIDE DAISY. Zones 4–6, 15–17, 22–24. Native of California, Oregon coast. Burns in hot sun inland. Basal leaves in clumps. Stout, hairy stems 10–12 in. high, topped by lavender flower heads 1½–2 in. across in spring, summer. Blue-green stems and foliage. Use in rock garden, in border, beside path. 'Arthur Menzies' is unusually compact, mat-forming selection with lavender pink flower heads.

E. karvinskianus. MEXICAN DAISY, SANTA BARBARA DAISY. Zones 8, 9, 12–24. Native to Mexico. Graceful, trailing plant 10–20 in. high. Leaves 1 in. long, often toothed at tips. Dainty flower heads ¾ in. across with numerous white or pinkish rays. Tolerates aridity. Use as ground cover in garden beds or large containers, in rock gardens, in hanging baskets, on dry walls. Naturalizes easily. Stands root competition well; invasive unless controlled. Often called vittadinia. The variety 'Moerheimii' is somewhat more compact than species, with slightly larger leaves and flower heads with a lavender tint.

E. speciosus. All zones. Native to Pacific Northwest coast. Erect, leafy stemmed, 2 ft. high. Flower heads 1–1½ in. across, with dark violet or lavender rays; summer bloom. *E. s. macranthus,* aspen daisy, is widespread through Rocky Mountain area. It has three to five flower heads to a stalk; stalks nod near top. Hybrids between *E. speciosus* and other species are available; these named sorts have larger flower heads and come in white and pink as well as the blue lavender of wild kinds.

ERIOBOTRYA

LOQUAT

Rosaceae

EVERGREEN TREES OR LARGE SHRUBS

ZONES VARY BY SPECIES

FULL SUN OR PARTIAL SHADE

BETTER WITH SOME WATER

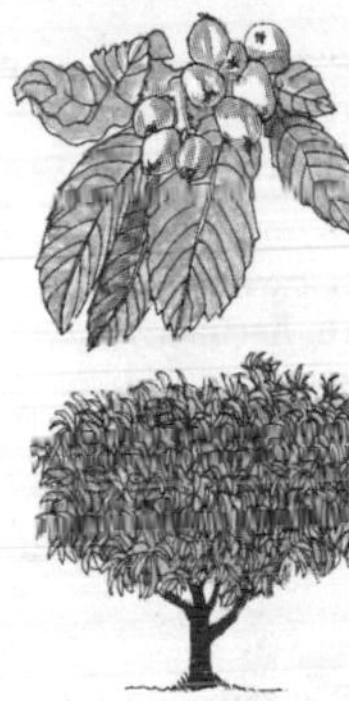

Eriobotrya japonica

Both kinds have large, prominently veined, sharply toothed leaves. One bears edible fruit. Attractive to birds.

E. deflexa. BRONZE LOQUAT. Zones 8–24. Shrubby but easily trained into small tree form. New leaves have bright coppery color that they hold for a long time before turning green. Leaves aren't as leathery or as deeply veined as those of *E. japonica;* they are shinier and more pointed. Garlands of creamy white flowers attractive in spring. No edible fruit. Good for espaliers (not on hot wall), patio planting, containers. Fast growing.

E. japonica. LOQUAT. Zones 4–24. Grows 15–30 ft. tall, equally broad in sun, slimmer in shade. Big, leathery, crisp leaves, stoutly veined and netted, 6–12 in. long, 2–4 in. wide, sharply toothed. They are glossy deep green above and show rust-colored wool beneath. New branches woolly; small, dull white flowers in woolly 3–6-in. clusters borne in fall. These are fragrant but not showy. Fruit 1–2 in. long, orange to yellow, with seeds (usually big) in center; flesh sweet, aromatic, and acid. Hardy to 20°F; has survived 12°F, but fruit often injured by low temperatures.

Plant in well-drained soil; will thrive with no irrigation when established but grows better with some moisture. Prune to shape; if you like the fruit, thin branches somewhat to let light into tree's interior. If tree sets fruit heavily, remove some while it's small to increase size of remaining fruit and to prevent limb breakage. Fireblight is a danger; if leaves and stems blacken from top downward, prune back 1 ft. or more into healthy wood. Discard prunings and sterilize shears with bleach between cuts. Use as lawn tree for sunny or shady spots; use as espalier on fence or trellis but not in reflected heat. Can be held in container for several years. Cut foliage good for indoor decorating. Plants draw bees.

Most trees sold are seedlings, good ornamental plants with unpredictable fruit quality; if you definitely want fruit, look for a grafted variety. 'Champagne', best in warm areas, has yellow-skinned, white-fleshed, juicy, tart fruit (March–May). 'Gold Nugget', best near coast, has sweeter orange fruit (May–June). 'MacBeth' has exceptionally large fruit with yellow skin, cream flesh (April–May). 'Thales' is a late yellow-fleshed variety.

ERICA

NAME, ZONES, ORIGIN	GROWTH HABIT, SIZE	LEAVES	FLOWER COLOR, SEASON	COMMENTS
Erica arborea TREE HEATH Zones 15–17, 21–24 Southern Europe, north Africa	Dense shrub or tree to 10–20 ft., with one or many trunks, often with heavy burl at base	Bright green, ¼ in. long. New growth lighter	White, fragrant. Mar.–May	Slow growing. Performs well enough in Zones 4–6 in years between big freezes. Burls are the "briar" used for making pipes
E. a. alpina	Dense, upright, fluffy-looking shrub to 6 ft.	As above	White. Mar.–May	Slow to reach blooming age, but free blooming. Slightly hardier than above
E. australis SOUTHERN HEATH Zones 5–9, 14–24 Spain, Portugal	Upright, spired, 6–10 ft.	Dark green	Rosy or red. Clustered at ends of shoots. Mar.–June	Needs protection in Northwest. There is a white form, 'Mr. Robert'
E. canaliculata (usually sold as **E. melanthera** and often called Scotch heather) Zones 15–17, 20–24 South Africa	Bushy, spreading, but with general spired effect. To 6 ft.	Dark green above, white beneath	Pink to rosy purple. Fall, winter	Pink-flowered form is sold as 'Rosea', reddish purple form as 'Rubra'. Excellent winter bloom in California. Sometimes called Christmas heather. Good choice for Zones 20–24. Cut flowers last for weeks, in water or out
E. c. 'Boscaweniana' (sometimes sold as **E. melanthera 'Rosea'**)	Upright bush or small tree to 18 ft.	As above	Pale lilac pink to nearly white. Winter, spring	Like *E. canaliculata*, good source of cut flowers
E. carnea (**E. herbacea**) Zones 2–10, 14–24 European Alps	Dwarf, 6–16 in. Upright branchlets rise from prostrate main branches	Medium green	Rosy red. Dec.–June	Unsightly unless pruned every year. This and its varieties tolerate neutral or slightly alkaline soil. Takes partial shade in hot-summer areas
E. c. 'Ruby Glow'	To 8 in.	Dark green	Deep ruby red. Jan.–June	One of richest in color
E. c. 'Springwood' ('Springwood White')	Spreading, to 8 in.	Light green	White; creamy buds. Jan.–Apr.	Toughest, fastest growing heather; one of neatest
E. c. 'Springwood Pink'	Spreading mound, to 10 in.	Bright green	Pure pink. Jan.–Apr.	New growth pinkish rust
E. c. 'Vivellii'	Spreading mound, to 1 ft.	Dark green; bronzy red in winter	Carmine red. Feb.–Mar.	Relatively tidy. Interesting for seasonal change in foliage color as well as for bloom
E. c. 'Winter Beauty' ('King George')	Bushy, spreading, compact, to 15 in.	Dark green	Deep, rich pink. Dec.–Apr.	Often in bloom at Christmas
E. ciliaris DORSET HEATH Zones 4–6, 15–17 England, Ireland	Trailing, 6–12 in.	Pale green	Rosy red. July–Sept.	Good for massing
E. c. 'Mrs. C. H. Gill'	Spreading, to 1 ft.	Dark green	Deep red. July–Oct.	Showy, bell-like flowers
E. c. 'Stoborough'	As above, but taller, to 1½ ft.	Medium green	White. July–Oct.	Free blooming, showy
E. cinerea TWISTED HEATH Zones 4–6, 15–17 British Isles, northern Europe	Spreading mound, to 1 ft.	Dark green, dainty	Purple. June–Sept.	Forms low mat; good ground cover
E. c. 'Atrosanguinea'	Low, spreading, bushy, to 9 in.	Dark green, dainty	Scarlet. June–Oct.	Dwarf, slow growing

ERICA

NAME, ZONES, ORIGIN	GROWTH HABIT, SIZE	LEAVES	FLOWER COLOR, SEASON	COMMENTS
E. c. 'C. D. Eason'	Compact, to 10 in.	Dark green	Red. May–Aug.	Outstanding; good summer flower display
E. c. 'P. S. Patrick'	Bushy, to 15 in.	Dark green	Purple. June–Aug.	Long, sturdy spikes; large flowers in summer
E. darleyensis 'Darley Dale' (E. mediterranea hybrida, E. purpurascens 'Darleyensis') Zones 2–10, 14–24	Bushy grower, to 1 ft.	Medium green	Light rosy purple. Nov.–May	Tough, hardy plant that takes both heat and cold surprisingly well. Tolerates neutral soils. In Northern California, most foolproof heath
E. d. 'Furzey'	Bushy, 14–18 in.	Dark green	Deep rose pink. Dec.–Apr.	Spreading, vigorous plant
E. d. 'George Rendall'	Bushy, 1 ft.	Medium bluish green	Deeper purple than 'Darley Dale'. Nov.–Apr.	New growth gold tinted
E. d. 'Silberschmelze' ('Molten Silver', E. d. 'Alba', 'Mediterranea Hybrid White')	Vigorous, 1½–2 ft.	Medium green	White, fragrant. Winter, spring	Easy to maintain
E. 'Dawn' Zones 4–9, 14–24	Spreading mound, 1 ft.	Green; new growth golden	Deep pink. June–Oct.	Excellent ground cover. Easy to grow. Hybrid between *E. ciliaris* and *E. tetralix*
E. lusitanica (E. codonodes) SPANISH HEATH Zones 5–9, 14–24 Spain, Portugal	Upright feathery shrub, to 6–12 ft.	Light green	Pinkish white, slightly fragrant. Jan.–Mar.	Remarkably profuse bloom. Needs sheltered spot in Northwest. One of best in Zones 20–24
E. mediterranea BISCAY HEATH Zones 4–9, 14–24 Ireland, France, Spain	Loose, upright, 4–7 ft.	Deep green	Lilac pink. Jan.–Apr.	Good background. Tolerates neutral soil. 'W. T. Rackliff' is pure white form with brown anthers
E. m. hybrida (see E. darleyensis 'Darley Dale')				
E. melanthera (see E. canaliculata)				
E. quadrangularis Zones 15–17, 20–24 South Africa	Stiff, upright shrub, to 2 ft.	Bright green	Tiny, rose or white. Late winter, early spring	Offered as pot plants or sold as cut branches. Often sold as *E. persoluta*
E. tetralix CROSS-LEAFED HEATH Zones 4–6, 15–17 England, northern Europe	Upright, to 1 ft.	Dark green, silvery beneath	Rosy pink. June–Oct.	Very hardy plant. New growth yellow, orange, or red. Best in moist, peaty soil, afternoon shade
E. t. 'Alba Mollis'	Upright, slightly spreading, to 1 ft.	Silvery gray	Clear white. June–Oct.	Foliage sheen pronounced in spring, summer
E. t. 'Darleyensis'	Spreading, open growth, to 8 in.	Gray green	Salmon pink. June–Sept.	Good color. Do not confuse with winter-flowering *E. darleyensis* (*E. purpurascens* 'Darleyensis')
E. vagans CORNISH HEATH Zones 3–6, 15–17, 20–24 Cornwall, Ireland	Bushy, open, to 2–3 ft.	Bright green	Purplish pink. July–Sept.	Robust and hardy

ERICA

NAME, ZONES, ORIGIN	GROWTH HABIT, SIZE	LEAVES	FLOWER COLOR, SEASON	COMMENTS
E. v. 'Lyonesse'	Bushy, rounded, to 1½ ft.	Bright, glossy green	White. July–Oct.	Best white Cornish heath
E. v. 'Mrs. D. F. Maxwell'	Bushy, rounded, to 1½ ft.	Dark green	Cherry pink or red. July–Oct.	Outstanding for color and heavy bloom; widely grown
E. v. 'St. Keverne'	Bushy, rounded, to 1½ ft.	Light green	Rose pink. July–Oct.	Heavy bloom. Compact if pruned annually
E. ventricosa Zones 15–17, 20–24 South Africa	To 6 ft., usually much less	Medium green, needlelike	Heavy spikes at tips of branches. Pale to medium pink, shiny. May–July	Occasionally sold as small pot plant in spring

ERIOGONUM

WILD BUCKWHEAT

Polygonaceae

ANNUALS, PERENNIALS, SHRUBS

⚘ ZONES VARY BY SPECIES

☼ FULL SUN

◐ ◑ NO WATER ON COAST, SOME INLAND

Eriogonum arborescens

Native to most areas of West (the few sold at nurseries are mostly native to California coast). Grow best in well-drained, loose, gravelly soil. Useful for covering dry banks, massing among rocks; pleasant specimen in rock gardens. Most available kinds withstand wind and heat well.

Individual blossoms are tiny, but flowers grow in long-stemmed or branched clusters—domed, flattish, or ball-like—popular among flower arrangers for dried bouquets. Clusters turn to shades of tan or rust as seeds ripen. If you leave clusters on plants, seeds will drop and produce volunteer seedlings. Transplant when they're small to extend planting or replace overgrown plants. Shrubby kinds get leggy after several years. You can do some pruning to shape if you start when plants are young, but if they've had no attention, it's better to replace them.

E. arborescens. SANTA CRUZ ISLAND BUCKWHEAT. Shrub. Zones 14–24. Native to Santa Cruz, Santa Rosa, and Anacapa islands, Southern California. Grows 3–4 (sometimes 8) ft. high, spreading to 4–5 ft. or more. Trunk and branches with shredding gray to reddish bark make attractive open pattern. Rather narrow, ½–1½-in.-long, gray-green leaves cluster at ends of branches. Long-stalked, flat clusters of pale pink to rose flowers, May–September.

E. cinereum. ASHYLEAF BUCKWHEAT. Shrub. Zones 14–24. Native to coastal bluffs and canyons of Southern California. Grows 2–5 ft. tall, with ash-colored, 1-in. leaves and pale pink flowers in ball-shaped clusters, July–September. Best planted in groups and given occasional summer water in hottest locations.

E. crocatum. SAFFRON BUCKWHEAT. Perennial. Zones 12–24. Native to Ventura County, California. Low, compact stems (to 1½ ft. high) and roundish, 1-in.-long leaves are covered with white wool. Sulfur yellow flowers in broad, flattish clusters, April–August.

E. fasciculatum. CALIFORNIA BUCKWHEAT. Shrub. Zones 8, 9, 12–24. Native to foothills of California (Santa Clara to San Diego counties) and desert mountain slopes of Southern California. Forms a clump 1–3 ft. high, spreading to 4 ft. Leaves narrow, ½–¾ in. long; may be dark green above, white and woolly beneath, or gray and hairy. White or pinkish flowers in headlike clusters, May–October. Good erosion control plant. 'Theodore Payne', lower growing, makes attractive green ground cover.

E. giganteum. ST. CATHERINE'S LACE. Shrub. Zones 14–24. Native to Santa Catalina and San Clemente islands. Differs from *E. arborescens* in its more freely branching habit; grayish white, broadly oval, 1–2½-in.-long leaves; and longer period of bloom.

E. grande rubescens (E. rubescens, E. latifolium rubescens). RED BUCKWHEAT. Perennial. Zones 14–24. Native to San Miguel, Santa Rosa, and Santa Cruz islands, Southern California. Woody based; branches tend to lie on ground, spreading to 1–1½ ft., with upright tips about 10–12 in. high. Gray-green, oval leaves 1–3½ in. long. Branch tips and sturdy upright branchlets are topped by headlike clusters of rosy red flowers in summer.

E. umbellatum. SULFUR FLOWER. Perennial. All zones; plants grow to timberline and above. Low, broad mats of woody stems set with 1-in. green leaves, white-felted beneath. In summer, 4–12-in. stalks carry clusters of tiny yellow flowers that age to rust. The variety 'Polyanthum' is 18 in. tall, 3 ft. wide, with an abundance of flowers.

ERIOSTEMON myoporoides

WAX FLOWER

Rutaceae

EVERGREEN SHRUB

⚘ ZONES 8, 9, 14–24

☼ ◐ SUN OR LIGHT SHADE

◐ TOLERATES SOME ARIDITY

Eriostemon myoporoides

Promising Australian shrub to 6 ft. tall, 8 ft. wide, densely foliaged to the ground with narrow, dark green leaves. Plant has aroma resembling pineapple. Inch-wide white, starlike flowers opening from pink buds completely cover bush over a long season. Long-lasting cut flower. Needs good drainage, prefers neutral or acid soil, and can withstand extended dry periods when well established. Best pruned hard while young to fatten it up.

ERODIUM reichardii (E. chamaedryoides)

CRANESBILL

Geraniaceae

PERENNIAL

⚘ ZONES 7–9, 14–24

☼ ◐ FULL SUN OR PARTIAL SHADE

◐ REGULAR WATER

Erodium reichardii

Native to Balearic Islands and Corsica. Dainty-looking but tough plant, forming dense foliage tuft 3–6 in. high, 1 ft. across. Long-stalked, roundish, dark green leaves ⅓ in. long with scalloped edges. Profuse, cup-shaped, ½-in.-wide flowers with white or rose pink, rosy-veined petals notched at tips, April–October. Good small-scale ground cover, rock garden plant. A double-flowered pink and a single white form exist. Plant in porous soil. *E. chrysanthum* has silvery foliage and pale yellow flowers, and *E. petraeum crispum (E. foetidum)* has white flowers with lavender veins and a conspicuous purple spot on one petal.

ERYNGIUM amethystinum

SEA HOLLY, AMETHYST ERYNGIUM

Apiaceae (Umbelliferae)

PERENNIAL

ALL ZONES

FULL SUN

TOLERATES SOME ARIDITY

Eryngium amethystinum

Erect, stiff-branched, thistlelike plant, 2–3 ft. high, blooming July–September. Striking oval, steel blue or amethyst, ½-in.-long flower heads surrounded by spiny blue bracts; upper stems also blue (flowers last long when cut, fresh or dried). Leaves sparse, dark green, deeply cut, spiny toothed. Plant in borders or fringe areas in deep sandy soil. Taprooted; difficult to divide. Make root cuttings; or sow seed in place, thinning seedlings to 1 ft. apart. Often self-sows.

ERYNGIUM FLOWERS NEED LONGER STEMS

Eryngium flowers have such dramatic form and unusual color, they call out to be used in arrangements. But their individual flower stems are too short (3–6 in.) to be seen in long-stemmed company. Cut florists' wire as needed, and fasten pieces to the stems with florists' tape. Eryngiums are everlastings; their stems won't need to be in water.

ERYSIMUM

WALLFLOWER

Brassicaceae (Cruciferae)

PERENNIALS AND BIENNIALS

ZONES VARY BY SPECIES

SUN OR LIGHT SHADE

LITTLE TO MODERATE WATER

Erysimum hieraciifolium

This genus swallowed up *Cheiranthus*, which included the old-fashioned biennial bedding-plant wallflowers and several choice perennials. All have the typical clustered four-petaled flowers that give the crucifers their name, but their habits and uses differ widely.

E. 'Bowles Mauve'. Zones 4–6, 14–17, 22, 23. One of the most useful and popular perennials where adapted. Massed erect stems with narrow gray-green leaves grow to 3 ft. tall, 6 ft. wide, each topped by an 18-in. narrow flower cluster of mauve.

Bloom is practically continuous; the plants, though perennial, may bloom themselves to death after several years. They look good with gray- and green-foliaged perennials and shrubs or in mixed "cottage" gardens. 'Wenlock Beauty' is similar but is smaller and has flowers that vary from buff to purple in a single spike. Moderate water.

E. cheiri (Cheiranthus c.). WALLFLOWER. Perennial, usually grown as a biennial, sometimes shrubby. Zones 4–6, 14–17, 22, 23. Branching, woody-based plants 1–2½ ft. tall, with narrow bright green leaves and broad clusters of fragrant flowers in yellow, cream, orange, red, brown, or burgundy, sometimes shaded or veined with contrasting color. Their blooming period fills the time slot between those of primroses and summer bedding plants. Need ample water. Sow seeds in spring for bloom the following year, or set out plants in fall. If faded blooms are cut and plants

shaped, they may behave as perennials in mild-winter regions. If plants are allowed to set seed, volunteers may appear.

E. hieraciifolium (E. alpinum). SIBERIAN WALLFLOWER. Perennial, usually grown as an annual. All zones. Branching plants 1–1½ ft. tall are covered with rich orange flowers in spring. Leaves are firm and narrow. In mild climates sow seed in fall for spring bloom; elsewhere sow in summer for well-established plants by fall. Moderate water. Often self-sows. Often sold as *Cheiranthus allionii* or *E. asperum*. 'Moonlight', with bright yellow flowers that open from red buds, is sometimes available as plants.

E. kotschyanum. Perennial treated as an annual in warm climates. Zones 1–11, 14–21. Light green leaves forming 6-in. mats produce deep yellow flowers on 2-in. stems. Use in rock gardens or mixed plantings of small perennials between paving stones. Moderate water. If plants hump up, cut out central portions, transplant them, and press original plant flat again.

E. linifolium. Zones 4–7, 14–17, 22, 23. Resembles 'Bowles Mauve' but smaller (to 2½ ft.), with broader leaves. Flowers open buff and turn to mauve, producing a two-tone effect. 'Variegatum' has leaves edged with white. Moderate water.

ERYTHEA. See BRAHEA   p. 189

ERYTHRINA

CORAL TREE

Fabaceae (Leguminosae)

DECIDUOUS OR NEARLY EVERGREEN TREES OR SHRUBS

ZONES VARY BY SPECIES

FULL SUN

INFREQUENT, DEEP WATERING IN DRY SEASON

Erythrina caffra

Many kinds; known and used chiefly in Southern California. Brilliant flowers from greenish white through yellow, light orange, and light red to orange and red. Thorny plants have strong structural value, in or out of leaf. Leaves divided into three leaflets. To eliminate too-rapid, succulent growth and limb breakage in larger species (*E. caffra, E. lysistemon, E. sykesii*), give little or no summer irrigation and prune after flowering.

E. acanthocarpa. TAMBOOKIE THORN. Deciduous shrub. Zones 19–24. To 3 ft. tall (rarely 6 ft.). Bluish green leaflets to 1½ in. are as broad as long. Spring flower spikes are 7 in. long, 6 in. thick, with scarlet, yellow-tipped flowers. Thorny plant grows from large, thick tuberlike root.

E. americana. Deciduous tree (but may be evergreen in mildest areas near coast). Zones 12, 13, 19–24. Native to Mexico; used as street tree in Mexico City. To 25 ft. tall. Resembles *E. coralloides* in habit and flowers.

E. bidwillii. Large deciduous shrub. Zones 8, 9, 12–24. To 8 ft., sometimes treelike to 20 ft. or more, wide spreading. Hybrid origin. Spectacular display—2-ft.-long clusters of pure red flowers on long, willowy stalks from spring until winter; main show in summer. Cut back flowering wood when flowers are spent. Very thorny, so plant away from paths and prune with long-handled shears.

E. caffra (E. constantiana). KAFFIRBOOM CORAL TREE. Briefly deciduous tree. Zones 21–24. Native to South Africa. Grows 24–40 ft. high, spreads to 40–60 ft. wide. Drops leaves in January; then angular bare branches produce big clusters of deep red-orange, tubular flowers that drip nectar. In March or earlier, flowers give way to fresh, light green foliage.

E. coralloides. NAKED CORAL TREE. Deciduous tree. Zones 12, 13, 19–24. Native to Mexico (some doubt about place of origin). To 30 ft. high and as wide or wider, but easily contained by pruning. Fiery red blossoms like fat candles or pine cones bloom at tips of naked, twisted, black-thorned branches, March–May. At end of flowering season, 8–10-in. leaves develop, give shade in summer, turn yellow in late fall before dropping. Bizarre form of branch structure when tree is out of leaf is almost as valuable as spring flower display. Sometimes sold as *E. poianthes.* ▶

E. crista-galli. COCKSPUR CORAL TREE. Deciduous shrub or tree. Zones 7–9, 12–17, 19–24. Native to rainy sections of Brazil. Unusual plant with habit all its own. In frost-free areas, becomes many-stemmed, rough-barked tree to 15–20 ft. high and as wide. In colder climates, dies to ground in winter but comes back in spring like perennial (cut back dead growth). First flowers form after leaves come in spring—at each branch tip a big, loose, spikelike cluster of velvety, birdlike blossoms in warm pink to wine red (plants vary). Depending on environment there can be as many as three distinct flowering periods, spring through fall. Cut back old flower stems and dead branch ends after each wave of bloom. Leaves 6 in. long, leaflets 2–3 in. long.

Erythrina crista-galli

E. falcata. Nearly evergreen tree. Zones 19–24. Native to Brazil and Peru. Grows upright to 30–40 ft. high. Must be in ground several years before it flowers (may take 10–12 years). Rich deep red (occasionally orange-red), sickle-shaped flowers in hanging, spikelike clusters at branch ends in late winter, early spring. Some leaves fall at flowering time.

E. humeana. NATAL CORAL TREE. Normally deciduous shrub or tree (sometimes almost evergreen). Zones 12, 13, 20–24. Native to South Africa. May grow to 30 ft. but begins to wear its bright orange-red flowers when only 3 ft. high. Blooms continuously from late August to late November, carrying flowers in long-stalked clusters at branch ends well above foliage (unlike many other types). Dark green leaves. *E. h.* 'Raja' is shrubbier and has leaflets with long, pointed "tails."

E. lysistemon. Deciduous tree. Zones 13, 21–24. Native to South Africa. Similar to *E. caffra* in size but slower growing. Light orange (sometimes shrimp-colored) flowers. Time of bloom varies greatly; may bloom intermittently from October to May, occasionally in summer. Many handsome black thorns. A magnificent tree of great landscape value. Very sensitive to wet soil. Sometimes erroneously sold as *E. princeps*.

Erythrina humeana

E. sykesii. Deciduous tree. Zones 19–24. Hybrid from Australia. Grows 24–30 ft.; spreading habit. Showy red flowers before leaves, January–March. Unlike preceding species, does not form pods.

ERYTHRONIUM

Liliaceae

CORMS

ZONES 1–7, 15–17

PARTIAL OR FULL SHADE

SUMMER WATER FOR GROWING PLANTS

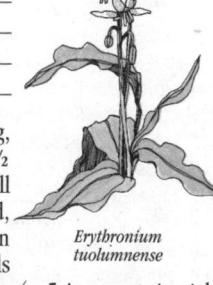
Erythronium tuolumnense

Most are native to West. Spring-blooming, dainty, nodding, lily-shaped flowers 1–1½ in. across, on stems usually 1 ft. high or less. All have two (rarely three) broad, tongue-shaped, basal leaves, mottled in many species. Plant in groups under trees, in rock gardens, beside pools or streams. Set out corms in fall, 2–3 in. deep, 4–5 in. apart, in rich, porous soil; plant corms as soon as you receive them, and don't let them dry out.

E. californicum. FAWN LILY. Leaves mottled with brown. Flowers creamy white or yellow with deeper yellow band at base.

E. dens-canis. DOG-TOOTH VIOLET. European species with purple or rose flowers 1 in. long; stems 6 in. high. Leaves mottled with reddish brown. Needs more sun than others. Specialists can supply named varieties in white, pink, rose, and violet.

E. hendersonii. Flowers deeply curled back at tips, 1½ in. across, light to deep lavender, deep maroon at base surrounded by white band. Leaves mottled.

E. revolutum. Similar to *E. californicum*, with mottled leaves, large rose pink or lavender flowers, banded yellow at base. 'Rose Beauty' and 'White Beauty' are choice varieties.

E. tuolumnense. Solid green leaves. Flowers golden yellow, greenish yellow at base. Robust, with stems 12–15 in. tall. 'Kondo' and 'Pagoda' are extra-vigorous selections.

ESCALLONIA

Saxifragaceae

EVERGREEN SHRUBS

ZONES 4–9, 14–17, 20–24

SUN NEAR COAST, PART SHADE INLAND

TAKE ARIDITY; BETTER WITH REGULAR WATER

Escallonia rubra

Native to South America, principally Chile. Wind hardy, clean looking, with glossy leaves. Clusters of flowers in summer and fall (nearly year-round in mild climates). May freeze badly at 10–15°F, but recover quickly. Will take direct coastal conditions and coastal winds. Tolerant of most soils but damaged by high alkalinity. Prune taller ones by removing one-third of old wood each year, cutting to the base; or shape into multitrunked trees. Prune after flowers fade. Tip-pinch smaller kinds to keep them compact.

Can be sheared as hedges, but this may sacrifice some bloom. Fast growing; good screen plants; attractive to bees. Foliage of some exudes resinous fragrance.

E. 'Apple Blossom'. See E. langleyensis

E. 'Balfouri'. See E. exoniensis

E. bifida (E. montevidensis). WHITE ESCALLONIA. Tall, broad shrub to 8–10 ft., useful as big screening plant or multitrunked small tree to 25 ft. Leaves dark green, glossy, 3–4 in. long. White flowers in large, rounded clusters at branch ends, late summer, fall. Many plants sold under this name are *E. illinita*, a smaller plant to 10 ft. tall with smaller flower clusters and pronounced resinous odor.

E. 'C. F. Ball'. See E. rubra

E. 'Compakta'. To 3 ft. high. Rose red flowers.

E. exoniensis. Name given to hybrids between *E. rosea* and *E. rubra*. Best selections are 'Balfouri', graceful plant to 10 ft. with drooping branchlets, narrow clusters of white, pink-tinted flowers; and 'Frades' (*E. 'Fradesii'*), compact growth to 5–6 ft. (lower with pinching). 'Frades' resembles *E. laevis*, but has smaller, glossy green leaves and prolific show of clear pink to rose flowers nearly year-round. Good as espalier.

E. 'Fradesii'. See E. exoniensis

E. 'Ingramii'. See E. rubra macrantha

E. 'Jubilee'. Compact 6-ft. shrub, densely leafy right to ground. Clustered pinkish to rose flowers bloom at intervals all year. Foliage inferior to that of *E. exoniensis*. Set 4 ft. apart for informal hedge or screen.

E. laevis (E. organensis). PINK ESCALLONIA. Leafy, dense-growing shrub to 12–15 ft. Leaves bronzy green. Pink to red buds open into white to pink flowers in short, broad clusters. Early summer bloom. Use like *E. bifida*. Leaves burn in beach plantings and in high heat of interior.

E. langleyensis. Name given to hybrids between *E. rubra* and *E. virgata*. Best-known selection is 'Apple Blossom', a dense-growing shrub to 5 ft., sprawling unless pinched back. Pinkish white flowers open from pink buds. Blooms all summer with peaks in late spring, early fall.

E. montevidensis. See E. bifida

E. 'Newport Dwarf'. Grows 2½ ft. tall, 4 ft. wide, with deep pink to red flowers over a long season.

E. organensis. See E. laevis

E. 'Pride of Donard'. Dense, rounded shrub wider than tall. Many stems end in clusters of rose pink flowers (plant blooms almost all year). Dark green, glossy leaves.

E

E. rosea. Shrub to 7 ft. with shiny, oval, 1½-in. leaves. Clustered white to red flowers in summer. Many closely related plants sold under this name; the commonest is probably a selection of *E. franciscana*, 10 ft. tall with tendency to throw out long, uneven branches. It has chocolate-colored bark and dark green leaves ½–1 in. long. Rosy pink flowers all summer long.

E. rubra. Upright, compact shrub 6–15 ft. tall. Leaves smooth, very glossy dark green. Red or crimson flowers in 1–3-in. clusters throughout warmer months. Much used as screen or hedge, especially near coast. Compact varieties are 'C. F. Ball' (to 3 ft. with some pinching) and 'William Watson', to 4 ft., with ruddy cerise flowers, spindly habit unless pruned. *E. r. macrantha* ('Ingramii') is large-flowered variety.

E. virgata. Partially deciduous shrub to 6 ft., with ¾-in. leaves and short clusters of pale rose or white flowers. 'Gwendolyn Anley' has flesh pink flowers. These are hardiest escallonias in frostiest parts of their hardiness range.

ESCHSCHOLZIA californica

| CALIFORNIA POPPY |
| *Papaveraceae* |
| PERENNIAL OFTEN GROWN AS ANNUAL |
| ✎ ALL ZONES |
| ☼ FULL SUN |
| ◊ ● SUMMER WATER EXTENDS BLOOM |

Eschscholzia californica

Native to California, Oregon. State flower of California. Free branching from base; stems 8–24 in. long. Leaves blue green, finely divided. Single flowers about 2 in. wide, with satiny petals; color varies from pale yellow to deep orange. Blooms close at night and on gray days.

California poppy is not the best choice for important, close-in garden beds: unless you trim off dead flowers regularly, plants go to seed and all parts turn straw color. But it can't be surpassed for naturalizing on sunny hillsides, along drives, or in dry fields, vacant lots, parking strips, or country gardens. Sow seed where plants are to grow; California poppies do not transplant well. Broadcast seed in fall on cultivated, well-drained soil in full sun; if rains are late, water to keep ground moist until seeds germinate. For large-scale sowing, use 3–4 lbs. of seed per acre. Birds like seeds.

There are also garden forms available in yellow, pink, rose, flame orange, red, cream, and white; Sunset strain has single flowers, Mission Bells semidouble flowers, and Ballerina semidouble flowers with frilled and fluted petals. The Silk strain has bronze-tinted foliage, semidouble flowers in the full color range. Single-color varieties are often available through seed catalogs. Among these are 'Cherry Ripe', 'Milky White', and 'Purple-Violet'.

E. caespitosa. Annual. Smaller than *E. californica;* garden variety 'Sundew' has densely tufted growth to 6 in. Bright yellow, 1-in. flowers. Edging, containers.

ESPOSTOA lanata

| PERUVIAN OLD MAN CACTUS |
| *Cactaceae* |
| CACTUS |
| ✎ ZONES 12–24 |
| ☼ ◗ FULL SUN OR LIGHT AFTERNOON SHADE |
| ● TOLERATES ARIDITY |

Espostoa lanata

Columnar cactus branching with age. Slow growing in pots, fairly fast to 8 ft. in open ground. Plant has light brown, bristly, ½–2-in.-long thorns, usually concealed in long, white hair that covers plant. Hair is especially long and dense near summit. Tubular, pink, 2-in.-long flowers, May–June. Protect from hard frosts.

EUCALYPTUS

| *Myrtaceae* |
| EVERGREEN TREES OR SHRUBS |
| ✎ ZONES 5, 6, 8–24 (SEE HARDINESS ON CHART) |
| ☼ FULL SUN |
| ◊ ● SUPREMELY TOLERANT OF ARIDITY |
| ▶ SEE CHART NEXT PAGE |

Eucalyptus citriodora

With few exceptions, native to Australia. Most widely planted nonnative trees in California and Arizona; for several hundred miles in parts of California you never lose sight of a eucalypt. First ones were planted in California in 1856. From 1870 on, they were widely planted for windbreaks, firewood, shade, and beauty. From 1904 to 1912 thousands of acres were planted in an ill-advised hardwood timber scheme. Eucalyptus remain popular landscaping trees. Reasons:

Great beauty. Some kinds are basically landscape trees or shrubs, with unimportant flowers. These kinds are grown for their attractive and functional form and texture. Others bear flowers as striking as roses or rhododendrons, or have foliage so handsome that florists sell it. Some species serve basic landscaping functions and produce pretty flowers, too. The chart indicates noteworthy features of over 50 different eucalyptus species.

Climate tolerance. Much of Australia has a desert, Mediterranean, or subtropical climate, as do sections of California and Arizona. Dozens of eucalyptus species are naturally adapted to our coast, coastal hills, valleys, and deserts—with or without irrigation. Except in the low deserts, most of these need no watering at all.

Few pests. Eucalyptus was a pest-free tree until 1984, when the eucalyptus longhorn beetle—one of the tree's native attackers in Australia—was observed in Southern California. Without its native predators to keep it in check, the beetle has become a serious pest, especially on stressed trees. Signs of infestation include oval holes, made by the beetles, leaving plant and branches dying with leaves still attached. Since 1988 the beetle has been in Northern California.

Eucalyptus ficifolia

For now, the best way to deal with the problem is good management. Avoid pruning from May to October. If any pruning cuts are absolutely necessary, seal them well to prevent sap flow, which attracts beetles. Freshly cut wood is a lure. If you observe tunnels under the bark of eucalyptus firewood, immediately burn or bury the wood. Remove dead or dying trees; bury logs or cover tightly with tarpaulins for at least 6 months. Keep eucalyptus firewood tightly covered, and do not transport it. Best hope for eventual control will come from introduced predatory insects.

Fast growth. A few types grow as fast as 10–15 ft. a year in early stages. Such growth rate is typically associated with short-lived trees, but not in this case; fast-growing tree eucalypts can live for at least a century if planted right.

Eucalypts are influenced through their lives by their condition at planting time and the kind of planting they get. Select the most vigorous-looking plants, not the biggest ones. Avoid those with many leafless twigs or evidence of hard pruning. If possible, do not buy plants with can-bound roots. If such plants are all you can get, do this: wash soil off roots, then spread roots out as straight and fanlike as possible in premoistened planting hole (place stem's old soil line ½–1 in. below grade level). Immediately fill in around fanned-out roots with moistened soil and

Eucalyptus nicholii

▶ page 287

EUCALYPTUS

NAME	HARDINESS	FORM AND SIZE	LEAVES AND BARK	FLOWERS AND FRUIT	BEST FEATURES AND HOW TO ENCOURAGE THEM
Eucalyptus albens WHITE BOX	22°F	Straight trunk, wide crown, fairly dense shade. To 30–80 ft.	Pale gray-green leaves. Pale bark	Clusters of small white flowers from whitish buds. Small fruits	Like *E. polyanthemos* but stronger growth in desert
E. baueriana BLUE BOX	10–18°F	Fuller-bodied substitute for *E. polyanthemos*	Leaves broader and rougher than those of *E. polyanthemos*	Same as *E. polyanthemos*	Attractive round tree when young; becomes tall and straight with age
E. caesia (*caesia* means "bluish gray")	22–25°F	Graceful, weeping, open habit as mallee or small, weak-structured tree. To 15–20 ft.	Gray-green, small leaves contrast with red stems. Bark white and mottled when young, curling when older	Outstanding dusty pink to deep rose flowers in loose clusters, blooming heavily late winter to early spring. Flowering scattered rest of year. Bell-shaped, 3/4-in. lavender-gray seed capsules	Not good in wind or in heavy soil. Use as thin screen in protected place. With pruning and training, use as espalier, shrub, or multi-trunked tree. Prune and stake to give body
E. camaldulensis (**E. rostrata**) RED GUM, RIVER RED GUM	12–23°F	Ultimately 80–120 ft. Form varies; typically has curved trunk, spreading crown, gracefully weeping branches	Long, slender, lance-shaped, medium green leaves, pendulous in varying degrees. Tan, mottled trunk	Unimportant white to pale yellow flowers in drooping clusters, summer. Followed by many rounded, pea-size seed capsules in long clusters. Not grown for flowers; structural tree	One of most planted eucalypts worldwide. Mighty tree for highways, broad streets, parks, skylines, even lawns, except in desert, where it gets chlorosis. Endures alkaline soil. Hardier than *E. globulus;* resprouts after 11°F freeze
E. campaspe SILVER-TOPPED GIMLET	18°F	Slender tree to 25–35 ft.	Silvery gray leaves. Copper brown, polished-looking mature bark	Flowers and fruit inconspicuous	Thrives under a wide variety of irrigation conditions. Can grow on 7-in. annual rainfall
E. cinerea (*cinerea* means "ash colored")	14–17°F	Medium-size tree, 20–50 ft. high, almost as wide. Irregular outline. Can be scrawny	Juvenile leaves gray-green, roundish, 1–2 in. long, in pairs. Mature leaves long. Furrowed bark	Small white flowers near stems in winter and spring, followed by small conical seed capsules. Grow for decorative juvenile foliage rather than flowers	Inclined to grow snakelike. Corrective pruning encourages and yields juvenile gray-foliaged branches. Fast growing. Withstands wind. Best in dry site or with fast drainage
E. citriodora LEMON-SCENTED GUM	24–28°F	One of most graceful of trees—slender, tall (75–100 ft.). Trunk usually straight, sometimes curved	Leaves long (3–7 in.), narrow, golden green, lemon-scented. Trunk and branches powder white to pinkish	Once tree gets up in the air, you'd need telescope to see flowers (lower 1/2 to 2/3 of tree is bare trunk). Blooms whitish, not distinctive, in clusters, mostly during winter. Seed capsules that follow are urn-shaped, 3/8 in. wide	Designer's tree. Enhances any architecture. Can grow close to walls, walks. Perfect for groves. Very fast growing. Weak trunk when young; stake stoutly. Cut back and thin often to strengthen. Tolerates much or little water. Tender to frosts
E. cladocalyx (**E. corynocalyx**) SUGAR GUM	23–28°F	Large, upright, graceful, round-topped, very open, 75–100 ft. high. Straight trunk	Oval or variably shaped leaves, 3–5 in. long, shiny, reddish. Tan bark peels to show cream patches	Creamy white flowers in dense 3-in. clusters, June–Aug. Oval seed capsules (3/8 in. wide). Planted for structure, not flowers	Dramatic skyline tree on Southern California coast. Puffy clouds of leaves separated by open spaces—like Japanese print. Tough. Variety 'Nana' to 20–25 ft.
E. conferruminata (usually sold as **E. lehmannii**) BUSHY YATE	25–28°F	Small tree, 20–30 ft., dense, flat-topped, wide spreading	Light green, long oval, 2-in. leaves. Some turn red in fall. Brown bark	Apple green flowers in big (4-in. wide), round clusters open from horn-shaped buds in clusters. Large, fused seed capsules remain on branches	Fast growing, densely leafed tree, very good for screening on coast or street tree with lower branches pruned. Unpruned, branches persist to ground
E. cornuta (*cornuta* means "horn shaped") YATE	22–25°F	Large-headed, spreading tree, to 35–60 ft. high. Attractive dense crown gives shade	Lance-shaped, shiny leaves, 3–6 in. long (young leaves round, gray). Bark peels in strips	Fingerlike buff caps of buds pushed off by opening flowers. Greenish yellow flowers make round, fuzzy clusters, 3 in. wide, summer. Clusters of round seed capsules with short horns	Useful for flowers, form, shade, and landscaping. Tolerates varying soil, water, climate conditions, even neglect. Not subject to wind breakage

EUCALYPTUS

NAME	HARDINESS	FORM AND SIZE	LEAVES AND BARK	FLOWERS AND FRUIT	BEST FEATURES AND HOW TO ENCOURAGE THEM
E. deglupta MINDANAO GUM	24–26°F	Erect, clean-trunked tree to 80 ft. or more	Dark green foliage. Bark flaking, strikingly colored in blue, green, yellow, red, purple	Flowers, fruit inconspicuous	Trunk is the spectacular feature. This jungle tree from the Philippines and New Guinea grows fast, endures light frost. Needs water
E. eremophila TALL SAND MALLEE	17–22°F	Multitrunked, small, bushy tree, 25 ft.	Dark green, narrow, lance-shaped, shiny leaves. Scaly bark	Round, yellow, fuzzy 1–2-in. flowers in clusters, June. Opening flowers push off long pointed caps. Cylindrical capsules, 1/4 in. wide	Good for banks, hillsides, beach areas. Not good in lawns. Better liked in Southern than in Northern California. Good desert plant
E. erythrocorys RED-CAP GUM	23–26°F	Small tree, 10–30 ft., best with multiple trunk; sprawling but attractive bush	Thick, shiny, 4–7-in., lance-shaped leaves, greener than most eucalyptus leaves. White trunk	Spectacular. Bright red caps tilt up and drop off to reveal yellow flowers in clusters like shaving brushes. Blooms any time, but heaviest fall to early spring. Cone-shaped seed capsules follow	Takes much water if drainage is good. Can be grown in lawn. To make dense multitrunked bush or tree, head back main shoots several times. Attractive in desert
E. erythronema RED-FLOWERED MALLEE	17–22°F	Mallee or small, bushy, crooked or sinuous tree, 10–25 ft.	Narrow, dull green leaves 1 1/2–3 in. long. Smooth bark in patches of pink, white, tan, pale green	Watermelon to deep red flowers, 1 in. wide, open from conical, pointed buds, 1 in. long, pinkish green to red. Conical, square-sided seed capsules, 1/2 in. wide	Trunk and flowers are its best features. You may have to thin some to make it presentable tree. Resists wind. Good near ocean. Recommended for desert
E. ficifolia RED-FLOWERING GUM	25–30°F	Usually single-trunked, round-headed tree to 40 ft. Compact crown. Can be multistemmed big bush	Leaves 3–7 in. long, shape and texture of rubber plant leaves. Bark red and stringy to gray and fibrous	Spectacular 1-ft. clusters of flowers in cream, light pink, salmon, orange, or light red (most common), all year, peaking July–Aug. Seed capsules 1 in. wide, like miniature dice cups	Not like other eucalypts. Prune off seed capsules from young trees so they won't pull branches down. Best on coast; seldom successful inland or in lawns. Unpredictable flower color from seed
E. formanii	15°F	Bushy, billowy big shrub or small tree to 15–30 ft.	Silvery to tan leaves, 2 1/2 in. long, 1/8 in. wide	Small white flowers are inconspicuous. Fruits small, rounded	Slow-growing tree of unusual interest in desert
E. globulus BLUE GUM	17–22°F	Tall, solemn trees of grandeur; reach 150–200 ft. Straight trunks. Heavy masses of foliage	Sickle-shaped, dark green leaves, 6–10 in. long. Young leaves oval, silvery, soft. Bark sheds	Flowers creamy white to yellow in winter and spring. Warty, ribbed, blue-gray seed capsules, 1 in. wide. Fruit drop added to leaf and bark litter makes tree very messy	Most common gum in California. Aromatic and great windbreak but too messy, greedy, and brittle for garden or city street. Needs deep soil, lots of room. Best on coastal slopes; poor in deserts
E. g. 'Compacta' DWARF BLUE GUM	17–22°F	Multibranched, bushy, shrublike tree, as high as 60–70 ft.	Same as *E. globulus*. Foliage persists to ground for 10–15 years. Becomes treelike later	Flowers and seed capsules same as on *E. globulus*	Lacks noble silhouette of *E. globulus* but is just as greedy, almost as messy. Good low windbreak in coastal areas—can be sheared to as low as 10 ft.
E. grossa COARSE-FLOWERED MALLEE	22–26°F	Multitrunked, spreading shrub, 9–15 ft. tall. Sometimes dense	Thick, glistening, deep green, 3-in., broad, oval leaves. Red-and-green stems	Noticeable yellow flowers in clusters open from bullet-shaped buds in spring and summer. Cylindrical seed capsules, 3/8 in. wide	Best feature is clean green foliage. Often erratic; can be made into dense hedge if pruned. Good desert choice
E. gunnii CIDER GUM	5–10°F	Medium to large, dense, vertical tree, 40–75 ft.	Mature leaves lance-shaped, 3–5 in. long. Smooth green-and-tan bark	Small creamy white flowers, April–June, from green, shiny, round buds. Seed capsules 1/4 in. wide, bell-shaped, in clusters	Strong, vigorous, tall grower. Healthy and vigorous looking. Good shade, windbreak, or privacy screen in cold areas (very hardy)
E. kruseana KRUSE'S MALLEE	25–28°F	Thin, open, angular shrub, almost ground cover; 5–8 ft. tall at most	Silver blue, round, 1-in. leaves like tiny *E. pulverulenta*. Smooth bark	Little (1/2-in.) yellow flowers along stems between round leaves. Flower bud caps cone-shaped. Seed capsules size and shape of small (1/4-in.) acorns	Attractive foliage and flowers on slow-growing shrub, small and dainty enough for Japanese garden. Conversation plant. Cut back frequently. Useful in desert gardens

EUCALYPTUS

NAME	HARDINESS	FORM AND SIZE	LEAVES AND BARK	FLOWERS AND FRUIT	BEST FEATURES AND HOW TO ENCOURAGE THEM
E. leucoxylon WHITE IRONBARK	14–18°F	Somewhat variable; usually slender, upright, open, with pendulous branches. Reaches 20–80 ft.	Gray-green, sickle-shaped leaves, 3–6 in. long. Bark sheds, leaving white to mottled trunk	White flowers intermittently, winter, spring. Goblet-shaped seed capsules, 3/8 in. wide. (*E. l.* 'Rosea' has pink flowers, larger capsules, may not come true from seed)	Free-flowering, fast-growing, moderate-size tree that tolerates adverse conditions including heavy soil, light rocky soil, heat, wind
E. l. megalocarpa 'Rosea' LARGE-FRUITED YELLOW GUM	14–18°F	Much-branched, shrublike tree. Variable 15–25 ft.	Gray-green leaves. Gray to pinkish trunk	Clear vivid crimson flowers borne profusely at early age. Goblet-shaped seed capsules, 3/4 in. wide	Very ornamental tree. Good in most soils, most sites, even near beach or in desert
E. macrocarpa (*macrocarpa* means "big fruited")	8–12°F	Erratic, sprawling shrub, 4–15 ft. Tries to be vine but stems are too stiff. Similar to *E. rhodantha*	Light gray-blue leaves, 2–5 in. long, round with definite point, set close to stem. Greenish white bark	Golf-ball-size gray buds (pointed at top) open to show flat-topped, round, fluffy flowers 4–7 in. wide. Usually pink; also white, red, or yellowish white (seedlings vary). No stems on flowers; grow right on branch. Flat-topped, bowl-shaped seed capsules, 3 in. wide	Sprawling plant good for seasonal display in dry, sunny place. Not for irrigated areas (overwatering causes blackening of leaves). New growth begins vertical, becomes horizontal when weighted down with buds and capsules. Stems tend to die back from pruning
E. maculata (*maculata* means "spotted")	19–23°F	Erect single-trunked tree, branching to make wide head. Graceful, strong. To 50–75 ft.	Dark green leaves, 3–6 in. long. Pearl gray bark patched dark red to violet	White flowers in branch-end clusters, 1–3 in. wide. Seed capsules urn-shaped, 1/2 in. wide, rough on outside. Not grown for flowers; landscaping tree	Good singly or in groves. Smooth, spotted trunks are usually quite handsome; vary in degree of spottiness. Best in sandy, well-drained soil
E. mannifera maculosa RED-SPOTTED GUM	20–25°F	Tall, slender tree, 20–50 ft. tall. Gracefully pendant branches sway prettily in wind	Leaves 1/2 in. wide, 4–6 in. long, light green with gray cast. Bark brown, gray, off white	Unimportant light-colored flowers open from pointed oval buds in clusters of 3–7; leave 1/2-in., goblet-shaped seed capsules	Landscaping tree to feature in place of honor. When mature, brownish and grayish bark flakes off in summer, leaving powdery white surface. Australian aborigines paint their faces with the white dust
E. megacornuta (*megacornuta* means "big horned")	20–23°F	Big shrub or small tree, 20–30 ft. Multistemmed or single-trunked. Spindly	Shiny, bronzy green leaves. Smooth, gray to tan bark	Clusters of kelly green flowers, 1 1/2 in. long, shaped like shaving brushes, open from buds like warty fingers. Clawlike capsules	Flower arrangers like 2-in.-long, bronzy green buds, flowers, and seed capsules. Form sometimes acceptable for landscaping
E. melliodora (*melliodora* means "honey scented")	18–20°F	Upright, graceful tree, 30–100 ft., with slightly weeping branches. Top fills in well	Boat- to sickle-shaped leaves, 2–6 in. long, grayish green. Old bark scaly, flaky, tan	Late-winter/early-spring flowers are off white, in clusters 1 1/2 in. wide; not showy but sweet smelling and attractive to bees. Seed capsules of 1/4 in., in clusters	Clean, well-mannered tree, very little litter. Good for shade tree, street tree, windbreak (takes wind very well). Form 'Rosea' has pink flowers
E. microtheca (*microtheca* means "tiny capsules") COOLIBAH	5–10°F	Bushy, round-headed tree to 35–40 ft. May have one or many trunks	Blue-green, ribbonlike leaves, 8 in. long. Smooth bark	Insignificant creamy white flowers. Seed capsules tiny (matchhead size) in clusters of 3–5. Seed capsules create no litter	Strong-looking, strong-growing tree of character. No breakage from wind. One of Arizona's best eucalypts
E. nicholii NICHOL'S WILLOW-LEAFED PEPPERMINT	12–15°F	Graceful, weeping tree to 40 ft. Upright main trunk. Spreading crown	Light green, very narrow leaves, 3–5 in. long. Mature foliage coarser. Bark deeply furrowed, reddish brown	Small, inconspicuous whitish flowers, mostly in summer. Very small, round seed capsules in roundish clusters	Garden or street tree. Beauty in fine-textured foliage, billowing, willowy form. Grows fast. Crushed leaves smell like peppermint. Too much water can cause chlorosis
E. orbifolia ROUND-LEAFED MALLEE	23–25°F	Large mallee of irregular, clambering habit. Not a tree	Leaves nearly round (slightly pointed), 2 in. long. Thin red bark	Little (1/2-in.-wide) yellow flowers in late spring. Round flower bud cap has point like Kaiser Wilhelm helmet	Ground cover in difficult sunny place; native to rocky desert. Espalier to show off round leaves and flowers. Slender, vinelike stems

E

EUCALYPTUS

NAME	HARDINESS	FORM AND SIZE	LEAVES AND BARK	FLOWERS AND FRUIT	BEST FEATURES AND HOW TO ENCOURAGE THEM
E. papuana GHOST GUM	22°F	Variable; can be short, crooked, 20-ft. tree with multiple trunks or 60-ft. single-trunked tree	Gray-green leaves, tinted purplish by frosts. Smooth white bark	Small white summer flowers. Fruit inconspicuous	White bark is its most striking feature. Does well in desert soils
E. pauciflora GHOST GUM	10–15°F	Tree. Branches spread to make crown as wide as tree is tall (40 by 40 ft.). Graceful, airy	White trunk and branches and narrow, gray-green, 3–6-in. leaves give it the name "ghost gum"	Insignificant flowers and little or no seed setting. Among other good points, ghost gum doesn't litter ground beneath it	White trunk and branches and open foliage make it good individual display tree. Takes wet or dry soil. Good in lawns. In youth, remove erratic branches
E. p. niphophila SNOW GUM	0–10°F	Small, wide-spreading, open tree to 20 ft. Trunk usually crooked	Silvery blue, lance-shaped, 1½–4-in. leaves. Smooth, white, peeling bark	Creamy white flowers in tight clusters 1½ in. wide, summer. Seed capsules round, ⅜ in. wide, very gray, also in tight clusters, close to stem	Acclaimed chiefly for hardiness and silvery look of leaves. Slow growing. Wind tolerant. Good on slopes. Can be picturesque
E. perriniana SPINNING GUM	10–15°F	Small, straggly tree, 15–30 ft. Best cut back as shrub	Juvenile leaves silvery, form circle around stem, spin on stem when dry	Many small white flowers in summer in clusters of 3. Seed capsules, also in clusters of 3, are cup-shaped, ¼ in. wide	Silvery foliage nice for arrangements. If you cut enough, silvery juvenile growth remains (mature leaves are long). Use as gray-leafed plant in border
E. platypus ROUND-LEAFED MOORT	23–26°F	Large bush or small tree, 20–30 ft. Many stems; may ultimately form one trunk	Dark, dull green leaves, round-ended, 1–2 in. long, rough. Smooth tan bark	Many flowers, red or green (2 forms), open at ends of flattened stems, make showy clusters 2 in. wide. Cluster of many ½-in., goblet-shaped seed capsules	Dense, fast-growing, pyramidal form, good for solid screening (space 12 ft. apart). Plants give general effect of stiff birches. Hummingbirds enjoy flowers. Good desert selection
E. polyanthemos SILVER DOLLAR GUM	14–18°F	Slender, erect tree, single or multistemmed, to 20–60 ft. Fairly fast growing	Juvenile leaves gray-green, oval or round, 2–3 in. Mature leaves lance-shaped. Bark mottled	Creamy white flowers in 1-in. clusters, spring and summer. Seed capsules are cylindrical cups, ½ in. wide, in clusters. Flowers incidental—grow tree for cut foliage or landscape	Popular landscaping and street tree. Excellent cut foliage. Select young trees carefully; some have leaves less round and gray than others. Grows almost anywhere. Not good in wet places
E. populnea (*populnea* means "poplarlike") BIMBLE BOX, POPLAR BOX	22°F	Grows 35–70 ft tall with short trunk and dense, roundish crown	Leaves thickish, round, deep green	Small white flowers	Leaves shimmer in wind
E. preissiana BELL-FRUITED MALLEE	24–26°F	Mallee—typically an open, many-stemmed shrub to 12 ft. Sometimes tree to 15 ft.	Oval leaves, 2–3 in. long, thick, dull bluish cast, red stems. Smooth gray bark	Showy. Round, flat yellow flowers 2–3 in. wide open from brown, globelike buds, 1 in. wide. Seed capsules cup-shaped, ¾ in. wide. Flower contrasts with leaf, trunk	First-rate flower producer that can hold its own as garden shrub. Cut flowers keep well. Blooms most heavily Jan.–Mar.
E. pulverulenta (*pulverulenta* means "powdered as with dust") SILVER MOUNTAIN GUM	15–21°F	Irregular, sprawling small tree or large shrub, 15–30 ft. Poor form unless pruned	Silver gray, shish kebab–style juvenile foliage (stems appear to go through leaves). Ribbony bark	Creamy white, ½-in., fuzzy flowers in clusters of 3 sandwiched between round leaves along stems. Fall to spring. Flowers are an extra, followed by ½-in.-wide, cup-shaped capsules	Use in garden as curiosity feature. Source of branches for arrangements. Cut back often to encourage and yield decorative juvenile leaf growth; mature leaves usually long and pointed
E. pyriformis PEAR-FRUITED MALLEE	25–28°F	Shrub or treelike shrub (mallee), 10–20 ft. Long, weak, rangy stems	Broad, oval, light green leaves 2–4 in. long. Light brown bark	Showy, large (2–3-in.-wide) flowers in clusters, late winter to early summer. May be red, pink, orange, yellow, or cream. Pear-shaped, 1-in. seed capsules	Collector's item. Sometimes an elegant, slender tree; sometimes a weak, rangy shrub. Flowers are best feature. Good performance in dry or sandy soil

E

▶

EUCALYPTUS

NAME	HARDINESS	FORM AND SIZE	LEAVES AND BARK	FLOWERS AND FRUIT	BEST FEATURES AND HOW TO ENCOURAGE THEM
E. rhodantha (*rhodantha* means "roselike") ROSE MALLEE	8–12°F	Erratic, sprawling shrub to 4–8 ft. Branches tend to grow horizontally	Light gray-blue leaves sometimes with greenish cast, 2–4 in. long, nearly round, close to stem. Greenish white bark	Buds same as *E. macrocarpa* but with shorter point on lid. Flowers, on 1–2-in.-long stems, same shape as those of *E. macrocarpa* but 3–5 in. wide and almost always carmine red. Capsules like those of *E. macrocarpa*	Sprawling plant good for almost continual flower display. For dry, sunny place and little water, same as *E. macrocarpa*. Better for spilling down slope than *E. macrocarpa* (follows terrain better). Put supports under branches to keep mud off. Makes good espalier
E. robusta SWAMP MAHOGANY	11–15°F	Tall, densely foliaged, ultimately round-headed. To 80–90 ft.	Dark green, leathery, shiny leaves 4–7 in. long. Rough, dark red brown, stringy bark	Attractive flowers for large tree: masses of pink-tinted, creamy white flowers any time, chiefly in winter. Cylindrical ³⁄₈-in. seed capsules in clusters	Big, strong tree performs well in moist or saline soil. Good for windy places at beach or inland. Windbreak. Attractive foliage. Darkest green eucalypt in deserts
E. rudis FLOODED GUM	12–18°F	Upright, spreading, often weeping, 30–60 ft. high. Robust	Mature leaves gray-green to green, lance-shaped, 4–6 in. long. Rough trunk	White flowers in clusters, spring and summer (not showy but good for large tree). Seed capsules ¼ in. wide	Good large shade tree or street tree. Tolerates valleys, beach, wind, much or little water, sandy and saline soil. Not good in desert unless on deep, gravelly soils with good drainage
E. saligna SYDNEY BLUE GUM	18–20°F	Tall, slender, shaftlike tree, dense when young, thins out later. To 60–80 ft.	Mature leaves medium green, 4–8 in. long, lance-shaped. Red to pinkish bark sheds	Flowers pinkish to cream in spring and summer, not showy. Smooth seed capsules, ¼ in. wide, in tight clusters 1 in. wide	Probably fastest growing ("fastest gum in the West"); if gal.-can plant not root-bound, can grow 10 ft. first year. Better near coast than inland. Can grow in lawns
E. sargentii SALT RIVER MALLET	22°F	Relatively short (25–30 ft.). Stout trunk or multiple trunks	Narrow green leaves to 4 in. long, ¼ in. wide. Dark trunk	Cream-colored flowers open from slender, long-horned buds in spring	Exceptionally tough, exceptionally salt tolerant
E. sideroxylon (often sold as **E. sideroxylon 'Rosea'**) RED IRONBARK, PINK IRONBARK	20–25°F	Varies: 20–80 ft. high, open or dense, slender or squat, weeping or upright	Slim blue-green leaves turn bronze in winter. Furrowed, nearly black trunk	Fluffy flowers, light pink to pinkish crimson, in pendulous clusters, mostly from fall to late spring. Seed capsules goblet shaped, ³⁄₈ in.	Use singly, as screen, or street or highway tree. Wide variation in individuals. Select trees that please you. Grows fast. Coast or inland. Gets chlorotic in wet adobe soils
E. spathulata NARROW-LEAFED GIMLET, SWAMP MALLEE	15–20°F	Small, erect, multitrunked tree, 6–20 ft.	Ribbonlike leaves 2–3 in. long. Smooth red bark	Cream-and-gold flowers open in summer from long, oval buds. Bell-shaped seed capsules	Versatile. Tolerates poor soil drainage. Bushy wind screen. Branches move nicely in breezes. Good desert plant
E. stellulata BLACK SALLY	12–18°F	Medium-size (20–50-ft.), spreading tree with pendulous branches	Broad elliptical leaves. Smooth gray bark changes to olive green	White to cream flowers, Oct.–Apr. Roundish seed capsules, size of small peas, in tight clusters along stem	Unusual colored bark. Nice spreading form. Good screening tree or shade tree
E. tetraptera SQUARE-FRUITED MALLEE	22–26°F	Shrub, 4–10 ft. (occasionally to 15 ft.). Straggly but interesting	Thick, rubbery, dark leaves, 4–5 in. long. Green to gray bark	Big (1½-in.) buds open to big, striking red flowers. Blooms almost continuously. Seeds, flanged squares, 1½ in. wide	A novelty with unusual form. Not for basic landscaping. Grows in sand. Wind resistant, salt tolerant. Prune to make bushy
E. torquata CORAL GUM	17–22°F	Slender, upright, narrow-headed, to 15–20 ft. Branches often droop from weight of flowers, seed capsules	Light green to golden green leaves, long and narrow or blunt and round. Rough, flaky bark	Flower buds are like little (¾-in.) Japanese lanterns. From them open beautiful flowers of coral red and yellow, on and off all year. Seed capsules ½ in. long, grooved	Grown for bloom (good cut flowers) and small size. Good as free-standing tree in narrow area or in grove. Stake and prune or head back to make it graceful. Select by plant form. Good in desert

EUCALYPTUS

NAME	HARDINESS	FORM AND SIZE	LEAVES AND BARK	FLOWERS AND FRUIT	BEST FEATURES AND HOW TO ENCOURAGE THEM
E. viminalis (*viminalis* means "long, flexible shoot") MANNA GUM	12–15°F	Tall, spreading patriarch tree to 150 ft.; drooping willowlike branches	Light green, narrow, 4–6-in.-long leaves. Trunk whitish; bark sheds	Little white flowers in long, thin, open clusters all year—usually too high to be seen. Small, roundish seed capsules	Can make significant silhouette. Grows best in good soil but can take poor soil. Needs room. For ranches, parks, highways, not small gardens. Creates debris
E. woodwardii LEMON-FLOWERED GUM	17–22°F	To 40 ft., with irregular growth	Gray leaves to 5 in. long, 2 in. wide	Flowers are lemon yellow puffs, spectacular fall to summer	Can grow on as little as 7-in. annual rainfall. Use lower plantings to mask bare base, awkward habit

E

irrigate heavily. If plants are top-heavy, cut back and stake (chart specifically prescribes staking for certain species).

Some descriptions in the chart recommend that you cut back plants to make them bushier or stouter. Do this between March and August (in areas where eucalyptus beetle is not a problem), preferably when tree has been in ground at least a year. If possible, cut back to just above side branch or bud. If you can't find such a growth point, cut right into smooth trunk; if plant is established, new growth will break out beneath cut. Later, come back and remove all excess new branches; keep only those that are well placed.

Best way to plant eucalyptus is directly from seed flats or seed pots. Seeding is as easy as with many annuals and perennials. Sow seed on flat of prepared soil in spring or summer. Keep flat shaded and water sparingly. When seedlings are 2–3 in. high, lift gently, separate, and plant into another flat of prepared soil, spacing 5 in. apart. Or transplant into gallon cans or cleaned 1-quart oil cans (puncture at bottom for drainage). Plant seedlings in 2–3 months when 6–12 in. high.

Eucalyptus polyanthemos

A eucalyptus tree in a suitable climate, properly planted and irrigated, is a vigorous, strong, and durable plant. Complete fertilizer is seldom needed, although iron often is required for eucalypts that chronically form yellow leaves. In the desert, eucalypts are especially subject to chlorosis in dense or shallow soils. Iron chelates added during the spring and fall growth flushes are helpful in young trees. Chlorosis can be brought on by overwatering; established trees can get by with infrequent watering. Newly planted trees may need water every day for their first week if the weather is hot and dry; thereafter, you may taper off to one or two waterings a week for the rest of the first growing season.

Eucalyptus preissiana

The chart gives approximate hardiness for each eucalyptus species listed, but it is important to remember that these temperatures are not absolute. In addition to air temperature, you must take into consideration the age of the plant (generally, the older, the hardier); the condition of the plant; the date of frost (24°F in November is more damaging than 24°F in January, after weeks of frosts); the duration of frost. If temperatures in your area are likely to fall within frost-damage range for certain species, plant it as a risk. If they regularly fall below given range, don't plant it. Occasional deep or prolonged freezes may kill even large trees. Do not be too hasty to remove them; they can sprout new growth from trunk or large branches, though heavy freeze damage may alter the tree's appearance. Delay removal or heavy pruning until summer

Eucalyptus rhodantha

(in areas where eucalyptus beetle is a problem, do not prune heavily from May to October; prune in earliest spring or late fall).

Most eucalypts have two conspicuously different kinds of foliage: the soft, variously shaped juvenile leaves, found on seedlings, saplings, and new branches that grow from stumps; and usually tougher adult or mature foliage. Where a species' juvenile foliage is significant, it is mentioned in the chart. Almost all eucalyptus leaves, juvenile and adult, have distinguishing pungent fragrance. Sometimes you must crush leaves to smell it. There is a common fragrance in all types, but various ones are additionally spiked with peppermint, lemon, medicinal aromas, or other scents.

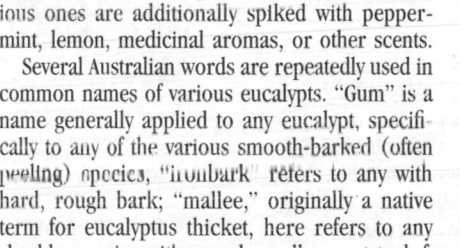

Eucalyptus sideroxylon

Several Australian words are repeatedly used in common names of various eucalypts. "Gum" is a name generally applied to any eucalypt, specifically to any of the various smooth-barked (often peeling) species; "ironbark" refers to any with hard, rough bark; "mallee," originally a native term for eucalyptus thicket, here refers to any shrubby species with round, swollen rootstock from which grow several slender stems; "marlock" refers to dwarf species; "messmate," an interesting name of no particular significance, is applied to several stringy-bark species; "peppermint" refers to any whose crushed leaves yield a peppermint odor, usually possessing finely fibrous bark; "yate" is a native word applied to certain species.

HANDSOME EUCALYPTS FOR SMALL GARDENS

Eucalyptus performs magnificently in lowland California and Arizona. The trees look handsome, and they need no watering at all once established. Many, however, become too big for small places. But each of the following can bring you a special form of eucalyptus beauty and not grow too big for a small garden: *E. ficifolia, E. microtheca, E. nicholii, E. spathulata,* and *E. torquata.*

More than 500 kinds of eucalyptus have been recorded in Australia. About 150 have been grown in California and Arizona, many as solitary representatives in arboretums.

California and Arizona don't have a monopoly on *Eucalyptus.* Gardeners in western Washington and Oregon can grow many. Safest for beginners in these milder-winter areas of the Northwest are *E. gunnii,* cider gum; and *E. pauciflora niphophila,* snow gum. Other choices are *E. perriniana,* spinning gum; and *E. stellulata,* black Sally.

FOR INFORMATION ON YOUR CLIMATE ZONE
PLEASE SEE PAGES 15–44

EUCOMIS

PINEAPPLE FLOWER

Liliaceae

BULBS

✀ ZONES 4–24

☼ ◑ SUN OR LIGHT SHADE

◉ SOME WATER IN SUMMER

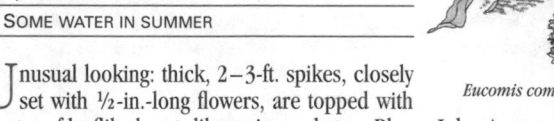
Eucomis comosa

Unusual looking: thick, 2–3-ft. spikes, closely set with ½-in.-long flowers, are topped with cluster of leaflike bracts like a pineapple top. Bloom July–August, but persisting purplish seed capsules carry on the show even longer. Garden or container plant, good cut flower. Need rich soil with plenty of humus. Divide when plants become crowded. Fairly easy to grow from spring-sown seed. Interesting potted plants.

E. bicolor. To 2 ft.; flowers green, each petal edged with purple. Attractive leaves 1 ft. long, 3–4 in. wide, with wavy edges.

E. comosa (E. punctata). Thick spikes 2–3 ft. tall are set with greenish white flowers tinged pink or purple. Stems are spotted purple at the base. Leaves grow to 2 ft. long and are less wavy than those of *E. bicolor.*

EUCRYPHIA

Eucryphiaceae

EVERGREEN OR SEMIEVERGREEN SMALL TREES

✀ ZONES 5, 6, 15–17

☼ ◑ TOLERATE SOME SHADE

◉ REGULAR WATER

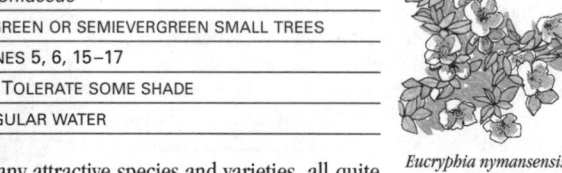
Eucryphia nymansensis

Many attractive species and varieties, all quite rare. The most frequently sold kinds in West have shiny evergreen leaves and 2½-in.-wide, pure white flowers with big tufts of yellow stamens in center. Give them neutral or slightly acid soil and shelter from strong winds. In Zones 5 and 6, protect young plants from temperatures below 15°F.

E. lucida. Slender evergreen tree to 30 ft. Smooth-edged, glossy leaves 1½–3 in. long. Fragrant white flowers in June, July. Native to Tasmania.

E. nymansensis. Group of hybrids between two species from Chile. 'Mt. Usher', best known, is small, columnar evergreen tree with toothed leaves, some simple, some divided into three to five leaflets 2–4 in. long. Flowers often double. 'Nymansay' is somewhat faster growing. Both bloom in August, September.

EUGENIA

Myrtaceae

EVERGREEN SHRUBS OR TREES, MOSTLY TROPICAL

✀ ZONES 21–24 (E. UNIFLORA)

☼ ◑ FULL SUN OR PARTIAL SHADE

◉ REGULAR WATER

Eugenia uniflora

Many species have been reclassified. For *E. myrtifolia, E. paniculata,* see *Syzygium paniculatum;* for *E. smithii,* see *Acmena smithii.*

E. uniflora. SURINAM CHERRY, PITANGA. Evergreen compact shrub or small tree. Very slow and open growth to 15–25 ft., usually to 6–8 ft., with equal spread. Leaves oval, to 2 in. long, glossy coppery green deepening to purplish or red in cold weather. White, fragrant flowers like little brushes, ½ in. across. Fruit, size of small tomatoes, changes color from green to yellow to orange to deep red, at which stage it is edible. Grow in well-drained soil. Best in moist atmosphere and sheltered spot. Can be sheared into hedge, but flowering and fruiting will be reduced. Prune to shape. Grafted varieties are sometimes available in Southern California.

EULALIA GRASS. See MISCANTHUS sinensis   p. 382

EUONYMUS

Celastraceae

EVERGREEN, DECIDUOUS SHRUBS; EVERGREEN VINES

✀ ZONES VARY BY SPECIES

☼ ◑ BEST IN FULL SUN OR LIGHT SHADE

◉ MODERATE WATER

Euonymus japonica

Evergreen kinds are highly valued for their foliage, texture, and form; they are almost always used as landscape structure plants, never for flower display. Some types display colorful fruit—pink, red, or yellow capsules that open to show orange-red seeds in fall and that attract birds. Climate adaptation is quite significant because of varying degrees of hardiness and susceptibility to mildew.

E. alata. WINGED EUONYMUS. Deciduous shrub. Zones 1–9, 14–16. Slow to medium growth to 7–10 ft. high, 10–15 ft. wide. Dense, twiggy, flat topped, with horizontal branching. Twigs have flat, corky wings that disappear on older growth. Dark green leaves turn rich rose red in fall. Inconspicuous flowers followed by sparse crop of bright orange-red fruit. Background, screen, or isolated plant; best against dark evergreens.

Variety 'Compacta' grows 4–6 ft. tall and equally wide, has less prominent wings. Use as screen or unclipped hedge.

E. fortunei. Evergreen vine or shrub. Zones 1–17. One of best broadleafed evergreens where temperatures drop below 0°F. Trails or climbs by rootlets. If plant is used as shrub, its branches will trail and sometimes root; allowed to climb, it will be spreading mass to 20 ft. or more. Prostrate forms can be used to control erosion.

In desert climates, takes full sun better than ivy *(Hedera).* Leaves dark rich green, 1–2½ in. long with scallop-toothed edges; flowers inconspicuous. Sun or full shade. Mature growth, like that of ivy, is shrubby and bears fruit; cuttings taken from this shrubby wood produce upright plants. Formerly *E. radicans acuta.*

E. radicans, once thought to be the species, was later classed as variety of *E. fortunei.* Zones 4–9, 14–17. Native to Korea, Japan. Many nurseries have not changed the names and still sell many varieties as forms of *E. radicans;* translate *radicans* to *fortunei* wherever you see it, except in *E. fortunei radicans.* The varieties of *E. fortunei* listed below are better known than the species itself.

'Canadale Gold'. Compact shrub with light green, yellow-edged leaves.

'Colorata'. PURPLE-LEAF WINTER CREEPER. Same sprawling growth habit as *E. f. radicans.* Leaves turn dark purple in fall and winter. Provides more even ground cover than *E. f. radicans.*

'Emerald Gaiety'. Small, dense-growing, erect shrub with deep green leaves edged with white.

'Emerald 'n Gold'. Similar to above, but with gold-edged leaves.

'Golden Prince'. New growth tipped gold. Older leaves turn green. Extremely hardy; good hedge plant.

'Greenlane'. Low, spreading shrub with erect branches, deep green foliage, orange fruit in fall.

'Ivory Jade'. Resembles 'Greenlane' but has creamy white leaf margins that show pink tints in cold weather.

E. f. radicans. COMMON WINTER CREEPER. Zones 4–9, 14–17. Tough, hardy, trailing or vining shrub with dark green, thick-textured, 1-in.-long leaves. Given no support, it sprawls; given masonry wall to cover, it does the job completely.

E. japonica. EVERGREEN EUONYMUS. Evergreen shrub. Zones 2–20. Upright, 8–10 ft. with 6-ft. spread, usually held lower by pruning or shearing. Flowers inconspicuous. Older shrubs attractive trained as trees with their curving trunks and umbrella-shaped tops. Can be grouped as hedge or screen. Leaves very glossy, leathery, deep green, 1–2½ in. long, oval to roundish.

This and its varieties are "cast-iron" shrubs where heat tolerance is important and soil conditions unfavorable. Notorious for mildew except in Zones 4–6, where plants grow well even in coastal wind and salt spray. To lessen risk of mildew farther south, locate plants in full sun, where air circulation is good. Since plants are also attacked by scale insects, thrips, and spider mites, it's a good idea to include them in your regular rose spray program for mildew and insects.

Variegated forms are most popular; they are among the few shrubs that maintain variegations in full sun in such hot-summer climates as Zones 8–14, 18–20. They are labeled in many ways; there may be some overlapping in names.

'Aureo-variegata'. Leaves have brilliant yellow blotches, green edges.

'Grandifolia'. Plants sold under this name have shiny dark green leaves larger than those of the species. Compact, well branched, good for shearing as pyramids, globes.

'Microphylla' *(E. j. pulchella)*. BOX-LEAF EUONYMUS. Compact, small leafed, 1–2 ft. tall and half as wide. Formal looking; usually trimmed as low hedge.

'Microphylla Variegata'. Like 'Microphylla', but with leaves splashed white.

'Silver King'. Green leaves with silvery white edges.

'Silver Princess'. Like 'Microphylla Variegata', but 3 ft. tall, 2 ft. wide, with larger leaves.

'Silver Queen'. Green leaves, creamy white edges.

EUPHORBIA

Euphorbiaceae

SHRUBS, PERENNIALS, ANNUALS, AND SUCCULENTS

ZONES VARY BY SPECIES

FULL SUN

LITTLE TO MODERATE WATER

SAP IS POISONOUS IN SOME SPECIES

Euphorbia characias wulfenii

What is called "flower" is really group of colored bracts. True flowers, centered in bracts, are inconspicuous. Many euphorbias are succulents; these often mimic cacti in appearance and are as diverse in form and size. Only a few are listed below, but specialists in cacti and succulents can supply scores of species and varieties.

E. amygdaloides. Clumping perennial. Zones 4–24. To nearly 3 ft., resembling a smaller *E. characias*. 'Purpurea' has foliage heavily tinted purple, with bright green inflorescence. *E. a. robbiae* is shorter, dark green in leaf, with yellow-green inflorescence. It tolerates shade and tree-root competition.

E. biglandulosa. See E. rigida

E. characias. Shrubby evergreen perennial. Zones 4–24. Upright stems make dome-shaped bush 4 ft. tall. Fairly drought resistant. Narrow, blue-green leaves crowded all along stems. Clustered flowers make dense, round to cylindrical masses of chartreuse or lime green in late winter, early spring. Color holds with only slight fading until seeds ripen; then stalks yellow and should be cut out at base. New shoots have already made growth for next year's flowers. *E. c. wulfenii (E. veneta)*, commonest form, has broader clusters of yellower flowers.

E. cotinifolia. CARIBBEAN COPPER PLANT. Shrub or tree. Zones 21–24. Can become a small tree in frost-free, warm spots, but is usually a multistemmed shrub. Long-stalked leaves to 4 in. long, 3 in. wide. *E. c.* 'Atropurpurea', the form commonly grown, has wine red leaves. Loose flower clusters have small white bracts. Likes heat, good drainage, average water; can't take frost. For a similar plant sometimes sold under this name, see *Synadenium grantii*.

E. epithymoides (E. polychroma). Perennial. All zones. Neatly rounded hemisphere of deep green leaves symmetrically arranged on closely set stems. Each stem ends in a branching, rounded cluster of tiny flowers surrounded by bright yellow bracts. Effect is of a 1–1½-ft. gold

mound suffused with green. Spring bloom. Displays good fall color (yellow to orange or red) before going dormant. Use in rock gardens, perennial borders.

E. griffithii. Perennial. Zones 4–9, 14–24. Erect stems to 3 ft., clad with narrow, medium green leaves and topped by clusters of brick red bracts. 'Fireglow' is the variety commonly sold. Spreads by creeping roots but is not aggressive.

E. heterophylla. MEXICAN FIRE PLANT. Summer annual. All zones. To 3 ft. tall. Bright green leaves of varying shapes, larger ones resembling those of poinsettia; flowers unimportant. In summer, upper leaves are blotched bright red and white, giving appearance of second-rate poinsettias. Useful in hot, dry borders in poor soil. Sow seed in place after frost danger is over.

E. lathyris. GOPHER PLANT, MOLE PLANT. Biennial. All zones. Legend claims that it repels gophers and moles. Stems have poisonous, caustic milky juice; keep away from skin and especially eyes, since painful burns can result. Juice could conceivably bother a gopher or mole enough to make it beat a hasty retreat. Grows as tall single stem to 5 ft. by second summer, when it sets cluster of unspectacular yellow flowers at top of stem. Flowers soon become seeds and plant dies. Leaves long, narrow, pointed, at right angles to stem and to each other. Grow from seed.

E. marginata. SNOW-ON-THE-MOUNTAIN. Summer annual. All zones. To 2 ft. Leaves light green, oval; upper ones striped and margined white, uppermost sometimes all white. Flowers unimportant. Used for contrast with bright-colored bedding dahlias, scarlet sage or zinnias, or dark-colored plume celosia. Before using in arrangements, dip stems in boiling water or hold in flame for a few seconds. Sow seed in place in spring, in sun or partial shade. Thin to only a few inches apart, as plants are somewhat rangy.

E. martinii. Perennial. Zones 4–24. Hybrid between *E. amygdaloides* and *E. characias*. Resembles a compact *E. characias*, with dense clusters of chartreuse, brown-centered "flowers."

E. milii (E. splendens). CROWN OF THORNS. Woody perennial or subshrub. Zones 21–24 in gardens; elsewhere as greenhouse or house plant or summer potted plant. Shrubby, climbing stems to 3–4 ft. armed with long, sharp thorns. Leaves roundish, thin, light green, 1½–2 in. long, usually found only near branch ends. Clustered pairs of bright red bracts borne nearly all year. Many varieties and hybrids vary in plant form, size, and color of bracts (yellow, orange, pink).

Train on small frame or trellis against sheltered wall or in container. Grow in porous soil, in full sun or light shade.

E. myrsinites. Perennial. All zones. Stems flop outward from central crown, then rise toward tip to 8–12 in. Leaves stiff, roundish, blue gray, closely set around stems. Flattish clusters of chartreuse to yellow flowers top stem ends in late winter, early spring. Cut out old stems as they turn yellow. Withstands cold, heat, and aridity, but is short lived in warm-winter areas. Use in rock gardens with succulents and gray-foliaged plants.

E. obesa. BASEBALL PLANT. Succulent. House plant or indoor/outdoor pot plant. Solid, fleshy, gray-green sphere (or short cylinder) to 8 in., with brownish stripings and brown dots that resemble stitching on a baseball. Flowers unimportant. Good drainage, bright light, warmth, no sudden temperature change. Moderate water; keep dryish in winter.

SECOND CHANCE FOR POINSETTIAS

Plants bloom only when they experience long nights. Starting in October, move them into a closet each night for 14 hours, then move them into light in the morning for a maximum of 10 hours. Continue this procedure for 10 weeks; you can have poinsettia blossoms by Christmas.

E. pulcherrima. POINSETTIA. Evergreen or deciduous shrub. Zones 13, 16–24; or indoors. Native to Mexico. Leggy, to 10 ft. tall or taller. Coarse evergreen leaves grow on stiffly upright canes. Showy part of plant consists of petal-like bracts; true flowers in center are yellowish, inconspicuous. Red single form most familiar; less well known are red doubles and forms with white, yellowish, pink, or marbled bracts. Bracts of these paler kinds often last until Easter. Poinsettia has typical milky euphorbia juice, but it is not poisonous; it is either completely harmless or at most mildly irritating to skin or stomach.

Useful garden plant in well-drained soil. Prune to prevent legginess. Grow as informal hedge in frostless areas; where frosty (not severely cold), plant against sunny walls, in sheltered corners, under south-facing eaves.

Where adapted outdoors, needs no special care. Give slightly acid soil. Thin branches in summer to produce larger bracts; prune them back at 2-month intervals for bushy growth (but often smaller flowers). To improve red color, feed every 2 weeks with high-nitrogen fertilizer, starting when color begins to show.

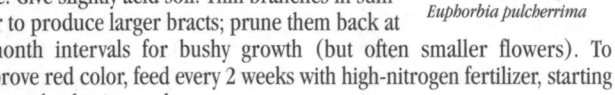

Euphorbia pulcherrima

To care for Christmas gift plants, keep plants in sunny window. Avoid sudden temperature changes. Keep soil moist; don't let water stand in pot saucer. When leaves fall in late winter or early spring, cut stems back to two buds, reduce watering to minimum. Store in cool place until late spring. When frosts are past, set pots in sun outdoors. They will probably grow too tall for indoor use next winter, but may survive winter if well sheltered. Start new plants by making late-summer cuttings of stems with four or five eyes (joints).

E. rigida (E. biglandulosa). Evergreen perennial or subshrub. Zones 4–24. Stems angle outward, then rise up to 2 ft. Fleshy, gray-green leaves to 1½ in. long are narrow and pointed, their bases tightly set against stems. Broad, domed flower clusters in late winter or early spring are chartreuse yellow fading to pinkish. After seeds ripen, stems die back and should be removed; new stems take their place. Showy display plant in garden or container. Tolerates aridity.

E. seguierana niciciana. Zones 4–24. Perennial. Resembles a delicate, fine-textured *E. characias*, to 18 in., with blue-gray, narrow, 1-in. leaves and chartreuse inflorescence.

E. tirucalli. MILKBUSH, PENCILBUSH, PENCIL TREE. Zones 13, 23, 24; house plant or indoor/outdoor plant anywhere. Tree or large shrub to possible 30 ft. tall in open ground, usually much smaller. Single or multiple trunks support tangle of light green, pencil-thick, succulent branches with no sign of a leaf. Flowers unimportant. Striking for pattern of silhouette or shadow. Thrives as house plant in driest atmosphere; needs all the light you can give it, routine soil, water, and feeding. Bleeds milky sap if cut.

E. veneta, E. c. wulfenii. See E. characias

Euphorbiaceae. The euphorbia family contains annuals, perennials, shrubs, and an enormous number of succulents. Most have milky sap, and many have unshowy flowers made decorative by bracts or bractlike glands. Poinsettia *(Euphorbia pulcherrima)* is the best-known example.

EURYA

Theaceae

EVERGREEN SHRUBS

✿ ZONES 4–6, 15–17, 21–24

◐ LIGHT SHADE

◆ MODERATE WATER

Eurya emarginata

Native to Japan. Grown for refined foliage. Yellowish green flowers are insignificant and ill smelling but are present only on old plants. Slow growing to 6–8 ft. but easily kept to 3–4 ft. by pruning to side buds or branches. Grow under same conditions as for azaleas.

E. emarginata. Branches rise at 45° angle from base of plant. Teardrop-shaped, dark green, leathery, ½-in.-long leaves are closely set on branches. *E. e. microphylla* has even tinier leaves—¼ in. long.

E. japonica. Leaves much larger (to 3 in. long) than those of *E. emarginata.* Cold weather gives them a purplish tint. 'Winter Wine' has more pronounced wine purple winter blush.

EURYOPS

Asteraceae (Compositae)

SHRUBBY EVERGREEN PERENNIALS

✿ ZONES 8, 9, 12–24

☀ FULL SUN

◆ LITTLE WATER ONCE ESTABLISHED

Euryops pectinatus

Native to South Africa. Leaves are finely divided; flower heads are daisylike. Long bloom season; cut back after flowering. Plants require excellent drainage. They thrive on buffeting ocean winds but are damaged by sharp frosts. Keep old blooms picked off; prune in June.

E. acraeus. Mounded growth to 2 ft. Leaves silvery gray, ¾ in. long. Inch-wide, bright yellow daisies cover plant in May and June. Native to high South African mountains; hardier to frost than others. Has been used as a rock garden plant in western Washington and Oregon.

E. pectinatus. To 6 ft. One of California's most widely planted shrubby perennials. Easy maintenance and extremely long flowering season make it a good filler, background plant, or low screen. Leaves are gray green, deeply divided, 2 in. long. Bright yellow, 1½–2-in.-wide daisies on 6-in. stems bloom most of the year. Cut back to side branches to control size as needed. 'Viridis' is identical, but with deep green leaves. 'Munchkin' is a dwarf 3 ft. tall, 4 ft. wide.

EUSTOMA grandiflorum (Lisianthus russellianus)

LISIANTHUS, TULIP GENTIAN, TEXAS BLUEBELL

Gentianaceae

BIENNIAL OR SHORT-LIVED PERENNIAL

✿ ALL ZONES

☀ FULL SUN

◆ REGULAR WATER

Eustoma grandiflorum

Native to high plains of the West, but garden forms introduced from Japan. Although hardy to cold, plant grows better and has longer stems where nights are warm. Best cut flowers are grown in greenhouses. In summer, clumps of gray-green foliage send up 1½-ft. stems topped by tulip-shaped, 2–3-in. flowers in purplish blue, pink, or white; plants bloom all summer if old blooms are cut off. Excellent cut flower. Buying started plants is easier, but eustoma can be grown with much care from dustlike seeds. Sprinkle seed on surface of potting soil; don't cover. Soak well; then cover the pot with glass or plastic. At four-leaf stage (about 2 months), transplant three or four plants into each 6-in. pot. Needs good garden soil, good drainage, average fertilizing. Use in pots, border, cutting garden. Often grown as annuals. Lion and Double Eagle strains have double flowers that look somewhat like roses. Heidi strain of F-1 hybrids are vigorous, long stemmed, and include a yellow in addition to other colors. 'Red Glass' has rose red flowers.

EVERLASTING. See HELIPTERUM   p. 319

EVOLVULUS glomeratus

BLUE DAZE

Convolvulaceae

TENDER PERENNIAL

✎ ZONE 24

☼ ◑ SUN OR LIGHT SHADE

● REGULAR WATER

Evolvulus glomeratus

Trailing stems to 20 in. are closely set with small gray-green leaves and spangled with small (less than 1 in. wide) blue morning glory flowers. Useful in hanging baskets. Often sold as *E. nuttallianus*.

EXACUM affine

GERMAN VIOLET, PERSIAN VIOLET

Gentianaceae

SUMMER ANNUAL; INDOORS OR IN COOL GREENHOUSE

◑ ● PARTIAL OR FULL SHADE

● ◐ REGULAR TO AMPLE WATER

Exacum affine

Small, rounded plant with egg-shaped, inch-long leaves and blue, sweet-scented, star-shaped flowers centered with tufts of bright yellow stamens. (A white variety is also available.) Plant seeds indoors in midwinter for summer bloom, in fall for spring bloom. Five plants in 5-in. pot make attractive showing. Needs rich soil.

EXOCHORDA

PEARL BUSH

Rosaceae

DECIDUOUS SHRUBS

✎ ZONES 3–9, 14–18; BEST IN ZONES 3–6

☼ FULL SUN

● REGULAR WATER

Exochorda racemosa

Loose, spikelike clusters of white, 1½–2-in.-wide flowers open from profusion of pearl-like buds. Flowers bloom about same time that roundish, 1½–2-in.-long leaves expand. Give plants ordinary garden soil. Prune after bloom to control size and form.

E. macrantha. Hybrid. The only variety available, 'The Bride', is a compact shrub to 4 ft. tall and as broad. Flowers in late April. Plant it beneath south- or west-facing windows.

E. racemosa (E. grandiflora). COMMON PEARL BUSH. Native to China. Loose, open, slender shrub to 10–15 ft. tall and wide. April bloom. In small gardens, trim it high to make upright, airy, multistemmed small tree. Resistant to oak root fungus.

Fabaceae. The pea family is an enormous group containing annuals, perennials, shrubs, trees, and vines. Many are useful as food (beans, peas), while others furnish timber, medicines, pesticides, and a host of other products. Many are ornamental.

The best known kinds—sweet peas *(Lathyrus)*, for example—have flowers shaped like butterflies, with two winglike side petals, two partially united lower petals (called the keel), and one erect upper petal (the banner or standard). Others have a more regular flower shape (bauhinias, cassias); still others have tightly clustered flowers that appear to be puffs of stamens, as in acacia and silk tree *(Albizia)*. All bear seeds in pods (legumes). Many have on their roots colonies of bacteria that can extract nitrogen from the air and convert it into compounds useful as plant food; clovers are a familiar example. This family was previously called Leguminosae.

Fagaceae. The beech family contains evergreen or deciduous trees characterized by fruit that is either a nut enclosed in a cup, as in oak *(Quercus)* and tanbark oak *(Lithocarpus densiflorus)*, or a burr, as in beech *(Fagus)* and chestnut *(Castanea)*.

FAGUS sylvatica

EUROPEAN BEECH

Fagaceae

DECIDUOUS TREE

✎ ZONES 1–9, 14–24

☼ BEST IN FULL SUN

● ◐ MODERATE TO LIGHT WATER

Fagus sylvatica

Beeches can reach 90 ft., although they're usually much shorter. Tree has a broad cone shape, with lower branches sweeping ground (unless pruned off). Smooth, gray bark contrasts well with dark, glossy foliage and looks handsome in winter. Leaves turn red brown in fall and hang on tree well into winter. Later, pointed winter buds and twig structure make lacy patterns; expanding new leaves have silky sheen. Little three sided nuts in spiny husks are edible but inconsequential; they often fail to fill out, especially on solitary trees.

Grow in any good garden soil. Salts in soil or water stunt growth, turn leaves brown. Woolly beech aphids cause little trouble except for dripping honeydew.

Glossy green leaves to 4 in. long. There are many garden varieties of European beech; some of the best are

'Asplenifolia'. Leaves narrow, deeply lobed or cut nearly to midrib. Delicate foliage on large, robust, spreading tree.

'Atropunicea'. COPPER BEECH, PURPLE BEECH. Leaves deep reddish or purple. Good in containers. Often sold as 'Riversii' or 'Purpurea'. Seedlings of copper beech are usually bronzy purple, turning bronzy green in summer.

'Fastigiata'. DAWYCK BEECH. Narrow, upright tree, like Lombardy poplar *(Populus nigra* 'Italica') in form; 8 ft. wide when 35 ft. tall. Broader in great age, but still narrower than species.

'Laciniata'. CUTLEAF BEECH. Narrow green leaves, deeply cut.

'Pendula'. WEEPING BEECH. Irregular, spreading form. Long, weeping branches reach to ground. Green leaves. Without staking to establish vertical trunk, it will grow wide rather than high.

'Purpurea Pendula'. WEEPING COPPER BEECH. Purple-leafed weeping form. Splendid container plant.

'Tricolor'. TRICOLOR BEECH. Green leaves marked white and edged pink. Slow to 24–40 ft., usually much less. Foliage burns in hot sun or dry winds. Choice container plant.

'Zlatia'. GOLDEN BEECH. Young leaves yellow, aging to yellow-green. Subject to sunburn. Good container plant.

FAIRY DUSTER. See CALLIANDRA eriophylla	**p. 196**
FAIRY LANTERN. See CALOCHORTUS albus, C. amabilis	**p. 199**
FAIRY LILY. See ZEPHYRANTHES	**p. 527**
FAIRY WAND. See DIERAMA	**p. 264**

F

F

FALLUGIA paradoxa

APACHE PLUME

Rosaceae

PARTIALLY EVERGREEN SHRUB

☀ ZONES 2–23

☀ FULL SUN

◯ NO WATER ONCE ESTABLISHED

Fallugia paradoxa

Desert plant native to mountains of east San Bernardino County, California; and to Nevada, southern Utah, Arizona, Colorado to western Texas, northern Mexico. Grows 3–8 ft. high, with straw-colored branches and flaky bark. Small, clustered, lobed leaves, deep green on top, rusty beneath. Flowers like single white roses (1½ in. wide) in April and May. Large clusters of feathery fruit follow; greenish at first, turning pink or reddish tinged later, they create a soft-colored, changing haze through which you can see rigid branch pattern. Needs gritty, well-drained soil.

FATSHEDERA lizei

Araliaceae

EVERGREEN VINE, SHRUB, OR GROUND COVER

☀ ZONES 4–10, 12–24

☀ ◑ ● FULL SUN ON COAST, SHADE INLAND

◐ ◐◐ REGULAR OR LOTS OF WATER

Fatshedera lizei

Hybrid between *Fatsia japonica* and *Hedera helix*, it shows characteristics of both parents. Highly polished, 6–8-in.-wide leaves with three to five pointed lobes look like giant ivy leaves, and plant sends out long trailing or climbing stems like ivy; but in form, it is shrubby like fatsia. Variety 'Variegata' has white-bordered leaves.

Leaves are injured at 15°F, tender new growth at 20–25°F; seems to suffer more from late frosts than from winter cold. Give it protection from hot, drying winds. Good near swimming pools.

Fatshedera tends to grow in a straight line, but it can be shaped if you work at it. Pinch tip growth to force branching. About 2 or 3 times a year, guide and tie stems before they become brittle. If plant gets away from you, cut it back to ground; it will regrow quickly. If you use it as ground cover, cut back vertical growth every 2–3 weeks during growing season. Grown as vine or espalier, plants are heavy, so give them strong supports. Even a well-grown vine is leafless at base. Because it is a hybrid between two genera, this shrubby vine has sometimes been called "botanical wonder."

FATSIA japonica
(Aralia sieboldii, A. japonica)

JAPANESE ARALIA

Araliaceae

EVERGREEN SHRUB

☀ ZONES 4–9, 13–24

◑ ● SHADE; SOME SUN IN COOL-SUMMER AREAS

● REGULAR WATER

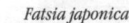

Fatsia japonica

Tropical appearance with big, glossy, dark green, deeply lobed, fanlike leaves to 16 in. wide on long stalks. Moderate growth to 5–8 ft. (rarely more); sparsely branched. Many roundish clusters of small whitish flowers in fall and winter, followed by clusters of small, shiny black fruit.

Grows in nearly all soils except soggy. Adapted to containers. If leaves are chronically yellow, add iron to soil. Wash occasionally with hose to clean leaves, lessen insect attack. Bait for snails, slugs. Established plants sucker freely; keep suckers or remove them with spade. Rejuvenate spindly plants by cutting back hard in early spring. Plants that set fruit often self-sow.

A natural landscaping choice where bold pattern is wanted. Most effective when thinned to show some branch structure. Year-round good looks for shaded entryway or patio. Useful near swimming pools. Variety 'Moseri' grows compact and low. 'Variegata' has leaves edged golden yellow to creamy white.

FEIJOA sellowiana
(Acca sellowiana)

PINEAPPLE GUAVA

Myrtaceae

EVERGREEN SHRUB OR SMALL TREE

☀ ZONES 7–9, 12–24

☀ FULL SUN

◐ ● TOLERATES MUCH ARIDITY AND LAWN WATER

Feijoa sellowiana

From South America. Hardiest of so-called subtropical fruits. Normally a large plant of many stems; reaches 18–25 ft. with equal spread if not trained or killed back by frosts. Oval leaves 2–3 in. long, glossy green above, silvery white beneath. Unusual inch-wide flowers have big tuft of red stamens and four fleshy white petals tinged purplish on inside. Petals edible; can be added to fruit salads. Blooms May or June. Attractive to bees and birds.

Fruit ripens 4–5½ months after flowering in Southern California, 5–7 months in cooler areas; production is low in deserts. Fruit is 1–4 in. long, oval, grayish green, filled with soft, sweet-to-bland, somewhat pineapple-flavored pulp. Plants grow well in valley heat, but fruit seems to have better flavor in cooler coastal areas. Fruit sometimes seen in markets as "feijoas" or "guavas."

Improved varieties 'Beechwood', 'Coolidge', and 'Nazemetz' are self-fertile, although cross-pollination will produce a better crop. Single plants of seedlings or other named varieties may need cross-pollination.

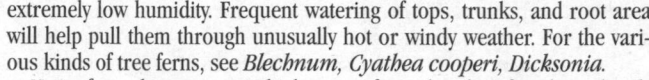

PINEAPPLE GUAVA TAKES SEVERAL FORMS

Feijoa sellowiana can take almost any amount of pruning or training to shape as espalier, screen, hedge, or small tree that resembles olive. Do most of the pruning or training in late spring.

FELICIA

Asteraceae (Compositae)

SHRUBS OR SHRUBBY PERENNIALS

🌗 ZONES VARY BY SPECIES

☼ FULL SUN

◊ ● WATER NEEDS VARY BY SPECIES

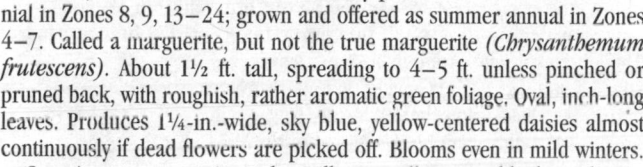

Felicia amelloides

Daisy relatives with (generally) blue flowers. Of the more than 80 species of this South African native, the following are grown in the West.

F. amelloides (F. aethiopica, Agathaea coelestis). BLUE MARGUERITE. Shrubby perennial in Zones 8, 9, 13–24; grown and offered as summer annual in Zones 4–7. Called a marguerite, but not the true marguerite (*Chrysanthemum frutescens*). About 1½ ft. tall, spreading to 4–5 ft. unless pinched or pruned back, with roughish, rather aromatic green foliage. Oval, inch-long leaves. Produces 1¼-in.-wide, sky blue, yellow-centered daisies almost continuously if dead flowers are picked off. Blooms even in mild winters.

Grow in pots or containers, let spill over wall or raised bed, or plant in any sunny spot in garden. Water regularly. Vigorous and likely to overgrow and look ragged; trim severely for cut flowers and prune back hard in late summer to encourage new blooming wood. One of most satisfactory perennials for warm regions.

Improved varieties include 'George Lewis', 'Midnight', and 'Rhapsody in Blue', all with very dark blue flowers; 'San Luis', 'San Gabriel', and 'Santa Anita', with extra-large (2½–3-in.), medium blue flowers; 'Jolly', 1-ft.-tall dwarf with medium blue flowers; and 'Astrid Thomas', compact grower with medium blue flowers that stay open at night. There is also a white-flowered variety.

F. fruticosa (Aster fruticosus, Diplopappus fruticosus). SHRUB ASTER. Evergreen shrub. Zones 8, 9, 14–24. Bushy, densely branched, 2–4 ft. tall, 3 ft. wide. Leaves narrow, dark green, ½–¾ in. long. Flowers lavender, profuse, to 1 in. across. April–June bloom. Prune after flowering. Needs no water once established.

FELT PLANT. See KALANCHOE beharensis	**p. 342**
FENNEL. See FOENICULUM vulgare	**p. 297**
FERNLEAF YARROW. See ACHILLEA filipendulina	**p. 138**
FERN-OF-THE-DESERT. See LYSILOMA microphylla thornberi	**p. 363**
FERN PINE. See PODOCARPUS gracilior	**p. 431**

FERNS. Large group of perennial plants grown for their lovely and interesting foliage. They vary in height from a few inches to 50 ft. or more, and are found in all parts of the world; most are forest plants, but some grow in deserts, in open fields, or near the timberline in high mountains. Most have finely cut leaves (fronds). They do not flower but reproduce by spores that form directly on the fronds.

Ferns are divided into several families, according to botanical differences. Such technical differences aside, these plants fall into several groups based on general appearance.

Most spectacular are tree ferns, which display their finely cut fronds atop a treelike stem. These need rich, well-drained soil, moisture, and shade (except in Zones 4–6, 17, 24, where they can take sun). Most tree ferns are rather tender to frost, and all suffer in hot, drying winds and in extremely low humidity. Frequent watering of tops, trunks, and root area will help pull them through unusually hot or windy weather. For the various kinds of tree ferns, see *Blechnum, Cyathea cooperi, Dicksonia.*

Native ferns do not grow as high as tree ferns, but their fronds are handsome and they can perform a number of landscape jobs. Naturalize them in woodland or wild gardens, or use them to fill shady beds, as ground cover, as interplantings between shrubs, or along a shady house wall. Many endure long, dry summers in California but look lusher if given ample summer water. Some ferns native to eastern United States grow well in Northwest and in Northern California; these take extreme cold and are usually deciduous. For native ferns, see *Adiantum, Asplenium, Athyrium, Blechnum, Dryopteris, Onoclea sensibilis, Osmunda regalis, Pellaea, Phyllitis, Polypodium, Polystichum, Pteridium, Woodwardia.*

Many ferns from other parts of the world grow well in the West; although some are house, greenhouse, or (in mildest climates) lathhouse subjects, many are fairly hardy. Use them as you would native ferns, unless some peculiarity of habit makes it necessary to grow them in baskets or on slabs. Some exotic ferns will be found under *Adiantum, Asplenium, Ctenitis, Cyrtomium, Davallia, Humata, Microlepia, Nephrolepis, Pellaea, Platycerium, Polypodium, Polystichum, Pteris, Pyrrosia, Rumohra, Woodwardia.*

All ferns look best if groomed: cut off dead or injured fronds near ground or trunk—but don't cut back hardy outdoor ferns until new growth begins, since old fronds protect growing tips. Feed frequently during growing season, preferably with light applications of organic-base fertilizer such as blood meal or fish emulsion. Mulch with peat moss occasionally, especially if shallow fibrous roots are exposed by rain or irrigation.

FEROCACTUS

BARREL CACTUS

Cactaceae

CACTI

🌗 ZONES 8–24

☼ FULL SUN

◊ NO WATER ONCE ESTABLISHED

Ferocactus cylindraceus

Medium to large cacti. Ribbed and formidably spiny; globular when young, cylindrical with increasing age.

F. cylindraceus (F. acanthodes). COMPASS BARREL CACTUS. Native to Southern California, Nevada, Baja California. Grows slowly to 8–9 ft. Yellow to orange, bell-shaped flowers, 3 in. across, bloom May–July. Grows faster on shady side of plant than on sunny side, producing curve toward the south.

F. wislizenii. FISHHOOK BARREL CACTUS. Native to Arizona, Texas, Mexico. Similar to above, with yellow or yellow-edged red flowers July–September. Hardy to near 0°F.

FESTUCA

FESCUE

Poaceae (Gramineae)

GRASSES

🌗 ALL ZONES, EXCEPT AS NOTED

☼ ☽ FULL SUN OR PARTIAL SHADE

● ◊ ● NOT MUCH WATER FOR GRASSES

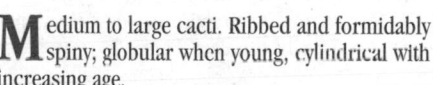

Festuca ovina 'Glauca'

Several of these grasses are used for lawns, erosion control, or pasture; others have use as ornamental plants. Lawn fescues are classified as fine or coarse.

F. amethystina, F. cinerea, F. glauca. These grasses form tight clumps of narrow bluish or grayish leaves. All are similar to *F. ovina* 'Glauca' in appearance, culture, and uses. (Indeed, *F. ovina* 'Glauca' may be the same plant as *F. amethystina* or *F. cinerea*). Named varieties abound; they vary in intensity of blue color and in height (from 6–18 in.).

F. californica. CALIFORNIA FESCUE. Zones 4–10, 14–24. Clumps of evergreen leaves 2–3 ft. tall produce flowering stems to 5 ft. or more in spring and early summer. Flowers fade to golden tan. Appreciates a little water when grown inland. Useful in natural plantings, on slopes, among boulders, with no-water native plants. Look for selections with bluish foliage.

F. elatior. TALL FESCUE. Coarse. Tall-growing (to 2½ ft.), clumping pasture grass also used for erosion control and supposedly low-water-use lawns. Tough blades, tolerance of compacted soils make it good play or sports lawn. Forms no runners, so plants must be close together to make dense turf; sow 8–10 pounds of seed per 1,000 sq. ft. in fall. After grass is 2–3 in. tall, soak deeply if rains fail; soak again to 1 ft. when blades begin to fold or curl. Feed lightly—monthly in summer, 3 times during fall, winter. Mow when 2 in. tall. Unmowed, makes excellent, deep-rooted erosion control on slopes, banks. 'Alta' is medium coarse and tough against wear. 'Fawn' has narrowest leaf, finest texture. 'Goars' is fairly tolerant of saline and alkaline soils. 'Kentucky 31' is best adapted to hot-summer climates. Finer-textured strains are used as lawn grasses, either alone or mixed with bluegrass.

F. ovina. SHEEP FESCUE. Fine. Low-growing (to 1 ft.), clumping grass with narrow, needle-fine, soft but tough leaves. *F. o. duriuscula*, hard fescue, is sometimes used as lawn grass. *F. o.* 'Glauca', blue fescue, forms blue-gray tufts 4–10 in. tall. Useful ground cover for sunny or partially shaded areas, on slopes or level ground. Needs little water in Zones 1–9, 14–24; as much as lawn grass in Zones 10–13. Cannot tolerate foot traffic. Clip back near to the ground after flowering or any time plants look shabby. Does not make solid cover and needs frequent weeding. Dig overgrown clumps, pull apart, and replant as small divisions. Set 6–15 in. apart, depending on desired effect.

F. rubra. RED FESCUE. Fine blades. Principal use is as lawn grass in blends with bluegrass or other lawn grasses. Blades narrow, texture fine, color dark green. Not fussy about soil; takes some shade. Used alone, tends to grow clumpy. Mow to 1½–2 in. tall. Common red fescue is sometimes called creeping red fescue; it is one of most shade tolerant of good lawn grasses. Two other creeping selections are sold as creeping red: 'Illahee', and 'Rainier'. *F. r. commutata*, Chewings fescue, tends toward clumpiness. Unmowed, red fescues make attractive meadow on slopes too steep to mow. They are also used to overseed Bermuda-grass lawns in winter.

FEVERFEW. See CHRYSANTHEMUM parthenium	**p. 228**
FIBER OPTICS PLANT. See SCIRPUS cernuus	**p. 481**

FICUS

Moraceae

EVERGREEN OR DECIDUOUS TREES, VINES, SHRUBS

☒ ZONES VARY BY SPECIES

☼ ☽ ● EXPOSURE NEEDS VARY BY SPECIES

◗ OUTDOOR KINDS NEED WATER UNTIL ESTABLISHED

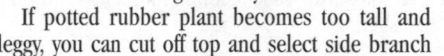
Ficus auriculata

Ornamental figs. The average gardener would never expect to find the commercial edible fig, small-leafed climbing fig, banyan tree, and potted rubber plant under one common heading—but they are classed together because they bear small or large figs (inedible in most species).

F. auriculata (F. roxburghii). Briefly deciduous. Zones 20–24. Native to India. Usually takes the form of large, spreading shrub or small tree to 25 ft. high and as wide. Full sun. Leaves are unusually large—broadly oval to round, about 15 in. across. New growth is interesting mahogany red, turning to rich green. Leaves have sandpapery texture. Large figs are borne in clusters on trunk and framework branches.

Can be shaped as small tree or espaliered. Beautiful in large container; good near swimming pools. Grow in wind-protected, sunny locations.

F. benjamina. WEEPING CHINESE BANYAN. Evergreen tree. Outdoors in Zones 13, 23, 24; indoor plant anywhere. Native to India. To 30 ft. high and broadly spreading. Leathery, poplarlike, 5-in.-long leaves densely clothe drooping branches in shining green. Red figs. Grow in sun or shade in frost-free, wind-protected locations. Probably best fig for heat tolerance in Zone 13 (damaged there by any frost but recovers quickly as weather warms). Often used as small tree in entryway or patio. Good as espalier or screen. In mildest climates, can be used as clipped hedge.

Ficus benjamina

Undoubtedly the most popular indoor tree, and one of most popular house plants. Thrives on rich, steadily moist (not wet) soil, frequent light feeding, and abundant light.

New plants are easy to start from semihardwood cuttings taken between May and July. Variety 'Exotica' has wavy-edged leaves with long, twisted tips; it is often sold simply as *F. benjamina*.

F. carica. EDIBLE FIG. See Fig, Edible

F. deltoidea (F. diversifolia). MISTLETOE FIG. Evergreen shrub. Outdoors in Zones 19–24; indoor plant anywhere. Native to Malaya. Grows very slowly to 8–10 ft. high. Interesting open, twisted branch pattern. Thick, dark green, roundish, 2-in. leaves are sparsely stippled with tan specks on upper surface and a few black dots below. Attractive, small, greenish to yellow fruit borne continuously. Most often grown in containers as patio and house plant. Grow in part shade or strong diffused light.

Ficus deltoidea

F. elastica. RUBBER PLANT. Evergreen shrub or tree. Outdoors in Zones 16, 17, 19–24; indoor plant anywhere. Native to India and Malaya. This is the familiar rubber plant found in almost every florist shop. One of most foolproof indoor pot subjects. Takes less light than most big indoor plants. Leaves are thick, glossy, leathery, dark green, 8–12 in. long by 4–6 in. wide. New leaves unfold from rosy pink sheaths that soon wither and drop. Can become 40-ft.-high tree in Zones 23, 24. As small tree or shrub, useful in shaded "tunnel" garden entrances. Comes back in 3 months when cut to ground by frost.

If potted rubber plant becomes too tall and leggy, you can cut off top and select side branch

Ficus elastica

to form a new main shoot or get a new plant by air layering top section. When roots form, cut branch section with attached roots and plant it in container.

F. e. 'Decora' (F. e. 'Belgica'). Considered superior of the species because of its broader, glossier leaves, bronzy when young.

F. e. 'Rubra'. New leaves are reddish and retain red edge as rest of leaf turns green. Grown as shrub or small tree in Zones 22–24.

F. e. 'Variegata'. Leaves are long, narrow, variegated yellow and green. Variegation is interesting when viewed close up in container, but as an outdoor tree, plant has an unhealthy look.

F. lyrata (F. pandurata). FIDDLELEAF FIG. Evergreen tree or large shrub. Outdoors in Zones 22–24. Native to tropical Africa. Dramatic structural form with huge, glossy-surfaced, dark green, fiddle-shaped leaves to 15 in. long and 10 in. wide, prominently veined. Highly effective as indoor pot plant. In protected outdoor position (sun or light shade), can grow to 20 ft. with trunks 6 in. thick. Good near swimming pools. To increase branching, pinch back when plant is young.

Ficus lyrata

F. macrophylla. MORETON BAY FIG. Huge evergreen tree. Zones 17, 19–24. Native to north New South Wales and Queensland, Australia. Grows to enormous dimensions. A tree in Santa Barbara planted in 1877 has spread of 150 ft., with massive buttressed trunk and surface roots. Blunt, oval, leathery leaves, 10 in. long and 4 in. wide, glossy green above, brownish beneath. Rose-colored leaf sheaths appear like candles at branch ends. Inch-long figs are purple spotted with white. Needs sun.

Although tender when young, acquires hardiness with size. Shows damage at 24–26°F. Plant only if you can give it plenty of room.

F. microcarpa (F. retusa). INDIAN LAUREL FIG. Evergreen tree. Zones 9, 13, 16–24. Native to India, Malaya. Both this and *F. m. nitida* are widely used along streets throughout Southern California and in San Francisco Bay area. They differ markedly in growth habit and appearance. Both perform best with some summer water. Sun.

F. microcarpa grows at a moderate rate to 25–30 ft. It has beautiful weeping form, with long, drooping branches thickly clothed with blunt-tipped, 2–4-in.-long leaves. Light rose to chartreuse new leaves, produced almost continuously, give tree pleasing two-tone effect. Slim, light gray trunk supporting massive crown may be concealed by lower trailing branches if these are not trimmed off.

F. m. nitida. Has dense foliage on upright-growing branches and is admirably suited to formal shearing. Leaves are clear lustrous green, similar in size to those of *F. microcarpa* but more pointed at base and apex. *F. m. nitida* may be pruned at almost any time of year to size or shape desired.

Where this tree is pest free, it is difficult to find a more satisfactory tree or tub plant for warm climates. Unfortunately, a thrips that attacks both the species and its variety has become established in California. This insect is difficult to control because it quickly curls new leaves, stippling them and causing them to fall. Best control: systemic insecticides. 'Green Gem' has thicker, darker green leaves and is apparently unaffected by thrips.

F. pumila (F. repens). CREEPING FIG. Evergreen vine. Zones 8–24. Native to China, Japan, Australia. A most unfiglike habit; it is one of few plants that attaches itself securely to wood, masonry, or even metal in barnacle fashion. Sun or shade.

In young stages, gives very little indication of its potential vigor. Delicate tracery of tiny, heart-shaped leaves frequently seen patterned against a chimney or stucco wall is almost certain to be *F. pumila*, but in this growth phase gives no hint of its powerful character at maturity. There is almost no limit to size of vine and area it will cover. Neat little leaves of juvenile growth ultimately develop into large (2–4 in. long), leathery, oblong leaves borne on stubby branches that bear large oblong fruit. In time, stems will envelop a 3- or 4-story building so completely that it becomes necessary to keep them trimmed away from windows.

It is safe to use this fig on houses if it is cut to the ground every few years; you may also control by removing fruiting stems from time to time as they form. Roots are invasive, probably more so than those of most other figs.

Because it is grown on walls, and thus protected, it is more often found in colder climates than any other evergreen fig. Will not climb on hot south or west wall—or, if it does grow there, will be unattractive yellow. Sometimes slow to begin climbing. Cut back to the ground soon after planting to make new growth that will take off fast.

F. p. 'Minima'. Slender, small-leafed variety. Another tiny variety sold as *F. p.* 'Quercifolia' has lobed leaves something like tiny oak leaves. 'Variegata' has creamy white markings.

F. religiosa. PEEPUL, BO-TREE. Briefly deciduous tree. Zones 13, 19, 21, 23, 24. Native to India. Large, upright; less spread than *F. macrophylla*. Foliage is quite open and delicate, revealing structure of tree at all times. Bark is warm, rich brown. Roundish, pale green leaves are rather crisp and thin textured, 4–7 in. long with long tail-like point. They move easily even in slightest breeze, giving foliage a fluttering effect. Foliage drops completely in April or May—a frightening experience for the gardener who has bought an "evergreen" fig. Sun.

F. retusa. See F. microcarpa

F. roxburghii. See F. auriculata

F. rubiginosa. RUSTYLEAF FIG. Evergreen tree. Zones 18–24. Native to Australia. Grows to 20–50 ft., with broad crown and single or multiple trunks. Dense foliage of 5-in. oval leaves, deep green above and generally rust colored and woolly beneath. Sun.

Does well in sand on coast and thrives in heat of interior valleys. A few trees in coastal gardens have developed hanging aerial roots that characterize many of the evergreen figs in tropical environments. Small-leafed form has been sold as *F. microphylla*.

F. r. australis varies from the species (if it varies at all) in having slightly less rusty leaves. Varieties 'El Toro' and 'Irvine' have exceptionally dark green leaves; 'Florida', widely distributed, has lighter green leaves. 'Variegata', with leaves mottled green and cream, is sometimes sold as a house plant.

SUDDEN LEAF-SHEDDING ON A FICUS BENJAMINA?

The problem is common. If the plant drops green leaves, the cause is probably insufficient water; try to keep soil evenly moist. If plant drops yellow leaves, it's usually the result of a move from another spot. In either case, fertilizer and/or too much water *will not* help and will probably make matters worse. Be patient: wait for nature to act.

FIG, EDIBLE

Moraceae

DECIDUOUS TREES

✿ ZONES 4–9, 12–24; ZONES 1–3, 10, 11, IN TUB

☼ FULL SUN

◊ IN GROUND, NEED NO WATER ONCE ESTABLISHED

Edible Fig

For ornamental relatives, see *Ficus*. Grow fairly fast to 15–30 ft., generally low branched and spreading; where hard freezes are common, fig wood freezes back severely and plant behaves as a big shrub. Can be held to 10 ft. in big container, or trained as espalier along fence or wall.

Trunks heavy, smooth, gray barked, gnarled in really old trees, picturesque in silhouette. Leaves rough, bright green, with three to five lobes, 4–9 in. long and nearly as wide. Casts dense shade. Winter framework, tropical-looking foliage, strong trunk and branch pattern make fig a top-notch ornamental tree, especially near patio where it can be illuminated from beneath. Protect container plants in winter. Fruit drop is problem immediately above deck or paving.

Not particular about soil. In Zones 4–7, trees planted near south walls or trained against them benefit from reflected heat. Cut back tops hard at planting. As tree grows, prune lightly each winter, cutting out dead wood, crossing branches, low-hanging branches that interfere with traffic. Pinch back runaway shoots any season. Avoid deep cultivation (may damage surface roots) and high-nitrogen fertilizers (stimulate growth at expense of fruit). 'Kadota', 'Mission' are resistant to oak root fungus.

Home garden figs do not need pollinating, and most varieties bear two crops a year. The first comes in June (July in Northwest) on last year's wood; the second and more important comes in August–November from current summer's wood. Ripe figs will detach easily when lifted and bent back toward the branch. Keep fruit picked as it ripens; protect from birds if you can. In late fall, pick off any remaining ripe figs and clean up fallen fruit. California pocket gophers love fig roots; to foil their attacks, plant young figs in ample wire baskets.

Varieties differ in climate adaptability; some thrive under cool coastal conditions, while others need prolonged high temperatures to bear good fruit. Familiar dried figs from the market are usually 'Calimyrna' or imported Smyrna figs. These require special pollinators (caprifigs) and special pollinating insect; not recommended for home gardens.

'Blue Celeste' ('Celeste', 'Celestial'). Hardy tree. Bronzy fruit tinged violet, pulp rosy amber; fruit resistant to spoilage, dries well on tree in California.

'Brown Turkey' ('San Piero'; sold in Northwest as 'Black Spanish'). Small tree; brownish purple fruit. Adaptable to most fig climates, Arizona

295

to Northwest. Good garden tree. Cut back hard to scaffold limbs to lessen fruit formation and subsequent fruit-drop mess.

'Conadria'. Choice thin-skinned white fig blushed violet; white to red flesh, fine flavor. Best in hot areas.

'Desert King'. Green fig with red flesh. Good in Northwest. One late-summer crop.

'Genoa' ('White Genoa'). Greenish yellow skin, amber to yellow flesh. Good quality, good home garden variety in California coastal and coastal valley gardens.

'Italian Everbearing'. Resembles 'Brown Turkey', but fruit is somewhat larger, with reddish brown skin.

'Kadota' ('White Kadota'). Tough-skinned fruit is greenish yellow in California's hot interior valleys (where tree bears best), green near coast. Commercial canning variety. Strong grower, needs little pruning. If given severe pruning, it will bear later, with fewer, larger fruit.

'Lattarula'. Also known as Italian honey fig. Green skin, amber flesh. Grown in Northwest, where it can ripen in summer and produce fall crops in good seasons.

'Mission' ('Black Mission'). Purple black fig for desert and all California gardens. Large tree.

'Neveralla'. Purple skinned, with amber flesh. Can ripen summer and produce fall crops in Northwest.

'Osborn Prolific'. Purplish brown fruit; good bearer in California coastal areas.

'Peter's Honey' ('Rutara'). Greenish yellow skin, amber flesh. Needs hot exposure in Northwest and coastal areas.

'Texas Everbearing'. Medium to large, mahogany to purple fruit with strawberry-colored pulp. Bears young and gives good crop in short-season areas of Southwest.

FILBERT

Betulaceae

DECIDUOUS NUT TREES

🌡 ZONES 2–7

☼ FULL SUN

● IRRIGATE SEVERAL TIMES IN A DRY SEASON

For ornamental relatives, see *Corylus*. More treelike in form (15–25 ft.) than ornamental forms of *Corylus*, the filbert *(C. maxima)* makes a handsome, well-structured, small tree for garden or terrace. From spring to fall, roundish and

Filbert

ruffle-edged leaves cast a pleasant spot of shade. Showy male catkins hang long and full on bare branches in winter. Crop of roundish to oblong nuts (ones sold in stores) comes as bonus in fall. A 10-year-old tree may yield up to 10 lbs. of nuts a year. Nuts form inside frilled husks.

Set out plants in late winter or early spring, in well-drained, deep soil. Tree tends to sucker; clear these out 3 or 4 times a year if you wish to maintain clear trunk. For a boundary hedgerow, plant mixed varieties 4 ft. apart and permit suckers to grow. Spray for aphids, bud mites, and filbert blight. Since cross-pollination is necessary, plant at least two varieties.

'Barcelona'. Slow or moderate growth to 18 ft. with greater spread. Roundish, large nuts.

'Butler'. Good pollinator for 'Barcelona' or 'Ennis'. Oval nuts of good flavor.

'Du Chilly'. Slow growth to 15 ft. with equal spread. Shoots grow at right angles to limbs. Large, long nut of high quality, slow to drop; nuts adhere to husks.

'Ennis'. Slow growth. Very productive. Large, round nuts. Pollinates and is pollinated by 'Butler'.

'Purpurea'. Ornamental variety with dark purple leaves. Thrives in Zone 17, but does not bear nuts there.

'Royal'. Slow growth to 18 by 18 ft. Large nuts of excellent flavor.

'White Aveline' and 'Daviana'. Varieties used as pollinators. Light-crop varieties with medium-size, high-quality nuts.

FILIPENDULA

Rosaceae

PERENNIALS

🌡 ZONES 1–9, 14–24

☼ ◐ FULL SUN ON COAST, LIGHT SHADE INLAND

● REGULAR WATER

Filipendula rubra 'Venusta'

Like related *Astilbe*, have plumes of tiny flowers above coarsely divided leaves that look like fern fronds. Dormant in winter. Use in borders or naturalistic plantings.

F. hexapetala. See F. vulgaris

F. purpurea. Pink plumes 3–4 ft. tall rise above maplelike 5–7-in. leaves.

F. rubra. QUEEN OF THE PRAIRIE. When given ample water and rich soil, can reach 8 ft. Plumes are pink; purplish pink in the variety 'Venusta'.

F. vulgaris (F. hexapetala). White plumes on 3-ft. stems rise above 10-in., fernlike leaves with 1-in. leaflets. Double-flowered 'Flore Pleno' has heavier-looking plumes.

FINOCCHIO. See FOENICULUM vulgare azoricum	p. 297
FIR. See ABIES	p. 130
FIRECRACKER FLOWER. See DICHELOSTEMMA ida-maia	p. 263
FIRETAIL. See ACALYPHA pendula	p. 135
FIRETHORN. See PYRACANTHA	p. 446
FIREWHEEL TREE. See STENOCARPUS sinuatus	p. 492

FIRMIANA simplex (F. platanifolia)

CHINESE PARASOL TREE

Sterculiaceae

DECIDUOUS TREE

🌡 ZONES 5, 6, 8, 9, 12–24

☼ ◐ FULL SUN OR MORNING SUN

○ NO WATER ONCE ESTABLISHED

Firmiana simplex

Native to China, Japan. Small (15–30 ft.), usually slow growing, with unique light gray-green bark. Trunk often has no side branches to 4–5 ft., where it divides into three or more slender, upright, slightly spreading stems that carry lobed, tropical-looking, 1-ft. leaves. Each stem looks as if it could be cut off and carried away as a parasol. Large, loose, upright clusters of greenish white flowers at branch ends in July. Interesting fruit looks like two opened green pea pods with seeds on margins. Goes leafless for long period in winter (unusual for tropical-looking tree).

Has been grown in mild-climate areas in all types of soil. Does well in patios and courtyards protected from wind. Useful near swimming pools.

| FISHTAIL PALM. See CARYOTA | p. 209 |
| FIVE-FINGER FERN. See ADIANTUM aleuticum | p. 140 |

Flacourtiaceae. This family of evergreen trees and shrubs (most of them tropical or subtropical) includes *Azara* and *Xylosma*.

FLAG. See IRIS	p. 332
FLAME PEA. See CHORIZEMA	p. 225
FLAME TREE. See BRACHYCHITON acerifolius	p. 189
FLAME VINE. See PYROSTEGIA venusta	p. 447

FOENICULUM vulgare

COMMON FENNEL

Apiaceae (Umbelliferae)

PERENNIAL HERB, GROWN AS SUMMER ANNUAL

ALL ZONES

FULL SUN

NO WATER EXCEPT F. V. AZORICUM

Foeniculum vulgare

Grows to 3–5 ft. Similar to dill, but coarser. Yellow-green, finely cut leaves; flat clusters of yellow flowers. Grows in light, well-drained soil. Start from seed where plants are to be grown; thin seedlings to 1 ft. apart. Use seeds to season bread; use leaves as garnish for salads, fish. Young leaves and seeds have slight licorice taste. Plant often grows as roadside or garden weed; is attractive until tops turn brown, and even then birds like the seeds.

F. v. azoricum. FINOCCHIO. Lower growing than the species, with larger, thicker leaf bases that are edible cooked or raw. Regular water.

> ### IT FEEDS BENEFICIAL INSECTS
>
> Common fennel is one of those prolific but valuable plants that provide pollen and nectar to beneficial insects during periods when those insects aren't feeding on plant-damaging insects and mites. The good guys sustained by common fennel include hover flies, lacewings, ladybird beetles, paper wasps, and soldier bugs.

FORESTIERA neomexicana

NEW MEXICAN PRIVET, DESERT OLIVE

Oleaceae

DECIDUOUS SHRUB

ALL ZONES

FULL SUN

GROWS FASTER WITH SOME WATER

Forestiera neomexicana

Native to New Mexico, Colorado, Arizona west to California. Little used outside arid regions. To 6–8 ft. tall, nearly as broad. Smooth, medium green leaves 1 to nearly 2 in. long. Flowers negligible. Egg-shaped, blue-black fruit, ¼ in. long, not always produced (some plants do not have both male and female flowers). Fairly fast growth makes it a good screening plant in arid climates.

FORSYTHIA

Oleaceae

DECIDUOUS SHRUBS

ZONES 2–16, 18, 19

FULL SUN

MODERATE WATER

Forsythia intermedia

Fountain-shaped shrubs; bare branches covered with yellow flowers February–April. During rest of growing season, medium green foliage blends well with other shrubs in border background. Lush green, rounded leaves with pointed tips. Branches can be forced for indoor bloom in winter. Use as screen, espalier, or bank cover, or in shrub border. Tolerates most soils; responds to fertilizer. Prune established plants after bloom by cutting to ground a third of the branches that have bloomed. Remove oldest branches and weak or dead wood.

F. intermedia. Hybrids between *F. suspensa* and *F. viridissima*. Most grow 7–10 ft. tall and have arching branches. 'Arnold Dwarf', 20–36 in. tall and to 6 ft. wide, has few, not especially attractive flowers, but it's a useful, fast-growing ground cover in hard climates. 'Beatrix Farrand', an upright grower to 10 ft. tall, 7 ft. broad, has branches thickly set with 2–2½-in.-wide, deep yellow flowers marked orange.

F. i. 'Karl Sax' resembles *F. i.* 'Beatrix Farrand' but is lower growing, neater, more graceful. *F. i.* 'Lynwood' ('Lynwood Gold') grows stiffly upright to 7 ft., with 4–6-ft. spread. Profuse tawny yellow blooms survive spring storms. *F. i.* 'Spectabilis' is dense, upright, vigorous shrub to 9 ft. with deep yellow flowers. *F. i.* 'Spring Glory' has heavy crop of pale yellow flowers.

F. ovata. KOREAN FORSYTHIA. Shrub to 4–6 ft., spreading wider. Profusion of bright yellow flowers in spring. Probably earliest to flower.

F. suspensa. WEEPING FORSYTHIA. Dense, upright growth habit to 8–10 ft. with 6–8-ft. spread. Drooping, vinelike branches root where they touch damp soil. Golden yellow flowers. Useful large-scale bank cover. Can be trained as vine; if you support main branches, branchlets will cascade. *F. s.* 'Fortunei' is somewhat more upright, more available in nurseries.

F. viridissima. GREENSTEM FORSYTHIA. Stiff-looking shrub to 10 ft. with deep green foliage, olive green stems, greenish yellow flowers. 'Bronxensis' is slow-growing dwarf form to 16 in. tall, for smaller shrub borders or ground cover. *F. v. koreana* (*F. koreana*), to 8 ft., has larger, brighter yellow flowers and attractive purplish autumn foliage.

FOTHERGILLA

Hamamelidaceae

DECIDUOUS SHRUBS

ZONES 3–9, 14–17

PARTIAL SHADE

MODERATE WATER

Fothergilla monticola

Grown principally for fall color, but small white flowers in brushlike, 1–2-in. clusters are pretty. Plant in peaty soil, partial shade—especially where summers are long and hot.

F. gardenii. DWARF FOTHERGILLA. Grows 2–3 ft. Inch-long flower clusters appear before leaves. Fall foliage intense yellow and orange red. The variety 'Mt. Airy' is taller, has deeper blue-green leaves, larger flower clusters, and better fall color. 'Blue Mist' also has bluish summer foliage.

F. major. Erect shrub to 9 ft. with roundish, 4-in.-long leaves turning yellow to orange to purplish red in autumn. Flowers appear with the leaves. Fall color early and good in San Francisco Bay area. ▶

F. monticola. Spreading plant to 3–4 ft. tall. Broadly oval leaves; flower clusters somewhat larger than those of *F. major.* Fall color from scarlet to crimson.

FOUNTAIN GRASS. See PENNISETUM setaceum   p. 410

FOUQUIERIA splendens

OCOTILLO
Fouquieriaceae
DECIDUOUS SHRUB
ZONES 10–13, 18–20
FULL SUN
NO WATER ONCE ESTABLISHED

Fouquieria splendens

Native to Mojave and Colorado deserts east to Texas and south to Mexico. Many stiff, whip-like gray stems 8–25 ft. high, heavily furrowed and covered with stout thorns. Fleshy, roundish, ½–1-in.-long leaves appear after rains, soon drop. Tubular, ¾–1-in.-long red flowers in attractive foot-long clusters after spring or summer rains. Can be used as screening, impenetrable hedge, or for silhouette against bare walls. Needs excellent drainage. Cuttings stuck in ground will grow.

FOUR O'CLOCK. See MIRABILIS jalapa   p. 381

FOXGLOVE. See DIGITALIS   p. 264

FRAGARIA chiloensis

WILD STRAWBERRY, SAND STRAWBERRY
Rosaceae
EVERGREEN GROUND COVER
ZONES 4–24
SUN AT COAST, SUN OR PART SHADE INLAND
LITTLE TO REGULAR WATER

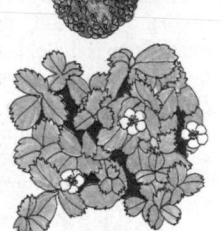
Fragaria chiloensis

Native of Pacific beaches and bluffs, North and South America. Forms low, compact, lush mats 6–12 in. high. Dark green, glossy leaves have three-toothed leaflets. Leaves take on red tints in winter. Large (1-in.-wide) white flowers in spring; bright red, ¾-in., seedy fall fruit attracts birds (fruit seldom sets in gardens). Plant rooted stolons in late spring or early summer. Nursery-grown plants can be planted any time. Set plants 1–1½ ft. apart. Needs annual mowing or cutting back (early spring) to force new growth, prevent stem buildup. Feed annually in late spring. In late summer, if leaves show yellowing, apply iron sulfate. For fruiting or garden strawberry, see Strawberry.

FRANCESCHI PALM. See BRAHEA elegans   p. 189

FRANCOA ramosa

MAIDEN'S WREATH
Saxifragaceae
PERENNIAL
ZONES 4, 5, 8, 9, 12–24
SUN HALF DAY OR DAPPLED SUN ALL DAY
MODERATE WATER

Francoa ramosa

Native to Chile. Spreading plant with basal clumps (up to 1–2 ft. across) of large leaves

with wavy margins. In midsummer, graceful, almost leafless flowering stems stand 2–3 ft. high; upper portions carry spikes of many pure white (occasionally pinkish) tiny flowers. Needs little fertilizer. Distribution seems mainly by neighborliness; more plants pass over back fences than through nurseries. In just a few years, plants increase in size enough that you can divide and replant fresh new segments from outside edges of clumps. *F. sonchifolia* is similar but with pink flowers.

Good companion for foxgloves, primroses, azaleas, camellias. Good cut flowers.

FRANGIPANI. See PLUMERIA rubra   p. 428

FRANKLINIA alatamaha (Gordonia alatamaha)

Theaceae
DECIDUOUS TREE
ZONES 2–6, 14–17
PARTIAL SHADE IN HOT-SUMMER AREAS
REGULAR TO AMPLE WATER

Franklinia alatamaha

Once native to Georgia, but apparently extinct in the wilds before 1800. Slender form, to 20–30 ft. high. Slow to moderate growth. Reddish brown bark with faint striping. Spoon-shaped leaves, 4–6 in. long, turn from bright green to scarlet in fall. White, 3-in.-wide flowers with center clusters of yellow stamens open from round white buds August–September, sometimes coinciding with fall foliage color. During wet autumns in Northwest, it blooms shyly. Give it a well-drained, rich, light, acid soil. Easy to grow from seed, blooming in 6–7 years. Use for contrast in azalea–rhododendron plantings. Unusual lawn or patio tree with right soil and exposure.

FRAXINELLA. See DICTAMNUS albus   p. 263

FRAXINUS

ASH
Oleaceae
DECIDUOUS TREES, ONE ALMOST EVERGREEN
ZONES VARY BY SPECIES
FULL SUN
WATER NEEDS VARY BY SPECIES

Fraxinus velutina 'Modesto'

Trees grow fairly fast, and most tolerate hot summers, cold winters, and many kinds of soil (including alkaline soil). Chiefly used as street trees, shade trees, lawn trees, patio shelter trees.

In most cases, leaves are divided into leaflets. Male and female flowers (generally inconspicuous, in clusters) grow on separate trees in some species, on same tree in others. In latter case, flowers are often followed by clusters of single-seeded, winged fruit, often in such abundance that they can be a litter problem. When flowers are on separate trees, you'll get fruit on female tree only if it grows near male tree.

F. americana. WHITE ASH. Deciduous tree. Zones 1–11, 14–17. Native to eastern United States. Grows to 80 ft. or more, with straight trunk and oval-shaped crown. Leaves 8–15 in. long with five to nine dark green, oval leaflets, paler beneath; turn purplish in fall. Needs some watering. Edges show burning in hot, windy areas. Male and female flowers on separate trees, but plants sold are generally seedlings, so you don't know what you're getting. If you end up with both male and female trees, you will get heavy crop of seed; both litter and seedlings can be problem. Seedless selections include 'Autumn Applause' and 'Autumn Purple', both with exceptionally good, long-lasting purple fall color; 'Champaign County', a dense grower; 'Rosehill', with bronzy red fall color; and 'Skyline', an upright oval with brown and purple fall color.

F. angustifolia (F. oxycarpa). Zones 3–9, 12–24. Compact, small-leafed, fine-textured ash with delicate, lacy look. Species is apparently not grown in the West, except in its variety 'Raywood', the Raywood ash or claret ash, a round-headed, compact, fast-growing tree 25–35 ft. tall with purple-red fall color, no seeds. Moderate water.

F. dipetala. FOOTHILL ASH. Deciduous tree or large shrub. Zones 7–24. Native to California foothills, Baja California. Treelike shrub to 6 ft. high or small tree to 18–20 ft. Aridity tolerant. Leaves 2–5½ in. long; occasionally undivided, but usually with three to nine leaflets about 1 in. long. White flowers in showy, branched clusters, March–June, followed by many 1-in.-long fruits.

F. excelsior. EUROPEAN ASH. Deciduous tree. All zones. Native to Europe, Asia Minor. Round-headed tree 60–80 ft. high, or may grow to 140 ft. Dormant buds black. Leaves 10–12 in. long, divided into 7–11 oval, toothed leaflets, dark green above, paler beneath; do not change color but drop while green. Water young trees.

F. e. 'Kimberly'. Especially valued as shade tree in Zones 1–3. A selected male variety that doesn't produce seed.

F. e. 'Pendula'. WEEPING EUROPEAN ASH. Spreading, rather asymmetrical, umbrella-shaped tree with weeping branches that reach ground.

F. 'Fan West'. Zones 1–14. Seedless hybrid between green ash (*F. pennsylvanica*) and Modesto ash (*F. velutina* 'Modesto'). Light olive green leaves, good branch structure, tolerates cold, desert heat, some aridity, and wind.

F. holotricha. Deciduous tree. Zones 4–24. Native to eastern Balkan Peninsula. Upright, rather narrow tree to 40 ft. Leaves of 9–13 dull green, 2–3-in.-long leaflets with toothed edges. Casts light, filtered shade. Leaves turn yellow in fall, dry up, and sift down into lawn or ground cover, thus lessening litter problem. Needs some water.

F. h. 'Moraine'. Selected variety; rounded head, produces few seeds. Good lawn tree—neat, symmetrical, uniform bright yellow in fall.

F. latifolia (F. oregona). OREGON ASH. Deciduous tree. Zones 4–24. Native to Sierra Nevada and along coast from Northern California to British Columbia. Grows to 40–80 ft. Leaves 6–12 in. long, divided into five to seven oblong to oval, light green, hairy or smooth leaflets; end leaflet to 4 in. long, larger than side leaflets. Male and female flowers on separate trees. Will grow in standing water during winter months. Needs no dry-season water.

F. ornus. FLOWERING ASH. Deciduous tree. Zones 3–9, 14–17. Native to southern Europe and Asia Minor. Grows rapidly to 40–50 ft. with broad, rounded crown 20–30 ft. wide. Supplies luxuriant mass of foliage. Leaves 8–10 in. long, divided into 7–11 oval, medium green, 2-in.-long leaflets with toothed edges. Foliage turns to soft shades of lavender and yellow in fall. In May, displays quantities of fluffy, branched, 3–5-in.-long clusters of fragrant white to greenish white blossoms followed by unsightly seed clusters that hang on until late winter unless removed. Water infrequently during dry season.

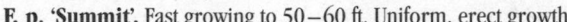

Fraxinus ornus

F. pennsylvanica (F. lanceolata). GREEN ASH, RED ASH. Deciduous tree. Zones 1–6. Native to eastern United States. Moderate grower to 30–40 ft., forming compact oval crown. Gray-brown bark; dense, twiggy structure. Leaves 10–12 in. long, divided into five to nine bright green, rather narrow, 4–6-in.-long leaflets. Male and female flowers on separate trees. Takes wet soil and severe cold, but foliage burns in hot, dry winds. Regular watering. Seedless varieties include 'Marshall' and 'Summit'; 'Bergeson', fast growing, cold tolerant; 'Emerald', yellow fall color; 'Patmore', tolerant of extreme cold; and 'Urbanite'.

F. p. 'Marshall'. MARSHALL SEEDLESS GREEN ASH. Selected male form with large, glossy, dark green leaflets. Fast grower with tapered crown.

F. p. 'Summit'. Fast growing to 50–60 ft. Uniform, erect growth.

F. quadrangulata. BLUE ASH. Deciduous tree. Zones 1–6. Native to central United States. Grows rapidly to 60–80 ft. or more. Branches distinctly square, usually with flanges along edges. Oval, dark green leaflets (7–11 per leaf), 2–5 in. long, with toothed edges. Foliage turns purplish in fall. Fruit may become litter problem if you have both female and male trees. Regular water.

F. uhdei. EVERGREEN ASH, SHAMEL ASH. Evergreen to semievergreen tree. Zones 9, 12–24. Native to Mexico. In mildest areas, leaves stay through winter; in colder areas, trees lose most or all foliage, but often only for a short time. Sharp frosts may kill back branch tips; serious damage at about 15°F or lower. Regular water, but tolerates aridity. A favorite in Southern California and low-elevation deserts. 'Majestic Beauty' has exceptionally large leaves, is more reliably evergreen than the species.

Grows fast to 25–30 ft. in 10 years; 40 ft. in 20 years; eventually 70–80 ft. or more. Upright, narrow tree when young; eventually takes on a spreading form as it grows older. Leaves divided into five to nine glossy dark green leaflets about 4 in. long, edged with small teeth. Foliage may burn if subjected to hot winds. Shallow rooted; encourage deeper rooting by watering deeply. Cut back any long, unsightly branches when tree is young. Eliminate deep crotches by pruning out weaker branches. Texas root rot sometimes causes dieback and will kill young trees, but established trees usually survive. Resistant to oak root fungus.

> ### ASH WHITEFLY
>
> First identified in 1988, these whiteflies are chalky white and ⅛ in. long. They colonize in great patches on undersides of ash leaves. Buy and release encarsia wasp; keep ground beneath infested plants clear of weeds; spray with insecticidal soap; keep infested plants well watered. Toxic sprays are all but useless.

F. u. 'Sexton'. SEXTON ASH. Forms very compact, rounded crown. Leaflets larger and deeper green than those of *F. uhdei*.

F. u. 'Tomlinson'. TOMLINSON ASH. Grows more slowly than species (18 ft. in 10 years). More upright and dense when young. Leaflets deep green and more leathery, with wavy-toothed margins.

F. velutina. ARIZONA ASH. Deciduous tree. Zones 8–24. Native to Arizona. Tree withstands hot, dry conditions and cold to about −10°F. Pyramidal when young; spreading, more open when mature. Leaves divided into three to five narrow to oval, 3-in.-long leaflets. Male and female flowers on separate trees.

F. v. coriacea. MONTEBELLO ASH. Zones 8, 9, 12–24. Native mostly to Southern California. Has broader, more leathery leaves than the species.

F. v. 'Modesto'. MODESTO ASH. Zones 3–24. Originated in Westside Park, Modesto, California. Vigorous form of Arizona ash. Grows to about 50 ft. with 30-ft. spread. Medium green leaflets, glossier than those of the species, turn bright yellow in fall.

In many areas, Modesto ash leaves get scorched look following a wet spring. This is caused by fungus disease called anthracnose. Prune out and dispose of infected wood—it can reinfect. Verticillium wilt is prevalent in agricultural areas; there is no control once it's started in young trees, but established trees often survive. In desert, subject to ash decline syndrome, an ailment of unknown origin. Keep trees vigorous; if any are lost, replace with 'Raywood' or Shamel ashes. Resistant to oak root fungus.

F. v. 'Rio Grande'. FAN-TEX ASH. Zones 8–24. Thrives in hot, dry climates and alkaline soils. Has very large, darker green, more succulent leaflets than Modesto ash; they unfold in early spring, turn golden yellow in late fall. Foliage resistant to wind burn.

FRECKLE FACE. See HYPOESTES phyllostachya   p. 328

PRACTICAL GARDENING DICTIONARY
PLEASE SEE PAGES 529–592

FREESIA

Iridaceae

CORMS

⚡ ZONES 8, 9, 12–24

☼ ☽ SUN OR PARTIAL SHADE

◐ WATER DURING GROWTH AND FLOWERING

Freesia Hybrid

Native to South Africa. Prized for rich fragrance of flowers. Slender, branched stems grow to 1–1½ ft., about same height as lowest leaves; stem leaves shorter. Flowers tubular, 2 in. long, in one-sided spikes. Older variety 'Alba' has fragrant white or creamy white blooms; newer, larger-flowered varieties with 1–1½-ft. stems are Tecolote and Dutch hybrids with white, pink, red, lavender, purple, blue, yellow, and orange flowers, mixed or in single-color-named varieties. Freesias will self-sow if faded flowers are not removed; volunteers tend to revert to cream marked with purple and yellow.

In mild climates, plant 2 in. deep (pointed end up) in fall in sunny, well-drained soil. Plants dry up after bloom, start growing again in fall; increase rapidly. In cold climates, plant 2 in. deep, 2 in. apart in pots; grow indoors in sunny window. Keep room temperature as cool as possible at night. Easily grown from seed sown in July–August; often bloom following spring. Good in rock gardens or for cutting. Flowering potted freesias are available all year; they have been grown from chilled and stored corms.

FREMONTODENDRON (Fremontia)

FLANNEL BUSH

Sterculiaceae (Bombacaceae)

EVERGREEN SHRUBS OR SMALL TREES

⚡ ZONES 7–24

☼ FULL SUN

◌ NEED NO DRY-SEASON WATER

Fremontodendron 'California Glory'

Fast growing to 6–20 ft. tall. Leathery leaves are dark green above, feltlike beneath. Yellow, saucerlike flowers. Conical seed capsules, covered with bristly, rust-colored hairs, persist; some consider them unsightly. Plants need excellent drainage; hillside planting is best. Roots shallow, so stake plants while young. Pinch and prune to shape. Usually short lived. Plant with other no-water shrubs like ceanothus.

F. 'California Glory'. Hybrid between *F. californicum* and *F. mexicanum*. To 20 ft. tall, possibly more. Flowers to 3 in. across, rich yellow inside, tinged red outside. Prolific bloom over long period.

F. californicum. COMMON FLANNEL BUSH. Native to foothills of Sierra Nevada and Coast Ranges, and Southern California mountains. Eye-catching show of lemon yellow, 1–1½-in.-wide flowers in May–June; flowers bloom all at once. Roundish unlobed or three-lobed leaves, 1 in. long.

F. 'Ken Taylor'. A hybrid, it grows to 5 ft. tall, considerably broader, and has somewhat cup-shaped golden flowers with orange reverse.

F. mexicanum. SOUTHERN FLANNEL BUSH. Native to San Diego County and Baja California. To 18 ft. Leaves have three to five distinct lobes, 1¼–3 in. long. Flowers are 1½–2½ in. wide, yellow often tinged orange. Blooms over longer period than *F. californicum*, but because flowers form among leaves, mass effect is not as showy.

F. 'Pacific Sunset'. Deep orange yellow flowers, 3½–4 in. wide. Peak bloom late April, May; sporadic bloom later.

F. 'San Gabriel'. Resembles *F.* 'California Glory', but leaves are more deeply cut (maplelike).

FRINGE BELLS. See SHORTIA soldanelloides   **p. 485**

FRINGECUPS. See TELLIMA grandiflora   **p. 503**

FRINGED WORMWOOD. See ARTEMISIA frigida   **p. 166**

FRINGE HYACINTH. See MUSCARI comosum   **p. 385**

FRINGE TREE. See CHIONANTHUS   **p. 224**

FRITILLARIA

FRITILLARY

Liliaceae

BULBS

⚡ ZONES 1–7, 15–17

☼ ☽ SUN OR LIGHT SHADE

◐ ◑ MOSTLY SUMMER-DRY PLANTS

Fritillaria imperialis

Native to Europe, Asia, North America; American species most numerous in West. Give variable performance in gardens; some kinds short lived. Unbranched stems 6 in.–4 ft. high, topped by bell-like, nodding flowers, often unusually colored and mottled. Use in woodland, rock garden, or as border plants. In fall, plant bulbs in porous soil with ample humus. Set smaller bulbs 3–4 in. deep; set largest (crown imperial) 4–5 in. deep. Most kinds should gradually dry out as foliage yellows, remain dry until late fall. Bulbs sometimes rest a year after planting or after blooming; use enough for yearly display.

F. imperialis. CROWN IMPERIAL. Stout stalk 3½–4 ft. tall, clothed with broad, glossy leaves. At top of stalk are clusters of large, drooping, bell-shaped flowers in red, orange, or yellow; tuft of leaves above flowers. Use in borders, containers. Bulb and plant have somewhat unpleasant odor.

F. lanceolata. CHECKER LILY. Western native. Stems 2½ ft. high with several whorls of leaves. Flowers are bowl-shaped, brownish purple bells mottled with yellow, greenish yellow, or purple spots.

F. meleagris. CHECKERED LILY, SNAKESHEAD. Nodding 2-in. bells on 1–1½-ft. stems. Showy flowers, checkered and veined with reddish brown and purple, bloom in late spring. Lance-shaped leaves are 3–6 in. long. There is a white form. Native to damp meadows in Europe, Asia; tolerates occasional flooding. Long lived in colder regions.

F. persica 'Adiyaman'. Stems 2–3 ft. tall carry up to 30 drooping, deep plum purple, 1-in. flowers on upper half. Foliage is grayish. Plant is hardy and easy to grow, but emerging stems need protection from late frosts in colder regions.

FUCHSIA

Onagraceae

EVERGREEN OR DECIDUOUS SHRUBS

⚡ ZONES VARY BY SPECIES

☽ PARTIAL SHADE

◐ ◑ IN POTS, NEED AMPLE WATER

Fuchsia hybrida
Double Type

Popular, showy-flowered fuchsias that come in hundreds of named varieties are forms of *F. hybrida*, and are discussed under that heading. Other species are grown almost entirely by collectors, but some are good for basic landscaping purposes.

F. arborescens. Zones 16, 17, 22–24. Big shrub to 18 ft. tall, with 8-in. leaves and large clusters of small, erect, pinkish or purplish flowers like lilacs in summer.

F. hybrida. HYBRID FUCHSIA. Here belong nearly all garden fuchsias. Zones 4–6, 15–17, 22–24 constitute finest climate in North America for growing fuchsias and region in which most varieties were developed. The next strip—Zones 2, 3, 7–9, 14, 20, 21—finds fuchsias grown, but with more difficulty. Outside those two strips, fuchsias are little known, grown as summer annuals in greenhouses or as house plants.

Fuchsias bloom from early summer to first frost. At least 500 varieties in West, with wide variety of combinations within color range. Sepals (top parts that flare back) are always white, red, or pink. Corolla (inside part of flower) may be almost any color possible within range of white, blue-violet, purple, pink, red, and shades approaching orange. Flowers have no fragrance, but hummingbirds visit them.

Fuchsias range in size from shelled-peanut size to giants as big as a child's fist. Within this range, some are single, meaning that there's just one layer of closely set petals in corolla; some are very double, with many sets of ruffled petals in corolla. Little-flowered types often have small leaves, and big-flowered types have large leaves.

Plant forms vary widely—from erect-growing shrubs 3–12 ft. high to trailing types grown in hanging containers. You can buy or train fuchsias in these forms: hanging basket, small shrub, medium shrub, large shrub, espalier, and standard (miniature tree shape).

Best environment. Fuchsias grow best in cool summer temperatures, in modified sunlight, and with much moisture in atmosphere and soil. If you live where fog rolls in on summer afternoons, any place in your garden will supply these conditions. Where summers are warm, windy, dry, or sunny, seek or create favorable exposure protected from wind and in morning sun or all-day dappled shade—a comfortable spot on hot summer afternoons. For containers or planting beds, soil mix should be porous (for aeration), water retentive, and rich in organic matter.

Watering. Water as often as you can. It's almost impossible to give too much water to thriving fuchsias in well-drained containers. Hanging-basket fuchsias need more watering than any other form. Fuchsias in ground can go longer between watering if drainage is good. In hot-summer climates, heavy mulching (1½–3 in. deep) helps maintain soil moisture. Frequent overhead sprinkling is beneficial in several ways: it keeps leaves clean, discourages pests, counteracts low humidity (especially important on windy days in inland climates). When foliage wilts in extreme heat regardless of watering, mist to cool it down.

Fuchsia hybrida
Single Type

Feeding. Apply complete fertilizer frequently. Light doses every 10 days – 2 weeks, or label-recommended feedings every month, will keep plants growing and producing flowers. You can almost see fertilizer take effect. Liquid fertilizers work well.

Growing from cuttings. You can take cuttings of favorite variety and grow them into flowering plants in a few months to a year. Cut 2–3-in. stem pieces (tips preferred) and put lower halves in damp sand to root.

Summer pruning and pinching. If plant is growing leggy, pinch out tips of branches whenever you can. Pinching forces growth into side branches, makes plant bushier. Pick off old flowers as they start to fade.

Spraying. Common pests in California are spider mites and whiteflies. They cause leaves to yellow and drop. Frequent overhead watering will discourage red spider mites; spray undersides of leaves with miticide to control them. In Northwest, aphids are worst pest. Spray to control, using any good general-purpose insecticide.

Winters in cold climates. Where frosts are light, fuchsias lose their leaves; sometimes tender growth is killed. Where freezes are hard, most plants die back to hard wood, sometimes to roots. A few varieties, including 'Royal Purple', 'Checkerboard', and 'Marinka', stand outdoor exposures in winter in Zones 4–7. In Northwest, best plan is usually to protect outdoor fuchsias by mounding 5–6 in. of sawdust over roots (tops will be killed), and to store potted plants in greenhouse or indoors (40–50°F is ideal) in damp sawdust. Keep soil moist (but not soggy) all winter.

Early spring pruning. Fuchsias everywhere need some pruning in early spring. In frost-free areas, cut out approximately the same volume of growth that formed the previous summer—leave about two healthy leaf buds on that growth. In mild-frost regions, cut out all frost-damaged wood and enough additional wood to remove most of the last summer's growth.

In cold-winter regions, prune plants lightly (remove leaves and twiggy growth) before storing them. In spring, prune out all broken branches and cut back into live wood.

F. magellanica. Zones 2–9, 14–24. Many arching, 3-ft.-long stems loaded with drooping, 1½-in.-long, red-and-violet flowers, July to frost. Flowers frequented by hummingbirds. Leaves are oval, in groups of two or three, ½–1 in. long. Where winters are mild, can reach 20 ft. trained against wall. Treat as perennial in cold-climate areas. Roots are hardy with mulching; tops will die back with the first hard frost.

F. procumbens. Zones 16, 17, 21–24. Prostrate, spreading fuchsia to 1 ft. high for containers, shady rock gardens. Leaves ½ in. long. Tiny flowers without petals in summer. Purple-tipped sepals pale orange marked green; anthers and pollen blue. Red berries, ¾ in. long, are showy.

F. thymifolia. Zones 14–17, 20, 24. Erect, spreading shrub 3–9 ft. tall, with leaves ½–1 in. long and a profusion of tiny, dangling white to pink flowers aging deeper pink. Pretty close up. Resistant to fuchsia mite.

F. triphylla. Zones 14–17, 20, 24. This West Indian species is seldom seen, but a hybrid descendant, 'Gartenmeister Bonstedt', is well known. It's a spreading, shrubby plant 2–3 ft. tall, with purplish leaf undersides and drooping clusters of intense orange-red, long-tubed flowers. It is somewhat more tender than most fuchsia hybrids but is said to be more tolerant of heat. Blooms all year in mildest climates. Protect from frost.

Fuchsia triphylla
'Gartenmeister Bonstedt'

THE FUCHSIA MITE

In the 1980s the fuchsia gall mite became a serious fuchsia pest in California. It distorts leaves and shoots. Cut off and destroy distorted tissue. Or plant mite-resistant fuchsias such as 'Carnival', 'Mrs. Victor Reiter', and 'Trumpeter', or many of the species fuchsias.

Fumariaceae. This family consists of annuals and perennials, usually with irregularly shaped flowers. *Corydalis* and *Dicentra* are examples. This family is considered by many to be included in the poppy family (Papaveraceae).

FUNKIA. See HOSTA p. 325

GAILLARDIA

Asteraceae (Compositae)

PERENNIALS AND ANNUALS

ALL ZONES

FULL SUN

LIGHT WATERING

Gaillardia grandiflora

Native to central and western United States. Low-growing plants with daisylike flowers in warm colors—yellow, bronze, scarlet. They thrive in heat, need good drainage. They are easy to grow from seed and fine for cutting and borders, and they often reseed.

G. grandiflora. BLANKET FLOWER. Perennial. To 2–4 ft. high. Developed from native species *G. aristata* and *G. pulchella*. Foliage roughish, gray green; flower heads 3–4 in. across, single or double. Much variation in flower color: warm shades of red and yellow with orange or maroon bands. Bloom in June until frost.

Plants flower first year from seed. Many strains and varieties are obtainable, including dwarf kinds and types with extra-large flowers. 'Goblin' is an especially good compact variety (1 ft. tall) with large, deep red flowers bordered in bright yellow.

▶

G. pulchella. Annual. Easy to grow. To 1½–2 ft. high. Flower heads 2 in. wide on long, whiplike stems in summer. Warm shades of red, yellow, gold. Leaves soft, hairy. Sow seeds in warm soil after frost danger is past.

G. p. 'Lorenziana'. Has no ray flowers (petals); instead, disk flowers are enlarged into little star-tipped bells, whole effect like balls of bright fluff. Double Gaiety strain (1½ ft.) has flowers that range from near-white to maroon, often with bicolors. Lollipop strain is similar, but 10–12 in. tall.

GALANTHUS

SNOWDROP

Amaryllidaceae

BULBS

☘ ZONES 1–9, 14–17

☼ ◐ SUN OR PARTIAL SHADE

● YEAR-ROUND MOISTURE

◊ G. NIVALIS BULB IS POISONOUS

Galanthus nivalis

Best adapted to cold climates. Closely related to and often confused with *Leucojum* (snowflake). White, nodding, bell-shaped flowers (one per stalk) with green tips on inner segments; larger outer segments pure white. Plants have two to three basal leaves. Use in rock garden or under flowering shrubs, naturalize in woodland, or grow in pots. Plant in fall, 3–4 in. deep, 2–3 in. apart, in moist soil with ample humus. Do not divide often; when needed, divide right after bloom.

G. elwesii. GIANT SNOWDROP. Globular, 1½-in.-long bells on 1-ft. stems; two or three leaves, 8 in. long, ¾ in. wide. January–February bloom in mild areas (where better adapted than *G. nivalis*); March–April in cold climates.

G. nivalis. COMMON SNOWDROP. Dainty 1-in.-long bells on 6–9-in. stems in earliest spring.

GALAX urceolata (G. aphylla)

Diapensiaceae

PERENNIAL

☘ ZONES 1–6

◐ ● PARTIAL OR FULL SHADE

● REGULAR WATER

Galax urceolata

Often used as ground cover, although it spreads slowly. Grow in acid soil with much organic material, preferably mulch of leaf mold. Space plants 1 ft. apart. Small white flowers on 2½-ft. stems in July. Leaves, in basal tufts, give plant its real distinction. They are shiny, heart shaped, 5 in. across; turn beautiful bronze color in fall. Leaves much used in indoor arrangements.

GALIUM odoratum (Asperula odorata)

SWEET WOODRUFF

Rubiaceae

PERENNIAL

☘ ZONES 1–6, 15–17

● SHADE

● ◓ REGULAR TO ABUNDANT WATER

Galium odoratum

Attractive, low-spreading perennial that brings to mind deep-shaded woods. Slender, square stems 6–12 in. high, encircled every inch or so by whorls of six to eight aromatic, bristle-tipped leaves. Clusters of tiny white flowers show above foliage in late spring and summer. Leaves and stems give off fragrant, haylike odor when dried; used to make May wine.

In the shade garden, sweet woodruff is best used as ground cover or edging along path. Will spread rapidly in rich soil with abundant moisture—can become a pest if allowed to grow entirely unchecked. Self-sows freely. Can be increased by division in fall or spring.

GALTONIA candicans

SUMMER HYACINTH

Liliaceae

BULB

☘ ZONES 8–24

◐ PARTIAL SHADE

● SOME SUMMER WATER

Galtonia candicans

Native to South Africa. Straplike leaves, 2–3 ft. long; stout 2–4-ft. stems topped in summer with loose, spikelike clusters of fragrant white flowers—drooping, funnel-shaped, 1–1½ in. long, with three outer segments often tipped green. Plant behind low, bushy plants. Plant bulbs 6 in. deep in rich soil in fall; they will grow well for many years without lifting, dividing. Where ground freezes, plant in spring; mulch deeply during winter or lift bulbs after foliage dies and store them at 55–60°F. Bait for slugs and snails.

GALVEZIA speciosa

ISLAND BUSH SNAPDRAGON

Scrophulariaceae

EVERGREEN SHRUB

☘ ZONES 14–24

☼ ◐ SUN NEAR COAST, LIGHT SHADE INLAND

◊ NO DRY-SEASON WATER ONCE ESTABLISHED

Galvezia speciosa

Native to Santa Catalina, San Clemente, and Guadalupe islands. Usually 3–5 ft. across, slightly less in height, but can climb or lean on other shrubs and reach 8 ft. Leaves are about 1 in. long, half as wide. Flowers scarlet, tubular, 1 in. long, clustering toward tips of branches. Bloom heaviest in midspring, but intermittent throughout year. Endures light or heavy soils if drainage is adequate. 'Firecracker' is a compact form with bright red flowers.

GARDENIA

Rubiaceae

EVERGREEN SHRUBS

☘ ZONES VARY BY SPECIES

☼ SUN ON COAST, FILTERED SHADE IN HOT VALLEYS

● MOIST SOIL

Gardenia jasminoides

White intensely fragrant flowers contrast sharply with shiny, leathery, dark green leaves. Double forms are classic corsage blooms.

G. jasminoides (G. augusta). Zones 7–9, 12–16, 18–23. Native to China. Glossy bright green leaves and double white, highly fragrant flowers. Though hardy to 20°F or even lower, plants fail to grow and bloom well without summer heat. They are hard to grow in adobe soils. Give northern or eastern exposure in desert.

Soil should drain fast but retain water, too; use plenty of peat moss or ground bark in conditioning soil. Plant high (like azaleas and rhododendrons) and avoid crowding by other plants and competing roots. Mulch plants instead of cultivating. Syringe plants in early morning except when in bloom—unless water is high in salts (residue from this water may burn leaves). Where water is poor, leach salts by monthly flooding. Feed every 3–4 weeks during growing season with acid plant food, fish emulsion, or blood meal. Treat chlorosis with iron sulfate or iron chelate. Prune to remove straggly branches, faded flowers. Use all-purpose spray or dust to control aphids, other sucking insects.

All are useful in containers or raised beds, as hedges, espaliers, low screens, or as single plants. Named varieties are

'August Beauty'. Grows 4–6 ft. high and blooms heavily, May–October or November. Large double flowers.

'First Love' ('Aimee'). Somewhat larger shrub than 'August Beauty', with a larger flower.

'Golden Magic'. Plants reach 3 ft. tall, 2 ft. wide in 2–3 years, eventually larger. Extra-full flowers open white, gradually age to deep golden yellow. April–September bloom, peaking in May.

'Kimura Shikazaki' ('Four Seasons'). Compact plant 2–3 ft. tall. Flowers similar to those of 'Veitchii', but slightly less fragrant. Extremely long bloom season—spring to fall.

'Mystery'. Best-known variety; has 4–5-in. double white flowers, May–July. Tends to be rangy. Needs pruning to keep it neat. In warm southwestern gardens may bloom through November. Can reach 6–8 ft.

'Radicans'. Grows 6–12 in. tall and spreads to 2–3 ft., with small dark green leaves and inch-wide summer flowers. Good small-scale ground cover, container plant. 'Radicans Variegata' has gray-green leaves with white markings.

'Veitchii'. Compact 3–4½-ft. plant with many 1–1½-in. blooms May–November, sometimes even during warm winter. Prolific bloom, reliable grower.

G. thunbergia. Zones 16, 17, 21–24. Native to South Africa. Angular-branched shrub to 10 ft. tall, 20 ft. wide. Leaves to 6 in. long, dark green (nearly black). Winter flowers long tubed, single, 3–4 in. across. Fragrant. Seems somewhat more tolerant of cool conditions and less than perfect soil than common gardenia, but tender to frost. With age, becomes more vigorous, flowers more profusely.

GARDENIA'S DEMANDS
Like a temperamental artist the gardenia has its own set of rules. Fawn over them and the plants give beauty. Ignore them and they yellow and die. For thriving gardenias, provide sun/warmth, regular water and feeding, good soil drainage, and morning dew or misting.

GARLAND FLOWER. See HEDYCHIUM coronarium p. 318

GARLIC

Liliaceae

BULB

☀ ALL ZONES

☼ FULL SUN

💧 REGULAR WATER

Garlic

For ornamental varieties, see *Allium*. Seed stores and some mail-order seed houses sell mother bulbs ("sets") for planting. In mild-winter areas, plant October–December for early summer harvest. Where winters are cold, plant early in spring. Break bulbs up into cloves and plant base downward, 1–2 in. deep, 2–3 in. apart, in rows 1 ft. apart. Harvest when leafy tops fall over; air-dry bulbs, remove tops and roots, and store in cool place. Giant or elephant garlic has unusually large (fist-sized) bulbs and mild garlic flavor. Same culture as regular garlic.

GARLIC CHIVES. See ALLIUM tuberosum p. 145

GARRYA

SILKTASSEL

Garryaceae

EVERGREEN SHRUBS

☀ ZONES VARY BY SPECIES

☼ ☽ SUN OR PARTIAL SHADE

◐ ◑ ● WATER NEEDS VARY BY SPECIES

Garrya elliptica

Pendulous male and female catkins on separate shrubs; male catkins are long, slender, and decorative. Both plants must be present to produce grapelike clusters of purple fruit on female plant.

G. elliptica. COAST SILKTASSEL. Zones 5–9, 14–21. Native to Coast Ranges from southern Oregon to San Luis Obispo County, California. Shrub to 4–8 ft. or small tree to 20–30 ft. Branches densely clothed with elliptical, wavy-edged leaves to 2½ in. long, dark green above, gray and woolly beneath. Clustered flower tassels December–February. Yellowish to greenish yellow male catkins are slender and graceful, 3–8 in. long; pale green, rather stubby female catkins are 2–3½ in. long. Female plants have clusters of purplish fruit that hang on June–September—even longer if not eaten by robins. Excellent foliage plant. Takes summer water. Use as screen, informal hedge, or display shrub. For unusually long catkins, plant male varieties 'Evie' (10 in.) or 'James Roof' (8 in.).

G. fremontii. FREMONT SILKTASSEL. Zones 4–10, 12, 14–17. Native to mountains of Washington, Oregon, California, Arizona. Differs from *G. elliptica* in its leaves—glossy, smooth edged, lively yellow green on both upper and lower surfaces. Catkins yellowish or purple; fruit purple or black. Grows 4–8 ft. high. Needs no dry-season water; takes heat, cold better than *G. elliptica*.

G. issaquahensis. Zones 4–7, 14–17. Hybrid between the preceding species. Male variety 'Pat Ballard' has 8-in. catkins with purple and yellow tints. Regular water.

GAS PLANT. See DICTAMNUS albus p. 263

GAULTHERIA

Ericaceae

EVERGREEN SHRUBS OR SHRUBLETS

☀ ZONES VARY BY SPECIES

☼ PARTIAL SHADE

● ROUTINE WATERING THROUGH DRY SEASON

Gaultheria shallon

All have urn-shaped flowers and berrylike fruit. They need woodland soil. Smaller kinds are favored for rock gardens, woodland plantings in Northwest. Larger kinds are good companions for other acid-soil shrubs such as rhododendrons and azaleas.

G. mucronata. Another name for plant better known as *Pernettya mucronata*. See *Pernettya mucronata*.

G. ovatifolia. Zones 1–7, 14–17. Native to mountains in Northern California to British Columbia, east to northern Idaho. Spreading, trailing, with upright branches to about 8 in. high. Oval, leathery dark green leaves, ¾–1½ in. long, nearly as wide. Tiny white to pinkish flowers in summer. Bright red berries ¼ in. wide in fall and winter are edible, wintergreen flavored. Small-scale ground cover in woodland.

G. procumbens. WINTERGREEN, CHECKERBERRY, TEABERRY. Zones 2–7, 14–17. Native to eastern United States. Creeping stems, upright branches to 6 in. with 2-in., oval, glossy leaves clustered toward tips. Small white summer flowers followed by scarlet berries. Leaves and fruit have flavor of wintergreen (or teaberry). Use as ground cover; plant 1 ft. apart.

G. shallon. SALAL. Zones 3–7, 14–17, 21–24. Native to Santa Barbara County, California, to British Columbia. In full sun and poor, dry soil, a tufted plant 1–2 ft. tall. In shade and good soil can reach 4–10 ft. Nearly round, glossy bright green leaves 1¾ – 4 in. long. White or pinkish, bell-like flowers on reddish stalks in loose, 6-in.-long clusters. Blooms March – June. Edible black fruits resemble large huckleberries but are bland in flavor. Birds like them.

In sun, good low-bank cover. In shade and acid soil, good companion for rhododendrons, azaleas, ferns. Only neglected plantings need pruning; cut back in April, remove dead wood, and mulch with leaf mold or peat moss. Cut branches are sold by florists as "lemon leaves."

GAURA lindheimeri

GAURA
Onagraceae
PERENNIAL
🌿 ALL ZONES
☼ FULL SUN
◐ LIGHT WATERING

Gaura lindheimeri

Native to Southwest. Grows 2¼ – 4 ft. high. Stalkless leaves, 1½ – 3½ in. long, grow directly on stems. Branching flower spikes bear many 1-in.-long white blossoms that open from pink buds closely set on stems. Long blooming period, with only a few blossoms opening at a time. Blossoms drop off cleanly when spent, but seed-bearing spikes should be cut to improve appearance and prevent overly enthusiastic self-sowing. Can take neglect. One of the few long-lived perennials in Southwest.

GAYFEATHER. See LIATRIS   p. 353

GAZANIA

Asteraceae (Compositae)
PERENNIALS OR SUMMER ANNUALS
🌿 ANNUALS, ALL ZONES; PERENNIALS, ZONES 8–24
☼ FULL SUN
◐ OCCASIONAL DRY-SEASON WATERING

Gazania 'Copper King'

Native to South Africa. Daisy flowers give daz-zling color display during peak bloom in late spring, early summer. In mild areas, they continue to bloom intermittently throughout the year. Gazanias grow well in almost any soil. Feed once in spring with slow-acting fertilizer. Divide plants about every 3 – 4 years. In cold areas, carry gazanias through winter by taking cuttings in fall as you would for pelargoniums.

There are basically two types: clumping and trailing. The clumping type (complex hybrids between a number of species) forms a mound of ever-green leaves—dark green above, gray and woolly beneath, often lobed. Flowers 3 – 4 in. wide, on 6 – 10-in.-long stems; they open on sunny days, close at night and in cloudy weather. You can buy clumping gazanias in sin-gle colors—yellow, orange, white, or rosy pink, with reddish purple petal undersides, often with dark blossom centers. Or you can get a mixture of hybrids (as plants or seeds) in different colors. Seed-grown kinds include Carnival (many colors, silver leaves); Chansonette (early blooming, com-pact; medium-size round flowers); Harlequin (many colors, eyed and banded); Mini-Star (compact, floriferous plants; named selections include 'Mini-Star Yellow', 'Mini-Star Tangerine'); Sundance (5-in. flowers, striped or banded); and Sunshine (big, multicolored flowers, gray foliage).

Named hybrids of special merit are 'Aztec Queen' (multicolored), 'Bur-gundy', 'Copper King', and 'Fiesta Red'; these are best used in small-scale plantings, although the last is sturdy enough for large expanses. 'Moon-glow' is double-flowered bright yellow of unusual vigor; its blossoms, unlike most, stay open even on dull days.

Clumping gazanias serve as temporary fillers between young, growing shrubs and as a replaceable ground cover for relatively level areas not sub-ject to severe erosion. Try in parking strips, as edgings along sunny paths, or

in rock gardens. Trailing gazanias (*G. rigens leucolaena*, formerly sold as *G. uniflora* or *G. leucolaena*) grow about as tall as clumping type, but spread rapidly by long trailing stems. Foliage is clean silvery gray; flowers are yellow, white, orange, or bronze. New, larger-flowered hybrids are 'Sun-burst' (orange, black eye) and 'Sunglow' (yellow). 'Sunrise Yellow' has large, black-eyed yellow flowers; leaves are green instead of gray. New hybrids are superior to older kinds in length of bloom, resistance to dieback. Trailing gazanias are useful on banks, level ground. Or grow them at top of wall and allow them to trail over. Attractive in hanging baskets.

GEIJERA parviflora

AUSTRALIAN WILLOW, WILGA
Rutaceae
EVERGREEN TREE
🌿 ZONES 8, 9, 12–24
☼ FULL SUN
◐◐ SUMMER WATER SPEEDS GROWTH

Geijera parviflora

Graceful, fine textured, to 25 – 30 ft. high, 20 ft. wide. Main branches sweep up and out, little branches hang down. Distant citrus relative; called Australian willow because its 3 – 6-in.-long, nar-row, medium green, drooping leaves give a kind of weeping willow effect. With age, produces loose clusters of unimportant small, creamy white flowers in early spring, early fall. Well-drained soil. Needs pruning only to correct form (much less pruning than willow). Quite pest free.

Has much of the willow's grace and the eucalyptus's toughness. Moder-ate growth rate; deep, noninvasive roots. Casts light shade. Plant singly as patio or street tree, or in colonies for attractive grove effect.

GELSEMIUM sempervirens

CAROLINA JESSAMINE
Loganiaceae
EVERGREEN VINE
🌿 ZONES 8–24
☼ FULL SUN
◐◐ LOOKS BEST IF WATERED REGULARLY
◆ ALL PARTS ARE POISONOUS

Gelsemium sempervirens

Shrubby and twining; moderate growth rate to about 20 ft. Clean pairs of shiny light green, 1 – 4-in.-long leaves on long, streamerlike branches make neat but not dense foliage pattern. On trellis, vine will cascade and swing in wind; makes delicate green curtain of branches when trained on house. Vine can get top-heavy; if it does, cut it back severely. Fragrant, tubular yellow flowers, 1 – 1½ in. long, in late winter, early spring. 'Plena' is a double-flowered form. Can be used as ground cover; keep trimmed to 3 ft. high.

GENISTA

BROOM
Fabaceae (Leguminosae)
DECIDUOUS OR EVERGREEN SHRUBS
🌿 ZONES VARY BY SPECIES
☼ FULL SUN
◐ NO DRY-SEASON WATER

Genista lydia

Leaves often small and short lived. Green branches give deciduous plants an evergreen look. Flowers yellow (rarely white or pink), sweet pea shaped. Less aggressive than other brooms (*Cytisus, Spartium*); will not run wild. Smaller kinds attractive in rock gardens, bank plantings. Need good drainage; tolerate rocky or infertile soil.

G. canariensis (Cytisus canariensis). CANARY ISLAND BROOM. Evergreen. Zones 8, 9, 14–24. Damages at 15°F but recovers quickly. Many-branched, upright shrub 6–8 ft. tall, 5–6 ft. wide. Bright green leaves divided into ½-in. leaflets. Bright yellow fragrant flowers at ends of branches spring and summer. The genista of florists. Grows like a weed and spreads by seedlings.

G. fragrans. This white-flowered species is not in nursery trade. Plants sold under this name are *G. spachiana*.

G. hispanica. SPANISH BROOM. Zones 2–22. Mass of spiny stems, with ½-in.-long leaves, to 1–2 ft. high and spreading wide. Golden yellow flowers in clusters at tips of stems, May–June.

G. lydia. Shrublet. Zones 4–6, 14–17. Often sold, erroneously, as *Cytisus lydia*. Grows to 2 ft. high, with spreading habit. Makes a good ground cover. Bright yellow flowers are borne in profusion at ends of shoots in June. This plant sets little seed.

G. monosperma. BRIDAL VEIL BROOM. Zones 16, 17, 22–24. Upright growth to 20 ft. high, 10 ft. wide, with slender, graceful, gray-green, almost leafless branches. Fragrant white flowers in late winter and spring.

G. pilosa. Zones 2–22. Fairly fast-growing prostrate shrub, ultimately to 1–1½ ft. with 7-ft. spread. Intricately branched, gray-green twigs. Roundish, ¼–½-in.-long leaves. Yellow flowers, May–June. 'Vancouver Gold' is best selection.

G. racemosa. See G. spachiana

G. sagittalis. Zones 2–22. Plants spread along ground. Upright, winged, bright green branchlets appear jointed. Rather rapid grower to 1 ft. high with wide spread. Makes sheet of golden yellow bloom, late spring and early summer.

G. spachiana (G. racemosa). Often sold as *G. fragrans*. Evergreen. Zones 7–9, 14–24. Similar to *G. canariensis*, but with larger leaflets and longer, looser flower spikes of yellow fragrant flowers in late spring. Naturalizes where adapted.

G. tinctoria. DYER'S GREENWEED, WOADWAXEN. Deciduous. All zones. Species grows to 6 ft. with undivided leaves to 2 in. long. 'Royal Gold', 2 ft. tall and as wide, is the only variety generally available.

GENTIANA

GENTIAN

Gentianaceae

PERENNIALS

⚡ ZONES 1–6, 14–17

☼ ◑ FULL SUN OR LIGHT SHADE

💧 AMPLE WATER

Gentiana acaulis

Low, spreading, or upright plants, generally with very blue tubular flowers. Most are hard to grow, but prized by rock garden enthusiasts. Need perfect drainage, lime-free soil. If they thrive, they produce some of richest blues in garden.

G. acaulis. Leafy stems to 4 in. tall. Leaves 1 in. long. Rich blue flowers 2 in. long in summer. Grows well; often fails to bloom.

G. asclepiadea. Upright or arching stems to 1½ ft. Leaves willowlike, 3 in. long. Flowers blue, 1½ in. long, in late summer, fall. Fairly easy to grow in cool border or rock garden.

G. clusii (G. acaulis clusii). Similar to *G. acaulis*. Flowers larger.

G. septemfida. Arching or sprawling stems 9–18 in. long. Oval leaves to 1½ in. long. Clusters of blue 2-in. flowers in late summer. Easy to grow.

G. sino-ornata. From 7-in. rosettes of bright green leaves come trailing stems that end in 2-in.-long flowers of brightest blue. Blooms in early fall. Fairly easy to grow in half shade.

Gentianaceae. The gentian family includes annuals and perennials from many parts of the world. Many have blue or purple flowers, including the gentians, Persian violet *(Exacum)*, and *Eustoma*.

Geraniaceae. The cranesbill family of annuals and perennials (the latter sometimes shrubby) includes true geranium, *Erodium* (perennial, rarely annual), and *Pelargonium* (perennial or shrubby).

GERANIUM

CRANESBILL

Geraniaceae

PERENNIALS

⚡ ZONES VARY BY SPECIES

☼ ◑ FULL SUN OR PARTIAL SHADE

💧💧💧 MOST NEED CONSTANT MOISTURE

Geranium pratense

Here we consider the true geraniums, hardy plants. Botanically, *Pelargonium* is the more common indoor/outdoor plant most people know as geranium. Several true geraniums have handsome, near-evergreen leaves and bloom over a long period in summer and fall. Flowers are attractive but not as showy as pelargonium "geranium." Borne singly or in clusters of two or three, flowers have five overlapping petals that look alike. (Pelargonium flowers have five petals also, but two point in one direction, while the other three point in opposite direction.) Colors include rose, blue, and purple; a few are pure pink or white. Leaves roundish or kidney shaped, lobed or deeply cut. Plants may be upright or trailing. Good plants in rock gardens, perennial borders; some are useful as small-scale ground covers.

G. argenteum. Zones 1–6. To 3–5 in. high. Densely covered with silky, silvery hairs. Leaves basal, with five to seven lobes, 1 in. across. Flowers June–July: pink with darker veins, 1¼ in. across, with notched petals.

G. cantabrigiense. All zones. Hybrid between *G. macrorrhizum* and *G. dalmaticum*. Similar to former, with pink flowers. 'Biokovo' is a similar hybrid with white flowers.

G. cinereum. All zones. To 6 in. tall, much wider, with deeply cut dark green leaves and inch-wide pink flowers with darker veining. 'Ballerina' has lilac pink flowers with purple veining; blooms over a long summer season. 'Flatman' has slightly larger flowers of a deeper color. *G. c. subcaulescens* has deep purplish red flowers with black centers.

G. clarkei 'Kashmir White'. Zones 3–9, 14–24. Grows 2 ft. tall, with finely cut leaves and 1½-in. white flowers veined with pink.

G. dalmaticum. All zones. Dwarf (6-in.) plant with 1½-in. glossy, finely cut leaves and bright pink 1-in. flowers. Useful in rock garden.

G. endressii. Zones 1–9, 14–24. Bushy, 1–1½ ft. high. Leaves 2–3 in. across, deeply cut in five lobes. Flowers rose pink, about 1 in. across; May–November. 'Wargrave Pink' is a more compact form with salmon pink flowers.

G. himalayense (G. grandiflorum). All zones. Wiry, branching stems 1–2 ft. high. Leaves roundish, five lobes, long stalked, 1¾ in. across. Flowers in clusters, lilac with purple veins and red-purple eye, 1½–2 in. across. Blooms all summer. 'Birch Double' ('Plenum') has double flowers of somewhat lighter shade.

G. ibericum. Zones 3–9, 14–24. To 2 ft. tall, with 4-in., deeply cut leaves and 2-in. lavender blue flowers with purple veining.

G. incanum. Zones 14–24. South African trailing ground cover plant 6–10 in. high, spreading. Least hardy of true geraniums. Spreads fast to make wide cushions of finely cut leaves; 1-in.-wide flowers of magenta pink appear spring to fall. Affected by hard frost; evergreen where frosts are light. Cut back every 2–3 years to keep neat. Little water.

G. 'Johnson's Blue'. Zones 3–9, 14–24. Hybrid geranium resembling *G. himalayense* but with more finely divided leaves. Flowers 2 in. wide, blue-violet, appearing spring to fall.

G. macrorrhizum. All zones. Plants 8–10 in. tall, spreading by underground roots. Flowers are magenta red; leaves with five to seven lobes are fragrant and have attractive autumn tints. Good ground cover plant for small areas but can overwhelm delicate smaller plants. Pink-and-white-flowered varieties exist. ▸

G. platypetalum. Zones 3–9, 14–24. Grows 16 in. tall, with dark violet blue flowers nearly 2 in wide. *G. magnificum,* a hybrid between this and *G. ibericum,* is a larger (2½ ft.) plant with somewhat larger flowers.

G. pratense. All zones. Common border perennial to 3 ft., branched above. Shiny green leaves, 3–6 in. across, cut in seven deep lobes. Flowers about 1 in. wide, typically blue, red veined; often vary in color. Blooms June–August. 'Mrs. Kendall Clark' has pale blue flowers with lighter veining.

G. 'Russell Pritchard'. Zones 3–9, 14–24. Clumps under 1 ft. tall, with 2-in. light green leaves and deep purplish pink ¾-in. flowers over a long period.

G. sanguineum. All zones. Grows 1½ ft. high; trailing stems spread to 2 ft. Leaves roundish, with five to seven lobes, 1–2½ in. across; turn blood red in fall. Flowers deep purple to almost crimson, 1½ in. across. May–August bloom. *G. s.* 'Album' is somewhat taller than the species and has white flowers. *G. s. striatum* (*G. s.* 'Prostratum', *G. lancastriense*), is a dwarf form, lower and more compact, with light pink flowers heavily veined with red (its seedlings may vary somewhat). It is an excellent rock garden or foreground plant.

G. wallichianum. Zones 1–9, 14–24. A foot tall and 3 ft. wide. Species has lilac flowers with a white eye; 'Buxton's Variety' has pure blue flowers. Blooms June to autumn.

WHICH IS REALLY A GERANIUM?

Gardeners use the word "geranium" to speak of ivy geraniums, fancy-leafed geraniums, common geraniums, and scented geraniums, all of which botanically are species of *Pelargonium*. Botanists define *Geranium* by the fact that all have five identical-looking overlapping petals in their flowers. See *Pelargonium* for its botanical definition.

GERBERA jamesonii

TRANSVAAL DAISY

Asteraceae (Compositae)

PERENNIAL

☒ ZONES 8, 9, 12–24

☼ ◑ FULL SUN, PARTIAL SHADE IN HOTTEST AREAS

💧 FUSSY ABOUT WATERING

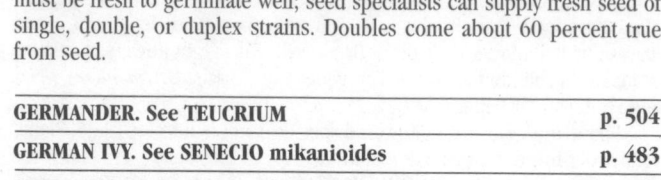

Gerbera jamesonii

Native to South Africa. Most elegant and sophisticated of daisies. Lobed leaves to 10 in. long spring from root crowns that spread slowly to form big clumps. Slender-rayed, 4-in. daisies (one to a stem) rise directly from crowns on 1½-ft., erect or slightly curving stems. Colors range from cream through yellow to coral, orange, flame, and red. Flowers are first rate for arrangements; cut them as soon as fully open and slit an inch at bottom of stem before placing in water. Blooms any time of year with peaks in early summer, late fall.

Needs good soil with excellent drainage. Where drainage is poor, grow in raised beds. Plant 2 ft. apart with crowns at least ½ in. above surface. Protect against snails and slugs. Water deeply and build a two-sided moat around plants to keep water and soil from washing over crowns, then allow soil to become nearly dry before watering again. Feed frequently. Keep old leaves picked off. Let plants remain until crowded; divide February–April, leaving two or three buds on each division. As house or greenhouse plant, grow in bright light with night temperature of 60°F.

Wild Transvaal daisy was orange red. Plants sold as hybrids are merely seedlings or divisions in mixed colors. Specialists have bred duplex and double strains. Duplex flowers have two rows of rays and are often larger (to 5–6 in. across) on taller (2–2½-ft.) stems. In doubles, all flowers are rays and flowers vary widely in form—some flat, some deep, some swirled, some bicolored. Happipot strain has 4-in. flowers on 6-in. stems. Double Parade strain has double flowers on 7–10-in. stems. Blackheart and Ebony Eyes strains have dark-centered flowers.

Plant as seedlings from flats, as divisions or clumps, or from cans. To grow your own from seed, sow thinly in sandy, peaty soil at 70°F. Water carefully; allow 4–6 weeks to sprout. Takes 6–18 months to flower. Seed must be fresh to germinate well; seed specialists can supply fresh seed of single, double, or duplex strains. Doubles come about 60 percent true from seed.

GERMANDER. See TEUCRIUM	p. 504
GERMAN IVY. See SENECIO mikanioides	p. 483
GERMAN STATICE. See GONIOLIMON tataricum	p. 309
GERMAN VIOLET. See EXACUM affine	p. 291

Gesneriaceae. The gesneriads are perennials, usually tropical or subtropical, grown for attractive flowers or foliage. Although a few are rock garden perennials, most are grown as house plants. African violet (*Saintpaulia*) and gloxinia (*Sinningia*) are examples.

GEUM

Rosaceae

PERENNIALS

☒ ALL ZONES

☼ ◑ SUN, PARTIAL SHADE IN HOT AREAS

💧 REGULAR WATER

Geum chiloense

Double, semidouble, or single flowers in bright orange, yellow, and red over long season (May to late summer) if dead blooms are removed. Foliage handsome; leaves divided into many leaflets. Plants evergreen except in coldest winters. Borders, cut flowers.

Ordinary garden soil; need good drainage. Grow from seed sown in early spring, or divide plants in autumn or early spring.

G. 'Borisii'. Plants sold under this name make 6-in.-high mounds of foliage and have foot-high leafy stems with bright orange-red flowers. Use in rock garden, front of border. True *G. borisii* has yellow flowers.

G. chiloense. Foliage mounds to 15 in. Leafy flowering stems, to 2 ft.; flowers about 1½ in. wide. Varieties: 'Fire Opal', semidouble orange-scarlet flowers; 'Georgenberg', to 10 in., with orange flowers over a long season; 'Lady Stratheden', double yellow; 'Mrs. Bradshaw', double scarlet; 'Princess Juliana', double copper.

G. triflorum. PRAIRIE SMOKE, OLD MAN'S WHISKERS. Native to western North America. Its 6-in. leaves have up to 30 leaflets. Flowering stems to 20 in. tall have nodding maroon flowers in clusters. Entire plant often furry. Seeds have long gray feathery "tails."

GHOST GUM. See EUCALYPTUS papuana, E. pauciflora	p. 285
GIANT GARLIC. See GARLIC	p. 303
GIANT REED. See ARUNDO donax	p. 167
GIANT SEQUOIA. See SEQUOIADENDRON giganteum	p. 484

GILIA

Polemoniaceae

SUMMER ANNUALS

☒ ALL ZONES

☼ FULL SUN

💧 LITTLE WATER

Gilia capitata

Western natives related to phlox. Useful and colorful in wild garden or in borders. In early spring, sow seed in open, well-drained soil. Thin plants to avoid crowding.

G. aggregata. See Ipomopsis

G. capitata. BLUE THIMBLE FLOWER. Slender plants 8–30 in. tall. Finely cut leaves. Flowers pale blue to violet blue with blue pollen, in dense clusters like pincushions, ½–1½ in. across, June–October.

G. rubra. See Ipomopsis

G. tricolor. BIRD'S EYES. Branching plant ranging from 10 to 20 in. tall. Finely cut leaves. Flowers ½ in. wide or wider, carried single or in clusters of two to five. Flower color varies from pale to deep violet, with yellow throat spotted purple; blue pollen. June–September.

GINGER. See ZINGIBER officinale	p. 528
GINGER LILY. See HEDYCHIUM	p. 318

GINKGO biloba

MAIDENHAIR TREE
Ginkgoaceae
DECIDUOUS TREE
ZONES 1–10, 12, 14–24
FULL SUN
WATER IN DRY SEASON UNTIL 10–20 FT. HIGH

Ginkgo biloba

Graceful, hardy tree, attractive in any season, especially in fall when leathery, light green leaves of spring and summer suddenly turn gold. Fall leaves linger (they practically glow when backlit by the sun), then drop quickly and cleanly to make golden carpet where they fall. Related to conifers but differs in having broad (1–4 in. wide), fan-shaped leaves rather than needlelike foliage. In shape and veining, leaves resemble leaflets of maidenhair fern, hence name. Can grow to 70–80 ft., but most mature trees are 35–50 ft. May be gawky in youth, but becomes well proportioned with age—narrow to spreading or even umbrella shaped. Usually grows slowly, about 1 ft. a year, but under ideal conditions can grow up to 3 ft. a year.

Plant only male trees (grafted or grown from cuttings of male plants); female trees produce messy, fleshy, ill-smelling fruit in quantity. Named varieties listed below are reliably male. Use as street tree, lawn tree. Plant in deep, loose, well-drained soil. Be sure plant is not root-bound in can. Stake young trees to keep stem straight; young growth may be brittle, but wood becomes strong with age. In general, ginkgos are not bothered by insects or diseases. Resistant to oak root fungus.

G. b. 'Autumn Gold'. Upright, eventually rather broad.

G. b. 'Fairmount'. Fast-growing, pyramidal form. Straighter main stem than 'Autumn Gold', requires less staking and tying.

GLADIOLUS

Iridaceae
CORMS
ALL ZONES
FULL SUN
REGULAR WATER

Gladiolus callianthus

All have sword-shaped leaves and tubular flowers, often flaring or ruffled, in simple or branching, usually one-sided spikes. Extremely wide color range. Bloom from spring to fall, depending on kind and time of planting. Superb cut flowers. Good in borders or beds behind mounding plants that cover lower parts of stems, or in large containers with low annuals at base. Plant in rich, sandy soil.

G. callianthus (Acidanthera bicolor). ABYSSINIAN SWORD LILY. Grows 2–3 ft. tall, with two to ten fragrant, creamy white flowers marked chocolate brown on lower segments. Flowers 2–3 in. wide, 4–5 in. long. Variety 'Murielae' is taller, with purple-crimson blotches. Both are excellent cut flowers. Same culture as garden gladiolus.

G. colvillei. BABY GLADIOLUS. Red-and-yellow hybrid, notable as ancestor of hybrid race called baby gladiolus. Latter have flaring, 2½–3¼-in. flowers in short, loose spikes on 1½-ft. stems. Flowers white, pink, red, or lilac, solid or blotched with contrasting color. May be left in ground from year to year and will form large clumps in border or among shrubs. Plant 4 in. deep, in October–November for May–June bloom in mild-winter areas (June–July in Northwest).

Summer-flowering grandiflora hybrids. GARDEN GLADIOLUS. Commonly grown garden gladiolus are a complex group of hybrids derived by variation and hybridization from several species. These are the best-known gladiolus, with widest color range—white, cream, buff, yellow, orange, apricot, salmon, red shades, rose, lavender, purple, smoky shades, and, more recently, green shades. Individual blooms as large as 8 in. across. Stems are 4–5 ft. tall.

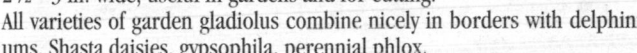

Gladiolus Hybrid

Newer varieties of garden gladiolus, up to 5 ft. tall, have sturdier spikes bearing 12–14 open flowers at a time. They are better garden plants than older varieties and stand upright without staking. Another group, called miniature gladiolus, grows 3 ft. tall, with spikes of 15–20 flowers 2½–3 in. wide; useful in gardens and for cutting. All varieties of garden gladiolus combine nicely in borders with delphiniums, Shasta daisies, gypsophila, perennial phlox.

High-crowned corms, 1½–2 in. wide, are more productive than older, larger corms (over 2 in. wide). Plant as early as possible to avoid damage by thrips. In frostless areas along Southern California coast, plant nearly all year. Along most of coast, growers plant every 15 days from January–March for succession of bloom. In Zones 12, 13, plant November–February to avoid heat during bloom. Plant April–June in Northwest, May–June where winters are severe. Corms bloom 65–100 days after planting.

If soil is poor, mix in complete fertilizer or superphosphate (4 lbs. per 100 sq. ft.) before planting; do not place fertilizer in direct contact with corms. Treat with bulb dust (insecticide-fungicide) before planting. Set corms about four times deeper than their height, somewhat less in heavy soils. Space big corms 6 in. apart, smaller ones 4 in. When plants have five leaves, apply complete fertilizer 6 in. from plants, water in thoroughly. Water regularly during growth. Control thrips and mites as necessary.

Cut flower spikes when lowest buds begin to open; keep at least four leaves on plants to build up corms. Dig corms when foliage starts to yellow; cut tops off just above corms. (In rainy areas, growers dig corms while leaves are still green to avoid botrytis infection.) Destroy tops; dry corms in shaded, ventilated area. In about 3 weeks, pull off old corms and roots, dust new corms with diazinon, and store at 40–50°F in single layers in flats or ventilated trays.

G. primulinus (G. dalenii). This 3-ft.-tall African species with hooded, primrose yellow flowers is rarely grown, but the name has been applied to its hybrids with other gladiolus. Strain called Butterfly gladiolus also belongs here. Flowers medium size, frilled, with satiny sheen, vivid markings in throat. Wiry 2-ft. stems bear as many as 20 flowers; 6–8 open at a time. Colors include bright and pastel shades and pure white.

G. tristis. Dainty gladiolus with 2½–3-in. flowers on slender 1½-ft. stems. Blooms are creamy to yellowish white, veined with purple; fragrant at night. *G. t. concolor* has soft yellow to nearly white flowers. Blooms March–April; hardy except in severe winters. Plant corms October–November.

FOR INFORMATION ON YOUR CLIMATE ZONE

PLEASE SEE PAGES 15–44

GLAUCIUM

HORNED POPPY, SEA POPPY

Papaveraceae

ANNUALS OR PERENNIALS

🌡 ZONES VARY BY SPECIES

☀ FULL SUN

💧 LIGHT WATERING

Glaucium flavum

Grow to about 2 ft. Gray-green leaves, lobed or finely cut. Individual flowers 2 in. wide, cup shaped, with four petals; short lived; but bloom season continues June–August. Flowers followed by unusually long (to 1 ft.), slender seed capsules. Grow with other gray plants or succulents.

G. corniculatum. Summer annual, all zones. Orange-red flowers with dark spot at base.

G. flavum. YELLOW HORNED POPPY. Perennial or biennial, Zones 8–24; grows as annual elsewhere. Orange to brilliant yellow flowers look varnished. Cut back to new basal leaves once a year.

GLECHOMA hederacea (Nepeta hederacea)

GROUND IVY

Lamiaceae (Labiatae)

PERENNIAL

🌡 ALL ZONES

☀ ◐ ● FULL SUN; ALSO TAKES SHADE

💧 REGULAR WATER

Glechoma hederacea

Trailing plant with neat pairs of round, scalloped, bright green or white-edged leaves 1½ in. across, spaced along stems. Small, trumpet-shaped blue flowers in spring and summer not especially showy. Sometimes planted as small-scale ground cover or used to trail from hanging basket. To 3 in. tall with stems trailing to 1½ ft., rooting at joints. Can become pest in lawns.

GLEDITSIA triacanthos

HONEY LOCUST

Fabaceae (Leguminosae)

DECIDUOUS TREE

🌡 ZONES 1–16, 18–20

☀ FULL SUN

💧💧 TAKES ARIDITY OR LAWN WATER

Gleditsia triacanthos

Fast growing with upright trunk and spreading, arching branches. To 35–70 ft. Leaves divided into many oval, ¾–1½-in.-long leaflets. Late to leaf out; leaves turn yellow and drop early in fall. Inconspicuous flowers followed by broad, 1–1½-ft.-long pods filled with sweetish pulp and roundish, hard seeds.

Tolerant of acid or alkaline conditions; hardy to cold, heat, wind. Does best in districts with sharply defined winters, hot summers. Good desert tree. A pod gall midge deforms leaves in some areas. No effective control. Good lawn tree. Leafs out late and goes dormant early, giving grass added sun in spring and fall. Small leaflets dry up and filter into grass, decreasing raking chores. Stake until good basic branch pattern is established. Not good in narrow area between curb and sidewalk: roots on old plants will heave paving. Don't plant if you need dense shade over long season.

Trunks and branches of species are formidably thorny, and pods make a mess; several garden varieties of *G. t. inermis* are thornless, have few or no pods.

Gleditsia triacanthos

'Halka'. Fast growing, forms sturdy trunk early, has strong horizontal branching pattern.

'Imperial'. Tall, spreading, symmetrical tree to about 35 ft. More densely foliaged than other forms; gives heavier shade.

'Moraine'. MORAINE LOCUST. Best known. Fast-growing, spreading tree with branches angled upward, then outward. Subject to wind breakage.

'Rubylace'. Deep red new growth. Subject to wind breakage.

'Shademaster'. More upright and faster growing than 'Moraine'—to 24 ft. tall, 16 ft. wide in 6 years.

'Skyline'. Pyramidal and symmetrical.

'Sunburst'. Golden yellow new foliage. Looks unhealthy unless combined with dark green or bronzy foliage. Defoliates easily in response to temperature changes, drought. Wind breakage. Showy against background of deep green foliage.

'Trueshade'. Rounded head of light green foliage.

GLOBE AMARANTH. See GOMPHRENA	**p. 309**
GLOBEFLOWER. See TROLLIUS	**p. 512**
GLOBE LILY, WHITE. See CALOCHORTUS albus	**p. 199**
GLOBE THISTLE. See ECHINOPS exaltatus	**p. 270**
GLOBE TULIP, PURPLE. See CALOCHORTUS amoenus	**p. 199**

GLOBULARIA

GLOBE DAISY

Globulariaceae

EVERGREEN PERENNIALS OR SHRUBS

🌡 ZONES VARY BY SPECIES

☀ FULL SUN

💧 SOME SUMMER WATER

Globularia indubia

Globe daisies are mat-forming or mounding plants with leathery leaves and small blue flowers gathered into tight, round heads on stalks standing above the foliage. They are not true daisies, although the flower heads resemble rayless daisies or small powder puffs.

G. cordifolia. Zones 1–9, 14–24. Woody-based perennial to 5 in. tall and a foot wide, with dark green leaves on creeping, rooting stems and blue flower heads in summer. Used in rock gardens.

G. indubia. Zones 8, 9, 14–24. Hybrid shrub forming a mound 1–2 ft. tall, 5 ft. wide, with lavender flower heads through summer and fall. Tough plant for hot, dry banks.

GLORIOSA DAISY. See RUDBECKIA hirta	**p. 470**

GLORIOSA rothschildiana

GLORY LILY, CLIMBING LILY

Liliaceae

TUBEROUS-ROOTED PERENNIAL

🌡 ZONE 24; OR GREENHOUSE OR CONTAINER PLANT

☀ ◐ SUN OR FILTERED SHADE

💧 WATER DURING GROWTH AND BLOOM

☠ ALL PARTS ARE POISONOUS

Gloriosa rothschildiana

Native to tropical Africa. Climbs to 6 ft. by tendrils on leaf tips. Lance-shaped leaves 5–7 in. long. Lilylike flowers 4 in. across with six wavy-edged, curved, brilliant red segments banded with yellow. Grow on terrace, patio; train on trellis or frame.

Set tuberous root horizontally about 4 in. deep in light, spongy soil. Start indoors or in greenhouse in February; set out after frosts. Feed with liquid fertilizer every 3 weeks. Dry off gradually in fall; store in pot, or lift tubers and store over winter. May survive outdoors in mild-winter areas, but likely to rot in cold, wet soil.

GOMPHRENA

GLOBE AMARANTH

Amaranthaceae

ANNUALS

✿ ALL ZONES

☼ ◑ FULL SUN, PARTIAL SHADE

⬤ INFREQUENT WATER

Gomphrena globosa

Stiffly branching plants 9 in.–2 ft. tall, covered in summer and fall with rounded, papery, cloverlike heads ¾–1 in. wide. These may be dried quickly and easily, retaining color and shape for winter arrangements. Narrow oval leaves are 2–4 in. long.

G. globosa. White, pink, lavender, or purple flower heads top 1-ft. stems. Dwarf varieties for use as edging or bedding plants are 9-in. 'Buddy' (purple) and 'Cissy' (white). 'Strawberry Fields' grows 2 ft. tall, has 1½-in. heads. Planted closely in large pots—six to a shallow 10-in. pot—makes a long-lasting living bouquet.

G. haageana. To 2 ft. tall, with heads of tightly clustered, bright orange bracts that resemble inch-wide pine cones. Tiny yellow flowers peep from the bracts. Sold as 'Haageana Aurea' or simply 'Orange'.

FOR GROWING SYMBOL EXPLANATIONS

PLEASE SEE PAGE 129

GONIOLIMON tataricum (Limonium tataricum)

GERMAN STATICE

Plumbaginaceae

PERENNIAL

✿ ALL ZONES

☼ FULL SUN

⬤ TOLERATES SOME DROUGHT

Goniolimon tataricum

Dense clumps of dark green, narrowly oval leaves arise from a woody rootstock. Leafless flower stalks arise to 1½ ft., forking repeatedly into a broad, domed cluster to 18 in. wide. Tiny flowers are light purplish to white. The entire inflorescence can be dried for winter flower arrangements. Plant is hardy to cold, heat.

Goodeniaceae. Members of this small family of perennials and shrubs come principally from the Southern Hemisphere, notably Australia. Flowers are irregularly lipped. Examples are *Dampiera* and *Scaevola*.

GOOSEBERRY

Saxifragaceae (Grossulariaceae)

DECIDUOUS SHRUBS

✿ ZONES 1–6, 17

☼ ◑ ⬤ SUN ON COAST, SHADE INLAND

⬤ WATER TO MAINTAIN GROWTH

Gooseberry

For ornamental relatives, see *Ribes*. Same culture as currant. Grown for pies, canning. Lobed, somewhat maplelike leaves. Fruit often striped longitudinally, decorative. 'Oregon Champion', 3–5-ft. thorny bush, is the preferred variety; green fruit. 'Pixwell', extremely hardy and with few thorns, has pink fruit. 'Poorman', favorite in Zones 1–3, has red fruit sweet enough to eat off bush. 'Welcome', as hardy as 'Poorman', has medium large, dull red fruit with tart flavor; plants are productive, nearly spineless.

GOURD

Cucurbitaceae

SUMMER ANNUAL VINES

✿ ALL ZONES

☼ FULL SUN

⬤ REGULAR DEEP WATERING

Gourd

Many plants produce gourds. One of most commonly planted is *Cucurbita pepo ovifera*, yellow-flowered gourd that produces great majority of small ornamental gourds in many shapes and sizes. May be all one color or striped. *Luffa aegyptiaca*, dish cloth gourd or vegetable sponge gourd, also has yellow flowers. Bears cylindrical gourds 1–2 ft. long, fibrous interior of which may be used in place of sponge or cloth for scrubbing and bathing. *Lagenaria siceraria (L. vulgaris),* white-flowered gourd, bears gourds 3 in.–3 ft. long. May be round, bottle shaped, dumbbell shaped, crooknecked, coiled, or spoon shaped.

All grow fast and will reach 10–15 ft. Sow seeds when ground is warm. Start indoors if growing season is short. Gourds need all the summer heat they can get to develop fruit by frost. If planting for ornamental gourd harvest, give vines wire or trellis support to hold ripening individual fruits off ground. Plant seedlings 2 ft. apart or thin seedlings to same spacing. You can harvest gourds when tendrils next to their stems are dead, but it's best to leave them on the vine as long as possible—until the gourds turn yellow or brown. They can even stay on the vine through frosts, but a heavy frost can discolor them. Cut some stem with each gourd so you can hang it up to dry slowly in a cool, airy spot. When thoroughly dry, preserve with coating of paste wax, lacquer, or shellac.

GRAPE

Vitaceae
DECIDUOUS VINES
↗ ZONES VARY BY VARIETY
☼ FULL SUN
◔ LITTLE IRRIGATION ONCE ESTABLISHED
▶ SEE CHART

Grape

For fruit, wine, shade. Single grapevine can produce enough new growth every year to arch over a walk, roof an arbor, form a leafy wall, or put an umbrella of shade over deck or terrace. Grape is one of few ornamental vines with dominant trunk and branch pattern for winter interest, bold-textured foliage, and colorful, edible fruit.

To get quality fruit you must choose a variety that fits your climate, train it carefully, and prune it regularly.

Two basic classes are European *(Vitis vinifera)*—tight skin, winelike flavor, generally high heat requirements, cold tolerance to about 5°F; and American *(V. labrusca)*—slipskin, "foxy" Concord-type flavor, moderate summer heat requirements, cold tolerance well below 0°F. Hybrids between classes are available; most are reasonably hardy, fall between parents in flavor.

Choosing the right variety is important, since varieties differ widely in hardiness and in heat requirements. Northwest is primarily American grape country; long warm-season areas of California, Arizona favor European varieties. Choose American grapes in short-season, high-elevation areas.

Ideal climate for most table grapes in California is that of California's Central Valley—a long season of high heat. Ideal climate in Northwest is in warmest parts of Columbia Basin. If your climate is cooler, or if growing season is shorter than ideal, look to early-ripening varieties.

Mildew is a serious disease of European grapes (most American varieties are immune). To control, dust vines with sulfur when shoots are 6 in. long, again when they are 12–15 in., then every 2 weeks until harvest. Vines growing near lawns may need additional dustings.

To control grape leafhopper in California, add diazinon dust to sulfur at time of third sulfur dusting, just before blooming time. In Northwest, dust with diazinon in June and again in August. Grape mealybugs may infest vines in Northwest. Control with dormant oil spray in late winter and with malathion in June.

Grape Pruning

1. December–March: Dig deep hole. Plant rooted cutting from nursery; leave only top bud exposed. Set stake for training. Mound soil over bud. Object is to secure deep rooting.

2. First year: Let vine sprawl, develop as many leaves as possible to manufacture food for the developing roots. This growth made by November. Leaves have fallen.

3. First winter: Prune vine to sturdiest cane; shorten it to 3 lowest buds. If cane is very vigorous, cut it at 2–3 ft., or at a good point for branching for arbor.

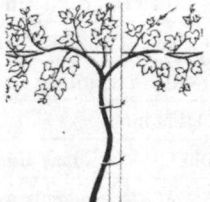

4. Second spring: When new shoots are 6–8 in. long, select 1 vigorous, upright shoot to form permanent trunk. Tie it loosely to the stake. Cut out all other shoots.

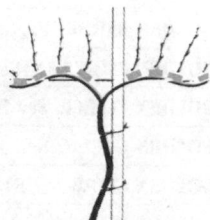

5. Second summer: When shoot reaches branching point, pinch out tip. Allow 2 strongest subsequent shoots to develop. Pinch out side shoots at 10 in.

6. Third winter: Cut spindly canes on arms back to old wood. Don't prune yet for fruit production; vines are too immature. For fruit, leave 2 buds on each cane.

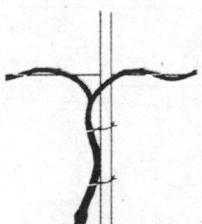

7. Third winter's finished product: On an arbor, arms would stretch out along roof level of structure. Length of arms determines size and permanent frame.

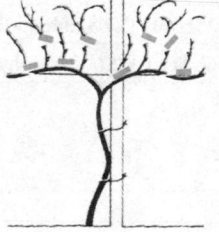

8. Fourth winter: These canes grew previous summer. To prune for fruit, cut out weak or crowding canes. Select sturdy canes 6–10 in. apart, cut each to 2 buds.

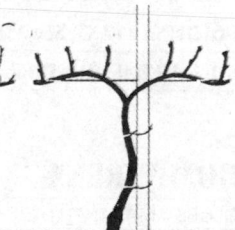

9. Fourth winter's finished product: Each bud will give 2 fruiting canes next summer. Following winter cut 1 out entirely, shorten the other to 2 buds. See Nos. 10, 11.

10. Fifth winter: These canes bore fruit the previous autumn. Cut 1 off at base. Branch at left already pruned. These short, thick branches are called spurs.

11. Fifth winter: Shorten remaining cane to 2 buds. These will give next year's fruiting canes. Pruning in subsequent years is the same.

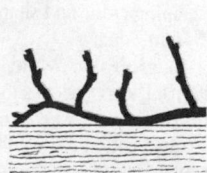

12. Well-pruned arm in its fifth year should look like this. Fruit spurs spaced approximately 6 in. apart, with 2 buds on each new cane at end of spurs.

GRAPE

VARIETY	ZONES	SEASON	PRUNING	COMMENTS
AMERICAN and AMERICAN HYBRID VARIETIES				
'Black Spanish'	1–3, 10, 11	Early midseason	Cane	Heavy annual producer of small black berries for juice, jelly. Tough, disease resistant
'Brilliant'	1–3, 10, 11	Very early	Cane	Light to dark red berries good for eating fresh. Very large leaves make it a good arbor vine
'California Concord' (see 'Pierce')				
'Campbell Early' ('Island Belle')	2–7, 17	Early	Cane	Dark purplish black with heavy bloom. High quality. Lacks foxy taste. Vine moderately vigorous. Excellent 'Concord' type where too cool for 'Concord'
'Canadice'	1–17	Early	Cane	Hardy vine produces small, light clusters of seedless red fruit with mild 'Concord' flavor
'Champanel'	1–14	Early	Cane	Large blue-black grape that holds well on vine. Takes heat, alkaline soil
'Concord'	1–3, 6–9, 14–16, 18–21	Midseason. Late in Northwest	Cane	Standard American slipskin. California's dry hot-summer areas are not to its liking. Fruit inferior to that grown in Northwest
'Concord Seedless'	1–3, 6–9	Midseason to late	Cane	Smaller berries than 'Concord', not as vigorous a vine
'Fredonia'	1–7, 17	Early	Cane	Large black berries with thick, tough skin. Similar to 'Concord' but larger. Vigorous vine, clean foliage. Excellent for arbors
'Golden Muscat' American hybrid	1–3, 6–9, 11–24	Early midseason	Cane	Golden green, with slipskin of American grapes but with 'Muscat' flavor. Hybrid of 'Muscat' and green American grape, 'Diamond'. Vigorous
'Himrod' ('Himrod Seedless') American hybrid	1–3, 5–7	Very early	Cane	Resembles 'Interlaken Seedless'
'Interlaken Seedless' American hybrid	1–7	Very early	Cane	Small, sweet, crisp, firm, greenish white berries. Tight skinned. Excellent flavor. Vine moderately vigorous, productive
'Moore Early'	1–3, 6, 7	Early	Cane	Medium clusters of large berries
'Niabell'	7–9, 14–16, 18–22	Early	Cane or spur	Large black berries similar to 'Concord' at its best. Excellent arbor grape. Vigorous and productive in wide range of climates. Succeeds in hot interiors where 'Concord' fails
'Niagara'	3, 6, 7	Midseason	Cane	Large, full clusters of medium to large green-gold berries. Sweet and juicy with strong foxy flavor. Attractive, vigorous vine, excellent for arbors
'Pierce'	7–9, 14–16, 18–21	Midseason	Cane	Called 'California Concord'. Berries larger, vine more vigorous than 'Concord'. Stands high heat better than 'Concord'
'Suffolk Red'	1–7, 17	Early	Cane	Seedless red grape with fine flavor. Fruit holds well on vine. Slight susceptibility to mildew
EUROPEAN VARIETIES				
'Black Monukka'	3, 7–9, 11–21	Early midseason	Cane or spur	Medium-size reddish black seedless berries in large, loose clusters. Popular home variety. One of hardiest European grapes
'Cardinal'	8, 9, 11–16, 18–21	Early	Spur, short cane	Large, deep red, firm, crisp. Slight 'Muscat' flavor when fully ripe. Heavy bearer. Thin some flower clusters off when shoots are 1–1½ ft. long

GRAPE

VARIETY	ZONES	SEASON	PRUNING	COMMENTS
EUROPEAN VARIETIES				
'Csaba' (**'Pearl of Csaba'**)	3, 6, 7	Very early	Spur	Small to medium, yellowish white, moderately firm, some 'Muscat' flavor. One of hardiest European types. Grown in central Washington
'Emperor'	8, 9, 18, 19	Late	Cane or spur	Large, reddish, very firm, crisp and crunchy. Neutral flavor
'Flame' (**'Flame Seedless'**)	6–9, 12–21	Early	Cane	Medium-size, light to medium red seedless grapes. Crisp, productive
'Italia' (**'Italian Muscat'**)	8, 9, 11–14, 18–20	Midseason	Spur	Large amber yellow berries. Crisp, with sweet 'Muscat' flavor, tender skin
'Lady Finger'	8, 9, 11–14, 18–20	Late midseason	Cane	Two varieties share this name: 'Olivette Blanche' and 'Rish Baba'. Grapes are greenish white, long, slender, with mild, sweet flavor
'Muscat' (**'Muscat of Alexandria'**)	8, 9, 11–14, 18, 19	Late midseason	Spur	Large, green to amber, round berries in loose clusters. Strongly aromatic. Renowned for its sweet, musky, aged-in-the-vat flavor
'Perlette'	3, 7–16, 18–21	Early	Spur	Earlier, larger, less sweet than 'Thompson Seedless'. Needs far less heat than most European varieties
'Ruby Seedless' (**'King's Ruby'**)	8, 9, 12–16, 18–20	Late midseason	Cane or spur	Large clusters of small to medium, red to reddish black seedless berries. Sweet dessert fruit; make good raisins
'Thompson Seedless'	8, 9, 11–14, 18, 19	Early to midseason	Cane	Small, sweet, mild flavored, greenish amber in big bunches. Widely planted but top quality in warm interior areas only
'Tokay'	8, 9, 14–16, 18–20	Late midseason	Spur	Brilliant red to dark red. Crackling crisp with distinctive winy flavor. Reaches perfection where summer heat is high but not excessive—Zone 14

GRASSES. The grasses in this book are either lawn or ornamental plants—except for corn, the only cereal commonly grown in home gardens. They are described under entries headed by their botanical names; to find these, check lists below. (All bamboos, which are grasses, are charted under Bamboo.)

Lawn grasses are *Agropyron,* wheatgrass; *Agrostis,* bent grass, redtop; *Bouteloua,* blue grama grass; *Buchloe,* buffalo grass; *Cynodon,* Bermuda grass; *Festuca,* fescue; *Lolium,* ryegrass; *Poa,* bluegrass; *Stenotaphrum,* St. Augustine grass; *Zoysia,* zoysia.

Ornamental grasses are *Arrhenatherum,* bulbous oat grass; *Arundo,* giant reed; *Briza,* rattlesnake grass; *Calamagrostis,* feather reed grass; *Chasmanthium,* sea oats; *Coix,* Job's tears; *Cortaderia,* pampas grass; *Deschampsia,* hair grass; *Elymus,* lyme grass; *Festuca,* fescue; *Hakonechloa,* Japanese forest grass; *Helictotrichon,* blue oat grass; *Imperata,* Japanese blood grass; *Milium effusum* 'Aureum', Bowles' golden grass; *Miscanthus,* eulalia grass, maiden grass, silver grass; *Muhlenbergia,* bamboo muhly, deer grass; *Pennisetum,* fountain grass; *Phalaris,* ribbon grass; *Setaria,* palm grass; and *Stipa,* feather grass, needle grass.

GRASS NUT. See TRITELEIA laxa p. 511

GRASS TREE. See NOLINA, XANTHORRHOEA pp. 391, 524

GREASEWOOD. See ADENOSTOMA fasciculatum p. 139

GRECIAN LAUREL. See LAURUS nobilis p. 349

GREEN CARPET. See HERNIARIA glabra p. 321

GREVILLEA

Proteaceae

EVERGREEN SHRUBS OR TREES

ZONES VARY BY SPECIES

FULL SUN, EXCEPT AS NOTED

MOST NEED NO DRY-SEASON WATER

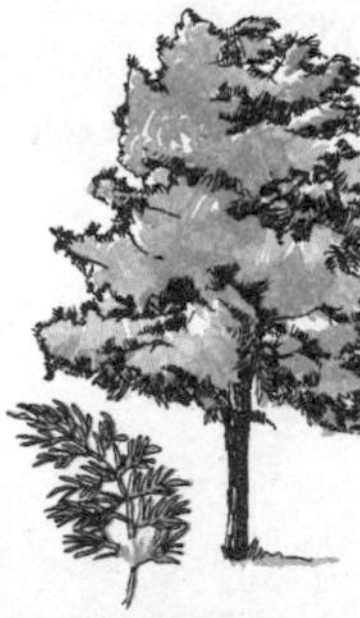

Grevillea robusta

Native to Australia. New species and hybrids appear frequently. Plants vary in size and appearance, but generally have fine-textured foliage and long, slender, curved flowers, usually in dense clusters.

Australia is extremely rich in *Grevillea* species (over 250) and hybrids, and many have great garden merit. Not all are widely available, and new introductions not mentioned here may show up in nurseries. Many cannot tolerate salt-laden soils, poor water quality, heavy summer irrigation, or heavy frost, but all are attractive enough to warrant some risktaking.

Like other members of the Protea family, they are sensitive to high levels of phosphorus in the soil. Fertilize lightly, and avoid fertilizers with high phosphorus content.

G. alpina. MOUNTAIN GREVILLEA. Highly variable in size and form. Zones 15–24. Most widely distributed form is 'East Grampians', a low, spreading shrub with inch-long bright green leaves and masses of red-and-yellow flowers from fall through spring.

G. banksii. Shrub or small tree. Zones 20–24. Often sold as *G. banksii forsteri*. To 15–20 ft. Leaves 4–10 in. long, deeply cut into narrow lobes.

Erect, 3–6-in.-long clusters of dark red flowers bloom sporadically throughout the year, heaviest in late spring. Showy used singly against high wall, near entryway, or grouped with other big-scale shrubs. Freezes at 24°F; takes wind.

G. 'Boongalla Spinebill'. Sprawling shrub. Zones 17–24. To 3 ft. tall, 10 ft. wide, with 6-in. deeply cut leaves, coppery on expanding, then deep green. Red flowers in toothbrush-shaped clusters nearly all year, heaviest in late winter. Can take some shade.

G. 'Canberra'. Shrub. Zones 8, 9, 12–24. Open, graceful growth to 8 ft. tall, 12 ft. wide. Bright green, needlelike, 1-in. leaves. Clusters of red flowers in spring and intermittently at other times.

G. 'Constance'. Shrub. Zones 8, 9, 12–24. Resembles 'Canberra' but broader in growth. Orange-red flowers in large clusters.

G. curviloba. Shrub to 6 ft., or ground cover spreading to 10–15 ft. Zones 14–24. Often sold as *G. tridentifera* or *G. biternata*. Leaves are finely divided, bright green. Flowers are cream colored, honey scented. To use as ground or bank cover, prune out stems that grow upright.

G. gaudichaudii. Prostrate plant. Zones 15–24. To 15 ft. across, with lobed oak-shaped leaves, bronzy while expanding, then dark green. Dark red flowers in toothbrush clusters. Needs occasional summer water (with good drainage), and takes sun or considerable shade.

G. lanigera. WOOLLY GREVILLEA. Shrub. Zones 15–24. Spreading, mounding plant 3–6 ft. tall, 6–10 ft. across. Closely set, narrow, ½-in. long leaves; general foliage effect gray green. Clusters of narrow, curved, crimson-and-cream flowers profusely carried in summer; attractive to hummingbirds. Good bank cover in hot, sunny areas; good transition between garden and wild areas. A low-growing form 2 ft. tall by 4 ft. wide is denser in growth, showier.

G. lavandulacea. LAVENDER GREVILLEA. Variable but highly desirable species. Zones 15–24. All have gray ½-in. leaves, dense growth. 'Billywing' grows 2½ ft. tall, 6 ft. wide, and has red-and-cream flowers in winter and spring. 'Penola' reaches 5 ft. or more, 8 ft. in width (more if unpruned). Flowers are deep rose red; blooms fall through spring. 'Tanunda' is lowest, densest selection, and makes a profuse show of coral pink flowers.

G. 'Noellii'. Shrub. Zones 8, 9, 12–24. Plant sold under this name reported to be a hybrid. To 4 ft. tall, 4–5 ft. wide. Densely foliaged; narrow, 1-in.-long, medium green glossy leaves. Clusters of pink-and-white flowers bloom for 6–8 weeks in early and midspring. Benefits from some water in the dry season.

Grevillea 'Noellii'

G. 'Red Hooks'. Wide-spreading shrub. Zones 16–24. To 12 ft. tall, possibly 18 ft. across, with finely cut 5-in. leaves and coral red toothbrush flowers produced late winter to late spring, with a scattering through the year.

G. robusta. SILK OAK. Tree. Zones 8, 9, 12–24. Fast growing to 50–60 (rarely 100) ft. Symmetrical, pyramidal when young. Old trees broad topped, picturesque against skyline, usually with a few heavy, horizontal limbs. Fernlike leaves are golden green to deep green above, silvery beneath. Heavy leaf fall in spring, sporadic leaf drop throughout year; frequent raking necessary. Large clusters of bright golden orange flowers in early spring; effective with jacaranda or with dark green background foliage.

Grows in poor, compact soils if not overwatered; takes fair amount of water in fast-draining soils. Brittle, easily damaged in high wind. Stake securely. To make sturdier branches and lessen wind damage, cut leading shoot back hard at planting time, shorten branches to well-balanced framework. Thrives in heat. Young trees damaged at 24°F; older plants hardy to 16°F.

Use for quick, tall screening or clip as tall hedge. One of lushest greens for low desert. Fast shade producer, showy tree for unused space far from hose bibb. Good temporary tree while you wait for slower, tougher-wooded tree to grow up.

G. 'Robyn Gordon'. Showy plant 6–7 ft. tall and as wide. Zones 16–24. Has hanging 6-in. clusters of bright red flowers through most of the year.

G. rosmarinifolia. ROSEMARY GREVILLEA. Compact shrub to 6 ft. tall, nearly as broad. Zones 8, 9, 12–24. Narrow, dark green, 1½-in.-long leaves (silvery beneath) somewhat like those of rosemary. Red-and-cream flower clusters (rarely pink or white) in fall and winter; scattered bloom in other seasons. Use as clipped or unclipped hedge in dryish places. Impervious to heat and aridity. A dwarf form 3 ft. tall, 6 ft. wide, blooms in waves throughout the year, most heavily spring and fall. Blossoms are pink-and-cream.

G. thelemanniana. HUMMINGBIRD BUSH, SPIDER-NET GREVILLEA. Shrub. Zones 9, 14–17, 19–24. Graceful, rounded, 5–8 ft. tall, equally wide. Dark green leaves 1–2 in. long, divided into narrow segments. Bright red flower clusters tipped yellow. Can bloom at any season. Water plants until established, then taper off. Somewhat temperamental. Plants airier, more open, less adapted to hedge and screen use than *G. rosmarinifolia*. Many forms exist. A dwarf gray-leafed variety is 6 in. tall, 6 ft. wide, and can trail over a walk or down a bank.

GREWIA occidentalis

LAVENDER STARFLOWER	
Tiliaceae	
EVERGREEN SHRUB	
✂ ZONES 8, 9, 12–24	
☀ FULL SUN	
💧 REGULAR WATER	

Grewia occidentalis

Usually sold as *G. caffra*. Native to South Africa. Fast-growing, sprawling habit. Tends to branch freely in flat pattern, making natural espalier if given some support. Becomes dense with pinching and pruning. Grows 6–10 ft. tall (sometimes higher), with equal spread if unstaked. Deep green, oblong, finely toothed leaves 3 in. long. Flowers are 1 in. wide, starlike, lavender pink with yellow centers. Blooms late spring with scattered bloom into autumn, especially if pruned after first heavy bloom. Plant against warm, sunny wall or fence. Can be planted 2 ft. apart and used as tall clipped hedge or screen. If upright growth is pruned out, can be used as bank cover. Can be trained and staked to make single-trunked tree or tied in place to cover arbor or trellis. Takes wind well. Needs iron if chlorotic. If plants become too large or woody for their situation, cut back hard, keeping one or two young basal branches to grow on for new framework.

GRISELINIA

Cornaceae	
EVERGREEN SHRUBS	
✂ ZONES 9, 14–17, 20–24	
☀ ◑ FULL SUN OR LITTLE SHADE	
💧 WATER DURING DRY SEASON	

Griselinia littoralis

Native to New Zealand. Upright form and thick, leathery, lustrous leaves. Flowers and fruit are insignificant. Always look well groomed. Good near swimming pools.

G. littoralis. A 50-ft. tree in New Zealand, but usually seen in California as 10-ft.-high shrub of equal spread. Leaves roundish, 4 in. long. With ample water it can reach 8 ft. in 3 years. Dense, compact screen or windbreak. Fine beach plant. Good espalier. Variety 'Variegata' has leaves marked with cream.

G. lucida. Slower growing, smaller, more open and slender than *G. littoralis*, with larger, 7-in.-long leaves. Excellent foliage plant for partial shade. Thrives in container. 'Variegata' has white markings on leaves.

G

GUNNERA

DINOSAUR FOOD

Gunneraceae

PERENNIALS

✔ ZONES 4–6, 14–17, 20–24

◐ PARTIAL SHADE

◉ CONTINUALLY MOIST SOIL

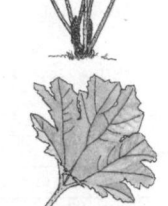

Gunnera tinctoria

Big, bold, awe-inspiring plants to 8 ft. high, with giant leaves (4–8 ft. across) on stiff-haired stalks 4–6 ft. long. Leaves are conspicuously veined, with lobed and cut edges. Given space (they need plenty) and necessary care, these plants can be the ultimate summertime conversation pieces. New sets of leaves grow each spring. In mild-winter areas, old leaves remain green for more than a year. Elsewhere, leaves die back completely in winter. Corncoblike 1½-ft. flower clusters form close to roots. Tiny fruits are red.

Soil must be rich in nutrients and organic material. Feed three times a year, beginning when new growth starts, to keep leaves maximum size. Give overhead sprinkling when humidity is low or drying winds occur. Use plants where they can be focal point in summer—beside a pool or dominating a bed of low, fine-textured ground cover. Makes confused scene when mixed with other plants with medium-size to large leaves.

G. manicata. Leaves carried fairly horizontally. Spinelike hairs on leaf stalks and ribs are red. Leaf lobes are flatter, lack frills of *G. tinctoria.*

G. tinctoria (G. chilensis). Most common species. Lobed leaf margins are toothed and somewhat frilled. Leaves held in bowl-like way, half upright and flaring.

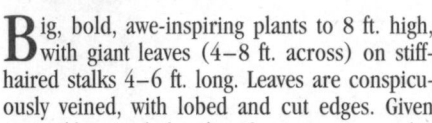

DINOSAUR FOOD

This edition of the *Western Garden Book* introduces that splendid common name for *Gunnera* (thanks to a curator of Seattle's Washington Park Arboretum). The two species listed here have an exotic, almost prehistoric look. The leaves are so large and primitive looking, you can easily imagine a giant reptile munching them.

GYMNOCLADUS dioica

KENTUCKY COFFEE TREE

Fabaceae (Leguminosae)

DECIDUOUS TREE

✔ ZONES 1–3, 7–10, 12–16, 18–21

◉ FULL SUN

◔ LITTLE WATER ONCE ESTABLISHED

Gymnocladus dioica

Native to eastern United States. Sapling grows very fast, but slows down at 8–10 ft. Tree ultimately reaches 50 ft. Narrowish habit in youth. Older tree is broader, with fairly few heavy, contorted branches. These, together with stout winter twigs, make bare tree picturesque. Leaves (1½–3 ft. long, divided into many leaflets 1–3 in. long) come out late in spring; they are pinkish when expanding, deep green in summer, yellow in autumn. Inconspicuous flowers are followed by 6–10-in.-long, flat, reddish brown pods containing hard black seeds. Established tree can take much heat and cold, poor soil. Effective for form in any cold-winter garden.

Gymnocladus dioica

GYPSOPHILA

Caryophyllaceae

ANNUALS AND PERENNIALS

✔ ZONES VARY BY SPECIES

◉ FULL SUN

◔ MODERATE WATER

Gypsophila repens

Much-branched slender-stemmed plants, upright or spreading, 6 in.–4 ft. tall, profusely covered in summer with small, single or double, white, pink, or rose flowers in clusters. Leaves blue green; few when plant is in bloom. Use for airy grace in borders, bouquets; fine contrast with large-flowered, coarse-textured plants. Dwarf kinds ideal in rock gardens, trailing from wall pocket, or over top of dry rock walls.

Add lime to strongly acid soils. Thick, deep roots of some perennial kinds difficult to transplant; do not disturb often. Protect roots from gophers, tender top growth from snails and slugs. For repeat bloom on perennial kinds, cut back flowering stems before seed clusters form.

G. cerastioides. Low plant. Zones 1–10, 14–21. Mat 3 in. tall, much broader, with gray leaves and clustered flowers varying from pink-veined white to pink. Use in rock garden, between paving stones.

G. elegans. Annual. All zones. Upright, 1–1½ ft. Lance-shaped, rather fleshy leaves to 3 in. long. Profuse single white flowers ½ in. or more across. Pink and rose forms available. Plants live only 5–6 weeks; for continuous bloom, sow seed in open ground every 3–4 weeks from late spring into summer.

G. paniculata. BABY'S BREATH. Perennial. Zones 1–10, 14–16, 18–21. Much branched to 3 ft. or more. Leaves slender, sharp pointed, 2½–4 in. long. Single white flowers about ¹⁄₁₆ in. across, hundreds in a spray, July–October. Variety 'Bristol Fairy' is improved form, more billowy, to 4 ft. high, covered with double blossoms ¼ in. wide. Florists' favorite variety is 'Perfecta', with larger flowers. Grow from root grafts or stem cuttings.

G. repens. Perennial. Zones 1–11, 14–16, 18–21. Alpine native 6–9 in. high, with trailing stems 1½ ft. long. Leaves narrow, less than 1 in. long. Clusters of small white or pink flowers in summer. Increase by cuttings in midsummer.

HABRANTHUS

Amaryllidaceae

BULBS

✔ ZONES 8, 9, 14–24

◉◐ SUN OR LIGHT SHADE

◔ WATER DURING GROWTH AND BLOOM

Bulbous plants somewhat resembling miniature amaryllis (*Hippeastrum*), with narrow, grassy leaves and trumpet-shaped flowers. Native from Mexico to Argentina, but many are widely grown in Texas and naturalized there. Where soil freezes, grow in pots. Set with bulb tops at soil level. Plants can withstand some aridity. Use in rock gardens or naturalize.

Habranthus robustus

H

H. andersonii (H. tubispathus). Flower stems reach 6 in., with inch-wide yellow flowers, coppery on the outside. 'Cupreus' is coppery orange. A bright yellow form with larger flowers is sold as *H. texanus*. Summer blooming.

H. robustus. Four-inch bright pink flowers are carried one or two to a stem. Bloom may occur any time from spring to fall.

HACKBERRY. See CELTIS p. 216

HAEMANTHUS katherinae
(Scadoxus multiflorus katherinae)

BLOOD LILY

Amaryllidaceae

BULB

🗲 ZONES 21–24

☼ LIGHT SHADE

💧 REGULAR WATER

Haemanthus katherinae

Tender South African plant closely related to amaryllis. Grow in pots in greenhouse or sunny room, move to terrace or patio for bloom in late spring or early summer. Large (4-in.-diameter), white bulb stained red (hence common name). Leaves broad, wavy edged, bright green, 12–15 in. long. Sturdy succulent stem 2 ft. tall, topped by large, round clusters of bright salmon red flowers that look like pom-poms, with protruding, showy red stamens.

Put one bulb in 10-in. pot in rich potting mix in winter or early spring. Set bulb with tip at soil surface; water sparingly, keep at 70°F. When leaves appear (8–10 weeks), move outdoors to sheltered, lightly shaded spot. Water thoroughly; feed monthly with complete fertilizer. Bait for snails. After bloom, gradually reduce watering; dry out plant in cool, protected place. Do not repot next season; add new mix on top or tip out root ball, scrape off some old soil, replace with fresh.

HAKEA

Proteaceae

EVERGREEN SHRUBS OR TREES

🗲 ZONES 9, 12–17, 19–24

☼ FULL SUN

◯ NO DRY-SEASON WATER

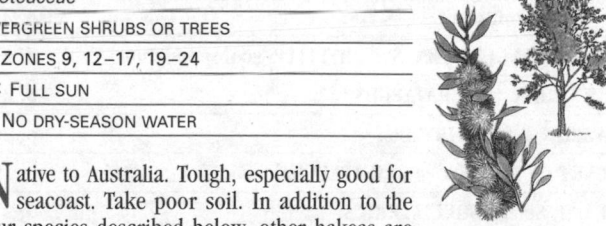
Hakea laurina

Native to Australia. Tough, especially good for seacoast. Take poor soil. In addition to the four species described below, other hakeas are offered from time to time by experimentally minded nurseries. Remarkably diverse in foliage and flower, all are quality shrubs or small trees for difficult sites.

H. laurina. SEA URCHIN, PINCUSHION TREE. Small, dense, rounded tree or large shrub to 30 ft. Narrow, gray-green, 6-in.-long leaves are often red margined. Showy flower clusters look like round crimson pincushions stuck with golden pins. Blooms in winter, sometimes in late fall. Stake young trees securely. Good small patio tree.

H. orthorrhyncha. BIRD BEAK HAKEA. Shrub 6 ft. by 6 ft., eventually larger, with dark green leaves like 6-in. pine needles. Clusters of bright red flowers form along mature wood. Useful screen or windbreak.

H. saligna. WILLOWLEAF HAKEA. Shrub to 8 ft.; rarely treelike to 20 ft. Narrow, gray-green leaves up to 6 in. long. Many clusters of small white flowers.

H. suaveolens. SWEET HAKEA. Dense, broad, upright shrub to 10–20 ft. tall. Stiff, dark green, 4-in. leaves, branched into stiff, needlelike, stickery segments. Small, fragrant white flowers in dense, fluffy clusters, fall

and winter. Useful, fast-growing barrier plant, background, or screen. Good with conifers. Can be pruned into tree form.

H. victoria. ROYAL HAKEA. Erect, narrow plant to 9 ft. tall, 5 ft. wide. Leaves broad, flat or slightly cupped, stemless, toothed, deep green beautifully netted with yellow and variegated with cream and orange. Flowers insignificant. Cut foliage dries well, lasts well in arrangements.

HAKONECHLOA macra
'Aureola'

JAPANESE FOREST GRASS

Poaceae (Gramineae)

PERENNIAL

🗲 ALL ZONES

☼ ● SHADE

💧 REGULAR WATER

Hakonechloa macra 'Aureola'

Graceful, slender, leaning or arching stems to 1½ ft. carry long, slender leaves with gold stripes. Effect is that of a tiny bamboo. Spreads slowly by underground runners. Needs good soil. Choice plant for woodland garden or for close viewing in a container.

HALESIA

Styracaceae

DECIDUOUS TREES

🗲 ZONES 2–9, 14–24

☼ PART SHADE

💧 REGULAR WATER

Halesia carolina

Both kinds give best flower display in areas of winter cold and grow best in cool, deep, humus-rich soil.

H. carolina (H. tetraptera). SNOWDROP TREE, SILVER BELL. Moderate growth to 20–50 ft. with 15–30-ft. spread, depending on climate. Rates high as flowering tree in May, when clusters of snow white, ½-in., bell-shaped flowers hang from graceful branches just as leaves begin to appear. Oval, finely toothed, 4-in.-long leaves turn yellow in fall. Interesting brown fruit with four wings hangs on almost all winter. Prune plant to a single stem when young or it will grow as a large shrub. Flowers show off best when you can look up into tree. Attractive as overhead planting for azaleas, rhododendrons.

H. monticola. MOUNTAIN SILVER BELL. Larger tree, 40–60 ft., with larger (3–6-in.) leaves than *H. carolina*.

HALIMIOCISTUS sahucii

Cistaceae

EVERGREEN SHRUB

🗲 ZONES 4–24

☼ FULL SUN

💧 VERY LITTLE WATER

Halimiocistus sahucii

Hybrid between *Halimium umbellatum* and *Cistus salviifolius*. Combines best characteristics of both parents. Densely foliaged with 1-in., narrow, gray-green leaves, it grows to 2 ft. high and spreads to 3 ft. or more. In summer, clusters of white, 1–2-in.-wide flowers with center tufts of yellow stamens almost hide foliage. Good in rock garden, on dry bank, or cascading over concrete retaining wall. Or plant on sunny side of house under wide eaves where rains seldom reach. Will not live in wet soil, and can be watered with other plants only if drainage is excellent. *H. wintonensis* is similar, but flowers have a purple spot at the base of each petal.

HALIMIUM

Cistaceae

EVERGREEN SHRUBLETS

◢ ZONES 7–9, 12–24

☼ FULL SUN

◖ VERY LITTLE WATER

Halimium lasianthum

Closely related to sunrose (*Helianthemum*) and sometimes sold under that name; cultural requirements and uses are the same. Halimiums grow 2–3 ft. high, have gray-green foliage, yellow flowers in loose clusters in spring.

H. lasianthum (Helianthemum formosum). Spreading plant with leaves ½–1½ in. long, ¼ in. wide. Flowers 1½ in. across, bright yellow with brownish purple blotch near base of petals.

H. ocymoides (Helianthemum ocymoides). Erect plant with leaves slightly narrower than those of above species. Flowers 1 in. wide, bright yellow, with black-and-purple blotch at base of petals.

H. umbellatum (Helianthemum umbellatum). Grows to 1½ ft. Leaves very narrow, resembling those of rosemary. Flowers ¾ in. across, white with yellow at petal bases, in 4–6-in.-long clusters.

Hamamelidaceae. The witch hazel family contains deciduous (rarely evergreen) trees and shrubs. Some have showy flowers (*Fothergilla, Hamamelis, Loropetalum*). Many of the deciduous kinds have brilliant fall color (*Liquidambar, Parrotia*).

HAMAMELIS

WITCH HAZEL

Hamamelidaceae

DECIDUOUS TREES OR LARGE SHRUBS

◢ ZONES VARY BY SPECIES

☼ ◖ SUN OR LIGHT SHADE

◖ REGULAR WATER

Hamamelis mollis

Yellow fall foliage. Fragrant yellow to red flowers with narrow, crumpled-looking petals in nodding few-flowered clusters. Plants need some peat moss, ground bark, or leaf mold in soil.

H. intermedia. Zones 4–7, 15–17. Group of hybrids between *H. mollis* and a Japanese witch hazel. Big shrubs (to 15 ft. high) with spreading habit. The following varieties are widely grown in Zones 4–7: 'Diane', bright red flowers, fine fall color; 'Jelena' (also known as 'Copper Beauty' and 'Orange Beauty'), spreading plant with large leaves, large yellow flowers heavily suffused with red, and fall foliage color of orange, red, and scarlet; 'Magic Fire' ('Fire Charm', 'Feuerzauber'), upright plant with blossoms in coppery orange blended with red; and 'Ruby Glow', erect, with coppery red flowers and fine fall color. Bloom season for all these is December–March.

H. mollis. CHINESE WITCH HAZEL. Zones 4–7, 15–17. Moderately slow-growing shrub to 8–10 ft. or (eventually) small tree to 30 ft. Branches in loose zigzag pattern. Roundish leaves, 3½–6 in. long; dark green and rough above, gray and felted beneath, turning good clear yellow in fall. Fragrant, 1½-in.-wide, rich golden yellow flowers with red-brown calyces bloom on bare stems, December–March. Effective against red brick or gray stone. Flowering branches excellent for flower arrangements.

H. virginiana. COMMON WITCH HAZEL. Zones 1–9, 14–16, 18–21. Native to eastern United States. Sometimes to 25 ft. tall but usually 10–15 ft. high; open, spreading, rather straggling habit. Moderately slow growing. Roundish leaves similar to those of *H. mollis* but not gray and felted beneath; turn yellow to orange in fall. Golden yellow, ¾-in.-wide blooms appear in October–November and tend to be lost in colored foliage.

HARDENBERGIA

Fabaceae (Leguminosae)

EVERGREEN SHRUBBY VINES

◢ ZONES VARY BY SPECIES

☼ ◖ SUN, PARTIAL SHADE IN HOT AREAS

◖ ◗ DO NOT OVERWATER

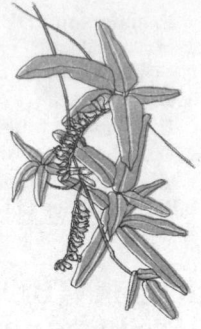

Hardenbergia comptoniana

Native to Australia. Grow at moderate rate to 10 ft., climbing by twining stems. Attractive flowers shaped like pea blossoms, several to many in clusters, late winter to early spring. Need light, well-drained soil. Provide support for climbing and cut back after bloom to prevent tangling. Good against trellises in large containers (use soil rich in organic matter). Subject to spider mites, nematodes; otherwise fairly free of pests and diseases.

H. comptoniana. LILAC VINE. Zones 15–24. Light, delicate foliage pattern; leaves divided in three to five dark green, narrow, 2–3-in.-long leaflets. Flowers violet blue, ½ in. long, in long, narrow clusters. Where temperatures drop below 24°F, shelter blossoms, buds, tender tops by planting under overhang.

H. violacea (H. monophylla). Zones 8–24. Coarser texture; leaves usually undivided, 2–4 in. long. Vining or shrubby. Flowers lilac or violet to rose or white. 'Happy Wanderer', pinkish purple, is a tough, hardy, vigorous selection. *H. v.* 'Rosea' has pink flowers.

> ### WAYS TO USE HARDENBERGIA
> Gardeners use this Australian native in the low elevations of California and Arizona to create a light, delicate pattern against the surfaces of low walls, fences, screens, and arches over gates. *Hardenbergia* can also be pegged down as a ground cover.

HEBE

Scrophulariaceae

EVERGREEN SHRUBS

◢ ZONES 14–24, EXCEPT AS NOTED

☼ ◖ FULL SUN ON COAST, PARTIAL SHADE INLAND

◖ REGULAR WATER

Hebe buxifolia

Closely related to *Veronica* and often still sold under that name. Native to New Zealand. Most are fast growers. Landscaping plants grown principally for form and foliage; some give good flower display. All do better in cool coastal gardens than in interior, where dry summer heat and winter frosts shorten their lives. Lower kinds are useful for edgings or ground cover; taller ones as shrubs near sea winds and salt air.

Good drainage is essential. Prune after bloom, shortening flowering branches considerably to keep plants compact.

H. andersonii. Hybrid between *H. speciosa* and *H. salicifolia*. Compact, to 5–6 ft. Leaves fleshy, deep green. Summer flowers in 2–4-in. spikes; white at base, violet at tip.

H. 'Autumn Glory'. Zones 5, 6, 14–24. Mounding, compact, 2 ft. high, 2 ft. wide. Oval leaves 1½ in. long. Many 2-in.-long, dark lavender blue flower spikes in late summer, fall.

H. buxifolia. BOXLEAF HEBE. Rounded, symmetrical habit. Eventually reaches 5 ft. tall; easily shaped into 3-ft. hedge. Deep green, ⅓-in.-long leaves densely cover branches. Small white flowers in headlike clusters in summer.

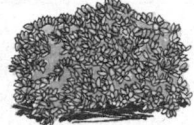
Hebe buxifolia

H. 'Carnea'. Grows 3–5 ft. tall. Deep green, willowlike leaves 2½ in. long. Rosy crimson flowers in 2½-in.-long spikes, August–September.

H. 'Coed'. Compact plant to 3 ft. tall and as broad. Reddish stems densely clothed with 1½-in.-long, dark green leaves. Blooms profusely May–August, bearing spikelike clusters of small, pinkish purple flowers.

H. 'Desilor'. Dense, rounded shrub to 3 ft. tall and as broad. Leaves somewhat smaller than those of *H. elliptica*. Flowers deep purple blue in 1½-in.-long clusters, May–October.

H. elliptica (H. decussata). Much-branched shrub 5–6 ft. high. Medium green leaves 1¼ in. long. Fragrant bluish flowers in 1½-in.-long clusters bloom in summer.

H. glaucophylla. Broad, compact, rounded shrub about 2 ft. wide. Roundish, blue-green, ½-in.-long leaves. White summer flowers in short, dense clusters. Use as low foundation plant or divider between sidewalk and lawn.

H. imperialis. See H. speciosa 'Imperialis'

H. 'Lake' ('Veronica Lake'). Dense shrub 3 ft. tall, with 1½-in., dark green leaves and abundant short spikes of lilac flowers in summer.

H. menziesii. Can reach 5 ft.; usually much lower. Narrow, closely spaced ¾-in.-long leaves are shiny bright green and slightly toothed. White flowers tinged lilac in short clusters; summer bloom. Spreading habit; good ground cover.

H. 'Patty's Purple'. To 3 ft. high. Stems wine red; leaves ½ in. long, dark green. Purple flowers on slender spikes in summer. Mass in groups or use to flower border.

H. 'Reevesii' (H. 'Evansii'). To 3 ft. high. Its 2-in.-long leaves are blend of dark green and reddish purple; reddish purple flowers bloom in summer.

H. speciosa. SHOWY HEBE. Dense, broad, spreading shrub 2–5 ft. high. Stout stems bear dark green, glossy leaves, 2–4 in. long. Reddish purple flowers in 3–4-in.-long spikes, July–September. *H. s.* 'Imperialis' has reddish foliage, magenta flowers in summer.

HEDERA

IVY
Araliaceae
EVERGREEN WOODY VINES
↗ ZONES VARY BY SPECIES
☼ ◐ ● ANY EXPOSURE
◌ ◑ ● WATER NEEDS VARY BY SPECIES

Hedera helix

Most widely planted ground cover in California; also often climbs on walls, fences, trellises. Sometimes planting does both—wall ivy spreads to become surrounding ground cover or vice versa. Ivy is dependable, uniform, neat. Holds soil, discouraging soil erosion and slippage on slopes. Roots grow deep and fill soil densely. Branches root as they grow, further knitting soil.

Ivy climbs almost any vertical surface by aerial rootlets—a factor to consider in planting against walls that must be painted. Chain link fence planted with ivy soon becomes wall of foliage.

Ivy must have shade in hot climates. Its only real shortcoming is monotony. All year long you get nothing from it but green or green and white (except in the case of *H. helix* 'Baltica').

Thick, leathery leaves are usually lobed. Mature plants will eventually develop stiff branches toward top of vine that bear round clusters of small greenish flowers followed by black berries. These branches have unlobed leaves; cuttings from such branches will have same kind of leaves and will be shrubby, not vining. Such shrubs taken from variegated Algerian ivy are called "ghost ivy." *H. helix* 'Arborescens' is another variety of that type.

You can grow regular ivy from cuttings, but many will die and growth will be very slow. Plants from pots grow much faster. Standard spacing: 1–1½ ft. Best planting time is early spring (March in California and Arizona, May in colder climates), but fall plantings, where winters are not excessively cold, require less water to get started.

When you plant, it is critical that soil be thoroughly premoistened; in addition, the ivy's roots must be moist and its tissues full of moisture (not wilted). Mix peat moss or ground bark into planting soil to a depth of 9–12 in., if possible. On steep slope, dig conditioner into each planting hole (6 in. deep, 6 in. wide). After spring planting, feed with high-nitrogen fertilizer. Feed again in August. For best possible growth, continue to feed in early spring and August of every year. In hot climates, the more water you give an ivy planting, the better it will hold up through summer.

Most ivy ground covers need trimming around edges (use hedge shears or sharp spade) 2 or 3 times a year. Fence and wall plantings need shearing or trimming 2 or 3 times a year. When ground cover builds up higher than you want, mow it with rugged power rotary mower or cut it back with hedge shears. Do this in spring so ensuing growth will quickly cover bald look.

Many trees and shrubs can grow quite compatibly in ivy. But small, soft, or fragile plants will never exist for long with healthy ivy—it simply smothers them.

Ivy can be a haven for slugs and snails. If your garden has these pests, put slug-snail poison in ivy often. Ivy also harbors rodents, especially when it is never cut back.

H. canariensis. ALGERIAN IVY. Zones 8, 9, 12–24. Shiny, rich green leaves 5–8 in. wide with three to five shallow lobes, more widely spaced along stems than on English ivy. Requires more moisture than English ivy.

H. c. 'Variegata'. VARIEGATED ALGERIAN IVY. Leaves edged with yellowish white; white edges are sometimes suffused with reddish purple in cold weather. Avoid extreme heat or desert sun.

H. colchica. PERSIAN IVY. Zones 7–9, 12–24. Evergreen, egg-shaped to heart-shaped leaves, 3–7 in. across, up to 10 in. long (largest leaves of all ivies). Best known for its variety 'Dentata', with faintly toothed leaves. 'Dentata Variegata' is marbled with deep green, gray green, and creamy white. Needs no water.

H. helix. ENGLISH IVY. All zones. Dull dark green leaves with paler veins are 2–4 in. wide at base and as long, with three to five lobes. Not as vigorous as Algerian ivy, better for small spaces. Best with regular water; tolerant of aridity.

H. h. 'Baltica'. Hardiest; has whitish-veined leaves half size of English ivy leaves. Turns purplish in winter. 'Bulgarica', also hardy, has larger leaves.

Many small- and miniature-leafed forms are useful for small-area ground covers, hanging baskets, and training to intricate patterns on walls and in pots. These varieties are also used to create topiary shapes— globes, baskets, animals—on wire frames. Some of small-leafed forms are 'Hahn's Self Branching', light green leaves, dense branching, part shade best; 'Conglomerata', slow-growing dwarf; 'Minima', leaves ½–1 in. across with three to five angular lobes. Other varieties are 'Buttercup', 'California', 'Fluffy Ruffles', 'Gold Dust', 'Gold Heart', 'Heart', 'Needlepoint', 'Ripple', 'Shamrock', and 'Star'.

FOR INFORMATION ON SELECTING PLANTS
PLEASE SEE PAGES 45–128

HEDYCHIUM

GINGER LILY	
Zingiberaceae	
PERENNIALS	
✿ ZONES 17, 22–24; INDOORS OR IN GREENHOUSE	
☀ LIGHT SHADE	
◉ MOIST SOIL	

Hedychium gardneranum

Foliage is handsome under ideal conditions. Leaves on two sides of stems but in a single plane. In late summer or early fall, richly fragrant flowers in dense spikes open from cone of overlapping green bracts at ends of stalks. Remove old stems after flowers fade to encourage fresh new growth. Useful in large containers but will not grow as tall as in open ground. Container plants can be moved out of sight when unattractive. Grow in soil high in organic matter. Frosts in mild areas can kill plants to ground, but new stalks appear in early spring. Useful next to swimming pools. Attractive with palms, ferns, other tropical-looking plants.

H. coronarium. WHITE GINGER LILY, GARLAND FLOWER. Native to India, Indonesia. Grows 3–6 ft. high. Leaves 8–24 in. long, 2–5 in. broad. Foliage usually unattractive in California because leaves will burn if plant is given enough heat to bloom well. White, wonderfully fragrant flowers in 6–12-in.-long clusters; good cut flowers.

H. gardneranum. KAHILI GINGER. Native to India. Grows to 8 ft. high; 8–18-in.-long leaves 4–6 in. wide. Clear yellow flowers with red stamens, in 1½-ft.-long spikes, tip branches from July to onset of cool weather.

H. greenei. Native to India. Grows to 5 ft., with orange-red flowers in 5-in. spikes.

HEDYSCEPE canterburyana

Arecaceae (Palmae)	
PALM	
✿ ZONES 17, 23, 24; INDOORS AND IN GREENHOUSE	
☀☀ SUN OR LIGHT SHADE	
◉ REGULAR WATER	

Hedyscepe canterburyana

Comes from Lord Howe Island in the South Pacific. Related to better-known Kentia palms (see *Howea*) but smaller, broader, and lower growing, with broader leaf segments and more arching, lighter green feather-type leaves. To 30 ft.

HELENIUM autumnale

COMMON SNEEZEWEED	
Asteraceae (Compositae)	
PERENNIAL	
✿ ALL ZONES	
☀ FULL SUN	
◉ LITTLE WATER	

Helenium autumnale

Many branching, leafy stems to 1–6 ft., depending on variety. Daisylike flowers summer to early fall—rays in shades of yellow, orange, red, and copper, surrounding brown, pompomlike center. Leaves 2–4 in. long, toothed. Flowers best where summers are hot. Trim off faded blossoms to encourage more blooms. Plants can take some neglect.

FOR INFORMATION ON YOUR CLIMATE ZONE
PLEASE SEE PAGES 15–44

HELIANTHEMUM nummularium

SUNROSE	
Cistaceae	
EVERGREEN SHRUBLETS	
✿ ALL ZONES	
☀ FULL SUN	
◉ DO NOT OVERWATER	

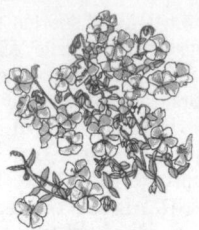

Helianthemum nummularium

Commonly sold under this name are a number of forms as well as hybrids between this species and others. They grow about 6–8 in. high and spread to 3 ft. Depending on the kind, the ½–1-in.-long leaves may be glossy green above and fuzzy gray beneath, or gray on both sides. Sunroses put on a delightful display of 1-in.-wide, clustered single or double flowers in lovely, sunny colors—flame red, apricot, orange, yellow, pink, rose, peach, salmon, and white. Plants bloom April–June in California and Arizona, May–July in Northwest. Each blossom lasts only a day, but new buds continue to open. Shear plants back after flowering to encourage fall bloom.

Let them tumble over rocks, give them a niche in a dry rock wall, or set them in a planter on a sunny patio. Use them at the seashore or in rock gardens. Allow them to ramble over gentle slope. If used as ground cover, plant 2–3 ft. apart. Plant in fall or early spring. Soil drainage must be good. In cold-winter areas, lightly cover plants with branches from evergreens in winter to keep foliage from dehydrating.

HELIANTHUS

SUNFLOWER	
Asteraceae (Compositae)	
ANNUALS AND PERENNIALS	
✿ ALL ZONES	
☀ FULL SUN	
◉ ◉◉ REGULAR TO MUCH WATER	

Helianthus annuus

Coarse, sturdy plants with bold flowers. All are tough, tolerant plants. Perennial kinds spread rapidly, may become invasive. Tall kinds not for tidy gardens. All bloom in late summer, fall.

H. annuus. COMMON SUNFLOWER. Annual. From this rough, hairy plant with 2–3-in.-wide flower heads have come many ornamental and useful garden varieties. Best-known form is coarse, towering (to 10 ft.) plant with small rays outside and cushiony center of disk flowers, 8–10 in. across. Usually sold as 'Mammoth Russian'. 'Sunspot' carries flowers of like size on 2-ft. plants. People eat the roasted seeds; birds like them raw and visit flower heads in fall and winter. For children, annual sunflowers are big and easy to grow and bring sense of great accomplishment. Sow seeds in spring where plants are to grow. Large-flowered kinds need rich soil, lots of water.

H. maximilianii. Perennial. Native to central and southwestern United States. Clumps of 10-ft. stems clothed with 8–10 in. narrow leaves have 3-in. yellow sunflowers in a narrow spire at the tops. These often peer over adobe walls in southwestern gardens.

H. multiflorus. Perennial. To 5 ft. with thin, toothed, 3–8-in.-long leaves and numerous 3-in.-wide flower heads with yellow centers. 'Loddon Gold' is double-flowered. Excellent for cutting.

H. salicifolius (H. orgyalis). Perennial. Clumps of tall (3–6-ft.) stems clothed with long, narrow, drooping leaves carry sheaves of long-stemmed yellow, 2-in. flower heads with brown centers.

H. tuberosus. JERUSALEM ARTICHOKE. Perennial. Also grown as a commercial crop; tubers are

Helianthus tuberosus

H

edible and sold in markets as "sunchokes." Plants 6–7 ft. tall, with bright yellow flower heads. Oval leaves 8 in. long. Spreads readily and can become pest. Best to harvest tubers every year and save out two or three for replanting. If controlled, makes a good, quick temporary screen or hedge.

A DOZEN SUNFLOWERS FOR CUT FLOWERS

Most of the large-flowered sunflowers grown for seed form one flower at the top of a stem. Branching forms produce many smaller flowers, good for arranging: 'Abendsonne', 'Autumn Beauty', 'California Black', 'Color Fashion', 'Luna', 'Primrose', 'Selma-Sonnen', 'Stella', 'Sungold', 'Sunlight', 'Sunspot', and 'Teddy Bear'.

HELICHRYSUM

Asteraceae (Compositae)	
ANNUALS AND PERENNIALS	
✂ ZONES VARY BY SPECIES	
☼ FULL SUN	
◐ ◆ WATER NEEDS VARY BY SPECIES	

Helichrysum bracteatum

Best known is the annual strawflower. Others are little known but choice perennials or subshrubs for landscape use.

H. bracteatum. STRAWFLOWER. Summer annual. All zones. Grows 2–3 ft. high with many flower heads. (Dwarf forms also available.) Known as "everlasting" because 2½-in. pompomlike flowers are papery and last indefinitely when dried. Also good in fresh arrangements. Flowers may be yellow, orange, red, pink, or white (seeds come in mixed colors). Alternate leaves 2–5 in. long. Plant seed in place in late spring or early summer (same time as zinnias). Once plants are well started, keep on dry side. Inclined to have dry leaves at base. Best for hillside or dry areas. 'Dargan Hill Monarch' and 'Diamond Head' are shrubby perennial forms for mild winter climates. Both have grayish green foliage and 3-in. golden yellow flower heads; the similar 'Cockatoo' has lemon yellow heads.

H. petiolare. LICORICE PLANT. Zones 16, 17, 22–24, sometimes grown as annual elsewhere. Woody-based plant with trailing stems to 4 ft., white-woolly inch-long leaves, insignificant flowers. Occasionally emits a licorice aroma. 'Limelight' has leaves of luminous light chartreuse; 'Variegatum', white markings. All are useful for trailing branches that thread through mixed plantings or mix with other plants in large pots, hanging baskets. For the so-called dwarf form, see *Plecostachys serpyllifolia*. Tolerates considerable aridity.

HELICTOTRICHON sempervirens
(Avena sempervirens)

BLUE OAT GRASS	
Poaceae (Gramineae)	
PERENNIAL	
✂ ALL ZONES	
☼ FULL SUN	
◆ REGULAR WATER	

Helictotrichon sempervirens

Evergreen, 2–3-ft. fountains of bright blue-gray, narrow leaves resemble giant clumps of blue fescue (*Festuca ovina* 'Glauca'), but are more graceful. Plants need full sun, good drainage. Combine with other grasses and broad-leafed plants, and with boulders in rock gardens. Pull out occasional withered leaves.

HELIOTROPE, GARDEN. See VALERIANA officinalis p. 516

HELIOTROPIUM arborescens
(H. peruvianum)

COMMON HELIOTROPE	
Boraginaceae	
PERENNIAL	
✂ ZONES 8–24; HOUSE PLANT OR SUMMER ANNUAL	
☼ ◐ PARTIAL SHADE IN HOT-SUMMER CLIMATES	
◆ AVOID OVERWATERING	
◆ ALL PARTS ARE POISONOUS	

Heliotropium arborescens

Rather tender old-fashioned plant grown for delicate, sweet fragrance of its flowers. In mild climates, it's a shrubby plant up to 4 ft. high. Flowers dark violet to white, arranged in tightly grouped, curved, one-sided spikes that form rounded, massive clusters. Veined leaves have darkish purple cast. If in pots, can be protected in winter and moved into patio or garden for spring and summer enjoyment. 'Black Beauty' and 'Iowa' are forms with deep purple flowers.

HELIPTERUM

EVERLASTING, SUNRAY	
Asteraceae (Compositae)	
ANNUALS AND PERENNIALS	
✂ ZONES VARY BY SPECIES	
☼ ◐ EXPOSURE NEEDS VARY BY SPECIES	
◆ ROUTINE WATERING	

Helipterum roseum

A large Australian genus, mostly annual but with some perennials. All have daisylike flower heads with papery 'petals' (ray florets) that retain their color and form when dried. Useful for winter arrangements and for garden color.

H. anthemoides. CHAMOMILE SUNRAY. Perennial. Zones 8, 9, 14–24. A compact, gray-green mound 1 ft. tall, 2 ft. wide, with foliage that has a chamomile scent when bruised. Bright red buds open to white daisies ½–1 in. across; bloom in late winter, with scattered bloom later. Part shade ideal inland, sun near coast.

H. roseum (Acroclinium roseum). PINK AND WHITE EVERLASTING, PINK PAPER DAISY. Annual. All zones. Top-notch flower for cutting, drying. Grows 2 ft. tall, with scanty, narrow foliage and 1–2-in. pink or white daisies. Grow in full sun in warm soil, sowing seeds after frost where plants are to grow. Thin to 6–12 in. apart.

HELLEBORUS

HELLEBORE	
Ranunculaceae	
PERENNIALS	
✂ ZONES VARY BY SPECIES	
◐ ● SHADE OR PARTIAL SHADE	
◐ ◆ ◆ ◆◆ WATER NEEDS VARY BY SPECIES	

Helleborus argutifolius

Distinctive, long-lived evergreen plants, blooming for several months in winter and spring. Basal clumps of substantial, long-stalked leaves, usually divided fanwise into leaflets. Flowers large, borne singly or in clusters, centered with many stamens. Good cut flowers; sear ends of stems or dip in boiling water, then place in deep, cold water.

Plant in good soil with lots of organic material added. Feed once or twice a year. Do not move often; plants reestablish slowly. Mass under high-branching trees on north or east side of walls, in beds bordered with ajuga, wild ginger, primroses, violets. Use in plantings with azaleas, fatsia, pieris, rhododendrons, skimmia, and ferns.

H. argutifolius (H. lividus, H. corsicus). CORSICAN HELLEBORE. Zones 4–24. Leafy stems to 3 ft. Leaves divided into three pale blue-green

H

319

leaflets with sharply toothed edges. (*H. lividus* has leaflets with smooth edges or only a few fine teeth.) Clusters of large, firm-textured light chartreuse flowers among upper leaves. In mild-winter climates, blooms late fall to late spring; in Northwest, blooms March–April. After shedding stamens, flowers stay attractive until summer. Best hellebore for Southern California. Neutral soil. Takes less water and more sun than other hellebores.

H. foetidus. All zones. Grows to 1½ ft. Attractive leaves—leathery, dark green, divided into 7–11 leaflets. Flowers 1 in. wide, light green with purplish margin; bloom February–April. Needs little or no dry-season water. Good with naturalized daffodils. Self-sows freely where adapted.

H. niger. CHRISTMAS ROSE. Zones 1–7, 14–17. Elegant plant to 1½ ft. tall, blooming December–April. Often planted in mild-winter climates but seldom thrives there. Lustrous dark green leaves divided into seven to nine leaflets with few large teeth. Flowers about 2 in. wide, white or greenish white turning purplish with age. Give it ample water.

H. orientalis. LENTEN ROSE. All zones. Much like *H. niger* in growth habit, but easier to transplant. Basal leaves with 5–11 sharply toothed leaflets. Blooms March–May. Flowering stems branched, with leaflike bracts at branching points and beneath flowers. Flowers white, greenish, purplish, or rose, often spotted or splashed with deep purple. Give it ample water. Lenten rose often sold as Christmas rose, but Lenten rose has different flower color and many small teeth on leaflets (few large teeth on those of Christmas rose). Lenten rose does better in Southern California than Christmas rose.

HELXINE. See SOLEIROLIA   p. 488

HEMEROCALLIS

DAYLILY

Liliaceae

DECIDUOUS OR EVERGREEN PERENNIALS

✔ ALL ZONES

☼ ◑ FULL SUN OR LIGHT SHADE IN HOTTEST AREAS

◔ WATER THOROUGHLY DURING BLOOM

Hemerocallis Hybrid

Large clumps of arching, sword-shaped leaves. Lilylike flowers in open or branched clusters at ends of generally leafless stems that stand well above foliage. Tuberous, somewhat fleshy roots. Older yellow, orange, and rust red daylilies have mostly been replaced by newer kinds; both tall and dwarf varieties are available.

Use in borders with bearded iris, Michaelmas and Shasta daisies, poker plant (*Kniphofia*), dusty miller, agapanthus. Mass on banks under high-branching, deciduous trees, along driveways and roadsides in country gardens. Group among evergreen shrubs, near pools, along streams. Plant dwarf daylilies in rock gardens, as edgings, low ground covers. Good cut flowers. Cut stems with well-developed buds; buds open on successive days, though each flower is slightly smaller than preceding one. Arrange individual blooms in low bowls. Snap off faded flowers daily.

Few plants are tougher, more persistent, or more pest free. Adapt to almost any kind of soil. Red-flowered daylilies need warmth to develop best color. Feed with complete fertilizer in spring and midsummer. Divide crowded plants in early spring or late fall.

H. fulva. TAWNY DAYLILY, COMMON ORANGE DAYLILY. Deciduous. To 6 ft. Leaves 2 ft. long or longer, 1 in. wide; tawny orange-red, 3–5-in.-long flowers bloom in summer. Old double-flowered variety 'Kwanso' superseded by newer, more handsome hybrids.

H. hybrids. Deciduous or evergreen. Modern hybrids grow 1–6 ft. tall, with flowers 3–8 in. across. Color range extends far beyond basic yellow, orange, rust red; includes shell pink, vermilion, buff, apricot, creamy white, many bicolors. Early, midseason, late varieties ensure bloom from May to September or October (in mild climates). Some varieties bloom twice a year (or even more often); some bloom in evening. 'Stella d'Oro',

2 ft. tall, produces bright yellow flowers throughout warm weather. Flowers single, semidouble, double; vary in shape from broad-petaled to narrow and twisted. Especially noteworthy are tetraploids ("tetras"), which have unusually heavy-textured flowers.

H. lilioasphodelus (H. flava). LEMON DAYLILY. Deciduous. To 3 ft. Leaves 2 ft. long. Fragrant, clear yellow, 4-in. flowers in June. Old-timer, worthwhile for fragrance and moderate size.

HEMLOCK. See TSUGA   p. 512

HEN AND CHICKENS. See SEMPERVIVUM tectorum   p. 482

HEN AND CHICKS. See ECHEVERIA elegans   p. 269

HERALD'S TRUMPET. See BEAUMONTIA grandiflora   p. 180

HERB-OF-GRACE. See RUTA graveolens   p. 470

HERBS. This category includes all plants that at some time in history have been considered valuable for seasoning, medicine, fragrance, or general household use. As you look through lists of plants, you can recognize certain herbs because they bear the species name *officinalis*—meaning sold in shops, edible, medicinal, recognized in the pharmacopoeia. Today's herb harvest is used almost entirely for seasoning foods.

Herbs are versatile. Some creep along the ground, making fragrant carpets. Others are shrublike. Many make attractive pot plants. However, many herbs do have a weedy look, especially next to regular ornamental plants. Many herbs are hardy and adaptable. Although hot, dry, sunny conditions with poor but well-drained soil are usually considered best for most herbs, some thrive in shady, moist locations with light soil rich in humus.

Following are lists of herbs for specific landscape situations:

Kitchen garden. This can be a sunny raised bed near the kitchen door, planter box near the barbecue, or part of the vegetable garden. Plant basic cooking herbs: basil (*Ocimum*), chives, dill (*Anethum graveolens*), sweet marjoram (*Origanum majorana*), mint (*Mentha*), oregano (*Origanum vulgare*), parsley, rosemary (*Rosmarinus*), sage (*Salvia officinalis*), savory (*Satureja*), tarragon (*Artemisia dracunculus*), thyme (*Thymus*). The connoisseur may wish to plant angelica, anise (*Pimpinella anisum*), caraway (*Carum carvi*), chervil (*Anthriscus cerefolium*), coriander (*Coriandrum sativum*), common fennel (*Foeniculum vulgare*).

Ground cover for sun. Prostrate rosemary, mother-of-thyme (*Thymus praecox arcticus*), lemon thyme (*T. citriodorus*), or woolly thyme (*T. pseudolanuginosus*).

Ground cover for shade or part shade. Chamomile (*Chamaemelum nobile*).

Ground cover for shade. Sweet woodruff (*Galium odoratum*).

Perennial or shrub border. Common wormwood (*Artemisia absinthium*), small burnet (*Poterium sanguisorba*), lavenders (*Lavandula*), monarda, rosemary, scented geraniums (*Pelargonium*).

Hedges. Formal clipped hedge—santolina, germander (*Teucrium*). Informal hedge—lavenders, winter savory (*Satureja montana*).

Herbs for moist areas. Angelica, mints, parsley, sweet woodruff.

Herbs for partial shade. Chervil, costmary (*Chrysanthemum balsamita*), lemon balm (*Melissa officinalis*), parsley, sweet woodruff.

Herbs for containers. Crete dittany (*Origanum dictamnus*), chives, costmary, lemon verbena (*Aloysia triphylla*), sage, pineapple sage (*Salvia elegans*), summer savory (*Satureja hortensis*), sweet marjoram, mints, small burnet.

EDIBLE HERB BOUQUETS

When cutting fresh herbs for the kitchen, don't worry about snipping more than you need. Put the extra cuttings in a vase of water and use them to decorate the table. They remain kitchen-useful as long as they stay perky (often a week or more). Basil, marjoram, mint, oregano, rosemary, sage, and thyme can be displayed and used this way.

Potpourris and sachets. English lavender, lemon balm, sweet woodruff, lemon verbena, monarda.

To dry leafy herbs for cooking, cut them early in day before sun gets too hot, but after dew has dried on foliage. (Oil content is highest then.) Leafy herbs are ready to cut from time flower buds begin to form until flowers are half open. (Exceptions: parsley can be cut any time; sage and tarragon may take on strong taste unless cut early in summer.) Don't cut perennial herbs back more than a third; annual herbs may be sheared back to about 4 in. from the ground. Generally you can cut two or three crops for drying during summer. Don't cut perennial herbs after September or new growth won't have chance to mature before cold weather.

Before drying, sort weeds and grass from herbs; remove dead or insect-damaged leaves. Wash off loose dirt in cool water; shake or blot off excess moisture. Tie woody-stemmed herbs such as sweet marjoram or thyme in small bundles and hang upside down from line hung across room. Room for drying herbs should be dark to preserve color; have good air circulation and warm temperature (about 70°F) for rapid drying to retain aromatic oils. If drying area is fairly bright, surround herb bundles with loose cylinders of paper.

For large-leafed herbs such as basil, or short tips that don't bundle easily, dry in tray with light wooden sides and window screen tacked to the bottom. On top of screen place double thickness of cheesecloth. Spread leaves out over surface. Stir leaves daily.

With good air circulation and low humidity, leafy herbs should be crumbly dry in a few days to a week. Strip leaves from stems and store whole in airtight containers—glass is best—until ready to use. Label each container with name of herb and date dried. Check jars first few days after filling to make sure moisture has not formed inside. If it has, pour out contents and dry for a few more days.

To gather seeds, collect seed clusters such as dill, anise, fennel, caraway when they turn brown. Seeds should begin to fall out when clusters are gently tapped. Leave a little of stem attached when you cut each cluster. Collect in box. Flail seeds from clusters and spread them out in sun to dry for several days. Then separate chaff from seed and continue to dry in sun for another 1½–2 weeks. Store seed herbs same way as leafy ones.

HERNIARIA glabra

GREEN CARPET, RUPTURE WORT

Caryophyllaceae

EVERGREEN PERENNIAL

⚡ ALL ZONES

☼ ◐ ● FULL SUN OR SHADE

● REGULAR WATER

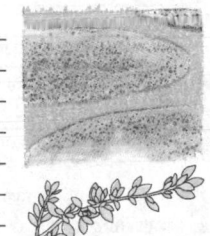
Herniaria glabra

Trailing plant under 2–3 in. tall with crowded, tiny, bright green leaves less than ¼ in. long. Bloom negligible. Foliage turns bronzy red in cold winters. Spreads well, but won't grow out of control; use it between stepping stones, on mounds, with rocks, or in parking strips. Endures occasional footsteps, but not constant traffic.

HESPERALOE parviflora

Agavaceae

EVERGREEN PERENNIAL

⚡ ZONES 10–16, 18–21

☼ FULL SUN

◊ NO DRY-SEASON WATER

Hesperaloe parviflora

Native to Texas, northern Mexico. Makes dense, yuccalike clump of very narrow, swordlike leaves 4 ft. long, about 1 in. wide. Pink to rose red, 1¼-in.-long, nodding flowers in slim, 3–4-ft.-high clusters bloom in early summer, with repeat bloom

frequent in milder climates. On older plants, spikes can reach 8–9 ft. Effective combined with other desert plants. Good large container plant with loose, relaxed look. *H. p. engelmannii* is similar to species, but its 1-in.-long flowers are more bell shaped.

HESPERIS matronalis

DAME'S ROCKET

Brassicaceae (Cruciferae)

PERENNIAL OR BIENNIAL

⚡ ALL ZONES

☼ ◐ SUN OR LIGHT SHADE

● REGULAR WATER

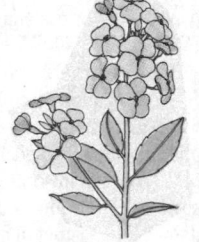
Hesperis matronalis

An old-fashioned, cottage-garden plant, freely branched, to 3 ft. tall and as broad, with 4-in. toothed leaves and rounded clusters of ½-in. four-petaled lavender to purple flowers. Flowers resemble those of stocks and are fragrant at night. Grows readily from seed and often self-sows. Old, woody plants should be replaced by young seedlings. White and double-flowering forms exist but are rare.

HETEROCENTRON elegans (Schizocentron elegans)

SPANISH SHAWL

Melastomataceae

PERENNIAL

⚡ ZONES 15–24

● SHADE

● REGULAR WATER

Heterocentron elegans

Creeping, vinelike habit. Oval leaves up to ½ in. wide with three well-marked veins. Leaves and stems often acquire a red color as the season advances. In summer, 1-in.-wide magenta flowers appear among the leaves; calyces remain after blossoms have withered. Needs protection from frost in Zones 15, 16, 18–20. When used as ground cover, plants in bloom give appearance of a carpet covered with bougainvillealike blossoms. Good subject for hanging baskets.

HETEROMELES arbutifolia (Photinia arbutifolia)

TOYON, CHRISTMAS BERRY, CALIFORNIA HOLLY

Rosaceae

EVERGREEN SHRUB OR SMALL TREE

⚡ ZONES 5–24

☼ ◐ FULL SUN OR PARTIAL SHADE

◊ TOLERATES ARIDITY; LOOKS BETTER IF WATERED

Heteromeles arbutifolia

Native to Sierra Nevada foothills, Southern California to Baja California, Coast Ranges. Dense shrub 6–10 ft. tall or multitrunked small tree 15–25 ft. tall; can be pruned to form small single-trunked tree. Thick, leathery, glossy dark green leaves 2–4 in. long with bristly, pointed teeth. Small white flowers in flattish clusters, June–July. Bright red (rarely yellow) berries in clusters, November–January; birds relish them. Bees also attracted to plant. *H. a. macrocarpa,* from Channel Islands, has larger berries. *Heteromeles* improves under cultivation. If trimmed to give abundance of year-old wood, it produces even more berries than in the wild. Valuable as screen or bank planting.

FOR GROWING SYMBOL EXPLANATIONS
PLEASE SEE PAGE 129

H

HEUCHERA

ALUM ROOT, CORAL BELLS

Saxifragaceae

PERENNIALS

ZONES VARY BY SPECIES

SUN; LIGHT SHADE IN HOTTEST AREAS

WATER NEEDS VARY BY SPECIES

Heuchera sanguinea

Compact, evergreen clumps of roundish leaves with scalloped edges. April–August, slender, wiry stems 15–30 in. high bear open clusters of nodding, bell-shaped flowers ¼ in. or more across, in carmine, reddish pink, coral, crimson, red, rose, greenish, and white. Use as edging in rock gardens, as ground cover; mass in borders, in front of shrubs. Flowers dainty, long lasting in cut arrangements, attractive to hummingbirds.

Divide clumps every 3 or 4 years in fall (in spring in colder areas). Use young, vigorous, rooted divisions; discard older, woody rootstocks. Sow seed in spring.

H. brizoides. All zones. Hybrids between *H. sanguinea* and other species. As seed-grown plants they are often called Bressingham Hybrids. Seed-grown plants come in white and shades of pink and red. 'Bressingham White' is a good white selection. Regular water.

H. maxima. ISLAND ALUM ROOT. Zones 15–24. Native to Channel Islands, Southern California. Foliage clumps 1–2 ft. across. Leaves roundish, heart shaped, lobed, shining dark green. Flowers whitish or pinkish; hundreds in each narrow, 1½–2½-ft.-long cluster. Blooms February–April. Good casual ground cover. Best with some summer water.

H. micrantha. All zones. Native to California, Washington, Oregon, Idaho. Adapts easily to garden conditions. Plant in protected spots in cold areas. Long-stalked, roundish leaves 1–3 in. long, hairy on both sides, toothed and lobed. Flowers whitish or greenish, about ⅛ in. long, in loose clusters on leafy, 2–3-ft. stems. Regular water.

H. 'Palace Purple'. All zones. Described variously as a form of *H. micrantha* or the very similar species *H. americana.* Maplelike leaves are rich brownish or purplish red. Plant grows 1½ ft. tall, keeps its color year round. Tiny flowers are white. Regular water.

H. sanguinea. CORAL BELLS. All zones. Native to Mexico and Arizona. Universal favorite. Makes neat foliage tufts of round, 1–2-in.-long leaves with scalloped edges. Slender, wiry stems 14–24 in. tall bear open clusters of nodding, bell-shaped, bright red or coral pink flowers. White, pink, crimson varieties available. Good edging for beds of delphinium, iris, lilies, peonies, roses. Regular water.

H. 'Santa Ana Cardinal'. Zones 14–24. Outstanding hybrid between garden forms of *H. sanguinea* and *H. maxima.* Unusually vigorous, free flowering. Clumps 3–4 ft. wide. Vibrant rose red flowers, 50–100 on a spike, on 2-ft. stems. Bloom season covers 3–5 months, lasts almost all year in mild areas. Best with some summer water.

HEUCHERELLA tiarelloides

Saxifragaceae

PERENNIAL

ZONES 1–9, 14–24

LIGHT SHADE

ROUTINE WATERING

Heucherella tiarelloides 'Bridget Bloom'

Hybrids between *Heuchera* and foam flower *(Tiarella cordifolia).* 'Bridget Bloom' is a dainty plant with low clumps of small roundish leaves. Flower stems a foot tall bear many tiny pink flowers in narrow plume effect. For woodland or shaded rock gardens.

PRACTICAL GARDENING DICTIONARY

PLEASE SEE PAGES 529–592

HIBBERTIA

Dilleniaceae

EVERGREEN SHRUBS AND VINES

ZONES VARY BY SPECIES

SUN OR PARTIAL SHADE

REGULAR WATER

Hibbertia cuneiformis

Most are native to Australia. Low-growing species for rock garden are worth looking for. One of these is *H. vestita,* 6 in. tall, 2–3 ft. wide, with tiny dark green leaves and comparatively large (1½-in.) bright yellow flowers.

H. cuneiformis (Candollea cuneiformis). Evergreen shrub. Zones 13, 15–24. Native to Australia. Pleasing appearance and substance, to 4 ft. and somewhat broader. Small, 1-in.-long, polished green leaves are tapered at base and toothed at tip. Flowers resembling clear yellow wild roses are carried all along new growth, March–June. Prune after flowering to control outline. Requires exceptionally fast drainage. Feed regularly. Resists wind well. Group with *Aster frikartii,* rockroses *(Cistus),* and sunroses *(Helianthemum).*

H. scandens (H. volubilis). GUINEA GOLD VINE. Evergreen vine. Zones 16, 17, 21–24. Native to Australia. Fast growing, shrubby, climbing by twining stems to 8–10 ft. In ideal climate, luxuriant foliage is handsome all year: waxy dark green leaves, 3 in. long by 1 in. wide. Clear bright yellow flowers, like single roses, first appear in May and continue to bloom into October.

Recovers quickly from burning by light frosts. Use as ground cover or to cover stone or tile walls. Good for small garden areas if trained on trellis or against low fence. Can also be grown in containers.

Hibbertia scandens

HIBISCUS

Malvaceae

SHRUBS, PERENNIALS, AND ANNUALS

ZONES VARY BY SPECIES

FULL SUN

REGULAR DEEP WATERING

Hibiscus rosa-sinensis

Five species are grown in the West—an annual, a perennial, two deciduous shrubs, and an evergreen shrub. In Hawaii and warmest areas of coastal Southern California, several more species are grown.

H. huegelii. See Alyogyne

H. moscheutos. PERENNIAL HIBISCUS, ROSE-MALLOW. Perennial. Zones 1–21. Hardy. To 6–8 ft. high. Stems rise each year; bloom starts in late June and continues until frost. Plants die down in winter. Oval, toothed leaves deep green above, whitish beneath. Flowers largest of all hibiscus; some reach 1 ft. across. Plants need protection from winds that may burn flowers. A 2-in.-deep mulch will help conserve moisture. Feed at 6–8-week intervals during growing season.

Named varieties grown from cuttings are sometimes available. Most are grown from seed, often flowering the first year if sown indoors and planted outdoors early. Southern Belle is tall (4-ft.) strain; 2–2½-ft.-tall strains are Disco Belle, Frisbee, and Rio Carnival. Flowers are 8–10 in. wide, in red, pink, rose, or white, often with red eye.

H. mutabilis. CONFEDERATE ROSE. Deciduous shrub. Zones 4–24. Shrubby or treelike in warmest climates, it behaves more like perennial in colder areas, growing flowering branches from woody base or short trunk. Leaves broad, oval, with three to five lobes. Summer flowers 4–6 in. wide, opening white or pink and changing to deep red by evening. Variety 'Rubrus' has red flowers.

H. rosa-sinensis. CHINESE HIBISCUS, TROPICAL HIBISCUS. Evergreen shrub. Zones 9, 12, 13, 15, 16, 19–24. House plant or indoor/outdoor plant in cold-winter areas. One of showiest flowering shrubs. Reaches 30 ft. in tropics, but seldom over 15 ft. tall in United States, even in mildest parts of California. Glossy foliage varies somewhat in size and texture depending on variety. Growth habit may be dense and dwarfish or loose and open. Summer flowers single or double, 4–8 in. wide. Colors range from white through pink to red, from yellow and apricot to orange. Although individual flowers last only a day, plant blooms continuously.

Plants require good drainage; to check, dig hole 1½ ft. wide and deep. Fill with water; if water hasn't drained in an hour, find another planting area, improve drainage, or plant in raised bed or container. Feed plants monthly (potted plants twice monthly) April–early September. Then let growth harden. Water deeply, frequently. All are susceptible to aphids.

TROPICAL HIBISCUS IN MAINLAND CLIMATES

Hibiscus need sun, heat, and protection from frost and wind. In warm inland areas, they usually grow best if partially shaded from hot afternoon sun. In Zone 17 they bloom only in warm, protected pockets. Where winter temperatures frequently drop below 30°F, even the hardier varieties need overhead protection. Where temperatures drop much lower, grow plants in containers and shelter them indoors over winter. Or grow them as annuals, setting out fresh plants each spring.

Can be used as screen planting, in containers, as espaliers, or as free-standing shrubs or small trees. To keep mature plants growing vigorously, prune out about a third of old wood in early spring. Pinching out tips of stems in spring and summer increases flower production. To develop good branch structure, prune poorly shaped young plants when set out in spring. A few of the many varieties sold in the West are

'Agnes Galt'. Big single pink flowers. Vigorous, hardy plant to 15 ft. Prune to prevent legginess.

'All Aglow'. Tall (10–15-ft.) plant has large single flowers with broad, gold-blotched orange petals, pink halo around a white throat.

'American Beauty'. Broad, deep rose flowers. Slow growth to 8 ft. tall. Irregular form.

'Bridal Veil'. Large pure white single flowers last 3–4 days. Plant 10–15 ft. tall.

'Bride'. Very large, palest blush to white flowers. Slow or moderate growth to open-branched 4 ft.

'Brilliant' ('San Diego Red'). Bright red single flowers in profusion. Tall, vigorous, compact, to 15 ft. Hardy.

'Butterfly'. Small, single bright yellow flowers. Slow, upright growth to 7 ft.

'California Gold'. Heavy yield of yellow, red-centered, single flowers. Slow or moderate growth to a compact 7 ft.

'Crown of Bohemia'. Double gold flowers; petals shade to carmine orange toward base. Moderate or fast growth to 5 ft. Bushy, upright. Hardy.

'Diamond Head'. Large double flowers in deepest red (nearly black red). Compact growth to 5 ft.

'Ecstasy'. Large (5–6-in.) single bright red flowers with striking white variegation. Upright growth to 4 ft.

'Fiesta'. Single bright orange flowers 6–7 in. wide; white eye zone at flower center edged red. Petal edges ruffled. Strong, erect growth to 6–7 ft.

'Fullmoon'. Double pure yellow flowers. Moderately vigorous growth to a compact 6 ft.

'Golden Dust'. Bright orange single flowers with yellow-orange centers. Compact, thick-foliaged plant 4 ft. tall.

'Hula Girl'. Large single canary yellow flowers have deep red eye. Compact growth to 6 ft. Flowers stay open several days.

'Itsy Bitsy Peach', 'Itsy Bitsy Pink', and 'Itsy Bitsy Red' are all tall (10–15-ft.) plants with small leaves and small (2–3-in.) single flowers.

'Jason Okumoto'. Semidouble scarlet-throated orange flowers surrounded by collar of large pink petals (blooms have a cup-and-saucer look). Grows 10–15 ft. tall.

'Kate Sessions'. Flowers large, single, broad petaled, red-tinged gold beneath. Moderate growth to 10 ft. Upright, open habit.

'Kona'. Ruffled double pink flowers. Vigorous, upright, bushy, to 15–20 ft. Prune regularly. 'Kona Improved' has fuller flowers of richer pink color.

'Kona Princess'. Small double pink flowers on a 6–7-ft. shrub.

'Morning Glory'. Single blush pink flowers changing to warmer pink with white petal tips. Grows 8–10 ft. tall.

'President'. Flowers single, 6–7 in. wide, intense red shading to deep pink in throat. Upright, compact, 6–7 ft. tall.

'Red Dragon' ('Celia'). Flowers small to medium, double, dark red. Upright, compact, 6–8 ft. tall.

'Ross Estey'. Flowers very large, single, with broad, overlapping petals of pink shading coral orange toward tips. Heavy-textured flowers last 2–3 days on bush. Vigorous grower to 8 ft. Leaves unusually large, ruffled, polished dark green.

'Vulcan'. Large single red flowers with yellow on back of petals open from yellow buds. Flowers often last more than a day. Compact grower, 4–6 ft. tall.

H. sabdariffa. ROSELLE, JAMAICA SORREL, JAMAICA FLOWER. Annual. All zones. Tall (4–5-ft.), narrowish plant. Leaves oval, with three to five lobes. Grown for fleshy red calyces that surround bases of yellow flowers. These calyces are used for making sauce, jelly, cool drinks, or teas; dried, they are known as Jamaica flowers. Their flavor is reminiscent of cranberry or currant. Plants need long, hot summer to ripen flowers; they do well in all interior valleys where frosts come late. Bloom begins as days shorten; early frosts prevent harvest. Grow like tomatoes; space plants 1½–2 ft. apart in rows. Can be used as narrow temporary hedge.

H. syriacus. ROSE OF SHARON, SHRUB ALTHAEA. Deciduous shrub. Zones 1–21. To 10–12 ft. tall, upright and compact when young, spreading and open with age. Easily trained to single trunk with treelike top. Leaves medium size, often with three lobes, coarsely toothed. Summer flowers single or double, 2½–3 in. across. Single flowers are slightly more effective, opening somewhat wider, but they produce many unattractive capsule-type fruits.

Established plants take some drought. Prune to shape; for bigger flowers, cut back (in winter) previous season's growth to two buds. Resistant to oak root fungus.

Best varieties, some of them hard to find, are: 'Albus', single pure white 4-in. flowers; 'Anemoniflora' ('Paeoniflora'), semidouble red with deeper crimson eye; 'Ardens', double purple; 'Blue Bird', single blue with deep red center eye; 'Blushing Bride', double bright pink; 'Boule de Feu', double deep violet pink; 'Coelestis', single violet blue with reddish purple throat; 'Collie Mullens', double purplish lavender; 'Lucy', double deep rose with red eye; 'Purpurea', semidouble purple with red center; 'Red Heart', single white with red center; and 'Woodbridge', single deep rose with red eye.

Newer selections are sterile triploids, which have a long blooming season and set few or no seed pods. They include 'Aphrodite', rose pink with deep red eye; 'Diana', pure white; 'Helene', white with deep red eye; and 'Minerva', ruffled lavender pink with reddish purple eye.

HIMALAYAN POPPY. See MECONOPSIS betonicifolia   **p. 377**

HINDU-ROPE PLANT. See HOYA carnosa   **p. 326**

HIPPEASTRUM

AMARYLLIS

Amaryllidaceae

BULBS

✿ ZONES 16, 17, 19, 21–24; OR INDOORS

☼ BRIGHT INDOOR LIGHT

◖ WATER UNTIL LEAVES BEGIN TO FADE

Hippeastrum Hybrid

Native to tropics and subtropics. Many species are useful in hybridizing, but only hybrids are generally available; these are usually sold as giant amaryllis or Royal Dutch amaryllis (though many are grown in South Africa or elsewhere). Named varieties or color selections in reds, pinks, white, salmon, near-orange, some variously marked and striped. Two to several flowers, often 8–9 in. across, form on stout, 2-ft. stems. Where plants are grown outdoors, flowers bloom in spring; indoors, they bloom just a few weeks after planting. Broad, strap-shaped leaves usually appear after bloom, grow through summer, disappear in fall.

Usually grown in pots. Plant November–February, in rich, sandy mix with added bonemeal or superphosphate. Allow 2-in. space between bulb and edge of pot. Set upper half of bulb above soil surface. Firm soil, water well, then keep barely moist until growth begins. Wet, airless soil causes root rot.

When flowers fade, cut off stem, keep up watering; feed to encourage leaf growth. When leaves yellow, withhold water, let plants dry out. Repot in late fall or early winter.

ACHIEVE EARLY INDOOR BLOOM WITH AMARYLLIS

A potted amaryllis bulb can be brought to bloom indoors in just a few weeks. Keep in a warm, dark place until rooted. Then move to a warm, lightly shaded place where air is not too dry. Increase watering as leaves form. Feed lightly every 2 weeks through flowering period.

HIPPOCREPIS comosa

Fabaceae (Leguminosae)

PERENNIAL GROUND COVER

✓ ZONES 8–24

☼ FULL SUN

◊ TOLERATES SOME ARIDITY

Hippocrepis comosa

Forms mat 3 in. high; spreads to 3 ft. Leaves divided into 7–15 medium green, oval, ¼–½-in.-long leaflets. Flowers golden yellow, sweet pea shaped, ½ in. long, in loose clusters of 5–12. Blooms in spring; some repeat bloom in summer. Takes poor soils, but lusher looking with good soil. Roots bind soil on steep banks. Bank cover, rock garden, small-scale lawn substitute (mow once just after flowers fade). Set 1 ft. apart. Takes light foot traffic.

| HOGAN CEDAR. See THUJA plicata 'Fastigiata' | p. 505 |

HOHERIA

Malvaceae

EVERGREEN TREES, DECIDUOUS TREES OR SHRUBS

✓ ZONES VARY BY SPECIES

☼ ◗ SUN OR PARTIAL SHADE

◖◗ KEEP ROOT AREA MOIST

Native to New Zealand. Leaves are bright green, leathery, toothed, 3–5 in. long, 1½–2 in. wide. Pure white flowers about 1 in. wide form in clusters among leaves.

H. glabrata. MOUNTAIN RIBBONWOOD. Deciduous tree or large shrub. Zones 5, 6. To 40 ft. high, usually much less. Attractive with azaleas or rhododendrons. Summer bloom.

H. populnea. NEW ZEALAND LACEBARK. Evergreen tree. Zones 4–6, 15–17, 21–24. In growth habit, as graceful as birch; in addition, it puts on good show of flowers from late summer into fall. Grows fast to eventual 50–60 ft., but enjoyable for many years as 20–30-ft., slender tree. Like birch, it's ideal for multiple planting and groves. Has deep, well-behaved

Hoberia glabrata

root system. Inner bark is interestingly perforated; in New Zealand, it is used for ornamental purposes. Rarely seen but worth seeking out for coastal gardens. Needs humid air to thrive, but dislikes cold ocean winds. Self-sows where adapted, and seedling volunteers could be a problem where tree is growing in ground cover.

HOLLY. See ILEX	p. 329
HOLLY FERN. See CYRTOMIUM falcatum	p. 256
HOLLYHOCK. See ALCEA rosea	p. 144
HOLLYLEAF CHERRY. See PRUNUS ilicifolia	p. 439
HOLLYLEAF REDBERRY. See RHAMNUS crocea ilicifolia	p. 453
HOLLYLEAF SWEETSPIRE. See ITEA ilicifolia	p. 335

HOLODISCUS

Rosaceae

DECIDUOUS SHRUBS

✓ ZONES VARY BY SPECIES

◗ PARTIAL SHADE

◊ VERY LITTLE WATER

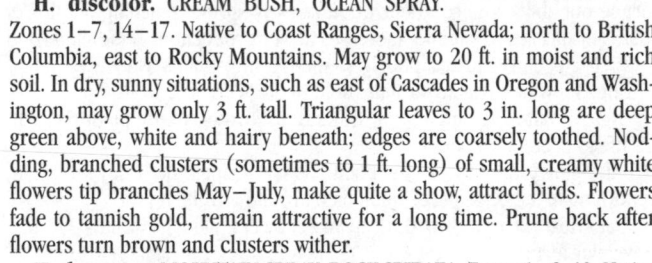

Holodiscus discolor

All are western natives. Use them as background in native plant gardens, or in rural low-maintenance gardens where they can fend for themselves.

H. discolor. CREAM BUSH, OCEAN SPRAY. Zones 1–7, 14–17. Native to Coast Ranges, Sierra Nevada; north to British Columbia, east to Rocky Mountains. May grow to 20 ft. in moist and rich soil. In dry, sunny situations, such as east of Cascades in Oregon and Washington, may grow only 3 ft. tall. Triangular leaves to 3 in. long are deep green above, white and hairy beneath; edges are coarsely toothed. Nodding, branched clusters (sometimes to 1 ft. long) of small, creamy white flowers tip branches May–July, make quite a show, attract birds. Flowers fade to tannish gold, remain attractive for a long time. Prune back after flowers turn brown and clusters wither.

H. dumosus. MOUNTAIN SPRAY, ROCK SPIRAEA. Zones 1–3, 10. Native to shady canyons in Rockies from Wyoming south. Generally smaller than *H. discolor* and with narrower flower clusters, but may reach 15 ft. Coarsely toothed leaves less than 1 in. long. Like *H. discolor*, is related to *Spiraea* and similar in appearance.

HOMERIA collina

Iridaceae

CORM

✓ ZONES 4–24

☼ ◗ SUN; PARTIAL SHADE IN HOTTEST AREAS

◊ WATER ONLY IF WINTER RAINS ARE INSUFFICIENT

Homeria collina

Branching or unbranched 1½-ft. stems bear 2½–3-in.-wide flowers in California poppy colors—golden yellow or muted orange. Corms planted in September or October send up a single floppy, grasslike leaf; flowers follow in March or April. Needs good drainage. Plants are dormant in summer. They multiply freely; dig when leaves fade, and share surplus.

HONEY BUSH. See MELIANTHUS major	p. 378
HONEY LOCUST. See GLEDITSIA triacanthos	p. 308
HONEYSUCKLE. See LONICERA	p. 360
HONG KONG ORCHID TREE. See BAUHINIA blakeana	p. 179

HORSERADISH

Brassicaceae (Cruciferae)

PERENNIAL

☘ ALL ZONES

☼ FULL SUN

● REGULAR WATER

Horseradish

A large, coarse, weedy-looking perennial plant grown for its large, coarse, white roots, which are peeled, grated, and mixed with vinegar or cream to make a condiment. Does best in rich, moist soils in cool regions. Grow it in some sunny out-of-the-way corner. Start with roots planted 1 ft. apart in late winter or early spring.

FRESH HORSERADISH

Through fall, winter, and spring, harvest pieces of horseradish roots from the outside of the root clump as you need them—that way you'll have your horseradish fresh and hot.

HOSTA (Funkia)

PLANTAIN LILY

Liliaceae

PERENNIALS

☘ ZONES 1–10, 12–21

☼ SUN ONLY IN COOL-SUMMER AREAS

● REGULAR WATER IN SUMMER

Hosta decorata

Their real glory is in their leaves—typically heart shaped, shiny, distinctly veined. Flowers come as a dividend: thin spikes topped by several trumpet-shaped flowers grow up from foliage mounds in summer, last for several weeks. Feeding once a year will bring on extra leafy splendor. Blanket of peat moss around plants will prevent mud from splattering leaves. Slugs and snails love hostas; bait 3–4 times a year. All forms go dormant (collapse almost to nothing) in winter; fresh new leaves grow from roots in early spring. Good in containers. In ground, plants last for years; clumps expand in size and shade out weed growth. Few plants have undergone so many name changes; to be quite sure you are getting the one you want, buy it in full leaf.

New garden varieties enter the scene in ever-increasing numbers; you'll find dwarf (6-in.) and giant (5-ft.) varieties, blue-leafed and gold-leafed types, and every gradation between. Many are available only from mail-order specialists. All are splendid companions for ferns and fernlike foliage plants such as *Dicentra*.

H. decorata (H. 'Thomas Hogg'). Plants to 2 ft. high. Oval leaves, 6 in. long, bluntly pointed at tips, green with silvery white margins. Lavender 2-in.-long flowers.

H. 'Honeybells'. Large grass green leaves. Fragrant lavender flowers on 3-ft. stems.

H. 'Krossa Regal'. Big bluish green leaves arch upward and outward to make a 3-ft. vase-shaped plant. Lavender flower spikes can reach 5–6 ft. in late summer.

H. lancifolia (H. japonica). NARROW LEAFED PLANTAIN LILY. Leaves dark green, 6 in. long; not heart shaped, but tapering into the long stalk. Pale lavender, 2-in.-long flowers on 2-ft. stems.

H. plantaginea (H. grandiflora, H. subcordata). FRAGRANT PLANTAIN LILY. Scented white flowers, 4–5 in. long, on 2-ft. stems. Leaves bright green, to 10 in. long.

H. sieboldiana (H. glauca). Blue-green leaves, 10–15 in. long, heavily veined. Many slender, pale lilac flowers nestle close to leaves. A showpiece plant near shaded pool or woodland path. The variety 'Frances Williams', sometimes called 'Gold Edge' or 'Gold Circle', makes clumps 4 ft. tall and as wide, with the typical blue-green leaves of the species boldly edged in yellow.

H. undulata (H. media picta, H. variegata). WAVY-LEAFED PLANTAIN LILY. Wavy-margined, 6–8-in.-long leaves are variegated white on green. Foliage used in arrangements. Pale lavender flowers on 3-ft. stalks.

H. ventricosa (H. caerulea). BLUE PLANTAIN LILY. Deep green, broad, prominently ribbed leaves. Blue flowers on 3-ft. stems.

HOUTTUYNIA cordata

Saururaceae

PERENNIAL

☘ ZONES 1–9, 14–24

☼◐● FULL SUN NEAR COAST, SHADE INLAND

● REGULAR WATER

Houttuynia cordata

Underground rhizomes send up 2–3-in. leaves that look much like those of English ivy, have odd scent of orange peel when crushed. Inconspicuous clusters of white-bracted flowers like tiny dogwood blossoms. Disappears completely in winter. Unusual ground cover. Can spread aggressively in wet ground. 'Variegata' ('Chameleon') has showy splashes of cream, pink, yellow, and red on foliage, is attractive in container or (curbed) in shady garden.

HOWEA

Arecaceae (Palmae)

PALMS

☘ ZONES 17, 21–24

● INDIRECT LIGHT INDOORS

● REGULAR WATER

Howea forsterana

Native to Lord Howe Island. These feather palms are the kentia palms of florists, and are usually sold under the name Kentia. Slow growing; with age, leaves drop to show clean, green trunk ringed with leaf scars. Plant under another plant when using outdoors.

Howeas are ideal pot plants—the classic parlor palms. Keep fronds clean and dust free to minimize spider mite problem.

H. belmoreana. SENTRY PALM. Less common than *H. forsterana*, smaller and more compact, with overarching leaves 6–7 ft. long. Withstands some watering neglect, drafts, dust.

H. forsterana. PARADISE PALM. Larger than *H. belmoreana*, with leaves to 9 ft. long and long, drooping leaflets.

HOYA

WAX FLOWER, WAX PLANT
Asclepiadaceae
HOUSE PLANTS
▨ ONE SPECIES GROWS OUTDOORS, ZONES 15–24
● SHADE
◗ WATER DEEPLY IN SUMMER, LET SOIL DRY, REPEAT

Hoya carnosa

Thick, waxy, evergreen leaves and tight clusters of small waxy flowers. Grown in sunny windows. Do best in rich, loose, well-drained soil. Bloom best when potbound; grown in pots even outdoors. Do not prune out flowering wood; new blossom clusters appear from stumps of old ones. Specialists list dozens of species and hybrids.

H. bella. House or greenhouse plant. Shrubby, small leafed, to 3 ft., with slender, upright branches that droop as they grow older. Tight clusters of purple-centered, white, ½-in. flowers in summer. Best in hanging basket.

H. carnosa. WAX FLOWER, WAX PLANT. Indoor plant or outdoors in Zones 15–24 with overhead protection—but even there it is quickly damaged by temperatures much below freezing. Vining to 10 ft. Leaves are oval, 2–4 in. long. Fragrant summer flowers in big, round, tight clusters; each ½-in.-wide blossom is creamy white, centered with five-pointed pink star. Red young leaves give extra color. In cool climates, let plant go dormant in winter, giving only enough water to keep plant from shriveling. Outdoors, in mild climates, train on pillar or trellis in shade; indoors, train on wire in sunny window. 'Variegata' has leaves edged with white suffused with pink; it is not as vigorous or hardy as the green form. 'Exotica' shows yellow-and-pink variegation. 'Krinkle Kurl' has crinkly leaves closely spaced on short stems; it is often sold as *H. c.* 'Compacta' or as Hindu-rope plant.

HUCKLEBERRY. See VACCINIUM ovatum, V. parvifolium	**p. 516**

HUMATA tyermannii

BEAR'S FOOT FERN
Polypodiaceae
FERN
▨ ZONES 17, 23, 24; INDOORS AND IN GREENHOUSE
◖ PARTIAL SHADE
● REGULAR WATER

Native to China. This small fern has furry, creeping rhizomes that look something like bear's feet. Fronds 8–10 in. long, very finely cut, rising at intervals from the rhizome. Like *Davallia* in appearance and uses, but slower growing.

Humata tyermannii

HUMBOLDT LILY. See LILIUM humboldtii	**p. 355**
HUMMINGBIRD BUSH. See GREVILLEA thelemanniana	**p. 313**
HUMMINGBIRD FLOWER. See ZAUSCHNERIA	**p. 527**

HUMULUS

HOP
Cannabaceae
PERENNIAL VINES
▨ ALL ZONES
☼ FULL SUN
◗ WATER DURING GROWTH

Humulus lupulus

Extremely fast growth. Large, deeply lobed leaves. Useful for summer screening on trellises or arbors.

H. japonicus. JAPANESE HOP. To 20–30 ft. Flowers do not make true hops. Variety 'Variegatus' has foliage marked with white. Flowers in greenish clusters like pine cones. Sow seeds in spring where plants are to grow. Roots are perennial; tops die back in fall.

H. lupulus. COMMON HOP. Perennial vine. This plant produces the hops used to flavor beer. Grow from roots (not easy to find in nurseries) planted in rich soil in early spring. Place thick end up, just below soil surface. Furnish supports for vertical climbing. Shoots appear in May and grow quickly to 15–25 ft. by midsummer. Leaves with three to five lobes, toothed. Squarish, hairy stems twine vertically; to get horizontal growth, twine stem tips by hand. Light green hops (soft, flaky, 1–2-in. cones of bracts and flowers) form in August–September. They're attractive and have fresh, piny fragrance. Cut back stems to ground after frost turns them brown. Regrowth comes the following spring. Tender hop shoots can be cooked as a vegetable.

H. l. neomexicanus (H. americanus). Native to central and southern Rockies; scarcely differs from the cultivated hop noted above.

HUNNEMANNIA fumariifolia

MEXICAN TULIP POPPY, GOLDEN CUP
Papaveraceae
PERENNIAL, USUALLY TREATED AS ANNUAL
▨ ALL ZONES
☼ FULL SUN
◊ NO WATER ONCE ESTABLISHED

Hunnemannia fumariifolia

Related to the California poppy (*Eschscholzia californica*). Bushy, open, 2–3 ft. high, with very finely divided blue-green leaves. Clear soft yellow, cup-shaped flowers with crinkled petals are about 3 in. across, bloom July–October. Showy plant in masses; striking with scarlet *Zauschneria californica* or with blues of ceratostigma, echium, or penstemon. Blooms last for a week in water if cut in bud. Plant from nursery containers or sow seed in place in warm, dry, sunny position; thin seedlings to 1 ft. apart. Reseeds. Plants need excellent drainage.

HYACINTH BEAN. See DOLICHOS lablab	**p. 266**
HYACINTHOIDES. See ENDYMION	**p. 272**

HYACINTHUS

HYACINTH
Liliaceae
BULBS
▨ ALL ZONES
☼◖ SUN OR HIGH SHADE
◗ WATER UNTIL FOLIAGE YELLOWS

Hyacinthus orientalis

As garden plants, best adapted in cold-winter climates. Bell-shaped, fragrant flowers in loose or tight spikes rise from basal bundle of narrow bright green leaves. All are spring blooming. Plant in fall. Where winters are cold, plant in September–October. In mild areas, plant October–December.

H. amethystinus. See Brimeura amethystina

H. azureus. See Muscari azureum

H. orientalis. COMMON HYACINTH. Grows to 1 ft., with fragrant, bell-shaped flowers in white, pale blue, or purple-blue. Two basic forms are the Dutch and the Roman or French Roman.

Dutch hyacinth, derived from *H. orientalis* by breeding and selection, has large, dense spikes of waxy, bell-like, fragrant flowers in white, shades of blue, purple, pink, red, cream, buff, and salmon. The size of the flower spike is directly related to the size of the bulb.

Biggest bulbs are desirable for exhibition plants or for potting; next largest size is most satisfactory for bedding outside. Small bulbs give smaller, looser clusters with more widely-spaced flowers. These are sometimes called miniature hyacinths. Set the larger bulbs 6 in. deep, smaller bulbs 4 in. Hyacinth bulbs have invisible barbs on their surfaces that can cause some people's skin to itch; after handling, wash hands before touching face or eyes.

Hyacinths look best when massed or grouped; rows look stiff, formal. Mass bulbs of a single color beneath flowering tree or in border. Leave bulbs in ground after bloom, continue to feed. Flowers tend to be smaller in succeeding years, but maintain same color and fragrance.

Choice container plants. Pot in porous mix with tip of bulb near surface. After potting, cover containers with thick mulch of sawdust, wood shavings, or peat moss to keep bulbs cool, moist, shaded until roots well formed; remove mulch, place in full light when tops show. Also grow hyacinths in water in special hyacinth glass, the bottom filled with pebbles and water. Keep in dark, cool place until rooted, give light when top growth appears; place in sunny window when leaves have turned uniformly green.

Roman or French Roman hyacinth (*H. o. albulus*) has white, pink, or light blue flowers loosely carried on slender stems; usually several stems to a bulb. Earlier bloom than Dutch hyacinths. These are well adapted to mild-winter areas, where they naturalize under favorable conditions. Where winters are cold, grow in pots for winter bloom.

HYDRANGEA

Hydrangeaceae (Saxifragaceae)

DECIDUOUS SHRUBS OR VINES

⚡ ZONES VARY BY SPECIES

☼ ◐ FULL SUN ON COAST, PARTIAL SHADE INLAND

● REGULAR WATER

Hydrangea macrophylla

Big, bold leaves and large clusters of long-lasting flowers in white, pink, red, or (under some conditions) blue. Summer, fall bloom. Flower clusters may contain sterile flowers (conspicuous, with large, petal-like sepals) or fertile flowers (small, starry petaled); or they may feature a cluster of small fertile flowers surrounded by ring of big sterile ones (these are called lace cap hydrangeas). Sterile flowers last long, often holding up for months, gradually fading in color. Effective when massed in partial shade or planted in tubs on paved terrace.

Easy to grow in rich, porous soil. Fast growing—prune to control size and form; cut out stems that have flowered, leaving those that have not. To get biggest flower clusters, reduce number of stems; for numerous medium-size clusters, nicely spaced, keep more stems.

H. anomala. CLIMBING HYDRANGEA. Deciduous vine. Zones 1–21. Climbs high by clinging aerial rootlets. Shrubby and sprawling without support. Roundish, 2–4-in.-long, green, heart-shaped leaves. Mature plants develop short, stiff, flowering branches with flat white flower clusters, 6–10 in. wide, in lace cap effect. *H. a. petiolaris (H. petiolaris)*, more common form in cultivation, differs hardly at all.

H. arborescens. SMOOTH HYDRANGEA. Deciduous shrub. Zones 1–21. Upright, dense to 10 ft. Oval, grayish green, 4–8-in. leaves. White flowers in 6-in. roundish clusters, June to frost; a few large sterile flowers. Much better is variety 'Grandiflora', with very large clusters made up of large sterile flowers. The variety 'Annabelle' is lower growing (to 4 ft.), yet produces enormous (to 12 in.) globular clusters of sterile white flowers throughout the summer.

H. macrophylla (H. hortensia, H. opuloides, H. otaksa). BIGLEAF HYDRANGEA, GARDEN HYDRANGEA. Deciduous shrub. Zones 2–9, 14–24. Symmetrical, rounded habit; grows to 4–8 or even 12 ft. Thick, shining, coarsely toothed leaves to 8 in. long; white, pink, red, or blue flowers in big clusters.

Great performer in areas where winters are fairly mild, but disappointing where plants freeze to ground every year (may never bloom under these conditions). Protect in Zones 2 and 3 by mounding soil or leaves over bases of plants.

There are hundreds of named varieties, and plants may be sold under many names. Florists' plants are usually French hybrids, shorter (1–3 ft. tall) and larger flowered than old garden varieties. Two varieties are unmistakable: 'Domotoi' has clusters of pink or blue double sterile flowers; 'Tricolor' (usually sold as 'Variegata'), a lace cap, has dark green leaves strongly marked with cream and light green.

H. paniculata 'Grandiflora'. PEEGEE HYDRANGEA. Deciduous shrub. Zones 1–21. Upright, of coarse texture. Can be trained as a 25-ft. tree, but best as a 10–15-ft. shrub. Leaves 5 in. long, turn bronzy in fall. Flowers in upright 10–15-in.-long clusters are white, slowly fading to pinky bronze.

H. quercifolia. OAKLEAF HYDRANGEA. Deciduous shrub. Zones 1–22. Broad, rounded shrub to 6 ft. with handsome, deeply lobed, oaklike, 8-in.-long leaves that turn bronze or crimson in fall. Creamy white flowers in open clusters, June. Pruned to ground each spring, it makes compact, 3-ft. shrub. Thinned out to well-spaced branches, it makes a distinguished container plant.

Hydrangea quercifolia

> ## BLUE OR PINK?
>
> Pink and red garden hydrangeas often turn blue or purple in acid soils. Florists grow French hybrids as pot plants, controlling flower color by controlling soil mix; blue-flowering plants from the florist may show pink flowers when planted in neutral or alkaline soil. Plants can be made (or kept) blue by applying aluminum sulfate to soil; plants can be kept red or made redder by liming the soil or applying superphosphate in quantity. Treatment is not effective unless started ahead of bloom.

Hydrangeaceae. This plant family includes several woody-stemmed plants formerly listed under Saxifragaceae.

Hydrophyllaceae. The waterleaf family, largely but not entirely native to North America, includes annuals, perennials, and a few shrubs. Many have flowers in crosier-shaped clusters. *Nemophila* and *Phacelia* are sometimes grown in gardens.

HYMENOCALLIS

Amaryllidaceae

BULBS

⚡ ZONES 5, 6, 8, 9, 14–24

☼ ◐ SUN OR PARTIAL SHADE

● WATER DURING GROWTH AND BLOOM

⬥ BULBS ARE POISONOUS

Clumps of strap-shaped leaves like those of amaryllis. In June and July, 2-ft. stems bear several very fragrant flowers; blooms resemble daffodils, but the center cup is surrounded by six slender, spidery, free segments. Unusual summer-blooming plants for borders or containers. Plant in rich, well-drained soil—in late fall or early winter in frostless areas, after frosts in colder climates. Set bulbs with tips 1 in. below surface. Dry off when foliage begins to yellow. Then dig and wash bulbs, dry in inverted position; do not cut off fleshy roots. Store in open trays at 60–75°F.

Hymenocallis narcissiflora

H. festalis. Free flowering, with four or more pure white flowers, the cup with very narrow curved segments. Leaves resemble those of *H. narcissiflora*. ▶

H. narcissiflora (Ismene calathina). BASKET FLOWER, PERUVIAN DAFFODIL. Leaves 1½–2 ft. long, 1–2 in. wide. White, green-striped flowers in clusters of two to five. Variety 'Advance' has pure white flowers, faintly lined with green in throat.

H. 'Sulfur Queen'. Primrose yellow flowers with light yellow, green-striped throat. Leaves like those of *H. narcissiflora*.

HYMENOCYCLUS. See MALEPHORA	p. 372
HYMENOLEPIS. See ATHANASIA	p. 171

HYMENOSPORUM flavum

SWEETSHADE
Pittosporaceae
EVERGREEN SMALL TREE OR LARGE SHRUB
✔ ZONES 8, 9, 14–23
☼ ☽ FULL SUN OR LIGHT SHADE
⬤ INFREQUENT, DEEP WATERING

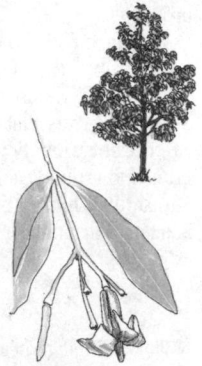

Hymenosporum flavum

Native to Australia. Slow to moderate growth to 20–40 ft. with 15–20-ft. spread. Graceful, upright, slender, open habit in first 10 years. Leaves shiny dark green, 2–6 in. long, 1–2 in. wide, with tendency to cluster near ends of twigs and branches. In early summer, bears clusters of yellow flowers with pronounced fragrance of orange-blossom honey.

Best away from coastal winds. Should have fast soil drainage, routine feeding. Early training is necessary, since branches spread out in almost equal threes, creating weak crotches that are likely to split. Strengthen branches by frequent pinching and shortening. As single tree, needs staking for several years. Attractive planted in small groves, in which case trees need no staking or training.

HYPERICUM

ST. JOHNSWORT
Hypericaceae
SHRUBS AND PERENNIALS, MOSTLY EVERGREEN
✔ ZONES 4–24, EXCEPT AS NOTED
☼ ☽ SUN NEAR COAST, PARTIAL SHADE INLAND
⬤⬤ TOLERATE ARIDITY; BETTER WITH SOME WATER

Hypericum calycinum

Best in mild, moist coastal areas. Open, cup-shaped, five-petaled flowers range in color from creamy yellow to gold, and have prominent sunburst of stamens in center. Neat leaves vary in form and color. Plants useful for summer flower color and fresh green foliage. Mass planting, ground cover, informal hedges, borders.

H. androsaemum. Shrub to 3 ft. tall, with stems arching toward the top. Leaves to 4 in. long, 2 in. wide. Clusters of ¾-in., golden yellow flowers at tops of stems and at ends of side branches. Blossoms followed by berrylike fruits—first red, then purple, then black. Useful as tall ground cover at edge of woods, shaded slopes, wild garden.

H. beanii (H. patulum henryi). To 4 ft., with light green, oblong leaves on graceful, willowy branches. Evergreen. Flowers brilliant golden yellow, 2 in. across, July–October. Good for low, untrimmed hedge, mass planting. Shabby winter appearance in cold-winter areas.

H. calycinum. AARON'S BEARD, CREEPING ST. JOHNSWORT. Evergreen shrub; semideciduous where winters are cold. Zones 2–24. Grows to 1 ft. tall; spreads by vigorous underground stems. Short-stalked leaves to 4 in. long; medium green in sun, yellow-green in shade. Flowers bright yellow, 3 in. across. Tough, dense ground cover for sun or shade; competes successfully with tree roots, takes poor soil. Fast growing, will control erosion on hillsides. Can invade other plantings unless confined. Plant from

flats or as rooted stems; set 1½ ft. apart. Clip or mow off tops every 2–3 years during dormant season.

H. coris. Evergreen subshrub. To 6–12 in. tall or taller. Leaves narrow, ½–1 in. long, in whorls of 4–6. Flowers yellow, ¾ in. across, in loose clusters. Blooms April–June. Good ground cover or rock garden plant.

H. frondosum. Zones 2–24. Native to Georgia. Evergreen or semievergreen in mild climates. Grows 1 ft. tall, twice as wide. Clusters of 1½-in., bright yellow flowers form at branch tips throughout summer. 'Sunburst' is a superior cutting-grown selection.

H. 'Hidcote' (H. patulum 'Hidcote'). Rounded shrub to 4 ft.; semievergreen in colder climates, where freezing keeps height closer to 2 ft. Leaves 2–3 in. long. Flowers yellow, 3 in. wide; blooms all summer.

H. kouytchense. Semievergreen. Twiggy, rounded shrub 1½–2 ft. tall, 2–3 ft. wide, with pointed oval, 2-in. leaves. Flowers golden yellow, 2–3 in. across, heavily produced July–August.

H. moseranum. GOLD FLOWER. Evergreen shrub or perennial. To 3 ft. tall where winters are mild; grows as hardy perennial in cold-winter areas. Moundlike habit with arching, reddish stems. Leaves 2 in. long, blue green beneath. Flowers golden yellow, 2½ in. across; borne singly or in clusters of up to five blossoms. Blooms June–August. Cut back in early spring. 'Tricolor' has gray-green leaves edged in white and tinged with pink.

H. patulum henryi. See H. beanii

H. reptans. Flat-growing shrublet that roots along ground. Leaves ¼–½ in. long, crowded along stems; flowers to 1¾ in. wide. Rock garden plant. Give protection from frosts in colder regions.

H. 'Rowallane'. Evergreen shrub. Upright to 3–6 ft., rather straggly growth. Flowers bright yellow, 2½–3 in. across, profuse in late summer and fall. Leaves 2½–3½ in. long. Remove older branches annually.

H. 'Sungold'. See H. kouytchense

HYPOCYRTA nummularia. See ALLOPLECTUS nummularia	p. 146

HYPOESTES phyllostachya (H. sanguinolenta)

FRECKLE FACE, PINK POLKA-DOT PLANT
Acanthaceae
HOUSE PLANT OR ANNUAL BEDDING PLANT
✔ ALL ZONES AS ANNUAL
☼ ☽ FULL SUN OR LIGHT SHADE
⬤ REGULAR WATER

Hypoestes phyllostachya

Can reach 1–2 ft. tall. Slender stems bear oval, 2–3-in.-long leaves spotted irregularly with pink or white. A selected form known as 'Splash' has larger spots. Blooms very rarely. For indoor use, plant in loose, peaty mixture in pots or planters. Feed with liquid fertilizer. Pinch tips to make bushy.

HYSSOP, ANISE. See AGASTACHE foeniculum	p. 142

HYSSOPUS officinalis

HYSSOP
Lamiaceae (Labiatae)
PERENNIAL HERB
✔ ALL ZONES
☼ ☽ FULL SUN OR LIGHT SHADE
⬤ INFREQUENT WATER

Hyssopus officinalis

Compact growth to 1½–2 ft. Narrow, dark green, pungent leaves; profusion of dark blue flower spikes, from July to November. There are also white- and pink-flowered forms.

IBERIS

CANDYTUFT

Brassicaceae (Cruciferae)

PERENNIALS AND ANNUALS

☀ ALL ZONES

☼ FULL SUN

● REGULAR WATER

Iberis sempervirens

These free-blooming plants bear clusters of white, lavender, lilac, pink, rose, purple, carmine, or crimson flowers from early spring to summer. Use annuals for borders, cutting; perennials for edging, rock gardens, small-scale ground covers, containers.

In fall (in mild areas) or early spring, sow seed of annuals in place or in flats. Set transplants 6–9 in. apart. Plant perennials in fall or spring; water deeply and infrequently. Shear lightly after bloom to stimulate new growth.

I. amara. HYACINTH-FLOWERED CANDYTUFT, ROCKET CANDYTUFT. Annual. Fragrant white flowers in tight, round clusters that elongate into hyacinthlike spikes on 15-in. stems. Narrow, slightly fuzzy leaves.

I. gibraltarica. Perennial. Resembles *I. sempervirens* but with flatter clusters of light pinkish or purplish flowers. Less hardy to cold.

I. sempervirens. EVERGREEN CANDYTUFT. Perennial. Grows 8 in. to 1 ft. or even 1½ ft. high, spreading about as wide. Leaves narrow, shiny dark green, good-looking all year. Flower clusters pure white, on stems long enough to cut for bouquets. Plants bloom early spring to June, but first flowers may appear as early as November in mild areas. Lower, more compact varieties are 'Little Gem', 4–6 in. tall; 'Purity', 6–12 in. tall, wide spreading; 'Snowflake', 4–12 in. tall, 1½–3 ft. wide. 'Snowflake' differs from species in its broader, more leathery leaves, larger flowers in larger clusters on shorter stems; it is extremely showy in spring and blooms sporadically all year in milder areas.

I. umbellata. GLOBE CANDYTUFT. Annual. Bushy plants 12–15 in. high. Lance-shaped leaves to 3½ in. long. Flowers in pink, rose, carmine, crimson, salmon, lilac, and white. Dwarf strains 'Dwarf Fairy' and 'Magic Carpet' grow to 6 in. tall, in the same colors.

ICE PLANT

Aizoaceae

SUCCULENT PERENNIALS, SUBSHRUBS, OR ANNUALS

☀ ZONES VARY

☼ FULL SUN

● WATER ENOUGH TO MAINTAIN GROWTH

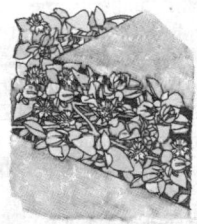

Delosperma

Once conveniently lumped together as *Mesembryanthemum*, but now classified under several new names. Where hardy, they are among the most useful and colorful ground covers. In cold-winter climates, use them as house plants, in summer-flowering window boxes, or in hanging baskets. Feed lightly when fall rains begin, again after bloom. All take most soils; won't take foot traffic.

Aptenia. Ground covers with small red flowers. Brightest green foliage in class.

Carpobrotus. Coarse, sturdy ice plants of beach and highway plantings.

Cephalophyllum. Slow spreading, hardy, showy flowers.

Delosperma. Good ground cover and bank cover.

Dorotheanthus. Annuals for summer bloom.

Drosanthemum. Profuse pink or purple flowers, useful on steep banks.

Lampranthus. Large flowering, brilliantly colorful as ground cover, in rock gardens.

Malephora. Ground covers that have good-looking foliage, long bloom season.

Mesembryanthemum. Annuals of little ornamental value are the only plants left here. One is sometimes seen as naturalized roadside planting in California.

Oscularia. Dainty form, fragrance.

ILEX

HOLLY

Aquifoliaceae

EVERGREEN SHRUBS OR TREES

☀ ZONES VARY BY SPECIES

☼ ☽ FULL SUN TO PARTIAL SHADE

● REGULAR WATER

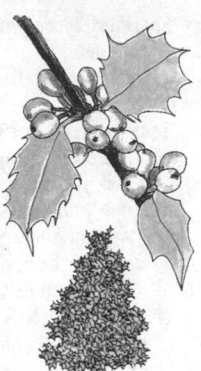

Ilex aquifolium

English holly is most familiar, but other species are becoming popular, especially in warmer, drier parts of the West. Hollies range from foot-high dwarfs to 50-ft. trees. Leaves may be tiny or large, toothed or smooth, green or variegated. Plants sold as Dutch holly are simply hollies without marginal spines. Berries may be red, orange, yellow, or black. Deciduous types of holly are rarely grown in the West.

Most holly plants are either male or female, and in general, both plants must be present for female to bear fruit. There are exceptions: some female holly plants will set fruit without pollination, and hormone sprays may induce berry set on female flowers. Safest way to get berries is to have plants of both sexes, or to graft male branch onto female plant. Male plants will have no berries.

Holly prefers rich, slightly acid, good garden soil with good drainage. (See descriptions for exceptions.) Add thick mulch rather than cultivating around plant. Attractive background plant, useful as barrier.

Scale and mealybugs can attack in all holly-growing areas. Holly bud moth and leaf miner need attention on English holly in Northwest. Two sprays a year generally give good control. Use an oil in late March for scale and bud moth; spray with systemics or malathion during May for leaf miner. Birds will eat fruit. Diseases rarely a problem to the home gardener.

I. altaclarensis 'Wilsonii' (I. wilsonii). WILSON HOLLY. Shrub or tree. Zones 3–24. Hybrid between English holly and a Canary Island species. One of best hollies, especially in warmer regions. Takes wind, almost any soil. Usually a 6–8-ft. shrub, but easily grown as 15–20-ft. single-stemmed tree. Evenly spine-toothed leaves to 5 in. long, 3 in. wide; thick, leathery, rich green. Heavy producer of bright red berries. Use as standard tree, espalier, shrub, screen, clipped hedge.

I. aquifolium. ENGLISH HOLLY, CHRISTMAS HOLLY. Shrub or tree. Zones 4–9, 12–24; at its best in Zones 4–6, 15–17. Occasionally seen in sheltered locations in colder climates. Native to southern and central Europe, British Isles. Slow growth to 40 ft., usually much less. Highly variable in leaf shape, color, and degree of spininess. Note that male plants do not have berries; females may or may not. Some varieties produce infertile berries without a pollinator, but these berries are usually small, slow to develop, and quick to drop. English holly needs protection from sun in hot, dry areas and requires soil conditioning where soils are alkaline. Resistant to oak root fungus. Best-known varieties include

'Angustifolia'. Grows as compact, narrow pyramid. Spiny leaves are ½ in. wide, 1½ in. long. Small, brilliant red berries.

'Balkans'. Hardiest of English hollies, this is grown from seed collected in the Balkan mountains. Upright plants with smooth, dark green leaves. Male and female (fruiting) forms are available.

'Big Bull'. Very ornamental male with large, nearly smooth-edged leaves.

'Boulder Creek'. Typical English holly with large leaves. Brilliant red berries.

'Ciliata Major'. Vigorous, erect holly with purple bark on young shoots. Large, olive-tinged dark green leaves are flat, long spined, with high gloss. Good berry producer.

'Ferox'. HEDGEHOG, PORCUPINE HOLLY. Male with sterile pollen. Twisted, fiercely spined leaves give it its common names.

'Fertilis'. Sets light crop of seedless berries without pollination.

'Gold Coast'. Male selection grown for bright yellow edging on its leaves. Dense growth to 6–8 ft.

'Little Bull'. Very ornamental compact male with small leaves.

'San Gabriel'. Bears seedless berries without pollination.

▶

'Sparkler'. Strong, upright grower. Heavy crop of glistening red berries at an early age.

'Teufel's Deluxe'. Exceptionally dark green leaves. Large, early-ripening red berries.

'Teufel's Zero'. Upright with long slender branches, weeping. Dark red berries ripen early. Unusually hardy.

'Van Tol'. Glossy green leaves. Early to mature. Large dark red berries.

Varieties with variegated leaves are also sold. Types with silver-edged leaves: 'Argenteo-marginata', 'Silvery', 'Silver Queen' (male), 'Silver King'. Silver-centered leaves: 'Argentea-mediopicta', 'Silver Star', 'Silver Milkmaid'. Gold-edged leaves: 'Aureo-marginata', 'Golden Queen' (male), 'Lily Gold'. Gold-centered leaves: 'Golden Milkmaid', 'Pinto'.

I. aquipernyi. Shrub or small tree. Zones 4–9, 14–24. Hybrid between *I. aquifolium* and *I. pernyi*. Varieties 'Brilliant' and 'San Jose' grow 8–10 ft. (possibly to 20 ft.), with cone-shaped habit and dense foliage. Leaves short stalked, densely set on branches, twice as large as those of *I. pernyi,* with few but very pronounced teeth. Heavy crop of red berries without pollination. Resistant to oak root fungus.

I. cornuta. CHINESE HOLLY. Shrub or small tree. Zones 4–24; best in Zones 8, 9, 14–16, 18–21. Needs long warm season to set fruit. Give it east or north exposure in desert climates. Dense or open growth to 10 ft. Typical leaves glossy, leathery, nearly rectangular, with spines at the 4 corners and at tip. Berries exceptionally large, bright red, long lasting. Great variation among varieties in fruit set, leaf form, spininess. In following list, all bear fruit without pollinator except those noted:

'Berries Jubilee'. Dwarf, dome-shaped plant with large leaves and heavy crop of large, bright red berries. Leaves larger, spinier than those of 'Burfordii', on much smaller plant.

'Burfordii'. BURFORD HOLLY. Widely planted in low-elevation California. Leaves nearly spineless, cupped downward. Useful as espalier.

'Carissa'. Extremely dwarf, dense grower with small leaves; smaller than 'Rotunda'. Use for small containers, low hedge. No berries.

'Dazzler'. Compact, upright growth. Glossy leaves have a few stout spines along wavy margins. Loaded with berries.

'Dwarf Burford' ('Burfordii Nana'). Resembles 'Burfordii' but is much smaller; 5-year-old plants not likely to exceed 1½ ft. in height, spread. Small (1½-in.), light green, spineless leaves, densely set.

'Femina'. Very spiny leaves. Good berry producer.

'Rotunda'. DWARF CHINESE HOLLY. Compact low grower. A 6-year-old may be 1½ ft. high and as wide. Does not produce berries. A few stout spines and rolled leaf margins between spines make medium light green leaves nearly rectangular.

'Willowleaf'. Large shrub or small tree with dense, spreading growth pattern. Long, narrow, dark green leaves. Good crop of dark red berries.

I. crenata. JAPANESE HOLLY. Shrub. Zones 2–9, 14–24. Looks more like a boxwood than a holly. Dense, erect, usually to 3–4 ft., sometimes to 20 ft. Narrow, fine-toothed leaves, ½–¾ in. long. Berries are black. Extremely hardy and useful where winter cold limits choice of polished evergreens for hedges, edgings. All grow best in slightly acid soil. Sun or shade. Varieties sold are

'Compacta'. Dense, compact form useful for untrimmed hedge.

'Convexa' (often sold as *I. c. bullata*). Compact and rounded shrub to 4–6 ft.; broader than tall. Leaves are ½ in. long, roundish with edges cupped downward. Handsome clipped or unclipped.

'Glory'. Small, dense grower; round bush with tiny leaves. Male plant (no fruit).

'Green Island'. Low and spreading, to 2 ft. high.

'Green Thumb'. Compact, upright to 20 in. Deep green leaves.

'Helleri'. Dwarf to 1 ft. high, 2 ft. wide.

'Hetzii'. Similar to 'Convexa', with larger leaves, more vigorous growth.

'Mariesii'. Smallest and slowest growing of Japanese hollies. Only 8 in. high in 10 years.

'Northern Beauty'. Resembles 'Hetzii' but is more compact.

I. dimorphophylla. OKINAWAN HOLLY. Shrub. Zones 16, 17, 19–24. Dwarf tropical evergreen holly with leaves less than 1 in. long, closely set with short spines. Red berries. Tender to frost.

I. 'Ebony Magic'. Shrub. Zones 4–9, 12–24. Hybrid evergreen holly of pyramidal form to 8–10 ft., with blackish purple bark and large orange-red berries.

I. glabra. INKBERRY. Shrub. Zones 3–24. Evergreen shrub with thick, dark green spineless leaves and black berries. Grows to 10 ft. The dwarf form 'Compacta', more widely available, grows to 4 ft., but can be sheared as a 2-ft. hedge.

I. latifolia. Tree. Zones 4–7, 15–17, 20–24. Native to China, Japan. Slow-growing, stout-branched tree to 50–60 ft. Largest leaves of all hollies: 6–8 in. long, dull dark green, thick and leathery, fine toothed. Large, dull red berries in large clusters.

I. meserveae. Shrubs. Zones 3–24. Hybrids between *I. aquifolium* and species from northern Japan. Apparently the hardiest of hollies that have true holly look. Dense, bushy plants 6–7 ft. tall with purple stems and spiny, blue-green, glossy leaves. Female forms include 'Blue Angel', 'Blue Girl', and 'Blue Princess'; male pollinators are 'Blue Boy' and 'Blue Prince'. 'China Boy' (male) and 'China Girl' (female) are taller (to 10 ft.).

I. 'Nellie Stevens'. Shrub. Zones 4–9, 14–24. Hybrid between *I. cornuta* and *I. aquifolium*. Leaves suggest both parents. Showy berries. Large, fast growing; can be trained as tree.

I. opaca. AMERICAN HOLLY. Tree. Zones 2–9, 15, 16, 19–23. Native to eastern United States. Slow-growing, pyramidal or round-headed tree to 50 ft. Leaves 2–4 in. long, dull or glossy green with spiny margins. Berries red, not as numerous as on *I. aquifolium.* Resistant to oak root fungus. Some of the many varieties are occasionally available in the West. They include 'Brilliantissima', 'East Palatka', 'Howard', 'Manig', 'Mrs. Sarver', 'Old Heavy Berry', 'Rosalind Sarver'.

I. pernyi. Shrub or small tree. Zones 4–9, 14–24. Slow growth to 20–30 ft. Glossy, square-based leaves closely packed against branchlets; leaves are 1–2 in. long, with one to three spines on each side. Red berries are set tightly against stem.

I. 'San Jose Hybrid'. Shrub or small tree. Zones 4–9, 14–24. Probably a variety of *I. koehneana* (hybrid between *I. aquifolium* and *I. latifolia*). To 15–20 ft. Resembles *I. altaclarensis* 'Wilsonii', but has somewhat longer, narrower leaves. Growth upright, berry production heavy.

I. vomitoria. YAUPON. Shrub or small tree. Zones 3–9, 11–24. Native to southeastern United States. Tolerates extremely alkaline soils better than other hollies. Large shrub or small tree to 15–20 ft. Often sheared into columnar form or grown as standard. Narrow, inch-long, dark green leaves. Tiny scarlet berries borne in profusion without pollinator. The following varieties are available:

'Nana'. DWARF YAUPON. Low shrub. Compact to 1½ ft. high and twice as wide. Refined, attractive. Formal when sheared.

'Pendula'. Weeping branches show to best effect when plant is trained as standard.

'Pride of Houston'. Large shrub or small tree, upright, freely branching. Use as screen or hedge.

'Stokes' ('Stokes Dwarf'). Dark green leaves, close set, compact. Smaller growing than 'Nana'.

IMMORTELLE. See XERANTHEMUM annuum   **p. 525**

IMPATIENS

BALSAM, TOUCH-ME-NOT, SNAPWEED

Balsaminaceae

PERENNIALS AND SUMMER ANNUALS

ZONES VARY BY SPECIES

☼ ◐ ● EXPOSURE NEEDS VARY BY SPECIES

● DON'T LET SOIL DRY OUT

Impatiens wallerana

Annuals grow best in sun, perennials in partial shade in all but coastal areas. Ripe seed capsules burst open when touched lightly and scatter seeds explosively.

I. balsamina. BALSAM. Summer annual. All zones. Erect, branching, 8–30 in. tall. Leaves 1½–6 in. long, sharply pointed, deeply toothed. Flowers large, spurred, borne among leaves along main stem and branches. Colors plain or variegated, in white, pink, rose, lilac, red. Compact, bushy, double camellia-flowered forms are most frequently used. Sow seeds in early spring; set out plants after frost in full sun (light shade in hot areas).

I. holstii. See I. wallerana

I. New Guinea hybrids. Perennials grown as summer annuals. All zones. A varied group of striking plants developed from number of species native to New Guinea, especially *I. hawkeri*. Plants can be upright or spreading; they usually have large leaves, often variegated with cream or red. Flowers are usually large (though not profuse); colors include lavender, purple, pink, red, orange. Best used as pot plants. Give ample fertilizer; need somewhat more light than conventional bedding impatiens. Many named kinds, ranging from spreading 8 in. to erect 2 ft. 'Sweet Sue' and 'Tango', with bronzed foliage and bright orange, 2–3-in. flowers, can be grown from seed, as can Spectra hybrids.

I. oliveri (I. sodenii). POOR MAN'S RHODODENDRON. Perennial. Zones 15–17, 21–24; elsewhere as greenhouse or indoor/outdoor container plant. Shrubby to 4–8 ft. tall, up to 10 ft. wide. Bears many slender-spurred lilac, pale lavender, or pinkish flowers 2¼ in. across. Glossy dark green leaves to 8 in. long in whorls along stems. Blooms in partial or deep shade. Along coast grows in full sun, takes sea breezes, salt spray. Inland, frosts kill it to ground; regrows in spring.

AMERICA'S NUMBER-ONE BEDDING PLANT

Impatiens wallerana does everything well and asks little. It's marvelously adaptable in shaded or semishaded landscapes; blooms prolifically from spring to late fall in beds, borders, pots, or hanging baskets.

I. sultanii. See I. wallerana

I. wallerana. BUSY LIZZIE. Perennial grown as summer annual. All zones. Includes plants formerly known as *I. holstii* and *I. sultanii*. Rapid, vigorous growth; tall varieties to 2 ft.; dwarf, 4–12 in. Dark green, glossy, narrow, 1–3-in.-long leaves on pale green, juicy stems. Flowers 1–2 in. wide, in scarlet, pink, rose, violet, orange, or white.

Useful for producing bright flowers for many months with begonias, fatsia, ferns, fuchsias, hydrangeas. Grow from seed, cuttings, or buy plants in six-packs or pots.

Space dwarf varieties 6 in. apart, big ones 12 in. apart. The need for shade varies: 2 hours a day on coast, 6 in inland valleys, 8 to 10 in mountains and deserts. Feed often enough to keep plants vigorous, plump, sassy. If plants overgrow, cut them back as close as 6 in.—it's a tonic. New growth emerges in a few days; flowers cover it in 2 weeks.

Strains exist in bewildering variety. Single-flowered kinds are best for massing or bedding; they nearly cover themselves with flowers. Doubles have attractive flowers like little rosebuds, but they don't match singles for mass show; use doubles in pots.

IMPERATA cylindrica 'Rubra' ('Red Baron')

JAPANESE BLOOD GRASS

Poaceae (Gramineae)

PERENNIAL

☀ ❁ ZONES 4–24

☀ ❁ SUN OR PARTIAL SHADE

💧 REGULAR WATER

Imperata cylindrica
'Rubra'

Clumping grass with erect stems 1–2 ft. tall, the top half rich blood red. Striking in borders, especially where sun can shine through blades. Completely dormant in winter. Spreads by underground runners.

INCARVILLEA delavayi

Bignoniaceae

PERENNIAL

☀ ALL ZONES

☀ ❁ SUN OR LIGHT SHADE

💧 REGULAR WATER

Incarvillea delavayi

Fleshy roots. Basal leaves 1 ft. long, divided into toothed leaflets. Stems to 3 ft., topped with clusters of 2 to 12 trumpet-shaped flowers 3 in. long and wide; rosy purple outside, yellow and purple inside. Blooms May–July.

Needs deep, porous soil; roots rot in winter in waterlogged soils. In extremely cold climates, lift and store roots as you would dahlias. Cover roots with soil; do not let them dry out.

IOCHROMA cyaneum

Solanaceae

EVERGREEN SHRUB

☀ ZONES 16, 17, 19–24

☀ BEST IN FULL SUN

💧 💧 GIVE PLENTY OF WATER

Iochroma cyaneum

To 8 ft. or more. Dull dark green, oval to lance-shaped leaves, 5–6 in. long. Clusters of purplish blue, tubular, drooping, 2-in.-long flowers in summer; flower color of seedlings may vary to purplish rose or pink. Buy plants in bloom to get color you want. Fast-growing, soft-wooded shrub that looks best espaliered or tied up against wall. Prune it hard after bloom; protect from hard frosts. Control measuring worms with insecticide. Sometimes called *I. lanceolatum, I. purpureum, I. tubulosum.*

IPHEION uniflorum (Brodiaea uniflora, Triteleia uniflora)

SPRING STAR FLOWER

Amaryllidaceae

BULB

☀ ZONES 4–24

☀ ❁ SUN OR PARTIAL SHADE

💧 ❁ NOT FUSSY ABOUT WATER

Ipheion uniflorum

Native to Argentina. Flattish, bluish green leaves that smell like onions when bruised. Spring flowers 1½ in. across, broadly star shaped, pale to deep blue, on 6–8-in. stems. Edging, ground cover in semiwild areas, under trees, large shrubs.

Plant in fall in any soil. Easy to grow; will persist and multiply for years. 'Wisley Blue' is a good bright blue selection.

IPOMOEA

MORNING GLORY

Convolvulaceae

PERENNIAL OR ANNUAL VINES

✐ ZONES VARY BY SPECIES

☼ FULL SUN

◖ LITTLE WATER ONCE ESTABLISHED

Ipomoea tricolor

Includes many ornamental vines and the sweet potato; does not include wild morning glory. Ipomoeas may self-sow, but they don't spread by underground runners.

I. acuminata (I. leari). BLUE DAWN FLOWER. Perennial. Zones 8, 9, 12–24. Vigorous, rapid growth to 15–30 ft. Leaves dark green; flowers bright blue, fading pink, 3–5 in. across, clustered. Use to cover large banks, walls. Blooms in 1 year from seed; grows from cuttings, divisions, and layering of established plants.

I. alba (Calonyction aculeatum). MOONFLOWER. Perennial vine grown as summer annual, as greenhouse plant in coldest climates. All zones. Fast-growing (20–30 ft. in a season); provides quick summer shade for arbor, trellis, or fence. Effective combined with annual morning glory 'Heavenly Blue'. Luxuriant leaves 3–8 in. long, heart shaped, closely spaced on stems. Flowers fragrant, white (rarely lavender pink), often banded green, 6 in. long and wide. Theoretically flowers open only after sundown, but will stay open on dark, dull days. Seeds are hard; abrade or soak 1–2 days for faster sprouting.

I. batatas. See Sweet Potato

I. nil. MORNING GLORY. Summer annual. All zones. Includes rare large-flowered Imperial Japanese morning glories and a few varieties of common morning glory, including rosy red 'Scarlett O'Hara'. Early Call strain comes in a number of colors and is useful where summers are short. For culture, see *I. tricolor.*

I. quamoclit (Quamoclit pennata). CYPRESS VINE, CARDINAL CLIMBER. Summer annual. All zones. Twines to 20 ft. Leaves 2½–4 in. long, finely divided into slender threads. Flowers are tubes 1½ in. long, flaring at mouth into five-pointed star; they are usually scarlet, rarely white.

I. tricolor. MORNING GLORY. Summer annual. All zones. Flowers showy, funnel shaped to bell-like, single or double, in solid colors of blue, lavender, pink, red, white, usually with throats in contrasting colors; some bicolored, striped. Most morning glories open only in morning, fade in afternoon. Bloom lasts until frost. Large, heart-shaped leaves.

Use on fence, trellis, as ground cover. Or grow in containers—train vine on stakes or wire cylinder or allow it to cascade. For cut flowers, pick stems with buds in various stages of development, place in deep vase. Buds open on consecutive days.

Sow seed in place in full sun after frost. To speed sprouting, notch seed coat with knife or file (some growers sell scarified seed), or soak in warm water for 2 hours. For earlier start, sow seeds indoors in small pots or plant bands. Set out plants 6–8 in. apart.

'Heavenly Blue' morning glory twines to 15 ft. Flowers 4–5 in. across, pure sky blue, yellow throat. A dwarf strain with white markings on the leaves is known as Spice Islands or simply as Variegated. Plants grow 9 in. tall and spill to 1 ft. in width. Colors include red, pink, blue, and bicolors.

IPOMOPSIS

Polemoniaceae

BIENNIALS OR SHORT-LIVED PERENNIALS

✐ ALL ZONES

☼ FULL SUN

◔ NO DRY-SEASON WATERING

Ipomopsis aggregata

Erect single stems, finely divided leaves, and tubular red (or yellow-and-red) flowers. They

are startling in appearance, best massed; individual plants are narrow. Sow seed in spring or early summer for bloom the following year.

I. aggregata (Gilia aggregata). Biennial. Native California to British Columbia, east to Rocky Mountains. To 2½ ft. tall. Flowers are red marked yellow (sometimes pure yellow), an inch or so long; borne in long, narrow clusters. June–September bloom.

I. rubra (Gilia rubra). Biennial or perennial. Native to southern United States. To 6 ft. tall. Flowers red outside, yellow marked red inside. Summer bloom.

IRESINE herbstii

BLOODLEAF

Amaranthaceae

EVERGREEN SHRUB

✐ ZONES 22–24

☼ FULL SUN

◉ REGULAR WATER

Iresine herbstii

Desirable for leaf rather than flower color. Stalked leaves are 1–2 in. long, oval to round, usually notched at tip; may be purplish red with lighter midrib and veins, or green or bronzed with yellowish veins. Leaf display best in summer, fall. Flowers inconspicuous. Good in containers. Except in mildest coastal climates, plant must be wintered indoors or treated as annual. Easy to propagate from cuttings taken in fall and grown for spring and summer display. Similar is *I. lindenii*, with red leaves pointed instead of notched at the ends.

Iridaceae. The large iris family includes many familiar (and unfamiliar) garden bulbs, corms, and fibrous-rooted perennials. Leaves are swordlike or grasslike, often in two opposing rows. Flowers may be simply arranged with six equal segments (crocus, for example) or highly irregular in appearance (as in iris).

IRIS

Iridaceae

BULBS AND RHIZOMES

✐ ALL ZONES, EXCEPT AS NOTED

☼ ◑ ● EXPOSURE NEEDS VARY BY SPECIES

◔ ◉ ◍ WATER NEEDS VARY BY SPECIES

Tall Bearded Iris

A large and remarkably diverse group of from 200 to 300 species, varying in flower color and form, cultural needs, and blooming periods (although the majority flower in spring or early summer). Leaves swordlike or grasslike; flowers showy, complex in structure. The three inner segments are petals, called "standards," and are usually erect or arching but, in some kinds, may flare to horizontal; the three outer segments are petal-like sepals, called "falls," and are at various angles from nearly horizontal to drooping.

Irises grow from bulbs or from rhizomes. In floral detail, there are three categories: bearded (each fall bears a caterpillarlike adornment), beardless (each fall is smooth), and crested (each fall bears a comblike ridge instead of a full beard).

Described here are the irises most available in the West. Tall bearded irises (and other bearded classes) are the most widely sold; many new hybrids are cataloged every year. Iris specialty growers abound. A small number offer various beardless classes and some species. Retail nurseries carry bulbous irises for fall planting; more and more are also selling Pacific Coast irises.

BULBOUS IRISES

Irises that grow from bulbs have beardless flowers. Bulbs become dormant in summer and can be lifted and stored until planting time in fall.

Dutch and Spanish irises. The species that parented this group come from Spain, Portugal, Sicily, and northern Africa. (Dutch irises acquired their name because the hybrid group was developed by Dutch bulb growers.) Flowers come atop slender stems that rise up from rushlike foliage. Standards are narrow and upright; oval to circular falls project downward. Colors include white, mauve, blue, purple, brown, orange, yellow, and bicolor combinations—usually with a yellow blotch on falls. Dutch iris flowers reach 3–4 in. across, on stems 1½–2 ft. tall; these are the irises sold by florists. Bloom period is March–April in warm climates, May–June in colder climates. Spanish irises are similar but have smaller flowers that bloom about 2 weeks after Dutch irises.

Dutch Iris

Plant bulbs 4 in. deep, 3–4 in. apart, in October–November, in full sun. Bulbs are generally hardy, but in coldest climates, mulch in winter. Give ample water during growth. After bloom, let foliage ripen before digging; store bulbs in cool, dry place for no more than 2 months before replanting. Dutch and Spanish irises are good in containers; plant five bulbs in a 5–6 in. pot.

The widely sold 'Wedgwood' is a Dutch hybrid hardy only in Zones 4–24. Large flowers are lavender blue with yellow markings, blooming earlier than others (generally coinciding with 'King Alfred' daffodils). Bulbs are larger than those of average Dutch hybrid. Vigorous foliage is best masked by bushy annuals or perennials that will mature later in the season.

English irises. Zones 1–6, 15–17, 21–24. The species (*I. latifolia*) from which named selections were made is native to the Pyrenees, where it grows in moist meadows. Early botanists first noticed the iris growing in southern England, to which it had been taken by traders. Flowers are similar in structure to Dutch and Spanish irises, but falls are broader and decorated with a hairline stripe of yellow. Colors include bluish purple, wine red, maroon, blue, mauve, white. Bloom time is early summer. Bulbs need cool, moist, acid soil; in fall, plant them 3–4 in. deep, 4 in. apart. Choose a partly shaded location in warm-summer areas, full sun where cool. Dig, store, and replant as for Dutch irises.

Reticulata irises. Bulbs covered by a netted outer covering give the group its name. These are classic rock garden and container plants, the flowers (like small Dutch irises) appearing on 6–8-in. stems in March–April (late January–early February in mild areas). Thin, four-sided blue-green leaves appear after bloom. Available species include *I. reticulata*, with 2–3-in. violet-scented flowers (purple, in the usual forms), and bright yellow–flowered *I. danfordiae*. Pale blue–flowered *I. histrio* (probably hardy only to Zone 6) and large-flowered, blue-and-yellow *I. histrioides* may be carried by some specialists. Far more common are named hybrids such as 'Cantab' (pale blue with orange markings), 'Harmony' (sky blue marked yellow), 'J. S. Dijt' (reddish purple).

Give bulbs well-drained soil and full sun. Plant 3–4 in. deep and as far apart in fall; water as necessary from fall through spring, but keep soil dry during the bulbs' summer dormant period. Dig and divide only when vigor, flower quality deteriorate.

RHIZOMATOUS IRISES

Irises that grow from rhizomes (thickened, modified stems) may have bearded, beardless, or crested flowers; among this rhizomatous group are the most widely grown types. Leaves are swordlike, overlapping each other to form flat fans of foliage.

Bearded irises. The most widely grown irises fall into the bearded group. Many species, varieties, and years of hybridizing have produced a vast array of beautiful hybrids. All have upright standards, flaring to pendant falls that have characteristic epaulettelike beards. Tall bearded irises are the most familiar of these, but they represent just one subdivision of the entire group.

Bearded irises need good drainage. They'll grow in soils from sandy to claylike, but in clay soils plant in raised beds or on ridges to assure drainage, avoid rhizome rot. Plant in full sun in cool climates; in hottest regions, they'll accept light shade during the afternoon. July–October is best planting period; plant during July–August in cold-winter zones, in September–October where summer temperatures are high. In mild coastal regions, plant throughout this period. Space rhizomes 1–2 ft. apart; set with tops just beneath soil surface, spreading roots well. Growth proceeds from the leafy end of rhizome, so point that end in direction you want growth initially to occur. For quick show, plant three rhizomes 1 ft. apart. Water to settle soil, start growth. Thereafter, water judiciously until new growth shows plants have rooted; then water regularly until fall rains or frosts arrive. If weather turns hot, shade newly planted rhizomes to prevent sunscald, possible rot. Where winters are severe, mulch new plantings to prevent heaving from alternate freezing, thawing.

From the time growth starts in late winter or early spring, water regularly until about 6 weeks after flowers fade; increases and buds for next year's flowers form during postbloom period. During summer, plants need less water: every other week in warm climates, monthly where summers are cool. For best performance, feed plants with moderate-nitrogen commercial fertilizer as growth begins in spring, then after bloom has finished. In cool, moist spring, leaf spot may disfigure foliage; use appropriate fungicide at first sign of infection. In fall (early to late, depending on climate) remove old and dry leaves.

Clumps become overcrowded after 3–4 years; quantity and quality of bloom decrease. Lift and divide crowded clumps at best planting time for your area. Save large rhizomes with healthy leaves, discard old and leafless rhizomes from clump's center. Break rhizomes apart or use a sharp knife to separate. Trim leaves, roots to about 6 in., let cut ends heal for several hours to a day before replanting. If replanting in the same soil, amend it with plenty of organic matter.

> ## DIRECTING BEARDED IRIS
> Rhizomes grow outward from the end with leaves; when planting, point that end in direction you want growth to take. For quick show, plant three rhizomes 1 ft. apart, two with growing ends pointed outward, the third aimed to grow into the space between them. On slopes, set rhizomes with growing end facing uphill.

Dwarf and median irises. These irises generally have flowers shaped like the familiar tall beardeds, but flower size, plant size, and stature are smaller. Median iris is a collective term for the categories standard dwarf, intermediate and border bearded, and miniature tall bearded.

Miniature dwarf bearded irises. Grow to 8 in. tall; flowers large for size of plant. Earliest to bloom of bearded irises (about 6 weeks before main show of tall beardeds). Hardy, need winter chill. Plants multiply quickly. Shallow root systems need moisture and feeding.

Standard dwarf bearded irises. Range 8–15 in. tall; flowers and plants are larger than miniature dwarfs, profuse bloom. Easier to grow than miniature dwarfs in western gardens but perform best with some winter chill.

Intermediate bearded irises. Grow 15–28 in., bear flowers 3–5 in. across. Flower later than dwarfs but 1–3 weeks before tall bearded irises. Most are hybrids between standard dwarfs and tall bearded varieties, resemble larger standard dwarfs rather than border beardeds. Some give second bloom in fall.

Border bearded irises. Grow 15–28 in. tall—proportionately smaller versions of tall beardeds in the same great range of colors and patterns. Bloom period is same as for tall bearded. ▶

Miniature tall bearded irises. Grow 15–28 in. high and flower with tall beardeds. But small flowers (2–3 in. wide), narrower foliage give them appearance of tall bearded irises reduced in every proportion. Good for cutting and arrangements—hence their original name, table irises.

Tall bearded irises. Among choicest perennials for borders, massing, cutting. Adapted in all climates, easy to grow. Flower in midspring, on branching stems 2½–4 ft. high. All colors but pure red and green; patterns of two colors or more, blends produce infinite variety. Countless named selections available. Modern hybrids often with flowers elaborately ruffled, fringed.

Remontant (or reblooming) tall bearded irises flower in mid- to late summer, fall, or winter, depending on variety and climate; some are nearly everblooming in mild climates. Plants need fertilizer, summer watering for best performance. Specialists' catalogs offer increasing numbers of remontant tall beardeds.

Aril and arilbred irises. The aril species and interspecies hybrids (characterized by an "aril," or collar, on their seeds) offer strange and often remarkably beautiful flowers on unattractive plants. Exacting cultural requirements. Most species come from semidesert areas of the Near East and central Asia; plants need limy soil, perfect drainage, full sun, and no summer water. Two main groups are *Oncocyclus,* in which a number of species have huge, nearly globular flowers in lavender, gray, silver, maroon, and gold, often intricately veined and stippled with deeper hues; and *Regelias,* which have smaller, narrower-petaled flowers, veined or unmarked. *Oncocyclus* are the most difficult to grow; somewhat easier are *Regelias* and hybrids between the two known as *Oncogelias.*

Arilbreds—hybrids between the arils and bearded irises—offer some of the arils' exotic beauty on plants nearly as easy to grow as tall beardeds, given well-drained, neutral to alkaline soil. Amount of aril ancestry can determine ease of culture: hybrids containing half aril ancestry or more usually are more demanding than those of one-quarter or three-eighths aril ancestry. Specialists' catalogs often state hybrid ancestries for this reason.

Beardless irises. Flowers in this group have smooth, "beardless" falls but otherwise differ considerably in appearance from one group or species to another. Rhizomes have fibrous roots (unlike fleshy roots of bearded types); most prefer or demand more moisture than bearded irises. Many can perform well from crowded clumps but will eventually need division. Timing varies; all should be dug and replanted quickly, keeping roots moist while plants are out of the ground.

Five hybrid groups contain the most widely sold beardless irises. Also described are three individual species (and their named selections) that have a place in western gardens.

Japanese irises. Zones 1–10, 14–24. Derived solely from *I. ensata* (formerly *I. kaempferi*), these irises feature sumptuous blossoms 4–12 in. across on slender stems to 4 ft. high. Flower shape is essentially flat. "Single" types have three broad falls and much-reduced standards, giving triangular flower outline; "double" blossoms have standards marked like the falls and about the same size and shape, resulting in circular flower outline. Colors are purple, violet, pink, rose, red, white—often veined or edged in contrasting shade. Plants have graceful narrow, upright leaves with distinct raised midribs.

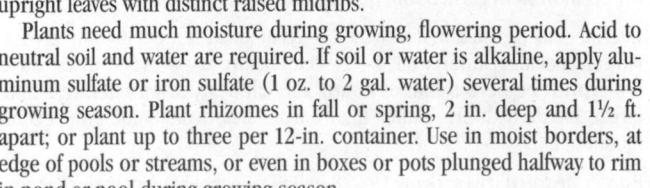

Iris ensata

Plants need much moisture during growing, flowering period. Acid to neutral soil and water are required. If soil or water is alkaline, apply aluminum sulfate or iron sulfate (1 oz. to 2 gal. water) several times during growing season. Plant rhizomes in fall or spring, 2 in. deep and 1½ ft. apart; or plant up to three per 12-in. container. Use in moist borders, at edge of pools or streams, or even in boxes or pots plunged halfway to rim in pond or pool during growing season.

Louisiana irises. Zones 3–24. Approximately four species from the lower Mississippi region and Gulf Coast compose this group of "swamp irises."

Graceful, flattish blossoms on stems 2–5 ft. tall, carried above and among leaves that are long, narrow, and unribbed. The range of flower colors and patterns is extensive—nearly the equal of tall beardeds.

Specialists offer a vast array of named hybrids; some may carry the basic species as well. *I. brevicaulis (I. foliosa)* has blue flowers with flaring segments carried on zigzag stems among the foliage. *I. fulva* has coppery to rusty red (rarely yellow) blossoms with narrow, drooping segments. *I. giganticaerulea* is indeed a "giant blue" (sometimes white) with upright standards and flaring falls; stems may reach 4 ft. or more, with foliage in proportion. *I. hexagona* also comes in blue shades with upright standards, flaring falls. *I. nelsonii,* a natural hybrid population derived from *I. fulva* and *I. giganticaerulea,* resembles the *fulva* parent in flower shape and color (but also including purple and brown tones) and approaches the *giganticaerulea* parent in size.

Plants thrive in well-watered, rich garden soil as well as at pond margins; soil and water should be neutral to acid. Locate in full sun where summer is cool to mild; choose light afternoon shade where summer heat is intense. Plant in late summer; set rhizomes 1 in. deep, 1½–2 ft. apart. Mulch for winter where ground freezes.

Pacific Coast irises. Zones 4–24. Eleven species native to Pacific Coast states constitute a homogeneous group within the genus *Iris.* From several species, breeders have developed hybrids in a broad range of colors and patterns; flowers may be white, blue shades, pink, copper, brown, maroon, violet—many with elaborate veining or patterning. Foliage is narrow, clumps are like coarse grass. Slender flower stems grow 8 in.–2 ft., depending on variety.

Best conditions are sun to light shade, well-drained soil, moderate to scant water in summer. Intense heat coupled with water and poor drainage can be fatal; in clay soil, grow in raised beds in organically amended soil. Plant from containers any time, though spring, fall are best. Timing is critical in digging and replanting. Best moment is when new roots are starting to form (scrape away soil at plant base to check); this ranges from early fall in colder regions to midwinter in mild-winter areas.

Several species prominent in the ancestry of hybrids are sold by specialists. *I. douglasiana* is native to California coast from Santa Barbara north into Oregon. Evergreen leaves 1½–2 ft. long; stems 1–2 ft., sometimes branched, with flowers from purple through blue shades to white, cream. Tolerates less-than-perfect conditions. *I. innominata* comes from northwestern California and southwestern Oregon. Evergreen leaves; 8–12-in. stems bear flowers in yellow, orange, lavender, purple, blended brown, many attractively veined. Best in mild-summer regions, woodland or rock garden planting. *I. tenax* from Washington and Oregon makes grassy clumps of 12-in. deciduous leaves. Flowers may be white, blue, purple, pink, cream, often veined in purple or brown. Best in regions with mild summer, some winter chill.

Siberian irises. Zones 1–10, 14–23. The most widely sold members of this group are named hybrids derived from *I. sibirica* and *I. sanguinea* (formerly *I. orientalis*). Clumps of narrow, almost grasslike leaves (deciduous in winter) produce slender stems up to 4 ft. (depending on variety), each bearing 2–5 blossoms with upright standards and flaring to drooping falls. Colors include white and shades of blue, lavender, purple, wine, pink, and light yellow.

Give plants full sun (partial or dappled shade where summer is hot), neutral to acid soil. Set rhizomes 1–2 in. deep, 1–2 ft. apart. In cold-winter regions, plant in early spring or late summer; in milder regions, plant in autumn. Water liberally from onset of growth until several weeks after bloom. Divide infrequently—when clumps show hollow centers—at best planting time for your region.

Specialists may offer various Sino-Siberian species. Most feature drooping falls, standards erect to flaring. Predominantly yellow colors are found in *I. forrestii* and *I. wilsonii;* predominantly purple to violet flowers occur in *I. chrysographes, I. clarkei,* and *I. delavayi.* These species and their hybrids perform best in Zones 4–6, 15–17, where climate is moist and relatively mild. Give plants good, acid soil, regular watering. Interesting hybrids between these species and Pacific Coast irises are called Cal-Sibes;

flowers resemble the Siberian parents but have expanded color range. Garden needs are the same as for Sino-Siberian types.

Spuria irises. In flower form, the spurias resemble Dutch irises. Older members of this group had primarily yellow or white-and-yellow blossoms; *I. orientalis* (universally known as *I. ochroleuca*) has naturalized in many parts of the West, its 3–5-ft. stems bearing white flowers with yellow fall blotches. Modern hybrids show a great color range: blue, lavender, gray, orchid, tan, bronze, brown, purple, earthy red, and near black—often with a prominent yellow spot on the falls. Flowers are held closely against 3–6-ft. stems, rising above handsome clumps of narrow, dark green leaves. Flowering starts during latter part of tall bearded bloom, continues for several weeks beyond. Plant rhizomes in late summer or early fall in rich, neutral to slightly alkaline soil where they'll get full sun to partial light shade. Set rhizomes 1 in. deep, 1½–2 ft. apart. Plants need ample moisture from onset of growth through bloom period but little moisture during summer. Divide clumps infrequently (not an easy task); mulch clumps for winter where temperatures reach –20°F or lower.

I. foetidissima. GLADWIN IRIS. Glossy evergreen leaves to 2 ft. make handsome foliage clumps. Stems 1½–2 ft. tall bear subtly attractive flowers in blue gray and dull tan; specialists may offer color variants in soft yellow, lavender blue, as well as a form with white-variegated leaves. Real attraction is large seed capsules that open in fall to show numerous round, orange-scarlet seeds; cut stems with seed capsules useful in arrangements. Grow in sun to shade in cool-summer regions, light or partial shade to full shade elsewhere. Extremely tolerant of aridity. Native to Europe.

I. pseudacorus. YELLOW FLAG. Impressive foliage plant; under best conditions, upright leaves may reach 5 ft. tall. Flower stems grow 4–7 ft. (depending on culture), bear bright yellow flowers 3–4 in. across. Selected forms offer ivory and lighter yellow flowers, variegated foliage, and plants with shorter and taller leaves. Plant in sun to light shade. Needs acid soil and more than average moisture; thrives in shallow water. Native to Europe but now found worldwide in temperate regions; seeds float, aiding plant's dispersal.

Several hybrids are excellent foliage plants with distinctive blossoms. All prefer ample water (but not pond conditions), sun to light shade. 'Holden Clough' perhaps has *I. foetidissima* as the other parent. Flowers, 3–4 in. across, are soft tan heavily netted with maroon veins; stems grow to 4 ft.; leaves reach 4–5 ft. but tips arch over. Two of its seedlings are similar but larger. 'Phil Edinger' grows to 4½ ft. with arching foliage; 4–5-in. flowers are brass colored, heavily veined in brown. 'Roy Davidson' is similar but flowers are dark yellow with fine brown veining and maroon thumbprint on falls.

I. unguicularis (I. stylosa). WINTER IRIS. Zones 4–24. Dense clumps of narrow, dark green leaves. Depending on variety and mildness of winter, flowers appear from November to March. Typical form has lavender blue blossoms elevated on 6–9-in. tubes that serve as stems. Named selections vary in flower color (lighter and darker lavender, orchid pink, white) and coarseness and length of foliage. Plants need neutral to acid soil, heat, and scant water during summer. In Zones 4–7, grow against sunny wall or house foundation to increase summer heat and to lessen winter cold. Divide overcrowded clumps in early fall (mild regions) or in late winter after flowering (in colder zones). To reveal flowers (usually partly concealed by foliage), cut back tallest leaves in September. Slugs attracted to flowers. Native to Greece, the Near East, northern Africa.

Crested irises. Botanically placed with beardless irises, they represent a transition between beardless and bearded: each fall bears a narrow, comblike crest where a beard would be in bearded sorts. Slugs, snails are especially attracted to foliage, flowers. Several tender species and hybrids form bamboolike stems carrying foliage fans aloft; flower stems to 2 ft. are widely branched, orchidlike sprays of fringed flowers in lavender to white with orange crests. These include *I. confusa, I. japonica, I. wattii,* and hybrids such as 'Nada' and 'Darjeeling'. Grow in sun where summer is cool, light shade elsewhere; plant in organically enriched soil. Regular water during growth. Reliable outdoors in Zones 17, 23, 24; in other zones, grow in containers and move to shelter over winter.

I. cristata. Zones 3–7, 15–17; hardy to –10°F. Leaves 4–6 in. long, ½ in. wide; slender, greenish rhizomes spread freely. Flowers white, lavender, or light blue with golden crests. Give light shade, organically enriched soil, regular water. Divide just after bloom or in fall after leaves die down.

I. tectorum. ROOF IRIS. Foliage fans to 12 in. tall look like bearded irises, but leaves are ribbed and glossy. Flowers suggest an informal bearded iris with fringed petals and crests in place of beards. Colors are violet blue with white crests, white with yellow crests; standards are upright at first, open out to horizontal as flower matures. Give plants organically enriched soil, light shade, regular water. Short lived in regions of hot, dry summers. Native to Japan where it is planted on cottage roofs. Its hybrid with a bearded iris, 'Paltec', will grow with bearded irises. Height is about 12 in., the lavender flowers suggesting a bearded iris with beards superimposed on crests.

ISOPOGON formosus

ROSE CONE FLOWER

Proteaceae

EVERGREEN SHRUB

❄ ZONES 15–24

☼ ◑ SUN OR LIGHT SHADE

💧 SOME SUMMER WATER

Isopogon formosus

Slender, erect shrub to 9 ft.; keep lower and broader by tip-pinching young plants. Stems densely clothed with finely divided leaves and topped by dense 2½-in. clusters of long, slender rosy purple flowers in late winter or spring. They keep well when cut, and cutting in bloom stimulates denser growth. Like most proteas, this shrub cannot tolerate high phosphorus level and should be fertilized lightly with nitrogen. Avoid watering when weather is hot.

ITEA ilicifolia

HOLLYLEAF SWEETSPIRE

Saxifragaceae

EVERGREEN SHRUB OR SMALL TREE

❄ ZONES 4–24

☼ ◑ TAKES SUN ON COAST; PART SHADE INLAND

💧 REGULAR WATER

Usually graceful, open, arching shrub, 6–10 ft. tall, rarely to 18 ft. Leaves glossy, dark green, oval, 4 in. long, spiny toothed. Small, greenish white, lightly fragrant flowers in nodding or drooping narrow clusters to 1 ft. long. Fall bloom.

Itea ilicifolia

Blooms sparsely where winters are mild. Inland, must have partial shade. Not a striking plant, but extremely graceful. Needs good soil. Good near pools or waterfalls, as espalier against dark wood or stone backgrounds. Good informal screen.

IXIA

AFRICAN CORN LILY
Iridaceae
CORMS
☘ ZONES 5–24
☼ FULL SUN
◊ NO DRY-SEASON WATER ONCE ESTABLISHED

Ixia maculata

Garden kinds are hybrids of several South African species, particularly *I. maculata*. Swordlike leaves, wiry stems 18–20 in. long, topped in May–June with spikelike clusters of 1–2-in., cup-shaped flowers in cream, yellow, red, orange, pink, all with dark centers. Long-lasting when cut. In mild areas, plant corms 3 in. deep in early fall; in Zones 5, 6, delay planting until after November 1. Set corms 4 in. deep. Apply protective mulch. Can be left in ground several seasons; when crowded, lift in summer, replant in fall. In mild climates, plants reseed freely and are quite drought tolerant. In coldest areas, grow in pots like freesias; plant 6–8 corms 1 in. deep in 5-in. pot. Keep cool after bringing indoors—not over 55°F night temperature.

IXIOLIRION tataricum (I. montanum)

Amaryllidaceae
BULB
☘ ZONES 5–24
☼ FULL SUN
◊ REGULAR WATER

Ixiolirion tataricum

Native to central Asia. Narrow, greenish gray leaves. Wiry, 12–16-in.-high stems bear loose clusters of violet blue, trumpet-shaped, 1½-in. flowers in late May–June. Plant in fall; set bulbs 3 in. deep, 6 in. apart. In cold areas, plant in warm, sheltered location, and mulch to protect leaves from severe frost in spring.

JACARANDA mimosifolia

JACARANDA
Bignoniaceae
DECIDUOUS TO SEMIEVERGREEN TREE
☘ ZONES 12, 13, 15–24
☼ FULL SUN
◊ INFREQUENT WATER

Jacaranda mimosifolia

Native to Brazil. Often sold as *J. acutifolia*. Grows 25–40 ft. high, 15–30 ft. wide. Open, irregular, oval headed; sometimes multitrunked or even shrubby. Finely cut, fernlike leaves, usually dropping in February–March. New leaves may grow quickly or branches may remain bare until tree flowers—usually in June, but bloom is possible any time from April to September. Blossoms lavender blue, tubular, 2 in. long, in many 8-in.-long clusters. White-flowered 'Alba' is sometimes seen; lusher foliage, longer blooming period, and sparser flowers. All forms have roundish, flat seed capsules, quite decorative in arrangements.

Plant is fairly hardy after it attains some mature, hard wood; young plants are tender below 25°F but often come back from freeze to make multistemmed, shrubby plants. Takes wide variety of soils but does best in sandy soil. Often fails to flower in path of ocean winds or where heat is inadequate. Resistant to oak root fungus.

Stake to produce single, sturdy trunk. Prune to shape. Usually branches profusely at 6–10 ft.

> ### JACARANDA'S MANY VIEWING ANGLES
>
> In hillside gardens, jacaranda makes a nice treetop to look down on from above (downslope from a deck, terrace, or window) or to view against the sky (planted on top of a knoll). But it's also widely used in flat valley floor gardens. A truly spectacular tree.

JACOBEAN LILY. See SPREKELIA formosissima	**p. 491**
JACOBINIA carnea. See JUSTICIA carnea	**p. 342**
JACOB'S LADDER. See POLEMONIUM caeruleum	**p. 431**
JADE PLANT. See CRASSULA argentea	**p. 247**
JAMAICA FLOWER, JAMAICA SORREL. See HIBISCUS sabdariffa	**p. 323**
JAPANESE ANGELICA TREE. See ARALIA elata	**p. 161**
JAPANESE ARALIA. See FATSIA japonica	**p. 292**
JAPANESE BLOOD GRASS. See IMPERATA cylindrica	**p. 331**
JAPANESE FELT FERN. See PYRROSIA lingua	**p. 447**
JAPANESE FLOWERING APRICOT, JAPANESE FLOWERING PLUM. See PRUNUS mume	**p. 443**
JAPANESE LACE FERN. See POLYSTICHUM polyblepharum	**p. 433**
JAPANESE PAGODA TREE. See SOPHORA japonica	**p. 488**
JAPANESE SNOWBALL. See VIBURNUM plicatum plicatum	**p. 519**
JAPANESE SNOWBELL, JAPANESE SNOWDROP TREE. See STYRAX japonicus	**p. 497**
JAPANESE SPURGE. See PACHYSANDRA terminalis	**p. 398**
JAPANESE SWEET SHRUB. See CLETHRA barbinervis	**p. 235**
JAPAN PEPPER. See ZANTHOXYLUM piperitum	**p. 527**

JASMINUM

JASMINE
Oleaceae
EVERGREEN OR DECIDUOUS SHRUBS OR VINES
☘ ZONES VARY BY SPECIES
☼ ☽ FULL SUN OR PARTIAL SHADE
◊ LARGE-LEAFED KINDS NEED WATER THE MOST

Jasminum nitidum

When one thinks of fragrance, jasmine is one of the first plants that comes to mind. Yet not all jasmines are fragrant, and star jasmine, one of the most fragrant plants commonly called jasmine, is not a true jasmine at all (it belongs to the genus *Trachelospermum*). All jasmines thrive in regular garden soil and need frequent pinching and shaping to control growth. Low-growing, shrubby kinds make good hedges.

J. angulare. SOUTH AFRICAN JASMINE. Evergreen vine. Zones 16–24. Leaves have three leaflets. Flowers in threes, white, over 1 in. wide, unscented.

J. floridum. Evergreen or partially evergreen, shrubby, sprawling, or half-climbing shrub. Zones 4–9, 12–24. To 3–4 ft. Leaves divided into three (rarely five) small leaflets, each ½–1½ in. long. Clusters of golden yellow, scentless, ½–¾-in. flowers over a long season in spring, summer, fall.

J. grandiflorum (J. officinale grandiflorum). SPANISH JASMINE. Semievergreen to deciduous vine. Zones 5–9, 12–24. Rapid growth to 10–15 ft. Glossy green leaves with five to seven leaflets, each 2 in. long. Fragrant white flowers, 1½ in. across, in loose clusters. Blooms all summer. Dry flowers stay on plant. Gives open, airy effect along fence tops or rails.

J. humile. ITALIAN JASMINE. Evergreen shrub or vine. Zones 5–10, 12–24. Erect, willowy shoots reach to 20 ft. and arch to make 10-ft. mound. Can be trained as shrub or, planted in a row, clipped as hedge. Light green leaves with three to seven leaflets, each 2 in. long. Clusters of fragrant, bright yellow, ½-in. flowers July–September. *J. h.* 'Revolutum' has larger, dull dark green leaves; flowers 1 in. across, up to 12 per cluster. Side clusters make even larger show.

J. ligustrifolium (J. leratii). PRIVET-LEAVED JASMINE. Evergreen vine. Zones 22–24. To 15 ft., with glossy privetlike leaves and white slightly fragrant flowers.

J. magnificum. See J. nitidum

J. mesnyi (J. primulinum). PRIMROSE JASMINE. Evergreen shrub. Zones 4–24; protected spots in Zone 3. Long, arching branches 6–10 ft. long. Leaves dark green with three lance-shaped, 2–3-in. leaflets; square stems. Flowers bright lemon yellow, to 2 in. across, semidouble or double, unscented. They are scattered singly through plant, November–April in mild-winter areas, and February–April in colder climates. Needs space. Best tied up at desired height and permitted to spill down in waterfall fashion. Use to cover pergola, banks, large walls. Can be clipped as 3-ft.-high hedge. In whatever form, plants may need occasional severe pruning to avoid brush-pile look.

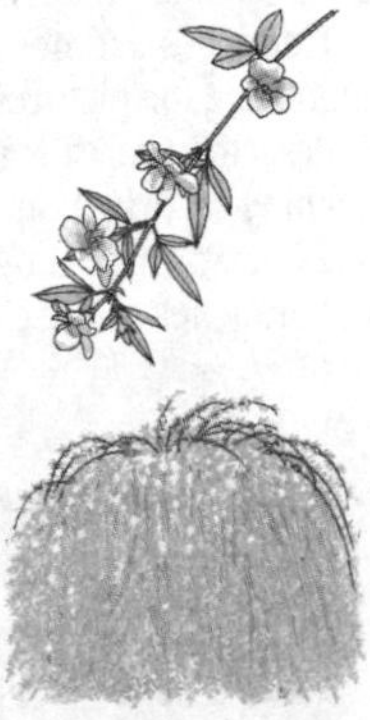
Jasminum mesnyi

J. multipartitum. AFRICAN JASMINE. Evergreen shrub. Zones 16–24. Sprawling growth 2–3 ft. tall, 10 ft. wide. Leaves have a single leaflet. Fragrant white flowers opening from pink buds at branch ends are divided into 8 to 12 narrow segments.

J. nitidum. ANGELWING JASMINE. Often sold as *J. magnificum.* Evergreen vine. Zone 13; semideciduous Zones 12, 16, 19–21. Needs long, warm growing season to bloom satisfactorily. Not reliably hardy below 25°F. Moderate growth to 10–20 ft. Leathery, uncut, glossy medium green leaves to 2 in. long. Very fragrant flowers shaped like 1-in.-wide pinwheels are borne in clusters of three in late spring and summer; flowers are white above, purplish beneath, purplish in bud. Responds well to drastic pruning. Shrubby ground cover. Good container plant.

J. nudiflorum. WINTER JASMINE. Deciduous viny shrub. Zones 3–21; best adapted in cooler climates. To 10–15 ft. with slender, willowy branches. Glossy green leaves with three leaflets. Yellow, 1-in. flowers January–March, before leaves unfold. Not fragrant. Train like *J. mesnyi.*

J. officinale. COMMON WHITE JASMINE, POET'S JASMINE. Semievergreen to deciduous twining vine. Zones 5–9, 12–24. Resembles *J. grandiflorum* but is taller (to 30 ft.), with smaller flowers (to 1 in. across). Somewhat more tender than *J. grandiflorum.*

J. parkeri. DWARF JASMINE. Evergreen shrub. Zones 5–9, 12–24. Dwarf, twiggy, tufted habit. To 1 ft. tall, 1½–2 ft. across. Leaves bright green, ½–1 in. long, made up of three to five tiny leaflets. Small, yellow, scentless flowers profusely borne in May–June. Good in rock gardens or pots.

J. polyanthum. Evergreen vine. Zones 5–9, 12–24. Fast climbing, strong growing to 20 ft. Finely divided leaflets. Dense clusters of fragrant flowers, white inside, rose colored outside; February–July in Zones 22–24, April–July in colder areas. Give regular summer watering; prune annually to prevent tangling. Use as climber, ground cover, in containers.

J. sambac. ARABIAN JASMINE. Evergreen shrub. Zones 13, 21, 23. In Hawaii also called pikake; favorite flower for leis and used in making perfume. In Asia, added to tea to make jasmine tea. Tender. To 5 ft. tall. Leaves undivided, glossy green, to 3 in. long. Flowers white, ¾–1 in. across, powerfully fragrant, in clusters. Grow as small, compact shrub on trellis or in container. The variety 'Grand Duke' has double flowers.

JERUSALEM ARTICHOKE. See HELIANTHUS tuberosus — **p. 318**

JERUSALEM CHERRY. See SOLANUM pseudocapsicum — **p. 488**

JERUSALEM SAGE. See PHLOMIS fruticosa — **p. 414**

JERUSALEM THORN. See PARKINSONIA aculeata — **p. 400**

JEWEL MINT OF CORSICA. See MENTHA requienii — **p. 379**

JICAMA. See PACHYRHIZUS erosus — **p. 398**

JOB'S TEARS. See COIX lacryma-jobi — **p. 237**

JOHNNY-JUMP-UP. See VIOLA tricolor — **p. 520**

JOJOBA. See SIMMONDSIA chinensis — **p. 486**

JONQUIL. See NARCISSUS jonquilla — **p. 388**

JOSEPH'S COAT. See AMARANTHUS tricolor — **p. 149**

JOSHUA TREE. See YUCCA brevifolia — **p. 525**

JUBAEA chilensis (J. spectabilis)

CHILEAN WINE PALM
Arecaceae (Palmae)
PALM
ZONES 12–24
FULL SUN
NO WATERING ONCE ESTABLISHED

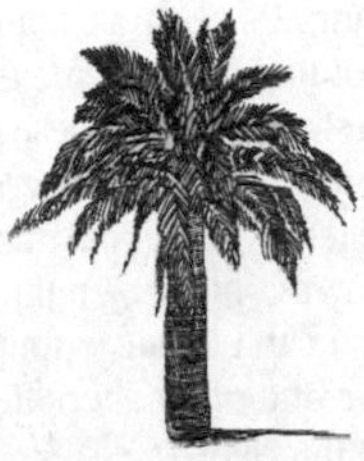
Jubaea chilensis

Slow grower to 50–60 ft. Feather type leaves can be 6–12 ft. long; flowers insignificant. Trunks are patterned with scars of leaf bases. Hardy for a palm (20°F).

JUDAS TREE. See CERCIS siliquastrum — **p. 219**

Juglandaceae. The walnut family consists of nut-bearing trees with leaves divided into many paired leaflets. Pecans and hickories *(Carya)*, walnuts *(Juglans)*, and wingnuts *(Pterocarya)* are examples.

JUGLANS. See WALNUT — **p. 521**

JUJUBE. See ZIZIPHUS jujuba — **p. 528**

JUNCUS

RUSH
Juncaceae
PERENNIALS
ZONES VARY BY SPECIES
SUN OR LIGHT SHADE
AMPLE WATER

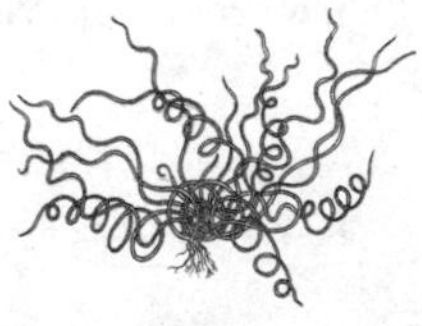
Juncus effusus 'Spiralis'

Rushes somewhat resemble grasses; specialists usually suggest planting them with grasses or aquatic plants. Leaflike stems are round, and tiny inconspicuous flowers are clustered at or near their tops. Use them at the edge of pond or stream or in the water, or among stones and pebbles.

J. effusus. SOFT RUSH. All zones. Stems are ⅛–¼ in. thick, up to 2½ ft. tall, medium green turning brown with frost. Erect at first, they arch somewhat toward tips. *J. e.* 'Spiralis' has stems that coil in spirals. Both are attractive in wet ground or pools.

J. patens. CALIFORNIA GRAY RUSH. Zones 8–24. Stems are stiffly erect, greenish gray. 'Elk Blue' is an epecially blue-gray selection.

J. polyanthemos. AUSTRALIAN SILVER RUSH. Zones 14–24. Stiffly erect gray-green stems reach to 4 ft. Slender, are easily moved about by breezes, lending motion to the garden.

JUNIPER MYRTLE. See AGONIS juniperina — **p. 143**

JUNIPERUS

JUNIPER
Cupressaceae
EVERGREEN SHRUBS AND TREES
☒ ALL ZONES
☼ ◗ SUN, PARTIAL SHADE ON COAST
◖ ◖ ◕ SOME SUMMER WATER IN HOT AREAS
▼ SEE CHART

Juniperus chinensis
'Torulosa'

Juniperus conferta

Coniferous plants with fleshy, berrylike cones. Foliage is needlelike, scalelike, or both. Junipers are the most widely used woody plants in West; there's a form for almost every landscape use. Western nurseries offer more than a hundred junipers with as many names. Junipers that do not tolerate extreme desert heat or mountain cold are not sold in these critical areas. In the chart, these offerings are grouped by common use and listed by botanical names with accompanying synonyms, nursery names, and common names. If you can't locate a juniper in the first column, look for one of its alternate names in the next column to the right.

The ground cover group includes types ranging from a few inches to 2–3 ft. If you are planning large-scale plantings, some of the taller junipers (such as Pfitzer) could be included in this group. Prostrate and creeping junipers are almost indispensable to rock gardens. As ground cover, space plants 5–6 ft. apart; for faster coverage, space plants 3–4 ft. apart and remove every other one when plants begin to crowd. In early years, mulch will help keep soil cool and weeds down. Or interplant with annuals until junipers cover.

Shrub types range from low to quite tall, from spreading to stiffly upright and columnar. You can find a juniper in almost any height, width, shape, or foliage color. Use columnar forms with care; they become quite large with age. Many serve well as screens or windbreaks in cold areas.

Juniperus horizontalis

Tree types are not widely used. They are tough and drought resistant, interesting for picturesque habit of trunk and branch.

Pests to watch for: spider mites (gray or yellow, dry-looking plants, fine webbing on twigs); aphids (sticky deposits, falling needles, sooty mildew); twig borers (browning and dying branch tips). Juniper blight causes twigs and branches to die back. Control with copper sprays in July, August.

MICROCLIMATE FOR JUNIPERS

These plants succeed in every type of soil the West offers—acid or alkaline, heavy or light. However, expect root rot (yellowing and collapse) if soil is waterlogged. Avoid planting junipers so close to lawn sprinkling systems that their roots stay wet. Well-established junipers can thrive on little or no summer water—except in hottest inland areas.

JUNIPER

NAME	ALSO SOLD AS	SIZE, HABIT	CHARACTERISTICS
GROUND COVERS			
Juniperus chinensis 'Parsonii' PROSTRATA JUNIPER	*J. squamata* 'Parsonii' *J. davurica* 'Parsonii' *J. prostrata*	To 1½ ft. by 8 ft. or more	Selected form. Slow growing. Dense short twigs on flat, rather heavy branches
J. c. procumbens JAPANESE GARDEN JUNIPER	*J. procumbens*	To 3 ft. by 12–20 ft.	Feathery yet substantial blue-green foliage on strong, spreading branches
J. c. procumbens 'Nana'	*J. procumbens* 'Nana' *J. procumbens* 'Compacta Nana' *J. compacta* 'Nana'	To 1 ft. by 4–5 ft. Curved branches radiating in all directions	Shorter needles and slower growth than *J. c. procumbens*. Can be staked into upright, picturesque shrub. Give it some protection in hot climates
J. c. 'San Jose'	*J. procumbens* 'San Jose' *J. japonica* 'San Jose' *J. c. procumbens* 'San Jose'	To 2 ft. by 6 ft. or more. Prostrate, dense	Dark sage green with both needle and scale foliage. Heavy trunked, slow growing. One of the best
J. c. sargentii SARGENT JUNIPER, SHIMPAKU	*J. sargentii* *J. sargentii viridis*	To 1 ft. by 10 ft. Ground hugging	Gray-green or green. Feathery. Classic bonsai plant. *J. c. sargentii* 'Glauca' has blue-green foliage; *J. c. sargentii* 'Viridis' has bright green foliage
J. communis saxatilis	*J. c. montana* *J. c. sibirica*	To 1 ft. by 6–8 ft. Prostrate, trailing	Variable gray, gray-green. Upturned branchlets like tiny candles. Native alpine
J. conferta SHORE JUNIPER	*J. conferta littoralis.* Plants so named may be a grower's selected form	To 1 ft. by 6–8 ft. Prostrate, trailing	Bright green, soft needles. Excellent for seashore and will stand valley heat if given moist, well-drained soil. 'Blue Pacific' is denser, bluer, more heat tolerant. 'Emerald Sea' is bright green
J. davurica expansa 'Aureovariegata'	*J. chinensis* 'Alba'	To 1½ ft. by 4–5 ft.	Slow growing, with heavy, horizontal branches, patches of creamy yellow. Variegations can burn in hot sun
J. d. e. 'Parsonii'	*J. prostrata* *J. squamata* 'Parsonii'	To 1½ ft. by 8 ft. or more	Dense, short twigs on heavy, horizontal branches

J

JUNIPER

NAME	ALSO SOLD AS	SIZE, HABIT	CHARACTERISTICS
GROUND COVERS			
J. horizontalis 'Bar Harbor' BAR HARBOR JUNIPER		To 1 ft. by 10 ft. Hugs ground	Fast growing. Feathery, blue-gray foliage turns plum color in winter. Foliage dies back in center to expose limbs as plant ages, especially in hot climates
J. h. 'Blue Chip'		To 1 ft. tall	Silvery blue foliage
J. h. 'Blue Mat'		9–12 in. by 6–7 ft.	Dense mat of gray-green foliage
J. h. 'Douglasii' WAUKEGAN JUNIPER		To 1 ft. by 10 ft. Trailing	Steel blue foliage turns purplish in fall. New growth rich green
J. h. 'Emerald Spreader'		To 6 in. tall	Dense, feathery, bright green foliage
J. h. 'Hughes'		To 6 in. tall	Showy silvery blue
J. h. 'Huntington Blue'		9–12 in. by 6–7 ft.	Dense, bright blue-gray foliage
J. h. 'Plumosa' ANDORRA JUNIPER	*J. depressa plumosa*	To 1½ ft. by 10 ft. Wide spreading	Gray-green in summer, plum color in winter. Flat branches, upright branchlets. Plumy
J. h. 'Prince of Wales'		To 8 in. tall	Medium green foliage turns purplish in fall
J. h. 'Turquoise Spreader'		To 6 in. tall	Dense turquoise green foliage
J. h. 'Wiltonii' BLUE CARPET JUNIPER	*J. h.* 'Blue Rug'	To 4 in. by 8–10 ft. Flattest juniper	Intense silver blue. Dense, short branchlets on long, trailing branches. Similar to *J. h.* 'Bar Harbor' but tighter; it rarely exposes limbs
J. h. 'Youngstown'		To 1 ft. by 6 ft.	Resembles *J. h.* 'Plumosa' but is flatter, more compact
J. h. 'Yukon Belle'		To 6 in. tall	Silvery blue foliage. Hardy in coldest climates
J. sabina 'Arcadia'		To 1 ft. by 10 ft.	Bright green, lacy foliage
J. s. 'Blue Danube'		To 1½ ft. by 5 ft.	Blue-green foliage
J. s. 'Broadmoor'		To 14 in. by 10 ft. Dense, mounding	Soft, bright green foliage
J. s. 'Buffalo'		8–12 in. by 8 ft. Lower than tamarix juniper. Very wide spreading	Soft, feathery, bright green foliage
J. s. 'Calgary Carpet'		6–9 in. by 10 ft.	Soft green foliage. Extremely cold hardy
J. s. 'Scandia'		To 1 ft. by 8 ft.	Low, dense, bright green
J. s. 'Tamariscifolia' TAMARIX JUNIPER, TAM	*J. tamariscifolia*	To 1½ ft. by 10–20 ft. Symmetrically spreading	Dense, blue-green. Widely used
J. scopulorum 'Blue Creeper'		To 2 ft. tall, 6–8 ft. wide	Spreading, mounding habit, bright blue-green color
J. squamata 'Blue Carpet'		To 1 ft. tall, 5 ft. wide. Spreading, mounding	Bright blue-gray foliage, slow growth
J. virginiana 'Silver Spreader'	*J. v. prostrata*	To 1½ ft. by 6–8 ft.	Silvery green, feathery, fine textured. Older branches become dark green

J

▶

JUNIPER

NAME	ALSO SOLD AS	SIZE, HABIT	CHARACTERISTICS
SHRUBS			
J. chinensis 'Armstrongii' ARMSTRONG JUNIPER		To 4 ft. by 4 ft. Upright	Medium green. More compact than Pfitzer juniper
J. c. 'Blaauw' BLAAUW'S JUNIPER, BLUE SHIMPAKU		To 4 ft. by 3 ft. Vase shaped	Blue foliage. Dense. Compact
J. c. 'Corymbosa Variegata' VARIEGATED HOLLYWOOD JUNIPER	*J. c.* 'Torulosa Variegata'	To 8–10 ft. Irregular cone	Variegation of creamy yellow. Growth more regular than Hollywood juniper
J. c. 'Fruitland'		To 3 ft. by 6 ft. Compact, dense	Like a Pfitzer juniper but more compact
J. c. 'Gold Coast'	*J.* 'Coasti Aurea'		Similar or identical to *J. c.* 'Golden Armstrong'
J. c. 'Golden Armstrong'		To 4 ft. by 4 ft. Full, blocky	Between golden Pfitzer and Armstrong juniper in appearance
J. c. 'Hetzii' HETZ BLUE JUNIPER	*J. c. hetzi glauca* *J. glauca hetzi*	To 15 ft. Fountainlike	Blue-gray. Branches spread outward and upward at 45° angle
J. c. 'Maneyi'		To 15 ft. Semierect, massive	Blue-gray. Steeply inclined, spreading branches
J. c. 'Mint Julep'		4–6 ft. by 6 ft. Vase shaped	Mint green foliage, arching branches
J. c. 'Pfitzerana' PFITZER JUNIPER		5–6 ft. by 15–20 ft. Arching	Feathery, gray-green. Sharp-needled foliage. 'Pfitzerana Aurea' is golden form
J. c. 'Pfitzerana Aurea' GOLDEN PFITZER JUNIPER		3–4 ft. by 8–10 ft.	Blue-gray foliage with current season's growth golden yellow
J. c. 'Pfitzerana Compacta' NICK'S COMPACT PFITZER JUNIPER		To 2 ft. by 4–6 ft. Densely branched	Compact. Gray-green foliage
J. c. 'Pfitzerana Glauca'		5–6 ft. by 10–15 ft.	Silvery blue foliage. Arching branches
J. c. 'Sea Green'		To 4–5 ft. by 4–5 ft. Arching, fountainlike	Compact, dark green
J. c. 'Torulosa' HOLLYWOOD JUNIPER	*J. c.* 'Kaizuka' is the proper name for this popular tree	To 15 ft. Irregular, upright	Rich green. Branches with irregular, twisted appearance. Give it enough room
J. sabina SAVIN JUNIPER		Creeping or shrubby plant to 4–6 ft. by 5–10 ft.	Dark green foliage. Exceedingly tough plant
J. s. 'Moor-Dense'		To 1½ ft. by 8 ft.	Resembles *J. s.* 'Broadmoor' but more dense. Has layered look
J. scopulorum 'Table Top Blue'		To 6 ft. by 8 ft.	Gray. Massive. Flat-topped
J. squamata 'Blue Star'		To 2 ft. by 5 ft.	Regular branching. Silver blue
J. s. 'Holger'		To 6 ft. by 6 ft.	Densely branched, broad, flat-topped. New growth yellow-tipped

J

JUNIPER

NAME	ALSO SOLD AS	SIZE, HABIT	CHARACTERISTICS
SHRUBS			
J. s. 'Meyeri' MEYER OR FISHBACK JUNIPER		6–8 ft. by 2–3 ft. Upright	Oddly angled stiff branches. Broad needles. Blend of green, gray, and reddish foliage
COLUMNAR TYPES			
J. chinensis 'Columnaris' CHINESE BLUE COLUMN JUNIPER	*J. c.* 'Columnaris Glauca'	12–15 ft.	Blue-green, narrow pyramid
J. c. 'Hetz's Columnaris'		12–15 ft.	Rich green. Dense column. Scale foliage predominant, branchlets threadlike
J. c. 'Robusta Green'		To 20 ft.	Brilliant green, dense-tufted column
J. c. 'Spartan'	*J. c. densaerecta* 'Spartan'	To 20 ft.	Rich green, dense column
J. c. 'Wintergreen'		To 20 ft.	Deep green, dense-branching pyramid
J. communis 'Compressa'		To 2 ft.	Dwarf, for rock gardens
J. c. 'Stricta' IRISH JUNIPER	*J. c. hibernica* *J. c. fastigiata*	12–20 ft.	Dark green. Very narrow column with closely compact branch tips
J. scopulorum 'Cologreen'			Narrow, bright green column
J. s. 'Gray Gleam'			Gray blue, symmetrical column. Slow grower
J. s. 'Green Ice'		To 15 ft. by 7–10 ft.	Dense branching, cold tolerance make it a good windbreak. Foliage is gray-green; younger foliage paler
J. s. 'Medora'		To 10 ft. by 2½ ft.	Slow growing, narrow, dense, bluish green
J. s. 'Moffetii'			Silvery green column
J. s. 'Pathfinder'		To 25 ft.	Gray-blue, upright pyramid
J. s. 'Welchii'			Silvery green. Very narrow spire
J. s. 'Wichita Blue'			Broad, silver blue pyramid
J. virginiana 'Cupressifolia' HILLSPIRE JUNIPER		15–20 ft.	Dark green, compact pyramid
J. v. 'Idyllwild'		To 15 ft. by 7 ft.	Broad pyramid with dark green foliage. Use for screening
J. v. 'Manhattan Blue'	*J. scopulorum* 'Manhattan Blue'	10–15 ft.	Blue-green, compact pyramid
J. v. 'Skyrocket'		10–15 ft.	Narrowest blue-gray spire
TREES			
J. californica CALIFORNIA JUNIPER		Shrubby or to 40 ft.	Yellowish to rich green. Useful in desert areas
J. deppeana pachyphlaea ALLIGATOR JUNIPER	*J. pachyphlaea*	Shrubby or to 60 ft.	Blue-gray foliage, strikingly checked bark like alligator hide
J. monosperma		To 40 ft.	Similar to *J. osteosperma*; bluish green

J

▶

JUNIPER

NAME	ALSO SOLD AS	SIZE, HABIT	CHARACTERISTICS
TREES			
J. occidentalis WESTERN JUNIPER		50–60 ft.	Massive, long-lived mountain native
J. osteosperma UTAH JUNIPER	*J. utahensis*	Shrubby or to 20–30 ft.	Yellowish green foliage. Adapted to high desert
J. scopulorum 'Tolleson's Blue Weeping'	*J. scopulorum* 'Repandens'	To 20 ft. or more, 10 ft. wide	Blue-green, drooping branchlets make a graceful weeping tree. 'Tolleson's Green Weeping' is similar, but dark green
J. virginiana EASTERN RED CEDAR		40–50 ft. or more	Conical dark green tree that turns reddish in cold weather

JUPITER'S BEARD. See CENTRANTHUS ruber **p. 216**

JUSTICIA

Acanthaceae

SUBTROPICAL SHRUBS

ZONES VARY BY SPECIES

EXPOSURE NEEDS VARY BY SPECIES

WATER NEEDS VARY BY SPECIES

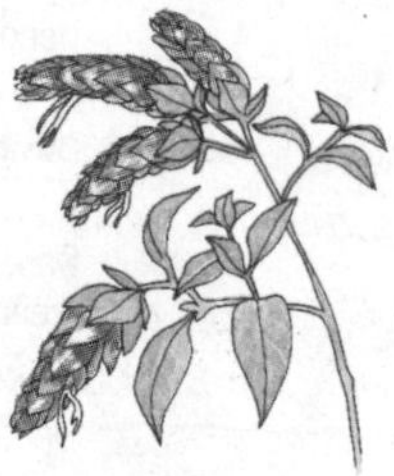

Justicia brandegeana

Includes plants formerly known as *Beloperone* and *Jacobinia.* Leaves are paired; flowers are tubular and tightly clustered.

J. brandegeana (Beloperone guttata). SHRIMP PLANT. Evergreen. Zones 12, 13, 15–17, 21–24; anywhere as indoor/outdoor plant or annual. Native to Mexico. Will grow to 3-by-4-ft. mound but can be kept much lower. Egg-shaped, apple green leaves to 2½ in. long often drop in cold weather or if soil is too wet or dry. Moderate water. Tubular white flowers spotted with purple are enclosed in coppery bronze, overlapping bracts to form compact, drooping spikes 3 in. long (lengthening eventually to 6–7 in.). Spike formation somewhat resembles large shrimp. Flowers attract birds. Plants will take sun, but bracts and foliage fade unless grown in partial shade. Variety 'Chartreuse' has chartreuse yellow spikes that sunburn more easily than those with coppery bracts. To shape plant, pinch continuously in early growth until compact mound of foliage is obtained, then let bloom. To encourage bushiness, cut back stems when flower bracts turn black. Good for pot or tub, for close-up planting near terraces, patios, entryways.

J. californica. CHUPAROSA, CALIFORNIA BELOPERONE. Deciduous. Zones 10–13. Native to edges of Colorado Desert to Arizona and northern Mexico. A low, gray-green shrub 2–5 ft. high, spreading to 4 ft. Arching branches appear almost leafless. Small, roundish, ¼-in. leaves. Bright red, tubular flowers, 1½ in. long in clusters, give good show of color in April–May. Full sun. Often freezes to ground in winter but comes back quickly in spring. Needs no dry-season water.

J. carnea (Jacobinia carnea). BRAZILIAN PLUME FLOWER. Evergreen shrub. Zones 8, 9, 13–24; indoor plant. Erect, soft-wooded, with veined leaves to 10 in. Dense clusters of pink to crimson, tubular flowers bloom on 4–5-ft. stems, midsummer to fall. Needs shade, rich soil, ample water. Cut back in early spring to encourage strong new growth. Tops freeze back at 29°F.

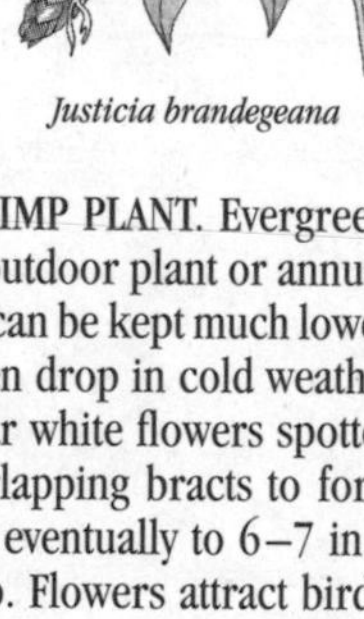

Justicia carnea

J. ghiesbreghtiana. See J. spicigera

J. leonardii. Shrub. Zones 12–24. To 3 ft. with velvety leaves to 6 in. long. Small clusters of 1½-in., scarlet flowers appear off and on through warmer weather. Often sold in California as *Anisacanthus thurberi,* a related plant. Full sun. No dry-season water.

J. spicigera. Shrub. Often sold as *J. ghiesbreghtiana* or, in Arizona, as *Anisacanthus thurberi.* Zones 12–24. To 6 ft., with smooth or velvety leaves and few-flowered clusters of 1½-in., orange or orange-red flowers. Full sun. No dry-season water.

KAFFIR LILY. See CLIVIA miniata, SCHIZOSTYLIS coccinea **pp. 236, 479**

KAHILI GINGER. See HEDYCHIUM gardneranum **p. 318**

KALANCHOE

Crassulaceae

SUCCULENTS

ZONES 17, 21–24

SUN, LIGHT SHADE, OR SHADE

VERY LITTLE WATER

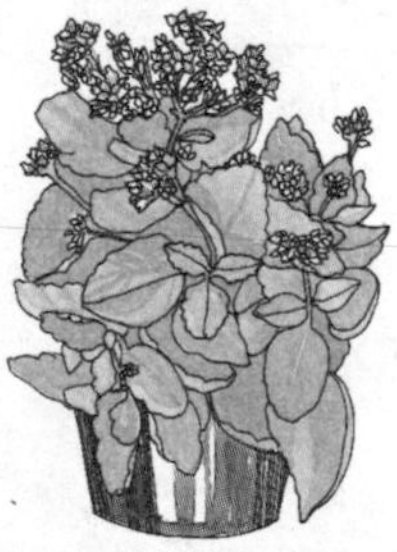

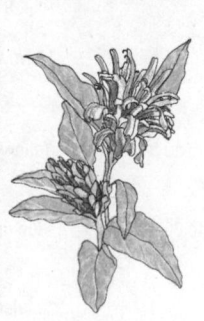

Kalanchoe blossfeldiana

Grown principally as house plants. Some hardy outdoors in mildest coastal regions, but safest even there with protection of lath, eaves, or other overhead structure. Shapes and sizes vary. Flowers fairly large, bell shaped, erect or drooping.

K. beharensis. FELT PLANT. Often sold as *Kitchingia mandrakensis.* Zones 21–24; house plant. Stems usually unbranched, to 4–5 ft., possibly 10 ft. Thick, triangular to lance-shaped leaves—usually six to eight pairs of them—at stem tips. Each leaf 4–8 in. or more long and half as wide, covered with a dense, feltlike coating of white to brown hairs. Flowers not showy; foliage strikingly waved and crimped at edges. Hybrids between this and other species differ in leaf size, color, and degree of felting and scalloping. Striking in big rock garden, raised bed, in sun or considerable shade.

K. blossfeldiana. House plant; some hybrids hardy Zones 17, 21–24. Fleshy, shiny dark green leaves edged red; smooth edged or slightly lobed, 2½ in. long, 1–1½ in. wide. Small bright red flowers in big clusters held above leaves. Hybrids and named varieties come in dwarf (6-in.) and extra-sturdy (1½-ft.) sizes and in different colors, including yellow, orange, salmon. 'Pumila' and 'Tetra Vulcan' are choice dwarf seed-grown selections. Blooms winter, early spring. Popular house plant at Christmas.

K. daigremontiana. MATERNITY PLANT. Upright, single-stemmed house plant 1½–3 ft. tall. Leaves fleshy, 6–8 in. long, 1¼ in. wide or wider, gray-green spotted red. Leaf edges are notched; young plants sprout in notches and may root on the plant. Clusters of small, grayish purple flowers.

K. manginii. Stems spreading or trailing, to 1 ft. long. Inch-long green leaves thick and fleshy. Drooping, bell-shaped, inch-long flowers are bright red. Hanging basket plant.

K. pinnata (Bryophyllum pinnatum). AIR PLANT. Fleshy stems eventually 2–3 ft. tall. Leaves also fleshy. First leaves to form are undivided and scallop edged; later ones divided into three to five leaflets, these also scalloped. Produces many plantlets in notches of scallops. Leaves can be removed and pinned to curtain, where they will produce plantlets until they dry up. Flower color ranges from greenish white to reddish. Likes moisture.

K. tomentosa. PANDA PLANT. House plant. Eventually 1½ ft. tall, branched. Leaves very fleshy, 2 in. long, densely coated with white, felty hairs. Leaf tips and shallow notches in leaves strongly marked dark brown.

K. uniflora. Trailing plant; inch-long, thick, fleshy leaves have a few scallops near rounded tips. Inch-long flowers are pinkish or purplish red. Hanging basket plant.

KALE and COLLARDS

Kale

Brassicaceae (Cruciferae)
VEGETABLES
ALL ZONES
SUN OR LIGHT SHADE
REGULAR WATER

Vegetable crops that live 1–2 years. The type of kale known as collards is a large, smooth-leafed plant like a cabbage that does not form a head. Planted in early spring or late summer, collards will yield edible leaves in fall, winter, and spring. 'Georgia' and 'Vates' are typical varieties. Collards are not widely grown in the West.

Slightly more popular are curly kales like 'Dwarf Blue Curled' and 'Dwarf Siberian'; these are compact clusters of tightly curled leaves. They make decorative garden or container plants as well as supplying edible leaves.

PRETTY AND EDIBLE

So called flowering kale (similar to flowering cabbage) has brightly colored foliage, especially toward centers of rosettes. Grow just like late cabbage. Harvest leaves for cooking by removing them from outside of clusters; or harvest entire plant.

KALMIA

Ericaceae
EVERGREEN SHRUBS
ZONES 1–7, 16, 17
EXPOSURE NEEDS VARY BY SPECIES
REGULAR WATER
LEAVES AND FLOWER NECTAR ARE POISONOUS

Kalmia latifolia

Related to rhododendron. All species have clusters of showy flowers with pleats formed by little pouches that hold the stamens.

K. latifolia. MOUNTAIN LAUREL, CALICO BUSH. Native to eastern United States. Slow growing to 6–8 ft. or more, with equal spread. Glossy, leathery, oval leaves, 3–5 in. long, dark green on top, yellowish green beneath. Clusters of pink buds open to pale pink flowers in apple blossom effect, May–June. Varieties range from white to near red. Named varieties come in red, white, and many shades of pink. Some show spots or bands of contrasting colors. 'Elf' is a dwarf variety. Flowers 1 in. across, in clusters to 5 in. across. Hardy well below 0°F. Shares rhododendron's cultural needs—moist atmosphere, partial shade, acid soil rich in humus. Has proved difficult to grow in Zones 16, 17 even under these conditions; seems to do better in containers there.

K. microphylla (K. polifolia microphylla). WESTERN LAUREL, ALPINE LAUREL. Low plant has spreading branches with erect branchlets, small leaves (dark green above, whitish beneath), and rounded clusters of extremely showy, ½-in., rose to purple flowers in summer. Full sun.

Typical high mountain form is 8–11 in. tall with leaves up to ¾ in. long. A taller variety, *K. m. occidentalis,* to 2 ft. tall and with slightly larger leaves, grows in coastal lowlands north to Alaska.

KALMIOPSIS leachiana

Kalmiopsis leachiana

Ericaceae
EVERGREEN SHRUB
ZONES 4–6, 14–17
PARTIAL SHADE
REGULAR WATER

Rhododendron relative native to mountains of southwest Oregon. Slow growing to 1 ft. tall, with 2-ft. spread. Many branches densely clothed with thick, dark green leaves. Blooms abundantly in early spring, with leafy clusters of ½-in., rose pink flowers. Takes same culture as rhododendron or azalea. Sometimes reblooms.

KERRIA japonica

Kerria japonica 'Pleniflora'

Rosaceae
DECIDUOUS SHRUB
ZONES 1–21
PARTIAL SHADE, SUN IN COOL AREAS
LITTLE WATER ONCE ESTABLISHED

Green branches give welcome winter color in cold areas. Open, graceful, rounded shrub to 8 ft., with 5–6-ft. spread. Leaves tooth edged, heavily veined, somewhat triangular, 2–4 in. long, bright green turning to yellow in fall. Flowers (March–May) like small, single yellow roses. Variety 'Pleniflora', the more commonly planted form, has double yellow, inch-wide flowers.

Give kerria room to arch and display its form. Remove suckers and prune heavily after bloom, cutting out branches that have flowered and all dead or weak wood. Cut green branches are a favorite subject in Japanese arrangements.

K

KNIPHOFIA uvaria (Tritoma uvaria)

RED-HOT POKER, TORCH-LILY, POKER PLANT

Liliaceae

PERENNIAL

⚘ ZONES 1–9, 14–24

☼ ◑ FULL SUN OR LITTLE SHADE

◊ NO DRY-SEASON WATER

Kniphofia uvaria

Native to South Africa. Has been in cultivation long enough to give rise to garden varieties with some range in size, color. Typical plant is coarse with large, rather dense clumps of long, grasslike leaves. Flower stalks (always taller than leaves) are about 2 ft. high in dwarf kinds, 3–6 ft. in larger kinds. The many drooping, orange-red or yellow, tubular flowers of the typical plant overlap, forming poker-like clusters 1 ft. long. Named varieties, in both dwarf and taller forms, come in soft or saffron yellow, creamy white, or coral. Flowers attract hummingbirds, are good in flower arrangements.

Blooms from spring through summer (exact flowering time varies). Cut out flower spikes after bloom. Cut old leaves at base in fall; new leaves will replace them by spring. Increase by root divisions. Useful in large borders with other robust perennials such as daylilies (*Hemerocallis*), *Echinops exaltatus*.

KNOTWEED. See POLYGONUM p. 432

KOCHIA scoparia

SUMMER CYPRESS

Chenopodiaceae

SUMMER ANNUAL

⚘ ALL ZONES

☼ FULL SUN

◗ REGULAR WATER

Kochia scoparia

Sow the seeds and thin the seedlings to make a low, temporary hedge, or separate them individually for their gently rounded form—like fine-textured coniferous shrubs. To 3 ft. Branches densely clothed with narrow, soft, light green leaves, making plants too dense to see through. Insignificant flowers. Tolerates high heat and will perform well in short-summer areas. Shear to shape if necessary.

K. s. trichophylla. MEXICAN FIRE BUSH, BURNING BUSH. Same as above, but foliage turns red at first frost. Can reseed profusely enough to become pest; hoe out unwanted seedlings when small.

KOELREUTERIA

Sapindaceae

DECIDUOUS TREES

⚘ ZONES VARY BY SPECIES

☼ FULL SUN

◊ ◗ ◗ WATER NEEDS VARY BY SPECIES

Koelreuteria paniculata

Small yellow flowers in large, loose clusters in summer. Colorful fruit is fat, papery capsules that seem to resemble clusters of little Japanese lanterns; used in arrangements.

K. bipinnata (K. integrifoliola). CHINESE FLAME TREE. Zones 8–24. Slow to moderate growth to 20–40 ft. or taller, spreading, and eventually flat topped. One- to 2-ft.-long leaves, divided into many oval leaflets, hold onto tree until December, then turn yellow for a short time before dropping. Capsules 2 in. long, orange, red, or salmon, showy in late summer and fall, in large clusters. Fruit formation not always dependable. Takes to most well-drained soils. Moderate watering. Stake and prune to develop high branching. Good patio shade tree, lawn tree, or street tree. Roots deep, not invasive. Good tree to plant under. A similar species, *K. elegans (K. formosana, K. henryi)*, is occasionally seen. It is less hardy and less widely sold.

K. paniculata. GOLDENRAIN TREE. Zones 2–21. Slow to moderate growth to 20–35 ft. with 10–40-ft. spread. Open branching, giving slight shade. Leaves to 15 in. long, with 7 to 15 toothed or lobed leaflets, each 1–3 in. long. Flower clusters in summer, 8–14 in. long. Fruit buff to brown in fall, hanging late. Takes cold, heat, no irrigation, wind, alkaline soil; needs regular watering when young. Prune to shape; can be gawky without pruning. Valuable as street, lawn, or terrace tree in difficult soils and climates. The variety 'Kew' or 'Fastigiata' is erect and narrow—3 ft. wide by 25 ft. tall.

KOHLRABI

Brassicaceae (Cruciferae)

VEGETABLE ANNUAL

⚘ ALL ZONES

☼ FULL SUN

◗ REGULAR WATER

Kohlrabi

Cool-season annual related to cabbage. The edible portion is an enlarged, bulblike portion of the stem, formed just above soil surface. Ordinary leaves grow above. Varieties are 'Early White Vienna' and 'Early Purple Vienna'—similar in size and flavor, differing only in skin color. Sow seed ½ in. deep in rich soil, about 2 weeks after average date of last frost. Follow first planting with successive plantings 2 weeks apart. In areas with warm winters, plant again in late fall and early winter. Space rows 1½ ft. apart; thin seedlings to 4 in. apart. Control aphids if necessary. Harvest when round portions are 2–3 in. wide; slice and eat raw like cucumbers or cook like turnips.

KOLKWITZIA amabilis

BEAUTY BUSH

Caprifoliaceae

DECIDUOUS SHRUB

⚘ ZONES 1–11, 14–20

☼ ◑ FULL SUN OR PARTIAL SHADE

◗ REGULAR WATER

Kolkwitzia amabilis

Growth upright, graceful to 10–12 ft., arching in part shade, denser and lower in full sun. Leaves gray green. Clusters of small, pink, yellow-throated flowers bloom heavily in May in California, June in Northwest and mountain states. Flowers followed by conspicuous pinkish brown, bristly fruit that prolongs color. Thin out after bloom; to enjoy the fruit, prune lightly in early spring, removing wood which has bloomed year before. Brown, flaky bark gradually peels from stems during winter.

KOREAN FORSYTHIA. See FORSYTHIA ovata   **p. 297**

KOREAN GRASS. See ZOYSIA tenuifolia   **p. 528**

KOWHAI. See SOPHORA tetraptera   **p. 489**

KUMQUAT. See CITRUS   **p. 232**

KUNZEA

Myrtaceae

EVERGREEN SHRUBS

☀ ZONES 16–24

☀ SUN

◊ ◖ LITTLE OR NO WATER ONCE ESTABLISHED

Large genus of Australian shrubs related to *Leptospermum* and *Callistemon*. Small flowers appear singly or crowded into bottlebrush clusters; all have fluffy stamens. All require good drainage, preferring sandy soil but tolerating well-drained clay.

Kunzea baxteri

K. affinis. Airy, open, spreading shrub to 6 ft. tall, 10 ft. wide, with bright green needlelike leaves and a big show of small (¼-in.) deep pink flowers. A good cut flower.

K. baxteri. SCARLET KUNZEA. Open, fast-growing shrub to 8 ft. tall and 10–20 ft. wide. Flowers are dark red, with yellow-tipped stamens, in 4-in. bottlebrush clusters. Bloom in winter and spring, with scattered flowers at other times.

Labiatae. See Lamiaceae	p. 346

LABURNUM

GOLDENCHAIN TREE

Fabaceae (Leguminosae)

DECIDUOUS LARGE SHRUBS OR SMALL TREES

☀ ZONES 1–10, 14–17

☀ ☽ AFTERNOON SHADE IN HOT AREAS

◖ MODERATE WATER

◊ SEEDPODS ARE POISONOUS

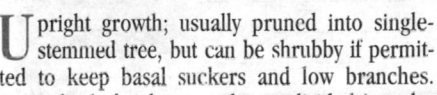

Upright growth; usually pruned into single-stemmed tree, but can be shrubby if permitted to keep basal suckers and low branches. Green bark, bright green leaves divided into three leaflets (like clover). Handsome in bloom: yellow, sweet pea–shaped flowers in hanging clusters (like wisteria).

Laburnum watereri

Well-drained soil. Subject to chlorosis in alkaline soils; use iron. Prune and trim regularly to keep plants tidy. Remove seedpods if possible, not only because they are toxic, but also because a heavy crop drains the plant's strength.

Use as a single tree in lawn or border; group in front of neutral background; or space regularly in long borders of perennials, rhododendrons, or lilacs.

L. alpinum. SCOTCH LABURNUM. To 30–35 ft. Flower clusters 10–15 in. long. Blooms in late spring. The variety 'Pendulum' has weeping branches.

L. anagyroides. COMMON GOLDENCHAIN. To 20–30 ft. high; often bushy and wide spreading. Flower clusters are 6–10 in. long in late spring. Like *L. alpinum*, it has a weeping variety, 'Pendulum'.

L. watereri. Hybrid between the two preceding species; has flower clusters 10–20 in. long. Most widely grown variety is 'Vossii', most graceful of the lot. Can be espaliered.

LACEBARK. See HOHERIA populnea	p. 324
LACE FERN. See MICROLEPIA strigosa	p. 381

FOR INFORMATION ON SELECTING PLANTS
PLEASE SEE PAGES 45–128

LACHENALIA

CAPE COWSLIP

Liliaceae

BULBS

☀ ZONES 16, 17, 24; OR INDOORS

☀ ☽ SUN, LIGHT SHADE IN HOT-SUMMER AREAS

◖ KEEP DRY DURING SUMMER

Native to South Africa. Usually grown in pots indoors or in greenhouses. Strap-shaped, succulent leaves, often brown spotted. Tubular, pendulous flowers in spikes on thick, fleshy stems bloom in winter, early spring. Plant in August or September; put six bulbs in 5–6-in. pot, setting 1–1½ in. deep to prevent flowering stems from falling over. Water and keep cool and dark until roots form and leaves appear. When growth becomes active, water thoroughly and bring plants into light. Keep cool (50°F night temperature). Feed when flower spikes show. When leaves start to yellow, gradually let plants dry out.

Lachenalia bulbiferum

L. aloides (L. tricolor). Flowers yellow, inner segments tipped red, outer tipped green, on stems 1 ft. tall or less. Usually two leaves to a plant, 1 in. wide, about as tall as or taller than flower stems. Variety 'Aurea' is bright orange yellow; 'Nelsonii', bright yellow tinged green; 'Pearsonii', slightly taller, yellow orange with reddish orange buds and flower bases.

L. bulbiferum (L. pendula). Basal leaves to 2 in. wide. Flowers 1½ in. long, coral red and yellow, purple tipped, in spikes 12–15 in. tall. 'Superba', improved form, has orange-red flowers.

L. contaminata. Leaves bright green, to 9 in. long, nearly erect. Flower spikes to 8 in. long, narrow, packed with roundish, ½-in. flowers in white tinged red or brown.

LADY BELLS. See ADENOPHORA liliifolia	p. 139
LADY FERN. See ATHYRIUM filix-femina	p. 171
LADY PALM. See RHAPIS	p. 453
LADY'S-MANTLE. See ALCHEMILLA mollis	p. 145
LADY'S SLIPPER. See PAPHIOPEDILUM	p. 400
LAGENARIA. See GOURD	p. 309

LAGERSTROEMIA indica

CRAPE MYRTLE

Lythraceae

DECIDUOUS SHRUB OR TREE

☀ ALL ZONES; SEE BELOW

☀ FULL SUN

◖ INFREQUENT, DEEP WATERING

Root hardy and sometimes treated as perennial in Zones 1–3. Hardy in Zones 4–6 but does not flower freely except in hottest summers; excellent in Zones 7–10, 12–14, 18–21. Generally a shrub in Zones 10, 11. Mildew is serious problem in Zones 15–17, 22–24. Native to China. Dwarf shrubby forms and shrub-tree forms, 6–30 ft. tall, are available. Slow growing as shrub, spreads as wide as high; trained as tree, becomes vase shaped with attractive trunk and branch pattern. Smooth gray or light brown bark flakes off to reveal smooth, pinkish inner bark.

Lagerstroemia indica

Spring foliage is light green tinged bronze red; mature leaves 1–2 in. long, oval, deep glossy green. Fall foliage is yellow, more rarely orange to red. Crinkled, crapelike, 1½-in. flowers in rounded, slightly conical clusters, 6–12 in. long, at ends of branches; smaller clusters form lower down on branches. Colors in shades of red, rose, deep or soft pink, rosy orchid, purple, white. Long flowering period, July–September.

Feed moderately. Where soil is alkaline or water high in salts, treat chlorosis or marginal leafburn by occasional leaching and applications of iron. Check mildew with sprays just before plants bloom. Prune in dormant season to increase flowering wood the next summer. Remove spent flower clusters and prune out small twiggy growth from dwarf shrub forms. On large shrubs and trees, cut back branches 1–1½ ft.

Many color selections are available. White: 'Glendora White'. Pink: 'Shell Pink' ('Near East'), 'Pink'. Red: 'Rubra', 'Watermelon Red', 'Watermelon Red Improved'. Other colors: 'Lavender', 'Select Purple', 'Majestic Orchid'. 'Peppermint Lace' has rose pink flowers edged with white. Dwarf, shrubby forms (to 5–7 ft.) include rose red 'Petite Embers', 'Petite Orchid', 'Petite Pinkie', 'Petite Plum', dark red 'Petite Red Imp', 'Petite Snow', and 'Petite Snow White'.

THE CRAPE MYRTLES WITH MILDEW RESISTANCE

The most mildew resistant are the Indian Tribes varieties, hybrids between *Lagerstroemia indica* and the otherwise unimportant *L. faurei*: 'Catawba', dark purple; 'Cherokee', bright red; 'Pecos', pink; 'Seminole', pink; and 'Zuni', dark lavender.

LAGUNARIA patersonii

PRIMROSE TREE, COW ITCH TREE

Malvaceae

EVERGREEN TREE

☀ ZONES 13, 15–24

☼ FULL SUN

💧 LITTLE WATER ONCE ESTABLISHED

Lagunaria patersonii

Native to South Pacific and Australia. Rather fast growth to 20–40 ft. Young trees narrow and erect; old trees sometimes spreading, flat topped. Densely foliaged. Thick, oval, 2–4-in.-long leaves are olive green above, gray beneath. Flowers hibiscuslike, 2 in. wide, pink to rose, fading to nearly white, in summer. Brown seed capsules hang on for a long time; flower arrangers like them because they split into five sections, revealing bright brown seeds. Handle carefully; pods also contain short, stiff fibers that can irritate skin.

Tolerates wide variety of soils and growing conditions. Resists ocean wind, salt spray; tolerates soils and heat of low deserts. Foliage burns at 25°F but recovers quickly. Best flowering under coastal conditions. Plant individually as garden tree or in groups as showy windbreak or screen. The selection 'Royal Purple' has purple flowers.

LAMB'S EARS. See STACHYS byzantina	p. 492
LAMB'S QUARTERS. See CHENOPODIUM album	p. 222

Lamiaceae. Members of the mint family of herbaceous plants and shrubs are easily recognized by their square stems, leaves in opposite pairs, and whorled flowers in spikelike, sometimes branched, clusters. Many of the group are aromatic; the family contains most of the familiar kitchen herbs, including basil *(Ocimum)*, mint *(Mentha)*, oregano *(Origanum)*, and sage *(Salvia)*. Many have attractive foliage or flowers (coleus, salvia). This family was previously called Labiatae.

LAMIASTRUM galeobdolon. See LAMIUM galeobdolon	p. 346

LAMIUM

DEAD NETTLE

Lamiaceae (Labiatae)

PERENNIALS

☀ ALL ZONES

● SHADE

💧 AMPLE WATER

Lamium maculatum

Leaves in opposite pairs are heart shaped, toothed, marked with white. Clustered flowers are pink, white, or yellow. All are vigorous growers that thrive in shade (some sun in fog belt). One species is used as a ground cover.

L. galeobdolon (Lamiastrum galeobdolon). YELLOW ARCHANGEL. Upright (to 2 ft.) perennial slowly spreads to form tight clumps. Yellow flowers are unimportant. 'Herman's Pride', best-known selection, has leaves evenly marked with white in streaks and spots.

L. maculatum. DEAD NETTLE, SPOTTED NETTLE. Running or trailing perennial used as a ground cover or in a hanging basket. To 6 in. tall, it spreads 2–3 ft. Its grayish green leaves have silvery markings. Flowers are pink. It is vigorous, even weedy, and is planted less frequently than its choicer varieties. These include 'Beacon Silver', which has silvery gray leaves with a green edge and pink flowers. 'White Nancy' is a 'Beacon Silver' with white flowers. 'Chequers' has pink flowers and green leaves with a white center stripe. These are useful in hanging baskets or for ground cover in shady areas, which they light up nicely. They need some grooming to remove old, shabby growth. Evergreen in mild climates but winter-deciduous elsewhere.

LAMPRANTHUS

ICE PLANT

Aizoaceae

SUCCULENT SUBSHRUBS

☀ ZONES 14–24

☼ FULL SUN

◐💧 LITTLE OR NO SUMMER WATER

Most of the blindingly brilliant ice plants with large flowers belong to this genus. Plants erect or trailing, woody at base; leaves fleshy and cylindrical or three-sided. Select in bloom for the color you want. Cut back lightly after bloom to eliminate fruit capsules, encourage new leafy growth. Good at seashore. Attract bees.

Lampranthus spectabilis

L. aurantiacus. To 10–15 in. tall. Gray-green, inch-long, three-sided leaves. Flowers (February–May) 1½–2 in. across, bright orange. Variety 'Glaucus' has bright yellow flowers; 'Sunman' has golden yellow flowers. Plant 15–18 in. apart for bedding, borders, low bank cover.

L. filicaulis. REDONDO CREEPER. Thin, creeping stems; finely textured foliage. Spreads slowly to form mats 3 in. deep. Small pink flowers in early spring. Use for small-scale ground cover, mound, or low bank cover.

L. productus. To 15 in. tall, spreading to 1½–2 ft. Gray-green, fleshy leaves tipped bronze. Purple flowers an inch wide. Blooms heavily January–April; scattered bloom at other times. Plant 1–1½ ft. apart.

L. spectabilis. TRAILING ICE PLANT. Sprawling or trailing, to 1 ft. tall, 1½–2 ft. wide. Gray-green foliage. Makes carpets of gleaming color, March–May. Flowers 2–2½ in. across, very heavily borne. Available in pink, rose pink, red, purple. Set plants 1–1½ ft. apart.

FOR INFORMATION ON YOUR CLIMATE ZONE
PLEASE SEE PAGES 15–44

LANTANA

Verbenaceae

EVERGREEN VINING SHRUBS; OR ANNUALS

ZONES 8–10, 12–22; SEE BELOW

FULL SUN

INFREQUENT, DEEP WATERING

Lantana montevidensis

Annuals in cold-winter climates; in Zones 8–10 and 14 they often persist but may need replacement after hard winter. Fast growing, valued for profuse show of color over long season—every month of the year in frost-free areas.

Get mildew in shade or continued overcast. Prune hard in spring to remove dead wood and prevent woodiness. Feed lightly. Too much water and fertilizer cuts down on bloom. Shrubby kinds used as substitutes for annuals in planting beds or containers, as low hedges or foundation shrubs. Spreading kinds are excellent bank covers, will control erosion. Effective spilling from raised beds, planter boxes, or hanging baskets. Crushed foliage has a strong, pungent odor that is objectionable to some people. Birds are attracted to the plants.

L. camara. One of two species used in hybridizing. Coarse, upright to 6 ft. Rough dark green leaves. Yellow, orange, or red flowers in 1–2-in. clusters.

L. montevidensis (L. sellowiana). The other species used in cross breeding. This one is sold at nurseries. A little hardier than *L. camara*, it's a well-known ground cover with branches trailing to as much as 3 or even 6 ft. Dark green leaves, 1 in. long, with coarsely toothed edges; sometimes tinged red or purplish, especially in cold weather. Rosy lilac flowers in 1–1½-in.-wide clusters. There is also a white-flowered form.

The following list gives some of the named kinds of lantana that are available. Some are merely forms of *L. camara*, or are hybrids between the forms. Others are hybrids between *L. camara* and *L. montevidensis*.

'Christine'. To 6 ft. tall, 5 ft. wide. Cerise pink. Can be trained into small patio tree.

'Confetti'. To 2–3 ft. by 6–8 ft. Yellow, pink, purple.

'Cream Carpet'. To 2–3 ft. by 6–8 ft. Cream with bright yellow throat.

'Dwarf Pink'. To 2–4 ft. by 3–4 ft. Light pink. Rather tender.

'Dwarf White'. To 2–4 ft. by 3–4 ft.

'Dwarf Yellow'. To 2–4 ft. and as wide as high.

'Gold Rush'. To 1½–2 ft. Rich golden yellow.

'Irene'. To 3 ft. by 4 ft. Compact. Magenta with lemon yellow.

'Lavender Swirl'. To 1½–2 ft. by 6–8 ft. Both lavender and white flowers.

'Lemon Swirl'. Slow growing to 2 ft. tall, 3 ft. wide. Yellow flowers, bright yellow band around each leaf.

'Radiation'. To 3–5 ft. and as wide as high. Rich orange red.

'Spreading Sunset'. To 2–3 ft. by 6–8 ft. Vivid orange red.

'Spreading Sunshine'. To 2–3 ft. by 6–8 ft. Bright yellow.

'Sunburst'. To 2–3 ft. by 6–8 ft. Bright golden yellow.

'Tangerine'. To 2–3 ft. by 6–8 ft. Burnt orange.

'White Lightnin'. To 1½–2 ft. by 6–8 ft. Pure white.

LAPAGERIA rosea

CHILEAN BELLFLOWER

Liliaceae

EVERGREEN VINE

ZONES 5, 6, 15–17, 23, 24

PARTIAL SHADE

REGULAR WATER

Lapageria rosea

The national flower of Chile. Likes high humidity, moderate summer temperatures. Slender stems twine to 10–20 ft. Leaves glossy, leathery, oval, to 4 in. long. Blooms scattered through late spring, summer, and fall. Beautiful, 3-in.-long, rosy red, pendant, bell-shaped flowers (frequently spotted with white) have unusually heavy, waxy substance; hold up as long as 2 weeks after cutting. Give it wind protection and loose soil with plenty of peat moss, ground bark, or sawdust. Protect from snails and slugs.

LARCH. See LARIX   p. 347

LARIX

LARCH

Pinaceae

DECIDUOUS CONIFERS

ZONES VARY BY SPECIES

FULL SUN

ACCEPT LAWN WATERING

Larix decidua

Slender pyramids with horizontal branches and drooping branchlets. Needles (½–1½ in. long) soft to touch, in fluffy tufts. Woody, roundish cones, ½–1½ in. long, are scattered all along branchlets. Notable for color in spring and fall and pattern in winter. In spring, new needle tufts are pale green and new cones bright purple red. In fall, needles turn brilliant yellow and orange before dropping. Winter interest is enhanced by many cones, which create a delightful polka-dot pattern against sky. Not particular about soils. Plant with dark evergreen conifers as background or near water for reflection. Larches attract birds.

L. decidua (L. europaea). EUROPEAN LARCH. Zones 1–9, 14–17. Moderate to fast growth to 30–60 ft. Summer color is grass green, lighter than the other species. In variety 'Pendula', branches arch out and down; branchlets hang nearly straight down.

L. kaempferi. JAPANESE LARCH. Zones 1–9, 14–19. Most frequently planted larch in West. Fast growing to 60 ft. or more but can be dwarfed in containers. Summer foliage is a soft bluish green.

L. occidentalis. WESTERN LARCH, TAMARACK. Zones 1–7. Native to Cascades of Washington and Oregon, eastern Oregon, northern Rocky Mountains. Needles sharp and stiff. Grows to 150–200 ft. as timber tree, 30–50 ft. in gardens.

LARKSPUR. See CONSOLIDA ambigua   p. 239

LARREA tridentata

CREOSOTE BUSH

Zygophyllaceae

EVERGREEN SHRUB

ZONES 10–13, 19

FULL SUN

TALLER, DENSER GROWTH WITH WATER

Larrea tridentata

One of most common native shrubs in deserts of southeastern California, Arizona, southern Utah, Texas, northern Mexico. Grows 4–8 ft. tall with many upright branches. Straggly and open in shallow, dry soil; attractive, dense, rounded but spreading where water accumulates. Leathery, yellow-green to dark green leaves divided into two tiny, ⅜-in.-long crescents. Gummy secretion makes leaves look varnished and yields distinctive creosote odor, especially after rain. Small yellow flowers off and on all year, followed by small roundish fruit covered with shiny white or rusty hairs. Give it fertilizer along with irrigation water to produce shiny dark green leaves. Use as wind or privacy screen, or trim into formal hedge. Sometimes sold as *L. divaricata*.

L

347

LATHYRUS

SWEET PEA

Fabaceae (Leguminosae)

ANNUAL OR PERENNIAL VINES

🌿 ZONES VARY BY SPECIES

☼ FULL SUN

◐ ◑ ● WATER NEEDS VARY BY SPECIES

Lathyrus odoratus

In this group is one of the best-known garden flowers—the delightfully fragrant and colorful sweet pea.

Throughout this book you will find flowers described as "sweet pea shaped." The flower of the sweet pea is typical of the many members of the pea family (Fabaceae). Each flower has one large, upright, roundish petal (banner or standard), two narrow side petals (wings), and two lower petals that are somewhat united, forming a boat-shaped structure (keel).

L. latifolius. PERENNIAL SWEET PEA. All zones. Strong-growing vine up to 9 ft., with blue-green foliage. Flowers usually reddish purple, often white or rose. Single colors—white and rose—sometimes sold. Long bloom season (June–September) if not allowed to go to seed. Plants grow with little care, tolerate aridity. May escape and become naturalized. Use as bank cover, trailing over rocks, on trellis or fence.

L. odoratus. SWEET PEA. Spring or summer annual. All zones. Bears many spikelike clusters of crisp-looking flowers with a clean, sweet fragrance, in single colors and mixtures. Color mixtures include deep rose, blue, purple, scarlet, white, cream, amethyst on white ground, salmon, salmon pink on cream. Sweet peas make magnificent cut flowers in quantity. Bush types offer cut flowers the same as vine types and require no training.

To hasten germination, soak seeds for a few hours before planting. Treat seeds with fungicide. Sow seeds 1 in. deep and 1–2 in. apart. When seedlings are 4–5 in. high, thin to not less than 6 in. apart. Pinch out tops to encourage strong side branches. Where climate prevents early planting or soil is too wet to work, start three or four seeds in each 2¼–3-in. peat pot, indoors or in protected place, and set out when weather has settled. Plant peat pots 1 ft. apart, thinning each to one strong plant. This method is ideal for bush types. Protect young seedlings from birds with wire screen. Set out bait for slugs and snails. Never let vines lack for water; soak heavily. To prolong bloom, cut flowers at least every other day and remove all seedpods. Regular monthly feeding with commercial fertilizer will keep vines vigorous and productive.

For vining sweet peas, provide trellis, strings, or wire before planting. Seedlings need support as soon as tendrils form. Freestanding trellis running north and south is best. When planting against fence or wall, keep supports away from wall to give air circulation.

The following describes vine-type sweet peas (grouped by time of bloom) and bush types.

Early flowering. (Early Flowering Multiflora, Early Multiflora, formerly Early Spencers.) The name "Spencer" once described a type of frilled flower (with wavy petals) that is now characteristic of almost all varieties. "Multiflora" indicates that the plants carry more flowers per stem than the old "Spencers" did. The value of early-flowering varieties is that they will bloom in midwinter when days are short. (Spring- and summer-flowering types will not bloom until days have lengthened to 15 hours or more.) Where winter temperatures are mild (Zones 12, 13, 17, 21–24), sow seeds in August or early September for late December or January bloom. Use these varieties for forcing in greenhouse. They are not heat resistant. Generally sold in mixed colors.

Spring flowering. (Spring-Flowering Heat-Resistant Cuthbertson Type, Cuthbertson's Floribunda, Floribunda-Zvolanek strain.) Both mixtures and single-color named varieties are available in seed packets. Wide color range: pink, lavender, purple, white, cream, rose, salmon, cerise, carmine, red, blue. Royal or Royal Family are somewhat larger flowered, more heat resistant than the others. In Zones 7–9, 12–24, plant between October and early January. Elsewhere, plant February–April (just as soon as soil can be worked).

Summer flowering. (Galaxy, Plenti-flora.) Available in named varieties and mixtures in wide color range. Heat resistant; bloom from early summer on. Large flowers, five to seven on long stems. Heat resistance is not enough for Zones 7–15, 18–21.

Bush type. The so-called bush-type sweet peas are strong vines with predetermined growth, heights. Unlike vining types that reach 5 ft. and more, these stop their upward growth at 1–2½ ft. All zones.

Bijou. To 1 ft. Full color range in mixtures and single varieties. Four or five flowers on 5–7-in. stems. Useful and spectacular in borders, beds, window boxes, containers. Not as heat resistant or as long stemmed as Knee-Hi; performs better in containers.

Cupid. Grows 4–6 in. tall, 1½ ft. wide. Trails on ground or hangs from container.

Jet Set. Bushy, self-supporting plants 2–3 ft. tall. All colors.

Knee-Hi. To 2½ ft. Large, long-stemmed flowers, five or six to the stem. Has all the virtues and color range of Cuthbertson's Floribundas on self-supporting, bush-type vines. Provides cutting-type flowers in mass display in beds and borders. Growth will exceed 2½ ft. where planting bed joins fence or wall. Keep in open area for uniform height. Follow same planting dates as for spring-flowering sweet peas.

Little Sweethearts. Rounded bushes, 8 in. tall, bloom over a long season. Full range of colors. Patio strain grows 9 in. tall. Snoopea (12–15 in.) and Supersnoop (2 ft.) need no support, come in full range of sweet pea colors.

L. splendens. PRIDE OF CALIFORNIA. Perennial vine to 8–10 ft. Zones 14–24. Each stem has clusters of three to ten deep red sweet peas, March–April. Native to chaparral in San Diego County and adjacent Baja California. Start from seed in pots in fall or spring; plant out in fall or winter. Needs little water first year or so, none once established. Long lived in dry, well-drained soil.

> ### GETTING SWEET PEAS OFF TO A FINE START
>
> In less-than-perfect soil, prepare ground for sweet peas like this: Dig trench 1–1½ ft. deep. Mix 1 part peat moss or other soil conditioner to 2 parts soil. As you mix, add complete commercial fertilizer according to label directions. Backfill trench with mix; plant seeds in it.

Lauraceae. The laurel family contains evergreen or deciduous trees and shrubs with inconspicuous flowers and (usually) aromatic foliage. Fruits are fleshy, containing a single seed. Examples are avocado, camphor (*Cinnamomum*), sweet bay (*Laurus nobilis*), and California laurel (*Umbellularia californica*).

LAUREL. See LAURUS nobilis, PRUNUS, UMBELLULARIA californica pp. 349, 439, 515

LAURENTIA fluviatilis (Isotoma fluviatilis)

BLUE STAR CREEPER

Campanulaceae (Lobeliaceae)

PERENNIAL GROUND COVER

🌿 ZONES 4, 5, 8, 9, 14–24

☼ ◑ FULL SUN OR PARTIAL SHADE

● REGULAR WATER

Laurentia fluviatilis

Creeping, spreading plant that grows only 2–3 in. tall. Pointed, oval leaves ¼ in. long give plant look of baby's tears (*Soleirolia*). Pale

L

blue, starlike flowers, slightly broader than the leaves, spangle plantings in late spring, summer, with a scattering at other times. Can take light foot traffic. Plant pieces 6–12 in. apart for cover within a year. Feed lightly once a month, spring to fall. Recently renamed *Pratia pedunculata*.

LAURUS nobilis

SWEET BAY, GRECIAN LAUREL

Lauraceae

EVERGREEN SHRUB OR TREE

✍ ZONES 5–9, 12–24

☼ ◖ FULL SUN OR PARTIAL SHADE

◔ LITTLE WATER ONCE ESTABLISHED

Laurus nobilis

Slow growth to 12–40 ft. Natural habit is compact, broad-based—often that of a multi-stemmed, gradually tapering cone. Leaves are leathery, aromatic, oval, 2–4 in. long, dark green; traditional bay leaf of cookery. Clusters of small yellow flowers are followed by ½–1-in.-long, black or dark purple berries.

Not fussy about soil but needs good drainage. Spray for black scale and laurel psyllid. Tends to sucker heavily. Dense habit makes it a good large background shrub, screen, or small tree. Takes well to clipping into formal shapes—globes, cones, topiary shapes, standards, or hedges. A classic formal container plant. 'Saratoga' has broader leaves and a more treelike habit, and is resistant to psyllid.

LAURUSTINUS. See VIBURNUM tinus   p. 519

LAVANDULA

LAVENDER

Lamiaceae (Labiatae)

EVERGREEN SHRUBS OR SUBSHRUBS

✍ ZONES VARY BY SPECIES

☼ FULL SUN

◔ LITTLE WATER

Native to Mediterranean region. Prized for fragrant lavender or purple flowers used for perfume, sachets. Grayish or gray-green aromatic foliage. Plant as hedge or edging, in herb gardens, or in borders with plants needing similar conditions—cistus, helianthemum, nepeta, rosemary, santolina, verbena.

Lavandula angustifolia

Need loose, fast-draining soil. Little or no fertilizer. Prune immediately after bloom to keep plants compact and neat. For sachets, cut flower clusters or strip flowers from stems just as color shows; dry in cool, shady place.

Interest in low-water-use plants has made the lavenders immensely popular. Because they have been in cultivation for centuries and tend to interbreed, many varieties and hybrids have arisen, and names are difficult to sort out. These names may not agree with those you see on nursery labels.

'Lavender Lady' grows quickly from seed, blooming the first year. Plants are dwarf (15 in.), with gray-green leaves and deep purple flowers.

L. angustifolia (L. officinalis, L. spica, L. vera). ENGLISH LAVENDER. Zones 4–24. Most widely planted. Classic lavender used for perfume and sachets. To 3–4 ft. high and wide. Leaves gray, smooth on margins, narrow, to 2 in. long. Flowers lavender, ½ in. long, on 1½–2-ft.-long spikes in July and August. Dwarf varieties: 'Compacta' ('Compacta Nana'), to 8 in. tall, 12–15 in. wide; 'Hidcote', slow growing to 1 ft. tall, with very gray foliage and deep purple flowers; 'Jean Davis', 1–2 ft. tall, with pale pink flowers; 'Munstead', most popular dwarf, 1½ ft. tall, with deep lavender blue flowers a month earlier than the species; 'Twickel Purple', 2–3 ft. high, with purple flowers in fanlike clusters on extra-long spikes. Attractive to bees.

L. dentata. FRENCH LAVENDER. Zones 8, 9, 12–24. To 3 ft. tall. Gray-green, narrow leaves, 1–1½ in. long, with square-toothed edges. Lavender purple flowers in short spikelike clusters, each topped with tuft of petal-like bracts. In mild-winter areas, blooms almost continually.

L. d. candicans. Has somewhat larger leaves than French lavender and dense, grayish white down on young foliage.

L. intermedia. Zones 4–24. Hybrids between *L. angustifolia* and *L. latifolia*. Plants listed here may also be sold as *L. angustifolia*. 'Grosso' has thick spikes of deep purple flowers. 'Provence' is the variety grown in France for perfumery. 'Fred Boutin' is a dense grower to 8 in., with woolly white 3-in. leaves. Flower stems are 1½ ft. tall.

L. lanata. Zones 8, 9, 12–24. Grows to 3 ft., with leaves 2 in. long, ½ in. wide. White woolly stems and leaves. Flower spikes are deep purple, 1–4 in. long.

L. latifolia. SPIKE LAVENDER. Zones 4–24. Much like English lavender in appearance, but with broader leaves and frequently branched flower stalks.

L. pinnata buchii, L. canariensis, L. multifida. Zones 16–24. Three very similar lavenders with deeply cut, almost fernlike leaves and tall flower stalks branching near the top, each branch carrying a short spike of deep purple flowers. They are nearly everblooming and are fine container subjects where frosts are frequent or severe.

L. stoechas. SPANISH LAVENDER. Zones 4–24. Stocky plant 1½–3 ft. tall, with narrow gray leaves ½–1 in. long. Flowers dark purple, about ⅛ in. long, in dense, short spikes, each topped with tuft of large, purple, petal-like bracts. Blooms in early summer. 'Otto Quast' has especially showy purple bracts.

LAVATERA

TREE MALLOW

Malvaceae

ANNUALS OR EVERGREEN SHRUBS

✍ ZONES VARY BY SPECIES

☼ FULL SUN

◔ ◔ LITTLE TO REGULAR WATER

Lavatera assurgentiflora

Lavatera is named after the Lavater family of Zurich, but for many the word means "easy to grow." The flowers resemble single hollyhocks.

L. assurgentiflora. Evergreen shrub. Zones 14–24. Native to Channel Islands but naturalized on California coastal mainland. Erect shrub to 12 ft., or treelike. Maplelike leaves 3–5 in. long, lobed and toothed. Rosy lavender, white-striped, 2–3-in.-wide flowers bloom almost throughout the year, heaviest from April to August. Resists wind, salt spray. Use as fast-growing windbreak hedge. Will reach 5–10 ft. and bloom first year from seed. Shear to keep dense.

L. maritima (L. bicolor). Evergreen shrub. Zones 8, 9, 14–24. Quick-growing to 6–8 ft., with gray-green 2½-in. maplelike leaves and a summer-long show of light pink 2–3-in. flowers with dark rose veining and a deep purple center. Open grower; cut back hard to keep it compact.

L. thuringiaca. Evergreen shrub. Zones 8, 9, 14–24. Resembles *L. maritima*, but growth is less open, leaves greener. Flowers are purplish pink, 3 in. across, nearly everblooming. The variety 'Barnsley' has lighter pink flowers paling to white centers. 'Rosea' has pink flowers.

L. trimestris. ANNUAL MALLOW. Annual. All zones. To height of 3–6 ft. from spring-sown seed. Leaves roundish, angled on upper part of plant, toothed. Flowers satiny, to 4 in. across; named varieties in white, pink, rosy carmine. July–September bloom if spent flowers are removed to halt seed production. Thin seedlings to allow ample room to spread. Colorful, fast-growing summer hedge or background planting. Compact (2–3-ft.) varieties include 'Mont Rose', rose pink; 'Mont Blanc', white; and 'Silver Cup', bright pink.

LAVENDER. See LAVANDULA   p. 349

LAYIA platyglossa

TIDYTIPS

Asteraceae (Compositae)

SPRING AND SUMMER ANNUAL

☑ ALL ZONES

☼ FULL SUN

◐ OCCASIONAL WATERINGS IF WINTER RAINS FAIL

Layia platyglossa

California native. Member of sunflower family. Often obtained in mixed wildflower packets or from native plant seed specialists. Rapid growth to 5–16 in. high. Flower heads about 2 in. across; the rays are light yellow with neatly marked white tips. Can grow in rather heavy soil but won't take standing water. Will naturalize on banks or other well-drained sites with poor soil and little competition from grasses. Give seedlings a good start by preparing soil as for any garden bed. Sow seeds in sunny place in autumn; water occasionally if winter rains fail.

LEEK

Liliaceae

ANNUAL VEGETABLE

☑ ALL ZONES

☼ FULL SUN

◐ NEVER LET DRY OUT

Leek

An onion relative that doesn't form distinct bulb. Edible, mild-flavored bottoms resemble long, fat green onions. Leeks need very rich soil. Best in cool weather. Sow in early spring; in cold-winter areas, sow indoors and set out plants in June or July. When plants have considerable top growth, draw soil up around fat, round stems to make bottoms white and mild. Plants grow 2–3 ft. high. Keep soil out of bases of leaves. Begin to harvest in late autumn. Where winters are cold, dig up plants with roots and plant them closely in boxes of soil in cool but frost-free location. Where winters are mild, dig as needed from late fall until spring. Any offsets may be detached and replanted. If leeks bloom, small bulbils may appear in the flower clusters. Plant for later harvest.

LEMAIREOCEREUS thurberi (Stenocereus thurberi)

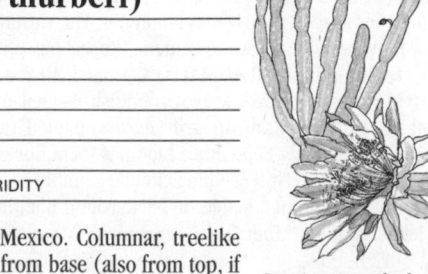

ORGANPIPE CACTUS

Cactaceae

CACTUS

☑ ZONES 12–24

☼ FULL SUN

◐ TOLERATES SOME ARIDITY

Lemaireocereus thurberi

Native to Arizona, Mexico. Columnar, treelike cactus branching from base (also from top, if injured). Dark green or gray-green stems, with 12–17 ribs, grow slowly to 15 ft. Spines black, ½–1 in. long. Has purplish, white-edged, 3-in. flowers, May–June. Needs excellent drainage. Night

blooming. Fruit 1½ in. long, red tinged olive green, filled with edible, sweet red pulp.

LEONOTIS leonurus

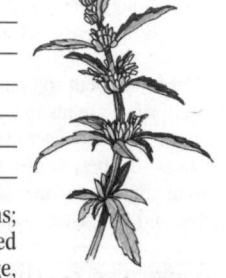

LION'S TAIL

Lamiaceae (Labiatae)

SHRUB

☑ ZONES 8–24

☼ FULL SUN

◐ LITTLE OR NO DRY-SEASON WATERING

Leonotis leonurus

Shrubby, branching, to 3–6 ft. Hairy stems; 2–5-in.-long leaves with coarsely toothed edges. Dense whorls of tubular, deep orange, 2-in.-long flowers covered with furlike coat of fine hairs. Blooms summer into fall. Striking if kept well groomed.

LEONTOPODIUM alpinum

EDELWEISS

Asteraceae (Compositae)

PERENNIAL

☑ ZONES 1–9, 14–24

☼ FULL SUN

◐ REGULAR WATER

Leontopodium alpinum

Short-lived, white, woolly plant 4–12 in. high, with small flower heads closely crowded on tips of stems; a collar of slender white, woolly leaves radiates out from below each flower head like the arms of a starfish. The tiny bracts of flower heads, also white and woolly, are tipped with black. Blooms June–July. Needs excellent drainage.

LEPTOSPERMUM

TEA TREE

Myrtaceae

EVERGREEN SHRUBS OR SMALL TREES

☑ ZONES 14–24

☼ FULL SUN

◐ ◐ NO WATER ON COAST; SUMMER WATER INLAND

Leptospermum laevigatum

Native to Australia, New Zealand. Soft and casual looking (never rigid or formal), partly because of branching habit. Substantial and useful landscape structure plants the year around. All make springtime display of flowers along stem among small leaves. The flowers (white, pink, or red) are basically alike, about ½ in. wide with petals arranged around hard central cone or cup. Single flowers look like tiny single roses. Petals fall to leave woody, long-lasting seed capsules about ¼ in. wide.

Need good soil drainage. Subject to chlorosis in alkaline soils. Sometimes succumb quickly to root troubles where drainage is poor. All take some surface shearing; in real pruning, cut back only to side branches, never into bare wood. Good near ocean.

L. horizontalis. Fast-growing, sprawling shrub 3–4 ft. tall, up to 15 ft. wide, with horizontal branches and drooping branchlets. Foliage is bright green, and summer to fall flowers are white. Good bank cover.

L. laevigatum. AUSTRALIAN TEA TREE. Large shrub or small tree. To 30 ft. high, often as wide. With the right soil—well drained, slightly acid—lives long and well with little care. Oval or teardrop-shaped, dull green to gray-green leaves to ³/₈ in. wide, 1 in. long. The plant has two growth habits depending on whether it is planted by itself or in a group. Solitary plants allowed to grow to full size develop picturesque character with muscular-looking, twisted, and gracefully curved, shaggy, gray-brown trunks up to 2 ft. across at the base. Equally handsome branches range out from trunk and carry canopies of finely textured foliage. Some pendulous branches weep down from the foliage canopies. Single white flowers appear in great numbers along branches in spring. Placed close together (1½–6 ft.) to make windbreak, thick natural screen, or clipped hedge, plants do not develop any visible branching character but do make solid bank of finely textured green foliage, highlighted in spring by white flowers.

THE TEA THAT PREVENTED SCURVY

Leptospermum scoparium and *L. laevigatum* are each called tea tree because, on his trips to New Zealand and Australia, Captain Cook had their leaves brewed into a tea to prevent scurvy among his crew. Such a tea might have been medicinal, but it doesn't taste very good. It can't compare to the infusion made from *Thea sinensis*.

L. l. 'Compactum'. Similar to species but smaller—to 8 ft. high, 6 ft. wide—and slightly more open and loose. Does not flower as heavily.

L. l. 'Reevesii'. Leaves are rounder, slightly bigger, and more densely set than those of *L. laevigatum*, and plant grows only 4–5 ft. high and wide. Heavier looking than either of the preceding two kinds.

L. nitidum 'Macrocarpum' (L. lanigerum 'Macrocarpum'). Shrub 6 ft. tall with reddish new growth, purplish bronze older foliage. Leaves are tiny and narrow—½ in. long, ⅛ in. wide. Spring flowers nearly 1 in. wide, chartreuse yellow with dark green disk.

L. rotundifolium (L. scoparium rotundifolium). Shrub to 6 ft. tall, 9 ft. wide. Variable size and habit, but usually with spreading, arching branches. Tiny leaves are roundish rather than needlelike. Spring flowers are large (1 in. wide) and vary from white to deep purplish pink. Extremely showy in bloom but has shorter bloom period than *L. scoparium*. 'Manning's Choice' is a selection with deep lavender pink flowers.

L. scoparium. NEW ZEALAND TEA TREE, MANUKA. Ground cover to large shrub. True species *L. scoparium* is of no interest in the West, but its many varieties are valuable. Not as bold of form or as serviceable in hedges and screens as the kinds listed above, but with showier flowers. Hardier than other species. Leaves are tiny (from almost needlelike and ¼ in. long to ⅛ in. wide and ½ in. long), pointed, densely set. Many white to pink flowers to ½ in. across in spring or summer.

L. s. 'Gaiety Girl'. Slow growing to 5 ft. Midspring flowers double, pink with lilac tint. Foliage reddish.

L. s. 'Helene Strybing'. Seedling of *L. s.* 'Keatleyi'; resembles parent except that flowers are somewhat smaller, much deeper pink.

L. s. 'Keatleyi'. Tallest (6–10 ft.), most open and rangy of *L. scoparium* varieties—and most inclined to develop picturesque habit. Single pink flowers, paler at edges, are extra large, sometimes as big as a quarter. Spring bloom; may repeat in summer.

L. s. 'Nanum Tui'. Low, rounded shrub to 2 ft. high. Single flowers light pink, darker at center.

L. s. 'Pink Cascade'. To 1 ft. tall by 3–4 ft. wide. Single pink flowers on sprawling, weeping branches. Attractive trailing over walls, among rocks.

L. s. 'Pink Pearl'. To 6–10 ft. Pale pink buds open to double blush pink to white flowers.

L. s. 'Red Damask'. To 6–8 ft. Dense in habit. Double ruby red flowers, red-tinged leaves. Heavy bloom from midwinter to spring.

L. s. 'Ruby Glow'. Compact, upright 6–8-ft. shrub with dark foliage. Double oxblood red flowers (¾ in. wide) in winter and spring, borne in great profusion—entire shrub looks red.

L. s. 'Snow White'. Spreading, compact plant 2–4 ft. high. Medium-size double white flowers with green centers, December to spring.

LETTUCE

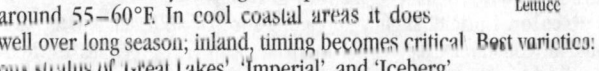

Asteraceae (Compositae)

ANNUALS

☀ SUMMER 1–7, 10, 11; COOL-SEASON, 8, 9, 12–24

☀ ☼ SUN ON COAST, LIGHT MIDDAY SHADE INLAND

● REGULAR WATER

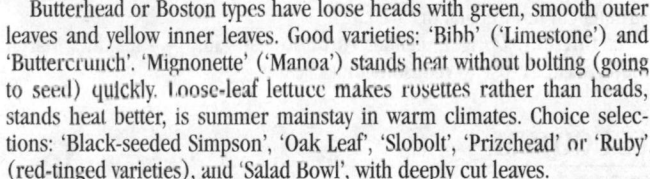

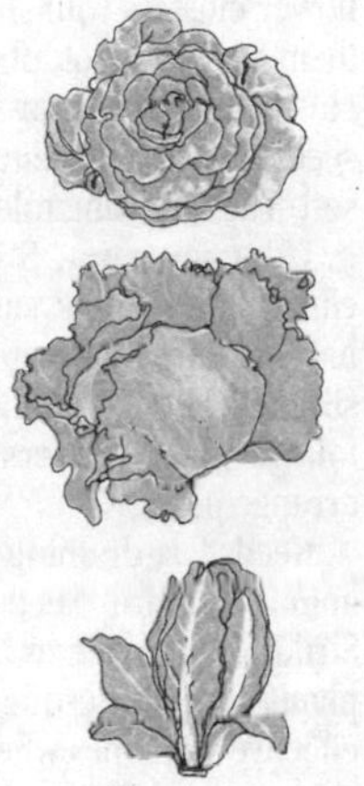

Lettuce

A short browse through a seed catalog, seed display rack, or nursery seedlings table reveals enough kinds of lettuce to keep your salad bowl crisp and colorful throughout your growing season. There are four principal types: Crisphead lettuce is the most familiar kind in markets, the most exasperating for home gardener to produce. Heads best when monthly average temperatures are around 55–60°F. In cool coastal areas it does well over long season; inland, timing becomes critical. Best varieties: various strains of 'Great Lakes', 'Imperial', and 'Iceberg'.

Butterhead or Boston types have loose heads with green, smooth outer leaves and yellow inner leaves. Good varieties: 'Bibb' ('Limestone') and 'Buttercrunch'. 'Mignonette' ('Manoa') stands heat without bolting (going to seed) quickly. Loose-leaf lettuce makes rosettes rather than heads, stands heat better, is summer mainstay in warm climates. Choice selections: 'Black-seeded Simpson', 'Oak Leaf', 'Slobolt', 'Prizehead' or 'Ruby' (red-tinged varieties), and 'Salad Bowl', with deeply cut leaves.

Romaine lettuce has erect, cylindrical heads of smooth leaves, the outer green, the inner whitish. Stands heat moderately well. Try 'White Paris', 'Parris Island', 'Dark Green Cos', or 'Valmaine'. Lettuces with bronzy to pinkish red leaves add color to a salad. 'Lollo Rosso', 'Red Sails', 'Red Oak Leaf', and 'Ruby' are loose-leaf varieties; 'Merveille des Quatre Saisons' and 'Perella Red' are butterheads; 'Rouge d'Hiver' is a romaine.

Lettuce needs loose, well-drained soil. Feed lightly and frequently. Sow in open ground at 10-day intervals, starting after frost as soon as soil is workable. Barely cover seeds; space rows 8–12 in. apart. Thin head lettuce or romaine to 1 ft. apart, carefully moving seedlings to extend the plantings. Loose-leaf lettuce can be grown 4 in. apart; harvest some whole plants as they begin to crowd.

In milder climates, make later sowings in late summer, fall. Where summers are very short, sow indoors, then move seedlings outdoors after last frost. Control snails, slugs, and earwigs with bait on the ground—not on the plants. Harvest when heads or leaves are of good size; lettuce doesn't stand long before going to seed, becoming quite bitter in the process.

PICKING LOOSE-LEAF LETTUCE

With this kind of lettuce you get three opportunities to harvest over a long period. Use the thinnings for salads; clip off just the outer leaves as you need them; finally, pull up whole plants. Finish harvesting when bloom stalks start to grow.

LEUCANTHEMUM. See CHRYSANTHEMUM p. 226

LEUCODENDRON

Proteaceae

EVERGREEN SHRUBS OR TREES

☀ ZONES 16, 17, 20–24

☀ FULL SUN

💧 SUMMER WATER

Leucodendron argenteum

Native to South Africa. Related to proteas. Male and female flowers are borne on separate plants. In some shrubby species, conelike male flower clusters with showy colored bracts beneath them have the look of giant daisies. Female flower clusters are less showy and develop into conelike seed clusters. All leucodendrons need good drainage; most prefer acid soil. The following tolerate neutral or mildly alkaline conditions.

L. argenteum. SILVER TREE. Young trees (the most spectacular in effect) are narrow and stiffly upright; mature trees, with tortuous, gray-barked trunk, have spreading, irregular silhouette. Can reach 40 ft. Silky, silvery white, 3–6-in.-long leaves densely cover the branches. This is a foliage plant; flowers and fruit are inconsequential. Foliage good for arrangements.

Needs fast-draining soil. Will not thrive in clay, alkaline soil, or soil with animal manure. Needs humid air; takes ocean winds but not dry winds. Striking appearance and cultural problems make it hard to use. Small plants are picturesque container subjects for 3–4 years. Larger plants are effective on slopes when combined with boulders, succulents, and pines in sheltered seaside gardens. Use singly or in groups.

L. discolor. Upright, slightly spreading shrub 4–8 ft. tall and as wide (smaller in container), its stems densely set with gray-green leaves. Red-centered gold inflorescences at stem tips in early fall or winter; these make striking cut flowers that dry well.

L. tinctum. Upright, slender shrub to 8 ft. tall, 3–4 ft. wide. March inflorescences rose to red, sometimes yellow.

LEUCOJUM

SNOWFLAKE

Amaryllidaceae

BULBS

☀ ZONES VARY BY SPECIES

☀ PARTIAL SHADE; SUN DURING BLOOM

💧 REDUCE WATER FOR SUMMER DORMANCY

Leucojum aestivum

Strap-shaped leaves and nodding, bell-shaped, white flowers with segments tipped green. Easy to grow and permanent. Naturalize under deciduous trees, in shrub borders or orchards, or on cool slopes. Plant 4 in. deep in fall. Do not disturb until really crowded; then dig, divide, and replant after foliage dies down.

L. aestivum. SUMMER SNOWFLAKE. All zones. Most commonly grown. Leaves 1–1½ ft. long. Stems 1½ ft. tall carry three to five flowers; variety 'Gravetye Giant' has as many as nine flowers to a stem. In mild-winter areas, blooms November through winter; blooms with narcissus in colder areas.

L. vernum. SPRING SNOWFLAKE. Zones 1–6; not successful in hot, dry climates. Leaves 9 in. long. Stems 1 ft. tall bear single large, nodding, white flowers in very early spring (late winter in warmer areas). Needs rich, moist soil.

FOR GROWING SYMBOL EXPLANATIONS
PLEASE SEE PAGE 129

LEUCOPHYLLUM

TEXAS RANGER, SILVERLEAF

Scrophulariaceae

EVERGREEN SHRUBS

☀ ZONES 7–24

☀ FULL SUN

💧 TOLERATES SOME ARIDITY

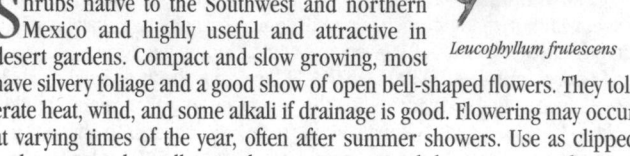

Leucophyllum frutescens

Shrubs native to the Southwest and northern Mexico and highly useful and attractive in desert gardens. Compact and slow growing, most have silvery foliage and a good show of open bell-shaped flowers. They tolerate heat, wind, and some alkali if drainage is good. Flowering may occur at varying times of the year, often after summer showers. Use as clipped hedges, massed as tall ground cover, or in mixed dry-country gardens.

L. candidum. VIOLET SILVERLEAF. To 4–5 ft. tall, with small (½-in.) silvery leaves and deep purple flowers. 'Silver Cloud' blooms heavily, and 'Thundercloud' is smaller (3–4 ft.).

L. frutescens. TEXAS RANGER, TEXAS SAGE, CENIZO. Grows to 6–8 ft., with silvery leaves and purple flowers. 'Compactum' is a dense grower to 3–4 ft. 'Green Cloud' has green leaves and deep violet flowers. 'White Cloud', with white flowers, has silvery foliage. 'Rain Cloud' is an erect grower.

L. laevigatum. CHIHUAHUAN SAGE. Grows 3–4 ft. tall and somewhat wider, with green leaves and blue-purple flowers.

LEUCOSPERMUM

PINCUSHION

Proteaceae

EVERGREEN SHRUBS

☀ ZONES 15–17, 21–24

☀ FULL SUN

💧 WATER EVERY 2–4 WEEKS ONCE ESTABLISHED

Leucospermum reflexum

South African shrubs related to *Protea;* see that entry for culture. Like proteas, these shrubs are difficult to grow, but extra effort is rewarded with spectacular flower clusters: many long, slender tubular flowers on a large thistlelike head. These make stunning cut flowers that last a month in water. Leaves are narrow ovals, stalkless and crowded along stems. Bloom peaks in late winter, early spring, but start earlier, last up to 6 months in mild winters. Well-established plants can take several degrees of frost; side buds will produce flowers even if main flower buds freeze.

L. nutans. NODDING PINCUSHION. Compact plants 4 ft. tall and as wide. Flower clusters 4 in. across; individual tube flowers, coral with yellow tips, curve gracefully outward, then inward again. Best kind for cut flowers.

L. reflexum. ROCKET PINCUSHION. Sprawling plant to 12 ft. tall with attractive gray foliage. Orange-rose, 4-in. heads; as flowers age, "pins" curl downward, giving shaggy look.

LEUCOTHOE

Ericaceae

EVERGREEN SHRUBS

☀ ZONES VARY BY SPECIES

☀ PARTIAL SHADE

💧 WATER NEEDS VARY BY SPECIES

☠ LEAVES AND NECTAR ARE POISONOUS

Leucothoe fontanesiana

Related to *Pieris.* All have leathery leaves and clusters of urn-shaped white flowers. Need acid, woodsy, deep soil; do best in woodland gardens or as facing for taller broad-leafed evergreens. Best used in masses; not especially attractive individually. Bronze-tinted winter foliage is a bonus.

L. davisiae. SIERRA LAUREL. Zones 1–7, 15–17. Grows in bogs and wet places in Trinity and Siskiyou mountains, Sierra Nevada. Upright shrub to 3½ ft. Oblong or egg-shaped leaves to 3 in. long, glossy rich green. White flowers in erect, 2–4-in.-long clusters. Blooms in summer. Water heavily.

L. fontanesiana (L. catesbaei). DROOPING LEUCOTHOE. Zones 4–7, 15–17. Borderline hardiness in Zones 1–3. Native to eastern United States. Slow grower to 2–6 ft.; branches arch gracefully. Leaves are leathery, 3–6 in. long; they turn bronzy purple in fall (bronzy green in deep shade). Spreads from underground stems. Drooping clusters of creamy white flowers resembling lily-of-the-valley in spring. Variety 'Rainbow', with leaves marked yellow, green, and pink, grows 3–4 ft. tall.

Requires summer water in first two or three summers but later can do with infrequent irrigation. Can be controlled in height to make 1½-ft. ground cover in shade; just cut older, taller stems to ground. Blooming branches are decorative cut flowers.

LEVISTICUM officinale

LOVAGE	
Apiaceae (Umbelliferae)	
PERENNIAL	
☀ ALL ZONES	
☼ FULL SUN	
💧 MODERATE WATER	

Levisticum officinale

This herb is sometimes grown for the celery flavor of its seeds, leaves, stems. Reaches 2–3 ft. tall, sometimes even 6 ft. Cut and divided, glossy deep green leaves; flattish clusters of small greenish yellow flowers. Grow from seeds or divisions.

LEWISIA

Portulacaceae	
PERENNIALS	
☀ ZONES 1–7, 14–17	
☼ ☼ FULL SUN OR LIGHT SHADE	
💧 LIGHT WATERING	

Lewisia tweedyi

Beautiful, often difficult plants for rock gardens, collections of alpine plants. All need excellent drainage; plant with fine gravel around crowns. Of the many offered by specialists, these are outstanding:

L. cotyledon. Native to Northern California and southern Oregon. Rosettes of narrow, fleshy, evergreen leaves bear 10-in. stems topped by large clusters of 1-in., white or pink flowers striped with rose or red. Spring to early-summer bloom is extremely showy. *L. c. howellii* is similar, but leaves are wavy edged and flowers somewhat larger. Same culture as *L. tweedyi*. Can be grown in pots in fast-draining sterilized soil or growing mixes.

L. rediviva. BITTERROOT. Native to mountains of the West. State flower of Montana. Fleshy roots; short stems with short, succulent, strap-shaped leaves to 2 in. long that usually die back before flowers appear (seemingly from bare earth) in spring. Flowers, borne singly on short stems, look like 2-in.-wide, rose or white water lilies. Not difficult if drainage is excellent.

L. tweedyi. Native to mountains, south central Washington. Stunning big, satiny, salmon pink flowers, one to three to a stem, bloom above fleshy, evergreen, 4-in. leaves. Needs perfect drainage around root crown to prevent rot. Prune out side growths.

LEYMUS. See ELYMUS	p. 272

LIATRIS

GAYFEATHER	
Asteraceae (Compositae)	
PERENNIALS	
☀ ZONES 1–10, 14–24	
☼ FULL SUN	
💧 💧 LIGHT TO REGULAR WATER	

Liatris spicata

Native to eastern and central United States. Showy plants. Basal tufts of narrow, grassy leaves grow from thick, often tuberous rootstocks. Tufts lengthen in summer to tall, narrow stems densely set with narrow leaves and topped by narrow plume of small, fluffy, rose purple (sometimes white) flower heads. Choice cut flowers.

These plants endure heat, cold, aridity, and poor soil. They are best used in mixed perennial borders, although the rosy purple color calls for careful placing to avoid color clashes.

L. callilepis. Plants grown and sold under this name by Dutch bulb growers are *L. spicata*.

L. spicata. To 6 ft., usually only 2–3 ft., with 15-in.-long flower plumes; each individual flower head to ⅓ in. wide. 'Kobold', a 2-ft. dwarf variety, is widely sold.

LIBERTIA

Iridaceae	
PERENNIALS	
☀ ZONES 8, 9, 14–24	
☼ ☼ SUN OR LIGHT SHADE	
💧 REGULAR WATER	

Libertia peregrinans

Iris relatives from New Zealand with swordlike leaves in fans and three-cornered flowers in clusters. Near the coast they like full sun; inland they require shade.

L. grandiflora. Bright green leaf fans reach 2 ft., with branching clusters of white ¾-in. flowers on 2½-ft. stems.

L. peregrinans. Leaves are narrow, stiffly erect, strikingly edged in brownish orange. Flowers are white. Plants form colonies by underground rhizomes. Leaves are especially attractive when backlit.

LIBOCEDRUS. See CALOCEDRUS	p. 198
LICORICE FERN. See POLYPODIUM glycyrrhiza	p. 433

LIGULARIA

Asteraceae (Compositae)	
PERENNIALS	
☀ ZONES VARY BY SPECIES	
☼ ☼ ● FULL SUN NEAR COAST, SHADE INLAND	
💧 REGULAR WATER	

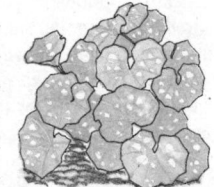

Ligularia tussilaginea 'Aureo-maculata'

Stately perennials with big leaves and yellow to orange daisy flowers. Some are hardy and winter dormant; one is less hardy and evergreen. All need rich soil. Hardy anywhere (with mulch in coldest winter climates), they perform poorly in poor soils and low humidity.

L. dentata. Zones 3–9, 15–17. Roundish leaves, heart shaped at the base, are more than 1 ft. wide. Orange-yellow daisies to 4 in. wide appear in midsummer to early fall on 3–5-ft. stalks. 'Desdemona' has deep purple leafstalks, veins, and leaf undersurfaces; upper surfaces are green. 'Othello', somewhat larger, has purple leaf undersurfaces.

L

L. stenocephala. Zones 3–9, 15–17. Usually represented by variety 'The Rocket'. Foot-wide leaves are deeply cut; yellow daisies form along tall, narrow spires to 5 ft.

L. tussilaginea (L. kaempferi, Farfugium japonicum). Zones 4–10, 14–24; house plant or indoor/outdoor plant. Speckled variety 'Aureo-maculata', leopard plant, has evergreen leaves 6–10 in. wide, thick and rather leathery, speckled and blotched with cream or yellow, nearly kidney shaped but shallowly angled and toothed. All leaves rise directly from rootstock on 1–2-ft. stems. Flower stalks, 1–2 ft. tall bear a few, 1½–2-in.-wide flower heads with yellow rays.

Choice foliage plant for shady beds or entryways. Good container plant. Tops hardy to 20°F; plants die back to roots at 0°F., put on new growth again in spring. Bait for snails and slugs. *L. t.* 'Argentea' has deep green leaves that are irregularly mottled, particularly on edges, with gray green and ivory white. 'Crispata' has curled and crested leaf edges.

LIGUSTRUM

PRIVET
Oleaceae
DECIDUOUS OR EVERGREEN SHRUBS OR SMALL TREES
⚡ ZONES VARY BY SPECIES
☼ ◑ SUN OR SOME SHADE
⬤ REGULAR WATER
◊ LEAVES, FRUITS CAUSE GASTRIC DISTRESS

Ligustrum lucidum

Most widely used in hedges. Can also be clipped into formal shapes and featured in tubs or large pots. One type is a common street tree. All have abundant, showy clusters of white to creamy white flowers in late spring or early summer. (Clipped hedges bear fewer flowers because most of the flower-bearing branches get trimmed off.) Fragrance is described as "pleasant" to "unpleasant" (never "wonderful" or "terrible"). Flowers draw bees. Small, blue-black, berrylike fruit follows blossoms. Birds eat fruit, thereby distributing seeds.

Most privets are easily grown in any soil. In some areas they are subject to lilac leaf miner, which disfigures leaves.

Nurseries sometimes misidentify certain privets. The plant sold as *L. japonicum* usually turns out to be the small tree *L. lucidum.* The true *L. japonicum* is available in two or more forms. The tall, shrubby kind is the true species; the lower-growing, more densely foliaged form is often sold as *L. texanum* and probably should be called *L. japonicum* 'Texanum'. The smaller-leafed hardy privets used for hedging are also often confused: *L. amurense, L. ovalifolium,* and *L. vulgare* look much alike, and any is likely to be sold as common privet—a name that belongs to *L. vulgare.*

L. amurense. AMUR PRIVET, AMUR RIVER NORTH PRIVET. Shrub. All zones. Deciduous in coldest areas, where it is much used for hedge and screen planting. Partially evergreen in milder climates but seldom planted there. Much like *L. ovalifolium* in appearance, but foliage is less glossy.

L. ibolium 'Variegata'. Semideciduous shrub. Zones 3–24. Variegated form of a hybrid between *L. ovalifolium* and another Japanese privet. Resembles *L. ovalifolium* but has bright green leaves with creamy yellow edges.

L. japonicum. JAPANESE PRIVET, WAX-LEAF PRIVET. Evergreen shrub. Zones 4–24. Dense, compact growth habit to 10–12 ft., but can be kept lower by trimming. Roundish oval leaves 2–4 in. long, dark to medium green and glossy above, distinctly paler to almost whitish beneath; have thick, slightly spongy feeling. Excellent plants for hedges or screens, or for shaping into globes, pyramids, other shapes, or small standard trees. Sunburns in hot spells. In areas of caliche soil, or where Texas root rot prevails, grow it in containers. Often sold as *L. texanum.*

L. j. 'Rotundifolium' (L. j. 'Coriaceum'). Grows to 4–5 ft. and has nearly round leaves to 2½ in. long. Partial shade in inland valleys.

L. j. 'Silver Star'. Leaves are deep green, with gray-green mottling and startling creamy white edges. Provides a good contrast to deep green foliage.

L. j. 'Texanum'. Very similar to species but lower growing (to 6–9 ft.), with somewhat denser, lusher foliage. Useful as windbreak.

L. lucidum. GLOSSY PRIVET. Evergreen tree. Zones 5, 6, 8–24. Makes a round-headed tree that eventually reaches 35–40 ft. Can be kept lower as a big shrub or may form multiple-trunked tree. Glossy, 4–6-in.-long leaves are tapered and pointed, dark to medium green on both sides. They feel leathery but lack the slightly spongy feel of *L. japonicum*'s leaves. Flowers in especially large, feathery clusters followed by profusion of fruit. Fine street or lawn tree. Can grow in narrow areas. Performs well in large containers. Or plant 10 ft. apart for tall privacy screen. Useful as windbreak.

Before planting this tree, carefully weigh the advantages listed above against the disadvantages. Eventual fruit crop is immense; never plant where fruits will fall on cars, walks, or other paved areas (they stain). Fallen seeds (and those dropped by birds) profusely sprout in ground cover and will need pulling. Many people dislike the flower's odor, and fruiting clusters are bare and unattractive after fruit drop.

L. ovalifolium. CALIFORNIA PRIVET. Semideciduous shrub, evergreen only in mildest areas. Zones 4–24. Inexpensive hedge plant, once widely used in California. Grows rapidly to 15 ft. but can be kept sheared to any height. Dark green, oval, 2½-in.-long leaves. Set plants 9–12 in. apart for hedges. Clip early and frequently to encourage low, dense branching. Greedy roots. Well-fed, well-watered plants hold leaves longest. Tolerates heat.

L. o. 'Aureum'. GOLDEN PRIVET. Leaves have broad yellow edges. Sold as *L. o.* 'Variegatum'.

L. 'Suwannee River'. Evergreen shrub. All zones. Reported to be hybrid between *L. japonicum* 'Rotundifolium' and *L. lucidum.* Slow growing to 1½ ft. tall in 3 years, eventually 3–4 ft.; compact habit. Leathery, dark green, somewhat twisted leaves; no fruit. Use in low hedge, foundation planting, containers.

L. 'Vicaryi'. VICARY GOLDEN PRIVET. Deciduous shrub. All zones. This one has yellow leaves, the color strongest on plants in full sun. To 3–4 ft. high. Best planted alone; color does not develop well under hedge shearing.

L. vulgare. COMMON PRIVET. Deciduous shrub. All zones. To 15 ft., unsheared. Light green leaves less glossy than those of *L. ovalifolium,* root system less greedy. Clusters of black fruit conspicuous on unpruned or lightly pruned plants. Variety 'Lodense' ('Nanum') is a dense, dwarf form that reaches only 4 ft. with equal spread.

LILAC. See SYRINGA	p. 499
LILAC VINE. See HARDENBERGIA comptoniana	p. 316

Liliaceae. The lily family contains hundreds of species of ornamental plants, as well as such vegetables as asparagus and the whole onion tribe. Most grow from bulbs, corms, or rhizomes. Flowers are often showy, usually with six equal-size segments.

LILIUM

LILY
Liliaceae
BULBS
⚡ ALL ZONES
◑ ROOTS IN SHADE; TOPS IN SUN OR FILTERED SHADE
⬤ NEVER LET ROOT ZONE DRY OUT

Lilium auratum

Most stately and varied of bulbous plants. For many years, only the species—the same plants growing wild in parts of Asia, Europe, and North America—were available, and many of these were difficult and unpredictable.

Around 1925, lily growers began a significant breeding program. They bred new hybrids from species with desirable qualities and also developed strains and varieties that were healthier, hardier, and easier to grow than the original species. They produced new forms and new colors; what is more important, they evolved the methods for growing healthy lilies in large quantities. Today, the new forms and new colors are the best garden lilies, but it is still possible to get some desirable species.

Lilies have three basic cultural requirements: deep, loose, well-drained soil; ample moisture year round (plants never completely stop growing); coolness and shade at roots, and sun or filtered shade at tops where flowers form.

Plant bulbs as soon as possible after you get them. If you must wait, keep them in a cool place until you plant. If bulbs are dry, place them in moist sand or peat moss until scales get plump and new roots begin to sprout.

In coastal fog belts, plant lilies in an open, sunny position, but protect them from strong winds. In warmer, drier climates, light or filtered shade is desirable.

Deep, well-drained soil that contains ample organic material will grow good lilies. If you want to plant lilies in heavy clay or soil that is very sandy and deficient in organic matter, you will need to add peat moss, ground bark, or sawdust. Spread a 3–4-in. layer of such material over surface; broadcast complete fertilizer (follow label directions for preplanting application) on top of it, then thoroughly blend both into soil as you dig to a depth of at least 1 ft.

Before planting bulbs, remove any injured portions and dust cuts with sulfur or a special antifungal seed and bulb disinfectant.

For each bulb, dig a generous planting hole (6–12 in. deeper than depth of bulb). Place enough soil at bottom of hole to bring it up to proper level for bulb (see next paragraph). Set bulb with its roots spread; fill in hole with soil, firming it in around bulb to eliminate air pockets. If your area is infested with gophers, you may have to plant each bulb in a 6-in.-square wire basket made of ½-in. hardware cloth. (The depth of the basket will depend on the planting depth.)

Planting depths vary according to size and rooting habit of bulb. General rule is to cover smaller bulbs with 2–3 in. of soil, medium-size bulbs with 3–4 in., and larger bulbs with 4–6 in. (but never cover Madonna lilies with more than 1 in. of soil). Planting depth can be quite flexible. It's better to err by planting shallowly than too deeply; lily bulbs have contractile roots that draw them down to proper depth. Ideal spacing for lily bulbs is 1 ft. apart, but you can plant as close as 6 in. for densely massed effect.

After planting, water well and mulch area with 2–3 in. of organic material to conserve moisture, keep soil cool, and reduce weed growth.

Lilies need constant moisture to about 6 in. deep. You can reduce watering somewhat after tops turn yellow in fall, but never allow roots to dry out completely. Flooding is preferable to overhead watering, which may help to spread disease spores. Pull weeds by hand if possible; hoeing may injure roots.

Viral or mosaic infection is a problem. No cure exists. To avoid it, buy healthy bulbs from reliable sources. Dig and destroy any lilies that show mottling in leaves or seriously stunted growth. Control aphids, which spread the infection. Control botrytis blight, a fungal disease, with appropriate fungicide. Control gophers; they relish lily bulbs.

Remove faded flowers. Wait until stems and leaves turn yellow before you cut plants back. At this point, withhold water somewhat but do not let soil become bone dry, since lilies never go completely dormant.

If clumps become too large and crowded, dig up, divide, and transplant them in spring or fall. If you're careful, you can lift lily clumps at any time, even in bloom.

Lilies are fine container plants. Place one bulb in a deep 5–7-in. pot or five in a 14–16-in. pot. First, fill pot one-third full of potting mix. Then place bulb with roots spread and pointing downward; cover with about an inch of soil. Water thoroughly and place in deep cold frame or greenhouse that is heated (in colder climates) just enough to keep out frost. During root-forming period, keep soil moderately moist. When top growth appears, add more soil mixture and gradually fill pot as stems elongate. Leave 1-in. space between surface of soil and rim of pot for watering. Move pots onto partially shaded terrace or patio during blooming period. Later, if you wish to repot bulbs, do so in late fall or early spring.

Although the official classification of lilies lists eight divisions of hybrids and a ninth division of species, the following are the lilies ordinarily available to western gardeners.

ASIATIC HYBRIDS

These are the easiest and most reliable for the average garden. Some have upward-facing flowers while others have horizontally held or drooping flowers. Stems are strong, erect, and short (1½ ft.) to moderate (4½ ft.) in height. Colors range from white through yellow and orange to pink and red. Many have dark spots or contrasting "halos." They are the earliest to bloom (June–July). Examples are 'Enchantment', orange red spotted with black; 'Impala', bright yellow; 'Pink Floyd', ivory pink banded with rose pink; and 'Sancerre', pure white and unspotted.

AURELIAN HYBRIDS

Derived from Asiatic species, excluding *L. auratum* and *L. speciosum*. They have trumpets or bowl-shaped flowers in July and August. Flowers range from white and cream through yellow and pink, many with green, brown, or purple shading on their outer surfaces. Plants are 3–6 ft. tall, and each stem carries 12–20 flowers.

ORIENTAL HYBRIDS

These are the latest to bloom (August) and the most exotic, with big (to 9 in.) fragrant flowers of white or pink, often spotted with gold and shaded or banded with red. Most are tall, with nodding flowers, but a few are dwarf and have upward-facing blooms. Examples are 'Casablanca', pure white; 'Pink Ribbons', light rose banded and spotted with deep rose; and 'Stargazer', rose red with white margins.

SPECIES AND VARIANTS

L. auratum. GOLD-BAND LILY. August or early September bloom on 4–6-ft. plants. Flowers fragrant, waxy white spotted crimson, with golden band on each segment.

L. candidum. MADONNA LILY. Pure white, fragrant blooms on 3–4-ft. stems in June. Unlike most lilies, dies down soon after bloom, makes new growth in fall. Plant while dormant in August. Does not have stem roots; set top of bulb only 1–2 in. deep in sunny location. Bulb quickly makes foliage rosette that lives over winter, lengthens to blooming stem in spring. Subject to diseases that shorten its life. Cascade strain, grown from seed, is healthier than imported bulbs. The lily of medieval romance, a sentimental choice for many gardeners.

Lilium candidum

L. cernuum. Only 12–20 in. tall, with lilac flowers often dotted dark purple. Summer blooming; perfectly hardy. Sun.

L. columbianum. COLUMBIA LILY, TIGER LILY. Dainty species bearing about 20–30 golden orange lilies on 2-ft. stems in July and August. Native from British Columbia to Northern California.

L. henryi. Slender stems to 8–9 ft. topped by 10–20 bright orange flowers with sharply recurved segments. Summer bloom. Best in light shade.

L. humboldtii. HUMBOLDT LILY. Native of open woodlands in Sierra Nevada. Grows 3–6 ft. tall. Nodding, recurved, bright orange flowers with large maroon dots. Early summer bloom. Larger, finer, easier to grow is *L. h. ocellatum (L. h. magnificum)*.

L. lancifolium (L. tigrinum). TIGER LILY. To 4 ft. or taller with pendulous orange flowers spotted black. Summer bloom. An old favorite. Newer tiger lilies are available in white, cream, yellow, pink, and red, all with black spots.

L. longiflorum. EASTER LILY. Very fragrant, long, white, trumpet-shaped flowers on short stems. Usually purchased in bloom at Easter as forced plant. Set out in garden after flowers fade. Sun or partial shade, good drainage. Stem will ripen and die down. Plant may rebloom in fall; in 1–2 years may flower in midsummer, its normal bloom season. Varieties include 'Ace', 1½ ft. tall; 'Tetraploid', 1–1½ ft. tall; 'Croft', 1 ft. tall; 'Estate', to 3 ft. Recent hybridization has yielded pink, yellow, and red offspring. Not for severe winter climates. Don't plant forced Easter lilies near other lilies; they may transmit a virus.

L. martagon. TURK'S CAP LILY. Purplish pink, recurved, pendant flowers in June and July on 3–5-ft. stems. This lily is slow to establish but is long lived and eventually forms big clumps. *L. m. album*, pure white, is one of the most appealing lilies. It is an ancestor of Paisley hybrids. ▶

L. pardalinum. LEOPARD LILY. California native. Recurved flowers orange or red orange shading to yellow, with brown spotting in center. Spring–summer bloom on stems 4–8 ft. high.

L. pumilum. A coral red lily that loves sun but needs shade for its roots. Each wiry, 1–1½-ft. stem carries 1–20 scented flowers. Blooms May–June.

L. regale. REGAL LILY. Superseded in quality by modern hybrid trumpet lilies but still popular and easy to grow. To 6 ft., with white, fragrant flowers in July.

L. speciosum. Grows 2½–5 ft. tall. Large, wide, fragrant flowers with broad, deeply recurved segments, August–September; white, heavily suffused rose pink, sprinkled with raised crimson dots. 'Rubrum', red; 'Album', pure white; also other named forms. Best in light and afternoon shade; needs rich soil with plenty of leaf mold.

L. tigrinum. See L. lancifolium

LILLY-PILLY TREE. See ACMENA smithii	**p. 138**
LILY. See LILIUM	**p. 354**
LILY-OF-THE-NILE. See AGAPANTHUS	**p. 141**
LILY-OF-THE-VALLEY. See CONVALLARIA majalis	**p. 239**
LILY-OF-THE-VALLEY SHRUB. See PIERIS japonica	**p. 418**
LILY-OF-THE-VALLEY TREE. See CLETHRA arborea, CRINODENDRON patagua	**pp. 235, 248**
LILY TURF. See LIRIOPE and OPHIOPOGON	**p. 358**
LIME. See CITRUS	**p. 231**
LIMEQUAT. See CITRUS	**p. 231**

LIMONIUM (Statice)

SEA LAVENDER

Plumbaginaceae

PERENNIALS, BIENNIALS, AND ANNUALS

✔ ZONES VARY BY SPECIES

☀ FULL SUN

💧 LITTLE WATER ONCE ESTABLISHED

Limonium perezii

Large, leathery basal leaves contrast with airy clusters of small, delicate flowers on nearly leafless, many-branched stems. Tiny flowers consist of two parts: an outer, papery envelope (the calyx) and an inner part, the corolla, which often has a different color. For spring–summer bloom, sow annual kinds indoors and move to garden when weather warms up. Or sow outdoors in early spring for later bloom. All tolerate heat and many soils but need good drainage. They often self-sow.

STATICE LASTS LONG FRESH OR DRIED

Cut these flowers for fresh bouquets after most flowers have finished blooming. For dried arrangements, cut after opening but before sun has faded them. With a rubber band, join several bunches together by stem bases. Hang bunches upside down in a dry spot out of bright sun (the garage is usually a good place) until flowers dry.

L. bonduellii. Summer annual or biennial. All zones. Grows 2 ft. tall, with 6-in. basal leaves lobed nearly to midrib. Flower stems are distinctly winged; calyx is yellow, tiny corolla deeper yellow.

L. latifolium. Perennial. Zones 1–10, 14–24. To 2½ ft. tall. Smooth-edged leaves to 10 in. long. Calyx is white and corolla bluish; white and pink kinds exist. Summer bloom. Vigorous plants may show a 3-ft.-wide haze of flowers.

L. perezii. Perennial. Zones 13, 15–17, 20–24. Often freezes in Zones 14, 18, 19. Rich green leaves up to 1 ft. long, including stalks. Summer bloom over long season. Calyx is rich purple and the tiny corolla white. Flower clusters may be 3 ft. tall, nearly as wide. First-rate beach plant. Often naturalizes along southern California coast. Damaged by 25°F temperatures, but useful even where it freezes out occasionally; nursery-grown seedlings develop fast.

L. sinuatum. Summer annual. All zones. Growth habit like *L. bonduellii*, with lobed leaves and winged stems, but calyx is blue, lavender, or rose and corolla is white. Widely grown as a fresh or dried cut flower.

L. suworowii. See Psylliostachys

L. tataricum. See Goniolimon

Linaceae. The flax family of annuals, perennials, and shrubs displays cup- or disk-shaped flowers with four or five petals. Flowers are often showy. Individually short lived, they appear over a long season. Examples are flax (*Linum*) and yellow flax (*Reinwardtia*).

LINARIA

TOADFLAX

Scrophulariaceae

PERENNIALS AND ANNUALS

✔ ZONES VARY BY SPECIES

☀ ◑ FULL SUN OR LIGHT SHADE

💧 MODERATE WATER

Brightly colored flowers that resemble small, spurred snapdragons. Very narrow, medium green leaves. Easy to grow. Best in masses; individual plants are rather wispy.

Linaria maroccana

L. cymbalaria. See Cymbalaria muralis

L. maroccana. BABY SNAPDRAGON, TOADFLAX. Summer annual; winter annual in Zones 10–13. To 1½ ft. Flowers in red and gold, rose, pink, mauve, chamois, blue, violet, and purple, blotched with different shade on the lip. Spur is longer than flower.

Fairy Bouquet strain is only 9 in. tall and has larger flowers in pastel shades. Northern Lights strain blooms in reds, oranges, and yellows as well as in bicolors. Blooms from June to September. Sow them in quantity for a show.

L. purpurea. Perennial. All zones. Narrow, bushy, erect growth to 2½–3 ft. Blue-green foliage and violet blue flowers. 'Canon Went' is a pink form. Summer blooming.

LINDEN. See TILIA	**p. 506**
LINGONBERRY. See VACCINIUM vitis-idaea minus	**p. 516**

LINNAEA borealis

TWINFLOWER

Caprifoliaceae

PERENNIAL

✔ ZONES 1–7, 14–17

☀ ◑ ● SUN NEAR COAST, SHADE INLAND

💧 REGULAR WATER

Native from Northern California to Alaska, Idaho, and much of Northern Hemisphere. Delicate, flat, evergreen mats with 1-in.-long, glossy leaves. Spreads by runners. Pale pink, paired, fragrant, trumpet-shaped flowers, ⅓ in. long on 3–4-in. stems. Collector's item or small-scale ground cover for woodland garden. Keep area around plants mulched with leaf mold to induce spreading.

Linnaea borealis

LINUM

FLAX	
Linaceae	
PERENNIALS AND ANNUALS	
☀ ALL ZONES	
☼ FULL SUN	
⬤ TOLERATES SOME ARIDITY	

Linum perenne

Erect, branching stems; narrow leaves; and abundant, shallow-cupped, five-petaled flowers blooming from late spring into summer or fall. Each bloom lasts but a day, but others keep coming. (The flax of commerce—*L. usitatissimum*—is grown for its fiber and seeds, which yield linseed oil.)

Use in borders; some naturalize freely in uncultivated areas. Light, well-drained soil. Most perennial kinds live only 3–4 years. Easy from seed; perennials also can be grown from cuttings. Difficult to divide.

L. flavum. GOLDEN FLAX. Perennial. Erect, compact, 12–15 in. tall, somewhat woody at base; grooved branches, green leaves. Flowers golden yellow, about 1 in. wide, in branched clusters, April–June. Often called yellow flax, a name correctly applied to closely related *Reinwardtia indica.* 'Compactum' is a smaller form.

L. grandiflorum 'Rubrum'. SCARLET FLAX. Annual. Bright scarlet flowers, 1–1½ in. wide, on slender, leafy stems 1–1½ ft. tall. Narrow, grayish green leaves. Also comes in a rose-colored form. Sow seed thickly in place in fall (in mild areas) or early spring. Quick, easy color in borders, over bulbs left in ground. Good with gray foliage or white-flowered plants. Reseeds but doesn't become a nuisance. Seed often included in wild flower seed mixtures.

L. narbonense. Perennial. Wiry stems to 2 ft. high. Leaves blue green, narrow. Flowers large (1¾ in. across), azure blue with white eye, in open clusters. Best variety, 'Six Hills', has rich sky blue flowers.

L. perenne. PERENNIAL BLUE FLAX. Most vigorous blue-flowered flax with stems to 2 ft., usually leafless below. Branching clusters of light blue flowers are profuse from May to September. Flowers close in shade or late in the day. Self-sows freely. *L. p. lewisii,* the western native flax, is similar but somewhat sturdier.

LION'S TAIL. See LEONOTIS leonurus	p. 350
LIPPIA citriodora. See ALOYSIA triphylla	p. 148
LIPPIA repens. See PHYLA nodiflora	p. 416

LIQUIDAMBAR

SWEET GUM	
Hamamelidaceae	
DECIDUOUS TREES	
☀ ZONES VARY BY SPECIES	
☼ FULL SUN	
⬤ WATER 1–2 TIMES A MONTH IN DRY SEASON	

Liquidambar styraciflua

Valuable for form, foliage, and fall color, easy culture. Moderate growth rate; young and middle-aged trees generally upright, somewhat cone shaped, spreading in age. Lobed, maplelike leaves. Flowers inconspicuous; fruits are spiny balls that ornament trees in winter, need raking in spring.

Give neutral or slightly acid, improved garden soil; chlorosis in strongly alkaline soils is hard to correct. Plant from containers or from ball and burlap; be sure roots are not can-bound. Stake well. Prune only to shape. Trees branch from ground up and look most natural that way, but can be pruned high for easier foot traffic.

Good street trees. Form surface roots that can be nuisance in lawns or parking strips. Effective in tall screens or groves, planted 6–10 ft. apart. Brilliant fall foliage. Fall color less effective in mildest climates or in mild, late autumns.

L. formosana. CHINESE SWEET GUM. Zones 4–9, 14–24. To 40–60 ft. tall, 25 ft. wide. Free-form outline; sometimes pyramidal, especially when young. Leaves with three to five lobes are 3–4½ in. across, violet red when expanding, then deep green. In Southern California, leaves turn yellow beige in late December or early January before falling. Farther north, leaves turn red. Variety 'Afterglow' has lavender purple new growth, rose red fall color.

L. orientalis. ORIENTAL SWEET GUM. Zones 5–9, 14–24. Native to Turkey. To 20–30 ft., spreading or round headed. Leaves 2–3 in. wide, deeply five-lobed, each lobe again lobed in lacy effect. Leafs out early after short dormant period. Fall color varies from deep gold and bright red in cooler areas to dull brown purple in coastal Southern California. Resistant to oak root fungus.

L. styraciflua. AMERICAN SWEET GUM. Zones 1–12, 14–24. Grows to 60 ft. (much taller in its native eastern United States). Narrow and erect in youth, with lower limbs eventually spreading to 20–25 ft. Tolerates damp soil; resistant to oak root fungus. Good all-year tree. In winter, branching pattern, furrowed bark, corky wings on twigs, and hanging fruit give interest; in spring and summer, leaves (3–7 in. wide, with five to seven lobes) are deep green; in fall, leaves turn purple, yellow, or red. Even seedling trees give good color (which may vary somewhat from year to year). For uniformity, match trees while they are in fall color or buy budded trees of a named variety, such as the following.

'Burgundy'. Leaves turn deep purple red, hang late into winter or even early spring if storms are not heavy.

'Festival'. Narrow, columnar. Light green foliage turns to yellow, peach, pink, orange, and red.

'Palo Alto'. Turns orange red to bright red in fall.

'Rotundiloba'. Lobes of leaves are rounded rather than sharp. Fall foliage is purple, and tree does not form seed balls.

LIRIODENDRON tulipifera

TULIP TREE	
Magnoliaceae	
DECIDUOUS TREE	
☀ ZONES 1–12, 14–23	
☼ FULL SUN	
⬤ AMPLE SUMMER WATER	

Liriodendron tulipifera

Native to eastern United States. Fast growth to 60–80 ft., with eventual spread to 40 ft. Straight columnar trunk, with spreading, rising branches that form tall pyramidal crown. Lyre-shaped leaves, 5–6 in. long and wide, turn from bright yellow green to bright yellow (or yellow and brown) in fall. Tulip-shaped flowers in late spring are 2 in. wide, greenish yellow, orange at base. Handsome at close range, they are not showy on the tree, being high up and well concealed by leaves. They are not usually produced until tree is 10–12 years old.

Give this tree room and deep, rich, well-drained neutral or slightly acid soil. Best out of prevailing winds. Control scale insects and aphids as necessary. Not bothered by oak root fungus.

Good large shade, lawn, or roadside tree. One of the best deciduous trees for Southern California; it turns yellow there most autumns. Spreading root system makes it hard to garden under. Columnar variety 'Arnold' is useful in narrow planting areas; it will bloom 2–3 years after planting. 'Majestic Beauty' (*L. t.* 'Aureomarginatum') has leaves edged with yellow. Moderate growth rate, size.

LIRIOPE and OPHIOPOGON

LILY TURF

Liliaceae

EVERGREEN GRASSLIKE PERENNIALS

✿ ZONES 5–10, 12–24 (L. SPICATA IN ALL ZONES)

☼ ◑ ● FULL SUN ON COAST, SHADE INLAND

◐ ◗ REGULAR TO AMPLE WATER

▼ SEE CHART

Liriope muscari

These two plants are similar in appearance: both form clumps or tufts of grasslike leaves and bear white or lavender flowers in spikelike or branched clusters (quite showy in some kinds). Last well in flower arrangements. Use as casual ground cover in small areas. Also attractive as borders along paths, between flower bed and lawn, among rock groupings, or in rock gardens. Grow well along streams and around garden pools. Try under bamboo or to cover bare soil at bases of trees or shrubs in large containers. None satisfactory as mowed lawn. Tolerate indoor conditions in pots or planter.

Plant in well-drained soil. Become ragged and brown with neglect. Cut back shaggy old foliage after new leaves appear. Plants don't need heavy feeding. Protect from snails and slugs. Increase plants by dividing in early spring before new growth starts.

Plants look best from spring until cold weather of winter. Extended frosts may cause plants to turn yellow; they take quite a while to recover. Can show tip burn on leaves if soil contains excess salts or if plants are kept too wet where drainage is poor.

LISIANTHUS. See EUSTOMA   p. 290

LIRIOPE and OPHIOPOGON

NAME	GROWTH FORM	LEAVES	FLOWERS	COMMENTS
Liriope muscari BIG BLUE LILY TURF	Forms large clumps but does not spread by underground stems. Rather loose growth habit, 1–1½ ft. high	Dark green. To 2 ft. long, ½ in. wide	Dark violet buds and flowers in rather dense, 6–8-in.-long spikelike clusters on 5–12-in.-long stems (resembling grape hyacinths), followed by a few round, shiny black fruits	Profuse flowers July–Aug. Flowers held above leaves in young plants, partly hidden in older plants. Many garden varieties. 'Lilac Beauty' has paler violet flowers
L. m. 'Majestic'	Resembles *L. muscari* but forms more open clumps and is somewhat taller growing	Similar to above	Dark violet flowers and buds in clusters that look somewhat like cockscombs on 8–10-in.-long stems	Heavy flowering. Clusters show up well, held above leaves on young plants
L. m. 'Silvery Sunproof'	Open growth, strongly vertical, partly arching, 15–18 in. high	Leaves with gold stripes that turn white as they mature	Lilac flowers in spikelike clusters rising well above foliage in early summer	One of the best for open areas and flowers
L. m. 'Variegata' (may be sold as **Ophiopogon jaburan 'Variegata'**)	Resembles *L. muscari*, but somewhat looser, softer	New leaves green, 1–1½ ft. long, edged with yellow, becoming dark green second season	Violet buds and flowers in spikelike clusters well above foliage. Flower stalk 1 ft. high	Does best in partial shade
L. spicata CREEPING LILY TURF	Dense ground cover that spreads widely by underground stems. Grows 8–9 in. high	Narrow (¼-in.-wide), deep green, grasslike leaves, soft and not as upright as those of *L. muscari*. 'Silver Dragon' has white-striped leaves	Pale lilac to white flowers in spikelike clusters barely taller than leaves	Hardy in all zones. Inland, it looks rather shabby in winter. To get best effect, mow every year in spring prior to new growth. Good ground cover for cold areas where *Ophiopogon japonicus* won't grow
Ophiopogon jaburan (often sold as **Liriope gigantea**)	Eventually forms large clump growing from fibrous roots	Dark green, somewhat curved, firm leaves 1½–3 ft. long, about ½ in. wide	Small, chalk white flowers in nodding clusters, somewhat hidden by leaves in summer. Metallic violet blue fruit	Does best in shade. Fruit is very attractive feature; good for cutting. *O. j.* 'Vittatus' has leaves striped lengthwise with white, aging to plain green. Similar, perhaps identical, is *Liriope muscari* 'Variegata', sometimes sold as *L. exiliflora* 'Vittata'
O. japonicus MONDO GRASS	Forms dense clumps that spread by underground stems, many of which are tuberlike. Slow to establish as ground cover	Dark green leaves ⅛ in. wide, 8–12 in. long. 'Nana' and 'Kyoto Dwarf' have half-sized leaves in tight clumps. Slow, sure spreader	Flowers light lilac in short spikes usually hidden by the leaves. Summer blooming. Fruit blue	In hot, dry areas, grow in some shade. Can be cut back. Easy to divide. Set divisions 6–8 in. apart. Roots will be killed at 10°F. Looks best in partial shade but will take full sun along coast
O. planiscapus 'Nigrescens' (**O. p. 'Nigricans'**, **O. p. 'Arabicus'**)	Makes tuft 8 in. high and about 1 ft. wide	Leaves to 10 in. long. New leaves green but soon turn black	White (sometimes flushed pink) in loose spikelike clusters in summer	Probably best grown in container, valuable as a novelty; black-leafed plants are rather rare

LITCHI chinensis

LITCHI, LITCHI NUT

Sapindaceae

EVERGREEN TREE

⚡ ZONES 21–24

☼ FULL SUN

⬤ REGULAR WATER

Litchi chinensis

Slow-growing, round-topped, spreading tree, 20–40 ft. tall. Leaves have three to nine leathery, 3–6-in.-long leaflets that are coppery red when young, dark green later. Inconspicuous flowers. When fruit is ripe, the brittle, warty rind surrounding it turns red. Fruit is sweet in flavor, juicy when fresh, raisinlike when dried.

Needs frost-free site, acid soil, moist air, nitrogen fertilizer. Has fruited in a few warm areas near San Diego. Look for named varieties if you're interested in fruit production. 'Brewster', 'Groff', 'Kwai Mi', 'Mauritius', and 'Sweet Cliff' are grown.

LITHOCARPUS densiflorus

TANBARK OAK

Fagaceae

EVERGREEN TREE

⚡ ZONES 4–7, 14–24

☼ ◑ FULL SUN OR LIGHT SHADE

⬤ LITTLE WATER ONCE ESTABLISHED

Lithocarpus densiflorus

Native to Coast Ranges from southern Oregon to Santa Barbara County, California. Reaches 60–90 ft. under forest conditions; in the open, tree is lower, broader, its lower branches sometimes touching the ground. Leathery, 1½–4-in., sharply toothed leaves are covered with whitish or yellowish wool upon expanding; later, they are smooth green above, gray green beneath. Tiny, whitish male flowers in large branched clusters have odd odor that some people find offensive. Acorns in burrlike cups. As street or lawn tree, it resembles holly oak (*Quercus ilex*), but has lusher foliage.

LITHODORA diffusa

Boraginaceae

PERENNIAL

⚡ ZONES 5–7, 14–17

☼ ◑ FULL SUN OR LIGHT SHADE

⬤ SOME SUMMER WATER

Lithodora diffusa

Prostrate, somewhat shrubby, slightly mounded, broad mass 6–12 in. tall. Narrow evergreen leaves, ¾–1 in. long; both foliage and stems are hairy. From May to June (and often later), plant sprinkled with brilliant blue, tubular flowers ½ in. long. Loose, well-drained, lime-free soil. Needs some summer watering. Rock gardens, walls. 'Heavenly Blue' and 'Grace Ward' are selected varieties. Formerly *Lithospermum diffusum* or *L. prostratum*.

LITHOPS

STONEFACE

Aizoaceae

SUCCULENTS, BEST GROWN INDOORS

☼ FULL SUN

⬤ LITTLE WATER IN SUMMER, NONE IN WINTER

Lithops

Among the best-known "living rocks" or "pebble plants" of South Africa. Shaped like inverted cones 2–4 in. high; tops are shaped like stones with a fissure across the middle. From this fissure emerge the large flower (resembling an ice plant flower) and new leaves. Many species, all interesting. Grow in pots of fast-draining soil.

LITHOSPERMUM. See LITHODORA p. 359

LIVINGSTONE DAISY. See DOROTHEANTHUS bellidiformis p. 267

LIVISTONA

Arecaceae (Palmae)

PALMS

⚡ ZONES 13–17, 19–24

☼ FULL SUN

⬤ WATER REGULARLY FOR LUXURIANT LOOK

Livistona australis

Native from China to Australia. These fan palms somewhat resemble *Washingtonia* but generally have shorter, darker, shinier leaves. All are hardy to about 22°F.

L. australis. In ground, grows slowly to 40–50 ft. Has clean, slender trunk with interesting-looking leaf scars. Dark green leaves 3–5 ft. wide. Good potted plant when young.

L. chinensis. CHINESE FOUNTAIN PALM. Slow growing; 40-year-old plants are only 15 ft. tall. Self-cleaning (no pruning of old leaves needed) with leaf-scarred trunk. Roundish, bright green, 3–6-ft. leaves droop strongly at outer edges.

L. decipiens. To 30–40 ft. in 20 years. Stiff, open head of leaves green on top, bluish beneath, 2–5 ft. across on long, spiny stems. Good in pots, gardens.

L. mariae. From hot, dry interior Australia. Grows slowly to 10–15 ft. Young or potted plants have attractive reddish leaves and leaf stems. Leaves 3–4 ft. wide.

LOBELIA

Campanulaceae (Lobeliaceae)

PERENNIALS OR ANNUALS

⚡ ZONES VARY BY SPECIES

☼ ◑ SUN OR PARTIAL SHADE

⬤ ⬤ ⬤ WATER NEEDS VARY BY SPECIES

☣ MOST CONTAIN POISONOUS ALKALOIDS

Lobelia erinus

Distinct differences separate the annual lobelia from the most familiar perennial kinds; the former is blue and spreading, the others red or blue and vertical. On all, tubular, lipped flowers resemble those of honeysuckle or salvia.

L. cardinalis. CARDINAL FLOWER. Perennial. Zones 1–7, 12–17. Native to eastern United States and to a few sites in mountains of the Southwest. Erect, single-stemmed, 2–4-ft.-high plant with saw-edged leaves set directly on the stems. Spikes of flame red, inch-long flowers. Summer bloom. A bog plant in nature, it needs rich soil and constant moisture through growing season. Crossbreeding with this and *L. splendens* (*L. fulgens*), which is closely related, has resulted in a number of hybrids. One of these, 'Queen Victoria', has deep purple-red foliage and scarlet flowers.

L. erinus. Summer annual. All zones. Popular and dependable edging plant. Compact or trailing growth habit with leafy, branching stems. Flowers, ¾ in. across, are light blue to violet (sometimes pink, reddish purple, or white) with white or yellowish throats. Blooms from early summer to frost; lives over winter in mild areas. Takes about 2 months for seed sown in pots to grow to planting-out size. Moist, rich soil. Self-sows where adapted. Trailing kinds make a graceful ground cover in large planters or in smaller pots; the stems, loaded with flowers, spill over the edges. ▶

L

'Cambridge Blue' has clear, soft blue flowers and light green leaves on compact 4–6-in. plant. 'Crystal Palace' has rich, dark blue flowers on a compact plant with bronze green leaves. Both take morning or late-afternoon sun inland. 'Rosamond' has carmine red flowers with white eyes. 'White Lady' is pure white. Three trailing varieties for hanging baskets or wall plantings are 'Hamburgia', 'Blue Cascade', and 'Sapphire'.

L. laxiflora. Perennial. Zones 7–9, 12–24. Mexican native. Narrow, erect, 2-ft. stems from creeping underground rootstocks bear narrow leaves and open clusters of tubular, orange red flowers over a long summer season. Once established, withstands considerable aridity and neglect; often persists in abandoned gardens.

L. syphilitica. Perennial. Zones 2–9, 14–17. Native to eastern United States. Leafy plants send up 3-ft. stalks set with blue flowers. Needs ample moisture, partial shade.

Lobeliaceae. See Campanulaceae	p. 203

LOBIVIA

Cactaceae

CACTI

☘ ZONES 16, 17, 21–24; OR INDOORS

☼ ◐ FULL SUN OR LIGHT SHADE

💧 AMPLE WATER IN SUMMER BLOOM AND GROWTH

Lobivia Hybrid

Small globular or cylindrical shapes with big, showy flowers in shades of red, yellow, pink, orange, purplish, lilac. Flowers sometimes nearly as big as plants, like flowers of *Echinopsis* but shorter, broader. Many species offered. Usually grown in pots by collectors. Give porous soil, occasional feeding. Can grow indoors; bring outside in warm weather.

LOBIVOPSIS

Cactaceae

CACTI

☘ ZONES 16, 17, 21–24

☼ ◐ BLOOM BEST IN FULL SUN

💧 WATER FREELY DURING BLOOM

Lobivopsis Hybrid

Hybrids between *Lobivia* and *Echinopsis*. Extremely free flowering with big, long-tubed flowers on small plants. Culture, hardiness same as for *Echinopsis*. Grow in fairly good-size pots (5-in. pot for a 3-in. plant); feed monthly in summer. Paramount Hybrids come in red, pink, orange, rose, and white. Some may show a dozen or more 6-in.-long flowers on a 3–4-in. plant. Keep cool and dry in winter.

LOBULARIA maritima

SWEET ALYSSUM

Brassicaceae (Cruciferae)

ANNUAL

☘ ALL ZONES

☼ ◐ BEST IN SUN, TOLERATES LIGHT SHADE

💧 BEST WITH REGULAR WATER

Lobularia maritima

Low, branching, trailing plant to 1 ft. tall. Leaves narrow or lance shaped, ½–2 in. long. Tiny, white, four-petaled flowers crowded in clusters; honeylike fragrance. Spring and summer bloom in cold regions; where winters are mild (Zones 10–24), blooms all year from self-sown seedlings. Seeds sometimes included in wildflower mixes or erosion-control mixes for bare or disturbed earth.

Easy, quick, dependable. Blooms from seed in 6 weeks; grows in almost any soil. Useful for carpeting, edging, bulb cover, temporary filler in rock garden or perennial border; between flagstones; in window boxes or containers. Attracts bees. If you shear plants halfway back 4 weeks after they come into bloom, new growth will make another crop of flowers, and plants won't become rangy.

Garden varieties better known than the species; these varieties self-sow too, but seedlings tend to revert to taller, looser growth; less intense color; smaller flowers. 'Carpet of Snow' (2–4 in. tall), 'Little Gem' (4–6 in.), and 'Tiny Tim' (3 in.) are good compact whites. 'Tetra Snowdrift' (1 ft.) has long stems, large white flowers. 'Rosie O'Day' (2–4 in.) and 'Pink Heather' (6 in.) are lavender pinks. 'Oriental Night' (4 in.) and 'Violet Queen' (5 in.) are rich violet purples.

LOCUST. See ROBINIA	p. 461
LOGANBERRY. See BLACKBERRY	p. 185

LOLIUM

RYEGRASS

Poaceae (Gramineae)

ANNUAL OR PERENNIAL LAWN GRASSES

☘ ALL ZONES

☼ FULL SUN

💧 WATER THROUGHOUT DRY SEASON

Lolium perenne

Not considered the choicest lawn grasses, but useful in special conditions and situations (lawns, pasture, soil reclamation). These are clumping, not running, grasses. To make tight turf, sow heavily. Ryegrass is often mixed with other lawn grass species for low-cost, large-area coverage in cool-summer climates. In Bermuda grass country, it is often sown in fall on reconditioned Bermuda lawns to give winter green.

L. multiflorum. ITALIAN RYEGRASS. Larger, coarser than perennial ryegrass. Basically an annual; some plants live for several seasons in mild climates. Fast growing, deep rooted. Hybrid between *L. multiflorum* and *L. perenne* is common or domestic ryegrass, often used as winter cover on soil or winter-dormant lawns.

L. perenne. PERENNIAL RYEGRASS. Finer in texture than above, deep green with high gloss. Disadvantages are clumping tendency and tough flower and seed stems that lie down under mower blades. Advantages are fast sprouting and growth. Best in cool-summer climates. 'Manhattan' is finer, more uniform. Other varieties are 'Pennfine', 'Derby', 'Yorktown', 'Loretta'. Mow at 1½–2 in., higher in summer.

LOMARIA. See BLECHNUM	p. 185
LONDON PRIDE. See SAXIFRAGA umbrosa	p. 478

LONICERA

HONEYSUCKLE

Caprifoliaceae

EVERGREEN OR DECIDUOUS SHRUBS OR VINES

☘ ZONES VARY BY SPECIES

☼ ◐ SUN; LIGHT SHADE INLAND

💧 MODERATE SUMMER WATER

Lonicera
hildebrandiana

Most kinds are valued for tubular, often fragrant flowers. Vining kinds need support when they are starting out. Most species need average summer water once established.

L. fragrantissima. WINTER HONEYSUCKLE. Deciduous shrub, partially evergreen in mild-winter areas. Zones 1–9, 14–24. Arching, rather stiff growth to 8 ft. Leaves oval, dull dark green above, blue green beneath, 1–3 in. long. Creamy white flowers, ⅝ in. long, on previous year's wood, in early spring to fall depending on climate. Flowers richly fragrant (like *Daphne odora*) but not showy. Berrylike red fruit. Can be used as clipped hedge or background.

L. heckrottii. GOLD FLAME HONEYSUCKLE, CORAL HONEYSUCKLE. Deciduous or semideciduous vine or small shrub. Zones 2–24. Vigorous to 12–15 ft., with oval, 2-in., blue-green leaves. Free blooming from spring to frost. Clustered 1½-in.-long flowers, bright coral pink outside and rich yellow within, open from coral pink buds. Train as espalier or on wire along eaves. Susceptible to aphids.

L. hildebrandiana. GIANT BURMESE HONEYSUCKLE. Fast-growing evergreen vine. Zones 9, 14–17, 19–24. Big plant with 4–6-in., oval, glossy dark green leaves on supple, ropelike stems. Blooms in summer: tubular, fragrant flowers up to 6–7 in. long that open white, then turn yellow to dull orange. Blossoms are slow to drop. Plants occasionally have dark green, inch-wide, berrylike fruit. Most widely planted honeysuckle in Southern California. Thin out older stems occasionally and remove some growth that has bloomed. Striking along eaves, on arbor or wall.

L. japonica. JAPANESE HONEYSUCKLE. Evergreen vine, partial or wholly deciduous in coldest regions. Zones 2–24. Rampant. Deep green, oval leaves; purple-tinged white flowers with sweet fragrance. Late spring, summer bloom.

Several varieties are grown, all better known than the species itself. *L. j.* 'Aureo-reticulata', goldnet honeysuckle, has leaves veined yellow, especially in full sun. *L. j.* 'Halliana', Hall's honeysuckle, most vigorous and widely grown, climbs to 15 ft., covers 150 sq. ft.; flowers pure white changing to yellow, attractive to bees. *L. j.* 'Purpurea', probably same as *L. j. chinensis*, has leaves tinged purple underneath and purplish red flowers that are white inside.

Of the above, *L. j.* 'Halliana' is the most commonly used as bank and ground cover, for erosion control in large areas; unless curbed, it can become a weed, smothering less vigorous plants. Needs severe pruning once a year to prevent undergrowth from building up and becoming fire hazard. Cut back almost to framework with shears. Train as privacy or wind screen on chain link or wire fence. Takes dryness pretty well when established; tolerates poor drainage. As ground cover, set 2–3 ft. apart.

L. nitida. BOX HONEYSUCKLE. Evergreen shrub. Zones 4–9, 14–24. To 6 ft. with erect, densely leafy branches. Tiny (½-in.), oval, dark green, shiny leaves. Attractive bronze to plum-colored winter foliage. Flowers (in June) are fragrant, creamy white, ½ in. long. Berries translucent, blue purple. Rapid growth, tending toward untidiness, but easily pruned as hedge or single plant. Takes salt spray; resistant to oak root fungus.

L. periclymenum. WOODBINE. Evergreen vine in mild-winter areas, deciduous elsewhere. Zones 2–24. Resembles *L. japonica* but is less rampant. Whorls of 2-in.-long, fragrant flowers in summer, fall. Blooms of 'Serotina' are purple outside, yellow inside; 'Berries Jubilee' has yellow flowers followed by profusion of red berries.

L. pileata. PRIVET HONEYSUCKLE. Semievergreen shrub. Zones 2–9, 14–24. Low, spreading, with stiff horizontal branches, to 3 ft. Dark green, 1½-in., privetlike leaves; small, fragrant white flowers in May; translucent violet purple berries. Good bank cover with low-growing euonymus or barberries. Does well at seashore.

L. sempervirens. TRUMPET HONEYSUCKLE. Evergreen or semievergreen twining vine, shrubby if not given support. Zones 3–24. Showy, unscented, orange-yellow to scarlet, trumpet-shaped flowers 1½–2 in. long, in whorls at ends of branches in summer. Scarlet fruit. Oval leaves, 1½–3 in. long, bluish green beneath.

A BIRD BANQUET

Shrubby honeysuckles offer an ongoing spring-to-fall bird banquet—nectar-bearing flowers for hummingbirds, succulent fruits, insects. The small red or purple fruits ripen in summer or autumn.

LOROPETALUM chinense

Hamamelidaceae

EVERGREEN SHRUB

ZONES 6–9, 14–24; BORDERLINE IN ZONES 4, 5

☼ ◑ SUN ON COAST, SUN OR PART SHADE INLAND

● REGULAR WATER

Loropetalum chinense

Generally 3–5 ft. tall, possibly up to 12 ft. in great age. Neat, compact habit, with arching or drooping tiered branches. Leaves roundish, light green, soft, 1–2 in. long. Occasional leaf turns yellow or red throughout the year for nice touch of color. Flowers white to greenish white, in clusters of four to eight at ends of branches. Each flower has four narrow, inch-long, twisted petals. Blooms most heavily March–April, but some bloom is likely to appear any time. The variety 'Rubrum' ('Razzleberri') has purplish leaves and bright rosy pink flowers.

Needs rich, well-drained soil. Subtly beautiful plant, good in foregrounds, raised beds, hanging baskets, woodland gardens, as ground cover. In Northwest, needs protection against hard freezes.

LOTUS

Fabaceae (Leguminosae)

SUBSHRUBS OR PERENNIALS

ZONES VARY BY SPECIES

☼ ◑ FULL SUN OR PARTIAL SHADE

● SOME SUMMER WATER

Lotus berthelotii

Trailing stems, often completely prostrate. Leaves divided into leaflets. Flowers sweet pea shaped, in shades of red to yellow. (For plants with common name "lotus," see *Nelumbo*.)

L. berthelotii. PARROT'S BEAK. Zones 9, 15–24. Trailing perennial with stems 2–3 ft. long, thickly covered with silvery gray foliage and very narrow, 1-in.-long, scarlet blossoms. Blooms June–July. Dies back in cold weather; suffers root rot in poor drainage. Space 2 ft. apart as ground cover; cut back occasionally to induce bushiness. Also very effective in hanging baskets, as cascade over wall or rocks.

L. corniculatus. BIRD'S FOOT TREFOIL. All zones. Goes dormant where winters are cold. Use as ground cover or coarse lawn substitute. Makes mat of dark green, cloverlike leaves. Forms clusters of small yellow flowers in summer and fall. Seedpods at top of flower stems spread like bird's foot, hence common name. Sow seeds or set out plants. Should be mowed occasionally.

L. maculatus 'Gold Flash'. Zones 9, 15–24. Resembles *L. berthelotii* but has bright yellow flowers with striking orange-red markings. *L. mascaensis* is similar. Both require the same care, grow in the same climate zones, and have the same uses as *L. berthelotii*.

L

LUMA apiculata

Myrtaceae

EVERGREEN SHRUB OR SMALL TREE

☘ ZONES 14–24

☼ FULL SUN

◐ ◑ LITTLE TO REGULAR WATER

Luma apiculata

Fast growth to 6–8 (possibly 20) ft. tall, equally wide. Old plants develop beautiful, smooth bark the color of cinnamon. Dense foliage; dark green, oval to roundish, ½–1-in.-long leaves close together. Flowers white to pinkish, a little more than ½ in. across, with four petals and a large brush of stamens in the center. Blue-black fruit less than ½ in. wide; it is edible but not especially tasty. Resembles common myrtle *(Myrtus)* but is denser and darker green. Also known as *Myrceugenella apiculata*, *Myrtus luma*.

LUNARIA annua (L. biennis)

MONEY PLANT

Brassicaceae (Cruciferae)

BIENNIAL

☘ ZONES 1–10, 14–24

☼ FULL SUN

◐ ◑ LITTLE OR NO WATER

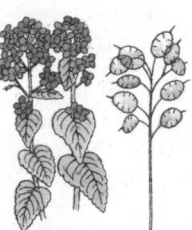

Lunaria annua

Old-fashioned garden plant, grown for the translucent silvery circles (about 1¼ in. across) that stay on flower stalks and are all that remain of ripened seedpods after outer coverings drop with seeds. Plants are 1½–3 ft. high, with coarse, heart-shaped, toothed leaves. Flowers resemble wild mustard blooms but are purple or white, not yellow.

Plant in an out-of-the-way spot in poor soil or in a mixed flower bed where shining pods can be admired before they are picked for dry bouquets. Tough, persistent; can reseed and become weedy.

LUNGWORT. See PULMONARIA   **p. 445**

LUPINUS

LUPINE

Fabaceae (Leguminosae)

PERENNIALS, SHRUBS, AND ANNUALS

☘ ZONES VARY BY SPECIES

☼ FULL SUN

◐ ◐ ◑ ◑ WATER NEEDS VARY BY SPECIES

Lupinus Russell Hybrid

Leaves are divided into many leaflets (like fingers of a hand). Flowers sweet pea shaped, in dense spikes at ends of stems. Many species native to western United States; occur in wide range of habitats, from beach sand to alpine rocks. Only best, easiest-to-grow kinds covered here; native plant seed specialists can supply many others.

All need good drainage but otherwise are not fussy about soil. Start from seed sown in winter or early spring.

L. arboreus. Shrub. Zones 14–17, 22–24. Native to California coastal areas. Grows 5–8 ft. tall. Flower clusters March–June, 4–16 in. long; usually yellow, but sometimes lilac, bluish, white, or some mixture of those colors. Little or no dry-season water. Striking beach plant.

L. argenteus. SILVERSTEM LUPINE. Perennial. All zones. Grows 8–24 in. tall. Stems with silvery hairs, leaves usually smooth. Flowers variable, usually blue, sometimes lilac or white. Native to Southwest and Rockies. Average water; tolerates summer aridity.

L. hartwegii. Summer annual. All zones. Native to Mexico. Grows 1½–3 ft. tall and comes in shades of blue, white, and pink. Easy to grow from seed sown in place in April or May. Flowers July–September. Needs some water.

L. nanus. SKY LUPINE. Spring annual. Zones 8, 9, 14–24. California native, 8–24 in. high; flowers rich blue marked white. Sow seeds in fall or winter for spring bloom. Sow California poppies with it for contrast. April–May flowers. Self-sows readily where it gets little competition. Excellent for barren banks. No dry-season water.

L. polyphyllus. Perennial. All zones. Native to moist places, Northern California to British Columbia. Grows 1½–4 ft. tall, with dense flower clusters, 6–24 in. long, in summer. Flowers blue, purple, or reddish. One important ancestor of the Russell Hybrids. Needs fair amount of water. Control aphids.

L. Russell hybrids. RUSSELL LUPINES. Perennials. Zones 1–7, 14–17. Large, spreading plants to 4–5 ft., with long, dense spikes of flowers, May–June. Little Lulu and Minarette strains are smaller growing (to 1½ ft.). Colors white, cream, yellow, pink, blue, red, orange, purple. Many bicolors.

Grow from seed or buy started plants from flats, pots. Striking border plant where summers aren't too hot and dry. Keep soil moist; give plants good air circulation to help avoid mildew. Often short lived.

HELP LUPINE SEEDS ALONG

Lupine seeds are hard coated and often slow to sprout. They will germinate faster if you soak them in hot water or scratch or nick the seed coats with a file before planting.

LYCHNIS

Caryophyllaceae

PERENNIALS AND ANNUALS

☘ ZONES VARY BY SPECIES

☼ ☽ FULL SUN OR LIGHT SHADE

◐ ◑ WATER NEEDS VARY BY SPECIES

Lychnis coronaria

Hardy, old-fashioned garden flowers, all very tolerant of adverse soils. The different kinds vary in appearance but all offer eye-catching color.

L. chalcedonica. MALTESE CROSS. Perennial. Zones 1–9, 11–24. Loose, open, growing 2–3 ft. high, with hairy leaves and stems. Keep moist. Scarlet flowers in dense terminal clusters, the petals deeply cut. June–July bloom. Plants effective in large borders with white flowers, gray foliage. There is a white variety, 'Alba'. Average water.

L. coeli-rosa (Silene coeli-rosa, Agrostemma coeli-rosa, Viscaria coeli-rosa). Summer annual. All zones. Single, saucer-shaped, 1-in. flowers cover foot-tall plants in summer. Blue and lavender are favorite colors; white and pink are also available, most with contrasting lighter or darker eye spot. Leaves long, narrow, and pointed. Good cut flowers with long bloom season. Sow seed March–April in rich soil. In Zones 8, 9, 12–24, sow in fall for winter, spring bloom. Keep moist.

L. coronaria. CROWN-PINK, DUSTY MILLER, MULLEIN PINK. Perennial or annual. All zones. Plants 1½–2½ ft. tall, with attractive, silky, white foliage and, in spring and early summer, magenta to crimson flowers a little less than an inch across. Effective massed. Endures infrequent watering. Reseeds copiously, but surplus plants are easily weeded out.

L. viscaria 'Splendens'. Perennial. Zones 1–9, 11–24. Compact, low, evergreen clumps of grasslike leaves to 5 in. long. Flower stalks to 1 ft. with

L

clusters of pink to rose, ½-in. flowers in summer. A double-flowered variety, 'Splendens Flore Pleno', is a good rock garden plant that lasts well when cut. Regular water.

LYCIANTHES rantonnei

PARAGUAY NIGHTSHADE

Solanaceae

EVERGREEN OR DECIDUOUS SHRUB OR VINE

✷ ZONES 12, 13, 15–24

☼ FULL SUN

◖ ◆ TOLERATES ARIDITY; BEST GROWTH WITH WATER

A freestanding plant makes 6–8-ft. shrub, but can be staked into tree form or, with support, grown as a vine to 12–15 ft. or more. Can also be allowed to sprawl as a ground cover. Informal, fast growing, not easy to use in tailored landscape. (If you use this plant there, prune it severely to keep neat.) Evergreen in mild winters; in severe cold, leaves drop and branch tips may die back. In Zones 12, 13, place on protected patio. Bright green, oval leaves to 4 in. long; violet blue, yellow-centered, 1-in.-wide flowers throughout warm weather, often nearly throughout year. Often sold as *Solanum rantonnetii*. Wild species has flowers only half as large. 'Royal Robe' is more compact, has a longer bloom season, and darker purple flowers than the species.

Lycianthes rantonnei

LYCORIS

SPIDER LILY

Amaryllidaceae

BULBS

✷ ZONES VARY BY SPECIES

☼ ◑ FULL SUN OR LIGHT SHADE

◆ WATER DURING GROWTH; KEEP DRY LATE SUMMER

Lycoris radiata

Narrow, strap-shaped leaves appear in spring, ripen and die down before bloom starts. Clusters of red, pink, or yellow flowers on bare stems up to 2 ft. tall in late summer, fall. Flowers are spidery looking, with long stamens and narrow, wavy-edged segments curved backward. Grow in garden beds, depending on hardiness, or as pot plants. Some kinds are tender, some half hardy. Bulbs available July–August. Set 3–4 in. deep (note exception for *L. squamigera*) in good soil. Don't disturb plantings for several years. When potting, set with tops exposed. Don't use pots that are too large, since plants with crowded roots bloom best.

L. africana (L. aurea). GOLDEN SPIDER LILY. Zones 16, 17, 19–24; indoor/outdoor container plants. September–October, bright yellow, 3-in. flowers.

L. radiata. Zones 4–9, 12–24. Best known and easiest to grow. Coral red flowers with gold sheen; 1½-ft. stems. 'Alba' has white flowers. Will take light shade. Give protection in cold-winter climates. Blooms August–September.

L. sanguinea. Zones 4–9, 12–24. To 2 ft. tall, with bright red to orange-red, 2–2½-in. flowers in fall.

L. sprengeri. Zones 4–9, 12–24. Similar to *L. squamigera*, but with slightly smaller purplish pink flowers.

L. squamigera (Amaryllis hallii). All zones. Funnel-shaped, fragrant, pink or rosy lilac, 3-in. flowers in clusters on 2-ft. stems. August bloom. Hardiest lycoris; overwinters in colder regions if bulbs are planted 6 in. deep in protected location, as against a south wall.

LYME GRASS. See ELYMUS   p. 272

LYONOTHAMNUS floribundus

CATALINA IRONWOOD

Rosaceae

EVERGREEN TREE

✷ ZONES 15–17, 19–24

☼ FULL SUN

◆ TOLERATES SOME ARIDITY

Native to Channel Islands off coast of Southern California. The species, with lobed or scallop-toothed leaves (not divided into leaflets), is seldom seen in cultivation; but *L. f. asplenifolius*, fernleaf Catalina ironwood, is well known. Moderate growth to 30–60 ft. with 20–40-ft. spread. Redwood-colored bark peels off in long, thin strips. Young twigs often reddish. The 4–6-in. leaves are divided into three to seven deeply notched or lobed leaflets, deep glossy green above, gray and hairy beneath. Small white blossoms in large, flat, 8–18-in. clusters stand out well from foliage but should be cut off when they fade; old clusters turn brown.

Lyonothamnus floribundus asplenifolius

Needs excellent drainage and should be pruned in winter to shape and control growth. Sometimes shows chlorosis in heavy soils. Easiest to grow near coast. Handsome in groves (like redwood); effective with redwood, Torrey pines.

LYSILOMA microphylla thornberi (L. thornberi)

FEATHER BUSH, FERN-OF-THE-DESERT

Fabaceae (Leguminosae)

SHRUB OR SMALL TREE

✷ ZONES 10, 12–24

☼ FULL SUN

◊ NO WATER ONCE ESTABLISHED

Native to foothills of Arizona's Rincon Mountains. To 12 ft. Evergreen in frostless areas, deciduous elsewhere. Makes broad canopy of finely cut bright green leaves somewhat like acacia. Sometimes killed by heavy frosts but usually comes back. Flowers tiny, white, in ½-in. heads, May–June. Seedpods flat, ridged, 4–8 in. long, 1 in. wide. Good informal background shrub, patio tree, transitional garden–desert planting.

Lysiloma microphylla thornberi

LYSIMACHIA

Primulaceae

VIGOROUS PERENNIALS

✷ ZONES VARY BY SPECIES

☼ ◑ ● SUN NEAR COAST, SHADE INLAND

◆ WATER ALL BUT LOOSESTRIFE

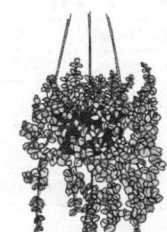

Three of these four vigorous perennials spread and should be policed as necessary lest they take over too much territory.

Lysimachia nummularia

L. ephemerum. Zones 3–10, 14–24. Grows to 3 ft.; a neat clump of leathery, gray-green foliage; long, slender clusters of long-lasting white flowers.

L. nummularia. MONEYWORT, CREEPING JENNY. Zones 1–9, 14–24. Evergreen creeping plant with long runners (to 2 ft.) that root at joints. Forms pretty light green mat of roundish leaves. Flowers about 1 in. across, yellow, form singly in leaf joints. Summer blooming. Best use is in corners where it need not be restrained. Will spill from wall, hanging basket. Good ground cover (plant 1–1½ ft. apart) near streams. 'Aurea' has yellow leaves, needs shade. ▸

L. procumbens. GOLDEN GLOBES. Zones 8, 9, 14–24. Trailing stems bend upward at tips. Leaves thick, to 2½ in. long. Branches end in clusters of bright yellow, inch-wide flowers opening from round buds. Spring bloom, with some scattered later. Use in hanging baskets or (with caution) as a ground cover.

L. punctata. LOOSESTRIFE. Zones 1–9, 14–24. To 4 ft. tall, 2 ft. wide, spreading freely by underground roots. Erect stems have narrow leaves in whorls, whorled yellow flowers on the top third. Useful at edge of wood or in outer garden borders. Can be invasive.

Lythraceae. The loosestrife family is represented in this book by *Cuphea*, *Lagerstroemia*, and *Lythrum*. *Lysimachia punctata*, whose common name is loosestrife, is in the primrose family.

LYTHRUM virgatum

PURPLE LOOSESTRIFE	
Lythraceae	
PERENNIAL	
☀ ALL ZONES	
☼ FULL SUN	
◐ NEEDS MUCH MOISTURE	

Lythrum virgatum

Showy magenta-flowered plant for pond margins or moist areas. Grows in 2-ft.-wide clumps. Stems are 2½–5 ft. tall, the upper 8–18 in. densely set with ¾-in. flowers in late summer, fall. Narrow leaves clothe lower stem. Hybrids known as 'Roseum Superbum', 'Morden's Pink', or 'Morden's Gleam' are grown in the West. Valued for cut flowers. In borders, tone down magenta by planting with white flowers. Garden varieties are often offered as varieties of *L. salicaria*, a similar plant.

> ### IN MOIST CONDITIONS, THEY BECOME WEEDS
> *Lythrum salicaria* and possibly *L. virgatum* are prone to scattering seed about and have become nuisances, displacing native vegetation in many parts of the Northwest and mountain states. Planting them is forbidden in some places and unwise wherever plants have reliable moisture through much of the year.

MACADAMIA

MACADAMIA NUT, QUEENSLAND NUT	
Proteaceae	
EVERGREEN TREES	
☀ ZONES 9, 16, 17, 19–24	
☼ FULL SUN	
◐ TOLERATES ARIDITY; BEST WITH SOME WATER	

Macadamia tetraphylla

Clean, handsome ornamental trees where frosts are light. Where best adapted (Zones 23, 24), produce clusters of hard-shelled, delicious nuts; pick them up as they fall from trees.

Best in deep, rich soil. Stake young trees. Prune to shape. Young plants tend to develop multiple trunks; eliminate the weaker ones and train the best to branch at 5 ft. above the ground. Yellow color in new growth flushes during winter is caused by cold and is not serious. Later growth will be green. You can plant a macadamia from a container any month of the year, but trees suffer less heat and water stress if planted in the fall. Expect nuts in 3–5 years.

Most trees are sold under the name *M. ternifolia*. They are nearly always one of the two species described below. 'Beaumont' ('Dr. Beau-mont'), 'Cooper', and 'Vista' are hybrids between the two species. Look for grafted, named varieties of proven nut-bearing ability. All are resistant to oak root fungus.

Both species reach 25–30 ft. tall or taller, 15–20 ft. wide (even larger when very old). Long (5–12-in.), glossy, leathery leaves. Mature foliage is durable and attractive for cutting. Small flowers in winter and spring are white to pink in dense, hanging, 1-ft. clusters.

M. integrifolia. SMOOTH-SHELL MACADAMIA. Best near coast. Leaves are smooth edged. Nuts ripen in late fall to May.

M. tetraphylla. ROUGH-SHELL MACADAMIA. Best inland. Spiny leaves. More open tree than *M. integrifolia*. Nuts have thinner shells, appear fall through February.

MACFADYENA unguis-cati

CAT'S CLAW, YELLOW TRUMPET VINE	
Bignoniaceae	
PARTLY DECIDUOUS VINE	
☀ ZONES 8–24	
☼ ◐ FULL SUN OR PARTIAL SHADE	
◐ LITTLE DRY-SEASON WATER ONCE ESTABLISHED	

Macfadyena unguis-cati

Climbs high and fast by hooked, clawlike, forked tendrils. To 25–40 ft. Leaves divided into two oval, glossy green, 2-in. leaflets. Blooms in early spring, bearing yellow trumpets to 2 in. long, 1¼ in. across.

Grows near coast but is faster growing and stronger where summers are hot—even on south walls in Zones 12, 13. Clings to any support—stone, wood, fence, tree trunk. Some are even seen clinging to undersides of freeway overpasses. Tends to produce leaves and flowers at ends of stems. Cut back some stems nearly to ground to stimulate new growth lower down; prune whole plant hard after bloom. Needs little dry-season water once established. Loses all leaves in cold winters. Formerly known as *Doxantha unguis-cati* or *Bignonia tweediana*.

MACKAYA bella

Acanthaceae	
EVERGREEN SHRUB	
☀ ZONES 15–24	
◐ ● PARTIAL OR FULL SHADE	
◐ ◑ LITTLE TO REGULAR WATER	

Mackaya bella

South African native; 4–5 ft. tall, sometimes much taller, with glossy, dark green leaves 4–5 in. long. In spring, produces 9–10-in.-long, loose clusters of pale lavender, 2-in. flowers with deep purple lines in the throat. Average soil.

MACLEAYA cordata
(Bocconia cordata)

PLUME POPPY	
Papaveraceae	
PERENNIAL	
☀ ALL ZONES	
☼ SUN AT LEAST HALF THE DAY	
◐ REGULAR WATER	

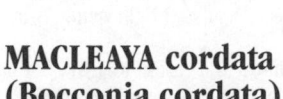
Macleaya cordata

Stately plant with 3-ft.-wide clumps of grayish green, deeply lobed leaves up to 10 in. wide. Branched flower stems to 7–8 ft. carry clouds of tiny, pinkish tan flowers. Plant thrives in good garden soil. Can crowd out smaller plants, so group with sturdy shrubs or plant alone.

M

MACLURA pomifera

OSAGE ORANGE

Moraceae

DECIDUOUS TREE

✎ ALL ZONES; MOSTLY GROWN IN ZONES 1, 3, 10–13

☼ FULL SUN

◊ NO WATER ONCE ESTABLISHED

Maclura pomifera

Fast growth to 60 ft. with spreading, open habit. Thorny branches. Leaves to 5 in. long, medium green. If there's a male plant present, female plants may bear inedible, 4-in. fruits (hedge-apples) that somewhat resemble bumpy, yellow-green oranges. Can stand heat, cold, wind, poor soil, moderate alkalinity. Easily propagated by seed, cuttings, root cuttings; easily transplanted. Useful as big, tough, rough-looking hedge or background. Prune to any size from 6 ft. up. Pruned high, becomes desert shade tree. Not bothered by oak root fungus.

MADAGASCAR JASMINE. See STEPHANOTIS floribunda   **p. 493**

MADAGASCAR PALM. See PACHYPODIUM lamerei   **p. 397**

MADAGASCAR PERIWINKLE. See CATHARANTHUS roseus   **p. 212**

MADEIRA VINE. See ANREDERA cordifolia   **p. 153**

MADRONE, MADRONA. See ARBUTUS menziesii   **p. 162**

MAGNOLIA

Magnoliaceae

DECIDUOUS OR EVERGREEN TREES AND SHRUBS

✎ ZONES VARY BY SPECIES

☼ ☽ FULL SUN; LIGHT SHADE IN DESERT REGIONS

● DEEP, THOROUGH WATERINGS

▶ SEE CHART NEXT PAGE

Magnolia soulangiana

Magnificent flowering plants with a remarkable variety of colors, leaf shapes, and plant forms. This list classifies magnolias by general appearance; the chart lists them alphabetically. New varieties and hybrids appear every year, but distribution is spotty in local nurseries. Mail-order specialists can supply many more kinds.

EVERGREEN MAGNOLIAS

To gardeners in California and Arizona, "magnolia" usually means *M. grandiflora*, the classic southern magnolia with glossy leaves and big, white, fragrant flowers. But it is something of a "sacred cow" in western gardens. On the one hand, it is loved for its pretty foliage and glorious flower display; it is also heat resistant and tolerant of damp soil. On the other hand, it requires maintenance and has limited uses. While it is generally considered a street or lawn tree, its surface roots have a tendency to lift walks, and its dense year-round shade prevents healthy lawn growth. Its big, hard, plasticlike leaves and other litter constantly fall from May through September. Furthermore, it is slow growing in heavy soil or with restricted root area. And although established trees can take some drought, they look their best only when amply supplied with water. Before making this choice, carefully consider your needs. Other evergreen magnolias are *M. delavayi*, *M. virginiana*, and *M.* 'Freeman'.

DECIDUOUS MAGNOLIAS WITH SAUCER FLOWERS

This group includes the saucer magnolia (*M. soulangiana*) and its many varieties, often erroneously called tulip trees because of the shape and bright colors of their flowers. Included here are the yulan magnolia (*M. denudata*) and lily magnolia (*M. liliiflora*). All are hardy to cold, thriving in various climates throughout the West—but early flowers of all forms are subject to frost damage, and all do poorly in hot, dry, windy areas. Related to these, but more tender to cold (and heat), are the big, spectacular oriental magnolias from western China and the Himalayas—*M. campbellii*, *M. dawsoniana*, *M. sargentiana robusta*, *M. sprengeri* 'Diva'. These are barely hardy in Zones 4 and 5, their early flowers subject to frost and storm damage.

DECIDUOUS MAGNOLIAS WITH STAR FLOWERS

This garden group includes *M. kobus*, *M. stellata* and its varieties (the star magnolias), and *M. salicifolia*. All are hardy, slow-growing, early-blooming plants with wide climatic adaptability.

OTHER MAGNOLIAS

Less widely planted is a group of magnolias that bloom as leaves appear or afterward but are generally considered foliage plants or shade trees. Among them are *M. acuminata*, a big shade tree with inconspicuous flowers; *M. hypoleuca* and *M. officinalis*, big trees with big leaves and large but not noticeable flowers; and the eastern American *M. fraseri* and *M. macrophylla*, middle-size trees with huge leaves and flowers.

MAGNOLIA CULTURE

For any magnolia, pick planting site carefully. Except for *M. grandiflora*, magnolias are hard to move once established, and many grow quite large. They never look their best when crowded and may be severely damaged by digging around their roots. They need moist, well-drained, rich, neutral or slightly acid soil. Add plenty of organic matter at planting time.

Magnolia grandiflora

Balled and burlapped plants are available in late winter and early spring; container plants are sold any time. Do not set plants lower than their original soil level. Stake single-trunked or very heavy plants against rocking by wind, which will tear the thick, fleshy, sensitive roots. Set stakes in planting hole before placing tree (to avoid damaging roots). If you plant your magnolia in a lawn, try to provide a good-size area free of grass for a watering basin. Water deeply and thoroughly, but do not drown the plants. Thick mulch will help hold moisture and reduce soil temperature. Surrounding grass will decrease reflected heat, but do not let grass invade watering basin. Keep root crown shaded and damp.

Prevent soil compaction around root zone by keeping foot traffic to a minimum. Prune only when absolutely necessary. Best time is right after flowering, and best way is to remove the entire twig or limb right to the base.

Damaging creatures and diseases are few. Watch for scale and aphids at any time and for spider mites in hot weather. Protect lower leaves of shrubby magnolias from snails and slugs. Magnolias are not immune to oak root fungus, but they seem somewhat resistant.

More bothersome are deficiency problems: chlorosis from lack of iron in alkaline soils, and nitrogen starvation. Iron chelates will remedy the first condition; fertilizer will fix the second. Burned leaf edges usually mean salt damage from overfertilizing, mineral salts in the soil, or salts in irrigation water. This last, a problem in Southern California, usually limits the success of magnolias in deserts. Regular, frequent, deep, heavy waterings help leach out salts and carry them to lower soil levels—if drainage is good. In the Northwest, late frosts may burn leaf edges.

Larger deciduous magnolias are at their best standing alone against a background that will display their flowers and, in winter, their strongly patterned, usually gray limbs and big, fuzzy flower buds. Smaller deciduous magnolias show up well in large flower or shrub borders and make choice ornaments in the oriental garden. All magnolias are excellent lawn trees.

Magnoliaceae. The magnolia family contains evergreen and deciduous trees and shrubs with large, showy flowers, usually with a large number of petals, sepals, and stamens. Tulip tree (*Liriodendron*), *Michelia*, and magnolia are examples.

M

MAGNOLIA

NAME	ZONES	TYPE	HEIGHT	SPREAD	AGE AT BLOOM	FLOWERS	USES, CHARACTERISTICS, COMMENTS
Magnolia acuminata CUCUMBER TREE	1–9, 14–21	Deciduous	60–80 ft.	25 ft.	12 yrs.	Small, greenish yellow, appear after leaves. Late spring, summer. Handsome reddish seed capsules, red seeds	Shade or lawn tree. Dense shade from glossy 5–9-in. leaves. Hardy to cold; dislikes hot, dry winds
M. a. cordata (M. cordata) YELLOW CUCUMBER TREE, YELLOW MAGNOLIA	4–9, 14–21	Deciduous	To 35 ft.	To 35 ft.	12 yrs.	Larger (to 4 in.), chartreuse yellow outside, pure yellow within; appear as leaves start to expand. Mild lemon scent	Slow-growing lawn or border tree for large properties. Lower, shrubbier than *M. acuminata*. Showier, but not ordinarily a tree you can walk or sit under. 'Elizabeth', a cross with *M. denudata*, is a shrubby tree with fragrant, light yellow blooms. 'Miss Honeybee', with pale yellow flowers, is a good selection
M. campbellii	6–9, 14–21	Deciduous	60–80 ft.	To 40 ft.	20 yrs. Grafts bloom younger. 'Iolanthe' has 10-in. flowers, but blooms when 2 ft. tall	Magnificent 6–10-in. bowls, deep rose outside, paler within. Central petals cupped over rose stamens. Very early flowering	Best in Zones 15–17. Plant in lee of evergreens to protect flowers from storm winds. Make it focus of garden and give it room. 'Alba', 'Strybing White' are white forms; 'Hendricks Park', 'Late Pink' are good pinks; 'Charles Raffill' has very large, bright pink flowers, white inside
M. dawsoniana DAWSON MAGNOLIA	4–9, 14–21	Deciduous	40–50 ft.	25–30 ft.	10 yrs. from grafts	Large (8–10 in.), white with rose shading. Narrow petals, slightly pendulous. Profuse bloom. Early flowering. Slight perfume	Big plant for big garden. Makes magnificent show; a little untidy close up. Very dark green leaves. Quite cold hardy when established; needs hardening off in fall. 'Chyverton' is selected salmon, fading pink
M. delavayi	7–9, 14–21	Evergreen	20–30 ft.	To 20 ft.	4–5 yrs.	Dull creamy white, 6–8 in. wide. Fragrant, short lived; shatter day they open. Long summer bloom	Foliage is the feature; leaves 8–14 in. long, 5–8 in. wide, stiff, leathery, gray-green, tropical looking. Use as single tree or giant shrub in lawn or large corner. Hard to train as single-stemmed tree
M. denudata (M. conspicua) YULAN MAGNOLIA	2–9, 14–24	Deciduous	To 35 ft.	To 30 ft.	6–7 yrs.	White, fragrant, sometimes tinged purple at base. Held erect; somewhat tulip-shaped, 3–4 in. long, spreading to 6–7 in. Early; often a few in summer	Tends toward irregular form—no handicap in informal garden or at woodland edge. Place it where it can be shown off against dark background or sky. Leaves 4–7 in. long. Cut flowers striking in oriental arrangements
M. fraseri (M. auriculata)	2–9, 14–21	Deciduous	To 50 ft.	20–30 ft.	10–12 yrs.	Creamy to yellowish white, 8–10 in. wide. Bloom May–June when leaves are full grown	Single lawn tree or woodland tree. Leaves 16–18 in. long, parchmentlike, in whorls at ends of branches. Effect is that of parasols. Rose red, 5-in. seed capsules showy in summer. Handsome dark brown fall color
M. 'Freeman'	4–12, 14–24	Evergreen	10–15 ft.	To 5 ft.	3–5 yrs. from grafts	White, 5 in. across, very fragrant. Summer	Narrow, dense, columnar evergreen tree for small gardens. Hybrid between *M. virginiana* and *M. grandiflora*. Leaves like those of *M. grandiflora* but smaller. One very old tree has reached 50 ft.
M. globosa	5–9, 14–21	Deciduous	To 20 ft.	To 20 ft.	10 yrs.	White, fragrant, cupped or globe-shaped, nodding or drooping. June	Use as big shrub in lawn, at woodland edge, above a wall (so people can look up into flowers). Leaves 5–8 in. long, half as wide, rusty and furry beneath. Tree tender when young

M

MAGNOLIA

NAME	ZONES	TYPE	HEIGHT	SPREAD	AGE AT BLOOM	FLOWERS	USES, CHARACTERISTICS, COMMENTS
M. grandiflora SOUTHERN MAGNOLIA, BULL BAY	4–12, 14–24	Evergreen	To 80 ft.	To 40 ft.	15 yrs., sometimes much less. 2–3 years from grafts or cuttings	Pure white, aging buff; large (8–10 in. across), powerfully fragrant. Carried throughout summer, fall	Street or lawn tree, big container plant, wall or espalier plant. Unpredictable in form and age of bloom. Grafted plants more predictable. Glossy, leathery leaves, 4–8 in. long. Does well in desert heat if out of wind. Needs warm wall or pocket in Zones 4, 5. Expect breakage, yearly pruning in Zones 6, 7. See general text for discussion
M. g. 'Edith Bogue'	4–12, 14–24	Evergreen	To 35 ft.	To 20 ft.	2–3 yrs. from grafts	As in *M. grandiflora*. Young plants slower to come into heavy bloom than some other varieties	Shapely, vigorous tree, one of hardiest selections of *M. grandiflora*. Has withstood −24°F. The one to try in coldest regions. Keep it out of strong winds
M. g. 'Little Gem'	4–12, 14–24	Evergreen	Slow to 15–20 ft.	To 10 ft.	2 yrs. from grafts	Small (5–6 in. wide)	Good in containers, as espalier, in confined area. Blooms young. Half-size foliage, rusty beneath. Branches to ground
M. g. 'Majestic Beauty'	4–12, 14–24	Evergreen	35–50 ft.	To 20 ft.	2 yrs. from grafts	Very large, to 1 ft. across, with 9 petals	Vigorous, dense branching street or shade tree of broadly pyramidal form. Leaves exceptionally long, broad, and heavy. Most luxuriant of southern magnolias. 'Timeless Beauty' is more erect, denser
M. g. 'Russet'	4–12, 14–24	Evergreen	Fast growth	To 20 ft	2 yrs. from grafts	Flattish, 10 in., last several days	Useful where fast, narrow evergreen tree is needed. Densely foliaged with narrow, glossy leaves with russet wool underneath
M. g. 'Samuel Sommer'	4–12, 14–24	Evergreen	30–40 ft.	To 30 ft.	Same as *M. grandiflora*	Very large and full; to 10–14 in. across, with 12 petals	Like the other grafted magnolias that bloom young, this will need pruning to become single-trunked tree. Can grow as multitrunked tree. Leaves large, leathery and glossy, with heavy, rusty red felting on underside; very dark green above. Fairly fast growing
M. g. 'San Marino'	4–12, 14–24	Evergreen	Slow to 25 ft.	To 20 ft.	Same as *M. grandiflora*	Profuse show of 4-in. flowers	Grow as large shrub, small round-headed tree, espalier. Densely foliaged to ground unless shaped
M. g. 'St. Mary'	4–12, 14–24	Evergreen	Usually 20 ft. Much larger in old age	To 20 ft.	Same as *M. grandiflora*	Heavy production of full-sized flowers on small tree	Fine where standard-sized magnolia would grow too large too fast. Left alone, it will form a big, dense bush. Pruned and staked, it makes a small tree. Good for espalier and pots
M. g. 'Victoria'	4–12, 14–24	Evergreen	To 20 ft.	To 15 ft.	2–3 yrs. from grafts	Same as *M. grandiflora*	Parent plant grew in Victoria, B.C. Withstands −10°F. with little damage, but plant out of wind. Foliage exceptionally broad, heavy, dark green. 'Pioneer' is as hardy
M. hypoleuca (M. obovata)	4–9, 14–21	Deciduous	To 50 ft.	To 25 ft.	15 yrs.	To 8 in. across, creamy, fragrant. Appear in summer after leaves expand	Only for big lawn or garden

M

MAGNOLIA

NAME	ZONES	TYPE	HEIGHT	SPREAD	AGE AT BLOOM	FLOWERS	USES, CHARACTERISTICS, COMMENTS
M. kobus KOBUS MAGNOLIA	2–9, 14–24	Deciduous	To 30 ft.	To 20 ft.	15 yrs.	White, to 4 in. across; early	Hardy, sturdy tree for planting singly on lawn or in informal shrub and tree groupings. 'Wada's Memory' (*M. kewensis* 'Wada's Memory') blooms young, grows faster, has bigger flowers, coppery red new growth. *M. k. borealis* is much larger (to 75 ft.), with larger (6-in.) leaves
M. k. stellata (see **M. stellata**)							
M. Kosar–De Vos Hybrids	2–9, 14–24	Deciduous	To 12 ft.	To 15 ft.	4–5 yrs.	'Ann' has dark purple flowers, pink inside. 'Betty' is lighter. 'Randy', a late bloomer, has purple flowers with white inside. 'Ricki' is larger flower. Compact 'Susan' has twisted petals	Use in shrub border or singly on lawn All are hybrids between *M. liliiflora* and *M. stellata* 'Rosea'
M. liliiflora LILY MAGNOLIA	2–9, 14–24	Deciduous	To 12 ft.	To 15 ft.	4–5 yrs.	White inside, purplish outside. Selections sold as 'Gracilis', 'Nigra', and 'O'Neill' are dark purple-red outside, pink inside. Blooms over long spring, summer season	Good for shrub border; strong vertical effect in big flower border. Spreads slowly by suckering. Leaves 4–6 in. long. 'Royal Crown', hybrid with *M. veitchii*, has pink, candle-shaped buds that open to 10-in. flowers. Good cut flower if buds taken before fully open
M. loebneri	2–9, 14–24	Deciduous	Slow to 12–15 ft.; can reach 50 ft.	12–15 ft.	3 yrs.	Narrow, strap-shaped petals like *M. stellata*'s; but fewer, larger. Plants bloom early and young	Hybrids between *M. kobus* and *M. stellata*. 'Ballerina' is white with faint pink blush; 'Leonard Messel' has pink flowers, deeper in bud; 'Merrill' ('Dr. Merrill') is a hardy, free-flowering white. Taller 'Spring Snow' has pure white flowers. Use in lawn or shrub border, at woodland edge
M. macrophylla BIGLEAF MAGNOLIA	2–9, 14–21	Deciduous	Slow to 50 ft.	To 30 ft.	12–15 yrs.	White, fragrant, to 1 ft. across, appearing May–July, after leaves are out	Show-off tree with leaves 1–2½ ft. long, 9–12 in. wide. Needs to stand alone. Striking foliage but hard to blend with other textures.
M. officinalis	4–9, 14–21	Deciduous	To 50 ft.	To 25 ft.	15 yrs.	To 8 in. wide, fragrant, creamy white, after leaves in May	Much like *M. hypoleuca*. Use for big, exotic-looking tree
M. salicifolia ANISE MAGNOLIA	2–9, 14–21	Deciduous	Slow to 18–30 ft.	To 12 ft.	2–10 yrs.	White, narrow petaled, to 4 in. across. Early	Usually upright with slender branches, graceful appearance. In front of trees, use as shrub border. Leaves (3–6 in. long) bronze red in fall. 'Kochanakee' and 'W. B. Clarke' are large flowered; bloom young and heavily. 'Miss Jack' has narrow, anise-scented leaves, blooms heavily
M. sargentiana robusta	5–9, 14–24	Deciduous	To 35 ft.	To 35 ft.	10–12 yrs.; 8–10 yrs. from grafts	Huge (8–12-in.), mauve pink bowls that open erect, then nod to horizontal. Early to midseason	One of most spectacular of flowering plants. Leaves 6–8 in. long. Not for hot, dry areas. Must have ample room and protection from stormy winds, which would tear early blooms. 'Caerhays Belle' and 'Marjory Gossler', hybrids of this and other large-flowered species, are vigorous trees with dinner plate–size pink flowers. Both are rare, choice

M

MAGNOLIA

NAME	ZONES	TYPE	HEIGHT	SPREAD	AGE AT BLOOM	FLOWERS	USES, CHARACTERISTICS, COMMENTS
M. sieboldii (sometimes sold as **M. parviflora**) OYAMA MAGNOLIA	4–9, 14–24	Decid-uous	6–15 ft.	6–15 ft.	5 yrs.	White, cup-shaped, centered with crimson stamens; fragrant. Begin blooming in May, extend over long period	Nice planted upslope or at top of wall so people can look into flowers. Good for small gardens. Buds like white Japanese lanterns. Leaves 3–6 in. long
M. soulangiana SAUCER MAGNOLIA (often erroneously called TULIP TREE)	1–10, 12–24	Decid-uous	To 25 ft.	To 25 ft. or more	3–5 yrs.	White to pink or purplish red, variable in size and form, bloom-ing before leaves expand. Generally about 6 in. across	Lawn ornament, anchor plant in big corner plantings. Hybrid of *M. denudata* and *M. liliiflora*. Seedlings highly variable; shop for named vari-eties. Foliage good green, rather coarse; leaves 4-6 in. (or more) long
M. s. 'Alba' (**M. s. 'Amabilis', M. s. 'Alba Superba'**)	1–10, 12–24	Decid-uous	To 30 ft.	To 25 ft. or more	3–5 yrs.	Large, suffused purple, opening nearly pure white. Early	Same uses as for *M. soulangiana*. Rather more upright in growth than most
M. s. 'Alexandrina'	1–10, 12–24	Decid-uous	To 25 ft.	To 25 ft. or more	3–5 yrs.	Deep purplish pink, white inside, large. Midseason	Same uses as for *M. soulangiana*. Large, rather heavy foliage. Late bloom helps it escape frosts in colder sections
M. s. 'Brozzonii'	1–10, 12–24	Decid-uous	To 25 ft.	To 25 ft. or more	3–5 yrs.	Huge, to 8 in. across. White, very slightly flushed at base. Early	One of handsomest whites. Large, vigorous plant
M. s. 'Burgundy'	1–10, 12–24	Decid-uous	To 25 ft.	To 25 ft. or more	3–5 yrs.	Large, well rounded; deep purple halfway up to petal tips, then lightening to pink. Early	San Francisco's Japanese Tea Garden has many of these, pruned to picturesque shapes
M. s. 'Coates'	1–10, 12–24	Decid-uous	To 25 ft.	To 25 ft. or more	3–5 yrs.	Large, attractive; resemble those of *M. liliiflora* 'Royal Crown'	Large, shrubby. Quick grower
M. s. 'Lennei' (**M. lennei**)	1–10, 12–24	Decid-uous	To 25 ft.	To 25 ft. or more	3–5 yrs.	Very large, globe-shaped, deep purple outside, white inside	Spreading, vigorous plant. Very late bloom helps it escape frosts in cold areas
M. s. 'Lennei Alba' (**M. lennei 'Alba'**)	1–10, 12–24	Decid-uous	To 25 ft.	To 25 ft. or more	3–5 yrs.	Like those of *M. s.* 'Lennei', but white in color, slightly smaller, earlier (midseason)	Spreading, vigorous plant
M. s. 'Lilliputian'	1–10, 12–24	Decid-uous	Smaller grower than others	To 25 ft. or more	3–5 yrs.	Pink and white, somewhat smaller than those of other *M. soulangiana* varieties. Late flowering	Good where a smaller magnolia is called for
M. s. 'Norbertii'	1–10, 12–24	Decid-uous	To 25 ft.	To 25 ft. or more	3–5 yrs.	White, stained purple on out-side. Late	Upright, dense habit
M. s. 'Pink Superba'	1–10, 12–24	Decid-uous	To 25 ft.	To 25 ft. or more	3–5 yrs.	Large, deep pink, white inside. Early	Best where late frosts are not a prob-lem. Identical to *M. s.* 'Alba' except for flower color
M. s. 'Rustica Rubra'	1–10, 12–24	Decid-uous	To 25 ft.	To 25 ft. or more	3–5 yrs.	Large, cup-shaped, deep reddish purple. Midseason	Tall, vigorous grower for large areas. More treelike than many varieties. Blooms somewhat past midseason. Big (6-in.) seedpods of dark rose
M. s. 'San Jose'	1–10, 12–24	Decid-uous	To 25 ft.	To 25 ft. or more	3–5 yrs.	Large, white flushed pink. Blooms Jan.–Feb.	Earliest *M. soulangiana*

M

MAGNOLIA

NAME	ZONES	TYPE	HEIGHT	SPREAD	AGE AT BLOOM	FLOWERS	USES, CHARACTERISTICS, COMMENTS
M. sprengeri 'Diva'	5–9, 14–24	Decid-uous	To 40 ft.	To 30 ft.	7 yrs. from grafts	To 8 in. wide, rose pink outside, white suffused pink with deeper lines inside. Scented. Early to midseason	One of brightest colors; erect, spectacular flowers. Buds more frost resistant than those of *M. sargentiana robusta*. Hybrids between this and *M. liliiflora* are 'Nigra' and 'Galaxy' (large purple flowers open late in spring); 'Spectrum (larger but fewer flowers). All are big shrubs that can be trained as small trees. Young plants broad, twiggy
M. stellata STAR MAGNOLIA	1–9, 14–24	Decid-uous	To 10 ft.	To 20 ft.	3 yrs.	Very early, white, with 19–21 narrow, strap-shaped petals. Profuse bloom in late winter, early spring. 'King Rose' has pink buds opening to white flowers with pink bases	Slow growing, shrubby; fine for borders, entryway gardens, edge of woods. Quite hardy, but flowers often nipped by frost in Zones 1–7. Fine texture in twig and leaf. Fair yellow and brown fall color
M. s. 'Centennial'	1–9, 14–24	Decid-uous	To 10 ft.	To 20 ft.	3 yrs.	Large (5 in.), white, faintly marked pink	Same uses as for *M. stellata*. Like an improved *M. s.* 'Waterlily'
M. s. 'Dawn'	1–9, 14–24	Decid-uous	To 10 ft.	To 20 ft.	3 yrs.	To 40–50 pink petals	Same uses as for *M. stellata*
M. s. 'Rosea' PINK STAR MAGNOLIA	1–9, 14–24	Decid-uous	To 10 ft.	To 20 ft.	3 yrs.	Pink buds; flowers flushed pink, fading to white	Same uses as for species. Place where you can see flowers from living or family room; they often bloom so early that you won't want to walk out to see them. In cold regions, plant these early-flowering sorts in a northern exposure to delay bloom as long as possible, lessen frost damage
M. s. 'Royal Star'	1–9, 14–24	Decid-uous	To 10 ft.	To 20 ft.	3 yrs.	White, 25–30 petals, bloom 2 weeks later than *M. stellata*'s	Same uses as for *M. stellata*. Faster growing
M. s. 'Rubra'	1–9, 14–24	Decid-uous	To 10 ft.	To 20 ft.	3 yrs.	Rosy pink	More treelike in form than other *M. stellata* varieties
M. s. 'Waterlily'	1–9, 14–24	Decid-uous	To 10 ft.	To 20 ft.	3 yrs.	White. Larger flowers than *M. stellata*'s; broader, more numerous petals	Faster growing than most star magnolias. Leaves modest in size (2–4 in. long); finer foliage texture than other magnolias
M. veitchii VEITCH MAGNOLIA	4–9, 14–24	Decid-uous	30–40 ft.	To 30 ft.	4–5 yrs.	Bloom early, before leaves. Rose red at base, shading to white at tips, to 10 in. across	Spectacular tree. Hybrid between *M. campbellii* and *M. denudata*. Fast growing and vigorous. Needs plenty of room and wind protection; branches are brittle. 'Rubra' has smaller, purple-red flowers
M. virginiana (M. glauca) SWEET BAY	4–9, 14–24	Decid-uous or semi-ever-green	To 50 ft. Usually less	To 20 ft.	8–10 yrs.	Nearly globular, 2–3 in. wide, creamy white, fragrant. June–Sept.	Prefers moist, acid soil. Grows in swamps in eastern U.S. Usually massive semievergreen shrub. Variable in leaf drop; some plants evergreen. Leaves grayish green, nearly white beneath, 2–5 in. long
M. wilsonii WILSON MAGNOLIA	4–9, 14–24	Decid-uous	To 25 ft.	To 25 ft.	10 yrs.	White, with red stamens, pendulous, 3–4 in. across, fragrant. May–June	Blooms at 4 ft. and tends to remain shrubby. Plant high on bank where people can look up at flowers. Best in light shade. Rich purple brown twigs and narrow, tapered leaves, 3–6 in. long with silvery undersides

M

MAHONIA

Berberidaceae

EVERGREEN SHRUBS

ZONES VARY BY SPECIES

EXPOSURE NEEDS VARY BY SPECIES

WATER NEEDS VARY BY SPECIES

Related to *Berberis* (barberry) and described under that name by some botanists. Easily grown; good looking all year. Leaves divided into leaflets that usually have spiny teeth on edges. Yellow flowers in dense, rounded to spikelike clusters, followed by blue-black (sometimes red), berrylike fruit. Generally disease resistant, though foliage is sometimes disfigured by small looper caterpillar. All attract birds.

Mahonia aquifolium

M. aquifolium. OREGON GRAPE. Zones 1–21. Native British Columbia to Northern California. State flower of Oregon. To 6 ft. or more with tall, erect habit; spreads by underground stems. Leaves 4–10 in. long, with five to nine very spiny-toothed, oval, 1–2½-in.-long leaflets that are glossy green in some forms, dull green in others. Young growth ruddy or bronzy; scattered mature red leaves through year (more pronounced in fall). Purplish or bronzy leaves in winter, especially in cold-winter areas or where plants are grown in full sun. Flowers in 2–3-in.-long clusters, March–May; edible blue-black fruit with gray bloom (makes good jelly).

Takes any exposure in most areas. Northern exposure best in Zones 12, 13 (where chlorosis is a problem); in Zones 9–14, 18–21, it looks best when grown in shade. Control height and form by pruning; cut to ground any woody stems that extend too far above mass (new growth fills in quickly). At first sign of caterpillar damage (lacelike perforations on leaves), spray with BTU (*Bacillus thuringiensis*). Needs little water.

For uniformity, plant a variety grown from cuttings or divisions. 'Compacta' averages about 2 ft. tall and spreads freely to make broad colonies. New foliage is glossy, light to coppery green; mature foliage is matte medium green. 'Orange Flame', 5 ft. tall, has bronzy orange new growth, glossy green mature leaves that turn wine red in winter.

Plant in masses as foundation planting, in woodland, in tubs, as low screen or garden barrier. Valuable for resistance to oak root fungus.

M. bealei. LEATHERLEAF MAHONIA. All zones. To 10–12 ft., with strong pattern of vertical stems, horizontal leaves. Leaves are over a foot long, divided into 7–15 thick, leathery, broad leaflets as much as 5 in. long, yellowish green above, gray green below, with spiny toothed edges. Flowers in erect, 3–6-in.-long, spikelike clusters at ends of branches in earliest spring. Powdery blue berries. Takes sun in fog belt; best in partial shade elsewhere. Plant in rich soil with ample organic material. Water generously. Truly distinguished plant against stone, brick, wood, glass.

M. fortunei. Zones 7–9, 14–24. Grows to 6 ft. Erect stems bear 10-in. dull matte green leaves with 7–13 spine-edged leaflets. Undersurface of leaves is yellowish green, strongly nerved. Yellow flowers in short clusters. Plant has an unusual stiff charm. Sun to light shade. Average water.

M. fremontii. DESERT MAHONIA. Zones 8–24. Native to deserts of Southwest. Erect habit, many stems, 3–12 ft. tall. Gray-green to yellowish green leaves with three to five thick, 1-in.-long leaflets; edges have very sharp, tough spines. Flowers in 1–1½-in.-long clusters, May–June; dark blue to brown fruit. Grow in full sun or light shade. Little water.

M. 'Golden Abundance'. Zones 1–21. Dense, heavily foliaged shrub, 5–6 ft. tall. Glossy green leaves with red midribs; heavy bloom and fruit set. Sun at coast to shade inland. Little water.

EXCELLENT SHRUB—BUT SHARP NEEDLES

Mahonia lomariifolia makes a dramatic plant for entry or shaded patio, against a shaded wall, or for a silhouetted lighting effect. Just don't place it so close to a walk that the sharp needles on its leaflets scratch passersby or get underfoot to distress barefoot walkers.

M. lomariifolia. Zones 6–9, 14–24. Showy plant with erect, little-branched stems to 6–10 ft. Young plants often have single, vertical unbranched stem; with age, plants produce more, almost vertical, branches from near base. Clustered near ends of these branches are horizontally held leaves to 2 ft. long. In outline, leaves look like stiff, crinkly, barbed ferns; each has as many as 47 thick, spiny, glossy green leaflets arranged symmetrically along both sides of central stem. Yellow flowers in winter or earliest spring grow in long, erect clusters at branch tips, just above topmost cluster of leaves. Powdery blue berries, appealing to birds, follow the flowers. Needs shade at least in afternoon to keep its deep green color. Prune stems at varying heights to induce branching. Regular water.

Mahonia lomariifolia

M. nervosa. LONGLEAF MAHONIA. Zones 2–9, 14–17. Native British Columbia to Northern California. Low shrub, 2 ft. (rarely 6 ft.) tall. Spreads by underground stems to make good cover. Clustered at stem tips are 10–18 in.-long leaves with 7–21 glossy, bristle-toothed, 1–3¾-in.-long, green leaflets. Creates the impression of a stiff, leathery fern. Yellow flowers in upright clusters 3–6 in. long, April–June. Blue berries. Best in shade; will take sun in cooler areas, becoming very compact. Woodland ground cover, facing for taller mahonias, low barrier planting. Some water.

M. nevinii. NEVIN MAHONIA. Zones 8–24. Native to scattered localities, Southern California. Many-branched shrub, 3–10 ft. tall, with gray foliage. Leaves with three to five leaflets, about 1 in. long, bristly or spiny. Flowers in loose, 1–2-in.-long clusters, March–May, followed by red berries. Sun or light shade, any soil, much or little water. Resistant to oak root fungus. Use individually or as screen, hedge, barrier. Rare in nature.

M. pinnata. CALIFORNIA HOLLY GRAPE. Zones 7–9, 14–24. Native southern Oregon to Southern California. Similar to *M. aquifolium*, but leaves are more crinkly and spiny, new growth often shows lots of red and orange, and plants may grow taller in ideal coastal conditions. Takes aridity better than *M. aquifolium*. In Zones 8, 9, 14, 18–21, it's best in light shade. For uniformity, plant selection 'Ken Hartman'.

M. repens. CREEPING MAHONIA. Zones 1–21. Native British Columbia to Northern California, eastward to Rocky Mountains. Creeps by underground stems. To 3 ft. tall with spreading habit. Dull bluish green leaves have three to seven spine-toothed leaflets, turn bronzy in winter. Yellow flowers, April–June, followed by blue berries in short clusters. Good ground cover in sun, partial shade. Needs little water.

MAIANTHEMUM dilatatum

FALSE LILY-OF-THE-VALLEY

Liliaceae

PERENNIAL

ZONES 1–9, 14–17

PARTIAL SHADE

NO DRY-SEASON WATERING

Maianthemum dilatatum

Native to Northern California, the Northwest. Also known as *M. bifolium* or *M. d. camtschaticum*. Creeping rootstocks send up neat, roundish, heavily veined leaves to 8 in. long, half as wide, on 2–6-in. stems. Foamy clusters of white flowers in spring are followed by red berries in summer. Attractive woodland ground cover, but capable of overwhelming delicate plant neighbors. Disappears in winter.

MALCOLMIA maritima

VIRGINIAN STOCK

Brassicaceae (Cruciferae)

SUMMER ANNUAL

✂ ALL ZONES

☼ FULL SUN

● REGULAR WATER

Malcolmia maritima

Grows to 8–15 in., single stemmed or branching from base, covered with nearly scentless, four-petaled flowers. Colors include white, yellow, pinks, lilacs, and magenta. Leaves are oblong. Sow in place at any time except in hot or very cold weather. As with sweet alyssum *(Lobularia maritima),* plant blooms only 6 weeks after seeds are sown. Does not readily reseed. Give it moderately rich soil. Good bulb cover.

MALEPHORA (Hymenocyclus)

ICE PLANT

Aizoaceae

SUCCULENTS

✂ ZONES VARY BY SPECIES

☼ FULL SUN

◊ NO WATER ONCE ESTABLISHED

Malephora luteola

Dense, smooth, gray-green to blue-green foliage highly resistant to heat, wind, exhaust fumes, fire. Widely used in streetside and freeway plantings. Plants flower over long season, but blooms are scattered rather than in sheets. Attractive to bees. For comparison with other ice plants, see Ice Plant.

M. crocea. Zones 11–24. Trailing plant to 6 in. high with smooth, gray-green foliage; sparse production of reddish yellow flowers nearly throughout year, heaviest in spring. Good on moderately steep slopes. One of the hardiest trailing ice plants. Plant 1–1½ ft. apart. *M. c. purpureo-crocea* has salmon flowers, bluish green foliage.

M. luteola. Zones 15–24. To 1 ft. Light gray-green foliage. Yellow flowers 1 in. wide, May through June and throughout the year. Bloom sparse.

MALUS

CRABAPPLE

Rosaceae

DECIDUOUS TREES, ONLY RARELY SHRUBS

✂ ZONES 1–21

☼ FULL SUN

● MODERATE WATER

▶ SEE CHART

Malus floribunda

Handsome pink, white, or red flowers and fruit that is edible, showy, or sometimes both. For crabapples used in jellies, see Crabapple. Ornamental crabapples include at least 200 named kinds, and new ones appear with each year's new catalogs. Chart describes most frequently used kinds.

Most types grow 6–30 ft. high. Leaves are pointed ovals, often fuzzy, from deep green to nearly purple. Longer lived than flowering peaches, hardier and more tolerant of wet soil than flowering cherries or other flowering stone fruits, flowering crabapples are among the most useful and least troublesome of flowering trees. Plant bare-root trees in winter or early spring; set out container plants any time. Good, well-drained garden soil is best, but crabapples will take rocky or mildly acid or alkaline soil. They take heat. Prune only to build good framework or to correct shape; annual pruning is not necessary.

Diseases and pests are few; fireblight can be a problem but usually is not. The same pests that affect apple also prey on crabapple; controls are simple. If you or your neighbors grow apples, or if you wish to use crabapples from your tree, spray to control codling moths. Scale, aphids, spider mites, and tent caterpillars may require spraying. Scab, powdery mildew, and crabapple rust are serious problems in the Northwest.

Malus sargentii

Northwestern varieties especially selected for disease resistance (particularly to scab) are 'Adams' (rounded tree to 20 ft., pink flowers, red fruit); 'Beverly' (spreading habit to 20 ft., pink flowers, red fruit); 'Liset' (spreading tree to 15 ft., rose flowers, purple leaves, maroon fruit); 'Robinson' (to 25 ft., deep pink flowers, purple leaves, red fruit); *M. sargentii* (see chart); *M.* 'Snowdrift' (see chart); and *M. yunnanensis* 'Veitchii' (upright, narrow to 20 ft., small white flowers, purple-brown fruit, orange and red fall color).

Crabapples are fine lawn trees and may be used in rows along driveways or walks. Planted near fences, they will heighten screening effect, provide blossoms and fruit, and still give planting room for primroses, spring bulbs, or shade-loving summer bedding plants. Good espaliers.

MALVA

MALLOW

Malvaceae

PERENNIAL OR BIENNIAL HERBACEOUS PLANTS

✂ ALL ZONES

☼ FULL SUN

● MODERATE WATER

Malva alcea

Related to and somewhat resembling hollyhock *(Alcea),* but bushier, with smaller, roundish leaves. Easy to grow; need good drainage, average soil. Grow from seed; usually bloom first year. Use in perennial borders or for a quick tall edging. Plants not long lived.

M. alcea. Perennial. Grows to 4 ft. tall, 2 ft. wide. Saucer-shaped, pink, 2-in.-wide flowers appear from late spring to fall. Common kind is the variety 'Fastigiata', which is a narrow grower that looks much like a hollyhock.

M. sylvestris. Perennial or biennial. Erect, bushy growth to 2–4 ft. Flowers 2 in. wide appear all summer. Common variety (often sold as *M. zebrina*) has pale lavender pink flowers with pronounced, deep purple veining. The variety 'Mauritiana' has deeper-colored flowers, often semidouble.

MAMMILLARIA

Cactaceae

CACTI

✂ ZONES 8–24

☼ FULL SUN

● REGULAR WATER IN SUMMER

Mammillaria

Small, cylindrical or globe shaped, either single stemmed or clustered. Plants mostly grow 2–6 in. high. Flowers generally small, arranged in circle near top of plant; red, pink, yellow, or white. Easy to grow in sun. These cacti are chiefly grown in pots by collectors. Specialists offer as many as a hundred species. For the plant sold as *M. vivipara,* see *Coryphantha.*

MALUS—CRABAPPLE

NAME	GROWTH RATE, HEIGHT, SPREAD	STRUCTURE	FOLIAGE	FLOWERS	FRUIT
Malus 'Almey'	Moderate, to 15 ft. by 15 ft.	Upright growth	Purplish to bronzy green. Susceptible to disease	Scarlet, white at base, single. Apr.	Scarlet, hangs on well
M. arnoldiana ARNOLD CRABAPPLE	Fairly rapid, 20 ft. by 30 ft.	Broad, spreading, with long, arching branches	Medium texture; fairly large leaf	Buds red. Flowers pink, fading white, fragrant, to 2 in.	Yellow and red. Sept.–Nov.
M. atrosanguinea CARMINE CRABAPPLE	Moderate, to 18 ft. by 18 ft.	Upright branches, drooping tips. Open, irregular	Purplish green, with more sheen than average crabapple	Fragrant, crimson to rose pink. Profuse. Late Apr.–May	Yellow aging to brown. Hangs on through winter in withered state
M. 'Coralburst'	Slow to 15 ft. by 10 ft.	Dense, rounded	Dense	Coral pink buds open to double rose pink flowers	Small, reddish orange
M. coronaria 'Charlotte'	Moderate, to 30 ft. by 30 ft.	Rounded, broad at base of crown	Dense	Pink, double, 2 in., fragrant. May	Large, green, sparsely produced
M. 'Dolgo'	Moderate, to 40 ft. by 40 ft.	Willowy, spreading; prune for good framework	Reddish green, dense. Good disease resistance	Profuse, white, single. Early spring	Cherrylike clusters of red, 1¼-in. fruit with good flavor. Aug.–Oct.
M. 'Dorothea'	Moderate, to 25 ft. by 25 ft.	Dense, rounded	Dense, finely textured	Double, 2-in., pink. May	Marble-size, bright yellow, effective
M. floribunda JAPANESE FLOWERING CRABAPPLE	Moderate, to 20 ft. by 30 ft.	One form is rounded, dense; the other is more upright	Dense, finely textured. Good disease resistance	Red to pink in bud, opening white. Extremely profuse	Small, yellow and red. Aug.–Oct.
M. 'Hopa'	Fast, to 25 ft. by 20 ft.	Upright branches spreading with weight of fruit	Dense, dark green with brownish cast. Subject to rust, scab, and fireblight	Fragrant, rose red, 1½-in., single. Apr. One of best in Southern California	Orange-red, coloring early. Profuse. Good for jelly
M. hupehensis (M. theifera) TEA CRABAPPLE	Moderate, to 15 ft. by 20 ft.	Rigid branches grow at 45° angles from short trunk	Dense on side branches, but these are spaced well apart	Deep pink buds. Flowers pink, fading white, fragrant. Early May	Not ornamental
M. 'Indian Magic'	Moderate, to 20 ft. by 15 ft.	Rounded, open	Dark green	Heavy show of rose to pink flowers opening from red buds	Fruit is red, turning to orange
M. ioensis 'Plena' BECHTEL CRABAPPLE	Moderate, to 25 ft. by 20 ft. 'Klehm's Improved Bechtel' is a better grower	Coarse branches, rather angular, eventually vase-shaped	Sparse, coarse, soft green	Large, very double, pink, fragrant. Resemble rambler rose	Rarely borne, green, not ornamental
M. 'Katherine'	Slow, to 20 ft. by 20 ft.	Loose and open	Dark green, not dense	Double, light pink fading white, very large—to 2¼ in. Alternate bloom: heavy one year, light the next	Dull red, not especially showy
M. micromalus (M. kaido) MIDGET CRABAPPLE (*kaido* is Japanese for "crabapple")	Slow, to 20 ft. by 15 ft.	One strain is upright and dense; the other is smaller with irregular branches	Dark green	Single, unfading pink, fragrant. Very profuse in Apr.	Red or greenish red, not showy
M. 'Oekonomierat Echtermeyer' (M. 'Pink Weeper') WEEPING CRABAPPLE	Moderate, to 15 ft. Spread depends on pruning	Weeping branches. Usually grafted high on a standard crabapple. Cut out branches that grow stiffly upright	Opening purplish, later bronzy green	Purplish red, 1½ in. wide, all along drooping branchlets	Purple-red, 1 in., effective in fall

M

MALUS—CRABAPPLE

NAME	GROWTH RATE, HEIGHT, SPREAD	STRUCTURE	FOLIAGE	FLOWERS	FRUIT
M. 'Pink Perfection'	Moderate, to 20 ft. by 20 ft.	Full, rounded crown	Thick, heavy, green; holds color to fall. Resists rust, mildew	Red buds open to large, double pink flowers	Yellow and insignificant
M. 'Pink Spires'	Moderate, to 15 ft. by 10 ft.	Narrow, upright growth	Red purple in spring, turning bronzy green. Good disease resistance	Rose pink	Small, purplish red
M. 'Prairifire'	Moderate, to 20 ft. by 20 ft.	Rounded	New foliage purplish red, aging dark green on red stems	Pinkish red	Dark red
M. 'Profusion'	Moderate, to 20 ft. by 20 ft.	Upright, spreading	Purple, maturing bronzy green	Purplish red buds, purplish pink flowers	Red
M. 'Purple Wave'	Moderate, to 10–15 ft. by 10 ft.	Spreading, broad headed	Dark purplish green	Large, single to semi-double, rose red fading to purplish pink	Dark purple-red, 1 in.
M. purpurea 'Aldenhamensis' ALDENHAM CRABAPPLE	Fast, to 20 ft. by 20 ft.	Somewhat irregular round head, dense	Purplish leaves and bark on twigs	Semidouble, purplish red, large. May, sometimes reblooming in fall	Purplish red, 1 in.
M. p. 'Eleyi' ELEY CRABAPPLE	Fast, to 20 ft. by 20 ft.	Irregular, open, graceful	Dark green, with reddish veins and stalks. Subject to apple scab	Wine red, 1¼ in. Apr.	Heavy bearer of ¾-in. purple-red fruit
M. 'Radiant'	Fast, to 20 ft. by 20 ft.	Broad, rounded crown	New foliage purple red, aging green	Deep red buds open to deep pink blooms	Bright red, ½ in. wide. Color in midsummer
M. 'Red Jade'	Moderate, to 15 ft. by 15 ft.	Long, slender, weeping branches. Charming, irregular habit	Dark green	Small, white. Profuse in Apr.–May	Heavy crop of bright red fruit holds late into fall, is showy on weeping branches
M. 'Red Silver'	Fast, to 15 ft. by 15 ft.	Irregular; branches angular with tips drooping slightly	Reddish or purplish bronze silvered with silky hairs	Deep wine red. Apr.	Dark purplish red, ¾ in. Good for jelly
M. 'Royalty'	Moderate, to 15 ft. by 15 ft.	Dense, moundlike crown	Same dark purple as purple-leaf plum. Extremely cold hardy. Resists scab	Single, purplish crimson	Dark red, nearly ¾ in. across
M. sargentii SARGENT CRABAPPLE	Slow, to 10 ft. by 20 ft.	Dense, broad shrub with zigzag branching	Dark green, often lobed at base. Good disease resistance	White, small, profuse, fragrant. Pink in *M. s.* 'Rosea'. Mid-May	Red, tiny, profuse, lasting late
M. 'Snowdrift'	Moderate, to 20–25 ft. by 20 ft.	Rounded, dense crown	Good green; scab resistant	Red buds open to single white flowers. Long bloom period	Orange-red, under ½ in. wide. Hangs on for a long time
M. 'Strathmore'	Moderate to fast, to 20 ft. by 10 ft.	Narrow, upright, pyramidal	Reddish purple leaves in summer, deepen to scarlet in fall. Subject to apple scab	Deep pink to reddish pink	Small, red
M. zumi calocarpa	Moderate, to 25 ft. by 15 ft.	Pyramidal, dense, branching; weeping branchlets	Densely foliaged; larger leaves lobed. Good disease resistance	Opening soft pink, fading white; fragrant. Late Apr.–early May	Small, ½ in., glossy, bright red. Holds on well into winter

MANDARIN ORANGE. See CITRUS   p. 231

MANDEVILLA

Apocynaceae

EVERGREEN OR DECIDUOUS VINES

☘ ZONES VARY BY SPECIES

☼ ☽ EXPOSURE NEEDS VARY BY SPECIES

◆ AMPLE WATER DURING GROWTH

Mandevilla
'Alice du Pont'

Known for showy flowers, the genus *Mandevilla* includes plants that were formerly known as *Dipladenia*. Saucer-shaped flowers open from tubular throats.

M. 'Alice du Pont' (M. splendens, M. amabilis, Dipladenia splendens, D. amoena). Zones 21–24; indoor and greenhouse plant. Evergreen vine to 20–30 ft., much less in pots or tubs (where it is usually grown). Twining stems produce dark green, glossy, oval leaves 3–8 in. long. Clusters of 2–4-in.-wide, pure pink flowers appear among leaves from April to November. Even very small plant in 4-in. pot will bloom. Plant in rich soil and provide frame, trellis, or stake for support. Pinch young plant to induce bushiness. Full sun in coastal areas, partial shade inland. Spray for spider mites.

M. boliviensis. Zone 24. Evergreen vine to 12 ft., or sprawling shrub to 3 ft. tall, 5 ft. wide. Glossy leaves; white flowers with yellow throats throughout the year. Full sun or partial shade.

M. laxa (M. suaveolens). CHILEAN JASMINE. Deciduous vine. Zones 4–9, 14–21. Twines to 15 ft. or more. Leaves are long ovals, heart shaped at base, 2–6 in. long. Clustered summer flowers are white, 2 in. across, trumpet shaped, powerfully fragrant (like gardenia). Sun, rich soil. If plant becomes badly tangled, cut it to ground in winter; it will bloom on new growth. Root hardy to about 5°F.

M. splendens (M. amabilis, M. 'Profusa', M. 'Red Riding Hood', M. sanderi). Evergreen vine. Zones 21–24; indoor and greenhouse plant. Lower growing, shrubbier than 'Alice du Pont', with deeper pink blooms. Full sun or partial shade. Superb hanging basket plant.

MANGIFERA indica

MANGO

Anacardiaceae

EVERGREEN TREE

☘ ZONES 23, 24

☼ FULL SUN

◆ MAINTAIN STEADY SOIL MOISTURE

Mangifera indica

Grows to large size in tropics. In mildest parts of Southern California it often survives for years but may remain shrubby and is likely to fruit only in most favored, frost-free locations. Yellow to reddish flowers in long clusters at branch ends. Fruits that follow are oval, to 6 in. long, green to reddish or yellowish, with large seeds and peach-flavored flesh with varnish or turpentine overtones. Leaves are large and handsome, often coppery red or purple at time of expanding, later dark green and 8–16 in. long. Needs steady moisture but tolerates fairly poor, shallow soils. Sap and juice can cause a skin rash in some susceptible people.

MANZANITA. See ARCTOSTAPHYLOS   p. 162

MAPLE. See ACER   p. 135

Marantaceae. The arrowroot family consists of tropical or subtropical herbaceous plants with fleshy rhizomes or tubers and highly irregular flowers. Most are grown for handsome foliage, a few for flowers. An example is *Calathea*.

MARGUERITE. See CHRYSANTHEMUM frutescens   p. 226

MARIGOLD. See TAGETES   p. 500

MARIGOLD, DESERT. See BAILEYA multiradiata   p. 174

MARIPOSA LILY. See CALOCHORTUS venustus   p. 199

MARJORAM. See ORIGANUM   p. 395

MARLBERRY. See ARDISIA japonica   p. 164

MARMALADE BUSH. See STREPTOSOLEN jamesonii   p. 497

MARRUBIUM vulgare

HOREHOUND

Lamiaceae (Labiatae)

PERENNIAL HERB

☘ ALL ZONES

☼ FULL SUN

○ NO WATER ONCE ESTABLISHED

Marrubium vulgare

Grows to 1–3 ft. Wrinkled, woolly, aromatic, gray-green leaves; whorls of white mintlike flowers on foot-long, branching stems. Grows in poor, sandy soil. Sow seeds in spring in flats; later transplant to 1 ft. apart. As garden plant it's invasive and rather weedy looking but can serve as edging in gray garden. Used for medicinal purposes and in candy. Foliage lasts well in bouquets.

MARSH MARIGOLD. See CALTHA palustris   p. 199

MASCAGNIA

ORCHID VINE

Malpighiaceae

DECIDUOUS VINES

☘ ZONES 12–24

☼ FULL SUN

◐ TOLERATE SOME ARIDITY

Mascagnia lilacina

Vines of Mexican origin used in the desert, where they bloom at hottest time of the year. Leaves in opposite pairs look like those of honeysuckle. Clusters of flowers are followed by oddly winged seedpods that somewhat resemble butterflies and are sometimes used in dried arrangements.

M. lilacina. LAVENDER ORCHID VINE. To 15–20 ft., with 1½-in. leaves and lilac blue flowers followed by inch-wide "butterflies." Hardy to 15–18°F; leaves drop at 22°F.

M. macroptera. YELLOW ORCHID VINE. To 15 ft., with 3-in. leaves and abundant bright yellow clustered flowers followed by conspicuous 2-in. yellow-green seedpods. Hardy to 22–24°F.

MASK FLOWER. See ALONSOA   p. 147

MASTERWORT. See ASTRANTIA   p. 171

MASTIC. See PISTACIA lentiscus   p. 425

MATILIJA POPPY. See ROMNEYA coulteri   p. 462

FOR INFORMATION ON SELECTING PLANTS
PLEASE SEE PAGES 45–128

M

MATRICARIA recutita (M. chamomilla)

CHAMOMILE

Asteraceae (Compositae)

SUMMER ANNUAL

☷ ALL ZONES

☀ FULL SUN

💧 LITTLE WATER ONCE ESTABLISHED

Matricaria recutita

This is the chamomile that yields a fragrant tea with overtones of pineapple. Plant grows 2–2½ ft. tall, with finely cut, almost fernlike foliage and daisylike white-and-yellow flower heads an inch wide or less. Grows easily in full sun and ordinary soil from seed sown in late winter or spring. Becomes naturalized. Dried flowers are the parts used in making tea.

Plants or seeds sold as *Matricaria* 'White Stars', 'Golden Ball', and 'Snowball' are varieties of *Chrysanthemum parthenium*. Chamomile sold as walk-on ground cover is *Chamaemelum nobile (Anthemis nobilis)*. Its flowers yield medicinal-tasting, rather bitter tea.

MATTEUCCIA struthiopteris

OSTRICH FERN

Polypodiaceae

FERN

☷ ZONES 1–10, 14–24

☀ ☽ 💧 SHADE; SUN IN COASTAL AREAS

💧 💧 BEST WITH AMPLE WATER

Matteuccia struthiopteris

Native to northern Europe and Asia. Hardy to extreme cold but indifferent grower in mild-winter areas. Clumps narrow at base, spread at top like a shuttlecock. Can grow to 6 ft. in moist, moderate climates but reaches only 1½–2 ft. in mountains where season is short, humidity low. Spreads slowly by underground rhizomes. Dormant in winter. *M. pensylvanica* (from eastern North America) is similar. Both are attractive woodland or waterside plants. Need rich soil.

MATTHIOLA

STOCK

Brassicaceae (Cruciferae)

BIENNIALS OR PERENNIALS GROWN AS ANNUALS

☷ ALL ZONES

☀ ☽ FULL SUN; CAN TAKE LIGHT SHADE

💧 WATER AS NEEDED

Matthiola incana

Stock has long been a favorite of western gardeners. All species have long, narrow gray-green leaves and luxuriant flowers in erect clusters.

M. incana. STOCK. Valued for fragrance, cut flowers, garden decoration. Leaves oblong to 4 in. long. Flowers single or double, 1 in. wide, in spikes. Colors include white, pink, red, purple, lavender, cream. Blues and reds are purple toned; yellows tend toward cream. Spicy-sweet fragrance.

Stock needs light, fertile soil; sun; good drainage; cool weather. Valuable winter flowers in Zones 8, 9, 12–24—there, set out plants in early fall for winter or early spring bloom. Plants take moderate frost but will not set flower buds if nights are too chilly; late planting means late flowers. Where rainfall is heavy, plant in raised beds to ensure good drainage, prevent root rot. In Zones 1–7, 10, 11, plant in earliest spring to get bloom before hot weather.

Many strains available. Column stock and Double Giant Flowering are unbranched, 2–3 ft. tall, and can be planted 6–8 in. apart in rows; ideal

for cutting. Giant Imperial strain is branched, 2–2½ ft. tall, comes in solid or mixed colors. Trysomic or Ten Weeks stock is branched, 15–18 in. tall. Trysomic Seven Weeks strain is 12–15 in. tall.

M. longipetala bicornis. EVENING SCENTED STOCK. Foot-tall plant with lance-shaped leaves to 3½ in. long. Small purplish flowers are inconspicuous by day, wonderfully fragrant at night. Full sun. Winter annual in low and intermediate desert.

MATTRESS VINE. See **MUEHLENBECKIA complexa**	p. 384
MAURANDYA scandens. See **ASARINA scandens**	p. 167
MAYBUSH, MAYDAY TREE. See **PRUNUS padus**	p. 443

MAYTENUS boaria

MAYTEN TREE

Celastraceae

EVERGREEN TREE

☷ ZONES 8, 9, 14–21

☀ FULL SUN

💧 💧 TOLERATES ARIDITY; IS LUSHER WITH WATER

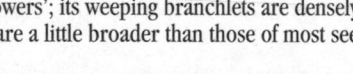

Maytenus boaria

Slow to moderate growth to an eventual 30–50 ft.; 20 ft. tall by 15 ft. wide at 12 years is typical. Long, pendulous branchlets hang down from branches, giving tree daintiness and grace. Habit and leaves (1–2 in. long) give tree the look of a small-scale weeping willow. Without deep watering, it will root voraciously near surface of soil and invade planting beds. Flowers and fruit inconspicuous.

Good drainage is crucial. Stake securely when planting. There will be much side growth; remove unwanted growth along trunk, or, if you wish, preserve some side branches for multiple trunk effect. Sometimes may show partial defoliation after cold snaps or at blooming time; recovery is rapid. Resistant to oak root fungus. For uniformity, plant cutting-grown variety 'Green Showers'; its weeping branchlets are densely clad with deep green leaves that are a little broader than those of most seedling trees.

A MAYTEN IN THE LANDSCAPE

It's better for a patio than a weeping willow (neater, less invasive roots). Can thrive in a lawn but may send up suckers, especially if roots are disturbed. Locate it to display its pattern—against walls in an entryway or on a patio, in a featured raised bed.

MAZUS reptans

Scrophulariaceae

PERENNIAL

☷ EVERGREEN, ZONES 14–24; DIES IN WINTER, 1–7

☀ ☽ SUN OR LIGHT SHADE

💧 REGULAR WATER

Mazus reptans

Slender stems creep and root along ground, send up leafy branches 1–2 in. tall. Leaves an inch long, narrowish, bright green, with a few teeth on edges. Flowers (spring, early summer) in clusters of two to five, purplish blue with white and yellow markings, about ¾ in. across. In shape, flowers resemble those of *Mimulus*. Rock gardens or small-scale ground cover; needs rich soil. Takes very light foot traffic.

| **MEADOW RUE.** See **THALICTRUM** | p. 504 |
| **MEADOW SAFFRON.** See **COLCHICUM** | p. 237 |

M

MECONOPSIS

Papaveraceae

PERENNIALS

⚘ ZONES VARY BY SPECIES

☼ ◐ ● EXPOSURE NEEDS VARY BY SPECIES

● SUMMER WATER

*Meconopsis
betonicifolia*

Ardent collectors and shade garden enthusiasts sometimes attempt the many species offered by specialist seed firms. Most are difficult, but the two listed here are not too hard to grow in the right climate.

M. betonicifolia (M. baileyi). HIMALAYAN POPPY. Zones 4–6, 17. Tall, leafy, short lived, 2–4 ft. tall, with hairy leaves and silky, 3–4-in.-wide poppies of sky blue or rosy lavender, centered with yellow stamens. Needs shade; humid air; coolness; loose, acid soil. Try it with rhododendrons.

M. cambrica. WELSH POPPY. Zones 1–9, 14–17. Short lived with 3-in., yellow or orange flowers on 1-ft. stems. Gray-green divided leaves. Full sun or light shade near coast, partial shade inland. Can take a little or a lot of summer water. Self-sows.

MEDITERRANEAN FAN PALM. See CHAMAEROPS humilis p. 221

MELALEUCA

Myrtaceae

EVERGREEN SHRUBS OR TREES

⚘ ZONES VARY BY SPECIES

☼ FULL SUN

◐ ● LITTLE OR NO WATER

*Melaleuca
linariifolia*

Narrow, sometimes needlelike leaves; clustered flowers with prominent stamens. Each cluster resembles a bottlebrush, and some melaleucas are called bottlebrushes, although that name is more generally applied to *Callistemon*. Clusters of woody seed capsules hang on for several years, forming odd, decorative cylinders around twigs and branches. Flowers attract birds.

Most melaleucas stand heat, wind, poor soil, limited moisture, and salt air. Most are vigorous and fast growing; control by cutting back selected branches to a well-placed side branch. Shearing makes plants dense and lumpish. Smaller melaleucas are good screening materials; some of the larger ones are useful as flowering or shade trees. Many have interestingly contorted branches and bark that peels in thick, papery layers.

Australia is home to 140 or more species, and it is likely that many of these will show up in western gardens. All are easy to grow.

M. armillaris. DROOPING MELALEUCA. Shrub or small tree. Zones 8, 9, 12–24. To 15–30 ft. Furrowed gray bark peels off in strips near base of trunk. Drooping branches. Light green, needlelike leaves to 1 in. long. Fluffy white flowers in 1–3½-in.-long spikes, spring to fall. Tough and adaptable, especially useful in sea winds. Clipped hedge or unclipped informal screen (prickly leaves a real deterrent); with training, a sprawling shrub or small tree.

M. decussata. LILAC MELALEUCA. Large shrub or small tree. Zones 9, 12–24. Grows 8–20 ft. tall with equal spread. Brown, shredding bark. Tiny (½-in.-long) leaves closely set on arching, pendulous branches. Lilac to purple flowers in 1-in. spikes, late spring to summer. Will stand some neglect. Use it to supply big masses of finely-textured, bluish foliage. Thinning will improve its appearance by showing off trunk, branch character.

M. elliptica. Shrub or small tree. Zones 9, 12–24. To 8–15 ft. high. Brown, shredding bark. Roundish, ½-in.-long leaves mostly at ends of fanlike branches. Large, showy, red to crimson bottlebrushes to 3½ in. long, on side branches, early spring to fall.

M. ericifolia. HEATH MELALEUCA. Shrub or small tree. Zones 9, 12–24. To 10–25 ft. Bark tan or gray, soft, fibrous. Dark green, needle-like, 1-in. leaves like those of heather. Yellowish white flowers in 1-in. spikes, early spring. Fast growing and tolerant of alkaline soil and poor drainage; good near beach. Attractive multitrunked tree.

M. hypericifolia. DOTTED MELALEUCA. Shrub. Zones 9, 12–24. Grows 6–10 ft. tall, with thin, peeling bark, drooping branches. Coppery green to dull green, 1¼-in. leaves; bright orange-red flowers in dense 2-in. clusters, late spring through winter (often hidden by foliage). Can be clipped into hedge but will bloom more profusely as informal, unclipped screen. Not suitable for planting right at beach although it takes ocean wind.

M. incana. GRAY HONEY MYRTLE. Shrub or small tree. Zones 8, 9, 12–24. Spreading, arching shrub with semiweeping branchlets. Foliage is gray and furry, creating a gray, smoky effect. Flowers are yellowish white, in small clusters. Natural habit is broad, to 9 ft. tall and wider, but shaping can create a handsome small tree.

M. linariifolia. FLAXLEAF PAPERBARK. Tree. Zones 9, 13–23. To 30 ft., with umbrellalike crown. White bark sheds in papery flakes. Slender branchlets. Bright green or bluish green, 1¼-in.-long leaves are stiff, needlelike. Numerous fluffy spikes of small white flowers in summer give effect of snow on branches. Young plants willowy, need staking until trunk firms up; prune out lower branches to shape.

M. nesophila. PINK MELALEUCA. Tree or large shrub. Zones 13, 16–24. Fast growth to 15–20 ft., possibly 30 ft. Grows naturally as small tree; unpruned, produces gnarled, heavy branches that sprawl or ascend in picturesque patterns. Thick, spongy bark. Gray-green, thick, roundish, 1-in. leaves. Roundish (to inch-wide) mauve flower brushes at branch ends, produced most of year, fade to white with yellow tips. Takes beach winds and spray; poor, rocky soil; desert heat; much or practically no water. Use as tree or big informal screen, or shear as hedge.

M. quinquenervia. CAJEPUT TREE. Tree. Zones 9, 13, 15–17, 20–24. Upright, open growth to 20–40 ft. Young branches pendulous. Trunk has thick, spongy, light brown to whitish bark that peels off in sheets. (You can use these sheets to line wire hanging baskets.) Leaves stiff, narrowly oval, pale green, shiny, 2–4 in. long. Young leaves have silky hairs. Foliage turns purple with light frost. Flowers yellowish white (sometimes pink or purple), in 2–3-in. spikes, summer and fall. Can take much or little water. Good street tree. Planted 8–10 ft. apart and thinned occasionally, trees make pleasant groves. Usually sold as *M. leucadendra.*

M. styphelioides. Tree. Zones 9, 13–24. To 20–40 ft. Pendulous branchlets; lacy, open growth habit. Thick, pale, spongy, light tan bark becomes charcoal with age, peels off in papery layers. Light green leaves to ¾ in. long, ¼ in. wide, sometimes twisted, prickly to touch. Creamy white flowers in 1–2-in. brushes, summer through fall. Thrives in any soil; resistant to oak root fungus. Good lawn tree. Best trained with multiple trunks.

MELAMPODIUM leucanthum

BLACKFOOT DAISY

Asteraceae (Compositae)

SHORT-LIVED PERENNIAL

⚘ ZONES 1–3, 10–13

☼ FULL SUN

● BLOOMS MORE HEAVILY WITH SOME WATER

*Melampodium
leucanthum*

Native to Arizona, New Mexico, Mexico, Texas. Foot-tall, foot-wide clumps of narrow gray leaves are topped by clouds of inch-wide daisies, white with yellow centers. Rays are broad and full; plant is showy when in bloom. In mild-winter climates, it blooms off and on during winter months and more heavily April–October—if given water. Where freezing temperatures are routine, expect spring and summer bloom only.

Plants need fast-draining soil; in nature, they grow principally in decomposed granite. If plants become too straggly for good looks, cut them back in autumn.

M

Melastomataceae. The melastoma family consists almost entirely of tropical shrubs and trees with strongly veined leaves and symmetrical flowers, such as Spanish shawl (*Heterocentron*), princess flower (*Tibouchina*).

MELIA azedarach

CHINABERRY

Meliaceae

DECIDUOUS TREE

▨ ZONES 6, 8–24

☼ FULL SUN

◐ LITTLE WATER

◈ FRUIT IS POISONOUS IF EATEN IN QUANTITY

Melia azedarach 'Umbraculiformis'

Spreading tree to 30–50 ft. high. Leaves 1–3 ft. long, cut into many narrow or oval, toothed, 1–2-in.-long leaflets. Loose clusters of lilac flowers in spring or early summer, fragrant in evening, followed by yellow, hard, berrylike fruit ½ in. across.

M. a. 'Umbraculiformis'. TEXAS UMBRELLA TREE. Less picturesque but far more common than the species, with a dense, spreading, dome-shaped crown and drooping leaves. Grows to 30 ft. Gives rich green color, dense shade in hottest, driest climates; grows even in poor alkaline soil. Leaves turn gold in autumn. Stands all but strongest ocean winds. Has brittle wood and sometimes suckers but is valuable where trees are hard to grow.

Meliaceae. The mahogany family, consisting largely of tropical trees and shrubs, contains two plants grown in the West: *Cedrela* and *Melia*. Both have finely divided leaves and clustered flowers.

MELIANTHUS major

HONEY BUSH

Melianthaceae

EVERGREEN SHRUB

▨ ZONES 8, 9, 12–24

☼ ◑ SUN; PARTIAL SHADE IN DESERT REGIONS

◌ ◐ ● TOLERATES ARIDITY OR REGULAR WATER

Melianthus major

Soft-wooded plant of rapid growth to 12–14 ft., but easily kept much lower. Stems slightly branched, upright or sprawling and spreading. Boldly patterned foliage: 1-ft.-long, grayish green leaves divided into nine to eleven strongly toothed leaflets (leaves have disagreeable smell when they are brushed or bruised). Foot-long spikes of reddish brown, 1-in.-long flowers in late winter, early spring. Adapts to most soils and most locations. To get tall plants, stake a few stems; for sprawling, bulky effect, shorten some stems in early spring before new growth begins. Needs grooming. Excellent when used as silhouette in raised beds, for sprawling over wall, in containers, with succulents or foliage plants.

M. minor. Rare plant occasionally seen at plant sales or in collectors' gardens. Leaves are much smaller (6–7 in.), on shorter (3-ft.) plants.

MELISSA officinalis

LEMON BALM, SWEET BALM

Lamiaceae (Labiatae)

PERENNIAL HERB

▨ ALL ZONES

☼ ◑ SUN OR PARTIAL SHADE

● REGULAR WATER

Melissa officinalis

Grows to 2 ft. Light green, heavily veined leaves with lemon scent. White flowers unimportant.

Shear occasionally to keep compact. Likes rich soil. Very hardy; self-sows, spreads rapidly. Propagate from seed or root divisions. Leaves used in drinks, fruit cups, salads, fish dishes. Dried leaves help give lemon tang to sachets, potpourris.

MELON, MUSKMELON, CANTALOUPE

Cucurbitaceae

ANNUALS

▨ ALL ZONES

☼ FULL SUN

◐ WATER MOST WHEN PLANTS ARE YOUNG

Melon

To ripen to full sweetness, a melon needs steady heat for 2½–4 months. Foggy or cool summer days don't help. Therefore, gardeners in cool-summer climates should plant melons in warmest southern exposures. In both cool-summer climates and interior short-summer climates, start plants indoors in peat pots a few weeks before last frost date; truly tropical plants, melons perish in even light frost. Black plastic mulch under melons warms soil, speeds harvest, helps keep melons from rotting. Plastic row covers permit earlier planting out of doors.

Melons need considerable space (dimensions described below). You can grow melons on sun-bathed trellises, but heavy fruit must be supported in individual cloth slings.

MELONS TELL YOU WHEN THEY'RE SWEET

Harvest muskmelon and 'Persian' melon when stems begin to crack away from melon end. Honeydew and 'Golden Beauty' casaba are ready when rinds turn yellow; Crenshaw turns mostly yellow but shows some green even when ripe. Also, smell the blossom end. Ripe melons have a pleasant, fruity perfume.

The true cantaloupe, a hard-shelled melon, is rarely grown in this country. Principal types grown here are muskmelons ("cantaloupes") and late melons. The former are ribbed, with netted skin and (usually) salmon-colored flesh; these are most widely adapted to various western climates. Good ones (best types for cooler climates) are 'Hale's Best'; 'Honey Rock'; and the hybrids 'Ambrosia', 'Mainerock' (early), 'Samson', and 'Saticoy'. Hybrids are superior to others in disease resistance and uniformity of size and quality. Small, tasty, highly perfumed melons from Mediterranean (and hybrids of these) are white-fleshed 'Ha-Ogen' and orange-fleshed 'Chaca' and 'Charentais'. Late melons ripen only where there is a long, hot, rather dry summer (Zones 8, 9, 12–14, 18, 19); members of this group are 'Persian', honeydew, 'Honey Ball', 'Golden Beauty' casaba, and Crenshaw.

Except as noted above, sow seeds two weeks after average date of last frost. Soil should be light and well drained. Melons are best planted on gently rounded mounds 6 ft. wide, a few inches high at center, and as long as your garden will permit. On south side of mounds make furrows 10 in. wide and 6 in. deep for irrigation. Water well until furrows are filled. Plant six or seven seeds about 1 in. deep, spaced within an 8–10-in. circle, 6 in. or so away from furrow. Space these circles (hills) 3 ft. apart. This system allows you to water roots without wetting foliage.

When plants are well established, thin each hill to the best two, and begin to train them away from furrow. Fill furrow with water from time to time, but do not keep soil soaked. Feed (again in furrow) every 6 weeks.

FOR INFORMATION ON YOUR CLIMATE ZONE

PLEASE SEE PAGES 15–44

M

MENTHA

MINT

Lamiaceae (Labiatae)

PERENNIAL HERBS AND GROUND COVERS

✂ ZONES VARY BY SPECIES

☼ ◑ SUN OR PARTIAL SHADE

● REGULAR WATER

Mentha spicata

Spread rapidly by underground stems. Can be quite invasive. Grow almost anywhere but perform best in light, medium-rich, moist soil. Contain in pot or box to keep in bounds. Propagate from runners. Keep flowers cut off. Replant every 3 years.

M. gentilis. GOLDEN APPLE MINT. All zones. To 2 ft. Smooth, deep green leaves, variegated yellow. Flowers inconspicuous. Use in flavoring foods. Foliage excellent in mixed bouquets.

M. piperita. PEPPERMINT. All zones. To 3 ft. Strongly scented, toothed, 3-in.-long leaves. Small purple flowers in 1–3-in. spikes. Leaves good for flavoring tea. *M. p. citrata,* orange mint, bergamot mint, grows to 2 ft. and has broad, 2-in.-long leaves, small lavender flowers. It is used in potpourris or in flavoring foods. Crushed leaves have slight orange flavor.

M. pulegium. PENNYROYAL. Zones 4–24. Creeping plant grows a few inches tall with nearly round 1-in. leaves. Small lavender flowers in tight, short whorls. Strong mint fragrance and flavor. Poisonous in large quantities but safe as a flavoring. Needs cool, moist site, with shade in hottest areas.

M. requienii. JEWEL MINT OF CORSICA. Zones 5–9, 12–24. Creeping, mat forming. Spreads at moderate to rapid rate, grows only ½ in. high. Tiny, round, bright green leaves give mossy effect. Tiny light purple flowers in summer.

Set divisions 6 in. apart for ground cover in sun or partial shade. Needs moisture; disappears during winter in colder areas. Delightful minty or sagelike fragrance when leaves are bruised or crushed underfoot.

M. spicata. SPEARMINT. All zones. To 1½–2 ft. Dark green leaves, slightly smaller than those of peppermint; leafy spikes of purplish flowers. Use leaves fresh from garden or dried, for lamb, in cold drinks, as garnish, in apple jelly.

M. suaveolens. APPLE MINT. All zones. Stiff stems grow 20–30 in. tall. Rounded leaves are slightly hairy, gray green, 1–4 in. long. Purplish white flowers in 2–3-in. spikes. Leaves have apple-mint fragrance. Usually sold as *M. rotundifolia. M. s.* 'Variegata', pineapple mint, has leaves with white markings, faint fragrance of pineapple.

MENTZELIA

BLAZING STAR

Loasaceae

PERENNIALS, BIENNIALS, AND ANNUALS

✂ ALL ZONES

☼ FULL SUN

◐ ● LITTLE OR NO SUMMER WATER

Mentzelia lindleyi

Native to desert or semidesert areas of western United States. They tolerate heat, wind, and poor soil but require good drainage. Star-shaped yellow blossoms are large and showy.

M. laevicaulis. Biennial or short-lived perennial grows to 3–3½ ft. Tall, rough, and ungainly. Narrow, 3–7-in.-long leaves. Spectacular pale yellow, 4-in.-wide stars open in the evening; plant is often called evening star. Best use is on bare banks, where it's perfectly at home.

M. lindleyi. Summer annual 1–4 ft. tall, usually narrow, sometimes spreading to 1½ ft. Light green, rough-textured leaves with short hairs. Flowers bright yellow with orange or reddish center ring and big brush of yellow stamens. Blooms from April to June. Sow seed in fall, winter, or earliest spring where plants are to bloom; give ample water until

plants come into bloom, then reduce or stop watering. Use alone or in wildflower mixtures.

MERREMIA aurea

YELLOW MORNING GLORY

Convolvulaceae

DECIDUOUS VINE

✂ ZONES 12–24

☼ FULL SUN

◐ TOLERATES SOME ARIDITY

Merremia aurea

Twines to 15 ft., with leaves divided into five leaflets and a fine show of golden yellow, 2–4-in. morning glories in summer. Tops are hardy to 26°F. Plant may be cut back to ground; it will sprout from a tuber.

MERTENSIA

Boraginaceae

PERENNIALS

✂ ZONES 1–21

● SHADE

◐ WATER DURING GROWTH AND BLOOM

Mertensia virginica

Resemble giant-size forget-me-nots (*Myosotis*) and are related to them. Plants appear and flower early, go dormant soon after seeding, usually before midsummer. Foliage usually smooth gray green or blue green. Flowers nodding, in loose, gradually uncoiling clusters, pink or lavender in bud opening to blue bells, sometimes with pinkish cast. Good with naturalized daffodils or with ferns, trilliums in woodland gardens.

M. ciliata. CHIMING BELLS, MOUNTAIN BLUEBELL. Native to damp places in Rocky Mountains. Grows 1–3 ft. tall, with ½–¾-in. flowers. Several other species grow in mountainous areas of the West; most are lower growing.

M. virginica. VIRGINIA BLUEBELLS. From eastern United States. Most widely planted species. Grows 1–2 ft. tall; flowers are 1 in. long. Widely available from mail-order bulb or plant catalogs.

MESCAL BEAN. See SOPHORA secundiflora   p. 488

MESEMBRYANTHEMUM crystallinum

ICE PLANT

Aizoaceae

SUMMER ANNUAL

✂ ALL ZONES

☼ FULL SUN

◐ ● LITTLE OR NO WATER ONCE ESTABLISHED

Mesembryanthemum crystallinum

The least ornamental of many plants commonly called *Mesembryanthemum* or ice plant, this is now considered the only true *Mesembryanthemum*. For other, showier kinds used as ground covers or ornamentals, see entry under Ice Plant.

M. crystallinum is a sprawling plant a few inches tall and several feet wide. Oval, flat, stalked, fleshy leaves grow up to 4 in. long, turn red in dry season. Leaves covered with tiny transparent blisters that glisten like flecks of ice. Foliage is edible and resembles New Zealand spinach. Inch-wide flowers white to pinkish. Easy to grow from seed. Plant has become wild in parts of California.

MESQUITE. See PROSOPIS   p. 438

M

METASEQUOIA glyptostroboides

DAWN REDWOOD

Taxodiaceae

DECIDUOUS CONIFER

🌿 ZONES 3–10, 14–24

☼ FULL SUN

💧 BEST IN MOIST, NOT BOGGY SOIL

Metasequoia glyptostroboides

Grows to 80–90 ft. high. Resembles coast redwood (*Sequoia sempervirens*) but differs in several ways. Cones are much smaller; leaves are soft to the touch and light, bright green, while coast redwood's are dark green and somewhat stiff. Dawn redwood's light brown branchlets turn upward; those of coast redwood usually stand out horizontally. Most important, foliage turns light bronze in autumn, then falls; coast redwood is evergreen.

Stands temperatures from −15°F to 105°F, but suffers winter wind damage in cold, dry areas. Salt winds cause foliage burn, as does hot sunlight in enclosed areas. Good in soil containing peat moss or leaf mold with good drainage; takes lawn watering well. Resistant to oak root fungus.

Best use is in groves, where it brings something of the redwood grove's beauty to cold-winter areas. However, also good for single planting—swelling buds and bright, silky new needles are a real treat in spring. Structurally interesting even when bare. Trunks of older trees show rugged, fluted bases. Grows very fast when young, sometimes 4–6 ft. a year in California, less in colder areas. Young tree grows satisfactorily in large tub or box.

METROSIDEROS excelsus (M. tomentosus)

NEW ZEALAND CHRISTMAS TREE, POHUTUKAWA

Myrtaceae

EVERGREEN TREE OR LARGE SHRUB

🌿 ZONES 17, 23, 24

☼ BEST NEAR COAST, BEACH

💧 TOLERATES NO WATER, OR SOME WATER

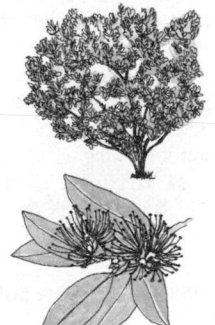

Metrosideros excelsus

Native to New Zealand. Grows to 30 ft. or more. Generally branches heavily from ground up; requires careful staking and pruning to bring into tree form. Leaves firm, leathery, densely spaced on branches; on young plants they are smooth, glossy green; on older plants they are dark green above, white and woolly underneath. Dark scarlet flowers, in big clusters covering ends of branches, bloom May–July (in December in New Zealand, hence common name "Christmas tree"). Along coast it rivals *Eucalyptus ficifolia* in flower color. There is a yellow-flowered variety, 'Aurea'. In humid coastside gardens old plants sometimes grow aerial roots that reach the ground.

"Pohutukawa" means "drenched with spray," which aptly describes the seashore conditions where wild plants grow. Water through the first two dry seasons; thereafter, it needs no irrigation. Useful lawn tree; good street tree, but if growing in narrow parking strip, can break sidewalk.

AN ARBOREAL "OLD SALT"

New Zealand Christmas tree really *can* take wind, salt spray, and other special conditions that come to big plants growing within the sound of surf (many other trees purported to grow there actually begin to fail in 5 years or so). This one is so thoroughly marine that it suffers inland—from dry air and frost.

MICHELIA

Magnoliaceae

EVERGREEN SHRUBS OR TREES

🌿 ZONES VARY BY SPECIES

☼ ◑ SUN; PARTIAL SHADE IN HOTTEST AREAS

💧 REGULAR WATER

Michelia doltsopa

Related to magnolias, but with numerous flowers borne among leaves rather than singly at ends of branches. All need rich soil.

M. champaca. Tree to 25–30 ft. Zones 16–24. Large (to 10 in.) glossy leaves and 3-in., many-petaled pale orange flowers off and on throughout the year, heaviest in winter and summer. Fragrance is legendary.

M. doltsopa. Large evergreen shrub or small tree. Zones 14–24. Tall tree in its native Himalayas. Has grown to 25 ft. in as many years in San Francisco. Varies from bushy to narrow and upright; choose plants for desired form and prune to shape. Leaves thin, leathery, dark green, 3–8 in. long, 1–3 in. wide. Flowers open January–March from brown, furry buds that form in profusion among leaves near branch ends. Flowers creamy or white, slightly tinged green at base of petals, 5–7 in. wide, fragrant, with 12–16 petals about 1 in. wide. They somewhat resemble flowers of saucer magnolia (*Magnolia soulangiana*).

M. figo (M. fuscata). BANANA SHRUB. Evergreen shrub. Zones 9, 14–24. Slow growth to 6–8 ft., possibly to 15 ft. Dense habit, with glossy, 3-in.-long, medium green leaves. Heavy bloom season March–May, but plants often show scattered bloom throughout the summer. Flowers 1–1½ in. wide, creamy yellow shaded brownish purple, resembling small magnolias. Notable feature is powerful, fruity fragrance; most people think it resembles smell of ripe bananas. Fragrance best in warm, wind-free spot. Choice plant for entryway or patio. The selection 'Port Wine' has rose to maroon flowers.

MICROBIOTA decussata

Cupressaceae

EVERGREEN SHRUB

🌿 ALL ZONES

☼ ◑ FULL SUN; LIGHT SHADE IN HOTTEST AREAS

💧 MODERATE WATER

Microbiota decussata

Native to Siberian mountains and hardy to any amount of cold. Neat, sprawling shrub that resembles a trailing arborvitae. Grows to 1½ ft. tall, 7–8 ft. wide, with many horizontal or trailing plumelike branches closely set with scalelike leaves. Foliage green in summer, turning purplish, reddish brown in winter. Bank cover.

MICROLEPIA

Polypodiaceae
FERNS
⚡ ZONES 17, 23, 24
● SHADE
◊ TOLERATE FAIRLY DRY SOIL

Microlepia strigosa

Sturdy plants useful for landscaping in mild climates. Both species described below can take fairly dry soil—drier than is usual for ferns.

M. firma. Native to India. Fronds dull green, delicately cut, triangular, to 3 ft. long. Surfaces densely hairy. Hardy to 28°F.

M. strigosa. LACE FERN. Native to tropical Asia. Robust fern with delicate fronds. Grows 2–3 ft. tall. Hardy to 28°F. Sometimes sold as *M. speluncae.*

MICROMERIA chamissonis. See SATUREJA douglasii	**p. 477**
MIGNONETTE. See RESEDA odorata	**p. 452**
MILFOIL. See ACHILLEA millefolium	**p. 138**

MILIUM effusum 'Aureum'

BOWLES' GOLDEN GRASS
Poaceae (Gramineae)
PERENNIAL GRASS
⚡ ALL ZONES
◐ LIGHT SHADE
● MAINTAIN CONSTANT SOIL MOISTURE

Milium effusum 'Aureum'

Attractive clumping grass to 2 ft. tall, usually less. Bright greenish gold leaves erect, then arching and weeping. Effective for spot of color in woodland garden, shaded rock garden.

MILKBUSH. See EUPHORBIA tirucalli	**p. 290**

MILLETTIA reticulata

EVERGREEN WISTERIA
Fabaceae (Leguminosae)
EVERGREEN VINE
⚡ ZONES 20–24
☼ FULL SUN
● REGULAR WATER

Millettia reticulata

Vigorous, twining vine that can reach great size. Shiny, leathery leaves divided into leaflets like those of wisteria; evergreen only in frost-free areas. Tight clusters of dark purple-red flowers in fall have odor of cedar and camphor. An extremely fast grower when established; if permitted to climb into trees, it can overwhelm them. Best use is as cover for large arbor, pergola, or chain-link fence.

MIMOSA. See ACACIA baileyana, ALBIZIA julibrissin	**pp. 132, 144**

FOR GROWING SYMBOL EXPLANATIONS
PLEASE SEE PAGE 129

MIMULUS

MONKEY FLOWER
Scrophulariaceae
PERENNIALS
⚡ ZONES VARY BY TYPE
☼ ◐ ● EXPOSURE NEEDS VARY BY TYPE
◊ ◑ ● WATER NEEDS VARY BY TYPE

Mimulus hybridus

Wide-ranging group of plants with widely differing needs. One is a short-lived perennial usually grown as an annual; the others are shrubby perennials. All have a funnel-shaped flower with two "lips," thought to resemble a grinning monkey face.

M. hybridus. All zones. Short-lived perennial grown as annual. Leaves are smooth and succulent; the 2–2½-in. flowers range in color from cream through rose, orange, yellow, scarlet, and brown, usually with heavy brownish maroon spotting or mottling. They need shade, ample moisture, and rich soil with a high organic content. In Zones 17 and 24 they can stand full sun. Use in spring gardens with ferns and primroses, or plant in hanging baskets or window boxes for close-up enjoyment. Sow in spring for summer bloom, or set out plants for early spring show.

The other plants were once classified as *Diplacus* and are still widely known by that name. These include *M. aurantiacus (D. aurantiacus)*, sticky monkey flower, a 4-ft. shrub with buff-orange 1½-in. flowers; *M. bifidus (D. grandiflorus)*, Plumas monkey flower, with large, pale yellow to peach flowers; *M. longiflorus (D. longiflorus)*, with cream to orange-yellow flowers; and its variety *M. l. rutilus*, with deep red flowers. All are California natives— aridity is part of their lives. Zones 8, 9, 14–24. Sun or part shade.

Mimulus longiflorus

More important are the hybrids derived from these species (often known as Verity hybrids after their originator). These are showy, no-water-needed plants for Zones 7–9, 14–24. They grow 1–4 ft. tall and bloom over a long period in late spring and summer. Narrow, glossy, dark green leaves are sometimes sticky, and the flowers are 1–3 in. long. Flowers range from white and cream to yellow, orange, copper, salmon, red, and maroon.

Prune in spring before growth starts. Pruned after first flowering, they often bloom again in fall or, with some water, repeatedly throughout the year. Give them sun or light shade and good drainage. Because plants are not long lived, take cuttings of your favorite plants; they easily root in moist sand.

MING ARALIA. See POLYSCIAS fruticosa	**p. 433**
MINT. See MENTHA	**p. 379**
MINT BUSH. See PROSTANTHERA	**p. 438**

MIRABILIS jalapa

FOUR O'CLOCK
Nyctaginaceae
PERENNIAL AND ANNUAL
⚡ PERENNIAL, ZONES 4–24; SUMMER ANNUAL, 1–3
☼ FULL SUN
◊ NO WATER ONCE ESTABLISHED

Mirabilis jalapa

Tuberous roots can be dug and stored like dahlia roots. Erect, many-branched stems grow quickly to form mounded clumps 3–4 ft. high and wide. Trumpet-shaped flowers, in red, yellow, or white with variations of shades between, open in midafternoon. Deep green, oval, 2–6-in.-long leaves and strong, bushy habit give plants the substance and character of shrubs (even though they are only temporary or seasonal). Jingles strain is lower growing than old-fashioned kinds, has elaborately splashed and stained flowers in two or three colors all at once. Sow seed in early spring for blooms from midsummer through fall. Reseeds readily.

M

MIRROR PLANT. See COPROSMA repens   p. 239

MISCANTHUS sinensis

EULALIA GRASS

Poaceae (Gramineae)

PERENNIAL GRASS

◪ ALL ZONES

☼ ◑ ● SUN OR SHADE

💧 HEAVY WATERING

Miscanthus sinensis

Tall (5–6-ft.), graceful, clumping grass to stand out in border or at focal points in garden. Grows in any soil. Plant turns tan or brown in winter and should be cut back before new growth starts in spring. Among many varieties are the following:

'Gracillimus'. MAIDEN GRASS. Slender, weeping leaves topped by loose, lacy, drooping, feathery, beige flower clusters that can be cut for fresh or dry arrangements.

'Morning Light'. White edges give leaves a silvery look.

'Variegatus'. Leaves striped lengthwise with white.

'Yaku Jima' ('Yakushima'). Smaller grower (3–4 ft.).

'Zebrinus'. Bands of yellow running across leaves.

MOCK ORANGE. See CHOISYA, PHILADELPHUS   pp. 225, 413

MODIOLASTRUM lateritium (Malvastrum lateritium)

TRAILING MALLOW

Malvaceae

PERENNIAL GROUND COVER

◪ ZONES 8, 9, 14–24

☼ FULL SUN

◊ NO WATER ONCE ESTABLISHED

Modiolastrum lateritium

Perennial with trailing stems that root as they spread. Roundish leaves, 2–3 in. across; flowers are 1½–2 in. wide, saucer shaped, salmon pink with pinkish orange center spot. Useful for holding soil on a bank or for ground cover (does not tolerate foot traffic). Tolerates poor soil, heat, much aridity. Only drawback is invasiveness; keep it away from more delicate plants.

MOLE PLANT. See EUPHORBIA lathyris   p. 289

MOLUCCELLA laevis

BELLS-OF-IRELAND, SHELL FLOWER

Lamiaceae (Labiatae)

SUMMER ANNUAL; WINTER ANNUAL IN DESERT

◪ ALL ZONES

☼ FULL SUN

💧 REGULAR WATER

Moluccella laevis

About 2 ft. high. Flowers are carried almost from base in whorls of six. Showy part of flower is large shell-like or bell-like, apple green calyx, very veiny and crisp textured; small white tube of united petals in center is inconspicuous. As cut flowers, spikes of little bells are attractive fresh (long lasting) or dried (be sure to remove unattractive leaves).

Needs loose, well-drained soil. Sow seeds in early spring or late fall; if weather is warm, refrigerate seeds for a week before planting. For long spikes, fertilize regularly.

MOMORDICA charantia

BALSAM PEAR, BITTER MELON

Cucurbitaceae

ANNUAL VINE

◪ ALL ZONES

☼ FULL SUN

💧 REGULAR WATER

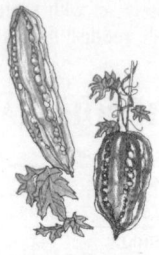

Momordica charantia

Deeply lobed leaves; white, fringed flowers 1 in. across. Fruit to 8 in. long, cylindrical with tapered ends, ridged and warty, bright yellow when ripe, splitting to show scarlet seeds. Immature fruits cherished in Oriental cooking despite bitter flavor. Ripe fruits showy, sometimes used in arrangements. Sprawls or climbs by tendrils. Sow seed when soil warms, feed generously, and provide a trellis or other support.

MONARDA

BEE BALM, OSWEGO TEA, HORSEMINT

Lamiaceae (Labiatae)

PERENNIALS

◪ ALL ZONES

☼ ◑ SUN; LIGHT AFTERNOON SHADE IN HOT AREAS

💧💧 REGULAR TO AMPLE WATER

Monarda didyma

Bushy, leafy clumps, 2–4 ft. tall, spread rapidly at edges but are not really invasive. Oval, 6-in.-long, dark green leaves have strong, pleasant odor like blend of mint and basil. In summer, stems are topped by tight clusters of long-tubed flowers much visited by hummingbirds. Plant 10 in. apart. Divide every 3–4 years. Not long lived where winters are warm, summers long and hot.

M. didyma. Scarlet flowers. Aromatic leaves to 4 in. long. Native to eastern United States. Garden selections and hybrids include scarlet 'Adam', pink 'Croftway Pink' and 'Granite Pink', lavender 'Violet Queen', and 'Snow White'. A very old variety, 'Cambridge Scarlet', is still widely grown. Scarlets are showiest and most typical.

M. fistulosa. Rosy lavender flowers. Takes moist or average soils. Native from eastern United States to Rocky Mountains.

MONDO GRASS. See OPHIOPOGON japonicus, under LIRIOPE and OPHIOPOGON	p. 358
MONEY PLANT. See LUNARIA annua	p. 362
MONEYWORT. See LYSIMACHIA nummularia	p. 363
MONKEY FLOWER. See MIMULUS	p. 381
MONKEY PUZZLE TREE. See ARAUCARIA araucana	p. 161
MONKSHOOD. See ACONITUM	p. 138

MONSTERA

Araceae

EVERGREEN VINES

◪ ZONES VARY BY SPECIES

◑ FILTERED SHADE

💧 REGULAR WATER

Monstera deliciosa

Related to philodendrons and resembling them in leaf gloss and texture. Most have cut and perforated foliage.

M. deliciosa. SPLIT-LEAF PHILODENDRON. Zones 16, 17, 21–24 or indoors. Eventually of great size if planted in open

M

ground bed in greenhouse or (in mildest areas) outdoors. Protect from frost; but if damaged, it recovers fairly quickly. Long, cordlike roots hanging from stems root into soil, help support plant on trees or on moss "totem poles." Leaves on youngest plants uncut; mature leaves heavy, leathery, dark green, deeply cut and perforated. Big plants may bear flowers something like callas, with a thick, 10-in. spike surrounded by a white, boatlike bract. Often sold as *Philodendron pertusum.*

Needs rich soil. For best results indoors, grow in container with good drainage, feed occasionally, and keep leaves clean. In poor light or low humidity, new leaves will be smaller. If tall plants get bare at base, replant in larger container and add younger, lower plant to fill in; or cut plant back and let new shoots start.

M. friedrichsthalii. SWISS CHEESE PLANT. Indoor and greenhouse plant. Leaves smaller, thinner in texture than those of *M. deliciosa;* edges are wavy, not deeply cut. Leaves are perforated by series of oval holes on either side of midrib.

HARVESTING MONSTERA FRUIT

If heat, light, and humidity are right, monstera flower spikes may ripen a year after bloom into edible fruits with a flavor reminiscent of banana, pineapple, and apple. The green, caplike rind knocks off easily when fruit is ripe, exposing the sticky fruit kernels; before that stage, the taste can be painfully caustic.

MONTANOA

DAISY TREE

Asteraceae (Compositae)

EVERGREEN SHRUBS OR SMALL TREES

✂ ZONES 16, 17, 20–24

☼ FULL SUN

● REGULAR WATER

Montanoa bipinnatifida

Give them good soil; groom by cutting off dead flower heads. Useful for winter flowers, tropical effects, background.

M. arborescens. To 12 ft. or more. Usually seen as multitrunked tree branching from base. Oval, 6 in. leaves are medium green, slightly toothed and rough textured. Covered with small, white, daisylike flower heads in winter. Needs little pruning.

M. bipinnatifida. To 7–8 ft. Boldly textured shrub with large, deeply lobed leaves. Flower heads to 3 in. across, mostly composed of white ray flowers to give double effect; some yellow in center of heads. Blooms all autumn, into early winter. Prune hard after bloom; new stems grow quickly.

M. grandiflora. Shrub to 12 ft., with large, deeply cut leaves; 3-in. daisies in fall, winter. Flowers smell like freshly baked cookies.

Moraceae. The mulberry family includes deciduous or evergreen trees, shrubs, and vines. Individual fruits are tiny and single-seeded but often aggregated into clusters. Fig *(Ficus)* and mulberry *(Morus)* are examples.

MORUS

MULBERRY

Moraceae

DECIDUOUS TREES

✂ ZONES VARY BY SPECIES

☼ FULL SUN

◖◆ WATER NEEDS VARY BY SPECIES

Morus alba

Leaves of variable form, size, and shape—often on same tree. Fruits look like miniature blackberries and are favored by birds. For home gardeners, however, the most important kinds are fruitless forms of *M. alba.*

M. alba. WHITE MULBERRY, SILKWORM MULBERRY. All zones. Fruit-bearing form grows to 20–60 ft., has inconspicuous flowers followed by sweet but rather insipid fruit that stains patios, clothing. 'Pendula' or 'Teas' Weeping' is a low-growing, strongly weeping variety; 'Chaparral' is another weeping mulberry (nonfruiting) with deeply cut, dark green leaves.

Fruitless forms are better for home gardens. They grow well in the desert and provide quick shade; they tolerate heat and alkaline soil and are resistant to Texas root rot. On the other hand, they produce pollen in prodigious amounts and, like fruiting forms, are subject to sooty canker disease. Take some aridity once established, but grow faster with water and feeding. Beach plantings in Southern California very successful. Difficult to garden under because of heavy surface roots. To 35 ft. tall with somewhat wider spread; often 20 ft. by 20 ft. in 3 years (slower in cool climates). 'Fan-San', 'Fruitless', 'Kingan', and 'Stribling' ('Mapleleaf') are good varieties.

Stake new plants carefully; they develop large crowns rather quickly, and these may snap from slender young trunks in high winds. For first few years, branches may grow so long that they droop from their own weight; shorten such branches to a well-placed, upward-growing bud. Do not prune heavy branches to stubs; these are likely either to rot or to furnish entry for sooty canker fungus.

M. nigra. BLACK or PERSIAN MULBERRY. Zones 4–24. To 30 ft., with short trunk and dense, spreading head. Takes some aridity once established. Heart-shaped leaves to 8 in. long. Fruit large, juicy, dark red to black. 'Black Beauty' is semidwarf (15 ft.).

M. papyrifera. See Broussonetia papyrifera

M

MUEHLENBECKIA

WIRE VINE

Polygonaceae

EVERGREEN VINES

⬥ ZONES VARY BY SPECIES

☼ ◐ SUN OR PARTIAL SHADE

💧 REGULAR SUMMER WATER

Muehlenbeckia axillaris

U nusual plants with thin, wiry stems, tiny leaves, and insignificant flowers. Each is capable of doing some useful and attractive creeping or climbing.

M. axillaris (M. nana). CREEPING WIRE VINE. Zones 3–9, 14–24. Small, dense, creeping plant to a few inches tall or mounding up to 1 ft. high, spreading by underground stems. Leaves ⅛ in. long, dark glossy green, closely spaced. Rock garden plant or small-scale ground cover. Deciduous where winter chill is pronounced. Translucent white fruits with black seeds can be attractive.

M. complexa. MATTRESS VINE, WIRE VINE. Zones 8, 9, 14–24. Vine climbs to 20–30 ft. or more, or sprawls when there is no support. Has a dense tangle of thin, black or brown stems. Leaves are variable in shape and are ⅛–¾ in. long. Tough vine for beach planting, also a good screen.

MUHLENBERGIA

Poaceae (Gramineae)

PERENNIAL GRASSES

⬥ ZONES VARY BY SPECIES

☼ ◐ FULL SUN OR LIGHT SHADE

◯ 💧 LITTLE TO NO WATER ONCE ESTABLISHED

Muhlenbergia rigens

T he two evergreen grasses described here require good drainage and are resistant to heat. Both are large and showy enough to stand out in the garden.

M. dumosa. BAMBOO MUHLY. Zones 8–24. Native to southern Arizona and northern Mexico. This odd but striking grass resembles a bamboo, carrying its narrow leaves and many branching flower clusters on slender woody stems. Without summer water it will grow to 3 ft.; with some it can reach 6 ft. Splendid container plant.

M. rigens. DEER GRASS. Zones 7–24. Native to much of California. Forms dense, tight clumps of narrow bright green leaves to 3 ft. tall (4 ft. with summer water). Evergreen even without summer water. Slender flower stalks are erect at first, then leaning; they can reach 6 ft.

MULBERRY. See MORUS	**p. 383**
MULLEIN. See VERBASCUM	**p. 517**
MULLEIN PINK. See LYCHNIS coronaria	**p. 362**

MURRAYA paniculata (M. exotica)

ORANGE JESSAMINE

Rutaceae

EVERGREEN SHRUB

⬥ ZONES 21–24

◐ BEST IN FILTERED SUN

💧 REGULAR WATER

Murraya paniculata

S ometimes grown as small single- or multi-trunked tree. To 6–15 ft. tall and wide. Open habit; graceful, pendulous branches with dark green, glossy leaves divided into three to nine oval, 1–2-in. leaflets. White, ¾-in., bell-shaped flowers have jasmine fragrance. Blooms late summer and fall, sometimes spring. Mature plants

have small red fruit. Needs rich soil, frequent feeding. Slowly recovers beauty after cold, wet winters. Good as hedge or filler; also for shaping. Fast growing; attracts bees. A dwarf variety is usually sold as *M. exotica*. It is slower growing, more upright and compact, to 6 ft. tall, 4 ft. wide. Leaves are lighter green; leaflets smaller, stiffer. Bloom is usually less profuse.

MUSA

BANANA

Musaceae

PERENNIALS, SOME TREELIKE IN SIZE

⬥ ZONES VARY BY SPECIES

☼ FULL SUN

💧 AMPLE WATER

Musa paradisiaca seminifera

F or most common bananas, see *Ensete*. Kinds described here include tall, medium, and dwarf (2–5-ft.) plants. All have soft, thickish stems and spread by suckers or underground roots to form clumps. Spectacular long, broad leaves are easily tattered by strong winds (protect outdoor plant from wind). Attractive near swimming pools. Give all types rich soil; feed heavily. Fast growing.

M. acuminata 'Dwarf Cavendish' (M. cavendishii, M. nana). Zones 21–24. Plants 6–8 ft. tall have leaves 5 ft. long, 2 ft. wide. Large, heavy flower clusters with reddish to dark purple bracts, yellow flowers. In warmest Southern California coastal gardens, can bear sweet, edible 6-in. bananas. Place near south wall. 'Enano Gigante' is similar in size and flavor; its young leaves have red markings. Some authorities place these fruiting varieties under *M. paradisiaca*.

M. ensete. See Ensete ventricosum

M. maurelii. See Ensete ventricosum 'Maurelii'

M. paradisiaca (M. sapientum). Zones 16, 19–24; root hardy but damaged by frost in Zones 9, 12–15. Many ornamental and edible forms. Most common type is often called *M. p. seminifera*. Grows to 20 ft., with leaves to 9 ft. Makes large clumps. Drooping flower stalk with powdery purple bracts; fruit (usually seedy and inedible) sometimes follows. Many varieties are available.

M. velutina. Zones 23, 24. Grows to 3–4 ft., with 3-ft. leaves that are green above, bronzy beneath. Upright pink bracts, orange flowers, velvety pink fruit.

Musaceae. The banana family consists of giant herbaceous plants that resemble palm trees; the bases of the enormous leaves form a false trunk. *Ensete* and *Musa* are grown in the West.

MUSCARI

GRAPE HYACINTH

Liliaceae

BULBS

⬥ ALL ZONES

☼ ◐ SUN OR LIGHT SHADE

◯ 💧 LITTLE OR NO SUMMER WATER

Muscari armeniacum

C lumps of narrow, grassy, fleshy leaves appear in autumn and live through cold and snow. Small, urn-shaped, blue or white flowers in tight spikes appear in early spring. Plant 2 in. deep in fall, setting bulbs in masses or drifts under flowering fruit trees or shrubs, in edgings and rock gardens, or in containers. Very long lived. Lift and divide when bulbs become crowded.

M. armeniacum. Bright blue flowers on 4–8-in. stems above heavy cluster of floppy foliage. 'Cantab' has clear light blue flowers and blooms later, is lower growing, has neater foliage. 'Blue Spike' has double blue flowers in a tight cluster at the top of the spike.

M. azureum (Hyacinthella azurea, Hyacinthus azureus). Something between hyacinth and grape hyacinth in appearance. The 4–8-in. stalks have tight clusters of bell-shaped (not urn-shaped), fragrant sky blue flowers.

M. botryoides. Medium blue flowers on 6–12-in. stems. 'Album' is white variety.

M. comosum. FRINGE or TASSEL HYACINTH. Unusual, rather loose cluster of shredded-looking flowers—greenish brown fertile ones, bluish purple sterile ones. Stems 1–1½ ft. high. Leaves about same length as stems, ³⁄₈–1 in. wide.

M. c. 'Monstrosum' (M. c. 'Plumosum'). FEATHERED or PLUME HYACINTH. Sterile violet blue to reddish purple flowers with finely divided and twisted segments. Stems 1–1½ ft. high.

M. latifolium. Largest, possibly showiest of grape hyacinths, it reaches 12 in., with deep indigo blue flowers. Plants have a single large leaf.

M. tubergenianum. Stems to 8 in. tall. Flowers at top of spike dark blue; lower flowers light blue.

MUSTARD

Brassicaceae (Cruciferae)
SUMMER ANNUALS
🔲 ALL ZONES
☼ FULL SUN
● WATER THOROUGHLY

Mustard

Curly-leaf mustards somewhat resemble curly-leaf kales in appearance. They are cooked like spinach or cabbage; young leaves are sometimes eaten raw in salads or used as garnishes. Fast and easy to grow; ready for the table in 35–60 days. Sow in early spring and make successive sowings when young plants are established. Plants thrive in cool weather but quickly go to seed in heat of summer. Sow in late summer for fall use. In mild winter areas, plant again in fall and winter. Thin seedlings to stand 6 in. apart in rows. Harvest outer leaves as needed. Mustard spinach, or tendergreen mustard, has smooth, dark green leaves. It ripens earlier than curly mustard and is more tolerant of hot, dry weather. 'Red Giant' or 'Chinese Red' has large, crinkled leaves with strong red shadings. Use when young as a salad green; older leaves are useful as boiled greens.

MYOPORUM

Myoporaceae
EVERGREEN GROUND COVERS, SHRUBS, SMALL TREES
🔲 ZONES VARY BY SPECIES
☼ FULL SUN
◐ ● WATER NEEDS VARY BY SPECIES
◈ FRUIT AND LEAVES CAN BE TOXIC

Myoporum laetum

Bell-shaped flowers attractive at close range but not showy; fruit small but colorful. Shiny dark green leaves with translucent dots. Tough and fast growing.

M. floribundum. Slender, open shrub or small tree. Zones 15–24. Has long, very narrow leaves drooping from horizontal branches. White flowers along branches in spring. Thrives in sun or some shade, with much or little water. Interesting as a piece of modern sculpture.

M. insulare. Shrub or tree. Zones 8, 9, 15–17, 19–24. Generally shrubby near coast, taller and more treelike inland. Grows to 20–30 ft. Leaves and flowers much like those of *M. laetum* but somewhat smaller. Fruit is bluish purple. Culture and uses same as for *M. laetum*. Needs little water.

M. laetum. Shrub or tree. Zones 8, 9, 14–17, 19–24. Temperatures in low 20s can inflict severe damage. Exceptionally fast growth to 30 ft. tall, 20 ft. wide. Dense foliage of rather narrow, 3–4-in.-long leaves. If allowed to assume natural habit, it's a broad-based, billowing mass of dark green.

Attractive multitrunked tree if staked and pruned; thin to prevent top-heaviness and wind damage. Summer flowers about ½ in. wide, white with purple markings, borne in clusters of two to six. Small reddish purple fruit is less toxic than the leaves.

Superb for seaside use—effectively blocks sound, wind, sun, blown sand. Needs some water. Can also make good ground cover; keep branches pegged down so they'll root and spread. Not good for tailored garden areas or near pools; some leaf drop at all times, invasive roots.

M. l. 'Carsonii'. Cutting-grown selection. Has darker, larger, broader leaves with fewer translucent dots; keeps its foliage right down to base of plant. Grows even faster than species.

M. 'Pacificum'. Shrub. Zones 16–24. Hybrid selection of extremely fast growth to 2 ft. tall, up to 30 ft. wide; as ground cover, can cover 100 square feet a year. Elongated oval, medium green leaves; small white flowers in summer. Best near coast, little water once established except in hot interior. Trim as needed; regrowth is rapid.

M. parvifolium (M. p. 'Prostratum'). Ground cover. Zones 8, 9, 12–16, 18–24. Bright green, ½–1-in. leaves densely cover plant. White summer flowers, ½ in. wide, are followed by purple berries. Grows to 3 in. high, 9 ft. wide. Plant 6–8 ft. apart. Plants will fill in within 6 months, branches rooting where stems touch moist ground. No traffic. Moderately aridity resistant but better with some summer water. Several selections are available: 'Burgundy Carpet' has red stems, purple new growth; 'Pink' has pink flowers; 'Putah Creek' is a vigorous selection to 1 ft. tall, 8 ft. wide.

MYOSOTIS

FORGET-ME NOT
Boraginaceae
PERENNIALS, BIENNIALS, AND ANNUALS
🔲 ALL ZONES
◐ BEST IN PARTIAL SHADE
● LOOKS BEST WITH REGULAR WATER

Myosotis sylvatica

Whether annual or perennial, forget-me-nots feature exquisite blue springtime flowers, tiny but profuse. The plants grow easily and thickly as a ground cover.

M. scorpioides. Perennial. Similar in most respects to *M. sylvatica*, but grows lower and blooms even longer, and roots live over from year to year. Flowers, ¼ in. wide, are blue with yellow centers, pink, or white. Bright green, shiny, oblong leaves. Spreads by creeping roots.

M. sylvatica. Annual or biennial. To 6–12 in. Soft, hairy leaves, ½–2 in. long, set closely along stem. Tiny, clear blue, white-eyed flowers to ⅓ in. wide loosely cover upper stems. Flowers and seeds profusely for a long season beginning in late winter or early spring. With habit of reseeding, will persist in garden for years unless weeded out. Often sold as *M. alpestris*. Improved varieties are available, best of which are 'Blue Ball' and 'Royal Blue Improved'.

MYRICA

Myricaceae
EVERGREEN OR SEMIEVERGREEN SHRUBS OR TREES
🔲 ZONES VARY BY SPECIES
☼ FULL SUN
● WATER NEEDS VARY BY SPECIES

Myrica californica

The species *M. californica* is from the Pacific Coast, *M. pensylvanica* from the Atlantic. They are grown in gardens for their attractive foliage.

M. californica. PACIFIC WAX MYRTLE. Evergreen shrub or tree. Zones 4–6, 14–17, 20–24. Native to coast and coastal valleys, Southern California to Washington. At the beach, it's a low, flattened mass; out of wind it's a big shrub or tree to 30 ft., usually with many upright trunks. In garden, one of best-looking native plants; its great

M

virtue is clean-looking foliage throughout the year. Branches are densely clad with tooth-edged, glossy, dark green leaves, paler beneath, 2–4 ½ in. long, about ½ in. wide. Spring flowers inconspicuous; fall fruits are purplish nutlets coated with wax, attractive to birds. Useful screen or informal hedge, 6–25 ft. tall. Can be used as clipped hedge. Aridity tolerant.

M. pensylvanica (M. caroliniensis). BAYBERRY. Deciduous or semievergreen shrub. Zones 4–7. Native to eastern United States. Dense, compact growth to 9 ft. Leaves to 4 in. long, narrowish, glossy green, dotted with resin glands, fragrant. Flowers inconspicuous. Fruit tiny, roundish, covered with white wax—the bayberry wax used for candles. Tolerates poor, sandy soil. Resistant to oak root fungus. Needs some water.

MYROBALAN. See PRUNUS cerasifera p. 442

Myrsinaceae. This plant family consists of evergreen shrubs and trees with (usually) inconspicuous flowers, attractive foliage and habit, and sometimes showy fruits. Representatives are *Myrsine* and *Ardisia.*

MYRSINE africana

AFRICAN BOXWOOD

Myrsinaceae

EVERGREEN SHRUB

☘ ZONES 8, 9, 14–24

☼ ☽ FULL SUN OR PARTIAL SHADE

◖ LITTLE WATER ONCE ESTABLISHED

Myrsine africana

Grows to 3–8 ft.; slightly floppy when young, but stiffens into dense, rounded bush easily kept at 3–4 ft. with pinching, clipping. Stems vertical; dark red, closely set with very dark green, glossy, roundish, ½-in. leaves (excellent cut foliage). Insignificant flowers.

Smog resistant; relatively pest free, although susceptible to red spider mites and, occasionally, brown scale. Good for low hedges, clipping into formal shapes, low backgrounds, foundations, narrow beds, containers.

Myrtaceae. The immense myrtle family of trees and shrubs is largely tropical and subtropical. Leaves are evergreen and often aromatic. Flowers are conspicuous thanks to large tufts of stamens, often showy. Fruits may be fleshy (*Feijoa*) or dry and capsular (*Eucalyptus*). Bottlebrush (*Callistemon*) and guava (*Psidium*) are two other familiar examples.

MYRTLE. See MYRTUS, VINCA pp. 386, 519

MYRTUS

MYRTLE

Myrtaceae

EVERGREEN SHRUBS

☘ ZONES 8–24

☼ ☽ HOT, BRIGHT SUN OR PARTIAL SHADE

◌ NO WATER ONCE ESTABLISHED

Myrtus communis

Included here are several of the most useful, basic evergreen shrubs for California and Arizona gardens.

M. communis. TRUE MYRTLE. Rounded form to 5–6 ft. high and 4–5 ft. wide; old plants can reach treelike proportions—15 ft. tall, 20 ft. across. Glossy bright green, pointed, 2-in. leaves, pleasantly aromatic when brushed or bruised. White, sweet-scented, ¾-in.-wide flowers with many stamens in summer, followed by bluish black, ½-in. berries. Any soil, but good drainage is essential—tip chlorosis occurs if drainage is poor. Good formal or informal hedge or screen. Can also be trained to reveal attractive branches.

M. c. 'Boetica'. Heavy, stiff, gnarled branches rise 4–6 ft. from base. Leaves large, leathery, very dark green, upward pointing, very fragrant. Popular in desert.

M. c. 'Buxifolia'. BOXLEAF MYRTLE. Small elliptical leaves.

M. c. 'Compacta'. DWARF MYRTLE. Slow-growing, small, compact plant densely set with small leaves. Very popular for low edgings and foundation plantings. Excellent for use as a low, compact, formal hedge.

M. c. 'Compacta Variegata'. VARIEGATED DWARF MYRTLE. Similar to 'Compacta', but leaves are edged in white.

M. c. 'Microphylla'. Dwarf myrtle with tiny, closely set leaves.

M. c. 'Variegata'. VARIEGATED MYRTLE. White-edged leaves.

M. luma. See Luma apiculata

M. ugni. See Ugni molinae

NAKED LADY. See AMARYLLIS belladonna p. 149

NANDINA domestica

HEAVENLY BAMBOO, SACRED BAMBOO

Berberidaceae

EVERGREEN OR SEMIDECIDUOUS SHRUB

☘ ZONES 5–24

☼ ☽ ● SUN OR SHADE; COLORS BETTER IN SUN

◌ ◌ ◖ BEST WITH REGULAR WATER; TAKES ARIDITY

Nandina domestica

Loses leaves at 10°F; killed to ground at 5°F, but usually recovers fast. *Nandina domestica* belongs to the barberry family but is reminiscent of bamboo in its lightly branched, canelike stems and delicate, fine-textured foliage.

Slow to moderate growth to 6–8 ft. (you can keep to 3 ft. by pruning oldest canes to ground). Leaves intricately divided into many 1–2-in., pointed, oval leaflets, creating lacy pattern. New foliage pinkish and bronzy red when it expands, turns to soft, light green. Picks up purple and bronze tints in fall; often turns fiery crimson in winter, especially in some sun and with some frost. Flowers pinkish white or creamy white in loose, erect, 6–12-in. clusters at branch ends, late spring or summer. Shiny red berries follow if plants are grouped; single plants seldom fruit heavily.

Needs some shade in low desert and hot valley regions. Best in rich soil, but roots can even compete with tree roots in dry shade. Apply iron sulfate or chelates to correct chlorosis in alkaline soils. Resistant to oak root fungus. Most useful for light, airy vertical effects as well as narrow, restricted areas. Good for hedge or screen, as tub plant, for bonsai. Dramatic with night lighting. Varieties include the following:

'Alba' ('Aurea'). White berries; light yellow foliage turns golden in fall.

'Compacta'. Lower growing than species (4–5 ft.), with narrower, more numerous leaflets; has very lacy look.

'Harbour Dwarf'. Low growing (1½–2 ft.), freely spreading. Underground rhizomes send up stems several inches from parent plants. Orange-red to bronzy red winter color. Good ground cover.

'Moyers Red'. Standard-size plant with broad leaflets. Brilliant red winter color in Zones 5–7.

'Nana' ('Nana Compacta', 'Nana Purpurea'). At least two plants are grown under these names; they are often mixed in nurseries, so select plants carefully to get the kind you want. Both grow about 1 ft. tall. One has coarse foliage (purplish green in summer, reddish purple in winter) with broad, somewhat cupped leaflets. Very slow to spread, it is best as container plant or as single plant among rocks or in prominent corner where its domelike growth may be emphasized. The other has finely cut leaves with narrow leaflets; it is green in summer, bright red in winter. It spreads fairly fast, making good small-scale ground cover.

'Umpqua Warrior'. Tallest and fastest growing of named forms, inclined to floppiness in its tallest stems. Large leaflets, good winter color.

'Woods Dwarf'. Rounded form to 3–4 ft. tall, densely foliaged, crimson orange to scarlet in winter.

NANKING CHERRY. See PRUNUS tomentosa p. 443

NARCISSUS

DAFFODIL

Amaryllidaceae

BULBS

✂ ALL ZONES

☼ ◑ SUN; LATE KINDS LAST WELL IN LIGHT SHADE

◔ WATER AS NEEDED DURING GROWTH AND BLOOM

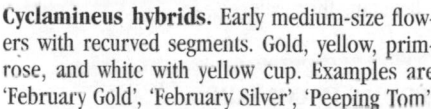

Narcissus—Daffodil

Most valuable spring-flowering bulbous plants for most regions of West. They are permanent, increasing from year to year; they are hardy in cold and heat; they are useful in many garden situations; they provide fascinating variety in flower form and color; and gophers won't eat them.

Leaves are straight and flat (strap shaped) or narrow and rushlike. Flowers are composed of ring of segments ("petals") that are at right angles to the trumpet or crown (also called cup) in center. Flowers may be single or clustered. Colors are basically yellow and white, but there are many variations—orange, red, apricot, pink, cream.

Flowers usually face sun; keep that in mind when selecting planting place. Use under trees and flowering shrubs, among ground cover plantings, near water, in rock gardens and patios, or in borders. Naturalize in sweeping drifts where space is available. Good in containers; fine cut flowers.

Plant bulbs as early in fall as obtainable. In Southern California and the deserts of Arizona, wait until November so soil can cool. Look for solid, heavy bulbs. Number One double-nose bulbs are best, Number One round, single-nose bulbs are second choice. Plant with 5–6 in. of soil over tops of bulbs (4–5 in. for smaller bulbs). Set bulbs 8 in. apart and you won't have to divide for at least 2–3 years.

Water well after planting; if fall rains are on schedule, further watering is usually unnecessary. Control snails and slugs; they relish leaves and flowers of all kinds of narcissus and are particularly abundant during the flowering season.

Let foliage ripen naturally after bloom. Lift and divide clumps of daffodils when flowers get smaller and fewer in number; wait until foliage has died down. Don't forcibly break away any bulbs that are tightly joined to mother bulb; remove only those that come away easily. Replant at once, or store for only a short time—preferably not over 3 weeks.

Following are the 11 generally recognized divisions of daffodils and representative varieties in each division.

Trumpet daffodils. Trumpet is as long as or longer than surrounding flower segments. Yellows are the most popular; old variety 'King Alfred' best known, top seller, although newer 'Unsurpassable' and 'William the Silent' are superior. White varieties include 'Mount Hood', 'Cantatrice', 'Empress of Ireland'. Bicolors with white segments, yellow cup, are 'Spring Glory', 'Trousseau'. Reverse bicolors like 'Spellbinder' have white cup and yellow segments.

Large-cupped daffodils. Cups are more than one-third the length of flower segments, but not as long as segments. Varieties include 'Carlton' and 'Carbineer', yellow; 'Ice Follies', white; 'Binkie' and 'Mrs. R. O. Backhouse', bicolors.

Small-cupped daffodils. Cups less than one-third the length of segments. Less widely available, for specialists.

Double daffodils. 'Golden Ducat'; 'Mary Copeland', white and bright red; 'White Lion', creamy white and yellow; 'Texas', yellow and orange scarlet; 'Windblown', white and pale lemon.

Narcissus—Double

Triandrus hybrids. Cups at least two-thirds the length of flower segments. Clusters of medium-size, slender-cupped flowers. 'Thalia' is a favorite white with two or three beautifully proportioned flowers per stem. 'Silver Chimes' has six or more yellow-cupped white flowers per stem.

Cyclamineus hybrids. Early medium-size flowers with recurved segments. Gold, yellow, primrose, and white with yellow cup. Examples are 'February Gold', 'February Silver', 'Peeping Tom'

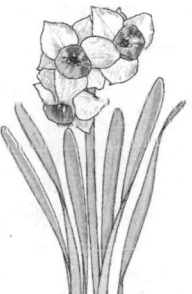

Jonquilla hybrids. Clusters of two to four rather small, very fragrant flowers. Yellow (like 'Trevithian' and 'Suzy'), orange, ivory.

Tazetta and Tazetta hybrids. These are polyanthus or bunch-flowered daffodils with small-cupped white and yellow flowers in clusters. Good double varieties are 'Cheerfulness' (white) and 'Golden Cheerfulness'. Division also includes

Narcissus tazetta 'Orientalis'

Narcissus Divisions (Groups)

Trumpet

Small Cupped

Large Cupped

Double

Cyclamineus Hybrid

Jonquilla Hybrid

Poeticus Narcissus

Split Cup

Triandrus Hybrid

Tazetta

'Geranium', paper white narcissus, and *N. tazetta* 'Orientalis' (Chinese sacred lilies). These last three, along with 'Cragford' (white, scarlet cup) and 'Grand Soleil d'Or' (golden yellow), can be grown indoors in bowls of pebbles and water. Keep dark and cool until growth is well along, then slowly bring into light.

Poeticus narcissus. POET'S NARCISSUS. White flowers with shallow, broad yellow cups edged red. 'Actaea' is largest.

Species, varieties, and hybrids. Many species and their varieties and hybrids delight the collector. Most are small; some are true miniatures for rock gardens or very small containers.

N. asturiensis. Very early miniature trumpet flowers on 3-in. stems. Usually sold as *N.* 'Minimus'.

N. bulbocodium. HOOP PETTICOAT DAFFODIL. To 6 in. tall, with little, upward-facing flowers that are mostly trumpet, with very narrow, pointed segments. Deep and pale yellow varieties.

N. cyclamineus. Backward-curved lemon yellow segments and narrow, tubular golden cup; 6 in. high.

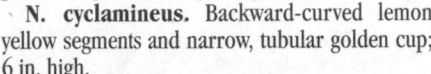

Narcissus bulbocodium

N. jonquilla. JONQUIL. Cylindrical, rushlike leaves. Clusters of early, very fragrant, golden yellow flowers with short cups.

N. triandrus. ANGEL'S TEARS. Clusters of small white flowers.

Miscellaneous. This group serves as a catch-all for a variety of new flower forms. Typical are 'Baccarat', light yellow with deeper yellow trumpet cut into six equal lobes; and 'Cassata', white with ivory split trumpet, the segments of which lie flat along the petals.

DAFFODILS IN CONTAINERS

For maximum show, set bulbs close together, the tips level with soil surface. Place pots in well-drained trench or cold frame and cover with 6–8 in. of moist peat moss, wood shavings, sawdust, or sand. Look for roots in 8–10 weeks (carefully tip soil mass from pot). Move pots with well-started bulbs to greenhouse, cool room, or sheltered garden spot to bloom. Keep well watered until foliage yellows; then plant in garden. You can sink pots or cans of bulbs in borders when flowers are almost ready to bloom, then lift containers when flowers fade.

NELUMBO (Nelumbium)

LOTUS
Nymphaeaceae
AQUATIC PLANTS
☀️ ALL ZONES
☀️◐ FULL SUN OR PARTIAL SHADE
💧 LOCATE IN PONDS, WATER GARDENS

These are water plants. If you acquire started plants in containers, put them in pond with

Nelumbo nucifera

8–12 in. of water over soil surface. If you get roots, plant in spring, horizontally, 4 in. deep, in 1–1½-ft.-deep container of fairly rich soil. Place soil surface 8–12 in. under water. Huge round leaves attached at center to leafstalks grow above water level. Large fragrant flowers, growing above or below leaves, form in summer. Ornamental woody fruit, perforated with holes like a salt shaker, good for dried arrangements. Roots should not freeze; where freezing is possible, cover pond or fill it deeper with water.

N. lutea (Nelumbium luteum). AMERICAN LOTUS. Similar to following but somewhat smaller in leaf and flower. Flowers are pale yellow.

N. nucifera (Nelumbium nelumbo). INDIAN or CHINESE LOTUS. Round leaves, 2 ft. or wider, carried 3–6 ft. above water surface. Pink, 4–10-in.-wide flowers carried singly on stems. Both tubers and seeds are esteemed in Chinese cookery, and the entire plant holds great religious significance for Buddhists. White, rose, and double varieties exist; dwarf forms suitable for pot culture are becoming available.

NEMESIA

Scrophulariaceae
PERENNIALS AND ANNUALS
☀️ ZONES VARY BY SPECIES
☀️ FULL SUN
💧 REGULAR WATER

Nemesia strumosa

These South African annuals and perennials are riotously colorful but somewhat touchy. To enjoy longer blooms, remove the fading flowers.

N. capensis (N. foetens). Zones 16–24. Somewhat shrubby evergreen perennial, deciduous in cold spells, 1 ft. tall and twice as wide. Leaves are narrow; the light pink flowers, ¾ in. across, have yellow throats and come in sprays. Cut off fading flower sprays for repeat bloom.

N. fruticans. Zones 16–24. Name uncertain. Shrubby evergreen perennial 1 ft. tall, 2 to 2½ ft. across. Lavender and pink vanilla-scented flowers bloom nearly continuously.

N. strumosa. Summer annual in all zones; winter–spring annual in Zones 15–17, 21–24. Plants sold under this name are usually hybrids between *N. strumosa* and *N. versicolor,* similar plants but with somewhat different color ranges. The hybrids include all colors except green, and many bicolors as well. Sow outdoors in spring in cold climates, spring or fall where winters are mild, or buy started plants. Time plantings of this rapid grower to avoid frost but bloom during cool weather. Likes rich, moist soil. Pinch to induce bushiness. Good bulb cover or hanging basket plant.

Several named strains are available in mixed colors. 'KLM' is a compact blue and white; 'Mello Red and White' is a showy bicolor.

N. versicolor. Summer annual in all zones; winter–spring annual in Zones 15–17, 21–24. Resembles *N. strumosa*, but color range contains more blue, yellow, and white.

NEMOPHILA

Hydrophyllaceae
ANNUALS
☀️ ALL ZONES
☀️◐ SUN OR PARTIAL SHADE
💧 MAINTAIN SOIL MOISTURE

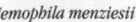

Nemophila menziesii

Often used as low cover for bulb beds. Broadcast seed in fall (mild winter regions) or early spring. Will reseed if growing conditions are ideal. Both are native to western United States.

N. maculata. FIVE-SPOT NEMOPHILA. To 6 in. tall; growth habit, foliage, flower size same as those of *N. menziesii.* Flowers white, with fine purple lines; small dots and one large dot appear on each of the five lobes.

N. menziesii (N. insignis). BABY BLUE EYES. To 6–10 in. tall; branching from base. Blooms as freely in gardens as it does in the wilds.

N

Cup-shaped spring flowers about 1 in. across are sky blue with whitish center. Leaves have rounded lobes. Short blooming period. Nice bulb cover.

NEODYPSIS decaryi

TRIANGLE PALM	
Arecaceae (Palmae)	
PALM	
✿ ZONES 20–24	
☀ ◑ FULL SUN OR PARTIAL SHADE	
◖ LITTLE WATER ONCE ESTABLISHED	

Neodypsis decaryi

Slow grower to 18–20 ft. Native to arid parts of Madagascar. Trunk is triangular in cross section because heavily keeled leaf bases grow in three ranks about the stem. Gray-green, featherlike fronds to 15 ft., strongly upright but arching at tips.

NEOREGELIA

Bromeliaceae	
BROMELIADS	
✿ ZONES 21–24; OR INDOORS	
◑ ● FILTERED SHADE OR STRONG INDIRECT LIGHT	
◖ KEEP WATER IN CUP AT BASE OF ROSETTE	

Neoregelia carolinae

Bromeliads with rosettes of leathery leaves, often strikingly colored or marked; short spikes of usually inconspicuous flowers are buried in hearts of rosettes. Need light, open, fast-draining planting mix that holds moisture but does not exclude air. Feed lightly. Grow in sheltered, frost-free gardens in Zones 21–24. Can be grown on tree branch with sphagnum moss around roots.

N. carolinae. Many narrow, shiny leaves 1 ft. long, 1½ in. wide. Medium green leaves turn rich red at base as plant approaches bloom. *N. c.* 'Tricolor' has leaves striped lengthwise with white. Center turns bright red.

N. spectabilis. PAINTED FINGERNAIL PLANT. Leaves 1 ft. long, 2 in. wide are olive green with bright red tips. Plant takes on bronzy color in strong light.

NEPETA

Lamiaceae (Labiatae)	
PERENNIALS, GROUND COVERS	
✿ ALL ZONES	
☀ FULL SUN	
◖ ◗ LITTLE TO MODERATE WATER	

Nepeta cataria

Vigorous, spreading plants of the mint family. Common names for both species relate to the attraction the plants have for domestic cats.

N. cataria. CATNIP. Perennial plant 2–3 ft. high with downy, gray-green leaves and clustered lavender or white flowers at branch tips in June. Easy grower in light soil; reseeds readily. Attractive to cats. Sprinkle its dried leaves over their food, or sew some into toy cloth mouse. Some people use it to flavor tea.

N. faassenii. CATMINT. Makes soft, gray-green, undulating mounds to 2 ft. high. Leaves aromatic and (like catnip) attractive to cats, who enjoy rolling in plantings. Lavender-blue, ½-in. flowers in loose spikes make display in early summer. If dead spikes prove unsightly, shear them back; this may bring on another bloom cycle. Set 1–1½ ft. apart for ground cover. Usually sold as *N. mussinii.*

N. hederacea. See Glechoma

NEPHROLEPIS

SWORD FERN	
Polypodiaceae	
FERNS	
✿ ZONES 8, 9, 12–24, AS NOTED; OR INDOORS	
◑ ● SHADE; BRIGHT INDOOR LIGHT	
◖ ◗ WATER WHEN SOIL SURFACE FEELS DRY	

Nephrolepis exaltata 'Bostoniensis'

Tough and easy-to-grow, they are the most widely used of all ferns for garden or house. For native western sword fern, see *Polystichum munitum.*

N. cordifolia. SOUTHERN SWORD FERN. Zones 8, 9, 12–24. Bright green, narrow, upright fronds in tufts to 2–3 ft. tall. Fronds have closely spaced, finely toothed leaflets. Roots often have small roundish tubers. Plant spreads by thin, fuzzy runners and can be invasive if not watched. Will not take hard frosts but is otherwise adaptable—easily moved; tolerant of poor soil, erratic watering. Can be used in narrow, shaded beds. Effective ground cover in sunny or shady tropical landscapes if adequately watered. In desert give light shade or morning sun. Often sold as *N. exaltata.*

N. exaltata. SWORD FERN. Zones 23, 24; or indoors. Taller (to 5 ft.) than *N. cordifolia,* and with fronds to 6 in. wide.

N. e. 'Bostoniensis'. BOSTON FERN. House plant. Spreading and arching in habit, with graceful, eventually drooping fronds. Classic parlor fern of 1890s. Many more finely cut and feathery forms exist; 'Fluffy Ruffles', 'Rooseveltii', and 'Whitmanii' are among best known. Northern light in cool room suits it. Plant in well-drained fibrous soil. Feed every month with dilute liquid fertilizer.

N. obliterata. House plant. From northwestern Australia. A selection called 'Kimberley Queen' has fronds to 3 ft. in length. Habit is stiffer, more erect than that of Boston fern, and plant is more tolerant of low humidity and both low and high light conditions.

NERINE

Amaryllidaceae	
BULBS	
✿ ZONES 5, 8, 9, 13–24	
☀ ◑ SUN OR PARTIAL SHADE	
◖ WATER DURING GROWTH AND BLOOM	

Nerine curvifolia 'Fothergillii Major'

Native to South Africa. Usually pot plants, but can grow outdoors year-round in mildest regions. Funnel-shaped flowers with six spreading segments bent back at tips, carried in rounded clusters on 1–2-ft. stems. Bloom August–January, depending on kind. Strap-shaped basal leaves appear during or after bloom.

Plant August–December. To grow outdoors, plant in sun in soil with good drainage; set bulb 3 in. deep. Do not disturb or divide for several years.

N. bowdenii. The hardiest; grows in milder parts of Northwest. Glossy green leaves 1 in. wide, 6–12 in. long. Flowers to 3 in. long, soft pink marked with deeper pink, in clusters of 8–12 on 2-ft. stems. Forms with taller stems, larger flower clusters come in deeper pink, crimson, and red. 'Crispa' is 1 ft. tall, has pale pink, wavy-edged segments; 'Pink Triumph', larger, is latest bloomer—in fall, as late as December in Southern California. ▶

POTTED NERINE, BLOOMING IN AUTUMN

In late summer or early autumn, put one bulb in 4-in. pot, or 3 in a 5–6-in. pot. Cover only lower half of bulb. Wait for signs of flower stalk before watering. Water through winter and spring. In May, move pot outdoors to lightly shaded spot. Withhold water from July until growth resumes. Do not repot until quite crowded.

N

389

N. curvifolia. Best known is variety 'Fothergillii Major', with clusters of 2-in.-wide, scarlet flowers overlaid with shimmering gold. Long stamens topped by greenish yellow anthers. Bloom stalks to 1½ ft.; leaves 1 ft. long.

N. filifolia. Leaves narrow, grassy, evergreen, 6–8 in. long. Flowers 1 in. wide, rose red with narrow, crinkled petals, in clusters of 8–12 on stems 1 ft. tall. Fast multiplier.

N. masonorum. Like *N. filifolia* but smaller, with 1-in.-wide flowers in clusters of 4–12 on 9-in. stems.

N. sarniensis. GUERNSEY LILY. Large clusters of iridescent crimson, 1½-in.-long flowers on 2-ft. stalks. Pink, orange scarlet, and pure white varieties. Green leaves, 1 ft. long, ¾ in. wide.

NERIUM oleander

OLEANDER

Apocynaceae

EVERGREEN SHRUB

ZONES 8–16, 18–24

☼ BEST IN HEAT AND STRONG LIGHT

◐ ● LITTLE OR NO WATER ONCE ESTABLISHED

✿ ALL PARTS ARE POISONOUS

Nerium oleander

One of the basic shrubs for desert and hot interior valleys. Moderate to fast growth; most varieties reach maximum height of 8–12 ft. and as wide. Ordinarily broad and bulky but easily trained into handsome single or many-trunked tree resembling (when out of bloom) an olive tree. Narrow, 4–12-in.-long leaves are dark green, leathery, and glossy, attractive all seasons; form with golden variegations in leaves is sometimes available. Flowers 2–3 in. across, clustered at twig or branch ends, May or June to October. Many varieties have fragrant flowers. Forms with double and single flowers are sold, with color range from white to shades of yellow, pink, salmon, and red. 'Sister Agnes', single white, is most vigorous grower, often reaching 20 ft. tall; 'Mrs. Roeding', double salmon pink, grows only 6 ft. tall and has proportionally smaller leaves, finer foliage texture than big oleanders. Double varieties exist in other colors, but all share a drawback: double flowers hang on after bloom and turn brown. 'Hawaii' is a single-flowered oleander with the same luscious color as 'Mrs. Roeding'; its flowers drop clean.

'Petite Pink' and 'Petite Salmon' can easily be kept to 3–4 ft. with moderate pruning and make excellent informal flowering hedges, though they are not as cold hardy as regular oleanders. 'Little Red', bright red, is completely hardy—as are the following, intermediate in size between dwarfs and full-size plants: 'Algiers', deep red; 'Casablanca', white; 'Ruby Lace', bright red with 3-inch, wavy-edged individual flower; and 'Tangier', soft pink. Even smaller (5–7 ft.) are red 'Marrakesh' and white 'Morocco'.

Oleanders are not at all particular about soil, tolerating poor drainage or soil with relatively high salt content. In shade or ocean fog, however, they produce weak or leggy growth and few flowers.

Prune in early spring to control size and form. Cut out old wood that has flowered. Cut some branches nearly to ground. To restrict height, pinch remaining tips or prune them back lightly. To prevent bushiness at base, pull (don't cut) unwanted suckers.

Chief insect pests are yellow oleander aphid (one spring spraying usually controls) and scale insects (spray at midsummer crawler stage). One disease is bacterial gall, which causes blackened, deformed flowers and warty growth and splitting on branches. Control by pruning out infected parts, making cuts well below visible damage—or completely remove infected plants.

Caution children against eating leaves or flowers; keep prunings, dead leaves away from hay or other animal feed; don't use wood for barbecue fires or skewers. Smoke can cause severe irritation.

Use as screens, windbreaks, borders for road or driveway, tubs, background plantings, small single or multitrunked trees. Use freely where deer are a problem—they don't touch it. Single white oleanders give cool look to hot-climate garden.

For a plant called yellow oleander, see *Thevetia*.

NERTERA granadensis (N. depressa)

BEAD PLANT

Rubiaceae

PERENNIAL

ZONES 17, 22–24; OR INDOORS

● SHADE

◐ KEEP SOIL MOIST, BUT NOT SOGGY

Nertera granadensis

Extremely tender, generally grown as house plant. Sometimes used as rock garden subject or small-scale ground cover. Prostrate habit. Tiny, smooth, rounded leaves make dense green mat an inch or so high; berrylike, ¼-in., bright orange fruit may last from midsummer into winter. Small green flowers are a lesser attraction. Plant in sandy loam with some leaf mold. Fine terrarium or dish-garden plant.

NET BUSH. See CALOTHAMNUS	**p. 199**
NEW MEXICAN PRIVET. See FORESTIERA neomexicana	**p. 297**
NEW ZEALAND BRASS BUTTONS. See COTULA squalida	**p. 246**
NEW ZEALAND BUR. See ACAENA microphylla	**p. 135**
NEW ZEALAND CHRISTMAS TREE. See METROSIDEROS excelsus	**p. 380**
NEW ZEALAND FLAX. See PHORMIUM	**p. 415**
NEW ZEALAND LAUREL. See CORYNOCARPUS laevigata	**p. 245**
NEW ZEALAND SPINACH. See SPINACH, NEW ZEALAND	**p. 490**
NEW ZEALAND TEA TREE. See LEPTOSPERMUM scoparium	**p. 351**

NICOTIANA

Solanaceae

TENDER PERENNIALS GROWN AS SUMMER ANNUALS

ALL ZONES EXCEPT AS NOTED

☼ ◑ FULL SUN OR PARTIAL SHADE

● REGULAR SUMMER WATER

✿ ALL PARTS ARE POISONOUS IF EATEN

Nicotiana alata

May live over in mild-winter areas. Upright-growing plants with slightly sticky leaves and stems. Usually grown for their fragrant flowers, which often open at night or on cloudy days; some kinds open during daytime. Flowers tubular, usually flaring at ends into five pointed lobes; grow near top of branched stems in summer. Large, soft, oval leaves. Some kinds reseed readily.

N. alata (N. affinis). Wild species is a 2–3-ft. plant with large, very fragrant white flowers that open toward evening. Seed is available. Selection and hybridization with other species have produced many garden strains that stay open day and night and come in colors ranging from white through pink to red (including lime green), but scent is not as strong as in the "unimproved" species.

Domino strain grows to 12–15 in. and has upward-facing flowers that can take heat and sun better than taller kinds. Nicki strain is taller (to 15–18 in.). The older Sensation strain is taller still—up to 4 ft.—and looks more at home in informal mixed borders than as a bedding plant. Fragrance is erratic. If fragrance—especially evening fragrance—is important, plant *N. a.* 'Grandiflora'.

N. glauca. TREE TOBACCO. Zones 7–24. Naturalized South American species. Shrubby or treelike to 20 ft.; bluish green leaves to 6 in. long and small yellow green flowers.

N. sylvestris. To 5 ft. Intensely fragrant, long, tubular white flowers grow in tiers atop a statuesque plant. Striking in a night garden.

NIEREMBERGIA

CUP FLOWER	
Solanaceae	
PERENNIALS	
▨ ZONES VARY BY SPECIES	
☼ FULL SUN	
◐ REGULAR WATER	

Nierembergia repens

Flowers are tubular but flare into saucerlike or bell-like cups. The first species listed here grows as a spreading mound; the other is a ground-covering mat.

N. hippomanica violacea (N. h. caerulea). DWARF CUP FLOWER. Zones 8–24. Grows to 6–12 in. high. Much-branched mounded plant. Stiff, very narrow, ½–⅔-in.-long leaves. Throughout the summer months the plants are covered with blue to violet, widely spreading, bell-like flowers almost an inch across. Trimming back plant after flowering to induce new growth seems to lengthen life. Dwarf cup flower is a good edging plant for semishade beds in desert regions. 'Purple Robe' is a readily available variety. 'Mont Blanc', to 6 in. tall, bears a profusion of white flowers.

N. repens (N. rivularis). WHITE CUP. Zones 5–9, 14–24. Prostrate 4–6-in. mat of bright green leaves covered in summer with white flowers of the same shape as those of dwarf cup flower, about an inch or more across. For best performance, don't crowd it with more aggressive plants.

NIGELLA damascena

LOVE-IN-A-MIST	
Ranunculaceae	
SPRING ANNUAL	
▨ ALL ZONES	
☼ ◑ FULL SUN OR PARTIAL SHADE	
◐ WATER DURING GROWTH AND BLOOM	

Nigella damascena

Branching, to 1–2½ ft. high. All leaves, even those that form collar under each flower, are finely cut into threadlike divisions. Blue, white, or rose flowers, 1–1½ in. across, are borne singly on ends of branches. Curious papery-textured, horned seed capsules give airiness in bouquet or in mixed border, are very decorative in dried bouquets. Sow seed on open ground. Plants quickly come into bloom in spring and dry up in summer. Will reseed. 'Miss Jekyll', with semidouble cornflower blue blossoms, is superior variety; 'Persian Jewels' is superior mixed strain.

NIGHT JESSAMINE. See CESTRUM nocturnum	p. 219
NIGHT PHLOX. See ZALUZIANSKYA capensis	p. 526
NIKAU PALM. See RHOPALOSTYLIS sapida	p. 459
NINEBARK. See PHYSOCARPUS	p. 417

NOLANA paradoxa

Nolanaceae	
ANNUAL	
▨ ALL ZONES	
☼ ◑ SUN OR LIGHT SHADE	
◐ BEST IN FAIRLY DRY SOIL	

Nolana paradoxa

Unusual plant from Chile that looks like a trailing sky blue petunia. Trailing stems bear 2-in.-long, ¾-in.-wide leaves and bright blue, 2-in. flowers with white throats. A variety is sold as 'Blue Bird' or *N. napiformis* 'Blue Bird'. Use as edging or in hanging basket. Withstands wide range of temperatures; needs good drainage.

NOLINA

Agavaceae	
EVERGREEN SHRUBS ✎	
▨ ZONES VARY BY SPECIES	
☼ FULL SUN	
◊ TOLERATE MUCH ARIDITY ONCE ESTABLISHED	

Nolina longifolia

Yucca and century plant relatives with narrow, tough, grassy leaves on a thick trunk. Desert or dry landscape plants. Tiny flowers are borne on showy, tall stalks.

N. longifolia. MEXICAN GRASSTREE. Zones 12–24. Native to central Mexico. In youth forms fountain of 3-ft.-long, 1-in.-wide grasslike leaves. In time, fountains top thick trunks 6–10 ft. tall, sometimes with a few branches.

N. parryi. Zones 8–24. Native to Southern California deserts. Smaller than above: 3-ft. trunk, leaves to 3 ft. long, ¾ in. wide.

NORFOLK ISLAND PINE. See ARAUCARIA heterophylla	p. 161

NOTHOFAGUS

SOUTHERN BEECH, FALSE BEECH	
Fagaceae	
EVERGREEN OR DECIDUOUS TREES	
▨ ZONES 5, 6, 14–17	
☼ FULL SUN	
◐ REGULAR WATER	

Nothofagus antarctica

Southern Hemisphere representatives of beech; many species grow in Chile, New Zealand, Australia. Small leaf size and open branch structure give all a graceful look. They require high humidity, neutral to acid soil, and good drainage. The nuts are so tiny as to be unnoticeable. Two Chilean species are available but scarce; evergreen species from Australia and New Zealand are rarely available.

N. antarctica. Deciduous tree to 50 ft. Closely set, oval, ½–1½-in. leaves line long, graceful shoots of young trees; open growth makes for handsome silhouette against a wall or the sky. Fast growth as a young tree; fills out with maturity but maintains graceful, frondlike branch structure.

N. dombeyi. Evergreen tree to 50–70 ft. Leaves to 1½ in. long, ½ in. wide, shiny dark green. Good tree for shading rhododendrons, azaleas; open branch structure admits filtered light.

N. obliqua. Deciduous tree to 100 ft.; leaves to 3 in. long. Fast growing.

Nyctaginaceae. The four-o'clock family contains annuals, perennials, shrubs, and vines in which the conspicuous elements of the flowers consist either of a showy calyx (rather than petals) or bracts. Examples are bougainvillea and four o'clock (*Mirabilis*).

NYMPHAEA

WATER LILY	
Nymphaeaceae	
AQUATIC PLANTS	
▨ ALL ZONES	
☼ PRODUCE FLOWERS IN SUN	
◐◐ LOCATE IN PONDS, WATER GARDENS	

Nymphaea

Leaves float and are rounded, with deep notch at one side where leaf stalk is attached. Showy flowers either float on surface or stand above it on stiff stalks. Cultivated water lilies are largely hybrids that cannot be traced back to exact parentage. There are hardy and tropical types. Hardy kinds come in white, yellow, copper, pink, and red. Tropical types add blue and purple; recent introductions include yellows and an unusual

N

391

greenish blue. Some tropicals in the white-pink-red color range are night bloomers; all others close at night.

Hardy kinds are easiest for beginners. Plant them February–October in mild-winter areas, April–July where freezes prevail. Set 6-in.-long pieces of rhizome on soil at pool bottom or in boxes at least 8 in. deep, placing rhizome in nearly horizontal position with bud end up. Top of soil should be 8–12 in. below water surface. Redwood containers can discolor water. Enrich soil with 1 lb. of complete dry fertilizer (3–5 percent nitrogen) for each lily. Groom plants by removing spent leaves and blooms. They usually bloom throughout warm weather and go dormant in fall, reappearing in spring. In very cold areas, protect as you would *Nelumbo*. Tropical kinds begin to grow and bloom later in summer but last longer, often up to first frost. Buy started tropical plants and set at same depth as hardy rhizomes. Tropical types go dormant but do not survive really low winter temperatures. They usually live longer where orange trees grow. Where winters are colder, store dormant tubers in damp sand over winter or buy new plants each year.

Nymphaeaceae. The water lily family consists of aquatic plants, usually with floating leaves and flowers. Lotus (*Nelumbo*) and water lily (*Nymphaea*) are examples.

Nyssaceae. Deciduous trees from Asia and North America. Two grown in the West are dove tree (*Davidia*) and *Nyssa*.

NYSSA sylvatica

SOUR GUM, TUPELO, PEPPERIDGE	
Nyssaceae	
DECIDUOUS TREE	
✂ ZONES 3–10, 14–21	
☼ FULL SUN	
◐ ◕ LITTLE OR MUCH WATER	

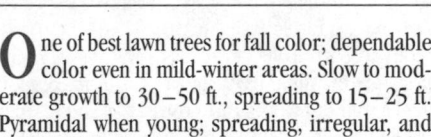

Nyssa sylvatica

One of best lawn trees for fall color; dependable color even in mild-winter areas. Slow to moderate growth to 30–50 ft., spreading to 15–25 ft. Pyramidal when young; spreading, irregular, and rugged in age. Crooked branches and twigs and dark, red-tinged bark make dramatic picture against winter sky. Dark green, glossy leaves 2–5 in. long, come out rather late in spring; turn hot, coppery red in fall before dropping. Flowers are inconspicuous. Bluish black fruit shaped like small olives is attractive to birds. Grows well in any soil. Tolerates poor drainage.

OCHNA serrulata (O. multiflora)

BIRD'S-EYE BUSH, MICKEY MOUSE PLANT	
Ochnaceae	
EVERGREEN SHRUB	
✂ ZONES 14–24	
◐ PARTIAL SHADE	
◔ TOLERATES ARIDITY ONCE ESTABLISHED	

Ochna serrulata

Slow, spreading growth to 4–8 ft. high and as wide. Oblong leaves, 2–5 in. long, are leathery, fine toothed, bronzy in spring, deep green later. Early summer flowers are size of buttercups; when yellow petals fall, sepals turn vivid red. Next, five or more green, seedlike fruits protrude from red center. They later turn glossy jet black, in strong contrast with red sepals; at this stage children see the configuration as eyes and ears of mouse. Slightly acid soil. Good in tub or box or as small espalier.

OCIMUM

BASIL	
Lamiaceae (Labiatae)	
SUMMER ANNUAL HERBS	
✂ ALL ZONES	
☼ FULL SUN	
◕ REGULAR WATER FOR SUCCULENT GROWTH	

Ocimum basilicum

One of the basic cooking herbs. Leaves in varying shades of green and purple. One type— 'Dark Opal'—is attractive enough for borders and mass plantings. Sow seed of any basil in early spring; make successive sowings 2 weeks apart to have replacements for the short-lived older plants. Or set out plants outdoors after frost. Space plants 10–12 in. apart. Fertilize once during growing season with complete fertilizer. Occasional overhead watering keeps foliage clean and bright. Keep flower spikes pinched out to prevent seeding, subsequent death of plant.

O. basilicum. SWEET BASIL. To 2 ft. Green, shiny, 1–2-in.-long leaves; spikes of white flowers. Forms with purple or variegated leaves have purple flowers. Most popular basil for cooking. Used fresh or dry, it gives a pleasant, sweet, mild flavor to tomatoes, cheese, eggs, fish, shellfish, poultry stuffing, salads. There is a dwarf, small-leafed kind that thrives in pots.

O. 'Dark Opal'. Large-leafed basil, known for its ornamental qualities. Dark purple bronze foliage; spikes of small lavender pink flowers. Grows 1–1½ ft. tall with spread of about 1 ft. Attractive in mass planting with dusty miller or 'Carpet of Snow' sweet alyssum.

OENOTHERA

EVENING PRIMROSE	
Onagraceae	
PERENNIALS AND BIENNIALS	
✂ ALL ZONES, EXCEPT AS NOTED	
☼ FULL SUN	
◔ LITTLE WATER	

Oenothera berlandieri

Valued for showy, four-petaled, silky early summer flowers. Bright yellow, rose pink, or white flowers. The plants grow in tough, rough places.

O. berlandieri (*O. speciosa childsii*). MEXICAN EVENING PRIMROSE. Perennial. During summer bloom period, profuse rose pink, 1½-in. flowers are carried on stems 10–12 in. high; stems die back after bloom. Blooms in daytime. Thrives with little or no care once established. Invasive if not controlled. Good ground cover for dry slopes, parking strips. There is a white-flowering form and a selection, 'Siskiyou', that is lighter pink, more compact, and more nearly everblooming.

O. caespitosa. TUFTED, FRAGRANT, or WHITE EVENING PRIMROSE. Zones 1–3, 7–14, 18–21. Grows 8 in. tall, 1–2 ft. wide, with gray-green fuzzy leaves and 3–4-in. fragrant white flowers that open in the evening, close in bright sunshine. Heavy bloom in early summer. Several subspecies, some with flowers that fade to pink.

O. hookeri. Biennial. Western native. To 2–6 ft. high. Bright yellow, 3½-in. flowers open late afternoon to sunrise. Hairy, elliptical leaves.

O. missourensis. Perennial. Prostrate, sprawling stems to 10 in. long. Soft, velvety, 5-in. leaves. Clear yellow flowers 3–5 in. across, in late spring or summer. One of most beautiful of evening primroses. Good rock garden subject.

O. stubbei. BAJA EVENING PRIMROSE. Perennial. Desert native that makes a 5-in.-deep mat of dark green foliage. Blooms in spring and sporadically throughout the year; yellow, 2½-in. flowers rise on individual stems 6–8 in. above foliage. Endures heat and drought but does better with occasional water. Grown in low and intermediate deserts. Often sold as *O. drummondii.*

O. tetragona. SUNDROPS. Perennial. Grows to 2 ft. with reddish stems and good green foliage. Daytime display of 1½-in.-wide, yellow blossoms throughout summer. Needs very little attention. Several varieties.

OKRA

Malvaceae
ANNUAL
✓ ALL ZONES
☼ FULL SUN
● REGULAR WATER

Okra

Warm-season annual vegetable that grows well under same conditions as sweet corn. Plant when ground begins to warm up. Soak seed 24 hours before planting to speed germination. Fertilize at least once in spring. Pods grow on large, erect, bushy plants with tropical-looking leaves. Harvest pods every 2 or 3 days. Best size is 1–3 in. long; overripe pods are tough, and they shorten plant's bearing life. In containers, variety 'Red River' has tropical look. In large tub in warm spot, a single plant can yield enough to make it worth growing.

OLD MAN CACTUS. See CEPHALOCEREUS senilis	**p. 217**
OLD MAN'S WHISKERS. See GEUM triflorum	**p. 306**

Oleaceae. The olive family contains trees and shrubs with leaves in opposite pairs and flowers with a four-lobed calyx and four-lobed corolla (they appear to have four petals). Privet *(Ligustrum)*, olive *(Olea)*, and lilac *(Syringa)* are typical.

OLEA europaea

OLIVE
Oleaceae
EVERGREEN TREE
✓ ZONES 8, 9, 11–24
☼ FULL SUN
◐ NO WATER ONCE ESTABLISHED

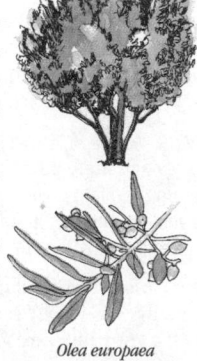

Olea europaea

Along with palms, citrus, and eucalyptus, olives stand out like regional trademarks along avenues and in gardens of California and southern Arizona. The trees' beauty has been appreciated in those areas since they were introduced to mission gardens for their oil.

Willowlike foliage is a soft gray green that combines well with most colors. Smooth gray trunks and branches become gnarled and picturesque in maturity. Trees grow slowly, eventually reaching 25–30 ft. high and as wide; however, young trees put on height (if not substance) fairly fast. Begin training early. For single trunk, prune out or shorten side branches below point where you want branching to begin, stake tree firmly, and cut

off basal suckers. For several trunks, stake lower branches or basal suckers to continue growth at desired angles. Large old olive trees can (with reasonable care) be boxed and transplanted with near certainty of survival.

Olive are most lush when growing in deep, rich soil, but will also grow in shallow, alkaline, or stony soil and with little fertilizer. They thrive in areas with hot, dry summers but also perform adequately in coastal areas. They take temperatures down to 15°F.

Olives withstand heavy pruning. Thinning each year shows off branch pattern to best advantage, and removing flowering-fruiting branches reduces or eliminates fruit crop, which is usually a nuisance.

Trees of fruiting varieties blacken and drop fruit late in the year. Without processing, the olives are inedible, and they can stain paving and harm a lawn if not removed. In addition to pruning, reduce crop by spraying with fruit-control hormones when tiny white flowers appear. Or spread tarpaulin at dropping time, knock off all fruit, and dispose of it. So-called fruitless varieties are not always reliably barren; see list.

These varieties are sold:

'Ascolana'. One of the commercial-grove kinds you can get as a specimen tree from a landscaping firm. Large fruit, small pit. Tree to 30 ft. high.

'Bonita'. Sold as fruitless (actually, has tiny fruit like privet's). Tree to 30 ft. high.

'Little Ollie'. Big, dense shrub (to 12 ft. high), very dark green, excellent as hedge or screen. Bears almost no fruit.

'Majestic Beauty'. Airy and fluffy looking, it's also suitable as a hedge or screen. Bears almost no fruit. Tree to 25 ft. high.

'Manzanillo'. Commercial-grove kind most often sold as specimen tree by landscaping firms. More spreading growth habit than most. Smallish, apple-shaped fruit. Tree to 30 ft. high.

'Mission.' Commercial-grove kind sold as specimen tree by landscaping firms. Hardier than the others. Tall tree with dense growth, to 40 ft. high.

'Sevillano'. Commercial-grove kind sold as specimen tree by landscaping firms. Oaklike form, to 35 ft. high.

'Skylark Dwarf'. Typically, multitrunked, large, compact shrub to 16 ft. Sets very small fruit crop in some years.

'Swan Hill'. Leaves are deep green in color. Tree to 30 ft. high. Bears no fruit. Little or no pollen—a boon to allergy sufferers.

'Wilsoni'. Spreading tree to 25 ft. high. Bears no fruit.

OLEANDER. See NERIUM oleander	**p. 390**
OLIVE. See OLEA europaea	**p. 393**

OLNEYA tesota

DESERT IRONWOOD
Fabaceae (Leguminosae)
EVERGREEN TREE
✓ ZONES 12, 13
☼ FULL SUN
◐ NO WATER ONCE ESTABLISHED

Olneya tesota

Grows slowly to 25–30 ft. with equal spread. Branches erect in youth, later spreading. Gray-green leaves, each with two spines at base, divided into many ¾-in. leaflets. In early summer, clusters of pinkish lavender, ½-in.-long, sweet pea–shaped flowers put on good show; 2-in.-long pods follow. Old leaves fall after bloom, with new ones replacing them quickly.

Name comes from extremely hard, heavy heartwood. Plant grows near washes where some deep water is usually available. Tree is deciduous in hard frosts and cannot endure prolonged freezes.

Onagraceae. Most members of the evening primrose family have flower parts in fours; otherwise, they are diverse in appearance and structure. Those that grow in western gardens are all annuals or perennials except for fuchsias. Many are western natives *(Clarkia, Gaura, Zauschneria).*

ONION

Amaryllidaceae

BIENNIALS GROWN AS ANNUALS

☑ ALL ZONES

☼ FULL SUN

● REGULAR WATER

Onion

Grow onions from seed or sets (small bulbs). Sets are easiest for beginners, but seed gives larger crop for smaller investment. In mild climates, sets can go in 1–1½ in. deep and 1–2 in. apart all winter long and through April. Where winters are cold, plant sets in earliest spring. Start pulling green onions in 3 weeks or so; any not needed as green onions can grow on for later harvest as dry onions when tops wither. Plant seed in early spring in rows 15–18 in. apart. Soil should be loose, rich, and well drained. When seedlings are pencil size, thin to 3–4 in. apart, transplanting thinnings to extend plantings. Trim back tops of transplants about halfway. In some areas, onion plants (field-grown, nearly pencil-size transplants or seedlings growing in pots) are available.

Onions are shallow rooted and need moisture fairly near the surface. Feed plants, especially early in season: the larger and stronger the plants grow, the larger the bulbs they form. Carefully eliminate weeds that compete for light, food, and water. When most of the tops have begun to yellow and fall over, dig bulbs and let them cure and dry on top of ground for several days. Then pull off tops, clean, and store in dark, cool, airy place.

Of the more familiar varieties, look for 'Crystal Wax Bermuda', 'Southport White Globe', and 'White Sweet Spanish' if you like white onions. Good yellow varieties are 'Early Yellow Globe', 'Yellow Globe Danvers', and 'Utah Sweet Spanish'. Fine red variety is 'Southport Red Globe'. An unusual onion is the long, red, very mild 'Italian Red' or 'Red Torpedo'. For ornamental relatives, see *Allium*.

ONOCLEA sensibilis

SENSITIVE FERN

Polypodiaceae

FERN

☑ ZONES 1–9, 14–24

☼ FULL SUN

◐ WET SOIL

Onoclea sensibilis

Native to eastern United States. Coarse-textured fern with 2–4-ft. sterile fronds divided nearly to midrib; fertile fronds smaller, with clusters of almost beadlike leaflets. Fronds come from underground creeping rhizome that can be invasive. Dies down in winter. Fronds seem coarse to many gardeners.

OPHIOPOGON. See LIRIOPE and OPHIOPOGON   p. 358

OPUNTIA

Cactaceae

CACTI

☑ ZONES VARY BY SPECIES

☼ FULL SUN

◌ ◑ LITTLE OR NO WATER ONCE ESTABLISHED

Opuntia microdasys

Many kinds, with varied appearance. Most species fall into one of two sorts: those having flat, broad joints or those having cylindrical joints. Members of the first group are often called prickly pear, the second group, cholla, but the terms are rather loose. Hardiness is variable. Flowers are generally large and showy. The fruit is a berry, often edible.

O. bigelovii. TEDDYBEAR CACTUS. Zones 11–24. Native to Arizona, Nevada, California, northern Mexico. Treelike plant of slow growth to 2–8 ft. Woody trunk covered with black spines. Branches cylindrical, easily detached, covered with vicious, silvery yellow spines. Flowers pale green, yellow, or white marked with lavender, 1–1½ in. wide. April bloom. Grows freely in hottest, driest deserts.

O. ficus-indica. Zones 8, 9, 12–24. Big shrubby or treelike cactus to 15 ft., with woody trunks and smooth, flat, green joints 15–20 in. long. Few or no spines, but has clusters of bristles. Yellow flowers 4 in. across, spring or early summer. Large, edible, red or yellow fruit, often sold in markets. Handle it carefully—bristles break off easily and are irritating. Use rubber gloves when peeling fruit, or impale fruit on a fork and strip skin carefully, avoiding bristly areas.

O. microdasys. BUNNY EARS. Zones 12–24. Native to Mexico. Fast growth to 2 ft. high, 4–5 ft. wide (much smaller in pots). Pads flat, thin, nearly round, to 6 in. across, velvety soft green with neatly spaced tufts of short golden bristles in polka-dot effect. *O. m.* 'Albispina' has white bristles. Small, round new pads atop larger old ones give plant silhouette of animal's head. Favorite with children.

ORANGE. See CITRUS	p. 231
ORANGE CLOCK VINE. See THUNBERGIA gregorii	p. 505
ORANGE JESSAMINE. See MURRAYA paniculata	p. 384
ORANGEQUAT. See CITRUS, Miscellaneous	p. 232

Orchidaceae. The orchid family is probably the largest in the plant kingdom, with nearly 800 genera and over 17,000 species. Relatively few are fixtures in western gardens, although fanciers keep large collections and specialist growers issue long lists. Flowers have an unusual shape: one or more petals united to form a lip, and the stamens, style, and stigma united into a single organ, the column.

Best known in the West are *Bletilla, Cattleya, Cymbidium, Epidendrum, Paphiopedilum, Phalaenopsis,* and *Pleione.*

Orchid growers' terms. Here are definitions of the orchid growers' terms you will encounter in this book.

Epiphytic. In nature epiphytic orchids cling to high branches of trees in tropical or subtropical jungles, deriving their nourishment from air, rain, and whatever decaying vegetable matter they can trap in their root systems.

Pseudobulb. Epiphytic orchids have thickened stems called pseudobulbs that store food and water and allow the plants to survive drought. These may be short and fat like bulbs or erect and slender. They vary from green to brown in color. Leaves may grow along pseudobulbs or from their tips.

Terrestrial. Some orchids (including most native orchids) are terrestrial and must grow in loose, moist soil rich in humus. They often occur in wooded areas but sometimes in open meadows as well. These orchids require constant moisture and food.

Sepals, petals, lip, and pouch. Segments of an orchid flower include three sepals and three petals; one of the petals, usually the lowest one, is called the lip. The lip is usually larger and more brightly colored than other segments. Sometimes it is fantastically shaped, with various appendages and markings. It may be folded into a slipperlike "pouch."

Rafts, bark. Nearly all orchids, terrestrial or epiphytic, are grown in pots. A few are grown on "rafts," slabs of bark or wood, or in baskets of wood slats; a few natives are grown in open ground.

Potting and growing. Potting materials for cattleyas (the most commonly grown orchids) will work for most epiphytic orchids: osmunda fiber, hapuu (tree fern stem), or ground bark. Most popular now is bark, which is readily available, easy to handle, and fairly inexpensive. Use fine grade for pots 3 in. or smaller, medium grade for pots 4 in. or larger. It's sensible to use ready-made mixes sold by orchid growers; these are blended for proper texture and acidity.

Water plants about once a week—when mix dries out and becomes lightweight. Feed with a commercial water-soluble orchid fertilizer once every 2 weeks during growing season. To provide humidity for plants in house, fill a metal or plastic tray with gravel and add just enough water to reach almost to top of gravel. Stretch hardware cloth over tray, leaving an inch between gravel and wire for air circulation. Set pots on top. Maintain water level.

Temperature requirements. This list classifies orchids according to temperature requirements. Many cool-growing orchids are hardy enough to grow outdoors in mild-winter areas; some are native to the West.

Temperate-climate orchids can be grown in pots on a window sill with other house plants, but will perform best if given additional humidity. An excellent method of supplying humidity is described in "Potting and growing," above. Most temperate-climate orchids can be moved outdoors in summer; place them in the shade of high-branching trees, on the patio, or in a lathhouse.

Warm-climate orchids need greenhouse conditions to provide the uniform warm temperatures and high humidity they require.

Cool-climate orchids: *Bletilla, Cymbidium, Epidendrum, Paphiopedilum* (green-leafed forms), *Pleione.* Some of these are hardy out of doors in mildest parts of California. Some are thoroughly hardy.

Temperate-climate orchids: *Cattleya, Epidendrum, Paphiopedilum* (mottled-leafed forms).

Warm-climate orchid: *Phalaenopsis.*

ORCHID CACTUS. See EPIPHYLLUM p. 273

ORCHID TREE. See BAUHINIA p. 179

ORCHID VINE. See MASCAGNIA, STIGMAPHYLLON pp. 375, 493

OREGANO. See ORIGANUM vulgare p. 395

OREGON BOXWOOD. See PAXISTIMA myrsinites p. 402

OREGON GRAPE. See MAHONIA aquifolium p. 371

OREGON MYRTLE. See UMBELLULARIA californica p. 515

ORGANPIPE CACTUS. See LEMAIREOCEREUS thurberi p. 350

ORIENTAL ARBORVITAE. See PLATYCLADUS orientalis p. 427

ORIENTAL GARLIC. See ALLIUM tuberosum p. 145

ORIENTAL POPPY. See PAPAVER orientale p. 400

ORIGANUM

Lamiaceae (Labiatae)

PERENNIALS

ZONES VARY BY SPECIES

FULL SUN

LITTLE WATER, EXCEPT AS NOTED

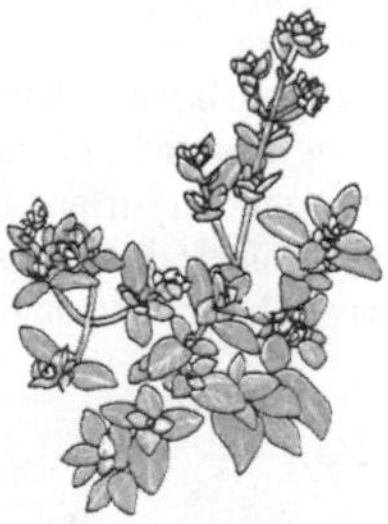

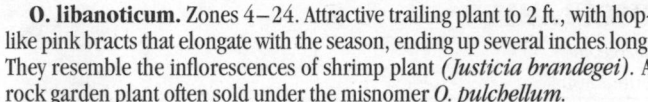

Origanum majorana

Mint relatives with tight clusters of small flowers and foliage with a strong, pleasant scent. Bracts in flower clusters overlap, giving effect of small pinecones. Not fussy about soil type.

O. dictamnus (Amaracus dictamnus). CRETE DITTANY. Perennial. Zones 8–24. Native to Mediterranean area. Aromatic herb with slender, arching stems to 1 ft. long. Thick, roundish, somewhat mottled, woolly white leaves to ¾ in. long. Flowers pink to purplish, ½ in. long; rose purple fruit in conelike heads. Blooms summer to fall. Shows up best when planted individually in rock garden, container, or hanging basket.

O. laevigatum. Zones 8–24. Sprawling, arching plant, with stems rooting at joints and branching clusters of purple flowers. 'Herrenhausen' has lilac pink flowers and purplish leaves in cool weather; 'Hopley's' has large heads of deep purplish pink flowers. Useful in dry gardens as bank or ground cover.

O. libanoticum. Zones 4–24. Attractive trailing plant to 2 ft., with hoplike pink bracts that elongate with the season, ending up several inches long. They resemble the inflorescences of shrimp plant *(Justicia brandegei).* A rock garden plant often sold under the misnomer *O. pulchellum.*

O. majorana (Majorana hortensis). SWEET MARJORAM. Summer annual in all zones; perennial herb in Zones 4–24. To 1–2 ft. Tiny, oval, gray-green leaves; spikes of white flowers in loose clusters at top of plant. Grow in fairly moist soil. Keep blossoms cut off and plant trimmed to prevent woody growth. Propagate from seeds, cuttings, or root divisions. It's a favorite herb for seasoning meats, salads, vinegars, casserole dishes. Use leaves fresh or dried. Often grown in container indoors on window sill in cold-winter areas.

O. onites. POT MARJORAM. Zones 8–24. To 2 ft. tall and as broad, with bright green aromatic leaves and flattish heads of tiny white or purplish flowers. Sometimes called Cretan oregano.

O. vulgare. OREGANO, WILD MARJORAM. All zones. Perennial herb. Upright growth to 2½ ft. Spreads by underground stems. Medium-size oval leaves; purplish pink blooms. Grow in medium rich soil; needs good drainage, average watering. Keep trimmed to prevent flowering. Replant every 3 years. Fresh or dried leaves are used in many dishes, especially Italian and Spanish ones. 'Compactum' is a few inches tall, spreads widely, and seldom flowers. It can be used as a ground cover.

ORNAMENTAL PEAR. See PYRUS p. 447

ORNITHOGALUM

Liliaceae

BULBS

ZONES 5–24

FULL SUN

WATER NEEDS VARY BY SPECIES

ALL PARTS ARE POISONOUS, ESPECIALLY THE BULB

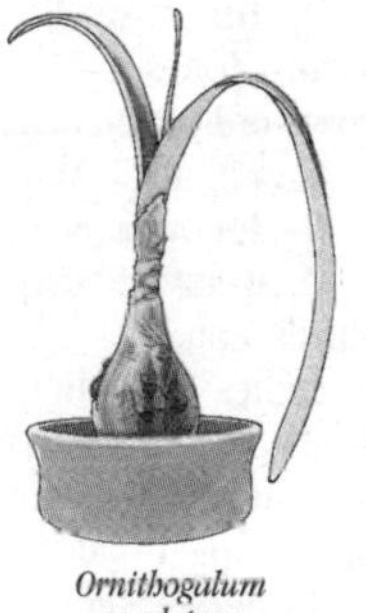

Ornithogalum caudatum

Leaves vary from narrow to broad and tend to be floppy. Flowers mostly star shaped, in tall or rounded clusters. Most bloom April–May. Use in borders or grow in pots.

O. arabicum. STAR OF BETHLEHEM. Handsome clusters of 2-in., white, waxy flowers with beady black pistils in centers. Stems 2 ft. tall. Floppy leaves to 2 ft. long, 1 in. wide, bluish green. Bulbs hardy except in coldest winters; in cool-summer climates, bulbs may not bloom second year after planting because they lacked sufficient heat. Wet-winter/dry-summer plant. Can be grown in pots. Excellent cut flower.

O. caudatum. PREGNANT ONION, FALSE SEA ONION. House plant. Grown for bulb and foliage rather than for tall wands of small green-and-white flowers. Strap-shaped leaves hang downward and grow to 5 ft. long. Big, gray-green, smooth-skinned bulb (3–4 in. thick) grows on, not in, the ground. Bulblets form under skin and grow quite large before they drop out and root. Hardy to 25°F; will lose leaves without occasional watering.

O. thyrsoides. CHINCHERINCHEE. Tapering, compact clusters of white, 2-in. flowers with brownish green centers. Leaves bright green, upright, 2 in. wide, 10–12 in. long. Flower stems 2 ft. high. Usually considered tender but has survived cold winters in sheltered southern or southwestern location when well mulched. Moderate water. Long-lasting cut flower.

O. umbellatum. STAR OF BETHLEHEM. Probably hardiest of group. May naturalize widely once it's established—can become pest. Clusters of 1-in.-wide flowers, striped green on outside, top 1-ft. stems. Grasslike leaves about as long as flower stems. Cut flowers last well but close at night. Give adequate water for good performance.

OSAGE ORANGE. See MACLURA pomifera p. 365

OSCULARIA

Aizoaceae	
SUBSHRUBS	
💧 ZONES 15–24	
☀ FULL SUN	
💧 LITTLE WATER	

Oscularia deltoides

Low plants with erect or trailing branches. To 1 ft. tall. Leaves very thick and fleshy, triangular, blue green with pink flush. Fragrant flowers to ½ in. across in late spring, early summer. Best in pots, hanging baskets, rock gardens, borders. Can be used for small-scale ground cover.

O. deltoides. Has purplish rose flowers.

O. pedunculata. Has paler, mauve pink flowers.

OSMANTHUS

Oleaceae	
EVERGREEN SHRUBS	
💧 ZONES VARY BY SPECIES	
☀ ◐ FULL SUN OR PARTIAL SHADE	
💧 LITTLE WATER ONCE ESTABLISHED	

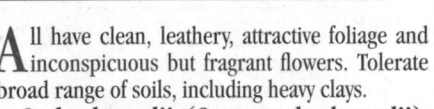

Osmanthus fragrans

All have clean, leathery, attractive foliage and inconspicuous but fragrant flowers. Tolerate broad range of soils, including heavy clays.

O. burkwoodii (Osmarea burkwoodii). Shrub. Zones 4–9, 14–17. Slow-growing to 6 ft. and as wide, with dense cover of 1–2-in. bright green, glossy, toothed leaves. Small, fragrant, white flowers in April, May. Useful as a hedge.

O. decorus. See Phillyrea decora

O. delavayi (Siphonosmanthus delavayi). DELAVAY OSMANTHUS. Shrub. Zones 4–9, 14–21. Slow growing, graceful, to 4–6 ft., with arching branches spreading wider. Leaves dark green, oval, to 1 in. long, with toothed edges. Clusters of four to eight white, fragrant flowers (largest of any osmanthus) in profusion, March–May. Attractive all year. Easily controlled by pruning. Good choice for foundations, massing. Handsome on retaining wall where branches hang down. In hot-summer areas, give partial shade.

O. fortunei. Shrub. Zones 5–10, 14–24. Hybrid between *O. heterophyllus* and *O. fragrans*. Slow, dense growth to eventual 20 ft. tall; usually seen at height of about 6 ft. Leaves are oval, hollylike, up to 4 in. long. Small, fragrant white flowers bloom during spring, summer.

O. f. 'San Jose'. Similar in appearance to species but has cream to orange flowers in October.

O. fragrans. SWEET OLIVE. Shrub. Zones 8, 9, 12–24. Moderate growth to 10 ft. and more with age. Broad, dense, compact. Can be pruned to upright growth where space is limited. Can be trained as small tree, hedge, screen, background, espalier, container plant. Pinch out growing tips of young plants to induce bushiness.

Leaves glossy, medium green, oval, to 4 in. long, toothed or smooth edged. Flowers tiny, white, inconspicuous except in their powerful, sweet, apricotlike fragrance. Bloom heaviest in spring and early summer, but plants flower sporadically throughout year in mild-winter areas. Young plants grow best in some shade but tolerate sun as they mature. In Zones 12, 13, grow in eastern or northern exposure.

O. f. aurantiacus. Leaves narrower and less glossy than those of *O. fragrans*. Concentrates its crop of wonderfully fragrant orange flowers in October.

O. heterophyllus (O. aquifolium, O. ilicifolius). HOLLY-LEAF OSMANTHUS. Shrub. Zones 3–10, 14–24. Useful as hedge.

'Goshiki'. Erect plant 3½ ft. tall to 5 ft. wide. New leaves have pinkish orange markings that mature to yellow variegations on dark green.

'Gulftide'. Similar to 'Ilicifolius' but more compact.

'Ilicifolius'. Dense, symmetrical upright growth to 6–8 ft., eventually to 20 ft. Leaves dark green, strongly toothed, hollylike, to 2½ in. long. Fragrant white flowers in fall, winter, early spring. Good for screen, background.

'Purpureus' ('Purpurascens'). Dark purple new growth, with purple tints through summer.

'Rotundifolius'. Slow growing to 5 ft. Roundish small leaves are lightly spined along edges.

'Variegatus'. Slow growing to 4–5 ft., with densely set leaves edged creamy white. Useful for lighting up shady areas.

OSMUNDA regalis

ROYAL FERN	
Osmundaceae	
FERN	
💧 ALL ZONES; BEST IN ZONES 4–6	
● SHADE	
💧 MOIST SOIL	

Osmunda regalis

Big, handsome fern with twice-cut fronds and large leaflets; coarser texture than that of most ferns. Fertile leaflets small, clustered at tips of fronds. Can reach 6 ft. Leaves die back in winter.

OSTEOSPERMUM

AFRICAN DAISY	
Asteraceae (Compositae)	
PERENNIALS OR EVERGREEN SUBSHRUBS	
💧 ZONES 8, 9, 12–24	
☀ FULL SUN	
💧 MODERATE WATER	

Osteospermum fruticosum

South African plants closely related to *Dimorphotheca* (Cape marigold) and often sold as such. Except for trailing perennial *O. fruticosum*, all are spreading, mounded shrubby plants bearing medium green foliage and a profusion of daisylike flowers over long season (best in spring, summer). Narrowish oval leaves, smooth edged or with a few large teeth, 2–4 in. long, are variable in size and shape, larger on young plants and vigorous young shoots. Flowers, on long stems, open only in sunlight.

Plants look best with good garden soil and care but will stand drought and neglect when established. Tip-pinching young plants induces bushiness; cutting back old, sprawling branches to young side branches keeps plants neat, often induces repeat bloom. Use in borders or mass plantings along driveways or paths, on slopes, in front of screening shrubs. Grow from seed or cuttings (named varieties from cuttings only).

O. barberae (Dimorphotheca barberae). To 2–3 ft. tall, a little wider. Flower heads 2–3 in. across. Rays pinkish lilac inside, with deep purplish blue stripes on reverse; dark purple-blue centers. Blooms from fall through spring, often through summer. Hybridizes freely, and seedlings vary in height and color. Most will be lavender pink.

WHY IS IT CALLED "FREEWAY DAISY"?

The popularity of *Osteospermum fruticosum* boomed in the late 1960s, when this perennial with cheerful white flowers was planted along freeways all over low-elevation California. Useful for large landscaping, it is a little coarse (and a bit ho-hum) for smaller home gardens.

O. 'Buttersweet'. Plant form resembles that of *O. barberae*. Flower heads have primrose yellow rays fading to cream near center, lavender to brownish zone at base, lavender blue to brownish center. Backs of rays yellow with pronounced brown stripe. Spring to frost.

O. ecklonis (Dimorphotheca ecklonis). Grows 2–4 ft. tall, equally broad. Long stems bear 3-in. flower heads with white rays (tinged lavender blue on backs), dark blue center. Blooms early summer to frost.

O

O. fruticosum (Dimorphotheca fruticosa). TRAILING AFRICAN DAISY, FREEWAY DAISY. Spreads rapidly by trailing, rooting branches. Rooted cutting will cover circle 2–4 ft. across in year; plants grow to 6–12 in. tall. Leaves shorter, thicker than those of other species. Blooms intermittently during year, most heavily from November to March. Heads to 2 in. across; rays lilac above, fading nearly white by second day, deeper lilac beneath and in bud; dark purple center. Good ground cover for sunny areas; good bank cover. Needs well-drained soil. Does well at seashore. If it gets too high, stacked, or weedy, mow or cut back in midsummer. Will spill over wall or grow in hanging basket (tip-pinch to induce bushiness). Used as annual (fall planting) in Zones 12, 13. 'Whirligig' has fantastic white-and-blue flower heads with spoon-shaped, white-tipped petals. Each petal is pinched in the middle to reveal its blue underside. White-flowering selections are common. 'African Queen', and 'Burgundy' are purple.

OSTRICH FERN. See MATTEUCCIA struthiopteris	p. 376
OSWEGO TEA. See MONARDA	p. 382
OTATEA. See BAMBOO	p. 174
OUR LORD'S CANDLE. See YUCCA whipplei	p. 526

OXALIS

Oxalidaceae

PERENNIALS; SOME GROW FROM BULBS OR RHIZOMES

⚡ ZONES VARY BY SPECIES

☼◐ SUN; LIGHT SHADE IN HOT-SUMMER AREAS

💧 REGULAR WATER

Leaves divided into leaflets; usually have three leaflets, like clover leaves. Flowers pink, white, rose, or yellow.

O. acetosella. WOOD SORREL, SHAMROCK. One of several plants known as shamrock. See Shamrock.

Oxalis oregana

O. adenophylla. Zones 4–9, 12–24. Dense, low (4-in.-high), compact tuft of leaves, each leaf with 12–22 crinkly, gray-green leaflets. Flowers are 1 in. wide, on 4–6-in. stalks, bell shaped, lilac pink with deeper veins, in late spring. Plant roots in fall. Needs good drainage. Good rock garden plant or companion to bulbs such as species tulips or the smaller kinds of narcissus, in pots or in the ground.

O. crassipes. Zones 8, 9, 12–24. Compact evergreen plant seems to bloom at all seasons. At top of 6–18-in.-high stalks are small pink flowers. Enough open at one time to be effective. There is a white-flowered form, *O. c.* 'Alba', and a blush pink one, *O. c.* 'Pinkie'.

O. hirta. Zones 8, 9, 14–24. Many upright, branching stems to 1 ft. high that gradually fall over with weight of leaves and flowers. Leaves cloverlike, small, set directly against stems or on very short stalks. General effect is feathery. Flowers (late fall or winter) are bright rose pink, 1 in. wide. Plant bulbs in fall. Good in rock gardens, hanging baskets.

O. lasiandra. Zones 8, 9, 12–24. Leaves wheel shaped, with as many as ten narrow leaflets. Foot-tall stems carry many dark red flowers slightly under 1 in. long.

O. oregana. REDWOOD SORREL, OREGON OXALIS. Zones 4–9, 14–24. Native to coastal forests from Washington to California. Creeping white roots send up velvety, medium green, cloverlike leaves 1½–4 in. wide on stems 2–10 in. high. Flowers to 1 in. across, pink or white veined with lavender, borne in spring, sometimes again in fall. Interesting ground cover for partial shade to deep shade in mild-winter/cool-summer areas. Good with ferns. Looks most lush when watered frequently.

O. pes-caprae (O. cernua). BERMUDA BUTTERCUP. Zones 8, 9, 12–24. Clusters of bright green cloverlike leaves (often spotted with dark brown) spring directly from soil in fall. Above them in winter and spring rise stems up to 1 ft. long topped with clusters of inch-wide, bright yellow flowers. This handsome plant is best grown in pots or baskets; it spreads rapidly by rhizomes and bulbs, and it can become a troublesome pest in an open garden.

O. purpurea (O. variabilis). Zones 8, 9, 12–24. Low growing (4–5 in. tall), with large cloverlike leaves and rose red flowers an inch across, November–March. Spreads by bulbs and rhizomelike roots, but is not aggressive or weedy. Plant bulbs in fall. Improved kinds sold under the name Grand Duchess; have larger flowers of rose pink, white, or lavender.

OXERA pulchella

Verbenaceae

EVERGREEN VINE OR VINING SHRUB

⚡ ZONES 22–24

☼ BEST UNDER HIGH-BRANCHING TREES OR LATH

💧 REGULAR WATER

Oxera pulchella

As a shrub, mounding to 6 ft. tall; with support, can be trained to 10 ft. Leaves leathery, glossy, very dark green, oblong, to 5 in. long. Clusters of white, waxy, 2-in., trumpet-shaped flowers give display of unusual quality at varying times of year. Refined appearance.

OXYDENDRUM arboreum

SOURWOOD, SORREL TREE

Ericaceae

DECIDUOUS TREE

⚡ ZONES 3–9, 14–17

☼ FULL SUN

💧 REGULAR WATER

Oxydendrum arboreum

Native to eastern United States. Slow growth to 15–25 ft., eventually to 50 ft. Slender trunk, slightly spreading head. Leaves 5–8 in. long, narrow, somewhat resemble peach leaves; bronze tinted in early spring, rich green in summer, orange and scarlet in autumn. Creamy white, bell-shaped flowers in 10-in.-long, drooping clusters at branch tips, late July–August. In autumn, when foliage is brilliant scarlet, branching clusters of greenish seed capsules extend outward and downward like fingers; capsules turn light silver gray and hang on late into winter.

Best known in areas with cool summers, well-defined winters. Requires acid soil. Not competitive—doesn't do well in lawns or under larger trees. Avoid underplanting with anything needing cultivation. Good shade tree for patio or terrace. Distinguished branch and leaf pattern, spring leaf color, summer flowers, fall color. Young plants are good container subjects.

OXYPETALUM caeruleum. See TWEEDIA caerulea	p. 514
PACHISTIMA. See PAXISTIMA	p. 402

PACHYPODIUM lamerei

MADAGASCAR PALM

Apocynaceae

HOUSE PLANT OR INDOOR/OUTDOOR SUCCULENT

☼ PART SHADE; BRIGHT INDOOR LIGHT

💧 WATER ONLY WHEN SOIL IS DRY

Pachypodium lamerei

Not a palm, though somewhat palmlike. Easy-to-grow succulent with impressive silhouette: succulent trunk 2–4 ft. tall (or more, with age) is unbranched, spiny, topped with a circle of strap-shaped leaves to 10 in. long, 1 in. wide. White flowers seldom seen. Needs excellent drainage. Cannot stand frost.

PACHYRHIZUS erosus

JICAMA
Fabaceae (Leguminosae)
ANNUAL VINE
⚡ ALL ZONES
☼ FULL SUN
💧 DO NOT LET ROOT ZONE DRY OUT
◊ SEEDS ARE POISONOUS IF EATEN

Pachyrhizus erosus

Grown for its edible root, which looks like a large brown turnip and tastes something like a water chestnut. Twining or scrambling vines are attractive, with luxuriant deep green foliage and pretty purple or violet flower clusters. Leaves have three leaflets, each the size of a hand; upright spikes of sweet pea–shaped flowers appear in late summer. Flowers should be pinched out for maximum root production, but you can allow seed for next year's crop to form on one or two plants. Needs long, warm growing season and rich garden soil. Sow seeds after danger of frost is past, 1–1½ in. deep, 6–12 in. apart in rows. Feed once or twice in early or midsummer. The roots or tubers will form as days begin to grow shorter; harvest them before first frost.

PACHYSANDRA terminalis

JAPANESE SPURGE
Buxaceae
EVERGREEN SUBSHRUB
⚡ ZONES 1–10, 14–21
◐ ● USE AS A GROUND COVER IN SHADE
💧 AMPLE WATER

Pachysandra terminalis

Spreads by underground runners. Stems reach 10 in. in deep shade, 6 in. in dappled shade. Leaves are rich dark green (yellowish in full sun), 2–4 in. long, in clusters atop stems. 'Variegata' has leaves edged with white. Small, fluffy spikes of fragrant white flowers in summer; white fruit follows.

Set 6–12 in. apart in rich, preferably acid soil. Feed during growing season for best color. May spread moderately but is not aggressive or weedy. Good transition between walks or lawns and shade-loving shrubs.

'Green Carpet' is lower growing, more compact, possibly hardier.

PAEONIA

PEONY
Paeoniaceae
TUBEROUS PERENNIALS, DECIDUOUS SHRUBS
⚡ ZONES VARY BY TYPE
☼◐ AFTERNOON SHADE IN HOT CLIMATES
● REGULAR SUMMER WATER

Paeonia
Single Type

Practically all garden peonies are hybrids. These fall into two principal classes, herbaceous and tree peonies. Nearly all of the former are descendants of *P. lactiflora*, a Chinese species.

Herbaceous peonies. Zones 1–11, 14–16. These perennials grow from thickened, tuberous roots; they are hybrids. Well-grown clumps reach 2–4 ft. tall and spread wider. Large, deep green, attractively divided leaves make effective background for spectacular mid- to late-spring flowers. These may be single (uncommon but very effective); single filled with mass of narrow, yellow, petal-like structures (Japanese type); semidouble; or fully double. Colors range from pure white through pale creams and pinks to red. Flowers may reach 10 in. across. Newer kinds have deeper reds and chocolate tones; there is even a pure yellow. Many have fragrance of old-fashioned roses.

Herbaceous peonies can grow in most soils, but because they are long lived, prepare soil well to at least 1½ ft. deep. Keep manure from direct contact with roots. Plant in early fall, being careful that eyes on tubers are no deeper than 2 in.; deeper planting may prevent blooming. Feed established clumps like other plants. Provide support for heavy flowers. Cut off stems carefully just below soil surface in fall after leaves turn brown. To control botrytis, which browns buds and spots leaves, spray with copper fungicide before buds open; cut out and destroy all withered buds, stems, and brown-spotted leaves.

Divide clumps only when absolutely necessary, in early fall. To divide, dig plants, cut off foliage, hose dirt from root cluster, and divide carefully into sections, each with at least three eyes (pink growth buds). Choice cut flowers and a mainstay of big perennial borders. Can be planted in bays of big shrub borders.

Tree peonies. Zones 2–12, 14–21. These deciduous shrubs are descendants of *P. suffruticosa*, a Chinese shrub to 6 ft. tall; yellow and salmon varieties are hybrids of this and *P. lutea*, a Tibetan plant with yellow flowers. Irregular, picturesque branching habit; plants grow 3–6 ft. tall, eventually as wide. Leaves large, divided, blue-green to bronzy green.

Flowers very large, up to 1 ft. across, single to fully double. Japanese types have single to double flowers held erect above foliage; silky petals range from white through pink and red to lavender and purple. European types have very heavy double flowers that tend to droop and hide their heads; colors are chiefly pinks and rosy shades. Hybrids with *P. lutea* have single to fully double flowers in yellow, salmon, or sunset shades; singles and semidoubles hold up their flowers best.

Paeonia
Double Type

Very hardy to cold and less dependent on winter chill than herbaceous peonies; can get botrytis in humid climates. Fragile blooms come in early to midspring and should be sheltered from strong winds. Plant in fall or earliest spring (from containers any time) in rich, deep, well-prepared soil away from competing tree roots. Plants are long lived, so take special pains to improve soil with peat moss or ground bark. Plant deep, setting plant several inches deeper than it grew in nursery can or growing field. To prune, remove spent flowers and cut back to live wood in spring when buds begin to swell. Many varieties are available, and some nurseries sell unnamed seedlings; select the latter in bloom to get desired form and color. Bare-root grafted plants are offered in winter, earliest spring.

CHOOSY ABOUT THEIR CLIMATES

Herbaceous peonies bloom well only when they experience a period of pronounced winter chill. Winter cold and summer heat are not problems, but flowers do not last well where spring days are hot and dry; in such areas, choose early-blooming varieties and give plants some afternoon shade and ample water. In Zones 1–7, where they grow best, they thrive in full sun.

PALMS. Most palms are tropical or subtropical; a few are surprisingly hardy (specimens are seen in Edinburgh, London, and southern Russia, as well as Portland and Seattle). Palms offer great opportunity for imaginative planting. In nature they grow not only in solid stands but also in company with other plants, notably broad-leafed evergreen trees and shrubs. They are effective near swimming pools.

P

Most young palms prefer shade and all tolerate it; this fact makes them good house or patio plants when they are small. As they grow, they can be moved into sun or partial shade, depending on the species. Growth rates vary, but keeping plants in pots usually slows growth of faster-growing kinds. If temperatures are in the 60s or higher, fertilize potted palms often; also wash them off frequently to provide some humidity and clean the foliage. Washing also dislodges insects, which (indoors, at any rate) are protected from their natural enemies and can increase at an unnatural rate.

To pot a palm, supply good potting soil, adequate drainage, and not too big a container. As with all potted plants, pot or repot a palm in a container just slightly larger than the one it's in.

Some shade-tolerant palms such as *Rhapis*, *Chamaedorea*, and *Howea* may spend decades in pots indoors. Others that later may reach great size—*Phoenix*, *Washingtonia*, *Chamaerops*—make charming temporary indoor plants but must eventually be moved.

To plant a palm of 5-gallon size in the ground, dig a hole 3 ft. wide and 8 in. deeper than the root ball. At bottom, place 1–2 cu. ft. of manure, fortified sawdust, or other organic amendment along with a handful or two of blood meal. Put 6-in. layer of soil over this, set palm, and fill around it with mixture of half native soil and half fortified sawdust, ground bark, or peat moss. Water well; continue watering throughout summer and fall. Give gallon-size palms the same treatment (scaled down proportionately).

Palms, even big ones, transplant easily in late spring or early summer. Since new roots form from base of trunk, root ball need not be large. New root system will form and produce lush new growth. During transplant of large palms, tie leaves together over center "bud," or heart, and secure the leaf mass to a length of 2-by-4 tied to trunk.

Palms need little maintenance; plants thrive with reasonably fertile soil and adequate water. All tropical palms do their growing during warm times of year. Winter rains wash them down and leach accumulated salts from soil. Washing with a hose is beneficial, especially for palms exposed to dust and beyond reach of rain or dew; it helps keep down spider mites and sucking insects that find refuge in the long leaf stems.

Feather palms and many fan palms look neater when old leaves are removed after they have turned brown. Make neat cuts close to trunk, leaving leaf bases. Some palms shed old leaf bases on their own. Others, including *Syagrus* and *Chamaedorea*, may hold old bases. You can remove them by slicing them off at the very bottom of base (be careful not to cut into trunk).

Many palm admirers say that dead leaves of *Washingtonia* should remain on the tree, the thatch being part of the palm's character. If you also feel this way, you can cut lower fronds in a uniform way close to trunk, but leave leaf bases, which present a rather pleasant lattice surface.

Here are nine roles that the right kinds of palms can fill (palms named in each listing are described under their own names elsewhere in this book):

Sturdy palms for park and avenue plantings and for vertical effects in large gardens: *Archontophoenix*, *Brahea*, *Jubaea*, *Livistona*, *Phoenix canariensis*, *P. dactylifera*, *P. loureiri*, *P. rupicola*, *Rhopalostylis*, *Sabal*, *Syagrus (Arecastrum)*, *Washingtonia*.

Small to medium-size palms for sheltered areas in frost-free gardens: *Archontophoenix*, *Caryota*, *Chamaedorea*, *Chamaerops*, *Chrysalidocarpus*, *Hedyscepe*, *Howea*.

Small to medium-size palms for gardens in areas of occasional frosts: *Brahea*, *Butia*, *Chamaedorea cataractarum*, *C. elegans*, *C. klotzschiana*, *C. seifrizii*, *Chamaerops*, *Livistona*, *Neodypsis*, *Phoenix roebelenii*, *Trachycarpus*.

Hardy palms for cold areas (those marked with asterisks have withstood very cold winters in various parts of the world): *Brahea armata*, *B. edulis*, **Chamaerops*, **Jubaea*, *Livistona*, **Phoenix canariensis*, *P. dactylifera*, *P. loureiri*, *Rhapis*, *Sabal mexicana*, *S. minor*, *S. palmetto*, **Trachycarpus*, *Washingtonia filifera*.

Frost becomes more damaging to palms as it extends its stay and is repeated. Light frosts for half an hour may leave no damage, but the same frost during a period of 4 hours may damage some palms, kill others. Simplest damage is burned leaf edges, but frost may affect whole leaves, parts of trunks, or crown. Damage in crown is usually fatal (though some have recovered). Hardiness is also a matter of size; larger plants may pass through severe frosts unharmed while smaller ones perish.

PALMS AND POOLS: PERFECT PARTNERS

Palms are ideal for landscaping beside swimming pools because they do not drop leaves. Mature plants of *Phoenix reclinata* or *Chamaerops humilis*, with their curved trunks, create a tropical illusion. But whether palm trunks are curved or upright or topped with fan or feather leaves, they can create beautiful mirror effects in the water.

Garden palms for seaside planting (the following are listed in order of their salt tolerance, most tolerant first): *Washingtonia robusta*, *Phoenix dactylifera*, *P. canariensis*, *P. reclinata*, *Chamaerops*, *Brahea edulis*, *Butia*, *Sabal blackburniana*, *S. palmetto*. Palms in Southern California beach plantings should be washed off occasionally to keep them free from salt accumulations.

Palms for inland and desert: *Brahea armata*, *Butia*, *Chamaerops*, *Livistona chinensis*, *L. mariae*, *Phoenix canariensis*, *P. dactylifera*, *P. loureiri*, *P. sylvestris*, *Sabal mexicana*, *S. minor*, *Washingtonia*.

Palms to grow under trees, lath, or overhangs; or indoors: *Archontophoenix*, *Caryota mitis*, *C. ochlandra*, *C. urens*, *Chamaedorea*, *Hedyscepe*, *Howea*, young *Livistona*, *Phoenix reclinata* (when young), *P. roebelenii*, *Rhapis*, *Rhopalostylis*, *Trachycarpus* (when young). Indoor palms should occasionally be brought outdoors into mild light.

Palms as ground covers: young palms, especially slow growers such as *Livistona chinensis* or *Chamaerops humilis*, can be used effectively as ground covers. They'll stay low from 5 to 10 years, especially if they're in low-maintenance gardens. When they get too tall, move them to a location where you need height.

Palms for night lighting: because of their stateliness and their spectacular leaves, all palms are good subjects for night lighting. You can backlight them, light them from below, or direct lights to silhouette them against light-colored building wall.

PANDOREA

Bignoniaceae

EVERGREEN VINES

🌱 ZONES 16–24

☼ ◑ FULL SUN NEAR COAST, PARTIAL SHADE INLAND

💧 MODERATE WATER

Pandorea jasminoides

Leaves divided into glossy oval leaflets; clusters of trumpet-shaped flowers. Climb by twining. They are attractive even out of bloom.

P. jasminoides (Bignonia jasminoides, Tecoma jasminoides). BOWER VINE. Fast to 20–30 ft. Slender stems, distinguished glossy medium to dark green foliage. Leaves have five to nine egg-shaped leaflets 1–2 in. long. Flowers white with pink throats, 1½–2 in. long, drop cleanly after June–October bloom. 'Alba' and the more vigorous 'Lady D' have pure white flowers; 'Rosea' has pink flowers with rose pink throats. There is a form with variegated leaves. Plant in lee of prevailing wind. Prolonged freezes will kill it.

P. pandorana (Bignonia australis, Tecoma australis). WONGA-WONGA VINE. Glossy foliage handsome in all seasons. Flowers smaller (to ¾ in. long), yellow or pinkish white, usually spotted brown purple in throat. Needs room to grow. Prune ends of branches heavily after spring bloom.

PAPAVER

POPPY

Papaveraceae

PERENNIALS AND ANNUALS

⚡ ZONES VARY BY SPECIES

☼ FULL SUN

⬤ ⬤ GET BY ON LITTLE WATER

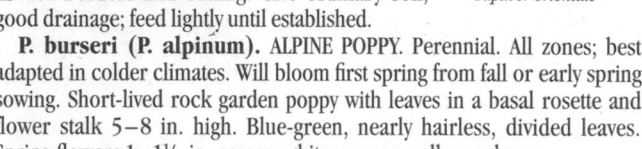
Papaver orientale

Poppies provide gay color in spring and summer for borders and cutting. Give ordinary soil, good drainage; feed lightly until established.

P. burseri (P. alpinum). ALPINE POPPY. Perennial. All zones; best adapted in colder climates. Will bloom first spring from fall or early spring sowing. Short-lived rock garden poppy with leaves in a basal rosette and flower stalk 5–8 in. high. Blue-green, nearly hairless, divided leaves. Spring flowers 1–1½ in. across, white, orange, yellow, salmon.

P. nudicaule. ICELAND POPPY. Perennial, grown as annual in warm-winter areas. All zones. Divided leaves with coarse hairs. Slender, hairy stems 1–2 ft. high. Cup-shaped, slightly fragrant flowers to 3 in. across, in yellow, orange, salmon, rose, pink, cream, or white. In mild climates, blooms winter and early spring from plants set out in fall. Where winters are cold, sow seed in earliest spring for summer bloom. To prolong bloom, pick flowers frequently. Several good strains available; Champagne Bubbles is most widely grown. Wonderland strain is lower growing (10 in.), sold in mixed or single colors—white to cream, pink, yellow, or orange. Oregon Rainbows has larger flowers in a wider color range, including bicolors and picotees. Excellent in the Northwest, it is less successful in warmer climates, producing a number of blind buds (buds that fail to open). Misato Carnival strain has 6-in. flowers on 2–3-ft. stems. Cover young plants with screen to protect them from birds. Poppies make excellent cut flowers; sear cut stem ends in flame before placing flowers in water.

P. orientale. ORIENTAL POPPY. Perennial. Zones 1–17. Short lived in warm-winter climates. Strong, bold plants to 4 ft. Coarse, hairy, divided leaves. Flowers single or double, 3–6 in. across, in brilliant and pastel shades. Many named varieties. Plants die back in midsummer; new leafy growth appears in early fall, lasts over winter, develops rapidly in warm weather. Baby's breath (*Gypsophila*) makes good summer filler.

P. rhoeas. FLANDERS FIELD POPPY, SHIRLEY POPPY. Summer annual. All zones. Slender, branching, hairy, 2–5 ft. high. Leaves short, irregularly divided. Flowers 2 in. or more across, single or double, in red, pink, white, orange, scarlet, salmon, bicolors. Selections with single scarlet flowers, black bases sold as 'American Legion' or 'Flanders Field'. Broadcast seed mixed with fine sand. Sow successively for bloom from spring through summer. Take cut flowers when buds first show color. Remove seed capsules (old flower bases) weekly to prolong the bloom season. Notorious self-sower.

Papaveraceae. The poppy family of annuals, perennials, and shrubs displays showy flowers usually borne singly. Examples are *Eschscholzia*, *Papaver*, and *Romneya*.

PAPAYA. See CARICA papaya   **p. 207**

PAPER MULBERRY. See BROUSSONETIA papyrifera   **p. 191**

PAPHIOPEDILUM

LADY'S SLIPPER

Orchidaceae

INDOOR AND COOL GREENHOUSE PLANTS

⬤ INDIRECT LIGHT

⬤ KEEP SOIL MOIST AT ALL TIMES

Paphiopedilum insigne

Sometimes sold as *Cypripedium,* these terrestrial orchids are native to tropical regions of Asia. The group includes large-flowered hybrids grown commercially for cut flowers. Blooms are perky, usually one to a stem, occasionally two or more. Many of them shine as if lacquered. Flowers may be white, yellow, green with white stripes, pure green, or a combination of background colors and markings in tan, mahogany brown, maroon, green, and white.

Graceful, arching foliage (no pseudobulbs) is either plain green or mottled. Plain-leafed forms usually flower in winter, mottled-leafed forms in summer. Most plants obtained from orchid dealers are hybrids.

In general, mottled-leafed forms do best with temperatures of about 60–65°F at night, 70–85°F during the day. Plain-leafed forms require nighttime temperatures of 55–65°F, 65–75°F during the day. They have no rest period. Combine equal parts ground bark and sandy loam for a good potting medium. Don't plant in oversize pot; plants thrive when crowded. Hardiest kinds can be grown in pots indoors, treated as house plants. They thrive in less light than most orchids require.

P. insigne. Polished flowers on stiff, brown, hairy stems any time from October to March. Sepals and petals green and white, with brown spots and stripes; pouch reddish brown. Hardy to brief exposures of 28°F.

PAPYRUS. See CYPERUS papyrus   **p. 255**

PARADISE PALM. See HOWEA forsterana   **p. 325**

PARKINSONIA aculeata

JERUSALEM THORN, MEXICAN PALO VERDE

Fabaceae (Leguminosae)

DECIDUOUS TREE

⚡ ZONES 8–24

☼ FULL SUN

◯ NO DRY-SEASON WATERING

Parkinsonia aculeata

Rapid growth at first, then slowing; eventually reaches 15–30 ft. high and wide. Yellow-green bark, spiny twigs, picturesque form. Sparse foliage; leaves 6–9 in. long, with many tiny leaflets that quickly fall in drought or cold. Numerous yellow flowers in loose, 3–7-in.-long clusters. Long bloom season in spring; intermittent bloom throughout year.

Tolerates alkaline soil. Stake young trees, train for high or low branching. Requires minimal attention once established. As shade tree, it filters sun rather than blocking it. Litter drop a problem on hard surfaces. Thorns, sparse foliage rule it out of tailored gardens. Flowering branches attractive in arrangements.

PARROT BEAK. See CLIANTHUS puniceus   **p. 236**

PARROTIA persica

PERSIAN PARROTIA

Hamamelidaceae

DECIDUOUS TREE OR LARGE SHRUB

⚡ ZONES 4–6, 15–17

☼ FULL SUN

⬤ ⬤ MODERATE WATER; ENDURES SOME ARIDITY

Parrotia persica

Native to Iran. Choice and colorful; attractive all seasons of year. Most dramatic display comes in fall: leaves usually turn from golden yellow to orange to rosy pink and finally scarlet. Slow growing to 30 ft. or more, but tends to be shrub or multitrunked tree to 15 ft. Bark attractive in winter: smooth, gray, flaking off to leave white patches. Thick foliage is made up of lustrous, dark green, oval, 3–4-in.-long leaves. Flowers with red stamens are in dense heads surrounded by woolly brown bracts; they appear in spring before leaves open, giving a hazy red effect.

P

To train as tree, stake and shorten lower side branches. Allow upper branches to take their wide-spreading habit. When tree reaches desired height, remove lower shortened side branches cleanly.

PARROT'S BEAK. See LOTUS berthelotii   p. 361

PARSLEY

Apiaceae (Umbelliferae)

BIENNIAL HERB TREATED AS ANNUAL

✓ ALL ZONES

☼ ◐ SUN; PARTIAL SHADE IF POSSIBLE

● REGULAR WATER

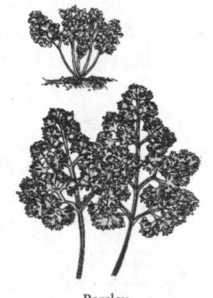

Parsley

Attractive edging for herb, vegetable, or flower garden. Plants are 6–12 in. high, with tufted, finely cut, dark green leaves. Attractive in boxes and pots. Use the leaves fresh or dried as seasoning, fresh as garnishes. Most satisfactorily grown anew every year. Buy plants at nursery or sow seed in place (April in Zones 1–7; December–May in Zones 8–11, 14–24; September–October in Zones 12, 13). Soak seed in warm water 24 hours before planting. Even then, it may not sprout for several weeks. According to an old story, parsley seeds must go to the devil and come back before sprouting. Thin seedlings to 6–8 in. apart.

> **THE SHOWY PARSLEY OR THE COOKING PARSLEY?**
> The Italian, flat-leafed parsley is the tastiest type for cooking. The curly varieties make the most attractive garnish and are appealing as a low border in a flower bed.

PARSNIP

Apiaceae (Umbelliferae)

BIENNIAL

✓ ALL ZONES

☼ FULL SUN

◉ MOIST SOIL

Parsnip

Needs deep, well-prepared, loose soil for long roots; roots of some varieties are 15 in. long. In cold-winter areas, plant seeds in late spring and harvest in fall; leave surplus in ground to be dug as needed in winter. In mild-climate areas, sow in fall and harvest in spring; in these areas, mature roots will continue to grow if they are left in ground, becoming tough and woody. Soak seeds in water 24 hours before planting to improve germination. Sow seeds ½ in. deep in rows spaced 2 ft. apart; thin seedlings to 3 in. apart.

PARTHENOCISSUS (Ampelopsis)

Vitaceae

DECIDUOUS VINES

✓ ALL ZONES, EXCEPT AS NOTED

☼ ◐ ● ANY EXPOSURE

● REGULAR WATER

Parthenocissus quinquefolia

Cling to walls by sucker discs at ends of tendrils. Superb and dependable fall leaf color, orange to scarlet. Flowers are insignificant. Attractive to birds. Think twice before planting them against wood or shingle siding; they can creep under it, and their clinging tendrils are hard to remove at repainting time.

P. henryana. SILVERVEIN CREEPER. Zones 4–9, 14–17. Resembles smaller (to 20 ft.), less aggressive *P. inserta*. Leaves formed by five leaflets, each 1–2½ in. long, which open purplish, turn dark bronzy green with pronounced silver veining and purple undersides. Color is best in shade, fades to plain green in strong light. Rich red autumn foliage. Clings to walls but needs some support to get started. Also good wall spiller, small-scale ground cover.

P. inserta. VIRGINIA CREEPER, WOODBINE. Western form of *P. quinquefolia*. Native to Rocky Mountains and eastward. Scrambles rather than clings: tendrils have few or no sucker discs.

P. quinquefolia. VIRGINIA CREEPER. Big, vigorous vine that clings or runs over ground, fence, trellis. Looser growth than *P. tricuspidata;* will drape its trailing branches over trellis. Leaves divided into five separate 6-in. leaflets with sawtoothed edges. Good ground cover on slopes; can control erosion. *P. q.* 'Engelmannii' has smaller leaves, denser growth.

P. tricuspidata. BOSTON IVY. Semievergreen in mild-winter areas. Glossy leaves variable in shape, usually three-lobed or divided into three leaflets, up to 8 in. wide. Clings tightly, grows fast to make dense, even wall cover. This is ivy of the Ivy League; covers brick or stone in areas where

Parthenocissus tricuspidata

English ivy freezes. Northern or eastern walls only in Zones 12, 13. Variety 'Beverly Brooks' has large leaves and good fall color, grows fast. Most leaves are divided into three leaflets. 'Green Showers' has large leaves, burgundy fall color. 'Lowii' has smaller (1½-in.), deeply lobed leaves. 'Veitchii' has small leaves, the younger ones purplish. Vine with leaves strongly resembling those of *P. tricuspidata* is *Ampelopsis brevipedunculata*.

PASPALUM vaginatum

SEASHORE PASPALUM

Poaceae (Gramineae)

LAWN GRASS

✓ ZONES 17, 24

☼ FULL SUN

● NEEDS LESS WATER THAN MOST LAWN GRASSES

Paspalum vaginatum

Native to southeastern United States. Makes an attractive lawn near coast; tolerates salty soil, heat, wear. Color is close to that of bluegrass, and lawns are pest free. In interior climates, it develops tough stems that turn brown after cutting. Mow to ¾ in. with a reel mower and feed only between late October and early May. Usually sold as sod, under names like Adalayd and Excalibre.

PASQUE FLOWER. See ANEMONE pulsatilla   p. 151

PASSIFLORA

PASSION VINE

Passifloraceae

EVERGREEN, SEMIEVERGREEN, OR DECIDUOUS VINE

✓ ZONES VARY BY SPECIES

☼ FULL SUN

● MODERATE WATER

Passiflora alatocaerulea

Climb by tendrils to 20–30 ft. Name comes from manner in which flower parts symbolize elements of the passion of Christ: the lacy crown could be a halo or crown of thorns; the five stamens, the five wounds; the ten petal-like parts, the ten faithful apostles. ▸

Vigorous, likely to overgrow and tangle; to keep plant open and prevent buildup of dead inner tangle, prune annually after second year, cutting excess branches back to base or juncture with another branch. Tolerant of many soils. Favorite food of caterpillars of gulf fritillary butterfly.

Use vines on trellises or walls for their vigor and bright, showy flowers; or use as soil-holding bank cover. In cold-winter climates, use as greenhouse or house plants, training plants on a trellis or winding them on hoops of wire for wreath effect.

P. alatocaerulea (P. pfordtii). Evergreen or semievergreen. Zones 12–24; root-hardy perennial in Zones 5–9. Hybrid between *P. alata*, *P. caerulea*. Best known, most widely planted, probably least subject to caterpillars. Leaves 3 in. long, three-lobed. Fragrant 3½–4-in. flowers, white shaded pink and lavender. Crown deep blue or purple. Blooms all summer. In colder areas, give it a warm place out of wind, against wall or under overhang. Mulch roots in winter. Forms no fruit.

P. caerulea. BLUE CROWN PASSION FLOWER. Evergreen or semievergreen. Zones 12–24; root-hardy perennial in Zones 5–9. Leaves smaller than those of *P. alatocaerulea,* five-lobed. Flowers smaller, greenish white; crown white and purple. Edible small, oval fruit with orange rind and red seeds.

P. edulis. PASSION FRUIT. Semievergreen. Zones 15–17, 21–24. Leaves three lobed, deeply toothed, light yellow green. Flowers white with white-and-purple crown, 2 in. across. Fruit produced in spring and fall: deep purple, fragrant, 3 in. long, delicious in beverages, fruit salads, sherbets. 'Nancy Garrison' is a hardier version. There is a yellow-fruited variety.

P. 'Incense'. Zones 5–24. Perennial. Hybrid between *P. incarnata* and an Argentinian species. Hardy to 0°F, even holding its foliage through short cold spells—deciduous otherwise. Flowers are 5 in. wide, violet with lighter crown, scented like sweet peas. Egg-shaped, 2-in. fruit; when ripe, it turns from olive to yellow green and then drops. Fragrant, tasty pulp.

P. jamesonii. Evergreen. Zones 14–24; especially good in Zones 17, 24. Glossy, three-lobed leaves. Long-tubed (to 4-in.) flowers are salmon to coral, profuse all summer. Fast bank, fence cover. This and similar plants are sold as 'Coral Seas'.

P. 'Lavender Lady'. Evergreen. Zones 16–24. Profuse show of 4-in. lavender purple flowers with deep violet crown of filaments.

P. mollissima. BANANA PASSION VINE. Evergreen. Zones 12–24. Soft green foliage; leaves three lobed, deeply toothed. Long-tubed pink to rose flowers 3 in. across. Yellow, 4–6-in.-long fruit. Rampant growth makes it a good bank cover, but a problem if planted with trees, shrubs.

P. vitifolia. Evergreen. Zones 16, 17, 23, 24. Grapelike 6-in. deep green leaves set off bright red flowers 3½ in. long. Summer blooming.

PASSION FRUIT. See PASSIFLORA edulis	**p. 402**
PASSION VINE. See PASSIFLORA	**p. 401**

PAULOWNIA tomentosa (P. imperialis)

EMPRESS TREE
Bignoniaceae
DECIGUOUS TREE
✿ ALL ZONES
☼ FULL SUN
● BEST WITH SOME SUMMER WATER

Paulownia tomentosa

Young trees may need protection in Zones 1–3; expect flowers only in Zones 4–9, 11–24. Somewhat similar to catalpa in growth habit, leaves. Fast growth to 40–50 ft. with nearly equal spread. Heavy trunk and heavy, nearly horizontal branches. Foliage gives tropical effect; leaves are light green, heart shaped, 5–12 in. long, 4–7 in. wide. If tree is cut back annually or every other year, it will grow as billowy foliage mass with giant-size leaves up to 2 ft.; however, such pruning will reduce flower production.

Brown flower buds the size of small olives form in autumn and persist over winter; they open before the leaves in early spring to form 6–12-in.-long upright clusters of trumpet-shaped, 2-in.-long, fragrant flowers of lilac blue with darker spotting and yellow stripes inside. Flowers are followed by 1½–2-in.-long seed capsules shaped like tops; these remain on tree with flower buds. Does not flower well where winters are very cold (buds freeze) or very mild (buds may drop off). In strong winds, leaves will be damaged. Bark tends to sunburn in Zones 7–14, 18–21. Plant where falling flowers and leaves are not objectionable. Not a tree to garden under because of dense shade, surface roots.

PAXISTIMA (Pachystima, Pachistima)

Celastraceae
EVERGREEN SHRUBS
✿ ZONES 1–10, 14–21
☼ ◑ FULL SUN NEAR COAST, PART SHADE INLAND
● ● MODERATE WATER; AMPLE IN HOT INTERIORS

Paxistima canbyi

Low growing with small, shiny, leathery leaves and insignificant flowers. Hardiness and compact habit make them useful as low hedges, edgings, ground cover. Best in well-drained soil.

P. canbyi. Native to mountains of eastern United States. Makes mat 9–12 in. tall. Narrow (¼-in.-wide), ¼–1-in.-long leaves, dark green turning to bronze in fall and winter.

P. myrsinites. OREGON BOXWOOD. Native to mountains in West. Dense growth to 2–4 ft. (usually much less); easily kept lower by pruning. More compact in sun. Larger leaves than *P. canbyi.*

PEA

Fabaceae (Leguminosae)
COOL-SEASON ANNUALS
✿ ALL ZONES
☼ FULL SUN
● REGULAR WATER

Pea

Easy crop to grow when conditions are right, and delicious when freshly picked. Peas need coolness and humidity and must be planted at just the right time. If you have space and don't mind the bother, grow tall (vining) peas on trellises, strings, or screen; tall peas reach 6 ft. or more and bear heavily. Bush types are more commonly grown in home gardens; they require no support. A good tall variety is 'Alderman'. Fine bush varieties are 'Green Arrow', 'Little Marvel', 'Morse's Progress No. 9', 'Freezonian', and 'Blue Bantam'. An unusually good vegetable (and one indispensable to oriental cooking) is edible-pod snow or sugar pea; 'Mammoth Melting Sugar' is a tall vining variety, 'Dwarf Gray Sugar' a bushy one. 'Sugar Snap' is an edible-pod pea with full complement of full-size peas inside; instead of shelling, you merely string and snap, just like green beans.

Peas need nonacid soil that is water retentive but fast draining. They are hardy and should be planted just as early in spring as ground can be worked. Where winters are mild and spring days quickly become too warm for peas, plant October–February, the later times applying where winters are coldest. Sow 2 in. deep in light soil, shallower (½–1 in.) in heavy soil or in winter. Moisten ground thoroughly before planting; do not water again until seedlings have broken through surface. Leave 2 ft. between rows and thin seedlings to stand 2 in. apart. Successive plantings several days apart will lengthen bearing season, but don't plant so late that summer heat will overtake ripening peas; most are ready to bear in 60–70 days.

Plants need little fertilizer, but if soil is very light give them one application of complete fertilizer. If weather turns warm and dry, supply water in furrows; overhead water encourages mildew. Provide support for climbing peas as soon as tendrils form. When peas begin to mature, pick all pods that are ready; if seeds ripen, plant will stop producing. Vines are brittle; steady them with one hand while picking with the other. Above all, shell and cook (or freeze) peas right after picking.

PEACH and NECTARINE

Rosaceae

DECIDUOUS FRUIT TREES

ZONES VARY BY VARIETY

FULL SUN

IN HOT SUMMERS, WATER WHILE FRUIT IS FORMING

SEE CHART NEXT PAGE

Peach

Peach (*Prunus persica*) and nectarine (*P. p. nucipersica*) trees look alike and have the same general cultural needs. Fruit of nectarines differ from those of peaches in two respects: they have smooth skins and, in some varieties, a slightly different flavor. In terms of landscaping and fruit growing, there are four kinds of peaches: flowering peaches, fruiting peaches, flowering-fruiting (dual-purpose) peaches, and genetic dwarf fruiting peaches that form large bushes. Here we consider the three groups of fruiting peaches. For strictly flowering peaches, see *Prunus*.

FRUITING PEACHES

A regular fruiting peach tree grows fast to 25 ft. high and as wide; well-pruned trees are usually less than 15 ft. tall and 15–18 ft. wide. The peach starts bearing large crops when 3–4 years old and reaches peak productivity at 8–12 years.

Peaches do best with some chilling in winter. The chilling requirement is usually given as the number of hours below 45°F a tree must experience during its dormant season to grow and bear satisfactorily. Only specially selected varieties do well in extremely mild-winter areas. Lack of winter chilling results in delayed foliation, little fruit, and eventual death of tree. The high desert satisfies chilling requirements, but late frosts make early-blooming varieties risky. Few are satisfactory in mild-winter areas of low desert. Peach trees also need clear, hot weather during the growing season; where spring is cool and rainy, they set few flowers, pollinate poorly.

Peaches require good drainage, a regular fertilizing program, and heavier pruning than any other fruit trees. When planting a bare-root tree, cut back to 2 ft. above ground. New branches will form below cut. After first year's growth, select three well-placed branches for scaffold limbs. Remove all other branches. On mature trees, in each dormant season, cut off two-thirds of previous year's growth by removing two of every three branches formed that year; or head back each branch to one-third its length. Or head back some branches and cut out others. Peach trees can be trained as espaliers.

Peaches and nectarines tend to form too much fruit even with good pruning. When fruit are about 1 in. wide, remove (thin) some of the excess. If growth becomes weak and leaves yellowish, feed with nitrogen fertilizer.

Protect all kinds of peaches and nectarines from peach leaf curl and peach tree borer. Two dormant sprayings, the first in November and the second in January before buds swell, will control leaf curl. Use fixed copper, Bordeaux mixture, or lime sulfur. Sprays combining oil and lime sulfur or fixed copper will control both scale insects and peach leaf curl. (See page 558 for other peach leaf curl controls.) Borers attack at or just below ground level. Pull away soil to expose 2–3 in. of roots. Spray with dursban every 3 weeks from early June to mid-August.

FLOWERING-FRUITING PEACHES

These dual-purpose peaches were developed in Southern California for regional conditions but are widely adapted and will grow in Zones 7–10, 12–22. Most likely to succeed in Zone 13 is 'Daily News Four Star'.

'Daily News Four Star'. Salmon pink double flowers. Highly colored red freestone with white flesh. Midseason.

'Saturn'. Large, deep pink double flowers. High-quality yellow-fleshed freestone. Midseason.

NATURAL DWARF PEACHES AND NECTARINES

Most dwarf fruit trees are grafts of standard varieties on dwarfing rootstocks. In the case of peaches and nectarines, the best dwarfs are genetic (natural) dwarf varieties. Look for the following varieties. All have medium-size fruit unless noted.

'Bonanza'. Peach. Blooms and bears fruit at 2 ft. high, 2 years old. Will eventually reach 6 ft. Semidouble rose pink flowers. Early red-blushed, yellow-fleshed freestone of bland flavor. Very low chilling requirement.

'Empress'. Peach. Semidwarf, reaching 4–5 ft. Pink to red skin. Yellow-fleshed clingstone of fine flavor. Early August.

'Garden Delight'. Nectarine. Slow to 5–6 ft. Large, yellow-fleshed freestone. Midseason.

'Garden Gold'. Peach. To 5–6 ft. Large, yellow-fleshed freestone. Late midseason.

'Golden Glory'. Peach. To 5 ft. Yellow-fleshed freestone. Golden skin with red blush. Heavy bearer. Mid- to late August.

'Golden Prolific'. Nectarine. Slow growing to 5 ft. Yellow-fleshed freestone. Yellow skin mottled with orange red. Midseason.

'Mono'. Nectarine. To 6 ft. Double pink flowers. Yellow-fleshed freestone. Two weeks earlier than 'Golden Prolific'.

'Nectar Babe'. Nectarine. High-quality yellow-fleshed freestone, dark red skin. Needs pollinator (any other dwarf peach or nectarine). Midseason.

> ### ALL THOSE PEACH VARIETIES DO ENTICE
> But many western gardens don't have space for a small peach orchard. Solution: plant three or four varieties in a single hole. Prune the new bare-root trees so that each retains just one primary branch and point those branches outward as you plant the trees in the hole.

'Nectarina'. Nectarine. To 5–6 ft. Skin deep red and yellow. Orange-fleshed freestone ripening in late July.

'Necta Zee'. Nectarine. High-quality yellow-fleshed semifreestone. Ripens in June.

'Pix Zee'. Peach. High-quality yellow-fleshed semifreestone. June.

'Red Sunset'. Nectarine. To 5 ft. Large, red skin, yellow flesh. Freestone. Self-fertile. June bearer.

'Sensation'. Peach. Yellow-fleshed freestone. To 6–8 ft. Early.

'Silver Prolific'. Nectarine. Slow growing to 5–7 ft. Yellow-fleshed freestone. Light yellow skin blushed red. Rich flavor. Midseason.

'Southern Belle'. Nectarine. To 5 ft. Yellow-fleshed freestone. Low chilling requirement. Midseason.

'Southern Flame'. Peach. To 5 ft. Yellow with red blush, yellow flesh. Freestone. Moderately low chilling requirement. Early midseason.

'Southern Rose'. Peach. To 5 ft. Yellow blushed red. Freestone. Needs little chilling. Midseason.

'Southern Sweet'. Peach. To 5 ft. Medium-size yellow fruit of good flavor. Freestone. Heavy bearer. Fairly low chilling requirement. Early ripening.

'Sunbonnet'. Nectarine. To 5 ft. Red skin, yellow flesh. Clingstone. Fairly low chilling requirement. Early midseason.

'Yosemite'. Peach. To 5–6 ft. Double pink flowers. Yellow flesh. Freestone. Ripens early, same time as 'Mono' nectarine.

PEANUT

Fabaceae (Leguminosae)

SUMMER ANNUALS

ALL ZONES

FULL SUN

REGULAR WATER UNTIL 2 WEEKS BEFORE HARVEST

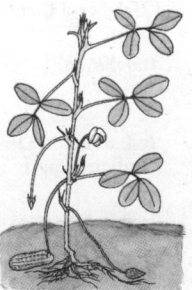

Peanut

Best production where summers are long and warm and soil is not acid. Tender to frost but worth growing even in cool regions. Plants resemble small sweet pea bushes 10–20 in. high. After

▶ page 407

PEACH and NECTARINE

NAME	ZONES	FRUIT	COMMENTS
PEACHES			
'Autumn Gold'	3, 6–9, 14–16	Medium to large yellow freestone. Yellow skin striped red. Good quality. Ripens late Sept.	Keeps well if picked firm-ripe
'Babcock'	15, 16, 19–24	White freestone, small to medium. Sweet flavor with some tang. Early	Needs little winter chilling. Old-timer
'Bonita'	15–24	Large yellow freestone with medium blush, firm flesh, fine flavor. Ripens in midseason	Bred for mild-winter areas
'Desertgold'	8, 9, 12, 13, 23	Medium-size yellow semiclingstone of good quality. Late Apr. or early May in low desert, early June in San Joaquin Valley	Very early bloom rules it out wherever spring frosts are likely
'Early Elberta' ('**Improved Elberta'**, '**Gleason Elberta'**, '**Lemon Elberta'**)	2–11, 14, 15	Superior in color and flavor to 'Elberta'. Freestone. Ripens 1 week earlier than 'Elberta'	Needs somewhat less heat and less winter chill than 'Elberta'; less subject to fruit drop. Thin well for good-size fruit
'Elberta'	1–3, 6–11, 14	Medium to large yellow freestone, skin blushed red, high quality. Midseason (later in Zone 6)	Needs good amount of winter chilling, high summer heat to ripen to full flavor
'Fairtime'	8, 9, 12, 13, 18–23	Large freestone, yellow blushed bright red. Good flavor. Ripens late	
'Fay Elberta' ('**Gold Medal'** in Northwest)	2, 3, 6–11, 14, 15, 18, 19	More colorful than 'Elberta', keeps a little better. Yellow-fleshed freestone. Ripens with 'Elberta'	Has large, handsome single flowers. Thin it well
'Flamecrest'	7–9, 14, 15, 18	Large freestone, yellow blushed red. Good flavor. Midseason	Vigorous tree
'Flavorcrest'	7–9, 14, 15, 18	Large, red over yellow, yellow flesh, semifreestone	Attractive flowers, moderately vigorous
'Flordaprince'	13, 18–24	Very early yellow peach; ripens late Apr., early May	Needs only 150 hours of chilling. Fruit becomes freestone when fully ripe
'Fortyniner'	5–9, 14–16, 18	Large yellow freestone. Bright red blush over yellow. Good to excellent flavor. Early midseason	Resembles 'J. H. Hale', the parent; about 1 week earlier
'Frost'	4–6	Medium-size freestone with red-blushed skin, yellow flesh	Resistant to peach leaf curl
'Gold Dust'	6–9, 11, 14–16	Yellow freestone, small to medium. High blush, good quality. Early	Quality best in Zones 8, 9, 14–18
'Golden Jubilee'	2, 3, 5, 6	Medium-size yellow freestone of fair flavor. Tender. Ripens 3 weeks before 'Elberta'	Good early peach in Zones 2, 3
'Halberta' ('**Hal-Berta Giant'**)	1–3, 6–11, 14, 18	Very large yellow freestone, very smooth skinned. Ripens with 'Elberta'	Needs pollinating; any other peach except 'J. H. Hale' or 'Indian Free' will do
'Halehaven'	1–3, 6–11, 14–16	Medium to large, highly colored yellow freestone. Ripens 2 weeks before 'Elberta'	Fine large yellow freestone to use fresh or canned. Flower and leaf buds are very winter hardy
'Indian Blood Cling' ('**Indian Cling'**)	1–3, 6–11, 14–16	Medium-size clingstone. Red skin. Flesh firm, yellow streaked red. Late	Old variety with small but devoted band of enthusiasts. Good for preserves
'Indian Free'	7–11, 14–16	Large, round, yellow freestone, deep red at pit. Tart until fully ripe. Late midseason. Another old favorite with a few loyal supporters	Needs pollinating by any other peach

P

PEACH and NECTARINE

NAME	ZONES	FRUIT	COMMENTS
PEACHES			
'J. H. Hale'	1–3, 7–11, 14–16	Very large, highly colored yellow freestone of high quality. Fine keeper. Ripens with 'Elberta'	Needs pollinating by any other peach except 'Halberta', 'Indian Blood Cling'
'July Elberta' ('Kim Elberta')	2, 3, 6–12, 14–16, 18, 19	Medium to large, yellow-fleshed freestone of high quality. Ripens a month before 'Elberta'	Prolific bearer. May need extra thinning to get size
'Melba'	2, 3, 10, 11	Large white freestone. Pale yellow skin. Sweet, juicy. Long ripening season	Sets fruit well in cold, unsettled spring weather
'Nectar'	7–11, 14–16	Medium to large white freestone of excellent flavor. Early midseason	Those who fancy white peaches consider it the best
'O'Henry'	7–10, 14–16, 18	Large yellow freestone of fine flavor. Skin blushed red, flesh streaked red. Ripens early Aug.	Good commercial and home garden tree
'Orange Cling' ('Miller Cling')	1–3, 7–12, 14–16, 18	Large, late clingstone with firm, deep yellow flesh	A favorite for home canning
'Polly'	1–3, 10	Medium-size white freestone. White skin blushed red. Juicy, excellent flavor. Late midseason	Tree and buds very hardy to cold
'Ranger'	3, 5–9, 14–16, 18	Medium to large, highly colored freestone, yellow fleshed. Good flavor. Early midseason, a month before 'Elberta'	Heavy fruit bud set. High yielder. Excellent early canner
'Redglobe'	3, 6–11, 14–16	Highly colored, firm-fleshed yellow freestone of good flavor. Three weeks before 'Elberta'	Good for canning or freezing. Sometimes sets light crop in Zone 6
'Redhaven'	3, 5, 12, 14–16	Brightly blushed yellow freestone. Long ripening season permits numerous pickings. Ripens 3–4 weeks ahead of 'Elberta'	Colors up early, so test for ripeness. Thin early and well. One of best for planting. 'Early Redhaven' ripens 2 weeks earlier
'Redskin'	1–3, 6–12, 14–16	Medium to large yellow freestone. Heavy red blush. Excellent quality fresh, canned, or frozen. Midseason	Productive tree. Needs only a little less winter chilling than 'Elberta'
'Reliance'	4–9	Yellow skin blushed dull medium red; soft yellow flesh of good flavor. Freestone. Ripens with 'Redhaven'	Has outstanding cold hardiness
'Rio Grande'	8–10, 15, 18–20	Medium to large yellow freestone. Red blush. Good quality. Early June	Medium-size productive tree with showy flowers
'Rio Oso Gem'	3, 7–9, 14, 15	Medium to large, yellow-fleshed freestone of excellent flavor. A week later than 'Elberta'	Small tree. Not vigorous. One of best
'Rubidoux'	18, 20	Medium to large yellow freestone with firm flesh. Good keeper. Late midseason	Developed specifically for Zones 18 and 20
'Shanghai'	14–16, 18–24	Medium-size white freestone. Red blush. Soft, juicy, very sweet flesh. Late midseason	Vigorous tree. Fruit too soft for canning, freezing. Very fine flavor
'Springcrest'	4–9	Small to medium, bright red over yellow. Good flavor	Semifreestone when fully ripe. Good early-ripening variety
'Springtime'	18–23	White semiclingstone of high color, mild flavor. Ripens late May, early June	One of earliest; sweet and juicy
'Strawberry Cling'	7–9, 14–16, 18–20	Large, creamy white marbled red. Clingstone. Flesh white, juicy, richly flavored. Early midseason	Favorite with home canners

P

PEACH and NECTARINE

NAME	ZONES	FRUIT	COMMENTS
PEACHES			
'Strawberry Free'	7–9, 14–16, 18–20	Medium-size white freestone. Medium blush, firm flesh, excellent flavor. Early midseason	Old favorite of those who like white peaches
'Summerset'	7–9, 14–16, 18, 19	Large yellow freestone with attractive red blush. Late	Firm flesh makes it good for canning, freezing. Vigorous, productive tree
'Tejon'	18–22	Small to medium semifreestone, very juicy, yellow flesh. Very early	Very low chilling requirement
'Tropi-berta'	8, 9, 14–16, 18–24	Large yellow freestone with red blush. Juicy; good flavor. Late midseason	Needs somewhat less chilling than 'Elberta'
'Ventura'	18–24	Medium-size, attractive yellow freestone. Very smooth skin. Midseason	Developed especially for Zones 18–24
'Veteran'	4–6	Medium-size yellow freestone of good flavor. Ripens 10 days earlier than 'Elberta'	Resembles 'Elberta' but rounder, less fuzzy. Sets fruit under adverse conditions
'White Heath Cling' ('Heath')	7–11, 14–16	Medium to large, firm-fleshed white clingstone of excellent flavor. Late	Distinctive flavor; a favorite for home canning
NECTARINES			
'Fantasia'	3, 7–9, 14–16, 18–22	Large freestone, bright yellow and red. Firm flesh. Ripens mid-July	Relatively low chilling requirement
'Flame Kist'	7–9, 14–16, 18–22	Large clingstone, yellow blushed red. Late	Resistant to cracking; thin out tree to bring sunshine in on fruit and improve color
'Flavortop'	3, 7–9, 14–16, 18, 19	Large freestone, red with yellow undertone. Good	Vigorous, productive tree
'Gold Mine'	7–9, 14–16, 18–24	Red-blushed, white-fleshed freestone. Late midseason. Tough skin, firm flesh; excellent for frozen halves	Low winter chilling requirement. Excellent, distinctive flavor
'Heavenly White'	7–9, 14–16, 18	Very large white-fleshed freestone of especially fine flavor. Midseason	Has been called a connoisseur's delight
'Independence'	7–9, 14–16, 18, 19	Large red freestone with yellow flesh of good flavor. Early	Moderately vigorous, productive tree
'Panamint'	7–9, 14–16, 18–24	Freestone with bright red skin, yellow flesh. Very good flavor. Midseason	Very low chilling requirement
'Pioneer'	7–9, 14–16, 18–23	Yellow overlaid with red. Flesh yellow touched with red. Freestone. Rich, distinctive flavor. Midseason	Large pink flowers
'Silver Lode'	7–9, 14–16, 18–20	White-fleshed freestone with scarlet-and-white skin. Early	Low chilling requirement
'Stanwick'	7–9, 14, 15	Greenish white shaded purple-red. White-fleshed freestone. Late	Excellent flavor. Good for freezing
'Stribling Giant Free'	7–9, 11	Large, highly colored, yellow-fleshed freestone of high quality. Early midseason	Beautiful fruit
'Stribling White Free'	7–9, 11, 14–16	Large, white blushed red. Sweet white flesh. Early	Good home orchard tree
'Sunred'	18–23	Medium-size, bright red semifreestone. Yellow flesh, good flavor. Very early	Best in warm-winter areas

P

bright yellow flowers fade, a "peg" (shootlike structure) develops at each flower's base, grows down into soil and develops peanuts underground. Soil must be light textured to admit penetration by pegs. Sandy soil is ideal.

Buy seeds (unroasted peanuts) from mail-order seed firms. Plant when soil warms up, setting nuts 2 in. deep in rows 3 ft. apart. Space shelled 'Jumbo Virginia' seeds 10 in. apart, 'Spanish' 4 in. apart (unshelled seeds of either variety 20 in. apart). Fertilize at planting time. In 110–120 days after planting, foliage yellows and plants are ready to dig; loosen soil, then pull up plants. Cure peanuts on vines in warm, airy place out of sunlight for 2–3 weeks, then strip from plants.

PEANUT CACTUS. See CHAMAECEREUS sylvestri　　　p. 220

PEAR (Pyrus communis)

Rosaceae

DECIDUOUS FRUIT TREES

☘ ZONES 1–11, 14–18

☼ FULL SUN

◐ ● MODERATE WATER DURING GROWING SEASON

▶ SEE CHART NEXT PAGE

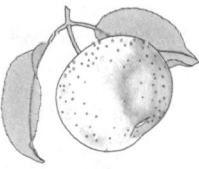
Pear

Pyramidal trees with strongly vertical branching; grow 30–40 ft. tall, sometimes more. Long lived. Leaves are leathery, glossy, bright green. Clustered white flowers are handsome in early spring. For ornamental relatives, see *Pyrus*.

Take damp, heavy soil better than most fruit trees; resistant to oak root fungus. Good looking enough for garden use and need little pruning when mature, but require spraying for codling moth, aphids, and other pests. Fireblight, which makes entire branches die back quickly, can be a serious problem. Cut out blighted branches well below dead parts; wash pruning tools with disinfectant between each cut.

Train trees early to good framework of main branches; then prune lightly to keep good form, eliminate crowding branches. Pears on dwarfing understock are good small garden trees, excellent espaliers.

PEAR, ORIENTAL or ASIAN

Rosaceae

DECIDUOUS TREES

☘ ALL ZONES

☼ FULL SUN

◐ ● MODERATE WATER DURING GROWING SEASON

Asian Pear

Descendants of two Asiatic species: *Pyrus pyrifolia (P. serotina)* and *P. ussuriensis*. Fruit differs from European pears in being generally round, gritty, crisp, and firm to hard. Asian pears are often called apple pears because of roundness and crispness, but they are not hybrids of these two fruits. All need pollination by a second variety or by 'Bartlett' European pear.

BEST WAY TO EAT AN ASIAN PEAR?

Peel thinly; slice in thin, crosswise pieces; and munch off the flesh around the core. This is a practical way to eat the entire fruit except the small, gritty core. Add a dash of salt or a squeeze of lime.

Because of their unpearlike texture and taste, fresh Asian pears should not be compared to European varieties, but they're especially valuable for cooking and mixing with other fruits and vegetables in salads. Culture is same as for other pears. Varieties available include 'Chojuro', 'Hosui',

'Ishiiwase', 'Kikusui', 'Niitaka', 'Nijisseiki' ('Twentieth Century'), 'Okusan-kichi' ('Late Korean'), 'Shinko', 'Shinseiki', 'Tsu Li', 'Ya Li', and 'Yakumo'.

PEARL BUSH. See EXOCHORDA　　　p. 291
PEASHRUB. See CARAGANA　　　p. 206
PECAN. See CARYA illinoensis　　　p. 209

PELARGONIUM

GERANIUM

Geraniaceae

SHRUBBY PERENNIALS

☘ ZONES 8, 9, 12–24; OR SUMMER OR INDOOR PLANT

☼ ◑ FULL SUN ON COAST, LIGHT SHADE INLAND

◐ ● WATER NEEDS VARY BY TYPE

Pelargonium domesticum

Although "geranium" is used as a common name for *Pelargonium*, botanically speaking, it's not really accurate. To the botanist, pelargoniums are evergreen or shrubby perennials that endure light frosts but not hard freezes and have slightly asymmetrical flowers in clusters. Most come from South Africa. A geranium, on the other hand, is one of many annual or perennial plants, most from the Northern Hemisphere, having symmetrical flowers borne singly or in clusters; some are weeds, some valued perennial border or rock garden plants.

To gardeners the pelargonium is a Lady Washington (Martha Washington) pelargonium. A geranium is an ivy geranium, a common geranium, or a scented geranium, all of which are species or varieties of *Pelargonium*. Gardeners also use the word "geranium" for both true geraniums and true pelargoniums.

Most garden geraniums can be divided among three species of *Pelargonium: P. domesticum*, Lady Washington pelargonium; *P. hortorum*, common geranium (this group also includes variegated forms usually referred to as fancy-leafed or colored-leafed geraniums); and *P. peltatum*, ivy geranium. In addition, many other species have scented leaves.

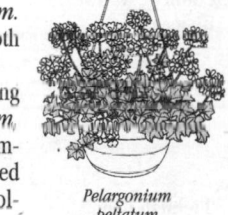
Pelargonium peltatum

Zones 17, 24 are ideal climates; next best are Zones 15, 16, 22, 23; possible but not as easy are Zones 8, 9, 12–14, 18–21. Elsewhere, a pelargonium or geranium is a summer bedding plant or house plant.

All geraniums do well in pots. Common geraniums grow well in garden beds; Lady Washington pelargoniums are also planted in beds but tend to get rangy. Some varieties of Lady Washington are used in hanging baskets. Ivy geraniums are good in hanging containers, in raised beds, and as a bank or ground cover. Use scented geraniums in close-up situations—in pots or in ground (in mild areas). For good bloom on potted geranium indoors, place it in a sunny window or in the brightest light possible.

Plant in any good, fast-draining soil. If soil is alkaline, add peat moss or nitrogen-fortified ground bark or sawdust to planting bed. Keep common and scented geraniums growing in ground slightly on dry side, watering when soil dries to about 1 in. below surface. In warm weather, deeply water Lady Washington pelargoniums once a week. Water ivy geraniums every 10 days–2 weeks. Geraniums of any kind in good garden soil need little feeding; if in light sandy soil, feed 2 or 3 times during active growing season.

Pelargonium crispum

Remove faded geranium flowers regularly to encourage new bloom. Pinch growing tips in early growth to force side branches. Prune after last frost, using tip cuttings to start new plants. With proper pinching and support, you can raise standard ("tree") or espalier geraniums. Geraniums in pots bloom best when somewhat pot-bound. When repotting, move plant to next larger pot. In warm weather, water common geraniums in pots

P

PEAR

NAME	CLIMATE ADAPTABILITY	FRUIT	COMMENTS
'Anjou', 'd'Anjou' ('Beurre d'Anjou')	A favorite late variety in Northwest, Northern California mountains	Medium to large, round or short necked, yellow to russeted yellow. Fine flavor, late ripening. Ripens after cold storage	Tree upright and vigorous. Tie down limbs for more consistent bearing. Moderately susceptible to fireblight. 'Red d'Anjou' is a red-skinned selection
'Bartlett'	Widely adaptable but not at its best in mild winters. In Southern California will succeed at high elevations or on cold canyon or valley floors	Medium to large, with short but definite neck. Thin skinned, yellow or slightly blushed, very sweet and tender. Standard summer pear of fruit markets	Generally sets fruit without pollination, but may require pollinator in cool California coastal areas and Northwest. Any variety except 'Seckel' will do. Tree form not the best; somewhat subject to fireblight. Nevertheless a good home variety
'Bosc' ('Beurre Bosc', 'Golden Russet')	Best in Northwest or at high altitudes farther south	Medium to large, quite long necked, interesting and attractive in form. Heavy russeting on green or yellow ground color. Fine flavor. Midseason. Firm flesh holds shape when cooked. Even though flesh is firm, fruit is juicy eaten fresh	Large, upright, vigorous tree. Needs pruning in youth. Highly susceptible to fireblight. Ripen fruit at room temperature after cold storage
'Cascade'	Pacific Northwest	Large, roundish; outstanding flavor. Late	Does not need cold storage to ripen
'Clapp Favorite'	Very hardy to cold; good garden tree in Northwest, intermountain areas	Resembles 'Bartlett'. Early, soft, sweet	Tree productive and shapely. Good foliage; highly susceptible to fireblight. 'Starkcrimson' and 'Super Red Clapp' are related red-skinned varieties
'Comice' ('Doyenne du Comice', 'Royal Riviera')	At its best in Hood River and Medford regions of Oregon and Santa Clara County, California	Large to very large, roundish to pear-shaped, thick-skinned, russeted greenish yellow, sometimes blushed. Superb flavor and texture. Late	Big, vigorous tree but slow to reach bearing age. Moderately susceptible to fireblight. Bears well only when soil, climate, and exposure are right. Bears better in Northwest with pollinator. Ripens best after cold storage
'Fan Stil'	Low winter chilling requirements, high tolerance to heat and cold. Grown in high desert	Medium-size, yellow with slight red blush. Crisp, juicy. Aug.	Vigorous, upright growth. Highly resistant to fireblight. Consistent bearer
'Flemish Beauty'	Grown in Northwest	Medium to large, roundish, yellow with pronounced red blush. Fine flavor. Early midseason	Large, productive, very hardy tree. Fruit best ripened off tree
'Flordahome'	Same as 'Fan Stil'	Small to medium, light green. Juicy, not too gritty. Early	Resistant to fireblight. With 'Hood', has lowest chilling requirement. Pollinate with 'Hood'
'Garber'	Same as 'Fan Stil'	Resembles 'Kieffer' but more rounded in form, lighter in color. Quality similar	Tree moderately vigorous, somewhat resistant to fireblight
'Hood'	Same as 'Fan Stil'	Large, yellow-green. Ripens a little later than 'Flordahome'	Vigorous tree, resistant to fireblight. Pollinate with 'Flordahome'
'Kieffer'	Same as 'Fan Stil'	Medium to large, oval, greenish yellow blushed dark red. Gritty in texture, fair in flavor. Best picked from tree and ripened at 65°F. Late	Asian pear hybrid; quite resistant to fireblight. Good pear for extreme climates
'Le Conte'	Same as 'Fan Stil'	Resembles 'Kieffer'. Roundish, gritty, late	Most tolerant to summer heat; somewhat resistant to fireblight
'Max-Red Bartlett'	Same as 'Bartlett'	Like 'Bartlett' except bright red in skin color and somewhat sweeter	Red color extends to twigs and tints leaves. Needs pollinator in Northwest
'Monterrey'	Same as 'Fan Stil'. Originated in Monterrey, Mexico	Large, apple-shaped, yellow skin. Flavor good; texture not too gritty. Aug.–Sept.	Probably cross between an Asian and a European pear
'Moonglow'	Wide climate tolerance	Somewhat like 'Bartlett' in looks. Juicy, soft. Flavor good. Ripens 2 weeks before 'Bartlett'	Tree upright, vigorous, very heavy bearer. Very resistant to fireblight

P

PEAR

NAME	CLIMATE ADAPTABILITY	FRUIT	COMMENTS
'Seckel' **('Sugar')**	Widely adaptable	Very small, very sweet, aromatic. Roundish to pear-shaped, yellow-brown. Flesh granular. Early midseason. A favorite for home gardens, preserving	Tree fairly resistant to fireblight, highly productive
'Sensation Red Bartlett'	Same as 'Bartlett'	Same fruit as 'Bartlett', but with bright red skin over most of fruit	Medium-size tree, less vigorous than 'Bartlett'
'Sure Crop'	Prolonged bloom period makes it safe bearer where spring frosts come late	Resembles 'Bartlett' in looks and flavor. Bears Aug.–Sept.	Consistent annual bearer. Fairly resistant to fireblight
'Winter Nelis'	Northwest; mountains, cold valley floors in Southern California	Small to medium, roundish, dull green or yellowish, rough. Very fine flavor. Late	Very fine keeper, fine for baking, but not attractive pear. Tree moderately susceptible to fireblight. Needs pollinator

every other day; Lady Washington pelargoniums may need daily watering. Tobacco budworm may be a problem in some areas. Control aphids and whiteflies on Lady Washington pelargoniums with all-purpose spray. Use a miticide to control red spider mites on ivy geraniums.

P. domesticum. LADY WASHINGTON PELARGONIUM, MARTHA WASHINGTON GERANIUM, REGAL GERANIUM. Erect or somewhat spreading, to 3 ft. More rangy than common geranium. Leaves heart shaped to kidney shaped, dark green, 2–4 in. wide, with crinkled margins, unequal sharp teeth. Large, showy flowers 2 in. or more across in loose, rounded clusters, in white and many shades of pink, red, lavender, purple, with brilliant blotches and markings of darker colors. Blooms in spring and summer.

Pelargonium graveolens

P. hortorum. COMMON GERANIUM, GARDEN GERANIUM. Most popular, widely grown. Shrubby, succulent stemmed, to 3 ft. or more; older plants grown in the open (in mild areas) become woody. Round or kidney-shaped leaves are velvety and hairy, soft to the touch, with edges indistinctly lobed and scallop toothed; most varieties show zone of deeper color just inside leaf margin. Some are plain green; others (color-leafed or fancy-leafed varieties) have zones, borders, or splashes of brown, gold, red, white, or green in various combinations. Some also have highly attractive flowers. Single or double flowers are flatter and smaller than those of Lady Washington, but clusters bear many more blossoms. Flowers are usually in solid colors. Many varieties in white and shades of pink, rose, red, orange, and violet. Blooms spring through fall.

Pelargonium hortorum

There are also dwarf-growing, cactus-flowered, and other novelty kinds. Tough, attractive geraniums for outdoor bedding can be grown from seed, flowering the first summer. Widely available strains are Diamond and Elite (quick to reach bloom stage, compact, need no pinching), Orbit (distinct leaf zoning; broad, rounded flower clusters), and Sprinter.

P. peltatum. IVY GERANIUM. Trailing plants to 2–3 ft. or longer. Leaves rather succulent, glossy bright green, 2–3 in. across, ivylike, with pointed lobes. Five to ten, 1-in. flowers in rounded clusters are white, pink, rose, red, and lavender, single or double. Upper petals may be blotched or striped. Many named varieties. Flat-grown plants for ground cover are usually labeled only by color. 'L'Elegante' has white-edged foliage; other varieties have white or yellow veins in leaves. Summer Showers strain may be grown from seed; it comes as a mixture of white, pink, red, lavender, and magenta.

Pelargonium tomentosum

P. tomentosum. PEPPERMINT-SCENTED GERANIUM. Large, 3–5-in.-wide, lobed leaves, velvety to the touch. Spreads to about 2–4 ft. Small white flowers in fluffy clusters. Use as ground cover in partial shade in frost-free gardens. Leafy branches draped over wall or hanging from basket are striking.

THE SMELL-GOOD GERANIUMS

The names of scented geraniums refer to their fragrances: lemon (*P. crispum*), lime (*P. nervosum*), rose (*P. graveolens*), peppermint (*P. tomentosum*) . . . the list goes on. Grow them for their fragrance or to flavor sauces or jellies. Species of *Pelargonium*, they reach 1–3 ft. tall with an equal spread. In summer they bear clusters of small white to pink blooms.

PELLAEA

CLIFF-BRAKE

Polypodiaceae

FERNS

🌿 ZONES VARY BY SPECIES

☼ FILTERED SHADE

💧 WATER LESS THAN MOST FERNS

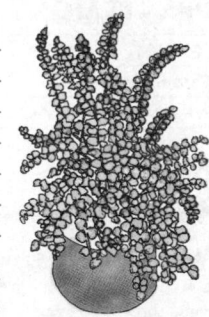
Pellaea rotundifolia

Small plants, not striking in appearance, but with charmingly detailed foliage. The first two, which are native to parts of the West, tolerate summer drought but look dry.

P. andromedifolia. COFFEE FERN. Zones 6–9, 14–24. Native to California, southern Oregon. Finely cut, gray-green to bluish green fronds on thin, wiry stalks. To 1½ ft. high.

P. mucronata. BIRD'S FOOT FERN. Zones 2–11, 14–24. Larger than *P. andromedifolia*, with gray-green, airy fronds and narrow leaflets arranged in groups of three.

P. rotundifolia. ROUNDLEAF FERN. Zones 14–17, 19–24. Small fern with spreading fronds to 1 ft. long. Nearly round leaflets, about ¾ in. across, are evenly spaced. Pretty fern for contrast with finer-textured ferns or to show off in pots, baskets, or raised beds. Hardy to 24°F.

P. viridis (P. adiantoides). Zones 14–17, 19–24. Fronds to 2 ft. long; fresh green leaflets oval to lance shaped. Ground cover, rock garden, containers. Hardy to 24°F.

P

PELTIPHYLLUM peltatum. See DARMERA peltata   **p. 259**

PENCILBUSH, PENCIL TREE. See EUPHORBIA tirucalli   **p. 290**

PENNISETUM

FOUNTAIN GRASS

Poaceae (Gramineae)

PERENNIAL GRASSES

✍ ZONES VARY BY SPECIES

☼ ◖ EXPOSURE NEEDS VARY BY SPECIES

◊ ● WATER NEEDS VARY BY SPECIES

Pennisetum setaceum

Fountain grasses are generally clump forming, with gracefully arching stems bearing fat, furry plumes at the ends. They are among the most graceful of ornamental grasses. Use them in containers, in perennial or shrub borders, as bank cover.

P. alopecuroides. Zones 3–24. The 3–4-ft. clumps of bright green foliage are topped by pinkish flower clusters. Leaves turn yellow in fall, brown in winter. 'Hameln' is smaller (2–3 ft.) and has white plumes. 'Moudry', to 3 ft., has black plumes. All thrive in sun or light shade and need some summer water in dry climates.

P. orientale. Zones 3–9. The 1–1½-ft. clumps of leaves are topped by many pinkish plumes that stand a foot or more above the foliage. Plumes mature to light brown and foliage turns straw color in winter. Growing conditions are the same as for *P. alopecuroides*.

P. setaceum. Perennial in Zones 8–24; annual elsewhere. Dense, rounded clump to 4 ft. In summer 3–4-ft. stems are topped by fuzzy coppery pink or purplish flower spikes. Use in dry locations, as in gravel beds, or as focal point in low ground covers. Any soil, full sun. Needs no irrigation and is dormant in winter. Seeds itself freely and threatens to crowd out native vegetation when planted near open country. To prevent seeding about in the garden, cut plumes before seeds mature. 'Rubrum', also known as 'Cupreum', has reddish brown leaves and dark plumes. It does not set seed.

PENNYROYAL. See MENTHA pulegium   **p. 379**

PENSTEMON

BEARD TONGUE

Scrophulariaceae

PERENNIALS, EVERGREEN SHRUBS AND SHRUBLETS

✍ ZONES VARY BY SPECIES

☼ ◖ FULL SUN; LIGHT SHADE IN HOT INTERIOR

● LITTLE WATER; BORDER KINDS NEED MORE

Penstemon heterophyllus purdyi

A few are widely grown; most are sold only by specialists. All have tubular flowers. Bright reds and blues are the most common colors, but there are penstemons in soft pinks through salmon and peach to deep rose, lilac, deep purple, white, and, rarely, yellow. Hummingbirds are attracted to flowers. Of some 250 species, most are native to western United States from Canada into Mexico—some on highest mountains; some in the desert; others in forest glades, foothills, and plains.

Need fast drainage; many kinds best in loose, gravelly soil. Usually short lived (3–4 years). In dry years or with little water, plants of wild species may thrive; if given too-rich soil and too much water, they may die quickly. Hybrids and selections tend to be easier to grow alongside regular garden plants.

P. ambiguus. PRAIRIE PENSTEMON, SAND PENSTEMON. Shrubby perennial. Zones 7–15, 18–21. To 2 ft., with very narrow leaves and broad (rather than tall) clusters of white to pink flowers that resemble phlox.

P. barbatus. Perennial. All zones. Native to mountains from Colorado and Utah to Mexico. Open, somewhat sprawling habit, to 3 ft. Bright green leaves, 2–6 in. long. Long, loose spikes of red flowers about 1 in. long; early summer bloom. Selections include 'Prairie Dusk', deep purple flowers on 2-ft. spikes; 'Prairie Fire', scarlet on 2½-ft. spikes; and 'Rose Elf', deep rose on 2½-ft. spikes. All are short lived in warm-winter areas, tolerate extreme cold.

P. centranthifolius. SCARLET BUGLER. Shrub. Zones 7–23. Gray foliage and bright red flames; 1–3 ft. tall.

P. cordifolius (Keckiella cordifolia). Evergreen shrub. Zones 8, 9, 14–24. Native to coast of Southern California. Loose branching, half climbing, with flexible, arching branches to 10 ft.; fuchsialike leaves ½–1½ in. long. Red, tubular flowers 1–1½ in. long, in dense clusters at tips of stems, April–June. Yellow-flowered forms exist.

P. davidsonii (P. menziesii davidsonii). Perennial. Zones 1–7. Native to high mountains of Sierra Nevada and western Nevada north to Washington. Mat-forming alpine to 3 in. high. Leaves oval, to ½–¾ in. long. Flowers violet blue, 1–1½ in. long, July–August. Ideal for gravelly slope in rock garden.

P. eatonii. FIRECRACKER PENSTEMON. Perennial. Zones 1–3, 7–13, 18–21. Grows 1½–3 ft. tall, with narrow, tubular, scarlet flowers in spring and early summer. Tolerates heat; best with a little summer water in hottest regions; requires perfect drainage.

P. gloxinioides. BORDER PENSTEMON, GARDEN PENSTEMON. Perennial treated as annual in cold-winter climates. All zones. Plants with this name are selections of *P. hartwegii* or hybrids between it and *P. cobaea*. Compact, bushy, upright stems to 2–4 ft. tall. Tubular flowers in loose spikes at ends of stems, in almost all colors but blue and yellow. Mass in borders or group with other summer-flowering plants.

Penstemon gloxinioides

Subject to root rot in heavy, wet soil. In mild climates, set out nursery-grown plants in fall for bloom in April. Older plants, if cut back after main bloom, flower again later in summer on side branches. Easy to grow from seed; several good mixed-color strains available. For plants in separate colors, make softwood cuttings from desirable plants. Some nurseries sell cutting-grown plants in separate colors.

Some named varieties are more reliably perennial than seed-grown plants. 'Apple Blossom' ('Huntington Pink') grows to 3 ft., has clear pink flowers. 'Firebird' is bright red, 'Garnet' dark red, 'Holly White' white, 'Lady Hindley' lavender, 'Midnight' dark purple, and 'Sour Grapes' purple with a pale throat.

P. heterophyllus purdyi. Perennial. Zones 6–24. Native to Sierra Nevada foothills and Coast Ranges of California. Stems upright or spreading, 1–2 ft. high. Narrow, pointed leaves 1–3 in. long. Blooms April–July, bearing spikelike clusters of flowers ranging from rosy lavender to intense gentian blue. Most nurseries stocking this plant sell it as 'Blue Bedder' penstemon.

P. palmeri. Perennial. Zones 10–13. Grows to 6 ft. tall, with thick grayish leaves and large, fragrant pink flowers. Difficult, needing excellent drainage.

P. parryi. PARRY'S PENSTEMON. Perennial. Zones 12, 13. Spikes of reddish pink flowers rise 2 ft. or more above clumps of smooth, gray-green foliage. Tender at higher desert elevations.

P. pinifolius. Shrublet. All zones. Spreading, 4–6 in. tall (rarely to 2 ft.), with crowded needlelike leaves ¾ in. long. Coral to scarlet, 1½-in.-long flowers. Rock garden, low border plant, or small-scale ground cover. 'Mersea Yellow' has bright yellow flowers.

P. pseudospectabilis. DESERT BEARD TONGUE. Perennial. Zones 10, 12–21. Shrubby plant 2–4 ft. tall with bluish green leaves whose bases clasp around the stems. Pinkish red flowers in spring, summer.

P. rupicola. Evergreen subshrub. Zones 1–7. Native to Cascades and Siskiyou Mountains. Trailing, much branched, to 4 in. high. Leaves roundish, blue green, fine toothed, ⅓–¾ in. long. Flowers bright rose

P

crimson, ½–1½ in. long, June–August. Gravel or perfectly drained soil is a must. Beautiful in rock gardens, in dry wall near miniature campanulas. Lesser-known, white-flowered form is available; it needs half shade, is somewhat harder to grow than species.

P. spectabilis. ROYAL BEARD TONGUE. Perennial. Zones 7, 14–23. The 2–4-ft. plants have blue or purplish flowers and smooth green or grayish green leaves that clasp around the stem.

P. strictus. ROCKY MOUNTAIN PENSTEMON. Perennial. Zones 1–3, 10–13. Multiple spires, 2 ft. or taller, of large, dark to brilliant blue-purple flowers in early summer. Very hardy.

P. superbus. Perennial. Zones 12, 13. Tall, 3–4 ft. or more, with gray-green leaves and deep rose to red flowers.

PENTAPTERYGIUM. See AGAPETES	p. 142

PENTAS lanceolata

STAR CLUSTERS

Rubiaceae

PERENNIAL USUALLY TREATED AS ANNUAL

✂ ALL ZONES

☼ FULL SUN

💧 REGULAR WATER

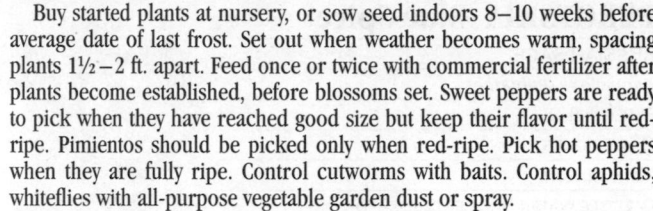

Pentas lanceolata

Spreading, multistemmed plant to 2–3 ft. tall. Leaves are long, somewhat hairy ovals; stems are topped by tight 4-in.-wide clusters of small, star-shaped flowers in white, pink, lilac, or red. Feed regularly. Remove dead flowers for a long bloom season. If growing as a house plant, give it as much sunlight as possible: set in a bright west or south window.

PEONY. See PAEONIA	p. 398
PEPINO. See SOLANUM muricatum	p. 488

PEPPER

Solanaceae

ANNUALS

✂ ALL ZONES

☼ FULL SUN

💧 INFREQUENT, DEEP WATERING DURING GROWTH

All peppers grow on 1½–2-ft.-tall handsome, bushy plants. Use plants as temporary low informal hedge, or grow and display them in containers. The two basic kinds of peppers are sweet and hot.

Bell Pepper

Sweet peppers always remain mild, even when flesh ripens to red. This group includes big stuffing and salad peppers commonly known as bell peppers; best known of these are 'California Wonder' and 'Yolo Wonder'. Hybrid varieties have been bred for early bearing, high yield, or disease resistance. Big peppers are also available in bright yellow and purple (purple types turn green when cooked). Other sweet types are thick-walled, very sweet pimientos used in salads or for cooking or canning; sweet cherry peppers for pickling; and long, slender Italian frying peppers and Hungarian sweet yellow peppers, both used for cooking.

Hot peppers range from tiny (pea-size) types to narrow, 6–7-in.-long forms, but all are pungent, their flavor ranging from the mild heat of Italian peperoncini to the near-incandescence of the 'Habañero'. 'Anaheim' is a mild but spicy pepper used for making canned green chiles. 'Long Red Cayenne' is used for drying; 'Hungarian Yellow Wax (Hot)', 'Jalapeño', and 'Fresno Chile Grande' are used for pickling. Mexican cooking utilizes an entire palette of peppers, among them 'Ancho', 'Mulato', and 'Pasilla'.

Buy started plants at nursery, or sow seed indoors 8–10 weeks before average date of last frost. Set out when weather becomes warm, spacing plants 1½–2 ft. apart. Feed once or twice with commercial fertilizer after plants become established, before blossoms set. Sweet peppers are ready to pick when they have reached good size but keep their flavor until red-ripe. Pimientos should be picked only when red-ripe. Pick hot peppers when they are fully ripe. Control cutworms with baits. Control aphids, whiteflies with all-purpose vegetable garden dust or spray.

PEPPERMINT. See EUCALYPTUS, MENTHA piperita	pp. 284, 379
PEPPERMINT TREE. See AGONIS flexuosa	p. 143
PEPPER TREE. See SCHINUS	p. 479
PEPPERWOOD. See UMBELLULARIA californica	p. 515
PERICALLIS cruenta. See SENECIO hybridus	p. 483

PERILLA frutescens

SHISO

Lamiaceae (Labiatae)

SUMMER ANNUAL

✂ ALL ZONES

☼ ☽ SUN OR LIGHT SHADE

💧 MODERATE WATER

Perilla frutescens

Sturdy, leafy plant to 2–3 ft. tall. Deeply toothed, egg-shaped leaves to 5 in. long. Kind most commonly seen has bronzy or purple leaves that look much like those of coleus. Leaves of Fancy Fringe strain are deeply cut and fringed, deep bronzy purple in color. Use leaves as vegetable or flavoring (they taste something like mint, something like cinnamon); fry long, thin clusters of flower buds as a vegetable in tempura batter. Extremely fast and easy to grow. In Asia, seeds are pressed for edible oil.

PERIWINKLE. See CATHARANTHUS, VINCA	pp. 212, 519

PERNETTYA mucronata (Gaultheria mucronata)

Ericaceae

EVERGREEN SHRUB

✂ ZONES 4–7, 15–17

☼ ☽ FULL SUN; PARTIAL SHADE INLAND

💧 REGULAR WATER

Pernettya mucronata

Compact growth to 2–3 ft. tall, spreading by underground runners to form clumps. Glossy, dark green, oval or narrow, ⅓–¾-in.-long leaves give finely textured look. Some leaves turn red or bronzy in winter. Tiny white to pink, bell-shaped flowers in late spring, followed by very colorful berries—purple, white, red, rose, pink, or near black—all with metallic sheen. Berries are fleshy, ½ in. across; they hold until knocked off by hard rain or frost, possibly until early spring. Plants set more fruit if you grow several for cross-pollination.

Acid, peaty soil. Full sun in cold-winter regions, partial shade where summers are long and hot. Can be invasive; control by pruning roots with spade. Tops often need regular pruning to stay attractive. Use as informal low hedge or border, in tubs or window boxes.

FOR INFORMATION ON SELECTING PLANTS

PLEASE SEE PAGES 45–128

P

PEROVSKIA 'Blue Spire'

RUSSIAN SAGE	
Lamiaceae (Labiatae)	
PERENNIAL	
⚘ ALL ZONES	
☼ FULL SUN	
⬤ LITTLE WATER ONCE ESTABLISHED	

Perovskia 'Blue Spire'

Woody-based, multistemmed plant to 3 ft. tall. Leaves gray green; lower ones finely cut, upper merely toothed, small. Lavender blue flowers in many-branched, slender, spikelike clusters that form a haze above the foliage. Long summer bloom if old flowers are trimmed off. Likes summer heat, winter chill. Dormant in winter. Hybrid between *P. atriplicifolia* and *P. abrotanoides*. Often sold as *P. atriplicifolia*.

PERSIAN VIOLET. See EXACUM affine   p. 291

PERSIMMON (Diospyros)

Ebenaceae	
DECIDUOUS FRUIT TREES	
⚘ ZONES VARY BY SPECIES	
☼ FULL SUN	
⬤ WATER NEEDS VARY BY SPECIES	

Persimmon

Two species are grown in the West, one a well-known fruit tree with outstanding ornamental qualities. Both are resistant to oak root fungus.

Oriental or Japanese persimmon *(Diospyros kaki)* grows in Zones 7–9, 14–16, 18–23; borderline in Zones 4–6; grows but rarely fruits in Zones 10–13. To 30 ft. or more with wide-spreading branches. New leaves soft, light green in spring, becoming dark green, leathery, broad ovals to 6–7 in. long, 2–3½ in. wide. In late autumn, leaves turn yellow, orange, or scarlet even in warm-winter climates. After leaves drop, orange-scarlet fruit lights tree for weeks; after fruit drops, handsome branch structure justifies featured spot in garden. Prune only to remove dead wood, shape tree, or open up too-dense interior. Only problem is fruit drop, common in young trees. To avoid it, be consistent in feeding and watering. Space deep irrigations so that root zone is neither too wet nor too dry. Feed plants in late winter or early spring; overfeeding with nitrogen causes excessive growth, excessive fruit drop. Mature plants usually bear consistently.

> ### TRY DRYING SOME PERSIMMONS
> To dry persimmon fruit, pick it when hard-ripe with some stem remaining. Peel and hang by string in sun until it shrivels. Dried fruit has a flavor something like a date or very high quality prune.

One of best fruit trees for ornamental use; good garden or small shade tree. Can be espaliered. Available varieties:

'Chocolate'. Brown-flecked, very sweet flesh.

'Fuyu'. Nonastringent even when underripe; firm fleshed (like an apple), reddish yellow, about size of baseball but flattened like tomato. Similar but larger is 'Gosho', widely sold as 'Giant Fuyu'.

'Hachiya'. Shapeliest tree for ornamental use. This variety yields big (4-in.-long, 2½–3-in.-broad), slightly pointed persimmons usually found in produce stores. Pick before fully ripe to save crop from birds, but allow to become soft-ripe before eating; astringent unless mushy.

'Tamopan'. Very large, turban shaped, astringent until fully ripe.

American persimmon *(Diospyros virginiana)* grows in Zones 3–9, 14–16, 18–23. Moderate-growing small tree to 20–30 ft. with broad, oval crown, and attractive gray-brown bark fissured into deep checkered pattern. Glossy, broad, oval leaves to 6 in. long. New foliage bronzy or reddish;

leaves turn yellow, pink, and red in fall. Fruit round, yellow to orange (often blushed red), 1½–2 in. wide, very astringent until soft-ripe, then very sweet. Moderate water.

PERUVIAN DAFFODIL. See HYMENOCALLIS narcissiflora   p. 328

PERUVIAN LILY. See ALSTROEMERIA   p. 148

PETREA volubilis

QUEEN'S WREATH	
Verbenaceae	
EVERGREEN VINE	
⚘ ZONES 19–24	
☼ FULL SUN	
⬤ REGULAR WATER	

Petrea volubilis

Grows to 40 ft., but can be kept much smaller. Deep green, rough-surfaced leaves. Stunning displays of purplish blue, star-shaped flowers in long, slender clusters, several times a year during warm weather. Flowers are individually small but profuse. Provide shelter in Zones 19–22.

PETUNIA hybrida

COMMON GARDEN PETUNIA	
Solanaceae	
TENDER PERENNIAL GROWN AS ANNUAL	
⚘ ALL ZONES	
☼ FULL SUN	
⬤ REGULAR WATER	

Petunia hybrida

Grown for summer bloom except in Zones 12 and 13, where it is planted in fall for color from spring to early summer. Fragrant flowers are single and funnel shaped to very double, in many colors from soft pink to deepest red, light blue to deepest purple, cream, yellow, and pure white. Leaves thick, broad, and slightly sticky to touch.

Plant in good garden soil. Single-flowered kinds tolerate alkalinity, will grow in poor soil if it's well drained. Plant 8–18 in. apart depending on size of variety. After plants are established, pinch back halfway for compact growth. Feed monthly with complete fertilizer. Near end of summer, cut back rangy plants about half to force new growth. In some areas, smog causes spots on leaves of seedlings—plants outgrow damage in clear periods. White-flowered kinds are most susceptible. Tobacco budworm may be a problem in some areas.

To most gardeners, petunias are of two main types: doubles or singles. Doubles are heavily ruffled, many-petaled flowers resembling carnations; singles are funnel shaped (either ruffled or smooth edged) with open throats. Both doubles and singles come as Grandifloras (very large flowers) or Multifloras (smaller but more numerous flowers).

F_1 hybrids, produced by crossing two different varieties, are more vigorous and more uniform in color, height, and growth habit than ordinary petunias. Most are hand-pollinated to produce seed and are thus somewhat more expensive than petunias grown from open-pollinated seed.

F_1 Hybrid Grandiflora. Sturdy plants, 15–27 in. high, 2–3 ft. across. Flowers usually single, ruffled or fringed, to 4½ in. across, in pink, rose, salmon, red, scarlet, blue, white, pale yellow, or striped combinations. Cascade, Countdown, and Supercascade series of petunias belong here; cascading growth habit makes them good for hanging baskets. Magic and Supermagic strains give heavy bloom on compact plants; large, single flowers are 4–5 in. across, in white, pink, red, blue. Double Hybrid Grandifloras with heavily ruffled flowers come in all petunia colors except yellow.

F_1 Hybrid Multiflora. Plants about same size as F_1 Hybrid Grandiflora, but flowers generally smooth edged and smaller (to 2 in. across), single or double. Neat, compact growth, ideal for bedding, massed planting. Many named varieties in pink, rose, salmon, yellow, white, blue. Resistant to botrytis disease, which disfigures blossoms and later foliage of other kinds in humid weather. Joy and Plum series of petunias belong in F_1 Hybrid Multiflora strain. Flowers single, satiny textured, to 2½ in. wide, in white, cream, pink, coral, red, blue. 'Summer Sun' is bright yellow petunia.

F_2 Hybrid Grandiflora and Multiflora. These petunias look like their F_1 seed parents but are variable in color and somewhat so in growth pattern.

Fluffy Ruffles. Strain has big flowers (to 6 in.) in a variety of colors.

PHACELIA campanularia

CALIFORNIA DESERT BLUEBELLS

Hydrophyllaceae

ANNUAL

✂ ALL ZONES

☼ FULL SUN

◉ DEEP WATERING EXTENDS BLOOMING SEASON

Phacelia campanularia

Native to California deserts. Adaptable to most well-drained soils. Grows to 6–18 in. tall, with egg-shaped, coarsely toothed leaves and loose clusters of inch-long, bell-shaped, deep blue flowers. Blooms in March and April. Sow where plants are to bloom in fall or earliest spring, or sow in pots and transplant while seedlings are very small.

PHAEDRANTHUS buccinatorius. See DISTICTIS buccinatoria   p. 265

PHALAENOPSIS

MOTH ORCHID

Orchidaceae

INDOOR AND GREENHOUSE PLANTS

☼ NEAR A WINDOW BUT NO DIRECT SUN

◉ MOIST POTTING MEDIUM AT ALL TIMES

Phalaenopsis

Epiphytic orchids with thick, broad, leathery leaves and no pseudobulbs. Long sprays of 3–6-in.-wide, white, cream, pale yellow, or light lavender pink flowers spring–fall; some are spotted, barred, or have contrasting lip color. Leaves are rather flat, spreading to 1 ft. long. Flower sprays may be 3 ft. long. Cut faded spray back to a node; a secondary spray may form.

Although very popular commercially, moth orchids are more for advanced amateurs than beginners. They require warmer growing conditions than most orchids (minimum of 60–70°F at night and 70–85°F during the day), fairly high humidity. Good location is near bathroom or kitchen window with light coming through a gauzelike curtain (foliage burns easily in direct sun). Give them same potting medium as for cattleyas. When cutting flowers, leave part of main stem so another set of flowers can develop from dormant buds. Many lovely, large-flowered hybrids. Some smaller-flowered new hybrids give promise of being easier to grow, taking somewhat lower nighttime temperatures.

PHALARIS arundinacea

RIBBON GRASS, GARDENER'S GARTERS

Poaceae (Gramineae)

DECORATIVE PERENNIAL GRASS

✂ ALL ZONES

☼ ☽ SUN OR PARTIAL SHADE

◉◉ GOOD IN MOIST SOILS

Phalaris arundinacea

Tough, tenacious grass that spreads aggressively by underground runners. Leaves form 2–3-ft. spreading clumps. Leaves are deep green

striped white, turning buff color in fall. Airy flower clusters are white, turning to pale brown.

'Dwarf Garters' is half as tall and spreads slowly; 'Fersey's Form' grows to 1½–2 ft., and the white variegation is strongly blushed with pink. Not aggressive.

PHASEOLUS caracalla. See VIGNA caracalla	**p. 519**
PHASEOLUS coccineus. See BEAN, SCARLET RUNNER	**p. 180**

PHILADELPHUS

MOCK ORANGE

Hydrangeaceae (Saxifragaceae)

DECIDUOUS SHRUBS, EXCEPT AS NOTED

✂ ZONES VARY BY SPECIES

☼ ☽ PARTIAL SHADE IN HOTTEST AREAS

◉ MODERATE WATER

Philadelphus lemoinei

White, usually fragrant flowers bloom in late spring (early summer for some species). Most are large, vigorous plants of fountainlike form with medium green foliage. Prune every year just after bloom, cutting out oldest wood and surplus shoots at base. Taller types are striking in lawns or as background and corner plantings; smaller kinds can be planted near foundations or used as low screens or informal hedges.

P. coronarius. SWEET MOCK ORANGE. Zones 1–17. Old favorite. Strong growing, 8–10 ft. tall. Oval leaves 1–4 in. long. Clusters of very fragrant, 1½-in.-wide flowers in June. 'Aureus' has bright golden leaves that turn yellow green in summer, does not grow as tall.

P. gordonianus. See P. lewisii

P. lemoinei. Zones 1–17. This hybrid includes many garden varieties, most to 5–6 ft. tall and all with very fragrant flowers in clusters. Leaves oval, to 2 in. long. Double-flowered 'Enchantment' is best-known variety.

P. lewisii. WILD MOCK ORANGE. Zones 1–17. Native to western North America. Erect and arching habit (tall race from west of the Cascades is often called *P. gordonianus*). Satiny, fragrant blooms nearly 2 in. across; oval leaves 2–4 in. long. Blooms June–July. Tolerates some aridity, especially the form native to California. State flower of Idaho. 'Goose Creek' is a double-flowered selection.

P. mexicanus. EVERGREEN MOCK ORANGE. Zones 8, 9, 14–24. Best used as vine or bank cover; long, supple stems with 3-in. evergreen leaves will reach 15–20 ft. if given support. Fragrant creamy flowers in small clusters bloom in spring and early summer, or intermittently.

P. purpureomaculatus. Zones 2–17. Group of hybrids including moderate-size shrubs with flowers showing purple centers. 'Belle Etoile' grows upright to 5 ft. tall; fragrant, fringed, single flowers to 2½ in. Oval leaves to 2 in. long.

P. virginalis. Zones 1–17. Another hybrid that has produced several garden varieties, usually with double flowers. Tall (6–8-ft.) varieties include 'Minnesota Snowflake' and 'Virginal', both double, and 'Natchez', with 2-in. single flowers. Lower growing are double 'Glacier' (3–4 ft.) and 'Dwarf Minnesota Snowflake' (2–3 ft.).

PHILLYREA decora (Osmanthus decorus)

Oleaceae

EVERGREEN SHRUB

✂ ZONES 4–9, 14–21

☼ ☽ SUN OR LIGHT SHADE

◉ LITTLE WATER ONCE ESTABLISHED

Phillyrea decora

Slow growth to 6–8 ft. Neat, glossy leaves 3–5 in. long, dark green above, yellowish green beneath. Small, pure white flowers, April–May.

P

Male and female flowers on different plants; if both sexes are present, small red fruit follows bloom, turning purplish black in late fall. Has foliage quality of camellia or skimmia.

PHILODENDRON

Araceae

EVERGREEN VINES AND SHRUBS, USUALLY INDOORS

✂ ZONES 8, 9, 12–24; SEE BELOW

☼ ● INDOORS OR OUTDOORS IN PARTIAL SHADE

◗ MOIST, NOT SOGGY, SOIL

Philodendron domesticum

Philodendrons are tough, durable, fast-growing plants grown for their attractive, leathery, usually glossy leaves. They fall into two main classes; the list that follows indicates the class of each species and variety.

Arborescent and relatively hardy. These become big plants 6–8 ft. high (sometimes higher) and as wide. They develop large leaves and sturdy, self-supporting trunks. They will grow indoors but need much more space than most house plants. They grow outdoors in certain milder climate zones; see individual descriptions. As outdoor plants, they do best in sun with shade at midday but can survive considerable shade. Use them for tropical jungle effects or as massive silhouettes against walls or glass. Excellent in large containers; effective near swimming pools.

Vining or self-heading and tender. These forms can only be house plants. There are many kinds, with many different leaf shapes and sizes. Vining types do not really climb and must be tied to or leaned against a support until they eventually shape themselves to it. The support can be almost anything, but certain water-absorbent columns (sections of tree fern stems, wire and sphagnum "totem poles," slabs of redwood bark) serve especially well because they can be kept moist, and moist columns help plants grow better. Self-heading types form short, broad plants with sets of leaves radiating out from central point.

Whether in containers or open ground, a philodendron should grow in rich, loose, well-drained soil. House plant philodendrons grow best in good light (but not direct sun) coming through a window. Feed lightly and frequently for good growth and color. Dust leaves of indoor plants once a month (commercial leaf polishes are available).

It's the nature of most philodendrons—especially when grown in containers—to drop lower leaves, leaving bare stem. To fix a leggy philodendron, you can air-layer leafy top and, when it develops roots, sever it and replant it. Or cut plant back to short stub and let it start over again. Often the best answer is to throw out an overgrown, leggy plant and replace it with a new one. Aerial roots form on stems of some kinds; push them into soil or cut them off—it won't hurt plant.

Flowers may appear on old plants if heat, light, and humidity are high; they resemble callas, with a boat-shaped bract surrounding a club-shaped, spikelike structure. Bracts are usually greenish, white, or reddish.

Here are the kinds. Note that the great favorite—the so-called split-leaf philodendron—is not a philodendron at all, but a *Monstera*.

P. bipinnatifidum. Arborescent. Zones 8, 9, 12–24. Deeply cut 3-ft. leaves on upright trunks (leaning with age). Old plants may develop greenish cream inflorescences like giant (to 12 in. long) callas.

P. cordatum. See P. scandens oxycardium

P. domesticum. Vining. Usually sold as P. 'Hastatum'. Fairly fast, open growth. Leaves 1 ft. long, arrow shaped, deep green. Subject to leaf spot if kept too warm and moist. A number of selections and hybrids have become available; these are more resistant to leaf spot and tend to be more compact and upright. Some, possibly hybrids with *P. erubescens,* have much red in new foliage and in leafstalks. 'Emerald Queen' is a choice deep green, 'Royal Queen' a good deep red.

P. 'Lynette'. Self-heading. Makes close cluster of foot-long, broadish, bright green leaves with strong patterning formed by deeply sunken veins. Good tabletop plant.

P. oxycardium. See P. scandens oxycardium

P. pertusum. See *Monstera deliciosa*. This is commonly sold as split-leaf philodendron.

P. scandens oxycardium. Vining. Most common philodendron, usually sold as *P. oxycardium* or *P. cordatum.* Heart-shaped, deep green leaves, usually 5 in. or less in length on juvenile plants, up to 1 ft. long on mature plants in greenhouses. Easily grown (cut stems will live and grow for some time in vases of water). Thin stems will trail gracefully or climb fast and high. Train on strings or wires to frame a window or hang from a rafter, or grow on moisture-retentive columns.

Philodendron scandens oxycardium

P. selloum. Arborescent. Zones 8, 9, 12–24. Hardiest big-leafed philodendron used outdoors. Deeply cut leaves to 3 ft. long. Variety 'Lundii' is more compact.

P. wendlandii. Self-heading. Compact clusters of 12 or more deep green, foot-long, broadly lance-shaped leaves on short, broad stalks. Useful where tough, compact foliage plant is needed for tabletop. P. 'Lynette' is similar.

PHLOMIS

JERUSALEM SAGE

Lamiaceae (Labiatae)

PERENNIALS OR SHRUBBY PERENNIALS

✂ ZONES 4–24, EXCEPT AS NOTED

☼ FULL SUN, EXCEPT AS NOTED

◗ LITTLE SUMMER WATER

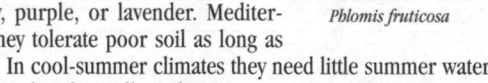

Phlomis fruticosa

Erect stems are set with whorls of tubular flowers in yellow, purple, or lavender. Mediterranean natives, they tolerate poor soil as long as drainage is good. In cool-summer climates they need little summer water. Where summers are hot they will need more.

P. fruticosa. Shrubby plant to 4 ft., with woolly, gray-green, 6–8-in. leaves. Yellow 1-in. flowers make ball-shaped whorls spaced along upper half of stems. Evergreen in mild winters. Resistant to oak root fungus. Plant with echinops, eryngium, helenium, helianthus, sages, lavenders in hillside or dry gardens. Cut back by half in fall to keep plants compact. With summer water, will produce several waves of bloom if cut back after each flowering. Can tolerate light shade.

P. lanata. Zones 7–24. Dense, compact, shrubby perennial to 2½ ft., with 1-in. woolly, wrinkled leaves and whorls of ½-in. yellow flowers. Nearly everblooming if old, faded stems are cut out.

P. russeliana. Spreads by runners, making clumps of large (to 8 in.), heart-shaped, furry leaves. Mats can be an effective weed-suppressing ground cover. Spikes with whorls of yellow flowers grow to 3 ft.

P. samia. Similar to *P. russeliana,* but with purplish pink flowers.

PHLOX

Polemoniaceae

PERENNIALS AND ANNUALS

✂ ZONES VARY BY SPECIES

☼ ◐ FULL SUN OR LIGHT SHADE

◗ MODERATE WATER

Phlox paniculata

Most are natives of North America. Plants in this group show wide variation in growth form. All have showy flower clusters. Grow in average garden soil unless otherwise noted.

P. carolina (P. maculata, P. suffruticosa). THICK-LEAF PHLOX. Perennial. Zones 1–14, 18–21. To 3–4 ft. tall. Early flowers about ¾ in. wide, in 15-in.-long clusters. Color varies from white, centered with pale

P

pink eye, to magenta. Shiny foliage, free from mildew and red spider mites (which often attack summer phlox). 'Miss Lingard' is excellent white-flowered variety to 3 ft. tall. 'Rosalinde' has pink flowers.

P. divaricata. SWEET WILLIAM PHLOX. Perennial. Zones 1–17. To 1 ft., with slender, leafy stems and creeping underground shoots. Leaves oval, 1–2 in. long, ¾ in. wide. Spring flowers in open clusters; bluish or pink-ish blue varying to white, ¾–1½ in. across, somewhat fragrant. Use in rock gardens, as bulb cover (see *Tulipa*). Light shade; good, deep soil. *P. d. laphamii* has best blue color. 'Fuller's White' is a white selection.

P. drummondii. ANNUAL PHLOX. Summer annual. All zones. Grows 6–18 in. tall, with erect, leafy stems more or less covered with rather sticky hairs. Flowers numerous, showy, in close clusters at tops of stems. Bright and pastel colors (no blue or orange), some with contrasting eye. Tall strains in mixed colors are Finest and Fordhook Finest. Dwarf strains (6–8 in. tall) include Beauty and Globe, both with rounded flowers, and starry-petaled Petticoat and Twinkle. Bloom lasts from early summer until frost if faded flowers are removed. Plant in spring in colder climates, in fall in mild areas of Southern California and desert. Give light, rich loam.

P. mesoleuca. CHIHUAHUAN PHLOX. Perennial. Zones 4–24. Grows 6 in. tall to 1½ ft. wide; growth tends to be straggly if plants are not tip-pinched. Flower color varies from cream to yellow, orange, and red. Likes heat, occasional summer water. Hardy to 0°F. Needs good drainage.

P. nivalis. TRAILING PHLOX. Perennial. Zones 4–7. Trailing plants form loose, 4–6 in. tall mats of narrow evergreen leaves. Big pink or white flowers in fairly large clusters in late spring or early summer. Excel-lent in rock gardens. 'Camla' is fine salmon pink variety.

P. paniculata. SUMMER PHLOX. Perennial. Zones 1–14, 18–21. Long lived. Thrives in full sun but in hottest areas colors may bleach. Leaves 2–5 in. long, narrow and tapering to slender point. Fragrant, 1-in.-wide summer flowers in large, dome-shaped clusters on 3–5-ft. stems. Colors include white, shades of lavender, pink, rose, or red; blooms of some types have a contrasting eye. Many named varieties. Mulch around plants to keep roots cool. Plants subject to mildew at end of blooming season. Divide plants every few years, replanting young shoots from outside of clump. Plants do not come true from seed; most tend toward uncertain purplish pink, though some may be attractive. Plant seed in fall.

P. stolonifera. CREEPING PHLOX. Perennial. Zones 1–17. Creeping, mounding plant to 6–8 in. tall with narrow evergreen leaves to 1½ in. long and a profusion of 1 in. flowers in spring. 'Blue Ridge' is lavender blue, 'Bruce's White' white, 'Sherwood Purple' deep lavender. Use in rock garden or front of border.

P. subulata. MOSS PINK. Perennial. Zones 1–17. Stiffish, ½-in., needlelike, evergreen leaves on creeping stems; forms mats to 6 in. tall. The ¾-in. flowers range in color from white through pink to rose and lavender blue. 'Candy Stripe' has white-and-pink striped flowers. Late spring or early summer bloom, according to climate. Makes sheets of bril-liant color in rock gardens. Ground cover. Grow in loose, not-too-rich soil. After flowering, cut back halfway.

P. suffruticosa. See P. carolina

PHOENIX

DATE PALM

Arecaceae (Palmae)

PALMS

🌡 ZONES VARY BY SPECIES

☀ FULL SUN, EXCEPT AS NOTED

💧 REGULAR WATER

Phoenix canariensis

Mostly large feather palms, but one is a dwarf. Trunks patterned with bases of old leafstalks. Small yellowish flowers in large, hanging sprays followed by clusters of often edible fruit (*P. dactylifera* bears dates of commerce). These palms hybridize freely, so buy from reliable nursery that knows seed or plant source.

P. canariensis. CANARY ISLAND DATE PALM. Zones 9, 12–24. Big, heavy-trunked plant to 60 ft. tall, with 50-ft. spread composed of a great many gracefully arching fronds. Grows slowly until it forms trunk, then speeds up a little. Young plants do well in pots for many years, looking something like pineapples. Grow on slopes, in parks and big spaces, along wide streets; not for small city lots. Hardy to 20°F. Slow to develop new head of foliage after hard-frost damage.

P. dactylifera. DATE PALM. Zone 9; warmer parts of Zones 11, 12–24. The date palm of Indio, California, and of Palm Springs golf courses; clas-sic palm of movie desert oases. Native to Middle East. Very tall (up to 80 ft.), with slender trunk and gray-green, waxy leaves; leaflets stiff and sharp pointed. Suckers from base; natural habit is clump of several trunks. Principal commercial variety in California is 'Deglet Noor'. Too stiff and large for most home gardens, but adapts to and does well in seaside, desert gardens. Leaves killed at 20°F but plants have survived 4–10°F.

Phoenix dactylifera

P. loureiri (P. humilis). Zones 9, 12–24. Resembles smaller, more slender and refined *P. canariensis*. Slow grower to 10–18 ft. tall. Leaves dark green, flexible, 10 ft. long. Good in containers or in the garden. Hardy to 20°F.

P. reclinata. SENEGAL DATE PALM. Zones 23, 24. Native to tropical Africa. Makes picturesque clumps from offshoots, with several curving trunks 20–30 ft. high. Offshoots can be removed to make single-trunked trees. Fertilize for fast growth. Expect trouble below 28°F.

P. roebelenii. PIGMY DATE PALM. Zones 23, 24; or house plant. Native to Laos. Fine-leafed, small-scale palm. One stem grows slowly to about 6 ft. Curved leaves form dense crown. Good pot plant. Does best in shade or partial shade, but not successful in dark indoor corners.

P. rupicola. CLIFF DATE PALM. Zones 17, 19–24. From India. As stately as *P. canariensis*, but much smaller, reaching only 25 ft. in height. Slender stem; lower leaves droop gracefully. Hardy to 26°F.

Phoenix roebelenii

P. sylvestris. SILVER DATE PALM. Zones 14–17, 19–24. Native to India. Hardy and beautiful date palm with single trunk to 30 ft., tapering from wide base to narrow top. Trunk covered with old leaf bases. Crown of gray-green leaves is thick and round. Hardy to 22°F.

HOW PALMS DATE

Young date palms won't bear fruit until 3–6 years after planting. What's more, since male and female flowers are borne on separate trees, you must plant not only a female date, but also a male to serve as a source of pollen. When male flowers open in spring, cut one from the tree and vig-orously shake it into a bag to collect the pollen. Dab the powdery yellow pollen on cotton swabs and loosely tie one to the end of each female flower. Wind will deposit the pollen.

PHORMIUM

NEW ZEALAND FLAX

Agavaceae

EVERGREEN PERENNIALS

🌡 ZONES 7–24; REGROW AFTER FREEZE IN 5, 6

☀ ☼ FULL SUN OR LIGHT SHADE

💧 TAKE LOTS OF WATER, OR A LITTLE

Phormium tenax
'Variegatum'

Big, dramatic plants composed of many sword-like, stiffly vertical leaves in fan pattern. Flow-ers dull red or yellow, 1–2 in. long, in clusters on stems that reach high above leaves. Use as point-of-interest display plant or near swimming pools. Sturdy, fast growing in

P

almost any soil or exposure—heat or cold, salt air or ocean spray. Take poor drainage to a point (in very poorly drained soil, crown rot can be problem). Subject to summer rot in low desert, but replacement plants set out in fall will grow quickly. Use as windbreak along coast; grow in containers anywhere. Increase by dividing large clumps.

P. colensoi (P. cookianum). Leaves 2½ in. wide, to 5 ft. long; less rigid than those of *P. tenax.* Flowers yellow or amber yellow, on 7-ft. spikes. Useful for its moderate size. With *P. tenax,* a parent of numerous hybrids.

P. tenax. NEW ZEALAND FLAX. Large, bold plant tending to spread. Leaves to 9 ft. long, up to 5 in. wide. Nursery plants in containers are deceptively small; allow enough garden room to accommodate mature plant. Reddish brown flower stalks bear many dark red to yellowish flowers. Variants in leaf color are available: 'Atropurpureum' is purple-red; 'Bronze' is brownish red; 'Rubrum' has deepest coloring, dark purplish red; 'Variegatum' has green leaves striped with creamy white. Little to no water once established.

Although *P. tenax* and its colored forms are widely used, a number of hybrids and selections with brightly colored leaves attract interest. These are smaller than *P. tenax* and better adapted to gardens of modest size. Some are prevailingly yellow or apricot ('Apricot Queen', 'Golden Sword', 'Yellow Wave'), while others are dark purplish bronze ('Bronze Baby', 'Dark Delight'). Many are dazzling, with stripings and edgings of red, apricot, cream, green, and bronze ('Maori Chief', 'Maori Maiden', 'Maori Queen', 'Maori Sunrise', and 'Sundowner'). Some are quite small ('Jack Spratt' and 'Tom Thumb'). These have the same water requirement as *P. tenax* but are less hardy to cold and heat. They are harmed by temperatures below 20°F and should have partial shade where temperatures are extremely high. Some tend to revert to green or bronze; remove such growths at the base to preserve original color. Use these forms for year-round color in perennial or shrub borders or on hillsides.

PHOTINIA

Rosaceae

EVERGREEN OR DECIDUOUS SHRUBS OR SMALL TREES

✎ ZONES VARY BY SPECIES

☼ FULL SUN

◐ ● BEST WITH MODERATE WATER

Attractive foliage and fruit color. Related to hawthorn, pyracantha. In Northwest, withhold water in late summer to ripen growth, lessen frost damage. Prune to shape; never allow new growth to get away and make long, bare switches. Use as screens, background. Attractive to birds.

Photinia fraseri

P. arbutifolia. See Heteromeles arbutifolia

P. fraseri. Evergreen shrub or small tree. Zones 4–24; Zones 2, 3, with protection. Moderate to fast growth to 10–15 ft., spreading wider. Leaves glossy dark green above, lighter beneath, 2–5 in. long. New growth bright bronzy red, showy. White flower clusters in early spring resemble those of *P. glabra* but are not followed by berries. Good espalier or small single-stemmed tree. Cut branches excellent in arrangements. Heat resistant; resists mildew where other kinds are susceptible. Sometimes chlorotic in Zones 12, 13. Control aphids. If *P. fraseri* is too large for your garden, try 'Indian Princess'—compact, dense, and half as tall (6-year-old plants are 5 ft. high). New foliage is more orange than red.

P. glabra. JAPANESE PHOTINIA. Evergreen shrub. Zones 4–24. Broad, dense growth to 6–10 ft. or more. Leaves oval, broadest toward tip, to 3 in. long. New growth coppery; scattered leaves of bright red give touch of color through fall and winter. Summer pruning will restrict size of plant to neat 5 ft. and give continuing show of new foliage. White flowers with hawthorn fragrance in 4-in.-wide clusters. Berries red, turning black. Prolonged freezes may set it back, but it usually recovers.

P. serrulata. CHINESE PHOTINIA. Evergreen shrub or small tree. Zones 4–16, 18–22. Broad, dense growth to 35 ft., but easily held to 10 ft. by 10 ft. Leaves stiff, crisp, deep green, to 8 in. long, prickly along edges. New

growth bright copper; scattered crimson leaves in fall, winter. Flowers white, in flat clusters 6 in. across, March–May. Bright red berries often last until December. May freeze badly in continued 0–10°F cold but usually recovers. Mildew can be expected almost anywhere. Needs little water once established. *P. s.* 'Aculeata' (often sold as *P. s.* 'Nova' or *P. s.* 'Nova Lineata') is more compact, has midrib and main leaf veins of ivory yellow.

P. villosa. Deciduous shrub or small tree. Zones 1–6. To 15 ft. tall, with spread of 10 ft. Leaves 1½–3 in. long, dark green. New foliage pale gold with rosy tints when expanding, bright red in fall. White flowers in 1–2-in.-wide clusters in midspring. Bright red fruit nearly ½ in. long.

PHYGELIUS

CAPE FUCHSIA

Scrophulariaceae

PERENNIALS

✎ ZONES 4–9, 14–24

☼ ◐ SUN OR LIGHT SHADE

● REGULAR WATER

Phygelius capensis

Woody-based perennials where winters are cold, these tend to be shrubby in warmer regions. Related to snapdragon and penstemon, but drooping flowers also suggest fuchsia. Plants grow 3–4 ft. tall and spread by underground stems or rooting prostrate branches. Flowers are tubular, curved, borne in loosely branched clusters at branch ends summer–fall. Prune to keep plants neat, and mulch roots where winters are cold. Species can be grown from seed; grow named varieties from cuttings or by layering branches.

P. aequalis. Flowers dusty rose, in pyramidal clusters. The variety 'Yellow Trumpet' has showy pale yellow flowers.

P. capensis. More sprawling in habit than the above, with more open clusters of pinkish red flowers. Hybrids between the two include 'African Queen', with orange-red flowers, and 'Moonraker', with pale yellow flowers.

PHYLA nodiflora (Lippia repens)

LIPPIA

Verbenaceae

PERENNIAL

✎ ZONES 8–24

☼ FULL SUN

◐ ● LOOKS BEST WITH REGULAR WATER

Phyla nodiflora

Creeps and spreads to form flat, ground-hugging mat sturdy enough to serve as lawn. Gray-green leaves to ¾ in. long. Small lilac to rose flowers in tight, round heads ½ in. across, spring to fall. Flowers attract bees; if you object to this, mow off tops. Dormant, unattractive in winter. Feed regularly, especially in early spring to bring it out of dormancy fast. Particularly useful in desert areas but subject to nematodes.

PHYLLITIS scolopendrium (Asplenium scolopendrium)

HART'S TONGUE FERN

Polypodiaceae

FERN

✎ ZONES 2–24

◑ ● PART TO FULL SHADE

● DIFFICULT WHERE SUMMERS ARE LONG AND DRY

Phyllitis scolopendrium

Native to Europe, eastern United States. Odd fern with undivided, strap-shaped leaves 9–18 in.

long. Fanciers collect various dwarf, crested, or forked varieties. Needs humus, some limestone chips if soil is poor in calcium. Difficult in desert and areas with poor water quality. Striking in woodland gardens, rock gardens, with rhododendrons and azaleas. Durable container plant; grows from tight crown, so may occupy same pot for many years.

PHYLLOSTACHYS. See BAMBOO p. 174

PHYSALIS

Solanaceae

PERENNIALS AND ANNUALS

❄ ALL ZONES

☼ ◐ SUN OR LIGHT SHADE

◗ MODERATE WATER

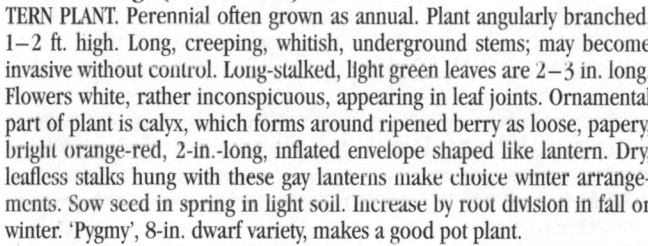
Physalis alkekengi

Fruit is surrounded by loose, papery husk (enlarged calyx of flower). First species below is ornamental; other two are edible.

P. alkekengi (P. franchetii). CHINESE LANTERN PLANT. Perennial often grown as annual. Plant angularly branched, 1–2 ft. high. Long, creeping, whitish, underground stems; may become invasive without control. Long-stalked, light green leaves are 2–3 in. long. Flowers white, rather inconspicuous, appearing in leaf joints. Ornamental part of plant is calyx, which forms around ripened berry as loose, papery, bright orange-red, 2-in.-long, inflated envelope shaped like lantern. Dry, leafless stalks hung with these gay lanterns make choice winter arrangements. Sow seed in spring in light soil. Increase by root division in fall or winter. 'Pygmy', 8-in. dwarf variety, makes a good pot plant.

P. ixocarpa. TOMATILLO. Annual of bushy, sprawling growth to 4 ft. Fruit about 2 in. wide, swelling to fill—or sometimes split—the baggy calyx. Fruit yellow to purple and very sweet when ripe, but usually picked green and tart and used (cooked) in Mexican cuisine.

P. peruviana. GROUND CHERRY, POHA. Tender perennial grown as annual. Bushy, 1½ ft. high. Leaves 2–4 in. long. Flowers bell shaped, ⅜ in. long, whitish yellow marked with five brown spots. Seedy yellow fruit is sweet, rather insipid; can be used for pies or preserves (remove papery husks before using in cooking). Grow in same way as tomatoes. Plants sprawl quite a bit and are slow to start bearing but are eventually productive where summers are long and warm. Several species resemble *P. peruviana*, including *P. pruinosa* and *P. pubescens*.

PHYSOCARPUS

NINEBARK

Rosaceae

DECIDUOUS SHRUBS

❄ ZONES 1–3, 10

☼ ◐ ● SUN OR SHADE

◗ MODERATE WATER

Physocarpus capitatus

These plants get their common name from their peeling bark, which often shows several layers. They resemble spiraeas and are closely related to them, bearing round clusters of tiny white flowers in spring or early summer.

P. capitatus. Native to mountains in the Northwest, Northern California, and northern Rocky Mountain states. To 8 ft. tall, with toothed and lobed 2-in. leaves and dense clusters of white flowers.

P. monogynus. MOUNTAIN NINEBARK. Rocky Mountain native; 3–4 ft. tall, with 1½-in. leaves and sparsely flowered clusters of pinkish to white flowers. Brilliant fall colors, mostly orange and red.

P. opulifolius intermedius. DWARF NINEBARK. Grows 4–5 ft. tall. Many white to pinkish flowers in each cluster. Reddish brown fall color. *P. o.* 'Luteus' has leaves that are yellow in sunlight, yellow green in shade. 'Dart's Gold' is similar.

PHYSOSTEGIA virginiana

FALSE DRAGONHEAD

Lamiaceae (Labiatae)

PERENNIAL

❄ ALL ZONES

☼ ◐ SUN OR PARTIAL SHADE

◗ REGULAR WATER

Physostegia virginiana

Slender, upright, leafy stems to 4 ft. Oblong, toothed leaves, 3–5 in. long, pointed at tip. Funnel-shaped, 1-in.-long flowers in dense 10-in. spikes, in glistening white, rose pink, or lavender rose. Summer bloom. Sometimes called obedience plant because flowers, if twisted on stem, remain in position. Spiky form useful in borders, cut arrangements. Combine with taller erigerons, *Scabiosa caucasica*, Michaelmas daisies. Stake taller stems to keep upright. Cut to ground after bloom. Vigorous and notably invasive; divide every 2 years to keep in bounds. 'Vivid', 2 ft. tall, has rose pink flowers. 'Summer Snow', an especially good white form, is least invasive.

PICEA

SPRUCE

Pinaceae

EVERGREEN SHRUBS OR TREES

❄ ZONES 1–6, 14–17, EXCEPT AS NOTED

☼ ◐ FULL SUN OR LIGHT SHADE

◗ INFREQUENT WATER, EXCEPT AS NOTED

Picea pungens 'Glauca'

These large cone-bearing trees take on pyramidal or cone shape. Many kinds have dwarf varieties that, where adapted, are useful in foundation plantings, rock gardens, and containers. Spruces have no special soil requirements. Dwarf forms need reasonably cool location. Birds are attracted to spruces.

Most trees are attacked by small, dull green aphids in late winter. Unless you check plants at that time to see if aphids are on foliage, the infestation may not be noticed until weather warms and needles start dropping. Start spraying in February and repeat monthly until May. Pine needle scale (flat and white) may cause sooty mold. Spray when scale insects are in crawler stage in May. In Rocky Mountain states, spruces may be bothered by spider mites and tussock moths.

Prune only to shape. If a branch grows too long, cut back to a well-placed side branch. To slow growth and make it more dense, remove part of each year's growth to force side growth. When planting larger spruces, don't place them too close to buildings, fences, or walks; they need space. Except in Zones 1–3, they can be grown in containers for years as living Christmas trees.

P. abies (P. excelsa). NORWAY SPRUCE. Native to northern Europe. Not as good as North American native spruces in Rocky Mountain states. Fast growth to 100–150 ft. Stiff, deep green, attractive pyramid in youth; in age, branchlets droop strongly, and oldest branchlets—nearest trunk—die back. Extremely hardy and wind resistant, Norway spruce is valued for windbreaks in cold areas. One of the best varieties it has produced is 'Sherwoodii', a rugged and picturesque shrub with compact but irregular growth habit. Parent tree, 60 years old, is 5 ft. tall and 10 ft. across.

P. brewerana. BREWER'S WEEPING SPRUCE. Zones 4–7, 14–17. To 100–120 ft. in its native Siskiyou Mountains in California and Oregon. Branchlets are pendulous, hanging vertically to 7–8 ft. or more. Rare in the wilds and in gardens. More tender than most spruces; requires much moisture and cool temperatures.

P. engelmannii. ENGELMANN SPRUCE. Densely pyramidal tree grows to 150 ft., native from southwest Canada to Oregon and Northern California, east to the Rockies. Resembles blue-green forms of Colorado spruce, but needles are softer and tree is not so spreading at base. Even 25-ft.

P

specimens will be densely branched to ground. Popular lawn tree in Rocky Mountain region.

P. glauca. WHITE SPRUCE. Native to Canada and northern United States. Conical tree to 60–70 ft., dense when young, with pendulous twigs and silver-green foliage. Best where winters are very cold.

P. g. 'Conica'. DWARF ALBERTA or DWARF WHITE SPRUCE. Compact pyramidal tree, growing slowly to 7 ft. in 35 years. Short, fine needles are soft to the touch, bright grass green when new, gray green when mature. Handsome tub plant—a miniature Christmas tree for many years. Also makes a fine small formal pyramid for garden. Thoroughly hardy to cold, but needs shelter from hot or cold drying winds and from strong reflected sunlight. Often sold as *P. albertiana.*

P. g. densata. BLACK HILLS SPRUCE. Slow-growing, dense pyramid; can reach 20 ft. tall in 35 years. Use it in containers, or plant it out in groves for screening or for alpine meadow effects.

P. pungens. COLORADO SPRUCE. Zones 1–10, 14–17. To 80–100 ft. Very stiff, regular, horizontal branches forming broad pyramid. Foliage varies in seedlings from dark green through all shades of blue green to steely blue. Often grown outside zones where it thrives; it survives but seldom looks its best. Spruce aphid is a serious pest in the Puget Sound area. For control, spray with acephate on March 1. Prefers dry soil. Varieties include

'Fat Albert'. Compact, erect, broad, formal-looking cone with blue color. Slow growth (to 10 ft. in 10 years) makes it a good living Christmas tree.

'Glauca'. COLORADO BLUE SPRUCE. Distinctive gray-blue color.

'Hoopsii'. Considered by many to be the bluest of spruces. Fast growing; needs early training to encourage erect, cone-shaped habit.

'Koster'. KOSTER BLUE SPRUCE. Bluer than 'Glauca', but growth habit sometimes irregular.

'Moerheimii'. Same blue as 'Koster', but tree has more compact and symmetrical shape.

'Pendula'. WEEPING BLUE SPRUCE. Gray blue, with weeping branchlets. Stake main trunk while plant is young.

'Thomsen'. Palest blue white of all spruces. Vigorous, symmetrical habit.

P. sitchensis. SITKA SPRUCE. Zones 4–6, 14–17. Native Alaska to California. Tall, pyramidal tree to 100–150 ft., with wide-spreading, horizontal branches. Short, thin needles are prickly to the touch, bright green and silvery white in color. Requires moist atmosphere and soil to look its best. Very subject to Cooley spruce gall, a conelike growth on new shoots caused by adelgids, a type of aphid. Treat as for scale.

PICKEREL WEED. See PONTEDERIA cordata p. 433

PIERIS

Ericaceae

EVERGREEN SHRUBS

✿ ZONES VARY BY SPECIES

☼ SOME SHADE, ESPECIALLY IN AFTERNOON

● REGULAR WATER

☠ LEAVES AND NECTAR ARE POISONOUS

Pieris japonica

Related to rhododendron and azalea, they have the same cultural needs and make good companion plants with their leathery leaves and clusters of small, white, urn-shaped flowers. Foliage and form are excellent all year. Flower buds in early winter look like strings of tiny greenish pink beads; these begin to open February–April. During (or just after) bloom, tinted new growth begins to appear.

Fairly easy to grow in coastal valleys of Northwest, these shrubs become increasingly fussy and are often less satisfactory south and inland. Where water is high in salts, they need careful leaching. Protect from wind for maximum beauty. Prune by removing spent flowers. Splendid in containers, in oriental and woodland gardens, in entryways where year-round quality is essential.

P. floribunda (Andromeda floribunda). MOUNTAIN PIERIS. Zones 2–9, 14–17, but needs protection in Zones 2, 3. Compact, rounded shrub

3–6 ft. tall, with elliptical, 1½–3-in. leaves, pale green when new, dull green when mature. Blossoms in upright clusters. Very hardy to cold; takes hotter, drier air than the others. Takes sun in Zones 4–6.

P. 'Forest Flame' (P. 'Flame of the Forest'). Zones 1–9, 14–17; satisfactory in Zones 2, 3 only if sheltered from drying winds and hot sun. Hybrid between *P. japonica* and a form of *P. forrestii* with especially bright red spring foliage; it combines new foliage brilliance of *P. forrestii* with some of the hardiness of *P. japonica.* Blooms profusely, with broader, heavier flower clusters than those of *P. japonica.* Grows 6–7 ft. tall and ultimately as wide.

P. forrestii (P. formosa forrestii). CHINESE PIERIS. Zones 5–9, 14–17. Dense, broad grower to 10 ft. tall with greater spread. Leaves shiny, leathery, dark green, to 6 in. long. New growth ranges from brilliant scarlet (in best forms) to pale salmon pink. Large, heavy clusters of tiny white flowers on branch tips in April, May. Buy when plants are making new growth; cutting-grown plants from best selections show their quality then. These may be offered as variety 'Bright Red'. Makes good espalier in shaded locations.

P. japonica (Andromeda japonica). LILY-OF-THE-VALLEY SHRUB. Zones 1–9, 14–17; in Zones 1–3, it requires generous watering, protection from sun and wind. Upright, dense, tiered growth to 9–10 ft. Mature leaves glossy dark green, 3 in. long; new growth bronzy pink to red. Drooping clusters of flower buds form in autumn and are attractive even before opening to white, pink, or nearly red flowers (February–May). Buds are often dark red. Responds well to frequent feeding—a must in heavy rainfall areas since leaching of nutrients will cause yellowing of foliage. Takes full sun in cool, humid climates, partial shade elsewhere. Many horticultural varieties, some rare. For unusual habit or foliage: 'Bert Chandler', with new foliage that turns from salmon pink through cream to white, then pale green; 'Compacta', smaller grower than parent; 'Crispa', smaller grower with wavy-edged leaves of great distinction; 'Mountain Fire', with fiery red new growth; 'Pygmaea', tiny dwarf less than 1 ft. tall, with very few flowers and narrow leaves 1 in. long or less; and 'Variegata', medium-size, slow-growing, compact plant with leaves prettily marked with creamy white, tinged pink in spring. 'Karenoma' and 'Spring Snow', compact 3–6-ft. plants, have the foliage quality of *P. japonica* combined with the upright flower clusters of *P. floribunda.*

These varieties are grown principally for flowers: 'Christmas Cheer', early-blooming bicolor in white and deep rose red, with rose red flower stalks; 'Coleman', pink flowers opening from red flower buds; 'Daisen', flowers similar to 'Christmas Cheer' but leaves are broader; 'Dorothy Wyckoff', white flowers from deep red flower buds; 'Pink', shell pink flowers fading white; 'Purity', late-blooming white flowers; 'Temple Bell', ivory white flowers and compact, tiered habit; 'Valley Rose', low growing, with pink-and-white flowers; 'Valley Valentine', deep red buds and flowers; and 'White Cascade', an extremely heavy flower producer.

P. taiwanensis. Zones 5–7, 14–17. Similar to *P. japonica*, but with somewhat larger, more erect flower clusters. Hybrid with *P. japonica*, 'Snowdrift', has unusually heavy pure white bloom.

PIGEON BERRY. See DURANTA repens p. 269

PIGGY-BACK PLANT. See TOLMIEA menziesii p. 507

PIMELEA

RICE FLOWER

Thymeleaceae

EVERGREEN SHRUBS

✿ ZONES VARY BY SPECIES

☼ ☀ SUN OR LIGHT SHADE

◗ ● WATER NEEDS VARY BY SPECIES

Pimelea prostrata

The rice flowers are daphne relatives from Australia and New Zealand. Flowers form in tight clusters at branch tips. Of the many species, only two are occasionally seen in the West.

P. ferruginea. PINK RICE FLOWER. Zones 16, 17, 21–24. Grows to 2 ft. tall, somewhat broader, with finely textured, glossy green leaves and magenta pink flower clusters 1½ in. wide in late winter through early summer. Demands frost protection, perfect drainage, and occasional summer water. Pruning after bloom keeps *P. ferruginea* compact. 'Bonne Petite' is a selected form.

P. prostrata. Zones 4–7, 14–17. Forms a gray, fine-leafed compact mat 3–6. in. tall, 1 ft. wide or more. Clusters of small, faintly fragrant, white four-petaled flowers are followed by white berries. Needs good drainage, neutral or acid soil, light feeding, regular water. Use in rock garden or as small-scale ground cover. Often sold as *P. coarctata.*

PIMPERNEL. See ANAGALLIS	**p. 150**

PIMPINELLA anisum

ANISE
Apiaceae (Umbelliferae)
ANNUAL HERB
✔ ALL ZONES
☼ FULL SUN
● REGULAR WATER

Pimpinella anisum

Bright green, toothed, basal leaves. Tiny white flowers in umbrellalike clusters on 2-ft. stems in June. Sow seed in place when ground warms up in spring. Grow in light soil. Does not transplant easily. Use fresh leaves in salads; use seeds for flavoring cookies, confections.

Pinaceae. Members of the pine family are evergreen trees with narrow, usually needlelike leaves and seeds borne on the scales of woody cones. Pines, firs, spruces, true cedars, larches, Douglas firs, and hemlocks are examples.

PINCUSHION FLOWER. See SCABIOSA	**p. 478**
PINCUSHION TREE. See HAKEA laurina	**p. 315**
PINDO PALM. See BUTIA capitata	**p. 193**
PINE. See PINUS	**p. 419**

PINEAPPLE

Bromeliaceae
BROMELIAD HOUSE PLANT; CAN BEAR FRUIT
☼ ◗ GREENHOUSE OR SUNNY ROOM
● REGULAR WATER

Pineapple

Plant is rosette of long, narrow leaves with sawtooth edges. To grow it, cut leafy top from market pineapple. Root base of top in water or mixture of damp sand and peat moss. When roots have formed, move to 7–8-in. pot of rich soil. Keep where temperatures stay above 68°F. Water when soil gets dry. Feed every 3–4 weeks with liquid fertilizer. Fruit forms, if you're lucky, in 2 years, on top of sturdy stalk at center of clump. Homegrown pineapple fruit is much smaller than commercial fruit. Sometimes available as house plant is a variety with foliage variegated in pink, white, and olive green.

PINEAPPLE FLOWER. See EUCOMIS	**p. 288**
PINEAPPLE GUAVA. See FEIJOA sellowiana	**p. 292**

PINUS

PINE
Pinaceae
EVERGREEN TREES, RARELY SHRUBS
✔ REGIONS VARY BY SPECIES
☼ FULL SUN
◖ ◗ MOST NEED LITTLE WATER
▶ SEE CHART NEXT PAGE

Pinus pinea

Pines are the great individualists of the garden, each species differing not only in its characteristics but also in the ways it responds to sun, wind, and soil type. The number of long, slender needles in a bundle and the size and shape of cones are the two chief characteristics by which pines are classified.

Generally speaking, soil need not be rich, but it should be well drained. Many pines naturally grow on rocky slopes or on sandy barrens where fertility is low but drainage excellent. They show effects of bad drainage or overwatering by general poor appearance and unusual number of yellowing needles, especially on older growth. Pines require little if any fertilizing; heavy feeding encourages too-rapid, rank growth. Most of the species with five needles to a bundle need watering.

Pines are vulnerable to air pollution, which causes abnormal needle drop and poor growth, and can kill trees. They are also subject to a number of pests, but healthy, well-grown plants will stay that way with comparatively little attention. Most five-needled pines are subject to a disease called white pine blister rust. Pines with two or three needles in a bundle are sometimes attacked by European pine shoot moth in Northwest (symptoms are distorted or dead new shoots). Aphids usually show their presence by sticky secretions, sooty mildew, yellowing needles. Engraver beetles sometimes bore into bark of Monterey, ponderosa, bishop, Coulter, beach, Aleppo, and Torrey pines in California. Healthy trees usually survive with little damage, but trees weakened by drought, smog, or mites and other pests often die. Birds like to feast on seeds contained in pinecones.

All pines can be shaped, and usually improved, by some pruning. To shape a pine in an oriental manner is tricky but not really difficult; it's just a matter of cutting out any branches that interfere with the effect, shortening other branches, and creating an upswept look by removing all twigs that grow downward. Cutting vertical main trunk back to well-placed side branch will induce side growth, and wiring or weighting branches will produce cascade effects.

It is unlikely that any one nursery will have all the pines described in the chart; in fact, any nursery that has even half of them is remarkably well stocked. Your nursery can help you locate the rare pines you may wish to try, and advise you concerning their adaptability to your climate zone and local insect, mite, disease, and environmental stress problems. Bonsai specialists and a few mail-order nurseries often stock a wide variety of pines.

SPRING PRUNING TO SHAPE A PINE TREE

To fatten up a rangy pine or to keep a young pine teddy-bear-chubby, cut back the candles of new growth by half (or even more) when the new growth begins to emerge in spring. Leave a few clusters untrimmed if you want growth to continue along a branch.

PINE

NAME, NATIVE HABITAT	GROWTH RATE, SIZE	GROWTH HABIT	NEEDLES AND CONES	CLIMATE ADAPTABILITY	COMMENTS
Pinus albicaulis WHITEBARK PINE High mountains of Canada, Washington, Oregon, Northern California, and western Nevada, and east into Idaho, Wyoming, Montana	Very slow to 20–40 ft., usually much less	Prostrate, spreading, or semiupright. Often multitrunked. In youth, slender and symmetrical	Needles: in 5s, 1½–3 in., dark green, dense. Cones: 3 in., roundish, purple	Hardy timberline tree. Does well east of Cascades in Northwest. Dislikes warm, low-elevation climates	Usually dug in mountains and sold by collectors as "alpine" conifer. Good for rock gardens, bonsai
P. aristata BRISTLECONE PINE High mountains of West; very local and widely scattered	Very slow to 45 ft., usually not more than 20 ft.	Dense, bushy, heavy trunked, with ground-sweeping branches. In youth, symmetrical, narrow crowned with mature look	Needles: in 5s, 1–1½ in., dark green, whitish beneath flecked with white dots of resin. Cones: 3½ in., dark purplish brown	Hardy. Does well at sea level in cool-summer areas of coastal California and along front range of Rocky Mountains. Variable in Northwest. Best in pot in Southern California	So slow growing it is good for years as container plant. Needles persist many years, making crown extremely dense. Sometimes called Rocky Mountain bristlecone pine
P. attenuata KNOBCONE PINE Northern and central Cascades in Oregon, Siskiyous, Sierra Nevada foothills in California, south to Baja	Rapid to 20–80 ft.	Open, irregular, and rough. In youth, rounded and regular. Some populations are far more dense, symmetrical. Habit depends on seed source	Needles: in 3s, 3–5 in., yellow-green. Cones: narrowly oval and asymmetrical, light brown, to 6 in.	Quite hardy; adaptable to most areas from Puget Sound south to Baja California	Very aridity tolerant when established. Grows well in poor soils. Holds its cones for many years
P. balfouriana FOXTAIL PINE California mountains: northern Coast Ranges and southern Sierra Nevada	Very slow to 20–50 ft.	In youth a symmetrical, narrow cone. Spreads more in maturity, with stout lower branches and irregular upper ones	Needles: in 5s, to 1½ in., glossy green in dense tufts at branch tips, lasting many years. Cones: narrow, cylindrical, drooping, to 5 in. long	Hardy; often timberline tree	Best planted as shrub; in much time can outgrow shrub status. Candidate for container, bonsai, rock garden
P. brutia (P. halepensis brutia) CALABRIAN PINE Eastern Mediterranean, southern Russia, southern Italy	Rapid, especially in youth, to 30–80 ft.	Denser, more erect than the related *P. halepensis,* closer to classic pine tree shape	Needles: in 2s, 5–6½ in. long, dark green. Cones: like *P. halepensis* but not stalked or bent back	Thrives in heat, drought, wind, indifferent soil. Cannot take temperatures much below 0°F	Faster growing, shapelier tree than *P. halepensis;* form is less interesting in maturity. Good possibilities as commercial Christmas tree
P. bungeana LACEBARK PINE Northern and central China	Slow to 75 ft.	Often multitrunked, spreading. Sometimes shrubby. Picturesque	Needles: in 3s, 3 in. long, bright green. Cones: 2–2½ in. long, yellowish brown	Hardy to subzero cold, tolerates heat of California's Central Valley	Smooth, dull gray bark flakes off like sycamore bark to show smooth, creamy white branches and trunk
P. canariensis CANARY ISLAND PINE Canary Islands	Fast, to 60–80 ft., sometimes shorter	In youth a slender, graceful pyramid. Later a tiered structure; finally a round-crowned tree	Needles: in 3s, 9–12 in., blue-green in youth, dark green when older. Cones: 4–9 in., oval, glossy brown	Tender in Northwest but good in Southern California and coastal Northern California. Has been severely damaged (even killed) at 10°F. Needles freeze at 20°F	Resistant to oak root fungus. Very young plants are gawky but soon outgrow their awkward phase. Aridity tolerant but needs water in Southern California
P. cembra SWISS STONE PINE Northern Asia, northern Europe	Extremely slow to 70 ft. or more	Spreading, short branches in narrow, dense pyramid; broad, open, and round-topped in age	Needles: in 5s, 3–5 in., dark green. Cones: 3½ in., oval, light brown	Very hardy (to –35°F). Good in Northwest and Rocky Mountain region	Resistant to white pine blister rust. Slow growth and dense, regular foliage make it a good plant for small gardens. Handsome in youth
P. cembroides MEXICAN PIÑON PINE Arizona to Baja California and northern Mexico	Slow to 10–25 ft.	Stout, spreading branches form round-topped head. In youth rather rangy	Needles: in 3s or 2s, 1–2 in., slender, dark green. Cones: 1–2 in., yellowish or reddish brown	Succeeds in Northwest west of Cascades, in California coastal and valley gardens, and in Rocky Mountains	Most treelike of piñons. Aridity resistant, good in desert soils

P

PINE

NAME, NATIVE HABITAT	GROWTH RATE, SIZE	GROWTH HABIT	NEEDLES AND CONES	CLIMATE ADAPTABILITY	COMMENTS
P. contorta BEACH PINE, SHORE PINE Coast from Mendocino County, California, to Alaska	Fairly fast to 20–35 ft.	Nursery-grown trees compact, pyramidal, somewhat irregular. Coast trees dwarfed, contorted by winds	Needles: in 2s, 1¼–2 in., dark green, dense. Cones: 1–2 in., light yellow-brown	Hardy anywhere but not at its best in hot, dry areas	Good-looking in youth. Densely foliaged, takes training well. One of best small pines for small gardens. Does well in containers
P. c. latifolia **(P. c. murrayana)** LODGEPOLE PINE, TAMARACK Blue Mountains of eastern Oregon, Cascades of Washington, throughout Rockies (in California and Oregon called **P. c. murrayana**)	Rather slow to 80 ft., sometimes 150 ft.; usually low, bushy tree in cultivation	In cultivation rather irregular, open-branched, attractive. Planted close together, trees are tall, slim-trunked. Solitary trees in mountains are heavy-trunked, narrow, and dense	Needles: in 2s, 1½–3 in., yellow-green. Cones: 1½ in., shiny brown, persist many years	Hardy	All forms of *P. contorta* excellent in small garden, wild garden, or large rock garden
P. coulteri COULTER PINE Dry, rocky California mountain slopes: Mt. Diablo, Mt. Hamilton, Santa Lucia ranges, and in Southern California, Baja California	Moderate to fast, 30–80 ft.	Shapely open growth; lower branches spread widely, persist. Sometimes develops several divergent leaders, producing "oak tree" shape	Needles: in 3s, 5–10 (even 14) in., deep green, stiff. Cones: 10–13 in., buff colored, heavy, persisting many years	Hardy. Adaptable to area west of Cascades. Resistant to heat, aridity, wind. Good in high desert	Excellent in gardens where not crowded. Too spreading for small gardens. Huge cones attractive but potentially dangerous around play areas, patios, parked cars
P. densiflora JAPANESE RED PINE Japan	Rapid when young. May reach 100 ft., usually much less	Broad, irregular head. Often develops two or more trunks at ground level	Needles: in 2s, 2½–5 in., bright blue-green or yellow-green, slender. Cones: 2 in., oval or oblong, tawny brown	Hardy to –20°F, but not tree for desert areas. Will not tolerate hot, dry, or cold winds	Handsome informal pine, especially multitrunked. Moderate shade for woodland gardens. 'Oculus-draconis', dragon eye pine, has 2 yellow bands on each needle; viewed endwise, branch has concentric green and yellow bands. 'Pendula' is dwarf, sprawling; good in rock gardens
P. d. 'Umbraculifera' TANYOSHO PINE Japan	Slow to moderate, 12–20 ft.	Broad, flat-topped, with numerous trunks from base. Spread greater than height	Same as *P. densiflora*	Same as *P. densiflora*. Has performed well in Denver	Gallon- and 5-gallon-size trees frequently bear cones. Good for containers, rock and oriental gardens
P. edulis **(P. cembroides edulis)** PIÑON, NUT PINE California's desert mountains; east to Arizona, New Mexico, and Texas; north to Wyoming	Slow to 10–20 ft.	Horizontal-branching tree. Bushy and symmetrical in youth; low, round or flat-crowned in age	Needles: usually in 2s, dark green, ¾–1½ in., dense, stiff. Cones: 2 in., roundish, light brown	Hardy. No water once established	Beautiful small pine for containers, rock gardens. Collected plants bring look of age into new gardens. Cones contain edible seeds (pine nuts)
P. eldarica AFGHAN PINE Southwestern Asia	Same as *P. brutia*	Same as *P. brutia*	Same as *P. brutia*	One of best desert pines, it also thrives near coast	Something of a mystery pine; may be *P. brutia* from Afghanistan and Pakistan. Christmas Blue is a selected blue-green strain
P. flexilis LIMBER PINE Mountains of northern Arizona, Utah, Nevada, southeastern California, and eastern slope of Rocky Mountains from Alberta to Texas. Grows at 5,000–11,000-ft. elevation	Slow, to 20–30 ft. in gardens	Thick trunk, open round top, many limber branches that may droop at decided angle to trunk	Needles: in 5s, to 3 in., slightly curved or twisted, dark green. Cones: to 5 in. long, ovoid-conic, buff to buff-orange	Hardy. Grows well on hot, dry, rocky slopes. Aridity tolerant	Smaller and more irregular at higher elevations. Young plants rather straggly appearing. Shapes well with shearing; can be used for bonsai. Susceptible to white pine blister rust. 'Vanderwolf's Pyramid' is a selection with a regular form and blue-green color

P

PINE

NAME, NATIVE HABITAT	GROWTH RATE, SIZE	GROWTH HABIT	NEEDLES AND CONES	CLIMATE ADAPTABILITY	COMMENTS
P. halepensis ALEPPO PINE Mediterranean region	Moderate to rapid, to 30–60 ft.	Attractive as 2-year-old; rugged character at 5 years; in age, open irregular crown of many short, ascending branches	Needles: usually in 2s, 2½–4 in., light green. Cones: 3 in., oval to oblong, reddish to yellow-brown	Semihardy. Thrives in desert heat, aridity, and wind; good at seashore. Tender when young; established trees can take near-zero temperatures	Useful in poor soils and arid climates. Handsomer trees can be found for easier climates. Standard desert pine. Can be bothered by mites in Southern California; temporary dieback in Tucson area
P. h. brutia (see **P. brutia**)					
P. heldreichii leucodermis (**P. leucodermis**) BOSNIAN PINE Balkans, Greece, Italy	Slow to 75 ft.	Erect, dense, oval to conical. Pale gray bark	Needles: in pairs, short, stiff, dark green, persisting 5–6 years. Cones: single or in 3s, 2–3 in. long, blue to bright brown	Very hardy to cold. Salt tolerant. Transplants well	Slow growth, dense habit, and salt tolerance make it a good landscape tree, especially near the sea
P. jeffreyi JEFFREY PINE Mountains of California, southern Oregon, western Nevada, Baja California	Moderate to 60–120 ft.	Symmetrical in youth, with straight trunk and short, spreading, often pendulous branches. Upper branches ascending; form open, pyramidal	Needles: in 3s, 5–8 in., blue-green. Cones: 6–12 in., reddish brown, oval. Cone doesn't feel prickly like *P. ponderosa*	Hardy. High-altitude tree that is not at its best in low areas. Aridity resistant. Slow growing in Seattle	Attractive in youth, with silver gray bark and bluish foliage. One of best natural bonsai trees. Furrows of bark have vanilla odor
P. lambertiana SUGAR PINE Sierra Nevada and California's higher Coast Ranges; high mountains of Southern California, Baja; north to Cascades of central Oregon	Slow in youth, then faster, to 200 ft. or more	Young trees narrow, open pyramids with spreading, rather pendulous branches. Old trees usually flat-topped with wide-spreading, open head	Needles: in 5s, 3–4 in., dark bluish green. Cones: 10–20 in., cylindrical, light brown	Hardy but temperamental. Grows well in Seattle	World's tallest pine. Susceptible to white pine blister rust but usually safe if no currants or gooseberry bushes (alternate hosts of blister rust) nearby
P. monophylla SINGLELEAF PIÑON PINE Southeastern California south to Baja California, east to Utah, Arizona	Very slow to 10–25 ft.	Young tree slender, symmetrical, narrow crowned. In maturity small, round-headed, with crooked trunk; open and broad-topped in age	Needles: usually carried singly, ¾–1½ in., gray-green, stiff. Cones: 2 in. long, wide, roundish, brown	Hardy and aridity resistant. Only piñon common in Southern California	Good bonsai or rock garden plant—or shrub of great character in dry, rocky places. Cones contain edible seeds (pine nuts)
P. montezumae MONTEZUMA PINE Mexico to Guatemala	Moderately fast. To 70 ft. or more in the wilds, usually much less in cultivation	Broad, fairly dense, with horizontal, somewhat drooping branches	Needles: in 5s, also in clusters of 3–8, to 1 ft., drooping gracefully; often bluish green. Cones: to 1 ft., yellow, reddish, or dark brown	Unlikely to survive low temperatures. Does well in San Francisco Bay Area. Substitute *P. wallichiana* in colder areas	Striking pine with unusually long needles
P. monticola WESTERN WHITE PINE Northern California, north to British Columbia, east to Montana	Fast first years, then slow to moderate to 60 ft.	Attractive, narrow, open crown in youth; in age, pyramidal form with spreading, somewhat drooping branches	Needles: in 5s, 1½–4 in., blue-green banded with white beneath, fine and soft. Cones: 5–11 in., light brown, slender	Very hardy	Susceptible to white pine blister rust throughout Northwest and Northern California
P. mugo (P. montana) SWISS MOUNTAIN PINE Mountains of Spain, central Europe to Balkans	Slow to variable heights	Variable. Prostrate shrub, low shrub, or pyramidal tree of moderate size	Needles: in 2s, 2 in., dark green, stout, crowded. Cones: 1–2 in., oval, tawny to dark brown	Hardy but suffers in desert heat	In nurseries, generally a bushy, twisted, somewhat open pine. *P. m. pumilio* is eastern European form, shrubby and varying from prostrate to 5–10 ft.

P

PINE

NAME, NATIVE HABITAT	GROWTH RATE, SIZE	GROWTH HABIT	NEEDLES AND CONES	CLIMATE ADAPTABILITY	COMMENTS
P. m. mugo MUGHO PINE Eastern Alps and Balkan states	Slow to 4 ft.	From infancy a shrubby, symmetrical little pine. May spread in age	Needles: darker green than *P. mugo.* Cones: a little shorter than those of *P. mugo*	Very hardy but, like *P. mugo,* suffers in desert heat	Widely used pines for low growth habit. Excellent pot plant. Pick plants with dense, pleasing form. Good in rock gardens
P. muricata BISHOP PINE Northern coast of California, Santa Cruz Island, northwestern Baja California	Rapid to 40–50 ft.	Open, pyramidal when young; dense, rounded in middle life; irregular in age	Needles: in 2s, 4–6 in., dark green, crowded. Cones: 2–3 in., borne in whorls of 3, 4, or 5; broadly oval, brown	Takes wind and salt air. Not reliably hardy in Northwest or interior	Many prefer it to *P. radiata* for slower growth rate, greater denseness in youth, better manners. *P. remorata* (Santa Cruz Island pine) and *P. cedrosensis* (Cedros Island pine) may belong here. First-rate windbreak tree
P. nigra (formerly **P. austriaca**) AUSTRIAN BLACK PINE Europe, western Asia	Slow to moderate, usually not more than 40 ft. in gardens	Dense, stout pyramid with uniform crown. Branches in regular whorls. In age, broad and flat-topped	Needles: in 2s, 3–6½ in., stiff, very dark green. Cones: 2–3½ in., oval, brown	Very hardy. Adaptable to winter cold and wind	Tree of strong character that will serve either as landscape decoration or as windbreak in cold regions. Resistant to oak root fungus
P. palustris LONGLEAF PINE Virginia and Florida and west to Mississippi, southeastern U.S. coast	Slow for 5–10 years, then fast to 55–80 ft.	Gaunt, sparse branches ascend to form open, oblong head	Needles: in 3s, to 1½ ft. on young trees, to 9 in. on mature trees. Dark green. Cones: 6–10 in., dull brown	Grows in Northern and Southern California. In native habitat can take frosts to 5°F but is used to warmer winters	Young plants look like fountains of grass. When taller, resemble green mops. Control chlorosis with iron chelates
P. parviflora JAPANESE WHITE PINE Japan and Taiwan	Slow to moderate, to 20–50 ft. or more	In open ground a broad pyramid nearly as wide as high	Needles: in 5s, 1½–2½ in., bluish green. Cones: 2–3 in. long, 1 in. wide, reddish brown	Hardy. Grows well in Seattle and in Northern California. Will survive −20°F	Widely used for bonsai or container plant. There are several dwarf and blue-gray forms, 'Glauca' among them
P. patula JELECOTE PINE Mexico	Very fast to 40–80 ft.	Symmetrical pyramid with widely spaced tiers of branches	Needles: in 3s, to 1 ft., grass green, slender, hanging down. Cones: to 4½ in., lustrous pale brown	Hardy to 15°F; a borderline case in Seattle or inland, thriving in coastal California	Graceful tree casts a light shade, provides handsome silhouette. One of the fastest-growing pines in the world. Treat for chlorosis. Resistant to oak root fungus
P. pinaster CLUSTER PINE, FRENCH TURPENTINE PINE, MARITIME PINE Atlantic coast of France, western Mediterranean, northern Africa	Very fast to 80–90 ft.	Spreading or sometimes pendulous branches forming pyramidal head	Needles: in 2s, 5–9 in., stiff, glossy green. Cones: 4–7 in., conic-oblong, borne singly or in clusters, glossy light brown	Hardy to 0°F. Best near coasts, in coastal valleys	Well adapted to sandy soil, ocean exposure. Used in San Francisco's Golden Gate Park to help bind sand dunes. May be weak-rooted when young
P. pinea ITALIAN STONE PINE Southern Europe and Turkey	Moderate to 40–80 ft.	In youth, a stout, bushy globe; in middle life, thick trunk topped with umbrella form of many branches. In age, broad and flat-topped	Needles: in 2s, 5–8 in., bright to gray-green, stiff. Cones: 4–6 in., glossy, chestnut brown, broadly oval	Hardy. Takes heat and aridity when established. Old trees hardy in Northwest, young ones tender. Good in California valleys and on coast; successful in Tucson	Excellent in beach gardens. Eventually too large for small gardens. Splendid roadside tree. Young trees are handsome, old trees striking. This is the pine of Rome and of Renaissance paintings, also the source of pignolias (pine nuts)
P. ponderosa PONDEROSA PINE, WESTERN YELLOW PINE British Columbia to Mexico and east to Nebraska, Texas, northeast Oklahoma	Moderate to rapid, to 50–60 ft. in 50 years, eventually to 150 ft. or more	In youth, straight-trunked and well-branched. Stately in age, with open branches in spirelike crown. Handsome plated bark	Needles: in 3s, 4–11 in., glossy yellow-green to dark green, firm, in clusters at branch ends. Cones: 3–5 in., light brown to red-brown, prickly	Very hardy, but not good in desert heat and wind	Bushy, attractive tree. Requires big gardens in age. Small ones make fine bonsai or large pot plants. *P. p. arizonica* has needles in 5s or 3s and 4s. *P. p. scopulorum* from Rockies has shorter needles, drooping branches

P

▶

PINE

NAME, NATIVE HABITAT	GROWTH RATE, SIZE	GROWTH HABIT	NEEDLES AND CONES	CLIMATE ADAPTABILITY	COMMENTS
P. radiata MONTEREY PINE Central California coast	Very fast to 80–100 ft.	Shapely, broad cone in youth, then drops lower branches to develop rounded or flattish crown	Needles: in 3s or 2s, 3–7 in., bright green. Cones: 3–6 in., lopsided, clustered, persisting many years	Widely planted in California even where poorly adapted. Not reliably hardy at temperatures below 15°F. Best where summers are cool. Not for high or low desert areas nor for California's Central Valley. Good in sea wind, but not in shallow soils	Very fast growing, 6 ft. a year when young, 50 ft. in 12 years. Often shallow-rooted, subject to blowdown. Prune to maintain denseness. In coastal California suffers many pests, smog damage, water molds. Keep healthy with occasional deep watering, feeding. Resists oak root fungus
P. roxburghii (P. longifolia) CHIR PINE, INDIAN LONGLEAF PINE Himalayan foothills	Medium fast to 60–80 ft. or more	Slender pyramid with long, drooping needles; later broad, spreading, with round-topped head	Needles: in 3s, 8–13 in., slender, light green. Cones: 4–7 in., ovoid-conic	Adapted to California coastal areas, lower Oregon coast. Succeeds in California's Central Valley and in Tucson	Rare pine. Similar in many ways to *P. canariensis*
P. sabiniana DIGGER, GRAY, or FOOTHILL PINE California foothills	Fast to 40–50 ft.	Wild trees in dry areas are sparse, open. Usually have forked trunks	Needles: in 3s, 8–12 in., gray-green, lacy. Cones: 6–10 in., with edible seeds	Though native to dry foothills and very resistant to aridity, thrives in Seattle	Unusual tree for large gardens. Bulky yet lacy, almost transparent crown. Offers little shade. Very ornamental
P. strobus WHITE PINE, EASTERN WHITE PINE Newfoundland to Manitoba, south to Georgia, west to Illinois and Iowa	Slow in seedling stage, then fast to 100 ft. or more	Symmetrical cone with horizontal branches in regular whorls. In age, broad, open, irregular	Needles: in 5s, 2–4 in., blue-green, soft. Cones: 3–8 in., slender, often curved	Hardy in any cold but burns in windy areas. Needs regular water supply	Finely textured and handsome in form and color. Subject to blister rust. 'Pendula' has weeping, trailing branches. 'Prostrata' is low, spreading shrub with trailing branches
P. s. 'Nana' DWARF WHITE PINE	Very slow to 3–7 ft.	Broad bush twice as wide as tall	As above but with shorter needles	Hardy wherever *P. strobus* grows successfully	Useful in containers or rock gardens
P. sylvestris SCOTCH PINE Northern Europe and Asia	Moderate to 70–100 ft.	Straight, well-branched pyramid in youth; irregular and picturesque in age, with drooping branches	Needles: in 2s, 1½–3 in., blue-green, stiff. Cones: 2 in., gray to reddish brown	Very hardy. Not for desert areas; often turns redbrown in cold winters, but recovers. Wind resistant	Popular as Christmas tree and in landscaping. Reddish bark, sparse foliage have own charm. Pick young trees for good green winter color; some turn yellowish, even with mild winter. Excellent in flower arrangements. Garden forms: dwarfs 'Nana' and 'Watereri', weeping 'Pendula'
P. s. 'Fastigiata'	Same as *P. sylvestris*	Dense, narrow column	Same as *P. sylvestris*	Same as *P. sylvestris*	Handsome, very densely foliaged plant
P. thunbergiana (P. thunbergii) JAPANESE BLACK PINE Japan	Fast to 100 ft. in Northwest. Slow to moderate, to 20 ft., in Southern California and desert	Spreading branches form broad, conical tree, irregular and spreading in age	Needles: in 2s, 3–4½ in., bright green, stiff. Cones: 3 in., brown, oval	Hardy. Widely planted in California, western Washington, Oregon. Grows well with watering in intermediate and high desert. 'Majestic Beauty' tolerates smog	Handsome tree in youth. Takes to pruning like cloth to scissors; shear it into Christmas tree form or make it into cascade. Excellent in planters or as bonsai. Often pruned to open, irregular shape as large container plant or giant bonsai
P. torreyana TORREY PINE California's San Diego coast and Santa Rosa Island	Fast to 40–60 ft., sometimes more	Broad, open, irregular, picturesque habit when exposed to sea winds	Needles: in 5s, 8–13 in., light gray-green to dark green. Cones: 4–6 in., chocolate brown	Native to the coast, but accepts inland, even high desert, conditions, with temperatures to 12°F. Tolerates aridity	Less open growth when grown in heavy soil. Don't prune: cut branches die back to trunk. Resistant to oak root fungus
P. wallichiana (P. griffithii, P. excelsa) HIMALAYAN WHITE PINE Himalayas	Slow to moderate; 40 ft. in gardens, 150 ft. in wild	Broad, conical	Needles: in 5s, 6–8 in., blue-green, slender, drooping. Cones: 6–10 in., light brown	Hardy to about –10°F. Poor performance in dry, hot areas	Resistant to blister rust. Eventually large, but good form and color make it good choice for featured pine in big lawn or garden

P

PISTACIA

PISTACHE

Anacardiaceae

EVERGREEN, SEMIEVERGREEN, OR DECIDUOUS TREES

☇ ZONES VARY BY SPECIES

☼ FULL SUN

◗ ◗ ◗ WATER NEEDS VARY BY SPECIES

D ivided leaves on all species. Flowers are not showy. Female trees will bear fruit after several years if male trees are nearby. Of species described, only *P. vera* bears edible fruit (nuts). Others are ornamental trees.

Pistacia chinensis

Verticillium wilt may strike established trees. Minimize susceptibility by planting in well-drained soil, watering deeply and as little as possible.

P. atlantica. MT. ATLAS PISTACHE. Semievergreen or deciduous. Zones 8–24. Slow to moderate growth to 60 ft. More regular and pyramidal than other pistaches, especially as young tree. Glossy medium green leaves with 7–11 narrow leaflets, rounded at tip. Fruit dark blue or purple. Needs good drainage. Takes desert heat and winds; established plants need no water. Holds its foliage very late—all winter in mild climate. Not widely grown as ornamental but is much used as understock for pistachio *(P. vera)*.

P. chinensis. CHINESE PISTACHE. Deciduous. Zones 4–16, 18–23; little grown in Zones 4–7. Moderate growth to 60 ft. tall, 50 ft. wide. Young trees often gawky and lopsided, but older trees become dense and shapely with reasonable care. Leaves with 10–16 paired leaflets 2–4 in. long by ¾ in. wide. Foliage colors beautifully in fall—scarlet, crimson, orange, sometimes yellow tones. Only tree to color scarlet in desert. Fruit on female trees bright red, turning dark blue.

Can take aridity or irrigation. Accepts moderately alkaline conditions, lawn watering (though verticillium wilt is a danger), or no summer watering at all (this only in deep soils). Resistant to oak root fungus. Stake young trees and prune them for the first few years to develop head high enough to walk under. Reliable tree for street, lawn, patio, or garden corner planting.

P. lentiscus. MASTIC. Evergreen. Zones 8, 9, 12–24. Dense shrub or small tree to 12 ft. Leathery leaves have four to six leaflets, ½ to 1½ in. long; inconspicuous flowers; and small red fruits that ripen to black. Useful as screening in hot, dry situations and poor soil. The source of mastic, an aromatic resin; needs no water once established.

P. vera. PISTACHIO, PISTACHIO NUT. Deciduous. Zones 7–12, 14, 15, 18–21. Broad, bushy tree to 30 ft. high, with one or several trunks. Leaves have three to five roundish, 2–4-in.-long leaflets. Fruit reddish, wrinkled, borne in heavy clusters. Inside husks are hard-shelled pistachio nuts. Be sure to include male tree in your planting. 'Peters' is the male variety most planted, 'Kerman' is principal fruiting (female) variety. When planting, avoid rough handling; budded tops are easily broken away from understock. Pistachios are inclined to spread and droop; stake them and train their branches to good framework of four or five limbs beginning at 4 ft. or so above ground. Established trees need little watering.

FOR INFORMATION ON YOUR CLIMATE ZONE
PLEASE SEE PAGES 15–44

PITHECELLOBIUM flexicaule

TEXAS EBONY

Fabaceae (Leguminosae)

EVERGREEN TREE

☇ ZONES 10–13

☼ FULL SUN

◗ INFREQUENT, DEEP WATERING

Pithecellobium flexicaule

N ative to Texas and Mexico, this tree is handsome in desert landscapes, where its dark green color is especially welcome. Don't plant near walks where thorns could cause problems.

Grows slowly to 20 ft. (possibly 30 ft.) tall, 15 ft. wide or more. Short, smooth, gray trunk; zigzagging thorny branches and twigs densely set with dark green leaves divided into ½-in. leaflets. Fragrant, creamy yellow flowers in short, feathery spikes appear in spring and early summer. Dark brown, 4–6-in.-long seedpods follow.

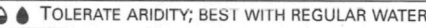

Pittosporaceae. The pittosporum family consists of evergreen shrubs, trees, and vines from Australia, New Zealand, and eastern Asia. Many have attractive flowers, foliage, or fruit. *Hymenosporum, Pittosporum,* and *Sollya* are representatives.

PITTOSPORUM

Pittosporaceae

EVERGREEN SHRUBS AND TREES

☇ ZONES VARY BY SPECIES

☼ FULL SUN TO HALF SHADE

◗ ◗ TOLERATE ARIDITY; BEST WITH REGULAR WATER

Pittosporum tobira

S ome forms have attractive fragrant flowers and some have pretty fruit, but as a group, pittosporums are valued most by westerners for their foliage and form. All make basic, dependable shrubs or trees—the kind of plants that can be a garden's all-year backbone. Some make good clipped hedges; all have pleasing outlines when left unclipped. Good as windbreaks.

Feed once each spring or summer with nitrogenous or complete fertilizer. All are susceptible to aphids and scale insects. Black sooty covering on leaves (mold growing on insects' honeydew secretions) is a sure sign of infestation.

P. crassifolium. Zones 9, 14–17, 19–24. Will grow to 25 ft. high in 8–10 years but can easily be kept 6–10 ft. high and 6–8 ft. wide with yearly pruning. Gray-green leaves, 1–2 in. long with rounded ends, densely set on branches. Clusters of little (¼-in.-wide) maroon flowers in late spring. Conspicuous fruit. Notably wind resistant; tolerates even salt-laden ocean winds. Good seaside plant. 'Compactum' is dense dwarf form growing 3 ft. tall or a bit taller, and as wide as it is high.

P. eugenioides. Zones 9, 14–17, 19–22. Excellent hedge plant or freestanding shade tree. Good as screen or background plant. Medium glossy, 2–4-in.-long leaves have distinctly wavy edges. Depending on environment, leaf color may be yellow green to medium green. On unpruned plants, clusters of fragrant, yellow, ½-in. flowers form in spring. To grow as hedge, plant gallon-can plants 1½ ft. apart in row. Force bushiness by shearing off 2–6 in. of plant tops several times each year between February and October. Begin clipping sides when necessary. As freestanding tree (to 40 ft. high, 20 ft. wide), develops handsome, curving gray trunk and lush foliage canopy. A form with creamy white edging on the leaves is smaller (to 10 ft.). It should have partial shade in very hot areas to prevent sunburn.

P. phillyraeoides. WILLOW PITTOSPORUM. Zones 8, 9, 12–24. Different from typical pittosporums: a weeping plant with trailing branches and deep, dusty green leaves, very narrow, 3 in. long. Grows slowly to 15–20 ft. high, 10–15 ft. wide. Always best standing alone; strong structure shouldn't be smothered by other foliage. Good by pool or patio. Small, yellow, bell-shaped, fragrant flowers borne along drooping branches in late winter, early spring, followed by deep yellow fruit. If drainage is poor, water very infrequently but deeply. Tolerates heat and aridity better than almost all other pittosporums and has even naturalized in some desert areas.

P. ralphii 'Green Globe'. Zones 17, 19–24. The parent species, which resembles *P. crassifolium*, is not grown commercially. 'Green Globe' is a dwarf version that grows 1½ ft. tall and as wide. Leaves are only ¼ in. long, bright green when first expanding, then gray green. Tiny, inconspicuous spring flowers are deep blackish purple.

P. rhombifolium. QUEENSLAND PITTOSPORUM. Zones 12–24. Slow-growing shrub or tree, to 15–35 ft. Glossy rich green leaves are nearly diamond shaped, to 4 in. long. Small white flowers in late spring. Growth is open enough that you can see the round, ½-in. fruit that follows: very showy, yellow to orange, in clusters from fall through winter. Fruit contrasts nicely with foliage. As small tree, well suited for lawn or patio (if litter of sticky fruit won't pose a problem). Or use several as a not-too-dense screen that needs little pruning. Resistant to oak root fungus.

P. tenuifolium (P. nigricans). Zones 9, 14–17, 19–24. Quite similar to *P. eugenioides* in most ways (size, growth habit, uses, culture), though it is more tolerant of beach conditions. Main difference is in leaves and twigs. This one has shorter (1–1½-in.), more oval leaves than *P. eugenioides;* leaf edges are less wavy, and color is deeper green. Small twigs and leaf stems are darker. Altogether, then, *P. tenuifolium* is more finely textured, darker, and a little denser than *P. eugenioides*. If pruning allows flowers to form, they will be dark purple, ½ in. wide, in clusters. There are varieties with bronzy purple foliage and variegated leaves.

P. tobira. TOBIRA. Zones 8–24; borderline in Zones 4–7. Broad, dense shrub or small tree, 6–15 ft. tall, rarely to 30 ft. Can be held to 6 ft. by careful heading back and thinning (*P. tobira* does not respond as well to shearing as do some other pittosporums). Clean-looking, dense foliage; leaves leathery, shiny dark green, 2–5 in. long, rounded at ends. Clusters of creamy white flowers at branch tips in early spring have fragrance of orange blossoms. Flowers become round, green fruit that turn brownish in fall and split to show orange seeds. Best for screens, massing, or individually as crooked-stemmed, freestanding small tree. Effective in containers. Variety 'Variegata', with gray-green leaves edged white, is smaller, usually growing to about 5 ft. high and as wide. Sometimes loses many leaves in winter. 'Turner's Variegated Dwarf' has gray-green leaves with creamy edges. 'Wheeler's Dwarf' has same handsome leaves as *P. tobira* but on very densely growing, 1–2-ft. shrub. Choice selection for foreground, low boundary plantings, or even small-scale ground cover. Good near swimming pools. 'Cream de Mint' is similar in size, but its gray-green leaves have white edging.

P. undulatum. VICTORIAN BOX. Zones 16, 17, 21–24; Zones 14 and 15 in frost-sheltered locations. Moderately fast growth to 15 ft., then slow to 30–40 ft. high, with equal width. Planted 5–8 ft. apart, can be kept to dense, 10–15-ft. screen by pruning (not shearing). Good background plant. Makes dense single or multitrunked, dome-shaped tree of great beauty. Leaves medium to dark green, glossy, wavy edged, 4–6 in. long. Fragrant creamy white flowers in early spring. Yellowish orange fruit opens in fall to show sticky, golden orange seeds that are messy on lawn or paving. Lawn tree or street tree, screen, or big container plant. Strong roots become invasive with age.

P. viridiflorum. CAPE PITTOSPORUM. Zones 15–17, 20–24. Shrub or tree to 25 ft. Leaves to 3 in. long, sharp pointed or blunt, often rolled in at edges. Flowers fragrant, yellowish green, in dense clusters. Orange-yellow fruit. Resembles large *P. tobira* and serves similar uses; also has great value as street tree or garden tree. Good as screen.

FOR GROWING SYMBOL EXPLANATIONS
PLEASE SEE PAGE 129

PLATANUS

PLANE TREE, SYCAMORE	
Platanaceae	
DECIDUOUS TREES	
✂ ZONES VARY BY SPECIES	
☼ FULL SUN	
◐ BEST WITH SOME DEEP WATERING IN SUMMER	

Platanus acerifolia

All grow large and have lobed, maplelike leaves. Older bark sheds in patches to reveal pale, smooth, new bark beneath. Brown, ball-like seed clusters hang from branches on long stalks through winter; prized for winter arrangements. Subject to blight (anthracnose), which causes early, continued leaf fall; *P. racemosa* especially susceptible. Rake up and dispose of dead leaves, since fungus spores can overwinter on them. Chlorosis may be a problem in desert.

P. acerifolia. LONDON PLANE TREE. Zones 2–24. Fast growth to 40–80 ft. with 30–40-ft. spread. Smooth, cream-colored upper trunk and limbs. Leaves are three- to five-lobed, 4–10 in. wide. Tolerates most soils, stands up beautifully under city smog, soot, dust, reflected heat. Can be pollarded to create dense, low canopy. Often sold as *P. orientalis*. Good street, park, or lawn tree. Used in lines and blocks for formal plantings in avenues, screens, masses. Watch for spider mites and scale. Powdery mildew can cause premature leaf drop some seasons. Scarce variety 'Yarwood' is somewhat resistant. 'Bloodgood' has some resistance to anthracnose.

P. occidentalis. AMERICAN SYCAMORE, BUTTONWOOD. All zones. Similar to *P. acerifolia;* new bark is whiter, tree is out of leaf longer. Very hardy. Occasionally grows with multiple or leaning trunks. Old trees near streams sometimes reach huge size and have heavy trunks.

P. racemosa. CALIFORNIA SYCAMORE. Zones 4–24. Native along streams in California foothills and Coast Ranges. Fast growth to robust 50–100 ft. Main trunk often divides into spreading or leaning secondary trunk. Attractive patchy, buff-colored bark. Smooth branches often gracefully twisted and contorted. Deeply lobed, yellowish green leaves 4–9 in. long. Susceptible to leaf miner, red spider mites. Leaves naturally turn dusty brown too early in autumn to be considered fall color. In mild coastal areas, brown leaves hang on until new leaf growth starts. In winter, the ball-like seed clusters hang three to seven together along single stalk. Tolerant of much heat, wind. With careful pruning it can be trained into picturesque multitrunked clump. For native or wild gardens or for big informal gardens generally.

P. wrightii (P. racemosa wrightii). ARIZONA SYCAMORE. Zones 10–12. To 80 ft. Native along streams and canyons in mountains of south and east Arizona. Needs regular water in dry season. Resembles *P. racemosa*, but leaves are more deeply lobed and seed clusters have individual stalks branching from common stalk.

PLATYCERIUM

STAGHORN FERN	
Polypodiaceae	
FERNS	
✂ ZONES VARY BY SPECIES	
◐ PARTIAL SHADE	
◑ LITTLE WATER; KEEP ON DRY SIDE	

Platycerium bifurcatum

In native habitat, tropical regions, they grow on trees; gardeners grow them on slabs of bark or tree fern stem, occasionally in hanging baskets or on trees. Give water only when slab or moss to which plant is attached is actually dry to the touch. Two kinds of fronds. Sterile ones are flat, pale green, aging to tan and brown; they support plant and accumulate organic matter to help feed it. Fertile fronds are forked, resembling deer antlers.

P. bifurcatum. Zones 15–17, 19–24. From Australia and New Guinea. Surprisingly hardy; survives 20–22°F with only lath structures for shelter. Fertile fronds clustered, gray green, to 3 ft. long. Makes numerous offsets that can be used in propagation. Often sold as *P. alcicorne.*

P. superbum. Zones 23, 24. From Australia. Fertile and sterile fronds both forked, the former broad but divided somewhat like moose antlers. To 6 ft. long. Protect from frosts. Don't overwater.

PLATYCLADUS orientalis (Thuja orientalis)

ORIENTAL ARBORVITAE
Cupressaceae
EVERGREEN SHRUB
✂ ALL ZONES
☼ BEST IN SOME SHADE
⬤ REGULAR WATER

Platycladus orientalis

Leaves scalelike, on twigs that are arranged in flat, vertical planes. Juvenile foliage needlelike; some varieties keep juvenile foliage throughout life. Small, fleshy cones become woody when ripe. Less hardy to cold than *Thuja occidentalis* (American arborvitae), but tolerates heat and low humidity better. In Rocky Mountains, grows best when in partial shade; shade during winter is especially helpful. Has survived well in nematode-infested soils. Give good drainage; protect from the reflected heat of light-colored walls or pavement. Blight of leaves and twigs in Northwest is easily controlled by copper sprays in early fall and by pruning out and destroying diseased growth. Spray for spider mites.

Widely used around foundations, by doorways or gates, singly in borders, or in formal rows. Most stay small, but some forms often end up bigger than the space they're meant for. Varieties include the following:

'Aureus' ('Aureus Nana', 'Berckmanii'). DWARF GOLDEN ARBORVITAE, BERCKMAN DWARF ARBORVITAE. Dwarf, compact, golden, globe shaped, usually 3 ft. tall, 2 ft. wide. Can reach 5 ft.

'Bakeri'. Compact, cone shaped, with bright green foliage.

'Beverlyensis'. BEVERLY HILLS ARBORVITAE, GOLDEN PYRAMID ARBORVITAE. Upright, globe shaped to conical; somewhat open habit. Branchlet tips golden yellow. In time, can reach 10 ft. tall, 10 ft. wide. Give it room.

'Blue Cone'. Dense, upright, conical; good blue-green color.

'Bonita' ('Bonita Upright', 'Bonita Erecta'). Rounded, full, dense cone to 3 ft. tall. Dark green with slight golden tinting at branch tips.

'Fruitlandii'. FRUITLAND ARBORVITAE. Compact, upright, cone-shaped shrub with deep green foliage.

'Minima Glauca'. DWARF BLUE ARBORVITAE. Grows 3–4 ft. tall and as wide. Blue-green foliage.

'Raffles'. Resembles 'Aureus' but is denser in growth, smaller, brighter in color.

'Westmont'. To 3 ft. tall, 2 ft. wide. Green foliage has yellow tips through the growing season.

PLATYCODON grandiflorus

BALLOON FLOWER
Campanulaceae (Lobeliaceae)
PERENNIAL
✂ ALL ZONES
☼ ☽ SUN NEAR COAST, LIGHT SHADE INLAND
⬤ MODERATE WATER

Platycodon grandiflorus

Upright branched stems to 3½ ft. Leaves light olive green, 1–3 in. long. Balloonlike buds open into 2-in.-wide, star-shaped flowers in blue violet, white, or soft pink. Blooms June–August if spent flowers (not entire stems) are removed.

Use in borders with astilbe, campanula, francoa, hosta, rehmannia. Protect roots from gophers. Completely dormant in winter; mark position to avoid digging up fleshy roots. (If you should dig up a root, replant it—or the pieces—at once. Most will grow.) Takes 2–3 years to get well established. Easy to grow from seed. Variety *P. g. mariesii* is dwarf form 1–1½ ft. high. 'Apoyama', 2–3-in. dwarf in pots, grows to size of *P. g. mariesii* in open ground. Flowers of 'Komachi' maintain their balloon shape, never opening fully. There are also plants with double flowers.

PLECOSTACHYS serpyllifolia

Asteraceae (Compositae)
SHRUBBY PERENNIAL
✂ ZONES 8, 9, 14–24
☼ FULL SUN
⬤ LITTLE WATER ONCE ESTABLISHED

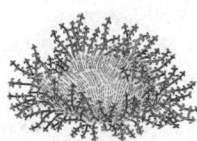

Plecostachys serpyllifolia

To 1½ ft. tall, spreading to twice as wide or more. Tiny, furry whitish leaves are closely packed along sprawling stems. Small, clustered, pinkish flowers less important than foliage. This plant has been sold as a dwarf form of *Helichrysum petiolare*, which it resembles in miniature. Attractive gray plant for ground or bank cover, large rock garden, or gray border.

PLECTRANTHUS

SWEDISH IVY
Lamiaceae (Labiatae)
PERENNIALS
✂ ZONES 22–24; OR IN LATHHOUSE OR GREENHOUSE
☼ ☽ ⬤ PARTIAL OR FULL SHADE
⬤ WATER WELL DURING GROWTH

Plectranthus oertendahlii

Leaves somewhat thickish, with scalloped edges and prominent veins. Small white or bluish flowers in spikes. Grow as ground cover on Southern California coast. Especially good trailing over wall or edge of planter or raised bed. As indoor or lathhouse plant, grow in hanging pot or wall container. Among easiest plants to grow. Will root in water or soil. Most people remove flower buds before bloom for more compact plants; alternative method is to allow plant to bloom, then cut it back afterward. Following are the best known of many species and varieties:

P. australis. Shiny dark green leaves. There are white-variegated forms.

P. coleoides 'Marginatus'. Somewhat less trailing in habit than others. Leaves green and gray green with cream edge.

P. oertendahlii. Leaf veins are silvery above, purplish beneath; leaf margins are purplish, scalloped.

PLEIONE

Orchidaceae
TERRESTRIAL ORCHIDS
✂ ZONES 5–9, 14–24
⬤ SHADE
⬤ KEEP ON DRY SIDE IN WINTER

Pleione bulbocodioides

Native to southeast Asia. Many species, all deciduous. Plant is a pseudobulb bearing one or two leaves. Leaves to 8 in. long in largest species, narrowly oval and pleated. Flowers, resembling those of cattleya, appear before foliage in early spring. Grow in pots with leaf mold or in peaty soil. Regular water during growth and bloom.

P. bulbocodioides (P. formosana). One or two 2½–3-in. flowers on 3–5-in. stem in spring. Lavender sepals and petals, paler lavender lip marked with brown and yellow.

PLUM and PRUNE

Rosaceae

DECIDUOUS FRUIT TREES

✎ ZONES VARY BY VARIETY

☼ FULL SUN

◊ BEST WITH SOME DEEP WATERING IN SUMMER

▶ SEE CHART

Plum

Varieties of edible plums and prunes commonly grown in the West are described in the chart. Noted beneath each variety is group to which it belongs—Japanese (*Prunus salicina*) or European (*P. domestica*). Damson plum (*P. insititia*) is often considered a type of European plum; it intercrosses with European plums freely.

Aside from Japanese and European plums, there is a third category, important only where climate is unusually severe. This is a complex group of hybrids involving Japanese plum, several species of native American wild plums, and the native sand cherry (*P. besseyi*). Originating in Canada, the Dakotas, and Minnesota, this group is exceptionally tolerant of cold and wind. Typical varieties are 'Compass', 'Pipestone', 'Sapa', 'Sapalta', and 'Waneta'. The fruit can be eaten fresh, cooked, or made into preserves. Pollination is often difficult with these hybrids; ask local nurseries about effective and available pollinators.

As orchard trees, both Japanese and European plums reach a height of 15–20 ft. with somewhat wider spread. Differences in growth habit are discussed below. All have white flowers. Leaves to about 3 in. long are broadly oval with serrated edges, turning tawny yellow in fall.

Fruit of Japanese plums ranges in color from green through yellow and brilliant red to deep purple black. In most cases, fruit is larger and juicier than that of European plums, with pleasant blend of acid and sugar. Most Japanese plums are used for fresh fruit only. European plums range in color from green and yellow to almost black. Prunes are European plums with a high sugar content and so may be sun-dried without fermenting at the pit. As fresh fruit, prunes are sweeter than other plums.

SOME PLUMS NEED TO BE THINNED

Heavy bearing of Japanese varieties results in much small fruit and, possibly, damage to the tree. Thin fruit drastically as soon as it is big enough to be seen, spacing them 4–6 in. apart. European plums and prunes do not require as much thinning as Japanese types do.

European plums and prunes bloom late and are better adapted than early-blooming Japanese plums to areas with late frosts or cool, rainy spring weather. Most European varieties have a moderately high chilling requirement that excludes them from extremely mild winter areas. You can grow plums in many soil types, but they do best in fertile, well-drained soil.

For larger fruit and vigorous growth, fertilize heavily. Orchardists give Japanese plums 1–3 lbs. of actual nitrogen a year, European plums 1–2 lbs.

Train young trees to vase shape. After selecting framework branches, cut back to lateral branches. If tree tends to grow upright, cut to outside branches; if it is spreading, cut to inside branches.

Japanese plums make tremendous shoot growth; rather severe pruning is necessary at all ages. Many varieties tend to produce excessive vertical growth; with these, shorten shoots to outside branchlets. European plums do not branch as freely, so selection of framework branches is limited. Prune to avoid formation of V-shaped crotches. Mature trees require little pruning—mainly to thin out annual shoot growth.

Pollination requirements are listed in the chart; the recommended pollinators are not the only ones possible, but those listed have worked.

Plumbaginaceae. The leadwort family consists of shrubs and perennials with clustered and funnel-shaped flowers. *Armeria*, *Ceratostigma*, and *Plumbago* are examples.

PLUMBAGO auriculata (P. capensis)

CAPE PLUMBAGO

Plumbaginaceae

SEMIEVERGREEN SHRUB OR VINE

✎ ZONES 8, 9, 12–24

☼ FULL SUN

◊ VERY LITTLE WATER ONCE ESTABLISHED

Plumbago auriculata

Unsupported, a sprawling, mounding bush up to 6 ft. tall, 8–10 ft. wide; with support, can reach 12 ft. or more. In Zone 12 it is usually a 2-ft. shrub. Fresh-looking, light to medium green leaves, 1–2 in. long. Inch-wide flowers in phloxlike clusters, varying (in seedling plants) from white to clear light blue. Select plants in bloom. Blooms mostly March–December, throughout year in warm, frost-free areas. Hot desert sun bleaches flowers. Good drainage is important. Young growth blackens and leaves drop in heavy frosts, but recovery is good. Prune out damaged growth after frost danger is past. In coldest climates, plant in spring so plants have greatest chance to become established before frosts. Propagate from cuttings. Slow to start but tough. Good cover for bank, fence, hot wall; good background and filler plant. 'Alba' is white-flowered variety. 'Royal Cape' is a cutting-grown selection with sky blue flowers. For other plants called plumbago, see *Ceratostigma*.

PLUMERIA

Apocynaceae

EVERGREEN OR DECIDUOUS SHRUBS OR SMALL TREES

✎ ZONES VARY BY SPECIES

☼ ☽ SUN NEAR COAST, PARTIAL SHADE INLAND

◊ KEEP ON DRY SIDE IN WINTER

Plumeria rubra

These handsome and useful plants have an open, gaunt character, with leathery, pointed leaves clustered near the tips of their thick branches. Clustered flowers are large, showy, waxy, very fragrant. All are easy to grow from cuttings. Tender to frost; won't take cold, wet soil. Grow in containers so that when frosts are expected, you can move plant indoors to bright window for continued bloom or to a frost-free garage or shed. Feeding late in year will result in soft growth that will be nipped by lightest frosts.

P. obtusa. SINGAPORE PLUMERIA. Evergreen shrub or small tree. Zone 24. Leaves dark green, 6 in. long, 2 in. wide, very glossy. White, fragrant, 2-in.-wide flowers bloom during warm weather. Very tender.

P. rubra. PLUMERIA, FRANGIPANI. Deciduous shrub or small tree. Zones 12, 13, 19, 21–24. Thick, pointed, 8–16-in.-long leaves drop in winter or early spring. Clusters of 2–2½-in.-wide flowers (red, purple, pink, yellow, or white) bloom June–November. Many varieties available in Southern California.

PLUM and PRUNE

NAME, GROUP	ZONES	POLLINATION	FRUIT	COMMENTS
'Autumn Rosa' **(Prunus salicina)** JAPANESE	7–12, 14–23	Self-fertile. Good pollinator for 'Mariposa'	Medium to large; purplish red skin, yellow flesh with red streaks. Very late	Ripens over long period, hangs well on tree
'Beauty' JAPANESE	7–10, 12, 14–20	Self-fertile; yield improved by pollination with 'Santa Rosa'	Medium-size; bright red skin, amber flesh with scarlet streaks. Good flavor. Very early	Fruit softens quickly
'Black Amber' JAPANESE	2–12, 14–20	'Santa Rosa', 'Late Santa Rosa'	Large, black, with yellow flesh, small pit, much like 'Friar'	Ripens 3 weeks ahead of 'Friar'
'Brooks' **(P. domestica)** EUROPEAN	2–12, 14–22	Self-fertile	Large; blue skin, yellow flesh. Good canned or dried. Midseason	Most reliable cropper in Northwest
'Burbank' JAPANESE	2–12, 14–20	'Beauty', 'Santa Rosa'	Large; red skin, amber yellow flesh. Excellent flavor. Midseason	Good choice in regions where hardiness to cold is important
'Casselman' JAPANESE	2, 3, 7–12, 14–22	Self-fertile	Resembles 'Late Santa Rosa' but is lighter in color and ripens later	Not subject to cracking of skin
'Damson' **('Blue Damson',** **P. insititia)** EUROPEAN	2–23	Self-fertile	Small; purple or blue-black skin, green flesh. Very tart flavor	Makes fine jam and jelly. Strains of this variety sold as 'French Damson', 'Shropshire'
'Elephant Heart' JAPANESE	2, 3, 7–12, 14–22	'Santa Rosa'	Very large; dark red skin, rich red flesh. Freestone, highly flavored. Midseason to late	Skin tart; some prefer these plums peeled. Long harvest season
'French Prune' **('Agen')** EUROPEAN	2, 3, 7–12, 14–22	Self-fertile	Small; red to purplish black skin. Very sweet and mild. Late	Standard drying prune of California. Suitable for drying or canning
'Friar' JAPANESE	2–12, 14–20	'Santa Rosa', 'Late Santa Rosa'	Large; black skin, amber flesh. Resists cracking and softens slowly after picking. Late midseason	Very vigorous, productive tree
'Golden Nectar' JAPANESE	7–12, 14–22	Self-fertile	Extra-large; yellow skin, yellow flesh, small pit. Excellent flavor. Midseason	Good keeping quality in storage or at room temperature
'Green Gage' **(P. d. italica)** EUROPEAN	2–12, 14–22	Self-fertile	Small to medium; greenish yellow skin, amber flesh. Good flavor. Midseason	Very old variety; still a favorite for eating fresh, cooking, canning, or making jam. Selected strain sold as 'Jefferson'
'Hollywood' **(see Prunus cerasifera** **'Hollywood' in Prunus–** **Flowering Plum chart)**				
'Howard Miracle' JAPANESE	7–10, 14–20	'Santa Rosa', 'Wickson'	Medium-size; yellow skin with red blush; yellow flesh with spicy, pineapplelike flavor. Midseason	More acid than most Japanese plums, but truly distinctive in flavor
'Imperial' **('Imperial Epineuse')** EUROPEAN	7–12, 14–18	'French Prune' or other European plums	Large; red-purple to black-purple skin, greenish yellow flesh. Sweet, highly flavored, fine quality. Late midseason	Excellent fresh. Makes a premium dried prune or canned product
'Italian Prune' **('Fellenburg')** EUROPEAN	2–12, 14–18	Self-fertile	Medium-size; sweet, purplish black. Late midseason	Standard for prunes in the Northwest. Excellent fresh and for canning. Can be dried. 'Early Italian' ripens 2 weeks earlier

P

PLUM and PRUNE

NAME, GROUP	ZONES	POLLINATION	FRUIT	COMMENTS
'Kelsey' JAPANESE	7–12, 14–18	Self-fertile	Large; green to greenish yellow skin splashed red; yellow, firm, sweet flesh. Nonjuicy. Late midseason	Holds for several weeks off tree
'Late Santa Rosa' JAPANESE	7–12, 14–22	Self-fertile	Medium to large; purplish crimson skin; amber flesh, red near skin. Tart-sweet, sprightly flavor. Late	Follows 'Santa Rosa' by a month
'Mariposa' ('Improved Satsuma') JAPANESE	7–12, 14–22	'Beauty', 'Santa Rosa', 'Late Santa Rosa', 'Wickson'	Large; purple-red skin, deep red flesh. Nearly freestone. Sweet flavor. Midseason	Good for cooking and eating
'Nubiana' JAPANESE	2–12, 14–20	Self-fertile	Large; deep purple-black skin, amber flesh. Sweet and firm. Midseason	Good for cooking and eating. Turns red when cooked. Good keeper
'President' EUROPEAN	2–12, 14–20	'Imperial'	Large; purplish blue skin, amber flesh. Attractive. Flavor not outstanding. Late	Used for cooking, eating fresh. Not for drying
'Queen Ann' JAPANESE	7–12, 14–18	'Santa Rosa', 'Wickson'	Large; dark purple, heart-shaped fruit; amber flesh. Rich flavor when fully ripe. Late	Holds shape well when cooked
'Santa Rosa' JAPANESE	2, 3, 7–12, 14–23	Self-fertile	Medium to large; purplish red skin with heavy blue bloom, flesh yellow to dark red near skin. Rich, pleasing, tart flavor. Early	Most important commercial and home variety. Good canned if skin is removed. Makes very strong vertical shoots. Shorten to outfacing branchlets
'Satsuma' JAPANESE	2–12, 14–22	'Beauty', 'Santa Rosa', 'Wickson'	Small to medium; dull deep red skin; dark red, solid, meaty flesh. Mild, sweet. Small pit. Early midseason	Preferred for jams and jellies. Sometimes called blood plum because of its red juice. Spreading habit. Tends to overbear, so thin fruit for best size
'Stanley' EUROPEAN	2–12, 14–22	Self-fertile	Large; purplish black skin, yellow flesh. Sweet and juicy. Midseason	Good canning variety; resembles larger 'Italian Prune'
'Sugar' EUROPEAN	2–12, 14–22	Self-fertile	Medium-size (somewhat larger than 'French Prune'). Very sweet, highly flavored. Early midseason	Good fresh, for home drying and canning. Trees tend to bear heavily in alternate years
'Wickson' JAPANESE	2–12, 14–22	'Beauty', 'Santa Rosa'	Large; showy, yellow, turning yellow red when ripe; firm yellow flesh. Fine flavor. Early midseason	Good keeper. Makes a fine-textured pink sauce

PLUM YEW. See CEPHALOTAXUS p. 217

POA

BLUEGRASS

Poaceae (Gramineae)

PERENNIAL AND ANNUAL GRASSES

✂ ZONES VARY BY SPECIES

☼ FULL SUN (EXCEPT FOR P. TRIVIALIS)

◗ ◖◗ NEEDS HEAVY DRY-SEASON WATERING

Poa pratensis

One is the best-known cool-season lawn grass; another is a sometimes-attractive weed; others are meadow grasses sometimes cultivated. Leaves of all have characteristic boat-prow tip.

P. annua. ANNUAL BLUEGRASS. All zones. Usually considered cool-season weed of lawns, it often furnishes much of the green in winter lawns.

Bright green, soft in texture, it would be attractive except for its seed heads and propensity to die off just when you need it—when rain lessens in late spring. Discourage it by maintaining thick turf of good grasses.

P. pratensis. KENTUCKY BLUEGRASS. Rich blue-green perennial lawn grass. Excellent in Zones 1–7; satisfactory but troublesome in Zones 8–11, 14–17; difficult in, and not recommended for, Zones 12, 13, 18–24. Many selections are available as seed or sod. Mow at 1½–2 in., higher in summer. Use alone or in mixture with other grasses.

P. trivialis. ROUGH-STALKED BLUEGRASS. Zones 1–11, 14–17. Finely textured, bright green perennial grass occasionally used in shady lawn mixtures for its tolerance of shade, damp soil.

Poaceae. The grass family is undoubtedly the most important plant family in terms of usefulness to humans. All the world's important grain crops are grasses; the bamboos (giant grasses) are useful in building and crafts. Many grasses are used in lawns or as ornamental annual or perennial plants. Some botanists use Gramineae as the family name for grasses.

PODOCARPUS

Podocarpaceae

EVERGREEN SHRUBS OR TREES

⚡ ZONES VARY BY SPECIES

☼ ◐ SUN OR PARTIAL SHADE

💧 BEST WITH REGULAR WATER

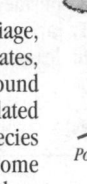

Podocarpus gracilior

Versatile plants grown for good-looking foliage, interesting form; adaptable to many climates, many garden uses. Good screen or background plants. Foliage generally resembles that of related yews *(Taxus),* but leaves of better-known species are longer, broader, and lighter in color. Some botanists now divide the following plants into three genera. New names are in parentheses.

Grow easily (if slowly) in ordinary garden soil and in containers. Sometimes troubled by chlorosis, especially in cold, wet, heavy soil.

P. elongatus. See *P. gracilior*

P. falcatus (Afrocarpus elongatus). Tree. Zones 8, 9, 14–24. Native to South Africa. Slow growth. Differs from *P. gracilior* in technical details. For culture and uses, see *P. gracilior.*

P. gracilior (Afrocarpus gracilior). FERN PINE. Tree, often grown as espaliered vine, even as hanging basket plant. Zones 8, 9, 12 (warmest areas), 13–24. Native to east Africa, where it grows to 70 ft. Old trees in California reach 60 ft. tall.

Habit and foliage vary with age of plant and method of propagation. Leaves on mature wood are closely spaced, soft grayish or bluish green, 1–2 in. long, narrow. Plants grown from cuttings or grafts taken from such wood have limber branches, are slow to make vertical growth, and have short bluish or grayish leaves. Such plants are often sold as *P. elongatus.* They are excellent for espaliering or for growing as vines along fences or eaves. With age they will become trees with single or multiple stems. Stake well to support heavy foliage masses.

The leaves of seedlings, vigorous young plants, and unusually vigorous shoots of mature plants differ from those on plants grown from cuttings or grafts: they are twice as long, more sparsely set on branches, and dark glossy green. In addition, seedlings are more upright in growth than plants grown from cuttings or grafts, and their branches will be less pendulous, more evenly spaced. Plants grown from seedlings are usually sold as *P. gracilior.* Stake these plants until strong trunk develops. With age, foliage will become more dense, and the leaves will be shorter and bluish or grayish green in color.

This is among the cleanest and most pest-free choices for street or lawn tree, patio or flower bed tree, espalier, hedge, big shrub, or container plant. Choice entryway plant or indoor/outdoor plant. Young plants sometimes used in dish gardens.

P. henkelii. LONG-LEAFED YELLOW-WOOD. Tree. Zones 8, 9, 14–24. Handsome, erect, slow-growing tree with masses of drooping foliage. Leaves 5–7 in. long, ⅓ in. wide; leaves are smaller on old trees in their native South Africa. Young trees are strikingly handsome.

P. macrophyllus. YEW PINE. Shrub or tree. Zones 4–9, 12–24. Has been grown in Zones 3, 11 with shelter from wind, hot sun, deep snow. More tolerant of heat, aridity than other species. Grows to 50 ft. high. Bright green leaves are 4 in. long and are broader than those of *P. gracilior.*

Grows indoors or out, in tubs or open ground. Generally narrow and upright but limber enough to espalier. Easily pruned to shape. Tub plant, large shrub, street tree or lawn tree (with staking and thinning), screen planting, topiary, clipped hedge.

P. m. maki. SHRUBBY YEW PINE. Shrub. Smaller, slower growing than yew pine (to 6–8 ft. in 10 years). Dense, upright form. Leaves to 3 in. long, ¼ in. wide. One of the very best container plants for outdoor or indoor use, and fine shrub generally.

P. nagi (Nageia nagi). Tree. Zones 8, 9, 14–24. Slow growth to 15–20 ft. (80–90 ft. in its native Japan). Branchlets drooping, sometimes

to a considerable length. Leaves 1–3 in. long, ½–1½ in. wide, leathery, smooth, sharp pointed. Takes considerable shade or sun, indoors or out. More treelike in youth than other species. Makes decorative foliage pattern against natural wood or masonry. Plant in groves for slender sapling effect. Excellent container plant.

P. nivalis. ALPINE TOTARA. Shrub. Zones 4–9, 14–17. Broad, low, spreading plant, eventually 2–3 ft. tall and 6–10 ft. wide. The dark olive green needles, ¼–¾ in. long, densely clothe branches. Resembles yew *(Taxus).* Attractive ground cover or large rock garden shrub.

P. totara. TOTARA. Tree. Zones 8, 9, 14–24. Reaches 100 ft. in New Zealand; likely to reach 25–30 ft. in gardens. Dense, rather narrow, with leathery, stiff, pointed, gray-green leaves to 1 in. long. General appearance like that of yew *(Taxus).*

PODRANEA ricasoliana

PINK TRUMPET VINE

Bignoniaceae

EVERGREEN VINE

⚡ ZONES 9, 12, 13, 19–24

☼ FULL SUN

💧 LITTLE TO REGULAR WATER

Podranea ricasoliana

Twining vine to 20 ft. Dark green leaves divided featherwise into three or four pairs of 2-in. leaflets. Open trumpet-shaped, 2–3-in.-wide summer flowers, pink veined red, in loose clusters at ends of new growth. Slow grower when young, speeding up as it matures. Likes heat, good drainage. May drop leaves in frost but can recover from root even if tops are frozen.

POHUTUKAWA. See METROSIDEROS excelsus	**p. 380**
POINCIANA. See CAESALPINIA	**p. 194**
POINSETTIA. See EUPHORBIA pulcherrima	**p. 289**
POISON OAK. See RHUS	**p. 460**
POKER PLANT. See KNIPHOFIA uvaria	**p. 344**

Polemoniaceae. The phlox family consists mostly of annuals and perennials, including many western wildflowers *(Gilia, Ipomopsis, Phlox).* One shrubby representative is *Cantua; Cobaea* is a vine.

POLEMONIUM

Polemoniaceae

PERENNIALS

⚡ ZONES 1–11, 14–17

◑ ● SHADE, HALF SHADE, UNDER TREES

💧 💧 BEST WITH FREQUENT WATER

Polemonium caeruleum

Lush rosettes of finely divided, fernlike foliage; clusters of bell-shaped flowers in summer. Combine with bleeding heart, campanulas, ferns, hellebores, hosta, and lilies. Need good drainage. Grow from seed, or divide after flowering or in spring. Many species are choice wildflowers from western mountains. Following are the two generally available in nurseries.

P. caeruleum. JACOB'S LADDER. Clusters of lavender blue, pendulous, 1-in.-long flowers on leafy, 1½–2-ft.-high stems.

P. reptans. Best known is its variety 'Blue Pearl', a dwarf, spreading plant 9 in. tall. Profuse display of blue flowers in April and May. Good in shaded, dampish rock garden.

P

POLIANTHES tuberosa

TUBEROSE

Agavaceae

TUBEROUS-ROOTED PERENNIAL

ZONES 15–17, 22–24

SUN OR PARTIAL SHADE

HEAVY WATERING IN GROWING SEASON

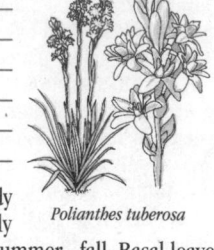

Polianthes tuberosa

Native to Mexico. Noted for powerful and heady fragrance. Flowers white, tubular, loosely arranged in spikelike clusters on stems to 3 ft., summer–fall. Basal leaves long, narrow, grasslike. Single forms are graceful, but double variety 'The Pearl' is most widely available. Long, slender, bulblike tubers always show a point of green if alive and healthy. In Zones 8, 9, and 14, plant in pots and move outdoors after frosts. Start indoors or plant outside after soil is warm. Plant 2 in. deep, 4–6 in. apart. Feed with acid-type fertilizer if soil or water is alkaline. Dry out when leaves yellow in fall; dig and store in a warm place. Or plant three tubers in 6-in. pot. Tubers will bloom year after year; divide clumps every 4 years.

POLYANTHUS. See PRIMULA polyantha   p. 437

POLYGALA

Polygalaceae

EVERGREEN SHRUBS OR SHRUBLETS

ZONES VARY BY SPECIES

SUN OR LIGHT SHADE

REGULAR WATER

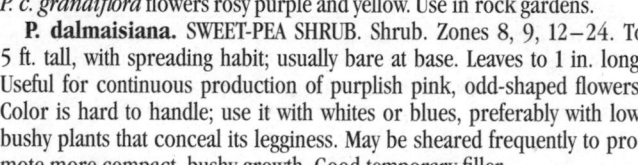

Polygala dalmaisiana

Flowers irregular, with slight resemblance to sweet peas. Many species exist; these two are grown in western gardens.

P. chamaebuxus. Shrublet. Zones 4–6. To 6–8 in. tall, spreading slowly by underground stems. Leaves dark green, 1–1½ in. long, shaped like those of boxwood. Flowers (April–May) creamy or yellow and white, sometimes with red. *P. c. grandiflora* flowers rosy purple and yellow. Use in rock gardens.

P. dalmaisiana. SWEET-PEA SHRUB. Shrub. Zones 8, 9, 12–24. To 5 ft. tall, with spreading habit; usually bare at base. Leaves to 1 in. long. Useful for continuous production of purplish pink, odd-shaped flowers. Color is hard to handle; use it with whites or blues, preferably with low, bushy plants that conceal its legginess. May be sheared frequently to promote more compact, bushy growth. Good temporary filler.

Polygonaceae. The buckwheat family consists of annuals, perennials, shrubs, trees, and vines. Flowers lack petals, but sepals are often showy. Stems are jointed. Fruit is small, dry, single seeded. *Eriogonum* is the best-known western representative. Other family members include rhubarb (*Rheum*), *Polygonum,* and *Antigonon.* (True buckwheat—the pancake flour kind—is *Fagopyrum,* a crop plant of no ornamental value.)

POLYGONATUM

SOLOMON'S SEAL

Liliaceae

PERENNIALS

ZONES 1–7, 15–17

WOODSY SHADE

FREQUENT WATER

Polygonatum biflorum

Arching, leafy stems grow from slowly spreading underground rhizomes. Greenish white, bell-shaped blossoms hang down beneath bright green leaves in spring. Plants disappear over winter. Attractive for form and flowers in woodland garden with ferns, hosta, wild ginger. Need loose, woodsy soil. Attractive in containers. For the western native false Solomon's seal, see *Smilacina.*

P. biflorum. Stems to 3 ft.; 1–3¾-in. flowers in clusters beneath 4-in. leaves.

P. commutatum. Stems possibly to 6 ft. Leaves to 7 in. long; two to ten flowers to a cluster. Considered to be a vigorous form of *P. biflorum.*

P. odoratum (P. japonicum). To 3½ ft. tall, with two-flowered clusters beneath 4–6-in. leaves. 'Variegatum' has leaves edged white.

POLYGONUM

KNOTWEED

Polygonaceae

EVERGREEN OR DECIDUOUS PERENNIALS OR VINES

ZONES VARY BY SPECIES

FULL SUN; A FEW TOLERATE SHADE

REGULAR WATER, EXCEPT AS NOTED

Polygonum cuspidatum compactum

Sturdy, sun-loving plants with jointed stems and small white or pink flowers in open sprays. Some kinds tend to get out of hand and need to be controlled.

P. affine. Evergreen perennial. Zones 4–9, 14–17. Tufted plant 1–1½ ft. tall. Leaves mostly basal, 2–4½ in. long, finely toothed, deep green turning to bronze in winter. Bright rose red flowers in dense, erect, 2–3 in.-long spikes, August–October. Informal border or ground cover. Sun or shade.

P. aubertii. SILVER LACE VINE. Deciduous in Zones 1–7, 10–12; evergreen in Zones 8, 9, 13–24. Rapid growing; can cover 100 sq. ft. in a season. Leaves heart shaped, glossy, wavy edged, 1½–2½ in. long. Flowers creamy white, small, in frothy mass from late spring to fall. Use as fast-growing screen on fences or arbors, on hillsides, at seashore. You can prune severely (to ground) each year; bloom will be delayed until August. Endures aridity.

P. baldschuanicum. BOKHARA FLEECEFLOWER. Deciduous vine. All zones. Much like *P. aubertii* in appearance, growth, vigor, and uses. Flowers, in large, drooping clusters, are pink, fragrant, and somewhat larger than those of *P. aubertii.*

P. capitatum. Evergreen perennial. Zones 8, 9, 12–24. Rugged, tough, trailing ground cover to 8 in. high, spreading to 20 in. Leaves 1½ in. long; new leaves dark green, old leaves tinged pink. Stems and flowers (in small, round heads) also pink. Blooms most of year. Leaves discolor and die below 28°F.

Good ground cover for uncultivated areas or for confined areas where its invasive roots can be held in check. Sun or shade—will even grow under pines. Will endure aridity. Seeds freely and can be grown as an annual where winters are cold.

P. cuspidatum (P. japonicum). JAPANESE KNOTWEED. Deciduous perennial. All zones. Tough, vigorous plant forming large clumps of red-brown, wiry, 4–8-ft. stems. Leaves nearly heart shaped, to 5 in. long. Greenish white blooms in late summer and fall. Extremely invasive; keep away from choice plants. Useful in untamed parts of garden. Cut to ground in late fall or winter. Often called bamboo or Mexican bamboo because of jointed stalks.

P. c. compactum (P. reynoutria). Fast-growing perennial ground cover 10–24 in. high with creeping roots. Can become a nuisance near choice plants. Stiff, wiry red stems. Pale green leaves, 3–6 in. long, heart shaped and red veined, turn red in fall. Plants die to ground in winter. Dense, showy clusters of small, pale pink flowers opening from red buds bloom in late summer. Ground cover for fringe areas of garden.

P. vacciniifolium. Evergreen perennial. Zones 4–7. Prostrate, with slender, leafy, branching stems radiating 2–4 ft. Leaves ½ in. long, oval and shining, turn red in fall. Rose pink late-summer flowers in dense, upright, 2–3-in. spikes on 6–9-in. stalks. Excellent bank cover or drapery for boulder in large rock garden. Increase by cuttings.

P

Polypodiaceae. The polypody family contains the vast majority of ferns. They differ from other ferns only in technical details concerning spore-bearing bodies (sporangia).

POLYPODIUM

Polypodiaceae

HARDY AND TROPICAL FERNS

⚡ ZONES VARY BY SPECIES

● SHADE

◐ ◑ ◕ ◓ WATER NEEDS VARY BY SPECIES

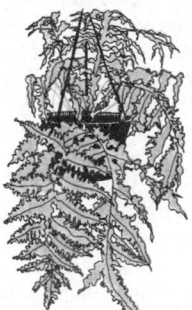

Polypodium aureum
'Mandaianum'

Widespread, variable group, some native to West. As with many ferns, reclassification has added new names; these appear in parentheses.

P. aureum (Phlebodium aureum). HARE'S FOOT FERN. Zones 15–17, 19–24; or indoor plant. From tropical America. Needs regular heavy watering. Big fern for hanging basket culture. Heavy brown creeping rhizomes, coarse blue-green fronds 3–5 ft. long. Fronds drop after frost, but plants recover fast. *P. a.* 'Mandaianum', sometimes called lettuce fern, has frilled and wavy frond edges. Both lettuce fern and the species are showy.

P. coronans. See Aglaomorpha coronans

P. glycyrrhiza (P. vulgare occidentale). LICORICE FERN. Zones 4–6, 14–24. Native to coastal strip from Alaska to California. Forms mats with creeping rhizomes. Fronds resemble smaller (to 1½ ft.) sword ferns. *P. hesperium (P. vulgare columbianum)*, which grows from Pacific Coast into Rocky Mountains, is smaller (to 10 in.). In the wilds, these ferns tend to grow on rocks or dead logs; in the garden, give them leaf mold or other organic material and shade (except right on the coast). Best with summer water but can survive without it.

P. heracleum. See Aglaomorpha heracleum

P. scouleri. LEATHERY POLYPODY. Zones 4–6, 15–17. Native along seacoast from British Columbia to California. Thick, glossy fronds may reach 1½ ft. long and 6 in. across at base. Often grows on trees and rocks, spreading slightly by short rhizomes. In the ground it tends to form clumps. Good for woodland gardens, naturalizing. Culture as for *P. glycyrrhiza*.

P. subauriculatum 'Knightiae' (Goniophlebium subauriculatum 'Knightiae'). KNIGHT'S POLYPODY. Zone 24; indoor and greenhouse plant. Long fronds (to 3 ft. or more and 1 ft. wide) with fringed edges droop gracefully. Makes spectacular hanging container specimen when well grown—like a magnified Boston fern. Outdoor plants shed old fronds in spring, quickly produce new ones. Routine house plant watering.

POLYSCIAS

Araliaceae

EVERGREEN SHRUBS USUALLY GROWN INDOORS

⚡ ZONES 21–24; OR INDOORS

◐ GOOD LIGHT BUT NO DIRECT SUNLIGHT

● FUSSY ABOUT TOO MUCH OR TOO LITTLE WATER

Polyscias fruticosa
'Elegans'

Like many other aralia relatives, they are grown for their handsomely divided leaves; flowers are unimportant and seldom produced outside tropics. As house plants they grow slowly, maintaining their shapeliness for many years. They are considered fussy, needing fresh air and just enough water but unable to tolerate drafts. Plants that fail usually do so because of overwatering or mite damage. Misting is useful, along with light feeding. If plant is doing well, don't move it. Polyscias appreciate warmth and humidity.

P. balfouriana (P. scutellaria 'Balfourii'). To 25 ft. tall. Leaves have three 2–4-in. toothed leaflets. Plain green form can grow out of doors in

Zones 21–24. 'Marginata', more common than species, has white-edged leaflets. 'Pennockii' has white to pale green leaflets that have irregular green spots.

P. fruticosa. MING ARALIA, PARSLEY PANAX. Grows 6–8 ft. tall. Leaves finely divided and redivided into multitude of narrow, toothed segments. 'Elegans' is small-growing, extremely densely foliaged variety.

P. guilfoylei 'Victoriae'. Compact grower with deeply slashed and cut leaflets with white edges.

POLYSTICHUM

Polypodiaceae

FERNS

⚡ ZONES 4–9, 14–24

● SHADE

● REGULAR WATER, EXCEPT AS NOTED

Polystichum munitum

Medium-size, evergreen fronds on hardy symmetrical plants. Among most useful and widely planted ferns in West, they blend well with other plants and are easy to grow.

P. acrostichoides. CHRISTMAS FERN. Evergreen to 2 ft., with once-divided leaves. Most useful for shaded sites in cold climates, but adapted elsewhere.

P. dudleyi. Native to Coast Ranges of Northern California. Resembles *P. munitum* but has broader, shorter, more finely cut fronds. Not always easy to find, but choice.

P. munitum. SWORD FERN. Native from California to Alaska and Montana. Most-seen fern of redwood forests. Leathery, shiny dark green fronds are 2–4 ft. long, depending on soil and available moisture. Fronds have medium coarse texture, are long lasting when cut. Old plants may have 75–100 fronds. Good for shady beds, along house walls, as large-scale ground cover, in mixed woodland plantings. Grows best in rich soil with organic matter. Established plants need little water.

P. polyblepharum. JAPANESE LACE FERN, TASSEL FERN. Handsome, dense, lacy. Resembles *P. setiferum* but is taller, darker green, somewhat coarser; fronds are somewhat more upright (to 2 ft.). Same culture, uses as *P. setiferum*. Usually sold as *P. setosum*.

P. setiferum. Low-growing fern with spreading, finely cut fronds, giving effect of dark green lace. Many cultivated varieties. 'Proliferum' makes plantlets on midribs of older fronds; these make for a dense, lacy plant and can be used for propagation. Northwestern specialists offer many fancy varieties as "English ferns." All are splendid in shaded rock gardens or for bedding with tuberous begonias and other shade plants.

POMEGRANATE. See PUNICA granatum	**p. 445**
POMPON TREE. See DAIS cotinifolia	**p. 257**

Pontederiaceae. The pickerel weed family contains aquatic or marsh plants with showy, usually blue, flowers, among them *Pontederia* and *Eichhornia*.

PONTEDERIA cordata

PICKEREL WEED

Pontederiaceae

AQUATIC PLANT

⚡ ALL ZONES

☼ ◐ SUN OR LIGHT SHADE

● LOCATE IN PONDS, WATER GARDENS

Pontederia cordata

Grown as companion to water lilies; best planted in pots of rich soil placed in 1 ft. of water. Long-stalked leaves stand well above water surface; these are heart shaped, to 10 in. long and

P

433

6 in. wide. Short spikes of bright blue flowers top 4-ft. (or shorter) stems. Gives wild-pond look to informal garden pool. Dormant in winter.

POPULUS

POPLAR, COTTONWOOD, ASPEN

Salicaceae

DECIDUOUS TREES

🌿 ZONES VARY BY SPECIES

☼ FULL SUN

💧 BEST WITH REGULAR DEEP WATERING

Populus nigra 'Italica'

All known for rapid growth. Eminently suitable for country places where fast growth, toughness, and low maintenance are considerations. Although most kinds can grow anywhere in the West, they are mostly grown and especially appreciated in the hot-summer/cold-winter interior regions. Appearance, performance poorer in mild-winter areas and near coast where temperature extremes are minimal. Some can go unwatered if roots grow deeply enough to tap water table or other underground water.

P. acuminata. LANCELEAF COTTONWOOD. All zones. Thrives at elevations to 7,500 ft. in Rocky Mountains. To 60 ft. tall, with egg-shaped, sharply pointed leaves to 4 in. long, glossy green above, pale beneath.

P. alba. WHITE POPLAR. All zones. Fast growth to 40–60 ft.; broad and wide spreading. The 5-in.-long leaves, usually with three to five lobes, are white and woolly underneath. A "lively" tree, even in light breezes, with flickering white and green highlights. Tolerates wide range of soils. Suckers profusely—an advantage if it is planted as windbreak, otherwise a problem.

P. a. 'Pyramidalis'. BOLLEANA POPLAR. Narrow, columnar form. Good for country windbreaks or sun screens. Suckers freely; may send up new shoots from roots many feet from main trunk. Usually sold as *P. bolleana*.

P. angustifolia. NARROWLEAF COTTONWOOD. All zones. Grows at elevations to 8,000 ft. To 60 ft. tall, with narrow leaves 5 in. long, 1½ in. wide.

STAY OUT OF ROOT TROUBLE

Do not plant any kind of *Populus* near pavement, sewer lines, septic tanks, or their leach lines. Also keep them out of lawns and small gardens. Their roots are invasive, and they form suckers.

P. balsamifera (P. candicans). BALM-OF-GILEAD. All zones. Fast to 30–60 ft.; broad topped. Suckers profusely. Triangular leaves 4½–6 in. long, 3–4 in. wide. Two seedless (hence cottonless) selections are 'Idahoensis' ('Idaho Hybrid') and 'Mojave Hybrid', similar fast-growing, large trees. The latter has nearly white bark. The species and all its selections thrive in Zones 11, 12, 13.

P. brandegeei (P. monticola). Zones 12, 13. Desert native tree to 40–60 ft. Resembles *P. fremontii* but has smooth, white bark like quaking aspen. Good for lining a long driveway.

P. canadensis. CAROLINA POPLAR. All zones. Fast growth to 40–150 ft. Triangular, tooth-edged leaves are 4 in. long. Deserves its bad reputation

for invading and breaking sewer lines. *P. c.* 'Eugenei' is somewhat narrower grower. 'Siouxland' is disease-resistant selection.

P. canescens 'Macrophylla'. All zones. Fast-growing, large tree with exceptionally large leaves (to 9 in. long on vigorous young shoots). Leaves white underneath, bark pale gray on older trees.

P. fremontii. WESTERN or FREMONT COTTONWOOD. Zones 7–24. Fast to 40–60 ft. or more. Yellow-green, triangular leaves are 2–4 in. wide, thick, glossy, and coarsely toothed; turn bright lemon yellow in fall, remain on tree practically all winter in Zones 12, 13. Small greenish yellow flowers in long, slender catkins appear before leaves. Female trees later bear masses of cottony seeds that blow about and become a nuisance; be sure to plant male trees (easily grown from cuttings). In desert, weekly watering is needed during hot weather if roots haven't tapped underground source. This is the cottonwood of desert waterholes and watercourses. 'Nevada' is a selected male (cottonless) variety.

P. nigra 'Italica'. LOMBARDY POPLAR. All zones. Fast to 40–100 ft. Beautiful columnar tree with upward-reaching branches. Suckers profusely; invasive roots are a problem. Indispensable to country driveways, valuable both as windbreak and skyline decoration. Bright green, triangular, 4-in.-long leaves turn beautiful golden yellow in fall. Subject to blight of branchlets in many areas. Healthy and attractive in cold, dry, interior climates. *P. n. thevestina* has white bark.

P. tremuloides. QUAKING ASPEN. Zones 1–7. Often tried in warmer areas, where it is usually short lived. Native throughout western mountains. Fast growing to 20–60 ft. Trunk and limbs smooth, pale gray green to whitish. Dainty, light green, round leaves flutter and quake in slightest air movement. Brilliant golden yellow fall color. Generally performs poorly or grows slowly at low elevations. Needs moist soil. Plants are occasionally offered in nurseries; some are collected, but many are raised from seed or cuttings. Good background tree for native shrubs and wildflowers. Apt to suffer from sudden dieback or from borers.

P. trichocarpa. BLACK COTTONWOOD. Zones 1–7. Native along mountain streams and wet lowlands of Coastal Ranges, California to Alaska. Tall, spreading tree to 40 ft. in 15 years, 150–180 ft. in age. Heavy limbed, with dark gray, furrowed bark; wood very brittle. Leaves 3–5 in. across, triangular, deep green above and distinctly silver beneath; attractive when ruffled by breeze. Male trees shed quantities of catkins; female trees release clouds of cottony seeds if male trees are present.

PORTULACA

PORTULACA, MOSS ROSE

Portulacaceae

SUMMER ANNUALS

🌿 ALL ZONES

☼ FULL SUN

💧 BEST WITH OCCASIONAL WATERING

Portulaca grandiflora

Low-growing, fleshy-leafed plants. One is widely grown for its flower display; the other is misunderstood—it's called a weed but can be used in cooking and salad making.

P. grandiflora. PORTULACA, MOSS ROSE. Useful warm-weather plants for brilliant color, from early summer until frost. Plants 6 in. high, 1½ ft. across. Leaves fleshy, succulent, cylindrical, pointed, 1 in. long. Trailing, branched reddish stems, also succulent. Flowers roselike, lustrous, in red, cerise, rose pink, orange, yellow, white, pastel shades. Flowers open fully only in sun, close in late afternoon. Available as single colors or mixes in either single-flowered or double (Prize Strain, Magic Carpet, Sunglo, Sunkiss) strains. Afternoon Delight and Sundance strains stay open longer in the afternoon than the earlier strains do.

Use on dry banks, in parking strips, rock gardens, gravel beds, patio insets, shallow containers, hanging baskets, among succulents, as edgings. Any soil; best in sandy loam. Sow seed in place after weather is warm, or plant flat-grown plants in late spring. Plants self-sow.

P. oleracea. PURSLANE. Essentially a weed with fleshy stems and fleshy leaves, tiny yellow flowers. Warm weather and heavy watering encourage its growth. Control by hoeing or pulling before it goes to seed. Don't allow pulled plants to lie about; they can reroot or ripen seed even if uprooted.

A strain called Wildfire has been offered both as *P. grandiflora* and *P. oleracea*. It is actually a strain of *P. umbraticola* and is popular in the Southwest and the Deep South. Plants have the broad, plump leaves of *P. oleracea*, but the bright single flowers may be red, white, yellow, pink, or orange. Plants are a few inches tall and spread to 2 ft. They make good hanging basket plants or quick, temporary ground cover. They like sun, heat, and average water.

PURSLANE A WEED?

The French call it pourpier, the Mexicans call it verdolaga, and both cultures use it in many culinary ways. You can use purslane in salad, soup, pork stew, tomato sauce, and scrambled eggs.

Portulacaceae. The portulaca family contains annuals, perennials, and a few shrubs, usually with succulent foliage and frequently with showy flowers. Examples are *Lewisia, Portulaca,* and *Portulacaria.*

PORTULACARIA afra

ELEPHANT'S FOOD

Portulacaceae

SUCCULENT

☀ HARDY IN ZONES 13, 16, 17, 22–24

☀ ◐ ● ANY EXPOSURE

◊ NO WATER ONCE ESTABLISHED

Portulacaria afra

Native to South Africa. Shrub with thick, juicy stems; to 12 ft. tall and nearly as wide, usually much smaller in pots. Looks a bit like jade plant *(Crassula argentea)* and is sometimes sold as "miniature jade plant," but it's faster growing and more loosely branched than jade plant, with more limber, tapering branches and smaller (½-in.-long) leaves. In South Africa, bears tiny pink flowers in clusters; seldom blooms in western United States.

Small plants are good, easy pot plants. Where hardy, can be used as fast-growing informal screen or unclipped hedge, or cut back as high-growing ground cover. Requires overhead protection in Zones 8, 9, 12, 14, 15, 18–21. Forms with variegated leaves ('Foliis Variegatis' and 'Variegata') are slower growing, smaller than species. Another form has larger, inch-long leaves. Same culture as for jade plant.

POTATO

Solanaceae

TUBEROUS-ROOTED PERENNIAL TREATED AS ANNUAL

☀ ALL ZONES

☀ FULL SUN

● MODERATE WATER

⬧ GREEN SKIN AND RAW SHOOTS ARE TOXIC

For ornamental relatives, see *Solanum.* Though not most widely grown of home garden vegetables, potatoes can be most satisfying. Two lbs. of

Potato

seed potatoes can give you 50 lbs. of potatoes for eating. The many diseases and pests that beleaguer commercial growers are not likely to plague home gardeners. Potatoes need sandy, fast-draining soil; tubers become deformed in heavy, poorly drained soil. For early crops, plant in spring as soon as soil can be worked, in midwinter where frosts are not severe; for fall and winter use, plant from mid-May to mid-June.

The above-ground potato plant is sprawling, bushy, and dark green with much-divided leaves somewhat like a tomato plant's. Clustered inch-wide flowers are pale blue. Round yellow or greenish fruit very rarely seen.

Buy certified (inspected, disease-free) seed potatoes from seed or feed store. Cut potatoes into chunky pieces with at least two eyes. These should be about 1½ in. square. Place chunks 4 in. deep and 1½ ft. apart. Do not plant if soil is very wet. After top growth appears, give plants an occasional soaking.

Dig early (or new) potatoes when tops begin to flower; dig mature potatoes when tops die down. Dig potatoes carefully to avoid bruises and cuts. Well-matured potatoes free of defects keep best in storage. Store in cool (40°F), dark place. Where ground doesn't freeze, late potatoes can remain in ground until needed. Dig before spring (or mild winter) temperatures start them into growth again.

Another method of planting is to prepare soil so surface is loose, plant potato eyes ½–1 in. deep, water well, and cover with 1–1½-ft. layer of straw, hay, or dead leaves; surround with fence of chicken wire to keep loose material from blowing away. Potatoes will form on surface of soil or just beneath, therefore requiring little digging. You can probe with your fingers and harvest potatoes as needed.

POTATO VINE. See SOLANUM jasminoides   p. 187

POTENTILLA

CINQUEFOIL

Rosaceae

EVERGREEN PERENNIALS OR DECIDUOUS SHRUBS

☀ ZONES VARY BY SPECIES

☀ ◐ SUN; PART SHADE IN HOT-SUMMER AREAS

◊ ● LITTLE TO MODERATE WATER

Potentilla fruticosa

Hardy plants useful for ground covers and borders. Leaves are bright green or gray green, divided into small leaflets. Small, mostly single, roselike flowers are cream to bright yellow, white or pink to red.

EVERGREEN PERENNIALS

These include creeping plants used as ground cover and sturdy clumping plants for use in rock gardens or perennial borders.

P. atrosanguinea. Zones 1–9, 14–24. Sprawling, mounding plant to 1½ ft. tall, 2 ft. wide, with foliage like furry strawberry leaves and red flowers over an inch wide. 'Gibson's Scarlet' has brilliant scarlet flowers.

P. nepalensis 'Willmottiae' (P. n. 'Miss Willmott'). All zones. Good performance near coast. Grows to 10 in. high; spreads to 1½ ft. Leaves divided fanwise into five roundish, 2–3-in.-long, green leaflets. Branching clusters of salmon pink, ½–1-in.-wide flowers. Borders, cut flowers.

P. tabernaemontanii (P. verna, P. v. 'Nana'). SPRING CINQUEFOIL. All zones. Dainty, bright green, tufted creeper 2–6 in. high. Leaves divided into five leaflets. Butter yellow, ¼-in.-wide flowers, borne in clusters of three to five, in spring and summer. Stands more moisture than other potentillas. May turn brown in cold winters. Fast-growing ground cover, bulb cover. Makes good lawn substitute for no-traffic situations. Smothers weeds effectively when well established. Although tough and persistent, this plant has suffered from a rust disease in some regions.

P. tonguei. All zones. Plant sold under this name is a hybrid between *P. nepalensis* and another species. Creeping plants with 1-ft.-long stems, leaves with three to five leaflets, and ½-in. apricot flowers with red centers. Use in rock garden or foreground of border. ▶

P

P. warrensii (P. warrenii). All zones. Name is properly *P. recta* 'Warrenii'. Grows to 15 in. tall, with leaves of five to seven leaflets. Bright yellow, 1-in.-wide flowers are profuse in May and June. Tolerates a wide range of soils. Sometimes sold as *P. warrensii macrantha*.

DECIDUOUS SHRUBS

The shrubby potentillas, most often sold as named forms of *P. fruticosa*, are native to northern latitudes everywhere, including the Cascades and Olympic and Rocky mountains. They perform well in Zones 1–21. All have leaves divided into three to seven leaflets; some are distinctly green on top, gray beneath, while others look more gray green. In full sun, all bloom cheerfully from June to October despite poor soil, heat, and little water. Best in well-drained soil with moderate water. Cut some of the oldest stems from time to time to make room for new growth. Here are some of the many varieties to be found in nurseries:

'Jackman's Variety'. Flowers bright yellow, to 1½ in. wide. Blooms profusely. To 4 ft. tall, somewhat wider.

'Katherine Dykes'. Can reach 5 feet but usually stays much lower, spreading at least as wide as it is high. Pale yellow, inch-wide flowers.

'Klondike'. Deep yellow, 1½–2-in.-wide flowers on dense-growing, 2-ft. shrub.

'Mount Everest'. Pure white, 1½-in.-wide flowers with yellow centers on upright, bushy plant to 4½ ft.

'Red Ace'. Bright red flowers with yellow reverse, 1½ in. wide. Reaches 2 ft. tall by 3–4 ft. wide. Flowers fade to yellow as they age (very quickly in hot-summer climates or under poor growing conditions).

'Sutter's Gold'. Grows 1 ft. high, spreading to 3 ft. Clear yellow flowers an inch wide.

'Tangerine'. Bright yellow-orange, 1½-in.-wide flowers on 2½-ft. shrub.

POTERIUM sanguisorba (Sanguisorba minor)

SMALL BURNET, SALAD BURNET

Rosaceae

PERENNIAL HERB

✔ ALL ZONES

☼ FULL SUN

◐ MODERATE WATER

Poterium sanguisorba

Grows to 8–12 in. Leaves with deeply toothed leaflets grow in rosette close to ground. Unusual thimble-shaped, pinkish white flowers borne on long stems.

Grows in poor soil with good drainage. Keep blossoms cut. Don't cut back plant more than half. Self-sows almost too freely if flowers are not cut. Also propagated from division of roots; divide each year. Good in containers. Leaves give cucumber aroma to salads, vinegar, cream cheese.

POTHOS aureus. See EPIPREMNUM aureum	p. 274
POT MARIGOLD. See CALENDULA officinalis	p. 195

PRATIA

Campanulaceae (Lobeliaceae)

PERENNIALS

✔ ZONES 4–9, 14–24

☼ ◐ ● SUN IN COOL AREAS, SHADE IN HOT ONES

◐ ◐◐ PREFER AMPLE WATER

Pratia angulata

Small perennial plants with creeping, branching stems that root at the joints. All are useful low ground covers where soil is reasonably rich and well drained, but they require constant moisture. If grown where summers are hot and dry, they require shade and frequent watering. In cool-summer areas they appreciate full sun. Small, closely set leaves and tolerance for an occasional footstep make them choice selections to use among stepping stones. They resemble baby's tears *(Soleirolia)* in appearance, but have attractive flowers.

P. angulata. New Zealand native with tiny roundish leaves on short stems and white or bluish white ¾-in. flowers on 2-in. stems. Flowers oddly shaped, with two-lobed upper lip, three-lobed lower lip. Can succeed in low desert if shade and moisture are ideal.

P. pedunculata (Isotoma fluviatilis, Laurentia fluviatilis). BLUE STAR CREEPER. Similar to the above, but leaves are practically stemless and the starlike pale blue flowers barely rise above the foliage mat. Blooms late spring and early summer, with scattered bloom at other times. Plant pieces 6–12 in. apart for cover within a year. Feed lightly once a month, spring to fall.

PREGNANT ONION. See ORNITHOGALUM caudatum	p. 395
PRICKLY PEAR. See OPUNTIA	p. 394
PRICKLY POPPY. See ARGEMONE	p. 165
PRIDE OF CALIFORNIA. See LATHYRUS splendens	p. 348
PRIDE OF MADEIRA. See ECHIUM fastuosum	p. 270
PRIMROSE. See PRIMULA	p. 436
PRIMROSE TREE. See LAGUNARIA patersonii	p. 346

PRIMULA

PRIMROSE

Primulaceae

PERENNIALS SOMETIMES TREATED AS ANNUALS

✔ ZONES 1–10, 12–24

☼ ◐ ● LIGHT SHADE; SUN ON COAST

◐ ◐◐ KEEP SOIL MOIST

▶ SEE CHART

Primula malacoides

Primula polyantha

Fanciers reserve the name "primrose" for *Primula vulgaris*, but gardeners generally use "English primrose" to refer to both this plant and Polyanthus primroses *(P. polyantha)*.

Out of some 600 species of primroses, only a few are widely adapted and distributed over the West. Long, hot summers and low humidity are limiting factors. But almost any primrose can be grown to perfection in the cool, moist climates of western Oregon and Washington and north coastal California. Most primroses are quite hardy; many thrive east of the Cascades and in the intermountain region. Some grow indoors.

Specialty nurseries, mainly in the Northwest, offer seeds and plants of many kinds of primroses. Fanciers exchange seeds and plants through primrose societies.

Primulaceae. The primrose family of annuals and perennials has single or variously clustered flowers with five-lobed calyxes and corollas. Examples are *Androsace, Cyclamen,* and *Primula.*

PRINCE'S FEATHER. See AMARANTHUS hybridus erythrostachys	p. 149
PRINCESS FLOWER. See TIBOUCHINA urvilleana	p. 506
PRIVET. See LIGUSTRUM	p. 354

PRACTICAL GARDENING DICTIONARY

PLEASE SEE PAGES 529–592

PRIMULA

NAME	ZONES	LEAVES	FLOWERS	COMMENTS
Primula acaulis (see **P. vulgaris**)				
P. alpicola MOONLIGHT PRIMROSE	1–6, 17	Long-stalked, wrinkled leaves forming dense clumps in time	Sulfur yellow, spreading, bell-shaped, in clusters on 20-in. stalk. Summer	Powerfully fragrant. Flowers sometimes white or purple. Somewhat tender in coldest areas
P. auricula AURICULA	1–6, 17, 22–24 (in shade, preferably in pots)	Evergreen rosettes of broad, leathery leaves, toothed or plain-edged, gray-green, sometimes with mealy, powdery coating that spots and runs in the rain	Clusters of white, cream, yellow, orange, pink, rose, red, purple, blue, or brownish; white or yellow eye. Fragrant. Early spring	Some choice named varieties have green or near-black flowers with rings of mealy powder, or rims of contrasting color
P. beesiana	1–6, 17	Long leaves taper gradually into leafstalk. Leaves (including stalks) reach 14 in.	Reddish purple, in 5–7 dense whorls on a 2-ft. flower stem. Mid- or late spring	Somewhat variable in color, but usually reddish purple with yellow eye. Very deep rooted; needs deep watering
P. bulleyana	1–6, 15–17	Like *P. beesiana*'s, but with reddish midribs	Bright yellow, from orange buds. Whorls open over long season mid- to late spring	Plants disappear in late fall; mark the spot. Older plants can be divided after bloom or in fall. Showy at woodland edge
P. denticulata	1–6	Leaves 6–12 in. long, only half grown at flowering time	Dense, ball-shaped clusters on foot-high, stout stems. Color ranges from blue violet to purple. Very early spring bloom	Pinkish, lavender, and white varieties are available. Not adapted to warm-winter areas
P. florindae	1–6, 17	Leaves broad, heart-shaped, on long stems	Up to 60 yellow, bell-shaped, nodding flowers top 3-ft. stems in summer. Most fragrant and latest-blooming primula (early July west of Cascades)	Will grow in a few inches of running water or in damp, low spot. Plants late to appear in spring. Hybrids have red, orange, or yellow flowers
P. japonica	1–6, 17	Leaves 6–9 in. long, to 3 in. wide	Stout stems to 2½ ft., each with up to five whorls of purple flowers with yellow eyes, May–July. 'Miller's Crimson' is excellent	White and pink varieties are obtainable. Needs semishade, lots of water
P. juliae hybrids (**Pruhonicensis hybrids**) JULIANA PRIMROSE	1–6, 14–17, 20–23	Tuftlike rosettes of bright green leaves	Borne singly (cushion type) or in clusters. Very early	Many named forms in white, blue, yellow, orange-red, pink, or purple. Excellent for edging, woodland, rock garden
P. malacoides FAIRY PRIMROSE, BABY PRIMROSE	8, 9, 12–24	Rosettes of soft, pale green, oval, long-stalked leaves 1½–3 in. long. Edges lobed and cut	Borne in loose, lacy whorls along numerous upright, 12–15-in. stems. White, pink, rose, red, lavender, Feb.–May	Winter–spring color in mild-winter areas of California and Arizona. Plant in Oct. or Nov. Under high-branching trees, with spring bulbs, in pots. Grown as annual; stands light frost. Indoors or cool greenhouse in cold climates
P. obconica	4–9, 15–24	Large, roundish, soft, hairy leaves on long, hairy stems; hairs (except those of Freedom strain) may irritate skin	Flowers 1½–2 in. wide in large, broad clusters on stems to 1 ft. tall. White, pink, salmon, lavender, and reddish purple. Nearly everblooming in mild regions	Perennial, best treated as annual. Use for bedding in shade where winters are mild, as house plant in cold regions
P. polyantha POLYANTHUS PRIMROSES (often called English primroses; this is a group of hybrids)	1–10, 12–24	Fresh green leaves in tight clumps	Flowers 1–2 in. across in large, full clusters on stems to 1 ft. high. Almost any color. Blooms from winter to early and mid-spring. Adaptable and brilliant. Treated as annuals in desert and other hot-summer areas	Fine, large-flowered strains are Clarke's, Barnhaven, Pacific, and Santa Barbara. Novelties include Gold Laced, with gold-edged mahogany petals. Miniature Polyanthus have smaller flowers on shorter stalks. All excellent for massing in shade, for planting with bulbs, or in containers

P

PRIMULA

NAME	ZONES	LEAVES	FLOWERS	COMMENTS
P. pulverulenta	1–6, 17	Leaves a foot or more long, deep green, wrinkled	Red to red-purple, purple-eyed, in whorls on 3-ft. stems thickly dusted with white meal	Bartley strain has flowers in pink and salmon range. A fine white with orange eye is available
P. sinensis CHINESE PRIMROSE	Greenhouse or indoor plant	Leaves on long stalks, roundish, lobed, toothed, soft, hairy, 2–4 in. long. Hairs may irritate skin	White, pink, lavender, reddish, coral; 1½ in. wide, many clustered on 4–8-in. stems. Stellatas have star-shaped flowers in whorls	Tender. Favorite European pot plant; imported seed available from specialists
P. veris COWSLIP	1–6, 17	Leaves similar to those of Polyanthus primroses	Bright yellow, fragrant, ½–1 in. wide, in early spring. Stems 4–8 in. high	Naturalize in wild garden or rock garden. Charming but not as sturdy as Polyanthus primroses
P. vialii **(P. littoniana)**	1–6, 17	Leaves to 8 in. long, 1½–2½ in. wide, hairy, irregularly toothed; disappear in winter	Violet blue, fragrant, ¼–½ in. across, opening from bright red calyxes. Stems erect, 1–2 ft. high. Dense, narrow spikes 3–5 in. long	Not long lived but quite easy from seed in cool-winter areas. Use in rock gardens
P. vulgaris **(P. acaulis)** PRIMROSE, ENGLISH PRIMROSE	1–6, 14–17, 21–24	Tufted; leaves much like those of Polyanthus primroses	Flowers borne singly; vigorous garden strains often have 2 or 3 to a stalk. Early spring bloom. White, yellow, red, blue, and bronze, brown, and wine	Double varieties available. Blues and reds especially desirable. Use in woodland or rock garden, as edging. Nosegay and Biedermeier strains are exceptionally heavy blooming

PROSOPIS

MESQUITE

Fabaceae (Leguminosae)

EVERGREEN OR DECIDUOUS TREES OR LARGE SHRUBS

⧄ ZONES 10–13

☼ FULL SUN

◊ ◖ DESERT PLANTS; TOLERATE SOME WATER

Native to deserts in the Southwest, Mexico, and South America, and among the toughest and most useful trees and shrubs for the desert. They are hardy elsewhere, but commonly found only in desert. The tendency to hybridize freely—and their differing appearance under differing cultural conditions—has made accurate identification of the various kinds difficult.

Prosopis glandulosa torreyana

The following species are similar in many ways although they do have significant differences. All have dark bark and spreading, picturesque branch canopies that cast light, airy shade. Leaves are composed of many tiny leaflets. Tiny, greenish yellow flowers in catkinlike spikes are followed by flat seedpods 2–6 in. long.

Trees may have one or many trunks; in poor, rocky soil and without water, they will be shrubby. In deep soil where taproots can reach groundwater, they can grow rapidly. They tolerate aridity, alkaline soil, and lawn watering. Many are spiny when young, but spines usually aren't a problem with older trees.

P. alba. ARGENTINE MESQUITE. Trees sold under this name are vigorous and fast growing, with erect single trunks and rather dense canopies of blue-green leaves. They are nearly evergreen, shedding old leaves as new ones appear in spring.

P. chilensis. CHILEAN MESQUITE. Two trees are sold under this name. The commonly sold type (probably a hybrid) is deciduous, with deep green foliage and a spreading crown of branches. The true species from Chile, also vigorous, has a more open foliage mass than the hybrid; it is evergreen in mild winters, deciduous in cold-winter areas. A cutting-grown thornless form of the latter is available.

P. glandulosa. HONEY or TEXAS MESQUITE. Deciduous tree with spreading habit, often with multiple trunks. Bright green leaves and drooping branchlets give it something of the look of California pepper tree (*Schinus molle*). *P. g. torreyana* ranges westward to California.

P. pubescens. SCREW BEAN. Deciduous shrub or tree to 25 ft. tall and broad, thorny branches, bluish green tiny leaflets, yellow spring flowers. Named for spirally twisted seedpods. Use as barrier shrub or prune as tree.

P. velutina (P. glandulosa velutina). ARIZONA MESQUITE. Like *P. glandulosa*, but smaller, shrubbier. Common tree in Arizona.

PROSTANTHERA

MINT BUSH

Lamiaceae (Labiatae)

EVERGREEN SHRUBS

⧄ ZONES 16, 17, 19–24

☼ FULL SUN

◖ OCCASIONAL SUMMER WATER

Prostanthera rotundifolia

Australian shrubs with fragrant, minty foliage and an enormous profusion of small flowers, usually in shades of purplish blue or white. They require excellent drainage. Although they tend to be short lived, they grow quickly and put on a good show. Prune carefully; avoid cutting into bare wood or any other hard pruning. There are many species; look for them at botanical garden plant sales or specialists' nurseries.

P. nivea induta. Upright, compact shrub to 6 ft. tall, 3 ft. wide, with narrow silvery leaves somewhat longer than 1 in. and blue flowers in spring. (*P. nivea* is a larger, more open shrub with white flowers.)

P. rotundifolia. To 6 ft. tall, 5 ft. wide, with small roundish leaves and purple-blue flowers. Among the selections being grown are 'Ghost Cave', with grayish green leaves and purple flowers; 'Glen Davis', with an especially profuse showing of dark purple flowers; and 'Rosea', to 3–4 ft., with dark green leaves and deep rose pink flowers.

P

PROTEA

Proteaceae

EVERGREEN SHRUBS

❄ ZONES 16, 17, 21–24

☼ FULL SUN

💧 UNIQUE SOIL AND WATER NEEDS

Protea cynaroides

Beautiful flowering plants from South Africa. Tubular flowers in large, tight clusters are surrounded by brightly colored bracts; effect is that of large, very colorful artichoke or thistle. Superb cut flowers, they hold their color for weeks and retain their shape even after fading.

Difficult to grow; definitely not for beginners. They need perfect drainage (preferably on slopes), protection from dry winds, good air circulation. Give moderate summer water until plants are established; thereafter, water only every 2–4 weeks. Most need acid soil; some accept alkaline soil. Smaller species will grow in containers. Young plants tender to cold; older plants of most species hardy to 25–27°F. They bloom in 3–4 years from seed but are not long-lived plants. Fertilize lightly with nitrogen; avoid fertilizers with phosphorus (plants will glut themselves, then die of the overdose). Small applications of iron can remedy chlorosis.

Some 150 species grow in South Africa. These two seem to do best here:

P. cynaroides. KING PROTEA. To 3–5 ft. tall with open, spreading habit. Leaves oval, leathery. Flower heads to 11–12 in. across. Bracts pale pink to crimson, flowers white (midsummer to winter, early spring). Needs regular watering throughout year. Can be grown in tubs.

P. neriifolia. To 10 ft., 6–8 ft. wide. Leaves narrow, shaped like oleander leaves. Flower heads (autumn, winter) 5 in. long, 3 in. wide. Bracts pink to salmon, with black, furry tips. Will take temperatures as low as 17°F and grow in alkaline soil.

Proteaceae. The protea family of evergreen shrubs and trees is characterized by leathery leaves and irregular, somewhat tubular flowers in spikelike clusters or heads often surrounded by showy colored bracts. Many are attractive (*Grevillea, Protea*); one has edible nuts (*Macadamia*).

PROVENCE BROOM. See CYTISUS purgans	**p. 256**
PRUNE. See PLUM and PRUNE	**p. 428**

PRUNELLA

SELF-HEAL

Lamiaceae (Labiatae)

PERENNIALS

❄ ALL ZONES

☼ ◑ SUN OR LIGHT SHADE

💧 REGULAR WATER

Prunella vulgaris

Creeping perennials forming low, dense mats of foliage from surface and underground runners. Tight spikes of gaping two-lipped mint flowers rise above the foliage on bare stems a few inches to 1 ft. tall. Names are much confused in nurseries and gardens, but all are much alike, being tough, tolerant plants with deep roots. They are useful for small-scale ground cover and can endure the occasional footfall but are too invasive to risk near choice, delicate rock garden plants.

P. grandiflora. Largest species, with 4-in. leaves and flower stalks rising to 8 in. Flowers are deep purple, but there are white, pink, and lilac varieties.

P. vulgaris. Common species, with 2-in. leaves. Flowers are purple or pink. A form called *P. v. incisa* has deeply cut leaves.

P. webbiana. Similar to *P. grandiflora,* but with shorter leaves. There are purple and pink varieties.

PRUNUS

Rosaceae

EVERGREEN OR DECIDUOUS SHRUBS OR TREES

❄ ZONES VARY BY SPECIES

☼ FULL SUN, EXCEPT AS NOTED

💧 MODERATE WATER, EXCEPT AS NOTED

▶ SEE CHARTS, PAGES 440–441, 442

Prunus cerasifera

Fruit trees that belong to *Prunus,* the "stone fruits," are described under their common names; see Almond, Apricot, Cherry, Peach and Nectarine, Plum and Prune.

The ornamentals may be divided into two classes: evergreens, used chiefly as structure plants (hedges, screens, shade trees, street trees); and deciduous flowering fruit trees and shrubs, closely related to the fruit trees mentioned above and valued for their springtime flower display as well as for attractive shape and for form and texture of foliage. The following alphabetical sections describe a wide variety of evergreen and flowering forms. The charts list flowering cherries and plums.

EVERGREEN FORMS

In addition to the familiar flowering fruit trees, *Prunus* contains several lesser-known but useful and attractive evergreen shrubs and trees.

P. caroliniana. CAROLINA LAUREL CHERRY. Shrub or tree. Zones 7–24. Native North Carolina to Texas. As upright shrub, it can be well branched from ground up and useful as formal, clipped hedge or tall screen to 20 ft. Can be sheared into formal shapes. Trained as tree, it will become broad topped and reach 35–40 ft. Attractive trained as multistemmed tree. Densely foliaged with glossy green, smooth-edged, 2–4-in.-long leaves. Small, creamy white flowers in 1-in. spikes, February–April. Fruit black, ½ in. or less in diameter. Denser, shorter varieties are 'Bright 'n Tight' and 'Compacta'.

Litter from flowers and fruit is problem when tree is planted over paved areas. Appearance best in coastal areas. Often shows salt burn and chlorosis in alkaline soils but does withstand desert heat and wind. Give it average soil; prune to shape. Needs no water once established.

P. ilicifolia. HOLLYLEAF CHERRY. Shrub or small tree. Zones 7–9, 12–24. Native to Coast Ranges and Baja California. Grows at moderate rate to 20–30 ft., usually broader than high. Mature leaves deep, rich green, 1–2 in. long, resemble holly leaves. Light green new leaves (March–May) contrast pleasantly with dark older foliage. Leaf color and size often vary from plant to plant. Creamy white, ½-in.-wide flowers in 3–6-in.-long spikes appear with new leaves in March. Round fruit, ½–¾ in. wide, turns from green to red, then reddish purple (never as dark or black as fruit of *P. lyonii*). Hybrids between this and *P. lyonii* appear frequently when plants are grown from seeds collected where both grow. Fruits of all these are edible, although the flesh is thin and the pit large.

P. ilicifolia can be grown in almost any soil but does best in coarse, well-drained types. May be attacked by whiteflies in moist, shady situations. Performs best in sun but will take light shade. Once established, it requires no irrigation in normal rainfall years. Growth rate and appearance are improved by deep but infrequent watering. Use as small tree, tall screen, or formal clipped hedge of any height from 3–10 ft. (space plants 1–1½ ft. apart, train as described under *Pittosporum eugenioides*). Like *P. lyonii,* has unusually high resistance to oak root fungus. Very large, old trees resemble California live oak (*Quercus agrifolia*).

P. laurocerasus. ENGLISH LAUREL. Large shrub or small tree. Zones 4–9, 14–24; best performance in Zones 4–6, 15–17. Hardy to 5°F; varieties listed below are hardier. Native from southeastern Europe to Iran. Generally seen as clipped hedge. As tree, fast growing to 30 ft. tall and as wide. Leaves leathery, glossy dark green, 3–7 in. long, 1½–2 in. wide. Creamy white flowers in 3–5-in.-long spikes in summer; often hidden by leaves. Small black fruit in late summer and fall. Where adapted, it's a fast-growing, greedy plant that's difficult to garden under or around. Ample watering and fertilizing will speed growth and keep treetop dense. Grows

▶ page 441

P

PRUNUS—FLOWERING CHERRY

NAME	ZONES	GROWTH HABIT, FOLIAGE	HEIGHT, SPREAD	FLOWERS, SEASON, COMMENTS
Prunus 'Accolade' (hybrid between **P. sargentii** and **P. subhirtella**)	2–9, 14–17	Small tree with spreading branches, twiggy growth pattern. Very vigorous	To 20 ft. or more, equally wide	Semidouble, pink, 1½ in. wide, in large drooping clusters. Early
P. campanulata TAIWAN FLOWERING CHERRY	7–9, 14–23	Graceful, densely branched, bushy, upright, slender small tree. Performs well in California climates where other flowering cherries fail	To 20–25 ft.; not as wide as high	Single, bell-shaped, drooping, in clusters of 2–5. Strong positive color—electric rose, almost neon purple-pink. Blooms early, along with flowering peach
P. 'Okame' (hybrid between **P. campanulata** and **P. incisa**)	4–9, 14–23	Upright, oval. Dark green, finely textured foliage. Yellow-orange to orange-red fall color	To 25 ft. tall, 20 ft. wide	Early single pink flowers
P. sargentii SARGENT CHERRY	1–7, 14–17	Upright, spreading branches form rounded crown. Orange-red fall foliage	To 40–50 ft. or more; not as wide as high	Single blush pink flowers in clusters of 2–4. Midseason. 'Columnaris' is more narrow and erect than typical *P. sargentii*
P. serrula BIRCH BARK CHERRY	1–7, 14–16	Valued for beauty of its bark— glossy mahogany red color	To 30 ft. and as wide	Small white flowers almost hidden by new leaves. Midseason
P. serrulata JAPANESE FLOWERING CHERRY	2–7, 14–20	The species is known through its many cultivated varieties. Best of these are listed below		
P. s. 'Amanogawa'	2–7, 14–20	Columnar tree. Use as you would small Lombardy poplar	To 20–25 ft. tall, 8 ft. wide	Semidouble, light pink with deep pink margins. Early midseason
P. s. 'Beni Hoshi' ('Pink Star')	2–7, 14–20	Fast grower with arching, spreading branches. Umbrella-shaped in outline	To 20–25 ft. high and as wide	Vivid pink single flowers with long, slightly twisted petals hanging below branches. Midseason
P. s. 'Kwanzan' ('Kanzan', 'Sekiyama')	2–7, 14–20	Branches stiffly upright, forming inverted cone	To 30 ft. high, 20 ft. wide	Large, double. Deep rosy pink in pendant clusters displayed before or with red young leaves. Midseason
P. s. 'Shirofugen'	2–7, 14–20	Wide horizontal branching	To 25 ft. and as wide	Double, long-stalked, pink, fading to white. Latest to bloom
P. s. 'Shirotae' ('Mt. Fuji')	2–7, 14–20	Strong horizontal branching	To 20 ft.; wider than high	Semidouble, pink in bud, white when fully open, purplish pink as flower ages. Early
P. s. 'Shogetsu'	2–7, 14–20	Spreading growth, arching branches	To 15 ft.; wider than high	Semidouble and very double, pale pink, often with white centers. Late
P. s. 'Tai Haku'	2–7, 14–20	Vigorous, with rounded crown. Good orange fall color	To 20–25 ft., equally wide	Largest blooms of any flowering cherry: pure white, 2½ in. wide, appearing with bronzy new foliage
P. subhirtella 'Autumnalis'	2–7, 14–20	Loose branching, bushy with flattened crown	To 25–30 ft. and as wide	Double, white or pinkish white in autumn as well as early spring. Often blooms in warm spells in Jan. and Feb.
P. s. 'Pendula' SINGLE WEEPING CHERRY	2–7, 14–20	Usually sold grafted at 5–6 ft. high on upright-growing understock. Graceful branches hang down, often to ground	Slow to 10–12 ft. and as wide	Single small pale pink blossoms in profusion. Midseason
P. s. 'Rosea' (usually sold as **P. s. 'Whitcombii'**)	2–7, 14–20	Wide-spreading, horizontal branching	To 20–25 ft., spreading to 30 ft	Buds almost red, opening to pink single flowers. Profuse, very early bloom. Northwest favorite

P

PRUNUS—FLOWERING CHERRY

NAME	ZONES	GROWTH HABIT, FOLIAGE	HEIGHT, SPREAD	FLOWERS, SEASON, COMMENTS
P. s. 'Yae-shidare-higan' DOUBLE WEEPING CHERRY	2–7, 14–20	Usually sold grafted at 5–6 ft. high on upright-growing under-stock. Graceful branches hang down, often to ground	Slow to 10–12 ft. and as wide	Double rose pink. Midseason
P. yedoensis YOSHINO FLOWERING CHERRY	2–7, 14–20	Curving branches; graceful, open pattern	Fast to 40 ft., with 30-ft. width	Single, light pink to nearly white, fragrant. Early
P. y. 'Akebono' (sometimes called **'Daybreak'**)	2–7, 14–20	Variety is smaller than species	To 25 ft. and as wide	Flowers pinker than those of *P. yedoensis*

best in partial shade in hot-summer areas, full sun elsewhere. Few pests. May be troubled occasionally by scale.

Stands heavy shearing but with considerable mutilation of leaves; best pruned not by shearing but by one cut at a time, removing overlong twigs just above a leaf. Maintenance of hedge is problem because of fast growth. Best used as tree or tall unclipped screen. Three dwarf forms of *P. laurocerasus* are sold: 'Mt. Vernon', 'Nana', and 'Otto Luyken'. All have leaf size reduced to match their 4–6-ft. (or less) height and spread.

P. l. 'Schipkaensis'. SCHIPKA LAUREL. Zones 2–9, 14–17. Smaller plant than species, with narrow leaves 2–4½ in. long.

P. l. 'Zabeliana'. ZABEL LAUREL. Zones 3–9, 14–21. This narrow-leafed variety has branches that angle upward and outward from base. Eventually reaches 6 ft., with equal or greater spread. More tolerant of full sun than *P. laurocerasus*. Use as low screen, divider, or big foundation plant. With branches pegged down, it makes an effective bank cover. Can be espaliered. In narrow strip between house and walk, half the branches will lie flat and rest will fan up the wall.

Prunus laurocerasus 'Zabeliana'

P. lusitanica. PORTUGAL LAUREL. Shrub or tree. Zones 4–9, 14–24. Native to Portugal and Spain. Slower growing than *P. laurocerasus*. Becomes densely branched large shrub 10–20 ft. high or multitrunked spreading tree to 30 ft. or more; trained to single trunk, it is used as formal street tree. Densely branching habit and attractive dark green foliage make it useful background plant. Glossy dark green leaves to 5 in. long. Small, creamy white flowers in 5–10-in. spikes extend beyond leaves in spring and early summer, followed by long clusters of bright red to dark purple, ⅓-in. fruit. Takes heat, sun, and wind better than *P. laurocerasus*. Needs little or no water once established.

P. l. azorica. Native to Azores and Canary Islands, where it grows 60–70 ft. high. In the West it grows into gigantic columnar bush 20 ft. high and 10 ft. wide. Exceptionally dark green and glossy foliage.

P. lyonii (P. integrifolia, P. ilicifolia integrifolia). CATALINA CHERRY. Shrub or tree. Zones 7–9, 12–24. Native to Channel Islands off Southern California. Dense shrub for clipped or informal hedges and screens. Or, trained as tree, it will reach 45 ft. tall, over 30 ft. broad, with trunk 6–8 in. in diameter. Leaves 3–5 in. long, dark green, smooth margined or faintly toothed. (Leaves of young plants are more definitely toothed and usually are similar to those of *P. ilicifolia*.) Creamy white flowers in clusters 4–6 in. long are borne in profusion in April and May. Black, large-stoned, ¾–1-in. cherries are sweet but insipid.

When *P. lyonii* is used as patio tree or street tree over sidewalks, its fallen fruit is objectionable. Needs little or no irrigation once established; may be short lived in heavy soil with regular garden watering. Seldom troubled by diseases, insects, or mites. May be attacked by whiteflies. Valuable as tall screen or hedge. Prune to hold to any height desired. Rates high in resistance to oak root fungus.

FLOWERING FRUIT TREES AND SHRUBS

Flowering cherry. These beautiful trees perform best in Zones 4–6, 15–17. Cold hardy enough for Zones 2 and 3, they suffer severe damage where winters are dry, sunny, and windy. Cultural needs of all varieties are identical. They require full sun and fast-draining, well-aerated soil; if your soil is heavy clay, plant in raised beds. Best with occasional summer water. Prune as little as possible. Cut while tree is in bloom and use branches in arrangements. Remove awkward or crossing branches. Pinch back the occasional overly ambitious shoot to force branching.

Pests and diseases are not usually a problem, though infestations of tadpole-shaped slugs and yellowish to greenish caterpillars may skeletonize leaves unless trees are sprayed with insecticide. Plants in heavy soil are sometimes subject to root rot (for which there is no cure) during winter. Affected tree usually will bloom, then send out new leaves that suddenly collapse. Use flowering cherries as their growth habit indicates. All are good trees to garden under. Large, spreading kinds make good shade trees. Smaller cherries are almost a necessity in oriental gardens.

Flowering nectarine. Zones 2–24. There is one important flowering nectarine: 'Alma Stultz'. It grows quickly to 20 ft. and as wide as high; in early spring, it is covered with deliciously fragrant, 2–2½-in.-wide, waxy-petaled flowers that look somewhat like azalea blossoms in rosy white shaded pink, the color deepening with age. White-fleshed fruit is sparsely produced. Plant appearance, cultural needs same as peach.

Flowering peach. Flowering peach is identical to fruiting peach in growth habit and height. But it's more widely adapted than fruiting peach—flowering peach can be grown in Zones 2–24. However, trees may be caught by late frosts in Zones 2, 10, and 11, and suffer from delayed foliation in 13, 23, 24. Heavy pruning necessary for good show of flowers. Cut branches back to 6-in. stubs at flowering time. Multibranched new growth will be luxuriant by summer's end and will flower profusely the following spring. Cultural requirements are same as for fruiting peaches. Place them where they will give maximum effect when in bloom and where they will be fairly unobtrusive out of bloom—behind evergreen shrubs, fence, or wall.

Some peach varieties produce showy blossoms and good fruit. These are described under Peach and Nectarine. The following varieties are strictly "flowering" in the sense that their blooms are showy and their fruit is either absent or worthless. Early-flowering varieties are best choices for regions with hot, early springs.

'Early Double Pink'. Very early.

'Early Double Red'. Deep purplish red or rose red. Very early and brilliant, but color likely to clash with other pinks or red.

'Early Double White'. Blooms with 'Early Double Pink'.

'Helen Borchers'. Clear pink, 2½-in.-wide flowers. Late.

'Icicle'. Double white flowers. Late.

'Late Double Red'. Later by 3–4 weeks than 'Early Double Red'.

'Peppermint Stick'. Flowers striped red and white; may also bear all-white and all-red flowers on same branch. Midseason. ▶

P

PRUNUS–FLOWERING PLUM

NAME	ZONES	GROWTH HABIT	FOLIAGE, FLOWERS, FRUIT
Prunus americana WILD PLUM, GOOSE PLUM	1–3, 10	Thicket-forming shrub or small tree to 15–20 ft. Extremely tough and hardy	Dark green foliage follows profusion of 1-in. clustered white flowers. Fruit yellow to red, to 1 in., sour but good for jelly
P. blireiana (hybrid between **P. cerasifera** 'Atropurpurea' and **P. mume**)	2–22	Graceful, to 25 ft. high, 20 ft. wide. Long, slender branches	Leaves reddish purple, turning greenish bronze in summer. Flowers double, fragrant, pink to rose, Feb.–Apr. Very little or no fruit
P. cerasifera CHERRY PLUM, MYROBALAN	2–22	Used as rootstock for various stone fruits. Will grow to 30 ft. and as wide	Leaves dark green. Flowers pure white, ¾–1 in. wide. Small red plums, 1–1¼ in. thick, are sweet but bland. Self-sows freely; some seedlings bear yellow fruit
P. c. 'Allred'	2–22	Upright, slightly spreading, 20 ft. tall, 12–15 ft. wide	Red leaves, white flowers. Red, 1¼-in.-wide, tart fruit is good for preserves, jelly
P. c. 'Atropurpurea' (**P. 'Pissardii'**) PURPLE-LEAF PLUM	2–22	Fast growing to 25–30 ft. high, rounded in form	New leaves copper red, deepening to dark purple, gradually becoming greenish bronze in late summer. White flowers. Sets heavy crop of small red plums
P. c. 'Hollywood' (hybrid between **P. c. 'Atropurpurea'** and Japanese plum **'Duarte'**)	2–22	Upright grower to 30–40 ft., 25 ft. wide	Leaves dark green above, red beneath. Flowers are light pink to white, Feb.–Mar. Good-quality red plums 2–2½ in. wide
P. c. 'Krauter Vesuvius'	2–22	Smaller growing than *P. c.* 'Atropurpurea', to 18 ft. high, 12 ft. wide; upright, branching habit	Darkest of flowering plums. Light pink flowers, purple-black leaves Feb.–Mar. Little or no fruit
P. c. 'Mt. St. Helens'	2–22	Upright, spreading, with rounded crown. Fast growth to 20 ft. by 20 ft.	A sport of 'Newport', it grows faster and leafs out earlier; it has richer leaf color and holds it later in summer
P. c. 'Newport'	2–22	To 25 ft. high, 20 ft. wide	Purplish red leaves. Single pink flowers. Will bear a little fruit
P. c. 'Purple Pony'	2–22	Genetic dwarf no taller than 10–12 ft. Available budded low or high	Deep purple foliage holds color throughout season. Pale pink single flowers. No fruit
P. c. 'Thundercloud'	2–22	More rounded form than *P. c.* 'Atropurpurea'. To 20 ft. high, 20 ft. wide	Dark coppery leaves. Flowers light pink to white. Sometimes sets good crop of red fruit
P. cistena DWARF RED-LEAF PLUM	2–22	Dainty, multibranched shrub to 6–10 ft. Can be trained as single-stemmed tree; good for planting in small patios	Purple leaves; white to pinkish flowers in early spring. Blackish purple fruit in July. 'Big Cis', a sport of *P. cistena*, grows to 14 ft. tall, 12 ft. wide. Form is dense, globular. Flowers are pink

'Weeping Double Pink'. Smaller than other flowering peaches, with weeping branches. Requires careful staking and tying to develop main stem of suitable height. Midseason.

'Weeping Double Red'. Similar to above, but with deep rose red flowers. Midseason.

'Weeping Double White'. White version of weeping forms listed above.

Flowering plum. Will grow in almost any soil. If soil is wet for long periods, plant in raised bed, 6–12 in. above grade. Expect attacks from aphids, slugs, caterpillars, spider mites. Spray with all-purpose fruit tree spray. Check trunk at and just below ground level for peach tree borers.

An adaptable and choice medium-size flowering trees for lawn, patio, terrace, or small street tree is *P. blireiana*. It also does well in planters and large tubs. In choosing plum to be planted in paved area, check its fruiting habits. When planting in a patio, prune to establish head at height to walk under. As tree develops, prune out crossing and inward-growing branches.

P. besseyi. WESTERN SAND CHERRY. Deciduous shrub. Zones 1–3, 10. To 3–6 ft. tall. White flowers in spring followed by sweet black cherries nearly ¾ in. in diameter. Used for pies, jams, jellies. Plants withstand heat, cold, wind, aridity.

P. fruticosa. Like *P. besseyi*, but 2–3 ft. tall, with smaller and red-purple fruit.

P. glandulosa. DWARF FLOWERING ALMOND. Deciduous shrub. Zones 1–10, 12, 14–19. Native to Japan, China. Much-branched, upright, spreading growth to 6 ft. tall. Leaves light green, narrow and pointed, to 4 in. long. Flowers, set close to slender branches, appear early, before leaves, and turn branches into long wands of blossoms. Species (seldom seen in gardens) has single pink or white flowers only ½ in. wide. Flowers of commonly available varieties are double, 1–1¼ in. across, resembling light fluffy pompom chrysanthemums. Variety 'Alboplena' has double white flowers; 'Sinensis' has double pink flowers. Prune back hard either just after blooming or when in bloom, using cut wands for arrangements. Can be used as flowering hedge.

P. maackii. AMUR CHOKECHERRY. Deciduous tree. Zones 1–3, 10. Native to Manchuria and Siberia; extremely hardy to cold and wind. To 25–30 ft. tall. Bark of trunk is yellowish and peeling, like birch bark.

Leaves strongly veined, rather narrow and pointed, to 4 in. long. Small white flowers in narrow clusters 2–3 in. long. Fruit is black, ¼ in. across.

P. mume. JAPANESE FLOWERING APRICOT, JAPANESE FLOWERING PLUM. Deciduous tree. Zones 2–9, 12–22. (Blooms may be frosted in Zones 2, 3.) Neither true apricot nor plum. Considered longest lived of flowering fruit trees, it eventually develops into gnarled, picturesque 20-ft. tree. Leaves to 4½ in. long, broadly oval. Flowers are small, profuse, with clean, spicy fragrance. Blooms January–February in mild areas, and February–March in cold-winter areas. Fruit is small, inedible. Prune heavily: let tree grow for a year, then prune back all shoots to 6-in. stubs. The next year, cut back half the young growth to 6-in. stubs; cut back other half the next year, and continue routine in succeeding years. Varieties include:

'Bonita'. Semidouble rose red.

'Dawn'. Large ruffled double pink.

'Peggy Clarke'. Double deep rose flowers with extremely long stamens and red calyxes.

'Rosemary Clarke'. Double white flowers with red calyxes. Very early; often in bloom New Year's Day in California.

'W. B. Clarke'. Double pink flowers on weeping plant. Effective large bonsai or container plant, focus of attention in winter garden.

P. padus. EUROPEAN BIRD CHERRY, MAYDAY TREE, MAYBUSH. Deciduous tree. Zones 1–3, 10. Moderate growth rate to 15–20 ft., occasionally taller, rather thin and open in habit while young. Dark, dull green oval leaves 3–5 in. long are among the first to unfold in spring. Small white flowers in slender, drooping, 3–6-in. clusters make big show in May, nearly hiding foliage. Small black fruit that follows is bitter but much loved by birds. Tolerates much cold.

P. tomentosa. NANKING CHERRY. Like *P. besseyi*, extremely tough, hardy fruiting shrub; grows 6–8 ft. tall. Scarlet, ½-in. fruit.

P. triloba. FLOWERING ALMOND. Deciduous small tree or treelike large shrub. Zones 1–11, 14–20. One of several plants known as flowering almond. Slow growth to 15 ft., usually 8–10 ft. with equal spread. Rather broad, 1–2½-in.-long leaves and double pink flowers 1 in. wide in very early spring. A white form is sometimes available. Hardy, small flowering plant of definite tree form. Also sold as multitrunked shrub.

P. virginiana. CHOKECHERRY. Deciduous shrub or small tree. Zones 1–3, 10. Leaves 2–4 in. long. After leaves have unfolded, tiny white flowers appear in slender, 3–6-in. clusters. Astringent fruit is ½–⅓ in. wide, dark red to black. Species gives good display of autumn foliage color. *P. v. demissa*, western chokecherry, is native to Pacific Coast, Sierra Nevada, Great Basin area, and northern Rockies. It tolerates heat and aridity. *P. v. melanocarpa*, black chokecherry, has smoother leaves and blacker, sweeter fruit. With normal garden watering it grows into 20–25-ft. tree. Its variety 'Canada Red' ('Shubert') has leaves that open green, then turn red as they mature. Tends to sucker freely.

PSEUDOLARIX kaempferi (Chrysolarix kaempferi)

GOLDEN LARCH

Pinaceae

DECIDUOUS CONIFER

✿ ZONES 2–7, 14–17

☼ FULL SUN

💧 REGULAR WATER

Pseudolarix kaempferi

Slow growing to 40–70 ft. high, often nearly as broad at base. Wide-spreading branches, pendulous at tips, grow in whorls to form symmetrical, pyramidal tree. Foliage has a feathery look; 1½–2-in.-long, ⅛-in.-wide, bluish green needles (golden yellow in fall) are clustered in tufts except near branch ends, where they are single. Cones and bare branches make interesting winter patterns. Give it an open spot sheltered from cold winds. Best in deep, rich, well-drained, acid or neutral soil. Fine for spacious lawns.

PSEUDOPANAX

Araliaceae

EVERGREEN SHRUBS OR TREES

✿ ZONES VARY BY SPECIES

☼ ◑ ● ANY EXPOSURE

💧 REGULAR WATER

Pseudopanax lessonii

Slow growing. Leaves of *P. crassifolius, P. ferox* highly variable. Young plants have long, narrow, spiny-toothed leaves; mature plants have divided or undivided leaves of no very remarkable shape. Young plants odd and decorative. Flowers inconspicuous.

P. crassifolius. LANCEWOOD. Zones 16, 17, 21–24. In time, a 50-ft. tree. Usually seen as single-stemmed plant 3–5 ft. tall with rigid, drooping leaves to 3 ft. long, less than 1 in. wide, strongly toothed, reddish bronze in color. Upright growth habit—good choice for narrow areas.

P. ferox. Zones 16, 17, 21–24. Eventually a 20-ft. tree. Young plants with strongly toothed leaves 1–1½ ft. long, 1 in. wide.

P. lessonii. Zones 17, 20–24. Moderate growth to 12–20 ft. tall. Effective multistemmed tree in open ground. Leaves dark green, leathery, divided into three to five leaflets 2–4 in. long. July–August flowers unimportant. Withstands wind. Excellent container plant.

PSEUDOSASA. See BAMBOO, p. 174

PSEUDOTSUGA

Pinaceae

EVERGREEN TREES

✿ ZONES VARY BY SPECIES

☼ ◑ FULL SUN; TAKES PART SHADE IN YOUTH

◔ 💧 LITTLE OR NO WATER ONCE ESTABLISHED

Pseudotsuga menziesii

The two species are quite similar but there's a great difference in status—the first is little known and the second is the most prominent tree in Pacific Northwest.

P. macrocarpa. BIGCONE SPRUCE. Zones 1–3, 10, 11, 18, 19. Native to Southern California. Stout trunked; grows to about 60 ft. tall. Needles similar to those of *P. menziesii*. Has much larger cones—4–7½ in. long, 2–3 in. wide; three-pronged bracts on cones barely protrude from each scale.

P. menziesii (P. taxifolia). DOUGLAS FIR. Zones 1–10, 14–17. Since pioneer days, northwesterners have been gardening under and near this magnificent native tree. Its entire range includes western Oregon, Washington, and parts of the Rocky Mountains and extends to Alaska and California (as far south as Fresno and Monterey counties).

Sharply pyramidal form when young; widely grown and cherished as Christmas tree. Grows 70–250 ft. in forests. Densely set, soft needles, dark green or blue green, 1–1½ in. long, radiate out in all directions from branches and twigs. Sweet fragrance when crushed. Ends of branches swing up. Pointed wine red buds form at branch tips in winter. These open in spring to apple green tassels of new growth that add considerably to tree's beauty. Reddish brown cones are oval, about 3 in. long, and have obvious three-pronged bracts. Unlike upright cone of true firs (*Abies*), these hang down. Best suited to its native areas or to areas with similar climates. Will grow in any except undrained, swampy soils. Can take wind. Resistant to oak root fungus. Environment influences its appearance. Where summers are dry, it is dense with shorter spaces between branches; where there is much moisture or too much shade, it tends to look awkward, thin, and gawky, especially as young tree. *P. m. glauca* is the common form in the Rocky Mountains; it usually has more bluish green needles than the species and is much hardier to winter cold than Pacific Coast trees. Compact, weeping, and other forms exist, but they are grown mostly in arboretums and botanical gardens.

PSIDIUM

GUAVA

Myrtaceae

EVERGREEN SHRUBS OR SMALL TREES

✿ ZONES VARY BY SPECIES

☼ FULL SUN

💧 INFREQUENT WATER ONCE ESTABLISHED

Psidium cattleianum

White flowers (composed principally of brush of stamens). Berrylike fruit, good in jellies, pastes. Best in rich soil.

P. cattleianum (P. littorale). STRAWBERRY GUAVA. Zones 9 and 14 (in sheltered locations), 15–24. Moderate, open growth to 8–10 ft. as shrub; can be trained as multitrunked, 10–15-ft. tree. Especially beautiful bark and trunk—greenish gray to golden brown. Leaves glossy green, to 3 in. long; new growth bronze. Fruit is dark red (nearly black when fully ripe), 1½ in. wide, with white flesh and a sweet-tart, slightly resinous flavor. *P. c.* 'Lucidum', yellow strawberry guava, or lemon guava, has yellow fruit, fairly dense growth.

P. guajava. GUAVA. Zones 23, 24. Taller than *P. cattleianum,* with strongly veined leaves to 6 in. long. Semideciduous briefly in spring; new leaves attractive salmon color. Fruit 1–3 in. across, with white, pink, or yellow flesh, musky and mildly acid flavor.

PSORALEA pinnata

BLUE PEA

Fabaceae (Leguminosae)

EVERGREEN SHRUB

✿ ZONES 16, 17, 19–24

☼ ◐ FULL SUN ON COAST, LIGHT SHADE INLAND

💧 REGULAR WATER

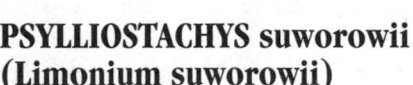

Psoralea pinnata

An open, rangy shrub to 6–10 ft., with needlelike but harmless, soft, bright green leaves and clusters of blue-and-white sweet pea–shaped flowers in spring and summer. Many think it resembles a flowering pine. Flowers have sweet scent of grape soda or chewing gum. Tip-pinching while young will help keep plant compact.

PSYLLIOSTACHYS suworowii (Limonium suworowii)

Plumbaginaceae

SUMMER ANNUAL

✿ ALL ZONES

☼ FULL SUN

💧 MODERATE WATER

Psylliostachys suworowii

Rosettes of narrow, 8-in.-long leaves produce 1½-ft.-tall spikes of lavender pink, tiny flowers. Spikes are very slender, single or branched, and cylindrical, reminiscent of slender, furry rats' tails. They are excellent in flower arrangements, fresh or dry.

Sow seed in pots or open ground seed bed when danger of frost is over; transplant to 1 ft. apart. The species' former name is *Statice suworowii.*

FOR INFORMATION ON SELECTING PLANTS

PLEASE SEE PAGES 45–128

PTERIDIUM aquilinum

BRACKEN

Polypodiaceae

FERN

✿ ALL ZONES

☼ ◐ FULL SUN TO MEDIUM SHADE

💧 TOLERATES SOME ARIDITY

◊ YOUNG FRONDS ARE POISONOUS

Pteridium aquilinum pubescens

Worldwide native. *P. a. pubescens* is native to West. Fronds coarse, much divided, rising directly from deep, running rootstocks. Grows from 2 ft. to as tall as 7 ft. under good conditions. Occurs naturally in many places and can be tolerated in untamed gardens, but beware of planting it: deep rootstocks can make it tough, invasive weed. Do not gather young fronds to cook as fiddleheads; they are a slow poison.

PTERIS

BRAKE

Polypodiaceae

FERNS

✿ ZONES VARY BY SPECIES

● SHADE

💧 MOIST, NOT SATURATED, SOIL

Small ferns of subtropical or tropical origin, mostly used in dish gardens or small pots; some are big enough for landscape use.

Pteris cretica

P. cretica. Zones 17, 23, 24. To 1½ ft. tall with comparatively few long, narrow leaflets. Numerous varieties exist: some have forked or crested fronds; others are variegated. Variety 'Wimsettii', light green form with forked tips on mature plants, is so dense and frilly that it doesn't look like a fern.

P. 'Ouvrardii'. Zones 17, 22–24. Dark green, 1–2½-ft.-tall fronds have extremely long, narrow, ribbonlike divisions.

P. quadriaurita 'Argyraea'. SILVER FERN. Zone 24. From India. Fronds 2–4 ft. tall, rather coarsely divided, heavily marked white. Showy, but the white markings seem out of place on ferns. Protect from frost and from snails.

P. tremula. AUSTRALIAN BRAKE. Zones 16, 17, 22–24. Extremely graceful, 2–4-ft. fronds on slender, upright stalks. Good landscape fern with excellent silhouette. Fast growing but tends to be short lived.

PTEROCARYA stenoptera

CHINESE WINGNUT

Juglandaceae

DECIDUOUS TREE

✿ ZONES 5–24

☼ FULL SUN

💧 INFREQUENT WATER

Pterocarya stenoptera

Fast to 40–90 ft., with heavy, wide-spreading limbs. Clearly shows its kinship to walnuts in its leaves: 8–16 in. long and divided into 11–23 finely toothed, oval leaflets. Foot-long clusters of small, single-seeded, winged nuts hang from branches. Good looking but has only one real virtue: it succeeds well in compacted, poorly aerated soil in play yards and other high-traffic areas. Aggressive roots make it unsuitable in garden or lawn. *P. fraxinifolia,* Caucasian wingnut, is similar, with slightly larger leaflets, longer nut clusters.

P

PTEROSTYRAX hispidus

EPAULETTE TREE
Styracaceae
DECIDUOUS TREE
ZONES 5–10, 14–21
FULL SUN
REGULAR WATER

Pterostyrax hispidus

Possibly reaches 40 ft., but more usually held to 15–20 ft. with 10-ft. spread. Trunk single or branched; branches open, spreading at top.

Light green leaves, gray green beneath, 3–8 in. long, rather coarse. Creamy white, fringy, lightly fragrant flowers in drooping clusters 4–9 in. long, 2–3 in. wide. Blooms in early summer. Gray, furry, small fruit in pendant clusters hangs on well into winter, is attractive on bare branches.

Prune to control shape, density. Best planted where you can look up into it—on bank beside path, above a bench, or in raised planting bed. It is a choice selection when planted at edge of woodland area or as focal point in large shrub border.

PTYCHOSPERMA macarthuri (Actinophloeus macarthuri)

Arecaceae (Palmae)
PALM
ZONES 23, 24
PARTIAL SHADE
LOOKS BEST WITH AMPLE WATER

Ptychosperma macarthuri

Native to New Guinea. Feather palm with several clustered, smooth green stems 10–15 ft. high. Soft green leaflets with jagged ends.

PULMONARIA

LUNGWORT
Boraginaceae
PERENNIALS
ZONES 1–9, 14–17
GOOD UNDER TREES
MOIST, POROUS SOIL

Pulmonaria saccharata

Long-stalked leaves mostly in basal clumps, with few on flower-bearing stalks. Funnel-shaped, blue or purplish flowers in drooping clusters from April to June. Use with ferns, azaleas, rhododendrons, blue scillas, pink tulips under spring-flowering trees. Creeping roots. All can be used as small-scale ground cover in shaded areas.

P. angustifolia. COWSLIP LUNGWORT. Tufts of narrowish, dark green leaves. Flowers dark blue, in clusters on 6–12-in. stems. Blooms in spring at same time as primroses. Divide in fall after leaves die down.

P. longifolia. Slender leaves to 20 in. long and deep green spotted silver. Variety 'Roy Davidson' has a long spring show of deep blue flowers fading to rose pink.

P. saccharata. BETHLEHEM SAGE. Grows to 1½ ft., spreads to 2 ft. White-spotted, roundish, evergreen leaves. Flowers reddish violet or white. 'Highdown' has sky blue flowers fading to soft pink; 'Sissinghurst White' has white flowers.

PULSATILLA. See ANEMONE pulsatilla p. 151

PUMMELO. See CITRUS, Miscellaneous p. 232

PUMPKIN

Cucurbitaceae
ANNUAL VINES
ALL ZONES
FULL SUN
WATER AT FIRST SIGNS OF WILTING

Pumpkin

The best variety to grow into a jumbo-size Halloween pumpkin is 'Atlantic Giant'. In late summer, slide wooden shingle under pumpkins to protect from wet soil (not necessary if soil is sandy).

Smaller pumpkins with finer-grained, sweeter flesh are 'Small Sugar' or 'Sugar'. Grow 'Trick or Treat' for its seeds; they have no hulls and can be roasted, salted, and eaten as nuts. 'Sweetie Pie' and 'Jack Be Little' are 3-in.-wide miniatures useful as decorations. 'Lumina' is a novelty white pumpkin with orange flesh. It weighs 10–12 lbs.

GROW A GIANT PUMPKIN

In early May, plant seeds 1 in. deep in 4-in. pots. Transplant seedlings to a sunny south-facing bed enriched with much compost. As plant grows, cut off all but two branches. When flowering begins, take off all but one flower on each branch (your aim: two branches with one pumpkin on each). Every 2 feet along each branch put a 4-in. mound of soil over branch so roots can form there. A single vine can cover 500 sq. ft. Lay a soaker hose beside vine to water it as needed.

PUNICA granatum

POMEGRANATE
Punicaceae
DECIDUOUS TREE OR SHRUB
ZONES 5–24; SEE BELOW
SUN FOR BEST BLOOM AND FRUIT
LITTLE WATER ONCE ESTABLISHED

Punica granatum

Showy flowers. Some varieties yield fruit. Narrow, glossy bright green to golden green leaves, bronzy new growth, brilliant yellow fall color except in Zone 24. All varieties tolerate great heat and will live and grow well in alkaline soil that would kill most plants. Plant against south or west wall in Zones 5 and 6.

'Chico'. DWARF CARNATION-FLOWERED POMEGRANATE. Compact bush can be kept to 1½ ft. tall if pruned occasionally. Double orange-red flowers over long season. No fruit. Excellent under lower windows, in containers, as edging.

'Legrellei' ('Madame Legrelle', 'California Sunset'). Dense 6–8-ft. shrub with double creamy flowers heavily striped coral red. No fruit.

'Nana'. DWARF POMEGRANATE. Dense shrub to 3 ft., nearly evergreen in mild winters. Blooms when a foot tall or less. Orange-red single flowers followed by small, dry, red fruit. Excellent garden or container plant; effective bonsai.

'Nochi Shibari'. Dark red double flowers.

'Tayosho'. Light apricot, fully double flowers.

'Wonderful'. Best-known fruiting pomegranate. Grow this variety as 10-ft. fountain-shaped shrub, tree, or espalier. Burnished red fruit in autumn follows orange-red single flowers up to 4 in. across. Will not fruit in cool coastal areas. Water deeply and regularly if fruit is important. Other fruiting varieties are rarely seen: 'Fleshman', 'King', 'Phil Arena's', and 'Utah Sweet' have pink flowers and sweet pink pulp.

PURPLE CONEFLOWER. See ECHINACEA purpurea p. 269

PURPLE HEART. See SETCREASEA pallida 'Purple Heart' p. 484

PUSCHKINIA scilloides

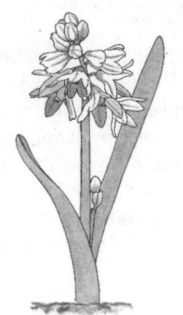

Liliaceae

BULB

◪ ALL ZONES

☼ ◑ SUN TO LIGHT SHADE

◖ TOLERATES SOME SUMMER DROUGHT

Puschkinia scilloides

Closely related to *Scilla* and *Chionodoxa*. Flowers bell-like, pale blue or whitish with darker, greenish blue stripe on each segment, in spikelike clusters on 3–6-in. stems. Leaves broad, strap shaped, upright, bright green, a little shorter than flower stems. Plant bulbs 3 in. deep, 3 in. apart in fall. Will grow for years without disturbance. Best in cold climates. *P. s. libanotica*, a more vigorous plant, is variety usually sold. *P. s.* 'Alba' has white flowers.

PUYA berteroniana

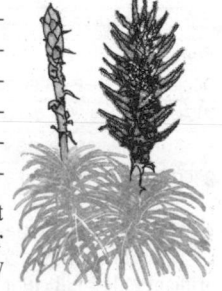

Bromeliaceae

EVERGREEN PERENNIAL

◪ ZONES 9, 13–17, 19–24

☼ FULL SUN

◖ LITTLE WATER ONCE ESTABLISHED

Puya berteroniana

Native to Chile. Big, spectacular flowering plant usually sold as *P. alpestris*. Massive flower clusters, resembling giant asparagus stalks as they develop, grow from crowded clump of 2-ft.-long, 1-in.-wide, swordlike, gray-green leaves with sharp tips and sharp-spined edges. Flower cluster, including stalk, reaches 4–6 ft. high. Blooms late April to early June. Cluster contains 2-in., bell-shaped flowers, metallic blue green and steely turquoise, accented with vivid orange anthers. Stiff, spiky branchlet ends protrude from cluster.

Use in rock gardens, on banks, or in large containers. Good with cactus, succulents, aloes. Takes poor soil.

PYRACANTHA

FIRETHORN

Rosaceae

EVERGREEN SHRUBS

◪ ZONES VARY BY SPECIES

☼ FULL SUN

◖◕ BEST WHERE SOIL IS NOT ALWAYS WET

Pyracantha coccinea

Grown widely for bright fruit, evergreen foliage, variety of landscape uses, and easy culture. All grow fast and vigorously with habit from upright to sprawling; nearly all have thorns. All have glossy green leaves, generally oval or rounded at ends, ½–1 in. wide and 1–4 in. long. All bear flowers and fruit on spurs along wood of last year's growth. Clustered flowers are small, fragrant, dull creamy white, effective because numerous.

Fruit varies in color, size, season, and duration. Some types color in late summer; others color late and hang on until cleared out by birds, storms, or decay in late winter. Control size and form by pinching young growth or by shortening long branches just before growth starts. Trim branches that have berried, cutting back to well-placed side shoot. Subject to fireblight, scale, woolly aphids, red spider mites. In coastal areas, apple scab is sometimes a problem in early spring and can nearly defoliate plants.

Use as espaliers on wall or fence, as barrier plantings, screens, rough hedgerows or barriers along roads. Can be trained as standards; often clipped into hedges or topiary shapes (which spoils their rugged informality and often their fruit crop). Low-growing kinds are good ground covers. If berry color is important, buy plants when in fruit. To eliminate old withered or rotted berries, dislodge with a water jet or an old broom.

P. angustifolia 'Gnome'. All zones except coldest parts of Zone 1. Dwarf, spreading, densely branched shrub, orange fruit. One of hardiest.

P. coccinea. All zones except coldest parts of Zone 1. Rounded bush to 8–10 ft. (20 ft. trained against wall). Flowers March–April; red-orange berries in October, November. Best known for its varieties 'Fiery Cascade' (to 8 ft.; orange berries turning red), 'Government Red' (red berries), 'Kasan' (red-orange, long-lasting berries), 'Lalandei' and 'Lalandei Monrovia' (orange berries), 'Lowboy' (low, spreading; orange berries), and 'Wyattii' (orange-red berries coloring early). Best species for cold-winter areas. 'Lalandei' is hardiest of all.

P. fortuneana (P. crenatoserrata, P. yunnanensis). Zones 4–24. Spreading growth to 15 ft. tall, 10 ft. wide. Limber branches make it good espalier plant. Berries orange to coral, lasting through winter. Variety 'Cherri Berri', 10 ft. tall, 8 ft. wide, has deep red berries that last through the winter. 'Graberi' has huge clusters of dark red fruit that colors in mid-fall, lasts through winter; growth more upright than species.

P. 'Mohave'. Zones 3–24. To 12 ft. tall and wide. Heavy producer of big orange-red fruit that colors in late summer and lasts into winter. One of reddest of the very hardy pyracanthas. Resistant to fireblight.

P. 'Red Elf'. Zones 4–9, 12–24. Low growing, compact, densely branched, with bright red fruit. Small enough for container culture. Less susceptible to fireblight than most pyracanthas. Apparently the same as plant sold as 'Leprechaun'.

P. 'Ruby Mound'. Zones 4–9, 12–24. Long, arching, drooping branches make broad mounds. Bright red fruit.

P. 'Santa Cruz' (P. 'Santa Cruz Prostrata'). Zones 4–24. Low growing, branching from base, spreading. Easily kept below 3 ft. by pinching out occasional upright branch. Red fruit. Plant 4–5 ft. apart for ground, bank cover.

P. 'Teton'. Zones 3–24. Columnar growth to 12 ft. tall and 4 ft. wide. Yellow-orange fruit. Resistant to fireblight.

P. 'Tiny Tim'. Zones 4–24. Compact plant to 3 ft. tall. Small leaves, few or no thorns. Berries red. Prune once a year when fruit begins to color, shortening any runaway vertical shoots. Informal low hedge, barrier, tub plant.

P. 'Victory'. Zones 4–24. To 10 ft. tall, 8 ft. wide. Dark red fruit colors late and holds on well.

P. 'Walderi' (P. 'Walderi Prostrata'). Zones 4–24. Low-growing (to 1½ ft., with a few upright shoots that should be cut out), wide-spreading ground cover plant with red berries. Plant 4–5 ft. apart for fast cover.

P. 'Watereri'. Zones 3–24. To 8 ft. tall, equally wide. Very heavy producer of bright red, long-lasting fruit. Northwest favorite.

P. 'Yukon Belle'. All zones. Dense, medium-size, semievergreen shrub with orange berries. Extremely hardy.

P

PYROSTEGIA venusta
(P. ignea, Bignonia venusta)

FLAME VINE

Bignoniaceae

EVERGREEN VINE

🌿 ZONES 13, 16, 21–24

☼ ☽ BEST IN SUN; TOLERATES SOME SHADE

💧 MODERATE WATER

Pyrostegia venusta

G rows fast to 20 ft. or more, climbing by tendrils. Leaves with oval, 2–3-in. leaflets. Orange, tubular, 3-in.-long flowers in clusters of 15–20 are impressive in fall, early winter. Any soil. Try against west wall.

PYRROSIA lingua

JAPANESE FELT FERN

Polypodiaceae

FERN

🌿 ZONES 14–17, 19–24

☼ ☽ SUN ON COAST, PARTIAL SHADE INLAND

💧 MODERATE WATER

Pyrrosia lingua

D ark green, broad, undivided, lance-shaped fronds with feltlike texture grow in dense clusters from creeping rootstocks. Fronds to 15 in. tall. Most often used in baskets, but makes choice ground cover for small areas. Slow grower. Crested and saw-edged forms are collectors' items.

PYRUS

ORNAMENTAL PEAR

Rosaceae

EVERGREEN OR DECIDUOUS SHRUBS OR TREES

🌿 ZONES VARY BY SPECIES

☼ FULL SUN

💧 MODERATE WATER

Pyrus kawakamii

F ruiting pear is described under Pear. Following are ornamental species. Most are subject to fireblight (see Pear).

P. betulifolia. Zones 2–9, 14–21. Erect, narrow, deciduous tree, 15–30 ft. tall, with arching branches. Leaves 1½–3 in. long, silver gray at first, maturing light green. Leaves flutter in wind like birch or aspen leaves. White flowers have purplish red stamens, open 3 weeks later than *P. calleryana.*

P. calleryana. Deciduous tree. Zones 2–9, 14–21. Grows to 25–50 ft. Strong horizontal branching pattern. Leaves 1½–3 in. long, broadly oval, scalloped, dark green, very glossy and leathery. Flowers clustered, pure white, ¾–1 in. wide. Very early bloom; in coldest areas, late freezes may destroy flower crop. Fruit very small, round, inedible. Fairly resistant to fireblight; rich purplish red fall color.

'Bradford', original introduction, has strongly horizontal limbs, has reached 50 ft. in height, 30 ft. in width. 'Aristocrat' is more pyramidal, with up-curving branches. 'Redspire' is similar, with yellow to red fall color. 'Capital' and 'Whitehouse' are narrowly columnar. 'Chanticleer' is narrow but not columnar, about 40 ft. tall by 15 ft. wide. 'Trinity' is a round-headed form. Newer varieties include 'Cleveland Select' and 'Stone Hill', both erect and dense growers to 30 ft., with good orange fall color.

P. communis. See Pear

P. kawakamii. EVERGREEN PEAR. Evergreen shrub or tree. Zones 8, 9, 12–24. Partially deciduous in coldest winters in coldest zones. Branchlets drooping; leaves glossy, oval, pointed. Clustered white flowers appear in sheets and masses in winter and early spring. Small, rare, inedible fruit.

Without support, evergreen pear becomes broad, sprawling shrub or, in time, a multitrunked small tree. With willowy young branches fastened to fence or frame, it makes a good-looking espalier. To make tree of it, stake one or several branches, shorten side growth, and keep staked until trunk is self-supporting. Beef up framework branches by shortening (when young) to upward-facing buds or branchlets. Established, well-shaped plants need little pruning or shaping. Heavily pruned evergreen pears, such as those espaliered on small frames, seldom flower.

Tolerant of many soils, easy to grow wherever it doesn't freeze. Spray for aphids and watch for fireblight, which can disfigure or destroy plants. Pyracantha is frequent source of infection.

P. pyrifolia (P. serotina). SAND PEAR, JAPANESE SAND PEAR. Deciduous tree. Zones 1–9, 14–21. Like common pear in appearance, but has glossier, more leathery leaves that turn brilliant reddish purple in fall. Fruit small, woody, gritty. Improved forms of this tree, *P. p. culta,* are grown for their fruit by the Japanese and are becoming popular in this country.

P. salicifolia 'Pendula'. WEEPING WILLOW–LEAFED PEAR. Deciduous tree. Zones 2–9, 14–21. To 25 ft. with weeping branches. White flowers appear in early spring, at the same time as silvery white leaves that slowly turn to silvery green. Fruit insignificant.

P. ussuriensis. Deciduous tree. Zones 1–3, 10; hardy to any cold, but flowers may be damaged by late freezes. Grows 20–30 ft. tall. Leaves roundish, glossy green turning bright red in fall. Flowers white, 1½ in. across. Fruit 1–1½ in. wide, yellow green, hard, inedible.

QUERCUS

OAK

Fagaceae

DECIDUOUS OR EVERGREEN TREES

🌿 ZONES VARY BY SPECIES

☼ FULL SUN

◌ 💧 DON'T WATER NATIVES; WATER PLANTED ONES

Quercus coccinea

W estern homeowners acquire oak trees in either of two ways. They may plant the trees themselves, starting from a nursery plant or an acorn (or a jay or squirrel may plant an acorn for them); or they may simply have a native oak tree, left from the days when the land was wild, on their property.

The method of acquisition is significant. An oak tree planted in a garden will grow vigorously and fast (1½–4 ft. a year). It probably will not experience trouble—whether it's a western native or not. Old wild trees, on the other hand, frequently cannot handle the surfeit of water and nutrients that they receive in a garden, and they must be given special treatment.

Special treatment for existing native oaks. If possible, do not raise or lower grade level between trunk and drip line. If you must alter grade, put a well around base of trunk so that grade level there is not changed. Never water within 4 ft. of trunk or allow water to stand within that area. Any of a number of sucking and chewing insects and mites feed upon existing native oaks. Most of the time these creatures are kept in check by other insects and mites, birds, and by insect-and-mite troubles that we don't even know about. Occasionally, though, an outbreak of some organism—usually oak moth larvae—gets bad enough to require artificial control. When that happens, call a commercial arborist or pest control firm to diagnose and treat the problem; oak trees are too big for home gardeners to reach with their limited spray equipment.

Oak root fungus (*Armillaria*) is often present in many California neighborhoods that once were oak forests or walnut groves. Get an arborist's advice on how to sustain infected trees. All old oaks, infected or not, can benefit from feeding and deep watering (fertilize and irrigate only out near drip line).

Old native oaks also benefit from periodic grooming to remove dead wood. However, arborists should not cut thick branches unless they have good reasons for doing so, since excessive pruning may stimulate succulent new growth that will be subject to mildew.

How to transplant an oak. Oak seedlings of any size up to 5–8 ft. seem not to suffer from having their vertical roots cut in transplanting if root ball is otherwise big and firm enough. Trees may wilt or lose leaves after roots are cut, but if watered well, should show new growth in 4–6 weeks. Oak seedlings from nursery containers usually will not show spiraling of taproots at bottom of containers. Better growers will cut a seedling's taproot when planting into a nursery container so the young oak will develop a branching root system.

How to train a young oak. By nature, many young oaks grow twiggy. Growth is divided among so many twigs that none elongate fast. To promote faster vertical growth, pinch off tips of unwanted small branches, meanwhile retaining all leaf surface possible to sustain maximum growth.

BEST OAKS FOR THE WEST

Among the oaks listed below, those native to the western United States or to the Mediterranean region need no watering after they are established (but water them through the first or second dry season).

Q. agrifolia. COAST LIVE OAK. Evergreen. Zones 5, 7–24. Native to Coast Ranges. Round-headed, wide-spreading tree to 20–70 ft. high, often with greater spread. Smooth, dark gray bark. Dense foliage of rounded, hollylike, 1–3-in.-long leaves, slightly glossy on upper surface. As planted tree from nursery or acorn, it can grow as high as 25 ft. in 10 years, 50 ft. in 25 years. Attractive green all year unless hit by oak moth larvae. Has greedy roots and drops almost all its old leaves in early spring just when gardening time is most valuable. Regardless of these faults, it's a handsome and worthwhile shade tree or street tree. Can be sheared into handsome 10–12-ft. hedge.

Quercus agrifolia

Q. bicolor. SWAMP WHITE OAK. Deciduous. Zones 1–3, 10. Medium to slow growth to 60 ft., rarely more. Leaves dark shiny green, up to 7 in. long, with shallow lobes or scallops, silvery white underneath. Bank of trunk and branches flakes off in scales. Tolerates wet soil; also thrives where soil is well drained.

Q. chrysolepis. CANYON LIVE OAK. Evergreen. Zones 5–9, 14–24. Native to mountain slopes and canyons of California, southern Oregon. Handsome round-headed or somewhat spreading tree to 20–60 ft., with smooth, whitish bark. Oval, 1–2-in.-long leaves are shiny medium green above, grayish or whitish beneath. Leaf edges are smooth or toothed. Acorn cups, covered with golden fuzz, look like turbans.

Q. coccinea. SCARLET OAK. Deciduous. All zones. Native to eastern United States. Moderate to rapid growth in deep, rich soil. Can reach 60–80 ft. High, light, open-branching habit. Leaves bright green, to 6 in. long, with deeply cut, pointed lobes. Leaves turn bright scarlet in sharp autumn nights (Zones 1–11, 14, 15, 18–20), but color less well where autumn is warm. Roots grow deep. Good street tree or lawn tree. Fine to garden under.

Q. douglasii. BLUE OAK. Deciduous. Zones 1–11, 14–24. Native to foothills around California's Central Valley. Low-branching, wide-spreading tree to 50 ft. high. Fine-textured light gray bark and decidedly bluish green leaves, shallowly lobed, oval, almost squarish. Good in dry, hot situations. Fall colors attractive—pastel pink, orange, yellow.

Q. emoryi. EMORY OAK. Evergreen. Zones 10–13. Handsome tree to 60 ft. (usually smaller in gardens), native to lower mountain slopes in Arizona, New Mexico, Texas, northern Mexico. Leathery, oval leaves, 2–3 in. long, sometimes turn golden just before new growth starts in late spring. Grows well in low desert, tolerates variety of soils. Needs periodic deep watering during summer.

Q. engelmannii. ENGELMANN OAK, MESA OAK. Evergreen. Zones 7–9, 14–21. Native to Southern California. Wide-spreading tree of character, to 60 ft. high. Leaves oval or oblong, 2 in. long, usually smooth edged. In its area, it has the same cherished native status as the coast live oak.

Q. frainetto. HUNGARIAN or ITALIAN OAK. Deciduous. Zones 2–12, 14–21. Tall tree with large (to 8 in. long, 4 in. wide), glossy deep green leaves with deeply cut lobes. Erect, shapely; takes aridity once established.

Q. gambelii (Q. utahensis). ROCKY MOUNTAIN WHITE OAK. Deciduous. Zones 1–3, 10. Grows slowly to 20–30 (rarely 50) ft., often in colonies from underground creeping root system. Leaves 3–7 in. long, half as wide, dark green turning to yellow, orange, or red in fall. Characteristic oak of Arizona's Oak Creek Canyon and Colorado foothills south of Denver.

Q. garryana. OREGON WHITE OAK, GARRY OAK. Deciduous. Zones 4–6, 15–17. Native from British Columbia south to Santa Cruz Mountains of California. Slow to moderate growth to 40–90 ft., with wide, rounded crown, branches often twisted. Bark grayish, scaly, checked. Leathery leaves 3–6 in. long, with rounded lobes; dark glossy green above, rusty or downy on lower surface. Casts moderate shade and has deep, nonaggressive root system—good shelter for rhododendrons (but don't plant them within 4 ft. of tree's trunk).

Q. ilex. HOLLY OAK, HOLM OAK. Evergreen. Zones 4–24. Native to Mediterranean region. Grows at a moderate rate to 40–70 ft. high, with equal spread. Leaves vary in shape and size, but are usually 1½–3 in. long, ½–1 in. wide, either toothed or smooth edged, dark, rich green on upper surface, yellowish or silvery below. Tolerates wind and salt air; will grow in constant sea wind, but tends to be shrubby there. Inland, growth rate can be moderately fast but varies with soil and water conditions. Good evergreen street tree or lawn tree where coast live oak is difficult to maintain, but lacks open grace of coast live oak. Can take hard clipping into formal shapes or hedges.

Q. kelloggii. CALIFORNIA BLACK OAK. Deciduous. Zones 5 (inland areas), 6, 7, 15, 16, 18–21. Native to mountains from southern Oregon to Southern California. Moderate growth rate to 30–80 ft. Dark, furrowed and checked bark. Handsome foliage; unfolding leaves are soft pink or dusty rose, becoming bright glossy green and turning yellow or yellow orange in fall. Leaves 4–10 in. long, 2½–6 in. wide, with deep lobes ending in bristly points. Good moderate-size tree for spring and fall color, winter trunk and branch pattern.

Quercus kelloggii

Q. lobata. VALLEY OAK, CALIFORNIA WHITE OAK. Deciduous. Zones 1–9, 14–24. Native to interior valleys, Sierra foothills, and Coast Ranges away from direct coastal influence. California's mightiest oak, often reaching 70 ft. or more, with equal or greater spread. Trunk and limbs massive, with thick, ashy gray, distinctly checked bark. Limbs are often picturesquely twisted; long, drooping outer branches sometimes sweep ground. Deeply lobed leaves, lobes rounded; 3–4 in. long, deep green above, paler beneath.

Quercus lobata

Tolerates high heat and moderate alkalinity in its native range. Best in deep soils where it can tap groundwater; in such situations, it can grow fast (2½–3 ft. a year). Magnificent tree for shading big outdoor living area (debris makes it difficult for beds of small plants or heavily used paved areas). This is the tree that gives much of California's Central Valley its parklike look.

"Oak balls" are lightweight, corky spheres about the size of tennis balls, black and tan when they fall. They result from insect activity but do not harm tree.

Q. macrocarpa. BUR OAK, MOSSY CUP OAK. Deciduous. Zones 1–11, 14–24. Native to eastern United States. Rugged looking, to 60–75 ft. high, 30 ft. wide. Leaves are glossy green above and whitish beneath, 8–10 in. long, broad at tip, tapered at base, deeply lobed. Large acorns form in mossy cups. Similar to *Q. bicolor* but faster growing, more tolerant of adverse conditions.

Quercus macrocarpa

Q. myrsinifolia. JAPANESE LIVE OAK. Evergreen. Zones 4–7, 14–24. A 30–50-ft. tree in its native China and Japan. Leaves 2½–4 in. long, narrow, toothed toward tips, glossy dark green. New foliage purplish. Unlike most oaks, it is graceful rather than sturdy and is not easily recognized as an oak unless seen with its acorns.

Q. palustris. PIN OAK. Deciduous. All zones. Native to eastern United States. Moderate to fairly rapid growth to 50–80 ft. Slender and pyramidal when young, open and round headed at maturity. Brownish gray bark. Lower branches tend to droop almost to ground; if lowest whorl is cut away, branches above will adopt same habit. Only when fairly tall will it have good clearance beneath lowest branches. Glossy dark green leaves are deeply cut into bristle-pointed lobes; in brisk fall weather, leaves turn yellow, red, and finally russet brown. Many hang on in winter.

Quercus palustris

Takes less aridity than most other oaks. Develops chlorosis in alkaline soils; treat with iron chelate. Needs ample water and good drainage. Stake young trees and give only corrective pruning. Plant where its spread will not interfere with walks, drives, or street traffic, or trim it often. Unlike western oaks, it is a fine tree for lawns.

Q. phellos. WILLOW OAK. Deciduous. Zones 1–4, 6–16, 18–21. Native to eastern United States. To 50–90 ft. Somewhat like pin oak in growth habit and spreading nature, this tree is grown and used the same way as pin oak. Smooth, gray bark. Leaves are not like those of other common oaks; they somewhat resemble willow leaves—2½–5 in. long, ⅓–1 in. wide, smooth edged. Foliage turns yellowish before falling; in warmer zones, dead leaves may hang on through winter. Of all oaks, willow oak has most delicate foliage pattern.

Quercus phellos

Q. robur. ENGLISH OAK. Deciduous. Zones 2–12, 14–21. To 90 ft., with rather short trunk and very wide, open head in maturity. Fairly fast growth. Leaves 3–4½ in. long, with three to seven pairs of rounded lobes. Leaves hold until late in fall and drop without much color change. Variety 'Fastigiata', upright English oak, is narrow and upright (like Lombardy poplar) when young, branches out to broad, pyramidal shape when mature. Other varieties are 'Skymaster' (broad pyramid to 50 ft. tall, half as wide, narrower in youth) and 'Westminster Globe' (round crown to 45 by 45 ft.).

Q. rubra (Q. r. maxima, Q. borealis). RED OAK, NORTHERN RED OAK. Deciduous. Zones 1–12, 14–24. Fast growth to 90 ft. Broad, spreading branches and round-topped crown. Leaves 5–8 in. long by 3–5 in. wide, with three to seven pairs of sharp-pointed lobes. New leaves and leaf stalks are red in spring, turning to dark red, ruddy brown, or orange in fall. Needs fertile soil and plenty of water. Stake young plants. High-branching habit and reasonably open shade make it a good tree for big lawns, parks, broad avenues. Its deep roots make it good to garden under.

Q. shumardii. SHUMARD RED OAK. Deciduous. Zones 4–9, 12, 14–17. Similar to scarlet oak (*Q. coccinea*), slightly less hardy. Fall color yellow to red. Tolerates acid, poorly drained soil.

Q. suber. CORK OAK. Evergreen. Zones 5–7 (with occasional winter damage), 8–16, 18–23. Native to Mediterranean region. Moderate growth rate to 70–100 ft. high and as wide. Trunk and principal limbs covered with thick, corky bark (cork of commerce). The toothed, 3-in. leaves are shiny dark green above, gray beneath. General

Quercus suber

effect is fine textured. Needs good drainage. Fairly tolerant of different soil types, but likely to yellow in alkaline soils. Established trees can take considerable aridity. One of best oaks for desert.

Good garden shade tree with interesting contrast between fairly light-textured foliage and massive, fissured trunk. Value as street tree or park tree diminishes when children find out how easy it is to carve bark.

Q. tomentella. ISLAND OAK. Evergreen. Zones 7–9, 14–17, 19–24. Native to California's Channel Islands. Tree to 60 ft., with slightly toothed leaves to 3 in. long, dark green above, grayish beneath. Acorns nearly 1 in. long. Symmetrical tree when well grown; some consider it the handsomest of California's evergreen oaks.

Q. vaccinifolia. HUCKLEBERRY OAK. Evergreen. Zones 4–7, 14–17. Native to mountains of California. Low (to 2 ft.), with sprawling stems and smooth-edged, gray-green leaves ¾–1¼ in. long. Sometimes planted in wild gardens, large rock gardens, mountain summer home gardens.

Q. virginiana. SOUTHERN LIVE OAK. Evergreen, partly or wholly deciduous in cold-winter regions. Zones 4–24. Native to eastern United States. Moderate to fast growth to eventual 60 ft., with broad, spreading, heavy-limbed crown twice as wide. Smooth-edged leaves 1½–5 in. long, shiny dark green above and whitish beneath. Thrives on water and does best in deep, rich soil. In hot interior climates, it's the most attractive of all evergreen oaks. Best oak for lawn planting in low desert. The fast-growing variety 'Heritage' is recommended for low desert areas.

Q. wislizenii. INTERIOR LIVE OAK. Evergreen. Zones 7–9, 14–16, 18–21. Native to Sierra foothills and east side of California's Central Valley. To 30–75 ft. high, often broader than high. Wide-spreading branches form dense crown. Oblong, glossy green leaves to 4 in. long, smooth or spiny edged. Handsome tree for parks and big lawns. Sparse, angular young plants fail to hint at tree's ultimate beauty.

GROW AN OAK FROM AN ACORN

Many of nature's creatures want to eat part of a sprouting/growing acorn. To frustrate them, dig a hole 6 in. deep and 6 in. across. Into it insert one end of an 18-in.-wide length of aluminum screening rolled into a 6-in.-diameter cylinder. Refill inside the screen-lined hole with soil. Plant an acorn sideways and cover it with 1 in. of soil (if a white root has developed, point it downward). Tie screen at top. If possible, water several times the first summer. After first summer, remove screen.

QUILLAJA saponaria

SOAPBARK TREE

Rosaceae

EVERGREEN TREE

ZONES 8, 9, 14–24

FULL SUN

LITTLE WATER ONCE ESTABLISHED

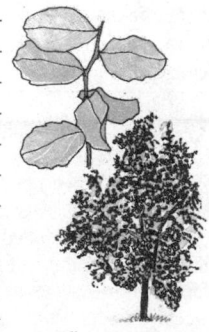

Quillaja saponaria

Usually to 25–30 ft.; occasionally to 60 ft. Young plant is a dense column foliaged right down to ground; old tree develops broad, flattened crown. Branchlets are pendulous, especially on younger plant, and general effect of young tree is that of narrow, bushy, weeping live oak. Leaves are 2 in. long, oval to nearly round, rather leathery, shiny green. White flowers are ½ in. across; handsome brown, 1-in. fruit opens into star form. Tends toward multiple trunks and excessive bushiness but responds quickly to pruning. Without firm staking and occasional thinning, younger tree may blow down in strong winds. Fairly tolerant of different soils. Good narrow screening tree. Can be pruned as tall hedge.

QUINCE, FLOWERING. See CHAENOMELES p. 220

QUINCE, FRUITING

Rosaceae

DECIDUOUS SHRUBS OR SMALL TREES

☑ ALL ZONES

☼ FULL SUN

◐ INFREQUENT WATER

Fruiting Quince

S low to 10–25 ft. Unlike flowering quince (*Chaenomeles*), fruiting quince has thornless branches. Generally overlooked by planters of flowering fruit trees and home orchard trees, yet its virtues make common quince worth considering as an ornamental. Its winter form can be dramatic in pattern of gnarled and twisted branches. In spring, it wears white or pale pink, 2-in.-wide flowers at tips of leafed-out branches. Attractive, oval, 2–4-in. leaves, dark green above, whitish beneath, turn yellow in fall. Fruit is yellow, fragrant. Quince is propagated by hardwood cuttings taken in late fall or winter.

Best in heavy, well-drained soil but tolerates wet soil. Avoid deep cultivation, which damages shallow roots and causes suckers. Prune only to form trunk and shape frame; thin out and cut back only enough to stimulate new growth. Do not use high-nitrogen fertilizer, as this results in succulent growth that is susceptible to fireblight. Remove suckers that sprout freely around the base of the tree; they rarely fruit and tend to weaken the tree.

Large, fragrant fruit is inedible when raw but useful in making jams and jellies. Fruit is also made into candy and blended with other fruits in pies. Ripens from late September to October. Some popular varieties are

'Apple' ('Orange'). Old favorite. Round, golden-skinned fruit. Tender orange-yellow flesh.

'Cooke's Jumbo'. Large yellowish green fruit with white flesh. Can be nearly twice the size of other quinces.

'Pineapple'. Roundish, light golden fruit. Tender white flesh; pineapple-like flavor.

'Smyrna'. Round to oblong fruit with lemon yellow skin. Strong quince fragrance.

QUINOA. See CHENOPODIUM quinoa	p. 222
RADICCHIO. See CHICORY	p. 223

RADISH

Brassicaceae (Cruciferae)

ANNUALS

☑ ALL ZONES

☼◐ FULL SUN; LIGHT SHADE IN WARM WEATHER

◐ REGULAR WATER

Radish

Y ou can pull radishes for the table 3 weeks after you sow the seed (the slowest kinds take 2 months). They need continual moisture and some added nutrients to grow well. Supply nutrients by blending rotted manure into soil before planting, or—about 10 days after planting—feed beside row as for carrots, or feed with liquid fertilizer. Sow seeds as soon as ground can be worked in spring and at weekly intervals until warm weather approaches. In mild areas, radishes also make a fall and winter crop.

Sow seeds ½ in. deep and thin to 1 in. apart when tops are up. Space rows 1 ft. apart. Most familiar kinds are short, round, red or red-and-white types like 'Cherry Belle', 'Crimson Giant', and 'Scarlet White-tipped'. These should be used just as soon as they reach full size. Slightly slower to reach edible size are long white radishes, of which 'Icicle' is best known. Late radishes 'Long Black Spanish' and 'White Chinese' grow 6–10 in. long, can be stored in moist sand in a frost-free place for winter use. The last named, along with 'Alpine Cross' and similar, very large, mild radishes, are sold as daikon (pronounced "dye-con").

RANGPUR LIME. See CITRUS, Sour-Acid Mandarin Oranges   p. 232

Ranunculaceae. The immense buttercup family numbers nearly 2,000 species, among them numerous ornamental annuals and perennials, including *Anemone, Aquilegia, Clematis, Delphinium, Helleborus, Ranunculus,* and many others. Many are poisonous if eaten.

RANUNCULUS

Ranunculaceae

TUBERS OR PERENNIALS

☑ ALL ZONES

☼ FULL SUN

◐ WATER DURING GROWTH

Ranunculus asiaticus

A very large group (up to 250 species of widely different habit and appearance), but the two listed are the only ones grown to any extent.

R. asiaticus. PERSIAN RANUNCULUS, TURBAN RANUNCULUS. Tuber. Leaves bright fresh green, almost fernlike. Flowers semidouble to fully double, 3–5 in. wide, in many shades of yellow, orange, red, pink, cream, and white. Large tubers produce many 1½-ft.-tall or taller stalks, 50–75 blooms (1–4 on each stalk). Popular strain is Tecolote Giants; you can purchase single colors or mixtures as well as picotee (edged) blends. Bloomingdale is dwarf (8–10-in.) strain. Use in borders with Iceland poppies, snapdragons, nemesias. Plant for follow-up color in daffodil beds. Superb cut flowers.

Planting time depends on climate: November in mild-winter areas, October in desert, November or mid-February in western Washington and Oregon. Later planting gives later bloom. Need perfect drainage, full sun. Set tubers (prongs downward) 6–8 in. apart, 2 in. deep (½–1 in. deep in heavy soil). Tubers come dry and hard but plump up after absorbing moisture. Water thoroughly after planting; unless weather is very hot and dry, do not water again until sprouts show (10 days–2 weeks). Tubers rot if overwatered before roots form. You can start tubers in flats of moist sand and plant them when sprouted and rooted. To protect young sprouts from birds, cover with netting. After blooms fade, let plants dry out; lift tubers, cut off tops, and store in dry, cool place. Nursery-grown seedlings are sold in some areas in fall. In coldest climates, grow ranunculus in greenhouse, plant after frosts. Early hot spells may shorten bloom period in such areas.

R. repens 'Pleniflorus'. CREEPING BUTTERCUP. Perennial. Vigorous plant with thick, fibrous roots and runners growing several feet in a season, rooting at joints. Leaves glossy, roundish, deeply cut, toothed. Flowers are fully double, button shaped, bright yellow, about 1 in. across, on stems 1–2 ft. high. Spring bloom. Ground cover in moist soil, filtered or deep shade. Can be invasive in flower beds and lawns. Single-flowered form, *R. repens,* is as aggressive or more so.

RAOULIA australis

Asteraceae (Compositae)

PERENNIAL CARPETING PLANT

☑ ZONES 4–9, 13–24

☼ FULL SUN

◐ MODERATE WATER

Raoulia australis

S tems up to 6 in. long form very close mats. Stems are hidden by small gray leaves that cover them completely. Inconspicuous pale yellow flowers in spring. Useful in dry rockery. Needs sandy soil, perfect drainage.

RAPHIDOPHORA aurea. See EPIPREMNUM aureum	p. 274
RAPHIOLEPIS. See RHAPHIOLEPIS	p. 453

R

RASPBERRY

Rosaceae

SHRUBS WITH BIENNIAL STEMS

◢ ALL ZONES; BEST IN ZONES 4–6, 15–17

☼ FULL SUN

◐ REGULAR WATER

Raspberry

Most popular and heaviest bearers are red raspberries. There are two types: summer-bearing raspberries, which bear once a year, in summer, on two-year-old canes; and fall-bearing (also called everbearing) raspberries, which bear twice on each cane—in autumn of the first year, then in summer of the second year. Both types bloom in loose clusters of white flowers. (There are also ornamental relatives. See *Rubus*.)

Raspberries need slowly warming, lingering springtime to reach perfection. In warmer zones outside of best raspberry climates, satisfactory production may come from plants grown in light shade. Well-drained soil is essential; if your soil is heavy clay, consider planting in raised beds. Slightly acid soil (pH 6 to 6.5) is ideal.

The best time to plant is in winter before growth starts. Set plants 2½–3 ft. apart in rows of 7–9 ft. apart and about an inch deeper than they grew originally. Cut back cane that rises from the roots, leaving only enough to serve as a marker (about 6 in.).

Summer-bearing plants should produce three to five canes the first year; these will bear the next year and should be cut out at ground level after fruiting. Second-year canes will come up all around the parent plant and even between hills and rows. Remove all except 5–12 closely spaced, vigorous canes that come up near the crown. Be sure to pull up all suckers away from the crown. Tie selected canes to top wire. In spring, before growth begins, cut them back to 4½–5½ ft. Fruit-bearing laterals will appear from these canes.

Fall-bearing raspberries differ slightly in pruning needs; these fruit in their first autumn on the top third of cane and in their second summer on the lower two-thirds of cane. Cut off the upper portion that has borne fruit and leave the lower portion to bear next spring. Cut out cane after it has fruited along its whole length.

In mild California climates, some growers have had success with handling fall-bearing raspberry canes as annuals. With this method, after canes finish fruiting, you cut all of them off as close to the ground as possible. In spring new canes appear and bear new crop. Use powerful rotary mower in large berry patch. Ease of maintenance helps make up for loss of earliest berries.

Plants need water especially during blossoming and fruiting. Feed at blossoming time. The following varieties are summer bearing unless otherwise indicated.

'Bababerry'. Spring and fall bearing. Needs little winter chill, stands heat well.

'Boyne'. Bred in Manitoba, it is hardy in all zones. Early bearer.

'Canby'. Large, bright red berries. Thornless, hardy.

'Cuthbert'. Medium-size berries of good quality.

'Durham'. Medium-size, firm berries of good quality. Fall bearing; starts to ripen 2 weeks before 'Indian Summer'.

'Fairview'. Variety for coastal Northwest. Bears young and heavily. Early variety of good quality.

'Heritage'. Small red berries are tasty, a bit dry. Bears in June and again in September.

'Indian Summer'. Small crops of large, red, tasty berries in late spring and again in fall; fall crop often larger.

'Latham'. Older, very hardy variety for intermountain areas. Late. Berries often crumbly. Mildews in humid-summer regions.

'Meeker'. Large, bright red, firm fruit on long, willowy laterals.

'Newburgh'. Hardy, late-ripening variety. Large light red berries. Takes heavy soil fairly well.

'New Washington'. Smallish fruit of high quality. Hardy, but needs well-drained soil.

'Puyallup'. For west of the Cascades. Large, soft berries with very good flavor. Midseason.

'Ranere' ('St. Regis'). Bears over a long season, from midspring to frost in California. Berries small, bright red. Needs steady irrigation for long bearing.

'September'. Medium to small berries of good flavor. Some fruit in June, good crop in fall.

'Sumner'. Hardy, with some resistance to root rot in heavy soils. Fine fruit. Early.

'Willamette'. Large, firm, dark red berries that hold color and shape well. Tasty novelty is 'Golden West', with yellow berries of excellent quality.

LIVING QUARTERS FOR RASPBERRIES

To arrange raspberries for easiest handling: train the vines on two horizontal wires, with the upper one 4–5 ft. above ground, the lower one 2½ ft. above ground.

RASPBERRY, BLACK or BLACKCAP

Rosaceae

SHRUBS WITH BIENNIAL STEMS

◢ BEST IN ZONES 4–6; FAIL TO THRIVE IN CALIFORNIA

☼ ◐ SUN OR LIGHT SHADE

◐ REGULAR SUMMER WATER

Black Raspberry

For ornamental relatives, see *Rubus*. Resemble regular red raspberry in many ways, but blue-black fruit is firmer and seedier, with a more distinct flavor. Plants do not sucker from roots; new plants form when arching cane tips root in soil. No trellis needed. Head back new canes at 1½–2 ft. to force laterals. At end of growing season, cut out all weak canes and remove canes that fruited during current season. In late winter or early spring, cut back laterals to 10–15 in. on strong canes, 3–4 in. on weak ones. Fruit is produced on side shoots from these laterals. If you prefer trellising, head new canes at 2–3 ft.

Varieties usually sold are 'Cumberland', an old variety; 'Morrison', large berry on productive vine; and 'Munger', most popular commercial variety. 'Sodus', purple raspberry, is a vigorous-growing hybrid of red and black raspberry; head new canes at 2½–3 ft.

RATIBIDA

Asteraceae (Compositae)

PERENNIALS

◢ ALL ZONES

☼ FULL SUN

◐ REGULAR WATER

Ratibida columnifera

Native to prairie and western states. Plants are stiffly erect, branched, roughly hairy, with deeply cut leaves. Flower heads resemble black-eyed Susans (*Rudbeckia*) but have fewer ray flowers and a round or cylindrical (rather than flat) central disc. Use in casual, natural-looking borders with grasses and other minimum-care perennials.

R. columnifera. MEXICAN HAT. To 2 ft. tall. Flowers have drooping ray flowers of yellow or brownish purple, and a tall columnar brown disc. Effect is that of a sombrero with drooping brim.

R. pinnata. PRAIRIE or YELLOW CONEFLOWER. Taller than *R. columnifera* (to 3 ft.), with yellow ray flowers and a nearly globular brown disc.

RATTAN PALM. See RHAPIS humilis   p. 453

REHMANNIA elata
(R. angulata)

Gesneriaceae

PERENNIAL EVERGREEN; CAN BE DECIDUOUS

☘ ZONES 7–10, 12–24

☼ ◑ ● SUN OR SHADE; BEST WITH SOME SHADE

● REGULAR WATER

Rehmannia elata

This plant's most impressive trait is its long bloom season: mid-April–November. Stalks rise to 2–3 ft., loosely set with 3-in.-long, tubular flowers that look something like big, gaping foxgloves. Common form is rose purple with yellow, red-dotted throat; there is a fine white-and-cream form that must be grown from cuttings or divisions. Coarse, deeply toothed leaves. Spreads by underground roots and forms big clumps. Easy to grow. Rich soil. Handsome and long-lasting as cut flowers. Deciduous in cold-winter areas.

REINWARDTIA indica
(R. trigyna)

YELLOW FLAX

Linaceae

PERENNIAL

☘ ZONES 8–10, 12–24

☼ ◑ SUN OR PARTIAL SHADE

● SOME DRY-SEASON WATER

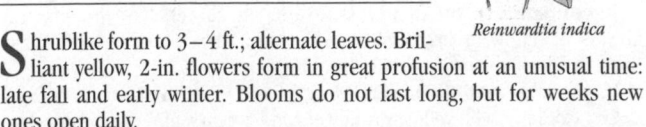

Reinwardtia indica

Shrublike form to 3–4 ft.; alternate leaves. Brilliant yellow, 2-in. flowers form in great profusion at an unusual time: late fall and early winter. Blooms do not last long, but for weeks new ones open daily.

Pinch to make more compact. Spreads by underground roots. Increase by rooted stems; divide in spring. Good choice for winter color in flower garden or with shrubs.

RESEDA odorata

MIGNONETTE

Resedaceae

SUMMER ANNUAL

☘ ALL ZONES

☼ ◑ SUN ON COAST, PARTIAL SHADE INLAND

● REGULAR WATER

Reseda odorata

To 1–1½ ft. tall; rather sprawling habit. Light green leaves. Not particularly beautiful plant, but well worth growing because of remarkable flower fragrance. Small greenish flowers tinged with copper or yellow, in dense spikes that become loose and open as blossoms mature. Flowers dry up quickly in hot weather. Sow seed in early spring—or late fall or winter in Zones 15–24. Successive sowings give long bloom period. Best in rich soil. Plant in masses to get full effect of fragrance, or spot a few in flower bed to provide fragrance to scentless plantings. Suitable for pots. Other forms have longer flower spikes and brighter colors, but they are less fragrant.

RETINISPORA pisifera. See CHAMAECYPARIS pisifera   **p. 220**

Rhamnaceae. The buckthorn family of shrubs and trees has small, usually clustered flowers and fruits that are either drupes (single seeded, juicy) or capsules. Western gardeners grow *Ceanothus, Rhamnus,* and *Ziziphus.*

RHAMNUS

Rhamnaceae

EVERGREEN OR DECIDUOUS SHRUBS OR TREES

☘ ZONES VARY BY SPECIES

☼ ◑ ● EXPOSURE NEEDS VARY BY SPECIES

◊ ● ● ● WATER NEEDS VARY BY SPECIES

Rhamnus californica

Small flowers in clusters are rather inconspicuous; plants are grown for form and foliage, occasionally for show of berrylike fruit.

R. alaternus. ITALIAN BUCKTHORN. Evergreen shrub. Zones 4–24. Fast, dense growth to 12–20 ft. or more, spreading as wide. Close planting or pruning will keep it narrow. Easily trained as multistemmed or single-stemmed small tree. Leaves oval to oblong, bright shiny green, ¾–2 in. long. Tiny, greenish yellow April flowers; black, ¼-in.-long fruit.

Easily sheared or shaped. Takes heat; you can either water it or not. Grows in full sun or partial shade. Valuable as fast screen or tall clipped hedge. Trained to single stem, makes good plant for tall screen above 6-ft. fence. *R. a.* 'Variegata' (*R. a.* 'Argenteovariegata'), with leaves edged in creamy white, is striking against dark background. Cut out plain green branches that occasionally appear; if you do not, they will quickly shade out and replace variegated foliage. 'John Edwards', vigorous, fast growing, and long lived, is a consistent cutting-grown variety.

R. californica. COFFEEBERRY. Evergreen shrub. Zones 4–24. Native to California, Arizona, New Mexico, southwest Oregon. May have low, spreading habit (especially if growing near ocean) or, in woodlands or hills, upright growth to 3–15 ft. Leaves 1–3 in. long, shiny dark green to dull green (depending on variety), paler beneath (in some forms gray and hairy beneath). Large berries green, then red, then black when ripe. 'Eve Case', a dense, compact form propagated from cuttings, grows 4–8 ft. tall with equal spread. Selected coastal form, *R. c.* 'Seaview', can be kept to 1½ ft. high, 6–8 ft. wide, if upright growth is pinched out. Both 'Eve Case' and 'Seaview' have foliage that is distinctly broader, flatter, brighter green than that of the species. Coffeeberries grow in full sun to half shade; they are not particular as to soil. Established plants need no water, but the broader-leafed varieties look better with some summer water.

R. cathartica. COMMON BUCKTHORN. Deciduous large shrub or small tree. Zones 1–3. To 15–20 ft. Leaves bright glossy green, 1–2½ in. long by half as wide, turning yellow before falling off in autumn. Short twigs often spine tipped. Fruit is black, ¼ in. thick. Useful hedge or small tree in coldest, driest areas. Full sun. Tolerates aridity, poor soil, wind.

R. crocea. REDBERRY. Evergreen shrub. Zones 14–21. Native to Coast Ranges, Lake County to San Diego County, California. To 2–3 ft. high and spreading, with many stiff or spiny branches. Leaves roundish, ½ in. long, glossy dark to pale green above, golden or brownish beneath, often finely toothed. Small bright red fruit, August–October. Full sun to partial shade; inland from its native territory, best with some shade. Needs just a little water each summer.

R. c. ilicifolia. HOLLYLEAF REDBERRY. Evergreen shrub. Zones 7–16, 18–21. Native to Coast Ranges and Sierra Nevada foothills, mountains of Southern California, Arizona, Baja California. Multistemmed or often treelike, to 3–15 ft. Leaves roundish, ½–1¼ in. long, spiny toothed. Good ornamental plant for dry banks or informal screen in hot-sun areas. No water once established.

R. frangula. ALDER BUCKTHORN. Deciduous shrub or small tree. Zones 1–7, 10–13. To 15–18 ft. tall. Leaves roundish, glossy dark green, 1–3 in. long, half as wide. Fruit turns from red to black on ripening. Sun to partial shade; established plants need only moderate summer watering. *R. f.* 'Columnaris', tallhedge buckthorn, grows 12–15 ft. tall, 4 ft. wide. Set 2½ ft. apart for tight, narrow hedge that needs minimum of trimming and can be kept as low as 4 ft.

R. purshiana. CASCARA SAGRADA. Deciduous shrub or small tree. Zones 1–9, 14–17. Native from Northern California to British Columbia and Montana. To 20–40 ft.; smooth, gray or brownish bark has medicinal value. Dark green, prominently veined leaves are elliptical, 1½–8 in. long, to 2 in. wide, usually somewhat tufted at ends of branches. Foliage turns good yellow in fall. Round black fruit attracts birds. Will grow in dense shade or full sun with ample water. Picturesque branching pattern.

RHAPHIDOPHORA aurea. See EPIPREMNUM aureum   p. 274

RHAPHIOLEPIS

Rosaceae

EVERGREEN SHRUBS

🌡 ZONES 8–10, 12–24; WORTH THE RISK, ZONES 4–7

☼ ◑ FULL SUN OR LIGHT SHADE

◌ ● ACCEPT INFREQUENT OR LAWN WATERING

Rhaphiolepis indica

These are among the most widely planted garden shrubs, for good reason: with their glossy, leathery leaves, and compact growth habit these shrubs make attractive dense background plantings, large-scale ground covers, low dividers, or informal hedges. And they offer more than the constant greenery of most basic landscaping shrubs. From late fall or midwinter to late spring, they carry a profusion of flowers ranging from white to near red. Dark blue, berrylike fruit (not especially showy) follows flowers. New leaves often add to color range with tones of bronze and red.

Most stay low. The taller kinds rarely reach more than 5–6 ft.; pruning can keep them at 3 ft. almost indefinitely. Prune from the beginning if you want sturdy, bushy, compact plants; pinch back tips of branches at least once each year, after flowering. For more open structure, let plants grow naturally and thin out branches occasionally. Encourage spreading by shortening vertical branches. Pinch side branches to encourage upright growth.

Note that in light shade they are less compact, produce fewer flowers than in full sun. They have few pest problems, although aphids occasionally attack. Fungus sometimes causes leaf spotting, especially during cold, wet weather—to control, destroy infected leaves, spray with fungicide, avoid overhead watering. In desert, plants will burn in reflected heat; they need some sheltering shade in Zone 13. Fireblight is a problem in some areas.

R. delacouri. Pink-flowered hybrid of *R. indica* and *R. umbellata*. To 6 ft. tall. Small pink flowers in upright clusters, October–May. Leaves smaller than most.

R. indica. INDIA HAWTHORN. White flowers tinged with pink are about ½ in. across. Leaves pointed, 1½–3 in. long. Plants grow 4–5 ft. high. Its varieties are widely grown and sold although the species is not. Varieties differ mainly in color of bloom and in size and form of plant; there is variation even within a variety.

Flower color is especially inconsistent: flowers in warmer climates and exposures are usually lighter; in general, bloom is paler in fall than in spring. Varieties include the following:

'Ballerina'. Deep rosy pink flowers. Stays low (not much taller than 2 ft.) and compact (no wider than 4 ft.). Leaves take on reddish tinge in winter. Tip-prune young plants for compact form.

'Clara'. White flowers on compact plants 3–5 ft. high, about as wide. Red new growth.

'Dancer'. Clear pink flowers. Dense. To about 4 ft. tall.

'Enchantress'. Rose pink flowers. Grows 3 ft. tall, 5 ft. wide. A white form is called 'White Enchantress'.

'Indian Princess'. Light pink flowers. To 3 ft. high.

'Jack Evans'. Bright pink flowers. To about 4 ft. tall, with wider spread. Compact and spreading. Leaves sometimes have purplish tinge.

'Spring Rapture'. Compact 4-ft.-tall plant with rose red single flowers.

'Springtime'. Deep pink flowers. Vigorous, upright growth can reach 4–6 ft. high.

R. 'Majestic Beauty'. Fragrant light pink flowers in clusters to 10 in. wide. Leaves 4 in. long. Larger in every detail than other rhaphiolepis; can reach 15 ft. Thought by some to be hybrid between *Rhaphiolepis* and *Eriobotrya*. Use as background shrub or small tree with single or multiple trunk. Stake tree form carefully until it has formed a sturdy trunk. Thin branches to reduce wind resistance and minimize chances of plant blowing down.

R. umbellata (R. u. ovata, R. ovata). Easily distinguished from *R. indica* by its roundish, leathery, dark green leaves, 1–3 in. long. White flowers about ¾ in. wide. Vigorous plants 4–6 ft. tall, sometimes to 10 ft. Thick and bushy in full sun. This plant is sometimes called Yeddo hawthorn. *R. u.* 'Minor' is a dwarf, slow-growing form.

RHAPIS

LADY PALM

Arecaceae (Palmae)

PALMS

🌡 ZONES VARY BY SPECIES

☼ ● LIGHT TO MEDIUM SHADE

● MODERATE WATER

Rhapis excelsa

Fan palms that form bamboolike clumps with deep green foliage. Trunks covered with net of dark, fibrous leaf sheaths. Slow growing, choice, expensive.

R. excelsa. LADY PALM. Zones 12–17, 19–24. Small, slow, 5–12 ft. tall, often much lower. Best in shade but will take considerable sun near the beach. In Zones 12–14 it needs shade, shelter from heat and cold. Well-drained soil. One of the finest container palms, it withstands poor light and neglect but responds quickly to better light and fertilizer. Hardy to 20°F.

R. humilis. RATTAN PALM, SLENDER LADY PALM. Zones 16, 17, 20–24. Tall, bamboolike stems (to 18 ft.) give charming, graceful, tropical air. Larger, longer-leafed palm than *R. excelsa;* less tolerant of sun. Hardy to 22°F.

R

RHIPSALIDOPSIS gaertneri (Schlumbergera gaertneri)

EASTER CACTUS

Cactaceae

HOUSE PLANT OR INDOOR/OUTDOOR PLANT

☘ ZONES 16, 17, 21–24 IN COVERED AREAS

☼ BRIGHT LIGHT INDOORS; HALF SHADE OUTDOORS

💧 REGULAR WATER

*Rhipsalidopsis
gaertneri*

For culture and general description, see *Schlumbergera*. Much like *S. bridgesii*, with the same drooping stems—but more upright, with more rounded stem joints. Bright red flowers to 3 in. long are upright or horizontal rather than drooping. Blooms April–May, often again in September. There are many varieties in shades of pink and red. Lathhouse or covered-terrace plant in Zones 16, 17, 21–24.

RHODODENDRON (includes Azalea)

Ericaceae

EVERGREEN OR DECIDUOUS SHRUBS, RARELY TREES

☘ BEST IN ZONES 4–6, 15–17; MANY EXCEPTIONS

☼ GENERALLY BEST IN FILTERED SHADE

💧 💧 CONSTANTLY MOIST SOIL AND HUMID AIR

☠ LEAVES ARE POISONOUS

*Rhododendron
'Trude Webster'*

Approximately 800 species belong to this huge group. The International Register lists more than 10,000 named varieties, of which perhaps 2,000 varieties are currently available. Botanists have arranged species into series and subseries; one of these series includes plants called azaleas.

The climate adaptation pattern of azaleas is quite different from that of rhododendrons. For example, evergreen azaleas are planted by the hundreds of thousands in Southern California, where rhododendrons are far less frequent and require more special attention. But gardeners in every climate of the West—except deserts and areas of coldest winters—can find ways to grow certain rhododendron varieties. Even some adventuresome desert gardeners have succeeded with container-grown plants.

Rhododendrons and azaleas have much the same basic soil and water requirements. They require acid soil. They need more air in the root zone than any other garden plants but, at the same time, they need a constant moisture supply. In other words, they need soil that is both fast draining and moisture retentive. Yellowing, wilting, and collapse of plants indicate root rot caused by poor drainage. Soils rich in organic matter have the desired qualities; improve your soil with liberal quantities of organic matter. Plant azaleas and rhododendrons with top of root ball slightly above soil level. Never allow soil to wash in and bury stems. Plants are surface rooters and benefit from a mulch such as pine needles, oak leaves, and wood by-products (for example, redwood or fir bark or chips). Never cultivate around these plants.

Sun tolerance of azaleas and rhododendrons differs by species and varieties. Too much sun causes bleaching or burning in leaf centers, though most can take full sun in cool-summer areas. Ideal location is in filtered shade beneath tall trees; east and north sides of house or fence are next best. Too-dense shade results in lanky plants that bloom sparsely. Fertilize when growth starts in spring, again at bloom time or right after; then feed monthly until August. Use commercial acid fertilizer and follow directions carefully; to be extra safe, cut portions in half and feed twice as often.

Both azaleas and rhododendrons need special attention where soil or water is high in dissolved salts—as it is in many areas in California. To avoid damage, plant in containers or raised beds and periodically leach the mix by heavy watering—enough to drain through mix 2 or 3 times. If leaves

turn yellow while veins remain green, plants have iron deficiency called chlorosis; apply iron chelate to soil or spray with iron solution.

Insects and diseases are seldom much of a problem. Root weevil larvae feed on roots. Adult weevils notch leaves but damage usually is minor. You can prevent larvae from developing in soil by applying diazinon, acephate, or carbaryl to soil and working it in to depth of 6 in. at planting time. Or you can kill adults as they emerge from soil (April–May). Use poison bait or spray plant and soil with acephate and repeat every 2 weeks until there is no sign of leaf feeding. The obscure root weevil (gray in color) can be a problem in western Oregon; control with malathion.

Wind and soil salts burn leaf edges; windburn shows up most often on new foliage, salt burn on older leaves. Late frosts often cause deformed leaves.

Prune evergreen azaleas by frequent pinching of tip growth from after flowering to August if you wish a compact plant with maximum flower production.

Prune large-flowered rhododendrons early in spring at bloom time if needed. Pruning in early spring will sacrifice some flower buds, but that is the best time for extensive pruning. Plant's energies will be diverted to dormant growth buds, which will then be ready to push out early in the growing season. Tip-pinch young plants to make them bushy; prune older, leggy plants to restore shape by cutting back to side branch, leaf whorl, or cluster of dormant buds. (Some varieties will not push new growth from dormant buds.) Clip or break off faded flower heads or spent clusters, taking care not to injure new buds and growth just beneath them.

KINDS OF RHODODENDRONS

Most people know rhododendrons as big, leathery-leafed shrubs with rounded clusters ("trusses") of stunning white, pink, red, or purple blossoms. But there are also dwarfs a few inches tall, giants that reach 40 or even 80 ft. in their native Southeast Asia, and a host of species and hybrids in every intermediate size, in a color range including scarlet, yellow, near-blue, and a constellation of blends of orange, apricot, and salmon.

The following sections list named varieties by categories, to give you some idea of their adaptability to different climates and garden roles. Many of them are described later. These are the generally available kinds, representing only a portion of the best rhododendrons grown in the West.

Ironclad hybrids for coldest winters. These can take temperatures to −25°F: 'America', *R. catawbiense* 'Album', 'English Roseum', *R. mucronulatum*, 'Nova Zembla', 'PJM'. Ironclad hybrids that also do well in Southern California: 'Anah Kruschke', 'Blue Ensign', 'Cunningham's White', 'Fastuosum Flore Pleno', 'Gomer Waterer', 'Mars', 'Pink Pearl'.

Northern California specials. Zones 15–17. These rhododendrons are too tender for Northwest gardens (many are fragrant): 'Countess of Haddington', 'Countess of Sefton', 'Else Frye', 'Forsterianum', 'Fragrantissimum'. These are commonly called Maddenii Hybrids. Good performers in California, rated low in Northwest: 'Anah Kruschke', 'Antoon Van Welie', 'Rainbow', 'Sappho', 'Van Nes Sensation'.

Vireyas for indoors and frost-free areas. The Vireya rhododendrons, from the tropics of Southeast Asia, manage nicely in California's frost-free and nearly frostless zones (17, 23, 24). They are also fine container plants (even indoors), so they can be grown in colder zones if brought inside for the winter. Typically, plants flower on and off throughout the year rather than in one blooming season, bearing waxy-textured flowers in exciting shades of yellow, gold, orange, vermilion, salmon, and pink, plus cream, white, and bicolors. Species, named hybrids, and unnamed seedlings are offered by some specialty growers.

Among the best you're likely to find are *R. aurigeranum*, a hybrid of *R. brookeanum* commonly listed as 'Gracile', *R. javanicum*, *R. konori*, *R. laetum*, *R. lochae*, *R. macgregorae*, and the hybrids 'George Budgen' (orange yellow), 'Ne Plus Ultra' (red), a *R. laetum–R. zoelleri* hybrid, and 'Taylori' (pink).

Widely adapted varieties. All of these are highly regarded, dependable, popular, easy to grow, just about anywhere in the designated zones: 'Anna Rose Whitney', 'Blue Ensign', 'Cotton Candy', 'Crest', 'Hallelujah', 'Loder's

White', 'Mrs. G. W. Leak' ('Cottage Gardens Pride'), 'Purple Splendour', 'Ramapo', 'The Hon. Jean Marie de Montague', 'Trude Webster'.

Low-growing species and hybrids. Although rhododendrons, these have the charm and general appearance of azaleas: *R. chryseum, R. impeditum, R. keiskei, R. moupinense, R. pemakoense*, 'Blue Diamond', 'Ocean Lake', 'Sapphire'.

Dwarfs and low growers. Distinctive foliage and bell-shaped or funnel-shaped flowers, not in typical trusses, mark these varieties: 'Bow Bells', 'Cilpinense', 'Ginny Gee', 'Patty Bee', 'Ramapo', 'Snow Lady'.

RHODODENDRON RATINGS AND HARDINESS

Each plant in the list that follows includes a two-number rating (3/3, for example) assigned by the American Rhododendron Society. Flower quality is shown first and shrub quality second; 5 is superior, 4 above average, 3 average, 2 below average, 1 poor.

The list also gives each plant a hardiness rating, which indicates minimum temperatures a mature plant can tolerate without serious injury. Heights given in the list are for plants 10 years old; older plants may be taller, and crowded or heavily shaded plants may reach up faster. Bloom seasons are approximate and vary with weather and location.

'A. Bedford'. 4/3. −5°F. Lavender blue with darker flare. Large trusses. To 6 ft. Late May.

'America'. 3/3. −25°F. Dark red. To 5 ft. tall and broad. Late.

'Anah Kruschke'. 2/3. −10°F. Lavender purple. Color not the best, but plant has good foliage, tolerates heat, is not fussy about soil. To 5 ft. May.

'Anna Rose Whitney'. 4/3. 5°F. Big, rich, deep pink trusses on compact, 5-ft. plant with excellent foliage. May.

'Antoon Van Welie'. 3/3. 5°F. Carmine pink. Big trusses of 'Pink Pearl' type on 6-ft. plant. Late May.

R. augustinii. 4/3. 5°F. Open, moderate growth to 6 ft. Leaves to 3 in. long. Flowers 2−2½ in. wide in clusters of three or four, blue or purple in best named forms. May.

'Autumn Gold'. 3/4. 0°F. Relaxed salmon blooms (not a full domed truss) that come late in the season. Well-branched plant with broad, rather upright growth to about 5 ft. It blooms young.

'Blaney's Blue'. 4/4. −5°F. Covered with pale blue flowers in midseason. To 4−6 ft.; growth is compact, dense, and rounded. Blooms young.

'Blue Diamond'. 5/4. 0°F. Compact, erect growth to 3 ft. Small leaves. Lavender blue flowers cover plant in April. Takes considerable sun in Northwest.

'Blue Ensign'. 4/3. −15°F. Lilac blue flowers have a striking dark spot in the upper petal. Compact, well-branched, rounded plant to 4 ft. Leaves tend to spot. Midseason bloom.

'Blue Peter'. 4/3. −10°F. Broad, sprawling growth to 4 ft.; needs pruning. Large trusses of lavender blue flowers blotched purple. May.

'Bow Bells'. 3/4. 0°F. Compact, rounded growth to 4 ft. Leaves rounded. Flowers bright pink, bell shaped, in loose clusters. May. New growth bronzy.

R. calophytum. 4/4. −5°F. Small, stocky tree, to 4 ft. Noted for big leaves—4 in. wide, 10−14 in. long. Trusses of white or pink flowers with deep red blotch. Protect from wind. March and April.

'Cary Ann'. 3/4. −5°F. Trumpet-shaped red flowers cover plant in midseason. Habit is low (3 ft.) and spreading; foliage looks good all year.

R. catawbiense 'Album'. 3/3. −25°F. Erect, to 5−8 ft. Pink buds open to white flowers with greenish blotch. Mid- to late-season bloom.

'Christmas Cheer'. 2/4. −5°F. Pink to white flowers in tight trusses. Can take full sun. To 3 ft. Early bloom (February−March) compensates for any lack in flower quality.

R. chryseum. 2/2. −15°F. Dwarf (1-ft.), densely branched plant with 1-in. leaves. Flowers are small, bright yellow bells, four or five to a cluster. April−May.

'Cilpinense'. 4/4. 5°F. Funnel-shaped flowers of apple blossom pink fading white; loose clusters nearly cover plants in March. Low, spreading growth to 2½ ft.; small leaves. Easy to grow. Effective massed. Protect blossoms from late frosts.

'Cinnamon Bear'. 5/5. −10°F. Rosy pink buds open to pink flowers. Midseason. Furry brown leaves an additional attraction. Low, dense, to 4 ft.

'CIS'. 4/2. 10°F. Flowers (in large trusses) are red in throat to cream yellow at edges of flower. To 3 ft. May.

'Cornubia'. 4/3. 15°F. Strong, upright growth to 7 ft. Blood red flowers in large clusters, February−March.

'Cotton Candy'. 4/4. 0°F. Large flowers in soft pink shades carried in tall trusses. Dark green foliage on medium-size plant. Early May.

'Countess of Haddington'. 4/4. 20°F. Light pink to white, waxy, tubular, fragrant flowers in compact trusses. To 5 ft. May.

'Countess of Sefton'. 3/3. 20°F. Large, tubular, fragrant, white flowers in loose trusses. Not as rangy as 'Fragrantissimum'. To 4 ft. Late April.

'Creamy Chiffon'. 5/4. 0°F. Salmon buds open into ruffled, double, creamy yellow flowers in midseason. Habit is low (to 3 ft.) and compact, leaves rounded.

'Crest'. 5/3. −5°F. Primrose yellow. Outstanding. To 5 ft. April, May.

'Cunningham's White'. 2/3. −15°F. To 4 ft. White with greenish yellow blotch. Hardy old-timer. Late May.

'Dora Amateis'. 4/4. −15°F. Semidwarf, rather small-foliaged plant; compact, spreading, good for foreground. Profuse bloomer with green-spotted white flowers. Early midseason.

'Elizabeth'. 4/4. 0°F. Several forms available. Broad grower to 3 ft. tall with medium-size leaves. Blooms very young. Bright red, waxy, trumpet-shaped flowers in clusters of three to six at branch ends and in upper leaf joints. Main show in April; often reflowers in October. Very susceptible to fertilizer burn, salts in water.

'Else Frye'. 5/3. 15°F. Long, limber growth makes this a natural for informal espalier. Considerable pinching needed for compact plant. Early-season flowers are white with pink flush and gold throats.

'English Roseum'. 3/4. −25°F. Lavender flowers with yellowish green blotch. Midseason. Erect shrub to 6 ft.

R. falconeri. 3/3. 5°F. One of the unusual tree rhododendrons (others not listed here). To 25 ft. high and wide. Leathery leaves 6−12 in. long, with reddish felted underside. Clusters of 2-in.-wide, creamy white to pale yellow flowers. Blooms when 15−20 years old, in early midseason.

'Fastuosum Flore Pleno'. 3/3. 10°F. Double mauve flowers in May. Dependable, hardy old-timer. To 5 ft.

R. forrestii repens. 3/3. 5°F. Low, spreading dwarf. To 6 in. Tubular, bright red flowers in small clusters, April−May. Not easy to grow. Needs perfect drainage.

'Forsterianum'. 5/4. 20°F. Tubular, frilled, fragrant white flowers tinted pink. March bloom; buds often damaged by frost in colder areas without overhead protection. Open, rangy growth to 5 ft. Attractive glossy, red-brown, peeling bark and medium-size, glossy leaves.

'Fragrantissimum'. 4/3. 20°F. Powerfully fragrant. Large, funnel-shaped white flowers touched with pink, April−May. Loose, open, rangy growth with medium-size, bright green, bristly leaves. With hard pinching in youth, a 5-ft. shrub. Easily trained as espalier or vine, reaching to 10 ft. or more. Can spill over wall. Grow as container plant in Northwest; overwinter indoors in bright but cool room.

'Furnival's Daughter'. 5/4. −5°F. Bright pink flowers with deep red blotch. Midseason. To 5 ft.

'Ginny Gee'. 5/5. −5°F. Striking 2-ft. plant is covered with 1-in. flowers in midseason. Blooms range from pink to white, with striped and dappled patterns. Leaves are small, growth dense. Early midseason.

Rhododendron
'Fragrantissimum'

'Golfer'. 4/5. −15°F. Bright pink flowers in midseason on a dense plant with silvery "fur" on leaves. Low, broad, to 1 ft.

'Gomer Waterer'. 3/4. −15°F. White flushed lilac. Hardy old-timer. To 5 ft. Late May.

'Halfdan Lem'. 5/4. −5°F. Luminous red trusses stand out against deep green foliage in midseason. Well shaped, vigorous, to 5 ft.

'Hallelujah'. 5/5. −15°F. Rose red flowers in midseason stand above beautiful, thick, forest green foliage. To 4 ft. Takes full sun; fine-looking plant with or without flowers. Very strong grower. ▶

'Hotei'. 5/4. 5°F. Canary yellow flowers backed by a prominent calyx come only when plant is 6−8 years old. Midseason. Habit is compact, to about 3 ft. Plant in well-drained soil only, since roots rot easily. Closest to a deep pure yellow.

R. impeditum. 2/3. 10°F. Twiggy, dwarf, dense shrub to 1 ft. with closely packed, tiny, gray-green leaves. Small flowers mauve to dark blue, April or May. Takes full sun in cooler areas. Needs excellent drainage to avoid root rot.

'Janet Blair'. 4/3. −15°F. Vigorous, tall and spreading. Ruffled pastel flowers blend pink, cream, white, and gold; large blossoms come in rounded trusses. Mid- and late-season bloom.

'Jean Marie de Montague'. 3/4. 0°F. Brightest scarlet red in May. Good foliage. To 5 ft.

'Johnny Bender'. 5/5. −5°F. Glossy dark green leaves set off blood red flower trusses. Midseason. To 4 ft.

'Lem's Cameo'. 5/4. 5°F. Flowers are a blend of apricot, cream, and pink. To 5 ft. Midseason.

'Lem's Monarch' ('Pink Walloper'). 5/5. 0°F. Pink flowers, darker at the edges, come in huge round trusses at midseason. Plant grows to 6 ft., takes on a treelike shape. Large, deep green leaves.

'Lem's Stormcloud'. 4/4. −15°F. Bright red flowers on large, erect trusses. Midseason. Grows to 5 ft.

'Leo'. 5/3. −5°F. Rounded to dome-shaped trusses are packed with rich cranberry red blooms. Midseason. Medium-size plant is well clothed in large dark green leaves.

Loderi Hybrids. 5/4. 0°F. Spectacular group with tall trusses of 6−7-in.-wide flowers in shades of pink or white. Fragrant; early May bloom. Informal, open growth to 8 ft., eventually much more. Too large for small garden. Slow to reach blooming age and not easy to grow. Difficult to maintain good foliage color. Best known are 'King George', with white flowers opening from blush buds; 'Pink Diamond', with blush flowers; and 'Venus', with shell pink flowers.

'Loder's White'. 5/5. 0°F. Big trusses of flowers are white tinged pink when they open, turn pure white as they mature. May. Shapely growth to 5 ft. Blooms freely even when young. Best white for most regions.

'Lord Roberts'. 3/3. −10°F. To 5 ft. Handsome dark green foliage and rounded trusses of black-spotted red flowers. Mid- to late-season bloom. Growth is more compact, flowers more profuse in sun.

R. macrophyllum (R. californicum). Coast rhododendron, western rhododendron. Unrated. 5°F. Native near coast, Northern California to British Columbia. Rangy growth to 4−10 ft., to 20 ft. in some locations. Leaves dark green, leathery, 2½−6 in. long; flower trusses rosy, rose purple, rarely white. May−June. Rarely sold; in Northwest, collect only with a permit.

'Madame Mason' ('Madame Masson'). 3/3. −5°F. White with light yellow flare on upper petal. Needs pruning to keep it compact. To 5 ft. Late May.

'Mars'. 4/3. −10°F. Dark red. Outstanding in form, foliage, flowers. To 4 ft. Late May.

'Molly Ann'. 4/5. −10°F. Rose-colored, upright trusses are set against round leaves on a compact 2-ft. plant. Midseason.

'Moonstone'. 4/4. −5°F. Flaring bells age from pale pink to creamy yellow. April. Attractive dense, dwarf growth to 2 ft. Leaves neat, small, rounded. Fine facing taller rhododendrons, as low foundation planting with 'Bow Bells'.

R. moupinense. 4/2. 0°F. Open, spreading. To 1½ ft. Small (1½-in.-long), oval leaves. White or pink flowers, spotted red. New spring foliage deep red. February−March.

'Mrs. Furnival'. 5/5. −10°F. Clear pink flowers with light brown blotch in upper petals, in tight, round trusses. Late May. Compact growth to 4 ft.

'Mrs. G. W. Leak' ('Cottage Gardens Pride'). 4/4. 5°F. Deep pink with deep brown flare on upper petals. Strong growth to 5 ft. May.

R. mucronulatum. 4/3. −25°F. Deciduous rhododendron with open growth to 5 ft. Makes up for bare branches by January−February flowering. Flowers generally bright purple; there is a pink form, 'Cornell Pink'.

'Nancy Evans'. 5/4. 5°F. Orange-tinged buds open to yellow in midseason. Each bloom is backed by a calyx that makes it look almost double. New foliage is bronzy. Compact growth to about 3 ft.

'Nova Zembla'. 3/3. −25°F. Profuse red flowers come late in the season, even in cold country. Takes heat. To about 5 ft.

'Ocean Lake'. 3/3. −5°F. Low, azalealike plant with flowers of deep violet. Early, midseason.

'Old Copper'. 4/4. 5°F. Copper orange flowers late in the season. Well-shaped plant to 5 ft.; can take more heat than most rhododendrons.

'Paprika Spiced'. 4/3. 0°F. Midseason flowers are a blend of yellow, pink, and orange, dotted with red. To 3 ft.

'Patty Bee'. 5/5. −10°F. Yellow, 2-in., trumpet-shaped flowers cover plant in midseason. Dense, moundlike growth to 1½ ft. Leaves are small, giving plant a finely textured look.

R. pemakoense. 2/3. 0°F. Compact, spreading. To 1½ ft. Leaves are small (1½ in. long); flowers pinkish purple, very free blooming. Useful in rock gardens. March−April.

'Pink Pearl'. 3/3. −5°F. Rose pink, tall trusses in May. To 6 ft. or more. Open, rangy growth without pruning. Dependable grower and bloomer in all except coldest climates.

'PJM'. 4/4. −25°F. To 4 ft. Takes heat as well as cold. Lavender pink blooms come early; foliage turns mahogany in winter.

'Purple Splendour'. 4/3. −10°F. Ruffled, deep purple blooms blotched black purple. Informal growth to 4 ft. Hardy, easy to grow. May.

R. racemosum. 3/3. −10°F. Several forms include 6-in. dwarf, 2½-ft. compact upright shrub, and tall 7-footer. Pink, inch-wide flowers in clusters of three to six all along stems, March−April. Easy to grow; sun tolerant in cooler areas.

'Rainbow'. 1/2. 0°F. Light pink center, carmine edges. Very showy. Heavy foliage. Strong growth to 5 ft. April bloom.

'Ramapo'. 3/4. −20°F. Violet blue flowers cover plant in midseason. Dense, spreading growth to 2 ft. in sun, taller in shade. New growth is dusty blue green. Fine for rockeries; good choice in California.

'Rosamundi'. 2/3. −5°F. Ball-like trusses of pink flowers appear early in season. Plant is slow growing, compact, to 4 ft. high and wide.

'Sapphire'. 4/4. 0°F. Small, bright blue, azalealike flowers in March, April. Twiggy, rounded, dense shrublet to 1½ ft. Foliage gray green, leaves are tiny.

'Sappho'. 3/2. −5°F. White with dark purple spot in throat. May. Easy to grow; gangly without pruning. To 6 ft.; use at back of border.

'Scarlet Wonder'. 5/5. −10°F. Outstanding dwarf (to 2 ft.) of compact growth. Shiny, quilted foliage forms backdrop for many bright red blossoms. Midseason.

'Scintillation'. 4/5. −15°F. Medium-size, compact plant covered in lustrous, dark green leaves. Rounded trusses carry gold-throated pink flowers.

'September Song'. 4/4. 0°F. Salmon-edged flowers shade into golden orange throats, giving trusses an overall orange look. Blooms young. Grows to 4 ft.; wider than tall. Midseason.

'Snow Lady'. 4/4. 0°F. White, black stamens. Wide, fragrant, flat flowers in clusters. To 3 ft. April.

'Susan'. 3/4. −5°F. Silvery lavender flowers in large trusses. May. Handsome foliage. To 4 ft.

'Taurus'. 5/4. 0°F. Brilliant red flowers with black spotting on upper lobes come in large, round trusses. Midseason bloom comes only after plants reach 4−6 years old. Vigorous, upright to 6 ft.; well covered with forest green leaves.

'Top Banana'. 4/4. 0°F. Clear, bright yellow. Midseason bloom. Upright, vase-shaped plant to 4 ft. Buds young (2 years).

'Trinidad'. 4/4. −20°F. Flowers are cream edged in red. Mid- to late-season bloom. To 4 ft.

'Trude Webster'. 5/4. −10°F. Huge trusses of clear pink flowers come in midseason on a strong 5-ft. plant. Fine plant habit, large leaves. One of the best pinks.

'Twilight Pink'. 4/4. 5°F. Apricot-and-pink flowers have large colored calyx. Midseason. To 5 ft.

'Unique'. 3/5. 5°F. Apricot buds open to deep cream, fade to light yellow; trusses tight, rounded. April, early May. Outstanding neat, rounded, compact habit. To 4 ft.

'Unknown Warrior'. 3/2. 5°F. Light soft red, fades quickly when exposed to bright sun. Easy to grow. To 4 ft. April.

R

'Van Nes Sensation'. 3/4. 0°F. Pale lilac flowers in large trusses. Strong grower. To 5 ft. May.

'Vulcan'. 3/4. −5°F. Bright brick red flowers in late May, early June. New leaves often grow past flower buds, partially hiding flowers. To 4 ft.

R. yakushimanum. 4/4. −20°F. Clear pink bells changing to white, about 12 in truss. Late May. Dense, spreading growth to 3 ft. New foliage gray felted; older leaves with heavy tan or white felt beneath. Selections range from 'Ken Janeck', a large (and large-leafed) form with very pink flowers, to 'Yaku Angel', with pink-tinged buds opening to pure white. There are also a number of hybrids that are as good in cold climates as they are in milder ones, among them 'Mardi Gras', "Mist Maiden", 'Yaku Sunrise', and 'Yaku Princess' (this last selection is part of a good series of hybrids, all with monarchic names).

RHODIES IN CLAY OR ALKALINE SOIL?

They don't like it. Planting in raised beds is the simplest way to give these plants the conditions they need. The finished bed should be 1–2 ft. above the original soil level. Liberally mix organic material into top foot of native soil, then fill bed above it with a mixture that's 50 percent organic material, 30 percent soil, 20 percent sand. This mixture will hold air and moisture while allowing alkaline salts to leach through.

KINDS OF EVERGREEN AZALEAS

The evergreen azaleas sold in the West fall into more than a dozen groups and species, though an increasing number of hybrids have such mixed parentage that they don't conveniently fit into any group. But group characteristics are rather variable. Here are several popular groups:

Belgian Indica. Zones 14–24. This is a group of hybrids originally developed for greenhouse forcing. Where lowest temperatures are 20–30°F, many of them serve well as landscape plants. They have lush, full foliage and profuse large blossoms during their flowering season. Among the most widely sold are 'Albert and Elizabeth', white and pink; 'California Sunset', salmon pink with white border; 'Chimes', dark red; 'Mardi Gras', salmon with white border; 'Mission Bells', red semidouble; 'Mme. Alfred Sanders', cherry red; 'Orange Sanders', salmon orange; 'Orchidiflora', orchid pink; 'Paul Schame', salmon; and 'Red Poppy'. 'Violetta', deep purple, and 'William Van Orange', orange-red, have pendant growth suitable for hanging baskets.

Beltsville Hybrids. Like the Glenn Dale Hybrids; hardy in Zones 4–9, 14–24. 'Casablanca Improved' is a large white single.

Brooks Hybrids. Zones 8, 9, 14–24. Bred in Modesto, California, for heat resistance, compactness, and large flowers. Best known are 'Madonna', white; 'My Valentine', rose; 'Pinkie', pink; and 'Red Wing'.

Gable Hybrids. Zones 4–9, 14–24. Developed to produce azaleas of Kurume type that take 0°F temperatures. In Zones 4–6, they may lose some leaves, but they bloom heavily from late April through May. Frequently sold are 'Caroline Gable', bright pink; 'Herbert', purple; 'Louise Gable', pink; 'Pioneer', pink; 'Purple Splendor', 'Purple Splendor Compacta', with less rangy growth; 'Rosebud', pink; and 'Rose Greeley', white.

Girard Hybrids. These originated from Gable crosses and are becoming increasingly popular in the West. Hardy in Zones 4–9, 14–24. Examples are 'Girard's Fuchsia', reddish purple; 'Girard's Hot Shot', orange red with orange-red fall and winter foliage; and 'Girard's Roberta', with 3-in. double pink flowers.

Glenn Dale Hybrids. Zones 4–9, 14–24. Developed primarily for hardiness, but they do drop some leaves in cold winters. Some are tall and rangy, others low and compact. Growth rate varies from slow to rapid. Some have small leaves like Kurumes; others have large leaves. Familiar varieties are 'Anchorite', orange; 'Aphrodite', pale pink; 'Buccaneer', orange red; 'Everest', white; 'Geisha', white, striped red; and 'Glacier', white.

Gold Cup Hybrids. Zones 14–24. Members of this group were originally called Mossholder-Bristow Hybrids. Plants combine large flowers of Belgian Indicas with vigor of Rutherfordianas. Good landscape plants where temperatures don't go below 20°F. Some popular varieties are 'Easter Parade', pink and white; 'Sun Valley', white; and 'White Orchid', white with red throat.

Greenwood Hybrids. Zones 4–7. Bred in Canby, Oregon, most of these are compact and hardy, with large double flowers. You can make them succeed in colder climates than they're bred for by keeping them from drying out: it's desiccation, not freezing, that does them in. Some of the most popular varieties are 'Greenwood Orange', 'Greenwood Rosebud', pink with a slight purple blush; 'Sherry', with very deep red flowers and maroon winter foliage; 'Silver Streak', with reddish purple flowers and white-edged leaves; and 'Sleigh Bells', with single white flowers.

Harris Hybrids. Zones 4–9, 14–22. These hybrids have grown mainly in the Pacific Northwest, though some California gardeners use them as well. The offspring of Glenn Dale, Kaempferi, and Satsuki azaleas, most of these extra-large-flowered plants bloom after midseason. 'Bruce Hancock', low, spreading to 4 ft., a good ground cover, has 3½-in., pink-edged flowers with white centers; 'Fascination' has 4½-in. red flowers with pink centers; and 'Rhonda Stiteler' has double pink flowers, leaves lightly variegated with yellow. All of these are worth looking for.

Kaempferi Hybrids. Zones 2–7. Based on *R. kaempferi*, the torch azalea, a hardy plant with orange red flowers. These are somewhat hardier than Kurumes, to −15°F, taller and more open in growth, nearly leafless in coldest winters. Flowers cover plants in early spring. Similar in every way to Vuykiana Hybrids. Among those sold are 'Fedora', salmon rose; 'Holland', late, large red; 'John Cairns', orange red; 'Palestrina', white.

Kurume. Zones 5–9, 14–24. Compact, twiggy plants, densely foliaged with small leaves. Small flowers are borne in incredible profusion. Plants mounded or tiered, handsome even out of bloom. Hardy to 5–10°F. Grow well outdoors in half sun. Many varieties available; the most widespread are 'Coral Bells', pink; 'Hexe', crimson; 'Hinocrimson', bright red; 'Hinodegiri', cerise red; 'Sherwood Orchid', red violet; 'Sherwood Red', orange red; 'Snow'; and 'Ward's Ruby', dark red.

Kurume Evergreen Azalea

North Tisbury Hybrids. Zones 4–9, 14–24. You can see a common, notable ancestry in most of these plants (*R. nakaharai*). Their low, spreading habit and extremely late bloom—into midsummer—make them naturals for hanging baskets and ground covers. Some of the best are 'Alexander', very hardy, with bronze foliage in fall and red-orange flowers; 'Pink Cascade', pink; and 'Red Fountain', with dark red-orange blooms around Fourth of July.

Pericat. Zones 4–9, 14–24. Hybrids originally developed for greenhouse forcing but as hardy as Kurumes and similar, although flowers tend to be somewhat larger. Varieties sold are 'Mme. Pericat', light pink; 'Sweetheart Supreme', blush pink; and 'Twenty Grand', rose pink.

Robin Hill Hybrids. Zones 4–9, 14–24. A large group that got its start more than 50 years ago. These medium-size plants flower late; large blooms have some resemblance to Satsukis. There are so many good ones—several with "Robin Hill" in their names—that it's hard to single out only a few. Try 'Betty Ann Voss', pink; 'Conversation Piece', pink with light center; 'Nancy of Robin Hill', pink with red blotch; 'Robin Hill Gillie', red orange.

Rutherfordiana. Zones 15–24. Greenhouse plants, good in garden where temperatures don't go below 20°F. Bushy 2–4-ft. plants with handsome foliage. Flowers intermediate between Kurume and Belgian Indica. Available varieties: 'Alaska', white; 'Constance', light orchid pink; 'Dorothy Gish', brick red; 'Firelight', rose red; 'L. J. Bobbink', orchid pink; 'Purity', white; 'Rose Queen', deep pink; and 'White Gish', pure white.

Satsuki. Zones 4–9, 14–24. Includes azaleas referred to as Gumpo and Macrantha hybrids. Hardy to 5°F. Plants low growing, some true dwarfs; many are pendant enough for hanging baskets. Large flowers late, often in June. Popular varieties: 'Bunkwa', blush pink; 'Flame Creeper', orange red; 'Gumpo', white; 'Gumpo Pink', rose pink; 'Hi Gasa', bright pink; 'Rosae-flora', rose pink; 'Shinnyo-No-Tsuki', violet red with white center.

Southern Indica. Zones 8, 9, 14–24. Varieties selected from Belgian Indicas for sun tolerance and vigor. Most take temperatures of 10–20°F, but some are damaged at 20°F. They generally grow faster, more vigorously, and taller than the other kinds. Many varieties are sold, among which are these popular ones: 'Brilliant', carmine red; 'Duc de Rohan', salmon pink; 'Fielder's White'; 'Formosa', brilliant rose purple, also sold as 'Coccinea', 'Phoenicia', 'Vanessa'; 'George Lindley Taber', light pink; 'Imperial Countess', deep salmon pink; 'Imperial Princess', rich pink; 'Imperial Queen', pink; 'Iveryana', white with orchid streaks; 'Little John', dense bush to 6 ft., with burgundy foliage and a few deep red flowers; 'Orange Pride', bright orange; 'Pride of Dorking', brilliant red; 'Southern Charm', watermelon pink, sometimes sold as 'Judge Solomon'; and 'White April'.

'Fielder's White'
Southern Indica
Evergreen Azalea

Vuykiana Hybrids. See description of Kaempferi Hybrids. Varieties sold: 'Blue Danube', violet blue; 'Vuyk's Rosy Red'; and 'Vuyk's Scarlet'.

R. mucronatum ('Indica Alba', 'Ledifolia Alba'). Zones 4–9, 14–24. Spreading growth to 6 ft. (but usually 3 ft.); large, hairy leaves. White or greenish flowers 2½–3 in. across, March–April. Variety 'Sekidera' ('Indica Rosea', 'Ledifolia Rosea') has white flowers flushed and blotched rose in February, March.

KINDS OF DECIDUOUS AZALEAS

Very few deciduous shrubs can equal deciduous azaleas in show and range of color. Their evergreen relatives can't match them in yellow, orange, and flame red range or in bicolor contrasts. They are at their best in Zones 4–7, 15–17. Also perform well in inland valley Zone 14 (even in full sun) if well watered. Deciduous types tend to be less particular about soil and watering than most evergreen sorts. Fall foliage color is often brilliant orange red to maroon.

Ghent Hybrids. Extremely hardy. Many will take −25°F temperatures. Upright growth variable in height. Flowers generally smaller than those of Mollis Hybrids. Colors include shades of yellow, orange, umber, pink, and red. May flowering.

Knap Hill–Exbury Hybrids. Plants vary from spreading to upright, from 4 to 6 ft. tall. Flowers are large (3–5 in. across), in clusters of 7–18, sometimes ruffled or fragrant, white through pink and yellow to orange and red, often with contrasting blotches.

Both Knap Hill and Exbury azaleas come from same original crosses; first crosses were made at Knap Hill, and subsequent improvements were made at both Exbury and Knap Hill. The "Rothschild" azaleas are Exbury plants. Ilam Hybrids are from same original stock, further improved in New Zealand.

A hundred or more named varieties are available in the Northwest and Northern California.

Knap Hill–Exbury
Deciduous Azalea

They make up perhaps half of all deciduous azaleas sold in the Pacific Northwest. If you want to be sure of color and size of flower, choose from named varieties. Some of the best are 'Cannon's Double', pink; 'Gibraltar', orange; 'Homebush', double deep pink; 'Klondyke', golden tangerine; and 'Oxydol', white with yellow markings. But don't consider all seedlings as inferior plants. Generally it's best to select seedlings in bloom.

Mollis Hybrids. Hybrids of *R. molle* and *R. japonicum*. Upright growth to 4–5 ft.; 2½–4-in. flowers in clusters of 7–13. Colors range from chrome yellow through poppy red. New growth has light skunky fragrance, but lovely yellow to orange fall foliage. Very heavy bloom in May.

Northern Lights Hybrids. Developed by the University of Minnesota, hardy to −40°F. Grow 2–4 ft. tall, produce ball-shaped trusses of fragrant, sterile flowers (they won't set seed) in late spring. Most widely available are 'Apricot Surprise', 'Orchid Lights', 'Rosy Lights', and 'White Lights'. Foliage can have the skunky odor of the hybrids' Mollis Hybrid ancestors.

Occidentale Hybrids. Hybrids between *R. occidentale* and Mollis Hybrids. Flowers 2½–4 in., plants to 8 ft. Colors from white flushed rose and blotched yellow to red with orange blotch.

Viscosum Hybrids. Hybrids between Mollis azaleas and *R. viscosum*. Deciduous shrubs with colors of Mollis but fragrance of *R. viscosum*.

R. japonicum. JAPANESE AZALEA. Hardy to −10°F. Upright, fast growth to 6 ft. Salmon red flowers, 2–3 in. wide, in clusters of 6–12. Variety *R. j. aureum* has rich yellow flowers. Blooms in May.

R. luteum (R. flavum). PONTIC AZALEA. To 8 ft. Fragrant flowers are single yellow with darker blotch. Blooms in May.

R. occidentale. WESTERN AZALEA. Hardy to −5°F. Zones 4–24. Native to mountains and foothills of California and Oregon. Erect growth to 6–10 ft. Funnel-shaped flowers in clusters, May–June. Color varies from white to pinkish white with yellow blotch; some are heavily marked carmine rose. Fragrant. Superior cutting-grown plants with variety names are scarce but available and worth looking for.

R. schlippenbachii. ROYAL AZALEA. Hardy to −20°F. Native to Korea. Densely branched shrub to 6–8 ft. Leaves in whorls of five at tips of branches. Large (2–4-in.), pure light pink flowers in clusters of three to six, April–May. A white form is also available. Good fall color: yellow, orange, scarlet, crimson. Protect from full sun.

R. vaseyi. PINKSHELL AZALEA. Hardy to −20°F. Upright, irregular, spreading to 15 ft. Light pink flowers in clusters of five to eight in May.

RHODOHYPOXIS baurii

Hypoxidaceae

BULBLIKE TUBER

✂ ZONES 4–7, 14–24

☼ FULL SUN

● REGULAR WATER

Rhodohypoxis baurii

Tufts of narrow, 2–3-in. leaves are nearly obscured by masses of 1-in., white, pink, or rose red flowers over a long spring–summer season. Dormant in winter. Tubers multiply quickly with good drainage, adequate water. In cold-winter climates, protect from winter rains with pane of glass or shingle. If grown in pots, turn pots on side in winter or store over winter in cold frame. Excellent plant for rock garden, stone sink garden, or pots.

RHODOPHIALA bifida

Amaryllidaceae

BULB

✂ ZONES 8, 9, 14–24

☼ SUN

● REGULAR WATER

Rhodophiala bifida

South American bulb resembling a small amaryllis (*Hippeastrum*), with a few foot-long leaves and a 1-ft. flower stalk bearing two to six bright red

R

2-in.-long flowers. Petals are narrow, but plants spread willingly and put on a fine show. It is considered by some to be *Hippeastrum advenum*.

RHOEO spathacea (R. discolor)

MOSES-IN-THE-CRADLE, MOSES-IN-THE-BOAT

Commelinaceae

PERENNIAL

ZONES 12–24; OR INDOORS

SUN OR SHADE

MODERATE WATER

Rhoeo spathacea

Stems to 8 in. high. Leaf tufts grow to 6–12 in. wide, with dozen or so broad, sword-shaped, rather erect leaves that are dark green above and deep purple underneath. Flowers are interesting rather than beautiful. Small, white, three-petaled, they are crowded into boat-shaped bracts borne down among leaves.

Best used as pot plant or in hanging basket. Tough plant that will take high or low light intensity and casual watering, low humidity and heat on a desert patio. Locate in sheltered spots in Zones 12–15, 18, 19. Avoid over-watering; keep water out of leaf axils. Variety 'Variegata' has leaves striped red and yellowish green.

RHOICISSUS capensis (Cissus capensis)

EVERGREEN GRAPE

Vitaceae

TUBEROUS-ROOTED EVERGREEN VINE

ZONES 10, 17, 21–24, OR INDOORS

SUN WITH SHADED ROOTS, OUTDOORS

REGULAR, THOROUGH WATERING

Rhoicissus capensis

Leaves roundish to kidney shaped, scallop toothed, something like those of true grape in size and appearance. New stems and leaves are a rosy rust color, covered with red hairs; mature leaves are strong light green tinged with copper, with rusty, hairy undersides. Flowers insignificant. Will take heavy shade as house plant. Good overhead screen or ground cover in milder regions. Slow growing.

RHOPALOSTYLIS

Arecaceae (Palmae)

PALMS

ZONES 17, 23, 24

SUN OR SHADE

REGULAR WATER

Feather palms with long, clean trunks marked with closely spaced rings. Moderate growth rate. Best in frost-free gardens.

R. baueri. From Norfolk Island. To 50 ft. tall; beautiful curving, arching leaves 6–9 ft. long.

Rhopalostylis sapida

R. sapida. NIKAU PALM, SHAVING BRUSH PALM. From New Zealand. Grows to 30 ft. Good container plant where small space dictates an upright palm. Feathers 4–8 ft. long stand upright from prominent bulge at top of trunk.

FOR GROWING SYMBOL EXPLANATIONS
PLEASE SEE PAGE 129

RHUBARB

Polygonaceae

PERENNIALS GROWN FROM RHIZOMES

ZONES 1–11, 14–24; BEST IN ZONES 1–11

COASTAL SUN; SOME SHADE INLAND

WATER FREELY DURING ACTIVE GROWTH

LEAVES ARE POISONOUS; USE STEMS ONLY

Rhubarb

In Zones 10, 11, they are treated as annuals and set out in fall for winter, spring harvest (plants tend to rot in heat of late spring, early summer). Big, elongated, heart-shaped, crinkled leaves and red-tinted leafstalks are showy enough to qualify for display spot in garden. Delicious leafstalks are used like fruit in sauces and pies. Flowers are insignificant, in spikelike clusters. Preferred varieties are 'Victoria', with greenish stalks, and 'Cherry' ('Crimson Cherry'), 'MacDonald', and 'Strawberry', all of which have red stalks.

Plant in late winter or early spring. Divisions should contain at least one bud. Soil should be deep, rich, and well drained. Place tops of divisions at soil line. Space divisions 3–4 ft. apart. Permit plants to grow 2 full seasons before harvesting. During next spring you can pull off leafstalks (to cook) for 4 or 5 weeks; older, huskier plants will take up to 8 weeks of pulling. Harvest stalks by grasping near base and pulling sideways and outward; cutting with knife will leave stub that will decay. Never remove all leaves from a single plant. Stop harvesting when slender leafstalks appear. After harvest, feed and water freely. Cut out any blossom stalks that appear.

RHUS

SUMAC

Anacardiaceae

EVERGREEN OR DECIDUOUS SHRUBS OR TREES

ZONES VARY BY SPECIES

FULL SUN

LITTLE TO NO WATER

Rhus typhina

Of the ornamental sumacs, deciduous kinds are hardy anywhere and thrive in poor soils. They tend to produce suckers, especially if their roots are disturbed by soil cultivation. Evergreen sumacs are not as hardy as the deciduous kinds, but they will grow in almost any soil as long as it is well drained (soggy soils may kill them).

R. aromatica. FRAGRANT SUMAC. Deciduous shrub. Zones 1–3, 10. Fast growing, 3–5 ft. tall, spreading much wider. Leaves divided into three leaflets, fragrant when brushed against or crushed. Tiny yellowish flowers in spring. Chief use: coarse bank cover, ground cover for poor, dry soils. Red fall color. Two available varieties are 'Low Grow' (to about 2 ft.) and 'Green Mound' (to 4 ft.).

R. cotinus. See Cotinus coggygria

R. glabra. SMOOTH SUMAC. Deciduous large shrub or small tree. Zones 1–10, 14–17. Native to eastern Oregon, eastern Washington, British Columbia, and eastward in North America. Upright to 10 ft., or sometimes treelike to 20 ft. In the wild, it spreads by underground roots to form large patches. Looks very much like *R. typhina,* but usually grows lower and does not have velvety branches. Needs little to no water.

Leaves are divided into 11–23 rather narrow, 2–5-in.-long, toothed leaflets, deep green above, whitish beneath; turn brilliant scarlet in fall. Inconspicuous greenish flowers followed by showy autumn display of scarlet fruit in conical clusters that last on bare branches well into winter. Garden use same as for *R. typhina. R. g. cismontana,* dwarf form that grows in Rocky Mountains, is 3–4 ft. tall, has smaller leaves with fewer leaflets. *R. g.* 'Laciniata' has deeply cut, slashed leaflets, for a fernlike appearance.

R. integrifolia. LEMONADE BERRY. Evergreen shrub. Zones 15–17, 20–24. Native to coastal Southern California, Channel Islands, and Baja California. Generally 3–10 ft. high and as wide, rarely treelike to 30 ft. Oval to nearly round, leathery, dark green leaves, 1–2½ in. long, with smooth

R

or shallowly toothed edges. White or pinkish flowers in dense clusters February–March, sometimes January–July. Small, flat, clustered fruit is reddish and gummy, with acid pulp that can be used to flavor drinks—hence common name.

Set out plants in fall or winter. *R. integrifolia* grows best near coast, where established plants need no water. Makes wonderful ground cover on rocky slopes exposed to salt-laden winds; one plant eventually sprawls over wide area, even down cliffs. In less windy places, use it as a tall screen or background. Makes excellent espalier against fences and walls. Can be trimmed to dense formal hedge and kept only 10 in. wide. Useful in erosion control. Very susceptible to verticillium wilt.

R. lancea. AFRICAN SUMAC. Evergreen tree. Zones 8, 9, 12–24. Slow growing to 25 ft. Open, spreading habit; graceful weeping outer branchlets. Leaves divided into three willowlike, dark green leaflets 4–5 in. long. Pea-size, berrylike, yellow or red fruit grows in clusters on female tree, can be messy on pavement. Because it can take high summer heat, *R. lancea* is popular in Zones 12, 13, although in the desert it needs some summer watering and is susceptible to Texas root rot. Hardy to 12°F.

Stake and prune to establish form you want. Makes attractive, airy tree with interesting branch pattern and effective dark red, rough bark. You can train it to a single trunk or let it grow as multitrunked tree that looks somewhat like olive. Also useful for screens, clipped hedges, or background plantings. Old plants easy to transplant if grown under dry conditions.

R. laurina. LAUREL SUMAC. Evergreen shrub. Zones 20–24. Native mostly to coastal foothills of Southern California and Baja California. Grows rapidly to 6–15 ft.; sometimes almost treelike, with rounded crown. Gets rangy unless pruned and trimmed. Attractive reddish branchlets. Laurel-like leaves, 2–4 in. long, light green, often with pink margins and pink leafstalks; foliage pleasantly aromatic. Small whitish flowers in dense, branched, 2–6-in.-long clusters bloom May–July, sometimes to December. Berrylike white fruit attracts birds. More tender to frost than *R. ovata* or *R. integrifolia*. Sometimes freezes in its native range but comes back quickly from stump. Useful as espalier plant or as clipped hedge. Good bank cover where frost is rare. Also called *Malosma laurina*.

ABOUT THE ITCHY RHUS SPECIES

Rhus includes poison oak and poison ivy. Both can cause severe dermatitis on contact; even breathing smoke from burning plants can be harmful. If either plant is on your property (the three-leaflet leaves turn bright red in fall), destroy it with chemical brush killer.

R. ovata. SUGAR BUSH. Evergreen shrub. Zones 7–24. Native to dry slopes away from coast in Southern California, Baja California, dry slopes in Arizona. Upright or spreading shrub 2½–10 ft. high. Glossy, leathery leaves, 1½–3 in. long, are somewhat trough shaped and pointed rather than rounded at the tips like those of *R. integrifolia*. White or pinkish flowers in dense clusters, March–May, followed by small, reddish, hairy fruit coated with sugary secretion. For culture and use, see *R. integrifolia*; *R. ovata* can substitute for *R. integrifolia* in inland areas. Can be used along coast but not where exposed to salt spray and sea winds. In desert, plant in fall or winter; hard to establish in hot weather.

R. trilobata. SQUAWBUSH, SKUNKBUSH. Deciduous shrub. Zones 1–3, 10. Similar in most details to *R. aromatica*, but scent of bruised leaves considered unpleasant by most people. Clumping habit makes it a natural low hedge. Brilliant yellow to red fall color.

R. typhina. STAGHORN SUMAC. Deciduous shrub or small tree. Zones 1–10, 14–17. Upright growing to 15 (sometimes to 30) ft., spreading wider. Very similar to *R. glabra*, but branches are covered with velvety short brown hairs, like deer's antler "in velvet." Leaves divided into 11–31 toothed, 5-in.-long leaflets, deep green above, grayish beneath; they turn rich red in fall. Tiny greenish flowers in 4–8-in.-long clusters, June–July, are followed by clusters of fuzzy crimson fruit that lasts all winter, gradually turns brown. *R. t.* 'Laciniata' has deeply cut leaflets; it doesn't grow quite as big as the species and is said to have richer color in fall.

Both *R. typhina* and *R. glabra* take extreme heat and cold and will grow in any except the most alkaline soils. Big divided leaves give tropical effect; when they turn color, show is brilliant. Bare branches make fine winter silhouette; fruit is decorative. Good among evergreens, where they can show off their bright fall foliage color. Can also grow in large containers.

RHYNCHOSPERMUM. See TRACHELOSPERMUM	**p. 509**
RIBBON GRASS. See PHALARIS arundinacea	**p. 413**

RIBES

CURRANT, GOOSEBERRY

Grossulariaceae (Saxifragaceae)

EVERGREEN OR DECIDUOUS SHRUBS

⧓ ZONES VARY BY SPECIES

☼ ☽ SUN OR PARTIAL SHADE

◐ ◑ ● WATER NEEDS VARY BY SPECIES

Ribes sanguineum

Those without spines are called currants; those with spines, gooseberries. A number of native species are ornamental; four are sold in nurseries. Fruit attracts birds. See Currant and Gooseberry for fruiting currants and gooseberries.

R. alpinum. ALPINE CURRANT. Deciduous shrub. Zones 1–3, 10. Spineless shrub 4–5 ft. tall (rarely taller) of dense, twiggy growth. Roundish, toothed and lobed leaves ½–1½ in. across appear very early in spring. Flowers and fruit inconspicuous. Good hedge plant. Water in dry season.

R. aureum. GOLDEN CURRANT. Deciduous shrub. All zones. Native to inland regions of West. Erect growth, 3–6 ft. tall. Light green, lobed, toothed leaves. Clusters of small, bright yellow spring flowers, usually with spicy fragrance, are 1–2½ in. long. Summer berries are yellow to red to black. Prefers moderate summer watering.

R. a. gracillimum, the less hardy California form (Zones 6–12, 14–24), lacks fragrance and its flowers fade to reddish orange.

R. indecorum. WHITE FLOWERING CURRANT. Deciduous shrub. Zones 7–9, 11, 14–24. Chaparral plant to 9 ft., with thickish scalloped leaves to 1½ in. long; a good winter show of small white flowers in pink-bracted clusters; and no spines. No summer water once established.

R. malvaceum. CHAPARRAL CURRANT. Deciduous shrub. Zones 6–9, 14–21. Spiny with hairy leaves and short clusters of pink-and-white flowers. No water once established.

R. nigrum. BLACK CURRANT. Deciduous shrub. Zones 1–7. Most varieties are banned because the plant is an alternate host to white pine blister rust, but the hybrid variety 'Consort' is immune to the disease. Thornless plants grow to 6 ft. Leaves are three-lobed, deep green, oddly scented. Drooping clusters of whitish flowers turn to juicy, shiny, black fruits with blackberry-currant flavor. Fruit used in jams, jellies, sauces. Provide some summer water.

R. odoratum. Deciduous shrub. All zones. Similar to *R. aureum* but native to the Midwest and high plains. Flowers have carnation fragrance. The variety 'Crandall' has large, shiny, black fruit with the rich, sweet-tart flavor of *R. nigrum.* Resistant to white pine blister rust. Water infrequently.

R. sanguineum. PINK WINTER CURRANT, RED FLOWERING CURRANT. Deciduous shrub. Zones 4–9, 14–24. Native to Coast Ranges from California to British Columbia. To 4–12 ft. tall. Leaves are 2½ in. wide, maple-like. Small, deep pink to red flowers, 10–30 to each drooping, 2–4-in.-long cluster, bloom March–June. Berries blue black, with whitish bloom. *R. s. glutinosum* (more southerly in origin) is the most common in nurseries; it has 15–40 flowers to a cluster, generally deep or pale pink. Needs some water away from the coast. 'Barrie Coate', 'Elk River Red', and 'King Edward VII' are selected red forms. Pink varieties are 'Claremont', two toned, pink aging to red; and 'Spring Showers', with 8-in. clusters. 'Album', 'Inverness White', and 'White Icicle' are good white varieties.

R. speciosum. FUCHSIA-FLOWERING GOOSEBERRY. Nearly evergreen shrub. Zones 8, 9, 14–24. Native near coast from Santa Clara County, California, south to Baja California. Erect, 3–6 ft. tall, with spiny, often bristly stems. Thick, green, 1-in. leaves resemble those of fruiting gooseberry. Drooping, deep crimson to cherry red flowers are fuchsialike, with long, protruding stamens. January–May bloom. Berries gummy, bristly. Excellent barrier planting. Sun near coast, light shade inland. Tolerates aridity but loses leaves from summer through fall (with a little summer water it is nearly evergreen).

Ribes speciosum

R. viburnifolium. CATALINA PERFUME, EVERGREEN CURRANT. Spreading evergreen shrub. Zones 8, 9, 14–24. Native to Catalina Island, Baja California. Low-growing plant. To 3 ft. tall and much wider (to 12 ft.). Low-arching or half-trailing wine red stems may root in moist soil. Leaves leathery, roundish, dark green, an inch across, fragrant (some say like pine, others like apples) after rain or when crushed. Light pink to purplish flowers, February–April; red berries.

Ground or bank cover for sun or half shade on coast, partial shade inland. Foliage turns yellow in hot sun. Spider mites are sometimes a problem in coastal areas. Needs no irrigation once established. Excellent ground cover under native oaks where watering is undesirable. To keep plants low, cut out upright-growing stems.

RICE PAPER PLANT. See TETRAPANAX *papyriferus*   p. 503

RICINUS communis

CASTOR BEAN	
Euphorbiaceae	
SUMMER ANNUAL	
✿ ALL ZONES	
☼ FULL SUN	
◑ ● BEST WITH REGULAR WATER	
◕ SEEDS (OR BEANS) ARE POISONOUS	

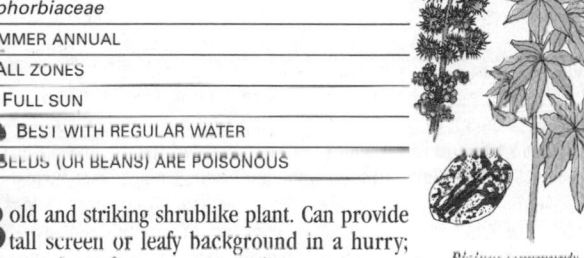

Ricinus communis

Bold and striking shrublike plant. Can provide tall screen or leafy background in a hurry; grows to 6–15 ft. in a season. Where winters are mild, will live over and become quite woody and treelike. Has naturalized in small areas in many climates.

Should not be planted in areas where small children play—the poisonous seeds are attractive. Foliage or seeds occasionally cause severe contact allergies as well. To prevent seed formation, pinch off the burrlike seed capsules while they are small.

Large-lobed leaves are 1–3 ft. across on vigorous young plants, smaller on older plants. Unimpressive small, white flowers are borne in clusters on foot-high stalks, followed by attractive prickly husks that contain seeds. Grown commercially for castor oil extracted from seeds. Many horticultural varieties: 'Zanzibarensis' has very large green leaves; 'Dwarf Red Spire' is lower-growing plant (to 6 ft.) with red leaves and seed pods.

RIVER RED GUM. See EUCALYPTUS *camaldulensis*   p. 282

ROBINIA

LOCUST	
Fabaceae (Leguminosae)	
DECIDUOUS SHRUBS OR TREES	
✿ ALL ZONES, EXCEPT AS NOTED	
☼ FULL SUN	
◔ NO WATER ONCE ESTABLISHED	
◕ BARK, LEAVES, AND SEEDS ARE POISONOUS	

Robinia pseudoacacia

Leaves divided like feathers into many roundish leaflets; clusters of sweet pea–shaped, white or pink flowers midspring

to early summer. Locusts are fairly fast growing and well adapted to dry hot regions. Will take poor soil. Drawbacks: wood is brittle, roots aggressive, plants often spread by suckers.

R. ambigua. Name given to hybrids between *R. pseudoacacia* and *R. viscosa,* a seldom-grown pink-flowering locust. The following are best-known varieties:

'Decaisneana'. To 40–50 ft. tall, 20 ft. wide. Flowers like those of *R. pseudoacacia* but pale pink.

'Idahoensis'. IDAHO LOCUST. Tree of moderately fast growth to shapely 40 ft. Flowers bright magenta rose in 8-in. clusters; one of showiest of locusts in bloom. Good flowering tree for Rocky Mountain gardens.

'Purple Robe'. Resembles 'Idahoensis' but has darker, purple-pink flowers, reddish bronze new growth; blooms 2 weeks earlier and over a longer period.

R. neomexicana. DESERT LOCUST. Zones 1–3, 7–11, 14–24. Shrub or small tree native from California's desert mountains to New Mexico. Clustered, inch-long, pink flowers.

R. pseudoacacia. BLACK LOCUST. Tree. Fast growth to 75 ft., with rather open and sparse-branching habit. Deeply furrowed brown bark. Thorny branchlets. Leaves divided into 7–19 leaflets 1–2 in. long. Flowers white, fragrant, ½–¾ in. long, in dense, hanging clusters 4–8 in. long. Beanlike, 4-in.-long pods turn brown and hang on tree all winter.

Robinia pseudoacacia

Because emigrants brought seeds with them from eastern United States, black locust is now common everywhere in West. In California's Gold Country it has gone native. With pruning and training in its early years, it is a truly handsome flowering tree—but it is so common, and so commonly neglected, that it's often overlooked.

Has been used as street tree, but not good in narrow parking strips or under power lines. Wood is extremely hard, tough; suckers are difficult to prune out where not wanted. Varieties include the following:

'Frisia'. Leaves yellow; new growth nearly orange. Thorns, new wood red.

'Pyramidalis' ('Fastigiata'). Very narrow, columnar tree.

'Tortuosa'. Slow growing, with twisted branches. Few flowers in blossom clusters.

'Umbraculifera'. Dense, round headed. Usually grafted 6–8 ft. high on another locust. Very few flowers.

ROCKCRESS. See ARABIS   p. 161

ROCKROSE. See CISTUS   p. 229

ROCK SPIRAEA. See HOLODISCUS *dumosus*   p. 324

RODGERSIA

Saxifragaceae	
PERENNIALS	
✿ ZONES 2–9, 14–17	
☼ ◑ SUN ON COAST, SHADE IN HOT-SUMMER AREAS	
● AMPLE WATER	

Rodgersia aesculifolia

Large plants with imposing leaves and clustered tiny flowers somewhat like those of astilbe. They need rich soil. Dormant in winter. Showy in woodland or bog gardens.

R. aesculifolia. To 6 ft. Leaves nearly round, divided like fingers of hand into five to seven toothed, 10-in. leaflets. White flowers.

R. podophylla. To 5 ft. Leaves divided into five 10-in. leaflets, green in spring, bronzy in summer. Creamy flowers.

R

ROMNEYA coulteri

MATILIJA POPPY	
Papaveraceae	
PERENNIAL	
✶ ALL ZONES	
☼ FULL SUN	
◊ ● RESPONDS TO WATER; TOLERATES ARIDITY	

Romneya coulteri

Native to Southern California, Baja California. Spectacular plant growing to 8 ft. or more. Stems and deeply cut leaves are gray green. White flowers up to 9 in. wide; five or six petals with texture of crepe paper surround a round mass of golden stamens. Fragrant. Blooms May–July, on into fall if watered. Flowers handsome in arrangements.

Use on hillsides as soil binder, along roadsides and in marginal areas, in wide borders. Invasive, spreading by underground rhizomes; don't plant near less vigorous plants. Tolerates varying soils (including loose, gravelly soil). Withhold summer irrigation to keep growth in check. Cut nearly to ground in late fall. New shoots emerge after first rains in winter. Although easy to grow once established, the plant is very difficult to propagate. Easiest way to grow more plants is to dig up rooted suckers from spreading roots, but you can try taking cuttings from thickest roots. To make seeds germinate, mix them with potting soil in a foil-lined flat, burn pine needles on top of flat for 30 minutes, water, and hope for sprouting.

> ## MATILIJA SEED SPROUTING IN NATURE
> In the wild, almost all Matilija poppies grow in disturbed soil, mostly road cuts and old landslides. That's where their reluctant seeds seem most able to germinate and grow.

ROSA

ROSE	
Rosaceae	
DECIDUOUS OR EVERGREEN SHRUBS	
✶ ALL ZONES, EXCEPT AS NOTED	
☼ ☼ FULL SUN OR LIGHT SHADE	
● REGULAR WATER, EXCEPT AS NOTED	

Hybrid Tea Rose
'Seashell'

The rose is undoubtedly the best-loved flower and most widely planted shrub in the West and all other temperate parts of the world. Although mostly deciduous, can be evergreen in mild climates. Centuries of hybridizing have brought us the widest possible range of form and color. There are foot-high miniatures, tree-smothering climbers, flowers the size of a thumbnail or a salad plate, and all possible variations in between. Red, pink, and white are traditional rose colors, but you also find cream, yellow, orange, and blended and bicolor flowers, as well as magenta, purple, lavender, and even tan and brown.

Growing roses is not difficult provided you choose types and varieties suited to your climate, buy healthy plants, locate and plant them properly, and attend to their basic needs—water, nutrients, any necessary pest and disease control, and pruning. Despite the delicate appearance of their blooms, roses are often quite resilient plants.

CLIMATE

Every year, the American Rose Society rates modern roses (and an increasing number of old roses) on a scale from 1 to 10. The higher the rating, based on a national average of scores, the better the rose. The highest rated roses are likely to perform well in most climates and so are good choices for novice growers. But a rating does not tell the entire story: a rose with a low rating may do especially well in certain regions but fail in others. The following general tips will help guide your selection.

In cool-summer areas, you should, if possible, avoid varieties having an unusually great number of petals. Many of these tend to "ball," opening poorly or not at all. Also, in the absence of heat, dark-colored flowers may appear "muddy" rather than clear and vibrant, while pastel colors seldom appear off-color or unattractive. The fog and overcast that create cool summers also encourage foliar diseases—primarily mildew, rust, or black spot. Choose varieties noted for disease resistance; then be sure to plant them in open areas where air circulation is good.

In hot-summer areas, rose plants still grow vigorously, but flowers open rapidly; some colors fade readily, and dark reds may sunburn. Varieties with few petals (under 30) may go from bud to flat-open blossom in several hours. Flowers with more petals take longer to open and stay attractive longer. Therefore, in hot-summer areas, all blooms last longer if plants receive midday or afternoon shade. Avoid planting roses where they will receive reflected heat from light-colored walls or fences—especially in southern or western exposures. Best flowering is always in spring and fall (and in winter, in mildest zones); summer flower production may drop markedly as plants approach dormancy during intensely hot weather.

In cold-winter areas (Zones 1–3), the widely marketed modern roses—hybrid teas, grandifloras, and floribundas—are not completely hardy; some form of winter protection is needed to guarantee their survival from year to year (see Winter protection, p. 464). Many of the old roses (usually those that flower in spring only) and a number of the species and their hybrids survive winters in Zones 1–3 with scant or no protection from the cold.

In any region, the best place to see roses suitable for your climate is a municipal or private rose garden. The varieties that are performing well are obviously good choices for your garden.

BUYING PLANTS

All roses are available as bare-root plants from late fall through early spring. In Zones 4–24, you may plant bare-root roses throughout winter. In Zones 1–3, either plant in fall before ground freezes (then protect plants over winter), or plant in early spring after soil has thawed.

The majority of modern roses sold are budded plants: growth eyes of the desired varieties are budded onto understock plants that furnish the root systems. The understocks are carefully selected to promote rapid top growth of the desired roses and make root systems capable of thriving in a wide range of soils and climates. However, many old roses, species and their hybrids, and virtually all miniatures are "own-root" plants raised from cuttings. Ultimately, it makes no difference whether the plant is budded or own-root: either can grow well and produce fine flowers. Budded plants do offer more uniform root quality than you find among own-root plants, and budded plants often are larger at time of purchase than are own-root ones. But both kinds will be equally husky within a year or two. Own-root roses have one advantage, however: if an own-root plant is killed to the ground by cold (or mowed down by accident), it will regrow from the roots as the rose you want, not as understock. Under similar conditions, regrowth from roots of the budded plant will be the understock rose rather than the desired variety.

Bare-root plants are the best buy, and they are graded 1, 1½, or 2 according to strict standards. Plants graded 1 and 1½ are the most satisfactory, number 1 being the best. Number 2 plants may take longer to develop into decent bushes than the huskier numbers 1 and 1½. Retail nurseries and mail-order suppliers of modern roses usually offer only number 1 plants, and they will often replace plants that fail to grow. Old roses, shrub roses, and species roses (most commonly available by mail order) may be offered as budded plants that conform to the numbered grading standards, but some growers offer own-root (not budded) plants that may or may not be up to number 1 size. Catalogs usually state what size of plant to expect.

During bare-root planting time, retail nurseries also may offer a selection of "boxed" roses with root systems encased in cardboard cartons. Supermarkets, discount stores, and some retail nurseries sell dormant roses that have roots encased in moist material and enclosed in long, narrow bags. These packaged roses may be good value, but you should buy them as soon as they appear for sale. Those that are displayed indoors on store shelves may be dried out or encouraged into premature growth by

R

the indoor heating. Be prepared, too, for a number of these bargain roses to be mislabeled.

If you wish to plant roses during their growing season, you can buy roses growing in containers. This way, you can see and evaluate unfamiliar varieties before purchase and quickly fill in gaps in your garden. But container roses are more expensive than bare-root plants. Best time to buy container-grown roses is in mid- to late spring—when plants are fairly well rooted in the containers and can be set out before stressful summer heat arrives. For standard bush and climbing roses, look for robust plants growing in large (preferably 5-gal.) containers; this guarantees that root systems will have received little or no pruning to fit the container. Also, try to buy only roses planted in containers toward the end of the most recent dormant season; they generally will be in better condition than plants that have been in containers for a year or more. Avoid plants showing considerable dead or twiggy growth. Miniature

Grandiflora Rose 'Camelot'

roses usually are sold in containers that range from 4-in. pots to 2-gal. cans. Healthy new growth and foliage are signs of a good miniature plant, regardless of container size.

The presence of a plant patent number on a variety's name tag is no assurance of quality. It simply means that for a variety's first 17 years in commerce, the patent holder receives a royalty on each plant sold. Many fine roses that bear no patent number on name tags once were patented but have been in commerce for longer than the 17-year patent lifespan.

LOCATION AND PLANTING

For best results, plant roses where they will receive full sun all day (exceptions noted under Climate, p. 462). Avoid planting where roots of trees or shrubs will steal water and nutrients intended for roses. To lessen any problem with foliar diseases, plant roses where air circulates freely (but not in path of regular, strong winds). Generous spacing between plants will also aid air circulation. How far apart to plant varies according to the growth habit of the roses and according to climate. The colder the winter and shorter the growing season, the smaller the bushes will be; where growing season is long and winters are mild, bushes can attain greater size. But some varieties are naturally small, others tall and massive—and those relative size differences will hold in any climate. In Zones 1–3, you might plant most vigorous sorts 3 ft. apart, whereas the same roses could require 6-ft. spacing in milder zones.

Soil for roses should drain reasonably well; if it does not, the best alternative is to plant in raised beds. Dig soil deeply, incorporating organic matter such as ground bark, peat moss, or compost; this preparation will help aerate dense clay soils and will improve moisture retention of sandy soils. Add complete fertilizer to soil at the same time, and dig supplemental phosphorus and potash into planting holes; this gets nutrients down at the level where roots can use them.

Healthy, ready-to-plant bare-root roses should have plump, fresh-looking canes (branches) and roots. Plants that have dried out slightly in shipping or in nursery can be revived by burying them, tops and all, for a few days in moist soil, sand, or sawdust. Just before planting any bare-root rose, it is a good idea to immerse entire plant in water for several hours to be certain all canes and roots are plumped up. Plant according to directions for bare-root planting (see page 565), making sure that holes are large enough that you can spread out roots without bending or cutting them back. Just before planting, cut back broken canes and broken roots to below breaks. Set plant in hole so that bud union ("knob" from which canes grow) is just above soil level. Even growers in Zones 1–3 find this successful, and plants produce more canes when planted this way, as long as plants are well protected during winter. After you have planted a rose and watered it well, mound soil, damp peat moss, or sawdust over bud union and around canes to conserve moisture. Gradually (and carefully) remove soil or other material when leaves begin to expand.

If you plan to plant new roses in ground where existing bushes have been growing for 5 or more years, dig generous (at least 18 in. by 18 in.) planting holes and replace old soil with fresh soil from another part of the garden. A condition known as "specific replant disease" inhibits growth of new roses planted directly in soil of established rose gardens.

ROUTINE CARE

All roses require water, nutrients, some pruning, and, at some point in their lifetimes, pest and disease control. (Exceptions are some antique and species roses that thrive on little water once established.)

Water. For best performance, the most popular garden roses need watering at all times during the growing season. Inadequate water slows or halts growth and bloom. Water deeply so that entire root system is moistened. How often to water depends on soil type and weather. Big, well-established plants need more water than newly set plants, but you will need to water new plants more frequently to get them established.

Basin flooding is a simple way to water individual rose plants, and if you have a drip irrigation system, many plants can be watered this way at one time. Overhead sprinkling, often practiced in hot, dry regions, helps remove dust and freshen foliage, and provides partial control for aphids and spider mites; on the minus side, it washes off spray residues, may leave mineral deposits on foliage if water is hard, and in some areas may encourage foliar diseases by keeping foliage and atmosphere damp. If you sprinkle, do it early in the day to be sure foliage dries off by nightfall. Even if you irrigate in basins, give plants an occasional sprinkling to clean dust off foliage.

Mulch, spread 2–3 in. deep, will help save water, prevent soil surface from baking hard, keep soil cool in summer, deter weed growth, and contribute to healthy soil structure (well aerated, permeable by water and roots).

Nutrients. Regular applications of fertilizer will produce the most gratifying results. In mild-winter climates, begin feeding established plants with complete commercial fertilizer in February. Elsewhere, give first feeding just as growth begins. Time fertilizer application in relation to bloom period. Ideal time to make subsequent feedings is when a blooming period has ended and new growth is just beginning for next cycle of bloom. Depending on expected arrival of freezing temperatures, stop feeding in late summer or fall, generally about 6 weeks before earliest normal hard frost. In Zones 1–3, last application may be around August 1; in Zones 4–7 and 10, last feeding may be from early to late September. In milder zones, fertilizing may continue until mid-October for crop of late fall flowers.

Dry commercial fertilizer, applied to soil, is most frequently used. A variation on that type is slow-release fertilizer that provides nutrients over prolonged period; follow directions on package for amount and frequency of applications. Liquid fertilizers are useful in smaller gardens utilizing basin watering. Most liquids can also be used as foliage fertilizers—sprayed on rose leaves, which absorb some nutrients immediately.

Pest and disease control. Certain controls usually are needed during the growing season.

Floribunda Rose 'Cathedral'

Principal rose pests are aphids, spider mites, and (in some areas) thrips. If you don't want to rely on natural predators, start controlling aphids when they first appear in spring and repeat as needed until they are gone or their numbers severely reduced. Spider mites are hot-weather pests capable of defoliating and weakening plants—especially those that are underwatered and weak. Thrips do their damage inside flower buds, discoloring petals or disfiguring them so that buds may not open. Contact insecticide sprays can't reach most thrips hidden in petals; systemic insecticides are more successful.

Powdery mildew, rust, and black spot are the Big Three of foliar diseases. First line of defense for all three is thorough cleanup of all dead leaves and other debris during the dormant season; this is simplest right after you have pruned plants. Then, before new growth begins, spray plants and soil with dormant-season spray of oil or lime sulfur (calcium polysulfide). This will destroy many disease organisms (as well as insect eggs) that might live over winter to reinfect plants in spring. During the growing season apply controls as needed; unchecked infections can weaken plants, especially if defoliation occurs from rust or black spot. ▶

Two other foliar diseases, anthracnose and downy mildew, can occur to a lesser extent on roses. Anthracnose is similar to black spot and responds to the same treatment. Downy mildew begins in the upper reaches of a plant after leaves have fully formed, appearing in moist weather when temperatures are below 80°F. Foliage of infected plants shows irregular, purplish blotches, then turns yellow (sometimes with patches of green remaining) and falls off. On stems, the fungus shows as purplish mottling; infected stems are likely to die by the end of the year without treatment. To combat downy mildew during the growing season, spray infected plants with a fungicide containing zinc and manganese. Where the disease has appeared, use a dormant spray containing zinc or copper after winter pruning and rose garden cleanup.

Polyantha Rose
'Margo Koster'

Chlorosis—evidenced by leaves turning light green to yellow while veins remain dark green—is not a disease but a symptom, usually of iron deficiency. It can be a major problem in Zones 12 and 13. Iron chelate corrects chlorosis most quickly; iron sulfate also is effective but slower to act.

Leaves that show irregular patterning in yellow or cream indicate that the plant is infected with a mosaic virus. Some plants show the virus consistently; others display symptoms just occasionally. Although plants may appear to grow with vigor, virus infection does impair overall strength and productivity—and it can make foliage unsightly. Fortunately, it is not transferable from plant to plant by insects or pruning; it is transmitted in propagation—from infected rootstock or budwood. Commercial rose producers now are diligently working to eliminate virused stock. If you have a virused plant that is growing poorly or is unattractive, remove it from the garden.

Pruning. Done properly each year, pruning will contribute to the health and longevity of your rose plants. Sensible pruning is based on several facts about the growth of roses. First, blooms are produced on new growth. Unless pruning promotes strong new growth, flowers will come on spindly outer twigs and be of poor quality. Second, the more healthy wood you retain, the bigger the plant will be; and the bigger the plant, the more flowers it can produce. Nutrients are stored in woody canes, so a larger plant is a stronger plant. Therefore, prune conservatively; never chop down a vigorous 6-ft. bush to 1½-ft. stubs unless you want only a few huge blooms for exhibition. (Exception: in Zones 1–3, where plant freezes back to its winter protection, you will remove dead wood in spring and may be left with equivalent of severely pruned plant.) Third, the best pruning time for most roses (certain climbers and shrub types excepted) is at the end of dormant season (January in mild climates to late February and early March in cold climates) when growth buds begin to swell. Exact time will vary according to locality.

General pruning guidelines. The following pruning practices apply to all roses except certain shrub and species roses. Special instructions for pruning those roses are included later in this section.

Use sharp pruning shears; make all cuts as shown in the Practical Gardening Dictionary under Pruning Cuts. Remove wood that is obviously dead and wood that has no healthy growth coming from it; branches that cross through the plant's center and any that rub against larger canes; branches that make bush appear lopsided; and any old and unproductive canes that strong new ones have replaced during past season. Cut back growth produced during previous year, making cuts above outward-facing buds (except for very spreading varieties: some cuts to inside buds will promote more height without producing many crossing branches). As a general rule, remove one-third to no more than one-half the length of previous season's growth (except in Zones 1–3, as noted above). The ideal result is a V-shaped bush with relatively open center.

If any suckers (growth produced from understock, not the rose variety growing on it) are present, completely remove them. Dig down to where suckers grow from understock and pull them off with downward motion; that removes growth buds that would have produced additional suckers in subsequent years. Let wound air-dry before you replace soil around it.

Be certain you are removing a sucker rather than a new cane growing from the bud union of the budded variety. Usually you can note a distinct difference in foliage size and shape, as well as in size of thorns, on sucker growth. If in doubt, let the presumed sucker grow until you can establish its difference from cane. A sucker's flowers will be different; a flowerless, climbing cane from a bush rose is almost certainly a sucker.

Consider cutting flowers as a form of pruning. Cut off enough stem to support flower in vase, but don't deprive plant of too much foliage. Leave on plant a stem with at least two sets of five-leaflet leaves. Prune to outward-growing bud or to five-leaflet leaf.

The most widely planted modern roses—hybrid teas and grandifloras—can be pruned successfully according to these guidelines. A few additional tips apply to five other popular types:

Floribunda, polyantha, and many shrub roses are grown for quantities of flowers, so amount of bloom rather than quality of individual flower is the objective. Cut back previous season's growth only by one-fourth, and leave as many strong new canes and stems as plant produced. Most produce more canes per bush than do hybrid teas and grandifloras. If you have a hedge of one variety, cut back all plants to uniform height.

Climbing roses may be divided into two general types: those that bloom in spring only (including a large category known as natural climbers, discussed in Climbing roses, p. 466), and those that bloom off and on in other seasons as well as in spring (including the very popular climbing sports of hybrid tea roses). All climbers should be left unpruned for the first 2–3 years after planting; remove only dead, weak, and twiggy wood, allowing plants to get established and produce their long, flexible canes. Most bloom comes from lateral branches that grow from long canes, and most of those flowering branches develop when long canes are spread out horizontally (as along a fence). Types that bloom only in spring produce strong new growth after they flower, and that new growth bears flowers the following spring. Prune these climbers just after they bloom, removing oldest canes that show no signs of strong new growth. Repeat-flowering climbers (many are climbing sports of bush varieties) are pruned at the same time you'd prune bush roses in your locality. Remove oldest, unproductive canes and any weak, twiggy growth; cut back lateral branches on remaining canes to within two or three buds from canes.

Pillar roses are not quite bush or climber. They produce tall, somewhat flexible canes that bloom profusely without having to be trained horizontally. Prune pillar roses according to general guidelines for bush roses.

Tree roses, more properly called "standards," are an artificial creation: a bush rose budded onto a 2–3-ft.-high understock stem. Be sure to stake trunk securely to prevent its breaking from weight of bush it supports. A ½-in. metal pipe makes good permanent stake; use cross tie between stake and trunk to hold them secure. General pruning guidelines apply, with particular attention to maintaining symmetrical plant.

Miniature roses should be pruned back to at least half the height they attained during the previous year, removing all weak and twiggy stems. Some growers prune miniatures severely—back to the lowest outward-facing growth buds on the previous year's new stems.

Winter protection. Where winter low temperatures regularly reach 10°F and lower, some winter protection is needed for nearly all modern roses. Low temperatures can kill exposed canes; repeated freezing and thawing will kill canes by rupturing cells; and winter winds can fatally desiccate exposed canes because plants are unable to replace moisture from frozen soil.

A healthy, well-ripened plant withstands harsh winters better than a weak and actively growing one. Prepare plants for winter by timing your last fertilizer application so that bushes will have ceased putting on new growth by expected date of first sharp frost. Leave the last crop of blooms on plants to form hips (fruits), which will aid the ripening process by stopping growth. Keep plants well watered until soil freezes.

After a couple of hard freezes have occurred and night temperatures seem to remain consistently below freezing, mound soil over base of each bush to height of 1 ft. Get soil from another part of garden; do not scoop soil from around roses, exposing surface roots. Cut excessively long canes back to about 4 ft.; then, with soft twine, tie canes together to keep them from whipping around in wind. When mound has frozen, cover it with evergreen boughs, straw, or other fairly lightweight material that will act as insulation to keep mounds frozen. Your objective is to prevent alternate freezing and thawing of mound (and canes it covers), maintaining plant at constant temperature of 15–20°F. A cylinder of wire mesh around soil mound will help keep it and insulating material in place.

Remove protection in early spring when you are reasonably certain hard frosts will not recur. Gradually remove soil mounds as they thaw; do it carefully to avoid breaking new growth that may have begun sprouting under the soil. Use of manufactured styrofoam rose cones eliminates the labor of mounding and unmounding; just a bit of soil around the cone's base plus a rock or brick on top will hold it in place over the bush. Disadvantages are cost and availability of cones; the need to cut rose down to fit cone over it, perhaps requiring more severe pruning than is usually necessary; moisture condensation inside cone as days begin warming. To avoid condensation problem, get cones with removable tops that can be opened on warm late-winter days.

You should mound climbing roses in same manner, but in addition you need to protect all of their canes. Where winter lows range from −10° to 5°F, wrap canes in burlap stuffed with straw for insulation. Where temperatures normally go below −10°F, remove canes from their support, gently bend them to ground, secure them in that position, and cover with soil. A wiser plan in such climates is to plant only climbers known to be successful in your area or reputed to be hardy in similar climates.

Standards (tree roses) may be insulated in the same manner as for climbers, but they still may not survive, since the head of the tree is the most exposed. Some rosarians wrap with straw and burlap, then construct a plywood box to cover the insulated plant. Others dig their standards each year and pack the roots loosely in soil or other medium in a cool garage, basement, or shed, then replant in spring. A simpler technique is to grow standards in large containers and move them in fall to cool shed or garage where temperatures won't drop below 10°F.

TYPES OF ROSES

A renewed interest in old roses, continued developments of new hybrids, and breeding programs directed toward producing landscape shrubs have led to a greatly expanded offering of roses to the gardening public. For convenience, the following sections describe three broad categories: modern roses, old roses, and species and species hybrids.

Modern roses. Types described below constitute the majority of roses offered for sale and planted by hundreds of thousands each year. Those that have been All-America Rose Selections, recognized on the basis of their performance in nationwide test gardens, are indicated by "AARS"; those with an asterisk (*) before their names are rated 8.0 or higher by the American Rose Society.

Hybrid teas. This, the most popular class of rose, outsells all other types combined. Flowers are large and shapely, generally produced one to a stem on plants that range from 2 ft. to 6 ft. or more, depending on the variety and climate. Many thousands of varieties have been produced since the first rose in the class, 'La France', appeared in 1867; hundreds are cataloged, and new ones appear each year. The most popular ones are listed in the following color groups:

Red. 'Chrysler Imperial' (AARS), *'Mr. Lincoln' (AARS), *'Olympiad' (AARS).

Pink. 'Bewitched' (AARS), 'Brigadoon' (AARS), *'Century Two', *'Color Magic' (AARS), *'Dainty Bess'(single), 'Duet' (AARS), *'First Prize' (AARS), *'Miss All-American Beauty' (AARS), 'Perfume Delight' (AARS), *'Royal Highness' (AARS), 'Secret' (AARS), 'Sheer Bliss' (AARS), *'Tiffany' (AARS), *'Touch of Class' (AARS).

Multicolors, blends. 'Broadway' (AARS), 'Chicago Peace', *'Double Delight' (AARS), *'Granada' (AARS), 'Just Joey', 'Medallion' (AARS), 'Rio Samba' (AARS), 'Seashell' (AARS), 'Voodoo' (AARS).

Orange, orange tones. 'Brandy' (AARS), *'Folklore', *'Fragrant Cloud', 'Tropicana' (AARS).

Yellow. *'Elina', 'Graceland', 'King's Ransom' (AARS), 'Oregold' (AARS), 'Midas Touch' (AARS), *'Peace' (AARS), 'Summer Sunshine', 'Sunbright'.

White. *'Garden Party' (AARS), 'Honor' (AARS), 'John F. Kennedy', *'Pascali' (AARS), *'Pristine'.

Lavender. 'Blue Girl', 'Blue Ribbon', 'Heirloom', *'Lady X', *'Paradise' (AARS).

Grandifloras. Vigorous plants, sometimes 8–10 ft. tall, with hybrid tea–type flowers borne singly or in long-stemmed clusters. Some are derived from crosses between hybrid teas and floribundas; others are just extravigorous, cluster-flowering segregates from ordinary hybrid tea ancestry. They're good for mass color effect, for number of cuttable flowers produced per plant, and as background or barrier plants.

Red. 'Love' (AARS), 'Olé'.

Pink, pink blends. *'Aquarius' (AARS), 'Camelot' (AARS), *'Earth Song', *'Pink Parfait' (AARS), *'Queen Elizabeth' (AARS), *'Sonia', *'Tournament of Roses' (AARS).

Orange, blends. 'Arizona' (AARS), 'Montezuma', 'Solitude' (AARS).

Yellow. *'Gold Medal'.

White. 'White Lightnin'' (AARS).

Lavender. 'Lagerfeld'.

Floribundas. Originally developed from hybrid teas and polyanthas (see below), these are noted for producing quantities of flowers in clusters on vigorous and bushy plants. Plant and flower sizes are smaller than those of most hybrid teas. Some have flowers of elegant hybrid tea shape; others are more informal. These are plants for providing mass color. Use for informal hedges, low borders and barriers, as container plants.

Red. *'Europeana' (AARS), 'Impatient', *'Sarabande' (AARS), *'Showbiz' (AARS), *'Trumpeter'.

Pink. *'Betty Prior', *'Bridal Pink', 'Cherish' (AARS), 'Gene Boerner' (AARS), 'Pleasure' (AARS), *'Sexy Rexy', 'Sweet Inspiration' (AARS), *'Sweet Vivien'.

Orange, blends. *'Apricot Nectar' (AARS), 'Cathedral', *'First Edition' (AARS), 'Gingersnap', 'Marina', *'Orangeade', 'Redgold' (AARS), *'Summer Fashion'.

Yellow. *'Sun Flare' (AARS), *'Sunsprite'.

White. *'Evening Star', *'French Lace' (AARS), *'Iceberg', *'Ivory Fashion' (AARS).

Lavender. *'Angel Face' (AARS), 'Intrigue' (AARS).

Polyanthas. Original members of this class appeared in the late 19th century, the result of crosses with *R. multiflora*. Small flowers (under 2 in. across) come in large sprays; plants are vigorous and usually low growing, nearly everblooming, and quite disease resistant. 'Margo Koster' has coral orange, very double flowers that resemble ranunculus; it has sported to produce color variants in white, pink, orange scarlet, and red. 'The Fairy' produces huge clusters of small, light pink flowers on a plant that can reach 4 ft. high. 'China Doll' is a knee-high plant with larger, deeper pink flowers in smaller clusters. With light pruning two 19th-century classics make sizable bushes that resemble bushy Noisettes (see under Old roses, p. 466). 'Cécile Brunner' (often called the Sweetheart Rose) has light pink flowers of perfect hybrid tea form; 'Perle d'Or' (sometimes called Yellow Cécile Brunner) is similar except for its apricot orange flower color.

Miniature roses. These are perfect replicas of modern hybrid teas and floribundas but plant size is reduced to 12–18 in. (grown in the ground) with flowers and foliage in proportion. Derived in part from *R. chinensis minima* (through its forms 'Rouletii' and 'Pompon de Paris'), they come in all colors of modern hybrid teas. Plants are everblooming. Grow them outdoors in containers, window boxes, and rock gardens or as border and bedding plants. You can grow them indoors: pot in rich soil in 6-in. (or larger) containers, and locate in a cool, bright window. Miniatures are hardier than hybrid teas but still need winter protection in Zones 1–3. Shallow roots demand regular water and fertilizer, mulch. Nearly all are own-root, cutting-grown plants.

Miniature Rose

Many new miniatures appear on the market each year. Among the best are these, all rated 8.5 or higher:

Red, orange. 'Orange Sunblaze', 'Peggy', 'Starina'.

Pink. 'Coral Sprite', 'Cupcake', 'Millie Walters', 'Pierrine', 'Pink Meillandina'.

Blends. 'Dreamglo', 'Earthquake', 'Jean Kenneally', 'Little Artist', 'Little Jackie', 'Loving Touch', 'Magic Carrousel', 'Minnie Pearl', 'Party Girl', 'Rainbow's End', 'Shortcake', 'Wow'.

Yellow. 'Morain', 'My Sunshine', 'Rise 'n' Shine'.

White. 'Pacesetter', 'Snowbride'.

Lavender, purple. 'Ruby Pendant', 'Winsome'.

Climbing roses. Modern climbing roses may be divided into two general categories: natural climbers (large flowered, except for miniatures) and climbing sports of bush roses (hybrid teas, grandifloras, floribundas, polyanthas, miniatures). Here are popular varieties of natural climbers:

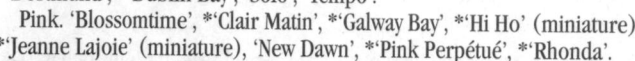

Climbing Rose 'Climbing Mrs. Sam McGredy'

Red. *'Altissimo' (single), 'Blaze', *'Don Juan', *'Dortmund', *'Dublin Bay', 'Solo', 'Tempo'.

Pink. 'Blossomtime', *'Clair Matin', *'Galway Bay', *'Hi Ho' (miniature), *'Jeanne Lajoie' (miniature), 'New Dawn', *'Pink Perpétué', *'Rhonda'.

Orange, blends. *'America' (AARS), *'Compassion', *'Handel', 'Joseph's Coat', *'Royal Sunset', 'Spectra'.

Yellow. 'Golden Showers' (AARS), 'Royal Gold'.

White. *'City of York', 'Lace Cascade', 'White Dawn'.

Here are popular varieties of climbing sports:

Red. 'Cl. Chrysler Imperial', 'Cl. Crimson Glory'.

Pink. 'Cl. Cécile Brunner' (polyantha), 'Cl. China Doll' (polyantha), 'Cl. Dainty Bess', 'Cl. First Prize', 'Cl. Queen Elizabeth'.

Orange, blends. 'Cl. Double Delight', 'Cl. Granada', 'Cl. Mrs. Sam McGredy', 'Cl. Peace'.

White. *'Cl. Iceberg'.

Shrub roses. Significant breeding is under way to develop roses for general landscape use. These are collectively known as shrub roses. Emphasis is on plants that will provide attractive floral displays (even good-looking individual blossoms), disease-resistant foliage, and individuals that will survive cold winters with no special protection. Mail-order rose specialists lead the way in offering these plants, but retail nurseries are offering them more and more. Here is an overview of types available:

Hybrid musk roses. These were developed in the first three decades of the 20th century from the multiflora rambler 'Trier', which was distantly descended from the musk rose through the Noisettes. The hybrid musks are large 6–8-ft. shrubs or small climbers that will perform well in dappled or partial shade as well as in sun. Most are nearly everblooming, with fragrant, clustered flowers in white, yellow, buff, pink shades, red. Popular varieties include 'Buff Beauty', buff apricot; 'Cornelia', coral; 'Felicia', pink; 'Kathleen', single pink, like apple blossoms; 'Penelope', salmon; 'Will Scarlet', red.

English roses. This is a rapidly expanding group of hybrids. England's David Austin has bred various old roses (albas, centifolias, gallicas) with modern roses in order to capture the forms and fragrances of old roses in repeat-flowering plants that offer the color range of modern hybrids. The group is extremely varied and includes low shrubs as well as plants that are determined to be climbers regardless of pruning. Choose varieties based on descriptions of performance in the West (where many grow much larger than they would in cold-winter regions). Many have Shakespearean or Chaucerian names; over 80 are in commerce. Popular varieties include 'Abraham Darby', pink-yellow-apricot blend, upright to climbing plant; 'Charles Austin', apricot, bushy plant; 'Fair Bianca', creamy white, spreading bush; 'Gertrude Jekyll', deep pink, tall and upright; 'Graham Thomas', rich yellow, tall plant; 'Mary Rose', rose pink, tall and upright; 'Othello', dusky dark red, tall bush or climber.

Ground cover roses. A number of European and American breeders are producing roses that spread their canes widely but build up to no more than 2 ft.—perfect for covering slopes, forming traffic-proof covers on level ground, or for container culture. Vigor, disease resistance, profusion of bloom are the hallmarks of these roses. Examples are 'Essex', 'Flower Carpet', 'Nozomi', 'Pink Bells', 'Rosy Carpet'.

Hardy roses. Two breeding programs have produced numerous varieties that will survive Rocky Mountain winters with virtually no special protection. Some of them resemble floribundas and grandifloras; ancestries include various hardy species plus modern hybrid teas and floribundas. Many of these feature country names: 'Country Dancer', 'Hawkeye Belle', 'Maytime', 'Prairie Princess'. Others are mostly larger shrubs to small climbers, derived in part from *R. rugosa;* most are cluster flowered, like large floribundas. Many are named for explorers: 'Alexander Mackenzie', 'Henry Kelsey', 'John Cabot', 'William Baffin'.

Patio roses. Larger than miniatures, smaller than floribundas, these plants (mostly of European origin) are bushy, profuse flowering, usually no more than 2 ft. tall. They're good providers of mass color as border and container plants. Examples are 'Amorette', white; 'Hakuun', white; 'Minilights', soft yellow; 'Pink Pollyanna', pink; 'Yellow Jacket', yellow.

Other shrub roses. Many modern shrub roses of complex ancestry can't be pigeonholed into categories according to species affiliation or specific characteristic. The plants may be spreading or upright, they are usually 3 ft. or greater in height, and their flowers come in small to large clusters. These includes such gems as 'Alchymist', 'Ballerina' (classed as hybrid musk but more like a giant polyantha), 'Erfurt', the various Meidiland roses ('Bonica', 'Pink Meidiland', 'Red Meidiland', 'White Meidiland'), 'Pearl Drift', 'Sally Holmes', and 'Sea Foam'. Check individual descriptions of catalog offerings to find appealing candidates that meet your specific landscape needs.

Old roses. Among rosarians, the dividing line between old and modern roses is 1867—the year that the first hybrid tea was introduced. Old roses are varieties that belong to the various rose classes that existed prior to 1867 (even though some varieties in these classes were introduced as late as the early 20th century). Old roses may be divided into two categories. The old European roses comprise the albas, centifolias, damasks, gallicas, and moss roses—the oldest hybrid groups derived from species native to Europe and western Asia. Most flower only in spring; many are hardy in Zones 1–3 with little or no winter protection. The second group contains classes derived entirely or in part from East Asian roses: Chinas, Bourbons, damask perpetuals, hybrid perpetuals, Noisettes, and teas. Original China and tea roses were brought to Europe from eastern Asia; 19th-century hybridizers greatly increased their numbers and also developed the other classes from crosses with European roses. Repeat flowering is a characteristic of these classes; hardiness varies; but nearly all need winter protection in coldest zones.

Alba roses. **R. alba.** WHITE ROSE OF YORK. Associated with England's War of the Roses. Spring flowers range from single to very double, white to delicate pink. Upright plants are vigorous and long lived, with green wood and handsome, disease-resistant gray-green foliage. Garden varieties include white 'Alba Semiplena' and these in shades of pink: 'Celestial', 'Great Maiden's Blush', 'Félicité Parmentier', and 'Königin von Dänemark'.

Centifolia roses. **R. centifolia.** CABBAGE ROSE. The roses often portrayed by Dutch painters. Plants are open growing with prickly stems, to 6 ft. tall, but stems arch with weight of blossoms. Intensely fragrant spring flowers typically are packed with petals, often with large outer petals that cradle a multitude of smaller petals within. Colors include white, pink shades. 'Rose des Peintres' is a typical rich pink cabbage rose; 'Paul Ricault' produces silken, deep pink flowers on an upright plant; 'Tour de Malakoff' is a tall, rangy plant with peonylike blossoms of pink fading to grayish mauve. Dwarf (3 ft. or less) varieties are 'Petite de Hollande', 'Pompon de Bourgogne', and 'Rose de Meaux'.

Damask roses. **R. damascena.** Plants reach 6 ft. or more, typically with long, arching, thorny canes and light or grayish green, downy leaves. The summer damasks flower only in spring; forms of these are cultivated to make attar of roses. Available varieties include 'Celsiana', blush pink; 'Leda', white with crimson markings; 'Mme. Hardy', white; and 'Versicolor'('York and Lancaster'), with petals that may be pink, white, or blend of pink and white. The autumn damask rose, *R. d.* 'Semperflorens' (*R. d. bifera*), flowers more than once in a year; slender buds open to loosely double, clear pink blossoms. This is the "Rose of Castile" of the Spanish missions.

Gallica roses. **R. gallica.** FRENCH ROSE. Fragrant spring flowers run from pink through red to maroon and purple shades. Plants reach 3–4 ft. tall with upright to arching canes bearing prickles but few thorns and dark green, often rough-textured leaves. Grown on their own roots, these plants will spread into clumps from creeping rootstocks. Historic *R. g.* 'Officinalis', known as the Apothecary Rose, is presumed to be the "Red Rose of Lancaster" from the War of the Roses; flowers are semidouble, cherry red, on a dense, medium-height plant. Its sport, *R. g.* 'Versicolor'—generally known as 'Rosa Mundi'—has pink petals boldly striped and stippled red. Other gallicas include 'Belle de Crécy', pink aging to violet; 'Cardinal de Richelieu', slate purple; 'Charles de Mills', crimson to purple; and 'Tuscany', dark crimson with gold stamens.

Moss roses. Two old rose classes—centifolia and damask—include variant types that feature mosslike, balsam-scented glands that cover unopened buds, flower stems, and sometimes even leaflets. The moss of centifolias is soft to the touch; that of damask mosses is more stiff and prickly. Flowers are white, pink, red, often intensely fragrant. 'Communis' and 'Centifolia Muscosa' (*R. centifolia* 'Muscosa') are typical pink centifolias with moss added; 'White Bath' is 'Centifolia Muscosa' done in white. Other available varieties are 'Comtesse de Murinais', pale pink to white; 'Gloire des Mousseux', deep pink; 'Mme. Louis Lévêque', salmon pink; 'Nuits de Young', dark red; 'William Lobb', dark red to purple. Repeat-flowering mosses include 'Alfred de Dalmas', creamy pink; 'Gabriel Noyelle', apricot; 'Henri Martin', red; and 'Salet', bright pink.

China roses. The first two China roses to reach Europe (around 1800) were really cultivated forms of *R. chinensis* that had been selected and maintained by Chinese horticulturists. Flowers were pink or red, under 3 in. across, in small clusters, on 2–4-ft.-high plants. 'Old Blush' ('Parson's Pink China'), one of the original two, is still sold; other available China roses include red 'Cramoisi Supérieur' ('Agrippina'), white 'Ducher', and crimson 'Louis Philippe'. China rose ancestry was the primary source of repeat-flowering habit in later 19th- and early 20th-century roses. Modern miniature roses owe their reduced stature to *R. chinensis minima*, presumably through its forms 'Pompon de Paris' and 'Rouletii'.

Bourbon roses. The original Bourbon rose was a hybrid between *R. chinensis* and the autumn damask (*R. damascena* 'Semperflorens'). Later developments were shrubs, semiclimbers, and climbers with flowers in white, pink shades, and red, mostly quite fragrant. Best known today are 'La Reine Victoria', 'Madame Ernst Calvat', 'Madame Pierre Oger', and 'Souvenir de la Malmaison' (all pink), and the supremely fragrant 'Madame Isaac Pereire' (magenta red). A famous Bourbon-China hybrid, 'Gloire des Rosomanes', gained widespread distribution as an understock (called "Ragged Robin") in commercial rose production. Occasionally it is offered as a hedge plant; growth is upright to fountainlike, with coarse foliage and semidouble, cherry red flowers throughout the growing season.

Damask perpetuals. This was the first distinct hybrid group to emerge, beginning around 1800, combining the China roses with old European rose types. Ancestries vary, but all appear to include China roses and the autumn damask (*R. damascena* 'Semperflorens'); generally they were known as Portland roses after the first representative, 'Duchess of Portland'. All are fairly short, bushy, repeat-flowering plants with centifolia- and gallica-like flowers. Among those sold are 'Comte de Chambord', cool pink; 'Duchess of Portland', crimson; 'Jacques Cartier', bright pink; and 'Rose du Roi', crimson purple.

Hybrid perpetuals. Before hybrid teas dominated the catalogs, these were *the* garden roses. Plants are big, vigorous, and hardy to about −30°F with minimal winter protection. Plants need more water and fertilizer than hybrid teas in order to produce repeated bursts of bloom. Prune high, thin out oldest canes, arch over remaining canes to encourage bloom in quantity, watch for rust. Flowers often are large (to 6 and 7 in.), full, and strongly fragrant; buds usually are shorter, plumper than standard hybrid tea buds. Colors range from white through pink shades to red and maroon. Varieties still sold include 'Frau Karl Druschki', white; 'Général Jacqueminot', cherry red; 'Mrs. John Laing', rose pink; 'Paul Neyron', deep pink, peonylike flower; 'Ulrich Brünner Fils', carmine red.

Noisette roses. The union of a China rose (*R. chinensis*) and the musk rose (*R. moschata*) produced the first Noisette rose, 'Champneys' Pink Cluster', a repeat-flowering shrubby climber with small pink flowers in medium-size clusters. Crossed with itself and China roses, it led to a race of similar roses in white, pink shades, and red; crossed with tea roses, it yielded large-flowered, climbing tea-Noisettes. Small-flowered Noisettes include 'Aimée Vibert Scandens', white; 'Blush Noisette', light pink; and 'Fellenberg', cherry red. Larger-flowered tea-Noisettes are 'Alister Stella Gray', yellow; 'Crepuscule', orange; 'Lamarque', white; 'Madame Alfred Carrière', white; 'Maréchal Niel', yellow; and 'Rêve d'Or', buff apricot.

Tea roses. A race of elegant, virtually everblooming, relatively tender roses best in Zones 6–9, 12–24. Plants are long lived, building on old wood and disliking heavy pruning. Flowers are in pastel shades—white, soft cream, light yellow, apricot, buff, pink, and rosy red; flower character varies, but many resemble hybrid teas in flower quality. In crosses with hybrid perpetuals, tea roses were parents of the first hybrid teas. Available varieties include 'Duchesse de Brabant', warm pink, tuliplike; 'Lady Hillingdon', saffron; 'Maman Cochet', creamy rose pink; 'Marie van Houtte', soft yellow and pink; 'Mlle. Franziska Krüger', pink and cream to orange; 'Monsieur Tillier', dark pink and brick red; and 'White Maman Cochet', creamy white shaded pink. The cross of a tea and the tea ancestor *R. gigantea* produced 'Belle Portugaise', ('Belle of Portugal'); a rampant, spring-flowering climber bearing large pale pink blossoms.

> ## UNFORGETTABLY FRAGRANT
> Many antique roses bear flowers that are among the most deliciously fragrant of all roses. Heavily perfumed 'La Reine', a hybrid perpetual, delivers choice petals for potpourri. 'Boule de Neige', a Bourbon, has white flowers that smell like cold cream. A single blossom of 'Sombreuil', a white-flowered climbing tea, can scent an entire room.

Species and species hybrids. Among this diverse assemblage of wild species and their hybrids are excellent shrub and climbing roses, useful for mass floral effect and for attractiveness of plant and foliage.

R. banksiae. LADY BANKS' ROSE. Evergreen climber (deciduous in cold winters). Zones 4–24. Vigorous grower to 20 feet or more. Aphid resistant, almost immune to disease. Stems have almost no prickles; glossy and leathery leaves have three to five leaflets to 2½ in. long. Large clusters of small, yellow or white flowers bloom in early to late spring, depending on zone. Good for covering banks, ground, fence, or arbor. The two forms sold are 'Lutea', with scentless, double yellow flowers; and *R. b. banksiae* ('Alba Plena' or 'White Banksia'), with violet-scented, double white flowers. 'Fortuniana' (*R. fortuniana*) sometimes is sold as the double white banksia; it differs in having thorny canes, larger leaves, and larger flowers that come individually rather than in clusters.

R. bracteata. Climbing shrub with large, single creamy white blossoms. Zones 4–24. Naturalized in southeastern United States. Its celebrated offspring is 'Mermaid', evergreen or semievergreen climber. Vigorous (to 30 ft.), thorny, with glossy, leathery, dark green leaves and many single, creamy yellow, lightly fragrant flowers, 5 in. across, in spring, summer, fall, and intermittently through winter in mildest zones. Tough, disease resistant, it thrives in sun or partial shade, on coast or inland. Plant 8 ft. apart for quick ground cover; or use to climb wall (will need tying), run along fence, or climb tree.

R. eglanteria (R. rubiginosa). SWEET BRIAR, EGLANTINE. Deciduous shrub or climber. All zones. Vigorous growth to 8–12 ft. Prickly stems. Dark green leaves are fragrant (like apples), especially after rain. Flowers single, pink, 1½ in. across, appearing singly or in clusters in late spring. Fruit red orange. Can be used as hedge, barrier, screen; plant 3–4 ft. apart and prune once a year in early spring. Can be held to 3–4 ft. Naturalized in some parts of West. Good hybrid forms: 'Lady Penzance', 'Lord Penzance'.

R. foetida (R. lutea). AUSTRIAN BRIER. Deciduous shrub. All zones. Slender, prickly stems 5–10 ft. long, erect or arching. Leaves dark green, smooth or slightly hairy; may drop early in fall. Flowers (May–June) are single, bright yellow, 2–3 in. across, with odd scent. This species and its well-known variety 'Bicolor', Austrian Copper rose, are the source of orange and yellow in modern roses. 'Bicolor' is a 4–5-ft.-tall shrub with brilliant coppery red flowers, their petals backed with yellow. Its form 'Persiana', Persian Yellow rose, has fully double, yellow blossoms.

R. foetida does best in warm, fairly dry, well-drained soil and in full sun. Needs reflected heat in Zones 4–6. Prune only to remove dead wood.

R. glauca (R. rubrifolia). Deciduous shrub. All zones. Foliage, not flower, is the main feature of this species: the 6-ft. plant is covered in leaves that combine gray green and coppery purple. Small, single spring flowers are pink, forming small, oval hips that color red in fall.

DISEASE-DEFIANT ROSES

Which of the popular floribundas, hybrid teas, and grandifloras are most resistant to black spot, powdery mildew, and rust? 'Olympiad' stands up to all three diseases better than just about any other modern rose, according to a *Sunset Magazine* survey of more than 300 western rosarians. For *black spot,* the top runners-up are 'Brandy', 'Iceberg', 'Pristine', and 'Gold Medal'. For *powdery mildew:* 'Gold Medal', 'Pristine', 'Honor', 'Voodoo'. And for *rust:* 'Gold Medal', 'Honor', 'Pristine', and 'Iceberg'.

R. harisonii. HARISON'S YELLOW ROSE. Deciduous shrub. All zones. Thickets of thorny stems to 6–8 ft.; finely textured foliage; flowers (in late spring) profuse, semidouble, bright yellow, fragrant. Occasionally reblooms in fall in warmer climates. Showy fruit. Hybrid between *R. foetida* and *R. spinosissima.* Very old rose that came west with pioneers and still persists in California's gold country and around old farmhouses. Vigorous growing, disease free, hardy to cold, and (once established) resistant to aridity. Useful deciduous landscaping shrub.

R. hugonis. FATHER HUGO'S ROSE, GOLDEN ROSE OF CHINA. Deciduous shrub. All zones. Dense growth to 8 ft. Stems arching or straight, with bristles near base. Handsome foliage; leaves deep green, 1–4 in. long, with 5–11 tiny leaflets. Flowers profusely May–June; branches become garlands of 2-in.-wide, bright yellow, faintly scented flowers. Useful in borders, for screen or barrier plantings, against fence, trained as fan on trellis. Will take high filtered afternoon shade. Prune out oldest wood to ground each year to shape plant, get maximum bloom.

R. laevigata. CHEROKEE ROSE. Evergreen climber. Zones 4–9, 12–24. Native to Southeast Asia but widely naturalized in southern United States, from which it gained its common name. Green stems with sharp, hooked thorns bear lacquered-looking, dark green leaves, each bearing three leaflets. Single white flowers appearing only in spring may reach 3½ in. across. Crossed with a tea rose, it produced 'Anemone', a mostly spring-flowering climber with soft, silvery pink, single flowers that resemble Japanese anemone blossoms. Its magenta pink sport is 'Ramona'.

R. moschata. MUSK ROSE. Deciduous shrub. Zones 4–24. Vigorous, arching plant is densely covered with matte-finish, mid-green foliage that turns butter yellow in late fall. Clustered, ivory white, single flowers appear in late spring, continuing through summer; scent is delicious, somewhat like honey. *R. m. plena* has double blossoms, though their effect is lessened because inner petals wither before outer ones.

R. moyesii. Deciduous shrub. All zones. Large, loose shrub is best as background plant or featured shrub-tree specimen. Spring bloom is a glorious display of bright red, single flowers to 2½ in. across, carried singly or in groups of two. A second display comes in fall, when the large, bottle-shaped hips ripen to brilliant scarlet. 'Geranium' is a selection with somewhat shorter, more compact growth and red flowers in clusters of up to

five. The hybrid 'Sealing Wax' offers pink flowers, also on a smaller and more compact bush.

From a hybrid tea crossed with a form of *R. moyesii,* 'Nevada' makes a large, arching shrub with light green leaves and dark stems. In spring, stems are covered with 4-in., pink-tinted, single white flowers, with lesser displays following later in the year. 'Marguerite Hilling' is a pink sport.

R. multiflora. Deciduous shrub. All zones. Arching growth on dense, vigorous plant 8–10 ft. tall and as wide. Susceptible to mildew, spider mites. Many clustered, small white flowers (like blackberry blossoms) in June; profusion of ¼-in. red fruit, much loved by birds, in fall. Promoted as hedge but truly useful for this purpose only on largest acreage—far too large and vigorous for most gardens. Spiny and smooth forms available; spiny form best for barrier hedge. Set plants 2 ft. apart for fast fill-in. Can help control erosion.

A number of distinctive climbing roses, known as multiflora ramblers, are hybrids of this species. Best known are several "blue ramblers": 'Bleu Magenta', crimson purple fading to gray violet; 'Rose-Marie Viaud', crimson purple to violet and lilac; 'Veilchenblau', maroon purple to gray lilac; and 'Violette', maroon purple to grayish plum.

R. roxburghii. CHESTNUT ROSE. Deciduous. Zones 2–24. Spreading plant with prickly stems 8–10 ft. long. Bark gray, peeling. Light green, very finely textured, ferny foliage; new growth bronze and gold tipped. Immune to mildew. Buds and fruit are spiny like chestnut burrs. Flowers—generally double, soft rose pink, very fragrant—appear in June. Normally a big shrub for screen or border, but if stems are pegged down it makes good bank cover, useful in preventing erosion.

R. rugosa. RAMANAS ROSE, SEA TOMATO. Deciduous shrub. All zones. Vigorous, very hardy shrub with prickly stems. To 3–8 ft. tall. Leaves bright glossy green, with distinctive heavy veining that gives them crinkled appearance. Flowers are 3–4 in. across and, in the many varieties, range from single to double and from pure white and creamy yellow through pink to deep purplish red, all wonderfully fragrant. Bright red, tomato-shaped fruit, an inch or more across, are edible but seedy and sometimes used in preserves.

All rugosas are extremely tough and hardy, withstanding hard freezes, wind, aridity, salt spray at ocean. They make fine hedges and will help prevent erosion. Foliage remains quite free of diseases and insects, except possibly aphids. Among most widely sold are 'Blanc Double de Coubert', double white; 'Frau Dagmar Hartopp', single pink; 'Hansa', double purplish red; 'Will Alderman', double pink. Two unusual rugosa hybrids are 'F. J. Grootendorst' and 'Grootendorst Supreme'; their double flowers with deeply fringed petals resemble carnations more than roses.

R. spinosissima (R. pimpinellifolia). SCOTCH ROSE, BURNET ROSE. Deciduous shrub. All zones. Suckering, spreading shrub 3–4 ft. tall. Stems upright, spiny, bristly, closely set with small, ferny leaves. Handsome bank cover on good soil; helps prevent erosion. Spring flowers white to pink, 1½–2 in. across; fruit dark brown to blackish. Its form 'Altaica' can reach 6 ft. tall, with larger leaves and 3-in. white flowers garlanding branches. Several hybrids are noteworthy. 'Stanwell Perpetual' produces blush pink, double blossoms from spring to fall on a mounding, twiggy plant with small, gray-green leaves. 'Frühlingsmorgen' is best known of several German hybrids; tall, arching bush bears large, single yellow flowers edged cherry pink and centered with maroon stamens. 'Golden Wings' makes a 6-ft. bush that flowers throughout the growing season; 4-in. blossoms are single, light yellow with red stamens.

R. wichuraiana. MEMORIAL ROSE. Vine. All zones; evergreen or partially evergreen in Zones 4–24. Trailing stems grow 10–12 ft. long in one season, root in contact with moist soil. Leaves 2–4 in. long, with five to nine smooth, shiny ¼–1-in. leaflets. Midsummer flowers are white, to 2 in. across, in clusters of six to ten. Good ground cover, even in relatively poor soil. Wichuraiana ramblers, produced in the first 20 years of this century, are group of hybrids between the species and various garden roses. Pink 'Dorothy Perkins' and red 'Excelsa' produce smothering spring displays of small, formless flowers that obscure the often-mildewed leaves. Larger, better-shaped flowers and glossy, healthier leaves are found in 'Albéric Barbier', creamy white; 'François Juranville', coral pink; 'Gardenia', light yellow; 'Paul Transon', coppery salmon; and 'Sander's White Rambler', white.

Rosaceae. The rose family contains an immense number of plants of horticultural importance. In addition to roses, family members include strawberries, bramble fruits, many flowering and fruiting trees, *Photinia*, *Pyracantha*, and *Spiraea*, as well as other ornamental trees, shrubs, and perennials.

ROSMARINUS officinalis

ROSEMARY

Lamiaceae (Labiatae)

EVERGREEN SHRUB, HERB

ZONES 4–24

FULL SUN

LITTLE OR NO WATER ONCE ESTABLISHED

Rosmarinus officinalis

Rugged, picturesque, to 2–6 ft. high. Narrow, aromatic leaves glossy dark green above, grayish white beneath. Small clusters of light lavender blue, ¼–½-in. flowers in winter, spring; bloom occasionally repeats in fall. 'Albus' has white flowers. Flowers attract birds, bees. Leaves widely used as seasoning.

Endures hot sun and poor soil, but good drainage is a must. Feeding and excess water result in rank growth, subsequent woodiness. Control growth by frequent tip pinching when plants are small. Prune older plants lightly; cut to side branch or shear.

Some taller varieties are useful as clipped hedges or in dry borders with native and gray-leafed plants. Greatest use for lower-growing varieties is as ground or bank covers. Set container-grown plants or rooted cuttings 2 ft. apart for moderately quick cover. Feed lightly, thin occasionally, and head back gently to encourage new growth. Useful in erosion control. Names are often mixed. Shop nurseries carefully and select plants that seem to fit your landscaping needs.

> ### ROSEMARY'S GREATEST ATTRIBUTE: ITS TOUGHNESS
> This popular Mediterranean native tolerates a wide range of growing conditions; it endures both hot sun and cool ocean spray and survives temperatures down to around 15°F. It thrives without irrigation, but in hot interiors sprinkle it occasionally to keep it looking fresh.

'Collingwood Ingram' *(R. ingramii)*. To 2–2½ ft. tall, spreading to 4 ft. or more. Branches curve gracefully. Flowers rich, bright blue violet. Tallish bank or ground cover with high color value.

'Corsican Prostrate'. Arching, spreading, 1–1½ ft., with dark blue flowers.

'Huntington Blue' ('Huntington Carpet'). Grows to 1½ ft. tall, spreads quickly yet maintains dense center. Pale blue flowers.

'Ken Taylor'. Resembles 'Collingwood Ingram' but lower growing, with greater tendency to trail.

'Lockwood de Forest' *(R. lockwoodii, R. forrestii)*. Resembles 'Prostratus', but has lighter, bright foliage and bluer flowers.

'Majorca Pink'. Erect shrub to 2–4 ft. with lavender pink flowers.

'Miss Jessup's Upright'. Erect plant to 4 ft. with violet blue flowers.

'Prostratus'. DWARF ROSEMARY. To 2 ft. tall with 4–8-ft. spread. Will trail over wall or edge of raised bed to make curtain of green. Pale lavender blue flowers.

'Tuscan Blue'. Rigid, upright branches to 6 ft. tall or taller grow directly from base of plant. Leaves are rich green, flowers blue violet. Makes an attractive tall, narrow screen.

Rubiaceae. This widespread and varied family contains herbs, shrubs, and trees with opposite or whorled leaves and (usually) clustered flowers. Among its members are *Bouvardia*, *Coffea* (coffee), *Gardenia*, and *Galium*.

RUBUS

BRAMBLE

Rosaceae

DECIDUOUS, EVERGREEN SHRUBS, GROUND COVERS

ZONES VARY BY SPECIES

FULL SUN OR LIGHT SHADE

INFREQUENT WATER

Rubus deliciosus

Best known for edible members blackberry and raspberry (see separate entries), the brambles include many ornamental plants, most of them without prickles or thorns.

R. deliciosus. ROCKY MOUNTAIN THIMBLEBERRY, BOULDER RASPBERRY. Deciduous shrub. Zones 1–5, 10. Graceful plant with arching, thornless branches; reaches 3–5 ft. Leaves bright green, nearly round, lobed. Flowers, 2–3 in. across, look like single white roses. May–June bloom. Fruit attracts birds. Good drainage, dryish soil. A hybrid between this species and *R. trilobus* is *R. tridel* 'Benenden', a large (8–10-ft.) shrub with arching branches and 2–3-in. white flowers.

R. pentalobus (R. calycinoides, R. fockeanus). Evergreen shrub, ground cover. Zones 4–6, 14–17. Creeping stems make a mat that spreads 1 ft. a year. Densely packed green leaves, ruffled, nearly round, 1½ in. across, look crinkled on upper surface, felty beneath. Some leaves turn red or bronze in winter or in full sun, greening again in moderate weather. Small white flowers resemble strawberry flowers; salmon-colored berries are edible. Plant needs good drainage and average soil. Use as an attractive ground cover or grow in a rock garden. Has some drought resistance, but stressed plants in full, hot sun will look unhappy. 'Emerald Carpet' is the selection usually seen.

RUDBECKIA

Asteraceae (Compositae)

PERENNIALS AND BIENNIALS

ALL ZONES

FULL SUN

MODERATE WATER

Rudbeckia hirta

Garden rudbeckias are descendants of wild plants from eastern United States. All are tough, easy-to-grow plants that thrive in any except soggy soils. Showy flowers are good for cutting and brighten summer and autumn borders.

R. fulgida. Perennials up to 3 ft. tall with branching stems and 5-in. leaves. Tough plants for summer bloom. 'Goldsturm' has 3-in. black-eyed Susan flowers.

R. hirta. GLORIOSA DAISY, BLACK-EYED SUSAN. Biennial or short-lived perennial; can be grown as annual, blooming first summer from seed sown in early spring. To 3–4 ft., with upright branching habit, rough, hairy stems and leaves. Daisylike single flowers 2–4 in. across, with orange-yellow rays and black-purple center.

Gloriosa Daisy strain has single daisies 5–7 in. wide in shades of yellow, orange, russet, or mahogany, often zoned or banded. 'Irish Eyes' has golden yellow flowers with light green centers that turn brown as they mature. 'Pinwheel' has mahogany-and-gold flowers. Gloriosa Double Daisy strain has somewhat smaller (to 4½-in.) double flower heads, nearly all in lighter yellow and orange shades. 'Marmalade' (2 ft.) and 'Goldilocks' (8–10 in.) are lower growing, can be used at front of border or as ground cover.

R. laciniata 'Hortensia'. GOLDEN GLOW. Perennial to 6–7 ft. tall. Spreads (sometimes aggressively) by underground stems. Leaves deeply lobed, light green. Flowers (summer and fall) double, bright yellow. Tolerates heat remarkably well. Good summer screen or tall border plant. Does not seed but spreads rapidly and is easily divided. Spray to control aphids. Variety 'Goldquelle' grows to 2½ ft., is less aggressive.

R. purpurea. See Echinacea

RUE. See RUTA graveolens	**p. 470**

RUELLIA

Acanthaceae
EVERGREEN SHRUBS
☘ ZONES VARY BY SPECIES
☼ ◐ FULL SUN OR LIGHT SHADE
○ ◐ ● WATER NEEDS VARY BY SPECIES

Ruellia peninsularis

Although some ruellias are hardy or tender perennials, most of those grown in the West are shrubs with opposite leaves and flaring bell-shaped flowers with five shallow lobes.

R. brittoniana. Zones 8, 9, 14–24. Mexican shrubby perennial naturalized in parts of the United States. To 3 ft., with narrow leaves and 2-in. blue flowers. 'Katie' is a dwarf (10–12 in.) herbaceous variety. Prefers sun and regular water.

R. californica. Zones 12, 13. Evergreen shrub 2–4 ft. tall with deep purple flowers following spring and summer rains. Drops leaves in cold spells or after protracted dry periods. Needs ample water until established, then little or no summer irrigation.

R. macrantha. Zones 21–24. Evergreen shrub to 3 ft. with paired dark green 4-in. oval leaves and clusters of 3–4 in. rose pink flowers with deeper pink veining. Sun or light shade, with regular water. Best as a container plant to be sheltered during frosty weather.

R. peninsularis. Zones 12, 13. Very similar to *R. californica* but with somewhat larger flowers. Both will drop leaves in sharp frosts, but can survive 20–25°F. Little summer water once established.

RUMOHRA adiantiformis

LEATHERLEAF FERN
Polypodiaceae
FERN
☘ ZONES 14–17, 19–24
☼ ◐ FULL SUN OR PARTIAL SHADE
● MODERATE WATER

Rumohra adiantiformis

Fronds are deep glossy green, triangular, finely cut, to 3 ft. tall. They are firm in texture and last well in arrangements. Hardy to 24°F. Usually sold as *Aspidium capense*.

RUPTURE WORT. See HERNIARIA glabra	**p. 321**

RUSCUS

BUTCHER'S BROOM
Liliaceae
EVERGREEN SHRUBLETS
☘ ZONES 4–24
◐ ● BEST IN SHADE; TOLERATE SOME SUN
○ ● TOLERATE ARIDITY OR REGULAR WATER

Ruscus hypoglossum

Unusual leafless plants with some value as small-scale ground cover, curiosity, or source of dry arrangement material and Christmas greens. Flattened leaflike branches do work of leaves and bear tiny greenish white flowers in centers of upper surfaces. If male and female plants are present, or if you have plant with male and female flowers, bright red (sometimes yellow), marble-size fruit follows flowers. Plants spread by underground stems. Tolerate competition from tree roots. Subject to chlorosis in desert.

R. aculeatus. To 1–4 ft. tall with branched stems. Spine-tipped "leaves" are 1–3 in. long, a third as wide, leathery, dull dark green. Fruit ½ in. across, red or yellow.

R. hypoglossum. To 1½ ft.; unbranched stems. "Leaves" to 4 in. long, 1½ in. wide, glossy green, not spine tipped. Fruit ¼–½ in. across. Spreads faster than *R. aculeatus*. Superior as small-scale ground cover.

RUSSELIA equisetiformis

CORAL FOUNTAIN
Scrophulariaceae
PERENNIAL
☘ ZONES 19–24; OR INDOORS
☼ ● SHELTERED LOCATION
● KEEP SOIL MOIST

Russelia equisetiformis

Hardy to about 32°F. Shrubby plant with trailing, bright green, practically leafless stems that look attractive spilling from a wall or hanging basket; stems can also be fastened to a trellis or wall. Many side branches bear a profusion of bright red, narrowly tubular flowers that look like little firecrackers; bloom lasts all spring and summer outdoors, goes on continuously in house or greenhouse. Needs regular fertilizing. Easy to propagate with pencil-size cuttings taken in spring.

RUSSIAN OLIVE. See ELAEAGNUS angustifolia	**p. 271**
RUSSIAN SAGE. See PEROVSKIA atriplicifolia	**p. 412**
RUTABAGA. See TURNIP and RUTABAGA	**p. 514**

Rutaceae. The rue family includes, besides rue (*Ruta*), a large number of perennials, shrubs, and trees, most important of which are the citrus clan. Most members of the family have oil glands in leaves or other plant parts and are aromatic. *Boronia*, *Choisya*, *Coleonema*, *Geijera*, and *Skimmia* are other important members.

RUTA graveolens

RUE, HERB-OF-GRACE
Rutaceae
PERENNIAL HERB
☘ ALL ZONES
☼ FULL SUN
○ ● LITTLE TO MODERATE WATER

Ruta graveolens

Aromatic, fernlike blue-green leaves; small, greenish yellow flowers; decorative brown seed capsules 2–3 ft. Rue is accorded herb status for its history and legend rather than for any use. It was once thought to ward off disease, to guard against poisons, and to aid the sight. It was also used to make brushes for sprinkling holy water.

Sow seeds in flats; transplant to 1 ft. apart. Good garden soil with additions of lime to strongly acid soil. Plant at back of border. Dry seed clusters for use in wreaths or swags. 'Jackman's Blue' is dense, compact, and fine gray blue in color. 'Blue Mound' and 'Curly Girl' are more compact.

RYEGRASS. See LOLIUM   p. 360

SABAL

PALMETTO
Arecaceae (Palmae)
PALMS
✎ ZONES 12–17, 19–24
☼ FULL SUN
◗ MODERATE WATER

Sabal palmetto

Native from North Carolina to South America. Large, slow-growing fan palms, some with trunks, some without. Large clusters of inconspicuous flowers appear among leaves when plants are mature. Hardy, withstanding 20–22°F, some even lower temperatures.

S. blackburniana (S. domingensis, S. umbraculifera). HISPANIOLAN PALMETTO. Largest palmetto, ultimately 80 ft. or more, with immense green fans 9 ft. across.

S. mexicana (S. texana). OAXACA PALMETTO. Leaf stems hang on trunk in early life, then fall to show attractive, slender trunk. Grows 30–50 ft. high.

S. minor. Leafy green palm, usually trunkless, but sometimes with trunk to 6 ft. Old leaves fold at base, hang down like closed umbrella.

S. palmetto. CABBAGE PALM. Also grows in Zone 10. Trunk grows slowly to 20 ft., much taller in its native southeastern states. Big (5–8-ft.) green leaves grow in dense, globular head.

SAFFLOWER. See CARTHAMUS tinctorius   p. 208

SAGE. See SALVIA   p. 473

SAGE, RUSSIAN. See PEROVSKIA   p. 412

SAGEBRUSH. See ARTEMISIA tridentata   p. 166

SAGINA subulata

IRISH MOSS, SCOTCH MOSS
Caryophyllaceae
PERENNIAL
✎ ZONES 1–11, 14–24
☼ ☽ FULL SUN OR PARTIAL SHADE
◗ REGULAR WATER

Sagina subulata

Of two different plants of similar appearance, *Sagina subulata* is the more common. The other is *Arenaria verna*, usually called *A. v. caespitosa*. Both make dense, compact, mosslike masses of slender leaves on slender stems. But *A. verna* has tiny white flowers in few-flowered clusters, while *S. subulata* bears flowers singly and differs in other technical details. In common usage, however, green forms of the two species are called Irish moss, and golden green forms (*A. v.* 'Aurea' and *S. s.* 'Aurea') are called Scotch moss.

Both *Sagina* and *Arenaria* are grown primarily as ground covers for limited areas. They're useful for filling gaps between paving blocks. In cool coastal gardens, they can seed themselves and become pests.

Although they look like moss, these plants won't grow well under conditions that suit true mosses. They need good soil, good drainage, and

occasional feeding with slow-acting, nonburning fertilizer. They take some foot traffic and tend to hump up in time; control humping by occasionally cutting out narrow strips, then pressing or rolling lightly. Control snails, slugs, cutworms. Cut squares from flats and set 6 in. apart for fast cover. To avoid lumpiness, plant so that soil line of squares is at or slightly below planted soil surface.

SAGO PALM. See CYCAS revoluta   p. 253

SAGUARO. See CARNEGIEA gigantea   p. 207

ST. AUGUSTINE GRASS. See STENOTAPHRUM secundatum   p. 493

ST. CATHERINE'S LACE. See ERIOGONUM giganteum   p. 278

SAINTPAULIA ionantha

AFRICAN VIOLET
Gesneriaceae
EVERGREEN PERENNIAL HOUSE PLANT
☼ ● FILTERED EARLY SUN, BRIGHT INDIRECT LIGHT
◖◗ WATERING IS AN ART; SEE BELOW

Saintpaulia ionantha

Probably most popular house plant in the United States. Fuzzy, heart-shaped leaves with smooth edges grow in rosettes up to 1 ft. wide. Pale lavender flowers grow in clusters of three or more. Hybrids and named varieties have leaves that are plain or scalloped, green or variegated; flowers are purple, violet, pink, white, or bicolored. Keep where temperatures average 60–70°F. Preferably humidity should be high; if house air is quite dry, increase humidity around plants by setting each plant on a saucer filled with wet gravel.

African violets won't take just any potting mix. They need acid conditions (use plenty of leaf mold); suitable soil conditioner such as builder's sand or vermiculite; good loam (preferably sterilized if you use garden soil); and small amount of slow-acting fertilizer such as bone meal or manure. One good mix is 3 parts leaf mold, 1 part loam, ½ part builder's sand, and small amount of bone meal. Don't use too large a pot—African violets bloom best when roots are crowded.

Water plants from top or below, but avoid watering crown or leaves. Wick-irrigated pots work well. Use water at room temperature or slightly warmer, wet soil thoroughly, let potting mixture become dry to the touch before watering again. Don't let water stand in pot saucers for more than 2 hours after watering plants. If plant is well established, feed—only when soil is moist—with slightly acid fertilizer once every 2–4 weeks. Propagate from seeds, leaf cuttings, or divisions. Most common pests are aphids, cyclamen mites, thrips, and mealybugs. Keep spent leaves and flowers plucked off.

SALAL. See GAULTHERIA shallon   p. 303

Salicaceae. The willow family consists of deciduous trees or shrubs with flowers in catkins and (generally) with silk-tufted seeds that blow about. Cottonwood, poplar, and willow are examples.

SALIX

WILLOW
Salicaceae
DECIDUOUS TREES OR SHRUBS
✎ ALL ZONES
☼ FULL SUN
◖◗ LOTS OF WATER

Salix babylonica

Fast growing. Will take any soil; most kinds will even tolerate poor drainage. All have invasive roots and are hard to garden under. Most are subject to tent caterpillars, aphids, borers, and spider mites.

Weeping willows are best used as single trees near stream or lake. With training, they can become satisfactory shade trees for patio or terrace. All leaf out very early in spring, hold leaves late (until Christmas in milder climates).

Shrubby willows are grown principally for their catkins ("pussy willows") or colored twigs, as screen plants, or for erosion control on stream or riverbanks. For this last purpose varieties native to the region are best.

The many species hybridize readily; as a result, names are much confused in the nursery trade.

S. alba tristis (S. babylonica aurea, S. 'Niobe'). GOLDEN WEEPING WILLOW. Tree. To 80 ft. or more, with greater spread. One-year-old twigs are bright yellow, quite pendulous. Leaves are bright green or yellow green, paler beneath. This tree is also known as *S. pendulina* and is considered a hybrid.

Left to go its own way, this (and other weeping willows) will head too low to furnish usable shade. Stake up main stem and keep it staked—right up to 15–18 ft. Shorten side branches and remove them as they lose their vigor; keep early growth directed into a tall main stem and high-branching scaffold limbs. This treatment will make a tree you can walk under. Subject to twig blight in Northwest; use copper spray on new foliage. Texas root rot a problem in desert.

S. alba vitellina is an upright form with brilliant yellow winter twigs. Hard pruning will keep tree size down and yield an abundance of twigs for winter color.

S. babylonica. WEEPING WILLOW. Tree. To 30–50 ft. with equal or greater spread. Smaller than golden weeping willow, with longer (3–6-in.) leaves and even more pronounced weeping habit. Greenish or brown branchlets. Train to be full-fledged weeper as described for *S. alba tristis*.

Variety 'Crispa' ('Annularis'), ringleaf or corkscrew willow, is an interesting oddity with leaves twisted and curled into rings or circles. It is somewhat narrower in spread than the species.

S. blanda (S. pendulina blanda). WISCONSIN WEEPING WILLOW. Tree. To 40–50 ft. or more, spreading wider. Less strongly weeping habit than *S. babylonica;* leaves broader, more bluish green. Fan giant blue weeping willow is resistant to borers and blight.

S. caprea. FRENCH PUSSY WILLOW, PINK PUSSY WILLOW. Shrub or small tree. To 25 ft. Broad leaves 3–6 in. long, dark green above, gray and hairy beneath. Fat, inch-long, pinkish gray, woolly catkins before leaves in early spring. Forces easily indoors and can be cut for winter arrangements. For large gardens that can spare room for unusual shrubs, or for naturalizing. Can be kept to shrub size by cutting to ground every few years. The variety 'Pendula', the Kilmarnock willow, is a small (to 8 ft.) tree with branches that trail to the ground.

S. discolor. PUSSY WILLOW. Shrub or small tree. To 20 ft., with slender, red-brown stems and bright green, 2–4-in.-long, oval leaves, bluish beneath. Catkins of male plants (usually the only kind sold) are the feature attraction—soft, silky, pearl gray, and up to 1½ in. long. Branches can be cut in winter for early bouquets.

S. gracilistyla. ROSE-GOLD PUSSY WILLOW. Upright spreading shrub. To 6–10 ft. tall; 2–4-in.-long, ½–1¼-in.-wide leaves are gray-green above, bluish green beneath. Plump, 1½-in.-long, furry gray catkins show numerous stamens with rose and gold anthers. Good-looking in garden or in arrangements. Cutting branches for indoor use will help curb shrub size; every 3 or 4 years, cut back whole plant to short stubs. You'll be rewarded by especially vigorous shoots with large catkins. *S. g. melanostachys* has black catkins with red anthers—weird but attractive in arrangements.

S. matsudana. HANKOW WILLOW. Tree. Upright, pyramidal growth to 40–50 ft. Leaves narrow, bright green, 2–4 in. long, ½ in. wide. Can thrive on less water than most willows. This plant and its varieties are popular in high desert.

S. m. 'Navajo'. GLOBE NAVAJO WILLOW. Large, spreading, round-topped tree to 70 ft. tall, equally wide. Tough and hardy.

S. m. 'Tortuosa'. TWISTED HANKOW WILLOW, CORKSCREW WILLOW. To 30 ft. high, with 20-ft. spread. Branches and branchlets fantastically twisted into upright, spiraling patterns, attractive in summer and showy even in winter. Use for silhouette value; cut branches good in arrangements.

S. m. 'Umbraculifera'. GLOBE WILLOW. To 35 ft. with equal spread. Round, umbrella-shaped head with upright branches, drooping branchlets.

S. purpurea. PURPLE OSIER, ALASKA BLUE WILLOW. Shrub. Grows to 10–18 ft. high with purple branches and dark green, 1–3-in.-long leaves that are markedly bluish underneath. Variety 'Gracilis' ('Nana'), dwarf purple osier, often seen in cold-winter regions, has slimmer branches and narrower leaves; it is usually grown as clipped hedge and kept 1–3 ft. high and equally wide. General effect is fine textured; color effect blue gray. Grows easily from cuttings. Good background plant.

S. udensis (S. sachalinensis 'Sekka'). Shrub or small tree. Leaves 2–4 in. long, ½ in. wide, green above, silvery beneath. Catkins silvery, up to 2 in. long. Big feature: flattened branches often 1–2 in. wide, twisted and curled, picturesque in arrangements.

SALPIGLOSSIS sinuata

PAINTED TONGUE
Solanaceae
SUMMER ANNUAL
✓ ALL ZONES
☼ FULL SUN
◖ MODERATE WATER

Salpiglossis sinuata

Upright, open habit, to 2–3 ft. tall. Sticky leaves and stems. Leaves to 4 in. long, narrowly oblong. Flowers much like petunias in shape and size (2–2½ in. wide), but more unusual in color—shades of mahogany red, reddish orange, yellow, purple and pink tones, marbled and penciled with contrasting color. Bolero (2 ft.), Friendship (15 in.), and Splash (2 ft.) are compact strains.

Best in rich soil; don't overwater. Pinch out tips of growing plants to induce branching. Best bloom in late spring and early summer, but plants will endure until frost. Good background plant for border; handsome cut flowers.

THE SEEDS NEED BABYING

Salpiglossis seeds are rather difficult to start, especially when sown directly in a garden bed. In late winter or early spring, plant in potting mixture in peat pots, several seeds to a pot. Keep in a warm, protected location; seeds should sprout in 7–10 days. Thin to one seedling per pot. Later, when young plants are well established and all danger of frost is past, plant in a sunny location.

SALSIFY

OYSTER PLANT
Asteraceae (Compositae)
HARDY BIENNIAL
✓ ALL ZONES
☼ FULL SUN
◖◖ MOIST SOIL

Salsify

Grown for its edible root, which looks something like parsnip and has creamy white flesh that tastes a little like oysters. Plant grows to 4 ft. tall; leaves are narrow, grasslike. Plant in rich, deep, sandy soil, spaded deep. Culture is same as for parsnips. It takes 150 days to grow to maturity. Cooked, mashed salsify, mixed with butter and beaten egg, can be made into patties and sautéed until brown to make mock oysters. If plant is allowed to overwinter, it will produce flower stalk topped by large head of lavender purple, dandelionlike flowers followed by white, cottony seeds.

SALVIA

SAGE

Lamiaceae (Labiatae)

ANNUALS, PERENNIALS, SHRUBS

🌡 ZONES VARY BY SPECIES

☼ MOST ENJOY FULL SUN

💧 MOST LIKE ARIDITY

▶ SEE CHART NEXT PAGE

Salvia officinalis

The sages, along with the grasses, became horticultural stars in the 1980s and 1990s. Botanical gardens and collectors have introduced scores of new species and selections from Mexico, South America, Eurasia, and Africa, along with superior forms of our native western species.

Some are annual bedding plants, others are border perennials, while still others serve as shrubs or ground cover. Flower colors range from white and yellow through pink to scarlet, from pale lavender to true blue and dark purple. What they have in common is a floral arrangement in which whorls of two-lipped flowers are either distinctly spaced along the flower stalks or so tightly crowded they appear as one dense spike. Inflorescences in some species are branched. Many are aromatic, some sweetly so, others flavorful, like garden sage. Some are strongly scented.

At least 60 species and an additional 40 to 50 selections are grown in the West. The chart on pages 474 and 475 lists 55 of the best.

SAMBUCUS

ELDERBERRY

Caprifoliaceae

DECIDUOUS SHRUBS OR TREES

🌡 ZONES VARY BY SPECIES

☼ ◑ SUN OR LIGHT SHADE

💧 MODERATE WATER

☠ BERRIES OF S. CALLICARPA ARE POISONOUS

Sambucus mexicana

In their natural state, these western natives are rampant, fast growing, wild looking. But they can be tamed to a degree. Use them in same way as spiraea or other large deciduous shrubs. In large gardens, they can be effective as screen or windbreak. To keep them dense and shrubby, prune hard every dormant season. New growth sprouts readily from stumps.

Elders are a confusing lot, and botanists in different regions tend to assign different names to the same plant. There are black-, blue-, and red-fruited elders; birds eat the fruit of all types, but red elderberries can cause nausea in humans if consumed raw in large quantities.

S. callicarpa (S. racemosa callicarpa). COAST RED ELDERBERRY, RED ELDERBERRY. Zones 4–7, 14–17. Native to coastal regions, Northern California to British Columbia. Shrub to 8 ft. or small tree to 20 ft. Leaves 3–6 in. long, divided into five to seven smooth, sharply toothed leaflets. Flowers creamy white, in dome-shaped clusters 2–5 in. across.

S. canadensis. AMERICAN ELDERBERRY. Zones 1–7, 14–17. Spreading, suckering shrub to 6–8 ft., seldom grown except in cold-winter climates. Almost tropical looking in foliage, each leaf having seven leaflets up to 6 in. long. Flat, creamy white flower clusters to 10 in. wide in summer are followed by purple-black fruit of good flavor. Fruit used for pies; both flowers and fruit used for wine. Needs hard pruning each year. In March, cut back all last year's growth to a few inches. Named fruiting varieties include 'Adams', 'Johns', and many more. Plant any two varieties for pollination.

Ornamental varieties include 'Aurea', with golden green foliage, golden in full sun; and 'Laciniata', cutleaf or fernleaf elder, with finely cut foliage.

S. mexicana (S. caerulea, S. glauca). BLUE ELDERBERRY. All zones. Native from California north to British Columbia, east to Rockies. Shrub 4–10 ft. tall or spreading tree to 50 ft. Leaves 5–8 in. long, divided into five to nine rather firm, toothed, 1–6-in.-long leaflets. Small white or creamy white flowers in flat-topped clusters 2–8 in. wide, April–August. Clusters of blue to nearly black, ¼-in. berries, usually covered with whitish powder. Berries edible, often used in jams, jellies, pies, and wine—if birds don't get them first. Forms from Southern California and desert states have fewer leaflets of grayer green, and berries are fewer, smaller, drier.

S. pubens. Zones 1–3. Shrubby, usually 2–4 ft. tall, possibly to 15 ft. Loose, tall flower clusters followed by bright red fruit later in season.

S. racemosa. RED ELDERBERRY, EUROPEAN RED ELDERBERRY. Zones 1–3. Native to northern latitudes in North America, Europe, Asia. Bushy shrub 8–10 ft. tall; leaves 3–6 in. long, divided into five or seven smooth, sharply toothed leaflets. Small, creamy white flowers in dome-shaped clusters to 2½ in. wide, May–July, followed by bright red berries. Golden variety with finely divided leaves is called 'Plumosa Aurea'.

SANGUINARIA canadensis

BLOODROOT

Papaveraceae

PERENNIAL

🌡 ZONES 1–6

● SHADE

💧 NEEDS DAMPNESS

Sanguinaria canadensis

This member of the poppy family gets its common name because of the orange-red juice that seeps from cut roots and stems. Big, deeply lobed grayish leaves. In early spring, 1½-in., white or pink-tinged flowers are borne singly on 8-in. stalks. For damp, shaded rock garden where it can spread. 'Multiplex' has double flowers.

SANSEVIERIA trifasciata

BOWSTRING HEMP, SNAKE PLANT, MOTHER-IN-LAW'S TONGUE

Agavaceae

EVERGREEN PERENNIAL

🌡 ZONES 13–24; PROTECTED LOCATIONS ZONE 12

◑ SHELTER FROM MIDDAY SUN

💧 INFREQUENT, DEEP WATERING

House plant everywhere. Often sold as *S. zeylanica*. Appreciated for thick, patterned leaves that grow in rosettes from thick rhizomes. Leaves 1–4 ft. tall, 2 in. wide, rigidly upright or spreading slightly at top, dark green banded gray-green. *S. t.* 'Laurentii' is identical, but with broad, creamy yellow stripes on leaf edges. Dwarf 'Hahnii' has rosettes of 6-in.-long, broad, triangular leaves, dark green with silvery banding. Plant piles up to make mass 1 ft. tall and wide. Good small potted plant or focus for dish garden.

Sansevieria trifasciata 'Laurentii'

▶ page 476

SALVIA

NAME, TYPE	ZONES	GROWTH HABIT	FLOWERS	COMMENTS
Salvia argentea SILVER SAGE Biennial	All zones	Flat 1-ft. rosette of white, furry, 6–8-in.-long leaves	Branched flowering stems to 4 ft., white, tinged pink or yellow	Use at front of border for striking foliage
S. azurea grandiflora **(S. pitcheri)** Perennial	1–11, 14–24	To 5 ft., with smooth or hairy 2–4-in. leaves	Gentian blue, ½-in. long, provide mass of color, summer to frost	Not always permanent in wet winters
S. blepharophylla Shrubby perennial	14–24	Mounding, spreading by underground stems, to 1½ ft. tall	Brilliant red, nearly everblooming	Provides midheight mass of color over a long period
S. cacaliifolia Perennial	14–24	Sprawling, to 3 ft. tall, much wider	Branching narrow clusters of pure blue, spring to fall	Appreciates some shade, ample water
S. chamaedryoides Perennial	8, 9, 14–24	Low, mounding, spreading by underground runners	Small silvery foliage mass a backdrop for bright blue flowers	Endures some aridity
S. clevelandii Shrub	10–24	Rounded shrub to 4 ft. Gray-green foliage has marvelous fragrance	Flowers lavender blue, in tall, open spires, fragrant, May–Aug.	Takes aridity. Look for choice compact named selections such as 'Allen Chickering' and 'Winifred Gillman'
S. coccinea Perennial, but usually a self-seeding annual	14–24	Bushy, to 2–3 ft., with dark green furry leaves	Flowers red, in 4-in spikes spring to fall	'Brenthurst' is a pink form
S. elegans PINEAPPLE SAGE Perennial	8–24	To 2–3 ft., light green leaves with fruity scent and taste	Red flowers in short spikes, autumn	Use leaves in cool drinks, fruit salads
S. farinacea MEALY-CUP SAGE Perennial grown as annual	All zones	Fast growth to 2–3 ft., grayish green leaves	Spikes of small blue flowers overtop mound	'Mina' (12 in.) and 'Victoria' (18 in.) are dwarfs
S. greggii AUTUMN SAGE Shrub	8–24	Erect, bushy, to 3–4 ft., with medium green leaves	Flowers in many colors—yellow to red to purple—late spring, summer; fall and winter in desert	Needs no irrigation near coast. Needs light shade, some water inland
S. guaranitica Shrubby perennial	8, 9, 14–24	Bushy, spreading, to 5 ft. tall, with dark green 5-in. leaves	Dark blue 2-in. flowers in 10-in. spikes summer to fall	Lush plant likes some shade, water. 'Argentina Skies' has pale blue flowers. Grow as an annual in colder climates
S. involucrata Shrubby perennial	8–24	Large plant (6 by 6 ft.), with dense foliage of velvety leaves	Foot-long clusters of rose pink flowers late summer, fall	For large gardens. Sun or light shade
S. leucantha MEXICAN BUSH SAGE Shrub	10–24	To 3–4 ft., with graceful arching stems, grayish green foliage	Long velvety purple spikes set with small white flowers arch outward summer and fall	Takes some aridity, sun or light shade. Cut old stems to the ground. Purple and pink forms exist
S. leucophylla PURPLE SAGE Shrub	8, 9, 14–17, 19–24	Erect or spreading shrub to 3–4 ft. tall, much wider, with white, woolly leaves	Summer flowers pink in long, open clusters	Chaparral plant; needs no irrigation once established. Use as bank cover. Selected forms are 'Point Sal' and 'Figueroa'
S. microphylla **(S. grahamii)** Shrub	8, 9, 14–24	Somewhat open, rounded shrub 3–5 ft. tall	Bright red flowers in 4–6-in. clusters	Bloom can be continuous in mild climates
S. muelleri Shrub	8, 9, 14–24	Resembles *S. greggii*, but lower, with narrow leaves	Short clusters of purple flowers spring–fall, longer in mild areas	Uses as in *S. greggii*
S. nemorosa Perennial	All zones	Narrow, erect plant to 3 ft. with narrow, 4-in. roughish leaves	Violet blue flowers in narrow spikes above foliage	Species rarely seen. 'East Friesland', 2½ ft., widely available. Pink flowering 'Rose Queen' is even lower, not so vigorous.

S

SALVIA

NAME, TYPE	ZONES	GROWTH HABIT	FLOWERS	COMMENTS
S. officinalis COMMON SAGE Perennial	All zones	To 2½ ft., with aromatic wrinkled gray-green leaves	Flowers blue, in short spikes above the foliage	All varieties good for seasoning. 'Berggarten', nonflowering, has biggest leaves, is longest lived; colored varieties are 'Icterina', yellow and green leaves; 'Purpurascens', purplish tints; and 'Tricolor', gray, white, and purplish pink. 'Nana' is a dwarf
S. patens GENTIAN SAGE Perennial	14–24	To 2–3 ft., compact, with large, long-stalked leaves	Flowers 2 in. long, pure blue, in clusters to 16 in. long	Perennial only in warm, well-drained sites. Grow as annual elsewhere
S. recognita Shrubby perennial	7–24	Leaves to 5 in. long, foliage mass low, gray-green	Flowers pink, atop 30–36-in. stalks	Summer bloom
S. regla Shrub	14–24	To 5 ft., possibly more, with bright green leaves	Flowers downy, 2 in. long, bright red or orange-red, with persistent orange calyx, spring through fall	'Huntington' form 3–4 ft. tall; 'Royal' much taller
S. roemeriana Perennial	8–24	Dense clump with soft 1-in. leaves	Flowers scarlet, in loose clusters on branching 1-ft. stalks, spring to fall	Tolerates sun, shade. Needs moderate water
S. sclarea CLARY Perennial or biennial	All zones	Rough, gray-green, highly aromatic leaves to 8 in. long	Flowers white to lilac in big branching clusters to 3 ft.	'Turkestanica' has pink flower stalks, white and pink flowers
S. sinaloensis Perennial	16, 17, 21 24	Low, spreading, 0–12 in. tall, with purplish tone	Flowers deep blue in short spikes	Rock garden plant. Appreciates shade, water
S. sonomensis Shrubby perennial	7, 14–24	Sprawling, mat-forming plant to 16 in. tall, much wider, with hairy leaves	Flowers lilac to blue in erect clusters	Ground cover for hot, dry banks. No summer water once established. Hard to maintain. Selection 'Dara's Choice', probably a hybrid, is easier
S. splendens SCARLET SAGE Perennial usually grown as annual	All zones	Branched plant 1–3 ft. tall, depending on strain or variety, with bright green foliage	Flowers scarlet, in tall, dense clusters; also available in pink, purple, white, in tall or dwarf strains	Grow from seed or buy young plants from nurseries. Effective with gray foliage
S. superba Perennial	All zones	Erect, branched, 2–3-ft. plants with narrow leaves, narrow erect flower spikes topping each stalk	Flowers violet blue or purple	Closely related to *S. nemorosa*. Plants often sold under either name are 'Blue Hills', dark blue, tall, nearly everblooming; 'Lubeca', tall, early flowering, deep violet; 'May Night', low growing, with deep blue flowers; 'East Friesland' and 'Rose Queen' (see under *S. nemorosa*)
S. uliginosa Perennial	8, 9, 14–24	Clumping plant with erect stems 6–7 ft. tall, with narrow, bright green, highly aromatic leaves	Flowers pale blue and white in erect, branched clusters to 5 in. long. Summer-long bloom. Hummingbird favorite	Plant spreads by rhizomes to make big clumps. Divide from time to time. Much or little summer water
S. verticillata LILAC SAGE Perennial	All zones	Clumps 1½–2 ft. tall composed of broad, hairy, heart-shaped leaves	Branched flower stalks to 2½ ft. carrying purple-blue flowers appear in spring, summer, early fall	Sun or light shade, average water
S. viridis **(S. horminum)** Annual	All zones	Single stemmed or branched plants to 1½ ft. tall	Flowers insignificant, but leaflike bracts in pink, white, or blue are showy. Long-lasting cut flowers fresh or dried	Claryssa is a superior strain

S

First common name comes from use of tough leaf fibers as bowstrings; second comes from leaf banding or mottling, which resembles some snakeskins; third probably comes from toughness of leaves and plants' persistence under neglect. Erect, narrow clusters of greenish white, fragrant flowers seldom appear. Indoors, plant will grow in much or little light, seldom needs repotting, and withstands considerable neglect—dry air, uneven temperatures, and light, capricious watering.

Other *Sansevieria* varieties and species are collectors' items; scores can be found in catalogs of succulent plant dealers.

SANTA BARBARA DAISY. See ERIGERON karvinskianus p. 275

SANTOLINA

Asteraceae (Compositae)

HERBS, EVERGREEN SUBSHRUBS

ALL ZONES

FULL SUN

LITTLE TO NO WATER

Santolina chamaecyparissus

These have attractive foliage, a profusion of little round flower heads, and stout constitutions. Good as ground covers, bank covers, or low clipped hedges. Grow in any soil. Both species are aromatic if bruised, and look best if kept low by pruning. Clip off spent flowers. Cut back in early spring. May die to ground in coldest areas, but roots will live and resume growth.

S. chamaecyparissus. LAVENDER COTTON. Can reach 2 ft., but looks best clipped to 1 ft. or less. Brittle, woody stems densely clothed with rough, finely divided, whitish gray leaves. Bright yellow, buttonlike flower heads in summer on unclipped plants. Plant 3 ft. apart as ground cover, closer as edging for walks, borders, foreground plantings. Replace if woodiness takes over. 'Nana' is a smaller version—1 ft. tall, 2–3 ft. wide.

S. ericoides. Grows 2–2½ ft. tall, with narrow, saw-edged dark green leaves, creamy button flowers at branch ends. 'Lemon Queen' is smaller, with deeper yellow flowers.

S. rosmarinifolius (S. virens). Similar to lavender cotton, but narrower, deep green leaves of striking texture; plants look something like puffs of green smoke. Creamy chartreuse flowers. Faster growing than *S. chamaecyparissus.*

SANVITALIA procumbens

CREEPING ZINNIA

Asteraceae (Compositae)

SUMMER ANNUAL

ALL ZONES

FULL SUN

LITTLE WATER ONCE ESTABLISHED

Sanvitalia procumbens

Not really a zinnia, but looks enough like it to fool most people. Plant grows only 4–6 in. high but spreads or trails 1 ft. or more. Leaves are like miniature (to 2-in.-long) zinnia leaves. Flower heads nearly 1 in. wide, with dark purple-brown centers and bright yellow or orange rays. Bloom lasts from midsummer until frost. Needs good drainage. Sow seeds from mid-March (low desert) to May or even June (where soil is slow to warm up). Good hanging basket or potted plants, temporary fillers in borders, slope and bank covers, edgings. Avoid overhead watering. 'Gold Braid' (yellow) and 'Mandarin Orange' are doubles.

Sapindaceae. The soapberry family contains trees and shrubs with (usually) divided leaves, clustered small flowers (sometimes showy), and fruit that is berrylike, often showy. Some have edible fruit. Examples are *Cupaniopsis, Dodonaea, Koelreuteria,* and *Litchi.*

SAPIUM sebiferum

CHINESE TALLOW TREE

Euphorbiaceae

DECIDUOUS TREE

ZONES 8, 9, 12–16, 18–21

FULL SUN

REGULAR WATER

Sapium sebiferum

To 35 ft. with dense round or conical crown of equal width. Outstanding fall color. Tends toward shrubbiness, multiple trunks, suckering, but easily trained to single trunk. In colder areas, unripened branch tips freeze back each winter; new growth quickly covers damage, but may require thinning. Leaves are poplarlike, roundish, tapering to slender point, light green. Foliage is dense, but general effect is airy; leaves flutter in lightest breeze. Tiny yellowish flowers in spikes at branch tips; fruit small, clustered, grayish white; they are covered by a waxy coating.

Hardy to 10–15°F. Grows in most soils, but does somewhat better in mildly acid conditions. Prune only to correct shape. Stake young plants securely. Good lawn tree or street tree, patio tree or terrace shade tree. Resistant to oak root fungus. Good screening against objectionable view. Gives light to moderate shade.

SHOP FOR SAPIUM FOR FLAMING COLORS

If a sapium tree lives in full sun and gets moderate autumn chill, its foliage can turn to a brilliant, translucent neon red, plum purple, yellow orange, or mixed colors. Select your tree while it is in fall color; some plants may show only an uninteresting purplish or yellow.

SAPONARIA

Caryophyllaceae

PERENNIALS

ZONES VARY BY SPECIES

FULL SUN

INFREQUENT WATER

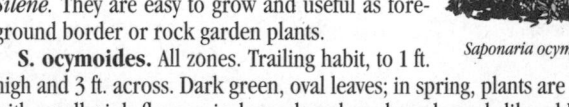

Saponaria ocymoides

The soapworts are generally low-growing perennial plants closely related to *Lychnis* and *Silene.* They are easy to grow and useful as foreground border or rock garden plants.

S. ocymoides. All zones. Trailing habit, to 1 ft. high and 3 ft. across. Dark green, oval leaves; in spring, plants are covered with small pink flowers in loose bunches shaped much like phlox. Any soil; easy to grow. Useful for covering walls and as ground cover.

S. pumilio (S. pumila). Zones 3–7, 14–17. Forms a small, tight cushion with relatively large purplish pink flowers borne singly on branch ends, making a ring of blossom around the base of the plant.

SAPOTE, WHITE. See CASIMIROA edulis p. 209

SARCOCOCCA

Buxaceae

EVERGREEN SHRUBS

ZONES 4–9, 14–24

PREFER SHADE, TAKE SUN ON COAST

LIGHT TO AVERAGE WATERING

Sarcococca ruscifolia

Native to Himalayas, China. Useful in landscaping shaded areas—under overhangs, in

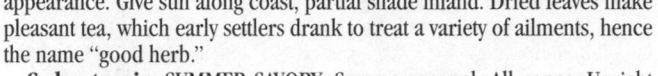

entryways, beneath low-branching, evergreen trees. They maintain slow, orderly growth and polished appearance in deepest shade. Grow best in soil rich in organic matter. Add peat moss, ground bark, or the like to planting bed. Scale insects only pests.

S. confusa. Similar to (and generally sold as) *S. ruscifolia.* However, latter has red fruit, while that of *S. confusa* is black.

S. hookerana humilis (S. humilis). Low growing, seldom more than 1½ ft. high; spreads by underground runners to 8 ft. or more. Dark green, glossy, narrow oval, pointed leaves (1–3 in. long, ½–¾ in. wide) closely set on branches. Tiny, fragrant white flowers, hidden in foliage in early spring, are followed by glossy blue-black fruit. Good ground cover in shade.

S. ruscifolia. Slow growth (6 in. a year) to 4–6 ft., with 3–7-ft. spread. Will form natural espalier against wall, branches fanning out to form dark patterns. Glossy, waxy, deep green, wavy-edged leaves, 2 in. long, densely set on branches. Flowers (in early spring) are small, white, nearly hidden in foliage, but fragrant enough to be smelled many feet away. Flowers are followed by red fruit.

SARGENT CHERRY. See PRUNUS sargentii p. 440

Sarraceniaceae. The pitcher plant family is easily identified by its leaves, which have been modified into hollow structures partially filled with liquid. These trap insects, which contribute to the plant's food supply. An example is *Darlingtonia*.

SASA. See BAMBOO p. 174

SASSAFRAS albidum

SASSAFRAS

Lauraceae

DECIDUOUS TREE

ZONES 3–9, 14–17

FULL SUN

REGULAR WATER

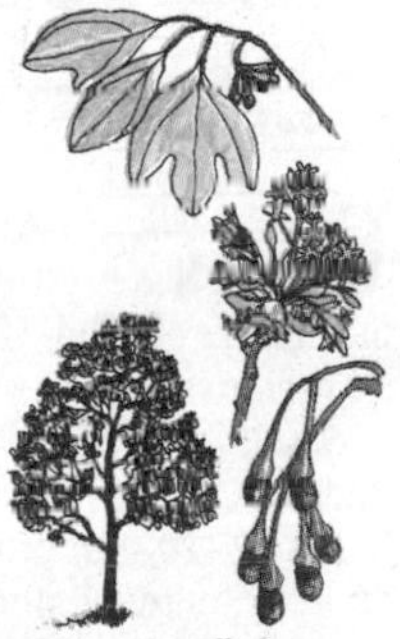

Sassafras albidum

Grows fast to 20–25 ft., then slower to eventual 50–60 ft. Dense and pyramidal, with heavy trunk and rather short branches. Sometimes shrubby. Pleasantly aromatic tree; bark of roots sometimes used for making tea. Leaves 3–7 in. long, 2–4 in. wide; oval, lobed on one side (mitten shaped), or lobed on both sides. Orange and scarlet fall color, better some years than others. Inconspicuous flowers. Best in sandy, well-drained soil; won't take long summer drought or alkaline soil. Hard to transplant. Suckers badly if roots are cut during cultivation.

SATUREJA

Lamiaceae (Labiatae)

ANNUALS OR SHRUBBY PERENNIALS

ZONES VARY BY SPECIES

EXPOSURE NEEDS VARY BY SPECIES

WATER NEEDS VARY BY SPECIES

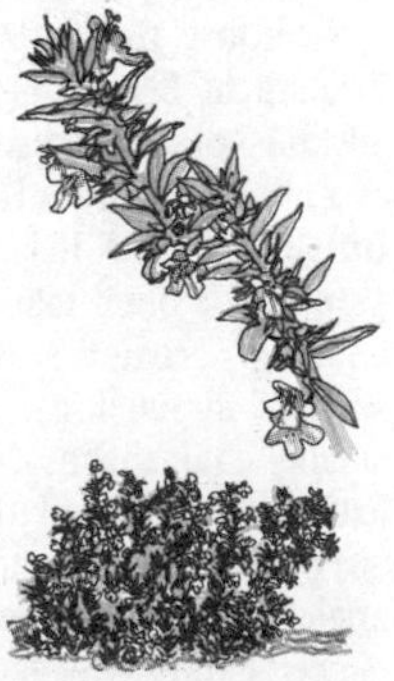

Satureja montana

Two of these aromatic plants serve many culinary purposes while the other has a long reputation as a medicinal or merely refreshing herb.

S. douglasii (Micromeria chamissonis). YERBA BUENA. Creeping perennial. Zones 4–9, 14–24. Native from Los Angeles County to British Columbia. Plant for which San Francisco was given its original name of Yerba Buena. Slender stems root as they grow, spreading to 3 ft. Roundish, 1-in.-long leaves with scalloped edges have strong minty scent. Small white or lavender-tinted flowers April–September. Needs rich, moist soil for best appearance. Give sun along coast, partial shade inland. Dried leaves make pleasant tea, which early settlers drank to treat a variety of ailments, hence the name "good herb."

S. hortensis. SUMMER SAVORY. Summer annual. All zones. Upright to 1½ ft. with loose, open habit. Rather narrow, ½–1½-in.-long, aromatic leaves. Delicate, ⅛-in.-long, pinkish white to rose flowers in whorls. Grow in light soil rich in humus. Full sun. Water moderately. Excellent container plant. Sow seed where plants are to be grown; thin to 1½ ft. apart. Use fresh or dried leaves as mild seasoning for meats, fish, eggs, soups, vegetables; favorite with beans (German name *Bohnenkraut* means "bean herb").

S. montana. WINTER SAVORY. Perennial or subshrub. All zones. Low, spreading, 6–15 in. high. Stiff, narrow to roundish, ½–1-in.-long leaves. Profusion of white to lilac, ⅜-in.-long blooms in whorls, attractive to bees. Grow in sun, in sandy, well-drained soil; give little to moderate water. Keep clipped. Space plants 1½ ft. apart in rows. Use as edging in herb border, or in rock garden. Use aromatic leaves fresh or dried. Clip at start of flowering season for drying. Not as delicate in flavor as summer savory.

SAUROMATUM venosum (S. guttatum)

VOODOO LILY

Araceae

TUBER

ZONES 5, 6, 8, 9, 12–24; OR INDOORS

SUN OR LIGHT SHADE

MODERATE WATER

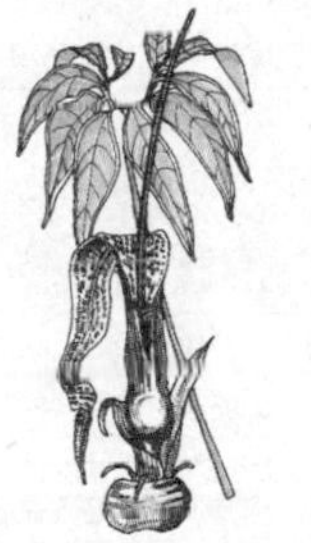

Sauromatum venosum

Flower is composed of 1-ft.-long bract, greenish yellow with deep purple markings, surrounding long, blackish purple central spike. Bloom has strong, unpleasant odor for a brief time after opening. Large, deeply lobed, fanlike, tropical-looking leaves on 3-ft. stalks appear after flowers. Tuber will bloom without planting if it is large enough; just place it on window sill or table. After bloom, plant in big pot or in garden. Loose, slightly acid soil. Also known as *Arum cornutum.*

SAVORY. See SATUREJA p. 477

SAXIFRAGA

SAXIFRAGE

Saxifragaceae

PERENNIALS

ZONES VARY BY SPECIES

EXPOSURE NEEDS VARY BY SPECIES

REGULAR WATER

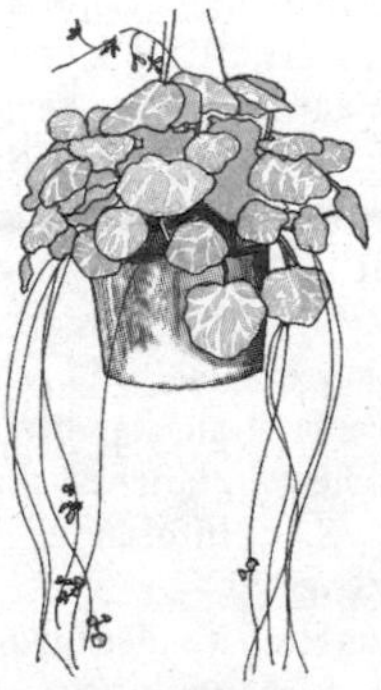

Saxifraga stolonifera

Some native to western mountains and foothills, most from Europe. They thrive best in rock gardens of Northwest, where specialists grow dozens of kinds. They require good drainage and light soil; they are easily rotted by soggy soil. Most saxifrages grow in full sun or light shade. The following grow in shade or part shade. Bergenias, once classified as saxifrages, are still often sold as such.

S. rosacea (S. decipiens, S. sternbergii). Zones 1–7, 14–17. Cushion-forming, spreading plant—typical "mossy saxifrage." Spreads fairly rapidly; narrow, fleshy leaves are divided into three to five narrow lobes. In Northwest, foliage turns crimson in late fall. In spring, flower stalks to 8–9 in. tall display wide-open white flowers. Afternoon shade best in cool-summer areas; shade essential where summers are hot. Many named varieties and hybrids exist, with flowers of pink, rose, and red. 'Carnival' has red flowers fading pink, then white.

S. stolonifera (S. sarmentosa). STRAW-BERRY GERANIUM. Zones 1–9, 14–24; house plant everywhere. Creeping plant that makes runners like strawberry. Nearly round, white-veined leaves to 4 in. across, pink underneath, blend well with pink azaleas. Flowers white, to 1 in. across, in loose, open clusters to 2 ft. tall. Used as house plant in hanging baskets or pots. Ground cover where hard freezes are infrequent. Shade or part shade, considerable moisture.

Saxifraga umbrosa

S. umbrosa. LONDON PRIDE. Zones 1–7, 14–17. Rosettes of green, shiny, tongue-shaped leaves 1½ in. long. Blooms in May, with open cluster of pink flowers on wine red flower stalk. Does best in shade. Good ground cover for small areas; effective near rocks, stream beds.

Saxifragaceae. Once this family included a number of shrubs, but these now occupy their own families—Hydrangeaceae, Philadelphaceae, and Grossulariaceae (currants and gooseberries). Remaining are a number of herbaceous plants including *Astilbe*, *Heuchera*, and of course *Saxifraga*.

SCABIOSA

PINCUSHION FLOWER

Dipsacaceae

ANNUALS, PERENNIALS

⚡ ZONES VARY BY SPECIES

☼ FULL SUN

💧 MODERATE WATER

Scabiosa columbaria

Stamens protrude beyond curved surface of flower cluster, giving illusion of pins stuck into a cushion. Easy to grow. Bloom begins in midsummer, continues until winter if flowers are cut. Good in mixed or mass plantings. Excellent for arrangements.

S. anthemifolia. Perennial. Zones 15–24. Rounded, shrubby, 1½–2 ft. tall or taller. Flower clusters to 2½ in. stand well above the foliage clump. Flowers are lavender blue or pink.

S. atropurpurea. PINCUSHION FLOWER, MOURNING BRIDE. Usually sold as *S. grandiflora*. Annual in all zones; may persist as perennial where winters are mild. Grows to 2½–3 ft. tall. Oblong, coarsely toothed leaves. Many long, wiry-stemmed flower clusters 2 in. across or more, in colors from blackish purple to salmon pink, rose, white.

S. caucasica. PERENNIAL PINCUSHION FLOWER. Perennial. All zones. To 2½ ft. high. Leaves vary from finely cut to uncut. Flower clusters 2½–3 in. across appear from June to frost. Depending on variety, color may be blue to bluish lavender or white. Excellent plant for cut flowers. Fama strain has branching stalks of 3-in. light blue flower heads with unusually large ray flowers around the edge.

S. columbaria. Perennial. Zones 4–24. Does particularly well in Zones 22–24. To 2½ ft. tall. Leaves gray green, finely cut. Flowers to 3 in. across; lavender blue, pink, white varieties.

S. ochroleuca. Biennial or short-lived perennial. All zones. To 2 ft. tall, with light yellow flowers.

S. stellata. Annual. All zones. To 1½ ft. with many heads of pale blue flowers that quickly turn to papery bronze drumsticks useful in dry arrangements.

SCADOXUS. See HAEMANTHUS katherinae **p. 315**

FOR INFORMATION ON YOUR CLIMATE ZONE
PLEASE SEE PAGES 15–44

SCAEVOLA 'Mauve Clusters'

Goodeniaceae

SHRUBBY PERENNIAL

⚡ ZONES 8, 9, 14–24

☼ FULL SUN

💧 TWO SOAKINGS A MONTH ARE ADEQUATE

Scaevola

Evergreen, nearly everblooming (in mild climates) ground cover or rock garden plant from Australia. Forms mats 4–6 in. tall, eventually 3–5 ft. across. Lilac mauve flowers in clusters are ½ in. wide, fan shaped (all petals on one side). Set plants 3 ft. apart for ground cover, or try in hanging basket. Needs little fertilizer, but iron sulfate deepens flower color. Other scaevolas from Australia can be found in nurseries. *S. aemula* 'Purple Fanfare' or 'Diamond Head' is a fleshy-stemmed, sprawling plant with 1½-in. lavender blue flowers produced along branches from spring through fall. Use as hanging basket plant or above a wall. 'Blue Wonder' is similar.

SCARLET LARKSPUR. See DELPHINIUM cardinale,
D. nudicaule **p. 260**

SCARLET WISTERIA TREE. See SESBANIA tripetii **p. 484**

SCHEFFLERA

Araliaceae

EVERGREEN LARGE SHRUBS, SMALL TREES

⚡ ZONES VARY BY SPECIES

☼◐ FULL SUN NEAR COAST, LIGHT SHADE INLAND

💧 ROUTINE WATERING

Schefflera actinophylla

Fast-growing, tropical-looking plants; long-stalked leaves divided into leaflets that spread like fingers of hand. Useful near swimming pools. All need rich soil.

S. actinophylla (Brassaia actinophylla). QUEENSLAND UMBRELLA TREE, OCTOPUS TREE, SCHEFFLERA. Zones 21–24; precariously hardy Zones 16–20 with protection of overhang. As garden plant, grows fast to 20 ft. or more. "Umbrella" name comes from way giant leaves are held. Horizontal tiers of long-stalked leaves are divided into 7–16 large (to 1-ft. long) leaflets that radiate outward like ribs of umbrella. "Octopus" refers to curious arrangement of flowers in narrow, horizontally spreading clusters to 3 ft. long. Color changes from greenish yellow to pink to dark red. Tiny dark purple fruit. Use for striking tropical effects, for silhouette, and for foliage contrast with ferns and other foliage plants. Cut out tips occasionally to keep plant from becoming leggy. Overgrown plant can be cut nearly to ground; it will branch and take better form.

As house plant, give standard rich potting mix, occasional feeding, bright light. Let mix become dry between waterings. Wash leaves occasionally; mist plants to discourage mites.

S. arboricola (Heptapleurum arboricolum). HAWAIIAN ELF SCHEFFLERA. Zones 23, 24. As outdoor plant can reach 20 ft. or more, with equal or greater spread, but easily pruned to smaller dimensions. Leaves dark green, much smaller than those of *S. actinophylla*, with 3-in. leaflets that broaden toward rounded tips. If stems are planted at angle, they continue to grow at that angle, which can give attractive multistemmed effects. Flowers clustered in flattened spheres 1 ft. wide, yellowish aging to bronze. General plant effect denser, darker, less treelike than *S. actinophylla*. Same care as for *S. actinophylla*. Loves humidity.

Schefflera arboricola

S. elegantissima (Dizygotheca elegantissima). House plant in juvenile form, evergreen garden shrub as mature plant. Zones 16, 17,

22–24. Leaves on juvenile plants are lacy looking, divided like fans into narrow (½-in.) leaflets with notched edges. Shiny dark green above, reddish beneath. As plants mature, leaflets grow to 1 ft. long, 3 in. wide.

As house plant it needs good light but not direct sunlight. Needs fast-draining, moisture-retentive soil. (Dry or waterlogged potting mix will cause leaf drop.) Feed monthly. Subject to pests indoors, but not outdoors. In mild climates it will thrive in a sheltered area, making a distinguished silhouette against a wall.

S. pueckleri (Tupidanthus calyptratus). Zones 19–24. To 20 ft., with single or multiple trunks. Leaves to 20 in. wide are divided fanwise into seven to nine glossy, bright green stalked leaflets 7 in. long, 2½ in. wide. Resembles *S. actinophylla,* but branches from base and is denser in growth. Care and uses are the same as for *S. actinophylla.*

SCHINUS

PEPPER TREE

Anacardiaceae

EVERGREEN TREES

ZONES VARY BY SPECIES

FULL SUN

WATER NEEDS VARY BY SPECIES

TOXICITIES ARE INVOLVED; SEE BELOW

Schinus molle

Commonly planted in lowland parts of California, Arizona. Pepper trees are praised by some gardeners, heartily disliked by others. Fruit attracts birds. The two species discussed here are quite different from each other. Leaves of both kinds can cause dermatitis.

S. molle. CALIFORNIA PEPPER TREE. Zones 8, 9, 12–24. Fast to 25–40 ft. tall and wide. Trunk of old tree is heavy and fantastically gnarled, with knots and burls that frequently sprout leaves or small branches. Bark is light brown, rough. Limbs heavy, branchlets light and gracefully drooping. Bright green leaves are divided into many narrow, 1½–2-in.-long leaflets. Numerous tiny, yellowish white summer flowers in drooping 4–6-in. clusters give way to pendant clusters of rose-colored berries in fall, winter. (Some trees have nearly all male flowers; these will not fruit.) Needs no water when established. Gets along with poor drainage. Plant in spring in Zones 8, 9, 14, to prevent sunburn damage to trunk, subsequent borer damage. Stake young plant; prune for high branching if you wish to walk under it. Subject to root rot diseases in infected soils—especially Texas root rot.

Some gardeners object to the tree's messy litter, scale infestation, and greedy surface roots; yet many newcomers to California consider it to be one of the state's most strikingly handsome trees. Probably the brightest green of desert-tolerant trees. Properly used, it is splendid. Don't plant it between sidewalk and curb, near house foundations, patio paving or entrances, in lawns, or near sewers or drains. Do plant along roads or rustic streets without curbs—if you can give it room to spread. A fine tree for shading play area or gravel-surfaced, informal lounging area. California pepper is a characteristic tree of mission gardens.

CALIFORNIA PEPPER AS A HEDGE

A different use for this familiar tree: plant 1-gallon size plants 2 ft. apart in a row. After a year's growth, head plants back to force side growth. Shear to make a graceful, billowy hedge.

S. terebinthifolius. BRAZILIAN PEPPER TREE. Zones 13, 14 (sheltered), 15–17, 19–24. Moderate growth rate to 30 ft., with equal spread. Differs from California pepper in its nonpendulous growth; in its darker green, coarser, glossy leaves with only 5–13 leaflets instead of many; and in bright red berries that are very showy in winter.

With little training, Brazilian pepper tree makes a broad, umbrella-shaped crown. Stake young trees well and prune to make fairly high

crown. Also popular as multitrunked tree. Variations in foliage and growth habit are often pronounced. When selecting tree, try to choose one that has rich foliage and that has already set berries. The dried berries are sold as pink peppercorns; some people are allergic to them. Eaten in quantity, the berries can cause gastric distress.

Feed and water infrequently and deeply to discourage surface roots. To reduce possibility of storm breakage, shorten overlong limbs and do some late-summer thinning so wind can pass through. Subject to verticillium wilt. Good shade tree for patio or small garden.

SCHIZANTHUS pinnatus

POOR MAN'S ORCHID, BUTTERFLY FLOWER

Solanaceae

ANNUAL

ZONES 1–6, 15–17, 21–24

FILTERED SHADE

REGULAR WATER

Schizanthus pinnatus

Grows to 1½ ft. high. Great quantities of small orchidlike flowers. Flowers have varicolored markings on pink, rose, lilac, purple, or white background and are quite showy against the ferny foliage. Sensitive to frost and to heat. Buy plants in pots, or start seeds indoors about 4 weeks ahead of planting time (germination is slow). Winter–spring annual in California; summer annual in Northwest. Combines well with *Primula malacoides* and cineraria, and has the same cultural requirements. Good container plant. Often grown in greenhouses and conservatories.

SCHIZOCENTRON elegans. See HETEROCENTRON elegans   **p. 321**

SCHIZOPHRAGMA hydrangeoides

Hydrangeaceae

DECIDUOUS VINE

ZONES 4–9, 14–17

PARTIAL SHADE

REGULAR WATER

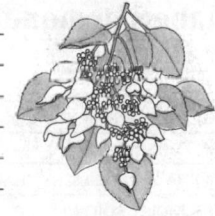

Schizophragma hydrangeoides

Resembles *Hydrangea anomala,* the climbing hydrangea. Climbs by holdfasts to 30 ft. Leaves are 3–5 in. long, oval, pointed, toothed. Broad clusters of flowers resemble lace cap hydrangeas, but the showy white parts are the enlarged (to 1½-in.) sepals of the outermost flowers. Use it in shaded areas to climb masonry walls or trees.

SCHIZOSTYLIS coccinea

CRIMSON FLAG, KAFFIR LILY

Iridaceae

RHIZOME

ZONES 5–9, 14–24

SUN, LIGHT SHADE IN HOT AREAS

WATER FREELY DURING GROWTH

Schizostylis coccinea

Narrow, evergreen leaves, 1½ ft. tall, resemble those of gladiolus. Spikes of showy, crimson, starlike, 2½-in. flowers on slender 1½–2-ft. stems in October–November. Variety 'Mrs. Hegarty' has rose pink flowers. Excellent cut flower spikes—each flower lasts 4 days, others follow. Add peat moss or leaf mold to soil. Divide overgrown clumps.

SCHLUMBERGERA

Cactaceae

CACTI

ZONES 16, 17, 21–24; OR INDOORS

OUTDOORS, GIVE HALF SHADE

REGULAR WATER

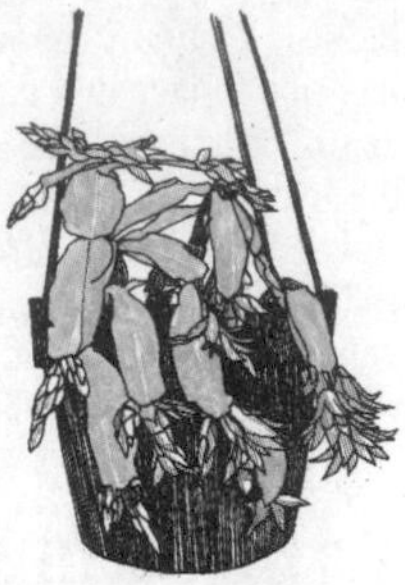

Schlumbergera bridgesii

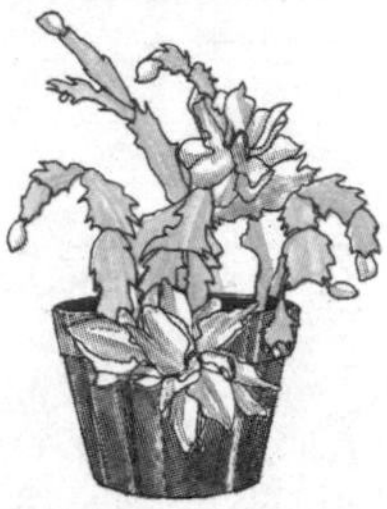

Schlumbergera truncata

In nature, these cacti live on trees like certain orchids. Plants often confused in nursery trade; many hybrids, selections differ principally in color. Remember, they come from the jungle—give them rich, porous soil with plenty of leaf mold and sand. Feed frequently—as often as every 7–10 days during growth and flowering—with liquid fertilizer.

S. bridgesii. CHRISTMAS CACTUS. Often sold as *Zygocactus truncatus*. Old favorite. Arching, drooping branches are made up of flattened, scallop-edged, smooth, bright green, spineless, 1½-in. joints. Grown right, plants may be 3 ft. across and may have hundreds of many-petaled, long-tubed, 3-in.-long, rosy purplish red flowers at Christmas time. To ensure bud set for late December bloom, keep plant where it will receive cool night temperatures (50–55°F) and 12–14 hours of darkness per day during November.

S. gaertneri. See Rhipsalidopsis gaertneri

S. truncata (Zygocactus truncatus). CRAB CACTUS. Joints 1–2 in. long, sharply toothed, with two large teeth at end of last joint. Short-tubed scarlet flowers with spreading, pointed petals, November–March. Many varieties in white, pink, salmon, orange.

SCHOENOPLECTUS tabernaemontanus 'Zebrinus'

ZEBRA RUSH

Cyperaceae

GRASSLIKE PERENNIAL

ZONES 5–24

SUN OR LIGHT SHADE

MOIST SOIL

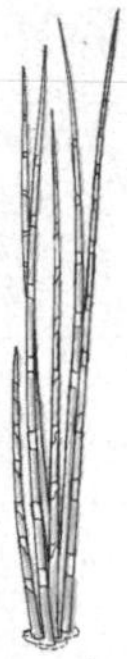

Schoenoplectus tabernaemontanus 'Zebrinus'

Zebra rush has simple, hollow, apparently leafless stems that are 2–4 ft. tall and banded horizontally with green and white. It will grow in several inches of water. Best used as a pool ornament. Striping tends to fade late in season, or in strong inland sun.

SCIADOPITYS verticillata

UMBRELLA PINE

Taxodiaceae

EVERGREEN TREE

ZONES 4–9, 14–24; BORDERLINE ZONES 1–3

SUN ON COAST; AFTERNOON SHADE INLAND

REGULAR WATER

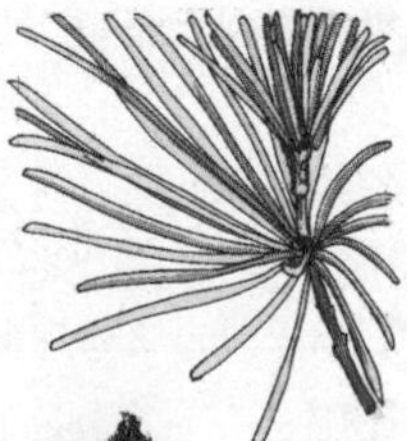

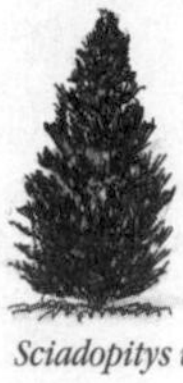

Sciadopitys verticillata

Grows to 100–120 ft. in its native Japan, but not likely to exceed 25–40 ft. in western gardens. Very slow grower. Young plant is symmetrical, dense, rather narrow; older plant opens up and branches tend to droop. Small, scalelike leaves grow scattered along branches, bunched at branch ends. At branch and twig ends grow whorls of 20–30 long (3–6-in.), narrow, flattened, firm, fleshy needles of glossy dark green (they radiate out like spokes of umbrella). In time, 3–5-in.-long woody cones may appear.

Plant in rich, well-drained, neutral or slightly acid soil. Watch for mites in hot, dry weather. Can be left unpruned or can be thinned to create oriental effect.

Choice decorative tree for open ground or container use. Good bonsai subject. Boughs are beautiful and long lasting in arrangements. These are trees for connoisseurs, scarce because of their slow growth. They deserve to be better known and more widely used.

SCILLA

SQUILL, BLUEBELL

Liliaceae

BULBS

ZONES VARY BY SPECIES

SUN DURING BLOOM

WATER DURING GROWTH AND BLOOM

ENTIRE PLANT IS POISONOUS

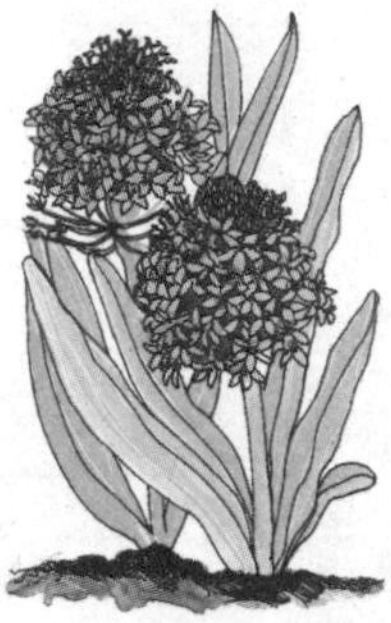

Scilla peruviana

All have basal, strap-shaped leaves and bell-shaped or starlike flowers in clusters on leafless stalks. Best planted in informal drifts among shrubs, under deciduous trees, among low-growing spring perennials. Good in pots, for cutting. Dormant in summer.

S. bifolia. All zones. First to bloom in early spring. Carries up to eight turquoise blue, inch-wide, starlike flowers on each 8-in. stem. White, pale purplish pink, and violet blue varieties. Plant 2 in. deep, 3–5 in. apart.

S. hispanica. See Endymion hispanicus

S. nonscripta. See Endymion non-scriptus

S. peruviana. PERUVIAN SCILLA. Outdoors all year in Zones 14–17, 19–24; in colder climates, grow in pots (1 to a 6-in. pot, 3 to a 9–10-in. pot). Despite its common name, Peruvian scilla is actually native to Mediterranean. Bluish purple, starlike flowers—50 or more in large, dome-shaped cluster, on 10–12-in. stalks. Long, floppy, strap-shaped leaves die down after flowers bloom in May–June. Plant 4–6 in. deep. Bulbs dormant only short time after leaves wither; replant then, if necessary.

S. siberica. SIBERIAN SQUILL. Zones 1–7, 10. Very early blooming, with loose spikes of intense blue flowers on 3–6-in. stems. 'Spring Beauty', with darker blue stripes, is choice. Also comes in white, purplish pink, and violet blue varieties.

S. tubergeniana (S. mischtschenkoana). All zones. Blooms in January, at same time as snowdrops *(Galanthus)*. Pale blue flowers, four or more to each 4-in. stalk; three or more stalks to each bulb. Plant bulbs 2–3 in. deep.

SCINDAPSUS pictus

Araceae

PERENNIAL VINE; INDOORS OR IN GREENHOUSE

BRIGHT (BUT NOT STRONG) INDOOR LIGHT

REGULAR WATER

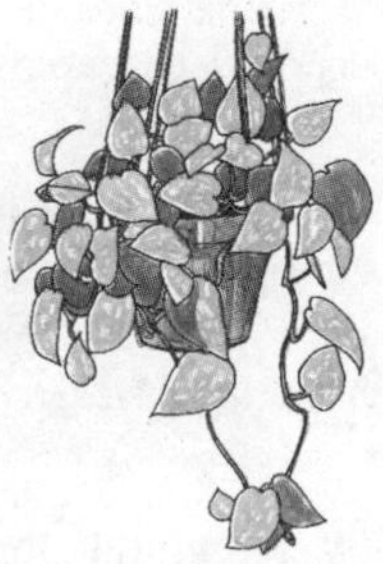

Scindapsus pictus

Resembles more familiar green-and-yellow pothos *(Epipremnum aureum)* in appearance, but the egg-shaped leaves are dark green mottled with gray-green. Leaves are also thinner in texture and usually somewhat larger (to 6 in., compared with 2–4-in. leaves of pot-grown pothos). Flowers insignificant. Variety 'Argyraeus' is most often grown; its markings are more prominent, larger, nearly silver, and leaves have a silky sheen. Needs same care as pothos and other philodendron relatives, but is fussier about drainage, good atmospheric humidity, watering, feeding, and light.

SCIRPUS cernuus
(Isolepis gracilis)

FIBER OPTICS PLANT

Cyperaceae

GRASSLIKE PERENNIAL

☘ ZONES 7–24

◑ PARTIAL SHADE

💧 AMPLE WATER

Scirpus cernuus

Grows to 6–10 in. high, usually less. Drooping, green, threadlike stems topped by small brown flower spikelets. Occasional division and resetting will keep it small. Ideal for edge of shallow pond; highly attractive for streamside effect in Japanese gardens. Good container plant.

SCOTCH BROOM. See CYTISUS scoparius	**p. 256**
SCOTCH HEATHER. See CALLUNA vulgaris	**p. 197**
SCOTCH MOSS. See SAGINA subulata	**p. 471**
SCREW BEAN. See PROSOPIS pubescens	**p. 438**

Scrophulariaceae. The figwort family consists principally of annuals and perennials. Most have irregular flowers, with four or five lobes often arranged as two lips. Some examples are *Antirrhinum* (snapdragon), *Calceolaria, Digitalis* (foxglove), *Nemesia, Penstemon*, and *Torenia.*

SEAFORTHIA elegans. See ARCHONTOPHOENIX cunninghamiana	**p. 162**
SEA HOLLY. See ERYNGIUM amethystinum	**p. 279**
SEA LAVENDER. See LIMONIUM	**p. 356**
SEA PINK. See ARMERIA	**p. 165**
SEA POPPY. See GLAUCIUM	**p. 308**
SEASHORE PASPALUM. See PASPALUM vaginatum	**p. 401**
SEASIDE DAISY. See ERIGERON glaucus	**p. 275**
SEA URCHIN. See HAKEA laurina	**p. 315**
SEA URCHIN CACTUS. See ECHINOPSIS	**p. 270**
SEDGE. See CAREX	**p. 206**

SEDUM

STONECROP

Crassulaceae

SUCCULENT PERENNIALS OR SUBSHRUBS

☘ ZONES VARY BY SPECIES

☀ ◑ ● FULL SUN TO CONSIDERABLE SHADE

💧 MOST TAKE LITTLE SUMMER WATER

Sedum rubrotinctum

They come from many parts of the world and vary in hardiness, cultural needs; some are among hardiest succulent plants. Some are tiny and trailing, others upright. Leaves fleshy, highly variable in size, shape, and color; evergreen unless otherwise noted. Flowers usually small, starlike, in fairly large clusters, sometimes brightly colored.

Smaller sedums are useful in rock gardens, as ground or bank cover, in small areas where unusual texture, color are needed. Some of the smaller types are prized by collectors of succulents, who grow them as potted or dish garden plants. Larger types good in borders or containers, as shrubs. Most propagate easily by stem cuttings—even detached leaves will root

and form new plants. Soft and easily crushed, they will not take foot traffic; otherwise they are tough, low-maintenance plants. Set ground cover kinds 10–12 in. apart.

S. acre. GOLDMOSS SEDUM. All zones. Evergreen plant 2–5 in. tall, with upright branchlets from trailing, rooting stems. Tiny light green leaves; clustered yellow flowers in middle or late spring. Extremely hardy but can get out of bounds, become a weed. Use as ground cover, between stepping stones, or on dry walls.

S. album. All zones. Often sold as *S. brevifolium.* Creeping evergreen plant 2–6 in. tall. Fleshy leaves ¼–½ in. long, light to medium green, sometimes red tinted. Flowers white or pinkish white. Ground cover. Roots from smallest fragment; beware of placing it near choice, delicate rock garden plants.

S. altissimum. See S. reflexum, S. sediforme

S. amecamecanum. See *S. confusum* for plant sold under this name. True *S. amecamecanum (Sedadia amecamecana)* resembles *S. confusum,* but is rare in gardens.

S. anglicum. All zones. Low, spreading plant 2–4 in. tall. Dark green, fleshy leaves to ⅛ in. long. Pinkish white spring flowers. Ground cover.

S. brevifolium. Zones 8, 9, 14–24. Native to Europe, North Africa. Tiny, slowly spreading plant to 2–3 in. high, with tightly packed, fleshy leaves less than ⅛ in. long. Gray-white leaves flushed with red; pinkish or white flowers. Sunburns in hot, dry places. Needs good drainage. Best in rock garden or with larger succulents in pots, containers, or miniature gardens.

S. confusum. Zones 8, 9, 14–24. Native to Mexico. Plant spreading, branching, 6–12 in. tall. Fleshy, shiny light green leaves, ¾–1½ in. long, tend to cluster in rosettes toward branch ends. Dense clusters of yellow flowers in spring. Good ground cover, but sometimes plagued by dieback in wet soils, hot weather; looks best during cooler weather. Use in borders, pots, or containers, as edging, in miniature gardens.

S. dendroideum. Zones 8, 9, 12, 14–24. Native to Mexico. To 2 ft. Branching, spreading plant with rounded, fleshy leaves 2 in. long, yellow-green, often bronze tinted. Flowers deep yellow, in spring and early summer.

S. d. praealtum (S. praealtum). Like the species but taller (it grows to 3–5 ft.), with lighter yellow flowers and less bronze tinting on leaves. Both plants good for low-maintenance informal hedge or space divider; especially useful along semirural streets or lanes where watering is difficult.

S. guatemalense. See S. rubrotinctum

S. kamtschaticum. All zones. Trailing stems to 12 in. long are set with thick, somewhat triangular 1–1½-in. slightly toothed leaves. Yellow flowers age to red. Used in colder climates as small-scale ground cover, stock garden plant.

S. lineare. All zones. Often sold as *S. sarmentosum.* Spreading, trailing, rooting stems to 1 ft. long, closely set with narrow, fleshy, light green leaves 1 in. long. Flowers yellow, star shaped, profuse in late spring, early summer. Ground cover. Vigorous spreader. 'Variegatum', with white-edged leaves, is favorite potted or herbarium plant.

S. morganianum. DONKEY TAIL, BURRO TAIL. Safely outdoors in Zones 17, 22–24; much used under protection of lath or eaves in Zones 13–16, 18–21. House plant everywhere. Makes long, trailing stems that grow to 3–4 ft. in 6–8 years. Thick, fleshy, light gray-green leaves overlap each other along stems to give braided or ropelike effect. Flowers (rarely seen) pink to deep red. Choice plant if well grown. Because it grows such long, pendulous stems, most practical place to grow it is in hanging pot or wall pot. In mildest areas near coast, try it at top of walls or high up in rock garden. Rich, fast-draining soil.

Sedum morganianum

Protect from wind and give half shade; water freely and feed 2 or 3 times during summer with liquid fertilizer. Relatives that have same culture and same uses: *S.* 'Burrito', with fat tails 1 in. thick composed of densely packed ½-in. leaves; giant donkey tail (often sold as *S. orpetii*), with somewhat shorter, thicker tails; and *Sedeveria* 'Super Giant Donkey Tail', with still thicker, shorter tails. ▶

S

S. oxypetalum. Zones 16, 17, 21–24. Native to Mexico. Grows to 3 ft. high, usually much less. Even tiny plant has look of a gnarled tree. Leaves 1–1½ in. long; flowers dull red, fragrant. Evergreen or semievergreen in mildest areas, deciduous elsewhere. Handsome pot plant.

S. reflexum. Zones 8–24. Often sold as *S. altissimum*. Much like *S. sediforme*, but with shorter leaves, yellow flowers. Ground cover.

S. rubrotinctum (S. guatemalense). PORK AND BEANS. Zones 8, 9, 12 (with a little shade and water), 14–24. Sprawling, leaning stems 6–8 in. tall. Leaves like jelly beans, ¾ in. long, green with reddish brown tips, often entirely bronze red in sun. Flowers reddish yellow. Easily detached leaves root readily. Rock garden or potted plant, small-scale ground cover.

S. sarmentosum. See S. lineare

S. sediforme (S. altissimum). Zones 8–24. Native to Mediterranean region. Spreading, creeping plant to 16 in. tall. Leaves light blue gray, fleshy, to 1½ in. long, narrow, closely set on stems. Flowers small, greenish white. Use in rock garden, for blue-green effects in carpet or pattern planting, as small-scale ground cover.

S. sieboldii. Zones 3–24. Native to Japan. Spreading, trailing, unbranched stems to 8–9 in. long. Fleshy leaves in threes, nearly round, stalkless, toothed in upper half, blue gray edged red. Plant turns coppery red in fall, dies to ground in winter. Each stem shows a broad, dense, flat cluster of dusty pink flowers in autumn. *S. s.* 'Variegatum' has leaves marked yellowish white. Beautiful rock garden or hanging basket plant. Light shade, occasional water in hot interior gardens.

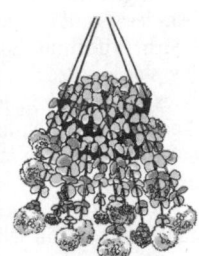

Sedum sieboldii

S. spathulifolium. All zones. Native from California's Coast Ranges and Sierra Nevada north to British Columbia. Leaves blue green tinged reddish purple, spoon shaped, fleshy, packed into rosettes on short, trailing stems. Flowers light yellow, spring–summer. Ground cover. 'Cape Blanco' is a selected form with good leaf color. 'Purpureum' has deep purple leaves. Good in sunny or partially shaded rock gardens. After it has rooted, it needs no water in cool-summer climates.

Sedum spathulifolium

S. spectabile. All zones. Native to China, Japan. Upright or slightly spreading stems to 1½ ft. tall, well set with blue green, roundish, fleshy, 3-in. leaves. Pink flowers in broad, dense clusters atop stems in late summer, autumn. Dies down in winter. 'Brilliant' has deep rose red flowers, 'Carmen' is soft rose, and 'Meteor', brightest, has carmine red flowers. Sun, average garden water. This plant and *S. telephium* are sometimes classified as *Hylotelephium*. Both species are showy over a long season; foliage, flowers, and developing seed heads are all attractive.

S. spurium. All zones. Evergreen perennial plant with trailing stems. Leaves thick, an inch or so long, nearly as wide, dark green or bronzy tinted. Flowers pink, in dense clusters at ends of 4–5-in. stems in summer. Garden variety called 'Dragon's Blood' has bronzy leaves and rosy red flowers. Rock garden, pattern planting subject, ground cover.

S. telephium. All zones. To 2 ft. Resembles *S. spectabile*, but leaves somewhat narrower. If stalks are not cut after bloom, 6-in., dome-shaped flower clusters turn to purple clusters of seeds on top of bare stalks. Garden varieties: 'Autumn Joy', to 2½ ft., with coppery rose blooms; 'Indian Chief', coppery red flowers. Average garden water.

FOR GROWING SYMBOL EXPLANATIONS

PLEASE SEE PAGE 129

S

SEMPERVIVUM

HOUSELEEK	
Crassulaceae	
SUCCULENTS	
⬙ ALL ZONES	
☼ ● SUN, SHADE IN DESERTS	
⬤ WATER ONLY TO PREVENT SHRIVELING	

Sempervivum tectorum

Evergreen perennial plants with tightly packed rosettes of leaves. Little offsets cluster around parent rosette. Flowers star shaped, in tight or loose clusters, white, yellowish, pink, red, or greenish, pretty in detail but not showy. Summer bloom. Blooming rosettes die after setting seed, but easily planted offsets carry on. Good in rock gardens, containers, even in pockets on boulders or pieces of porous rock. Good drainage. Many species, all good.

S. arachnoideum. COBWEB HOUSELEEK. Native to Europe. Tiny gray-green rosettes, ¾ in. across, of many leaves joined by fine hairs that give a cobweb-covered look to plant. Spreads slowly to make dense mats. Bright red flowers on 4-in. stems; seldom blooms.

S. tectorum. HEN AND CHICKENS. Rosettes gray green, 4–6 in. across, spreading quickly by offsets. Leaves tipped red brown, bristle pointed. Flowers red or reddish in clusters on stems to 2 ft. tall. Easy to grow in rock gardens, borders, pattern planting.

SENECIO

Asteraceae (Compositae)	
PERENNIALS, SHRUBS, VINES	
⬙ ZONES VARY BY SPECIES	
☼ ◐ ● EXPOSURE NEEDS VARY BY SPECIES	
⬤ ⬤ ⬤ WATER NEEDS VARY BY SPECIES	

Senecio cineraria

Daisy relatives that range from garden cineraria and dusty miller to vines, shrubs, perennials, succulents, even a few weeds. Succulents are often sold as *Kleinia*, an earlier name.

S. cineraria. DUSTY MILLER. Shrubby perennial. All zones (needs protection Zones 1–3). Spreading plant to 2–2½ ft.; woolly, white leaves cut into many blunt-tipped lobes. Clustered heads of yellow or creamy yellow flowers at almost any season. Plant gets leggy unless sheared occasionally. Easy to grow; needs only light watering. Use in combination with bright-flowered, sun-loving annuals and perennials. Striking in night garden.

S. confusus. MEXICAN FLAME VINE. Evergreen or deciduous vine. Zones 13, 16–24. Sometimes grown as annual or perennial in colder climates. Twines to 8–10 ft. in frost-free areas; dies back to ground in mild frost, comes back fast from roots. Leaves light green, rather fleshy, 1–4 in. long, ½–1 in. wide, coarsely toothed. Daisylike flowers in large clusters at ends of branches, ¾–1 in. wide, startling orange-red with golden centers. 'Sao Paulo' is deeper orange, almost brick red.

Blooms all year where winters are mild. Sun or light shade; moist, light soil. Use on trellis, column, to cascade over bank or wall, or in hanging basket.

S. greyi (Brachyglottis greyi). Evergreen shrub. Zones 5–9, 14–24. Spreading plant that grows 4–5 ft. high. Stiff, slightly curving stems bear 3½-in.-long, leathery leaves of gray green outlined in silvery white. Blooms profusely in summer; 1-in.-wide, yellow daisies in 5-in.-wide, flattish clusters contrast effectively with gray foliage.

Full sun, not-too-rich soil, good drainage, little or moderate water. Prune yearly to remove oldest or damaged growth, stimulate new wood. Attractive with geraniums, zauschneria, cistus, rosemary, purple- or red-leafed shrubs. Cut branches effective in arrangements, especially with scarlet and orange flowers; long lasting.

Senecio greyi

S. hybridus (S. cruentus, Pericallis cruenta). CINERARIA. Annual or house plant. May persist or reseed in Zones 16, 17, 22–24. Valuable for bright colors in cool, shady places; not for hot, dry climates. Most commonly grown are the large-flowered, dwarf kinds generally sold as Multiflora Nana or Hybrida Grandiflora. These are compact, 12–15-in.-tall plants with lush, broad, green leaves. Broad clusters of daisies 3–5 in. wide cover top of plant. Will self-sow where adapted. Colors range from white through pink and purplish red to sensational blues and purples, often with contrasting eyes or bands. Bloom late winter and early spring in mild regions, spring and early summer elsewhere. Plants sold as *Cineraria stellata* are taller (to 2½–3 ft.), with looser clusters of smaller, starlike daisies; these often self-sow in shaded gardens that get regular (even if infrequent) irrigation.

Senecio hybridus

Frost is a hazard to fall-planted cinerarias; plant in spring or protect by planting under shrubs, trees, overhang, or lath. Plant in shade in cool, moist, loose, rich soil. Water generously and often, but avoid soggy soil. Principal pests are leaf miners, spider mites, slugs, snails.

To grow in large pots for patio display, begin by setting transplants in 3–4-in. pots in mixture of rich soil, leaf mold, sand. After several weeks (or before they become pot-bound), shift into 5–6-in. pots. Feed every 2 weeks with liquid fertilizer. Never let plants dry out.

Effective in mass plantings or combined with ferns, tuberous or other begonias, foliage plants. Use to decorate lanais, shaded terraces, sitting areas. Usually discarded after bloom.

S. leucostachys. See S. vira-vira

S. macroglossus. KENYA IVY, NATAL IVY, WAX VINE. Evergreen vine. House plant. *S. macroglossus* can grow out of doors in Zones 12, 13, if given north or east exposure. 'Variegatum' has leaves sharply splashed with creamy white. Twining or trailing vine with thin, succulent stems and thick, waxy or rubbery leaves 2–3 in. across. Leaves are shaped like ivy leaves with three, five, or seven shallow lobes. Flowers are tiny yellow daisies. Grow in sunny window and water only when soil becomes dry.

S. mandraliscae (Kleinia mandraliscae). Succulent perennial. Zones 12, 13 (protected spots), 16, 17, 21–24 (full sun). Somewhat shrubby, with branches to 1–1½ ft. tall, spreading wider. Leaves cylindrical, 3–3½ in. long, slightly curved, strikingly blue gray. Widely used as a ground cover where blue-gray effect is desired. Takes some water or aridity.

Senecio mandraliscae

S. mikanioides. GERMAN IVY. Perennial vine. Zones 14–24. Evergreen in mildest areas, deciduous elsewhere. Twines to 18–20 ft. Leaves roundish, with five to seven sharply pointed lobes, ivylike, ½–3 in. long. Winter flowers are small yellow daisies without rays. Trailer in window boxes, or screening vine. Plant in sun to semishade. Water sparingly. Has become a weed in coastal California where it can grow into or smother choicer plants.

S. petasitis. VELVET GROUNDSEL, CALIFORNIA GERANIUM. Perennial or shrubby perennial. Zones 15–17, 21–24, greenhouse plant anywhere. Bulky plant 6–8 ft. tall or more, equally wide. Leaves evergreen, tropical looking, large, lobed, fanlike, velvety to touch, to 8 in. across. Blooms in midwinter, with large clusters of small, daisylike, bright yellow flowers standing well above mass of plant. Best in sheltered locations in full sun. Needs ample water, some feeding. Prune hard after bloom to limit height and sprawl. Can be kept 2–4 ft. tall in big pots or tubs. Good filler in tropical garden.

S. serpens (Kleinia repens). Succulent perennial. Zones 16, 17, 21–24. Like *S. mandraliscae*, but grows 1 ft. tall, has 1½-in.-long, light gray or bluish leaves.

Senecio serpens

S. vira-vira (S. leucostachys, S. cineraria 'Candissimus'). Subshrub. Zones 3–24. To 4 ft. tall; broad, sprawling habit. Leaves like those of *S. cineraria* but whiter and more finely cut into much narrower, pointed segments. Creamy white summer flowers are not showy. In full sun brilliantly white, densely leafy; in partial shade looser, more sparsely foliaged, with larger, greener leaves. Tip-pinch young plants to keep them compact. Needs light watering.

WILL THE REAL DUSTY MILLER PLEASE STAND UP?

Many plants answer to the name; all have whitish, silvery, or grayish foliage, grow in full sun, and need little water. Four plants are sold by this common name in western nurseries; the best known is *Centaurea cineraria*. Two are species of *Senecio*: *S. vira-vira* and *S. cineraria*. The fourth, less well known, is *Artemesia stelleriana*.

SENSITIVE FERN. See ONOCLEA sensibilis **p. 394**

SENTRY PALM. See HOWEA belmoreana **p. 325**

SEQUOIA sempervirens

COAST REDWOOD

Taxodiaceae

EVERGREEN TREE

☀ ZONES 4–9, 14–24

☀ ☼ ● FULL SUN, PARTIAL SHADE WHEN YOUNG

💧 REGULAR WATER

Sequoia sempervirens

Native to parts of Coast Ranges from Curry County, Oregon, to Monterey County, California. Tallest of the world's trees, and one of West's most famous native trees (equally famous is its close relative *Sequotadendron*, giant sequoia or big tree). Fine landscaping tree—fast growing (3–5 ft. a year), substantial, pest free, and almost always fresh looking and woodsy smelling.

Its red-brown, fibrous-barked trunk goes straight up (unless injured). Nearly parallel sides on redwood's trunk indicate tree has fared well (if redwoods struggle, they develop trunks with noticeable taper). Branchlets hang down slightly from branches. Flat, pointed, narrow leaves (½–1 in. long) grow in one plane on both sides of stem like feathers. Leaves are medium green on top, grayish underneath. Small round cones are 1 in. long.

One of best growing places is in or directly next to a lawn, since redwood thrives on generous watering (in 10–20 years, however, tree may defeat lawn). Away from lawns it needs occasional feeding and regular summer watering (at least for first 5 years). Resistant to oak root fungus.

Here's a planting mix recipe for a 1- or 5-gallon-size redwood. It makes a redwood grow well in just about any soil—especially useful in Zones 7–9, 14–16, 18–24. Dig a hole 1½ ft. wide and 3 ft. deep. Pile the excavated soil and thoroughly mix into it 1 lb. of iron sulfate and 2 cubic ft. of cattle manure. Throw the blended mix back into the hole and saturate it (to leach out salts and ammonia). After mix dries enough to be workable, remove enough from the center to make room for the root ball. Use removed mix to make a watering dike about 10 in. out from the tree trunk.

Troubles the tree encounters are mostly physiological: (1) not enough water or hot, dry sites make it sulk and grow slowly; (2) too much competition from bigger trees and structures makes it grow lanky, thin, and open; (3) lack of available iron makes needles turn yellow every summer, especially on new growth—apply iron sulfate or chelated iron. (It's normal for oldest leaves to turn yellow, then brown, and then drop in late summer and early fall; it is normal for short twigs to brown and fall also.)

Count on branch spread at base (tip to tip) of 14–30 ft. Centuries-old natives surpass 350 ft. in height, but 70–90 ft. seems to be most to expect in one gardener's lifetime; trees can reach this height in 25 years. ▶

S

Redwoods vary greatly in form, texture, and color. Some are dense and some are open; some are pendulous, others bristly; foliage colors may be any shade from light green to deep blue green and blue gray; branch angles vary from a slight up-tilt to straight out from the trunk and cupping a little at the outer ends to almost straight down. These characteristics are determined mostly by heredity—a tree will have them all its life.

Until the 1970s, all redwoods at nurseries were grown from seed, with each seedling inheriting a slightly different set of characteristics. But since then, named varieties have been available, vegetatively propagated, with certain definite growth and color characteristics.

'Aptos Blue' has dense blue-green foliage on nearly horizontal branches with branchlets hanging down. 'Majestic Beauty' has densely set blue-green foliage. 'Santa Cruz' has light green foliage, soft texture, branches pointing slightly down. 'Soquel' has fine texture, somewhat bluish green foliage, horizontal branches that turn up at tips, and a sturdy, stout trunk with little suckering. 'Los Altos' has deep green foliage of heavy texture on horizontal, arching branches. 'Filoli' and 'Woodside', similar, possibly identical varieties, are distinctively blue—almost like blue spruce. These need careful training when young to establish good form. Other varieties are 'Majestic Beauty' (dense, blue green) and a silvery blue variety, 'Simpson's Silver'.

Variety 'Adpressa' ('Albo-Spica') is a dwarf for rock garden use—up to 3 ft. high and 6 ft. wide; its new growth is tipped white, which deepens to green as summer advances.

WAYS TO USE REDWOODS

Use *Sequoia sempervirens* singly as a shade tree, tree to look up into or hang a swing from, or tree to be seen from two blocks away. Plant several in a grove or in a 40-ft.-diameter circle—inside it's cool, fragrant, and a fine spot for fuchsias, begonias, and people on hot summer days. For grove or circle planting, space trees 7 ft. apart. To make a beautiful hedge, plant trees 3–4 ft. apart and top at least once a year.

SEQUOIADENDRON
giganteum (Sequoia gigantea)

BIG TREE, GIANT SEQUOIA
Taxodiaceae
EVERGREEN TREE
✎ ALL ZONES
☼ FULL SUN
◐ INFREQUENT, DEEP WATERING

Sequoiadendron giganteum

Native to west slope of the Sierra Nevada from Placer County to Tulare County. Most massive trunk in the world and one of the tallest trees, reaching 325 ft. in height with 30-ft. trunk diameter. It has always shared fame and comparisons with its close relative, the coast redwood (*Sequoia*). Horticulturally, however, similarities are rather few.

Although tolerant of cold and varying climatic conditions, giant sequoia is subject to fungus diseases that can disfigure or kill it outside its natural habitat. It seems more successful in colder interior climates than near the coast.

Dense foliage of giant sequoia (more bushy than that of coast redwood) is gray green; branchlets are clothed with short, overlapping, scalelike leaves with sharp points. It's a somewhat prickly tree to reach into. Dark reddish brown cones, 2–3½ in. long. Bark is reddish brown and generally similar to that of coast redwood.

Giant sequoia is hardier to cold than coast redwood. It grows a little more slowly—2–3 ft. a year. It also needs less water. Plant in deep soil.

Primary use is as featured tree in large lawn (roots may surface there in due time) or other open space. Trees hold lower branches throughout

their long youth and are likely to get too broad for the small garden. In essence, then, giant sequoia is easier to grow than coast redwood and more widely adaptable to cold, dry climates, but it doesn't have as many landscape uses. Variety 'Pendulum' has drooping branches and must be staked to coax it into vertical habit.

SERVICEBERRY. See AMELANCHIER   **p. 150**

SESBANIA tripetii
(Daubentonia tripetii)

SCARLET WISTERIA TREE
Fabaceae (Leguminosae)
DECIDUOUS SHRUB OR SMALL TREE
✎ ZONES 7–9, 12–16, 18–23
☼ FULL SUN AND WARM SPOT IN GARDEN
◐ MODERATE WATER

Sesbania tripetii

Native to Argentina. Neither a wisteria nor a tree, and flower color is more burnt orange than scarlet. Fast growing to 8–10 ft. high and 6–8 ft. wide, with fernlike leaves. Showy, drooping clusters of yellow and orange-red, sweet pea–shaped flowers from May through summer; winged, four-angled pods follow. To prolong flowering, remove pods as they form.

Prune severely in early spring to thin and shorten side branches to stubs. Not long-lived plant and appears a little out of place with glossy-leafed, refined plants, but valued for exciting color and quick effects. Most often seen trained into flat-topped standard tree on 6-ft. trunk. Can be grown in containers, blooming quite heavily in 1-ft. pots.

SETARIA palmifolia

PALM GRASS
Poaceae (Gramineae)
PERENNIAL
✎ ZONES 14–24
☼ ◐ SUN OR LIGHT SHADE
◐ REGULAR WATER

Setaria palmifolia

This tropical-looking grass has long (1–3-ft.), wide (2–3-in.), pleated, deep green leaves in clumps 3–6 ft. tall. Plants are evergreen in mild climates but freeze in the upper 20s, resprouting if roots do not freeze. Use along walks or in woodland plantings for tropical look. Where adapted it can seed itself and become a pest; remove flowers before seeds ripen.

SETCREASEA pallida
'Purple Heart'

PURPLE HEART
Commelinaceae
PERENNIAL
✎ ZONES 12–24
☼ ◐ LIGHT SHADE, SUN FOR BEST COLOR
◐ MODERATE WATER

Setcreasea pallida 'Purple Heart'

Freezes, recovers from roots in Zones 12–18; house plant anywhere. Stems a foot or more high, inclined to flop over. Leaves rather narrowly oval and pointed, strongly shaded with purple, particularly underneath. Use discretion in planting, or the vivid foliage may create a harsh effect (pale or deep purple flowers are inconspicuous). Pinch back after bloom. Plant is generally unattractive in winter. Frosts may kill tops, but in warm weather recovery is fast.

S

SHADBLOW. See AMELANCHIER   p. 150

SHALLOT

Liliaceae

SMALL ONIONLIKE BULB

⬚ ALL ZONES

☼ FULL SUN

💧 💧💧 AVERAGE TO HEAVY WATERING

Shallot

Prized in cooking for its distinctive flavor. Plant either sets (small dry bulbs) or nursery plants in fall in mild climates, early spring in cold-winter areas. Leaves 1–1½ ft. high develop from each bulb. Tiny lavender or white flowers sometimes appear. Ultimately 2–8 bulbs will grow from each original bulb. At maturity (early summer if fall planted, late summer if spring planted), bulbs are formed and tops yellow and die. Harvest by pulling clumps and dividing bulbs. Let outer skin dry for about a month so that shallots can be stored for 4–6 months.

Some seed firms sell sets; nurseries with stocks of herbs may sell growing plants. If you use sets, plant so that tips are just covered. Golden brown skins of Dutch shallots enclose white cloves. Coppery skins of red shallots conceal purple cloves.

SHAMROCKS. Around St. Patrick's Day, nurseries and florists sell "shamrocks." These are small potted plants of *Medicago lupulina* (hop clover, yellow trefoil, black medick), an annual plant; *Oxalis acetosella* (wood sorrel); or *Trifolium repens* (white clover), both perennials. The last is most common.

All have leaves divided into three leaflets, symbolic of the Trinity. They can be kept on a sunny window sill or planted out, but they have little ornamental value and are likely to become weeds.

SHASTA DAISY. See CHRYSANTHEMUM maximum   p. 226

SHELL FLOWER. See ALPINIA zerumbet,
MOLUCCELLA laevis   pp. 148, 382

SHELL GINGER. See ALPINIA zerumbet   p. 148

SHE-OAK. See CASUARINA   p. 211

SHEPHERDIA argentea

SILVER BUFFALOBERRY

Elaeagnaceae

DECIDUOUS SHRUB

⬚ ZONES 1–3, 7, 10, 14–24

☼ FULL SUN

◌ NO WATER ONCE ESTABLISHED

Shepherdia argentea

Native to many western habitats, from the plains of Canada and the Midwest to California. Spreading, suckering shrub grows 5–6 ft. tall (rarely to 12 ft.) with spine-tipped branchlets. Longish oval leaves to 1 in., silvery on both upper and lower surfaces. Plant either male or female; if both are present, latter bear ¼-in. berries of bright red or orange, sour but edible and used for jams and jellies. Flowers not showy. Good plant for attracting birds. Withstands any amount of cold and wind, takes most soils (including considerable alkali).

SHIBATAEA. See BAMBOO   p. 174

SHIMPAKU. See JUNIPERUS chinensis sargentii   p. 338

SHISO. See PERILLA frutescens   p. 411

SHOOTING STAR. See DODECATHEON   p. 266

SHORTIA

Diapensiaceae

PERENNIALS

⬚ ZONES 1–7

● SHADE

💧 💧💧 AVERAGE TO HEAVY WATERING

Shortia galacifolia

Beautiful small evergreen plants. Spread slowly by underground stems. Need acid, leafy, or peaty soil. Grow with azaleas or rhododendrons.

S. galacifolia. OCONEE BELLS. Forms clump of round or oval, glossy green leaves 1–3 in. long, with scallop-toothed edges. Single, nodding white bell, 1 in. wide, with toothed edges, tops each of the many 4–6-in.-high stems in March–April.

S. soldanelloides. FRINGE BELLS. Round, coarsely toothed leaves form clumps similar to those of *S. galacifolia*, but flowers are pink to rose in color, with deeply fringed edges.

S. uniflora 'Grandiflora'. Like *S. galacifolia* but with indented and wavy-edged leaves and flowers that are large fringed bells of clear soft pink.

SHRIMP PLANT. See JUSTICIA brandegeana   p. 342

SHUNGIKU. See CHRYSANTHEMUM coronarium   p. 226

SIBERIAN WALLFLOWER. See ERYSIMUM hieraciifolium   p. 279

SIDALCEA malviflora

CHECKERBLOOM

Malvaceae

PERENNIALS

⬚ ZONES 4–9, 14–24

☼ SUN

💧 REGULAR WATER

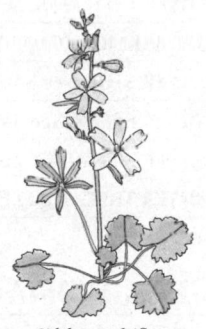

Sidalcea malviflora

Checkerblooms are low, sprawling perennials with roundish leaves to 2½ in. across. Stems rise toward their tips to show 1–2-in. flowers like miniature hollyhocks in bright or lavender pink, usually with white or purple veining. With water, plants will bloom all summer. Without, they go dormant and reappear with fall rains. Garden varieties like 'Elsie Heugh' can reach over a yard in height and show flowers that range from white to red. *S. candida*, from the high plains, is hardier, to 2½ ft., with inch-wide white flowers in narrow upright clusters.

SILENE

Caryophyllaceae

PERENNIALS

⬚ ZONES VARY BY SPECIES

☼ ◑ SUN, PARTIAL SHADE

◌ 💧 💧 💧💧 WATER NEEDS VARY BY SPECIES

Silene californica

Many species, some with erect growth habit, others cushionlike. Most species are used as rock garden plants.

S. acaulis. CUSHION PINK, MOSS CAMPION. Zones 1–11, 14–16, 18–21. Mosslike mat of bright green, narrow leaves about ⅝ in. long. Reddish purple flowers, ½ in. across, borne singly, March–April. Good choice for gravelly, damp but well-drained spot in rock garden. ▶

S. alpestris (S. quadrifolia). Zones 1–9, 14–24. Low, creeping perennial to 8 in. tall. For rock garden use. Moderate water. Produces a fine show of small double white flowers in spring, with scattered bloom later.

S. californica. CALIFORNIA INDIAN PINK. Zones 7–11, 14–24. Native to California and southern Oregon foothills. Loosely branching plant to 6–16 in. tall. Foliage somewhat sticky. Flaming red, 1¼-in.-wide flowers, with petals cleft and fringed, bloom during spring. *S. californica* is occasionally sold in seed packets. Needs well-drained soil; let it dry off in the summer months.

S. coeli-rosa. See Lychnis coeli-rosa

S. schafta. MOSS CAMPION. Zones 1–9, 14–16, 18–21. Forms tufts of upright-growing, rather wiry stems to 6–12 in. high. Leaves are small and tongue shaped. Rose purple flowers, one or two to each blossomed stalk, bloom from late summer into autumn. Water moderately.

S. uniflora (S. vulgaris maritima). All zones. Moderate water. Low, cushion-forming perennial with gray-green foliage and an abundance of white flowers, each of them nearly enclosed by a balloonlike inflated calyx.

SIMMONDSIA chinensis

JOJOBA, GOATNUT

Buxaceae

EVERGREEN SHRUB

✂ ZONES 10–13, 19–24

☼ FULL SUN AND HEAT

◊ LITTLE WATER

Simmondsia chinensis

Native to the deserts of Southern California, Arizona, and Mexico. Dense, rigid-branching, spreading shrub 3–6 (rarely to 16) ft. tall. Dull gray-green, leathery leaves are 1–2 in. long, to ½ in. wide. Flowers are inconspicuous. Male and female blooms are borne on different plants; if both are present, female plants bear edible, nutlike fruit about ¾ in. long. Flavor like filbert, slightly bitter until cured.

High oil content of fruit gives plant commercial value as crop for marginal land. Such plantings are chancy in soil infested with verticillium or Texas root rot.

Young plant rather tender; when established, will take 15°F. Of particular value as clipped hedge, foundation planting in desert garden.

SINNINGIA speciosa (Gloxinia speciosa)

GLOXINIA

Gesneriaceae

TUBER

✂ PATIO OR HOUSE PLANT

☼ ● BRIGHT LIGHT INDOORS; SHADE OUTDOORS

◊ SEE INSTRUCTIONS BELOW

Sinningia speciosa

Leaves oblong, dark green, toothed, fuzzy, 6 in. or longer. Flowers are spectacular—large, velvety, bell shaped, ruffled on edges, in blue, purple, violet, pink, red, or white. Some flowers have dark dots or blotches, others contrasting bands at the flower rims. Leaves occasionally white veined. Tubers usually available December–March. Plant 1 in. deep in rich, loose mix. Water sparingly until first leaves appear; increase watering after roots form. Apply water around base of plant; don't water on top of leaves. When roots fill pot, shift to larger pot. Feed regularly during growth.

After bloom has finished, gradually dry off plants and store tubers in cool dark place with just enough moisture to keep them from shriveling, or store tubers, soil and all, in pots until new growth starts. Repot in January–February.

SISYRINCHIUM

Iridaceae

PERENNIALS

✂ ZONES 4–24

☼ ◐ SUN OR LIGHT SHADE

◊ ● TOLERATE SOME ARIDITY OR SOME WATER

Sisyrinchium bellum

Related to iris. Narrow, rather grasslike leaves. Small flowers, made up of six segments, open in sunshine. Pretty but not showy, best suited for informal gardens or naturalizing.

S. bellum. BLUE-EYED GRASS. Native to coast of California. To 4–16 in. tall. Narrow green or bluish green leaves. Flowers purple to bluish purple, ½ in. across, bloom early to midspring. Several named forms, many of them dwarf, are available.

S. californicum. YELLOW-EYED GRASS. Native to coast of California and Oregon. Dull green leaves, broader, slightly taller than those of blue-eyed grass. Yellow flowers open May–June. Can grow in wet, low, or poorly drained places.

S. macounii. Native to Northwest. Grows 12–20 in. tall with short, broad leaves and blue, 1-in. flowers. Plant sold as *S. macounii* 'Album' (probably a form of *S. bellum*) has inch-wide white flowers on 6-in. stems.

S. striatum. Larger than other sisyrinchiums; attractive gray-green leaves are irislike, 1 ft. long, up to 1 in. wide. Spikelike flower clusters grow to 2½ ft., with many pale yellow, brown-streaked, ½-in. flowers in spring. Useful for foliage clumps of gray, with old leaves fading to black.

SKIMMIA

Rutaceae

EVERGREEN SHRUBS

✂ ZONES 4–9, 14–22; BEST IN ZONES 4–6, 17

☼ LIGHT TO MODERATE SHADE

◊ REGULAR WATER

Skimmia japonica

Slow growing and compact, with glossy, rich green leaves neatly arranged. In April and May, tiny white flowers open from clusters of pinkish buds held well above foliage. Red hollylike fruit in fall and through December if pollination requirements are met. When massed, forms level surface of leaves; individual plants are dense mounds.

No special soil requirement in Northwest. In California's alkaline soils, add at least 50 percent peat moss or the like to planting soil. In the Northwest, skimmia is attacked by a skimmia mite that gives leaves sunburned look. Also expect attacks by thrips and red spider mites. Water mold is a problem in hot regions. Good shrub under low windows, beside shaded walks, flanking entryways, in containers. Blends well with all shade plants.

S. foremanii. Hybrid between *S. japonica* and *S. reevesiana.* Resembles *S. japonica* but is more compact, with broader, heavier, darker green leaves. Seems to take Northern California conditions better than either parent. Plants may be male, female, or self-fertile.

S. japonica. Variable in size. Slow growth to 2–5 ft. tall, 3–6 ft. wide. Leaves 3–4 in. long, an inch wide, oval, blunt ended, mostly clustered near twig ends. Flowers fragrant, in 2–3-in. clusters. Female plants bear bright red berries if male plant present; berries are attractive enough to be worth the effort of planting both male and female shrubs. Form with ivory white berries is available. *S. j.* 'Macrophylla' is a male form—rounded, spreading shrub to 5–6 ft., with large leaves and flowers.

S. reevesiana (S. fortunei). Dwarf, dense-growing shrub 2 ft. tall. Self-fertile, with dull crimson fruit. Fragrant flowers.

SKUNKBUSH. See RHUS trilobata p. 460

SKY FLOWER. See DURANTA repens, THUNBERGIA grandiflora pp. 269, 505

SMILACINA racemosa

FALSE SOLOMON'S SEAL

Liliaceae

PERENNIAL

ZONES 1–7, 14–17

SUN TO SHADE

WATER DURING SPRING GROWTH

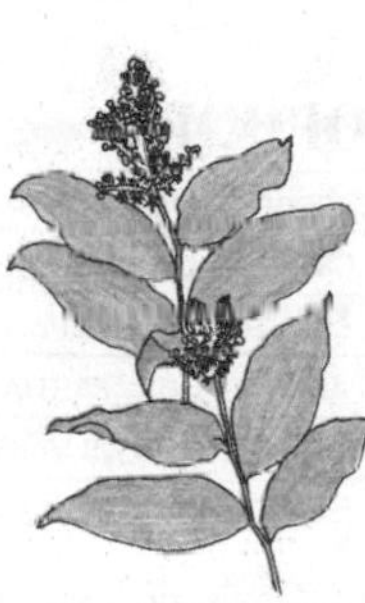

Smilacina racemosa

Commonly seen in shaded woods—California to British Columbia, east to Rockies. Grows 1–3 ft. tall. Each single, arching stalk has several 3–10-in.-long leaves, hairy beneath. Stalks topped by fluffy, conical clusters of small, fragrant, creamy white flowers in March–May, followed by red, purple-spotted berries. Most common form in the West is *Smilacina amplexicaulis,* with leaves sheathing stem at base.

SMOKE TREE. See COTINUS coggygria, DALEA spinosa pp. 245, 258

SNAIL VINE. See VIGNA caracalla p. 519

SNAKE PLANT. See SANSEVIERIA trifasciata p. 473

SNAKESHEAD. See FRITILLARIA meleagris p. 300

SNAPDRAGON. See ANTIRRHINUM majus p. 154

SNAPWEED. See IMPATIENS p. 330

SNEEZEWEED. See HELENIUM autumnale p. 318

SNOWBALL, FRAGRANT. See VIBURNUM carlcephalum p. 518

SNOWBELL. See STYRAX p. 497

SNOWBERRY. See SYMPHORICARPOS p. 498

SNOWDROP. See GALANTHUS p. 302

SNOWDROP TREE. See HALESIA carolina p. 315

SNOWFLAKE. See LEUCOJUM p. 352

SNOW GUM. See EUCALYPTUS pauciflora niphophila p. 285

SNOW-IN-SUMMER. See CERASTIUM tomentosum p. 217

SNOW MYRTLE. See CALYTRIX alpestris p. 200

SNOW-ON-THE-MOUNTAIN. See EUPHORBIA marginata p. 289

SOAPBARK TREE. See QUILLAJA saponaria p. 449

SOCIETY GARLIC. See TULBAGHIA violacea p. 512

Solanaceae. Members of the potato family bear flowers that are nearly always star or saucer shaped and five petaled; fruits are berries or capsules. Plants are frequently rank smelling or even poisonous, but many are important food crops—eggplant, pepper, potato, tomato. Others are garden annuals, perennials, shrubs, or vines—*Browallia, Cestrum, Nicotiana,* and *Petunia,* to name a few.

SOLANDRA maxima

CUP-OF-GOLD VINE

Solanaceae

EVERGREEN VINE

ZONES 17, 21–24; ALSO SEE BELOW

SUN; SHADE ROOTS IN HOT INLAND VALLEYS

REGULAR, DEEP WATERING

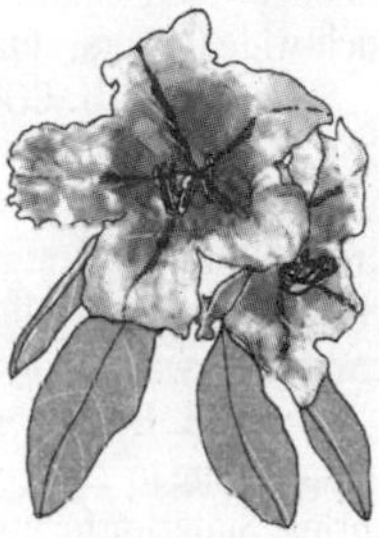

Solandra maxima

Usually sold as *S. guttata.* Fast, sprawling, rampant growth to 40 ft. Fasten to support. Large, broad, glossy leaves 4–6 in. long. Blooms February–April and intermittently at other times. Bowl-shaped flowers are 6–8 in. wide, golden yellow striped brownish purple.

Prune to induce laterals and more flowers. Can be cut back to make rough hedge. Takes salt spray directly above tide line; stands wind, fog. Use on big walls and pergolas, along eaves, or as bank cover. For easy viewing inside the big flowers, encourage growth low on plant by tip-pinching. This vine is spectacular trained along swimming pool fence. Provide overhead protection against cold in Zones 15, 16, 18–20.

SOLANUM

Solanaceae

EVERGREEN AND DECIDUOUS SHRUBS AND VINES

ZONES VARY BY SPECIES

SUN OR PARTIAL SHADE

LITTLE TO MODERATE WATER

MANY SPECIES ARE POISONOUS, MOST SUSPECT

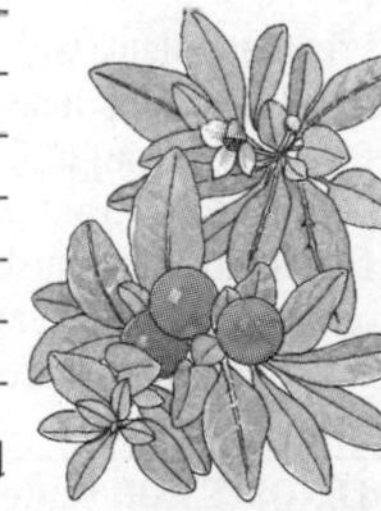

Solanum pseudocapsicum

In addition to potato and eggplant (described under those names), *Solanum* includes a number of ornamental plants. Ordinary garden care suits most of them.

S. aviculare. Evergreen shrub. Zones 17, 21–24. Grows fast to 6–10 ft.; deeply cut, smooth deep green leaves to 1 ft. long. Purple 1-in. flowers.

S. crispum. Evergreen vine. Zones 8, 9, 12–24. Climbs to 12 ft. (sometimes shrubby), with leaves to 5 in. long, often wavy edged, and 4-in. clusters of star-shaped fragrant lilac blue flowers with yellow centers. Yellow fruit may be poisonous. May lose leaves in hard frost. The variety 'Glasnevin' has deeper blue flowers in larger clusters.

S. jasminoides. POTATO VINE. Evergreen or deciduous vine. Zones 8, 9, 12–24. Fast growth to 30 ft.; twining habit. Leaves 1½–3 in. long, evergreen in milder winters, medium to purplish green. Flowers pure white, or white tinged blue, an inch across, in clusters of 8–12. Nearly perpetual bloom; heaviest in spring. Grown for flowers or for light overhead shade. Cut back severely at any time to prevent tangling, promote vigorous new growth; control rampant runners that grow along ground. ▶

S. muricatum. PEPINO. Evergreen perennial. Zones 17, 24; with shelter in Zones 15, 16, 20–23, but fruiting inconsistent there. Sprawling plant to 2 ft. tall, several feet across. Bright green leaves are 3 in. long. Blue flowers are followed by football-shaped, greenish yellow fruit striped with purple. Fruit weighs from 4 oz. to 1 lb. and tastes like a cross between melon and cucumber. Named varieties grown from cuttings. Grow like tomatoes.

S. pseudocapsicum. JERUSALEM CHERRY. Evergreen shrub. Zones 23, 24; potted or container plant for indoor use, outdoor summer decoration in all zones. Grows 3–4 ft. high. Foliage deep green; leaves 4 in. long, smooth, shiny. White, ½-in.-wide flowers. Fine show of scarlet (rarely yellow), ½-in. fruit like miniature tomatoes, October–December. Fruit may be poisonous. Usually grown as annual. In Zones 23, 24, blooms, fruits, and seeds itself through year. The many dwarf strains (to 1 ft. high) are more popular than taller kinds, have larger fruit (to 1 in.).

S. rantonnetii. See Lycianthes rantonnei

S. seaforthianum. BRAZILIAN NIGHTSHADE. Vine. Zones 16, 21–24. Evergreen in mildest winter areas. Leaves to 8 in. long, some undivided, others divided featherwise into leaflets. Clusters of violet blue, star-shaped, inch-wide flowers; small red fruits edible only to birds.

S. wendlandii. COSTA RICAN NIGHTSHADE. Deciduous vine. Zones 16, 21–24. Tall, twining vine with prickly stems. Leaves larger than those of other species (4–10 in. long), lower ones divided into leaflets. Leaves drop in low temperatures even without frost. Slow to leaf out in spring. Big clusters of 2½-in., lilac blue flowers. Use to clamber into tall trees, to cover a pergola, to decorate eaves of large house.

S. xantii. Evergreen shrub. Zones 7–9, 14–24. California native. Erect or sprawling to 2 ft., leaves to 1¾ in. long, purple 1-in. flowers late winter, spring. Superior forms seen in California native plant gardens.

SOLEIROLIA soleirolii
(Helxine soleirolii)

BABY'S TEARS, ANGEL'S TEARS	
Urticaceae	
PERENNIAL	
✎ ZONES 4–24	
◐ ● SHADE; SOME SUN NEAR COAST	
◖ ◗ WATER CAREFULLY THROUGH DRY SEASON	

Soleirolia soleirolii

Creeping plant with tiny round leaves makes lush, 1–4-in.-high, medium green mats. Flowers inconspicuous. Tender, juicy leaves and stems are easily injured, but aggressive growth habit quickly repairs damage. Roots easily from pieces of stem and can become an invasive pest.

Freezes to black mush in hard frosts, but comes back. Cool-looking, neat cover for ferns or other shade-loving plants. Can be used to carpet terrariums or space under greenhouse benches. There is a golden green variety.

SOLENOSTEMON scutellarioides. See COLEUS hybridus   p. 238

SOLIDAGO

GOLDENROD	
Asteraceae (Compositae)	
PERENNIALS	
✎ ALL ZONES	
◐ ◑ FULL SUN OR LIGHT SHADE	
◖ MODERATE WATER	

Solidago

Not as widely known and grown in far West as Rockies and eastward. A few can be grown here. Varieties of garden origin are sometimes sold. They grow 1–3 ft. high (sometimes to 5 ft.), with characteristic goldenrod plume of yellow flowers topping leafy stems. Varieties differ chiefly in size and in depth of

yellow shading. 'Golden Mosa', to 3 ft., has light yellow flowers the color of "mimosa" (*Acacia baileyana*). Plants grow best in not-too-rich soil. Good meadow planting with black-eyed Susan and Michaelmas daisies, or can be used in border for summer–fall color.

SOLLYA heterophylla
(S. fusiformis)

AUSTRALIAN BLUEBELL CREEPER	
Pittosporaceae	
EVERGREEN SHRUB OR VINE	
✎ ZONES 8, 9, 14–24	
◐ ◑ SUN NEAR COAST, PARTIAL SHADE INLAND	
◖ ◗ LOOKS BEST WITH REGULAR WATER	

Sollya heterophylla

Grows 2–3 ft. tall as loose, spreading shrub; given support and training, climbs to 6–8 ft. Foliage light and delicate; leaves narrow, glossy green, 1–2 in. long. Clusters of ½-in.-long, brilliant blue, bell-shaped flowers appear through most of summer. 'Alba' has white flowers.

Give frequent pruning to fatten it up. Dies if drainage is poor. Spray to control scale insects. Will grow under eucalyptus trees. Use as ground cover, border planting, along steps, on half-shaded banks. Plant over low wall, where its branches can spill downward. Good container plant.

SOLOMON'S SEAL. See POLYGONATUM   p. 432

SOPHORA

Fabaceae (Leguminosae)	
DECIDUOUS OR EVERGREEN TREES OR SHRUBS	
✎ ZONES VARY BY SPECIES	
◐ ◑ FULL SUN, PARTIAL SHADE	
◖ ◗ WATER NEEDS VARY BY SPECIES	
◈ SEEDS OF S. SECUNDIFLORA ARE POISONOUS	

Sophora japonica

Leaves divided into numerous leaflets. Drooping clusters of sweet pea–shaped flowers are followed by pods bearing seeds.

S. arizonica. Evergreen shrub. Zones 10, 11 (possibly), 12, 13. To 6–10 ft. Gray-green foliage, clusters of lavender, 1-in. flowers. Takes heat, needs occasional deep irrigation. Slow growing.

S. japonica. JAPANESE PAGODA TREE, CHINESE SCHOLAR TREE. Deciduous tree. All zones. Unreliable bloom where summers are cold and damp. Moderate growth to 20 ft.; from this point it grows slowly to 40 ft., with equal or greater spread. Young wood smooth, dark gray green. Old branches and trunk gradually take on rugged look of oak. Dark green, 6–10-in. leaves divided into 7–17 oval, 1–2-in.-long leaflets. Long, open, 8–12-in. clusters of yellowish white, ½-in.-long flowers, July–September. Pods are 2–3½ in. long, narrowed between big seeds in bead necklace effect. Not fussy about soil, water; no special pests or diseases. Resistant to oak root fungus. 'Regent' is exceptionally vigorous, uniform grower. One of best spreading trees for giving shade to lawn or patio. Good tree for Rocky Mountain area, but subject there to damage from ice storms.

S. secundiflora. MESCAL BEAN, TEXAS MOUNTAIN LAUREL. Evergreen shrub or tree. Zones 8–16, 18–24. Can be trained into 25-ft. tree with short, slender trunk or multiple trunks, narrow crown, and upright branches. Very slow growth, especially in cool-summer regions. Leaves 4–6 in. long, divided into seven to nine glossy, dark green, oval leaflets, 1–2 in. long. Blooms February–April; inch-wide, violet blue, wisterialike, sweet-scented flowers are carried in drooping 4–8-in. clusters. A white-flowered form rarely appears. Silvery gray, woody, 1–8-in.-long seed pods open on ripening to show the bright red poisonous ½-in. seeds. Remove

S

pods before they mature. Thrives in heat and alkaline soil, but needs good drainage and some water. Choice small tree for street, lawn, or patio. Untrained, it is good large screen, bank cover, or espalier.

S. tetraptera. KOWHAI, YELLOW KOWHAI. Evergreen or deciduous shrub or small tree. Zones 15–17. Slow growing to 15–20 ft. Slender, open, rather narrow tree which drops its leaves in spring just before blooming. Leaves 3–6 in. long, divided into 20–40 tiny leaflets. Flowers bright golden yellow, 2 in. long, in hanging clusters of four to eight. Seed pods with four wings, narrowed between seeds, grow 2–8 in. long. Does not take aridity and low humidity. Well-drained soil, regular watering.

SORBARIA sorbifolia (Spiraea sorbifolia)

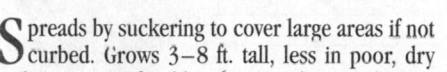

FALSE SPIRAEA

Rosaceae

DECIDUOUS SHRUB

ZONES 1–10, 14–21

SUN OR LIGHT SHADE

TOLERATES ARIDITY; LOOKS BEST IF WATERED

Sorbaria sorbifolia

Spreads by suckering to cover large areas if not curbed. Grows 3–8 ft. tall, less in poor, dry soil. Leaves are fernlike, 6–12 in. long, with up to 23 toothed, deep green leaflets. Stems topped in summer by branching clusters (to 1 ft. long) of tiny white flowers. These should be cut off after they have faded. Effect is lush, almost tropical, especially in rich, moist soil. Thin clumps drastically or cut back near ground in earliest spring; plant blooms on new wood.

SORBUS

MOUNTAIN ASH

Rosaceae

DECIDUOUS TREES, RARELY SHRUBS

ZONES 1–10, 14–17

SUN OR LIGHT SHADE

MODERATE WATER

Sorbus aucuparia

Grown for finely cut, somewhat fernlike foliage, clustered white flowers, and bright, inedible fruit. All stand winter cold, can endure strong winds, low humidity, extreme heat. Need good drainage. Where adapted, good small garden tree or street tree, though fruit can be messy over paving. Fruit is generally red, but white, pink, and golden kinds are occasionally available. All are attractive to birds. Some may be difficult to transplant. Cankers a problem when trees are under stress. Watch for fireblight.

S. alnifolia. KOREAN MOUNTAIN ASH. Unlike others, has simple, undivided leaves like those of alder. Broad, dense tree, eventually to 60 ft., with small, loose clusters of flowers, red-and-yellow fruit, yellow to orange fall color.

S. aucuparia. EUROPEAN MOUNTAIN ASH. Moderate to rapid growth to 20–30 ft. with 15–20-ft. spread; may grow much larger. Sharply rising branches make dense, oval to round crown. ('Black Hawk' is columnar in form.) Leaves have 9–15 leaflets to 1–2 in. long, dull green above, gray green below, turning yellow, orange, or red in fall. Flat, 3–5-in.-wide clusters of tiny white flowers bloom in late spring; these are followed by orangered, berrylike, ¼-in. fruit that colors in midsummer and may hang until spring unless birds eat it. Fruit especially attractive against background of conifers. 'Cardinal Royal' has especially large bright red berries that color early. Although grown in Zones 14–17, it is rarely successful there.

S. hupehensis. Eventually 50 ft. tall, usually much less. Leaves to 7 in. long, with four to eight pairs of 1–2-in. leaflets. Fruit clusters are white or coral red; the form in cultivation is fireblight-resistant 'Coral Cascade', with red fruit and red fall foliage.

S. hybrida. Erect tree to 20–30 ft. tall; leaves are divided into leaflets at the base, but tips are merely lobed, like oak leaves. Fruit is red, ½ – ⅝ in. across.

S. reducta. Shrub ½–2 ft. tall, 3 ft. wide, spreading by underground runners. Leaves to 4 in. long, with four to seven pairs of leaflets. Spring flowers white, in loose clusters. Fruit pink. Rock garden shrub or bonsai.

S. thuringiaca. Tree to 40 ft. tall. Hybrid between European mountain ash and a species with undivided leaves. Leaves either deeply lobed and toothed, or having one pair of leaflets beneath a large terminal leaflet. Spring flowers are white, in clusters 3–5 in. wide. Berries bright red, ¼ – ⅜ in. in diameter.

S. tianshanica. TURKESTAN MOUNTAIN ASH. Large shrub or small tree to 16 ft. Leaves 5–6 in. long, with 9–15 leaflets to 2 in. long, ½ in. wide. Loose, 3–5-in.-wide clusters of ¾-in. flowers are followed by bright red fruit. Neat form, slow growth; excellent plant for small garden. 'Red Cascade' is a compact, oval-crowned variety.

SPARAXIS tricolor

HARLEQUIN FLOWER

Iridaceae

CORM

ZONES 9, 12–24

FULL SUN

MODERATE WATER

Sparaxis tricolor

Native to South Africa. Closely related to ixia and similar to it in uses and culture. Swordshaped leaves; small, funnel-shaped flowers in spikelike clusters on 1-ft. stems. Flowers come in yellow, pink, purple, red, and white. Usually blotched and splashed with contrasting colors. Blooms over long period in late spring. Use in borders, rock gardens, containers, for cutting. Plant in fall; set corms 2 in. deep, 2–3 in. apart.

SPARMANNIA africana

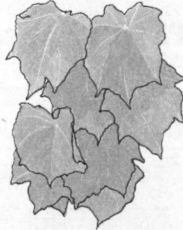

AFRICAN LINDEN

Tiliaceae

EVERGREEN SHRUB, TREE, HOUSE PLANT

ZONES 15–24

SUN OR SHADE

REGULAR WATER

Sparmannia africana

Fast to 10–20 ft., usually as thicket, multitrunked from base, especially if frosted back or pruned to control size; slower, smaller in container or as house plant. Dense, coarse foliage. Leaves broad, angled, to 9 in. across, light green, heavily veined, velvety with coarse hairs. Flowers white with brush of yellow stamens, 1–1½ in. across, clustered, borne in midwinter to early spring. ▶

S

489

Feed regularly. Susceptible to spider mites. Prune heavily every few years to give desired height and control legginess. Best used for furnishing bulk and mass near entryways, screening, combining with tropical foliage plants. Big leaves, easy cleanup make it a good choice near pools. Easily propagated by cuttings.

SPARTIUM junceum

SPANISH BROOM

Fabaceae (Leguminosae)

EVERGREEN SHRUB

ZONES 5–24

FULL SUN

DOES BEST WITH LITTLE WATER

ALL PARTS ARE POISONOUS

Spartium junceum

Grows to 6–10 ft., forming a shrub of many green, erect, almost leafless stems. Bright yellow, fragrant, 1-in.-long flowers in clusters at branch ends bloom continuously from July to frost in north, March–August in south. Flowers followed by hairy seed pods.

Gaunt-looking woody shrub, but pruning will fatten it up. Takes poor, rocky soil. Has naturalized many places in West. Good rough bank cover with native shrubs, but where best adapted is capable of crowding out desirable native plants.

In Southern California (especially Zone 24), Spanish broom is extremely subject to caterpillars in summer; by fall, they often leave plants without flowers or stems. (Stems may resprout at base in winter.) Aphids are a problem at blooming time.

SPATHIPHYLLUM

Araceae

EVERGREEN PERENNIALS

GOOD INDOOR LIGHT BUT NO HOT WINDOWS

AVERAGE OR MUCH WATER

Spathiphyllum
'Mauna Loa'

Dark green leaves are large, oval or elliptical, and narrowed to a point, erect on slender leaf stalks that rise directly from soil. Flowers resemble calla lilies or anthuriums—central column of closely set tiny flowers surrounded by leaflike white flower bract.

Loose, fibrous potting mixture; weekly feedings of dilute liquid fertilizer. One of the few flowering plants that grow and bloom readily indoors. Many varieties include 'Mauna Loa', 3½ ft.; 'St. Mary', 6 ft.; 'Silver Streak', 1½ ft., with matte-finished leaves with a silvery midrib; 'Supreme', 2½ ft.; 'Tasson', 2 ft. (considered by some the surest bloomer); and 'Wallisii', 20 in. 'Silver Streak' has insignificant flowers, but foliage is attractive.

SPATHODEA campanulata

AFRICAN TULIP TREE

Bignoniaceae

EVERGREEN TREE, DECIDUOUS WITH FROST

ZONES 21–24

FULL SUN

MODERATE WATER

*Spathodea
campanulata*

Fast growing. Glossy leaves divided into four to eight pairs of leaflets. Branches end in clusters of spectacular tulip-shaped, 4-in., orange-scarlet flowers edged with yellow; typical bloom time is spring, but flowers may appear in any season. Plant grows rapidly and

blooms young, but can be devastated by frosts. Give good drainage and a warm site. Can reach 40–70 ft., but such height is unlikely in California because of frost damage.

SPINACH

Chenopodiaceae

ANNUAL VEGETABLE

ALL ZONES

FULL SUN

AMPLE WATER

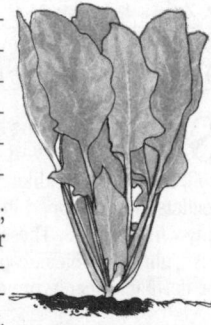

Spinach

Sow to mature during fall, winter, and spring; long daylight of late spring and heat of summer make it go to seed too fast. It requires rich, fast-draining soil. Make small sowings at weekly intervals to get succession. Space rows 1½ ft. apart.

After seedlings start growing, thin plants to 6 in. apart. One feeding will encourage lush foliage. When plants have reached full size, harvest by cutting off entire clump at ground level.

SPINACH, NEW ZEALAND

Tetragoniaceae

PERENNIAL OR SUMMER ANNUAL

ALL ZONES; PERENNIAL IN ZONES 15–17, 21–24

FULL SUN

FREQUENT, DEEP WATERING

New Zealand Spinach

Cook and serve it like spinach. Can be harvested through warm season; real spinach comes in cool season. You harvest greens from plants by plucking off top 3 in. of tender stems and attached leaves. A month later new shoots grow up for another harvest. Plants are spreading, 6–8 in. high; evergreen in mild-winter areas, they go dormant in heavy frosts. Sow seed in early spring after frosts. Feed 1 or 2 times a year with complete fertilizer. Though heat tolerant, also thrives in cool, damp conditions at shore and is often seen growing wild.

SPIRAEA

Rosaceae

DECIDUOUS SHRUBS

ZONES 1–11, 14–21

SUN OR LIGHT SHADE

MODERATE WATER

Spiraea bumalda
'Anthony Waterer'

Easy to grow in all kinds of soil. Form, height, and flowering season vary; all provide generous quantities of white, pink, or red flowers.

Prune according to form and time of bloom. Those with loose, graceful look need annual renewal of new growth. Remove the old wood that has

S

produced flowers—cutting it back to ground. Most shrubby types require less severe pruning. Prune spring-flowering kinds when they finish blooming—or better yet, cut flowering branches for arrangements; they have graceful lines and last well. Prune summer-flowering species in late winter or very early spring.

S. bumalda. Blooms June to fall. Includes hybrids between *S. japonica* and *S. albiflora.* Varieties include 'Anthony Waterer', 2–3 ft. tall, with flat-topped, bright carmine flower clusters and maroon-tinged foliage; 'Froebelii', similar, but taller (3–4 ft.), with rosy red flower clusters; 'Goldflame', like 'Froebelii' but with bronzy leaves that turn yellow as they expand; and 'Limemound', dense and dwarf, with pink flowers and lime green leaves that turn orange red in fall.

S. cantoniensis (S. reevesiana). DOUBLE BRIDAL WREATH. Upright, to 5–6 ft., with arching branches. Small dark green leaves turn red in fall. White flowers wreathe branches in June and July. Pinch back occasionally to limit growth.

S. douglasii. WESTERN SPIRAEA. Suckering, clump-forming shrub 4–8 ft. tall. Native West Coast to Rocky Mountains. Leaves are dark green above, velvety white beneath; pale to deep pink flowers form 8-in.-tall clusters at branch ends in July and August. Useful for wild plantings near streams.

S. fritschiana. Low-growing, compact shrub to 2–3 ft., with an early crop of flat-topped white flower clusters above dark green foliage.

S. japonica. Upright-growing shrub with flat clusters of pink flowers to 8 in. wide at branch tips. Varieties, better known than the species, include 'Fortunei', taller, with markedly saw-toothed leaves and pink summer flowers; 'Alpina' and 'Little Princess', under 20 in. tall, with long summer bloom in pink; and 'Shirobana', 2–3 ft. tall, with flowers of white, pink, and red on same plant.

S. nipponica tosaensis 'Snowmound'. Compact, spreading plant, 2–3 ft. tall with a profusion of white flowers in early summer.

S. prunifolia 'Plena'. BRIDAL WREATH SPIRAEA, SHOE BUTTON SPIRAEA. Graceful, arching branches on a 6-by-6-ft. plant. Small dark green leaves turn rich red in fall. Small double white flowers like tiny roses line branches in April and May.

S. thunbergii. Showy, billowy, graceful shrub with many arching branches. To 5 ft. Blue-green leaves turn soft reddish brown in fall; round clusters of small single white flowers appear all along branches in April.

S. trilobata 'Swan Lake'. Like a smaller bridal wreath. Grows as tall as 3–4 ft., gives massive show of tiny white flowers in May and June.

S. vanhouttei. Widely planted hybrid between *S. cantoniensis* and *S. trilobata.* Forms a 6-ft. fountain of arching branches covered with white flower clusters in June and July.

SPLIT-LEAF PHILODENDRON. See MONSTERA deliciosa   **p. 382**

SPREKELIA formosissima

JACOBEAN LILY, ST. JAMES LILY, AZTEC LILY

Amaryllidaceae

BULB

☒ ZONES 9, 12–24

☼ FULL SUN

◗ REGULAR WATER

Sprekelia formosissima

Often sold as *Amaryllis formosissima.* Native to Mexico. Foliage looks like that of daffodils. Stems 1 ft. tall, topped with dark crimson blooms resembling orchids: three erect upper segments and three lower ones rolled together into tube at base, then separating again into drooping segments. Plant in fall, setting bulbs 3–4 in. deep and 8 in. apart. Blooms 6–8 weeks after planting. Most effective in groups. In mild climates, may flower several times a year, with alternating moisture and drying out. Where winters are cold, plant outdoors in spring; lift plants in fall when foliage yellows and store over winter (leave dry tops on). Or grow in pots

like amaryllis *(Hippeastrum)*, giving slightly cooler conditions. Repot every 3–4 years.

SPRING STAR FLOWER. See IPHEION uniflorum   **p. 331**

SPRUCE. See PICEA   **p. 417**

SPURGE, JAPANESE. See PACHYSANDRA terminalis   **p. 398**

SQUASH

Cucurbitaceae

ANNUAL VEGETABLES

☒ ALL ZONES

☼ FULL SUN

◗ REGULAR WATER

Crookneck Squash

These edible annuals come in two forms. Those that are harvested and cooked in the immature state are called summer squash; this group includes scalloped white squash, yellow crookneck and straightneck varieties, and cylindrical, green or gray zucchini or Italian squash. The other is winter squash. Its varieties have hard rinds and firm, close-grained, fine-flavored flesh. They store well and are used for baking and for pies. They come in a variety of shapes—turban, acorn, and banana are a few—and a variety of sizes and colors.

Many summer squash grow on broad, squat bushes rather than on vines; these help save garden space. 'Early Summer Crookneck' and 'Early Prolific Straightneck' are good yellow summer squash. 'Early White Bush' (white) and 'Scallopini Hybrid' (green) are fine-scalloped varieties. 'Ambassador Hybrid', 'Aristocrat Hybrid', and 'Burpee Hybrid' are productive zucchini varieties. Zucchini and scalloped squash also come in golden yellow variants. Novelties include 'Gourmet Globe', a round, striped zucchini, and 'Kuta', a whitish squash that can be eaten like summer squash at 6 in. or permitted to ripen into a 1-ft. winter squash.

WHEN TO HARVEST SUMMER SQUASH?

When they are still small and tender. You should be able to pierce rind easily with your thumbnail. A common complaint with summer squash is that immature fruit rot at the blossom end while still tiny. The usual reason is that the blossoms have not been pollinated, due to poor weather, lack of bees, or lack of open male blossoms.

Fall and winter squash for storing are the small 'Bush Table Queen', 'Acorn', 'Butternut', and 'Buttercup', and the large 'Hubbard', 'Blue Hubbard', and 'Jumbo Pink Banana'. Spaghetti squash looks like any other winter squash, but when you cook (bake or boil) and open it, you find that the flesh is made up of long, spaghettilike strands. It has a nutty flavor.

Bush varieties of summer squash can be planted 2 ft. apart in rows. If planted in circles ("hills"), they need more room, so space hills 4 by 4 ft. Runner-type winter squash needs 5-ft. spacing in rows, 8 by 8 ft. in hills. Roots will need ample water, but keep leaves and stems as dry as possible; irrigate in basins or furrows. Late squash should stay on vines until thoroughly hardened; harvest these with an inch of stem and store in cool (55°F), frost-free place.

SQUAWBUSH. See RHUS trilobata   **p. 460**

SQUILL. See SCILLA   **p. 480**

SQUIRREL'S FOOT FERN. See DAVALLIA trichomanoides   **p. 259**

FOR INFORMATION ON SELECTING PLANTS
PLEASE SEE PAGES 45–128

S

STACHYS byzantina (S. lanata, S. olympica)

	LAMB'S EARS
	Lamiaceae (Labiatae)
	PERENNIAL
🌿	ALL ZONES
☀ ☽	SUN OR LIGHT SHADE
💧	INFREQUENT WATER

Stachys byzantina

Soft, thick, white-woolly, rather tongue-shaped leaves grow densely on spreading, 1–1½-ft. stems. Flower stalks with many whorls of small purplish flowers form in June–July, but plant is most useful for foliage effect. Rain smashes it down, makes it mushy. Frost damages leaves. Cut back in spring.

Use for contrast with dark green and different-shaped leaves such as those of strawberry or some sedums. Good edging plant for paths, flower bed borders; highly effective edging for bearded iris. Excellent ground cover under high-branching oaks.

The variety 'Silver Carpet' does not produce flowers. Spikelike flower clusters are attractive but become dowdy when they fade. You can either cut them off near the ground or tear them out with your hands; plenty of leaf rosettes will remain behind.

STACHYURUS praecox

	Stachyuraceae
	DECIDUOUS SHRUB
🌿	ZONES 4–6 BEST; ALSO 14–17
☀ ☽	FULL SUN OR LIGHT SHADE
💧 💧	REGULAR TO AMPLE WATER

Stachyurus praecox

Slow to 10 ft., with spreading, slender, polished chestnut brown branches. Pendulous flower stalks 3–4 in. long, each with 12–20 unopened buds, hang from branches in fall–winter. These open in February–March into pale yellow or greenish yellow, bell-shaped flowers ⅓ in. wide. Berry-like fruit in August–September. Bright green, toothed leaves, 3–7 in. long, taper to sharp tip. Leaves often somewhat sparse. Fall color pleasant (but not bright) rosy red and yellowish. Grow under deciduous trees to shelter winter buds from heavy freezes.

STACKHOUSIA monogyna

	Stackhousiaceae
	PERENNIAL
🌿	ZONES 8, 9, 14–24
☀ ☽	SUN OR PARTIAL SHADE
💧	A LITTLE SUMMER WATER

Stackhousia monogyna

Australian perennial. It makes clumps of erect stems to 18 in. tall and 3 ft. wide, with narrow bright green leaves. Narrow clusters of white flowers form at the top of the stems and elongate to an eventual 2 ft. Flowering lasts for months. Plant should never go completely dry; it appreciates some shade in hot inland gardens.

STAGHORN FERN. See PLATYCERIUM	p. 426

STAPELIA

	STARFISH FLOWER, CARRION FLOWER
	Asclepiadaceae
	SUCCULENTS
🌿	ZONE 24; ZONES 12, 13, 16–23 WITH SHELTER
☀	FULL SUN
💧	MODERATE WATER

Plants resemble cacti, with clumps of four-sided, spineless stems. Flowers (summer) are large, fleshy, shaped like five-pointed stars; they usually have elaborate circular fleshy disk in center. Most smell like carrion, but odor is not usually offensive on plants blooming outside in summer. They need cool, dry rest period in winter. Best managed in pots. Good desert succulent, tolerating extreme heat.

Stapelia variegata

S. gigantea. Grow this plant as a remarkable novelty. Stems 9 in. tall. Flowers 10–16 in. wide, fringy edged, brown purple marked yellow.

S. variegata. Most common. Stems to 6 in. Flowers to 3 in. across, yellow heavily spotted and barred dark purple brown. There are many hybrids and color variants. Flowers not strongly scented. Plant can take light frost.

STAR BUSH. See TURRAEA obtusifolia	p. 514
STAR CLUSTERS. See PENTAS lanceolata	p. 411
STARFISH FLOWER. See STAPELIA	p. 492
STAR JASMINE. See TRACHELOSPERMUM	p. 509
STAR OF BETHLEHEM. See CAMPANULA isophylla, ORNITHOGALUM arabicum	pp. 204, 395
STAR TULIP. See CALOCHORTUS uniflorus	p. 199
STATICE. See LIMONIUM	p. 356

STENOCARPUS sinuatus

	FIREWHEEL TREE
	Proteaceae
	EVERGREEN TREE
🌿	ZONES 16, 17, 20–24
☀	FULL SUN
💧 💧	OCCASIONAL DEEP WATERING

Stenocarpus sinuatus

Slow to 30 ft., with a spread of 15 ft. Foliage dense, shiny. Leaves on young plant to 1 ft. long, lobed like oak leaves; on older plant, leaves are smaller and usually unlobed. Tubular, 2–3-in., scarlet-and-yellow flowers arranged in clusters like spokes of wheel. Has been adopted by Rotary Club as mascot. Plant will not bloom until established for several years. Bloom season varies; plant may flower at any time, but early fall is usually peak season. Blooms sometimes come out of the trunk's bark, giving most unusual effect.

Rather tender, especially when young. Best in deep, rich, well-drained, acid soil. Prune to shape in early years. Where climate, soil, and water are right, it can be a showy flowering tree for use near patio or terrace. Good lawn tree. Good near swimming pools; has little leaf drop. Beautiful juvenile leaves make it popular as an indoor potted plant.

STENOCEREUS thurberi. See LEMAIREOCEREUS thurberi	p. 350
STENOLOBIUM stans. See TECOMA stans	p. 503

STENOTAPHRUM secundatum

ST. AUGUSTINE GRASS

Poaceae (Gramineae)

PERENNIAL LAWN GRASS

🌡 ZONES 12, 13, 18–24

☀☽ SUN, ENDURES SHADE

💧💧 MODERATE TO AMPLE WATER

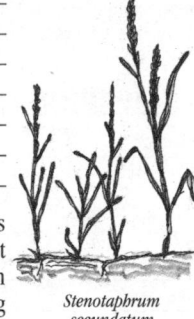

Stenotaphrum secundatum

Tropical or subtropical coarse-textured grass that spreads fast by surface runners that root at joints. Leaves dark green, up to ³/₈ in. wide, on coarse, wiry, flattened stems. Turns brown during short winter dormancy, can creep into flower beds or other plantings, requires power mower to deal with heavy blades, produces thick thatch. On the plus side, it is easily removed from flower beds because of shallow roots, tolerates much wear, has few pests, and is fairly salt tolerant. Plant from sod, plugs, or stolons. Mow 1 in. high once a week.

Will grow in Zones 14–16, but long dormant season limits use. Needs somewhat less water than bluegrass. A variegated form exists and is sometimes seen as a hanging basket plant.

STEPHANOTIS floribunda

MADAGASCAR JASMINE

Asclepiadaceae

EVERGREEN VINE

🌡 ZONES 23, 24; HOUSE PLANT ANYWHERE

☼ ROOTS IN SHADE, TOPS IN FILTERED SUN

💧 REGULAR WATER

Stephanotis floribunda

Moderate growth to 10–15 ft. (more if grown in open ground). Can be kept small in pots. Waxy, glossy green leaves to 4 in. long. Funnel-shaped flowers are white, waxy, very fragrant, 1–2 in. long in open clusters. Blooms June through summer as outdoor plant; grown indoors and properly rested by some drying out, will bloom 6 weeks after resuming growth. Favorite flower in bridal bouquets.

Needs warmth, support of frame or trellis. As indoor/outdoor plant, feed liberally, but dry out somewhat before bringing indoors. Grow in bright light out of direct sun. Watch for scale, mealybugs.

STERCULIA. See BRACHYCHITON p. 189

Sterculiaceae. The sterculia family of shrubs and trees has flowers in which the calyx (usually bowl shaped and five lobed) replaces the corolla as the conspicuous element. Examples are *Brachychiton* and *Firmiana*.

STERNBERGIA lutea

Amaryllidaceae

BULB

🌡 ALL ZONES

☼ SUN

💧 LITTLE OR NO SUMMER WATER

Sternbergia lutea

Narrow, 6–12-in. leaves appear in fall simultaneously with flowers and remain green for several months after blooms have gone. Golden yellow, 1½-in.-long flowers resemble large crocuses on 6–9-in. stems, provide a pleasant autumn surprise in borders, in rock gardens, near pools. Good cut flowers. Plant bulbs as soon as available—August or September. Set 4 in. deep, 6 in. apart, in sun. In coldest climates, give sheltered location. When bulbs become crowded, lift, divide, and replant in August.

STEWARTIA

Theaceae

DECIDUOUS SHRUBS OR TREES

🌡 ZONES 4–6, 14–17, 20, 21

☼☽ SUN OR PARTIAL SHADE

💧 💧💧 REGULAR TO AMPLE WATER

Stewartia koreana

These are all-season performers: distinctive pattern of bare branches in winter, fresh green leaves in spring, white flowers like single camellias in summer, and colored foliage in autumn. Slow growing. Best in acid soil with high content of organic matter.

S. koreana. KOREAN STEWARTIA. Tree. To 20–25 ft.; may eventually reach 50 ft. Rather narrow pyramidal habit. Leaves dark green, to 4 in. long, somewhat silky underneath, turning orange or orange red in fall. Blooms in June–July: white flowers with yellow-orange stamens, to 3 in. across, on short stalks among leaves. Possibly a variety of Japanese stewartia.

S. monadelpha. TALL STEWARTIA. Tree. To 25 ft., with upward-angled slender branches, 1½–2½-in.-long leaves. Summer flowers 1½ in. across, the stamens with violet anthers. Outstanding red leaf color in fall.

S. ovata. MOUNTAIN STEWARTIA. Shrub or small tree. To 15 ft. Slender habit. The 2½–5-in., grayish green leaves turn brilliant orange in fall. Three-inch flowers with frilled petals bloom in summer. *S. o. grandiflora* has 4-in. flowers with lavender anthers. It will bloom even as a young plant.

S. pseudocamellia. JAPANESE STEWARTIA. Tree. Grows to 60 ft. Leaves 1–3 in. long, turning bronze to dark purple in fall. July–August flowers to 2½ in. across, with orange anthers.

STIGMAPHYLLON

ORCHID VINE

Malpighiaceae

EVERGREEN OR PARTIALLY DECIDUOUS VINES

🌡 ZONES VARY BY SPECIES

☼ ROOTS IN SHADE

💧💧 AMPLE WATER

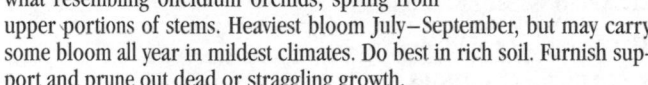

Stigmaphyllon ciliatum

Tall twiners of fairly fast growth to 20–30 ft. Leaves borne in pairs. Long-stalked clusters of bright yellow flowers of irregular shape, somewhat resembling oncidium orchids, spring from upper portions of stems. Heaviest bloom July–September, but may carry some bloom all year in mildest climates. Do best in rich soil. Furnish support and prune out dead or straggling growth.

S. ciliatum. Zones 19–24. Foliage open and delicate, and plants easily kept small. Leaves heart shaped, 1–3 in. long, with a few long, bristly teeth on edges. Clusters of three to seven flowers 1½ in. across.

S. littorale. Zones 15–24. Larger, coarser vine than *S. ciliatum*, with larger (to 5 in. long) oval leaves and larger clusters (10–20) of smaller flowers (1 in. across). Extremely vigorous; can climb to tops of tall trees.

STIPA

FEATHER GRASS, NEEDLE GRASS

Poaceae (Gramineae)

PERENNIAL GRASSES

🌡 ZONES VARY BY SPECIES

☼ SUN

💧 💧 💧 WATER NEEDS VARY BY SPECIES

Feather or needle grasses have large, open, airy inflorescences that can impart lightness and motion to the garden. Of the 150 or so species, three have special merit. ▶

Stipa gigantea

S. gigantea. GIANT FEATHER GRASS. Zones 4–9, 14–24. Clumps of narrow, arching leaves grow 2 to 3 ft. tall. Open, airy sheaves of yellowish flowers shimmer in a broad cloud reaching to 6 ft. in height and breadth. Needs ample water until well established, after which it can tolerate some extended dry spells.

S. pulchra. PURPLE NEEDLE GRASS. Zones 5, 7–9, 11, 14–24. One of the native bunch grasses that once covered much of California's Central Valley and foothills. Foliage clumps are 1–1½ ft. tall, flowering stems to 3 ft. Purplish flowers with long (to 4 in.) bristles mature, along with leaves, to golden yellow in summer. Plants remain dormant until winter rains. Use in wild garden.

S. tenuissima. MEXICAN FEATHER GRASS, TEXAS NEEDLE GRASS. Zones 4–24. Very thin bright green leaves form erect clumps that arch outward toward the top. Numerous thin flowering stems divide and redivide into almost hairlike fineness, green at first, then golden. Single or scattered clumps are effective among ground cover or boulders, on slopes. Larger plantings can create effective erosion control. Water regularly, but soil should dry out between irrigations. Can self-sow in irrigated gardens.

STOCK. See MATTHIOLA p. 376

STOKESIA laevis

STOKES ASTER
Asteraceae (Compositae)
PERENNIAL
ZONES 1–9, 12–24
SUN
REGULAR WATER

Stokesia laevis

Rugged and most adaptable plant. Much branched, with stiff erect stems 1½–2 ft. high. Smooth, firm-textured, medium green leaves, 2–8 in. long, spiny, toothed at bottom. Asterlike flower heads in blue, purplish blue, or white, 3–4 in. across. Composed of button of small flowers in center, surrounded by ring of larger flowers. Blooms summer, early autumn. Leafy, curved, finely toothed bracts surround tight flower buds. Several varieties; 'Blue Danube' is selected form. Good in pots. Long-lasting cut flower.

STONECRESS. See AETHIONEMA p. 141
STONECROP. See SEDUM p. 481
STONEFACE. See LITHOPS p. 359
STORAX, CALIFORNIA. See STYRAX officinalis californicus p. 497

S

STRANVAESIA davidiana

Rosaceae
EVERGREEN SHRUB OR SMALL TREE
ZONES 4–11, 14–17
SUN
MODERATE WATER

Stranvaesia davidiana

Informal, wide-spreading, 6–20 ft. high; moderate growth rate. Leaves oblong, smooth edged, to 4 in. long; new foliage reddish. Some leaves turn bronze or purple in late fall and winter—good foil for clusters of showy red berries that form at same time. White flowers in 4-in. clusters bloom in June.

Best if given plenty of room, not-too-rich soil. In hot interior gardens, protect from hot winds. Subject to fireblight. Looks good with strong-growing native plants, or as screen or background. Berried branches are handsome as holiday cut foliage.

S. d. undulata (S. undulata). Lower growing than the species, to irregularly shaped 5-ft. shrub. New foliage and branch tips are colorful bronzy red. Leaves are wavy along edges.

STRAWBERRY

Rosaceae
PERENNIALS
ALL ZONES
SUN
FREQUENT, DEEP SOAKINGS
SEE CHART

Strawberry

Plants are 6–8 in. tall, spreading about 1 ft. across with long runners. Toothed, roundish, medium green leaves, white flowers. Plant strawberries in well-drained, fairly rich soil.

You'll find that strawberries are often labeled as day neutral, everbearing, or June bearing. June-bearing types produce one crop per year, in late spring or early summer. Plant these for preserving or freezing, since they give you all their fruit at once. Generally speaking, June-bearing types are the highest-quality strawberries you can grow.

Everbearing kinds include the day neutrals, which flower and set fruit with little regard for day length. Instead of coming all at once, the everbearing harvest tends to peak in early summer, then continue on (often unevenly) through fall; the exact fruiting pattern depends on the variety.

To harvest just a few berries, you can simply plant a dozen or so plants, spaced 14–18 in. apart, in sunny patch within flower or vegetable garden, or even in boxes or tubs on patio.

To bring in big crop of berries, plant in rows. If soil is heavy or poorly drained, set plants in rows along raised mounds 5–6 in. high and 28 in. from center to center. Use furrows between mounds for irrigation and feeding. Set plants 14–16 in. apart.

If your soil drains well or if furrow irrigation would be difficult, plant on flat ground, 14–18 in. apart, in rows 1½ ft. apart, and irrigate by overhead sprinkler. Flat-ground method is best where salinity is a problem. Strawberries are difficult to grow in desert or other regions where soil and water salinity are very high.

In Northwest, most gardeners set plants 2–3 ft. apart in rows 4–5 ft. apart, let runners fill in until plants are 7–10 in. apart, then keep additional runners pinched off. Keep the rows 20–30 in. wide.

Planting season is usually determined by when your nursery can offer plants. In mild-winter areas, plants set out in late summer or fall produce a crop the following spring. Other than that, rule is to plant in early spring. Everbearers will give summer and fall crop from spring plantings; pinch off earliest blossoms to increase plant strength.

Set plants carefully; crown should be above soil level, topmost roots ¼ in. beneath soil level (buried crowns rot; exposed roots dry out). Mulch to keep down weeds, conserve moisture, keep berries clean.

Strawberry plants are in special need of water in bearing season. In summer-arid areas they may need water every 2 or 3 days if soil is sandy, every 7–10 days if soil is heavy. In humid Northwest, early berries may ripen without irrigation, but everbearers will need summer water.

Feed plants twice a year—once when growth begins, again after first crop. In California and Southwest, nitrogen is especially necessary. Northwest growers usually apply superphosphate at planting time and use complete fertilizers high in phosphorus.

Most varieties are reproduced by offset plants at ends of runners. You can (a) pinch off all runners, which will give large plants and small yields of big berries; or (b) permit offset plants to grow 7–10 in. apart or even closer, which will give heavy yields of somewhat smaller berries. When your plants have made enough offsets, pinch off further runners. (Some varieties make few or no offsets.)

Strawberries are subject to botrytis (fruit rot), red stele (root rot), yellows (virus), and verticillium wilt (soil-borne fungus). Spray or dust to control aphids and spider mites; do not use chemicals if fruit has set. Control

STRAWBERRY

NAME	DESCRIPTION	ADAPTABILITY	RESISTANCE
'Benton'	June-bearing variety that produces a good crop of firm, flavorful berries	Outstanding in Northwest, especially in mountain and intermountain areas	Virus tolerant, mildew resistant
'Brighton'	Everbearing. Showy flowers and big, beautiful berries make this good for hanging baskets. Fruit flavor not as intense as many others	Best in California, but hardy enough for mountain and intermountain states	Resists verticillium wilt and viruses; some mildew resistance
'Chandler'	Everbearing. Large berries, excellent flavor, good texture, juicy	Grows well in California, particularly Santa Barbara County and south	Some resistance to leaf spot
'Douglas'	June bearing. Heavy producer of early, flavorful berries. Grows and flowers in low temperatures	At its best in California	Resistant to viruses and leaf spot, but gets botrytis; gets red stele in Pacific Northwest
'Fern'	Everbearing. Sweet, medium-size, wedge-shaped berries are good fresh, canned	Good throughout the West, except in coldest regions east of the mountains	Susceptible to viruses, red stele
'Fort Laramie'	Everbearing. Good yield of large, bright red berries over long season. Excellent flavor	Tolerates −30°F without mulch. Hardy in mountain states, high plains	
'Hecker'	Everbearing. Smallish berries are very flavorful, a little soft	Bred on the mild California coast; like 'Fort Laramie', can handle extreme cold	Good virus and wilt resistance, but gets red stele
'Hood'	Berry is large, cone-shaped, bright red. Bears same time as 'Northwest'. Fine for jam, fresh use. Not best freezer	Similar to 'Northwest'	Resists mildew
'Lassen'	Medium-large berry with spring and fall crops. Use fresh or for freezing	Good in Southern California, inland valleys. Takes warm winters	Moderate resistance to alkalinity. Highly subject to yellows
'Northwest'	Big, good-looking berry for use fresh, frozen, in preserves. June–July in Northwest	Popular in Washington, Oregon	Resistant to yellows. Susceptible to red stele; give good drainage
'Ogallala'	Everbearing. Hybrid with wild Rocky Mountain berry	Cold tolerant. Blossoms fairly frost resistant	
'Olympus'	Average-size light red fruit in midseason. No runners; vigorous plants bear on branching crowns	Good in southwestern Washington and northwestern Oregon	Some botrytis resistance. Resists red stele where best adapted; susceptible in northwestern Washington
'Ozark Beauty'	Everbearing. Large, long-necked berries. Mild, sweet flavor. Produces many runners	Wide climate adaptability. Tolerates much cold	
'Puget Beauty'	Sweet, glossy red. Good fresh, frozen, and for jam. Main crop in June; light crop in Aug.	Good variety for heavy soils in Northwest	Some resistance to red stele and mildew
'Quinault'	Everbearing. Fruit is large, attractive, tasty, rather soft. Good producer of runners	Developed for Northwest	Resistant to viruses and red stele, but susceptible to botrytis
'Rainier'	Good-size red berries that hold size throughout long main crop season. Fine flavor; fine home garden variety. Vigorous plant producer	Best in Northwest, west of Cascades	Fair tolerance to root rot
'Selva'	Everbearing. First flush of fruit comes as late as July, but produces heavily through fall. Fruit huge for day-neutral type, very sweet	Perfectly hardy; great in California, not so good in the Northwest	Gets red spider mites, leaf spotting in mild parts of the Northwest, but appears to be red stele resistant
'Sequoia'	Medium to large red fruit. Tastiest of modern strawberries. Prolific. Bears for many months	Developed in and for coastal California, but with wide climate adaptability, even in coldest winters	Resistant to alkalinity, yellows, and most leaf diseases
'Shuksan'	Medium-size, dark red, soft, mealy berries in midseason	Cold hardy, tolerant of alkalinity. Good east of Cascades	Resistant to botrytis

S

STRAWBERRY

NAME	DESCRIPTION	ADAPTABILITY	RESISTANCE
'Tillikum'	Everbearing. Because it's such a heavy producer, its soft berries are small. Flavor is mild	Best in western Oregon and Washington	Good virus tolerance, no problem with mildew
'Tioga'	Yield, size, and appearance better than 'Lassen'	Grows well in all strawberry areas of California	Resistant to yellows. Susceptible to wilt
'Totem'	June bearing. Productive; juicy, flavorful fruit is on the soft side	Good, flavorful berries for western Oregon, Washington, but since it flowers early, late frosts can impair fruit set	Resistant to red stele; virus tolerant. Holds berries up off ground, so fruit rot is rarely a problem
'Tristar'	Everbearing. Large fruit has best flavor of any everbearing type but 'Quinault'. Bears well the first year	Good throughout the West	Resists red stele and mildew, but moderately susceptible to viruses

snails and slugs. Replace plants every 3 years (everbearers every other year). Use your own runner-grown plants only if they are disease free.

See variety chart for choices in regular strawberries. 'Pink Panda', a hybrid between a strawberry and a potentilla, has typical strawberry foliage and an occasional tasty berry, but is grown chiefly for its inch-wide pink flowers borne from spring through fall. Grow it in sun or light shade, as ground cover, edging, or hanging basket plant.

WILD STRAWBERRIES

Wild strawberries, or *fraises de bois,* are worthwhile garden plants even though it takes many of them to produce much. The runnerless plants bear numerous tiny, fragrant, tasty berries from spring to fall. Raise from seed sown in early spring. Extend plantings by dividing older plants. Often naturalize in partially shaded, well-watered gardens. Attractive informal low edging plant. Several varieties are offered.

STRAWBERRY GERANIUM. See SAXIFRAGA stolonifera   p. 478

STRAWBERRY TREE. See ARBUTUS unedo   p. 162

STRAWFLOWER. See HELICHRYSUM bracteatum   p. 319

STRELITZIA

BIRD OF PARADISE

Strelitziaceae

EVERGREEN PERENNIALS

✿ ZONES VARY BY SPECIES

☼ ◗ FULL SUN ON COAST, LIGHT SHADE INLAND

◖ REGULAR WATER

Tropical plants of extremely individual character. Both species are good to use by pools; they make no litter and seem to withstand some splashing.

Strelitzia reginae

S. nicolai. GIANT BIRD OF PARADISE. Zones 22–24; with protection, Zones 12, 13. This one is grown for its dramatic display of leaves (similar to those of banana plants); flowers are incidental. Treelike, clumping, many stalks to 30 ft. Gray-green, leathery, 5–10-ft. leaves are arranged fanwise on erect or curving trunks. Floral envelope is purplish gray, flower is white with dark blue tongue.

Feed young plants frequently to push to full dramatic size, then give little or no feeding. Goal is to acquire and maintain size without lush growth and need for dividing. Keep dead leaves cut off and thin out surplus growth. Endures temperatures to 28°F

S. reginae. BIRD OF PARADISE. Outdoors in Zones 22–24; under overhangs where heat can be trapped, Zones 9, 12–21. Damaged at 28–29°F and recovers slowly; do not attempt where frost is likely. This one is grown for its spectacular flowers, startlingly like tropical birds. Orange, blue, and white flowers on long, stiff stems bloom intermittently throughout year, but best in cool season. Extremely long lasting. Official city flower of Los Angeles. Trunkless plants grow 5 ft. high with leathery, long-stalked, blue-green, 1½-ft.-long leaves, 4–6 in. wide. Benefits greatly from frequent and heavy feedings. Divide infrequently, since large crowded clumps bloom best. Good in containers.

STREPTOCARPUS

CAPE PRIMROSE

Gesneriaceae

EVERGREEN PERENNIALS

✿ ZONES 17, 22–24; HOUSE PLANTS ANYWHERE

☼ ◗ SHADE OR PART SHADE

◖ ◖◖ REGULAR TO HEAVY WATERING

Streptocarpus Hybrid

Related to gloxinias (*Sinningia*) and African violets and look something like a cross between the two. Leaves are fleshy, sometimes velvety. Flowers are trumpet shaped, with long tube and spreading mouth. Long bloom season; some flower intermittently all year. Indoors, handle like African violets. Many species and hybrids of interest to fanciers; most widely available kinds are hybrids.

Large-flowered hybrids (Giant hybrids). Clumps of long, narrow leaves and 1-ft.-tall stems with long-tubed, 1½–2-in.-wide flowers in white, blue, pink, rose, red, often with contrasting blotches. Usually bloom after 1 year from seed.

Nymph series. Long-blooming plants grown from leaf cuttings. 'Constant Nymph', medium blue, is best known; other named sorts available in purple, rose, red, white, pink. Flowers resemble those of Large-flowered hybrids.

Wiesmoor hybrids. Flowers fringed and crested, to 4–5 in. wide, on 2-ft. stems. Grow from seed.

S. saxorum (Streptocarpella saxorum). Unlike other species; shrubby, much-branched perennial that makes a spreading mound of furry, gray-green, 1½-in.-long, fleshy leaves. Long-stemmed flowers appear in waves over much of year, pale blue and white, 1½ in. wide. Makes splendid hanging container plant. Give African violet conditions, perhaps a bit more light. Among the hybrids, 'Concord Blue', with large flowers, blooms continuously.

STREPTOSOLEN jamesonii

MARMALADE BUSH

Solanaceae

EVERGREEN VINING SHRUB

ZONES 17, 23, 24

SUN OR PARTIAL SHADE

REGULAR WATER

Streptosolen jamesonii

To 4–6 ft. tall and as wide (to 10–15 ft. trained against wall, bank, trellis). Leaves ribbed, oval, 1½ in. long. Flowers are 1 in. across, carried in large, loose clusters at branch ends. Color ranges from yellow to brilliant orange, but most types have orange flowers. Main bloom season April–October (in most frost-free parts of Zones 23, 24, plants are occasionally everblooming, with good display in midwinter). Grow in warm spot with fast drainage. Protect in Zones 13, 15, 16, 18–22. In colder areas, protect plant from frost; cut back dead wood after last frost, thin and prune to shape. Good hanging basket plant (needs some protection from hottest sun). Strikingly effective spilling over a wall or lining garden stairs.

Styracaceae. The storax family includes trees and shrubs with bell-shaped, usually white flowers. Members are *Halesia*, *Pterostyrax*, and *Styrax*.

STYRAX

Styracaceae

DECIDUOUS TREES, SHRUBS

ZONES VARY BY SPECIES

FULL SUN OR PARTIAL SHADE

WATER NEEDS VARY BY SPECIES

Styrax japonicus

Pretty white bell-like flowers in hanging clusters. All deserve to be better known for their subtly attractive and fragrant flowers.

S. japonicus. JAPANESE SNOWDROP TREE, JAPANESE SNOWBELL. Tree. Zones 3–10, 14–21. Slow to moderate growth to 30 ft. Slender, graceful trunk; branches often strongly horizontal, giving the tree a broad, flat top. Leaves oval, scallop edged, to 3 in. long; turn from dark green to red or yellow in fall. White, faintly fragrant flowers ¾ in. long hang in clusters on short side branches in June. Leaves angle upward from branches while flowers hang down, giving parallel green and white tiers.

Needs reasonably good, well-drained garden soil. Needs plenty of water. Prune to control shape; tends to be shrubby unless lower side branches suppressed. Splendid tree to look up into; plant it in raised beds near outdoor entertaining areas, or on high bank above path. Roots are not aggressive. 'Pendula' is a rare shrubby variety with weeping branches. 'Pink Chimes' is rarer still; it has pink flowers on a normal-size tree.

S. obassia. FRAGRANT SNOWBELL. Tree. Zones 3–10, 14–21. To 20–30 ft. tall, rather narrow in spread. Roundish leaves 3–8 in. long, deep green. White June flowers fragrant, ¾–1 in. long, carried in drooping, 6–8-in. clusters at ends of branches. Culture same as for *S. japonicus*. Good against background of evergreens, or for height and contrast above border of rhododendrons and azaleas. Regular water.

S. officinalis californicus (S. californica). CALIFORNIA STORAX. Zones 8, 9, 14–24. Shrub to 4–12 ft. Native to foothills of Sierra Nevada, inner Coast Ranges. Trunks gray, leaves 1–2 in. long, green above, gray underneath. Flowers (April–June) fragrant, white, drooping in clusters of two or three, about an inch long. *S. o. fulvescens*, similar, is native to mountains of Southern California. Endures aridity, heat, rocky soil.

SUCCULENTS. Strictly speaking, a succulent is any plant that stores water in juicy leaves, stems, or roots to withstand periodic drought. Practically speaking, fanciers of succulents exclude such fleshy plants as epiphytic orchids and include in their collections many desert plants (yuccas, puyas) that are not fleshy. Although cacti are succulents, common consent sets them up as a separate category (see Cactaceae).

Most succulents come from desert or semidesert areas in warmer parts of the world. Mexico and South Africa are two very important sources. Some (notably sedums and sempervivums) come from colder climates, where they grow on sunny, rocky slopes and ledges.

Succulents are grown everywhere as house plants; in milder western climates, many are useful and decorative as landscaping plants, either in open ground or in containers. When well grown and well groomed, they look good all year, in bloom or out. Although considered low-maintenance plants, they look shabby if neglected; they may live through extended drought but will drop leaves, shrivel, or lose color. Amount of irrigation needed depends on summer heat, humidity of atmosphere. Plants in interior valleys may need water every 1–2 weeks; near the coast, water less. Give plants just enough water to keep them healthy, plump of leaf, and attractive.

One light feeding at start of growing season should be enough for plants in open ground. Larger-growing and later-blooming kinds may require additional feeding.

Some succulents make good ground covers. Some are sturdy and quick growing enough for erosion control on large banks. Other smaller kinds are useful among stepping stones or for creating patterns in small gardens. Most of these come easily from stem or leaf cuttings, and a stock can quickly be grown from a few plants. See *Echeveria*, ice plant, *Portulacaria*, *Sedum*, *Senecio*.

Large-growing succulents have decorative value in themselves. See *Aeonium*, *Agave*, *Aloe*, *Cotyledon*, *Crassula*, *Dudleya*, *Echeveria*, *Kalanchoe*, *Portulacaria*, *Yucca*.

Many succulents have showy flowers. For some of the best, see *Aloe*, some species of *Crassula*, *Hoya*, ice plant, *Kalanchoe*.

Some smaller succulents are primarily collectors' items, grown for odd form or flowers. See smaller species of *Aloe*, *Ceropegia*, *Crassula*, *Echeveria*, *Euphorbia*, *Lithops*, *Stapelia*.

A few words of caution to growers of succulents:

Not all succulents like hot sun; read species descriptions carefully. Some do not thrive in interior valley or desert summer heat, even if given some shade.

Variety of forms, colors, textures offers many possibilities for handsome combinations, but there's a fine line between successful grouping and jumbled medley. Beware of using too many kinds in one planting. Mass a few species instead of putting in one of each.

You can combine succulents with other types of plants, but plan combinations carefully. Not all plants look right with them. Consider also different cultural requirements.

S

SWEET POTATO

Convolvulaceae

VEGETABLE

🗡 ZONES 8, 9, 14, 18–21; 12, 13 IF WELL WATERED

☼ FULL SUN

💧 AVERAGE WATER

Sweet Potato

This vegetable is the thickened root of a trailing tropical vine closely related to morning glory (*Ipomoea*). Requires long frost-free season; much space; well-drained, preferably sandy loam soil; and considerable work in getting started. The tubers are, moreover, tricky to store. All in all, only devoted gardeners will take trouble to order plants from specialist growers. Mark off rows 3 ft. apart and ditch between them to form planting ridges 6–9 in. high. Set shoots with roots 5–6 in. deep so that only stem tips and leaves are exposed. Plants should be 14–16 in. apart. Harvest before first frost; dig carefully to avoid cutting or bruising roots. Dry in sun, then cure by storing 10–14 days in dry place at temperatures between 85 and 95°F. Then store in cool place (not below 55°F) to await use. Sometimes grown for its attractive foliage; handsome vine in hanging basket.

Leaves of sweet potato are variable in shape; some are simply heart shaped, others variously cut or lobed. One ornamental variety called 'Blackie' has deep purple leaves on purple stems.

To Grow Sweet Potato Vine as House Plant

Push three toothpicks firmly into sweet potato at equal distances around tuber to support potato within the rim of a water glass. Adjust water level so it just touches the tuber. Sprouts will grow from the tuber and in 6 weeks you'll have a lush vine with attractive foliage. Vine will grow until tuber shrivels. If nothing happens after several weeks, your sweet potato probably has been treated to prevent sprouting.

SWISS CHARD

Chenopodiaceae

LEAF VEGETABLE

🗡 ALL ZONES

☼ FULL SUN

💧 WATER TO MAINTAIN GROWTH

Swiss Chard

One of the easiest and most practical of vegetables for home gardens. Sow big, crinkly, tan seeds ½–¾ in. deep in spaded soil, any time from early spring to early summer. Thin seedlings to 1 ft. apart. About 2 months after sowing (plants are generally 1–1½ ft. tall) you can begin to cut outside leaves from plants as needed for meals. New leaves grow up in center of plants. Yield all summer and seldom bolt to seed (if one does, pull it up and throw it away). In desert, plant in fall; doesn't stand up to summer heat there.

Regular green-and-white chard looks presentable in flower garden. 'Rhubarb' chard has red stems, reddish green leaves and makes attractive plant in garden beds or containers. Its leaves are valuable in floral arranging and tasty when cooked, too—sweeter and stronger flavored than green chard. Both leaves and leaf stalks are edible, but best cooked separately. Stems take longer to cook. Swiss chard is actually a form of beet.

SYAGRUS romanzoffianum

QUEEN PALM

Arecaceae (Palmae)

PALM

🗡 ZONES 12, 13, 15–17, 19–24

☼ FULL SUN

💧 REGULAR WATER

Syagrus romanzoffianum

South American palm with exceptionally straight trunk to 50 ft. Arching, bright glossy green leaves 10–15 ft. long break in high wind. Grows quickly with fertilizer. Subject to mites; wash young plants frequently. Damaged at 25°F, but has recovered from 16°F freeze. Formerly known as *Arecastrum romanzoffianum*.

SYMPHORICARPOS

SNOWBERRY, CORALBERRY

Caprifoliaceae

DECIDUOUS SHRUBS

🗡 ZONES VARY BY SPECIES

☼ ◐ ● EXPOSURE NEEDS VARY BY SPECIES

◊ NO DRY-SEASON WATER ONCE ESTABLISHED

Symphoricarpos albus

North American natives. Low growing, often spreading by root suckers. Small, pink-tinged or white flowers in clusters or spikes. Attractive round, berrylike fruit remains on stems after leaves fall; nice in winter arrangements, attracts birds. Best used as wild thicket in sun or shade for erosion control on steep banks.

S. albus (S. racemosus). COMMON SNOWBERRY. All zones. Upright or spreading shrub 2–6 ft. tall. Leaves roundish, dull green, ¾–2 in. long (to 4 in. and often lobed on sucker shoots). Pink flowers May–June;

S

white, ½-in.-wide fruit from late summer to winter. Best fruit production in sun. Not a first-rank shrub, but useful in its tolerance of poor soil, urban air, and shade. Withstands neglect.

S. chenaultii. All zones. Hybrid of garden origin. Resembles *S. orbiculatus,* but red fruit is lightly spotted white and leaves are larger. *S. c.* 'Hancock' is 1-ft. dwarf valued as woodland ground or bank cover. High shade.

S. mollis. CREEPING SNOWBERRY, SPREADING SNOWBERRY. Zones 4–24. Like *S. albus,* but usually less than 1½ ft. high, earlier flowering, fewer flowers, smaller fruit. Spreads like ground cover. Best in partial shade.

S. orbiculatus (S. vulgaris). CORAL BERRY, INDIAN CURRANT. All zones. Resembles *S. albus,* but with profusion of small purplish red fruit in clusters. These are bright enough and plentiful enough to provide a good fall–winter show. Full sun.

SYMPHYTUM officinale

COMFREY	
Boraginaceae	
PERENNIAL	
☀ ◑ ALL ZONES	
☀ ◑ FULL SUN OR PARTIAL SHADE	
◐ REGULAR WATER	
⬥ LEAVES CONTAIN A POISON, SHOULD NOT BE EATEN	

Symphytum officinale

Deep-rooted, clumping perennial to 3 ft. Basal leaves 8 in. or more in length, upper leaves smaller, all furry with stiff hairs. Flowers not showy, ½ in. long, usually dull rose, sometimes white, creamy, or purple. Leaves can be dried as medicinal tea, but use only with directions from a herbalist. Leaves grow all year in coastal Southern California. Plant goes dormant elsewhere. To keep leaf production high, cut out flowering stalks and mulch each spring with compost. Grow from root cuttings.

Although comfrey has a long history as a folk remedy, think hard before establishing it in your garden. Plant spreads freely from roots and is difficult to eradicate. Herb enthusiasts claim that comfrey accumulates minerals, enriches compost.

SYNADENIUM grantii

Euphorbiaceae	
EVERGREEN SHRUB	
☀ ZONES 21–24; HOUSE PLANT ANYWHERE	
☀ FULL SUN	
◐ MODERATE WATER	
⬥ STEMS CONTAIN MILKY, POISONOUS SAP	

Synadenium grantii

Can reach 12 ft. in warm, frost-free location, but is usually much lower. Thick stems are clothed with dark green leaves to 7 in. long and half as wide. More widely grown than the species is *S. g.* 'Rubra', with deep purplish red leaves. Flowers are insignificant. Resembles *Euphorbia cotinifolia,* but easily distinguished by leaves that taper toward the main stems and are stalkless; leaves of *E. cotinifolia* have long stalks. Showy container plant.

SYRINGA

LILAC	
Oleaceae	
DECIDUOUS SHRUBS, RARELY SMALL TREES	
☀ ZONES VARY BY SPECIES	
☀ SUN	
◐ ◐ WATER DURING BLOOM AND GROWTH	

Syringa vulgaris

Best known are common lilac (*S. vulgaris*) and its many named varieties, but there are other species of great usefulness. Best where winter brings pronounced chill, but some bloom well with light chilling. Light shade in hottest areas. All like alkaline soil; in areas where soils are strongly acid, add lime and cultivate into soil beneath drip line of plants. Control growth during early years by pinching and shaping. Flower buds for next year form in pairs where leaves join stems. After bloom, remove spent flower clusters just above points where buds are forming. Heavy pruning results in loss of much of next year's bloom. Thin out dead and weak wood at same time.

Renovate old, overgrown plants by cutting a few of oldest stems to the ground each year. Leaf miner, scale, and stem borer are the only important pests; bacterial blight, leaf spot, downy mildew are occasional problems.

S. chinensis (S. rothomagensis). CHINESE LILAC. Zones 1–11, 14–16, 18–21. Hybrid between common and Persian lilacs. Moderate growth rate to 15 ft., usually much less. More graceful than common lilac, with finer-textured foliage. Airy, open clusters of fragrant rose purple flowers in May (April in warmer zones). Profuse bloom. Does well in mild-winter, hot-summer climates. Variety 'Alba' has white flowers.

S. hyacinthiflora. Zones 1–12, 14–16, 18–22. Hybrids between common lilac and *S. oblata,* a Chinese species. 'Excel' and 'Grace McKenzie' (both single lilac) can bloom as early as March 1. Other varieties are 'Alice Eastwood' (double magenta), 'Blue Hyacinth' (single lavender blue), 'Clarke's Giant' (single lavender blue, large flowers), 'Esther Staley' (single magenta), 'Gertrude Leslie' (double white), 'Pocahontas' (single purple), 'Purple Heart' (single purple), and 'White Hyacinth' (single white).

S. josikaea. HUNGARIAN LILAC. Zones 1–11, 14–16, 18–21. Dense, upright growth to 12 ft. Dark green foliage. Flowers lilac purple, slightly fragrant, in narrow clusters 4–7 in. long. Blooms in May (April in warmer zones).

S. laciniata (S. persica laciniata). Zones 1–12, 14–16, 18–21. Moderate growth to 8 ft. tall, open habit, good rich green foliage color. Leaves to 2½ in. long, divided nearly to midrib into three to nine segments. Many small clusters of fragrant lilac flowers in April, May.

S. patula (S. palibiniana, S. velutina). KOREAN LILAC. Zones 1–9, 14–16. Dense, twiggy growth to eventual 8–9 ft., but stays at 3 ft. many years. Flowers pink to lavender, in clusters to 5 in. long. Blooms April–May. Sometimes grafted high to make 3-ft. standard tree. 'Miss Kim' is dwarf (to 3 ft.) lavender blue variety.

S. persica. PERSIAN LILAC. Zones 1–12, 14–16, 18–21. Graceful, loose form to 6 ft., with arching branches and 2½-in.-long leaves. Many clusters of fragrant pale violet flowers appear all along branches in May (April in warmer zones).

S. prestoniae. Zones 1–12, 14–16. To 10–15 ft. tall. Group of extra-hardy hybrids developed in Canada. Medium to large shrubs that bloom on new spring growth after other lilacs have finished. 'Isabella' (single lilac), 'Jessica' (single violet), 'Nocturne' (blue); and 'Royalty' (purple to violet) are good selections. For 'James MacFarlane' (sometimes sold as member of this group), see *S. swegiflexa.*

S. reticulata (S. japonica, S. amurensis japonica). JAPANESE TREE LILAC. Large shrub easily trained as single-stemmed 30-ft. tree. Zones 1–12, 14–16. Bark smooth, something like cherry in its gloss. Large leaves (to 5 in. long). White flower clusters to 1 ft. appear in late spring, early summer. Flowers showy, but not fragrant; they smell like privet flowers. Useful small shade or street tree in difficult climates.

S. swegiflexa. Zones 1–9, 14–16. To 12 ft. Single pink flowers open from deep reddish buds. Clusters to 8 in. long. Blooms 3 weeks after common lilac. Sometimes sold as pink pearl lilac. Hybrid between two hardy Chinese species, *S. reflexa* and *S. sweginzowii.* 'James MacFarlane' is best-known variety.

S. vulgaris. COMMON LILAC. Zones 1–11. In Zones 12–16, 18–22, plants often bloom irregularly because of failure to break dormancy after mild winters. It was once recommended that plants be gradually but completely dried off beginning in August. It is now felt that such treatment can harm the plant, possibly kill it. Water may be restricted at this time, but should always be available. To accept mild winters and perform exceptionally well in Zones 18–22, the Descanso Hybrids were developed in Southern California. Best known is 'Lavender Lady' (lavender); other varieties are 'Blue Skies' and 'Blue Boy' (blue), 'Chiffon' (lavender), 'Forrest

K. Smith' (light lavender), 'Sylvan Beauty' (rose lavender), and 'White Angel' (or 'Angel White').

Common lilacs can eventually reach 20 ft. tall, with nearly equal spread. Leaves roundish oval, pointed, dark green, to 5 in. long. Pinkish or bluish lavender flowers ('Alba' has pure white flowers) in clusters to 10 in. long or more. Flowers in May; fragrance is legendary. Excellent cut flowers. Lilac fanciers swear these are more fragrant than newer varieties.

Varieties, often called French hybrids, number in the hundreds. They generally flower a little later than species and have larger clusters of single or double flowers in wide range of colors. Singles are often as showy as doubles, sometimes more so. All lilacs require 2–3 years to settle down and produce flowers of full size and true color. Here are just a few of the many choice varieties:

'Charles Joly' (double dark purplish red), 'Miss Ellen Willmott' (double pure white), 'Ludwig Spaeth' (single reddish purple to dark purple), 'President Lincoln' (single Wedgwood blue), 'President Poincare' (double two-tone purple), 'Sensation' (single wine red with white picotee edge), 'William Robinson' (double pink).

Hybrids between *S. vulgaris* and *S. oblata* are called *S. hyacinthiflora* by some experts. These bloom earlier than the French hybrids by a week or 10 days. 'Blue Hyacinth' and 'Clarke's Giant' (blue) and 'Esther Staley' (deep pink) are typical. See *S. hyacinthiflora*.

SYZYGIUM

Myrtaceae

EVERGREEN SHRUBS OR TREES

☀ ZONES VARY BY SPECIES

☀ ◐ BEST IN SUN, TOLERATE SHADE

● REGULAR WATER

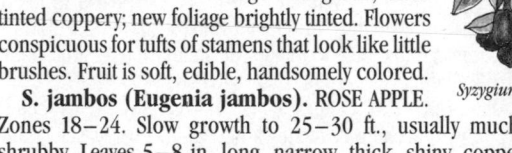

Syzygium paniculatum

Closely related to *Eugenia* and usually sold as such in nurseries. Foliage rich green, often tinted coppery; new foliage brightly tinted. Flowers conspicuous for tufts of stamens that look like little brushes. Fruit is soft, edible, handsomely colored.

S. jambos (Eugenia jambos). ROSE APPLE. Zones 18–24. Slow growth to 25–30 ft., usually much smaller and shrubby. Leaves 5–8 in. long, narrow, thick, shiny, coppery green; new growth pinkish. Greenish white flower brushes 2–3 in. across in clusters at branch ends. Spring bloom. Fruit greenish or yellow (sometimes blushed pink), 1–2 in. wide; sweetish, with mild flavor, fragrance of rose water. Slow growth means little or no pruning.

S. paniculatum (Eugenia myrtifolia, E. paniculata). BRUSH CHERRY, AUSTRALIAN BRUSH CHERRY. Zones 16, 17, 19–24. Unclipped, a handsome, narrowish tree, to 30–60 ft. tall. Single or multitrunked, with dense foliage crown. Usually clipped into formal shapes and hedges, and a most popular hedging, background, and screening plant in mild, nearly frost-free areas. Young foliage reddish bronze; mature leaves oblong, 1½–3 in. long, rich glossy green, often bronze tinged. Flowers creamy, ½ in. wide. Fruit is rose purple, showy, ¾ in. long, edible but insipid. Psyllids (sucking insects) are hard to control.

Will not stand heavy frost; foliage burns at 25–26°F, and even old plants may die if temperature drops much lower. Thrives in well-drained garden soil. Hedges need frequent clipping to stay neat, and heavy root systems make it hard to grow other plants nearby; new red foliage, showy fruit make it worth the effort. Don't plant where dropping fruit will squash on pavement.

Variety 'Monterey Bay' is a larger-leafed selection that displays bronzy coloring over a longer period. 'Compacta' is smaller, denser in growth. Popular hedging plant. 'Brea' and 'Globulus' are also dwarf and compact, with bronzy amber foliage color. Tiniest of all is 'Teenie Genie'; it grows very slowly to 4 ft. 'Red Flame' has new growth of exceptionally bright red.

FOR INFORMATION ON YOUR CLIMATE ZONE
PLEASE SEE PAGES 15–44

TABEBUIA

Bignoniaceae

BRIEFLY DECIDUOUS, SOMETIMES EVERGREEN TREES

☀ ZONES 15, 16, 20–24

☀ FULL SUN

● REGULAR WATER

Tabebuia chrysotricha

Fast growth to 25–30 ft. Showy, 2–4-in.-long, trumpet-shaped flowers grow in rounded clusters that become larger (up to 23 flowers) and more profuse as trees mature. Leaves dark olive green, usually divided into three to seven leaflets arranged like fingers of hand.

Useful as patio trees or as free-standing flowering trees for display. Tolerate many soils and degrees of maintenance, but respond well to feeding. Good drainage essential. Stake while young and keep plants to single leading shoot until 6–8 ft. tall, then allow to develop freely. Hardy to about 24°F.

T. chrysotricha. GOLDEN TRUMPET TREE. Sometimes sold as *T. pulcherrima*. Rounded, spreading growth to 25 ft. Leaves with five leaflets (2–4 in. long, 1–2 in. wide); young twigs, undersides of leaves covered with tawny fuzz. Flowers are 3–4 in. long, golden yellow, often with maroon stripes in throat. Bloom heaviest April–May, when trees lose leaves for brief period. Sometimes blooms lightly at other times with leaves present. Blooms young.

T. impetiginosa (T. ipe). PINK TRUMPET TREE. More erect, larger growing. Leaves dark green, smooth; usually evergreen. Flowers 2–3 in. long, lavender pink with white throat banded with yellow. Blooms late winter, sometimes again late summer to fall. Does not bloom as a young tree.

TAGETES

MARIGOLD

Asteraceae (Compositae)

SUMMER ANNUALS, PERENNIALS

☀ ZONES FOR PERENNIALS VARY BY SPECIES

☀ FULL SUN

● REGULAR WATER, EXCEPT AS NOTED

Tagetes erecta

Robust, free-branching, nearly trouble-free plants ranging from 6 in. to 4 ft. tall, with flowers from pale yellow through gold to orange and brown maroon. Leaves finely divided, ferny, usually strongly scented. Summer annuals in all zones. Plants will bloom early summer to frost if old flowers are picked off; in desert, they bloom best in fall, until frost. Handsome, long-lasting cut flowers; strong scent permeates a room, but some odorless varieties are available. Easy to grow from seed, which sprouts in a few days in warm soil; to get earlier bloom, start seeds in flats or buy flat-grown plants. Smog will damage tender young plants, but they toughen up. University tests discount the widely held belief that marigold roots can entrap, destroy, or repel nematodes.

T. erecta. AMERICAN MARIGOLD, AFRICAN MARIGOLD (often sold as tall marigold). Annual. All zones. Original strains were plants 3–4 ft. tall with single flowers. Modern strains more varied; most have fully double flowers. They range from dwarf Guys and Dolls and Inca series (12–14 in.) through Galore, Lady, and Perfection (16–20 in.) to Climax (2½–3 ft.). Novelty tall strains are Odorless and First Whites (28–30 in.). 'Snowbird' (1½ ft.) is a white marigold with uniform habit and color. Triploid hybrids, crosses between African and French marigolds, have exceptional vigor, long bloom season. Generally shorter than other *T. erecta* strains, with enormous profusion of 2-in. flowers. They range from the 10-in. Nugget to the 12–14-in. Fireworks, H-G, Solar, and Sundance. Avoid overhead watering on taller kinds, or stems will sag and perhaps break.

T. filifolia. IRISH LACE. Annual. All zones. Mounds of bright green, finely divided foliage, 6 in. tall and as wide, resemble unusually fluffy round ferns. Used primarily as edging plant for foliage effect, but tiny white flowers in late summer and fall are attractive.

T

T. lemmonii. Shrubby perennial. Zones 8–10, 12–24. Native from southeastern Arizona (where it can reach 3 ft.) to southern Mexico and Central America, where it is a shrub to 6 ft. or taller, spreading as wide as it's high. Finely divided 4-in. leaves are aromatic when brushed against or rubbed—a strongly fragrant blend of marigold, mint, and lemon. To some people the odor of the foliage is too strong; it will not trouble you if you don't brush against the plant. Golden orange flower heads are carried in broad sheaves at branch ends. Bloom is scattered throughout the year, heaviest winter–spring. Damaged by frost in open situations; cut back to remove damaged growth or to correct shape and limit size. Takes aridity.

T. lucida. MEXICAN TARRAGON. Perennial in Zones 8, 9, 12–24 (but usually grown as an annual); annual elsewhere. Single, usually unbranched stems grow to 2–2½ ft. Narrow, uncut, smooth dark green leaves have strong scent and flavor of tarragon. Unimpressive yellow flowers are less than ½ in. wide.

T. patula. FRENCH MARIGOLD. Annual. All zones. Varieties from 6–18 in. tall, in flower colors from yellow to rich maroon brown; flowers may be fully double or single, and many are strongly bicolored. Best for edging are the dwarf, very double Janie (8-in.), Bonanza (10-in.), and Hero (10–12-in.) series in a range of colors from yellow through orange to red and brownish red. The Aurora and Sophia series have flowers that are larger (2½ in. wide) but not as double.

T. tenuifolia (T. signata). SIGNET MARIGOLD. Annual. All zones. Infrequently planted. Smaller flower heads than French marigold, but incredibly profuse in bloom. Finely cut foliage. Golden orange 'Golden Gem' ('Ursula') and bright yellow 'Lemon Gem' both grow 8 in. tall.

MAKE A TALL MARIGOLD PLANT STAND STRAIGHT
To make tall marigold plants stand as firmly as possible (perhaps stoutly enough not to need staking), dig planting holes extra deep, strip any leaves off lower 1–3 in. of stem, and plant with stripped portion below soil line.

TAMARIX

TAMARISK
Tamaricaceae
DECIDUOUS SHRUBS AND TREES
☀ ZONES VARY BY SPECIES
☀ FULL SUN
◊ ◖ TOLERATE LONG PERIODS OF DRYNESS

Tamarix aphylla

In deserts of California and Arizona, they have no equal in resistance to wind and aridity, and they will grow in saline soils that are toxic to other plants. Nurseries can't keep them in containers long because they form deep taproots. But they are easy to grow from ½–1-in.-thick cuttings set in place and kept watered.

There is much confusion in labeling of tamarisks in the nurseries and among botanists; these plants are difficult to classify. Leaves and flowers are individually tiny, and hand lens is necessary to see flower details. Gardeners are concerned with three kinds—evergreen-appearing, spring-flowering, and spring-through-summer-flowering trees.

Spring-flowering tamarisks are hardy and adapted in all zones. Fast growth to 6–15 ft., depending on culture. Graceful, airy, arching branches with reddish bark. Pink flowers in clusters on branches of previous year.

Prune after bloom in spring to maintain graceful effect, limit height, and produce new flowering wood.

T. africana. Spring-flowering tree. All zones. Flowers bloom in upright, 1–2-in.-long clusters of white or pale pink. *T. parviflora* is often sold and used under this name in California.

T. aphylla (T. articulata). ATHEL TREE. Evergreen-appearing tree. Widely used in Zones 10–13; useful in some difficult situations in Zones 7–9, 14–24. Heavily damaged at 0°F but comes back rapidly. Excellent windbreak tree. Fast growth from planted cuttings to 10 ft. or more in 3 years; eventually 30–50 ft. and more in 15 years with deep soil and water.

Greenish jointed branchlets give tree its evergreen appearance. Takes on grayish look in late summer where soils are saline, because of secretions of salt. True leaves are minute. White to pinkish, very small flowers grow in clusters at ends of branches in late summer, but tree is not as spectacular in bloom as other tamarisks. Not a good selection for highly cultivated gardens; its roots are too competitive.

T. chinensis (T. pentandra, T. ramosissima). SALT CEDAR. Spring-through-summer-flowering tree or huge shrub. Hardy in Zones 4–24, usually planted in Zones 10–13. To 20–30 ft., with white, cream, pink, or purple flowers. Has resistance to heat and cold, as well as high salt tolerance—all qualities that make it a successful weed. Widely seen in desert regions, but disliked because its aggressive spreading and deep, thirsty roots displace native vegetation. Efforts are being made to wipe it out in many desert areas.

T. parviflora. Often sold as *T. tetrandra;* sold as *T. africana* in California. Spring-flowering tree. All zones. Profuse display of pink, four-petaled flowers that turn to tan, then brown; prune hard after bloom.

TANACETUM

Asteraceae (Compositae)
PERENNIAL HERBS
☀ ZONES VARY BY SPECIES
☀ FULL SUN
◊ ◖ FAIR TOLERANCE OF ARIDITY

Tanacetum vulgare

Most kinds of *Tanacetum* have finely divided leaves (often highly aromatic), and clusters of daisylike flower heads. Some have gray to nearly white foliage.

T. balsamita. See Chrysanthemum balsamita

T. coccineum. See Chrysanthemum coccineum

T. densum amanii. Zones 3–24. Sometimes sold as *Chrysanthemum haradjanii.* Low-growing plant spreading slowly to make broad mats. Leaves are finely cut, silvery white, featherlike in appearance. Small yellow flower heads appear a few inches above the mat. Use in rock garden, as small-scale ground cover in bright, sunny area with good drainage. Can withstand some dry spells when established. One of the whitest plants.

T. parthenium. See Chrysanthemum parthenium

T. ptarmiciflorum. See Chrysanthemum ptarmiciflorum

T. vulgare. TANSY. All zones. Coarse garden plant to 3 ft. with finely divided bright green aromatic (some say smelly) leaves, and small yellow button flowers. Thin clumps yearly to keep in bounds. No longer used medicinally, though still grown in herb gardens. *T. v. crispum,* fern-leaf tansy, to 2½ ft., has finely cut foliage, is more decorative than the species.

Taxaceae. The yew family contains needle-leafed evergreens with single-seeded fruit surrounded by a fleshy coat. Yew (*Taxus*) and California nutmeg (*Torreya*) are examples.

Taxodiaceae. The taxodium family contains evergreen (rarely deciduous) coniferous trees, usually with small cones containing two to six seeds on each scale. Bald cypress and Montezuma cypress (*Taxodium*) give the group its name. Includes *Cryptomeria,* redwood, and giant sequoia.

TAXODIUM

Taxodiaceae

DECIDUOUS OR EVERGREEN TREES

⚎ ZONES VARY BY SPECIES

☼ FULL SUN

◌ ◌ ◖ ● ◖ TOLERATE DRY TO WET SOIL

Taxodium distichum

Conifers of great size bearing short, narrow, flat, needlelike leaves in graceful sprays. Cones are scented. One of these trees is native to the Southeast, the other to Mexico; both adapt widely to colder and drier climates.

T. distichum. BALD CYPRESS. Deciduous tree. Zones 2–9, 14–24. Also thrives in wet places in Zones 10, 12, 13. Can grow into 100-ft.-tall, broad-topped tree in the wild, but young and middle-aged garden trees are pyramidal. Foliage sprays delicate and feathery; leaves about ½ in. long, narrow, and of pale, delicate, yellow-toned green. Foliage turns bright orange brown in fall before dropping. Any soil except alkaline. Takes extremely wet conditions (lawns and even swamps), but also will tolerate rather dry soil. No particular pests or diseases. Requires only corrective pruning—removal of dead wood and unwanted branches. Outstanding tree for streambank or edge of lake or pond.

T. mucronatum. MONTEZUMA CYPRESS. Evergreen tree in mild climates; partially or wholly deciduous in cold regions. Zones 5, 6, 8–10, 12–14. Has strongly weeping branches. Fast grower in its youth; with ample water will reach 40 ft. in 14 years, and is likely to reach eventual 75 ft. in gardens. Growth of established plants is slow under dry conditions. Extremely graceful, fine-textured evergreen for large lawns.

TAXUS

YEW

Taxaceae

EVERGREEN SHRUBS OR TREES

⚎ ZONES 3–9, 14–24, EXCEPT AS NOTED

☼ ◐ ● SUN TO SHADE

◖ LITTLE WATER ONCE ESTABLISHED

◆ FRUIT (SEEDS) AND FOLIAGE ARE POISONOUS

Taxus baccata 'Stricta'

Conifers, but instead of cones they bear fleshy, scarlet (rarely yellow), cup-shaped, single-seeded fruit. In general, yews are more formal, darker green, and more tolerant of shade and moisture than most cultivated conifers. Slow growing, long lived, tolerant of much shearing and pruning. Excellent for hedges, screens.

Easily moved even when large, but slow growth makes big plants a luxury item. Take many soil conditions, but will not thrive in strongly alkaline or strongly acid soils. Reflected light and heat from hot south or west wall will burn foliage. Even cold-hardy kinds show needle damage when exposed to dry winds, very low temperatures. Only female plants produce berries, but many do so without male plants nearby. The few pests include vine weevils, scale, and spider mites. All yews benefit from being washed off with water from hose every 2 weeks during hot, dry weather.

T. baccata. ENGLISH YEW. Slow growth to 25–40 ft., with wide-spreading branches forming broad, low crown. Needles ½–1½ in. long, dark green and glossy above, pale underneath. Red fruit has poisonous seeds. Garden varieties are far more common than the species.

T. b. 'Adpressa'. Usually sold as *T. brevifolia*, which is really the native western yew. Wide-spreading, dense shrub grows to 4–5 ft. high; leaves about ½ in. long.

T. b. 'Aurea'. More compact than the species. New foliage is golden yellow spring to autumn, then turns green.

T. b. 'Repandens'. SPREADING ENGLISH YEW. Long, horizontal, spreading branches make 2-ft.-high ground cover. Useful low foundation plant. Will arch over wall.

T. b. 'Stricta' ('Fastigiata'). IRISH YEW. Makes column of dark green. Slow growing to 20 ft. or higher. Needles larger than those of English yew. Many crowded upright branches tend to spread near top, especially in snowy regions or where water is ample, growth lush. Branches can be tied together with wire. Plants that outgrow their space can be reduced by heading back and thinning; old wood sprouts freely. Striking against big wall, in corner plantings, or as background planting.

T. b. 'Stricta Variegata'. Like Irish yew, but leaves show yellowish white variegations.

T. brevifolia. WESTERN or OREGON YEW. Zones 1–6, 14–17. Native to moist places, California north to Alaska, inland to Montana. Tree of loose, open growth to 50–60 ft. with dark yellowish green needles 1 in. or less in length. Not common in nature and difficult to grow. Most plants sold under this name are *T. baccata* 'Adpressa' or *T. cuspidata* 'Nana'.

T. cuspidata. JAPANESE YEW. Zones 1–6, 14–17. Tree to 50 ft. in Japan. Most useful yew in cold-winter areas east of the Cascades. Varieties will grow in shaded areas of Rocky Mountain gardens. Usually grown as compact, spreading shrub. Needles ½–1 in. long, usually in two rows along twigs, making flat or V-shaped spray. Foliage dark green above, tinged yellowish underneath.

T. c. 'Capitata'. Plants sold under this name are probably ordinary *T. cuspidata* in its upright, pyramidal form. Dense, slow growth to 10–25 ft. Can be held lower by pinching new growth. Fruits heavily.

T. c. 'Nana'. Often sold as *T. brevifolia*. Grows 1–4 in. a year, to 3 ft. tall, spreads to 6 ft. in 20 years. Low barrier or foundation plant.

T. media. Group of hybrids between Japanese and English yew. Intermediate between the two in color and texture.

T. m. 'Brownii'. Slow-growing, compact, and rounded yew eventually to 4–8 ft. tall. Good for low, dense hedge.

T. m. 'Hatfieldii'. Broad columnar or pyramidal yew of good dark green color. Grows 10 ft. or taller.

T. m. 'Hicksii'. Narrow, upright yew, slightly broader at center than at top and bottom; to 10–12 ft.

TECOMA

Bignoniaceae

LARGE SHRUBS OR SMALL TREES

⚎ ZONES 10, 12, 13, 21–24

☼ FULL SUN

◖ LITTLE WATER

Various trumpet vines once lumped together as *Tecoma* now have different names. What remains is a showy large shrub or small tree.

Tecoma stans

T. australis. See Pandorea pandorana
T. capensis. See Tecomaria capensis
T. jasminoides. See Pandorea jasminoides
T. stans (Stenolobium stans). YELLOW BELLS, YELLOW TRUMPET FLOWER, YELLOW ELDER. Evergreen shrub or small tree. In mildest-winter areas, can be trained as tree. Where frosts are common, it is usually a large shrub. Much of wood may die back in winter, but recovery is quick in warm weather: rapid, bushy growth to 20 ft. Leaves divided into 5–13 toothed, 1½–4-in.-long leaflets. Flowers (June–January) bright yellow, bell shaped, 2 in. across, in large clusters. Needs heat, deep soil, fairly heavy feeding. Cut faded flowers to prolong bloom; prune to remove dead and bushy growth. Showy mass in large garden. Boundary plantings, big shrub borders, screening. Takes very little water.

Tecoma stans

T. s. angustata, with narrow leaflets, is kind best adapted to Zones 12, 13; it needs less water and feeding. June–October bloom.

TECOMARIA capensis (Tecoma capensis)

CAPE HONEYSUCKLE
Bignoniaceae
EVERGREEN VINE OR SHRUB
ZONES 12, 13, 16, 18–24; PROTECTED IN 14, 15
SUN OR LIGHT SHADE
LITTLE WATER ONCE ESTABLISHED

Tecomaria capensis

Native to South Africa. Can scramble to 15–25 ft. if tied to support. With hard pruning, a 6–8-ft. upright shrub. Leaves divided into many glistening dark green leaflets. Total foliage effect is informal and fine textured. Brilliant orange-red, tubular, 2-in. blossoms grow in compact clusters, October through winter.

Needs good drainage. Takes heat, wind, salt air. Use as espalier, bank cover (especially good on hot, steep slopes), coarse barrier hedge.

Variety 'Aurea' has yellow flowers and lighter green foliage; it's smaller growing and less showy. Requires more heat to perform well.

TEDDYBEAR CACTUS. See OPUNTIA bigelovii   p. 394

TELLIMA grandiflora

FRINGE–CUPS
Saxifragaceae
PERENNIAL
ZONES 4–9, 14–17
FULL SUN TO PART SHADE
WATER DURING GROWTH

Tellima grandiflora

Creeping rootstocks send up roundish, lobed leaves to 4 in. across on leaf stalks up to 8 in. long. Leaves are light green, softly hairy, somewhat like those of piggyback plant *(Tolmiea)*. Small, urn-shaped flowers with tiny fringed petals open green, age to deep red; these are not showy but are attractively disposed along tall (to 2½ ft.), slender stems.

Evergreen where winters are mild, deciduous in colder parts of its native range—central California north to southern Alaska. Choice with ferns in woodland garden.

FOR GROWING SYMBOL EXPLANATIONS
PLEASE SEE PAGE 129

TERNSTROEMIA gymnanthera (T. japonica)

Theaceae
EVERGREEN SHRUB
ZONES 4–9, 12–24
SUN ON COAST, FULL SHADE IN DESERT
AVERAGE TO MUCH WATER

Ternstroemia gymnanthera

Takes a long time to reach 6–8 ft. and is usually seen as rounded plant 3–4 ft. tall and 4–6 ft. wide. Its appeal lies in its glossy, leathery foliage. Red-stalked, rounded oval to narrow oval leaves are 1½–3 in. long, bronzy red when new; when mature, they turn deep green to bronzy green to purplish red, depending on season, exposure, and plant itself. In deep shade it tends to be dark green; with some sun, leaves may be bronzy green to nearly purple red. Red tints are deeper in cold weather.

Summer flowers are ½ in. wide, creamy yellow, fragrant but not showy. Fruit (uncommon on small plants) resembles little yellow to red-orange holly berries or cherries, splits open to reveal shiny black seeds.

Leaves turn yellow if soil isn't acid enough—feed with acid plant food. Pinch out tip growth to encourage compact growth. Use as basic landscaping shrub, informal hedge, tub plant. Good near pools. Grows well and blends well with camellias (to which it is related), azaleas, nandina, pieris, ferns. Cut foliage keeps well.

TETRAPANAX papyriferus (Aralia papyrifera)

RICE PAPER PLANT
Araliaceae
EVERGREEN SHRUB
ZONES 15–24
SUN, SHADE; MIDDAY SHADE WHERE HOT
REGULAR WATER

Tetrapanax papyriferus

Fast growing to 10–15 ft., often multitrunked. Big, bold, long-stalked leaves are 1–2 ft. wide, deeply lobed, gray green above, white-felted beneath, carried in clusters at ends of stems. Fuzz on new growth irritates if it gets in eyes or down the neck. Tan trunks often curve or lean. Big, branched clusters of creamy white flowers on furry tan stems show in December.

Young plant sunburns easily, older plant adapts. Seems to suffer only from high winds (which break or tatter leaves) and frost (foliage severely damaged at 22°F, but recovers fast from freezes, often puts up suckers to form thickets). Digging around roots stimulates sucker formation; suckers may arise 20 ft. from parent plant. Use as silhouette against walls, in patios; combine with other sturdy, bold-leafed plants for tropical effect. Name comes from the thick pith of the stems, used to make Chinese rice paper.

TETRASTIGMA voinieranum (Cissus voinierana)

Vitaceae
EVERGREEN VINE
ZONES 13 (SHADE ONLY), 17, 20–24
ROOTS NEED SHADE, TOPS CAN GET SUN
LITTLE WATER

Tetrastigma voinieranum

Climbs by tendrils or covers ground rapidly to 50–60 ft. Thick, fleshy stems. New growth covered with silvery fuzz. Leaves glossy, dark green, up to 1 ft. across, divided fanwise into three

T

to five oval, leathery leaflets with toothed edges. Flowers and fruit are rarely seen. Feed until well established. Good eave-line decoration. Large-scale bank or ground cover in Zones 17, 23, 24. Good near swimming pools.

TETRATHECA thymifolia

Tremandraceae	
EVERGREEN SHRUB	
🌿 ZONES 16, 17, 21–24	
☼ LIGHT SHADE	
💧 SOME SUMMER WATER	

This 2-ft. shrub sends up a number of slender stems clothed with small dark green leaves. Small (½-in.), drooping, rose pink, bell-shaped flowers line branches from late winter through spring. This Australian shrub is a fine plant for small containers or rock gardens.

Tetratheca thymifolia

TEUCRIUM

GERMANDER	
Lamiaceae (Labiatae)	
EVERGREEN SHRUBS OR SUBSHRUBS	
🌿 ZONES VARY BY SPECIES	
☼ FULL SUN	
💧 LITTLE WATER ONCE ESTABLISHED	

Tough plants, enduring poor, rocky soils. They can't stand wet or poorly drained soils but will take ordinary watering where drainage is good.

Teucrium chamaedrys

T. chamaedrys. All zones. Low growing (1 ft. tall), spreading to 2 ft., with many upright, woody-based stems densely set with toothed, dark green, ¾-in.-long leaves. In summer, red-purple or white, ¾-in. flowers form in loose spikes (white-flowered form is looser). Attractive to bees. Use as edging, foreground, low clipped hedge, or small-scale ground cover. To keep neat, shear back once or twice a year to force side branching. As ground cover, set plants 2 ft. apart.

T. c. 'Prostratum'. Leaves and flowers are similar to those of *T. chamaedrys,* but growth habit is very prostrate (4–6 in. high and spreading to 3 ft. or more).

T. cossonii majoricum. Zones 8, 9, 14–24. Low mound a few inches tall with narrow gray leaves and a nearly unending show of small rosy purple flowers in dense heads. Good rock garden plant.

T. fruticans. BUSH GERMANDER. Zones 4–24. Loose, silvery-stemmed shrub to 4–8 ft. tall and as wide or wider. Leaves 1¼ in. long, gray-green above, silvery white beneath, giving overall silvery gray effect. Lavender blue, ¾-in.-long flowers in spikes at branch ends through most of year. Thin and cut back in late winter, early spring.

Use as an informal hedge, against a fence or screen, in mass at end of lawn area, but far enough from sprinklers to avoid overwatering. Attractive with reddish- or purplish-leafed plants. 'Azurea' has deeper blue flowers than the species. 'Compactum' grows to 3 ft., is relatively narrow and dense in habit, and has deep blue flowers.

TEXAS MOUNTAIN LAUREL. See SOPHORA secundiflora	**p. 488**
TEXAS RANGER, TEXAS SAGE. See LEUCOPHYLLUM frutescens	**p. 352**
TEXAS UMBRELLA TREE. See MELIA azedarach 'Umbraculiformis'	**p. 378**

FOR INFORMATION ON SELECTING PLANTS
PLEASE SEE PAGES 45–128

THALICTRUM

MEADOW RUE	
Ranunculaceae	
PERENNIALS	
🌿 ALL ZONES	
☼ LIGHT SHADE	
💧 REGULAR WATER	

Thalictrum aquilegifolium

Basal foliage clumps resemble those of columbines; sparsely leafed stems on most species are 3–6 ft. tall, topped by airy clusters of small flowers in summer. Give wind-protected location. Most kinds short lived in Southern California. Superb for airy effect; delicate tracery of leaves and flowers is particularly effective against dark green background. Pleasing contrast to sturdier perennials. Foliage good in flower arrangements.

T. aquilegifolium. Grows 2–3 ft. tall. Bluish green foliage. White, lilac, or purple flowers.

T. delavayi 'Hewitt's Double'. Grows 5 ft. or more, with dark-colored stems and double flowers of lilac.

T. dipterocarpum. CHINESE MEADOW RUE. To 3–6 ft. Lavender to violet flowers, yellow stamens. Long lived everywhere.

T. minus. A somewhat variable species. The form most often sold reaches 3 ft. when in flower. Bluish green foliage; yellow flowers, consisting mostly of stamens.

T. rochebrunianum. Clumps grow to 4–6 ft. tall. White flowers with pale yellow stamens. Variety *T. r.* 'Lavender Mist' has lavender flowers.

Theaceae. The tea family consists of evergreen or deciduous trees and shrubs with leathery leaves and five-petaled flowers that have a large number of stamens. *Camellia, Franklinia,* and *Stewartia* are important representatives.

THEA sinensis. See CAMELLIA sinensis	**p. 203**

THEVETIA

Apocynaceae	
EVERGREEN SHRUBS, SMALL TREES	
🌿 ZONES VARY BY SPECIES	
☼ FULL SUN	
💧 REGULAR WATER	
☠ ALL PARTS ARE POISONOUS	

Fast-growing plants with narrow leaves and showy, funnel-shaped, yellow or apricot flowers in clusters. *Thevetia* thrive in heat and can take very little frost.

Thevetia peruviana

T. peruviana (T. neriifolia). YELLOW OLEANDER. Zones 12 (with careful protection), 13, 14 (sheltered locations), 21–24. Fast growth typically to 6–8 ft. or more. Leaves 3–6 in. long, very narrow, with edges rolled under. Leaves are deep green, glossy, with inconspicuous veins. Fragrant flowers bloom any time (mostly June–November); yellow to apricot, 2–3 in. long, in clusters at branch ends.

Best with good drainage. Shallow rooted. Protect from wind or prune to lessen wind resistance. Can be grown (with training) as 20-ft. tree or pruned into 6–8-ft. hedge, background planting, or screen. In cold-winter areas, mound dry sand 6–12 in. deep around base of stem. If top is frozen, new growth will bloom same year.

T. thevetioides. GIANT THEVETIA. Zones 12, 13 (with winter protection), 22–24. Fast, open growth to 12 ft. tall, 12 ft. wide. Leaves, darker green than those of *T. peruviana,* resemble oleander leaves but are corrugated, heavily veined beneath. Flowers brilliant yellow, to 4 in. across, in large clusters, June–July and into winter. Desert heat wilts summer flowers.

THRIFT. See ARMERIA	**p. 165**

THUJA

ARBORVITAE

Cupressaceae

EVERGREEN SHRUBS OR TREES

⚡ ZONES VARY BY SPECIES

☼ ◑ SUMMER SHADE IN HOT-SUMMER AREAS

⬤ ⬤ ⬤ TAKE LITTLE TO MUCH WATER

Thuja plicata

Neat, symmetrical, even, geometrical plants that run to globes, cones, or cylinders. Scalelike leaves in flat sprays; juvenile foliage feathery, with small, needlelike leaves. Small cones with few scales. Foliage in better-known varieties is often yellow green or bright golden yellow. Sometimes spelled "Thuya."

T. occidentalis. AMERICAN ARBORVITAE. Tree. Zones 2–9, 15–17, 21–24. Native to eastern United States. Upright, open growth to 40–60 ft. with branches that tend to turn up at ends. Leaf sprays bright green to yellowish green. Foliage turns brown in severe cold, will scorch badly in winter in coldest, windiest Rocky Mountain gardens unless plants are shaded, watered. Needs moist air to look its best. Spray for red spider mites.

The species itself is seldom seen, but certain garden varieties are fairly common. Among them, taller kinds make good unclipped or clipped screens. Lower-growing kinds often planted around foundations, along walks or walls, as hedges. Some good varieties are

'Brandon'. Fast growth to 12–15 ft. tall, 3–4 ft. wide. Useful as screen.

'Douglasii Pyramidalis'. Tall, vigorous green pyramid of fairly fast growth.

'Emerald' ('Emerald Green', 'Smaragd'). Neat, dense growing, cone-shaped plant that holds its color through the winter.

'Fastigiata' ('Pyramidalis', 'Columnaris'). Tall, narrow, dense, columnar plant to 25 ft. high, 5 ft. wide; can be kept lower by pruning. Good plant for tall (6-ft. or more) hedges and screens, especially in cold regions and damp soils. Set 4 ft. apart for neat, low-maintenance screen.

'Globosa' ('Little Gem', 'Little Giant', and 'Nana' are similar varieties). GLOBE ARBORVITAE, TOM THUMB ARBORVITAE. Dense, rounded, with bright green foliage. Usually 2–3 ft. tall, equal spread, eventually larger.

'Little Gem' ('Pumila'). Dense, dark green; slow growth to 2 ft. tall, 4 ft. across. Larger in great old age.

'Little Giant'. Dwarf, slow growing, globular, dark green.

'Nana'. Small, round, dense, to 1½–2 ft. in height.

'Nigra'. Tall, dense, dark green cone.

'Rheingold' ('Improved Ellwangeriana Aurea'). Cone-shaped, slow-growing, bright golden plant with a mixture of scalelike and needlelike leaves. Even very old plants seldom exceed 6 ft.

'Umbraculifera'. Globe shaped in youth, gradually becoming flat topped. At 10 years it should be 4 by 4 ft.

'Woodwardii'. Widely grown dense, globular shrub of rich green color. May attain considerable size with age, but it's a small plant over reasonably long period. If you can wait 72 years, it may be 8 ft. high by 18 ft. wide.

'Yellow Ribbon', to 8–10 ft. tall, 2–3 ft. wide, with bright yellow foliage throughout the year.

T. orientalis. See Platycladus

T. plicata. WESTERN RED CEDAR. Tree. Zones 1–9, 14–24. Native from coastal Northern California north to Alaska and inland to Montana. Plants from inland seed are hardy anywhere in West; those from coastal seed less hardy to cold. Can reach over 200 ft. in coastal belt of Washington, but usually much less in gardens. Slender, drooping branchlets, set closely with dark green, scalelike leaves, form flat, graceful, lacy sprays. Cones are ½ in. across, cinnamon brown. Single trees are magnificent on large lawns, but lower branches spread quite broadly and trees lose their characteristic beauty when these are cut off. A few varieties are

'Aurea'. Younger branch tips golden green.

'Fastigiata'. HOGAN CEDAR. Very dense, narrow, erect; fine for tall screen.

'Hillieri'. Irregularly shaped dense, broad shrub with thick, short, heavy branches.

'Stoneham Gold'. Dense, slow-growing dwarf; new growth orange.

'Striblingii'. Dense, thick column 10–12 ft. tall, 2–3 ft. wide. For moderate-height screen planting or use as an upright sentinel.

THUJOPSIS dolabrata

FALSE ARBORVITAE, DEERHORN CEDAR, HIBA CEDAR

Cupressaceae

EVERGREEN TREE

⚡ ZONES 3–7, 14–17

☼ ◑ FULL SUN; PARTIAL SHADE IN ZONES 14, 15

⬤ ⬤ NEEDS SOME SUMMER WATER

Thujopsis dolabrata

Pyramidal, coniferous, often shrubby, of very slow growth to 50 ft. high. Foliage resembles that of *Thuja*, but twigs are coarser, glossy, branching in staghorn effect. Best where summers are cool, humid. Plant as single tree where foliage details can be appreciated. Slow growth makes it good container plant. 'Nana' is a dwarf variety; 'Variegata' has white branch tips.

THUNBERGIA

Acanthaceae

PERENNIAL VINES

⚡ ZONES VARY BY SPECIES

☼ ◑ SUN NEAR COAST, PARTIAL SHADE INLAND

⬤ REGULAR WATER

Thunbergia alata

Noted for showy flowers. Tropical in origin, but some are hardy in milder parts of California and Zone 13. Others grow fast enough to bloom the first season and thus to be treated as annuals.

T. alata. BLACK-EYED SUSAN VINE. Perennial, grown as summer annual. May live over in Zones 23, 24. Small, trailing or twining plant with triangular, 3-in. leaves. Flowers are flaring tubes to 1 in. wide, orange, yellow, or white, all with purple black throat. Start seed indoors, set plants out in good soil in sunny spot as soon as weather warms. Use in hanging baskets or window boxes or as ground cover; or train on strings or low trellis.

T. battiscombei, T. erecta. Shrubs or vines. Zones 16, 21, 24. Similar if not identical, these grow to 6 ft. with large (3-in.) velvety dark blue trumpet flowers with orange or cream throats.

T. grandiflora. SKY FLOWER. Zones 16, 21–24. Vigorous twiner to 20 ft. or more, with lush, green, 8-in., heart-shaped leaves. Slightly drooping clusters of tubular, flaring, 2½–3-in., delicate pure blue flowers. Blooms fall, winter, spring. Takes a year to get started, then grows rapidly. Comes back to bloom in a year if frozen. Use to cover arbor, lathhouse, or fence; makes dense shade. There is a white variety. *T. laurifolia* is nearly identical to *T. grandiflora* in appearance and needs.

T. gregorii (T. gibsonii). ORANGE CLOCK VINE. Zones 21–24; warm lathhouse or greenhouse in Zones 13, 16, 17; or grow as summer annual. Twines to 6 ft. tall or sprawls over ground to cover 6-ft. circle. Leaves 3 in. long, toothed, evergreen. Flowers tubular, flaring, bright orange, borne singly on 4-in. stems. Blooms nearly all year in mildest areas, in summer where winters are cool. Plant 3–4 ft. apart to cover wire fence, 6 ft. apart as ground cover. Plant above wall, over which vine will cascade, or grow in hanging basket. Showy and easy to grow.

T. mysorensis. Zones 16, 21–24. Tall-climbing vine with spectacular hanging clusters of gaping flowers that are red on the outside, yellow within. Clusters can reach several feet in length. Vine should be trained to overhead pergola or other support to permit flowers to hang unimpeded.

T

THYMUS

THYME
Lamiaceae (Labiatae)
GROUND COVERS, ERECT SHRUBBY PERENNIAL HERBS
⚡ ALL ZONES
☼ ◑ FULL SUN TO LIGHT SHADE
◐ SOME SUMMER WATER IN HOTTEST AREAS

Foliage usually heavily scented. Plants attract bees. Grow in warm, light, well-drained soil that is fairly dry. Restrain plants as needed by clipping back growing tips. Propagate from cuttings taken early in summer, or sow seed. Plant ground cover kinds 6–12 in. apart in fall or spring.

Thymus vulgaris

T. citriodorus. LEMON THYME. Small shrub, 4–12 in. tall, erect or spreading. Tiny leaves (to ³/₈ in.) have lemon scent. Flowers palest purple. Variegated forms are 'Argenteus' (silver) and 'Aureus' (gold).

T. herba-barona. CARAWAY-SCENTED THYME. Ground cover. Fast growing; forms thick, flat mat of dark green, ¼-in.-long leaves with caraway fragrance. Rose pink flowers in headlike clusters.

T. lanuginosus. See T. pseudolanuginosus

T. praecox arcticus (T. serpyllum, T. drucei). MOTHER-OF-THYME, CREEPING THYME. Ground cover. Forms flat mat, the upright branches 2–6 in. high. Roundish, ¼-in.-long, dark green, aromatic leaves. Small purplish white flowers (white in one form) in headlike clusters, June–September. Good for small areas or filler between stepping stones where foot traffic is light. Soft and fragrant underfoot. Leaves can be used in seasoning and in potpourris. Rose red variety is sold as 'Reiter's'.

T. pseudolanuginosus (T. lanuginosus). WOOLLY THYME. Ground cover. Forms flat to undulating mat 2–3 in. high. Stems densely clothed with small, gray, woolly leaves. Seldom shows its pinkish flowers. Plants become slightly rangy in winter. Use in rock crevices, between stepping stones, to spill over bank or raised bed, to cover small patches of ground.

T. vulgaris. COMMON THYME. Shrubby perennial herb. To 6–12 in. high. Narrow to oval, ¼-in.-long, fragrant, gray-green leaves. Tiny lilac flowers in dense whorls, June–July. Low edging for flower, vegetable, or herb garden. Good container plant. Use leaves fresh or dried for seasoning fish, shellfish, poultry stuffing, soups, vegetables, vegetable juices.

T. v. 'Argenteus'. SILVER THYME. Has leaves variegated with silver.

TI PLANT. See CORDYLINE terminalis　　　　　**p. 240**

TIARELLA

FOAMFLOWER, SUGAR-SCOOP
Saxifragaceae
PERENNIALS
⚡ ZONES VARY BY SPECIES
● SHADE
◐ REGULAR WATER

Clump-forming perennials spread by rhizomes (and by stolons, or runners, in *T. cordifolia*). Leaves spring directly from the rhizome. Flower stems narrow, erect, with many small white (sometimes pinkish) flowers. Useful in shaded rock gardens; make pretty ground covers but will not bear foot traffic.

Tiarella wherryi

T. cordifolia. FOAMFLOWER. Zones 1–9, 14–24. Foot-wide clumps of light green, 4-in. leaves show red and yellow fall color. Flower stalks 12 in. tall. Spreads rapidly by rhizome and stolons.

T. trifoliata unifoliata (T. unifoliata). SUGAR-SCOOP, WESTERN FOAMFLOWER. Zones 3–7, 14–17. Leaves are dark green, deeply cut and toothed. Evergreen except in coldest part of its range. Small white flowers in upright clusters are followed by little fruits that resemble sugar scoops.

T. wherryi. Zones 1–9, 14–24. Much resembles *T. cordifolia* but has no stolons and is slower to spread. Flower clusters somewhat more slender.

TIBOUCHINA urvilleana (T. semidecandra)

PRINCESS FLOWER, PLEROMA
Melastomataceae
EVERGREEN SHRUB OR SMALL TREE
⚡ ZONES 16, 17, 21–24; SHELTERED IN 14, 15
☼ ◑ BEST WITH ROOTS IN SHADE, TOP IN SUN
◐ REGULAR WATER

Tibouchina urvilleana

Native to Brazil. Fast, rather open growth up to 5–18 ft. Branch tips, buds, new growth shaded with velvety, orange, and bronze red hairs. Oval, velvety, 3–6-in.-long green leaves are strongly ribbed, often edged red; older leaves add spots of red, orange, or yellow, especially in winter. Brilliant royal purple, 3-in.-wide flowers in clusters at ends of branches appear intermittently May–January. Best in somewhat acid, well-drained soil. Protect from strong wind. Minimize legginess by light pruning after each bloom cycle, heavier pruning in early spring. Resprouts quickly after heavy pruning. Pinch tips of young plants to encourage bushiness. Feed after spring pruning and lightly after each bloom cycle. If buds fail to open, look for geranium (tobacco) budworm.

TIDYTIPS. See LAYIA platyglossa　　　　　**p. 350**

TIGER FLOWER. See TIGRIDIA pavonia　　　　　**p. 506**

TIGRIDIA pavonia

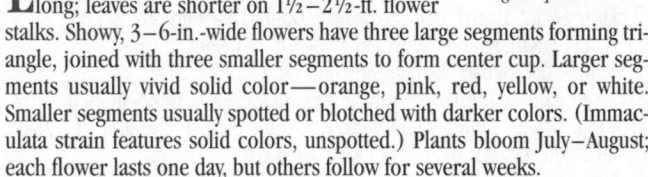

TIGER FLOWER, MEXICAN SHELL FLOWER
Iridaceae
BULB
⚡ ALL ZONES
☼ ◑ SUN ON COAST, AFTERNOON SHADE INLAND
◐ CAN DRY OFF AFTER FLOWERING

Tigridia pavonia

Leaves narrow, ribbed, swordlike, 1–1½ ft. long; leaves are shorter on 1½–2½-ft. flower stalks. Showy, 3–6-in.-wide flowers have three large segments forming triangle, joined with three smaller segments to form center cup. Larger segments usually vivid solid color—orange, pink, red, yellow, or white. Smaller segments usually spotted or blotched with darker colors. (Immaculata strain features solid colors, unspotted.) Plants bloom July–August; each flower lasts one day, but others follow for several weeks.

Plant after weather warms in rich, porous soil. Set 10–12 bulbs 2–4 in. deep, 4–8 in. apart. Or plant 6–8 bulbs in 9-in. pot. During active growth, water regularly and feed every 2 weeks with mild solution of liquid fertilizer. In colder areas, dig and store after foliage ripens. Break bulbs apart just before planting in spring. Plants in open ground require division every 3–4 years. Easily grown from seed; may bloom first year. May be necessary to control red spider mites; start while leaves are a few inches tall.

TILIA

LINDEN
Tiliaceae
DECIDUOUS TREES
⚡ ZONES VARY BY SPECIES
☼ FULL SUN
◐ REGULAR WATER, EXCEPT AS NOTED

Dense, compact crowns. Used for street and park planting in Europe. Small, quite fragrant, yellowish white flowers in drooping clusters. Give deep, rich soil. Growth slow to moderate. Young

Tilia cordata

trees need staking and shaping; older trees only corrective pruning. Aphids can cause disagreeable drip of honeydew and sooty mildew.

T. americana. AMERICAN LINDEN, BASSWOOD. Zones 1–17. To 40–60 ft. with 20–25-ft. spread. Straight trunk; dense, compact, narrow crown. Heart-shaped, dull dark green leaves to 4–6 in. long, 3–4 in. wide (sometimes larger). Loose clusters of fragrant, yellowish white flowers in June–July. 'Redmond' is a pyramidal form with glossy foliage.

T. cordata. LITTLE-LEAF LINDEN. Zones 1–17. To 30–50 ft. with 15–30-ft. spread. Form densely pyramidal. Leaves 1½–3 in. long, equally broad or broader, dark green above, silvery beneath. Flowers in July. Excellent medium-size lawn tree or street tree. Given space to develop its symmetrical crown, it can be a fine patio shade tree (but expect bees in flowering season). It is the hardiest linden. 'Chancellor', 'Glenleven', 'Greenspire', 'June Bride', and 'Olympic' are selected forms. 'June Bride' has an especially heavy show of flowers.

T. euchlora. CRIMEAN LINDEN. Zones 1–17. To 25–35 ft., perhaps eventually to 50 ft., almost as wide. Branches slightly pendulous. Leaves oval or roundish, 2–4 in. long, rich glossy green above, paler beneath. Yellowish white flowers in July. Use in same way as little-leaf linden—form is broader, shade and foliage less dense. 'Redmond' is pyramidal in habit.

T. tomentosa. SILVER LINDEN. Zones 1–21. To 40–50 ft. high, 20–30 ft. wide. Light green, 3–5-in.-long leaves, silvery beneath, turn and ripple in the slightest breeze. Needs no dry-season water when well established.

Tiliaceae. The linden family of trees and shrubs includes *Grewia*, *Sparmannia* (African linden), and *Tilia*.

TILLANDSIA

Bromeliaceae

PERENNIALS

✎ ZONES 22–24; HOUSE PLANTS ANYWHERE

☼ ☽ ● EXPOSURE NEEDS VARY BY SPECIES

◍ ● WATER NEEDS VARY BY SPECIES

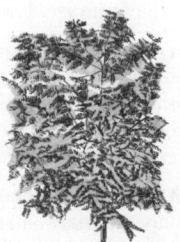
Tillandsia cyanea

Bromeliads grown in pots of fast-draining, loose soil mix or as epiphytes on tree branches or slabs of bark. The best known is *T. usneoides*, the "Spanish moss" of southern United States. Similar is Arizona native *T. recurvata*. Leaf rosettes of some are bright green, of others gray and scaly or scurfy. Bright green ones need water. Gray ones require bright light and little water. They are often mounted on plaques of wood or bark and used as wall ornaments indoors or outside (where hardy). Let potting mix dry out between waterings.

T. cyanea. Rosette of bright green, arching, 1-ft. leaves produces showy flower cluster, a flattened plume of deep pink or red bracts from which violet blue flowers emerge one or two at a time for a long period.

T. ionantha. Miniature rosettes of 2-in.-long leaves covered with a silvery gray fuzz. Small, tubular flowers are violet; at bloom time, center of rosette turns red. Tough and undemanding plant.

T. lindenii (*Vriesea lindenii*). Like *T. cyanea*, but plume is green or green marked rose. As with other bromeliads, each rosette produces just one long-lasting inflorescence. Offsets replace original plant.

TIPUANA tipu

TIPU TREE

Fabaceae (Leguminosae)

DECIDUOUS OR SEMIEVERGREEN TREE

✎ ZONES 12 (WARMEST AREAS), 13–16, 18–24

☼ FULL SUN

◍ SOAK YOUNG TREES OFTEN, OLD ONES LESS

Fast growing to 25 ft.; can reach 35–50 ft. eventually. Hardy to 25°F; well-ripened wood

Tipuana tipu

will take 18°F with minor damage. Broad silhouette with flattened crown that is usually wider than high; can be pruned to umbrella shape to make narrower, denser crown. Leaves divided into 11–21 oblong, 1½-in.-long, light green leaflets. Blooms June–July, bearing clusters of apricot to yellow, sweet pea–shaped flowers. Blooms followed by 2½-in. pods. Any soil except strongly alkaline. Flowers best in warm-summer areas out of immediate ocean influence. Good street tree or lawn tree. Useful shade canopy for patio or terrace, although flower litter can be slight nuisance.

TITHONIA rotundifolia (T. speciosa)

MEXICAN SUNFLOWER

Asteraceae (Compositae)

PERENNIAL GROWN AS SUMMER ANNUAL

✎ ALL ZONES

☼ FULL SUN

◍ CAN TAKE SOME ARIDITY

Tithonia rotundifolia

Husky, gaudy, rather coarse plant; rapid growth to 6 ft. tall. Spectacular 3–4-in.-wide flower heads with orange-scarlet rays and tufted yellow centers bloom July to frost. Inflated hollow stems; cut with care for bouquets to avoid bending stalks. Velvety green leaves. Sow seed in place in spring, in not-too-rich soil. Tolerates heat; good choice for desert gardens. 'Torch', lower-growing variety (to 4 ft.) makes bushy summer hedge.

| TOADFLAX. See LINARIA | **p. 356** |
| TOBIRA. See PITTOSPORUM tobira | **p. 426** |

TOLMIEA menziesii

PIGGY-BACK PLANT

Saxifragaceae

HOUSE PLANT

✎ ZONES 5–9, 12–24; HOUSE PLANT ANYWHERE

☼ ● GOOD GROUND COVER FOR SHADE

◍ ◍ TOLERATES WET SOIL

Tolmiea menziesii

Native to Coast Ranges from Northern California northward to Alaska. Chief asset is abundant production of attractive 5-in.-wide basal leaves—shallowly lobed and toothed, rather hairy. Leaves can produce new plantlets at junction of leaf stalk and blade. Tiny, rather inconspicuous reddish brown flowers top 1–2-ft.-high stems. As house plant, needs filtered light, cool temperatures, frequent watering. Mealybugs, spider mites are occasional pests. Makes handsome hanging basket plant. Start new plants any time of year. Take leaf with plantlet and insert in moist potting mix so base of plantlet contacts soil.

| TOMATILLO. See PHYSALIS ixocarpa | **p. 417** |

TOMATO

Solanaceae

FRUITING VEGETABLES

✎ ALL ZONES

☼ FULL SUN

◍ ◍ LITTLE TO MUCH WATER

Tomato

Easy to grow and prolific, tomatoes are just about the most widely grown of all garden plants, edible or otherwise. Amateur and commercial growers have varying ideas about how best to grow tomatoes; if your

T

own particular scheme works, continue to follow it. But if you're a novice or you're dissatisfied with previous attempts, you may find the following useful.

First, choose varieties suited to your climate that will yield the kind of tomatoes you like on the kind of vines that you can handle. (Though the tomato plant is really a sprawling plant incapable of climbing, it is commonly referred to as a "vine.") Plant a few each of early, midseason, and late varieties for production over a long period.

To grow your own tomato plants from seed, sow in early March in pots of light soil mix or in a ready-made seed starter (sold at garden supply stores). Cover seed in pots with ½ in. of fine soil. Firm soil over seeds. Keep soil surface damp. Place seed container in cold frame or sunny window. (A temperature of 65–70°F is ideal, although a range of 50°F at night to 85°F in the day will give acceptable results.) When seedlings are 2 in. tall, transplant them into 3- or 4-in. pots. Keep in sunny area until seedlings reach transplant size.

The time to plant tomato seedlings, whether grown from seed (above) or purchased from a nursery or garden store, depends on where you live. Plant in February or early March in Zones 12, 13; April, May, or early June in Zones 7–9, 14–24; May or early June in Zones 1–6, 10, 11. Typically, six plants can supply a family with fresh fruit and some for processing.

Plant in a sunny location in well-drained soil. Space plants 1½–3 ft. apart (staked or trained) to 3–4 ft. apart (untrained). Make planting hole extra deep. Set seedlings in hole so lowest leaves are just above soil level. Additional roots will form on buried stem and provide stronger root system.

When selecting tomato varieties, you may find some noted as determinate, others as indeterminate. Determinate types are bushier and not as suitable for staking or trellising. Indeterminate ones are more vinelike, need more training, and generally have a longer bearing period.

Tomato management and harvest will be most satisfying if you train plants to keep them mostly off the ground (left alone, they will sprawl and some fruit will lie on soil, often causing rot, pest damage, and discoloration). Most common training method for indeterminate varieties is to drive a 6-ft.-long stake (at least 1- by 1-in. size) into ground a foot from each plant. Tie plants to these stakes as they grow.

Slightly easier in the long run, but more work at planting time, is to grow each plant in wire cylinder made of concrete reinforcing screen (6-in. mesh). Form cylinder with 1½-ft. diameter. Screen is manufactured 7 ft. wide, which is just right for cylinder height; most indeterminate vines can grow to top of such a cylinder. Put stakes at opposite sides of cylinder and tie cylinder firmly to them. As vine grows, poke protruding branches back inside cylinder every week. Reach through screen to pick fruit.

IRRIGATED TOMATOES TASTE WATERY

Dry-farmed tomatoes (no irrigation or close to it) concentrate flavor. Dry farming works best in clay or clay-loam soil that gets at least 20 in. of rainfall. In fall, plant cover crop of beans, rye, and vetch. About a month before last rain, cut down cover crop, leave it on soil as a mulch, loosen soil, and plant tomatoes through the cut cover crop. Remove each plant's lower leaves and plant up to the top set. Space plants 6 ft. apart. Water deeply. Let plants sprawl. Water again only if plants droop. Harvest when ripe—and enjoy!

For a novelty, you may also plant in a large suspended container and let vine cascade down (quite useful and practical with small-fruited tomatoes).

Irrigate tomato plants often during early part of the season, less frequently after fruit begins to ripen. Tomato plants are deep rooted, so water heavily when you do water. If soil is fairly rich, you won't need to fertilize at all. But in ordinary soils, give light application of fertilizer every 2 weeks from the time first blossoms set until end of harvest.

If diseases or insects trouble or threaten tomatoes, protect plants with all-purpose vegetable dust or spray—a mixture that contains both an insecticide and a fungicide.

If your plants grow, set fruit, and then shrivel, wilt, and die, they may have been sabotaged by gophers. If no gopher evidence is found, plants probably are suffering from verticillium or fusarium wilt or both. Pull and dispose of such plants. Diseases live over in soil, so the next year plant in different location and try one of the wilt-resistant varieties suited to your climate. Some tomato problems—leaf roll, blossom-end rot, cracked fruit—are physiological, usually corrected (or prevented) by maintaining uniform soil moisture. A mulch will help.

If you have done everything right and your tomatoes have failed to set fruit in the spring, use hormone spray on blossoms. Tomatoes often fail to set fruit when night temperatures drop below 55°F. In chilly-night areas, select cold-tolerant varieties (especially small-fruited strains). Fruit-setting hormone often speeds up bearing in the earlier part of the season. Tomatoes can also fail to set fruit when temperatures rise above 100°F, but hormones are not effective under those conditions.

Harvest fruit when it is fully red and juicy; keep ripe fruit picked to extend season. When frost is predicted, harvest all fruit, both green and partly ripe. Store at 58°F and bring into 70°F to ripen as needed.

TOMATO VARIETIES

Following are kinds of tomatoes you can buy as seeds or started plants—listings are arranged according to fruit and vine types. Several varieties are valued especially for their resistance to verticillium or fusarium wilt. Varieties with VF after their names tolerate verticillium and fusarium; those marked VFN also tolerate nematodes. Additional keys to disease resistance include FF (resistant to Race 1 and Race 2 fusarium), T (tobacco mosaic virus), A (alternaria leaf spot), and L (septoria leaf spot).

Main crop or standard tomatoes. 'Ace' and 'Ace' types are large tomatoes of very fine flavor that bear well in California's interior and inner coastal valleys. 'Pearson' and 'Pearson Improved' will set fruit under wide range of temperatures and produce well in California's coastal and interior valleys. 'Stone' is a late-maturing variety with globular scarlet fruit on large vines; it is a Southern California favorite. 'Manalucie' is another good main crop variety for warm areas. 'Pritchard' produces fairly early main crop and is useful in northwestern gardens.

Early tomatoes. "Early" means more than early harvest. Early varieties set fruit at lower night temperatures than midseason or late varieties; most will ripen fruit in cool-summer climates. Name 'Earliana' covers several varieties such as 'Early Market', 'First Early', 'Morse's 498', and 'Pennheart'. 'Early Girl' gives high yield of medium–small tomatoes beginning early and lasting through season. Early types grown in Oregon and Washington include 'Bonny Best', 'John Baer', and 'Valiant', all large-vine types; and 'Willamette', a small-vine type.

Cool-summer tomatoes. Where summers are cool, nurseries offer locally adapted varieties. In Seattle, there's 'Seattle Best of All'; in San Francisco, 'Early Girl' seems to perform better than the traditional 'Frisco Fogger'.

Hybrid tomatoes. Hybrid vigor makes these tomatoes grow more strongly and rapidly, and produce larger and more uniform fruit than other varieties. And except for the large-fruited kinds, they produce fruit in climate extremes. Well-known hybrids include 'Beefmaster' (VFN); 'Burpee Hybrid', a medium to large main crop variety; 'Big Boy', a very large, thick, round red tomato; 'Better Boy' (VFN); 'Wonder Boy'; and 'Spring Giant' (VF).

Yellow-orange tomatoes. 'Jubilee' and 'Sunray' are strikingly handsome golden orange tomatoes. They taste just like good red tomatoes and look good too, especially sliced and mixed with sliced red tomatoes. (There are even white tomatoes: 'New Snowball' and 'White Beauty' are interesting novelties with very low acid content.)

Large-fruited tomatoes. These are home gardener's specials. They are poor shippers. Among the best are 'Ponderosa', 'Beefsteak' ('Crimson Cushion'), 'Big Boy', 'Big Girl' (VF), 'Beef-master' (VFN), 'Bragger', 'Spring Giant' (VF). Fruit is large, broad, rather shallow, meaty, and mild. All varieties need moderate heat and rarely thrive in cool-night or coastal areas.

Small-fruited tomatoes. Ripe fruit is size of large marbles or small plums, but vines of small-fruited tomatoes, trained against a wall, will reach 8 ft. and spread almost as wide. These varieties set fruit well under greater climate extremes than do larger-fruited varieties. Shapes and colors

T

are indicated by their names: 'Red Cherry', 'Red Plum', 'Red Pear', 'Yellow Cherry', 'Yellow Pear', 'Yellow Peach'. Extra-heavy producers of small, very sweet tomatoes are 'Sugar Lump', 'Sweet 100', and 'Sweet Million'. 'Basket Pak' produces tomatoes to 1½ in. wide. Dwarf varieties for pots or containers are 'Tiny Tim', 'Small Fry' (VFN), 'Pixie', 'Toy Boy', 'Patio', 'Salad Top', 'Tumbling Tom', 'Early Salad', 'Atom'. Smallish, extra-meaty tomatoes with little seed pulp are often grown for making tomato paste and purée. These include 'Roma' and 'San Marzano'.

TOONA sinensis. See CEDRELA sinensis	**p. 214**
TORCH-LILY. See KNIPHOFIA uvaria	**p. 344**

TORENIA fournieri

WISHBONE FLOWER	
Scrophulariaceae	
SUMMER ANNUAL	
◰ ALL ZONES	
☼ ◑ SUN NEAR COAST, PARTIAL SHADE INLAND	
◓ LOTS OF WATER	

Torenia fournieri

Compact, bushy, to 1 ft. high. Light blue flowers with deeper blue markings and bright yellow throats look like miniature gloxinias. Stamens arranged in wishbone shape. White-flowered form also available. Blooms summer, fall. Sow seed in pots; transplant to garden after frosts. Use in borders, pots, window boxes.

TORREYA californica

CALIFORNIA NUTMEG	
Taxaceae	
EVERGREEN TREE	
◰ ZONES 7–9, 14–24	
☼ ◑ FULL SUN OR PARTIAL SHADE	
◓ OCCASIONAL WATERING	

Torreya californica

Conifer native to cool, shaded canyons in California mountain regions below 4,500 ft. elevation. Slow growing to 15–50 ft. with trunk 1–3 ft. in diameter. Wide, open pyramidal crown, dome-like with age. Branches are horizontal, slender, somewhat drooping at tips. Leaves dark green with two whitish bands underneath, flat, rigid, sharp pointed, 1¼–2½ in. long, ⅛ in. wide, in flat sprays. Plumlike fruit is pale green with purplish markings.

TOTARA. See PODOCARPUS totara	**p. 431**
TOUCH-ME-NOT. See IMPATIENS	**p. 330**
TOWER OF JEWELS. See ECHIUM wildpretii	**p. 270**
TOYON. See HETEROMELES arbutifolia	**p. 321**

TRACHELIUM caeruleum

Campanulaceae (Lobeliaceae)	
PERENNIAL	
◰ ZONES 7–9, 14–24; ANNUAL ELSEWHERE	
☼ FULL SUN	
◓ MODERATE WATER	

Trachelium caeruleum

Grows to 2½ ft. tall and as wide; clumps of stems are clothed with narrow, sharply toothed dark green leaves and

topped by broad, dome-shaped clusters of tiny bluish violet flowers (good for cutting) over a long season. Sown early, will bloom first year; may self-sow in mild climates. Tough, undemanding plant.

TRACHELOSPERMUM (Rhynchospermum)

STAR JASMINE	
Apocynaceae	
EVERGREEN VINES OR SPRAWLING SHRUBS	
◰ ZONES VARY BY SPECIES	
☼ ◑ FULL SUN, PARTIAL SHADE IN HOT AREAS	
◓ REGULAR WATER	

Trachelospermum jasminoides

Used as ground covers, spillers, or climbers. They are among the most versatile and useful of shrubby plants.

T. asiaticum. Zones 6–24. Twines to 15 ft. or sprawls on the ground with branchlets rising erect. Leaves smaller, darker, duller green than those of *T. jasminoides*; flowers smaller, creamy yellow or yellowish white, fragrant, blooming April–June.

T. jasminoides. STAR JASMINE. Zones 8–24. One of most widely used plants in California and Arizona. Given support, is twining vine to 20 ft.; growth rate slow at first but eventually moderately fast. Without support and with some tip-pinching, a spreading shrub or ground cover 1½–2 ft. tall, 4–5 ft. wide. New foliage glossy light green; mature leaves lustrous dark green, to 3 in. long.

White, sweet-scented flowers to 1 in. across, profuse in small clusters on short side branches. Blooms June–July; May–June in desert. Attractive to bees. Fragrance most notable on warm still evenings. Rare variety *T. j.* 'Variegatum' has leaves variegated with white.

To grow as bank or ground cover, set plants 1½–3 ft. apart (depending on how fast you want cover). Cut back upright shoots. Feed in spring, late summer. Spray if necessary for scale, mealybugs, red spider mites. Keep well watered and weeded. In 3–4 years, growth is thick enough to discourage most annual weeds.

Use in raised beds or entry gardens, for edging along walks or drives, as extension of lawn, or as ground cover under trees and shrubs that need summer water.

TRACHYCARPUS

Arecaceae (Palmae)	
PALMS	
◰ ZONES VARY BY SPECIES	
☼ FULL SUN	
◓ REGULAR WATER	

Trachycarpus fortunei

Fan-leafed palms of moderate size and great hardiness. Characteristic blackish fiber grows on upper portions of all but oldest trunks.

T. fortunei. WINDMILL PALM. Sometimes sold as *Chamaerops excelsa*. Zones 4–24; indoor potted palm anywhere. Native to China. Hardy to 10°F or lower. Moderate to fast growth to 30 ft. in warm-winter areas. Trunk is dark, usually thicker at top than at bottom, covered with dense, hairy-looking fiber. Leaves 3 ft. across on toothed, 1½-ft. stalks. Sometimes becomes untidy and ruffled in high winds.

T. martianus. Zones 15–17, 19–24. Native to Himalayas. Hardy to 22°F. Slower growing, taller, more slender than *T. fortunei.* Trunk covered with fiber only at top, ringed with leaf scars.

T. takil. Zones 15–17, 19–24. Native to western Himalayas. Very slow grower with heavy, inclined trunk. Can reach 20 ft., but is dwarf for many years.

T

TRACHYMENE coerulea (Didiscus coeruleus)

BLUE LACE FLOWER

Apiaceae (Umbelliferae)

SPRING OR SUMMER ANNUAL

⚍ ALL ZONES

☼ SUN BUT WON'T TAKE MUCH HEAT

● REGULAR WATER

*Trachymene
coerulea*

To 2 ft. tall. Numerous small, lavender blue flowers in 2–3-in.-wide, flat-topped clusters that are quite lacy in appearance, as are divided leaves. Sow seeds in place in early spring for summer bloom.

TRADESCANTIA

Commelinaceae

PERENNIALS

⚍ ZONES VARY BY SPECIES

◑ ● BEST IN STRONG LIGHT, NO DIRECT SUNLIGHT

● ●● MODERATE TO WET

*Tradescantia
fluminensis*

Most are long-trailing, indestructible plants often grown indoors, or outdoors as ground cover for shaded areas. Usually used as potted plants or hanging basket plants; these can also be used as ground covers, but are likely to prove invasive. Long-stemmed, rambling kind often called inch plant or wandering Jew—a name also often applied to related *Callisia* and especially *Zebrina*.

T. albiflora. WANDERING JEW, GIANT INCH PLANT. Zones 12–24. Trailing, or sprawling and rooting at joints. Leaves 2–3 in. long. Flowers small, white. 'Albovittata' has leaves finely and evenly streaked with white; 'Aurea' ('Gold Leaf') has chartreuse yellow foliage; 'Laekenensis' ('Rainbow') has bandings of white and pale lavender. Variegated forms are unstable and tend to revert to green; keep solid green growth pinched out. Easiest care in well-drained soil with average water. Trailing stems will live a long time in water, rooting quickly and easily. Renovate overgrown plants by cutting back severely or by starting new pots with fresh tip growth.

T. blossfeldiana. Zones 12–24. Fleshy, furry stems spread and lean, but do not really hang. Leaves to 4 in. long are shiny dark green above, purple and furry underneath. Flowers showier than those of most trailing or semitrailing tradescantias: clusters of furry purplish buds open into ½-in., white-centered pink flowers.

T. fluminensis. WANDERING JEW. Zones 12–24; house plant everywhere. Prostrate or trailing habit. Fast growing. Succulent stems have swollen joints where 2½-in.-long, dark green, oval or oblong leaves are attached ('Variegata' has leaves striped yellow or white). Tiny white flowers are not showy. Easy to grow. In mild-winter areas can be grown in shade as ground cover. Excellent for window boxes and dish gardens. A few stems placed in glass of water will live for a long time and will even grow.

T. navicularis. CHAIN PLANT. House plant. Compact plant with short, barely trailing branches packed with fleshy, folded, brownish purple leaves. Miniature plants form along stems, detach for propagation. Tiny purple-red flowers. Treat as succulent.

T. sillamontana. House plant. Short trailing or ascending branches with 2–2½-in. leaves densely coated with soft white fur. Tiny rose purple flowers. Avoid overwatering.

T. virginiana. SPIDERWORT. Usually sold as *T. andersoniana*. All zones. Grows in clumps 1½–3 ft. tall, with long, deep green, erect or arching grasslike foliage. Three-petaled flowers open for only a day, but buds come in large clusters and plants are seldom out of bloom during summer. Named garden varieties come in white and shades of blue, lavender, purple, pink, to near red. Takes wet soil. Propagate by division.

TRAILING AFRICAN DAISY. See OSTEOSPERMUM fruticosum   p. 397

TRAILING MALLOW. See MODIOLASTRUM lateritium	p. 382
TRANSVAAL DAISY. See GERBERA jamesonii	p. 306
TREE FERN. See BLECHNUM, CYATHEA cooperi, DICKSONIA	pp. 185, 253, 263
TREE MALLOW. See LAVATERA	p. 349
TREE-OF-HEAVEN. See AILANTHUS altissima	p. 143
TREE TOMATO. See CYPHOMANDRA betacea	p. 255

TRICHOSTEMA lanatum

WOOLLY BLUE CURLS

Lamiaceae (Labiatae)

EVERGREEN SHRUB

⚍ ZONES 14–24

☼ FULL SUN

◌ ESTABLISHED PLANTS NEED NO IRRIGATION

Trichostema lanatum

Native to dry, sunny slopes of Coast Ranges, California. Much-branched, 3–5-ft.-high, neat plant. Narrow, 1¼–2-in.-long leaves, pungently aromatic when bruised, are shiny dark green on upper surface, white and woolly beneath; leaf edges are rolled under. Flowers, in separated clusters along a long stalk, are blue with conspicuous arching stamens. Stalks and parts of flowers are covered with blue, pink, or whitish wool. Blooms April–June; throughout summer and early fall if old flower stems are cut back. Needs excellent drainage.

TRICUSPIDARIA dependens. See CRINODENDRON patagua   p. 248

TRICYRTIS

TOAD LILY

Liliaceae

PERENNIALS

⚍ ZONES 1–9, 14–17

◑ PARTIAL SHADE

●● AMPLE WATER

Tricyrtis hirta

Woodland plants that resemble false Solomon's seal (*Smilacina*) in foliage. Complex flowers are heavily spotted, not showy. Need soil with plenty of organic material.

T. formosana. To 2½ ft. tall, with green leaves mottled with deeper green. Clusters of brown or maroon buds open to inch-wide white flowers spotted purple. Fall bloom.

T. hirta. To 3 ft., with white, purple-spotted flowers set all along the stems in leaf joints. Late summer, fall bloom.

TRIFOLIUM

CLOVER

Fabaceae (Leguminosae)

PERENNIALS

⚍ ZONES VARY BY SPECIES

☼ ◑ FULL SUN OR PARTIAL SHADE

◌ WATER WELL UNTIL ESTABLISHED

*Trifolium
repens*

Scores of species, most of them field crops. Two are perennials of garden importance as lawns or lawn substitutes. Leaves have three (rarely a lucky four) leaflets.

T. fragiferum. STRAWBERRY CLOVER. Zones 4–24. O'Connor's Legume, an Australian strain of this forage crop, is used as a ground or

T

bank cover for its deep rooting (6–7 ft.) and tolerance of heat, aridity, and moderate salinity. Sow seed at 2–8 oz. per 1,000 sq. ft. With average water, makes 6–7-in. mat of green.

T. repens. WHITE CLOVER, WHITE DUTCH CLOVER. All zones. Sometimes used to mix with lawn grass or dichondra seed. Useful for deep rooting and ability to take nitrogen from air and put it into the soil through root bacteria action. Can stain clothing of children who play on it; white flower heads attract bees. Prostrate stems root freely and send up lush cover of three-part leaves with ¾-in. leaflets. *T. r. minus* is one of the shamrocks.

TRILLIUM

WAKE ROBIN

Liliaceae

PERENNIALS

ZONES VARY BY SPECIES

SHADE

NEVER LET PLANTS COMPLETELY DRY OUT

Trillium ovatum

Early spring–blooming plants. Whorl of three leaves tops each stem, and from center of these springs a single flower with three maroon or white petals. Plant the thick, deep-growing, fleshy rhizomes in shady, woodsy location. Let them alone; they will gradually increase.

T. chloropetalum (T. sessile californicum). Zones 4–9, 14–17. Western native. To 1–1½ ft. high. Flower, with greenish white to yellowish petals about 2½ in. long, sits without a stalk on the three 6-in.-long, mottled leaves. *T. c. giganteum* has deep maroon petals.

T. grandiflorum. Zones 1–6. Stout stems 8–18 in. long; leaves can be 2½–6 in. long. Flower is stalked, nodding, white aging to rose.

T. ovatum (T. californicum). Zones 1–6, 14–17. Western native similar to *T. grandiflorum* but with narrower petals; flowers are usually upright on stalks. Effective in shady part of wildflower garden or among ferns, azaleas, or Polyanthus primroses.

TRINIDAD FLAME BUSH. See CALLIANDRA tweedii   p. 196

TRISTANIA

Myrtaceae

EVERGREEN TREES

ZONES 19–24

FULL SUN

LITTLE OR NO WATER ONCE ESTABLISHED

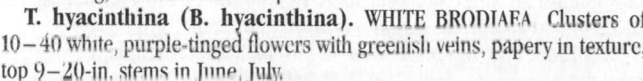

Tristania conferta

Related to eucalyptus. The two species grown in California are of manageable size, and both have brightly colored, shedding bark in addition to handsome evergreen foliage.

T. conferta (Lophostemon confertus). BRISBANE BOX. Moderate to fast growth rate to 30–60 ft. Trunk and limbs resemble those of madrone, with reddish brown bark peeling away to show smooth, light-colored new bark underneath. Growth habit is rather upright, crown eventually broad and rounded. Leaves are 4–6 in. long, oval, leathery, bright green; they tend to cluster toward tips of branchlets. White to creamy, ¾-in.-wide flowers in clusters of three to seven in summer. Fruit is woody capsule something like that of eucalyptus. 'Variegata' has brilliant yellow leaf markings.

Takes almost any soil, but young plant gets better start with good soil. Pinch and prune to get more twiggy growth. Not bothered by insects or diseases, but chlorosis is sometimes a problem in Los Angeles area. Good street tree or lawn tree.

T. laurina (Tristaniopsis laurina). Slow-growing, rather formal-looking small tree or shrub. Trees 8 years old are 10 ft. tall and 5 ft. across, with remarkably dense and rounded crown. Trunk is covered with mahogany-colored bark that peels to show satiny white new bark. Leaves to 4 in. long, usually narrow, but varying to somewhat broader, heavy textured, glossy medium green. Clusters of small yellow flowers are borne in sufficient profusion to put on good show in late spring or early summer. Fruit similar to that of *T. conferta* but smaller (only ¼ in. across). Young plant is densely shrubby and can be kept that way with a little pinching. May be trained, like olives, as multistemmed trees. To make a single-stemmed tree, stake plant and shorten side branches. Remove shortened side branches when treelike growth pattern is established; thereafter, only light shaping will be necessary. Good tub plant. Variety 'Elegant' has broad leaves that open red and hold color until shaded by newer growth; they then turn green.

Both species and variety make excellent tall screens or boundary and background plantings.

TRITELEIA

Amaryllidaceae

CORMS

ALL ZONES

SUN

NO WATER ONCE ESTABLISHED

Triteleia laxa

Plants under this name were formerly known as *Brodiaea*. General descriptions and culture are same as for *Brodiaea*, which differs only in technicalities.

T. grandiflora (Brodiaea douglasii, B. grandiflora). Flowering stalk to 2 ft. tall; many 1¼-in.-long, blue to white trumpets.

T. hyacinthina (B. hyacinthina). WHITE BRODIAEA. Clusters of 10–40 white, purple-tinged flowers with greenish veins, papery in texture, top 9–20-in. stems in June, July.

T. ixioides (B. ixioides). PRETTY FACE, GOLDEN BRODIAEA. Flower stalk to 2 ft.; flowers 1 in. long, golden yellow with purple-black midrib and veins.

T. laxa (B. laxa). GRASS NUT, ITHURIEL'S SPEAR. Flower stalk to 2½ ft.; purple-blue, 1½-in. trumpets.

T. 'Queen Fabiola'. Flower stalk to 2½ ft. tall; flowers deep violet. Good cut flower.

T. tubergenii. Flower stalk to 2½ ft. tall; flowers light blue.

T. uniflora. See Ipheion uniflorum

TRITOMA uvaria. See KNIPHOFIA uvaria   p. 344

TRITONIA (Montbretia)

Iridaceae

CORMS

ZONES 9, 13–24

SUN

WATER DURING BLOOM

Tritonia crocata

Native to South Africa. Related to freesia, ixia, and sparaxis. Narrow, sword-shaped leaves. Branched flower stems carry short, spikelike clusters of brilliant flowers. After blooming period, foliage dies down. Good in rock gardens, borders, pots. Long-lasting cut flowers.

T. crocata. Often called flame freesia. Flower stems to 1–1½ ft. Flowers orange red, funnel shaped, 2 in. long. *T. c. miniata* has bright red blooms; 'Princess Beatrix' has deep orange flowers. Others come in white and shades of pink, salmon, yellow, and apricot.

T. hyalina. Flowers bright orange; narrower segments than *T. crocata*, with transparent area near base. More dwarf than *T. crocata*.

T

511

TROLLIUS

GLOBEFLOWER

Ranunculaceae

PERENNIALS

✓ ALL ZONES

☼ ● SHADE OR PARTIAL SHADE

● REGULAR WATER

Shiny, finely cut, dark green leaves. Yellow to orange flowers resemble those of ranunculus. Bloom season late spring to late summer. Subject to aphids. Valuable for bringing bright color to shady area; particularly happy choice near garden pool. Excellent cut flowers.

Trollius ledebouri

T. europaeus. To 1–2 ft. tall. Flowers yellow, 1½ in. across. Some varieties are orange.

T. ledebouri. Plant so called by nurseries grows to 2 ft. tall. Flowers gold orange, 2 in. across. 'Golden Queen' reaches 4 ft., has 4-in. flowers.

TROPAEOLUM

NASTURTIUM

Tropaeolaceae

PERENNIALS OR ANNUALS

✓ ANNUAL IN ALL ZONES; PERENNIAL IN 15–24

☼ ☼ SUN OR LIGHT SHADE

● REGULAR SUMMER WATERING

Tropaeolum majus

Distinctive appearance, rapid growth, and easy culture are three of nasturtiums' many strong points. Less conspicuous, but odd and pretty, is *T. peregrinum,* the canary bird flower.

T. majus. GARDEN NASTURTIUM. Two main kinds. Climbing types trail over the ground or climb to 6 ft. by coiling leaf stalks; dwarf kinds are compact, up to 15 in. tall. Both have round, shield-shaped, bright green leaves on long stalks. Broad, long-spurred flowers have a refreshing fragrance, come in colors ranging through maroon, red brown, orange, yellow, and red to creamy white. Young leaves, flowers, and unripe seed pods have peppery flavor like watercress and may be used in salads.

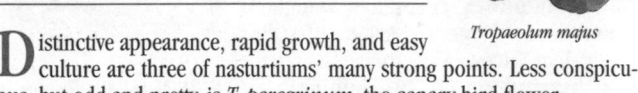

A WALL OF NASTURTIUMS

In fall, plant seed in a triangular pattern 6 in. out from a fence. Run string trellising from top of the fence to a headerboard alongside the row of seeds. Vines climb the strings and create a beautiful orange floral wall in spring. Water regularly and feed vines weekly with fish emulsion until flowering. After flowering, let vines go to seed, then cut them back, allowing seeds to drop in place. They'll come back the next year.

Easy to grow in most well-drained soils; best in sandy soil. Sow early spring. Grows and blooms quickly, often reseeds itself. In Zones 12 and 13, plant seeds in fall; plants will bloom from winter until heat of late spring. Has naturalized in some Zone 17 areas. Needs no feeding in average soils.

Climbing or trailing kinds will cover fences, banks, stumps, rocks. Use dwarf kinds for bedding, to cover fading bulb foliage, for quick flower color in ground or in pots. Good cut flowers.

Dwarf forms are most widely sold. You can get seeds of mixed colors in several strains, or a few separate colors, including cherry rose, mahogany, gold. Both single- and double-flowered forms are available.

T. peregrinum. CANARY BIRD FLOWER. Climbs to 10–15 ft. Leaves are deeply five-lobed. Flowers ¾–1 in. across, canary yellow, frilled and fringed, with green curved spur. Light shade, moist soil.

TRUMPET CREEPER, TRUMPET VINE. See CAMPSIS   p. 203

TSUGA

HEMLOCK

Pinaceae

CONIFEROUS EVERGREEN TREES AND SHRUBS

✓ ZONES 1–7, 14–17, EXCEPT AS NOTED

☼ SUN, OR PART SHADE AS NOTED

● BEST WITH AMPLE WATER

These are mostly gigantic trees with unusually graceful foliage. Branches horizontal to drooping; needlelike leaves flattened and narrowed at the base to form distinct, short stalks. Small, medium brown cones hang down from branches. Best in acid soil, high summer humidity, protection from hot sun and wind.

Tsuga canadensis

T. canadensis. CANADA HEMLOCK. Zones 3–7, 17. Dense, pyramidal tree to 90 ft. tall in its native eastern states, much smaller here. Has tendency to grow two or more trunks. Outer branchlets droop gracefully. Dark green needles, white banded beneath, about ½ in. long, are mostly arranged in opposite rows on branchlets. Oval cones about ¾ in. long grow on short stalks. Fine lawn tree or background planting. Can be clipped into outstandingly beautiful hedge, screen. One variety, 'Pendula', Sargent weeping hemlock, is low, broad plant 2–3 ft. high and twice as wide, with pendulous branches; it is good in large rock gardens. Many other dwarf or pendulous varieties exist. Dwarf 'Gentsch White' has white tips on new growth.

T. heterophylla. WESTERN HEMLOCK. Native along coast from Alaska to Northern California, inland to northern Idaho and Montana. Handsome tree with narrow, pyramidal crown. Grows fairly fast to 125–200 ft. high. Somewhat drooping branchlets and fine-textured, dark green to yellowish green foliage give fernlike quality. Short needles (¼–¾ in. long) with whitish bands beneath grow in two rows. Many 1-in. cones droop gracefully from branch tips. Picturesque large conifer for background use, hedges, or screens.

T. mertensiana. MOUNTAIN HEMLOCK. Native to high mountains from Alaska south through the higher Sierra Nevada in California and to northern Idaho and Montana. Grows to 50–90 ft. high in the wilds but is much shorter and slower growing in home gardens. Blue-green foliage with a silvery cast; ½–1-in.-long needles grow all around stems to give branchlets plump, tufty appearance. Cones 1½–3 in. long. Trees at timberline frequently grow in horizontal or twisted fashion. Slow growing under lowland conditions. Thrives on cool slope with plenty of organic matter in soil. Least adapted to lowland, hot-summer areas. Decorative in large rock garden. Good for containers, bonsai. Give part shade in Zone 14.

TUBEROSE. See POLIANTHES tuberosa   p. 432

TULBAGHIA

Amaryllidaceae

PERENNIALS

✓ ZONES 13–24

☼ FULL SUN

● REGULAR WATER

Frost damage at 20–25°F with quick recovery. Many narrow leaves grow from central point to make broad clumps. Clusters of star-shaped flowers rise above clumps on long stems. Evergreen in mild climates.

Tulbaghia violacea

T. fragrans. Leaves to 12–14 in. long or longer, 1 in. wide, gray green. Fragrant, lavender pink flowers, 20–30 on 1½–2-ft. stalk. Blooms in winter. Good cut flower.

T. violacea. SOCIETY GARLIC. Leaves bluish green, narrow, to 1 ft. long. Flowers rosy lavender, 8–20 in cluster on 1–2-ft. stems. Some bloom most of year, with peak in spring and summer. Leaves, flower stems have onion or garlic odor if cut or crushed. Unsatisfactory cut flower for this reason (but can be used as seasoning). One form has creamy stripe down the center of each leaf. Variety 'Silver Lace' has white-margined leaves. 'Tricolor' has leaves edged in white suffused in spring with pink.

TULIPA

TULIP

Liliaceae

BULBS

✂ ALL ZONES

☀ SUN DURING BLOOM

● REGULAR WATER DURING GROWTH, FLOWERING

Darwin Hybrid Tulip

Best adapted to cold-winter climates. Tulips vary considerably in color, form, height, and general character. Some look stately and formal, others dainty and whimsical; a few are bizarre. Together, the species (the same as those growing in the wilds) and hybrids provide color March–May in the garden, in containers, and for cutting.

Use larger tulips in colonies or masses with low, spring-blooming perennials such as arabis, aubrieta, aurinia, iberis, or *Phlox divaricata*, or with annuals such as forget-me-not, sweet alyssum, pansies, or violas. Plant smaller, lower-growing species in rock gardens, near paths, in raised beds, or in patio or terrace insets for close-up viewing. Tulips are superb container plants. More unusual kinds, such as Double Early, Rembrandt, and Parrot strains, seem more appropriate in containers than in garden.

Can be planted under deciduous trees that leaf out after tulips fade (good practice in hot-summer areas). Light shade helps prolong bloom of late-blooming kinds. Good light should come from overhead; otherwise, stems will lean toward light source. Rich, sandy soil is ideal, although tulips will grow in any good soil with fast drainage. Plant bulbs 2½ times as deep as they are wide, and 4–8 in. apart depending on ultimate size of plant. Plant bulbs in October except where weather is still warm.

Gophers, field mice, and aphids consider tulips a great delicacy. To protect from rodents, plant bulbs in baskets of ¼ in. wire mesh. To control aphids, spray twice a month in growing season or use systemic insecticide.

Tulips have been classified into many divisions; the most important of these are listed below, in approximate order of bloom.

Single Early tulips. Large single flowers of red, yellow, or white grow on 10–16-in. stems. Much used for growing or forcing indoors in pots. Also grown outdoors, blooming in March to mid-April, except in warm-winter climates.

Double Early tulips. Double peonylike flowers to 4 in. across bloom on 6–12-in. stems. Same colors, same bloom season as Single Early tulips. In rainy areas, mulch around plants or surround with ground cover to keep mud from splashing short-stemmed flowers. In colder climates, effective massed in borders for early bloom.

Darwin hybrids. Spectacular group bred from Darwin tulips and huge, brilliant species *T. fosterana*. Bloom before Darwins; have enormous, brightly colored flowers on 24–28-in. stems. Most are in scarlet orange to red range; some have contrasting eyes or penciling; some measure 7 in. across. Pink, yellow, and white varieties exist.

Mendel tulips. Single flowers grow on stems to 20 in. tall. Bloom after Single Early and Double Early kinds, before Darwin tulips. Shades of white, rose, red, orange, yellow.

Triumph tulips. Single flowers on medium-tall (20-in.), sturdy stems. Bloom earlier than Darwin tulips and (like Mendel tulips) are valuable in providing continuity of bloom.

Darwin tulips. Most popular of late April–May-flowering tulips. Graceful, stately plants with large oval or egg-shaped flowers, square at base, usually with stems to 2½ ft. tall. Clear, beautiful colors of white, cream, yellow, pink, red, mauve, lilac, purple, maroon, and near black.

Breeder tulips. Large oval to globular flowers on stems to 35 in. tall. May blooming. Unusual colors include orange, bronze, purplish, mahogany—often overlaid with flush of contrasting shade. Called Breeders because Dutch growers once grew them primarily to breed the much-admired "broken" (variegated) tulips.

Lily-flowered tulips. Once included in Cottage division; now separate group. Flowers are long and narrow, with long, pointed segments. Graceful, slender stemmed, fine in garden (where they blend well with other flowers) or for cutting. Stems 20–26 in. tall. May blooming. Full range of tulip colors.

Cottage tulips. Often called May-flowering tulips. About same size and height as Darwins. Flower form variable, long oval to egg shaped to vase shaped, often with pointed segments. May blooming.

Double Late tulips (often called Peony-flowered). Large, heavy blooms like peonies. They range from 18–22 in. tall; flowers may be damaged by rain or wind in exposed locations.

The ten divisions above have recently been reclassified (and somewhat simplified), and you may now find tulips sold under the following names:

Single Early and Double Early. The earliest large tulips.

Triumph and Darwin hybrids. Midseason bloomers.

Single Late or May-flowering. Now includes Darwin and Cottage classes.

Double Late, Lily-flowered, and Parrot classes wind up the season. Novelty tulips (described below) include Rembrandt, Bizarre, Bybloems, and Parrot types.

Rembrandt tulips, Bizarre tulips, Bybloems (Bijbloemens). Because the streaks and variegations on these tulip flowers are caused by a transmittable virus, they can no longer be imported and should not be planted. Tulips now sold as Rembrandts are multicolor tulips of genetic, not viral origin.

Parrot tulips. May-flowering tulips with large, long, deeply fringed and ruffled blooms striped and feathered in various colors. Many have descriptive names, e.g., 'Blue Parrot', 'Red Parrot'. Good in containers, unusual cut flowers.

Three fairly new novelty groups include: Fringed tulips, variations from Single Early, Double Early, and Darwin tulips, finely fringed on edges of segments; Viridiflora tulips, 10–20 in. tall, flowers edged or blended green with other colors—white, yellow, rose, red, or buff; and Multiflowered, three to six flowers on each 20–27-in. stem, flowers white, yellow, pink, and red, May bloom.

Seven divisions include varieties and hybrids of *T. fosterana*, *T. greigii*, and *T. kaufmanniana*, and another division that includes all other species. Most important are

Hybrids and varieties of *T. fosterana*, including huge, fiery red variety 'Red Emperor' ('Mme. Lefeber'), 16 in. tall.

Varieties and hybrids of *T. greigii* resemble those of *T. kaufmanniana*, with leaves usually heavily spotted and streaked with brown.

Varieties and hybrids of *T. kaufmanniana*, 5–10 in. tall, very early blooming, in white, pink, orange, and red, often with markings, some with leaves patterned brown.

Most species tulips—wild tulips—are low growing and early blooming with shorter, narrower leaves than garden hybrids, but there are exceptions. Generally best in rock gardens or wild gardens where plantings can remain undisturbed for many years. Those noted as being "easy" are also good container subjects.

Outstanding species are

T. acuminata. Flowers have long, twisted, spidery segments of red and yellow on 1½-ft. stems. May. Easy.

T. batalinii. Single, soft yellow flowers on 6–10-in. stems. Very narrow leaves. April.

▶

T. clusiana. LADY or CANDY TULIP. Slender, medium-size flowers on 9-in. stems. Rosy red on outside, white inside. Easy; grows well in mild-winter areas. Give sheltered position in colder areas. April–May.

T. c. chrysantha (T. stellata chrysantha). To 6 in. tall. Outer segments rose carmine, shading to buff at base; inner, bright yellow. April.

T. eichleri. Big scarlet flowers with black bases margined buff on 1-ft. stems. Blooms late March.

T. greigii. Scarlet flowers 6 in. across, on 10-in. stems. Foliage mottled or striped with brown. Early flowering.

T. kaufmanniana. WATERLILY TULIP. Medium-large creamy yellow flowers marked red on outside and yellow at center. Stems 6 in. tall. Very early bloom. Easy, permanent in gardens. Many choice named varieties.

T. linifolia. Scarlet, black-based, yellow-centered flowers on 6-in. stems in late April. Handsome with *T. batalinii.*

T. praestans. Cup-shaped, orange-scarlet flowers, two to four to 10–12-in. stem, in early April. Variety 'Fusilier' is shorter, has four to six flowers to a stem.

T. saxatilis. Fragrant, yellow-based pale lilac flowers open nearly flat, one to three to each 1-ft. stem. Early bloom. Good in warm-winter areas.

T. stellata chrysantha. See T. clusiana chrysantha

T. sylvestris. Yellow, 2-in. flowers, one or two on 1-ft. stem. Late flowering. Good in warm-winter areas.

T. tarda (T. dasystemon). Each 3-in. stem has three to six upward-facing, star-shaped flowers with golden centers and white-tipped segments.

T. turkestanica. Vigorous tulip with up to eight flowers on each slender, 1-ft. stem. Flowers slender in bud, star shaped when open, gray green on outside, off-white with yellow base inside. Early March bloom. Easy.

Tulipa kaufmanniana

TULIPS IN MILD-WINTER CALIFORNIA

Buy bulbs from a well-stocked garden center offering varieties selected for the area. Refrigerate them in paper bags (away from ripening fruit) 6 weeks before planting. Plant between Christmas and mid-January. Before planting, mix low-nitrogen granular fertilizer into soil. Plant bulbs at equal depths under 4–6 in. of soil. Water once after planting, sparingly until leaves emerge, then generously.

TULIP TREE. See LIRIODENDRON tulipifera, MAGNOLIA soulangiana **pp. 357, 369**	
TUPELO. See NYSSA sylvatica **p. 392**	
TUPIDANTHUS calyptratus. See SCHEFFLERA pueckleri **p. 479**	

TURNIP and RUTABAGA

Brassicaceae (Cruciferae)

BIENNIAL VEGETABLES

☀ ALL ZONES

☼ FULL SUN

💧 REGULAR WATER

Turnip

Although turnips are best known for roots, foliage of turnips is also a useful green vegetable. Different varieties give a nice choice of colors (white, white topped with purple, creamy yellow) and shapes (globe, flattened globe). Rutabaga is a tasty kind of turnip with large yellowish roots. It's a late-maturing crop that stores well in the ground; turnips are quick growing and should be harvested and used as soon as they are big enough. Roots are milder flavored if soil is kept moist, become more pungent under drier conditions.

In cold-winter areas, plant turnips or rutabagas in April for early summer harvest, or in July or August for fall harvest. In mild-winter areas, grow as winter crop by planting September–March.

TURRAEA obtusifolia

STAR BUSH

Meliaceae

EVERGREEN SHRUB

☀ ZONES 22–24; PROTECTED, 15, 16, 19–21

☼ LIGHT SHADE

💧 INFREQUENT, DEEP WATERING

Turraea obtusifolia

Native to South Africa. Slow growth to 4–5 ft. tall, 4 ft. wide; many drooping branchlets, some lower branches nearly prostrate. Leaves 2 in. long, dark green, glossy, polished. Many star-shaped, narrow-petaled, pure white flowers, 1½ in. across, in loose clusters. Long bloom season reaches peak in September, October. Temperamental: needs good drainage and either light shade of high branches or eastern exposure without strong reflected heat. Hardy to 26°F.

TWEEDIA caerulea (Oxypetalum caeruleum)

Asclepiadaceae

ANNUAL, PERENNIAL, VINE

☀ ZONES 14–24

☼ SUN

💧 REGULAR WATER

Tweedia caerulea

Can be a perennial subshrub or twiner to 3 ft. It can also be grown as an annual, flowering in late summer from early-sown seed. Tip-pinch young plants to force branching. Leaves are 4 in. long and the blue star-shaped 1-in. flowers grow along the stems and at the top. They are good for cutting.

TWINFLOWER. See LINNAEA borealis **p. 356**	
TWINSPUR. See DIASCIA **p. 262**	

UGNI molinae (Myrtus ugni)

CHILEAN GUAVA

Myrtaceae

EVERGREEN SHRUB

☀ ZONES 14–24

☼ SUN NEAR COAST, PART SHADE IN HOT AREAS

💧 REGULAR WATER

Ugni molinae

Slow to moderate growth to 3–6 ft. tall. Scraggly and open in youth, it matures into compact, rounded plant. Foliage is dark green with bronze tints; leaves are oval, leathery, ½ in. long, whitish beneath, with edges slightly rolled under. White, rose-tinted flowers in late spring, early summer; they are principally little brushes of stamens. Purplish or reddish, pleasant-tasting, ½-in. fruit follows; it smells like baking apples and can be used fresh or in jams and jellies.

Neutral to acid soil. Tidy, restrained plant for patios, terraces, near walks and paths where passersby can pick and sample fruit, enjoy its fragrance.

Ulmaceae. The elm family contains trees and shrubs, usually deciduous, with inconspicuous flowers and fruit that may be nutlike, single-seeded and fleshy, or winged. Elm, hackberry, and zelkova are representative.

ULMUS

ELM

Ulmaceae

DECIDUOUS OR PARTIALLY EVERGREEN TREES

☘ ZONES VARY BY SPECIES

☼ FULL SUN

💧 BEST WITH REGULAR WATER

Ulmus americana

Easy to grow in any fairly good soil; will survive in most poor ones. Root systems are aggressive and close to surface; you'll have trouble growing any other plants under these trees. Branch crotches often narrow, easily split. Many of the larger elms are tasty to leaf beetles, bark beetles, leafhoppers, aphids, and scale, making them either time consuming to care for or messy (or both). Dutch elm disease, formerly a problem in the East, reached western states in the 1970s.

U. americana. AMERICAN ELM. Zones 1–11, 14–21. Fast-growing tree that can reach 100 ft. or more with nearly equal—sometimes even greater—spread. Form is stately, with stout trunk dividing into many upright main branches at same height; outer branches are pendulous, silhouette vase shaped. Rough-surfaced, toothed leaves are 3–6 in. long. Leafs out very late where winters are mild. Yellow fall color. Pale green, papery seeds in spring blow about, are messy.

Grows best in deep soil, with 70–75-ft. circle to spread in. Roots send up suckers, can make thickets; will lift pavement if crowded. Leaf and bark beetles weaken and disfigure trees; scale causes drip and sooty mildew. Until the 1970s the only really recommendable use for such a tree was for very large gardens, out-of-the-way places, on broad boulevards unencumbered by utility lines, or in parks. Since then its attack by Dutch elm disease in the West has ruled out recommendation for planting anywhere.

U. carpinifolia. SMOOTH-LEAFED ELM. Zones 1–11, 14–21. To 100 ft. Wide-spreading branches, weeping branchlets. Leaves 2–3½ in. long, shiny deep green above. Culture, uses, precautions as for American elm.

U. glabra. SCOTCH ELM. Zones 1–11, 14–21. To 120 ft. tall. Does not sucker. Leaves 3–6 in. long, oval, sharply toothed, rough surfaced, on very short stalks. Old trees sometimes seen, but scarcely grown now. Variety 'Camperdownii', Camperdown elm, generally 10–20 ft. tall, has weeping branches that reach to ground, making tent of shade.

U. hollandica. DUTCH ELM. Zones 1–11, 14–21. To 100 ft. or more. Suckers freely. Includes hybrids between Scotch and smooth-leafed elms.

U. parvifolia. CHINESE ELM, CHINESE EVERGREEN ELM. Often sold as *U. p.* 'Sempervirens'. Zones 8, 9, 12–24. Evergreen or deciduous according to winter temperatures and tree's individual heredity. So-called evergreen elm usually sold as 'Sempervirens'; this may be evergreen most winters, lose its leaves in unusual cold snap (new leaves come on fast). Fast growth to 40–60 ft., with 50–70-ft. spread. Often reaches 30 ft. in 5 years. Extremely variable in form, but generally spreading, with long, arching, eventually weeping branchlets. Trunks of older trees have bark that sheds in patches somewhat like sycamore. Leaves leathery, ¾–2½ in. long, ⅓–1⅓ in. wide, oval, evenly toothed. Round fruit forms in fall.

Stake young trees until trunks can carry weight of branches. Stake and head leading shoot higher than other shade trees to compensate for weeping. Rub or cut out small branches along trunk for first few years. Shorten overlong branches or strongly weeping branches to strengthen tree scaffolding. Older trees may need thinning to lessen chance of storm damage. Little bothered by pests or diseases except Texas root rot in desert. Good for patio shade in milder portions of West. Useful for sun screening. With careful pruning, useful as a street tree. Varieties are 'Brea', with larger leaves, more upright habit; and 'Drake', with small leaves, weeping habit. Both are more or less evergreen. 'True Green' has small deep green leaves, is round headed, more evergreen. Word of caution: Siberian elm (*U. pumila*) is sometimes sold as Chinese elm. Siberian elm flowers in spring, has stiffer habit and thinner, less glossy leaves.

U. procera. ENGLISH ELM. Zones 1–11, 14–21. To 120 ft. Suckers profusely. Tall trunk with broad or tall, dense crown of branches. Foliage

holds dark green color later in fall than American elm. Same precautions apply to this tree as to American elm.

U. pumila. SIBERIAN ELM. All zones; most useful in Zones 1–3, 10, 11. To 50 ft. Leaves ¾–2 in. long, ⅓–1 in. wide, dark green, smooth. Extremely hardy and tough, enduring cold, heat, aridity, and poor soil. As fast-growing tree, it is suitable for windbreaks or shelterbelts. Has brittle wood, weak crotches, and is not a desirable tree. Root system troublesome in gardens, but possibly useful in holding soil against wind or water erosion. Papery, winged seeds disperse seedlings over wide area.

UMBELLULARIA californica

CALIFORNIA LAUREL, CALIFORNIA BAY, OREGON MYRTLE, PEPPERWOOD

Lauraceae

EVERGREEN TREE

☘ ZONES 4–10, 12–24

☼ ☽ FULL SUN OR PARTIAL SHADE

○ NO WATER ONCE ESTABLISHED

Umbellularia californica

Native to southwestern Oregon, California Coast Ranges, lower elevations of Sierra Nevada. In the wilds, it varies from a huge, gumdrop-shaped shrub (on windy hillsides near coast) to a tall and free-ranging tree 75 ft. high and over 100 ft. wide (in forests). Leaves are 2–5 in. long, ½–1 in. wide, pointed at tip, medium to deep yellow green and glossy on top, dull light green beneath.

Tiny yellowish flowers in clusters give plant yellowish cast in spring. They are followed by olivelike, inedible green fruit that turns purple. Each fruit contains a large seed, and volunteer seedlings occasionally turn up in suburban gardens; they can be transplanted if no more than 6 inches tall.

In gardens, California laurel tends to grow slowly (about 1 ft. a year) to 20–25 ft. high and as wide. Grows best and fastest in deep soil with ample water, but tolerates many other conditions, including aridity. Will grow in deep shade and ultimately get big enough to become shade maker itself (casts very dense shade unless thinned). Always neat. Good for screening, background plantings, or tall hedges. Often multitrunked. Good patio or street tree. Expect heavy autumn fallout of yellow to tan leaves.

UMBRELLA PINE. See SCIADOPITYS verticillata	**p. 480**
UMBRELLA PLANT. See CYPERUS alternifolius	**p. 255**
UMBRELLA TREE, QUEENSLAND. See SCHEFFLERA actinophylla	**p. 478**
URBINIA agavoides. See ECHEVERIA agavoides	**p. 269**

Urticaceae. The nettle family, best known for stinging nettles (*Urtica*), also contains such ornamentals as baby's tears (*Soleirolia*).

VACCINIUM

Ericaceae

EVERGREEN AND DECIDUOUS SHRUBS

☘ ZONES VARY BY SPECIES

☽ PARTIAL SHADE

💧 MODERATE WATER

Vaccinium ovatum

Excellent ornamental shrubs with clusters of bell-shaped flowers and colorful, edible fruit that attracts birds. All require acid soil and ample leaf mold, peat moss, or ground bark. Good woodland garden subjects.

V. corymbosum. See Blueberry

V. moupinense. Zones 4–7, 14–17. Native to western China. Evergreen shrub to 2 ft. with tiny bright green leaves that emerge with a bronzy cast. Flowers are reddish, fruit purple black.

V

▶

V. ovatum. EVERGREEN HUCKLEBERRY. Evergreen shrub. Zones 4–7, 14–17. Native Santa Barbara County north to British Columbia. Erect shrub to 2–3 ft. in sun, to 8–10 ft. in shade. Young plants spreading, older plants taller than wide, compact. Leathery, lustrous dark green leaves, ½–1¼ in. long; bronzy new growth. Flowers (March–May) are white or pinkish. Black berries with whitish bloom, good in pies, jams, jellies, syrups. Can be trimmed into hedge or grown in container. Cut branches popular for arrangements.

V. parvifolium. RED HUCKLEBERRY. Deciduous shrub. Zones 2–7, 14–17. Native to Sierra Nevada and Northern California Coast Ranges to Alaska. Slow growth to 4–12 ft., rarely 18 ft. Thin, green branches with spreading or cascading habit provide intricate, filmy winter silhouette. Light green leaves are thin, oval, ½–¾ in. long, light green. Greenish or whitish flowers, fine for arrangements, bloom April–May. Clear, bright red, showy berries for jams, jellies, pies. Needs highly acid humus soil.

V. vitis-idaea. COWBERRY, FOXBERRY. Evergreen shrub. Zones 2–7, 14–17. Slow growth to 1 ft. tall, spreading by underground runners to 3 ft. Leaves glossy, dark green, ⅓–1 in. long; new growth often brightly tinged red, orange. Clustered white or pinkish flowers bloom in May. Sour red berries, something like tiny cranberries, are esteemed for preserves, syrups. Handsome little plants for small-scale ground cover, informal edging around larger acid-soil plantings. Good in wet areas. With ample water, will take full sun in cool-summer areas. *V. v. minus,* lingonberry, is smaller, with leaves ⅛–½ in. long. Attractive container plant.

Valerianaceae. The valerian family of perennial herbs (rarely shrubs) has clustered small flowers. False valerian (*Centranthus*) and valerian are the only representatives in western gardens.

VALERIANA officinalis

VALERIAN, GARDEN HELIOTROPE

Valerianaceae

PERENNIAL HERB

☀ ALL ZONES

☼ ☽ SUN OR PARTIAL SHADE

◐ ● TAKES ARIDITY, LOOKS BEST WITH SOME WATER

Valeriana officinalis

Both true heliotrope (*Heliotropium*) and red valerian (*Centranthus ruber*) are more common than *Valeriana officinalis.* Tall, straight stems grow to about 4 ft. high; most leaves remain fairly close to ground. Leaves are light green, borne in pairs that are further divided into eight to ten pairs of narrow leaflets. Tiny, fragrant flowers are white, pink, red, or lavender blue, in rounded clusters at ends of stems. Plant spreads and can become invasive. Roots are strong smelling. Start new plants from seeds or divisions. Grow in mixed herb or flower borders but don't allow it to crowd other plants. Use cut flowers in arrangements.

VALLOTA speciosa (Cyrtanthus purpureus, C. elatus)

SCARBOROUGH LILY

Amaryllidaceae

BULB

☀ ZONES 16, 17, 23, 24

☼ ☽ LIGHT SHADE, FULL SUN ON COAST

● REGULAR WATER DURING GROWTH AND BLOOM

Vallota speciosa

Native to South Africa. Strap-shaped evergreen leaves are 1–2 ft. long. Clusters of bright orange-vermilion, funnel-shaped, 2½–3-in.-wide flowers grow on 2-ft. stalks. Blooms summer and early fall. White-flowered form rarely available. Survives outdoors where frosts are very light and infrequent, even succeeding in competition with tree roots. Excellent pot plant. Plant June–July or just after flowering. Set bulbs with tips just below surface. Plant blooms best when roots are crowded. Fertilize monthly during active growth. Water regularly except during semidormant period in winter and spring, but never let plant dry out completely.

VANCOUVERIA

Berberidaceae

DECIDUOUS AND EVERGREEN PERENNIALS

☀ ZONES VARY BY SPECIES

☼ GROW IN TREE-SHADED BEDS

◐ ● LITTLE SUMMER WATER EXCEPT IN ZONES 14–16

Vancouveria planipetala

These close relatives of *Epimedium* have the same uses in garden. Leaves are divided into numerous leaflets. Flowers in late spring, early summer. Attractive ground cover. Cut foliage is attractive in bouquets.

V. chrysantha. Evergreen. Zones 5, 6, 14–17. Native to Siskiyou Mountains. To 8–16 in. tall. Bronzed, gray-green leaves, 1½ in. long and wide. Small yellow flowers, 4–15 to the stalk, each flower ½ in. wide.

V. hexandra. Deciduous. Zones 4–6, 14–17. Native to coastal forests from Northern California to Washington. To 4–16 in. tall. Leaflets are 1–2½ in. long, light green; fresh appearance all summer. Flower stalks usually topped with three drooping white flowers to ½ in. across, petals and sepals sharply bent backward.

V. planipetala (V. parviflora). INSIDE-OUT FLOWER. Evergreen, can be deciduous in cold-winter areas. Zones 4–6, 14–17. To 2 ft. tall. Light to medium green, 1½-in. leaflets, shallowly lobed. White flowers are even smaller than those of *V. hexandra* but are carried in clusters of 25–50.

VANILLA TRUMPET VINE: See DISTICTIS laxiflora   p. 265

VARIEGATED GINGER. See ALPINIA sanderae   p. 148

VAUQUELINIA californica

ARIZONA ROSEWOOD

Rosaceae

EVERGREEN SHRUB OR SMALL TREE

☀ ZONES 10–13

☼ FULL SUN

○ NO WATER ONCE ESTABLISHED

Vauquelinia californica

Upright, sometimes rather contorted growth to as much as 20 ft., with dark gray to reddish brown bark. Lance-shaped leaves with lightly toothed edges, to 3 in. long and ½ in. wide, leathery bright green with slightly woolly undersides. White, ¼-in.-wide, five-petaled flowers grow in loose, flattened clusters at branch tips in late spring. Woody seed capsules, about ¼ in. long, develop in summer, persist through fall, winter. Rather open-growing shrub or small tree.

VELTHEIMIA bracteata

Liliaceae

BULB

☀ ZONES 13, 16–24

☼ PARTIAL SHADE

● AS NEEDED DURING GROWTH AND BLOOM

Veltheimia bracteata

Native to South Africa. There is some name confusion in the nursery trade; some plants sold as *V. capensis* or *V. viridifolia* are really *V. bracteata.* True *V. capensis* has bluish green leaves and pale pink flowers, while *V. bracteata* has pinkish purple flowers and shiny deep green, wavy-margined leaves to 1 ft. long, 3 in. wide. It is probable that all sold are *V. bracteata* or a variety of it. Foliage makes *V. bracteata* a beautiful plant even when not in bloom. Flowers appear in winter and early spring: heavy clusters of green-tipped, tubular, drooping blooms, resembling those of red-hot poker (*Kniphofia*), on 1-ft., stout, brown-marked stems. Set bulbs with upper third above surface. Increase light and warmth as growth begins. Fertilize every 2 weeks through growing season. Protect from wind. Give winter shelter in Zones 13, 16–22.

VELVET GROUNDSEL. See SENECIO petasitis   p. 483

VERBASCUM

MULLEIN
Scrophulariaceae
BIENNIALS, PERENNIALS
✱ ALL ZONES
☼ FULL SUN
◐ NEED LITTLE WATER; BETTER WITH SOME

Stately, summer-blooming plants. Broad leaves closely set on stems. Shallow-dished flowers in straight spikes. A large group, some weedy. Self-sow freely. Start biennial sorts from seed in spring; sow in place or in containers (transplant to ground when 2 in. high). *V. thapsus*, common mullein, is attractive roadside weed.

Verbascum bombyciferum 'Arctic Summer'

V. blattaria. MOTH MULLEIN. Biennial. Low clumps of smooth, dark green, cut or toothed leaves. Flower spikes 1½–2½ ft. high with pale yellow or white blooms, purple stamens. Flowers open with morning light.

V. bombyciferum 'Arctic Summer'. Biennial. Foot-high rosettes of furry, gray green, oval leaves. Powdery white stems to 6 ft. or more bear yellow, 1½-in. flowers.

V. chaixii. Leaves less conspicuously furry than the preceding, to 12 in. long. Flowering spikes erect, narrow, often branched, to 3 ft. tall. 'Album', most widely grown variety, has white flowers with bluish center.

V. dumulosum. Perennial. Dwarf, to 1 ft., with velvety white leaves and spikes of yellow, purple-eyed flowers in midsummer. A hybrid, 'Letitia', has a long summer bloom season.

V. olympicum. Perennial. Stems to 5 ft. high. Large white leaves, 2 ft. or more long, with soft, downy hairs. Bright yellow, 1-in. flowers clustered in many long spikes.

V. phoeniceum. PURPLE MULLEIN. Perennial. Stems 2–4 ft. high. Leaves smooth on top, hairy on underside. Purple flowers in slender spikes half the height of plant or more. The Cotswold Hybrids are similar to the species and come in shades of pink, white, purple, and cream.

VERBENA

Verbenaceae
PERENNIALS, SOME GROWN AS ANNUALS
✱ ZONES VARY BY SPECIES
☼ FULL SUN
◑◐ WATER NEEDS VARY BY SPECIES

Verbena peruviana

They need heat to thrive. Set 2 ft. apart for ground cover; growth is fast. These species adjust effectively to planting in parking strips, along driveways, and on dry banks, walls, and crevices where they display color all summer. All like good air circulation, dislike wet foliage.

V. bipinnatifida. Perennial. All zones. Native from western Great Plains to Mexico. Grows 8–15 in. tall. Finely divided leaves; blue flowers all summer. Spreads by self-sowing in most climates. Needs little water.

V. bonariensis. Perennial. Zones 8–24. Airy, branching stems carry many spikes of purple flowers to 3–6 ft. Leaves are mostly basal. Plant's

see-through quality fits it for foreground as well as background planting. In cold climates treated as an annual. Needs little water once established.

V. gooddingii. Short-lived perennial. All zones. Native to Southwest. To 1½ ft. high, spreading. Oval, deeply cut leaves. Heads of flowers, usually pinkish lavender, top short spikes. Sow in early spring for summer bloom. Can reseed where moisture is adequate. Good performer in desert heat.

V. hybrida (V. hortensis). GARDEN VERBENA. Short-lived perennial in Zones 8–24; usually grown as annual. Many-branched plants 6–12 in. high and spreading 1½–3 ft. Oblong, 2–4-in.-long leaves are bright green or gray green, with toothed margins. Flowers in flat, compact clusters, 2–3 in. wide. Colors include white, pink, bright red, purple, blue, and combinations. Romance (6 in.) and Showtime (10 in.) are superior strains. 'Showtime Trinidad', deep rose pink, is hardy enough to withstand light frosts. Less chance of mildew if you water deeply and not too often. If used as perennial, prune severely in winter or early spring. Good ground cover in Zones 12, 13, if Bermuda grass can be kept out of it.

V. peruviana (V. chamaedryfolia). Perennial, often grown as annual. Zones 8–24. Spreads rapidly, forms very flat mat. (Planted 2 ft. apart, can make solid cover in a season.) Leaves are neat, small, closely set. Flat-topped flower clusters on slender stems lavishly cover foliage. In original form, corolla tube is white, spreading lobes rich scarlet. Hybrids spread somewhat more slowly, have slightly larger leaves and stouter stems, and are available in several colors: 'Starfire' (red); 'Appleblossom', 'Cherry Pink', 'Princess Gloria', 'Little Pinkie', 'Raspberry Rose', 'St. Paul' (pink and rose tones); many purplish varieties; and a fine pure white. Especially popular in Southern California and the desert. Modest water.

V. pulchella gracilior. MOSS VERBENA. Perennial. Zones 8–24. Finely cut leaves, rose violet to pink flowers. A form that is widely sold as *V. tenuisecta* has white flowers. Little water.

V. rigida (V. venosa). Perennial. All zones. Spreading plants that can be 10–20 in. tall. Leaves rough, dark green, 2–4 in. long, strongly toothed. Lilac to purple-blue flowers in cylindrical clusters on tall, stiff stems summer and fall. Useful in low-maintenance gardens. Can be grown as annual; blooms in 4 months from seed. Needs little water.

V. tenera maonettii. Creeping perennial. Zones 8–24. Leaves cut to midrib and lobes cut again. Flat clusters of pink flowers with distinct white margins. Average water.

VERBENA, LEMON. See ALOYSIA triphylla   p. 148

Verbenaceae. The immense verbena family contains annuals, perennials, shrubs, and a few trees and vines. Leaves are usually opposite or in whorls, flowers in spikes or spikelike clusters. Fruit may be berries or nutlets. *Clerodendrum, Lantana, Verbena,* and *Vitex* are examples.

VERONICA

SPEEDWELL
Scrophulariaceae
PERENNIALS
✱ ALL ZONES
☼ FULL SUN
◐ MOST NEED REGULAR WATER

Veronica prostrata

Handsome plants ranging from 4 in. to 2½ ft. in height. Small flowers (¼–½ in. across) are massed to display effectively the white, rose, pink, pale or deep blue color. Use in sunny borders and rock gardens. Prostrate, mat-forming kinds will tolerate less frequent watering than bushy kinds. For shrubby plants sold as *Veronica*, see *Hebe*.

V. grandis holophylla. Many stems to 2 ft. high are densely clothed with dark green, glossy leaves. Long stalks of rich deep blue flowers show above foliage.

V. hybrids. These include a number of midsummer-blooming, upright bushy perennials from 10 to 18 in. high. Choice varieties: 'Barcarole', to

V

10 in. tall, rose pink flowers; 'Crater Lake Blue', prostrate with flower stems to 10 in. tall, bright blue flower spikes; 'Icicle', 15–18 in. tall, white flower spikes; 'Sunny Border Blue', 1½ ft. tall, a choice blue with a long bloom season.

V. longifolia subsessilis. Clumps of upright stems to 2 ft. tall topped by close-flowered spikes of deep blue flowers about ½ in. across in midsummer. Stems are leafy and rather closely set with narrow, pointed leaves.

V. pectinata. Forms prostrate mats that spread by creeping stems that root at joints. Roundish, ½-in.-long leaves with scallop-toothed or deeply cut edges. Flowers are profuse, deep blue with white center, in 5–6-in. spikes among the leaves. Good as a rock plant or in wall crevices.

Veronica Hybrid

V. prostrata (V. rupestris). Has tufted, hairy stems, some of which are prostrate. Leaves ½–¾ in. long. Flower stems to 8 in. high are topped by short cluster of pale blue flowers. 'Heavenly Blue' is almost entirely prostrate, with flower stems reaching up to 6 in. high. Bright blue flowers.

V. repens. Shiny green, ½-in.-long leaves clothe prostrate stems, give mosslike effect. Flowers ¼ in. wide, lavender to white in few-flowered clusters in spring. Takes some shade. Good as a small-scale ground cover, paving plant, or cover for small bulbs.

V. saturejoides. Many-tufted stems spread by creeping roots. Roundish, ½-in.-long leaves closely overlap on stems. Dark blue flowers in short, compact spikes appear in May. Fine rock plant.

V. spicata. Much like *V. longifolia subsessilis* but less robust and with shorter flower spikes. Miniature variety 'Nana' grows 6 in. high, with violet blue flowers June–July.

VIBURNUM

Caprifoliaceae

DECIDUOUS OR EVERGREEN SHRUBS, SMALL TREES

ZONES VARY BY SPECIES

SUN OR PART SHADE

MOST NEED REGULAR WATER

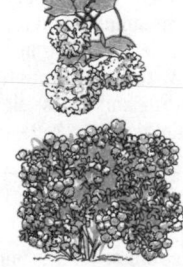

Viburnum opulus 'Roseum'

Large and diverse group of plants with clustered, often fragrant flowers and clusters of single-seeded, often brilliantly colored fruit much liked by birds. Some are valuable for winter flowers. They tend to fall into groups determined by landscape use.

Evergreen viburnums used principally as foliage plants are *V. davidii*, *V. japonicum*, and *V. rhytidophyllum*. Evergreen viburnums used as foliage and flowering plants are *V. suspensum*, *V. rigidum*, *V. tinus*.

Partially deciduous viburnums grown for their flowers are *V. burkwoodii* and *V. macrocephalum macrocephalum*. They are nearly evergreen in mild climates and have showy flowers.

Deciduous viburnums grown for fragrant flowers are *V. bodnantense*, *V. burkwoodii* 'Chenault', *V. carlcephalum*, *V. carlesii*, *V. farreri*, and *V. juddii*. Deciduous viburnums for showy flowers, fall leaf color include *V. lentago*, *V. opulus* (also has showy fruit), *V. o.* 'Roseum', *V. plicatum plicatum*, *V. p. tomentosum*, *V. prunifolium*, *V. trilobum*.

With few exceptions noted in descriptions, viburnums tolerate alkaline and acid soils. They do well in heavy, rich soils. Useful near swimming pools. Many have wide range in climate adaptability; note *V. burkwoodii* and *V. tinus* 'Robustum'. Most evergreen kinds look better with some protection from sun where summers are hot and long. Prune to prevent legginess; some evergreen kinds can be sheared. Aphids, thrips, spider mites, and scale are likely problems. Use an all-purpose insecticide-miticide spray in early spring at two-week intervals. Keep sulfur sprays off foliage.

V. bodnantense. Deciduous shrub. Zones 4–9, 14–24. To 10 ft. or more. Oval leaves 1½–4 in. long are deeply veined, turn dark scarlet in fall. Flowers deep pink fading paler, very fragrant, in loose clusters October– April. Fruit red, not showy. This plant is a hybrid; there are several vari-

eties. Best known is 'Dawn' ('Pink Dawn'). Flower buds freeze in coldest Northwest winters.

V. burkwoodii. Deciduous shrub in coldest areas, nearly evergreen elsewhere. Zones 1–12, 14–24. To 6–12 ft. tall, 4–5 ft. wide. Leaves to 3½ in. long, glossy dark green above, white and hairy beneath; purplish in cold weather. Very fragrant white flowers open from dense 4-in. clusters of pink buds. Blooms February–March. Fruit blue black, not showy. Early growth is straggly; mature plants are dense. Can be trained as espalier.

V. b. 'Chenault' (V. chenaultii). Deciduous shrub. Zones 1–9, 14–24. To 4–6 ft. tall, 3–4 ft. wide. Leaves and flowers are much like those of *V. burkwoodii*, though plant is more compact, more deciduous.

V. carlcephalum. FRAGRANT SNOWBALL. Deciduous shrub. Zones 1–11, 14–24. To 8–10 ft. tall, 4–5 ft. wide. Leaves dull grayish green, downy beneath, 2–3½ in. long. Flowers long-lasting, waxy white, fragrant; bloom in dense 4–5-in. clusters in spring, early summer. No fruit. Showy as common snowball (*V. opulus* 'Roseum') but has added fragrance.

V. carlesii. KOREAN SPICE VIBURNUM. Deciduous shrub. Zones 1–11, 14–24. To 4–8 ft. tall, 4–5 ft. broad. Leaves are like those of *V. carlcephalum*. Flowers pink in bud, opening white, in 2–3-in.-wide clusters, sweetly fragrant, March–May. Blue-black fruit in summer. Loose, open habit. Best in part shade during summer, in sun during spring, winter.

V. davidii. Evergreen shrub. Zones 4–9, 14–24. Grows to 1–3 ft. tall, 3–4 ft. wide. Leaves are glossy dark green, deeply veined, to 6 in. long. White flowers in 3-in.-wide clusters open from dull pinkish red buds; not showy. Metallic turquoise blue fruit.

Use as foundation shrub, in foreground plantings, with ferns, azaleas, other acid soil plants in part shade. Extremely valuable in Zones 4–6, 17.

V. dilatatum. LINDEN VIBURNUM. Deciduous shrub. Zones 3–9, 14–16. Compact shrub to 6 ft., possibly 10 ft. tall. Leaves nearly round, 2–5 in. long, gray green. Flowers are tiny, creamy white, in 5-in.-wide clusters in early summer. Showy bright red fruits are produced best where summers are warm; they ripen in September, hang on into winter.

V. farreri (V. fragrans). Deciduous shrub. Zones 4–9, 14–24. To 10–15 ft. tall and as wide. Smooth green leaves are oval, heavily veined, 1½–3 in. long; turn soft russet red in fall. Fragrant white to pink flowers in 2-in. clusters, November–March. Blossoms will stand to 20–22°F, freeze in colder temperatures. Fruit bright red. Prune to prevent leggy growth. *V. f.* 'Album' (*V. f.* 'Candidissimum') has pure white flowers. *V. f.* 'Nanum' is lower growing (to 2 ft.), with pink flowers.

V. japonicum. Evergreen shrub or small tree. Zones 5–10, 12, 14–24. To 10–20 ft. tall. Leaves are leathery, glossy dark green, to 6 in. long. Sparse bloom in spring: fragrant white flowers in 4-in. clusters. Red fruit is sparse but very attractive. Big, bulky shrub or small tree for background plantings. Best with some shade in warmer areas. Control aphids.

V. juddii. Deciduous shrub. Zones 3–9, 14–24. To 4–8 ft. tall. Hybrid. More spreading and bushy than *V. carlesii*, but otherwise similar to it.

V. lentago. NANNYBERRY. Deciduous shrub or small tree. Zones 1–9, 14–21. Will grow as single-trunked tree up to 30 ft. or as massive shrub to lesser height. Creamy white spring flowers in flat clusters to 4–5 in. across. Edible fruit red at first, changing to blue black. Glossy foliage turns purplish red in fall. Grows in shade as well as sun. Use as large background shrub, small tree. Good in shade of taller trees, at woodland edge.

V. macrocephalum macrocephalum (V. m. 'Sterile'). CHINESE SNOWBALL. Deciduous shrub in coldest areas, nearly evergreen elsewhere. Zones 1–9, 14–24. To 12–20 ft. tall, with broad, rounded habit. Leaves oval to oblong, dull green, 2–4 in. long. Spectacular big, rounded flower clusters to 6–8 in. are composed of sterile flowers. Blooms April–May. No fruit. Good for espaliers, display.

V. opulus. EUROPEAN CRANBERRY BUSH. Deciduous shrub. Zones 1–9, 14–24. To 10–20 ft. Lobed dark green leaves shaped like maple leaves; 2–4 in. long and wider, turn red in fall. Blooms in May: white flower clusters 2–4 in. across, rimmed with ¾-in.-wide, white sterile flowers in lace cap effect. Large, showy red fruit. Needs careful spraying to control aphids. Varieties include

'Aureum'. To 10 ft. Golden yellow foliage needs some shade to prevent sunburn. Red fruit.

'Compactum'. Same as *V. opulus* but smaller: 4–5 ft. high and wide.

'Nanum'. Dwarf form of *V. opulus*. To 2 ft. tall, 2 ft. wide. Needs no trimming as low hedge. Can take poor, wet soils. No flowers, fruit.

'Roseum' (*V. o.* 'Sterile'). COMMON SNOWBALL. To 10–15 ft. Resembles *V. opulus*, but flower clusters resemble snowballs: 2–2½ in. across, composed entirely of sterile flowers (so no fruit).

V. plicatum plicatum (V. tomentosum 'Sterile'). JAPANESE SNOWBALL. Deciduous shrub. Zones 1–9, 14–24. To 15 ft. tall and as wide. Oval, dull dark green, strongly veined leaves 3–6 in. long. Turn purplish red in fall. Snowball clusters of white sterile flowers 2–3 in. across, borne in opposite rows along horizontal branches, May. Less subject to aphids than *V. opulus*. Horizontal branching pattern, fall color, flowers all attractive.

V. p. tomentosum. DOUBLEFILE VIBURNUM. Resembles plant above, but flat flower clusters are 2–4 in. wide, edged with 1–1½-in.-wide sterile flowers in lace cap effect. Fruit red, showy, not always profuse. Selections include 'Cascade', a smaller grower; 'Mariesii', with larger sterile flowers; 'Shasta', with even more horizontal habit (6 ft. tall, 12 ft. wide); and 'Watanabe', a dwarf (4- by 6-ft.), nearly everblooming variety.

V. prunifolium. BLACK HAW. Deciduous shrub. Zones 1–9, 14–21. Upright to 15 ft. and spreading as wide. Can be trained as small tree. Common name comes from dark fruit and plant's resemblance to hawthorn (*Crataegus*). Oval leaves, to 3 in. long and finely toothed, turn red in autumn. Abundant clusters of creamy white flowers in spring are followed by edible blue-black fruit to ½ in. long in fall, winter. Use as dense screen or barrier, attractive specimen shrub, or small tree. Best in sun.

V. rhytidophyllum. LEATHERLEAF VIBURNUM. Evergreen shrub. Zones 2–9, 14–24. Narrow, upright shrub to 6–15 ft. tall; fast growing in colder areas, slow in Zones 18–24. Leaves narrowish, to 4–10 in. long, deep green and wrinkled above, densely fuzzy underneath. Off-white spring flowers in 4–8-in.-wide clusters. Fruit scarlet, turning black. Cold hardy, but tattered looking where cold winds blow. Striking to some, to others coarse. Hybrids include 'Alleghany', 'Pragense', and 'Willowwood', all similar to the parent.

Viburnum rhytidophyllum

V. rigidum. CANARY ISLAND VIBURNUM. Evergreen shrub. Zones 15–24. Resembles *V. tinus* but has larger flower clusters, larger leaves to 6 in. long. Grows upright to 6–10 ft. with equal or greater spread. Flowers in late winter, early spring are followed by blue fruit that later turns black. Uses same as for *V. tinus*.

V. sargentii 'Onondaga'. Zones 2–9, 14–24. Deciduous shrub with erect, rounded form to 6 ft. Leaves emerge deep maroon and hold a maroon tinge when mature. Late spring lace cap flowers are white tinged purple.

V. suspensum. SANDANKWA VIBURNUM. Evergreen shrub. Risky in coldest winters Zones 8–10; reliable in Zones 12–24. To 8–10 ft. tall and as broad. Leathery, oval, 2–4-in.-long leaves; glossy deep green above, paler beneath. Flowers white, in loose 2–4-in. clusters in early spring. Fragrance objectionable to some people. Fruit red turning black, not long lasting. Takes sun or shade. Once established, needs no water. Serviceable screen, hedge, with dense foliage. Watch for thrips, spider mites, aphids.

V. tinus. LAURUSTINUS. Evergreen shrub or small narrow tree. Zones 4–10, 12, 13 (in coolest locations), 14–23. To 6–12 ft. tall, half as wide. Leaves dark green, oval, leathery, slightly rolled under at edges, 2–3 in. long. New stems wine red. Tight clusters of pink buds open to white flowers, November–spring. Lightly fragrant. Bright metallic blue fruit lasts through summer. Dense foliage right to ground makes it good plant for screens, hedges, clipped topiary shapes. Mildews near ocean. Watch for mites.

V. t. 'Dwarf'. Similar to above, but grows only 3–5 ft. tall, equally wide. Low screens, hedges, foundation plantings.

V. t. 'Lucidum'. SHINING LAURUSTINUS. Leaves larger than those of *V. tinus*; plant less hardy, but more resistant to mildew near coast.

V. t. 'Robustum'. ROUNDLEAF LAURUSTINUS. Leaves coarser, rougher than those of *V. tinus*; flowers less pink. More resistant to mildew. Makes excellent, small narrow tree.

V. t. 'Spring Bouquet'. Also sold as *V. t.* 'Compactum'. Foliage is slightly smaller, darker green than that of *V. tinus*. Plant is fairly compact, upright to about 6 ft.; good for hedges.

V. t. 'Variegatum'. Zones 4–9, 14–23. Like *V. tinus*, but leaves are variegated with white and pale yellow.

V. trilobum. CRANBERRY BUSH. Deciduous shrub. Zones 1–11, 14–20. To 10–15 ft. tall. Leaves are much like those of *V. opulus*; turn red in fall. Lace cap flowers and fruit (edible) similar to those of *V. opulus*. Less susceptible to aphid damage than *V. opulus*. 'Compactum' grows to 6 ft.; 'Wentworth' has large, showy, edible red berries.

VICTORIAN BOX. See PITTOSPORUM undulatum   p. 426

VIGNA caracalla (Phaseolus caracalla)

SNAIL VINE
Fabaceae (Leguminosae)
PERENNIAL VINE
✁ ZONES 12–24
☼ FULL SUN
◑ REGULAR WATER

Vigna caracalla

Looks like pole bean in foliage and appearance. Climbs to 10–20 ft. Flowers (spring and summer) are fragrant, cream marked purple or pale purple. Common name comes from twisted keel petals, which are coiled like snail shell. Odd and pretty. Cut to ground when frost kills tops. Summer screen or bank cover. Sometimes sold as *Phaseolus gigantea*.

VINCA

PERIWINKLE, MYRTLE
Apocynaceae
EVERGREEN PERENNIALS
✁ ZONES VARY BY SPECIES
◐ ● BEST IN SHADE
◑ MODERATE WATER

Vinca minor

Trailing habit; used as ground covers and for rough slopes and otherwise unused areas. Can be extremely invasive in areas that are sheltered and forested.

V. major. Zones 5–24. Long, trailing stems root as they spread, carry many 1–3-in., somewhat broad-based, oval, dark green, glossy leaves (white-variegated form also common). Short flowering branches with lavender blue flowers 1–2 in. across. Will mound up 6–12 in., possibly to 2 ft. high. Tough plant, quite easy to grow. Takes sun if watered generously. As ground cover, shear close to ground occasionally to bring new growth.

V. minor. DWARF PERIWINKLE. All zones; in Zones 1–3, 7, 10–13, grow only in shade. Perfect miniature of *V. major*, except leaves are more often oblong, have shorter stalks, are more closely spaced. Also requires more care—two or three good soakings per month and feeding several times a year. Lavender blue flowers an inch across; also forms with white, double blue, and deeper blue flowers and with variegated foliage.

V. rosea. See Catharanthus roseus

VIOLA

VIOLA, VIOLET, PANSY
Violaceae
PERENNIALS; SOME TREATED AS ANNUALS
✁ ZONES VARY BY SPECIES
☼ ◑ FULL SUN ON COAST, SOME SHADE INLAND
◑ RICH, MOIST SOIL

Viola wittrockiana

Botanically speaking, violas, pansies, and violets are all perennials belonging to genus *Viola*. However, pansies and violas are generally treated as annuals, especially in mild-winter areas. Violets need shade from hot afternoon sun; in desert and other hot-summer climates, plant in full shade.

Violas and pansies are invaluable for winter and spring color in mild regions, from spring through summer in cooler areas. They provide mass color in borders and edgings, as ground covers for spring-flowering bulbs, and in containers outdoors. Pansies also give colorful displays in pots and boxes. Sweet violets are notorious hosts to spider mites.

PANSIES WITH A SOFT GREEN COMPANION

Try interplanting pansies from six-packs with plants of chamomile (*Chamaemelum*) also from six-packs. The chamomile grows fastest at first, filling in around the still-gangly young pansy plants. Then, for months, both display together—the chamomile's light green as a soft, friendly filler among the flowering pansies. Shear the chamomile if it gets too big.

V. alba. PARMA VIOLET. Zones 4–9, 14–24. Small, sweetly fragrant, double blue-purple flowers. Resembles *V. odorata* in plant form and growth habit. Give it rich soil, cool location, regular water. Individual plants send out runners that form new crowns. Use as small-scale ground cover in woodland gardens.

V. cornuta. VIOLA, TUFTED PANSY. All zones. Tufted plants 6–8 in. high. Smooth, wavy-toothed, ovalish leaves. Purple, pansylike flowers, about 1½ in. across, have slender spur. Modern strains and varieties have larger flowers with shorter spurs, in solid colors of purple, blue, yellow, apricot, ruby red, and white. Crystal strain has especially large flowers in clear colors.

In mild-winter climates, sow seed of violas in late summer, set out plants in fall for color from late winter or early spring to summer. In cold regions, sow seed in September or early spring; transplant September-sown seedlings to cold frame, keep there over winter, set plants outside in spring. Named varieties of violas such as 'Maggie Mott' and 'Pride of Victoria' also increased by division or cuttings.

V. hederacea. AUSTRALIAN VIOLET. Zones 8, 9, 14–24. Tufted plant 1–4 in. high, spreads by stolons at slow to moderate rate to several feet in time. Leaves kidney shaped. Flowers, ¼–¾ in. across, nearly spurless, are white or blue fading to white at petal tips. Summer bloom; plant goes dormant at about 30°F. Use as ground cover in shade or in sun with abundant water.

V. labradorica. Perennial. All zones. Tiny violet 3 in. tall or less, with roundish, 1-in. leaves tinged purple and tiny lavender blue flowers in spring. Spreads aggressively by runners and can invade choice small perennials. Useful for small-scale ground cover in shade or for filler between stepping stones or paving blocks.

V. odorata. SWEET VIOLET. All zones. The violet of song and story. Tufted, long runners root at joints. Leaves dark green, heart shaped, toothed on margins. Flowers are fragrant, short spurred, deep violet, bluish rose, or white. Large, long-stemmed (to 6 in.), deep purple 'Royal Robe' is widely used. 'Royal Elk' has single, fragrant, long-stemmed violet-colored flowers; 'Charm' grows in clumps, has small white flowers; 'Rosina' is pink flowered. Plant size varies from 2 in. for smallest varieties to 8–10 in. for largest. Plants spread by runners at moderate rate. Take full sun near coast and in cool-summer areas. Remove runners and shear rank growth in late fall for better spring flower display. For heavy bloom, feed in very early spring, before flowering, with complete fertilizer.

V. priceana. See V. sororia

V. sororia (V. priceana). CONFEDERATE VIOLET. All zones. Leaves, blossoms rise directly from sturdy rootstock. Leaves are somewhat heart shaped, to 5 in. wide. Flowers ½–¾ in. across, white, heavily veined with violet blue, flat-faced like pansies. Self-sows readily; best in woodland garden. Good ground cover among rhododendrons.

V. tricolor. JOHNNY-JUMP-UP. Annual or short-lived perennial. All zones. To 6–12 in. tall with oval, deeply lobed leaves. Tufted habit. Purple-

and-yellow flowers resemble miniature pansies. Color forms available in blue or in mix including yellow, lavender, mauve, apricot, red. Spring bloom. Self-sows profusely.

V. t. hortensis. See V. wittrockiana

V. wittrockiana (V. tricolor hortensis). PANSY. All zones. Excellent strains with flowers 2–4 in. across, in white, blue, mahogany red, rose, yellow, apricot, purple; also bicolors. Petals often striped or blotched; Crown and Crystal Bowl strains have unblotched flowers. Plants grow to about 8 in. high. F_1 and F_2 hybrids more free flowering, heat tolerant.

Sow pansy seed from mid-July to mid-August. In mild-winter areas, set out plants in fall for bloom from late winter or early spring to summer. In cold sections, transplant seedlings into cold frame, set out plants in spring; or sow seed indoors in January or February, plant outdoors in spring. Or plant nursery plants in spring. To prolong bloom, pick flowers (with some foliage) regularly, remove faded blooms before they set seed. In warmer climates, plants get ragged by midsummer and should be removed.

VIOLET. See VIOLA	p. 519
VIOLET TRUMPET VINE. See CLYTOSTOMA callistegioides	p. 236
VIRGINIA BLUEBELLS. See MERTENSIA virginica	p. 379
VIRGINIA CREEPER. See PARTHENOCISSUS inserta, P. quinquefolia	p. 401
VIRGINIAN STOCK. See MALCOLMIA maritima	p. 372
VISCARIA coeli-rosa. See LYCHNIS coeli-rosa	p. 362

Vitaceae. The grape family contains vines that climb by tendrils and produce berries. Grape, Boston ivy, and Virginia creeper are the best-known representatives.

VITEX

CHASTE TREE

Verbenaceae

DECIDUOUS AND EVERGREEN SHRUBS OR TREES

🌡 ZONES VARY BY SPECIES

☼ SUN

◖ ● TOLERATE ARIDITY; BEST WITH WATER

Vitex agnus-castus

Of the 250 species, only the following 2 species are grown in the West. Both have divided leaves and clustered flowers.

V. agnus-castus. CHASTE TREE. Deciduous shrub or small tree. Zones 4–24. Growth is slow in cold climates, fast in warmer areas. Size varies from 6 ft. in Northwest to 25 ft. in low desert. Habit broad and spreading, usually multitrunked. Leaves are divided fanwise into five to seven narrow, 2–6-in.-long leaflets that are dark green above, gray beneath. Conspicuous 7-in. spikes of lavender blue flowers in clusters appear in summer and fall.

Tolerates many types of soils, but requires plenty of summer heat for richly colored, profuse bloom. In rich, moist soils it grows luxuriantly, but has paler flowers. Good for summer flower color in shrub border. If trained high, makes good small shade tree. Resistant to oak root fungus. Varieties are 'Alba', white flowers; 'Latifolia' (sometimes sold as *V. macrophylla*), sturdy, with large leaflets; and 'Rosea', pinkish flowers.

V. lucens. NEW ZEALAND CHASTE TREE. Evergreen tree. Zones 16, 17, 22–24. Slow to moderate growth to 40–60 ft. Divided leaves with three to five shining, glossy, corrugated-looking, roundish, 5-in.-long leaflets. Pink winter buds open to lavender pink, 1-in. flowers in loose clusters. Bright red fruit resembles small cherries. Needs deep, rich soil and protection from frost while young. Luxuriant near coast; tolerates sea breezes.

VITIS. See GRAPE	p. 310
VOODOO LILY. See SAUROMATUM venosum	p. 477

VRIESEA

Bromeliaceae

PERENNIALS

☀ ZONES 22–24; HOUSE PLANTS ANYWHERE

☼ STRONG LIGHT BUT NOT DIRECT SUN

💧 WATER LEAF BASES, DAMPEN MOSS

Vriesea hieroglyphica

Bromeliads with rosettes of long, leathery leaves and oddly shaped flower clusters. Grow as epiphytes in pockets of sphagnum moss on branches or in pots of loose, highly organic mix. Mist if grown in hot, dry rooms. Feed lightly and often.

V. hieroglyphica. Rosettes of 30–40 leaves, each 3 ft. long, 3 in. wide, dark green with pronounced cross-banding of blackish purple. Greenish flower spike with dull yellow flowers.

V. lindenii. See Tillandsia lindenii

V. splendens. FLAMING SWORD. Rosettes of up to 20 dark green, 1½-ft. leaves barred transversely with blackish purple. Flower stalk like a 1½–2-ft.-wide feather of bright red bracts from which small yellow flowers emerge. 'Chantrierei' is brightly colored selection.

WAKE ROBIN. See TRILLIUM p. 511

WALDSTEINIA fragarioides

BARREN STRAWBERRY

Rosaceae

GROUND COVER

☀ ZONES 2–9, 14–17

☼☼ FULL SUN TO LIGHT SHADE

💧 REGULAR WATER

Waldsteinia fragarioides

Evergreen strawberrylike plant 2–3 in. high, spreading to 6–8 in. Leaves have three wedge-shaped leaflets to 2 in. long, glossy green turning bronze in fall. Yellow, five-petaled spring flowers to ¾ in. across.

WALLFLOWER. See ERYSIMUM cheiri p. 279

WALNUT (Juglans)

Juglandaceae

DECIDUOUS TREES

☀ ZONES VARY BY SPECIES

☼ FULL SUN

💧💧 WATER NEEDS VARY BY SPECIES

Walnut

Usually large and spreading, with leaves divided into leaflets. Oval or round nuts in fleshy husks. English walnut (*J. regia*) is a well-known orchard tree in many parts of the West; American native species are sometimes planted as shade trees with incidental bonus of edible nuts or are used as understock for grafting English walnut.

J. californica. SOUTHERN CALIFORNIA BLACK WALNUT. Zones 18–24. Native to Southern California. Treelike shrub or small tree to 15–30 ft., usually with several stems from ground. Leaves 6–12 in., with 9–19 leaflets to 2¼ in. long. Roundish, ¾-in. nuts have good flavor but extremely hard, thick shells. Tree is not commercially grown, but worth saving if it grows as native. Takes aridity and poor soil. Resistant to oak root fungus.

J. cinerea. BUTTERNUT. Zones 1–9, 14–17. Native to eastern United States. To 50–60 ft., with broad, spreading head. Resembles black walnut (*J. nigra*), but is smaller; leaves have fewer leaflets; nuts are oval or elongated rather than round. Flavor is good, but shells are thick and hard. Needs only moderate amount of summer water.

J. hindsii. CALIFORNIA BLACK WALNUT. Zones 5–9, 14–20. Native to scattered localities in Northern California. To 30–60 ft. tall, with single trunk and broad crown. Leaves have 15–19 leaflets, each 3–5 in. long. Widely used as rootstock for English walnut in California. Needs no summer water and is resistant to oak root fungus.

J. major (J. rupestris major). NOGAL, ARIZONA WALNUT. Zones 10, 12, 13. Native to Arizona, New Mexico, northern Mexico. Broad tree to 50 ft. Leaves have 9–13 leaflets. Round, small, thick-shelled nuts in husks that dry on tree. Takes desert heat and wind; needs deep soil, some water.

J. nigra. BLACK WALNUT. Zones 1–9, 14–21. Native to eastern United States. High-branched tree grows to 150 ft. (usually not over 100 ft. in the West) with round crown, furrowed blackish brown bark. Leaves have 15–23 leaflets, each 2½–5 in. long. Nuts 1–1½ in. across, thick shelled and very hard, but with rich flavor. Big, hardy shade tree for big places. Fairly tolerant of aridity. Don't plant near vegetable or flower gardens, rhododendrons, or azaleas; black walnut inhibits these plants' growth, either through root competition or by secreting a substance that inhibits growth of other plants. Long dormant season.

J. regia. ENGLISH WALNUT. Zones 4–9, 14–23; some varieties in Zones 1–3. Native to southwest Asia, southeast Europe. To 60 ft. high, with equal spread; fast growing, especially when young. Smooth, gray bark on trunk and heavy, horizontal or upward-angled branches. Leaves with five to seven leaflets, rarely more, 3–6 in. long. The tree is hardy to –5°F, but certain varieties are injured by late and early frosts in colder regions.

CARS AND WALNUT TREES: BAD NEWS

English and California black walnut trees are notorious as hosts to aphids. The pests and their honeydew exudation are inevitable, so you should not plant either tree where branches will arch over a patio or automobile parking place.

English walnut should be planted as landscape tree only on large lots. It's out of leaf a long time, messy when in leaf (drip and sooty mildew from aphid exudations), and messy in fruit (husks can stain). Needs deep soil and deep watering. Keep other plants beyond drip line where feeder roots grow. Many people are allergic to the wind-borne pollen.

Established plants can exist with no water, but in dry-summer areas need deep, regular watering for top-quality nuts. Old plants need pruning only to remove dead wood or correct shape. Young plants grow fast, should be trained to make central leading shoot and branch high enough for comfortable foot traffic. Shorten overlong side branches.

Spray for aphids, scale insects, codling moths, spider mites. Walnut husk fly attacks husks, making them adhere to and disfigure nuts. Control with repeated malathion sprays.

Walnut husks open in fall, dropping nuts to ground. Hasten drop by knocking nuts from tree. Pick up nuts immediately. Remove any adhering husks. Dry in single layer spread out in airy shade until kernels become brittle; then store.

In Zones 1–3, grow walnuts described as Carpathian or Hardy Persian. Most offered are seedlings, but grafted, named varieties do exist. 'Ambassador' is hardy to –25°F. In Zones 4–7, 'Adams', 'Cooke's Giant Sweet', 'Franquette', 'Idaho', and 'Mayette' bloom late enough to escape spring frosts, yield high-quality nuts. Gardeners in Zones 8, 9 can grow 'Carmelo', 'Cooke's Giant Sweet', 'Drummond', 'Eureka', 'Hartley', 'Payne', 'Idaho', or 'Serr' (bears at early age). Best varieties for Zones 14–16 are 'Carmelo', 'Concord', 'Cooke's Giant Sweet', 'Franquette', 'Hartley', 'Mayette', 'Payne', 'Serr', and 'Wasson'. In Zones 18–20, grow 'Drummond', 'Payne', or 'Placentia'. In Zones 21–23, best choice is 'Placentia'. Variety 'Laciniata', with deeply cut leaflets, is occasionally sold.

WANDERING JEW. See CALLISIA, TRADESCANTIA, ZEBRINA pendula pp. 196, 510, 527

WARMINSTER BROOM. See CYTISUS praecox p. 256

WASHINGTONIA

Arecaceae (Palmae)

PALMS

☀ ZONES 8, 9, 10 (WARMER PARTS), 11–24

☀ FULL SUN

◐◑ WITHSTAND ARIDITY BUT THRIVE ON MOISTURE

Washingtonia robusta

Native to California, Arizona, northern Mexico. Fan-shaped leaves. Following two species are the most widely planted palms in California.

W. filifera. CALIFORNIA FAN PALM. Fast grower to 60 ft. In native stands in Southwest deserts, it always grows near springs or other moist spots. Long-stalked leaves stand well apart in open crown. As leaves mature, they bend down to form a petticoat of thatch that develops in straight lines, tapering inward toward trunk at lowest edge of petticoat. Trunk is much more robust than that of its Mexican cousin, even though that cousin's specific name is *robusta*. Hardy to around 18°F.

Use young trees in containers. In landscape, can serve as street or parkway planting, in groves, or in large gardens as single trees or in groups.

W. robusta. MEXICAN FAN PALM. Taller (to 100 ft.), more slender, more widely sold than California fan palm. Leaf stalks are shorter, with distinguishing reddish streak on undersides. More compact crown, rougher thatch. Fast growing. Old plants take on natural curvature; young ones started at an angle will grow upright to produce a bend. Hardy to 20°F. Takes poor soil but grows faster where soil is good.

> ## ONE OF L.A.'S SIGNATURE PALMS
>
> This very tall palm with its long, skinny trunk is widely seen as an avenue tree in Southern California. Notable ones line Ocean Ave. in Santa Monica. Also, from the western half of the Santa Monica freeway you see in the middle distance many more of those parallel rows—down both sides of aging residential blocks.

WASHINGTON THORN. See CRATAEGUS phaenopyrum   p. 248

WATERCRESS

Brassicaceae (Cruciferae)

PERENNIAL

☀ ALL ZONES

☀◑ SUN OR PARTIAL SHADE

◑ GROWS NATURALLY IN RUNNING STREAMS

Watercress

You can plant seed in flats or pots and transplant seedlings to moist banks, where they will grow rapidly. Or insert cuttings of watercress from the market into wet soil in or near the stream; these root readily. Be quite certain the stream is free from pollution before planting out in such a location. Watercress can also be grown in wet place in garden. Or grow it in pots of soil placed in tub of water; water should be changed at least weekly by running hose slowly into tub. Plant grows to 10–15 in. with small, roundish leaflets. Flowers are insignificant.

WATER HAWTHORN. See APONOGETON distachyus   p. 154

WATER HYACINTH. See EICHHORNIA crassipes   p. 271

WATER LILY. See NYMPHAEA   p. 391

WATERMELON

Cucurbitaceae

ANNUAL

☀ ALL ZONES

☀ FULL SUN

◑ REGULAR WATER

Watermelon

Needs a long growing season, more heat than most other melons, and more space than other vine crops—space hills (circles of seed) 8 ft. by 8 ft. Other than that, culture is as described under Melon. If you garden in a commercial watermelon-growing area—Zones 8, 9, 12–14, 18–21—choose any variety that suits your fancy. If your summers are short or cool (Zones 1–6, 15–17, 22–24), choose a fast-maturing ("early") variety. Those listed in catalogs and on seed packets at 70–75 days to harvest are best.

WATSONIA

Iridaceae

DECIDUOUS AND EVERGREEN PERENNIALS

☀ ZONES 4–9, 12–24

☀ FULL SUN

◐◑ LITTLE TO MODERATE WATER

Watsonia pyramidata

Gardeners in Zones 1–3 can experiment growing them like gladiolus, lifting and storing corms over winter. Native to South Africa. Flowers are smaller, generally more tubular than gladiolus, on taller, branched stems. They grow in fall and winter and hence are of limited use where winters are severe. All are good cut flowers. Plant in late summer or early fall; plants produce foliage in autumn. Stake tall stems of pot-grown plants. In mild climates, they can remain undisturbed for many years. Lift overcrowded clumps in summer after bloom; divide and replant as quickly as possible.

W. beatricis. Evergreen. Leaves 2½ ft. long; July–August, flowers 3 in. long, bright apricot red, on somewhat branched, 3½-ft. stems. Selected hybrids in colors from peach to nearly scarlet.

W. pyramidata. Deciduous. Blooms late spring, early summer. Rose pink to rose red, 2½-in. flowers in spikelike clusters on branched, 4–6-ft. stems. Leaves are 2½ ft. long, 1 in. wide. Many excellent large-flowered hybrids in pink, white, lavender, and red.

WATTLE. See ACACIA   p. 131

WAXFLOWER, GERALDTON. See CHAMELAUCIUM uncinatum   p. 221

WAX FLOWER, WAX PLANT. See HOYA   p. 326

WAX MYRTLE, PACIFIC. See MYRICA californica   p. 385

WAX VINE. See SENECIO macroglossus   p. 483

WEDELIA trilobata

Asteraceae (Compositae)

PERENNIAL

☀ ZONES 12, 13, 21–24

☀◑ FULL SUN OR LIGHT SHADE

◑ REGULAR WATER

Wedelia trilobata

Trailing plant that roots wherever stems touch damp earth. Fleshy evergreen leaves are dark glossy green, to 4 in. long and half as wide, with a few coarse teeth or shallow lobes toward tips. Inch-wide flower heads resemble tiny yellow zinnias or marigolds. Blooms

W

nearly throughout the year in sun; blooms sparsely in shade. Spreads fast by creeping, rooting stems; easily propagated by lifting rooted pieces or by placing tip cuttings in moist soil. Best in sandy, fast-draining soils but will take others if drainage is acceptable. Reasonably salt tolerant. Killed to ground by frost, it makes fast comeback. Tolerates high heat of desert. Plant 1½ ft. apart, feed lightly. Cut back hard if plantings mound up or become stemmy.

WEIGELA

Caprifoliaceae

DECIDUOUS SHRUBS

ZONES 1–11, 14–17

FULL SUN TO PARTIAL SHADE

MODERATE WATER

Weigela florida

Valuable for voluminous flower display late in spring season (May–June in Northwest, earlier in California). Funnel-shaped flowers grow singly or in short clusters all along previous season's shoots. When weigelas finish blooming, their charm fades—they aren't attractive out of bloom. Most are rather coarse leafed and stiff, becoming rangy unless pruned.

After flowering, cut back branches that have bloomed to unflowered side branches. Leave only one or two of these to each stem. Cut some of the oldest stems to ground. Thin new suckers to a few of the most vigorous. A simpler method you can employ every other year is to cut back entire plant about halfway just after blooms fade. Resulting dense new growth will provide plenty of flowers the next spring. Use as backgrounds for flower borders, as summer screens, in mixed shrub borders.

W. 'Bristol Ruby'. To 6–7 ft. tall, nearly as wide. Ruby red flowers in late spring; some repeat bloom midsummer and fall.

W. florida (W. rosea). Fast growth to 8–10 ft. tall. Flowers pink to rose red, 1 in. long, in May and June.

W. f. 'Minuet'. Dwarf (2–3 ft.) shrub with purplish leaves and flowers that blend red, purple, or yellow.

W. f. 'Red Prince'. Hardy 6-ft. plant with nonfading red flowers.

W. f. 'Variegata'. Bright green foliage variegated with cream. Popular and showy.

W. 'Java Red'. Compact, mounding plant to 6 ft. or wider. Deep pink flowers open from red buds. Foliage deep green tinted purple.

W. middendorffiana. Dense, broad shrub to 3–4 ft. tall. Dark green leaves 2–3 in. long, 1–1½ in. wide, wrinkled. Flowers (April, May) are sulfur yellow marked orange, an inch long and as wide, clustered at ends of branches. Best in cool, moist place; less rugged than other weigelas.

W. 'Newport Red'. Also sold as *W.* 'Vanicekii', 'Cardinal', 'Rhode Island Red'. To 6 ft. tall, with brilliant red flowers 1–1½ in. across in May–June.

W. praecox. Similar to *W. florida* but blooms several weeks earlier and grows to about 6 ft. tall. Flowers pink to rose with yellow throats.

WESTRINGIA fruticosa

Lamiaceae (Labiatae)

EVERGREEN SHRUB

ZONES 8, 9, 14–24

SUN

LITTLE TO MODERATE WATER

Westringia fruticosa

Native to Australia. Spreading, rather loose growth to 3–6 ft. tall, half again as wide. Leaves medium green to gray green above, white beneath, slightly finer and filmier in texture than rosemary leaves. Small white flowers February through spring in colder areas, all year in milder climates. 'Wynyabbie Gem' produces light purplish flowers most of the year. Needs light, well-drained soil. Good near coast; wind tolerant. Effective on sunny banks and in borders with lavender; charming with *Podocarpus gracilior*.

WISTERIA

Fabaceae (Leguminosae)

DECIDUOUS VINES

ALL ZONES

FULL SUN OR PARTIAL SHADE

WATER YOUNG ONES WELL, OLDER ONES LESS

Wisteria sinensis

Twining, woody vines of great size, long life, and exceptional beauty in flower. So adaptable they can be grown as trees, shrubs, or vines.

Wisterias are not fussy about soil, but they need good drainage. In alkaline soil, watch for chlorosis and treat with iron chelates or iron sulfate.

Pruning and training are important for bloom production and control of plant's size, shape. Let newly set plants grow to establish framework you desire, either single or multitrunked. Remove stems that interfere with desired framework, pinch back side stems and long streamers, rub off buds that develop on trunk for single-trunked specimens. For multiple

W

trunks, select as many vigorous stems as you wish and let them develop. If plant has only one stem, pinch it back to encourage others to develop. Remember that main stem will become good-size trunk, and that weight of mature vine is considerable.

Tree wisterias can be bought ready trained; or you can train your own. Remove all but one main stem and stake this one securely. Tie stem to stake at frequent intervals, using plastic tape to prevent girdling. When plant has reached height at which you wish head to form, pinch or prune out tip to force branching. Shorten branches to beef them up. Pinch back long streamers and rub off all buds that form below head. Replace stakes and ties as needed. Wisterias can be trained as big shrubs or multistemmed, small, semiweeping trees; permit well-spaced branches to form the framework, shorten side branches, and nip long streamers. Unsupported plants make vigorous bank cover.

Young plants should be well fed; blooming-size, established plants flower better with less food and water. Prune blooming plants every winter, cutting back or thinning out side shoots from main or structural stems and shortening back to two or three buds the flower-producing spurs that grow from these shoots. You'll have no trouble recognizing fat flower buds on these spurs.

In summer, cut back long streamers before they tangle up in main body of vine; save those you want to use to extend height or length of vine and tie them to support—eaves, wall, trellis, arbor. If old plants grow rampantly but fail to bloom, withhold all nitrogen fertilizers for an entire growing season (buds for the next season's bloom are started in early summer). If that fails to produce bloom the next year, you can try pruning roots in spring—after you're sure no flowers will be produced—by cutting vertically with spade into plant's root zone.

WISTERIA SHOPPING TIP

To get wisteria off to a good start, buy cutting-grown, budded, or grafted plants; seedlings may not bloom for years. With budded or grafted plants, watch for suckers during the first few years and remove them, or they may take over.

W. floribunda. JAPANESE WISTERIA. Often sold as *W. multijuga.* Leaves are 12–16 in. long, divided into 15–19 leaflets. Violet or violet blue, fragrant flowers in 1½-ft. clusters appear with leaves in April–May. Flowers begin to open at base of cluster, gradually open toward tip, prolonging bloom season but making less spectacular burst of color than Chinese wisteria. Long clusters give extreme beauty of line. Many varieties obtainable in white, pink, and shades of blue, purple, lavender, usually marked with yellow and white. 'Longissima' ('Macrobotrys') has long (1½–3-ft.) clusters of violet flowers; 'Longissima Alba' bears white flowers in 2-ft. clusters. 'Ivory Tower' is similar. A good lavender pink variety is 'Rosea'. 'Plena' has very full clusters of double, deep blue-violet flowers. Japanese wisteria blooms best in full sun.

W. sinensis. CHINESE WISTERIA. Most widely planted throughout West. Leaves divided into 7–13 leaflets. Plants bloom before leaves expand in April–May. Flower clusters are shorter (to 1 ft.) than those of Japanese wisteria, but make quite a show by opening nearly full length of cluster at one time. Violet blue, slightly fragrant. Will bloom in considerable shade. *W. s.* 'Alba' is white-flowered form. 'Caroline' and 'Cooke's Special' are grafted forms.

W. venusta. SILKY WISTERIA. Often sold as *W. v.* 'Alba'. Broad leaves and leaflets have silky hairs. Individual flowers are white, very large, long-stalked, in short, heavy clusters that open all at once. Profuse bloom when leaves begin to open in April. Plant in full sun for best bloom. *W. v.* 'Violacea' has fragrant, purple-blue flowers. Older plants (especially in tree form) remarkably profuse in bloom.

WOODWARDIA fimbriata

GIANT CHAIN FERN	
Polypodiaceae	
LARGE, STRONG-GROWING FERN	
☀ ZONES 4–9, 14–24	
◐ ● HIGH-TREE SHADE	
● MOIST PLACES	

Woodwardia fimbriata

Often sold as *W. chamissoi* or *W. radicans.* Native from British Columbia to Mexico. The largest native fern, it can reach 9 ft. tall in wet coastal forests. Fronds twice cut, rather coarse in texture, with strong upright or spreading silhouette. Use near pool or brook, against shaded wall, in woodland gardens. Slow to establish if dug from clumps; nursery plants are vigorous and rapid. Ultimately withstands neglect.

XANTHORRHOEA

GRASS TREE	
Liliaceae	
PERENNIALS	
☀ ZONES 12–24	
☼ FULL SUN	
○ NO WATER ONCE ESTABLISHED	

Xanthorrhoea preissii

Native to Australia. Dense tufts of narrow, long, grasslike leaves radiate out from top of thick, woody, nearly black, slow-growing stem. White flowers grow in dense, narrow spike on tall stem. Best used with yuccas, century plants, succulents in dry, loose, sandy soil.

X. preissii. BLACKBOY. Stem is slow growing, but in age may reach 15 ft. Leaves 2–4 ft. long, about ⅛ in. wide. Flower spike 1–3 ft. long, on stem of equal length.

X. quadrangulata. Trunk reaches several feet high. Leaves 1½ ft. long. Spike and its stem may reach 12–15 ft.

XANTHOSOMA

Araceae	
CORMLIKE TUBERS	
☀ ZONES 12, 13, 16, 17, 21–24	
☼ WARM FILTERED SHADE	
● AMPLE WATER	

Tropical foliage plants related to *Alocasia.* All have big, arrow-shaped leaves on long stalks. Flowers clustered on spike surrounded by calla-like bract (spathe), usually greenish or yellowish

Xanthosoma violaceum

and more curious than attractive. Rich soil, ample water. Use with ferns, begonias, schefflera. Humus soil. Protect from hard frosts.

X. sagittifolium. Trunklike stem to 3 ft. Dark green leaves 3 ft. long on 3-ft. stems. Spathes greenish white, 7–9 in. long.

X. violaceum. Stemless, forming clumps by offsets. Leaves to 2 ft. long, 1½ ft. wide, dark green above, lighter beneath, with purplish veins and margins, powdery appearance. Purple, 2½-ft. leaf stalks with heavy, waxy, bluish or grayish cast. Large, yellowish white spathes.

XERANTHEMUM annuum

COMMON IMMORTELLE

Asteraceae (Compositae)

SUMMER ANNUAL

🗹 ALL ZONES

☼ FULL SUN

● REGULAR WATER

Xeranthemum annuum

Grows to 2½ ft. tall. Everlasting flower; fluffy heads of papery bracts up to 1½ in. across in pink, lavender, white, shades of violet purple. Scant foliage is silvery green. Sow seed in spring in place. Accepts almost any soil. Cut flowers dried for winter bouquets.

XYLOSMA congestum (X. senticosum)

Flacourtiaceae

EVERGREEN OR DECIDUOUS SHRUB OR SMALL TREE

🗹 ZONES 8–24

☼ ◐ SUN OR FILTERED SHADE

◖ ● LOOKS BEST WITH MODERATE WATERING

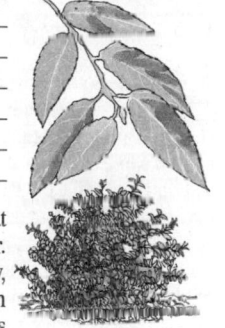
Xylosma congestum

Usually a loose, graceful, spreading shrub that grows to 8–10 ft. tall and as wide or wider. Height can be easily controlled. Leaves are shiny, yellowish green, long-pointed oval in shape, clean and attractive. New growth bronzy. Flowers insignificant, rarely seen. Some plants are spiny.

Left alone, plants develop angular main stem that takes its time zigzagging upward. Meanwhile, side branches grow long and graceful, arching or drooping, sometimes lying on the ground. Variety 'Compacta' grows more slowly, reaches half the size of species.

Adaptable to most soils; heat tolerant. Moderate feeding. Spray as necessary to control occasional scale or red spider mites. Apply iron chelates or iron sulfate for chlorosis.

One of the handsomest, easiest, and most versatile of the all-foliage, landscape structure plants. Unattractive appearance in nursery cans (especially in winter, when plants may be nearly bare of leaves) and slow start in ground may discourage the gardener. Plants actually are hardy to 10°F, but may lose many (or all) leaves in sharp frosts. Plant normally sheds many old leaves in April when new growth begins. Frost at that time will kill new growth. Well-established plants usually evergreen except in coldest seasons, and new leaves come fast.

Use as single or multitrunked tree, arching shrub, ground or bank cover (prune out erect growth), espalier on wall or fence, clipped or unclipped hedge (twine long branches together to fill in gaps faster), container shrub in large (1½-ft.-wide or wider) container.

YUCCA

Agavaceae

EVERGREEN PERENNIALS, SHRUBS, TREES

🗹 ZONES VARY BY SPECIES

☼ FULL SUN

◖ ● PERIODIC DEEP SOAKINGS HELP

Yucca whipplei

Yuccas grow over much of North America, and hardiness depends on species. All have clusters of tough, sword-shaped leaves and large clusters of white or whitish flowers. Some are stemless, while others reach tree size. Best in well-drained soil. Useful near swimming pools.

Group with agaves, cacti, or succulents in desert gardens, or grow with various softer-leaved tropical foliage plants. Taller kinds make striking silhouettes, and even stemless species provide important and vertical effects when in bloom. Some have stiff, sharp-pointed leaves; keep these away from walks, terraces, and other well-traveled areas. (Some people clip off the sharp tips with nail clippers.)

Young plants of some species can be used as indoor plants. They withstand dry indoor atmosphere and will grow well in hot, sunny windows. Buy gallon-can size or smaller; set out in garden ground when plants become too large for the house. Successful indoors are *Y. aloifolia* (but beware of sharp-pointed leaves), *Y. elephantipes, Y. filamentosa, Y. gloriosa, Y. recurvifolia.*

Y. aloifolia. SPANISH BAYONET. Zones 7–24. Native to southern United States. Slow growth to 10 ft. or more; trunk either single or branched, or sprawling in picturesque effect. Sharp-pointed leaves to 2½ ft. long and 2 in. wide densely clothe stems. Leaves are dark green; in *Y. a.* 'Variegata', they are marked yellow or white. White flowers (sometimes tinged purple) to 4 in. across in dense, erect clusters to 2 ft. tall. Summer bloom. Sharp-spined leaf tips a hazard if plant is near walkway.

Y. baccata. DATIL YUCCA. All zones. Native to deserts of Southern California and Nevada to Colorado, Texas. Grow as single stemless rosettes or in clumps with short, leaning trunks to 3 ft. Leaves 2 ft. long, 2 in. wide. Flowers (May–June) fleshy, red-brown outside, white inside, in dense clusters 2 ft. long. Fleshy fruit was eaten by Indians in the early West.

Y. brevifolia. JOSHUA TREE. Zones 8–24. Native to deserts of Southern California, Nevada, Utah, Arizona. Tree of slow growth to 15–30 ft. with heavy trunk and few, heavy branches. Short, broad, sword-shaped leaves clustered near ends of branches. Old, dead leaves hang on. Flowers (February–April) greenish white, in dense, foot-long clusters.

Collected plants sometimes available; nursery plants are very slow to make trunks. Best in dry, well-drained soil in desert gardens. Difficult under average garden conditions.

Y. elata. SOAPTREE YUCCA. Zones 7–24. Native to Arizona, New Mexico, west Texas, northern Mexico. Slow growth to 6–20 ft. with single or branched trunk. Leaves to 4 ft. long, ½ in. wide. White summer flowers bloom in tall spikes. ▶

Y

Y. elephantipes (Y. gigantea). GIANT YUCCA. Zones 12, 13 (protected from sun, hard frosts), 16, 17, 19–24. Native to Mexico. Fast growing (to 2 ft. a year), eventually 15–30 ft. tall, usually with several trunks. Leaves 4 ft. long, 3 in. wide, dark rich green, not spine tipped. Striking silhouette alone or combined with other big-scale foliage plants; out of scale in smaller gardens. Large spikes of creamy white flowers in spring. Does best in good, well-drained soil with ample water.

Y. filamentosa. All zones. Native to southeastern United States. Much like *Y. flaccida*, but with stiffer, narrower leaves, narrower flower clusters. Variety 'Bright Eagle' has leaves margined in creamy white.

Y. flaccida. Zones 1–9, 14–24. Native to southeastern United States. Stemless. Leaves to 2½ ft. long, 1 in. wide, with long, loose fibers at edges of leaves. White flowers in tall, branching clusters to 4–7 ft. or more in height. Lightly fragrant in the evening. One of hardiest, most widely planted in colder regions.

Y. gloriosa. SPANISH DAGGER, SOFT-TIP YUCCA. Zones 7–9, 12, 13 (protected from frost, reflected heat), 14–24. Much like *Y. aloifolia*, generally multitrunked to 10 ft. tall. Blooms late summer. Leaf points soft, will not penetrate skin. Good green color blends well with tropical-looking, lush plants. Easy garden plant, but overwatering may produce black areas on leaf margins. There is a variegated form.

Y. recurvifolia (Y. pendula). Zones 7–10, 12–24. Native to southeastern United States. Single, unbranching trunk to 6–10 ft. tall, or lightly branched in age. Can be cut back to keep single trunked. Spreads by offsets to make large groups. Leaves, 2–3 ft. long, 2 in. wide, beautiful blue-gray-green, are spine tipped, sharply bent downward. Leaf tips bend to touch, are not dangerous. Less stiff and metallic looking than most yuccas. Flowers (in June) are large and white, in loose, open clusters 3–5 ft. tall. Easy to grow under all garden conditions.

Y. rostrata. Zones 7–24. Native to Mexico, extreme southwestern Texas. Notable feature is the trunk, 6–12 ft. tall, 5–8 in. thick, covered with soft gray fuzz (fibers remaining from old leaf bases). Needle-pointed leaves to 2 ft. long, ½ in. wide. White flowers in 2-ft. clusters on a 2-ft. stalk.

Y. schidigera (Y. mohavensis). Zones 10–24. Native to deserts of California, Nevada, Arizona, Baja California. Trunk 3–12 ft. tall, single or branched. Tough, sharp-tipped leaves 2–3 ft. long, 1–2½ in. wide, yellowish green. Creamy or purple-tinted flowers (April–May) in 2-ft. clusters.

Y. whipplei. OUR LORD'S CANDLE. Zones 2–24. Native to Southern California mountains, California coast, Baja California. Stemless, with dense cluster of rigid, gray-green leaves 12–21 in. long. These are needle tipped; don't plant where people can walk into them. Flowering stems to 6–14 ft. long. Drooping, bell-shaped, 1–2-in., creamy white blossoms in large, branched spikes 3–6 ft. long. Plants die after blooming and producing seed; new plants come from seeds or offsets.

ZALUZIANSKYA capensis

NIGHT PHLOX
Scrophulariaceae
PERENNIAL OR ANNUAL
☘ ZONES 15–24
☼ SUN
◖ REGULAR WATER

Zaluzianskya capensis

Perennial where frosts are light and infrequent, this plant can be grown as an annual if seeds are sown indoors or in the greenhouse in earliest spring, and planted out later. A wispy plant to 18 in. with narrow 2-in. leaves, it is valued for the fragrance (notable only at night) of the narrow, clustered 2-in. dark red flowers with white interiors.

Zamiaceae. This family is closely related to the Cycadaceae, differing only in technical details; both families are generally considered to be cycads. *Ceratozamia, Dioon,* and *Zamia* are representatives.

ZAMIA pumila (Z. furfuracea)

Zamiaceae
CYCAD RELATIVE
☘ ZONES 21–24; HOUSE PLANT ANYWHERE
◐ STRONG LIGHT WITH OVERHEAD SHADE
◖ REGULAR WATER

Zamia pumila

Native to Florida, Mexico. Short (6-in.) or completely buried trunk and 2–4-ft.-wide crown of leaves. Each leaf has up to 13 pairs of oval leaflets with inrolled edges. Effect is that of a coarse, leathery fern. Slow growing, choice container plant. Needs light feeding.

ZANTEDESCHIA

CALLA
Araceae
RHIZOMES
☘ ZONES 5, 6, 8, 9, 14–24
☼ ◐ SUN NEAR COAST, PARTIAL SHADE INLAND
◑ ◖ THRIVE ON HEAVY WATERING

Zantedeschia aethiopica

Native to South Africa. Basal clumps of long-stalked, shiny, rich green, arrow- or lance-shaped leaves, sometimes spotted white. Flower bract (spathe) surrounds central spike (spadix) that is tightly covered with tiny true flowers.

Common calla tolerates many soils. Nearly evergreen in mild areas, deciduous where winters are cold. Set rhizomes 4–6 in. deep, 1–2 ft. apart.

Golden, red or pink, and spotted callas need slightly acid soil, moderate water with drainage, and a resting season. Plant 2 in. deep, 1 ft. apart. In mild climates, they survive in well-drained, open-ground beds. If drainage is poor or frosts heavy, dry off gradually in late summer, dig, and store at 40–50°F in dry soil, sawdust, or peat moss. To grow in pots, set 2 in. deep (1 rhizome to 6-in. pot) and water sparingly until leaves appear. Then water freely, feed weekly with mild solution of complete fertilizer. Reduce watering after bloom to dry off plants, then withhold entirely until new growth begins.

Z. aethiopica. COMMON CALLA. Forms large clump of leaves 1½ ft. long, 10 in. wide. Pure white or creamy white, 8-in.-long spathes on 3-ft. stems appear mostly spring and early summer. 'Green Goddess' is a robust variety with large spathes that are white at the base, green toward the tip. 'Hercules', larger than species, has big spathes that open flat, curve backward. 'Childsiana' is 1 ft. tall. 'Minor' grows 1½ ft. tall, with 4-in. spathes.

Z. albomaculata. SPOTTED CALLA. Grows to 2 ft. Leaves spotted white. Spathes 4–5 in. long, creamy yellow or white with purplish crimson blotch at base. Spring–summer bloom.

Z. elliottiana. GOLDEN CALLA. To 1½–2 ft., with bright green, white-spotted leaves 10 in. long by 6 in. wide. Spathes 4–5 in. long, changing from greenish yellow to rich golden yellow, June–July. Tolerates full sun, even in hot-summer areas.

Z. pentlandii. Resembles *Z. albomaculata*, but leaves are unspotted and large spathes (to 5 in. long) are deep golden yellow with a purple blotch at the base.

Z. rehmannii. RED or PINK CALLA. To 1–1½ ft., with narrow, lance-shaped, unspotted green leaves 1 ft. long. Pink or rosy pink spathes to 4 in. long. Blooms May. 'Superba', a deeper pink, improved variety, is generally sold rather than species. Hybrids of this and other callas available; flowers range through pinks and yellows to orange and buff tones, with some purplish and lavender tones on yellow grounds.

ZANTHOXYLUM piperitum

JAPAN PEPPER

Rutaceae

DECIDUOUS SHRUB OR SMALL TREE

✓ ZONES 6–9, 14–17

☼ FULL SUN

◖ MODERATE WATER

Zanthoxylum piperitum

Dense, to 20 ft. Leaves 3–6 in. long, divided into 7–11 oval, 2-in.-long leaflets. Prickly main leaf stalk. Form sometimes seen in California nurseries has yellow main leaf stalk, yellow blotches at base of each leaflet. Green flowers are inconspicuous. Small, black, aromatic fruit is ground and used as seasoning in Japan.

ZAUSCHNERIA (Epilobium)

CALIFORNIA FUCHSIA, HUMMINGBIRD FLOWER

Onagraceae

PERENNIALS OR SUBSHRUBS

✓ ZONES 2–10, 12–24

☼ FULL SUN

◖ LITTLE TO NO WATER ONCE ESTABLISHED

Zauschneria californica

These California natives can take dry, hot summers and will produce many pretty red flowers against gray foliage from summer to fall, but they never will become completely domesticated. Most grow a bit rangy, spread into other garden beds with invasive roots, go to seed and reseed themselves, and become twiggy and ungroomed through the winter. Use them in full sun in informal gardens, at summer cabins, on banks or hillsides. All have leaves that are ½–1½ in. long, gray or gray green, and narrow, and bright scarlet flowers, trumpet shaped and 1½–2 in. long. The flowers attract birds. *Zauschneria* have been reclassified as *Epilobium*, a change not welcomed by native plant enthusiasts.

Z. californica. Stems upright or somewhat arching, 1–2 ft. tall. Plants sometimes shrubby at base. Evergreen in mild-winter climates. There are pure white forms.

Z. c. latifolia (Z. septentrionalis). Often sold as *Z. latifolia* 'Etteri'. Perennial that makes mats of closely set stems about 6 in. high. Dies to ground in winter. There is a bright pink variety named 'Solidarity Pink'.

Z. cana. Stems woody at base, sprawling. Foliage dense; leaves very narrow, silvery. Evergreen in mild-winter climates.

ZEBRA PLANT. See CALATHEA zebrina p. 195

ZEBRINA pendula

WANDERING JEW

Commelinaceae

HOUSE PLANT

◑ MUCH INDOOR LIGHT

◖ REGULAR WATER

Zebrina pendula

Has much the same growth habit and leaf shape as *Tradescantia fluminensis* but is not as hardy. Small clusters of flowers are purplish rose and white. Known mostly in its variegated forms. *Z. p.* 'Quadricolor' has purplish green leaves with longitudinal bands of white, pink, and carmine red; 'Purpusii' has leaves of dark red or greenish red. Other varieties add white, pink, and cream to prevailing colors. When selecting a location indoors, remember that variegated plants need more light than all-green ones.

ZELKOVA serrata

SAWLEAF ZELKOVA

Ulmaceae

DECIDUOUS TREE

✓ ZONES 3–21

☼ FULL SUN

◖ WATER DEEPLY TO ENCOURAGE DEEP ROOTING

Zelkova serrata

A good shade tree, it grows at moderate to fast rate, eventually to 60 ft. or higher, and equally wide. Smooth, gray bark like that of beech. Leaves similar to those of elm (2–3½ in. long by 1½ in. wide) but rougher textured, with sawtooth margins. Carefully train young trees to develop strong framework—head back excessively long pendulous branches to force side growth, thin competing branches to permit full development of the strongest. Fall foliage color varies from yellow to dark red to dull reddish brown. Three grafted selections are sold; 'Halka', the fastest growing, resembles American elm more than do 'Green Vase' and 'Village Green'.

ZENOBIA pulverulenta (Andromeda speciosa)

Ericaceae

DECIDUOUS SHRUB

✓ ZONES 4–7, 14–17

◑ PARTIAL SHADE

◖◖ UNIFORMLY MOIST SOIL

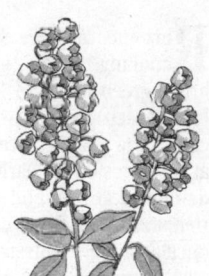

Zenobia pulverulenta

Native to southeastern United States. Slow growth to 2–4 ft., possibly 6 ft. Open, loose growth. Leaves pale green, 1–2 in. long, half as wide, new growth heavily dusted with bluish white powder in pearly gray effect. White, bell-shaped, ½-in.-wide flowers grow in loose clusters at ends of branches. Blooms June–July in Northwest. Sometimes spreads by underground stems. Related to heaths and heathers; needs acid soil.

ZEPHYRANTHES

ZEPHYR FLOWER, FAIRY LILY

Amaryllidaceae

BULBS

✓ ZONES 1–9, 12–24

☼ FULL SUN

◖ KEEP SOIL ALTERNATELY WET AND DRY

Zephyranthes candida

Bright green, rushlike leaves. Funnel-shaped flowers with six segments appear singly on hollow stems, usually in late summer or early fall, often all year. In wild, flowers appear after a rain (hence, often called rain lily). Use in rock garden or foreground of border. Good in pots. Plant late summer or early fall; set bulbs 1–2 in. deep, 3 in. apart. In cold climates, plant in spring and lift in fall; or mulch heavily over winter.

Z. ajax. Hybrid between *Z. candida* and *Z. citrina*. Free flowering, light yellow. Evergreen. Leaves to 8 in. long.

Z. candida. Large clumps of rushlike, glossy evergreen leaves to 1 ft. long. Crocuslike flowers 2 in. long, glossy textured, pure white outside, tinged rose inside, borne singly on stems as long as leaves; blooms in late summer, autumn. Can take light shade.

Z. citrina. Fragrant, lemon yellow, 2-in. flowers on 10-in. stems.

Z. grandiflora. Rose pink, 4-in.-wide flowers like small amaryllis; 8-in. stems. Leaves 1 ft. long, show with flowers in late spring, early summer.

Z. hybrids. 'Alamo' has deep rose pink flowers flushed yellow. 'Apricot Queen', low growing, has yellow flowers stained pink. 'Prairie Sunset' has large, light yellow flowers suffused with pink that appear after rain or a watering. 'Ruth Page' is rich pink. Available from mail-order specialists.

ZEPHYR FLOWER. See ZEPHYRANTHES p. 527

Zingiberaceae. The ginger family contains tropical or subtropical perennials with fleshy rhizomes and canelike stems clothed with sheathing leaf stalks; usually bear large leaves. Flowers are irregular in form, in spikes or heads, often showy or with showy bracts. Many are aromatic or have fragrant flowers. Includes *Alpinia, Hedychium,* and *Zingiber.*

ZINGIBER officinale

TRUE GINGER

Zingiberaceae

PERENNIAL WITH THICK RHIZOMES

✷ ZONES 9, 14–24

☼ SHADE FROM HOTTEST SUN

⬤ WATER HEAVILY AFTER GROWTH STARTS

Zingiber officinale

Rhizomes are the source of ginger used in cooking. Stems 2–4 ft. tall. Narrow, glossy bright green leaves to 1 ft. long. Summer flowers (rarely seen) are yellowish green, with purple lip marked yellow; not especially showy. Ginger needs heat and humidity. Buy roots (fresh, not dried) at grocery store in early spring; cut into 1–2-in.-long sections with well-developed growth buds. Let cut ends dry, then plant just underground in rich, moist soil. Water cautiously until top and root growth are active. Feed once a month. Plants are dormant in winter; rhizomes may rot in cold, wet soil. Plant with tree ferns, camellias, fuchsias, begonias. Harvest roots at any time—but allow several months for them to reach some size.

ZINNIA

Asteraceae (Compositae)

SUMMER ANNUALS, PERENNIAL

✷ ALL ZONES

☼ FULL SUN

◐ ⬤ WATER ON GROUND, NOT OVERHEAD

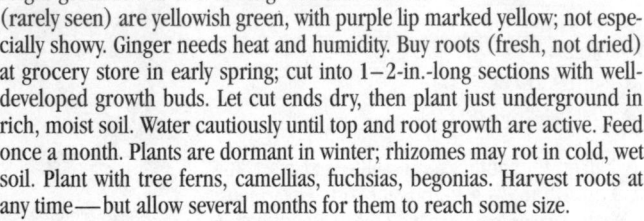

Zinnia elegans

Long-time garden favorites for colorful, round flower heads in summer and early fall. Hot-weather plants, they do not gain from being planted early, but merely stand still until weather warms up. Subject to mildew in foggy places, if given overhead water, and when autumn brings longer nights, more dew and shade. Sow seeds where plants are to grow (or set out nursery plants) May–July. Give good garden soil, feed generously. Most garden zinnias belong to *Z. elegans.*

Z. angustifolia. Annual. Compact plants to 8 in. tall. Leaves very narrow. Inch-wide flower heads orange, each ray with a paler stripe. Blooms in 6 weeks from seed, continues late into fall. 'Classic' 8–12 in. tall, to 2 ft. wide. Can be perennial in mild winters. Good in hanging baskets.

Z. elegans. Annual. Plant height ranges from 1–3 ft., leaves to 5 in., flower head size from less than 1 in. to as much as 5–7 in. across. Forms include full doubles, cactus flowered (with quilled rays), and crested (cushion center surrounded by rows of broad rays); colors include white, pink, salmon, rose, red, yellow, orange, lavender, purple, and green.

Many strains are available, from dwarf plants with small flowers to 3-ft. sorts with 5-in. blooms. Extra dwarf (to 6 in. tall) are the Mini series and Thumbelina strain. Other small-flowered kinds on larger (1-ft.) but still compact plants are Cupid and Buttons; still taller (to 2 ft.) but small flowered are the Lilliputs. Dreamland and Peter Pan strains have 3-in. blooms on bushy dwarf plants to 1 ft.; Whirligig has large bicolored flowers on 1½-ft. plants. Large-flowered strains with 2–3-ft. plants include Border

Beauty and Burpeeana California Giants, Dahlia-flowered, Giant Cactus–flowered, Ruffles, State Fair, and Zenith. 'Rose Pinwheel', a single (daisy-type) rose pink zinnia, represents a breakthrough: a hybrid between *Z. elegans* and *Z. angustifolia,* it is apparently resistant to mildew. Grows 1½ ft. tall, 2 ft. wide; has 2½–3-in. flowers.

Z. grandiflora. Perennial. Native to high plains, the Southwest, Mexico. Grows to 10 in. tall, spreads by seeds or runners. Leaves narrow (⅛ in. wide), to 1 in. long. Flower heads orange eyed, bright yellow, 1½ in. wide. Blooms spring–fall if watered, but needs little or no water once established.

Z. haageana. Annual. Plants compact, 1–1½ ft. tall; 3-in. leaves narrower than on common zinnias. Double strains Persian Carpet (1 ft. tall) and Old Mexico (16 in. tall) have flowers in mahogany red, yellow, and orange, usually mixed in the same flower head. Colorful, long blooming.

ZIZIPHUS jujuba

CHINESE JUJUBE

Rhamnaceae

DECIDUOUS TREE

✷ ZONES 7–16, 18–24

☼ FULL SUN

⬤ DEEP WATERING DURING GROWING SEASON

Ziziphus jujuba

Slow to moderate growth to 20–30 ft. Branches spiny, gnarled, somewhat pendulous. Leaves glossy bright green, 1–2 in. long, with three prominent veins. Clusters of small yellowish flowers in May–June. Shiny, reddish brown, datelike fruit in fall has sweet, applelike flavor; candied and dried, fruits resemble dates.

Tree is deep rooted and takes well to desert conditions, tolerating drought, saline and alkaline soils. Grows better in good garden soil. Thrives in lawns. No serious pests, but subject to Texas root rot in deserts. Prune in winter to shape, encourage weeping habit, or reduce size. Attractive silhouette, foliage, fruit, and toughness make it a good decorative tree, especially for high desert. Foliage turns a good yellow in fall.

Fruit of seedlings is ½–1 in. long. Two cultivated varieties are 'Lang' (1½–2-in.-long fruit, bears young) and 'Li' (2-in.-long fruit).

ZOYSIA

Poaceae (Gramineae)

PERENNIAL GRASSES

✷ ZONES VARY BY SPECIES

☼ ◐ THRIVE IN SUN, TOLERATE SOME SHADE

◐ ⬤ NEED LITTLE WATER FOR GRASSES

Zoysia tenuifolia

They tend to spread slowly, are fairly deep rooted. Dormant and straw colored during the winter; turn green in spring. Use for lawns, ground covers. Plant using sod, sprigs, stolons, or plugs. (Stolons give much faster cover than plugs.) Cut lawns ¾ in. high.

Z. japonica 'Meyer'. MEYER ZOYSIA. Zones 12, 13. Resembles bluegrass. Turns brown earliest in winter, turns green latest in spring.

Z. matrella. MANILA GRASS. Zones 8, 9, 12–14, 18–24. Also similar to bluegrass in appearance. Holds color a little better than 'Meyer'.

Z. tenuifolia. KOREAN GRASS. Hardy in Zones 8, 9, 12–24; best in Zones 18–24. Creeping, fine textured, bumpy. Makes a beautiful grassy meadow or gives mossy oriental effect in areas impossible to mow or water often. The farther inland, the longer the dormant season.

Z. t. 'Emerald'. EMERALD ZOYSIA. Zones 8, 9, 12–14, 18–24. Wiry, dark green, prickly-looking turf. Dense, wiry blades hard to cut. More frost tolerant than other zoysias.

ZUCCHINI. See SQUASH p. 491

ZYGOCACTUS. See SCHLUMBERGERA p. 480

Practical Gardening
DICTIONARY

Gardening successfully in the West requires a knowledge of techniques and materials, and an appreciation for the versatility of the plants that grow here. But it also demands a basic understanding of plant growth and its integral relationship to climate, soil, water, sunlight, nutrients, and the other organisms—both good and bad—that populate our gardens.

On the next 64 pages, you'll find definitions of common gardening terms; information on techniques, materials, tools, plant groups, and pests (animals, insects, diseases, and weeds); and all the helpful tips and illustrated step-by-step guidelines you'll need to garden successfully.

Acid Soil

An acid soil is one with a pH below 7. See Soil pH (p. 576).

Actual

In such phrases as "actual nitrogen," "actual" refers to the amount of the specified nutrient (by weight) contained in a fertilizer. For example, we sometimes recommend applying a certain amount of actual nitrogen. To find out how to calculate "actual" nutrient contents from fertilizer labels, see the illustration below.

Aeration

Loosening or puncturing the soil by mechanical means to increase water penetration and air permeability is called aeration. Aerating can be as simple as cultivating around newly planted seedlings with a trowel or, in the case of lawns,
can involve use of a gas-powered machine that removes small cores of soil from the turf. The response to aeration is generally improved plant growth.

Alkaline Soil

An alkaline soil is one with a pH above 7. See Soil pH (p. 576).

Annual

A plant that completes its life cycle in a year or less is called an annual. Seed germinates and the plant grows, blooms, sets seed, and dies—all in one growing season. Examples are most marigolds *(Tagetes)* and zinnias. The phrase "grow as an annual" or "treat as an annual" means to sow seed or set out plants in spring after the last frost, enjoy the plants from spring through fall, and pull them out or let the frosts kill them at the end of the year. Some plants that mild-winter (Zones 8–24) gardeners treat as annuals are planted in fall, grow and bloom during winter and spring, and then are killed by summer heat.

Think of annuals as the real workhorses of the garden. Their lives are short, but that brief lifetime is extremely productive. Annuals can bloom literally for months, from the moment the plants are mature enough to bear flowers until they are cut down by frost. In areas of no or mild frosts (Zones 8–24), certain annuals can brighten even a winter garden with blossoms.

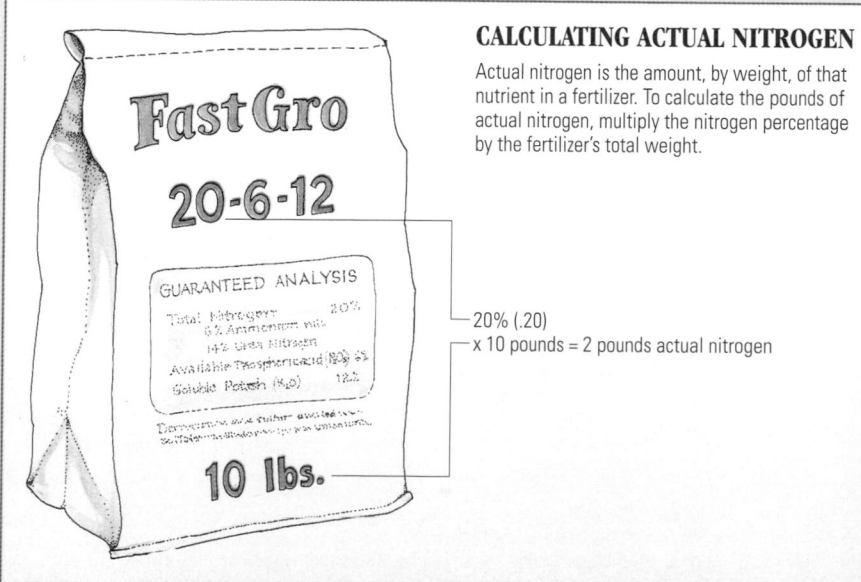

CALCULATING ACTUAL NITROGEN

Actual nitrogen is the amount, by weight, of that nutrient in a fertilizer. To calculate the pounds of actual nitrogen, multiply the nitrogen percentage by the fertilizer's total weight.

Fast Gro
20-6-12

GUARANTEED ANALYSIS
Total Nitrogen   20%
  6% Ammonium nitr.
  14% Urea Nitrogen
Available Phosphoric acid (P₂O₅) 6%
Soluble Potash (K₂O)   12%

20% (.20)
x 10 pounds = 2 pounds actual nitrogen

10 lbs.

B

Good soil, the foundation on which a successful annual planting is built, requires some advance preparation. Whether sowing seeds or setting out small plants, first refer to the soil preparation advice under Planting Techniques: Seeds (p. 563).

Planting and timing. Many gardeners prefer to sow their own annual seeds; you'll find guidelines for seed sowing under Planting Techniques: Seeds (p. 563). Or you can buy a wide selection of popular types and varieties already started at nurseries—sold in small individual containers, in packs of four or six, or in flats. The handling of these plants is discussed under Planting Techniques: Annuals and Perennials (p. 564).

In the mild-winter zones (8–24), there are two principal times of year for planting annuals: early spring, for those that bloom in late spring, summer, and fall (warm-season annuals); and late summer or fall, for the winter and early-spring bloomers (cool-season annuals). Both are periods of moderately cool temperatures preceding the sort of weather that favors development of annuals. Gardeners in cold-winter zones (1–7) can plant only in early spring.

The summer-flowering annuals need to establish roots before really warm days come along to hasten growth and bloom. Winter-blooming annuals should be set out while days are still warm enough for good plant growth but nights are lengthening. Winter annuals set out while days are longer than nights may perish or rush to maturity as stunted, poorly established plants. Favorite annuals are listed according to seasons of bloom in the charts beginning on page 52.

The secret to success with annual plantings is to keep the plants growing steadily. The keys to plant growth are watering, fertilizing, and grooming.

Watering. Sprinkling is an effective way to water annuals, although the spray of water may topple tall or weak-stemmed plants. An economical and thorough way to water annuals grown in rows or in block beds is to irrigate in furrows between the rows. With a small bed of annuals, you may be able to hoe up a shallow dike around the bed and irrigate by flooding. Drip irrigation, using any of the various sorts of emitters available, offers a range of watering options. Mulching helps conserve water and reduce weeds. See Watering (p. 585) for detailed information on techniques.

Fertilizing. Mixing a complete fertilizer into the soil before planting annuals generally supplies enough nutrients to last at least half the growing season. In cold-winter zones (1–7), an application of fertilizer after bloom is under way will tide annuals through their season. Where winters are warmer and the growing season for annuals is correspondingly longer, give plants another fertilizer application in late summer.

If you didn't add fertilizer to your soil before planting annuals, give plants an application of a high-nitrogen complete fertilizer about 2 weeks

after planting; then follow with a second application about 6 weeks after the first. In warmest zones, where growing seasons are longest, a third application may be in order 6 to 8 weeks after the second. For more about fertilizers, see Fertilizers (p. 543), and Nutrients, Basic (p. 556).

Grooming. To keep blooms coming all season long, you have to interrupt nature's seed-producing process by removing old blossoms before the plant can begin seed formation.

Anthracnose. See Leaf Spot   p. 554

Ants

By themselves, ants are not serious garden pests, although some types may damage young seedlings. However, they are closely associated with honeydew produced by sucking insect pests and are often the most visible clue that the pest is present. Ants can also interfere with the effectiveness of biological controls (p. 533). See Aphids (next entry) for control measures.

Aphids

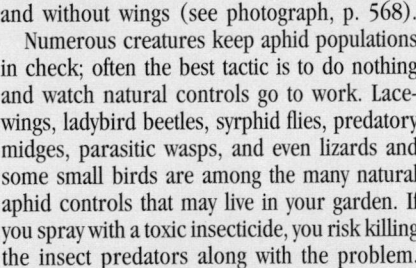

Aphids are soft, oval, pinhead- to match-head-size insects that cluster together on young shoots, buds, and leaves. They come in various colors— including green, pink, red, and black—with and without wings (see photograph, p. 568).

Numerous creatures keep aphid populations in check; often the best tactic is to do nothing and watch natural controls go to work. Lacewings, ladybird beetles, syrphid flies, predatory midges, parasitic wasps, and even lizards and some small birds are among the many natural aphid controls that may live in your garden. If you spray with a toxic insecticide, you risk killing the insect predators along with the problem.

Controls. Fortunately, you can get rid of most aphids with a blast of water from the hose. For greater effectiveness, wash them off with an insecticidal soap; the soap kills aphids but won't linger to harm other insects later.

The most troublesome aphids curl leaves around themselves or stay in protected places (inside a head of cabbage, for example). The best control for these aphids is anticipation: if you had them last year, expect them this year; hose or wash them off when the aphid colony is young and leaves are still open. You can also prevent aphids from reaching vegetables by planting under floating row covers (p. 573).

A dormant oil spray is effective in killing overwintering eggs of many species of aphids on trees and shrubs. On herbaceous plants, clean up old

plant debris before growth starts in spring. If an aphid infestation is severe, spray with insecticidal soap, pyrethrum, rotenone, diazinon, malathion, or (on nonedible plants) acephate.

Ants often maintain aphid colonies, fighting off parasites and predators to feed on the sticky honeydew aphids produce. Getting rid of the ants often permits natural aphid controls to reestablish themselves. To keep ants out of plants, encircle trunks with bands of a sticky ant barrier, put out diazinon or chlorpyrifos granules, or use poisonous ant baits.

Backfill

Backfill soil is returned to a planting hole after a plant's roots have been positioned. Unless the native soil is heavy clay or very sandy, most plants will become established faster if backfill is simply the soil dug out to create the planting hole. In problem soils, mix the backfill with some organic soil amendments (p. 575) to improve its texture.

Balled-and-Burlapped

Sometimes abbreviated B-and-B, balled-and-burlapped shrubs and trees are sold by some nurseries from late fall to early spring. The name comes from the large ball of soil around the roots, which is wrapped in burlap to hold it together. B-and-B plants usually cannot be offered bare-root. See Planting Techniques: Trees and Shrubs (p. 566) for planting instructions.

Bare-Root

In winter and early spring, nurseries offer many deciduous shrubs and trees, and some perennials, with all soil removed from their roots. For planting instructions, see Planting Techniques: Trees and Shrubs (p. 565) or Perennial (p. 559).

Bedding Plant

Plants (mainly annuals) suitable for massing in beds for their colorful flowers or foliage are called bedding plants.

Beneficial Insects. See Visual Guide to Identifying Biological Controls   p. 533

Bermuda Grass

A fine-textured and fast-growing perennial, Bermuda grass is a well-established lawn grass and the second most difficult garden weed at low elevations in California, Arizona, and New Mexico. Native to warm areas of the Old World, Bermuda grass spreads underground by rhizomes and aboveground by seeds and stolons. If not carefully confined, its rhizomes and stolons invade shrubbery and flower beds and can be difficult to eradicate once they are established.

Controls. If stray clumps do turn up in flower beds, pull or dig them up before they form sod. Be sure to remove all of the underground stem; otherwise, it can start new shoots. Or spray with fluazifop-butyl or sethoxydim, which can be applied over some ornamentals (check the label). Where patches are too big to be dug out of a lawn, apply glyphosate in summer or fall as Bermuda grass slows its growth (avoid desirable plants nearby). Repeat applications may be necessary.

Biennial

Plants called biennials complete their life cycle in 2 years. Two familiar biennials are foxglove *(Digitalis)* and Canterbury bells *(Campanula medium)*. Typically, you plant seeds in spring or set out seedling plants in summer or fall. The plants bloom the following spring, then set seed and die.

Bindweed

Also called wild morning glory, bindweed grows in open, exposed areas—usually in loam to heavy clay—throughout the West, but it is especially bothersome for gardeners in the Northwest, Northern California, and the mountain states. Bindweed crawls over the ground and twines over and around other plants, competing with them for nutrients and light. Its flowers appear in summer or early fall, before the plant goes dormant for winter.

When you pull bindweed, the stems break off, but frequently the deep roots and underground stems remain. The more you break it, the more it sprouts. If allowed to go to seed, bindweed becomes nearly impossible to control: its hard-coated seeds can sprout after lying dormant in the soil for years.

Controls. In midsummer, at the plant's peak growth but before it sets seed, spray isolated patches with glyphosate; repeat applications may be needed. If bindweed is intertwined with desirable plants, carefully paint its leaves with a herbicide.

Biological Pest Control. See Visual Guide to Identifying Biological Controls; and Pest Management   pp. 533, 559

Bird Protection

Most gardeners see birds as friends rather than enemies, but certain birds (crows in particular) at certain times can be nuisances: they eat newly planted seeds, tender seedlings, transplants, fruits, nuts, or berries.

Reflectors, fluttering objects, and scarecrows may reduce damage briefly, but birds soon become accustomed to them and resume their activities. The only surefire solution to bird depredation is to use screen or nylon or plastic netting material.

Broad-mesh netting (¾-inch) is popular for trees because it easily lets in air, water, and sunlight. Enclose fruit trees with nets 2 or 3 weeks before fruit ripens; tie nets off where the lowest branches spring from the trunk. Remove netting to harvest.

For protecting sprouting seedlings and maturing vegetables, floating row covers (p. 573) are the easiest to use because they need no supports. Other options—which need to be supported with stakes and string, in tent fashion—are fine-mesh screen and nylon netting. If crows are the problem, chicken wire folded into a tent shape over the rows will provide protection.

Blackberry

Of the three kinds of blackberries common in the Pacific Northwest, 'Himalaya' is the predominant one. It grows wild in pastures and along highways, thriving in the mild, moist climates of western Oregon and Washington  (where gardeners name it as a top pest). It can turn up in flower beds, gravel paths, or lawns.

The roots are perennial, but the canes are biennial: they grow one year and flower and form fruit the next. Blackberry spreads rapidly by underground runners and seeds; birds eat the ripe, shiny berries in late summer and scatter the seeds willy-nilly across the landscape.

Controls. Pull out young plants in spring, before feeder roots develop. Cut back established plants during the summer growing season, when foliage is green (it's easier to dispose of fresh than dry). Wear heavy gloves; use a pick and shovel to dig up as many roots as possible.

Paint fresh shoots with glyphosate when 6 to 12 inches tall (spray only in isolated areas). Retreatment is usually necessary to control plants growing from dormant seeds, old and incompletely killed roots, and root crowns. Triclopyr can also be effective.

Black Spot. See Leaf Spot; and Visual Guide to Identifying Plant Problems   pp. 554, 569

Blanching

Tying outer leaves over the inner head or leaves of a plant to produce a lighter color or a milder flavor is termed blanching. It is most often done to keep heads of cauliflower white.

Bolt

Annual flowers and vegetables that grow quickly to flowering stage at the expense of good overall development are said to bolt. This happens most often when plants are set out too late in the year or when unseasonably hot weather rushes growth.

Bonsai

Bonsai (the word is Japanese) is one of the fine arts of gardening: growing carefully trained, dwarfed plants in containers selected to harmonize with the plants. The objective is to create in miniature scale a tree or landscape; often the dwarfed trees take on the appearance of very old, gnarled specimens. To get the desired effect, bonsai craftspeople meticulously wire and prune branches and trim roots.

Botanical Name

The Latin scientific name of a plant is its botanical name. Unlike common names, of which an individual plant may have many, a plant has only one botanical name, which it shares with no other. (The same common name—for example, dusty miller—may represent three or four different plants.) Asking for a plant by its botanical name (as listed in the Western Plant Encyclopedia) assures you of getting the plant you want. See also Plant Classification (p. 561).

Bracts

Modified leaves called bracts may grow just below a flower or flower cluster (not all flowers have bracts). Bracts are usually green, but in some cases they are conspicuous and colorful, constituting what people regard as "flowers"; examples are bougainvillea, dogwood, and poinsettia.

Broadcast

To broadcast means to scatter seed by hand over the soil surface. See Planting Techniques: Seeds (p. 563).

Broad-Leafed

The phrase "broad-leafed evergreen" refers to a plant that has green foliage all year but

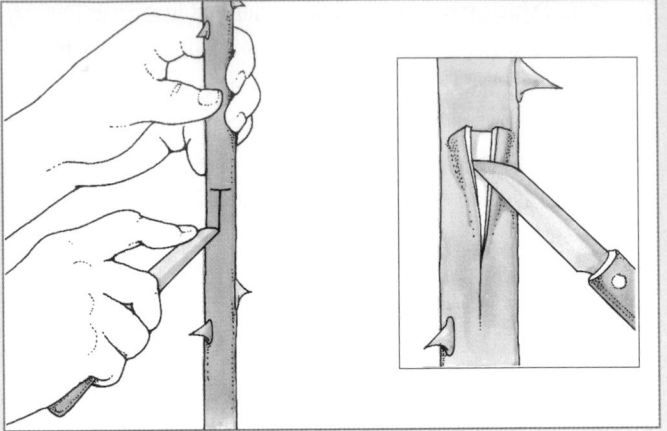

BUDDING

1 T-budding is fairly easy for the novice. Make T-shaped cut in branch ¼ to ½ inch in diameter; top of T should extend about one-third the distance around stem. Gently pry up corners where cuts meet.

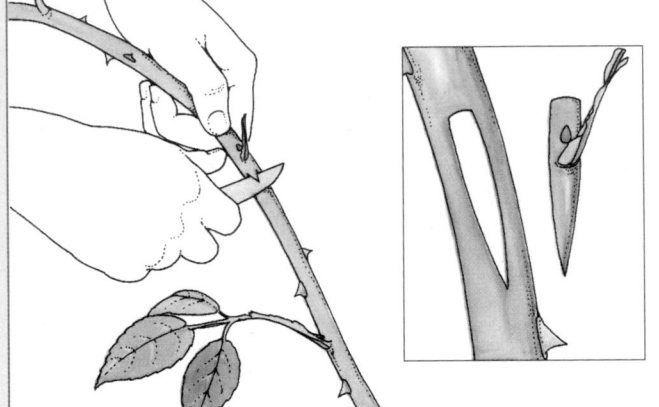

2 Cut shield-shaped patch containing bud from selected bud-wood plant. Begin about ½ inch below bud and finish about 1 inch above it; leave a bit of wood attached to back of bud shield.

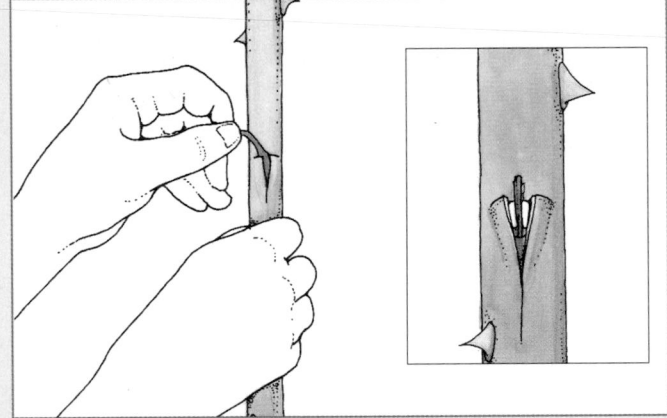

3 Push bud shield down between flaps of T-cut, being careful not to damage the bud. Cut off top of shield even with horizontal cut of the T; all of shield should fit beneath bark flaps.

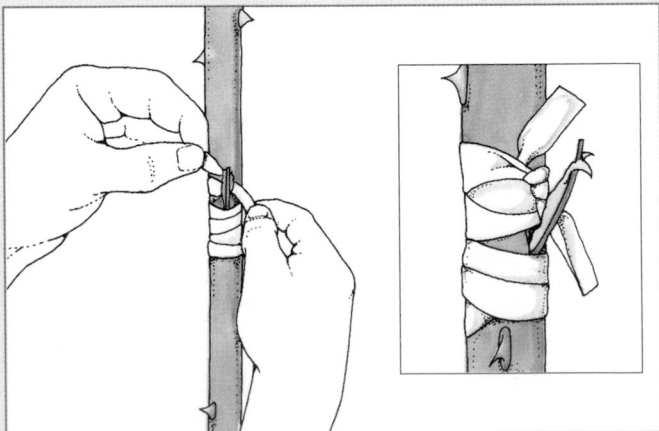

4 Bind the operation snugly with plastic tape, starting beneath the bud and finishing above it so that tape overlaps in shingle fashion. Only bud itself should be exposed.

is not an evergreen conifer (such as a juniper) with needlelike or scalelike foliage. A broadleafed weed is any weed that is not a grass.

Bud

The word "bud" has several definitions. A flower bud is one that develops into a blossom. A growth bud may be at the tip of a stem (terminal) or along the sides of a stem (lateral); these buds will produce new leafy growth (see Plant Anatomy and Growth, p. 561). To bud a plant is to propagate by a process similar to grafting (see Budding, next entry).

Budding

Budding is a method of propagation in which a bud (the scion) from one plant is inserted into the bark of another related plant, usually a rootstock. This technique is commonly used to grow specific varieties of fruit trees and roses on desirable rootstocks.

Budding accomplishes the same result as grafting, but it is considerably easier to do and, for the novice, is more likely to be successful. In summer or early fall, when plants are actively growing, insert a growth bud from one plant under the bark of another plant of a related kind. If the plants are compatible and if you do the budding carefully, the bud will unite with the stem into which it was inserted. Throughout fall and winter, the bud will remain plump but dormant; it will begin to grow in spring when all buds on the plant have a growth spurt. At that time, cut off the stem at a point just above the growing bud you inserted. See illustration.

Bud Union

The part of a plant where top growth joins with the understock, generally 1 to 6 inches above the roots, is its bud union. It is an enlarged knob from which all major stems grow.

Bulbs

Bulbs are a very specialized group of perennial plants. Following popular usage, we call a number of plants bulbs that are not true bulbs—corms, rhizomes, tubers, and tuberous roots (see The Five Bulb Types illustration, pp. 534–535). But whether true bulbs or bulblike plants, they all hold a reserve of nutrients in a thickened underground storage organ. This reserve almost guarantees that the bulb you purchase in summer or fall will bloom the following spring: all the nutrients the plant needs to complete its life cycle are in storage, waiting for the right combination of moisture and soil temperature to trigger the cycle's beginning phase.

Planting. Although the bulb you purchase from a nursery or commercial specialist is likely to be a sure first-season performer, performance in subsequent years will depend on

▶ page 534

Visual Guide to Identifying
BIOLOGICAL CONTROLS

U sing living organisms such as beneficial insects to destroy garden pests is called biological control. It is an effective way to reduce plant damage without using strong chemicals or sprays. Here are beneficial insects that are either common in western gardens or can be released to reduce pest populations. Also described are other organisms that kill insect pests and a natural hormone product that hopelessly confuses them. For more information, see Pest Management (p. 559).

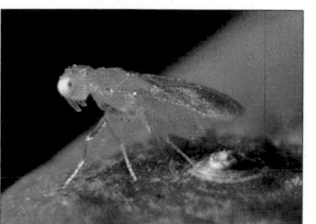

Scale Parasites
One tiny parasitic wasp *(Aphytis melinus)* attacks and kills red scale and other types of hard scale. *Metaphycus helvolus* attacks black scale and other hemispherical scales

Cryptolaemus Beetle
The larvae and adults of the Cryptolaemus beetle, a ladybird-beetle relative, feed on mealybugs.

Lacewings
Commonly found in gardens, both lacewing larvae and adults feed on a variety of insects and mites.

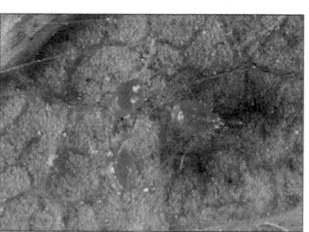

Predator Mites
Various species of mites feed on spider mites and sometimes thrips but do no damage to plants.

Fly Parasites
Tiny wasps (many species) that lay their eggs in the pupae of several types of flies, including houseflies, are very effective and most useful in controlling flies on ranches or farms.

Ladybird Beetle
The ladybird beetle (or ladybug, as most people know it) occurs naturally in gardens. Larvae *(left)* and adults feed on aphids, mealybugs, small worms, spider mites, and similar soft-bodied insects. Releasing ladybird beetles in your garden is usually not effective because they fly away. They also migrate annually. If you do release them, do so in the evening because daylight encourages flight.

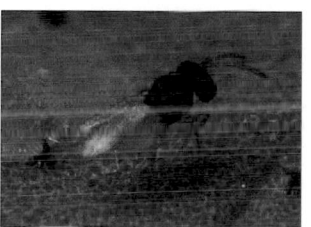

Whitefly Parasite
Several species of small wasps attack immature stages of whiteflies. Control of the greenhouse whitefly using *Encarsia formosa* requires average temperatures above 75°F. The wasps are most effective in greenhouses. A related species that is not commercially available has been released in California to control ash whitefly.

Trichogramma Wasps
Larvae of the tiny trichogramma wasp develop within the eggs of caterpillars and eat their way out, destroying the eggs. Adult wasps fly off to find new eggs to parasitize. Repeated releases are usually necessary to reduce a caterpillar infestation.

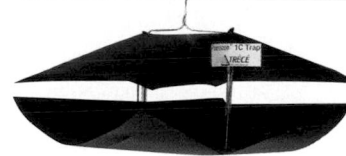

Semiochemicals
Insects use semiochemicals to communicate. Two general groups are commercially available: pheromones, which affect communications between insects, and kairomones, which affect feeding behavior. Both can be used to attract insects: sometimes to trap (possibly to monitor pest levels for precise timing of sprays) or confuse an insect pest; at other times, to lure beneficials into the garden. Semiochemicals are very target specific and are available for several common pests.

Parasitic Nematodes
Parasitic nematodes include several species of microscopic worms that seek out and eat their way into more than 250 soil-dwelling pests, such as grubs, weevils, sod webworms, and carpenter worms. Read directions carefully. Soil conditions and release techniques must be right for effectiveness.

Bacillus thuringiensis (BT)
The bacteria BT controls caterpillars (including worms like budworms). After eating BT-treated leaves, caterpillars die within 2 to 3 days. BT can be used on all food crops up to harvest. Mixing it in alkaline water (pH 8 or higher) reduces its effectiveness. Apply it when caterpillars are small; reapply in 3 to 14 days. The strain for most caterpillars is *B. t. kurstaki.* Other available strains include *B. t. israeliensis* for mosquitoes and *B. t. 'San Diego'* for Colorado potato beetle and elm-leaf beetle. BT is sold under several trade names.

C

THE FIVE BULB TYPES

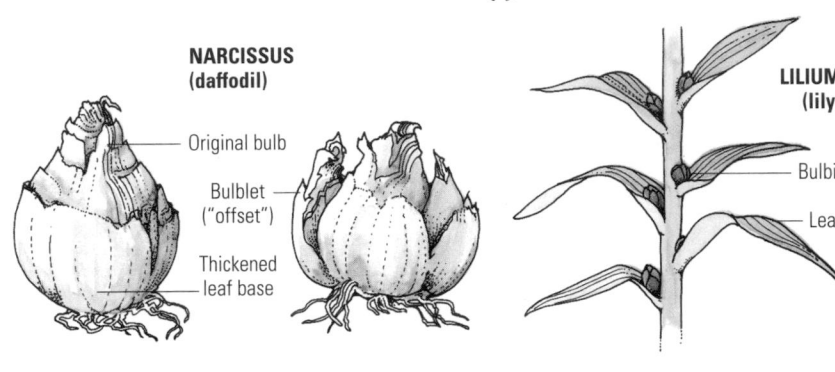

True bulb and bulblet. A true bulb is a short underground stem (on solid basal plate) surrounded by modified fleshy leaves (scales) that protect and store food for use by the embryonic plant. Outer scales are dry and form papery covering (tunic).

The new bulb (often called an offset) is formed from a lateral bud on the basal plate; the old bulb may die or, like daffodils, keep coming back each year. Bulblets can be separated from the mother bulb and replanted to increase stock of the original plant. Bulbils are small bulbs that form in the axils of leaves, in flowers, or on stems of certain bulbous plants.

ALLIUM (onion)
- Tunic
- Fleshy leaves (scales)
- Embryonic plant
- Basal plate
- Roots

NARCISSUS (daffodil)
- Original bulb
- Bulblet ("offset")
- Thickened leaf base

LILIUM (lily)
- Bulbil
- Leaf

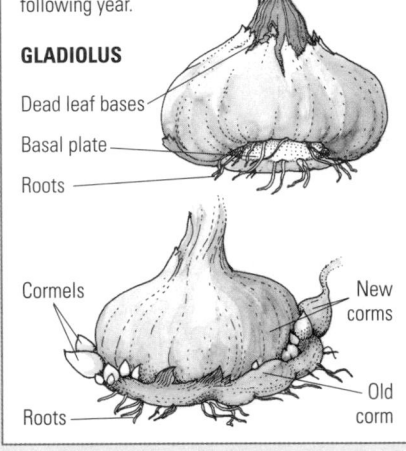

Corm and cormel. A corm is a swollen, underground stem base—solid tissue (in contrast to bulb scales) but with a basal plate from which roots grow. Growth point is on the corm's top; many corms have tunics that consist of dried bases of previous season's leaves. An individual corm lasts just one year. New corms form from axillary buds on the top of an old corm as it completes its growth cycle. Fingernail-size cormels will take 2 to 3 years to flower; larger corms should bloom the following year.

GLADIOLUS
- Dead leaf bases
- Basal plate
- Roots
- Cormels
- New corms
- Old corm
- Roots

the care you give it. As always, proper care begins with the soil. Most bulbs prefer soil that drains well yet retains a certain amount of water. See Soils (p. 576).

In planting true bulbs and most corms, the rule of thumb is to dig a hole about three times as deep as the bulb's greatest diameter. (To determine planting depths for the other "bulbs," see individual plant descriptions in the Western Plant Encyclopedia.) If you will be planting many bulbs in one bed, it may be easier to dig a trench or to excavate the bed to the desired planting depth than to dig individual holes.

Fertilizer. This is the time to add a complete fertilizer, including phosphorus and potassium. Ones with controlled-release nitrogen are very effective. (See Fertilizers, p. 543.) If you plant bulbs in individual holes, dig up to a tablespoonful of fertilizer into the soil at the bottom of each hole, then cover with about 2 inches of soil and plant the bulb. Otherwise, dig fertilizer into the bottom of the trench or excavated bed.

Water. When all the bulbs are set in place and covered with soil, soak the area thoroughly. In some regions this initial watering, along with subsequent rain, will supply all the moisture bulbs will need until their leaves poke above the soil surface. But if you live in an arid climate or have an unusually dry winter, you will need to soak the bulbs periodically throughout the winter and into the blooming season. Summer-flowering bulbs need watering at least until they finish blooming.

The roots of bulbs grow below the depth at which you planted, so water, to do them any

good, must penetrate deep into the soil. (See Watering, p. 585, for specific advice on watering practices.) Mulching (p. 555) is also beneficial.

Care. Bulb plantings established for a year or more may benefit from application of a nitrogen fertilizer at the start of the growing season (as recommended for perennials, p. 559). But the crucial moment for applying fertilizer comes after the blooms have faded.

When a bulb has finished flowering, much of its supply of stored nutrients is depleted. It must replenish those nutrients if it is to perform well the next year. For this reason, it is essential to leave the foliage on the plant, even if it begins to look unsightly, until it has yellowed and can be pulled off easily. The leaves continue to manufacture food for the plant (see Plant Anatomy and Growth, p. 561). Cutting them off prematurely amounts to removing the next year's blossoms—or at least reducing their quantity and quality.

Furthermore, fertilizer application at this time helps bulbs form not only next year's flowers but also new bulbs that will increase the planting. Phosphorus and potassium—the nutrients emphasized in "bulb food"—are most useful now, although they must reach the root zone to be fully effective (see Nutrients, Basic, p. 556). In an established planting, you may be able only to scatter fertilizer over the soil surface, scratch it in, and hope that some phosphorus and potassium will reach the roots. Where bulbs are spaced far enough apart or in rows, you may be able to get fertilizer deep into the soil by digging narrow trenches or holes

8 inches deep, placing fertilizer at the bottom, and then filling with soil.

Caliche

A soil condition found in some areas of the arid Southwest, caliche is a deposit of calcium carbonate (lime) beneath the soil surface. For help in dealing with it, see Hardpan (p. 550).

Cambium. See Plant Anatomy and Growth p. 561

Catkin

A catkin is a slender, spikelike, and often drooping flower cluster.

Chelate

A chelate (pronounced key-late) is a complex organic substance that holds micronutrients (see Nutrients, Basic, p. 556), usually iron, in a form available for absorption by plants. Iron chelates, for example, are often used to cure chlorosis (p. 535).

Chilling Requirement

Many deciduous shrubs and trees (fruit trees in particular), bulbs, and perennials need certain amounts of cold weather in winter to grow and bloom well the following year. Where winters are mild and these plants do not get the necessary winter chill, their perfor-

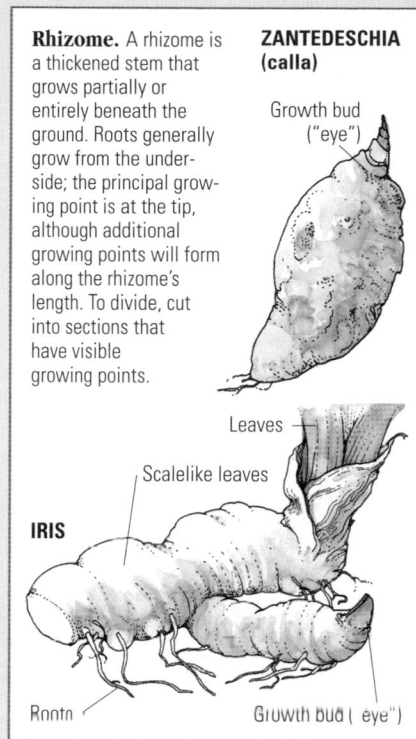

Rhizome. A rhizome is a thickened stem that grows partially or entirely beneath the ground. Roots generally grow from the underside; the principal growing point is at the tip, although additional growing points will form along the rhizome's length. To divide, cut into sections that have visible growing points.

ZANTEDESCHIA (calla)

Growth bud ("eye")

Leaves

Scalelike leaves

IRIS

Roots

Growth bud ("eye")

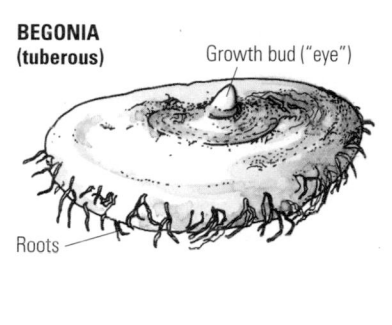

Tuber. A tuber is a swollen, underground stem base, like a corm, but it lacks the corm's distinct organization. There is no basal plate, so roots can grow from all sides; multiple growth points are distributed over the upper surface—each is a scalelike leaf with a growth bud in its axil. An individual tuber can last for many years. Some (*Cyclamen*, for example) continually enlarge, but never produce offsets; others (such as *Caladium*) form protuberances that can be removed and planted separately. Divide tubers by cutting into sections that have growth buds.

BEGONIA (tuberous)

Growth bud ("eye")

Roots

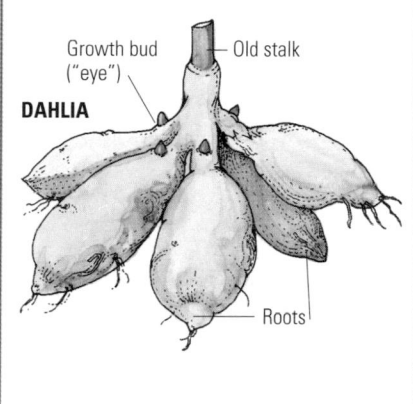

Tuberous roots. Tuberous roots are actual roots (rather than stems) that are specialized to store nutrients. In a full-grown dahlia, daylily, or other tuberous-rooted plant, the roots grow in a cluster, with the swollen tuberous portions radiating out from a central point. Growth buds are at the bases of old stems rather than on the tuberous roots. To divide, cut apart so that each division contains both roots and part of the stem's base with one or more growth buds.

Growth bud ("eye")

Old stalk

DAHLIA

Roots

mance is often disappointing: plants leaf out late, fail to flower or fruit well, and often decline in health and vigor even to the point of dying. With some of these plants (apples and lilacs, for example), varieties have been developed that require less winter cold than is normal for the type. Gardeners in milder-winter areas should choose varieties with low chilling requirements. (Chilling requirement is measured in hours required at temperatures below 45°F.)

Chlorosis

A systemic condition in which a plant's newer leaves turn yellow, chlorosis is usually caused by a deficiency of iron. (It occasionally results from lack of another mineral, such as zinc.) If the deficiency is mild, areas of yellow show up between the veins of the leaves, which remain a dark green (see photograph, p. 569). In severe or prolonged cases, the entire leaf turns yellow. Iron deficiency is only occasionally the result of a lack of iron in the soil; more frequently it is the result of some other substance (usually lime) making the iron unavailable to the plant.

To correct chlorosis, treat the soil with iron sulfate or with iron chelate (the latter has the important ability to hold iron in a form that is available to plants). Plants can also be treated with foliar sprays containing iron.

Cold Protection

A t high elevations where soil freezes hard and temperatures drop below zero, tender

plants will not thrive. But many gardeners do grow roses, and a few attempt broad leafed evergreens: boxwood, *Euonymus*, holly, *Pieris*, and rhododendrons. All these plants need help to survive harsh winters.

With roses, which are basically deciduous, the aim is to keep roots and bud union alive and to preserve as many live canes as possible. For detailed instructions on winter protection for roses, see page 464.

Some broad-leafed evergreens will survive fairly low temperatures but succumb to windburn and sunburn when low temperatures, strong sun, and cold, drying winds combine forces. The greatest damage occurs when these plants transpire water from their leaves but can't replace the moisture because water in the soil is frozen.

Careful selection of garden location minimizes damage to broad-leafed evergreens. Locate these plants where bright sun—especially in early morning—will not strike frozen plants. To avoid rupturing plant tissues, thawing should be gradual. Above all, keep soil moist and unfrozen with a thick mulch.

To protect an exposed broad-leafed evergreen, shelter it with burlap, lath, plywood, Styrofoam, or cardboard secured on its windward side. A palisade of evergreen boughs stuck in the ground around the plant will offer further protection. See also Frost Protection (p. 546).

Cole Crops

A group of vegetables belonging to the cabbage family, cole crops include broccoli, Brus-

sels sprouts, cabbage, kohlrabi, and cauliflower. They perform best in cool growing conditions.

Complete Fertilizer

A ny plant food that contains all three of the primary nutrient elements—nitrogen, phosphorus, and potassium—is a complete fertilizer. See Fertilizers (p. 543).

Compost

W ell-made compost is a soft, crumbly, brownish or blackish substance resulting from decomposition of organic material. It has limited value as a nutrient source but great value as an organic soil amendment (p. 575). Composting takes time, effort, and space. But if you have a ready supply of plant waste or a small garden that could be supplied by a continually maintained compost pile, the time and effort might be well spent. Remember, though, that a poorly maintained compost pile will be slow to yield its reward and may also breed flies and give off an obnoxious odor.

In its simplest and least efficient form, composting consists of piling up grass clippings, leaves, and other garden debris—plus vegetable kitchen refuse—and permitting them to decompose. In 6 weeks to 6 months, depending on temperature, moisture, and size of materials, the compost will have broken down sufficiently for use.

Composters. For the average garden, a better system is to stack the material for composting to

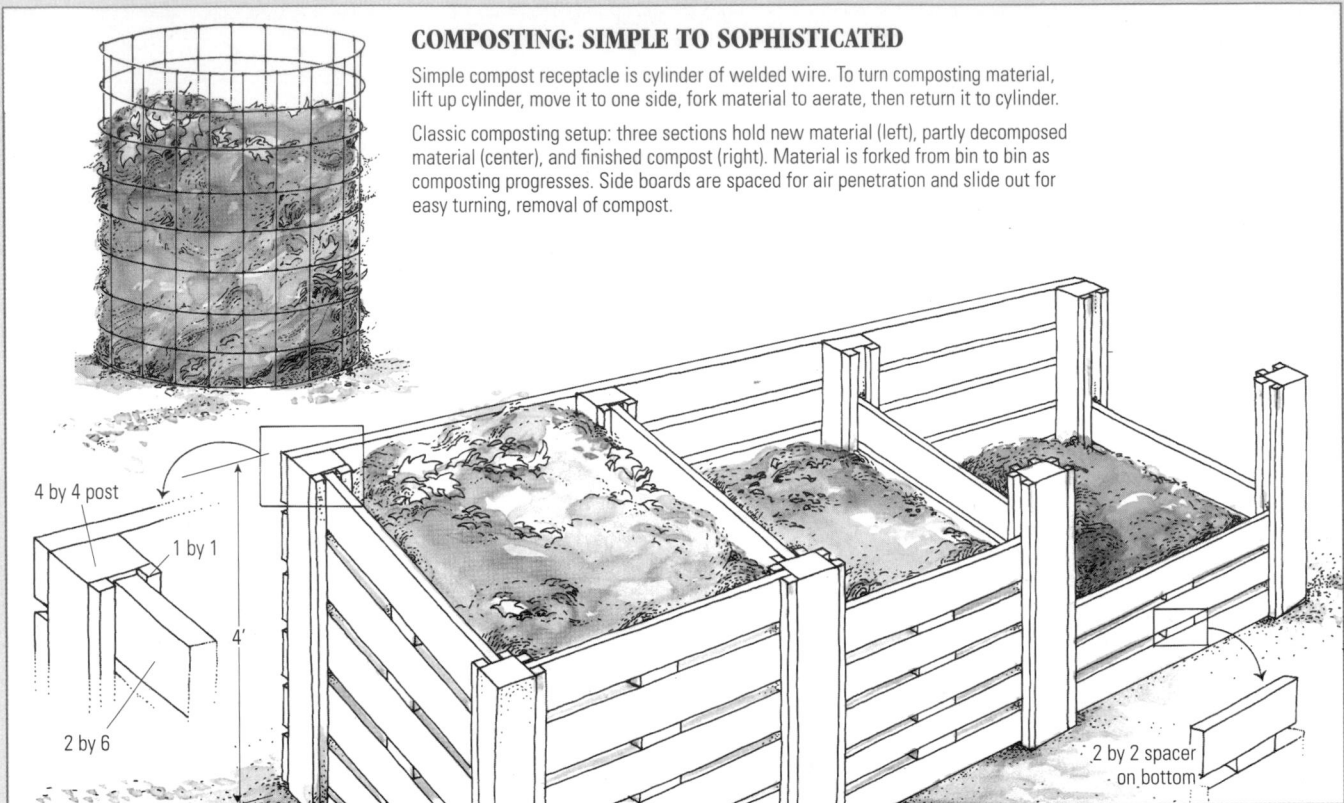

COMPOSTING: SIMPLE TO SOPHISTICATED

Simple compost receptacle is cylinder of welded wire. To turn composting material, lift up cylinder, move it to one side, fork material to aerate, then return it to cylinder.

Classic composting setup: three sections hold new material (left), partly decomposed material (center), and finished compost (right). Material is forked from bin to bin as composting progresses. Side boards are spaced for air penetration and slide out for easy turning, removal of compost.

4 by 4 post

1 by 1

4'

2 by 6

2 by 2 spacer on bottom

a height of 4 to 6 feet inside an enclosure that has openings in its sides through which air can penetrate. A slatted bin or a wire-mesh cylinder (see illustration) will do the trick. Turn the piled-up material at least once a week to aerate the mass and to relocate pieces in various stages of decomposition. (Compost decomposes more rapidly in the heat and moisture of the pile's interior than on the outside.) Thoroughly moisten the pile as needed; it should be about as wet as a squeezed-out sponge. Adding a few handfuls of complete fertilizer with every sizable load of raw material hastens decomposition. Compost additives—or boosters, as they are sometimes called—have proven to be of little benefit.

A more sophisticated composting operation uses three receptacles, as shown in the illustration. Placing the receptacles side by side makes it simple to fork or shovel material from bin to bin. Prefabricated composters are also available for purchase.

Because large, coarse pieces decompose slowly, chop them up before adding them to the pile or omit altogether. A good mixture consists of green and dried materials in about equal proportions.

The serious composter might consider purchasing a compost grinder. Chopping up everything from leaves to thumb-thick branches into uniformly small fragments, these machines are a great aid to people who live beyond the service area of garbage collectors—particularly those who are prevented by ordinance from burning debris.

Conifer

Conifer is a more precise word for the plants many people call evergreens, such as cedars, cypresses, junipers, and pines. Leaves on most are narrow and needlelike or tiny and scalelike. Not all conifers are evergreen, but all bear seeds in cones or modified conelike structures.

Container Gardening

Container plants generally require more attention than plants growing in the ground, but their potential advantages may make the extra care worthwhile. For the gardener with just a balcony or a paved patio, planting in containers is the only way to have a garden. And even those with garden space can use container plants to bring seasonal flowers onstage when colorful and remove them when past their prime. Other plants have such handsome foliage that they deserve to be grown in containers so they can be appreciated at close range throughout the year.

Container culture also lets you enjoy plants that aren't entirely suited to your garden conditions. You can grow acid-soil plants in regions where native soil is alkaline and plants that demand fast drainage even if your garden soil is clay. Plants too tender for your climate can be moved to shelter when cold weather comes, and plants sensitive to winter cold or summer heat may function well as container subjects indoors.

The routine extra attention container plants need falls into three categories: soil prepara-

tion, watering, and fertilizing. These plants also require periodic transplanting and replanting.

Soil mixes for containers. Container plants need soil that is porous and well drained but that retains moisture. The soil must allow roots to grow easily, and it must drain fast enough that roots don't suffocate in soggy soil. Yet the soil should retain enough moisture so that continuous watering isn't necessary.

Even the best garden soils fail to satisfy container soil requirements: in containers, garden soil inevitably forms a dense mass that roots can't penetrate easily, and it remains soggy for too long after watering. For these reasons, gardeners growing container plants turn to potting mixes.

Bagged soil mixes. You can purchase packaged potting mixes that are ready to use directly out of the bag. Formulations (listed on the bags) vary somewhat from brand to brand, but none contain actual soil. Look for a mix high in bark, forest materials, or sphagnum peat plus vermiculite. A 2-cubic-foot bag of potting mix will fill a planter box 36 by 8 by 10 inches; it will also be enough to transplant 8 to 10 plants from 1-gallon nursery containers to separate 10- or 12-inch pots.

Homemade soil mixes. If you prefer to mix your own potting soil—or if you are planning a large-scale operation that would be too costly using packaged mixes—you can purchase the basic component materials and combine them yourself. There are countless possible formulations, but they all combine organic material (bark, peat moss, leaf mold, compost) and mineral matter (soil, sand, perlite, vermiculite) in proportions that produce the desired porosity, drainage, and moisture retention.

One time-honored basic container mixture consists of 1 part good garden soil (not clay), 1 part sand (river or builder's sand) or perlite, and 1 part peat moss or nitrogen-stabilized bark. For plants that prefer acid soil (such as rhododendrons, azaleas, and heather), alter the above mix to 2 parts peat moss or nitrogen-stabilized bark.

The use of soil-less mixes lessens the danger from soilborne diseases. But these mixes dry faster than those containing soil, and they will need more frequent fertilizer applications due to leaching from frequent watering. For a quantity of soil-less mix, combine ⅔ cubic yard of nitrogen-stabilized bark (or peat moss) and ⅓ cubic yard washed 20-grit sand; add to this 6 pounds of 0-10-10 dry fertilizer and 10 pounds dolomite or dolomitic limestone. For ways to increase the water retention of a potting soil, read about Soil Polymers (p. 576).

Watering. In hot, dry, windy weather you may need to water actively growing plants more than once a day; when the weather is cool, still, and overcast or if plants are semidormant, weekly (or even less frequent) watering may suffice. Test with your fingers: it's time to water if the soil is dry beneath the surface.

To water thoroughly, apply water over the entire soil surface until it flows out the pot's drainage holes. This guarantees moistening the entire soil mass and also prevents any potentially harmful salts from accumulating in the soil mix.

Note: If water comes out the drainage holes too fast, check to see if it is just running down the inside surface of the container and not through the soil. A root ball that has become too dry can shrink away from the sides of the container; when that happens, water will run around the root ball without penetrating it. To correct the problem, set the container in a tub of water and soak the plant until bubbles stop rising. If that method isn't practical, cork the container's drainage holes and then water the plant. Remove corks after the soil is soaked.

Fertilizing. Heavy and thorough watering leaches out plant nutrients from container soils, so regular fertilizer applications are required for best plant growth. Use either liquid or dry fertilizer according to label directions. The slow-release dry fertilizers, which release nutrients steadily over a period of time, don't need to be applied as often as other fertilizers. With other types, light and frequent applications give best results.

Transplanting. Shift a plant to a larger container when its root system fills the container in which it is growing; usually the first sign of this is roots protruding from drainage holes. Gener-

ally speaking, container plants should be shifted to a slightly larger container rather than to a much larger one, because you want to keep the soil mass fairly well filled with roots (unused soil in a container can stagnate and become a haven for potentially harmful organisms). With fast-growing plants, it's safe to shift to a definitely larger container. And you can always put a number of small plants in a large container—their combined root systems will occupy the total soil mass.

When moving a plant to a larger container, select a new container that allows an inch or two of fresh soil on all sides of the root mass. If the plant's root ball appears compacted, cut it vertically with a sharp knife to encourage roots to move out into the new soil in the larger container. Make at least four equally spaced cuts

TRANSPLANTING CONTAINER-GROWN PLANTS

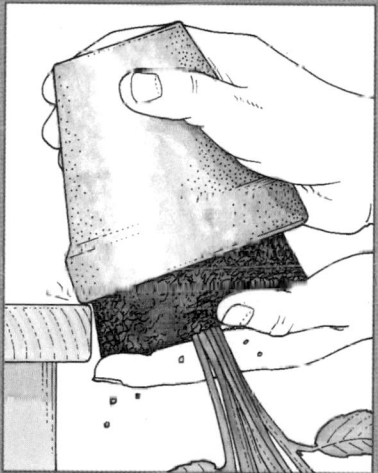

1 Tap pot gently against edge of workbench to free root ball. Pull apart coiled roots.

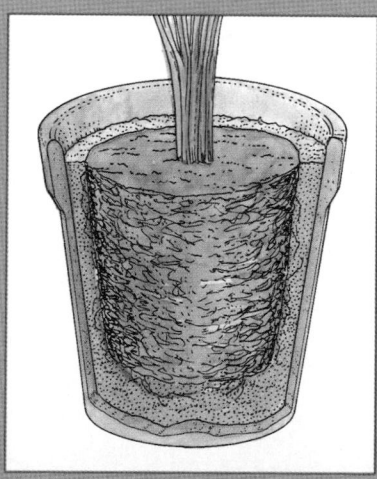

2 Set root ball into new pot partially filled with soil; top of root ball should be about an inch below pot's rim. Add soil around edges, firming lightly. Water thoroughly.

about ¼ to 1 inch deep, depending on root ball size.

To keep an older plant in the same large container indefinitely, you can periodically root-prune the plant. During the plant's dormant period, gently turn it out of the container. Shave off an inch or two of the outer root mass on all sides and on the bottom with a sharp knife; then replant in the same container with fresh soil mix around and underneath the roots. See illustration.

Cool-Season Plants

Plants that thrive in cool weather are referred to as cool-season plants. They include some vegetables (cole crops, lettuce, spinach, peas), annual flowers (pansies, violas, calendula), and lawn grasses (bluegrass, tall fescue). See also Vegetable Gardening (p. 581), Annual (p. 529), and Lawns (p. 551).

Corm

Technically, a corm is a thickened underground stem capable of producing roots, leaves, and flowers during the growing season. See Bulbs (p. 532) and The Five Bulb Types illustration (pp. 534–535).

Cover Crops

Sometimes referred to as "green manure," a cover crop is dug into the soil in early spring to return valuable organic matter and nitrogen to the soil. Legumes such as clover, cowpeas, and vetch are the commonest cover crops.

Crabgrass

An infamous summer annual, crabgrass grows well in hot, damp areas. This shallow-rooted weed thrives in lawns and flower beds that receive frequent surface watering, in underfed lawns, and in poorly drained fields.

Seeds germinate in early spring in Southern California, later in Northern California. As the plant grows, it branches out at the base; stems can root where they touch the soil. Seed heads form in mid- to late summer. As crabgrass declines in fall, it turns purplish, becoming especially noticeable in lawns.

In flower beds, pull crabgrass before it makes seeds. Keep lawns well fertilized and vigorous to provide tough competition for weeds; to dry out crabgrass roots, water lawns deeply

C

but not frequently. In late winter or early spring, apply a granular pre-emergent herbicide—such as DCPA (Dacthal)—with a fertilizer spreader. Lawn care combination products include other effective controls. Use fluazifop-butyl or sethoxydim in ornamental plantings.

Crown

The crown of a tree is its entire branch structure, including foliage. In another usage, "crown" refers to the point at which a plant's roots and top structure join (usually at or near the soil line).

Cultivate

Cultivating is the process of breaking up the soil surface, often removing weeds in the process. It aerates the soil and improves plant growth. Increased aeration due to cultivation also allows the soil to warm earlier in spring and dry faster in wet weather.

Cuttings

Most gardeners who have propagated new plants have started cuttings from plant stems, roots, or leaves. Stem cuttings are of three types—softwood, semihardwood, and hardwood—depending on the maturity of the cutting material.

Softwood and semihardwood cuttings. Softwood cuttings, taken from spring until late summer, are the easiest and quickest-rooting stem cuttings. You take them during the active growing season from soft, succulent, flexible new growth. The steps are outlined in the illustration. You take semihardwood cuttings after the active growing season or after a growth flush, usually in summer or early fall. Growth is then firm enough that a sharply bent twig snaps (if it just bends, the stem is too mature for satisfactory rooting).

In addition to deciduous and evergreen shrubs and trees, many herbaceous or evergreen perennials may be propagated by softwood or semihardwood cuttings.

Choices of rooting medium are several, but all allow for easy water penetration and fast drainage. Pure sand (builder's sand or river sand) is the simplest medium but requires the most frequent watering. Better are half-and-half mixtures of sand and peat moss or of perlite and peat moss, or perlite or vermiculite alone.

Loss of water through the leaves that remain on the cuttings is the greatest threat to softwood and semihardwood cuttings. To minimize this water loss, provide a greenhouse atmosphere—high humidity—for the cuttings while they are striking roots. The easiest way is to place a plastic bag over the cuttings and container, then tie it around the container to confine humid air within the bag. Ventilate any of these improvised greenhouses for a few minutes every day or two.

When new growth forms on the cuttings, you can be fairly sure that they have rooted and can be transplanted.

Hardwood cuttings. Hardwood cuttings are best made during the fall-to-spring dormant season from wood of the previous season's growth.

SOFTWOOD CUTTINGS

Take softwood and semihardwood cuttings during the growing season; cut below a leaf, remove lower leaves, dip cut in rooting hormone, then plant. Maintain high humidity around cutting (see text).

HARDWOOD CUTTINGS

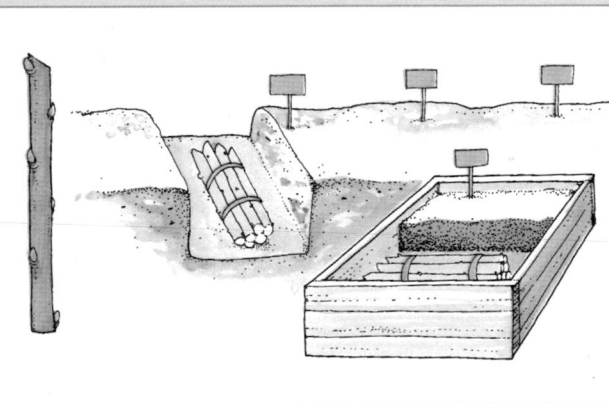

Take hardwood cuttings at onset of dormant season; make cut below a leaf bud, dip cut in rooting hormone. Refrigerate over winter in Zones 1–3; bury in a trench or soil-filled box outdoors in warmer climates.

LEAF CUTTINGS

Leaf cuttings will increase many succulents, African violets, *Sansevieria*, *Begonia*, and other plants. With some, cut veins and lay leaf flat on soil; others will grow from part of leaf inserted in soil.

ROOT CUTTINGS

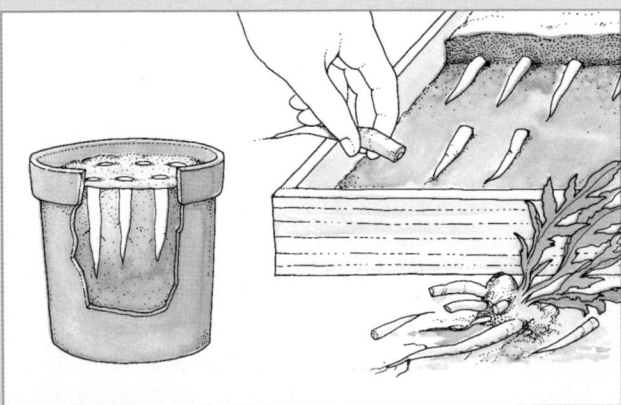

To make root cuttings, cut pencil- to finger-thick sections of roots; place them on their sides and cover with soil, or insert upright in soil with tops just at soil surface. Moisten, cover with plastic, and place in shade.

Many deciduous shrubs and trees can be increased from cuttings taken during the dormant season. See the illustration.

Hardwood cuttings may take longer to root and start growth than softwood cuttings, so you will want to put your hardwood cuttings where they can remain undisturbed.

During the winter the lower ends of the cuttings will begin to form calluses from which roots will grow. When weather starts to warm as spring approaches, dig out the cuttings and plant them in the open ground or in containers. Cuttings must be planted top side up; to be sure, make the top cut slanted, the bottom cut square.

Leaf cuttings. Some plants will root successfully from a leaf or portion of a leaf. See the illustration. New plants will sprout from the base of each leaf section or from the cut veins.

Root cuttings. Any plant that produces sprouts from its roots will grow from root cuttings. The technique is shown in the illustration. Check cuttings every week for moisture and for sprouts; remove the covering when growth shows.

Cutworms

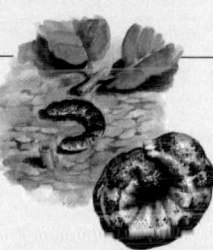

A large variety of hairless larvae of night-flying moths make up the diverse group called cutworms. They feed at night and on overcast days, and most can cut off young plants at the ground—hence, their name. In the daytime, they hide in the ground, curled up.

Barriers. Susceptible seedlings should be protected from cutworms by putting a physical barrier around each seedling the day it sprouts or the day you plant it. One simple barrier is a cutoff milk carton sleeve: sink it 1 inch below soil level, allow 2 inches above, and provide at least an inch of space between the sleeve and the plant. As an extra precaution, put petroleum jelly or a sticky ant barrier on the upper edge.

Some cutworms crawl up into plants and eat buds, leaves, and fruit. One way to keep them out is to spread a sticky ant barrier around the base of each susceptible plant. If you have too many plants to easily employ barriers, try handpicking cutworms at night. Or try trapping them by placing cardboard, plywood, wide boards, or heavy paper sacks in garden paths. During daylight, lift the traps and destroy the worms that have taken refuge beneath.

Cutworms in lawns. These are more difficult to eradicate. Your clue to infestation in grass or dichondra is small bare patches that grow rapidly in size day by day. If you're not sure the damage is from cutworms, drench a square yard with 1 tablespoon of dishwashing soap diluted in a gallon of water. That should bring the cutworms to the surface. Sometimes you can also see them with a flashlight at night.

Biological and chemical controls. Parasitic nematodes (p. 533) are the first line of defense against cutworms. *Bacillus thuringiensis* has limited effectiveness. To control seedling-eating cutworms, try dusting the ground where they feed with carbaryl; for cutworms in lawns, apply diazinon, chlorpyrifos, or carbaryl.

Damping Off

In the most conspicuous type of damping off (a disease that can be caused by a number of different organisms), the stem of a seedling collapses at or near the soil surface, and the seedling topples. In some woody seedlings, infected plants may remain alive and standing for a while. Another type rots the seedling before it emerges from the soil or causes the seed to decay before sprouting.

Professional horticulturists practice careful sanitation, pasteurizing their soil mixes. Home gardeners can take the following steps to reduce the occurrence of damping off:

■ Buy seeds that have been treated with a fungicide, or dust them with one before planting.

■ Provide good air circulation and ventilation (especially if growing seedlings indoors) to keep tops of seedlings dry and standing moisture to a minimum.

■ Sow seeds or root cuttings in an inert (sterile) material rather than in garden soil. Vermiculite, perlite, pumice, sand, sphagnum moss, and sterilized commercial mixes are all safe—at least the first time they are used.

You also can reduce problems by not planting too deeply or too close together and by avoiding overwatering.

A number of chemical fungicides help control damping off. Look for products that contain captan, or other properly labeled fungicides. But realize that one product may not be effective against all damping-off organisms. If one product doesn't work, switch to another.

Dandelion

Familiar as a lawn weed throughout the West, dandelion is particularly troublesome in gardens in the Northwest and the mountain states. It grows from a deep, fleshy taproot that often breaks (and can regrow) when the weed is pulled out and spreads by dispersing wind-borne seeds and by sprouting root crowns. Flowering begins in spring and often continues until frost; in mild weather, seeds can germinate year-round.

Pull out young plants before the taproot has a chance to grow deep into the soil. On lawns, apply 2,4-D in spring and fall. Spray isolated plants with glyphosate or another properly registered herbicide.

Deciduous

Any plant that sheds all of its leaves at one time each year (usually in fall) is deciduous.

Deer Protection

With their soulful eyes and graceful gait, deer may be pleasant to watch, but they can make a garden ragged in no time by nipping off flower heads and nibbling tender leaves and new shoots. As wild plants dry out, deer spend more time looking for food in gardens on the fringes of suburbia. They develop browsing patterns, visiting tasty gardens regularly—most often in the evening. Fond of a wide array of flowering plants, especially roses, deer will eat foliage or fruit of nearly anything you grow for your table. For a list of plants deer usually ignore, see page 106.

Physical controls. Fencing is the most certain protection. On level ground, a 7-foot woven-wire fence will usually keep deer out, although some determined deer can jump even an 8-foot fence. A horizontal "outrigger" extension on a fence makes it harder for a deer to jump it. On a slope, you may need to erect a 10- to 11-foot fence to guard against deer jumping from higher ground. Because deer can jump high or jump wide—but not simultaneously—some gardeners have had success with a pair of parallel 5-foot fences, with a 5-foot-wide "no-deer's-land" between.

If you don't fancy a fortress garden, focus on individual plants (or areas). Put chicken-wire cages around young plants and cylinders of wire fencing around larger specimens. Cover raised beds with mesh, and use floating row covers (p. 573) on vegetables. It sometimes helps to keep a zealous (and vocal) watchdog in the yard, particularly during evening and nighttime hours.

Chemical controls. Commercial repellents can work if sprayed often enough to keep new growth covered and to replace what rain and watering wash away (though some repellents may make sticky, unsightly spots on flowers and foliage). Do not apply repellents to edible portions of plants unless approved by the label; some are not safe to eat. Some gardeners repel deer by hanging small cloth bags filled with blood meal among their plants; disadvantages are that blood meal attracts dogs and smells unpleasant when wet.

Defoliation

The unnatural loss of a plant's leaves, usually to the detriment of the plant's health, is called defoliation. It may result from high winds that strip foliage away; intense heat (especially if accompanied by wind) that critically wilts leaves; drought; unusually early or late frosts that strike a plant still in active growth or just beginning growth; or severe damage by chemicals, insects, or diseases.

Dethatch

The process of removing dead stems (thatch) that build up beneath certain ground covers and lawn grasses is known as dethatching. It can be done by hand with a thatching rake or, in the case of lawns, with a gas-powered dethatcher, also called a vertical mower. It's usually performed in fall or early spring on cool-season lawns and in late spring for warm-season grasses. Followed up with fertilizer, the result is healthier, more vigorous growth.

Dieback

In dieback, a plant's stems die, beginning at the tips, for a part of their length. Causes are various: not enough water, nutrient deficiency, plant not adapted to climate in which it is growing, or severe insect, mite, or disease injury.

Diseases

Different kinds of organisms cause plant diseases. Most leaf, stem, and flower diseases result from bacteria, fungi, or viruses. The most prevalent soilborne diseases are caused by fungi.

Sometimes disease results from plants interacting with unfavorable environmental factors, such as air pollution, a deficiency or excess of nutrients or of sunlight, or the wrong climate (too hot, too cold, too dry, too wet). For information on symptoms and treatments of the most common nutrient deficiencies and excesses, see Chlorosis (p. 535) and Soil Salinity (p. 576), respectively. Exposure and climate preferences are spelled out for each plant listed in the Western Plant Encyclopedia. This discussion focuses on the various diseases that are caused by organisms.

Bacterial diseases. Bacteria are single-celled micro-organisms that are unable to manufacture their own food (as green plants do); those bacteria that cause plant diseases must obtain their nutrients from the host plants.

Fungal diseases. Certain multicellular branching, threadlike organisms called fungi obtain their food parasitically from green plants, causing diseases in the process. Many fungi produce great numbers of tiny reproductive bodies called spores, which can be carried by wind or water from leaf to leaf and from plant to plant. Each spore, under the right conditions, will germinate and grow—producing new infections. Fungus diseases are among the most widespread of plant maladies, but many are controllable by good sanitation, use of fungicides, and cultural practices.

Viral diseases. Ultramicroscopic viruses are capable of invading plant tissue and reproducing in it, usually at the expense of the host plant. Viruses may produce such symptoms as abnormalities in growth, color variegation of foliage, or "breaking" (color distortion) of blossoms.

In agriculture—especially among beans, citrus, sugar beets and cane, grapes, cucumbers, squash, potatoes, and tomatoes (to cite just a few)—virus-induced diseases are a serious threat because they affect vigor and productivity. In the home garden, a viral infection may or may not be detrimental. Undesirable viruses are those that cause an unattractive mottling on leaves or that stunt and yellow foliage; in some diseases, such as rose mosaic, the virus causes a striking foliage variegation but does not significantly reduce plant vigor. Some attractive plants—such as the various tulips that have bizarrely striped flowers and the variegated-leaf abutilon—owe their variegation to a virus.

There is no home cure at this time for a virus-infected plant, but you can reduce chances of a virus spreading to other plants in two ways. First, remove from your garden any plants that are severely stunted or mottled. Second, try to

---

DISEASE CONTROL

The first line of defense against plant diseases is prevention. Whenever possible, choose disease-resistant plants; make sure that planting locations and conditions don't encourage disease-producing organisms that are troublesome in your region.

Numerous packaged products are available for control of diseases. They can be categorized as preventatives (products that prevent diseases from occurring but are ineffective in controlling them once they are established), eradicants (materials that help control diseases—many simply protect new growth—once they are established), and systemics (materials that move inside the plant and act as preventatives, eradicants, or both). The controls described here are the ones most useful and commonly available. Several other products—generally less widely sold—are mentioned in the entries for the specific diseases they control.

The product descriptions that follow mention the common diseases each product controls, but these are usually just a few of the diseases listed on the product labels. (You may find a disease listed on a product label but not mentioned in these descriptions; that is because other products described for that disease usually are more effective.) You should also know that fungicide registrations change rapidly. Some products listed here may no longer be available or be labeled for the disease or plant mentioned. Check labels carefully.

Some products will control a disease on one plant but not on another; moreover, some products can do damage if applied to inappropriate plants. Read product labels carefully to be sure your plant is listed.

- **Benomyl (Benlate):** Systemic, wettable powder effective against many plant diseases. Future registration limitations are possible.

- **Captan:** Dust or wettable powder for prevention or eradication of damping off, leaf spots, and many other fungal diseases. Future registration limitations are possible.

- **Chlorothalonil (Daconil):** Multipurpose liquid fungicide for prevention of diseases on lawns, fruits, vegetables, and ornamentals.

- **Copper compounds:** A group of general-purpose fungicides and bactericides, most often used to prevent fireblight, peach leaf curl, and shot hole diseases.

- **Lime sulfur (calcium polysulfide):** Liquid preventative for various leaf spots, peach leaf curl, and powdery mildew. Often used as a dormant spray. Also controls some mites, scale insects, and thrips.

- **Sulfur:** Dust or wettable powder; one of the oldest fungicides. Used to prevent powdery mildew, scab, and rust.

- **Triadimefon (Bayleton):** Wettable powder; systemic for prevention or eradication of powdery mildew, rust, and some lawn diseases; also effective against azalea petal blight.

- **Triforine (Funginex):** Liquid systemic for prevention and eradication of powdery mildew, rust, black spot, and a variety of other diseases. You must wear goggles and a face mask when using it.

Controls are listed alphabetically by generic name (name on the product label under "active ingredients") or common name; trade name (where different from generic name) appears in parentheses.

DIVIDING

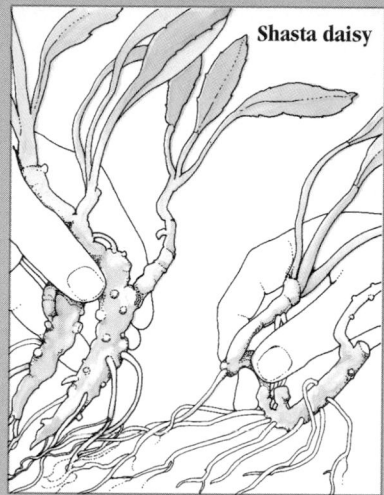

Shasta daisy

Iris

Daylily

Dividing is an easy way to increase stock of many perennials and bulblike plants. Pull apart individual plants of clump-forming perennials (such as daylilies and Shasta daisies); break or cut apart separate plants of rhizomes (such as iris), some bulbs, and tuberous-rooted plants.

control the insects that carry viruses. Aphids are most efficient in spreading different kinds of viruses; leafhoppers and thrips can be vectors, too. And humans may spread viruses by vegetatively propagating virus-infected plants or by handling tobacco while working around plants (thereby spreading tobacco mosaic virus, which affects many plants in addition to tobacco).

Divided Leaf

A leaf is said to be divided when it is separated into sections entirely or nearly to its stalk. In the first case, the sections are called leaflets; in the second, they are called lobes.

Dividing

The easiest way to propagate perennials, bulbs, and shrubs that form clumps of stems with rooted bases is by dividing. In fact, to keep these plants healthy and strong, it's necessary to divide them periodically. Each rooted segment or division is actually a plant in itself or is capable of becoming a new plant.

Division generally is done in autumn or early spring, when plants are dormant. In most climate zones, fall is the best time to divide perennials that bloom in spring or early summer, whereas early spring is better for those that blossom in late summer and autumn. But in the coldest zones, the spring-blooming perennials must be divided in early fall so that their roots will have a chance to grow before the coldest weather sets in.

To divide deciduous and semideciduous perennials, prune the foliage back to about 4 inches from the ground. With evergreen perennials, leave all young, healthy foliage, but remove all dead leaves. (See illustration, left.) Perennials that form a taproot and grow from a compact crown are best propagated by making stem cuttings (see Cuttings, p. 538) or by sowing seeds.

When decline in flower quantity and quality signals overcrowding of bulbs and bulblike plants (p. 532), let foliage ripen thoroughly before digging and separating the bulbs. Replant in well-prepared soil or store until the appropriate planting time.

Dormancy

The annual period when a plant's growth processes greatly slow down, dormancy occurs in many plants with the coming of winter, as days grow shorter and temperatures, colder.

Dormant Spray

An insecticide or a fungicide applied to a plant during the season it is not putting on new growth is a dormant spray. Usually including, or composed only of, a dormant oil, a dormant spray is a very effective way to kill overwintering insects and disease and reduce the necessity for multiple sprays during the growing season. Dor-

mant sprays are often used on fruit trees; see the illustration below for instructions.

SPRAYING DORMANT TREES

If diseases and insects have troubled your fruit or shade trees in the past, spray them while leafless (dormant). Use horticultural oil mixed with either lime sulfur or fixed copper. For complete coverage, spray branches (A), crotches (B), trunk (C), and ground within drip line (D).

Double Digging

A soil preparation approach, double digging helps to amend soil on the upper level and to break up soil on the lower level to allow roots to grow deeper. The classic procedure:

- Dig a trench one spade deep; set soil aside alongside trench.

- Dig down one spade's depth further in the same trench, mixing amendments with soil in lower level.

- Dig second trench by first; mix in amendments. Move amended soil to first trench.

- In second trench, dig one spade's depth more; mix in amendments.

- Continue to dig trenches in the same way. ▶

SIMPLIFIED DOUBLE DIGGING

Remove spade's depth of soil; put it around sides. Spade soil amendments into next layer. Mix same kind of amendments into excavated soil as you replace it. Soil will be high at first.

Another, simpler method of double digging is shown in the illustration.

Double Flower

A double flower has an indefinite (usually large) number of petals that give the blossom an unusually full appearance. Many fruit trees with double flowers, including varieties of pomegranate, plum, and cherry, do not produce fruit. They are commonly grown as ornamentals.

Drainage

Drainage refers to the movement of water through the soil in a plant's root area. When this happens quickly, the drainage is "good" or "fast," and the soil is "well drained"; when it happens slowly, the drainage is said to be "slow" or "bad," and the soil is "poorly drained." For plants to grow, water must pass through the soil. Plant roots need oxygen as well as water, and soil that remains saturated deprives roots of necessary oxygen. Fast drainage (water disappears from a planting hole in 10 minutes or less) is typical of sandy soils; slow drainage (water still remains in planting hole after several hours) is found in clay soils and where hardpan exists. Refer to Soils (p. 576) for more information on soil types and drainage.

Drip Line

The circle that could be drawn on the soil around a tree directly under the tips of its outermost branches is called a drip line. Rainwater tends to drip from the tree at this point. The term is used in connection with feeding, watering, and grading around existing trees and shrubs.

Drought

Technically, a drought is a period of time during which a region gets less than what is considered normal precipitation. The word has been, and probably always will be, more appropriate in the East and Midwest than in the far West.

In the Midwest and East, historically, every dry period has ended with the return of adequate rainfall. Such a period, with a beginning and an end, is a drought. But in the permanently arid West, the land is forever in a state of inadequate precipitation for local needs, so the midwestern and eastern sense of the word "drought" as a temporary, abnormal condition is inappropriate in the West.

In heavily populated regions of the arid West, water is imported, usually over considerable distances, by pipelines and canals from reservoirs fed by rivers that are, themselves, fed by mountain streams. These populated areas depend on distant wintertime snowfall and rainfall for their supply of water. In years when precipitation is lower than normal and those reservoirs cannot provide adequate amounts of water, gardeners in irrigated arid areas must turn to a wide variety of water conservation approaches (p. 583). And as the West's population continues to grow, placing greater demands on limited water supplies, water conservation will become an everyday fact of life.

Drought Resistant, Drought Tolerant

Plants that can withstand long periods with little or no water, plants that have relatively low water requirements, or plants that are well adapted to the arid West are often described as drought resistant or drought tolerant. However, because water requirements vary greatly from plant to plant and from region to region (a plant that needs little water under cool coastal conditions may need a lot more in warmer inland areas), the phrases are often ambiguous and usually inappropriate. Soil conditions, exposure, degree of establishment, length of time without water, and other factors also affect a plant's water needs, its appearance, and its survival.

Dust

Dust defines a type of insecticide or fungicide—one so finely ground that it is dust—as well as its method of application. Applied in early morning when the air is still, the dust makes a large cloud, and the particles slowly settle as a thin, even coating over everything. The advantage of dusting over spraying is convenience: no mixing, fast application, and easy cleanup.

Dutch Elm Disease

A devastating disease for decades confined to the East and Midwest, Dutch elm disease (abbreviated DED) spread slowly across the United States to reach the West in the early 1970s.

DED is spread primarily by the elm bark beetle, although it can also spread from infected trees to nearby healthy ones by natural root grafting. Normal transmission starts with beetle larvae that overwinter in dead and dying elm trees. When the young beetles emerge in spring, the sticky fungus spores adhere to their bodies; as the beetles migrate to healthy new elm growth to feed, they spread the fungus. The fungus spores begin to grow in feeding wounds, and the fungus moves through the water-conducting system of the tree. The first symptom of infection is usually wilted foliage (because water conductivity is interrupted); then leaves turn yellow and fall, and the tree dies.

DED is incurable at present, but sometimes its progress can be slowed. Removal of trees showing infection may help save other trees. (Do not save wood from infected trees.) If you have an elm you suspect has DED, call your county agricultural agent and report the symptoms. The agent should then advise you on the best course of action to take.

Earwigs

Gardeners in all the western climates except the desert have problems with earwigs. In the San Francisco Bay area and along the Northern California coast, they are often second only to snails and slugs in damaging gardens.

Earwigs will eat almost any soft materials. One common food is insects—such as aphids—which means that earwigs can be an important natural control of plant pests. Unfortunately, earwigs also feed on soft parts of plants, such as flower petals and corn silks. A large earwig population can significantly damage desirable plants.

Earwigs hide during the day but are active at night. When dawn comes, they scurry back into tight, cozy places. You can trap earwigs by providing the type of tight-fitting, moist shelter in which they like to spend the day. At night, put moistened rolled-up newspapers, rolls of corrugated cardboard, or short sections of garden hose on the ground; in the morning, dispose of the accumulated insects. You can also trap earwigs in a short cat food or tuna fish can filled with ½ inch of vegetable oil. Place several cans around the yard. Dispose of them as they fill.

Or you can buy earwig bait, which usually contains propoxur or carbaryl as the killing ingredient, and spread it around nonedible plants. If the lure in the bait is fish oil, however, it can also attract pets, which may be harmed by the active ingredient.

Epiphyte

Epiphytes grow on another plant for support but receive no nourishment from the host plant. Familiar examples of these plants are cattleya orchids and staghorn ferns. Epiphytes are often mistakenly called parasites; true parasites steal nourishment from the host.

Erosion Control

Many types of plants (see p. 93 for a list), certain landscape fabrics, and heavy mulches like straw can be used alone or in combination to prevent the erosion of soil by heavy rains or fast moving water. When dealing with steep construction cuts or burned hillsides, it's best to get expert help. Your local cooperative extension office can offer advice or recommend a soil engineer.

Espalier

A tree or shrub trained so that its branches grow in a flat pattern—against a wall or fence, on a trellis, along horizontal wires—an espalier may be formal and geometric or informal. The illustration below shows several espalier forms. For plants that espalier well, see page 78.

Established

A plant that is firmly rooted and producing a good growth of leaves is said to be established. Remember that an established plant needs time to re-establish itself after you transplant it.

Evapotranspiration

Abbreviated ET, evapotranspiration is the amount of water that transpires through a plant's leaves combined with the amount that evaporates from the soil in which the plant is growing. Measured in inches, ET can be used as a guideline for how much water a specific type of plant needs per day, per week, or per year. See its application for Lawns (p. 551).

Evergreen

An evergreen plant never loses all its leaves at one time. See also Broad-Leafed (p. 531) and Conifer (p. 536).

Eye

An undeveloped growth bud, an eye will ultimately produce a new plant or new growth. The eyes on a potato will, when planted, produce new potato plants. "Eye" is synonymous with one definition of Bud (p. 532).

Family. See Plant Classification   p. 561

Female Plant

A plant that produces fruit or seed but does not produce pollen is called a female plant.

Fertilize

In popular usage, fertilize has two definitions. To fertilize a flower is to apply pollen (the male element) to the flower's pistil (the female element) for the purpose of setting seed. (See Pollination, p. 570.) To fertilize a plant is to apply nutrients (plant food, usually referred to as fertilizer).

For fertilizer recommendations for specific plant types, see the appropriate entry in the Western Plant Encyclopedia.

Fertilizers

A visit to a nursery may reveal a bewildering selection of fertilizers for a variety of specified uses and with differing formulas. There are granular types packaged in cartons and sacks and liquid ones in bottles. An understanding of the basic fertilizer types will clear the confusion and help you select a product that meets your plants' needs.

The first distinction to draw is between dry and liquid forms. There are further differences between complete, simple, special-purpose, and organic fertilizers and between controlled-release, tablet, and combination products. The illustrations on pages 544 and 545 show several application methods.

Dry fertilizers. The majority of fertilizers sold are dry. You sprinkle or spread them onto a lawn; sprinkle them onto the soil around plants and scratch, rake, or dig them in; or apply them in subsurface strips. Dissolving when they contact water, the dry granules begin their fertilizing action quickly. But, depending on the fertilizer, they can last for several months.

Liquid fertilizers. Although the most widely sold fertilizers are the solid types, liquid fertilizers have certain attributes that recommend their use:

■ They are easy to use, especially on container plants.   ▶

POPULAR ESPALIER PATTERNS

Espalier training can take a number of different forms, as shown.

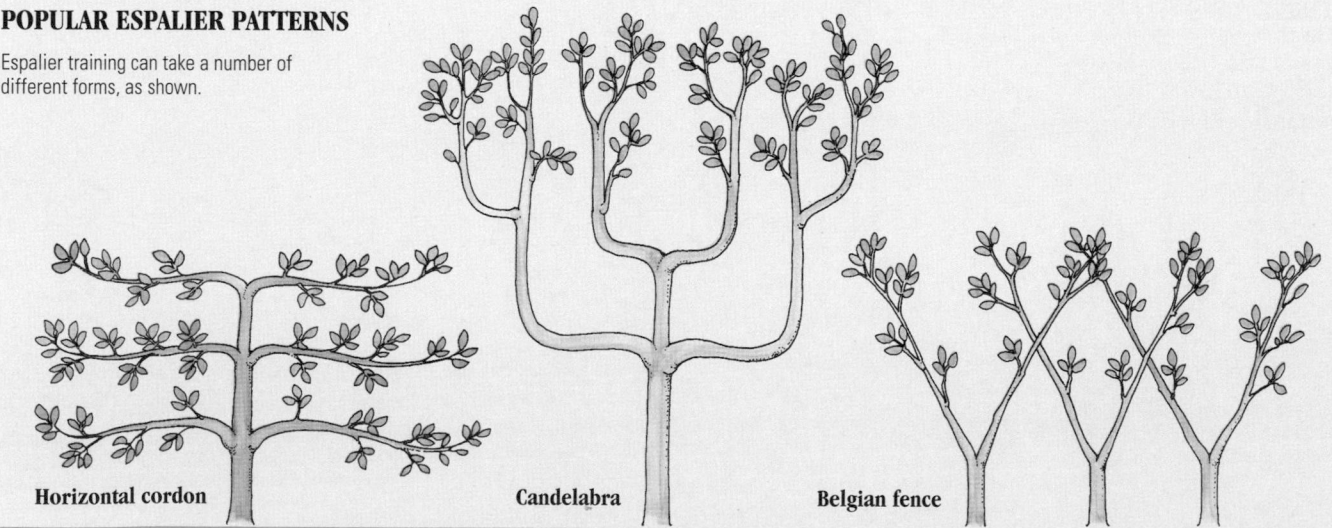

Horizontal cordon   Candelabra   Belgian fence

THREE WAYS TO FERTILIZE TREES

Surface feeding. In sandy soil or wet climates, broadcast granular fertilizer on the surface, by hand or using a spreader. Soak it in thoroughly with a sprinkler.

Root plug. With a soil-sampling tube or pipe, make 6- to 12-inch-deep holes 2 to 3 feet apart. Pour granular fertilizer into holes, fill with soil, and water well.

Root feeder. Insert a root feeder with a fertilizer tablet attached 6 to 12 inches deep every 4 to 6 feet; turn feeder on for about 5 minutes in each hole.

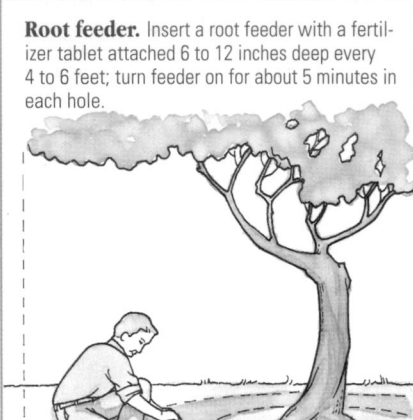

■ There is no risk of burning a plant as long as you follow label directions for dilution.

■ The nutrients are available to the roots immediately.

Liquids are less practical than solids for large-scale use because they cost more and must be reapplied more often (their nutrients in solution leach through the root zone more rapidly).

Available in a variety of different formulations, liquid fertilizers include complete formulas and special types that offer just one or two of the major nutrients. All are made to be diluted with water: some are concentrated liquids; others are powder or pellets. Some liquid fertilizers are sold in ready-to-use, hose-end sprayers. Formulations for lawns may include herbicides for weed control.

Growers of container plants often use liquid fertilizers at half the strength and twice the frequency recommended so that plants receive a steadier supply of nutrients.

Foliar fertilizers. Some nutrients, particularly nitrogen in urea form and micronutrients (see Nutrients, Basic, p. 556), can be absorbed quickly through plant leaves. Many liquid or water-soluble fertilizers include rates for foliar feeding on their labels. In general, actively growing plants show the best response. But remember, foliar feeding is a quick fix and not a substitute for soil feeding. To avoid burning plant leaves, first make sure plants are well watered; don't apply foliar fertilizers if temperatures will rise above 85°F.

Complete fertilizers. Any fertilizer that contains all three of the primary nutrient elements—nitrogen (N), phosphorus (P), and potassium (K)—is called a complete fertilizer. Many fertilizer manufacturers put their product's N, P, and K percentages on the label, right under the product name, in big numbers—for example, 10-8-6. Without looking at the fine print under Guaranteed Analysis (always listed somewhere on a fertilizer label), you know that the fertilizer contains 10 percent total nitrogen, 8 percent phosphate (P_2O_5), and 6 percent potash (K_2O). See illustration on page 545.

There are fertilizers with many different nutrient ratios on the market. Even when the percentages are the same on two different products, the formula by which one manufacturer arrives at its ratio can differ from others. (See Nutrients, Basic, p. 556.) The higher the numbers in the analysis, the stronger or more concentrated the fertilizer is (a 22-6-4 formula contains twice as much nitrogen as does an 11-6-4 fertilizer). And the higher the concentration (of N especially), the less you apply at one time.

Complete fertilizers are most useful when you work them into the soil where active roots can take up the phosphorus and potassium. If you want only the benefits of nitrogen, choose a nitrogen-only simple fertilizer.

Simple fertilizers. Simple fertilizers contain just one of the three major nutrients. Most familiar are the nitrogen-only types, such as ammonium sulfate (21-0-0), but you can find phosphorus-only and potassium-only fertilizers

THREE WAYS TO FERTILIZE VEGETABLE TRANSPLANTS

Work dry fertilizer into soil with spading fork before planting.

Side-dress with narrow bands of dry fertilizer 5 to 6 inches from plants.

Liquid-feed in watering basins. (This is the most precise way to apply.)

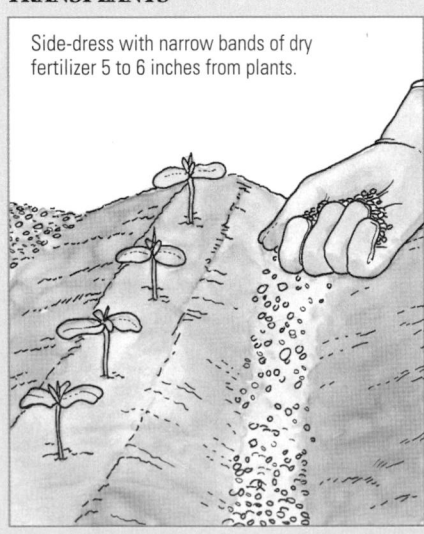

as well. Falling between the two extremes are "incomplete" types that contain two of the three major elements: N and P, N and K, or P and K.

Special-purpose fertilizers. Some packaged fertilizers are formulated for specific types of plants—"camellia food," "rhododendron and azalea food," and "rose food," for example. The camellia and rhododendron-azalea fertilizers belong to an old, established group, the acid fertilizers. The other fertilizers packaged for certain plants do not have as solid a background of research (compare, for example, the NPK ratios of three different brands of "tomato food").

All chemical fertilizers except calcium nitrate reduce the pH of soil by producing acids as they decompose. Those that are especially acid producing are labeled "acid fertilizers" and are useful on acid-loving plants. They also are good for general-purpose fertilizing in alkaline-soil regions, to reduce alkalinity.

Organic fertilizers. The word "organic" simply means that the nutrients contained in the product are derived solely from the remains, part of the remains, or a by-product of a once-living organism. Cottonseed meal, blood meal, bonemeal, hoof-and-horn meal, and manures are examples of organic fertilizers. (Urea is a synthetic organic fertilizer—an organic-like substance manufactured from inorganic materials.) Most of these products packaged as fertilizers will have their NPK ratios stated on the package labels. Usually, an organic fertilizer is high in just one of the three major nutrients and low in the other two, although some are chemically fortified with the other nutrients. In general, the organics release their nutrients over a fairly long period. The potential drawback is that they may not release enough of their principal nutrient at a time to give the plant what it needs for best growth. Because they depend on soil organisms to release the nutrients, most organic fertilizers are effective only when the soil is moist and warm enough for the soil organisms to be active.

Although manure is a complete organic fertil-

izer, it is low in N, P, and K. Nutrient content varies according to the animal species and its diet, but an NPK ratio of 1-1-1 is typical. Manures are best used as mulches or as soil conditioners, but only after they have been aged or composted. Many fresh manures have a high salt content, which will burn plants.

Controlled-release fertilizers. The beadlike granules of controlled-release fertilizers are balls of complete fertilizer coated with resin, sulfur, or another permeable substance. When the granules are moistened, as in normal watering, some of the fertilizer diffuses through its coating into the surrounding soil—a little bit with each watering—until the encapsulated fertilizer is used up. Some products are effective for 3 to 4 months; others, for 8 or more months. Scratch or dig the pellets into the soil so that they are covered. These are particularly useful

for fertilizing container plants, which need frequent nutrient replenishment due to leaching from frequent watering.

Sticks, stakes, and tablets. Some fertilizers are compressed into hard cylinders or tablets; you push or hammer the sticks or stakes into the soil or drop the tablets into holes. Dissolving slowly in the presence of water, they yield nutrients gradually, sometimes for a year or more. These products are convenient for getting phosphorus and potassium to the regions of active root growth of established shrubs and trees.

Combination products. You can buy fertilizers combined with insecticides (chiefly for roses) or with weed killers, fungicides, or moss killers (all for lawns). These products are appropriate if you need the extra ingredient every time you fertilize; if not, it is more economical to buy it separately. Herbicides included in some combination products can damage plants whose roots are growing into areas where the product is applied. Read labels carefully.

Fire, Landscaping for

Wildfires are common in many parts of the arid West, especially in foothill and mountainous areas. Unfortunately, many of these areas are heavily populated, and wildfires frequently result in loss of life and property. Although *everything* burns in a high-intensity fire, you can reduce the chances of fire destroying your home. Experts recommend the following:

- **Maintain a clear space around your home.** Ideally, the first 30 feet from your house should be clear of vegetation, but this is often not possible. If planted, it should be with plants that are not highly flammable (most are low-growing ground covers) and watered regularly to maintain a high moisture content. From 30 to 70 feet, plant low-fuel-volume herbaceous perennials, such as gazania, poppy, and common yarrow. Keep watered and green all year, or let dry out and cut back. The next 30 feet should be free of highly combustible plants and kept pruned to reduce the buildup of dead wood.

- **Trim trees and shrubs near your house.** Trim tree limbs to 20 feet or more above the ground. Cut branches back to 15 to 20 feet from the house. Thin crowns of clustered trees, keeping trees 10 feet apart. Along the driveway, clear overhanging tree branches and prune bushy shrubs for fire-truck access.

- **Reduce fuel load.** Prune out all dead branches and remove dead plants. Cut grasses to about 4 inches after they turn brown. Cut back woody native chaparral yearly. Clear leaf litter from ground, rooftops, and gutters.

- **Select and position plants wisely.** Plants should be chosen not only for their low growth habit, low fuel volume, and high moisture content, but also for their aridity

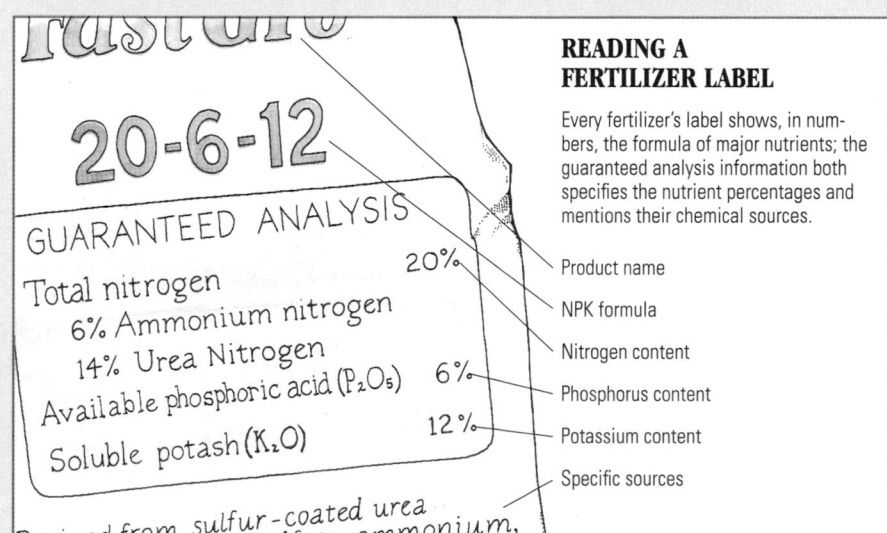

READING A FERTILIZER LABEL

Every fertilizer's label shows, in numbers, the formula of major nutrients; the guaranteed analysis information both specifies the nutrient percentages and mentions their chemical sources.

- Product name
- NPK formula
- Nitrogen content
- Phosphorus content
- Potassium content
- Specific sources

20-6-12

GUARANTEED ANALYSIS

Total nitrogen 20%
  6% Ammonium nitrogen
  14% Urea Nitrogen
Available phosphoric acid (P_2O_5) ... 6%
Soluble potash (K_2O) ... 12%

Derived from sulfur-coated urea

tolerance, deep-rooting habit, and compatibility with other plants in your garden and your native environment. Your local nursery staff or cooperative extension office can help you select plants. Arrange plants in islands and avoid creating a fire ladder, where flames can easily jump from plant to plant to house.

■ **Use fire-resistant building materials.** Check local codes for appropriate roofing materials. Consider using wood substitutes for fences and decks.

Fireblight

Troublesome in all of the West, fireblight is worst at high elevations and along the eastern slope of the Rocky Mountains. It affects only the plants in the pome tribe of the rose family. When a flowering shoot of an apple, cotoneaster, crabapple, hawthorn, pear, pyracantha, quince, or toyon dies suddenly and looks as though it has been scorched by fire (see photograph, p. 569), fireblight probably is the culprit.

The bacteria that cause fireblight survive in blighted twigs and cankers. During moist weather—especially in early spring, when temperatures are above 60°F—the bacteria are carried to blossoms by splashing water, flies, and other insects. Once in the blossoms, they are spread to other flowers by honeybees. Infection progresses from the blossoms down the shoots into the larger limbs, where dark, sunken cankers form. Infection also can enter a plant through any fresh wound in the foliage.

Controls. Wherever fireblight is a persistent problem, avoid growing susceptible plants, or if you continue to grow them, take regular control measures. To protect blossoms from infection, spray at 4- or 5-day intervals during the flowering season with a fixed copper–based spray (or agricultural streptomycin, if available).

To control the bacteria once it has appeared, prune out and burn the diseased twigs and branches. On a small branch, make the cut 4 to 6 inches below the infection; on larger branches, make cuts at least 12 inches below blighted tissue. Disinfecting pruning shears between cuts is probably of little value.

Flat

A shallow box or tray used to start cuttings or seedlings is called a flat.

Foliar Fertilizer

A foliar fertilizer is one applied in liquid form to a plant's foliage in a fine spray. The nutrients it contains are absorbed through the plant's leaves. See Fertilizers (p. 543).

Forcing

Forcing is the process of hastening a plant along to maturity or a marketable state or of growing a plant to the flowering or fruiting stage out of its normal season. This is usually done by growing it in a greenhouse, where temperature, humidity, and light can be controlled.

Formal

The term "formal" means regular, rigid, and geometric. In gardening, it is variously applied to flowers, methods of training, and styles of garden design. A formal double flower, as in some camellias, consists of layers of regularly overlapping petals. Examples of formal plant training are rigidly and geometrically structured espaliers (p. 543) and evenly clipped hedges. Formal gardens are those laid out in precise geometric patterns.

Frond

In the strictest sense, fronds are the foliage of ferns. Often, however, the word is also applied to the leaves of palms and is even used to designate any foliage that looks fernlike.

Frost

The most common type of frost occurs when low temperatures and humidity combined with clear, still nights cause surfaces (such as leaves or ground) to cool faster than the surrounding air, causing moisture to condense and freeze. Depending on the species of plant, the time of year, and the condition of the plant, a frost may or may not damage it. Because plants are actively growing in early fall and late spring, frosts at these times tend to be most damaging.

Frost Protection

Virtually no place in the West is completely free from the threat of frost. From the dip below freezing that may hit San Diego once or twice in a decade to the occasional Big Freeze that sweeps down on Seattle, these periodic deviations from the norm can wreak havoc on a landscape. Established plants that reach the limit of their cold tolerance in a particular zone's typical winter weather may suffer extensive damage—or they may die. Fortunately, there are ways to prepare for the occasional big chill and avert potential disaster in your garden.

Know your plants. Use trees, screen and hedge plants, and shrubs that are hardy enough for the extremes of your climate zone. Use the chancy or tender plants as fillers, as summertime display plants, in borders, or in areas of secondary interest. Locate these plants in sheltered sites, or grow them in containers and move them to sheltered sites when the weather turns cold.

Know your garden. Learn your garden's microclimates: discover which areas are warm and which are cool. Most dangerous for marginally hardy plants (and all tender vegetation) are stretches of open ground exposed to the air on all sides, particularly to the north. Hollows and low, enclosed areas that catch cold air as it sinks and hold it motionless also are poor choices. For iffy plants, the safest areas are under overhanging eaves (the best protection), lath structures, or branches of evergreen trees. Slopes from which cold air drains freely are safer than hollows and valley or canyon floors.

South-facing walls absorb heat during the day and radiate it at night, warming nearby plants. The warmest location of all is a south-facing wall with an overhang (see illustration). It gives maximum protection against frost, and in cool-summer/mild-winter climates, it supplies the warmth needed to stimulate buds, blossoms, and fruit of heat-loving plants such as bougainvillea, hibiscus, fig, and evergreen magnolia.

Condition plants and soil for frosts. Feed and water while plants are growing fastest, in late spring and early summer. To discourage production of new growth that would not have time to mature before cold weather hits, taper

GARDEN MICROCLIMATES

Garden microclimates are influenced by hills and hollows, points of the compass, and structures. Cold air moves downslope to the lowest point but will collect if flow is impeded by fences, walls, or structures.

Winter sun

Cold air collects

Cold air drains

Coldest spot   N ⟷ S   **Warmest spot**

off nitrogen feeding in late summer. Actively growing plants are more susceptible to cold than are dormant or semidormant plants. Reducing water helps harden growth, but soil around plants should be moist at the onset of the frost season; moist soil holds and releases more heat than dry soil does.

Some hardy plants have early blossoms that are damaged by spring frosts. Try to delay bloom of deciduous magnolias and some early rhododendrons beyond the time of heavy frosts by planting them with a north exposure or in the shade of high-branching deciduous trees.

Be especially watchful for frosts early in fall or in spring after growth is under way. These are much more damaging than frosts that occur while plants are semidormant or dormant. The warning signs are still air (tree branches motionless, smoke going straight up); absence of cloud cover (stars easily visible, very bright); low humidity (windshields and grass dry); and low temperature (45°F or less at 10 P.M.). If you notice these danger signs at bedtime, move any at-risk container plants under a porch roof or eaves or into a garage. Shelter any such plants that are in the ground; use burlap or plastic film—even evergreen boughs will help—secured over frames or stakes so that the covering material does not touch the plant. (Freezing is likely where the material touches foliage.) Remove coverings during the daytime.

After a frost. If plants have been damaged by frost, don't hurry to prune them. Premature trimming may stimulate new, tender growth that will be nipped by later growth. And you may mistake still-alive growth for dead. Wait until new growth begins in spring; then remove only wood that is clearly dead.

Fungicide

Any material applied to plants to control fungus diseases is called a fungicide. See Diseases (p. 540).

Galls

Galls are growths on plant leaves and stems (see photograph, p. 568). Cause is usually abnormal cell growth stimulated by sucking insects like aphids or reactions to infection from fungus, bacteria, or virus. Prune off infested growth.

Genus. See Plant Classification   p. 561

Geranium (Tobacco) Budworm, Corn Earworm

The geranium budworm (properly, the tobacco budworm) is a first-rank garden pest in California and has appeared in damaging numbers in some mountain regions outside California. It is closely related to the corn earworm.

Both are larvae of stout-bodied, dull-colored, night-flying moths.

The typical geranium budworm lives through the winter as a pupa in the soil. Then, in late

GERMINATION OF A SEED

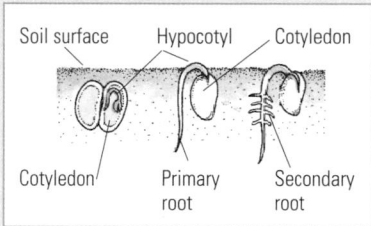

Soil surface — Hypocotyl — Cotyledon

Cotyledon — Primary root — Secondary root

When conditions such as moisture, heat, and light are just right, the seed germinates.

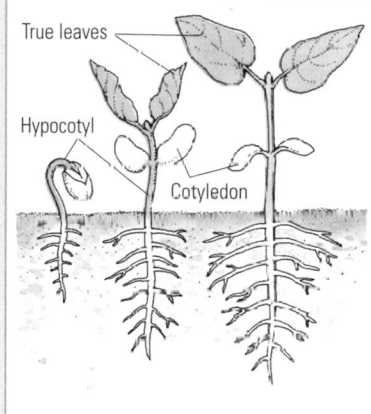

True leaves

Hypocotyl

Cotyledon

Some familiar plants—grasses, corn, orchids, lilies—have only one cotyledon and are called monocots. Plants with two cotyledons are called dicots.

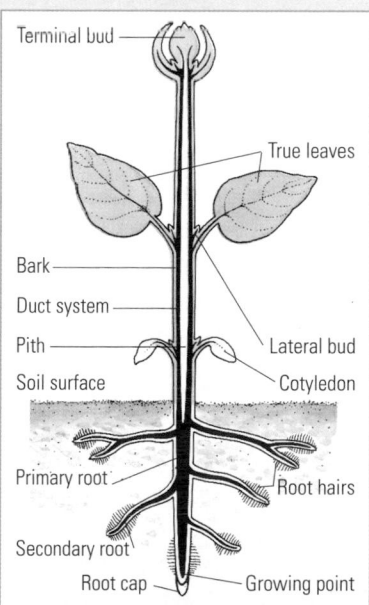

Terminal bud

True leaves

Bark
Duct system
Pith
Soil surface

Lateral bud
Cotyledon

Primary root

Root hairs

Secondary root

Root cap — Growing point

Germinating seed has primary root and cotyledons. Cotyledons sustain plant until true leaves and secondary roots appear.

April or May, a mature gray moth emerges and lays eggs on geranium buds—one egg per bud. From the egg hatches a very small worm, which enters and feeds on the geranium bud (or on a rosebud or petunia bud). As the worm grows, it consumes the bud and moves on to the rest of the plant, taking on the color of the plant tissue it eats. Once you see a hole in a bud, pick the bud, squash it, and discard it; this may destroy the young worm, which already will have damaged the potential blossom. For heavy infestations—where worms have outgrown the protective covering of flower buds—spray with *Bacillus thuringiensis*, pyrethrins, carbaryl, or acephate. Repeat weekly as needed. For ways to control corn earworm, see Corn (p. 241).

Germination

The sprouting of a seed is called germination. The process is explained in the illustration.

Girdling

The choking of a branch by a wire, rope, or other inflexible material, girdling occurs most often in woody plants that have been tightly tied to a stake or support. As the tied limb increases in girth, the tie fails to expand in diameter and cuts off supplies of nutrients and water to the part of the plant above the tie. If girdling goes unnoticed, the part of the plant above the constriction will die. The word "girdling" also applies to an encircling cut made through the bark of a trunk or branch to improve fruiting.

Gopher. See Pocket Gophers   p. 567

Grafting

Although many different grafting methods have been devised, all involve uniting a short length of stem—the scion—with a stock. The stock plant may be either a pencil-slim seedling to be grafted near ground level or an old fruit tree to be grafted at the top of its trunk or on its major limbs. Cleft grafting (see illustration, p. 548) is popular for converting old fruit and nut trees to new varieties.

With any grafting, it is crucial to align scion cambium with stock cambium. When that is done, the two cambiums will unite, the cuts will callus over, and the scion will be ready to grow. Use a very sharp knife to make all cuts; the cleaner the cuts, the better the chance for a successful union. When the operation is completed, cover the union with some sort of sealing agent to keep air from getting to the area.

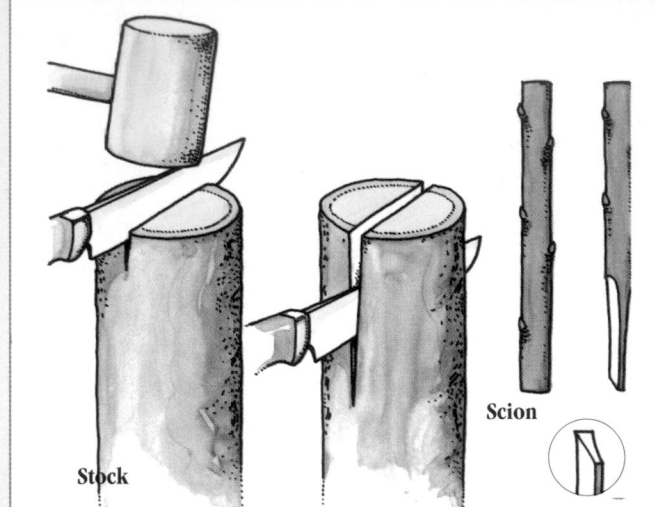

Stock

Scion

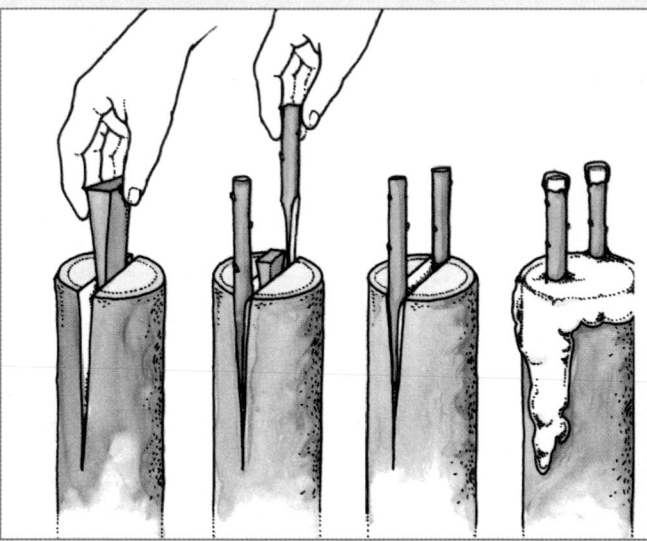

CLEFT GRAFTING

1 Prepare stock by splitting it several inches through a smooth, straight-grained section (so the split will be even). Shape one end of the scion into a long, gradually tapering wedge; outside edge of wedge should be slightly thicker than the inside (as shown in cross-section diagram).

2 Use a wedge to hold open the split in the stock while you work. Insert the scion (or two, as illustrated) into the stock, carefully placed so that cambium layers of stock and scions match. After the scions are properly placed, cover the entire union with grafting wax.

Grasshoppers

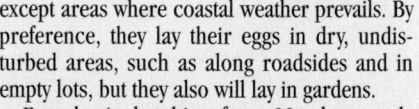

During their periodic outbreaks, grasshoppers own much of the West—except areas where coastal weather prevails. By preference, they lay their eggs in dry, undisturbed areas, such as along roadsides and in empty lots, but they also will lay in gardens.

Eggs begin hatching from March to early June, depending on temperature and climate. Newly hatched nymphs resemble adults but are smaller and lack wings; these nymphs feed voraciously, sometimes stripping entire areas bare. When they mature and develop wings, they fly out and find new feeding areas.

Controls. When you are cultivating in fall, winter, and early spring, watch for and destroy egg clusters, which contain up to 75 cream or yellow rice-shaped eggs. In spring and early summer, while grasshoppers are still young and wingless, they are most vulnerable to chemicals and baits. Use malathion, diazinon, acephate, carbaryl, chlorpyrifos, or bran-and-carbaryl bait. Grass-

hoppers roost at night in hedges, tall weeds, and shrubs. Observe their evening behavior to locate roosting sites, then spray in these areas after dark.

Your best defense against large numbers of grasshoppers may be to protect desirable plants with floating row covers (p. 573) or netting.

In summer, when grasshoppers are mature and less vulnerable to chemicals, handpick them in early morning.

The disease-producing organism *Nosema locustae* causes grasshoppers to produce fewer eggs. Over large areas—on a ranch, for example—applying this commercially packaged material can help reduce grasshopper problems in later years.

Greenhouses

The ultimate in climate modification is a greenhouse. In such a structure, of glass or plastic, you can control temperature, humidity, and day length. Greenhouses are useful for

■ Wintering plants that are too tender for the normal outdoor winter low temperatures

■ Starting seeds of annuals and vegetables early so that plants can be set out in the garden as soon as weather permits

■ Starting cuttings and seeds that require the growth stimuli a greenhouse can provide

■ Raising vegetables and flowers out of season (particularly when outside conditions are too cold), or maturing them earlier than would be normal if they were planted outdoors

■ Growing specialty plants (orchids and tropical plants, for example) that cannot be grown outdoors because temperature or humidity or both are unfavorable

A greenhouse may be a simple lean-to constructed of plastic, a small bay window attachment on a house window, or a more elaborate separate structure with precise controls for regulation of heat, humidity, ventilation, and water.

Ground Bark

The bark of trees, ground up or shredded for use as a mulch or soil amendment, is known as ground bark. It may have other names in some areas.

Ground Covers

Gardeners select ground covers to blanket a prescribed area of soil and create a uniform appearance. The area may be just a 4- by 4-foot patch beneath a tree or it may run to an acre or more. The best-known ground cover is, of course, grass; you'll find information on choosing lawn grasses beginning on page 551. Other ground covers include perennials, shrubs, and vines—particular types that produce a relatively even surface (which may be as low as turf or as tall as 3 feet). Some matlike plants can be walked upon, although none will take the amount of foot traffic a lawn will tolerate.

Choosing a ground cover. Is the ground you want to cover level or sloping, sunny or shady, small or large in extent? Do you want a cover that will act as a barrier, or do you want to be able to walk across it? Will the ground cover have the space all to itself, or will it flow around shrubs, landscape boulders, or trees? And what about appearance: Do you prefer foliage only or green punctuated by colorful flowers or fruits? Answers to these questions will help you select the ground cover you need. Consider also the relationships that will exist between the ground cover and the adjacent landscape; take into account foliage textures and colors, as discussed in Selecting Shrubs (p. 575). Use the lists beginning on page 115 as a guide to more than 100 of the West's most popular ground-cover plants.

General guidelines for planting and care of ground covers depend on whether the plants are perennials, shrubs, or vines. Each group has special requirements.

G

Planting and care of perennials. Many perennial ground-cover plants root as they spread, in time forming dense, interlacing carpets; examples are *Vinca minor* and *Arctotheca calendula*. Others spread much more slowly as they increase from clumps (*Liriope, Convallaria majalis*). Still another sort behaves more as a nonwoody shrub does, sending spreading branches out from the plant's base (*Nepeta faassenii, Iberis sempervirens*).

For all perennial ground covers, prepare the soil as recommended for sowing seeds (p. 563). Perennials that root as they spread may be sold in flats of rooted cuttings or in packs of small plants; those that spread from clumps generally appear in individual small pots or in 1-gallon containers. Spacing depends on the spread of the mature plant (see Western Plant Encyclopedia). Mulch plantings to conserve moisture, suppress weeds, and present a neat appearance while young plants develop. As plantings mature, some may need periodic shearing or light cutting back for neatness.

Planting and care of shrubs. Among the low-growing shrubs used for ground covers, you'll find three types: those that send out horizontal branches from a central point; those that begin at a central point but root from branches as they spread; and those—typified by *Hypericum calycinum*—that increase their territory by underground runners. Plants are sold in 1-gallon cans, small pots, or flats of rooted cuttings. Spacing depends on the ultimate spread of the plant (see Western Plant Encyclopedia). It typically ranges from 6 to 12 inches to more than 3 feet. If you plant rooted cuttings or plants from small pots, prepare the soil as directed for

sowing seeds (p. 563); for 1-gallon container plants, follow the instructions for Plants in Containers (p. 565) under Planting Techniques: Trees and Shrubs. Apply mulch. As plantings mature, you may have to head back branches that grow above the desired foliage surface or that spread too far; you may also need to restrict the spread of those that increase by underground runners.

Planting and care of vines. Among vines used as ground covers are some that spread by rooting branches, such as ivy and euonymus, but most spread far and wide by extending their branches from a central point. Those vines that root as they spread may be sold in flats as rooted cuttings; most vines, however, are available in 1-gallon (or larger) containers. Planting and mulching directions are the same as for shrubs (above). As plants grow, you may need to do some untangling, thinning, or directing of growth to achieve even coverage. Mature plants may call for periodic heading back or shearing to maintain evenness and limit spread.

Ground Squirrels

Throughout the West, ground squirrels are especially troublesome in gardens that border fields or wild land. The California ground squirrel is the most common kind in California, western Oregon, and southwestern Washington (see illustration). It lives in

burrows, usually 2½ to 4 feet underground, where it stores food, raises young, and hides from its chief predators: foxes, hawks, and owls.

During spring and summer, the ground squirrel scurries around most actively in mid-morning or late afternoon (except in very hot weather), nibbling through tomato patches, digging up bulbs, gnawing roots and bark, and climbing trees after fruits and nuts.

Controls. Methods of control include using a baited (with a walnut, almond, or slice of orange tied to the trigger) box-type gopher trap placed outside the burrow. Anticoagulant types of poison bait are more effective with less effort. Baits should be placed in one or more bait stations near the squirrel burrows and must be available to the squirrel for at least a week to achieve maximum control. Before you try any of these approaches, check with your county agent or farm advisor: laws in some areas prohibit catching certain kinds of ground squirrels.

Metal guards around tree trunks can keep ground squirrels out of trees. Protect bulb beds with a cover of fine-mesh chicken wire.

Growing Season

Specifically, the number of days between the average date of the last killing frost in spring and the average date of the first killing frost in fall is called the growing season. Used in general terms, the phrase also describes the period of time a plant is actively growing and not dormant.

Gypsum. See Soil Amendments, Inorganic
p. 575

PLANTING AND CARE OF GROUND COVERS ON SLOPES

Sloping land frequently is prime territory for ground-cover planting: it is too steep to mow or to cultivate easily, and it is prone to erosion in the rainy season. The list on page 93 recommends ground-cover plants that are well adapted to life on an incline and can control soil erosion.

Planting technique. On a gentle slope, follow general Planting Techniques for the plant type, starting on page 563. On more steeply sloping land, however, the simplest method is to create a terrace for each plant, as shown in the illustration. These terraces create individual watering basins, but the high planting keeps the crowns of the plants from becoming saturated during waterings or buried if soil gradually washes downslope into the basin.

Care and training. Applying water is the most important aspect of care, at least when plants are young and becoming established. For sloping land, a drip irrigation setup (p. 586) provides the most thorough watering of each plant while minimizing or eliminating problems with water runoff or soil erosion that can result from watering with sprinklers.

After the ground cover is planted and watered in and a drip system is in place, mulch the entire area.

If you have planted vining plants to cover a bare slope, you may need to periodically untangle the growing stems and, more important at first, train some stems to grow upslope to achieve faster cover. To pin stems in place, use short lengths of wire bent into a U like a croquet wicket.

PLANTING ON A SLOPE

On a steep slope, set out plants on individual terraces with crowns high and watering basins behind the plants.

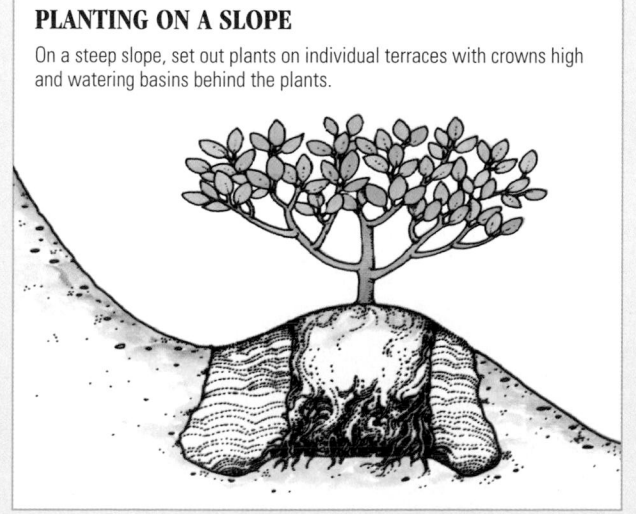

Harden Off

Hardening off is the process of adapting a plant that has been grown in a greenhouse, indoors, or under protective shelter to full outdoor exposure. Over a week or more, the plant is exposed to increasing intervals of time outdoors, so that when it is planted in the garden it can make the transition with a minimum of shock. "Hardened off" also refers to a plant's ability to withstand cold. See Frost Protection (p. 546).

Hardpan

A tight, impervious layer of soil, hardpan can cause trouble if it lies at or near the surface. Such a layer can be a natural formation—in the Southwest, the commonest natural hardpan layer is called caliche—or it can be created, such as when builders spread excavated subsoil over the surface and then drive heavy equipment over it. If the subsoil has a clay content and is damp while construction is going on, it can dry to a bricklike hardness. A thin layer of topsoil may conceal hardpan, but roots cannot penetrate the hard layer and water cannot drain through it. Planting holes may become water tanks: plants will fail to grow, be stunted, or die.

Planting in hardpan. If the hardpan layer is thin, you may be able to improve the soil by having it plowed to a depth of 12 inches or more. If plowing is impractical, you can drill through it with a soil auger when planting. See illustration. If the layer is too thick, a landscape architect can help you with a drainage system, which might involve sumps and drain tiles. To improve the soil over large planting areas, dig up the area to a depth of 18 inches or so with heavy equipment, then add organic matter and thoroughly mix it in. As a beneficial extra step, you can then grow a crop of some heavy-rooting grass, and after it grows, rotary-till it into the soil as additional organic material.

If drainage problems prove especially difficult or costly to surmount, consider installing raised beds for most of your garden plantings. Fill them with good, well-aerated soil, and make them deep enough to allow for root growth.

PLANTING OVER HARDPAN

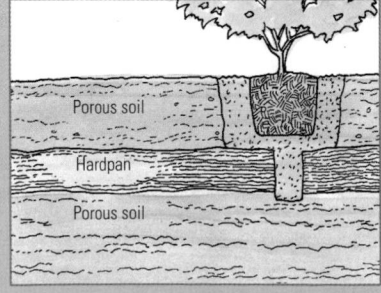

For thin hardpan under shallow soil, dig down from planting hole to hardpan. Drill or chip to porous soil below. Backfill with porous soil.

Hardy

A plant's hardiness is its resistance to, or tolerance of, frost or freezing temperatures (as in "hardy to −20°F"). The word does not mean tough, pest resistant, or disease resistant. A half-hardy plant is hardy in a given situation in normal years but may freeze in coldest winters.

Heading Back

Cutting a 1-year-old shoot back to a bud or cutting an older branch or stem back to a stub or tiny twig is called heading back. See Pruning (p. 570).

Heavy Soil

A rather imprecise term, "heavy soil" refers to dense soil made up of extremely fine particles packed closely together. The term is used interchangeably with "clay" and "adobe." See Soils (p. 576).

Heeling In

Heeling in is a means of preventing roots of bare-root plants from drying out before you can set the plants out in the garden. The simplest approach is to dig a shallow trench, lay the plant on its side so that its roots are in the trench, and then cover the roots with soil, sawdust, or another material, moistened to keep the roots damp.

Herb

The general term "herb" describes a variety of plants valued for their flavor, fragrance, or medicinal purposes.

Herbaceous

Herbaceous, the opposite of woody, describes a plant with soft (nonwoody) tissues. In the strictest sense, it refers to plants that die to the ground each year and regrow stems the following growing season. In the broadest sense, it refers to any nonwoody plant—annual, perennial, or bulb.

Herbicide

A herbicide is a chemical used to destroy undesirable plants. See Weed Control (p. 589).

Honeydew

Aphids, scales, and whiteflies, as well as several other sucking insects, secrete a sticky substance called honeydew; certain ants and fungi feed on honeydew, adding to the mess. Often honeydew from a tree will drip onto whatever is below: car, patio, or other plants. See entries for individual pests for control measures.

Horticultural Oil

A horticultural oil is a refined oil sprayed on plants to control insects. See Pest Management (p. 559).

House Plants

Plants that you keep indoors need careful attention to soil preparation, watering, and fertilizer application. The basics are outlined under Container Gardening (p. 536). Additional information appears below.

Soil. Container soil for house plants should be composed entirely of sterile materials—such as a prepared potting soil mix or a soil-less mix you make yourself. Potentially harmful organisms in garden soils pose a great threat to plant health when confined with roots in a limited soil mass and in the warmth and low light levels of a home.

Water. The best water for house plants is rainwater, but most people rely instead on water from the tap—which is usually satisfactory unless it contains quantities of harmful salts or is artificially softened with sodium. If you have a water softener, draw water for your house plants from an outside tap. If you must use softened water (or water that is high in alkaline salts), leach house plants completely about once a month. Thoroughly flush water through the soil several times, or set each plant in a sink or tub and let a trickle of water run through it for a while.

Light. Give house plants good light, but avoid the searing sun that comes through south and west windows. Unless you set plants back from such windows or moderate the sunlight with thin curtains, stick to a northern or eastern exposure. Plants grown for their flower display generally need more light than plants grown for foliage alone.

Humidity. Low humidity is the bane of most house plants, and low humidity goes hand in hand with heated rooms. Best places for plants are the cooler (but adequately lit) spots around the house; the higher humidity in bathrooms and kitchens favors growth. Avoid at all costs placing plants near hot-air registers.

Humus

The soft brown or black substance formed in the last stages of decomposition of animal or vegetable matter is called humus. Common usage, however, incorrectly applies the term to almost all organic materials that will eventually decompose into humus—sawdust, ground bark, leaf mold, and animal manures, for example.

Hybrid. See Plant Classification   p. 561

Insecticide

An insecticide is a material that kills or repels insects. See Pest Management (p. 559).

Iron Chelate. See Chelate   p. 534

Irrigation. See Watering   p. 585

Kikuyu Grass

A perennial grass, kikuyu can make a useful lawn in some coastal areas but is a tough weed in others. Spreading rapidly by rhizomes and stolons, it eventually forms an impenetrable mat of wiry stems (see photograph, p. 590). Leaves are medium green and covered with fine hairs. To control kikuyu outside lawns, apply glyphosate.

Landscape Fabrics

Various fibrous or plastic materials called landscape fabrics can be rolled over the ground before planting to reduce growth of weeds and soil erosion. Use an old knife to make small X-shaped holes in the fabric for planting. Landscape fabrics are more attractive when covered with an organic mulch.

Lath

In gardening, lath designates any overhead plant protecting structure (originally a roof of spaced laths) that reduces the amount of sunlight that reaches plants beneath or protects them from frost.

Lawn Problems. See Visual Guide to Identifying Lawn Problems   p. 553

Lawns

The irrigated, mowed lawn became a basic landscaping element in the arid West early in the 20th century, when dams, pipelines, and electric pumps began to make water abundant. Now, in much of the West, a burgeoning population is stretching the limits of that supply. Water conservation has assumed a sense of urgency, and attention has focused on the water needs of lawns—revealing that our favored turf grasses (Kentucky bluegrass, ryegrass, fescues, bent grasses) require more water per square foot than almost any other kind of garden plant. Further research also has revealed that as much as half the water used by a typical single-family residence is applied outdoors—mostly to lawns—and that most homeowners apply at least twice as much water as their lawns actually need.

Minimizing water use on lawns. These startling facts have led many western communities to concentrate outdoor water conservation programs on providing more precise lawn-watering guidelines. Founded on evapotranspiration (ET)—a weather-based, localized measurement of how much water a plant uses and how much evaporates from the soil—these guidelines indicate the average amount of water your lawn needs on a daily, weekly, or seasonal basis. For lawn-watering guidelines for your area, contact your local water department or cooperative extension office.

Various alternatives to lawns are presented under Water Conservation (p. 583). If, however, a lawn is a necessary component of your landscape (as a play surface, for example), consider these options: minimizing lawn size; choosing a grass adapted to your climate; installing a sprinkler system tailored to your lawn; and automating watering with an electronic controller and moisture sensor (see information on electronic devices, p. 584) so that the turf will receive no more than the minimum amount of water it needs for good appearance.

Lawn care. Any good lawn—even if it is of less-thirsty grasses—demands a great amount of labor in preparation and care. You must prepare the soil well, carefully sow seeds or plant live plants (sod, plugs, stolons), and then pamper the young lawn while it becomes established. Thereafter, routine maintenance involves mowing, watering, fertilizing, and controlling weeds and pests. Here we focus on selecting grass type; information on watering begins on page 585. More information on individual grasses appears under Grasses (p. 312) in the Western Plant Encyclopedia. For detailed information on lawn care consult the Sunset book *Lawns*. For help solving lawn problems, see the Visual Guide to Identifying Lawn Problems (p. 553).

Lawn grasses. Climate should dictate your choice of a lawn grass in two ways. The first is water. If the water supply is sufficient (especially in areas where summer rain is common), you can consider one of the high water-consumers such as bluegrass, ryegrass, bent grass, or fine-textured fescue. Where water is scarce or the supply is unpredictable, choose from among the less-thirsty grasses.

The second climate factor to consider is temperature. Your summer heat and winter cold will direct you to either cool-season or subtropical grass types, as explained below.

Cool-season grasses. Cool-season grasses withstand winter cold, but most types languish in hot, dry summers. They are best adapted to the Northwest, to regions where marine influence tempers summer heat, and to parts of the Rocky

---

SECRETS OF A GREAT-LOOKING LAWN

Here are some tips for keeping a lawn healthy without wasting water.

- **Keep it small.** A small lawn takes less work, time, and money to care for than a big one. It also demands less water. How much lawn do you really need? Studies show that for most activities, 600 square feet is plenty. Keep it a simple geometric shape so you can irrigate without overspray, and keep it fairly level to minimize runoff.

- **Choose the right grass.** Read the lawn grasses information on this page and the next to select a grass that is adapted to your climate.

- **Water efficiently.** To encourage deep rooting and to conserve water, irrigate lawns as deeply and infrequently as possible. In mild climates, twice a week should be adequate. In hotter climates, you may have to water more often. Check with local water agencies for evapotranspiration guidelines. Water less in cool months.

    Step on the grass. If the blades don't spring back from your footprint, it's time to water. You can also poke the soil with a screwdriver; if it doesn't penetrate easily, the lawn probably needs water (or the soil is compacted).

Many sprinklers apply water faster than the soil can absorb it. To prevent runoff, water in cycles. Let the sprinklers run until just before runoff or puddling occurs (often in 10 or 15 minutes); repeat the cycle in an hour. Adjust sprinklers so they don't overshoot onto paving.

To improve water penetration and reduce runoff, aerate and dethatch your lawn once a year.

- **Fertilize regularly.** Lawns are heavy feeders and require regular applications of high-nitrogen fertilizers. In the desert, iron may also be beneficial. Cool-season lawns should be fed throughout fall and spring. Feed warm-season lawns in the warm months of late spring and summer. If you cut back on watering because of drought, hold back on fertilizing, too.

- **Mow often.** To keep a lawn healthy, mow the grass when it's about a third taller than the recommended height. Grass is weakened if it grows too long between mowings. Shorter clippings can be left on the lawn to decompose and add nitrogen to the soil. Set mowers to cut at these heights: hybrid Bermuda, 1 inch tall; tall fescue and bluegrass, 2 to 3 inches; fine fescue, 1½ to 2½ inches; perennial rye, 1½ to 2 inches.

Mountains area, where there is usually abundant summer rainfall.

These grasses are started from seeds sold either in blends of several different grasses or as individual types. Lawns of a single grass type will be the most uniform in appearance, most clearly expressing the characteristic you desire (fine texture or toughness, for example). The chief disadvantage of homogeneous lawns is that they may be wiped out by a pest infestation or disease to which they are susceptible or by extreme weather (drought or unusually high temperatures, for example). A blend of several kinds of grasses is safer. Those that survive to maturity will be the one, two, or three that do best given your soil conditions, climate, and maintenance practices.

When buying seed, consider both the kind of lawn you want and the cost to cover your area. Don't be fooled by the cost per pound. Choice, fine-leafed blends contain many more seeds per pound than do coarse, fast-growing blends; therefore, seeds of fine-textured grasses will cover a greater area per pound.

Subtropical grasses. Unlike the cool-season types, subtropical grasses grow vigorously during hot weather and go dormant in cool or cold winters. But even in their brown or straw-colored winter phase, they maintain a thick carpet that keeps mud from being tracked into the house. If you find their winter brownness offensive, they can be either dyed green or over-seeded with certain annual cool-season grasses that will stay green during mild winters.

The better subtropical grasses are grown from stolons, sprigs, plugs, or sod. Common Bermuda, hybrid Bermuda, and *Zoysia japonica* may be available in seed form, but seeding results are unsatisfactory and therefore the seeds are not widely offered. The hybrid Bermudas and St. Augustine grass cover quickly from runners; most zoysias are relatively slow. (Faster-growing zoysias are now becoming available as sod.) All can crowd out broad-leafed weeds. Hybrid Bermudas require frequent, close mowing and thatch removal.

"Water-conserving" grasses. Lawn grasses that thrive on less water than traditional Kentucky bluegrass can be broken up into three groups.

The first group is represented by the tall fescues, cool-season grasses that are grown from seed or sod planted in October. Although slightly coarser in texture than bluegrass, turf-type tall fescues stay green year-round and are the turf of choice where a cool-season grass is desired. Newer dwarf tall fescue varieties have the added advantage of reducing mowing.

The second group of "water-conserving" grasses is made up of several specialties of the Rocky Mountains and high plains—wheatgrass (*Agropyron*), blue grama grass (*Bouteloua*), and buffalo grass (*Buchloe*). Although widely used in high-elevation areas (Zones 1–3), they are still being tested in mild-winter areas. Each is described in the Western Plant Encyclopedia.

The third group consists of warm-season or subtropical grasses (see previous column), such as hybrid Bermuda. Thriving in hot summer weather, warm-season grasses can form an attractive turf on at least 20 percent less water than Kentucky bluegrass.

Layering

In layering, a method of propagating plants, a branch is rooted while it is still attached to a

GROUND LAYERING

Pebble

1 Select a low, flexible branch that can be bent into shallow hole. Cut halfway through it, put pebble in cut, and stake tip upright.

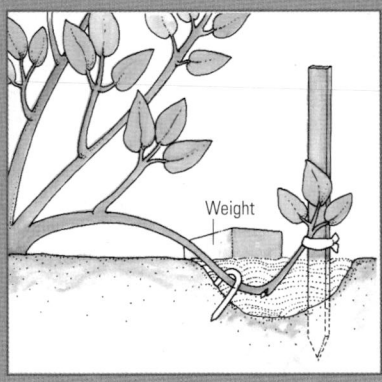

Weight

2 Secure prepared branch in shallow hole, using wire pin if needed. Brick or rock on soil also helps hold branch in place.

AIR LAYERING

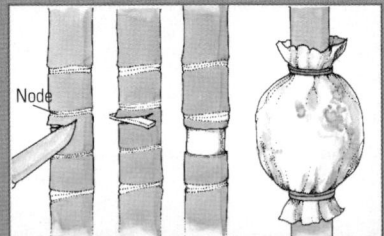

Node

Begin air layering below a node. Make a slanting cut (inserting matchstick to keep it open) or remove ring of bark. Dust cut with rooting hormone, encase in damp moss, and wrap with polyethylene to keep moss moist.

plant. The two layering methods—ground layering and air layering—tend to be slow to produce results, but with some hard-to-root plants layering is more likely to be successful than is propagating from cuttings (p. 538). Because you don't remove the branch from the parent plant until it has formed roots, the original plant continues to keep the layer alive.

Ground layering. The technique for ground layering is shown in the illustration. Keep the soil around the layer moist, as you would for any cutting. When you are sure roots have formed (it may take more than a year; gently dig around the cut to check), cut the new plant free from the parent plant, dig it up, and move it to its intended location.

Air layering. The principle of air layering is the same as that of ground layering; the difference is that air layering is used for branches higher on a plant. It is especially useful with some large house plants. The technique is shown in the illustration.

If the rooting is successful, you'll see roots appearing in the sphagnum moss after several months. Then you can sever the newly rooted stem from the mother plant and pot it or plant it out on its own. At that time it is usually wise to halve the number of leaves—to prevent excessive loss of moisture through transpiration while the newly independent plant establishes itself. If no roots form, the branch will callus where it was cut, and new bark will eventually grow over the cut area.

Leaching

To understand leaching, think of brewing tea or coffee: when you pour hot water through tea leaves or ground coffee, you are leaching. You leach soil with water when you want to remove excess salts (see Soil Salinity, p. 576). In high-rainfall areas, rainwater leaches good as well as bad substances from the soil.

Leader

In a single-trunked shrub or tree, the leader is the central, upward-growing stem.

Leafburn

Leafburn occurs when there is damage to or destruction of a leaf's tissues from sunlight, chemicals (in the soil or on the leaves), strong wind, or lack of water. It usually starts as burnt-looking, dried-out tissue around the edges of the leaves. In bad cases, the whole leaf can dry out. Leafburn is very common among Japanese maples and azaleas.

Leaf-Cutting Bees

Even though the leaf-cutting bee is extremely efficient at pollinating the flowers of alfalfa,

▶ page 554

L

Visual Guide to Identifying
LAWN
PROBLEMS

The best advice for avoiding serious lawn problems is to keep your lawn healthy. Do this by following proper cultural techniques: watering, mowing, fertilizing, aerating, and dethatching on a regular basis. This page will help you correctly identify the more common lawn problems. For help identifying weeds in your lawn, see the Visual Guide to Identifying Weeds (pp. 590–591). For more information on lawn care, see page 551.

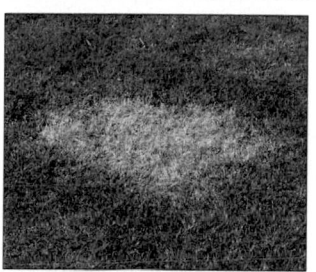

Problem: Small brown dead spots on the lawn.

Cause, Solution: If dead spots are circled by dark green grass, they may be caused by dog urine. If not, a gasoline spill from a power mower may be the cause. To prevent further damage, try to keep dogs off the lawn and fuel the mower on a paved surface. To repair damage, water area heavily to leach out salts or gasoline. Remove dead patch, along with 3 to 4 inches of soil beneath it. Fill hole with fresh soil; patch it with a fresh piece of sod, or reseed.

Problem: Small circular patches of dark green grass surrounding areas of dead or light-colored grass. Mushrooms may or may not be present.

Cause, Solution: Fairy ring, a fungus disease common in lawns growing in soil high in organic matter or including wood debris (boards or dead roots). To control, apply a nitrogen fertilizer and keep the lawn wet for 3 to 5 days. Aerate. There are no chemical controls.

Problem: Lawn has an uneven, washboard look with wavy ridges running in one direction.

Cause, Solution: Usually caused by running a power mower in the same direction every time you mow. Alternate mowing directions. It can also be caused by an unbalanced mower.

Problem: Bluegrass or ryegrass lawn has a yellowish to reddish brown color throughout. Small reddish pustules form in circular or elongated groups on older leaf blades and stems; blades eventually shrivel and die.

Cause, Solution: Rust. The best solution is to apply a high nitrogen fertilizer, water, and mow more frequently. Several fungicides are labeled for control.

Problem: Yellow patches showing up in St. Augustine and zoysia grass lawns (also possible in bluegrass and creeping bent grass), especially in dry or drought-stressed locations. Patches eventually die.

Cause, Solution: Chinch bugs, small (1/4-inch) gray-black insects that suck plant juices from grass blades, especially in hot weather. To confirm, push a bottomless can into the soil just where the grass is beginning to turn brown. Fill can with water. If lawn is infested, chinch bugs will float to the surface. Diazinon and chlorpyrifos are chemical controls.

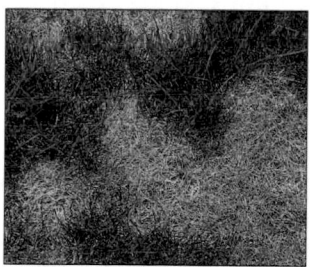

Problem: Lawn looks striped or mottled yellow and dark green, often with brown dead streaks near edges.

Cause, Solution: Uneven fertilizer application: Parts of the lawn that received the right amount of fertilizer turn dark green, but portions that didn't, turn yellow. Areas that got too much burn and turn brown. To prevent streaking with a drop spreader, overlap wheel tracks so that no grass goes unfed. Burned areas along edges are usually caused by double dosing. To prevent, apply fertilizer around outside edges of lawn first, then go back and forth across middle. When you come to the edges, turn spreader off as you make the turn over part already fed.

Problem: Small dead patches in spring gradually enlarge as summer progresses. Whitish to buff-colored moths fly around lawn in a zigzag pattern at night.

Cause, Solution: Sod webworms. Larvae (gray caterpillars) feed on grass blades. To confirm, drench area of lawn with solution of 1 tablespoon dishwashing soap diluted in 1 gallon water. Larvae will come to surface. Treat if there are 15 or more webworms per square yard. Proper lawn care—watering, aeration, and dethatching—will reduce damage. Chlorpyrifos and diazinon are chemical controls.

Problem: Distinct, irregularly shaped brown patches. Symptoms most severe in late summer. Sections of dead turf can be pulled up like sod.

Cause, Solution: White grubs (beetle larvae) feeding on grass roots. Usually about 1 to 1 1/2 inches long, the grubs curl into a C-shape when exposed. Parasitic nematodes are the biological control. Chlorpyrifos and diazinon are chemical controls. Treat if there is more than one grub per square foot.

it is looked upon as a prime garden trouble-maker in some mountain and desert regions. As these bees gather materials for nest building, they cut disks from the foliage or petals of certain plants to line their nests (see photograph, p. 568). The bees seem to prefer rose and bougainvillea leaves, although they also cut disks from developing rosebuds. Avoid these plants if leaf-cutting bees are known to be a problem in your area.

Although leaf-cutting bees may temporarily disfigure some favorite garden plants, their activity doesn't really damage healthy plants. Be philosophical: agriculture benefits from these pollinating insects; the tradeoff is some leaves and flowers.

Leaflet

Completely separated divisions of a leaf are called leaflets. They may be arranged like the fingers of a hand (palmate, fanwise) or like the divisions of a feather (pinnate, featherwise).

Leaf Mold

Partially decomposed leaves—leaf mold—can be dug into the soil as an organic amendment. Oak leaf mold is the most familiar.

Leaf Rollers

The two most common leaf rollers—a group of larval garden pests—are the fruit-tree leaf roller and the oblique-banded leaf roller. Despite its name, the fruit-tree species feeds on oaks as well as fruit trees.

In spring, summer, or fall, adult moths can lay egg clusters, which they cover with a waterproof cement. In some species, the eggs hatch early and overwinter in cracks in the bark of the host tree; other species don't hatch until spring. For the first few weeks after hatching, while the green larvae are about the size of long rice grains, they eat day and night. Then, when they are about half grown, they begin to hide during the daytime by folding leaves together (see photograph, p. 568); at night they crawl out and feed on the plant. When disturbed, they thrash about violently.

At some point in maturity, the larvae pupate. From the pupa—a light brown or green segmented cylinder within the rolled-up leaf—emerges the adult moth. The oblique-banded leaf roller produces one or two generations a year; the fruit-tree leaf roller, just one.

Controls. A number of parasitic insects usually keep populations of leaf rollers low. Light infes-

tations are easy to take care of physically: just pick off and destroy rolled leaves, or squash leaf rollers in place.

Use sprays only when leaf rollers threaten serious damage. The favored control is *Bacillus thuringiensis;* the surest chemical sprays are diazinon, carbaryl, and acephate.

Leaf Scar

Usually a rounded or crescent-shaped mark on a branch, a leaf scar indicates where a leafstalk was once attached.

Leaf Spot

Red, brown, yellow, or black spots on leaves and stems may be found on a number of different plants. On some *Prunus* plants, the spots drop out, leaving a "shot hole" appearance. Sometimes spots enlarge and coalesce, and then infected leaves drop; severe infections can defoliate some plants.

These symptoms represent several different diseases, including anthracnoses, black spot (familiar to rose growers), and scab, which affects some fruits. The fungus spores that cause these diseases are airborne or waterborne. Because the spores need free moisture to germinate, these diseases are far less serious in low-rainfall areas than they are in Zones 4 to 6 and 17. Some types of leaf-spot fungi, activated by moisture during the winter rainy period, affect evergreen plants in the three coastal states.

The source of these diseases is mainly live infected plants, although some disease-producing organisms can overwinter in plant refuse. Thorough garden cleanup each winter is important to lessen or eradicate infection. In addition, various fungicides may be labeled for use as sprays to control infections: benomyl, captan, and triforene.

Three particular leaf-spot diseases are troublesome enough to warrant further explanation.

Anthracnose. Anthracnose fungi infect leaves and tender shoots as they emerge in spring; these fungi also infect older leaves, on which they produce large, irregular brown blotches and cause premature dropping of leaves (see photograph, p. 569.) The fungi also cause twig dieback and canker on small branches; these blighted twigs and cankers will be a source of infection the following spring. Spores are spread by rain and by sprinkling; hence, the disease is most severe in wet springs and is checked by dry weather.

Your first attempt at control should be to eliminate sources of future infection: prune out all infected twigs and branches, if feasible. To prevent infection in spring, use benomyl (on ash trees) or chlorothalonil. Spray when leaves unfold, then two or three more times at 2-week intervals. Consult a commercial sprayer for help.

Some anthracnoses are very difficult to control, and sometimes it is necessary to live with them—especially if the disease affects a large

or favorite plant. But the best approach is to grow plants that resist the disease. Among susceptible trees such as ash, Chinese elm, and sycamore, resistant cultivars are available.

Black spot. Black spot thrives where humidity runs high and summer rainfall is common. It is especially troublesome on roses in the Northwest and is an increasing problem in California. The fungus appears on leaves and stems as roughly circular spots of black with fringed edges, usually circled with yellow (see photograph, p. 569). In severe cases, the plant will defoliate; unchecked infections, with repeated defoliation, can seriously weaken the host plant.

The black-spot fungus lives through winter in lesions on canes and on old leaves on the ground. In spring the fungus again becomes active and produces spores, which are then spread by splashing water to new leaves. Preventive control consists of sanitation: clean up and destroy (burn or discard) old leaves in winter. Rose growers often have good luck controlling black spot with weekly applications of a baking soda—summer oil spray. To make the solution, mix 2 teaspoons baking soda and 2 teaspoons summer oil in a gallon of water. Otherwise, in spring, spray new foliage with triforene (the favorite of most rose growers), benomyl, or chlorothalonil. Repeat sprayings will be needed as long as weather conditions favor the fungus's development.

Scab. Scab produces disfiguring lesions on apple and crabapple fruits and, when severe, can also cause defoliation. Another kind of scab occurs on loquats, pyracanthas, and toyons; still another infects willows. Scab is most prevalent in high-rainfall regions. The scab fungus (as well as the fungus that causes black spot on roses) differs from other leaf-infesting fungi in that the dark spots on leaves represent fungus growth on the foliage rather than dead tissue.

For control of scab on deciduous trees, spray just before flower buds open with benomyl or wettable sulfur. Spray again when blossoms show color and again when three-quarters of the blossom petals have fallen. Whenever possible, try to avoid the problem by planting scab-resistant varieties of apple and crabapple. Scab on evergreen ornamentals is more difficult to control. Thoroughly spray with benomyl as needed; clean up all infected foliage debris.

Light Soil

The opposite of "heavy soil," the imprecise term "light soil" refers to soil composed of relatively large particles loosely packed together. The term is often synonymous with "sandy soil." See Soils (p. 576).

Loam

Gardeners call soil that is rich in organic material, does not compact easily, and drains well after watering loam. It is the ideal soil. See Soils (p. 576).

Macronutrients

Basic nutrients required by plants in relatively large amounts are called macronutrients. See Nutrients, Basic (p. 556).

Male Plant

A plant that produces pollen but does not produce fruit or seed is called a male plant. See Pollination (p. 570).

Manure

Manure is an organic material excreted by animals that is used as a fertilizer and an amendment to enrich the soil. See Soil Amendments, Organic (p. 575).

Mealybugs

Closely related to scale insects, mealybugs have an oval body with overlapping soft plates and a white, cottony covering (see photograph, p. 569). Unlike most scales, a mealybug can move around—at a very slow crawl. These pests suck plant juices, causing stunting or death. Often a black, sooty mold grows on the honeydew they excrete.

Mealybugs are prime house plant pests everywhere; outdoors, they are especially troublesome in Zones 15 to 17 and 22 to 24. For any infestation indoors or for a minor infestation outdoors, daub mealybugs with a cotton swab dipped in rubbing alcohol. Outdoors, hose plants with jets of water (or insecticidal soap) every 2 to 4 weeks to remove adult mealybugs, their eggs and young, and the black mold, which deters beneficial insects. Ants have the same symbiotic relationship to mealybugs as to aphids and scale insects; see Aphids (p. 530) for control.

Natural predators, such as ladybird beetles, can help control mealybugs—as can some commercially available predators such as Cryptolaemus beetles and lacewings. Cryptolaemus beetle larvae are "sheep in wolves' clothing": they look like mealybugs but have chewing mouth parts and a ropey wax covering. See Visual Guide to Identifying Biological Controls (p. 533).

When mealybug infestations are heavy, spray with malathion, diazinon, acephate, or horticultural oil.

Microclimate

The climate of a small area or locality (such as a backyard or portion of it)—as opposed to that of a larger area, like a *Sunset Western Garden Book* climate zone—is called a microclimate. The ability to recognize microclimates around your home—or if necessary, to create them—will influence which plants you choose and how well they grow in a particular area. Microclimates are influenced by hills and hollows, points of the compass, and structures. See also Frost Protection (p. 546).

Micronutrients

Mineral elements required in small amounts for healthy plant growth are micronutrients. See Nutrients, Basic (p. 556).

Mites

To the naked eye, mites look like tiny specks of red, yellow, or green; in reality, they are tiny spider relatives (each has eight legs). Spider mites are especially troublesome in interior regions. The first (and sometimes only) sign of spider mite damage is yellow-stippled leaves (see photograph, p. 569). But there are many reasons for leaf yellowing. To confirm that mites are the problem, hold a piece of white paper beneath the stippled leaves and sharply rap the stem from which they are growing. If mites are present, the blow will knock some onto the paper—where they will look like moving specks. Some mites also make fine webbing across leaves (especially on the undersides) and around stems. Citrus bud mites (see photograph, p. 568) distort lemon fruit and foliage in coastal areas. Control measures are rarely necessary.

Spider mite controls. If the plant is small, you might jet it thoroughly with water to wash off the mites; insecticidal soap added to a water spray will increase the spray's effectiveness. Dust that settles on leaves encourages mites, so continual hosing helps keep mite populations down. Increased humidity also helps. Drought-stressed plants are more prone to mites.

Many natural predators keep mites in check most of the time. Some of these predators—lacewing larvae and five different species of predatory mites—are bred and sold by biological control companies (see p. 533).

If you can't wash the plant or if washing is not effective, try spraying. Summer horticultural oils are especially effective because all stages of mites, including eggs, are killed. Sulfur can also be effective—but don't use in combination with oil sprays (it can be toxic to plants). If infestation is severe, outside California try dicofol (not registered in California).

Moles

Notorious pests in good soils throughout the West, moles have short forelegs pointing outward; large, flattened hands; and claws for digging tunnels. Townsend's mole—common in the Pacific states west of the Sierra–Cascades chain of mountains—has velvety blue-black fur and a nearly hairless tail and snout.

Moles are primarily insectivorous, eating earthworms, bugs, and larvae, and only occasionally nibbling greens and roots. Irrigation and rain keep them near the soil surface, where they do the most damage as they tunnel: heaving plants from the ground, severing tender roots, and disfiguring lawns. A mole's main runways, which are used repeatedly, are usually from 6 to 10 inches underground and are frequently punctuated with volcano-shaped mounds of excavated soil. Shallower burrows, created while feeding, are used for short periods and then abandoned.

Controls. Trapping is the most efficient way to control moles. The spear- or harpoon-type trap is the easiest to set because you simply position the trap above the soil. A scissor-jaw trap must be carefully set into the main runway (probe with a sharp stick to find it); a wily mole will spring, heave out, or walk around a faultily set trap.

Due to their feeding habits, moles are very difficult to control with poison baits. And moles, like gophers, are difficult to control with toxic gas. To be successful with this method, place gas "mole bombs" directly in the main runways and block all holes. Be persistent with follow-up treatments.

You can dispatch a mole with a shovel blade, but you may wait a long time for a mole to appear. Your chances are best at dawn. If you see a mole scuttling along below ground (you'll notice the ground surface heaving), try the two-shovel method: block the runway in front of the mole with one shovel blade, and dig out the creature with the other.

Mulch

Any loose, usually organic material placed over the soil—such as ground bark, sawdust, straw, or leaves—is a mulch. The process of applying such materials is called mulching. A mulch can serve various functions. It may reduce evaporation of moisture from soil, reduce or prevent weed growth, insulate soil from extreme or rapid changes of temperature, prevent mud from splashing onto foliage and other surfaces, protect falling fruit from injury, or make a garden bed look tidy.

M

NATURALIZING BULBS

A number of bulbs, corms, and tubers can be planted in meadow, field, or light woodland situations where they will perform year after year as though they were wildflowers. By choosing bulbs that adapt to naturalizing and that thrive in your climate and location, you can enjoy an annual display with little more effort than it takes to plant them.

Selecting. Careful choice is the key to success with naturalizing. Read the description of each candidate in the Western Plant Encyclopedia to see if your choices will thrive under the conditions you can provide. Note especially the requirements for sun or shade. Also check moisture needs: Will the selected bulbs survive without supplemental water, or will you have to provide water during the dry months?

Planting. To achieve a naturalistic effect, plant bulbs in drifts, informal plant masses that appear to spread naturally from densely populated areas into more open areas. (See illustration.) If you plant spring-flowering bulbs in a grassy field or meadow you will mow, try to delay mowing the bulbs' area until bulb foliage has begun to yellow.

Flower size and quantity may decrease after bulbs have been in place for a number of years and become overcrowded. After flowering and foliage ripening, dig the bulbs, divide if needed, and replant when the time is right.

PLANTING BULBS IN DRIFTS

2 Plant each bulb where it falls—some in clusters, some farther apart. Bury each at correct depth for its species.

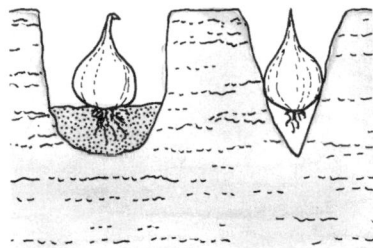

1 Toss handfuls of a single kind of bulb over the planting area, varying their density. Repeat with a second and third kind, if you like.

3 In hard ground, loosen the base of each hole so bulb rests on fine soil (left), not above an air pocket.

Naturalize

To plant out randomly, without a precise pattern, and leave in place to spread at will is called naturalizing. Some plants have the capability to naturalize, meaning that they can spread or reseed themselves, growing as wildflowers do.

Nitrogen. See Nutrients, Basic   p. 556

Node

The joint in a stem where a leaf starts to grow is a node. The area of stem between joints is the internode.

Nutgrass, Yellow

An upright perennial weed that thrives in moist areas, yellow nutgrass can be identified by its bright green ¼-inch-wide leaves with a conspicuous midvein. Its flowerhead is golden brown (see photograph, p. 591). Small, roughly round tubers, or nutlets, may be found at the root tips. Nutgrass spreads by tubers or seed. Control can be difficult. Try glyphosate or another appropriately labeled herbicide.

Nutrient Deficiency

If soil drains well, has ample water, is neither too acid nor too alkaline, yet still fails to sustain plant growth well, it may be deficient in nutrients—most likely nitrogen.

Nutrients, Basic

In addition to light, air, water, and space for roots, growing plants need a supply of nutrients—elements necessary to carry out their life processes. Six nutrients, called macronutrients, are needed in relatively large amounts. The most commonly deficient macronutrient for all plants is nitrogen (chemical symbol N). Two others, phosphorus (P) and potassium (K), are often needed for annual plants, bulbs, and shallow-rooted perennials, including turf, but seldom needed for trees and deep-rooted shrubs and vines. These three nutrients are the basis for commercial fertilizers.

Micronutrients, so-called because they are needed by plants only in infinitesimal quantities, are present in adequate amounts in most soils. Their availability to some plants may be inadequate, however, due to soil pH or another soil problem.

Nitrogen. The most commonly deficient nutrient, nitrogen, is not a mineral and hence is not present in the minute particles of soil from which plants derive their phosphorus, potassium, and other elements. All nitrogen must come from other sources: organic matter, air, water, or fertilizers. In nature, nitrogen comes primarily from decomposing organic material, which is generally in very short supply in western soils—especially in the drier regions. Rainfall carries nitrogen from the atmosphere into the soil. Some groundwater may also contain nitrogen. In addition, specialized nitrogen-fixing bacteria that live on the roots of certain plants (legumes in particular) extract nitrogen from air between soil particles.

Plants use large quantities of nitrogen to form proteins, chlorophyll, and enzymes needed for plant cells to live and reproduce. When nitrogen is deficient, leaves yellow from their tips toward the stem, the plant yellows from the bottom upward, and growth is stunted (see photograph, p. 569).

Nitrogen can be absorbed by plant roots as nitrate, ammonium, or urea. Nitrate is soluble. Consequently, it can be easily lost by the leaching action of irrigation and rainfall. The ammonium ion, in contrast to nitrate, does not move through the soil with water. If applied to the soil surface, it must be converted to nitrate by soil organisms before it will move into the root zone. Urea is unique in that it moves with water, is converted to ammonium ion, and stays in the root zone until converted to nitrate. At that point it can be leached from the soil. Soil organisms also need nitrogen to thrive, and they, too, place demands on the available supply. For these reasons, many plants need supplemental nitrogen from time to time to grow as well as we expect them to.

Nitrogen fertilizers. The first of the three numbers shown on a fertilizer label indicates the percentage of nitrogen. In the natural course of events (with no supplemental fertilizer), nitrogen that comes into the soil as dead plant or animal material must undergo several chemical changes before it takes on the nitrate form plant roots can use. If a fertilizer's label says that all or most of the nitrogen contained is in either nitrate or nitric form, nitrogen will be released quickly and plants will be able to use it immediately. But if most of the nitrogen is in the ammonium form (ammonium sulfate, for example), nitrogen release will be slower—taking anywhere from 2 weeks to 3 months—but should be more sustained once it starts.

Ammonium nitrate consists of half ammonium nitrogen and half nitric nitrogen; it therefore yields some of its nitrogen quickly and some slowly. Organic nitrogen—as in blood meal and IBDU (isobutylidene diurea)—first must go through a conversion to ammoniac nitrogen, which then is converted to nitrogen in the nitrate form. These are the slowest acting of the nitrogen sources. As a nitrogen source, organic matter is no more beneficial than inorganic sources because, ultimately, it is absorbed in the nitrate form. Organic fertilizers do, however, contribute organic matter to the soil, which can improve soil texture. See Soil Amendments, Organic (p. 575).

Note: If you add organic matter to your soil as a conditioner, the matter may be high in carbon compared with nitrogen. Soil organisms working to digest the high-carbon material may then compete with plants for the limited amounts of nitrogen available in the soil. For this reason, high-carbon (high-cellulose) soil conditioners—such as sawdust, wood shavings, ground bark, and straw—require special handling. One choice is to shop for and buy those materials in fortified form (with nitrogen already added to the material so that the organisms of decomposition will not take any nitrogen from the soil). If you get unfortified material, mix a nitrogen fertilizer with it.

Phosphorus. The second percentage of the three on a fertilizer label indicates the amount of phosphorus (expressed as phosphate, P_2O_5, and listed as available phosphoric acid) the product contains. Phosphorus availability is low in most soils; it does not move readily through the soil for roots to absorb. Soil particles that contain phosphorus ions release them "reluctantly" to the microscopic film of water (soil solution) surrounding them.

The phosphoric acid in a fertilizer ionizes in the soil to form phosphate compounds. Some of these compounds are useful to plants; others are so insoluble that plants cannot use them. When a phosphate fertilizer is simply spread on the soil and watered in, the phosphoric acid binds chemically to the mineral particles in only the top inch or two of soil. This means that surface applications of phosphorus fertilizers are largely ineffective, because they reach only surface roots. In western soils, trees and shrubs almost never respond to applications of phosphorus.

For shallow-rooting annuals and perennials, including turfgrass and bulbs, many soils do not have sufficient amounts of phosphorus.

The most effective way to apply a fertilizer containing phosphorus is to concentrate it where roots can get at it. When you plant a lawn, annuals, or perennials (including bulbs), dig in superphosphate or a complete fertilizer that contains phosphorus as well as nitrogen and potash. Thoroughly mix the amount suggested in the label directions into what you estimate will be the root area for a few years to come. For seed planting, place the fertilizer beside the seed rows, a couple of inches to one side and a couple of inches below the seed level (following fertilizer label directions for amount per foot of row).

Potassium. The third percentage on a fertilizer label represents potassium (expressed as potash, K_2O). This element is described in various ways, such as "available or soluble potash" or "water-soluble potash." Plants remove from the soil more potassium than any other nutrient except nitrogen and calcium.

Potassium exists naturally in the soil in several forms, but plants can't use most of the natural soil potassium, even though it may be abundant. About 1 percent of the total soil potassium, called exchangeable potassium, acts as an important source for plants.

Potassium fertilization is often needed for annuals and perennials, but in most soils trees and shrubs seldom respond to its addition. Potassium deficiencies occur in soils that are acid, sandy, low in organic matter, and low in nutrient-holding capacity. If you suspect potassium deficiency on a woody plant, confirm it with your county cooperative extension agent or a knowledgeable nursery person.

Like phosphorus, potassium is effective only if placed near roots, in their anticipated growth paths.

Calcium, magnesium, sulfur. Some fertilizers contain the important macronutrients calcium, magnesium, and sulfur; others do not. These elements are usually present in the soil in adequate supply, except that many soils of the high-rainfall areas of the Pacific Northwest have a sulfur deficiency. There, sulfur can be readily leached away, just as nitrogen is. If you live in these areas, apply additional sulfur regularly to annual crops and lawns for optimum performance.

Calcium and sulfur often enter the soil in other kinds of garden products: lime (calcium), lime-sulfur fungicide and soil conditioner (calcium and sulfur), gypsum (calcium and sulfur), superphosphate (sulfur), and soil sulfur used for acidifying alkaline soils.

Calcium plays a fundamental part in cell manufacture and growth—most roots must have some calcium right at the growing tips. Magnesium forms the core of every chlorophyll molecule in the cells of green leaves. And sulfur acts with nitrogen in making new protoplasm for plant cells; it is just as essential as nitrogen, but its deficiency in the soil is not so widespread.

Iron, zinc, manganese. If soil is highly alkaline, as some soils in low-rainfall areas are, plants may not be able to absorb enough of these micronutrients. Gardeners can buy products to put on soil or spray on leaves to correct the deficiency. Some of these products are chelated—meaning that the iron, zinc, or manganese is in a form that can be used by the roots and is not susceptible to the fixing (a chemical binding process) that makes the native iron, zinc, or manganese unavailable.

Iron is essential to chlorophyll formation. Zinc and manganese seem to function as catalysts, or "triggers," in the utilization of other nutrients.

Oak Moths

The pale brown California oak moth can damage oaks in Zones 7 to 9 and 14 to 24; it can be a major problem in coastal California, particularly around the San Francisco and Monterey bays.

The tan, inch-wide moths lay eggs in live oak trees twice a year (three times if winters are unseasonably mild). The first generation of larvae hatch in November and overwinter on live oak leaves, growing and eating more as weather warms in spring. About an inch long, full-sized worms have bulbous brown heads and olive green bodies with distinct black and olive or yellow stripes (see photograph, p. 568). The moths emerge from their pupae in June and July, and their offspring larvae eat leaves again from late July to October. The worms aren't a problem every year; populations may become heavy enough to defoliate trees for 2 or 3 years in a row and then almost disappear for several years. ▶

Controls. In late March or April, look for the telltale little green pellets—the droppings of feeding larvae—falling from live oaks. Even if the worm population is heavy, trees may get by without treatment and suffer no real damage beyond unsightliness. However, if you can't tolerate the loss of shade or the rain of droppings on patios, walks, and people, have the tree sprayed by a professional (it takes a high-pressure rig to reach the top of most mature oak trees).

Commercial spray operators commonly use *Bacillus thuringiensis* (BT), carbaryl, or acephate. BT won't harm natural predators and parasites (and there are many), but it must be applied as soon as worms are large enough to eat completely through leaves. As worms grow larger, they become more difficult to kill with BT. Carbaryl and acephate, on the other hand, kill all sizes of worms quickly, but both are highly toxic to bees.

Oak Root Fungus

Oak root fungus (*Armillaria mellea*) can destroy a variety of woody garden plants, especially in low-elevation, nondesert regions of California. First symptoms may be dull or yellowed leaves and/or sparse foliage. Leaves may wilt and entire branches die; eventually, the affected plant succumbs.

To verify a problem as oak root fungus, check under the bark of the stem or trunk (or large roots) at or below ground level: between the bark and the hard wood, you'll find a mat of whitish fungus tissue. In late autumn or early winter, clumps of tan mushrooms may appear around infected plants (see photograph, p. 569). The fungus kills its host by gradually decaying the roots and moving into the main stem, where it girdles the plant; the aboveground part of the plant shows distress because its supply of water and nutrients is reduced and finally cut off.

Controls. You may be able to save lightly infected trees—or at least prolong their lives—by removing soil from their bases, exposing the juncture of roots and trunk or stems to the air, and cutting out all destroyed and infected tissue. More often, though, the disease runs its full course despite remedial action. The fungus lives for many years in the root systems of plants it has killed; roots of susceptible plants that contact infected roots will be invaded by the fungus. If you intend to replace a victim with a susceptible tree or shrub, thoroughly remove all infected roots from the soil. It's better to choose replacement plants such as the following: *Acacia longifolia,* Japanese maple, ginkgo, jacaranda, *Mahonia aquifolium,* and nandina.

Offset

Some mature perennials may send out from their base a short stem, at the end of which a small new plant develops. The new plant is an offset. Some familiar examples are hen and chicks *(Echeveria)*, hen and chickens *(Sempervivum)*, and strawberry. See also Stolon (p. 578).

Organic Gardening

In simplest terms, organic gardening means using only materials derived from living things to grow plants. Such materials include organic fertilizers, soil amendments, and pest controls. The goals of organic gardening are to minimize impact on the environment, to reduce risks to people enjoying the garden, and to produce the healthiest food possible. However, the word "organic" is often considered a synonym for "safe," which is not always the case. Some organic pesticides, such as nicotine sulfate and rotenone, are toxic. Others, like pyrethrins, can cause allergic reactions in humans. Still others kill beneficial insects like bees as well as plant pests.

Organic Matter

Any material originating from a living organism—peat moss, ground bark, compost, or manure, for example—that can be dug into soil to improve its condition is referred to as organic matter. See Soil Amendments, Organic (p. 575).

Oxalis, Yellow

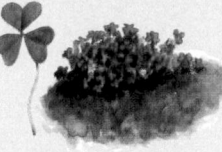

A very aggressive weed, yellow oxalis thrives all over the West in sun or shade; gardeners in Central and Southern California rate it especially troublesome. It spreads quickly by seed. Seedlings start out from a single taproot, which soon develops into a shallow, spreading, knitted root system. Yellow flowers are followed by elongated seed capsules that open like popcorn as they dry, shooting seeds as far as 6 feet. In mowed lawns, clumps generally stay low and tight. In flower beds, they grow rangier and tangle up with desirable plants.

Control is difficult. Dig out small plants, or carefully spot-treat isolated plants with glyphosate. Once you have removed or killed plants, oryzalin is an effective pre-emergence control. Various herbicides included in lawn-care products also help control oxalis. Check labels carefully.

A vigorous, well-fertilized lawn provides tough competition for oxalis. Frequent surface watering encourages the shallow-rooted weed; water less frequently and more deeply.

Peach Leaf Curl

Named for its most widely grown host plant, the peach leaf curl fungus also infects nectarines. In early spring the emerging new leaves thicken and pucker along their midribs, producing the characteristic curling. The curled and distorted leaves may be tinged with red, pink, yellow, or white (see photograph, p. 568); later in the season, they may become covered with white spores that can be carried by the wind to other leaves or plants. Lodging in and on the buds of next year's growth, these spores become the source of next year's infection. By midsummer the curled leaves usually fall, and trees then produce new leaves. Successive years of infection severely weaken a tree and decrease or eliminate fruit production.

The fungus overwinters on and in buds and on old, infected leaves, developing most rapidly during cool, moist winter or spring weather. Actual infection takes place when the bud scales (protective coverings on growth buds) first crack open—as early as December or as late as March, depending on the year, variety, and region. If buds swell early, they are susceptible to infection for several months, until active growth starts. Once leaf differentiation takes place, plants are resistant to infection.

Controls. For best control, protect buds with fungicide until they begin to swell. Spray with fixed copper (wettable powder) or lime sulfur; make the first application around the first of the year and follow up with two more applications at 3- to 4-week intervals. Do not spray after buds have opened. You also can control infection by covering trees with plastic during rainy weather; this is easiest with genetic dwarf varieties. Picking off the whitish leaves on isolated plants may also stop the spread of peach leaf curl.

Peat Moss

A highly water-retentive, spongy organic soil amendment, peat moss is the partially decomposed remains of any of several mosses. It is somewhat acid in reaction, adding to soil acidity. Sphagnum peat moss is generally considered to be highest in quality. There is a sedge peat, not composed of mosses, which is not necessarily acid.

Perennial

A perennial is a nonwoody plant that lives for more than 2 years. The word is frequently used to refer to a plant whose top growth dies each winter and regrows the next spring, but some perennials keep their leaves all year.

Perennials are as diverse an assortment of plants as you'll find under one collective heading, yet all will have two traits in common: (1) unlike shrubs, they are not woody and (2) unlike annuals, they live from year to year. Typically, a perennial has one blooming season each year, from only a week to more than a month long.

After blooming, the plant may put on new growth for the next year; it may die down and virtually disappear until the time is right, some months later, for growth to resume; or it may retain much the same appearance throughout the year.

Some perennials store reserve food for the next season in specialized underground tissues. These plants are discussed separately under Bulbs (p. 532).

Many of the popular perennials are grown for the beauty of their flowers, and any attractive foliage is merely a bonus. Conversely, a smaller group of perennials—artemisias, for example—are grown for their foliage alone, the flowers being inconsequential or even unattractive. Some perennials have evergreen foliage and are attractive throughout the year.

Garden uses. Like annuals, perennials provide color masses, but unlike annuals, they will bloom several years in a row without having to be dug up and replanted. Perennials are thus more permanent than annuals but less permanent than flowering shrubs. In fact, their semipermanence is a definite selling point. You can leave perennials in place for several years with little maintenance beyond annual cleanup, some fertilizing, and routine watering; but if you want to change the landscape, perennials are easy to dig up and replant—much more so than the average flowering shrub.

Planting. For instructions on planting most perennials, see Planting Techniques: Annuals and Perennials (p. 564). A number of popular perennials (irises, daylilies, peonies, oriental poppies) and perennial fruits and vegetables (asparagus, rhubarb, and strawberries) are sold in nurseries or by mail as bare-root plants during their dormant periods. The roots of these bare-root perennials should be kept moist until planting. They also benefit from a several hours' soak in water before planting. For handling mail-order perennials, see illustration.

Before planting dormant, bare-root perennials, prepare the soil well, as recommended under Planting Techniques: Seeds (p. 563), and be sure to set out each plant at its proper depth; refer to individual entries in the Western Plant Encyclopedia for specific planting information. Be sure to spread roots out well in the soil, gently firm soil around them, and then water thoroughly to establish good contact between roots and soil. See illustration.

Care of established perennials. Feed perennials with a nitrogen fertilizer just prior to the normal growth cycle—in fall or late winter to early spring. Repeat after bloom.

With perennials that are periodically dug up, divided, and replanted, you can renew phosphorus and potassium when you prepare the soil for replanting. But even the "permanent" perennials, such as peonies, may appreciate replenishment of these nutrients from time to time. The best way to apply them is to use a complete fertilizer high in phosphorus and potassium: carefully dig it in, apply it in deep trenches, or use fertilizer stakes or tablets (see Fertilizers, p. 543).

Routine watering during the growth and bloom periods will satisfy most perennials. Exceptions are noted in the Western Plant Encyclopedia as preferring dry or unusually wet soil.

After a perennial has finished blooming, remove the old blossoms to prevent the plant's energy from going into seed production.

Later in the season (usually in fall), remove dead growth to minimize overwintering diseases and eliminate hiding and breeding places for insects, snails, and slugs.

In cold-winter regions (Zones 1–3), many gardeners routinely mulch their perennials to protect them from alternate freezing and thawing. After the ground first freezes, apply a lightweight mulch that won't pack down into a sodden mass. Straw is one popular choice; evergreen boughs are good where available.

Digging, dividing, and replanting. Over time many perennials grow into such a thick clump that performance declines because the plants are crowded. When this happens, dig up the clump during its dormant period and divide it. See instructions under Dividing (p. 541).

Perlite

Perlite is a mineral expanded by heating to form very lightweight, porous white granules useful in container soil mixes to enhance moisture and air retention.

Pest Management

The notion of pest control—where control implies eradication—has been superseded by the concept of pest management. The management concept acknowledges that many perceived "problems" are natural components of gardens: the presence of pests doesn't necessarily spell trouble. In a diversified garden, most insect pests are kept in check by natural forces (such as predators and weather). If pests reach damaging levels, however, temporary intervention may be needed to restore a balance.

Because of this natural system of checks and balances in a garden, it makes sense to determine which form of intervention will return the situation to a normal balance with the least risk of destroying helpful (as well as harmless) organisms that maintain the equilibrium. Action choices range from doing nothing (giving nature a chance to correct the imbalance), or using restraints (washing plants, or repelling or physically destroying the damagers), to biological controls (improving the helpful side of nature's control system), and, as a last choice, chemical controls.

More and more gardeners are turning to physical restraints and biological controls (see Visual Guide to Identifying Biological Controls, p. 533) as a first line of defense against garden pests because they want natural gardens that are safer for children, pets, and wildlife. Yet almost all horticulturists acknowledge the need for at

P

PLANTING A BARE-ROOT, MAIL-ORDERED PERENNIAL

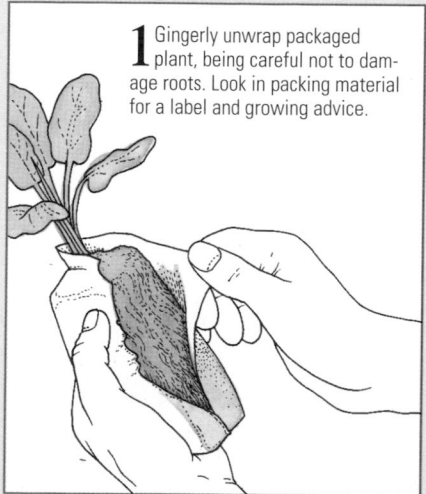

1 Gingerly unwrap packaged plant, being careful not to damage roots. Look in packing material for a label and growing advice.

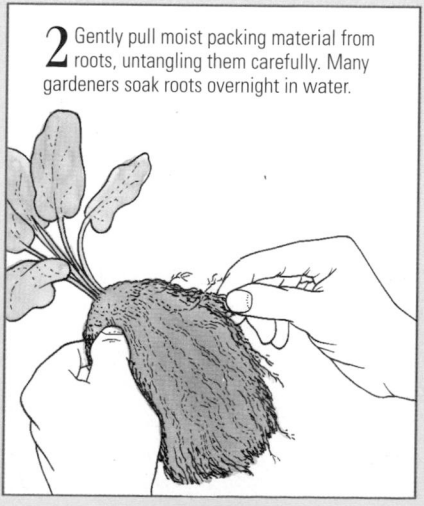

2 Gently pull moist packing material from roots, untangling them carefully. Many gardeners soak roots overnight in water.

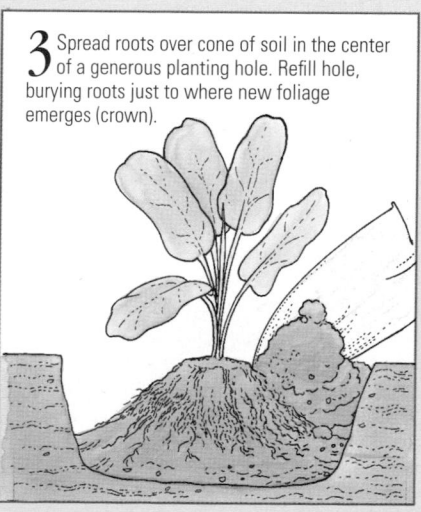

3 Spread roots over cone of soil in the center of a generous planting hole. Refill hole, burying roots just to where new foliage emerges (crown).

least occasional treatment with chemical controls. This approach—the preferred use of natural and mechanical controls, plus chemicals as a discretionary second choice—is called integrated pest management (IPM). Increasingly, IPM is being used in parks, city landscapes, and greenhouses.

The IPM approach. The following points explain how to implement IPM in your own garden.

- **Select well-adapted plants.** Choose plants that are adapted to your area and that are resistant to your region's pest and disease problems. Plants stressed by inhospitable climate or from lack of water or nutrients are more vulnerable to damaging organisms than are their healthy, well-cared-for counterparts.

- **Adjust planting time.** If by planting early you can avoid a sure-thing pest, do so. Spider mites are most troublesome when the weather

---

INSECTICIDES

Insecticides carry one or more active ingredients in a liquid, powder, or granular form. Their availability is constantly shifting. New products continue to be developed and marketed. Existing products may be withdrawn from sale for home use if research reveals hazards to health or the environment.

On the label of each product is a list of plants and pests on which the control is registered for use. It is illegal to apply the control to a plant or pest not listed on the label.

- **Azadirachtin (neem).** A botanical insecticide from the African neem tree *(Azadirachta indica)*, this liquid spray is nontoxic to mammals; it stops feeding of many insects and prevents normal growth of immature insects. Neem has limited registration in some states.

- **Baygon (propoxur).** Common in earwig baits and wasp and hornet sprays, propoxur should not be used on edible crops.

- **Bendiocarb.** A dust, bendiocarb controls crawling pests (such as earwigs, pillbugs, and sowbugs) and some soil pests, including root weevils. It is not registered in all western states.

- **Contact dusts.** Differing from insecticidal dusts, these powdered materials cling to, scratch, and destroy the waxy exterior of some pests. Diatomaceous earth, boric acid, and silica aerogels are among the most useful, but they can be hazardous to humans if inhaled.

  Use natural-grade, properly labeled diatomaceous earth to discourage ants, slugs, and snails. Boric acid, usually a dust or powder, is also available as a spray or paste and in baited traps. Silica aerogels dehydrate an insect's body, killing it. In the garden, apply as a dust for ants, fleas, and ticks.

- **Diazinon.** A broad-spectrum insecticide also widely used to control various lawn pests, diazinon is the only chemical control for soil pests in vegetable gardens. It is toxic to bees and birds.

- **Dursban (chlorpyrifos).** A control for certain borers in shade trees, lawn insects, and many other pests of ornamental plants, chlorpyrifos should not be used on vegetables.

- **Kelthane (dicofol).** Designed to control spider mites, dicofol may be found as one of the ingredients in multipurpose insecticides. It is not registered in California.

- **Malathion.** A broad-spectrum insecticide for use on both edible and ornamental crops, malathion is toxic to honeybees.

- **Mesurol (methiocarb).** An effective control for slugs and snails, methiocarb will also kill earthworms. It is not for use around edible crops.

- **Metaldehyde.** The most common slug and snail control, metaldehyde is usually the active ingredient in various baits and is also contained in some liquids. It may be used around vegetable and fruit crops, but it loses effectiveness in moist weather and after waterings. It can be toxic to pets.

- **Oil sprays.** Special, highly refined oils smother insects and their eggs. "Dormant oils" are used during winter for control of insects that overwinter on deciduous plants. "Summer oils" can be used after leaves have emerged and on woody evergreen plants such as citrus. Use in summer to control aphids, pear psylla, scale insects, mites, and eggs of some insects. Oils can burn sensitive leaves; test-spray on a small area of plant first.

- **Pyrethrum/pyrethrins.** Pyrethrum is a natural insecticide derived from *Pyrethrum* daisies. It is effective against many insects (especially quick knockdown of flying ones) but will break down within a few hours after exposure to sunlight. Pyrethrins are specific chemicals derived from the *Pyrethrum* daisy. Pyrethroids are synthetic versions, which are more toxic and last longer in the environment.

- **Rotenone.** A botanical insecticide derived from South American plants, rotenone dust is commonly used to control chewing insects on vegetables. It is fairly toxic to mammals (especially hogs) and extremely toxic to fish.

- **Ryania.** A botanical insecticide derived from the powdered stem of a tropical shrub, ryania acts as a stomach poison, controlling codling moth, citrus thrips, corn earworm, and asparagus beetle. It is gentle on beneficials.

- **Sabadilla.** Made by grinding seeds of the sabadilla lily, this control acts as a stomach and contact poison against caterpillars, leafhoppers, and thrips. It has low toxicity to people but is highly toxic to birds. Sabadilla has limited registration in California.

- **Sevin (carbaryl).** This insecticide, commonly used in vegetable gardens, is effective against most chewing insects but generally not effective against sucking insects. It often increases problems with the latter pests by destroying their natural predators. Carbaryl is highly toxic to honeybees and earthworms.

- **Soaps.** These mixtures of special fatty acids are of low toxicity to humans but will control most small insects and mites. They are safe for use on edible plants and fast acting, but have no residual effectiveness. Soaps injure some plants. They are most effective in soft water. Once dry, soaps will not kill beneficials.

- **Sulfur.** Finely ground sulfur mixed with clay, talc, and gypsum is dusted over plants (or sometimes diluted with water and sprayed) to control mites, psyllids, and certain mildews. Never use when temperature will exceed 90°F.

- **Systemics.** These pesticides are absorbed by a plant's foliage or roots; insects that pierce the plant's external tissues and ingest the juices or chew the leaves are killed. Sprayed on the foliage, some systemics also kill insects on contact. Widely available are Cygon (apply to leaves or soil), Disyston (apply to leaves or soil), and Orthene (acephate) (apply only to leaves; toxic to bees). None can be used on edible crops.

- **Thiodan (endosulfan).** This broad-spectrum insecticide is particularly effective against thrips, aphids, borers, fuchsia mites, and whiteflies. Its use is restricted in some areas.

Packaged pesticides are listed alphabetically by trade name or common name; the generic name, which you will find under "active ingredients" on the product label, appears in parentheses when it differs from the trade name.

P

turns hot; plant beans early to avoid them. Keep records of planting dates and temperatures so you can make adjustments from season to season.

- **Try mechanical controls.** Hand-picking, traps, barriers, floating row covers, or a strong jet of water can reduce or thwart many pests, especially in the early stages of a potential problem. Cleanup of plant debris can remove the environment in which certain pests and diseases breed or overwinter.

- **Accept minor damage.** A totally pest-free garden is neither possible nor desirable. Allow natural control methods to play the major role in maintaining a healthy balance between pests and the beneficial (plus the harmless) insects and creatures that are normal garden components.

- **Solarize the soil.** Using the sun to heat the soil before planting is an effective way to reduce or eliminate soil-inhabiting pests. Just before the hottest time of the year (usually mid-July) and well before fall planting, till soil and remove weeds. Water soil, then lay 1½- to 2-mil clear plastic over it; anchor edges with soil. Leave in place for 4 to 6 weeks.

- **Use less toxic alternatives.** Release or encourage beneficial insects; use soaps, horticultural oils, botanical insecticides (such as natural pyrethrins), and one of several packaged forms of *Bacillus thuringiensis;* see the Visual Guide to Identifying Biological Controls (p. 533) for further explanation of these products. Realize that beneficial insects may take a while to reduce the pests they prey upon, and that you may have to use nonchemical controls at more frequent intervals than you would chemical controls. And although many natural insecticides have a relatively low impact on the environment, they can be harmful to humans if used carelessly. Follow label instructions exactly.

- **Use chemical preparations prudently.** Occasionally you will need to use a chemical control—especially for management of diseases (p. 540). Before you purchase a chemical control and begin applying it, be sure you have correctly identified the problem. Only use a pesticide to solve a problem if both the pest and the plant it is preying on are listed on the pesticide's label. If you are at all uncertain, ask at a reputable local nursery or contact the nearest cooperative extension agent. Follow label directions exactly. For help identifying specific plant problems, see pages 568–569.

Biological controls. A number of living organisms can provide some measure of pest control. Many occur naturally in gardens (and may be eliminated by unwise pesticide use). For information on beneficial insects—insects that prey on garden insect pests—and other biological controls, see page 533.

Petals. See Plant Anatomy and Growth p. 561

Phosphorus. See Nutrients, Basic p. 556

Pillbug, Sowbug

These two familiar creatures have sectioned shells and seven pairs of legs. Pillbugs roll up into black balls about the size of a large pea; sowbugs are gray and cannot roll up as tightly. Their principal food is decaying vegetation, but they also will eat very young seedling plants and the skins of melons, cucumbers, squash, and berries—particularly if the fruits are overripe and have a break in the skin.

Mulching and composting encourage pillbugs and sowbugs. If you sprout seeds near a compost pile or in heavily composted soil, you may get some pillbug and sowbug damage. You can apply carbaryl to the seedlings or to the ground where the pests are active. Or lift fruit off the ground on top of small saucers or boards, plastic mulch, or landscape fabric.

Pinching Back

Using thumb and forefinger to nip off the tips of branches is called pinching back. This basic pruning technique (p. 571) forces side growth, making the plant more compact and dense. It is especially useful with annuals, house plants, and shrubs.

Plant Anatomy and Growth

Knowledge about how plants grow is an important key to becoming a successful gardener. This background will make all aspects of plant culture more understandable. The box below explains the anatomy of a flower; the illustration on the next page outlines the basics of plant growth.

Plant Classification

Botanists have classified the world's plants into an orderly, ranked system reflecting similarities among them. The plant kingdom is broken down into groups that are less and less inclusive: division, class, order, and then the groups defined on the next page, which are the ones of most significance to gardeners. ▶

ANATOMY OF A FLOWER

Among flowering plants, blossom form varies enormously. But this diversity obscures the fact that all flowers share a basic structural plan and that the structural elements always appear in the same order. The illustration shows a schematic flower and its parts, which are described below.

- **Receptacle** is the point where floral parts are attached to the tip of the specialized stem that bears the flower.

- **Sepals** make up the outer circle, or ring, of floral parts. Collectively, the sepals are known as the calyx.

- **Petals** form the next circle of flower parts, just inward from the sepals. In showy flowers, it is usually the petals that make the display. Petals may be separate, as in camellias and roses, or united into tubular, cupped, or bell-like shapes, as in rhododendrons and petunias. Collectively, the petals are called the corolla (and the calyx and corolla together are known as the perianth).

- **Stamens,** positioned inward from the petals, contain the male reproductive elements. Typically a stamen consists of a slender stalk (the filament) topped by an anther (most often a yellow color). The latter contains grains of pollen, which is the male element needed to fertilize the flower for it to produce seeds. See Pollination (p. 570).

- **Pistils,** found in the center of a flower, bear the female reproductive parts. Each pistil typically consists of an ovary at the base (in which seeds will form following pollination) and a stalklike tube called the style that rises from the ovary. The style is topped by a stigma, the part that receives the pollen.

A complete flower—a term that describes most of the flowers we grow—comprises all the parts described above. An incomplete flower lacks one or more of the floral parts, but those it does contain appear in the order listed. For more information on flowers and flower parts, see Single Flower (p. 574) and Double Flower (p. 542).

ANATOMY OF A COMPLETE FLOWER

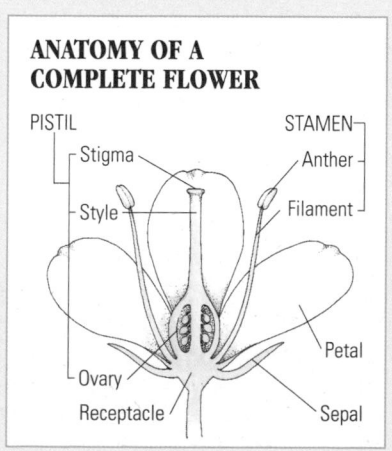

PISTIL — Stigma — Style — Ovary — Receptacle
STAMEN — Anther — Filament — Petal — Sepal

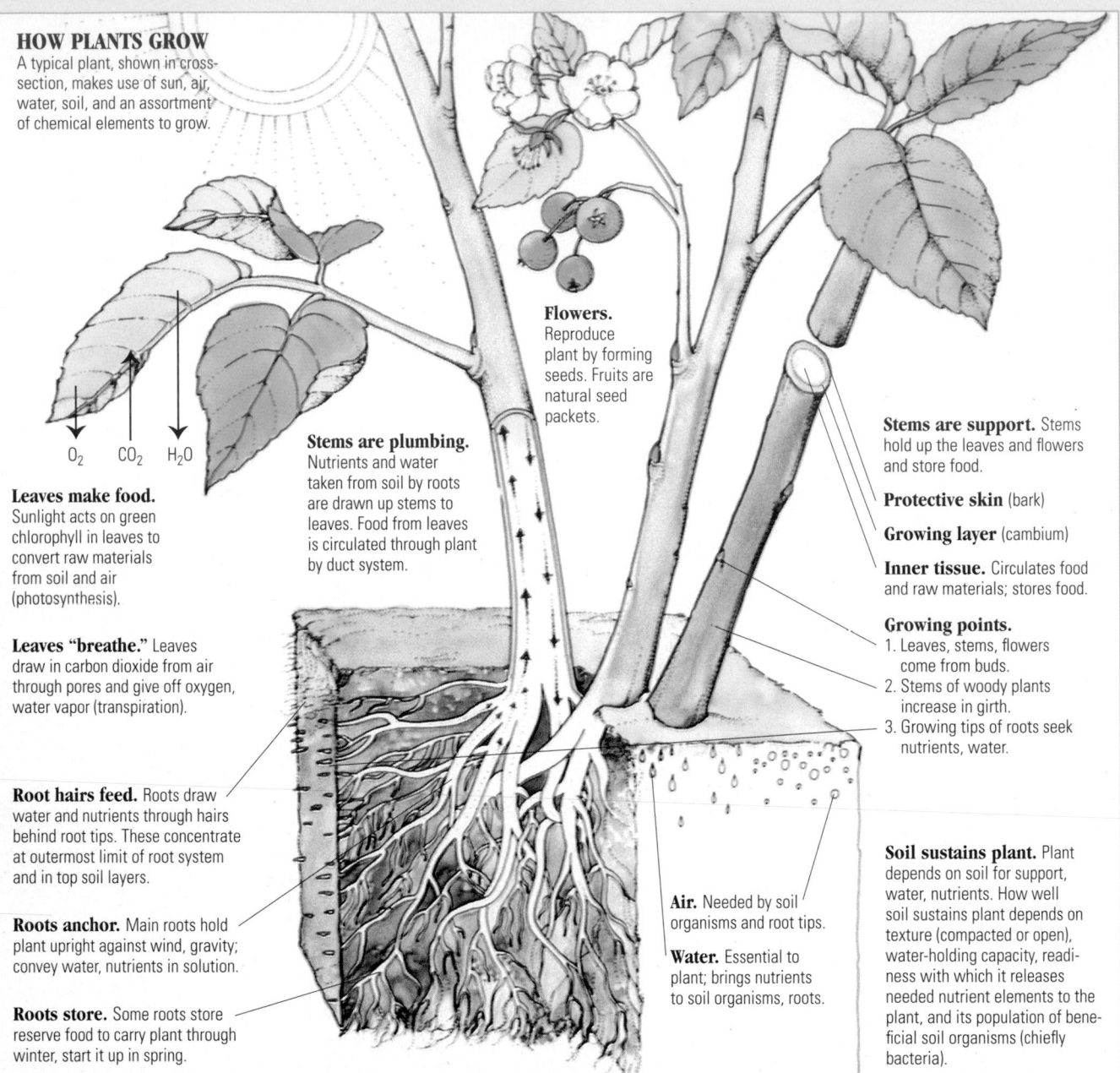

HOW PLANTS GROW

A typical plant, shown in cross-section, makes use of sun, air, water, soil, and an assortment of chemical elements to grow.

O_2 CO_2 H_2O

Leaves make food. Sunlight acts on green chlorophyll in leaves to convert raw materials from soil and air (photosynthesis).

Leaves "breathe." Leaves draw in carbon dioxide from air through pores and give off oxygen, water vapor (transpiration).

Root hairs feed. Roots draw water and nutrients through hairs behind root tips. These concentrate at outermost limit of root system and in top soil layers.

Roots anchor. Main roots hold plant upright against wind, gravity; convey water, nutrients in solution.

Roots store. Some roots store reserve food to carry plant through winter, start it up in spring.

Stems are plumbing. Nutrients and water taken from soil by roots are drawn up stems to leaves. Food from leaves is circulated through plant by duct system.

Flowers. Reproduce plant by forming seeds. Fruits are natural seed packets.

Air. Needed by soil organisms and root tips.

Water. Essential to plant; brings nutrients to soil organisms, roots.

Stems are support. Stems hold up the leaves and flowers and store food.

Protective skin (bark)

Growing layer (cambium)

Inner tissue. Circulates food and raw materials; stores food.

Growing points.
1. Leaves, stems, flowers come from buds.
2. Stems of woody plants increase in girth.
3. Growing tips of roots seek nutrients, water.

Soil sustains plant. Plant depends on soil for support, water, nutrients. How well soil sustains plant depends on texture (compacted or open), water-holding capacity, readiness with which it releases needed nutrient elements to the plant, and its population of beneficial soil organisms (chiefly bacteria).

Family. Each plant belongs to a family, members of which share certain broad characteristics that are not always immediately evident. The rose family, for instance, includes such diverse plants as the rose, the apple tree, and the familiar perennial *Geum*. Many family names end in *-aceae* (Orchidaceae, Asteraceae, Liliaceae).

Genus. A plant family is divided into groups of more closely related plants; each group is called a genus (the plural is "genera"). Sometimes a family contains only one genus: for example, Ginkgoaceae contains only the genus *Ginkgo*. At the other extreme, the composite family (Compositae) contains around 950 genera. The first word in a plant's botanical name is the name of the genus to which it belongs: for example, *Ginkgo, Liquidambar, Primula*.

Species. Each genus is subdivided into groups of individuals called species; the second word in a plant's botanical name designates the species. Each species is a generally distinct entity, reproducing from seed with only a small amount of variation. Species in a genus share many common features but differ in at least one characteristic.

Subspecies, variety. A third word in a botanical name indicates a subspecies or variety. In the strictest sense, a subspecies is more inclusive than a variety. "Subspecies" is often used to denote a geographical variant of a species, but in general usage, "subspecies" and "variety" have become virtually interchangeable. Subspecies or varieties retain most characteristics of their species while differing in some particu-

lar way, such as flower color or leaf size. The name may appear in either of two ways: *Juniperus chinensis sargentii* (a subspecies) or *Juniperus chinensis* 'San Jose' (a variety).

Horticultural variety (clone or cultivar). Varieties often are of hybrid origin. They are usually listed by genus name followed by cultivar name, as *Rosa* 'Chrysler Imperial'. Some have been found as wild plants but have been perpetuated by cuttings or other means of vegetative propagation.

Hybrid. A hybrid is a distinct plant resulting from a cross between two species, subspecies, varieties, cultivars, strains—or any combination of the above—or even between two plants from different genera. Some occur in the wild, but more often hybrids are deliberate crosses.

P

Strain. Many popular annuals and some perennials are sold as strains, such as State Fair zinnias. Plants in a strain usually share similar growth characteristics but are variable in some way—usually in flower color.

Planting

Proper planting techniques depend on the type of plant—annual, perennial, shrub, tree, and so on—and how the plant is sold or propagated—as seed, bare-root, or in containers. Special techniques for various types of plants and planting approaches are explained in the entries that follow. To get plants off to a good start, you should also have an understanding of Soils (p. 576) and Soil Amendments (p. 575). Planting techniques for bulbs can be found under the alphabetical listing (p. 532).

Planting Techniques: Seeds

In nature, seeds are scattered randomly from seed-bearing plants. And scattering, or broadcasting, seeds is a common method for planting seeds of lawn grasses and sometimes of wildflowers. To plant seeds of most garden plants, though, the gardener sows seeds more carefully in the open ground or in some sort of container.

You can buy seeds of most ornamental plants in three different forms. The traditional packaging is the seed packet: with a picture of the flower, fruit, or plant on the outside, the loose seeds within. You also can buy packets or packages of pelletized seeds: each seed is coated, like a small pill, to make handling and proper spacing easier. The third form is seed tapes—strips of biodegradable plastic in which seeds are embedded, properly spaced for growing to maturity. You just unroll the tape in a prepared furrow and cover it with soil. In all three cases, you will find planting instructions on the package.

In the open ground. One advantage of sowing seeds directly in the earth is that you usually avoid the need to transplant. The seeds germinate and grow into mature plants in one place. You may need to thin seedlings to prevent overcrowding, filling in a few sparse spots with thinned plants. But most of the seedling plants will need no handling once they break ground.

Gardeners commonly choose between two seed-sowing methods—broadcasting and row planting—depending on the results desired. Seeds planted in rows will probably need to be thinned later.

Broadcasting. Native wildflowers will make a reasonably good show if simply scattered—in time to catch fall rains—where they are to grow. But they will do even better if the ground is first cleared of weeds and grasses and prepared a bit by tilling and by adding organic amendments. If you plan to broadcast seeds in drifts or patterned plantings, or if you wish to sow a broad area with tough, easy-to-grow plants (such as sweet alyssum or California poppies), you can achieve a more even distribution by mixing the seed with several times its bulk of fine sand. After you have scattered the seeds—or seed-and-sand mixture—rake lightly, then carefully sprinkle the area with water. Cover the area with a very thin mulch (p. 555) to prevent the soil from crusting and to hide the seeds from predators. (Be prepared, though, for some loss to birds and, perhaps, to rodents.)

Most garden annuals and vegetables also can be sown in place, but they will benefit from a bit more attention than simple broadcasting calls for. With a fork, spade, or rotary tiller, prepare the seedbed, working in soil amendments (p. 575) and a complete fertilizer (read the label and apply the recommended amount). Smooth the prepared soil with a rake and moisten it well a few days before you intend to plant (if rains don't do the watering for you). Then follow the sowing and covering directions outlined for broadcasting.

Row planting. If you intend to grow vegetables or annuals in rows, prepare the soil as described previously. But you can omit the fertilizer and apply it, instead, at seeding time in furrows 1 inch deeper than the seeds and 2 inches on either side of the seed row (again, consult label recommendations for the proper amount of fertilizer per foot of row). Follow the seed packet instructions for optimum planting depth and spacing of the rows, and lay them out in a north-south direction so that both sides will receive equal sunlight during the day. Use a hoe, rake, or stick to form the furrow; for perfectly straight rows, use a board or a taut string as a guideline. See illustration.

To sow seeds or seed pellets from packets, one of two methods will work best. Either tear off a small corner of the packet and tap the seeds out as you move the packet along the furrow or prepared seedbed; or pour a small quantity of seed into your palm, and then scatter pinches of seed as evenly as possible.

Thinning. When seedlings appear, thin excess plants (if necessary) so that those remaining are spaced as directed on the seed packet. Bare seeds scattered in furrows almost always come up too thickly; pelletized seeds are easier to sow at the proper spacing, and seed tapes do the spacing for you. Thin seedlings while they are still small. If you wait too long to thin them, plants will develop poorly, and it will be more difficult to remove one without disturbing those around it. Work quickly but gently, replanting the surplus seedlings elsewhere as you go.

In flats and containers. Many plants get off to a better start when they are sown in containers and later transplanted into place in the garden. Most nurseries stock seedling plants in flats or other containers, ready for you to plant. But you can start your own seedlings indoors or in a greenhouse—or in any location that is warmer than the out-of-doors and has adequate light. See illustration on next page.

TWO WAYS TO PLANT STRAIGHT

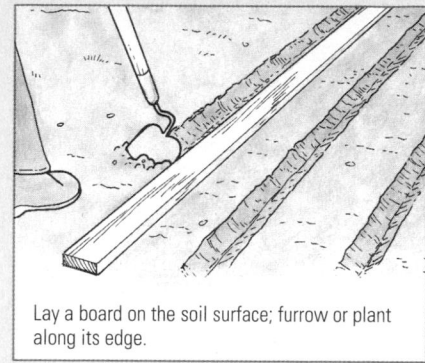

Lay a board on the soil surface; furrow or plant along its edge.

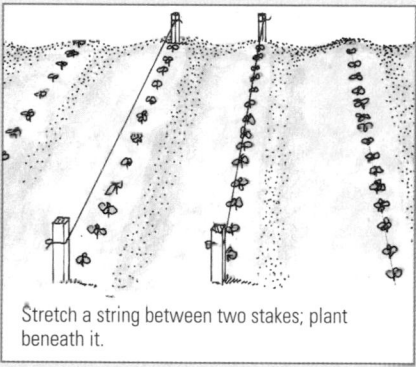

Stretch a string between two stakes; plant beneath it.

Choosing a container. Almost anything that will hold soil and has provision for drainage will do for a seed starting container. Plastic or wooden nursery flats will accommodate the largest number of seeds; other choices are clay or plastic pots, peat pots, aluminum foil pans (the sort sold for kitchen use), Styrofoam or plastic cups, cut-down milk cartons, or shallow wooden boxes that you can make yourself.

Remember to punch holes for drainage in the bottom of any container that holds water; if you make your own wooden flats or boxes, leave about a ¼-inch space for drainage between the boards that form the container's bottom.

If you use containers that have held plants before, give them a thorough cleaning to avoid the possibility of infection by damping-off fungi, which destroy seedlings. A vigorous scrubbing followed by a few days of drying in the sun usually suffices.

Choosing a planting mix. Unless you plan a large-scale seed-planting operation, it's easiest to buy a prepared planting mixture for starting seeds. Nurseries carry a variety of such mediums—look for labels that say "potting soil." See Container Gardening (p. 536).

Sowing in a container. Gently firm the mixture into the container and level it off about ¾ to 1 inch from the top of the container. If the mixture is powdery dry, water it thoroughly and wait a day or two to plant. Very fine seeds can be broadcast over the surface and covered with sand; larger seeds can either be planted in shallow furrows scratched into the surface or be poked in individually. Always remember that

P

SOWING SEEDS IN CONTAINERS

For small seeds like lettuce, first mix 1/4 package with 2 tablespoons sand. Scatter over moist potting mix in flat or aluminum pan with holes punched in bottom. Sprinkle with soil, firm, and water lightly. Set in protected area with bright light. Keep moist.

For large seeds like Swiss chard, sow in furrows made with a small stake. Sow according to label directions and water lightly. Set in protected area with bright light. Keep moist.

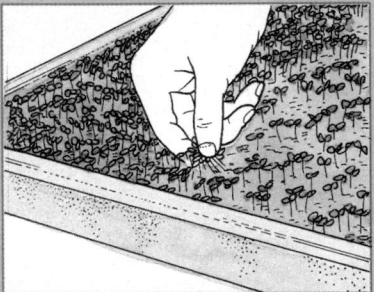

Thin seedlings of small, scatter-sown seeds (top drawing) to about 1 to 2 inches apart by snipping with scissors or pinching off with fingers.

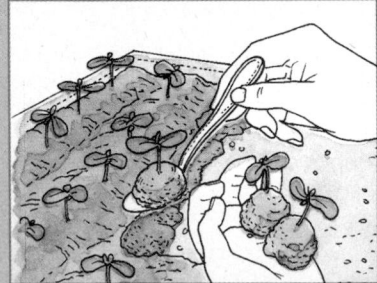

Transplant when seedlings have at least their second set of leaves. Scoop out with a kitchen spoon. Water regularly. If it's hot, shade plants.

seeds should be planted no deeper than recommended on packet labels; a good general rule is to cover seeds to a depth equal to twice their diameter. Cover seeds with the proper amount of prepared mixture, press down gently but firmly, and then water. Direct watering of the soil surface can sometimes dislodge the seeds. Instead, place the container in a tub, sink, or bucket containing a few inches of water. The planting mix in the container will absorb enough water within a few hours. Thereafter, keep the seeding mixture moist but not soaking wet.

For slow-sprouting seeds or for plants whose seedlings develop slowly, you can sow seeds in a pot, and then tie a clear plastic bag around it. Place the pot where it receives good light but not direct sunlight. Air can get through the plastic, but water vapor cannot get out; seedlings will have enough moisture to complete germination without further watering. If you use this technique, be sure that your planting mixture is sterile and that the container has not been used for planting before.

Transplanting seedlings. When the new seedlings have developed their second set of true leaves, it's time to transplant or thin them. If you don't need many plants, you can thin them in place. Give them enough "elbowroom" (1½ to 2 inches between them) to grow larger before you plant them out in the garden. But if you want to save most of the plants that have germinated, you will need to transplant them to larger containers for growth to planting-out size. Preferably, transplant them into individual pots or cups; then when you plant out in the garden, they'll suffer a minimum of root disturbance.

First transplanting. Fill a new container with moist planting mix. Loosen the soil around the seedling plants (a kitchen fork or spoon is handy for this), and carefully lift out a seedling. Or lift a clump of seedlings and gently tease individual plants apart from the tangled mass of roots. Handle a seedling by its leaves to avoid bruising or crushing its tender stem. With a pencil, poke a hole in the new container's planting mix, place the seedling in the hole, and firm the soil around it. Water the transplant right away. Do this for each seedling plant until all are transplanted. Keep these plants out of direct sunlight for a few days, until they have adjusted.

Final transplanting. A few weeks to a month after the initial transplant, the seedlings should be ready to plant in the garden. During that month, you can help their development by watering once with a half-strength liquid fertilizer solution or by sprinkling lightly with a slow-acting fertilizer.

Planting Techniques: Annuals and Perennials

Busy gardeners often forgo the pleasures of seed planting and buy seedlings of annuals, vegetables, and perennials at the nursery. Many of these plants—as well as some ground covers and hedge plants—are sold in plastic cell-packs, individual plastic pots, peat pots, and flats. Some perennials, perennial vegetables, and strawberries may also be sold bare-root during their dormant seasons; for planting instructions, see page 559.

You'll get the best results from small plants in pots and flats if you prepare the soil well, as you would for sowing seeds (see p. 563). Be sure not to let these plants dry out while they're waiting to be planted. For all small plants, plant so that the tops of their root balls are even with the soil surface.

From cell-packs. Plants in plastic cell-packs, with each plant in an individual cube of soil, are easy to remove. Push down with your thumb on the bottom of a soil cube, and remove the root ball with the other hand. See illustration, next page. If there is a mat of interwoven roots at the bottom of the root ball, tear it off—the plant will benefit from its removal. Otherwise, loosen the roots by pulling apart the bottom third of the root ball.

From pots. Plants in individual pots can be dislodged by placing one hand over the top of the container, with the plant stem between index and middle fingers, and then turning the container upside down. The plant and its root ball should slip out of the container into your hand.

From peat pots. If the plant is in a peat pot, plant it pot and all; the roots will grow through the pot. But make sure that the peat pot is moist before you plant it. A dry peat pot takes up moisture slowly from the soil, so roots may be slow in breaking through it. This can stunt the plant's growth or cause roots within the peat pot to dry out completely. Several minutes before transplanting, set the peat pot in a shallow container of water. Also be sure to cover the top of a peat pot with soil, because exposed peat acts as a wick to draw moisture out of the soil. If covering the peat would bury the plant too deeply, break off the top of the pot to slightly below the plant's soil level.

From flats. For plants in flats, a putty knife or spatula is a handy transplanting tool: separate the plants in the flat by cutting straight down around each one. Many gardeners prefer to separate individual plants out of flats gently with their fingers; they lose some soil this way, but keep more roots on the plant. If you work quickly, there will be little transplant shock.

Planting Techniques: Trees and Shrubs

At all times of the year, you can purchase trees and shrubs for immediate planting: bare-root in the dormant season, balled-and-burlapped generally in the cooler months, and planted in containers the year around.

Bare-root plants. In winter and early spring, you can buy bare-root plants at many retail nurseries and receive them from mail-order nurseries. A great many of the deciduous plants are available bare-root: fruit and shade trees, deciduous flowering shrubs, roses, grapes, and cane fruits.

Why go out in the cold and wet of winter to buy and set out bare-root plants when you can wait until spring, summer, or fall and plant the same plants from containers? There are two valid reasons:

■ You save money. Typically, a bare-root plant costs only 40 to 70 percent of the price of the same plant purchased in a container later in the year.

■ The manner in which a bare-root tree or shrub is planted makes it establish itself faster and often better than it would if set out later from a container.

The advantage of bare-root planting is that, when you set out the plant, you can refill the planting hole with the backfill soil that you dug from the hole: the roots will grow in only one kind of soil. In contrast, when you plant from a container or balled-and-burlapped, you put two soils, usually with different textures, in contact with each other. The two different kinds of soil can make it difficult to get uniform water penetration into the rooting area.

Planting techniques. For successful bare-root planting, the roots should be fresh and plump, not dry and withered. Even if roots appear fresh and plump, it's a good idea to soak the root system overnight in a bucket of water before you plant.

Dig the planting hole broad and deep enough to accommodate roots easily without cramping, bending, or cutting them to fit. But cut back any broken roots to healthy tissue. In areas with shallow or problem soils, a wider hole will speed establishment. Follow the illustrations on page 566 to dig the planting hole and set out the bare-root plant.

After the initial watering, water bare-root plantings conservatively. Dormant plants need less water than actively growing ones, and if you keep the soil too wet, new feeder roots may not form. Check soil periodically for moisture (using a trowel, fingers, soil-sampling tube, or any pointed instrument) and water accordingly: if the root zone soil is damp, the plant doesn't need water.

When weather turns warm and growth becomes active, you will need to water more frequently. Do not overwater: check soil for moisture, as mentioned above, before watering. If hot, dry weather follows planting, shade the new plant at least until it begins to grow. And be patient—some bare-root plants are slow to leaf out. Many will not do so until a few warm days break their dormancy.

PLANTING FROM CELL-PACKS

1 Poke plants out of cell-pack by pushing on bottom of individual cell; let gravity help. If tight, run a knife between side of container and soil.

2 Lightly separate matted roots. If there's a pad of coiled-up white roots at the bottom, cut it off so roots will grow outward into soil.

3 Without squeezing roots, position plant in generous planting hole. Form a watering basin around each plant. Water each one separately, with a gentle flow that won't disturb soil or roots.

Plants in containers. Plants grown in containers are popular for many reasons. Most broadleafed evergreen shrubs and trees—the West's landscaping specialties—are only offered growing in containers, and you can buy these plants in cans in all seasons. Available in a variety of sizes and prices, they are easy to transport and needn't be planted immediately. Furthermore, you can buy a container plant in bloom or fruit and see exactly what you are getting.

When shopping for container-grown plants, look for plants that have a generally healthy, vigorous appearance and good foliage. The root system should be unencumbered—that is, not badly tangled or constricted by the plant's own roots. Two signs of a seriously rootbound plant are roots protruding above the soil level and husky roots growing through the container's drainage holes. When selecting young trees, feel for circling roots around the trunk in the top two inches of soil. Additional indicators of crowded roots: plants that are large for the size of their containers, leggy plants, and dead twigs or branches. If you find any of these signs, look for another plant.

Removing plants from containers. Nurseries sell plants in a variety of containers—metal cans (1- and 5-gallon are standard sizes), plastic or fiber pots, clay pots, and wooden boxes for large specimen shrubs and trees. With straight-sided metal cans, have the cans slit down each side. The best time to cut cans is just before you plant, but you may prefer to have the cans cut at the nursery before taking the plants home. Handle cut edges with care. If planting is delayed, keep the plants in a cool place (out of hot sun) and water often enough to keep roots moist (water gently so that you don't wash out soil). With tapered metal cans and plastic containers, you can easily knock the plants out of their containers; sharp taps on the bottom and sides will loosen the root ball so that the plant will slide out easily. With fiber pots, it's often easier to tear the pots away from the root ball. ▶

P

THE PLANTING HOLE

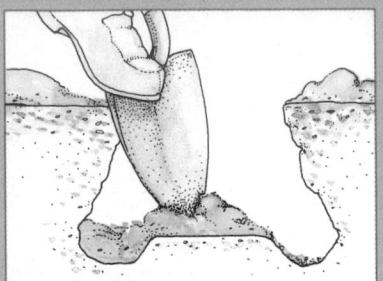

All tree and shrub planting begins with digging a hole. Dig it so that sides taper outward into the soil and are roughened, not smoothly sculpted (use a spading fork to dig, or to roughen shovel-dug sides); this lets roots penetrate more easily into surrounding soil. To prevent or minimize settling of the plant after planting and watering, make the hole a bit shallower than the root ball or root system of the plant it will receive, then dig deeper around edges of the hole's bottom. This leaves a firm plateau of undug soil to support plant at proper depth.

Planting techniques. Follow the steps shown in the illustration on page 567 to set out plants from containers. After completing step 1, cut off any outside roots that seem to be permanently kinked. Set plant in hole, spread roots, and fill in around roots with unamended backfill, firming with your fingers until hole is about half full. Water thoroughly to eliminate air pockets. Finish filling the hole; then go to step 3. After planting, pump the plant up and down slightly to settle wet soil around the roots, and check to see that the top of the root ball remains about 2 inches above soil grade.

Balled-and-burlapped plants. Certain plants have roots that won't survive bare-root transplanting. Instead, they are dug with a ball of soil around their roots, the soil ball is wrapped in burlap (or another sturdy material), and the wrapping is tied with twine to keep the ball intact. These are called balled-and-burlapped (or B-and-B) plants. Available in this fashion are some deciduous shrubs and trees, such evergreen shrubs as rhododendrons and azaleas, and various conifers.

Treat B-and-B plants carefully: don't use the trunk as a handle; and don't drop them, because the root ball could shatter, exposing the roots. Cradle the root ball well by supporting the bottom with one or both hands. If it is too heavy for one person to carry, get a friend to help you carry it in a sling of canvas or stout burlap.

Note: Many B-and-B plants are grown in clay or fairly heavy soil that will hold together well when the plants are dug up and burlapped. If your garden soil is medium to heavy in texture (heavier loam to clay), you can plant without amending the soil you return to the planting hole (called backfill soil). But when the B-and-B soil is more dense than the soil of your garden, there can be a problem in establishing the plant: its dense soil will not absorb water as quickly as the lighter garden soil around it. In such situations the soil ball around your B-and-B plant can become dry even when the garden soil is kept moist. To avoid this problem, amend the backfill as explained in the planting instructions that follow.

Planting techniques. Dig a hole twice as wide as the root ball and follow the instructions in the illustration on page 567. If the root ball is wrapped in burlap or another biodegradable fabric, you can leave it in place. But if a synthetic material encases the root ball, carefully remove it so that the roots can grow into the surrounding soil. Then fill the hole half full with backfill soil, firming it with your fingers or a stick.

If your soil is light to medium (and your B-and-B soil is heavier), mix one shovelful of organic amendment to each three shovelfuls of backfill soil. This will improve the water retention of the backfill soil, creating a transition zone between root ball and garden soil. Use peat moss, ground bark, nitrogen-fortified sawdust, or similar organic amendments—but not animal manures.

If you are setting out a B-and-B plant in a windy location, you should stake it. Drive the stake firmly into the soil beneath the planting hole on the side of the plant that faces the prevailing winds.

During the first couple of years after planting, pay close attention to watering—especially if the root-ball soil is heavier than your garden soil. Keep the surrounding garden soil moist (but never continuously soggy) so that the roots will grow out of the root ball into the surrounding soil as fast as possible.

Note: If a root ball becomes dry, it will shrink, harden, and fail to absorb water. Where there's a great difference between garden soil and root-ball soil, you can achieve better water penetration if you carefully punch holes in the root ball with a pointed instrument ¼ to ½ inch wide. Or use a root irrigator (see Watering Devices, p. 586). After several years, when roots have grown out and become established in your garden soil, the difference between soil types won't matter.

Plant Problems. See Visual Guide to Identifying Plant Problems p. 568

Pleaching

In pleaching, a method of training plant growth, branches are interwoven and plaited together to form a hedge or an arbor. Subsequent pruning merely maintains a neat, rather formal pattern. Trees that can be pleached include beech, apple, peach, and pear.

PLANTING BARE-ROOT...

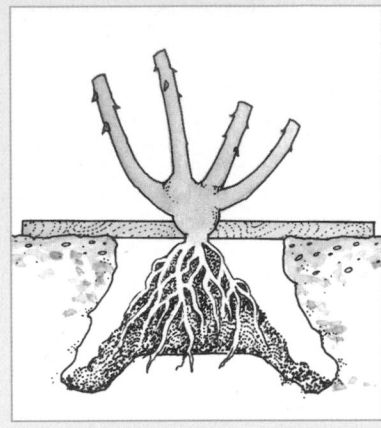

1 Make a firm cone of soil in hole. Spread roots over cone, positioning plant at same depth as (or slightly higher than) it was in growing field; use stick to check depth.

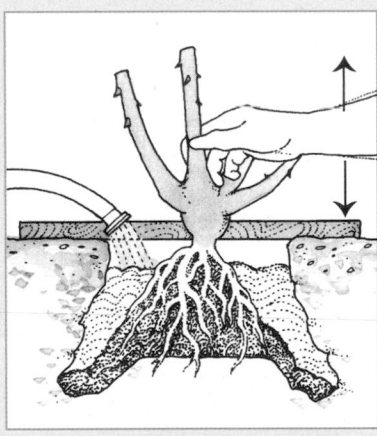

2 Fill in backfill soil nearly to top, firming it with your fingers as you fill. Then add water. If plant settles, pump it up and down, while soil is saturated, and raise it to proper level.

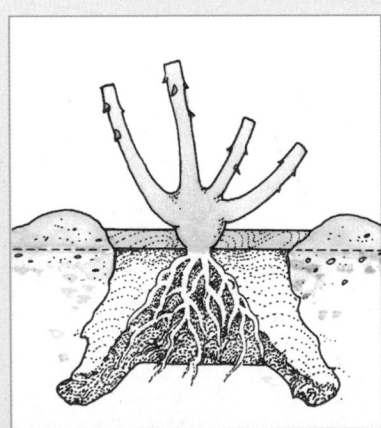

3 After plant is watered in and correct level has been established, fill in any remaining soil. When growing season begins, make ridge of soil around hole to form a watering basin.

...FROM A CONTAINER

1 Roots of container plants may have become coiled or matted. Spray soil off the outer few inches of root ball; then loosen and uncoil circling or twisted roots.

2 Spread roots out over firm plateau of soil, then add unamended backfill soil. Top of root ball should be about 2 inches above surrounding soil.

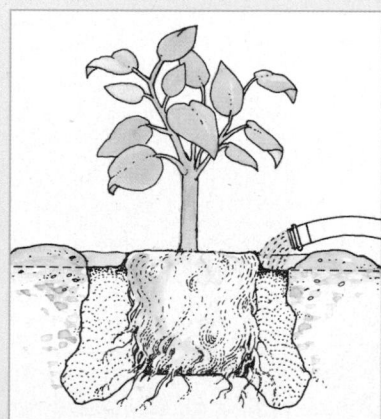

3 Make berm of soil to form watering moat. Irrigate gently—water should remain in moat rather than flood basin; objective is to keep trunk base dry.

...OR BALLED-AND-BURLAPPED

1 Set balled-and-burlapped plant into planting hole, placing root ball on firm plateau of undug soil; top of root ball then should be about 2 inches above surrounding soil.

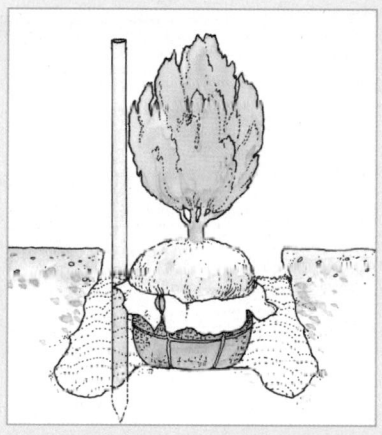

2 Untie burlap and spread it out to uncover about half of root ball. Drive stake into soil alongside root ball before filling hole with backfill.

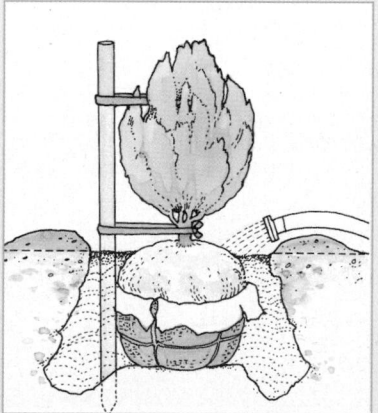

3 After firming in backfill soil, make berm of soil to form watering moat. Gently water in plant; then loosely tie plant to stake. Burlap will slowly decay.

Pocket Gophers

Pocket gophers are serious pests in many areas of the West, and in coastal California they rank among the top three garden pests. Like little bulldozers, they dig out a network of tunnels—usually 6 to 18 inches below the surface—with strong, clawed forefeet. Tunnels near the surface are for gathering food; deeper ones are for sleeping, storing food, and raising young. Gophers eat roots, bulbs, and sometimes entire plants by pulling them down into their burrows. Well suited to burrow life, they have small eyes and ears that don't clog with dirt, and the flexibility needed to turn around in tight spaces.

The first sign of gopher trouble often is a fan-shaped mound of fresh, finely pulverized earth in a lawn or flower bed; this soil is a by-product of burrowing operations, brought to the surface through short side runs opening off the main burrow. A plug of earth is used to close the hole.

Controls. Trapping is the most efficient method of catching gophers. Avoid the temptation to place a single trap down a hole. Your chances of catching a gopher are much greater when you dig down to the main horizontal runway connecting with the surface hole and place two traps in the runway, one on either side of your excavation. Attach each trap to a stake on the surface with a chain or wire (this prevents a trapped gopher from dragging the trap farther into a burrow). The Macabee trap is the most effective. Box-type traps also work and are easier to set, but they require a larger hole to be dug for insertion.

When the traps are in place, plug the hole with a ball of carrot tops, fresh grass, or other tender greens; their scent attracts gophers. Next, place a board or soil over the greens and the hole to block all light. Check traps frequently, and clear tunnels if the gopher has pushed soil into the traps. Be persistent: a clever gopher may avoid your first traps.

Poison baits are very effective for the control of trapwise gophers. Probe for the deep burrows with a rod or sharp stick, insert bait, and close the hole. These baits are hazardous to other living things, so be sure not to spill any on the ground. And although poisoning of dogs and cats from eating poisoned gophers is rare, it can happen.

If your garden is subject to ongoing invasion by gophers from neighboring fields or orchards —or if all your trapping efforts fail—you can protect roots of young plants by lining the sides and bottom of planting holes with light-gauge chicken wire or hardware cloth.

P

Visual Guide to Identifying
PLANT
PROBLEMS

Problems on plant leaves are often difficult to diagnose— there are so many possible causes, including insects, disease organisms, nutritional deficiencies, and cultural practices. Yet identifying the cause properly is the most important step in finding a solution. These pages will help you identify common maladies on plant leaves, so that you can refer to the entry for the pest to determine effective control measures. Also be sure to read Pest Management (p. 559).

EATEN LEAVES

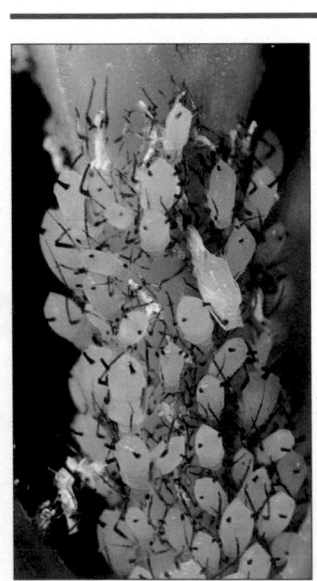

Slugs, Snails
Irregular holes   p. 574

Leaf-Cutting Bees
Scalloped edges
p. 552

Root Weevils
Notches in leaf edges   p. 573

Squash Bugs
Eaten, wilted leaves   p. 577

Oak Moth Adult (top), Larvae
Irregular holes   p. 557

DISTORTED LEAVES, STEMS, AND FRUIT

Citrus Bud Mites
Distorted fruit, buds   p. 555

Thrips (above), Leaf Rollers (below)
Rolled or distorted leaves pp. 579, 554

Aphids
Distorted new leaves   p. 530

Peach Leaf Curl
Curled, distorted leaves   p. 558

Galls
Unusual growths   p. 547

WILTED AND DISCOLORED LEAVES

Powdery Mildew
Wilted leaves coated with white powder p. 570

Mealybugs
White cottony masses p. 555

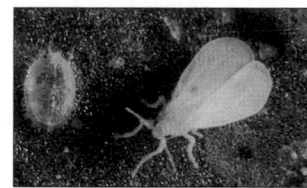

Whiteflies
Whitish specks on leaf undersides p. 589

Mites
Yellow stippling p. 555

Nitrogen Deficiency
Yellow leaves p. 556

Iron Deficiency (Chlorosis)
Yellow leaves, green veins p. 535

Oak Root Fungus
Dull yellow leaves, wilting, entire dead branches, possibly brown mushrooms at base in early winter p. 558

Anthracnose
Irregular blotches of dead tissue, dropping leaves p. 554

Oak Root Fungus–Resistant Plants

A plant may be resistant to oak root fungus until it is weakened by insects, drought, or other cultural problems—then it will become infected.

Acacia longifolia	Erica arborea	Persimmon
Acer palmatum	Eucalyptus camaldulensis	Phlomis fruticosa
Arbutus menziesii	Fraxinus velutina 'Modesto'	Pinus halepensis
Avocado	Ginkgo biloba	Pistacia chinensis
Brachychiton populneus	Liquidambar orientalis	Plum, Japanese
Carpenteria californica	Magnolia	Prunus lyonii
Celtis occidentalis	Mahonia aquifolium	Sambucus canadensis
Cercis	Mahonia nevinii	Walnut, California black
Cotinus coggygria	Nandina domestica	Wisteria sinensis

Scale
Bumps on stems, leaves p. 574

Black Spot
Black spots with fringed edges p. 554

Fireblight
Dry, scorched leaves p. 546

Verticillium Wilt
Leaf dieback p. 582

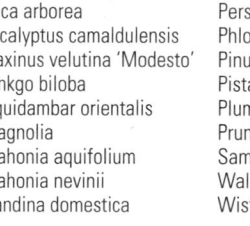

Rust
Yellow-to-orange pustules on leaf undersides p. 574

Sooty Mold
Black sticky mold on leaves p. 576

ments, by improving aeration and water penetration, also improve the efficiency of these organisms in making nitrogen available.

The final product of the action by soil bacteria and other organisms on organic materials is humus. By binding minute clay particles into larger crumbs, this soft, sticky material improves aeration and drainage. And in sandy soil, humus remains in pore spaces and helps hold water and nutrients.

Types of amendments. Because all organic materials are continuously being decomposed by soil organisms, even the best of soils will benefit from periodic applications of organic amendments. Included among organic soil amendments are ground bark, peat moss, leaf mold, sawdust and wood shavings, manure, compost (p. 535), and many other plant remains.

When you add organic amendments to your soil, be generous and mix them deeply and uniformly. For the most marked improvement, add a volume equal to 25 to 50 percent of the total soil volume in the cultivated area. Mix in thoroughly, either by spading and respading or by rotary-tilling. The mixing will add air to the soil, and amendments will help keep it there.

Cautions. Organisms that break down organic materials need nitrogen to sustain their own lives. If they cannot get all the nitrogen they require from the organic material itself, they will draw upon any available nitrogen in the soil. This, in effect, "steals" the nitrogen that is vital to plants' roots; the result can be a temporary nitrogen depletion and reduced plant growth.

To raw wood shavings, ground bark, straw, or manure containing much litter (such as straw or sawdust), you will need to add nitrogen. After application, use 1 pound of ammonium sulfate for each 1-inch-deep layer of raw organic material spread over 100 square feet. A year later, apply half as much ammonium sulfate, and in the third and fourth years, use one-fourth as much.

Liberal and prolonged use of organic matter can significantly lower soil pH—that is, increase its acidity. Where soil already is neutral or acid, this can result, over a period of time, in an overly acid soil. A simple soil test (see entry on this page) will reveal your soil's pH.

Soil pH

Soil pH is a measurement of one aspect of the soil's chemical composition: the concentration of hydrogen ions (an ion is an electrically charged atom or molecule). The relative concentration of hydrogen ions is represented by the symbol pH followed by a number. A pH of 7 means that the soil is neutral, neither acid nor alkaline. A pH below 7 indicates acidity; one above 7 indicates alkalinity. The surest way to determine your soil's pH is to have the soil tested. See Soil Test (this page).

Acid soil. Most common in regions where rainfall is heavy, acid soil is often associated with sandy soils and soils high in organic matter. Most plants grow well in mildly acid soil, but highly acid soil is inhospitable.

In the West, overly acid soils are common in western Washington, in western Oregon, and along the north coast of California. Add lime to such soils only if a soil test indicates that it is needed and only in the quantity recommended by your county agricultural agent. If you attempt to raise your soil's pH with lime, be sure that any fertilizers you use thereafter do not have an acid reaction.

Alkaline soil. Common in regions with light rainfall, alkaline soil is high in calcium carbonate (lime) or certain other minerals, such as sodium. Many plants grow well in moderately alkaline soil; others, notably camellias, rhododendrons, and azaleas, will not thrive there because the alkalinity reduces the availability of particular elements necessary for their growth.

Large-scale chemical treatment of highly alkaline soil is expensive and complex. A better bet is to plant in raised beds or containers, using a good prepared soil mix.

Soils that are only slightly alkaline will support many garden plants. They can be made to grow acid-loving plants with liberal additions of peat moss, ground bark, or sawdust; fertilization with acid-type fertilizers; and periodic applications of chelates (see Chlorosis, p. 535).

Deep watering can help lessen alkalinity but is advisable only if the soil drains quickly.

Soil Polymers

Superabsorbent polymers are a recent development that can increase water retention of soils. Particularly useful in potting mixes, these gel-like polymers absorb hundreds of times their weight in water; in potting soil, the gel holds both water and dissolved nutrients for plant roots to use. Because the gel retains water that normally drains from the soil, plants still have a source of moisture when their potting soil becomes dry. This lets you stretch intervals between waterings. And plants grow better because the gel eliminates the wide fluctuations of moisture that can occur between waterings. Polyacrylamide gel is the longest-lasting kind. Mix the dry material with water to expand the particles; then add to potting mix in the proportion recommended by the manufacturer—usually about 1 pint gel to 6 pints potting mix.

Soils

An understanding of your soil is perhaps the most important aspect of gardening. It will guide you in watering and fertilizing your plants—in other words, in caring for them.

Soil is a mass of mineral particles mixed with air, water, and living and dead organic matter. The size (texture) and arrangement (structure) of the mineral particles greatly influence a soil's water- and nutrient-holding capacity, aeration, and ease of workability. The basic soil structure and texture—together with its pH and its content of organic matter, air, and nutrients—determine a soil's quality. For a discussion of soil texture and structure, see next page.

Soil Salinity

An excess of salts (salinity) in the soil is a widespread problem in arid parts of the West. These salts may be naturally present in the soil or they may come from water (especially softened water, which has a high sodium content), from fertilizers and chemical amendments, and from manures with high salt content. Where these salts are not leached through the soil by high rainfall or deep irrigation, they reach high concentrations in the root zone, inhibiting germination of seeds, stunting growth, and producing "salt burn"—scorched and yellowed leaves or browned and withered leaf margins.

Periodic, thorough leaching of the soil with water will lessen its salt content; but for effective leaching, drainage must be good.

Soil Test

A soil analysis will disclose your soil's pH (acidity or alkalinity) and also can reveal nutrient deficiencies. In some western states, the agricultural extension service can test your soil; if not, it should be able to direct you to commercial soil laboratories that can make such analyses. Many nurseries sell soil-test kits that can indicate definite problems.

Sooty Mold

A common black mold (see photograph, p. 569) that grows on leaves and twigs of trees and shrubs, sooty mold occurs when a fungus grows on honeydew secreted by sap-sucking insects such as aphids and scale. Wash or wipe the mold from leaves. Control the insects.

Sowbug. See Pillbug, Sowbug   p. 561

Species. See Plant Classification   p. 561

Specimen

As used by nursery staff, the term "specimen" refers to a tree or shrub large enough to make an immediate, significant contribution to a planting. "Specimen" may also refer to a single large plant in a conspicuous location.

Sphagnum

Various mosses native to bogs are called sphagnum. Much of the peat moss sold in the West is composed partly or entirely of decomposed sphagnum. These mosses also are collected live and packaged in whole pieces, fresh or dried. They are used for lining hanging baskets, and for air layering (p. 552).

SOIL TEXTURE AND SOIL STRUCTURE

Clay particles are the smallest mineral component of a soil, sand particles are the largest, and silt represents the intermediate size. Clay and sand give their names to two soil types. A combination of the three particle sizes forms the basis for the soil called loam. See illustration.

Clay soils. Also called adobe, gumbo, or just "heavy" soils, clay soils are composed of microscopically small mineral particles. These tiny particles are flattened and fit closely together; pore spaces between particles (for air and water) also are small. But because small clay particles offer the greatest surface area per volume of all soil types, clay soils can contain the greatest volume of nutrients in soluble or exchangeable form (see Nutrients, Basic, p. 556). When clay soils get wet, drainage—the downward movement of water—is slow. This means that loss of soluble nutrients by leaching also is slow. And because of its high density, clay soil is the slowest to warm in spring.

Sandy soils. Sandy soils have comparatively large particles that are cube-shaped rather than flattened. The particle size and shape allow for much larger pore spaces between particles than clay soils have; consequently, sandy soils contain a lot of air, drain well, and warm quickly. In a given volume of sandy soil, the surface area of particles is less than that in the same volume of clay. The volume of soluble and exchangeable nutrients in sandy soil is therefore correspondingly less. And because sandy soil drains quickly, and hence leaches out nutrients faster than clay, plants in sand need watering and fertilizing more often than those in clay.

Loam. Loam is a gardener's term for soil intermediate between clay and sand. It contains a mixture of clay, silt, and sand particles, and in addition, is well supplied with organic matter. Thus loam—a compromise between the extremes of clay and sand—is the ideal gardening soil: draining well (but not too fast drying), leaching only moderately, and containing enough air for healthy root growth.

SOIL PARTICLES AND SOIL TYPES

Size of mineral particles determines a soil's texture and designates its type. Loam—a mixture of particle sizes and organic matter—is considered ideal garden soil.

Clay
Less than
1/12,500 in.
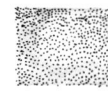

Silt
Up to
1/500 in.

Fine sand
Up to
1/250 in.
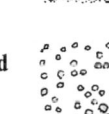

Medium sand
Up to
1/50 in.

Largest sand particles
1/12 in.
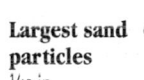

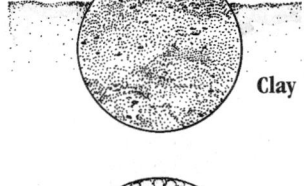
Clay

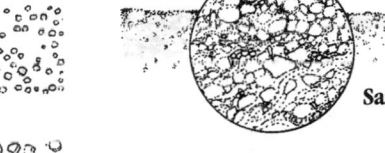
Sand

Loam

Spike

A flowering stem with flowers directly attached (without any short flower stems) along its upper portion is a spike. The flowers open in sequence, beginning at the bottom of the spike. Familiar examples are *Gladiolus* and red-hot poker (*Kniphofia*). The term is often applied loosely to flower clusters that resemble spikes—especially to racemes, which differ in that each individual flower has its own short stem.

Spore

A spore is a simple type of reproductive cell capable of producing a new plant. Certain kinds of plants (such as algae, fungi, mosses, and ferns) reproduce by spores.

Sport

A mutation—a spontaneous variation from the normal pattern—is called a sport. In horticulture, a sport is usually seen as a branch that differs noticeably from its parent plant. Examples include the spurred apple varieties that occur as limb sports on standard apple varieties and camellias propagated from branches that have shown changes in color or form of flowers.

Spotted Spurge

A demon in warm weather, the very aggressive summer annual spotted spurge grows from a shallow taproot in exposed areas such as sparse lawns, garden walks, and flower beds. It spreads fast; in as little as a month, each plant can produce several thousand seeds in clusters of tiny pinkish seed capsules. Oblong ¼- to ⅜-inch leaves have reddish green undersides. Cut stems exude a milky juice. Plants turn red-orange and decline in fall (especially noticeable in lawns) as temperatures drop. Seeds germinate as early as January in Palm Springs, and seedlings start active growth when temperatures climb in spring.

Control is difficult. Hoe out isolated plants early, before they produce seed, or spray them with glyphosate. On lawns (except dichondra), use a pre-emergence broad-leafed herbicide appropriately labeled to control spotted spurge. Watch for small plants in areas that have had problems in past years. A vigorous, well-fertilized lawn provides tough competition for spotted spurge. For cool-season lawn grasses, mowing the grass higher helps to discourage this weed.

Spur

Some fruit trees, particularly apples and cherries, bear their blossoms on a specialized short twig called a spur. Spurs are also short and saclike or long and tubular projections from a flower. The columbine (*Aquilegia*) is a familiar flower with pronounced spurs. Spurs can arise from either sepals or petals.

Squash Bugs

About ⅝ inch in length, squash bugs are a problem on many plants of the squash family, particularly in high desert and mountain areas. Damage is usually greatest on winter squash and pumpkin plants: the bugs can cause leaves to wilt completely and also will damage the fruit (see photograph, p. 568). Summer squash, melons, and cucumbers are seldom affected.

In spring, adult bugs lay their eggs on squash leaves. If you find a mass of hard brown eggs crowded together on a leaf underside, destroy them. Squash bugs spend nights under flat objects, so put out boards in the evening; in

S

Visual Guide to Identifying
WEEDS

Uninvited and usually unattractive, weeds poke their scruffy leaves up into flower beds and lawns, ramble freely around the garden stealing moisture and nutrients from ornamental plants, and make a garden look unkempt. Some of them even jump fences to invade native plant habitats. Use this visual guide to help you identify common western weeds. For controls, see the guidelines here, where provided, the individual weed entry, or Weed Control (p. 589).

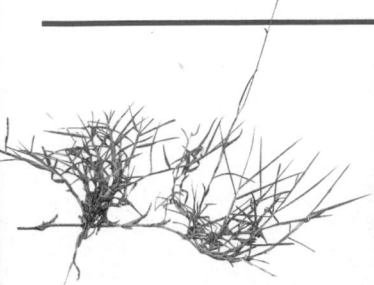

Bermuda Grass
Warm-season grass that spreads by seed or underground runners   p. 530

Dandelion
Edible, broad-leafed weed common to beds and lawns   pp. 258, 539

Yellow Oxalis
Broad-leafed weed that thrives in sun or shade; deep taproot makes it hard to control   p. 558

Crabgrass
Well-known grassy weed common in lawns and beds; thrives in warm, wet soil   p. 537

Purslane *(Portulaca oleracea)*
Prostrate, broad-leafed weed with fleshy leaves and small yellow flowers   pp. 435, 573

Poison Oak
Vining, deciduous shrub that causes skin irritation; look for specifically labeled herbicides and note cautions   p. 460

Spotted Spurge
Low-growing, rapidly spreading broad-leafed weed that reproduces prolifically by seed   p. 577

Scarlet Pimpernel *(Anagallis)*
Annual, broad-leafed weed with reddish flowers; easily hoed or pulled   p. 150

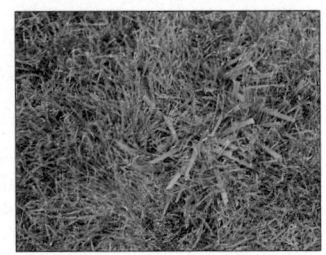

Quack Grass
Aggressive perennial weed in gardens and lawns; herbicides are the most effective control

Kikuyu Grass
A vigorous perennial grass, sometimes used as a turf in coastal areas; spreads readily by underground stems   p. 551

Common Mallow
Deep-rooted, broad-leafed weed; mature plants hard to pull, so hoe or pull when young, or use appropriate herbicide

Annual Bluegrass *(Poa annua)*
Common annual weed in lawns; easy to pull or hoe elsewhere   p. 430

Black Medic, Burclover
Two similar, low, spreading, broad-leafed weeds with small yellow flowers, usually annual, that are common in under-fertilized lawns and gardens; pull young weeds, increase nitrogen fertilizer in lawns

Annual Sowthistle
Upright, broad-leafed weed with yellow flowers and puffball seed heads; pull or hoe young plants

Nettleleaf Goosefoot
Annual, broad-leafed weed with greenish flower clusters; pull or hoe young plants

Common Groundsel
Upright, broad-leafed perennial with small yellow flowers and puffball seed heads; hoe or pull young plants

Bindweed
Vining, broad-leafed weed with white flowers; tough to control because of its long-lived seeds and deep taproots
p. 531

Nutsedge (Nutgrass)
Grasslike perennial common to wet areas; yellow or purple flowering forms   p. 556

WORST WAIST-HIGH WEEDS

Many plants introduced into western gardens for ornamental use have jumped the garden fence and proliferated. Uncontrolled by the pests that plagued them in their native habitats, they threaten, in some areas, to crowd out the native flora of our parks and rural areas. Notorious examples are pictured here.

Sharp mattocks have proven the best tools for extirpating pampas grass; use them to chop off plants just below the soil surface—pampas grass will not resprout from the roots. Seedlings can be hand-pulled.

Young broom plants are not too difficult to pull up by hand (use a rocking motion). Give older plants the mattock treatment. Pull seedlings as soon as you spot them.

Blackberry spreads rapidly by underground runners; birds eat the ripe berries and scatter the seeds. For controls, see Blackberry, p. 531.

Herbicides are generally not accepted in ecology-minded communities, but if they are accepted in your location, see Weed Control, p. 589.

Pampas Grass

Scotch Broom

Blackberry

WEED CONTROL WITH HERBICIDES

Caution is the byword in using any chemical herbicide. Carefully read (and follow) label directions not only for application but also for the plants on which the product may be used (those not harmed by its proper application). The herbicide user can be held responsible for damage to neighboring properties resulting from uses not specified on the product label. If you have a particularly bad weed problem, consider contacting a commercial weed sprayer. They have a larger arsenal of sprays available.

Pre-emergence. Pre-emergence herbicides work by inhibiting growth of germinating weed seeds and very young seedlings. Apply them to weed-free soil; if weeds are already present, thoroughly remove the weeds or kill them with a translocated herbicide (see below). Common pre-emergents include:

- **DCPA (Dacthal).** Controls annual grasses and some broad-leafed weeds. Can be used on a wide variety of ornamental plantings, including turf.

- **EPTC (Eptam).** Controls a number of grasses and broad-leafed weeds among ornamental plants. Must be incorporated into soil immediately to reduce loss through vaporization.

- **Oryzalin (Surflan).** Controls annual grasses and many broad-leafed weeds (including spotted spurge and yellow oxalis) in some turf grasses and ornamental plantings.

- **Simazine.** Controls a wide variety of broad-leafed and grassy weeds among ornamentals and some crops. Effect is long-lasting—could nearly fit into the Total Soil Cleanup category. Not recommended for desert regions or sandy soils.

- **Trifluralin.** Controls many grasses and annual broad-leafed weeds in ornamental plantings.

Postemergence. Two types of weed killer act on growing weeds and other unwanted vegetation. The contact herbicides are effective when they touch the plant. Translocated herbicides must be absorbed by the plant, which they kill by interfering with plant metabolism; these are slower to show effectiveness than the contact kinds. Common post-emergents include:

- **Fluazifop-butyl.** Translocated. Controls actively growing grassy weeds; best results when weeds are healthy and you add a surfactant (spreader-sticker) to the mixture. Can be sprayed over many ornamentals; see product label.

- **Glyphosate.** Translocated. Controls a great variety of actively growing vegetation: grasses, perennial weeds, woody plants (including poison oak); repeat application sometimes needed on perennial and woody plants. Effectiveness may be enhanced by addition of a surfactant (spreader-sticker).

- **Herbicidal soap (Superfast).** Contact. Made from selected fatty acids, like insecticidal soaps. Degrades quickly. Provides quick top-kill. Works best against annual weeds.

- **Sethoxydim (Poast).** Translocated. Controls annual grasses (but not annual bluegrass or hard fescue) in ornamental plantings. Should be applied at particular stage of weed growth; needs addition of an oil-based surfactant (spreader-sticker) to be effective.

- **Triclopyr (Brush-b-gon).** Translocated. Used on hard-to-kill brush and weeds, such as blackberry and poison oak.

Total soil cleanup. Chemicals for total soil cleanup (prometon is the most common) have a broader-spectrum toxicity than the previous herbicides and/or a significant longevity in the soil. They are often misused. Follow the special application procedures outlined on the product label.

Packaged controls are listed alphabetically by generic name (the name you will find on the product label under "active ingredients") or common name; trade name (where different from generic name) appears in parentheses.

Standard controls. Nature keeps whitefly populations in check most of the time: tiny wasp species (p. 533) are parasites of the nymphs and pupae, and some predatory creatures feed on them. When you spray with a chemical insecticide, you may also kill those parasites and predators—resulting in an increase of whiteflies. So before you decide to use a chemical control, consider these options:

- Eliminate highly susceptible plants from your garden.

- Hose off infested plants, hitting both sides of all leaves to wash off adults and crawlers (newly hatched nymphs); repeat every few days. Insecticidal soap can be more effective than water, and it is less harmful than insecticides to natural enemies.

- Place yellow cards or stakes covered with sticky material among infested plants. The color attracts adult whiteflies; the sticky material captures and holds them.

- Buy and release in your garden a commercially reared natural parasite: *Encarsia formosa* wasps. They are parasites of the greenhouse whitefly (common species) and will kill them in a greenhouse or outdoors.

- On plants like squash, get rid of old, nonproductive yellow leaves in the center of the plant. These leaves carry many whitefly nymphs.

On edible plants, use pyrethrins or malathion. On nonedible plants, you can use systemics, neem, chlorpyrifos, or summer oils. Increase spray effectiveness by spraying at night, while whiteflies are resting.

Recent outbreaks of introduced species of whitefly, including the ash whitefly, are not effectively controlled with chemical sprays. Instead, massive releases of parasitic wasps by state agencies have been successful in bringing these annoying pests down to reasonable levels.

Cool-climate controls. In cool climates—including all of Colorado and areas to the north and northwest—whiteflies don't overwinter outdoors; all garden infestations originate from indoor plants or are imported as transplants. Inspect greenhouse and indoor plants and eliminate any whiteflies you find. When you buy new plants for your garden—particularly bedding plants, which may have started their lives in a greenhouse—carefully examine the undersides of leaves for the nymphs.

Whorl

Whorls are composed of three or more leaves, branches, or flowers growing in a circle from a joint (node) on a stem or trunk.

Xeriscape

Derived from *xeros*, Greek for "dry," Xeriscape is a patented name that stands for water-conserving landscapes.

RESOURCE DIRECTORY

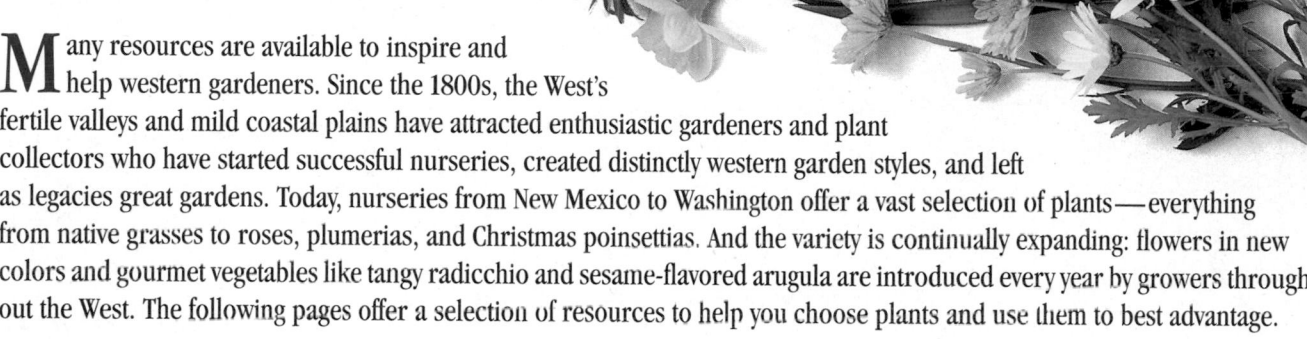

Many resources are available to inspire and help western gardeners. Since the 1800s, the West's fertile valleys and mild coastal plains have attracted enthusiastic gardeners and plant collectors who have started successful nurseries, created distinctly western garden styles, and left as legacies great gardens. Today, nurseries from New Mexico to Washington offer a vast selection of plants—everything from native grasses to roses, plumerias, and Christmas poinsettias. And the variety is continually expanding: flowers in new colors and gourmet vegetables like tangy radicchio and sesame-flavored arugula are introduced every year by growers throughout the West. The following pages offer a selection of resources to help you choose plants and use them to best advantage.

Botanical Gardens, Arboretums, and Estate Gardens

Scattered around the West are many fine gardens, open to the public, that range in size from a city block to hundreds of acres. Some were planted by early collectors such as Elia J. "Lucky" Baldwin, whose turn-of-the-century estate on the old Rancho Santa Anita formed the nucleus of the Arboretum of Los Angeles County, and the late opera diva Ganna Walska, whose estate in Santa Barbara, California, displays novelties such as giant topiary animals.

Some public gardens mimic wild land; others are carefully tailored formal gardens or museum-style displays of labeled plants. If you're planting a new garden or adding to an established one, a visit to a public garden can give you ideas to use at home, like show-stopping flower combinations, innovative ways to plant vegetable beds, and interesting container plantings. Before you purchase new plants, you can see which plants are best for your area and what they look like when fully grown.

Mail-Order Catalogs

Western nurseries and garden centers, too numerous to list in this resource directory, offer a wide variety of plants and seeds throughout the year. But sooner or later adventurous gardeners may want to try growing novelties such as blue potatoes or chocolate-colored bell peppers. Many mail-order sources specialize in unusual or tough-to-find varieties. The Native Seeds/SEARCH catalog, for instance, lists brown tepary beans (favored for vegetarian pâtés), chiltepines (wild chilies best described as small round firecrackers), and a native California sunflower with lemon yellow flowers. Some mail-order catalogs provide growing tips, recipes, or pieces of gardening wisdom among their listings.

Most catalogs tantalize readers into making unplanned purchases, but keep in mind that impulse buying is a surefire way to end up with a mishmash of a landscape. Our advice for great performance and the most value for your dollar? Be a smart shopper. Before you buy plants or seeds, form a clear idea of your needs by assessing the space you are planning to plant, the amount of sunlight it receives, and its soil conditions. Think about potential plant combinations and consider compatible bloom times and the plants' colors and heights as well as the frequency of watering and fertilizing they require. Also, estimate how many plants you'll need.

Once you know your needs, read the catalog's plant descriptions carefully. Catalog language combines solid information with consumer marketing. As a result, you can expect some jargon. Here's a sampling of catalog phrases and their meanings:

"Start seeds indoors" describes seeds that require more care than usual. They may germinate slowly or need more warmth, or the seedlings may demand extra time or attention prior to their planting outdoors. Many perennials fall into this category.

When a vegetable is proclaimed "novel" or "unusual" or has "unique" color or shape, you know flavor and texture are secondary. "Giant" is a clue that vegetables so described may be better mounted above the fireplace than tossed into a winter stew.

Watch out for anything "vigorous." The term implies that the vine, shrub, or vegetable in question is ready and able to outcompete most plants in its path. If space is limited, look for compact, bush, or dwarf varieties.

Plants that "self-sow readily" are usually annuals and biennials (but could be trees or shrubs) that you plant once and have forevermore. Each year a new crop of seeds germinates and grows without any help from you. Depending on the plant and your attitude, it may become a weed or a favorite companion.

"Sow in place" usually means that the plant doesn't survive transplanting well. It's a wise directive to follow when given.

Scientific Plant Names

In public gardens, nurseries, and catalogs, you'll most likely encounter Latin plant names. To learn what they mean and why they are important, see pages 604–605. How do you pronounce them? For guidelines, see pages 606–607.

BOTANICAL GARDENS
and Arboretums

Strybing Arboretum and Botanical Gardens

Botanical gardens and arboretums are important resources for home gardeners. They display plants from around the world and from their own regions, often in landscape situations. They may have demonstration gardens packed with flowers, fruits, and vegetables or displays featuring irrigation devices, mulches, fencing, or paving. Many offer classes or seminars in gardening techniques, operate horticultural libraries, and sell hard-to-find plants. Some are living plant laboratories that oversee the propagation and preservation of endangered plants. Below we list the major (and a few less well known) botanical gardens and arboretums around the West that we have visited. Hours are subject to change.

ARIZONA

The Arboretum at Flagstaff
Box 670
Woody Mountain Road
Flagstaff, AZ 86002
(520) 774-1441
Open Monday through Saturday 10 to 3; also open Sunday noon to 3, April through September
Specialty: high-elevation, low-rainfall plants
Ten developed acres on 200 acres of ponderosa pine forest land (elevation 7,150 feet) display plants of the Colorado Plateau—northern Arizona, northeastern New Mexico, southern Colorado, and southern Utah—in view of the San Francisco Peaks.

The Arizona Sonora Desert Museum
2021 N. Kinney Road
Tucson, AZ 85743
(520) 883-2702 (recorded information); (520) 883-1380
Open daily 8:30 to 5:30 October through February; 7:30 to 6 March through September
Specialty: plants and animals of the Sonoran Desert
This living museum encompasses more than 25 developed acres on a total of 88 acres, including demonstration gardens where you can see plants such as palo verdes and salvias that are well adapted to desert gardens. An enclosed garden contains hummingbirds and is landscaped with plants that attract them. Other exhibits feature animals of the desert, such as bighorn sheep, coyotes, prairie dogs, mountain lions, and reptiles.

The Boyce Thompson Arboretum
Superior, AZ 85273
Located 60 miles east of Phoenix (3 miles west of Superior) on Highway 60
(602) 689-2811 (recorded information)
Open daily 8 to 5; closed Christmas Day
Specialty: plants adapted to the Sonoran Desert
The steep red cliffs of Magma Ridge provide a dramatic backdrop for demonstration gardens and 2 miles of nature trails on this arboretum's 35 acres. Plants adapted to southern Arizona's Sonoran Desert, as well as plants native to the Chihuahuan Desert, are displayed. The Main Loop Trail is especially scenic: it winds through a section of the rugged ridge and back through a cool, shaded riparian habitat populated by plants like Chilean palo verdes.

The Desert Botanical Garden
1201 N. Galvin Parkway
Phoenix, AZ 85008
(602) 941-1225
Open 7 A.M. to 10 P.M. summer, 8 A.M. to 8 P.M. winter
Specialty: plants of the Sonoran Desert
Displays on 145 acres of landscaped grounds focus mainly on plants and ecology of the Sonoran Desert. Trails snake among many kinds of cacti, including giant saguaros. Other displays feature plants native to deserts of Mexico, Australia, and Africa. October through May is the best time to visit. Wildflowers add seasonal color.

Tucson Botanical Gardens
2150 N. Alvernon Way
Tucson, AZ 85712
(520) 326-9255
Open daily 8:30 to 4:30; closed major holidays
Specialty: planting ideas for desert gardeners
Five acres of display areas and gardens include the Sensory Garden, which invites exploring by touch, smell, and taste; the Spring Wildflower Garden; and the Backyard Bird Garden. In the Xeriscape Garden plants are grouped by water needs. March and April are the gardens' most colorful months.

CALIFORNIA

Arboretum of Los Angeles County
301 N. Baldwin Avenue
Arcadia, CA 91007-2697
(818) 821-3222
Open daily 9 to 4:30; closed Christmas Day
Specialties: plants from around the world, demonstration gardens
Demonstration gardens and greenhouses are scattered throughout these 127 acres of lush landscaped grounds, where boisterous peacocks wander. Plants are grouped

according to regions of origin. Among them are many that are being tested for suitability to Southern California's climate. Palm-edged Baldwin Lake and an 1880s Queen Anne cottage are popular backdrops for films and television.

Fullerton Arboretum
California State University, Fullerton
1900 Associated Road
Fullerton, CA 92634-9480
(714) 773-3579
Open daily 8 to 4:45; closed major holidays
Specialties: fruit trees, California natives, plants by region
A 26-acre oasis that displays plants from around the world, many of them arranged into major plant groupings: Temperate Zone, Tropical Zone, and Arid Zone. Included are plants from Australia, South Africa, and South America, as well as California chaparral and foothills natives, a deciduous fruit orchard, a citrus plot, and plants such as Catalina cherry from the California Channel Islands.

The Huntington Botanical Gardens
1151 Oxford Road
San Marino, CA 91108
(818) 405-2141
Open Tuesday through Friday 1 to 4:30, Saturday and Sunday 10:30 to 4:30; closed major holidays
Specialty: plants from around the world
More than 150 meticulously landscaped acres, showcasing one of the country's finest collections of plants, surround the former mansion of the late railroad tycoon Henry E. Huntington. The plants—many of them rare—are displayed in separate gardens: the Jungle Garden, the Palm Garden, the 12-acre Desert Garden (which contains a large outdoor collection of cacti and succulents), and the Camellia Garden, Rose Garden, and Japanese Garden. A Shakespeare Garden features annuals and bulbs mentioned in the playwright's works.

Quail Botanical Gardens
230 Quail Gardens Drive
Encinitas, CA 92024
Off I-5 north of San Diego
(619) 436-3036
Open daily 8 to 5; closed Thanksgiving, Christmas, and New Year's Day
Specialties: bamboos, cycads, palms

Over 30 acres of trails, gardens, pools. Frost-free conditions favor the growth of tropical fruits. Exhibits include a native-plant demonstration garden, two desert gardens, and a compost demonstration site.

Rancho Santa Ana Botanic Garden
1500 N. College Avenue
Claremont, CA 91711
(909) 625-8767
Open daily 8 to 5; closed major holidays
Specialty: California native plants
California native trees, shrubs, perennials, and bulbs grow throughout the garden's 86-acre site, which was once a Spanish rancho. Many are shown in residential settings (*Fremontodendron* espaliered against a fence, for example); others grow in natural chaparral, forest, woodland, and desert settings.

Arboretum of Los Angeles County

The Huntington Botanical Gardens

Santa Barbara Botanic Garden
1212 Mission Canyon Road
Santa Barbara, CA 93105
(805) 682-4726
Open weekdays 9 to 5, weekends 9 to 6, March through October; closes an hour earlier November through February
Specialty: California native plants

This 65-acre garden at the foot of the Santa Ynez Mountains has more than a thousand species of California native plants. Five miles of trails (explore with self-guided maps or docents) crisscross habitats ranging from oak woodland to wildflower meadow. A home demonstration garden offers ideas for gardening with Southern California native plants that tolerate aridity and are suited to fire-prone areas. Garden shop is sizable.

South Coast Botanical Garden
26300 Crenshaw Boulevard
Palos Verdes Peninsula, CA 90274
(310) 544-6815
Open daily 9 to 5; closed Christmas Day
Specialties: ideas for home gardeners, plants from around the world
More than 87 acres of gardens on a site that was once a diatomite mine. Trails wind through a diverse collection of trees, flowering plants, demonstration gardens; there is also an herb garden.

Strybing Arboretum and Botanical Gardens
Golden Gate Park
Ninth Avenue and Lincoln Way
San Francisco, CA 94122
(415) 661-1316
Open weekdays 8:30 to 4:30, weekends and holidays 10 to 5
Specialties: plants from around the world, home demonstration gardens
In this 70-acre arboretum, plants are displayed both in residential settings and in labeled collections. A 3½-acre native plant section uses rocks, plant groupings, and low soil undulations to mimic creek beds and craggy terrain. In spring, it's carpeted with blooming poppies, Pacific iris, and meadowfoam.

UC Botanical Garden
200 Centennial Drive
Berkeley, CA 94720
(510) 642-3343
Open daily 9 to 4:45; closed Christmas Day
Specialty: California native plants
More than 2,500 native plants fill 11 acres of this 34-acre garden about ¾ mile up Strawberry Canyon from Memorial Stadium. About 3 miles of primary trails wander among plant collections from six continents; non-native collections take up about two-thirds of the garden. Conservatory houses tropical plants.

UC Davis Arboretum

University of California at Davis
Davis, CA 95616
On La Rue Road, just off Old Davis Road,
UCD campus

(916) 752-2498

Open daily

Specialty: trees and shrubs for dry gardens

Native and exotic trees—especially species that thrive in the Central Valley's hot, dry climate—provide plenty of shade throughout 150 developed acres on the 200-acre grounds. In the central section, native plants such as lupines and poppies put on a bloom show in spring.

UC Irvine Arboretum

University of California at Irvine, North Campus
Irvine, CA 92717

(714) 856-5833

Open Monday through Saturday 9 to 3; closed holidays

Specialty: South African bulbs

Twelve-acre garden with fine collection of plants from dry-climate regions. Several borders are devoted to South African bulbs like amaryllis, iris, babiana, ixia, and dietes.

UC Riverside Botanic Gardens

University of California at Riverside
Riverside, CA 92521

(909) 787-4650

Open daily 8 to 5; closed major holidays

Specialty: plants from around the world

Plants from various parts of the world are arranged by microclimates and plant communities. Among them are rare fruits and desert plants like yucca and jojoba. Self-guided tour follows some 4½ miles of trails. This outdoor classroom spans rocky slopes, dry creek beds, and other scenic land.

UC Santa Cruz Arboretum

University of California at Santa Cruz
High Street
Santa Cruz, CA 95064

(408) 427-2998 (recorded information)

Open daily 9 to 5

Specialty: plants from Australia, New Zealand, and South Africa

Rugged and young compared with its counterparts at other California universities, this arboretum is nevertheless a horticulturally rich repository for plants from countries across the Pacific that have Mediterranean climates similar to California's. In the Australian section, curving paths wind through tall trees (including many eucalypts) and shrubs such as grevillea and banksias. Proteas with big, colorful flower heads are highlights in the South African section.

COLORADO

Denver Botanic Garden

1005 York Street
Denver, CO 80206-3799

(303) 331-4000

Open Wednesday through Friday 9 to 5, Saturday through Tuesday 9 to 8; closed Christmas Day and New Year's Day

Specialty: alpine rock garden plants

Denver Botanic Garden

Set in the heart of the city with an exhilarating westward view of the Rocky Mountains, this 20-acre landscape is a year-round haven for plant enthusiasts. In the tropical conservatory, brilliant bougainvilleas and orchids challenge winter doldrums. Small theme gardens include a Japanese garden, plains garden, and formal herb garden. A 1-acre alpine rock garden features some 3,500 species of plants from the world's mountains. It's most colorful in May.

OREGON

Berry Botanic Garden

11505 S.W. Summerville Avenue
Portland, OR 97219

(503) 636-4112 (reservations, directions)

Open daily 8 to 5; closed Sundays November through February

Specialties: alpines, Pacific Northwest natives, rhododendrons

Woods and rockeries make up this 6-acre garden begun in 1938 by Northwest plant collector Rae Selling Berry. Displays feature plants from other parts of the world, as well as Pacific Northwest natives. January is a fine time to see winter bloomers like Chinese witch hazel; bulbs create a splash in spring, followed in early summer by primroses and wildflowers.

Hoyt Arboretum

400 S.W. Fairview Boulevard
Portland, OR 97221

(503) 823-3655

Grounds open daily dawn to dusk; visitor center open daily 9 to 3

Specialty: conifers, shrubs

Trails crisscross this 175-acre site through collections of trees from around the world as well as the Pacific Northwest. Along the Redwood-Spruce Trail, Northwest natives such as Brewer's weeping spruce fill the air with their woodsy scents. In spring, flowering cherries and magnolias are cloaked in bloom. Fall brings flaming glory to the arboretum's poplars, persimmons, and maples.

Leach Botanical Garden

6704 S.E. 122d Avenue
Portland, OR 97236

(503) 761-9503

Open Tuesday through Saturday 9 to 4, Sunday 1 to 4

Specialty: Pacific Northwest natives

More than 1,500 kinds of plants (including some 125 Northwest natives) grow in this 9-acre garden begun in the 1930s by botanist Lilla Leach. Most are arranged in natural habitats—a dry native woodland, a riparian area, and a rock garden, for example. Visit in spring to see the garden's azaleas, camellias, and wildflowers in bloom.

UTAH

Red Butte Garden and Arboretum/ State Arboretum of Utah

University of Utah
300 Wakara Way
Salt Lake City, UT 84133

(801) 581-5322; (801) 581-4747 (information hotline)

Open Tuesday through Sunday 10 A.M. to sunset April through October; closed Mondays and Tuesdays November through March

Wildflowers, flowering shrubs, and a large collection of dwarf conifers are among the displays on 25 acres of developed gardens.

WASHINGTON

Bellevue Botanical Garden
12001 Main Street
Box 7081
Bellevue, WA 98008
Located in Wilburton Hill Park
(206) 541-3755
Open daily 10 to 6

This 36-acre garden may be the region's youngest garden (it opened in 1992), but it offers plenty of ideas for Northwest gardeners. It's organized into separate garden "rooms," including a 7-acre rhododendron garden and a ground cover garden, joined by a ½-mile loop trail that begins at the visitor center. Highlights include a 300-foot perennial border—at its bloom peak in late spring—and a water-wise garden.

Washington Park Arboretum
2300 Arboretum Drive East
Seattle, WA 98112
Just off Lake Washington Boulevard East
(206) 543-8800
Open daily 7 a.m. to dusk
Specialty: plants for western Washington

More than 200 acres of trees, shrubs, and bulbs. In January, plants like wintersweet and witch hazel dot the landscape with color and spice the air with fragrance. But mid-spring brings an explosion of blooms from flowering cherry trees, dogwoods, azaleas, and magnolias. In fall, leaves of Japanese maples and other deciduous trees in the Woodland Garden are ablaze with color.

HAWAII

Honolulu Botanical Gardens
Head office: Foster Botanical Garden
50 N. Vineyard Boulevard
Honolulu, HI 96817
(808) 522-7060
Open daily 9 to 4; closed Christmas and New Year's Day
Specialties: vary according to site

Five separate gardens, located in different parts of Oahu, are operated by Honolulu Botanical Gardens. Foster Botanical Garden, on 13 acres in downtown Honolulu, displays orchids and large old tropical trees like Mindanao gum. Koko Crater

Bellevue Botanical Garden

Botanical Garden, which displays dryland plants in a wild setting, occupies the crater of an extinct volcano. Wahiawa Botanical Garden, a cool rain-forest habitat, straddles a 27-acre wooded gulch in Wahiawa, 13 miles northwest of Honolulu. And Ho'omaluhia, tucked against Oahu's windward cliffs, is a 400-acre garden of shrubs and trees—including one of the world's largest mango trees—from different regions of the tropical world. Lili'uokalani Botanical Garden, on 7 acres near downtown Honolulu, is a new site for native Hawaiian plants.

Lyon Arboretum
3860 Manoa Road
Honolulu, HI 96822
(808) 988-7378
Open Monday through Saturday 9 to 3
Specialty: plants from the world's tropical regions

Lyon Arboretum

Koko Crater Botanical Garden

This lush, junglelike, 194-acre garden tucked back in the upper Manoa Valley is a treasure trove of exotics from around the world. Paths wind through towering palms and majestic trees with vines scrambling up their trunks. A small ethnobotanical garden displays plants used by the earliest Hawaiians for food, medicine, and building materials. Conservation of endangered native plants is an important focus at this garden.

National Tropical Botanical Garden
Box 340
Lawai, HI 96765
(808) 332-7361
Call for opening times
Specialties: tropicals and native Hawaiian plants

The nation's only congressionally chartered tropical botanical garden. Located in a verdant valley near Poipu, the 186-acre garden contains the world's largest collection of native Hawaiian plants, many rare and endangered.

Waimea Arboretum and Botanical Garden
59-864 Kamehameha Highway
Haleiwa, HI 96712
(808) 638-8655
Open daily 10 to 5:30
Specialties: tropicals and native Hawaiian plants

This 100-acre garden straddles a coastal valley on Oahu's windward side. Paths wander among tropical plants from around the world. The Hibiscus Evolution Garden shows the development of modern hybrid hibiscus from a few true species and hybrids of unknown origin.

BRITISH COLUMBIA

University of British Columbia Botanical Garden
6804 S.W. Marine Drive
Vancouver, B.C., Canada V6T 1Z4
(604) 822-4208
Open daily 10 to 6 mid-March to mid-October
Specialties: alpines, rhododendrons, and magnolias

Seventy acres of plants that thrive in Northwest gardens. Giant Asian lilies are stunners in summer; espaliered fruit trees are also interesting. The ¾-acre Food Garden, a patchwork of raised beds, displays cool- and warm-season vegetables.

ESTATE GARDENS
and Other Historic
Public Gardens

Filoli

The West is filled with monuments to its colorful history. Among them are grand old estates left to posterity by pioneering gardeners and plant collectors and living museums that celebrate plants and animals of this region and beyond. Such public gardens are often rich in ideas that gardeners can take home, and they offer the opportunity to view plants tested by time. The gardens are listed by state.

CALIFORNIA

Blake Garden
70 Rincon Road
Kensington, CA 94707
(510) 524-2449
Open Monday through Friday 8 to 4:30; closed university holidays
Specialty: Mediterranean plants
This Mediterranean garden surrounds an Italianate-style house used by the president of the University of California at Berkeley. The garden on the 10½-acre property is run by the university's landscape architecture department. Formal gardens surround a reflecting pool shaded by southern magnolia trees. Dryland plants from the Mediterranean area, South Africa, and South America thrive on a sunny west slope, against the backdrop of San Francisco Bay.

Descanso Gardens
1418 Descanso Drive
La Cañada, CA 91011
(818) 952-4400
Open daily 9 to 4:30; closed Christmas Day
Specialties: camellias, roses
Many camellias the size of large trees bloom mostly January through March on this site, which began as a private estate called Rancho del Descanso, "Ranch of Rest." The garden's 165 acres, about half of which are cultivated, also contain an international rosarium, a California native plant garden on 15 acres of slope, and a Japanese garden where azaleas and wisteria bloom beside streams and a tea house. Bulbs are another spring highlight: the tulip display typically includes 10,000 bulbs.

Filoli
Cañada Road
Woodside, CA 94062
(415) 364-2880
Open Tuesday through Saturday plus second Sunday of each month mid-February through first Saturday in November; call for times and reservations
Specialties: spring bulbs, roses, rhododendrons
Magnificent formal gardens surround a stately, 36,000-square-foot Georgian manor house on this 654-acre estate about 25 miles south of San Francisco. Walls and hedges divide the 16-acre gardens into individual garden rooms, including a sunken garden with lily pond; the Wild Garden, where tall oaks shelter rhododendrons;

The Living Desert

and the Rose Garden, which contains more than 500 bushes. Midspring is a grand time to visit; bloom erupts then from masses of tulips, spring annuals, flowering fruit trees, and a huge old wisteria.

The Living Desert
47900 Portola Avenue
Palm Desert, CA 92260
(619) 346-5694
Open daily 9 to 5 (last admission 4:30); closed Christmas Day
Specialty: plants and animals of the Southwest deserts
More than 1,200 acres include protected, preserved natural desert; some 20 acres of developed gardens; demonstration gardens; trails; a plant nursery; and live desert animals in realistic settings. Plants on display include tall California fan palms and groves of smoke trees.

Lotusland
695 Ashley Road
Santa Barbara, CA 93108 (mailing address)
(805) 969-9990 weekdays 9 to noon (reservation office)
Tours available by reservation only Wednesday through Saturday 10 and 1:30 mid-February to mid-November; space is limited
Specialty: plants from around the world in novel settings
A one-stop botanical tour of the world, this 37-acre estate was the home of the late Ganna Walska, an eccentric Polish opera diva and a passionate plant collector. Manicured paths lead through 13 distinctive

gardens, including a garden that features plants with bluish foliage, an aloe garden that surrounds a pool edged with abalone shells, a cycad garden containing more than 370 specimens, and a water garden featuring water lilies and lotuses.

Lummis Home State Historic Monument

200 E. Avenue 43
Los Angeles, CA 90031

(213) 222-0546

Open Friday through Sunday noon to 4

Specialty: Mediterranean and California native plants

Mature sycamore trees, oaks, and California bay trees create a leafy backdrop for this historic stone house built by Charles Lummis and called El Alisal, "The Place of the Sycamores." Around them on the 1.8-acre site is a garden that Lummis began and tended until his death in 1928; since renovated, the garden now displays dry-climate plants from around the world. It's at its most colorful in spring, when ceanothus and wildflowers bloom, and summer, when crape myrtles put out their papery flowers.

San Diego Zoo

Box 551
San Diego, CA 92112
Located at the northwest corner of Balboa Park

(619) 231-1515

Opening hours vary

Specialty: exotic plants and animals

This is one of the finest zoological gardens in the world, a preserve for plants (more than 6,500 species) as well as animals that's organized according to bioclimatic zones. Tiger River is a 3-acre junglelike garden that approximates an Asian rain forest. Palms, bamboos, and many other exotic plants line its 1,500-foot path.

Sherman Library and Gardens

2647 E. Pacific Coast Highway
Corona Del Mar, CA 92625

(714) 673-2261

Open daily 10:30 to 4

Specialty: flowering annuals

Colorful annuals, hanging baskets, and plants from around the world are displayed in this garden, which covers a city block. Shaded patios show off grand collections of begonias and fuchsias in full flower. Ferns, orchids, and bromeliads thrive in the climate-controlled Tropical Conservatory.

Theodore Payne Foundation

10459 Tuxford Street
Sun Valley, CA 91352

(818) 768-1802; (818) 768-3533 (wildflower hotline March through June)

Open Wednesday through Sunday 8 to 4:30; summer hours vary; call ahead; closed major holidays

Specialties: natives, wildflowers

This nonprofit organization dedicated to the preservation and use of wildflowers and native plants oversees a nursery and garden on the site's 21 acres. In spring, Wildflower Hill is in brilliant bloom; demonstration gardens provide landscaping ideas.

WASHINGTON

Bloedel Reserve

7571 N.E. Dolphin Drive
Bainbridge Island, WA 98110
45 minutes from downtown Seattle

(206) 842-7631

Open Wednesday through Sunday; closed on national holidays; reservations required

Specialty: garden "rooms"

Gardens on 150 acres are crisscrossed by native woodland and dotted with meadows. The moss garden, reflection pool, bird marsh, English landscape, and Japanese garden offer glimpses of the styles that influence Northwest garden design.

Lakewold

On Gravelly Lake, 8 miles south of Tacoma

(206) 584-3360

Open Thursday through Monday 10 to 4 April through September; also open Monday, Thursday, and Friday 10 to 3 October through March; reservations required for guided tours only

Specialty: many plants in formal settings

This 10-acre lakeside garden, started in the 1920s and developed over more than a half century, has a formal look: boxwood parterres, a rose-covered tea house, and a knot garden of handsomely interwoven herbs.

Ohme Gardens

3327 Ohme Road
Wenatchee, WA 98801
3 miles north of Wenatchee near junction of Highways 2 and 97

(509) 662-5785

Open daily 9 to 6, April 15 through October 15 (to 7 during summer)

Specialty: alpine rock garden plants

This 9-acre garden reflects the commitment of two generations of the Ohme family, who have created a natural-looking landscape of beauty and tranquillity. Paths wind among rocky outcrops and up hillsides that are most colorful when sweeps of thyme and sedum bloom (beginning in April).

Rhododendron Species Botanical Garden

2525 S. 336th Street
Federal Way, WA 98007

(206) 661-9377

Opening hours vary

One of the most extensive collections of rhododendron species in North America. Covers some 24 acres and displays more than 400 species, many rare. Peak bloom is from late March to mid-May.

Butchart Gardens

BRITISH COLUMBIA

Butchart Gardens

800 Benvenuto Avenue
Brentwood Bay, Victoria,
B.C., Canada V8M 1J8

(604) 652-4422

Opening hours vary

Specialty: flowering plants of all kinds

This 50-acre garden is considered one of the top tourist destinations in the Northwest. It was started in 1904 by Robert and Jenny Butchart in an old limestone quarry. In midspring, hundreds of bulbs bloom; in summer, hanging baskets overflow with flowers, and beds blaze with color against a backdrop of blooming trees, shrubs, and a pond.

MAIL-ORDER SUPPLIERS

Antique roses

Tulips swirled with color like ribbon candy, watermelons splashed with yellow spots, red tomatoes with yellow stripes, red-brown cosmos that smell like chocolate: these are just a few of the varieties that you may not find readily available in nurseries. But you can order them by mail. Among the hundreds of mail-order suppliers that have sizable catalogs, some old faithfuls continue to offer flowers and vegetables from A to Z. These top the list below. But an increasing number of suppliers are specialists—of antique roses, bulbs, fruits, native plants or grasses, ornamentals, seeds of gourmet herbs and vegetables, or heirloom and open-pollinated (nonhybridized) seeds.

Western specialists are emphasized throughout the lists. Some suppliers east of the Rockies are also included because they offer especially large or unusual selections of bulbs or seeds. Call or write to the companies for current catalog prices. Addresses and phone numbers are subject to change.

FLOWERS AND VEGETABLES FROM A TO Z

Jackson & Perkins
Box 1028
Medford, OR 97501
(800) 292-4769; (503) 776-2000
Roses of every kind and color, plus perennials, garden accessories, and gifts. Free plant care instructions with purchase.

Park Seed Company
Cokesbury Road
Greenwood, SC 29647
(800) 845-3369; (803) 223-7333
Seeds, plants, bulbs, nearly 2,000 varieties of flowers and vegetables.

Stokes Seeds, Inc.
Box 548
Buffalo, NY 14240
(716) 695-6980
Annuals for sun and shade, herbs, perennials, and vegetables, including Chinese varieties.

Thompson & Morgan, Inc.
Box 1308
Jackson, NJ 08527-0308
(800) 274-7333
Rare and unusual varieties of annuals, bulbs, perennials, vegetables, and grasses.

W. Atlee Burpee Company
300 Park Avenue
Warminster, PA 18974
(800) 888-1447
Seeds of flowers and vegetables; also lilies, fruit trees, and tools.

Wayside Gardens
Hodges, SC 29695
(800) 845-1124
Unusual and hard-to-find perennials, bulbs (including tulips, daffodils, lilies), grasses, ornamental shrubs, trees, and vines. Varied collection of roses, including antique and David Austin English roses.

Sweet peas

White Flower Farm
Box 50
Litchfield, CT 06759-0050
(203) 496-9600
Begonias, dahlias, and lilies; also perennials, ornamental shrubs such as lilac and rose, and some fruit trees.

ANTIQUE ROSES

Heirloom Old Garden Roses
24062 N.E. Riverside Drive
St. Paul, OR 97137
(503) 538-1576; fax (503) 538-5902
Catalog includes albas, Bourbons, damasks, hybrid musks, Noisettes; substantial collection of David Austin English roses.

Heritage Rose Gardens
16831 Mitchell Creek Drive
Fort Bragg, CA 95437
Lists more than 200 old roses.

Mendocino Heirloom Roses
Box 670
Mendocino, CA 95460
(707) 877-1888; (707) 937-0963
An eclectic list includes antique and species roses on their own roots and a few newer roses, such as some from the 1920s and 30s.

Roses of Yesterday and Today
802 Brown's Valley Road
Watsonville, CA 95076-0398
(408) 724-3537
Old and rare varieties of garden roses.

Vintage Gardens
2227 Gravenstein Highway South
Sebastopol, CA 95472
(707) 829-2035
Antique and extraordinary roses: hybrid perpetuals, Bourbons, Portlands, teas, Chinas, Noisettes. Ramblers, climbers; also old hybrid teas, floribundas, miniatures.

BULBS, TUBERS, AND CORMS

Suppliers advise ordering bulbs as early as possible to obtain best selection.

A & D Peony and Perennial Nursery
6808 180th SE
Snohomish, WA 98290
(360) 668-9690
Daylilies, peonies, hostas, and perennials.

Aitken's Salmon Creek Garden
608 N.W. 119th Street
Vancouver, WA 98685
(360) 573-4472
Iris of all kinds, bearded and beardless.

B & D Lilies
330 P Street
Port Townsend, WA 98368
(360) 385-1738; fax (360) 385-9996
Asiatic and Oriental hybrids, trumpets, and species lilies, and daylilies.

Cooley's Gardens
Box 126—WG
Silverton, OR 97381
Iris, 300 varieties.

Dutch Gardens
Box 200
Adelphia, NJ 07710
(908) 780-2713
Bulbs of all kinds for spring or summer bloom: anemones, crocus, iris, daffodils, dahlias, fritillarias, hyacinths, lilies, tulips.

Grant E. Mitsch, Novelty Daffodils
Box 218
Hubbard, OR 97032
(503) 651-2742
Novelty daffodils; develops own hybrids.

Lilium 'Casablanca'

Roris Gardens
8195 Bradshaw Road
Sacramento, CA 95829
(916) 689-7460
Iris, many shapes and colors.

Schreiner's Gardens
3625 Quinaby Road
Salem, OR 97303
(503) 393-3232
Bearded iris, including tall, dwarf, median, and arilbreds.

Swan Island Dahlias
Box 700
Canby, OR 97013
(503) 266-7711; fax (503) 266-8768
Dahlias of all kinds, colors, flower forms, and sizes.

Van Bourgondien Bros.
Box 1000
245 Farmingdale Road, Route 109
Babylon, NY 11702-0598
(800) 622-9997
Bulbs of many kinds, including amaryllis, daffodils, tuberous begonias, peonies, tulips, dahlias, Asiatic and Oriental lilies; also a large selection of perennials.

Tulip and hyacinth bulbs

VanLierop Bulb Farm
13407 80th Street East
Puyallup, WA 98372-3608
(206) 848-7272
Many kinds of crocus, daffodils, hyacinths, tulips, and other bulbs. Selection includes Tazetta and poeticus daffodils, species tulips, and snowflakes *(Leucojum)*. Orders guaranteed February 1 through June 1; fall bulb sales offered September 15 through October 30.

FRUITS, NUTS, AND BERRIES

Northwoods Nursery
27635 S. Oglesby Road
Canby, OR 97013
(503) 266-5432; fax (503) 266-5431
Fruits of all kinds.

Raintree Nursery
391 Butts Road
Morton, WA 98356
(360) 496-6400
Hundreds of edible plants from all over the world, including fruits, nuts, and berries of all kinds. Specializes in disease-resistant varieties for home gardeners.

NATIVES AND GRASSES

Desert Moon Nursery
Box 600
Veguita, NM 87062
(505) 864-0614
Agaves, yuccas, other desert succulents, cacti, desert perennials like blackfoot daisy and penstemons, wildflowers, shrubs, and trees.

Greenlee Nursery
301 E. Franklin Avenue
Pomona, CA 91766
(909) 629-9045
Large selection of ornamental and native grasses of all kinds. Catalog includes tips on planting and care.

Las Pilitas Nursery
Las Pilitas Road
Santa Margarita, CA 93453
(805) 438-5992
California natives. List includes perennials such as heucheras and salvias; as well as shrubs like baccharis, buckwheats, and ceanothus; and trees like oaks.

DEMYSTIFYING
Scientific
Plant Names

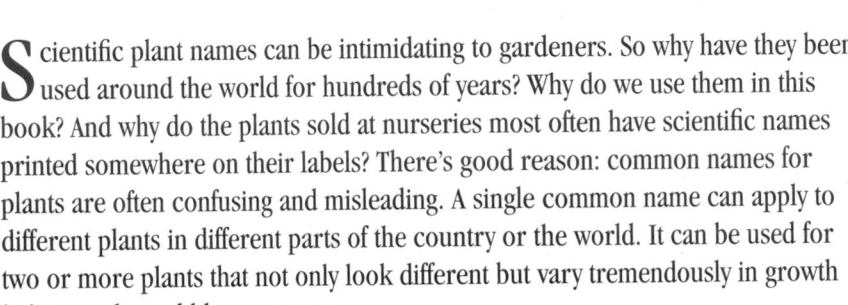

Campsis radicans

S cientific plant names can be intimidating to gardeners. So why have they been used around the world for hundreds of years? Why do we use them in this book? And why do the plants sold at nurseries most often have scientific names printed somewhere on their labels? There's good reason: common names for plants are often confusing and misleading. A single common name can apply to different plants in different parts of the country or the world. It can be used for two or more plants that not only look different but vary tremendously in growth habit, needs, and bloom season.

Scientific Names Are Precise

Scientific names are more precise than common names. If you tell a nursery you want to buy a dusty miller, for example, you might be asked: "Which one?" A number of plants answer to the name. They're all perennials with silvery foliage, but *Centaurea cineraria* has big, yellow thistlelike flowers; *Senecio vira-vira* has white flowers; *Senecio cineraria* has small yellow flowers; and *Lychnis coronaria* has magenta to crimson flowers.

Other plants with the same common

Rudbeckia hirta

name often are not at all similar. "Blackeyed Susan," for example, applies to a golden-flowered perennial (*Rudbeckia hirta*) and to a vine most often planted as a summer annual (*Thunbergia alata*). "Angel's tears" is a bulb grown for its clusters of white flowers (*Narcissus triandrus*) and is also a ground cover with inconspicuous flowers (*Soleirolia soleirolii*).

Thunbergia alata

Ornamentals and weeds may bear the same common name. "Spanish broom" is either a tidy, 2-foot shrub with yellow flowers (*Genista hispanica*) or a rangy, 6- to 10-foot shrub (*Spartium junceum*) that runs wild across many parts of the West.

So the real reason for learning scientific names is a practical one: they provide the most accurate means we have for putting a verbal handle on a plant. You can't be sure what you are getting unless you order a plant by its scientific name.

Scientific Names Offer Clues

Scientific names, if you break them down, can tell you something about the plants. The first part of a scientific name is the genus name, which is usually a classical name. The second part is the species name, which is usually a descriptive word and often simple to decipher.

Descriptive words used again and again in species names are listed opposite. When you know the meanings of these words, many names become easy to understand and helpful in identifying plants. *Sollya heterophylla,* for example, combines *hetero* (heterogeneous or various) with *phylla* (leaves) to mean "various-size leaves." Some of the leaves are lanceolate and others oblong.

The common names that are direct translations are among the easiest to remember. Bigleaf hydrangea (*Hydrangea macrophylla*) does have large leaves. *Macro* means large, *phylla* means leaves.

Some of the scientific names are so much like English words that there is no question as to their meaning. *Prostratum, compacta, deliciosa, fragrans,* and *pendula* all say something immediately recognizable.

A GUIDE TO BOTANICAL NAMES

Color of Flowers or Foliage

albus—white

argenteus—silvery

aureus—golden

azureus—azure, sky blue

caeruleus—dark blue

caesius—blue-gray

candidus—pure white, shiny

canus—ashy gray, hoary

cereus—waxy

citrinus—yellow

coccineus—scarlet

concolor—one color

croceus—yellow

cruentus—bloody

discolor—two colors, separate colors

glaucus—covered with gray bloom

incanus—gray, hoary

luteus—reddish yellow

pallidus—pale

purpureus—purple

rubens, ruber—red, ruddy

rufus—ruddy

Dodonaea viscosa 'Purpurea'

Form of Leaf (*folius*—leaves or foliage)

acerifolius—maplelike

angustifolius—narrow

aquifolius—spiny

buxifolius—boxwood-like

ilicifolius—hollylike

laurifolius—laurel-like

parvifolius—small

populifolius—poplarlike

salicifolius—willowlike

Lavandula angustifolia 'Hidcote'

Shape of Plant

adpressus—pressing against, hugging

altus—tall

arboreus—treelike

capitatus—headlike

compactus—compact, dense

confertus—crowded, pressed together

contortus—twisted

decumbens—lying down

depressus—pressed down

elegans—elegant, slender, willowy

fastigiatus—branches erect and close together

humifusus—sprawling on the ground

humilis—low, small, humble

impressus—impressed upon

nanus—dwarf

procumbens—trailing

prostratus—prostrate

pumilus—dwarf, small

pusillus—puny, insignificant

repens—creeping

reptans—creeping

scandens—climbing

Where It Came From

The suffix *-ensis* (of a place) is added to place-names to specify the habitat where the plant was first discovered.

africanus—of Africa

alpinus—of the Alps

australis—southern

borealis—northern

campestris—of the field or plains

canadensis—of Canada

canariensis—of the Canary Islands

capensis—of the Cape of Good Hope area

chilensis—of Chile

chinensis—of China

hispanicus—of Spain

hortensis—of gardens

indicus—of India

insularis—of the island

japonicus—of Japan

littoralis—of the seashore

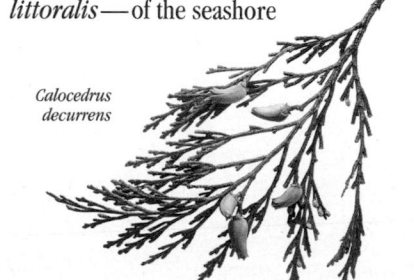

Calocedrus decurrens

montanus—of the mountains

riparius—of riverbanks

rivalis, rivularis—of brooks

saxatilis—inhabiting rocks

Plant Parts

dendron—tree

flora, florum, flori, florus—flowers

phyllus, phylla—leaf or leaves

Cestrum elegans

Zephyranthes grandiflora

Elaeagnus pungens

Ligustrum japonicum

Passiflora caerulea

Brachychiton acerifolius

Plant Peculiarities

armatus—armed

baccatus—berried, berrylike

barbatus—barbed or bearded

campanulatus—bell or cup shaped

ciliaris—fringed

cordatus—heart shaped

cornutus—horned

crassus—thick, fleshy

decurrens—running down the stem

densi—dense

diversi—varying

edulis—edible

floridus—free flowering

Hydrangea macrophylla

fruticosus—shrubby

fulgens—shiny

gracilis—slender, thin, small

grandi—large, showy

-ifer, -iferus—bearing or having; e.g., *stoloniferus*, having stolons

imperialis—showy

laciniatus—fringed or with torn edges

laevigatus—smooth

lobatus—lobed

longus—long

macro—large

maculatus—spotted

micro—small

mollis—soft, soft-haired

mucronatus—pointed

nutans—nodding, swaying

obtusus—blunt or flattened

officinalis—medicinal

-oides—like or resembling; e.g., *jasminoides*, like a jasmine

patens—open, spreading growth

pinnatus—constructed like a feather

platy—broad

plenus—double, full

plumosus—feathery

praecox—precocious

pungens—piercing

radicans—rooting, especially along the stem

reticulatus—net-veined

retusus—notched at blunt apex

rugosus—wrinkled, rough

saccharatus—sweet, sugary

sagittalis—arrowlike

scabrus—rough feeling

scoparius—broomlike

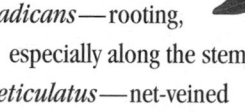
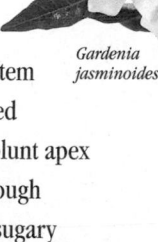

Gardenia jasminoides

OUR SPELLING	AS IN
a	hat, hand
ay	baby
ah	hall
ai	air
e	met, bed
ee	we
i	tin
ye	wine
o	hot
oe	romance
u	must, burr
oo	rumor
ew	human
uh	comma, consider, sinister, vapor, minus

PRONUNCIATION GUIDE

Scientific names are the universal language for plants, but they are pronounced differently in various parts of the world, even among English-speaking countries. Because these names come from Latin and Greek, there is no absolute, approved, obligatory pronunciation for them —we say them as we choose. What follows is a list of the most-often-used ways to say many scientific plant names.

Abutilon

A

Abelia—uh-BEE-lee-uh
Abutilon—uh-BEW-tuh-lon
    Acacia—uh-KAY-shuh
    Acer—AY-sir
    Achillea—ak-il-LEE-uh
    Achimenes—uh-KIM-muh-neez
    Aconitum—ak-oe-NYE-tuhm
    Actinidia—AK-ti-NID-ee-uh
    Adiantum—ad-ee-AN-tuhm
    Aesculus—ES-keew-luhs
    Agapanthus—ag-uh-PAN-thuhs
    Agave—ah-GAH-vay
    Ageratum—ah-JER-ah-tum
      (usually pronounced
      ad-juh-RAY-tuhm)
    Ailanthus—uh-LAN-thuhs
    Ajuga—uh-JEW-guh
    Alstroemeria—al-struh-MEE-ree-uh
    Amaryllis—am-uh-RIL-is
    Anemone—uh-NEM-uh-nee

Aconitum
    Anthurium—an-THU-ree-uhm
Aquilegia—ak-wuh-LEE-jee-uh
Arabis—AIR-uh-bis
Aralia—uh-RAY-lee-uh
Arctostaphylos—ark-toe-STAF-i-luhs
Arctotheca—ark-toe-THEE-kuh
Artemisia—AHR-tuh-MEE-zee-uh
Aspidistra—as-puh-DIS-truh
Astilbe—as-STIL-bee
Atriplex—AT-rip-lex

B

Babiana—bab-ee-AN-uh
Baccharis—BAK-uh-ris
Bauhinia—boe-HIN-ee-uh
Berberis—BUR-buh-ris
Bergenia—bur-GEN-ee-uh
Betula—BET-ew-luh

Bougainvillea

Bougainvillea—boo-guhn-VIL-ee-uh
Buddleia—BUD-lee-uh

C

Caladium—kuh-LAY-dee-uhm
Calceolaria—kal-see-oe-LAIR-ee-uh
Calendula—kuh-LEN-dew-luh
Callistemon—ka-lis-STEE-muhn
Callistephus—ka-LIS-tee-fuhs
Calochortus—kal-oh-COR-tuhs
Campanula—kam-PAN-ew-luh
Carpenteria—CAHR-pen-TEER-ee-a
Cattleya—KAT-lee-uh
Ceanothus—see-uh-NO-thuhs
Celosia—see-LOW-she-uh
Centaurea—sen-tah-REE-uh
Ceratonia—sair-uh-TONE-ee-uh
Ceratostigma—sair-uh-toe-STIG-muh
Cercidium—sir-CID-ee-uhm
Cercis—SIR-suhs
Chamaecyparis—kam-uh-SIP-uh-ris
Cheiranthus—kye-RAN-thuhs
Chionanthus—kye-oe-NAN-thuhs
Chlorophytum—klor-oe-FYE-tum
Choisya—SHOY-zee-uh
Clematis—KLEM-uh-tis
Cleome—KLEE-oe-mee
Clivia—KLYE-vee-uh
Cocculus—COC-ew-lus
Colchicum—KAHL-chik-uhm
Convallaria—con-va-LAIR-ee-uh
Convolvulus—kon-VOL-vew-luhs
Coreopsis—kor-ee-OP-suhs
Cotinus—koe-TYE-nuhs
Cotoneaster—koe-toe-nee-AS-tuhr
Crataegus—kruh-TEE-guhs
Crocosmia—kroe-KOZ-mee-uh
Cuphea—KEW-fee-uh
Cymbidium—sim-BID-ee-uhm
Cynoglossum—sin-oh-GLOS-uhm

D

Daboecia—dab-EE-shee-uh
Daphne—DAFF-nee
Deutzia—DOOT-zee-uh or DOYT-zee-uh
Dieffenbachia—deef-uhn-BAK-ee-uh
Dizygotheca—diz-uh-GOTH-ik-uh
   or diz-uh-goe-THEE-kah
Dracaena—druh-SEE-nuh
Dryopteris—drye-OP-ter-uhs
Duchesnea—dew-KEZ-nee-uh

E

Echeveria—ek-uh-VAIR-ee-uh
Echinacea—ek-uh-NAY-see-uh
Echinops—EK-uh-nops
Echium—EK-ee-uhm
Elaeagnus—el-ee-AG-nuhs
Epidendrum—ep-uh-DEN-druhm
Epiphyllum—ep-uh-FIL-uhm
Equisetum—ek-wuh-SEE-tuhm
Eremurus—er-uh-MEWR-uhs
Erica—ee-RYE-kuh (correct,
   but universally pronounced AIR-ik-uh)
Erigeron—ee-RIJ-uh-ron
Erythrina—air-i-THRYE-nuh
Eschscholzia—eh-SCHOELT-see-uh
Eucalyptus—ew-kuh-LIP-tuhs
Euonymus—ew-ON-uh-mus
Exacum—EK-suh-kuhm
Exochorda—ek-so-KOR-duh

F

Fatshedera—fats-HED-uh-ruh
Feijoa—fay-HOE-uh
Ficus—FYE-kuhs
Forsythia—for-SITH-ee-uh
Fragaria—fra-GAIR-ee-uh
Fraxinus—FRAK-suh-nuhs
Fuchsia—FEW-shee-uh

G

Gaillardia—gay-LAHR-dee-uh
Gazania—guh-ZAY-nee-uh
Genista—jen-NIS-tuh
Gentiana—jen-shee-AY-nah
Gerbera—GUR-bur-uh
Geum—JEE-uhm
Gleditsia—gluh-DIT-see-uh
Gomphrena—gom-FREE-nuh
Grevillea—gruh-VIL-ee-uh
Gypsophila—jip-SOF-uh-luh

H

Hamamelis—ham-uh-MEE-luhs
Hebe—HEE-bee
Hedera—HED-uh-ruh
Helianthemum—hee-lee-AN-thuh-muhm
Helianthus—hee-lee-AN-thuhs
Heliopsis—hee-lee-OP-suhs
Heliotropium—hee-lee-oe-TROE-pee-uhm
Hemerocallis—hem-uh-roe-KAL-uhs
Heteromeles—het-uh-roe-MEE-leez
Heuchera—HEW-kuh-ruh
Hibiscus—hye-BIS-kuhs
Hippeastrum—hip-ee-AS-truhm
Hosta—HAHST-uh
Hydrangea—hye-DRAIN-jee-uh
Hymenocallis—hye-muh-noe-KAL-uhs
Hypericum—hye-PEER-ik-uhm

I

Iberis—eye-BEE-ruhs
Ilex—EYE-lex
Impatiens—im-PAY-shuns
Ipomoea—ip-oe-MEE-uh
Iresine—ir-uh-SYE-nee

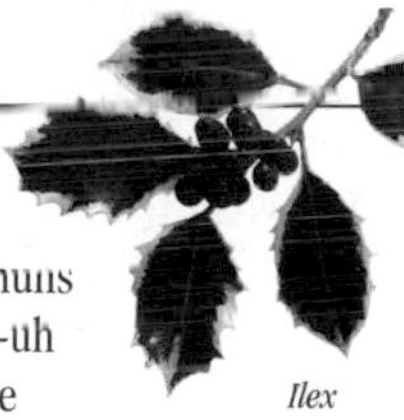

Ilex

J

Jacaranda—jak-uh-RAN-duh
Jasminum—JAZ-muh-nuhm
Juniperus—joo-NIP-uh-ruhs

K

Kalanchoe—kal-an-KO-ee
Kniphofia—nip-HOE-fee-uh
Kochia—KO-kee-uh
Koelreuteria—kell-rew-TEE-ree-uh
Kolkwitzia—koel-KWIT-zee-uh

L

Lagerstroemia—lay-gur-STREE-mee-uh
Lathyrus—LATH-uh-ruhs
Leptospermum—lep-toe-SPUR-muhm
Liatris—lie-AT-ruhs
Liriodendron—lear-ee-oe-DEN-druhn
Liriope—leer-EYE-oh-pee
Lobelia—loe-BEE-lee-uh
Lonicera—lo-NIS-uh-ruh

Lychnis—LIK-nis
Lysimachia—lye-suh-MAY-kee-uh

M

Malus—MAY-lus
Mandevilla—man-duh-VIL-uh
Matthiola—ma-thee-OE-luh
Maytenus—MAY-te-nuhs
Melaleuca—mel-uh-LOO-kuh
Metrosideros—MET-roe-SID-uh-ruhs
Mimulus—MIM-ew-luhs
Musa—MEW-zuh
Myosotis—mye-oh-SO-tuhs
Myrica—mi-RYE-kuh

N

Nandina—nan-DEE-nuh
Narcissus—nahr-SIS-uhs
Nerine—nuh-RYE-nee
Nerium—NEE-ree-uhm
Nicotiana—ni-koe-shee-AY-nuh
Nierembergia—nee-rem-BURG-ee-uh
Nyssa—NIS-uh

O

Olea—O-lee-uh
Osmanthus—oz-MAN-thuhs
Osteospermum—os-tee-oe-SPUR-muhm
Oxalis—OK-sal-uhs
Oxydendrum—OK-see-DEN-druhm

P

Pachysandra—pak-ee-SAN-druh
Papaver—puh-PAY-vur
Parthenocissus—PAHR-thuh-noe-SIS-uhs
Pelargonium—pel-ahr-GOE-nee-uhm
Pennisetum—pen-uh-SEE-tuhm
Penstemon—PEN-stuh-muhn
Philadelphus—fil-uh-DEL-fuhs
Photinia—foe-TIN-ee-uh
Phyla—FYE-luh
Phyllostachys—FIL-oe-STACK-ees
Physalis—FYE-suh-luhs
Picea—pye-SEE-uh
Pieris—pee-AIR-uhs
Pinus—PYE-nuhs
Pittosporum—pit-TOS-poe-ruhm,
   pit-toe-SPOER-uhm
Platanus—PLAT-uh-nuhs
Platycladus—plat-i-CLAD-uhs
Podocarpus—poe-doe-KAR-puhs
Polianthes—pol-ee-AN-thez
Polygonatum—pol-ee-GON-uh-tuhm
Portulaca—por-tew-LAK-a
Potentilla—poe-ten-TIL-uh
Primula—PRIM-ew-luh
Protea—PROE-tee-uh or proe-TEE-uh
Pseudotsuga—soo-doe-TSOO-guh
Pyrostegia—pye-roe-STEE-jee-uh
Pyrus—PYE-ruhs

Q

Quercus—KWER-kuhs

R

Ranunculus—ra-NUN-kew-luhs
Rhaphiolepis—raf-ee-OL-uh-pis or
   raf-ee-o-LEP-uhs
Rhoeo—REE-oe
Romneya—ROM-nee-uh
Rosmarinus—ros-muh-RYE-nuhs
Rudbeckia—rud-BECK-ee-uh

Rosmarinus

S

Salpiglossis—sal-pi-GLOS-sis
Sanvitalia—san-vi-TALE-ee-uh
Scabiosa—skay-bee-OH-suh
Schefflera—SHEF-luh-ruh
Schizanthus—ski-ZAN-thuhs
Scilla—SIL-luh
Sempervivum—sem-per-VYE-vuhm
Senecio—suh-NEE-shee-oe
Sequoia—suh-QUOY-uh
Sinningia—si-NIN-jee-uh
Solandra—soe-LAN-druh
Soleirolia—soe-lee-uh-ROE-lee-uh
Spiraea—spye-REE-uh
Strelitzia—stre-LIT-see-uh
Syngonium—sin-GOE-nee-uhm

T

Tagetes—tuh-JEE-teez
Taxodium—taks-OF-dee-uhm
Thuja—THOO-yuh
Thymus—TYE-muhs
Tibouchina—tib-oo-KYE-nuh
Tigridia—tye-GRID-ee-uh
Tolmiea—tol-MEE-uh
Trachelospermum—tra-kee-lo-SPER-muhm
Tradescantia—trad-es-KAN-shee-uh
Trichostema—trik-oe-STEE-mah
Tropaeolum—tro-PEE-oh-luhm
Tsuga—TSOO-guh

V

Vaccinium—vak-SIN-ee-uhm
Vancouveria—van-koo-VEE-ree-uh
Verbascum—vur-BAS-kuhm
Verbena—ver-BEE-nuh
Vinca—VING-kuh
Vitex—VEE-teks

Vinca minor

W–Z

Weigela—wye-JEE-luh
Xylosma—zye-LOZ-muh
Zantedeschia—zan-tuh-DES-kee-uh
Zephyranthes—zef-i-RAN-theez
Zizyphus—ZIZ-uh-fuhs
Zoysia—ZOY-see-uh

INDEX
Gardening Terms and Topics

INDEX
Scientific and Common Names

Italic page numbers refer to pages on which there are relevant photographs. The **boldface** page number after each scientific name refers to the plant's encyclopedia entry. The page number after a common name also refers to the encyclopedia entry; to find more page references to a common name, look under the scientific name in parentheses.

Acknowledgments

SUNSET CONSULTANTS, 40th Anniversary Edition

Pacific Northwest:
Mark Albright
Arthur L. Antonelli
Wilbur Bluhm
Ron Brightman
Charles A. Brun
Tonie Fitzgerald
Bill Hielscher
Donald G. Howse
Bill Janssen
Mareen Kruckeberg
Russell Link
Nicola Luttropp
Craig McConnell
Ray McNeilan
Warren Manhart
Robert Norton
George Pinyuh
Melody Putnam
Diana Reeck
Robert L. Stebbins
George Taylor
Ted Van Veen

Rocky Mountain States:
Whitney Cranshaw
Ray Daugherty
Ginny McCamant
Kevin Mosley
Larry Sager
Lauren Springer

Southwest:
Mark Dimmitt
Ron Gass
Warren Jones
Michael W. Kilby
Terry Mikel
Carol Shuler

California and Nevada:
Maile Arnold
Dan Atkin
Michael Barclay
Tim Barnett
Mike Bodger
R. A. Brendler
Steve Brigham
Dorthy Bunch
William J. Carlos
Ann Chandler
Barrie Coate
Michelle Comeau
Richard Cowles
Dave Cudney
Dan Davids
Angela Dellavalle
Barbara Deutsch
Clyde Elmore
John and Cathy Etheridge
Susan Frommer
Rhonda Gildersleeve
Richard Harris
Eric A. Johnson
Elizabeth McClintock
Glenn McGourty
Rex Marsh
Jim Marshall
Luen Miller
Robert Morris
Kathy Musial
Eric Oglesby
Robert Raabe
Richard Schell
M. Nevin Smith
Ray Sodomka
John Steiner
Mathew Tekulsky
Paul Vossen
Judy Wigand
Christine Wotruba

Weldon Owen would like to thank the following for their contributions to this 40th Anniversary Edition.

Cartographic production: Barton Wright. **Database design:** Carol Sionkowski. **Design assistance:** Barbara Geisler, Rob Roehrick. **Location scouting:** Jane Hudon, Michaele Thunen. **Computer production:** Ruth Jacobson, Joan Lloyd, Joan Olson, Lori Robinson, Karen Teague, Liz Vaughn, Lisa Zamarin. **Photography editing assistance:** Heather Cogswell. **Technical support:** Phoebe Bixler, Pamela Seawell, David Walton. **Editorial consulting:** editcetera. **Copyeditors:** Frances Bowles, Beverley DeWitt, Nancy Palmer Jones, Virginia Rich, David Sweet. **Proofreaders:** Mu'frida Bell, Desne Border, Kathryn Chetkovich, Ruth Flaxman, Marcella Friel, Wendy Mattson, Karen Stough. **Manuscript processing:** Frances Malamud-Roam.

Sunset's special thanks to those consultants who contributed to the development of previous editions of the *Western Garden Book,* and to the illustrators of the previous edition, whose work forms the heart of the new encyclopedia and dictionary.

SPECIAL CONSULTANTS: Bob Cowden, Walter L. Doty, Elsa Uppman Knoll. **Pacific Northwest:** Bob Badger, Noble Bashor, Bruce Briggs, Ralph Byther, Andrew A. Duncan, Roger Gossler, Harold Greer, L. Keith Hellstrom, Harold T. Hopkins, Anton S. Horn, Stott Howard, Wallace K. Huntington, Francis J. Lawrence, Whitney Lawrence, John Mitsch, Patrick P. Moore, Earl L. Phillips, Wallace M. Ruff, Ellie Sather, George Schenk, R. M. Snodgrass, Eleanor Stubbs. **California and Nevada:** A. D. Ali, William Aplin, John Boething, Gerald Bol, Worth Brown, Charles Burr, John Catlin, Philip E. Chandler, Francis Ching, Stephen Cohan, Clifford Comstock, Al Condit, Jerry C. Davids, Donald F. Dillon, Roger Duer, Morgan Evans, Percy Everett, Everett Farwell, Stan Farwig, George Haight, Richard A. Haubrich, Don Hodel, Barbara Joe Hoshizaki, Colin Jackson, Myron W. Kimnach, Carlton Koehler, Frederick M. Lang, Andrew T. Leiser, Peter J. Lert, Robert Ludekens, James M. Lyons, Arthur H. McCain, Rod McLellan, Ralph D. McPheeters, Mildred Mathias, Ray Miller, Craig Minor, Dennison Morey, Bill Moynier, Howard D. Ohr, Hadley Osborne, Glenn Park, Owen Pearce, Dennis Perry, Eleanor Philp, Robert G. Platt, Harold Prickett, Chris Rosmini, Robert H. Ruff, Roy Rydell, Saratoga Horticultural Foundation, R. H. Sciaroni, George Harmon Scott, Joe Seals, Lily Singer, Ted Sjulin, L. K. Smith, Soil and Plant Laboratory, Inc., Vernon T. Stoutemyer, Strybing Arboretum, Peter Sugawara, Harold Swanton, John Van Barneveld, Rod Whitlow, James Wilson, Donald R. Wooley, Carl Zangger. **Rockies and Southwest:** James Behnken, William M. Brown, Jr., Rodney Engard, Boyce Foerman, Stan Heathman, Dick Hildreth, Richard Hine, Panayoti Kelaidis, James Klett, David Langston, Irene Mitchell, Ernest F. Reimschussel, Jackie H. Richner, Michael Rowland, Bill G. Scott, Harvey F. Tate, Larry F. Watson, Gayle Weinstein, Ric Wogisch.

ILLUSTRATORS: Lois Lovejoy, Mary Davey Burkhardt, Ireta Cooper, Dennis Nolan.

If you would like to order additional copies of any of our books, call us at 1 (800) 759-0190 or check with your local bookstore.

Photography Credits

For pages with six or fewer photographs, each image has been identified by its position on the page: Left (L), center (C), or right (R); top (T), middle (M), or bottom (B). On other pages, such as those in "A Guide to Plant Selection" or the Dictionary Visual Guides, photographs are identified by their position in the grid (shown right). Photographs on the page edge are designated "tab"; those on the back cover, "back".

L	LC	RC	R
1	1	1	1
2			
3			
4			
5			

Val Atkinson: 41 M. **M. Badgley:** 533 L1, L2, L3, LC2, LC3, RC1, RC2, R1, R2, LC1, R3; 568 L3, LC2, RC1, RC2, R1, R2, R3, R4; 569 L1, L3, LC1, RC1; 590 LC1, R1; 591 R1, R2. **T. Boyden:** 569 LC3; 590 RC3. **Ron Boylan:** 590 R2. **Gary Braasch:** 22 T. **Marion Brenner:** 4 RC; 8 tab; 9 L1, R2, tab; 10 tab; 11 B, tab; 12 T; 29 TL, TR; 46 L2; 47 R5; 48 L4; 49 L1, L3, L4, L5, R5; 50 L1, L2, L3, R4; 51 R5; 52 L1, L2, L3, L5, R3, R4; 53 L3; 55 L1, R3; 56 L1; 59 L2; 60 L3, R3; 61 R3; 62 L1, R1; 64 L3, R2; 65 R2; 66 L4; 67 L2, L3, R2; 70 R3; 71 R3; 73 L1; 74 L2, L4, R3; 75 L2, L4, R3; 78 L2, L3; 79 L3; 80 L2; 82 L3, R2; 83 L1; R2; 84 L2, R1; 85 R2; 86 R3; 87 R2; 91 R1, R4; 93 R3; 94 L2, L5, R2; 95 L1, L4; 96 L1, L2, L3, L5, R1, R2, R3, R4; 97 R3; 98 R5; 101 L2, L5; 102 L1, L4; 103 R1; 104 L2, L3, R1, R2, R3, R4, R5; 105 L1, R1, R2, R4; 106 L2, L3, L4, R2, R3; 107 L1, L3, R1, R2, R3, R4, R5, R6; 108 L1, L2, L3, L5, R2, R3, R4, R5; 109 L2, L4, L5, R1, R3, R4, R5; 110 L2, L3, L4, R1, R3, R4, R5; 111 L1, L2, L3, L4, R1, R2, R4, R5; 112 L2, L3, R3; 113 L1, R1, R4; 114 L6; 119 L3, L4; 120 L2, L4, L5, R2, R3; 123 L2, L3; 124 L3; 126 L4, L5, R2, R3; 127 R2; 128 L2, L5, R4; 605 LC1, RC2; 606 TL. **Kathy Brenzel:** 9 R5; 58 R4; 599. **Richard Brown:** 41 B. **Lisa Butler:** 14 M; 17 T; 72 L1, L2, L3, L4, R1, R2, R4; 73 R4; 83 R4; 85 R3. **Peter Christiansen:** 593; 601 B. **Steven Cohan:** 33 B. **Ed Cooper:** 25 B; 28 T; 29 B; 43 T; 123 L1. **R. Cowles:** 553 R2; 568 LC7; 569 L2, L4, RC2, R2; 590 L1, RC2, L3, R3. **Crandall & Crandall:** 553 LC2, RC2, RC3; 568 LC3, RC3; 569 LC2, RC3; 590 RC1. **Whitney Cranshaw:** 568 L1, L2; 590 RC4. **Rosalind Creasy:** 11 R. **D. Cudney:** 591 L1, L2, LC1, LC2, RC1, RC2, R3, R4. **Claire Curran:** 4 L, R; 7; 9 R4; 33 T; 36 BL, BR; 39 T; 43 BL; 46 L3; 47 R1; 48 L2, L5, R2, R3, R4, R5; 49 R1; 50 R2; 51 L1, L2, L5, 52 L4, R1; 53 L1, L2, L4, L5, L6, R2, R3, R4, R5; 54 R1; 55 L3, L4, L5, R5; 57 R1; 58 L4; 59 L1, L3, L4, R1, R5; 60 R2; 63 L1, L2, R2; 65 L2, R5; 66 L2, L3; 67 L4, L5, R1, R5; 68 L2, L3, L5, R1, R2, R3, R4; 69 L1, L2, L3, L4, R2, R3, R5; 73 R1, R2, R3; 74 L3, R1, R5; 75 L1, L3, LC3, LC4, R2; 76 L3; 79 L2; 80 L3, L4, R2; 81 L4, L5, R1, R2, R3, R4; 82 R3, R4; 83 L5; 84 R3; 85 L4, R4; 86 L2, L3; 88 L2, L3, L4, R2, R3, R4; 89 L1, L2, R1, R2, R3, R4; 91 L2; 93 L1, L2, L3, L4, R2; 94 R4, R5; 95 L2, R1, R4; 97 L5, R5; 98 L2, L3, R3, R4; 99 L1, L2, R1, R3, R4; 100 L1, L2, R1, R4; 101 L1, L4, R3, R4, R5; 102 L2; 105 L3, R5; 108 R1; 109 R2; 110 L5; 112 R4; 113 L3; 119 R1, R4; 120 L1, R1; 121 L1, L3, L4, R1, R3, R4; 122 L1, L2, L3, L4, L5, R1, R2, R3, R4, R5; 123 R3; 124 R4, L4, R1, R3, R4; 125 L2, L4, L5, R2; 126 R5; 128 L1; 591 L3; 595 T, B; 601 T; 604 TL, BL; 605 RC1, RC3, LC3. **William Dewey:** 8T; 13 BL; 26 T; 32 T; 33 ML; 36 T; 37 B, T; 85 L1, L5; 86 L4, R1; 87 L1, L2, L4, L5, R1, R3, R4, R5; 100 R2; 101 R2; 102 R1, R2; 103 L3, R5; 112 L1; 114 L3; 119 L1. **Craig Engle:** 113 L5; 124 R2. **E. Ferguson:** 590 LC2. **Joe K. Hale (Zephyr Pictures):** 39 BR. **Saxon Holt:** 8 B; 12 B; 25 TR; 26 B; 46 L1, L4, L5; 47 L2, L3, L4, R4; 50 R3; 51 R1, R2, R3, R4; 56 L2, L4, R1, R2, R3, R4; 57 L3, R3; 58 L2, L3, R1, R3; 59 R2; 62 R3; 64 R1; 69 R4; 78 L1, L4, R2; 79 L4; 83 L3; 85 L3; 91 L3; 92 R4, R5; 94 R1; 107 L2; 112 R2; 113 R2; 127 R5; 128 R2, R5; 594; 598 B. **Verna Johnston:** 25 TL. **B. Knoop:** 553 L1, RC1; 590 L2. **Michael Landis:** 56 L5; 57 R2. **Jim McCausland:** 22 M; 82 L1. **David McDonald:** back TL, BR; 4TL, TR; 12 tab; 13 tab; 14 tab; 17 B; 19 T; 21 B; 46 R1, R4; 47 R2, R3; 48 L3; 52 R2; 54 L4, R3; 55 L2, R2, R4; 60 L2, L4; 61 R4, R5; 62 L2, L4, L5, R4; 63 R1, R3, R4; 64 L2, L5; 65 L3, R1, R3, R4; 66 R4; 70 L2, L3, L4, R1, R2; 71 L1, L2, L3, L4, L5, R1, R2, R5; 72 R3; 75 LC2; 78 R3, R4; 79 R1, R4; 81 L1; 84 L4; 89 L3; 90 R1, R2, R3, R4; 91 L1, R3, R5; 92 L1, L2, L3, L4, R2; 95 R5; 97 L2, L5, R1, R2; 102 R4; 103 R2; 104 L4; 112 L5, R5; 113 L2, L4, R5; 114 L4, L5, R1, R2, R4; 115 L2, L3, L4, L5, R2, R3; 116 L1, L3, L4, R1, R2, R3, R4, R5; 117 L2, L3, L4, L5, R1, R4; 118 L1, L3, L4, L5, R1, R2, R3; 119 R3; 120 R5; 125 R4; 128 R3; 591 RC3, R5; 596; 597 T; 605 LC2. **Andrew McKinney:** 13 T. **Charles Mann:** back LB, RC; 6; 7 tab; 9 L2; 13 BR; 41 TL, TR; 43 BR; 45 T; 46 R3; 48 L1, 49 R2; 50 L5; 51 L3; 57 L1, L2, R4; 58 R2; 59 R3; 60 R1; 60 R4; 61 L1, L2, L3, R1; 63 L4; 65 L1; 66 R3, 70 L1; 72 L5; 73 L2, L3, L4; 74 L5, R2; 75 LC1, R4; 76 L1, L2, L4, L5, R1, R2, R3, R5; 77 L1, L2, L3, L4, L5, R1, R2, R3, R4, R5; 79 R3; 80 R4; 81 L2; 84 L1, L3, R2; 86 R5; 90 L2, L3, L4; 94 L3, L4; 96 L4, 97 L3, R4; 98 L1, R2; 99 L3, R2; 100 L3; 102 L5, R3; 103 L1, L4, L5, R4; 109 L3; 114 L2; 117 R2, R5; 118 R4; 123 L4, R2; 124 L1, L2; 125 R3; 126 L1, L3; 127 L1, L2, L3, R1, R4; 128 L3. **Scott Millard:** 39 M. **Don Normark:** 14 B. **Bart O'Brien:** 32 B. **Shep Ogden:** 602. **Jerry Pavia:** 56 L3; 58 L1; 71 R4, R6; 115 L1. **Joanne Pavia:** 67 R4. **Karl Petzke:** 2, 623. **Norman A. Plate:** 10 B; 54 L5, R2; 55 R1; 597 M, B; 598 T; 600 T, B; 603 C. **Rob Proctor:** 14 T; 19 B. **Scotts Co.:** 553 L2, L3, R1. **David Stubbs:** 9 R3. **K. Bryan Swezey:** 25 TM. **Keith Warren:** 22 B. **Darrow Watt:** 28 B, M; 54 L2; 80 L1; 533 LC1; 603 L, R. **Stephen Whalen (Zephyr Pictures):** 39 BL. **Peter Whiteley:** 10 T, TR; 88 R1. **Doug Wilson:** back TR; 4 LC; 9 R1; 46 R2; 47 L1; 49 R3; 54 L3; 63 L3; 64 L4, R3, R4; 66 R1; 82 L4; 83 R1; 85 R1; 86 R2; 92 R1; 94 R3; 95 R2; 105 L2; 114 R3. **Tom Woodward:** 3; 5; 45 B, BC; 48 R1; 49 L2, R4; 50 L4, R1, R5; 51 L4; 53 R1, R6; 54 L1; 57 R5; 59 R4; 60 L1, R5; 61 R2, R6; 62 L3, R2, R5; 63 R5; 64 L1; 66 L1, R2; 67 L1, R3; 68 L1, L4, R5; 69 R1; 74 L1, R4; 75 L5, R1; 78 L5, R1; 79 L1, R2; 80 R1, R3; 81 L3, R5; 82 L2, R1; 83 L2, L4, R3, R5; 84 R4; 85 L2; 86 L1, L5, R4; 87 L3; 88 L1; 90 L1, L5; 91 R2; 92 R3; 93 R1, R4; 94 L1; 95 L3, R3; 97 L1, L4; 98 L4, R1; 99 L4; 100 L4, R3; 101 L3, R1; 102 L3, R5; 103 L2, R3; 104 L1; 105 R3; 106 L1; 107 L4; 108 L4; 109 L1; 110 L1, R2; 111 R3; 112 L4, R1; 113 R3; 114 L1, R5; 115 R1; 116 L2, L5; 117 L1, R3; 118 L2, R5; 119 L2, R2; 120 L3, R4; 121 L2, L5, R2; 123 R1; 124 R5; 125 L1, L3, R1; 126 L2, R1, R4; 127 L4, R3; 128 L4, R1; 569 R1, RC4, R3; 604 TC, TR, BR; 605 L1, R1, R2; 606 BL, R; 607 L, TR, BR. **Tom Wyatt:** back LC. **Linda Yonker:** 21 T.

The photographers for this edition would also like to recognize the following gardens and thank their respective staffs in general and specific advisors in particular for help throughout their work on this project.

Pacific Northwest: Park Tilford Gardens (Todd Major); Van Dusen Botanical Garden (Christine Chevaldave); **Southern California:** Balboa Park (Kathy Puplava); California State University at Fullerton Arboretum (Rico Montenegro); Sherman Library and Gardens; Arboretum of Los Angeles County (Jim Bauml); Descanso Gardens; The Huntington Botanical Gardens (Kathy Musial); Roger's Gardens; Tree of Life Wholesale Nursery (Mike Evans); **San Francisco Bay Area:** Blake Garden; Strybing Arboretum; University of California Botanical Garden (Daniel Campbell).